De Franceschi / Schulze

Harmonizing Digital Contract Law

Harmonizing Digital Contract Law

The Impact of EU Directives
2019/770 and 2019/771
and the Regulation of Online Platforms

A Handbook

edited by

Alberto De Franceschi
Reiner Schulze

2023

Published by
Nomos Verlagsgesellschaft mbH & Co. KG, Waldseestraße 3-5, 76530 Baden-Baden, Germany,
email: vertrieb@nomos.de

Co-published by
Verlag C.H.Beck oHG, Wilhelmstraße 9, 80801 München, Germany,
email: bestellung@beck.de

and

Hart Publishing, Kemp House, Chawley Park, Cumnor Hill, Oxford, OX2 9PH, United Kingdom,
online at: www.hartpub.co.uk

Published in North America by Hart Publishing,
An Imprint of Bloomsbury Publishing 1385 Broadway, New York, NY 10018, USA
email: mail@hartpub.co.uk

ISBN 978 3 7560 0605 2 (NOMOS Print)
ISBN 978 3 7489 4141 5 (NOMOS ePDF)
ISBN 978 3 406 81091 6 (C.H.BECK)
ISBN 978 1 5099 5604 3 (HART)

First Edition 2023
© Nomos Verlagsgesellschaft mbH & Co. KG, Baden-Baden 2023. Overall responsibility for manufacturing (printing and production) lies with Nomos Verlagsgesellschaft mbH & Co. KG.

This work is subject to copyright. All rights are reserved, whether the whole or part of the material is concerned, specifically those of translation, reprinting, re-use of illustrations, broadcasting, reproduction by photocopying machine or similar means, and storage in data banks. Under § 54 of the German Copyright Law where copies are made for other than private use a fee is payable to »Verwertungsgesellschaft Wort«, Munich, Germany.

Preface

"Harmonizing Digital Law" has become a crucial task for European and national legislation in view of the challenges of the "digital revolution" for the European Union and for its Member States. The implementation of the 2019 "Twin Directives" on the sale of goods and the supply of digital content and services represents one of the most important steps on this path so far. In addition to the harmonization of Member States law, the emergence of a uniform law of the EU is becoming more and more important with regard to the challenges of digitization, as recently shown in particular by the Internet Platform Regulation.

In view of these changes at European and national level, 40 legal scholars from all Member States of the European Union have come together in this volume to examine the impact of European legislation on the development of private law in Europe. 27 country reports present the impact of the Twin Directives in the Member States on the basis of common questions. A number of other contributions analyse the overarching features of harmonization, the contours and effects of legal unification with regard to the Internet Platform Regulation, and the further perspectives of EU legislation in face of digital and sustainability challenges.

This volume was prepared by a conference in Ferrara on 9 and 10 June 2022, where the authors of the contributions could exchange their thoughts and coordinate their work. It was no easy undertaking that, following this meeting, the large number of participants completed the Country reports and other contributions for the volume in synchrony and ensured the timely publication. We would like to express our sincere thanks to all authors for this great cooperation.

We would also like to thank the University of Ferrara and its staff for making the conference possible in a way that was impressive for all involved, as well as Nomos Verlag and in particular its responsible editor Matthias Knopik for their commitment to the production of the volume.

Ferrara and Münster, March 2023   *Alberto De Franceschi and Reiner Schulze*

CONTENTS

List of Authors IX
Harmonizing Digital Contract Law – an Introduction 1

I.
THE IMPACT OF EU DIRECTIVES 2019/770 AND 2019/771

Austria 33
Belgium 69
Bulgaria 89
Croatia 117
Cyprus 139
Czech Republic 167
Denmark 191
Estonia 211
Finland 229
France 249
Germany 273
Greece 301
Hungary 319
Ireland 357
Italy 381
Latvia 409
Lithuania 425
Luxembourg 449
Malta 471
The Netherlands 491
Poland 513
Portugal 527
Romania 541
Slovakia 581
Slovenia 605
Spain 625
Sweden 649

II.
DIGITAL SERVICES AND THE NEW PLATFORMS REGULATION

Some major issues of EU Regulation 2019/1150 on promoting fairness and transparency for business users of online intermediation services 681
The EU Digital Services Act and EU Consumer Law 705
The Impact of the EU Digital Markets Act on Contract Law 715

III.
RESHAPING CONTRACTS IN THE DIGITAL AGE

Digital Content Regulation as Building Block of the Private Law Harmonization 729
Smart Contracts 739
The Impact on Private Law of the Product Policy Initiatives under the European Green Deal 751

List of Authors

Laura Aade is a doctoral researcher at the University of Luxembourg. Her research explores the intersection of European consumer protection and platform governance. Prior to joining the University of Luxembourg, Laura was a member of the Maastricht Law & Tech Lab, where she provided research support and helped coordinate numerous interdisciplinary projects related to consumer protection, content monetization, and platform governance. Laura graduated from the United Nations University (cum laude) with a Master's in Public Policy and Human Development specializing in Governance of Innovation, and holds a Bachelor of Law in European Law from Maastricht University.

Zuzana Adamová, PhD. (Slovakia), is a Director of the Intellectual Property and Information Technologies Law Department at Trnava University (Slovakia). She is also a Senior Associate in the Advocate Office Petkov&Co. (Attorneys at Law). She is an expert within the Arbitration Centre for Alternative Domain Names Dispute Resolution (EISi) deciding disputes according to ADR rules for domain '.sk'. In the past she worked at the Civil and Commercial Law Department at Trnava University and was a visiting scholar at Max Planck Institute for Innovation and Competition in Munich.

Esther Arroyo Amayuelas is Full Professor of Civil Law at the University of Barcelona and EU Private Law Jean Monnet Chair at the same University from 2015-2018 and 2019-2022.

Kaspars Balodis is Professor of Civil Law at the University of Latvia and Judge of the Supreme Court of the Republic of Latvia. Previously, he served as a Justice of the Constitutional Court of Latvia. Before joining the Civil department of the Supreme Court, he was an attorney at law in Riga. At the University, he teaches courses in civil and commercial Law. His research interests include commercial law (including company law) as well as various aspects of contract law.

Wojciech Bańczyk, Ph.D., assistant at the Chair of Civil Law, Jagiellonian University in Kraków, UJ director of the American Law Program at The Catholic University of America in Washington D.C. and UJ, attorney at law. Winner of the first prize of the General Counsel to the Republic of Poland contest for the best master theses on court law and scholarships of DAAD, Foundation of Polish Science, Polish Ministry of Science and Higher Education. Member of European Society of Comparative Legal History, European Law Institute. Investigator of National Science Centre, DPWS and German Federal Bank grants. Interested in contract law, inheritance law.

Jean-Sébastien Borghetti is professor of private law at Paris-Panthéon-Assas Université in France. He specialises in tort and contract law, both in a domestic and a comparative perspective.

Mireille M. Caruana is Senior Lecturer and Head of Department of Media, Communications and Technology Law within the Faculty of Laws, University of Malta. Her research interests encompass data privacy and consumer protection law, as well as exploring the intersection of law and artificial intelligence, consistently maintaining a focus on emerging technologies and their implications throughout. She was awarded her PhD from the University of Bristol in 2014. She graduated Doctor of Laws from the University of Malta in 2002 and was called to the bar (Advocate) in Malta in 2003. She is a member of the University Research Ethics Committee and the Board of the Centre for Distributed Ledger Technologies.

Alberto De Franceschi is Full Professor of Private Law and Digital Law at the University of Ferrara, Global Law Professor of Digital Law at the Katholieke Universiteit Leuven and Visiting Professor of EU Digital Law at the Zhejiang University, Hangzhou. He served as an expert to the Italian Ministry of Justice for the adoption and implementation of the EU Directives 2019/770 on Supply of Digital Content and Digital Services and 2019/771 on the Sales of Goods. He is Delegate of Italy at UNCITRAL Group IV on E-Commerce, G7, UNIDROIT and the Hague Academy of International Law. He is co-editor of the "Journal of European Consumer and Market Law" and of "The Italian Law Journal". He is Member of the Academia Europaea. His research deals with Law of Obligations and Contracts, with focus on digital economy and sustainability.

Laurynas Didžiulis is a docent at Vilnius University teaching civil law of property and contracts. From 2014 he holds a PhD in private enforcement of EU financial regulation and was recognized as an exceptional junior scholar in 2016. He is an author of several books and articles on various issues of Lithuanian civil law. He is an advocate of civil law and a recommended arbitrator at Vilnius Court of Commercial Arbitration. Before joining the Lithuanian Bar he has worked almost six years in the Supreme Court of Lithuania.

Philipp Fabbio is a Full Professor of Law at the University of Perugia and an attorney at law in Rome, Italy. His research focuses on the fields of competition and intellectual property law. He has taught as a Visiting Professor at Chicago-Kent College of Law – IIT, Loyola University of Chicago, Wuhan University and Regensburg University. He regularly gives conference lectures on IP and competition law topics, in Italy and abroad.

Ádám Fuglinszky, LL.M. (Heidelberg) and PhD (Hamburg) is ordinary professor of civil law and comparative law at Eötvös Loránd University (ELTE) Law School, Budapest, Hungary. His research interests are contract and tort law (in a comparative perspective), legal transplants and European private law. Besides monographs and commentaries he published several papers on Articles 74 and 79 CISG as legal transplants and on comparative law in general (RabelsZ, ERCL, JICL, ZEuP, JETL). He is member of the editorial board of ERPL and of the advisory board of Journal of Civil Law Studies (LSU).

Juanita Goicovici is Associate Professor of Consumer Law, Data Protection Law, and Business-to-Consumer Contracts at the Faculty of Law of the Babes-Bolyai University of Cluj-Napoca (Romania). She served as a national rapporteur for the study "Collective redress in the Member States of the European Union" commissioned by the European Parliament's Policy Department for Citizens' Rights and Constitutional Affairs at the request of the Committee on Legal Affairs (2018). In 2016, she served as a national rapporteur for the "Study on all mandatory rules applicable to contractual obligations in contracts for sales of tangible goods sold at a distance and, in particular online" (European Commission, DG Justice and Consumers).

Friedrich Graf von Westphalen, attorney-at-law, Lohmar, professor at the University of Bielefeld.

List of Authors

Hans Christoph Grigoleit received his legal education at the Universities of Tübingen and Munich (1984-1989). He then achieved an LL.M. from the University of Miami (1990), obtained his doctorate in 1996 and his habilitation in 2003 at the University of Munich. In his PhD-thesis he dealt with "Pre-Contractual Information Liability" (1996) while his habilitation study concerned "Shareholder Liability" (2003). After his first teaching position as a professor at the University of Regensburg (2003-2009), he returned to the University of Munich in 2009, where he has since been holding a Chair for Private Law, Commercial Law, Corporate Law and Theory of Private Law.

Geraint Howells is Executive Dean for Business, Public Policy and Law at the University of Galway. Previously he was Professor of Commercial Law at Manchester University, where he remains a visiting professor. He has been Dean of Law at the City University of Hong Kong and Head of the Law Schools in Manchester and Lancaster. He has published extensively on consumer law, product liability and European private law and was a member of the Acquis group developing common principles of European contract law and tort law. A former President of the International Association of Consumer Law, he edited the Consumer Law Journal for many years and is Series Editor for Routledge's Markets and Law series.

Jiří Hrádek is an Assistant Professor at the Department of Civil Law at the Faculty of Law of Charles University and an in-house lawyer. He graduated in law from the Faculty of Law of Charles University (2002). Jiří Hrádek studied at the University of Hamburg (2000-2001), in the LLM programme at the Eberhard-Karls-University in Tübingen (2002-2003) and in the post-graduate programme of the Charles University (2002-2009). In 2002 and 2003 he completed research stays at the European Centre of Tort and Insurance Law (ECTIL) in Vienna; in 2007 he received an internship at the European Commission, DG Health and Consumer Protection. Jiří Hrádek specialises in civil and procedural law, with a special focus on tort law and consumer law. He is the author of a book on pre-contractual liability, co-author of commentaries on the Czech Civil Code, the Czech Civil Procedure Code and book on Delict Law.

Bert Keirsbilck is a Professor of Law at the Faculty of Law and Criminology of KU Leuven. He lectures in Commercial Law, EU Law and European Economic Law in Brussels, Leuven and Kortrijk. He is a co-director of Consumer Competition Market (CCM). Bert is a co-author of '*Commercial Practices and Consumer Contracts*' (in Dutch) and a co-editor of the CCM series. Recent research focuses on sustainable production and consumption, circular economy and servitisation.

Marco B.M. Loos is professor of Private Law, in particular of European consumer law, at the Amsterdam Centre for Transformative Private Law (ACT) of the University of Amsterdam. Loos specialises in European and Dutch contract law and European and Dutch consumer law. He publishes regularly on subjects of European consumer law, including standard contract terms, digital content, consumer sales, and enforcement of consumer law. His list of publications and his list of ancillary activities is available at https://www.uva.nl/en/profile/l/o/m.b.m.loos/m.b.m.loos.html.

Christiana Markou is an Associate Professor at the European University Cyprus and a practising lawyer at the law firm C. Markou & Co LLC. She holds an LLB (Hons.) from the University of Sheffield (UK) and an LLM in International, Commercial and European Law. She also holds PhD in Law from the University of Lancaster (UK). She is a legal researcher involved in funded research in various areas, including consumer protection. She also deals with civil litigation and legal consultancy. Following a nomination by the Embassy of the United States of America, in recognition of her expertise in data protection law, she has participated in the premier professional exchange programme of the US State Department, the International Visitors Leadership Program (IVLP) of January 2020. She publishes in international scientific publications (journals and edited books), and one of her main publications is her book on *Consumer Protection, Automated Shopping Platforms and EU Law (Routledge, 2019)*. She is also a member of the Expert Group for the EU Observatory on the Online Platform Economy.

Plamena Markova is a policy adviser to a Bulgarian Member of the European Parliament focusing on budgetary policies, EU funding and budgetary control (CONT & BUDG committees). Plamena has a legal background in International and European Law with a Bachelor of Laws from The Hague University with a semester abroad at LUISS Guido Carli University and a Master of Laws from King's College London specialising in EU law. Plamena's interests lie in the field of European consumer law in which she authored and co-authored academic publications.

Emilia Mišćenić, Dr. Iur. (KFU Graz), LL.M. (Saarland) is an Associate Professor at the Faculty of Law of the University of Rijeka. She is an awarded scientist in her field of expertise. In 2011, she obtained the Croatian National Science Award, in 2012 the Award of the University of Rijeka Foundation, in 2013 the Recognition of the Croatian Ministry of Science, Education and Sports and in 2020 the Award of the Republic of Croatia 'Ivan Filipović' for her outstanding academic and professional results. Her scientific work has been recognised and cited by Advocate Generals in cases C-453/10, Pereničová et Perenič, C-319/20, Meta Platforms Ireland and as a member of the COVID-19-Consumer Law Research Group in C-407/21, UFC, Que choisir and CLCV AG.

Jorge Morais Carvalho is Associate Professor and Vice-Dean at the NOVA School of Law (Portugal), Coordinator of the LLB, Director of the NOVA Consumer Lab, Researcher at CEDIS (Centre for Research & Development on Law and Society), Editor of the EuCML – Journal of European Consumer and Market Law. Author (or co-author) of about 140 books and scientific articles in the areas of consumer law, contract law, and consumer alternative dispute resolution. Participation in about 180 seminars, conferences, and scientific colloquia in Argentina, Brazil, Cape Verde, Chile, England, Italy, Mozambique, Peru, Poland, Portugal, and Spain.

Damjan Možina is a Professor of oivil and commercial Law at the University of Ljubljana/Faculty of Law. His research interests include the areas of law of obligations, European Private Law and the Law of State Liability for damage.

Jori Munukka is a Full Professor of Law at Stockholm University. His research focuses on the fields of general private law and real estate law. He used to assist the Ministry of Justice in the analysis of and negotiations on the proposed Common European Sales Law and was appointed expert in the Swedish legislative inquiry preparing the transposition of the Twin directives.

Elise Poillot is full professor of Droit Civil and director of the Consumer Law Clinic at the University of Luxembourg. Her fields of research are, in a national comparative and EU perspective, consumer law, contract law, and legal education. More recently her research focuses on the transformation of the concept of "droit civil" in civil law jurisdictions and on the impact of data protection on consumer law. On these topics she has extensively written monographs and articles. She regularly presents the development of EU jurisprudence in consumer law in the *Recueil Dalloz* and in the *Journal de Droit Européen*.

Katarzyna Południak-Gierz, Ph.D., assistant professor at the Chair of Civil Law, Faculty of Law and Administration Jagiellonian University in Kraków. Her scientific interests focus on the interplay between private law and technology. She researches private law reaction towards use of personalization techniques in consumer contracts, especially in insurance sector, and the possibility of using Big-data fueled granularity to increase ecological efficiency of sales law.

Jernej Renko is a teaching assistant for civil and commercial law at the University of Ljubljana, Faculty of Law. He completed his undergraduate and master's studies at University of Ljubljana, Faculty of Law, his LL.M. degree at the Humboldt University of Berlin and is currently pursuing his doctorate at University of Ljubljana, Faculty of Law. His research interests are mainly in the areas of contract, consumer, and tort law, especially their application in the context of emerging digital technologies.

Hugo-Maria Schally holds a doctorate of law from the University of Graz/Austria and is a graduate of the Vienna Diplomatic Academy. He worked for the United Nations Development Programme, the Austrian Ministry for Foreign Affairs and the Organisation for Security and Cooperation in Europe before joining the European Commission. He was most recently responsible for the development and implementation of the EU Circular Economy Action Plan and for the collaboration with international environmental organisations and multilateral environmental agreements. He currently serves as EU lead negotiator in negotiations under the Convention on Biological Diversity and for a new Global Agreement on Plastics.

Hans Schulte-Nölke (*1963); Law Studies at University of Münster; Member of Graduate College of Legal History in Frankfurt/Main; Doctorate (1994); Second State Examination/Qualification for Judicial Office (1995); Postdoctorate at University of Münster (1995-1997); Grant as Visiting Scholar at Radboud University Nijmegen (1998-1999), Habilitation (2000); Chair of Private Law at University of Bielefeld (2001-2008); Chair of Civil Law, European Private and Commercial Law, Comparative Law and European Legal History at University of Osnabrück (since 2008); Director of European Legal Studies Institute; Professor of German Law at Radboud University Nijmegen (since 2013); Member of: Academia Europaea (MAE), American Law Institute.

Reiner Schulze is Professor of German and European civil law and Director of the Centre of European Private Law at the University of Münster (Germany). His main research interests are in the field of European trade and consumer protection law; the law of obligations (in particular contract law and tort law) and international contract law; and history of European Community law. He is a founding member of the European Law Institute; a honorary member of the Spanish "Real Academia de Jurisprudencia y Legislación"; a member of the Italian "Accademia Nazionale dei Lincei"; and of the Academia Europaea.

List of Authors

Karin Sein is a Professor of Civil Law and the Deputy Head of the Institute of Private Law in the Faculty of Law of the University of Tartu, Estonia. Her main research interests cover domestic and European contract law, consumer law, private international law and digital law. During 2018-2021, she was the PI of a scientific project funded by the Estonian Research Council concentrating on consumer contract law in the Digital Single Market. She has provided expertise for the Estonian Ministry of Justice on implementing European consumer protection directives into Estonian law. During the Estonian EU Presidency in 2017, she was acting as a Chair for the Council Working Group on Contract Law.

Rita Simon, LL.M., is a senior researcher at the Institute of State and Law, and has focused on consumer protection and sustainable consumption from a comparative perspective since 2017. She studied law at ELTE in Budapest and holds a LL.M. degree (2001) and a Ph.D. in European Competition Law from the University of Cologne (2005). She worked for various German institutions, such as the Centre for European Integration Studies in Bonn and the Eastern Law Institute at the University of Cologne and served as an associate in the Bureau for Civil Law Codification at the Hungarian Ministry of Justice. Between 2011 and 2021 she worked at the Centre for Comparative Law at Charles University. She is a Member of the European Law Institute.

Marie Jull Sørensen is associate professor at the Department of Law at Aalborg University, Denmark. She has written several articles and book contributions in the area of consumer law. Her research covers for example the implementation of EU consumer law into Danish law, the challenges of online marketplaces and the duty for national courts to apply consumer law ex officio. She has participated in Consumer Law Pro and is a reporter on the E-justice Portal. She chairs the Nordic Hub of the European Law Institute and is currently co-reporter on the ELI-project on automated decision-making.

Evelyne Terryn is full professor at the KU Leuven and teaches consumer law, commercial law and company law, she is guest professor at UHasselt. Evelyne studied law at the KU Leuven (master and PhD), at King's College London and Oxford (MJur). She is co-director of the research institute CCM – Consumer Competition Market (law.kuleuven.be/ccm). Her research focuses on commercial law and (European) consumer law – with a specific interest in making consumer law more sustainable. She is also sustainability coordinator within the KU Leuven Kulak management committee and a practicing lawyer (Kortrijk bar).

Zafeirios Tsolakidis was born in Athens in 1977. He graduated and received his doctorate with merits from the Law School of National & Kapodistrian University of Athens. He is an Associate Professor of Civil Law at the National & Kapodistrian University of Athens Law School, where he teaches General Principles of Civil Law, Law of Obligations, Family Law, as well as Banking Law, Real Estate Law and Methodology of Law (in Postgraduate courses). Author of 6 books (among which "Compensation in precontractual liability", and "Contractual and Delictual Liability for Assistants") and more than 35 articles in Legal Journals.

Sjef van Erp is Head of the Private Law Department at the University of Amsterdam, Emeritus Professor at Maastricht University, Visiting Professor at Trento University. He is also Deputy-Justice at the Court of Appeals 's-Hertogenbosch. Professor Van Erp is co-founder and former Vice-President of the European Law Institute (ELI) and he is currently the President of the International Association of Legal Science. He is a member of the American Law Institute (ALI) and titular member of the International Academy of Comparative Law. Prof. Van Erp is co-founder and editor of the European Journal of Comparative Law and Governance and he is also co-founder and editor-in-chief of the European Property Law Journal.

Klaus Viitanen is LL.D. and Docent in Commercial Law. He worked 35 years in the University of Helsinki (Finland) where he specialized in Commercial Law and Civil Procedural Law.

Fidelma White is a Senior Lecturer at the School of Law, University College Cork, Ireland, where she teaches and researches on consumer and commercial law. Dr. White also engages in the public policy debate. In 2021, she was invited by the Attorney General to contribute to the development and drafting of new consumer legislation, that culminated in the Consumer Rights Act 2022, which inter alia, transposes the 2019 "Twin Directives" on the sale of goods, and digital content and digital services (in Parts 2 and 3, respectively) into Irish law.

Brigitta Zöchling-Jud is a professor at the Department of Private Law and, since October 2020, Dean of the Faculty of Law of the University of Vienna. Her research focuses on the law of obligations and inheritance, consumer contract law, banking law as well as European and international private law. She has been involved in legislative projects of the Federal Ministry of Justice on several occasions, which include the implementation of the DCD and the SGD in Austria. She is admitted to the bar of Cologne and the bar of Vienna and is active as an arbitrator and a legal expert.

Fryderyk Zoll, doctor honoris causa (West-Ukrainian National University in Ternopil), professor at the Chair of Civil Law, Jagiellonian University in Kraków and the European Legal Studies Institute, University of Osnabrück; leading researcher of numerous Polish, German, EU grants; member of numerous academic associations; vice-chairperson of the Committee for the Defence of Democracy (KOD) regional board in Lesser Poland; past member of the European Law Institute Executive Committee, Common Frame of Reference and Committee of Acquis Group drafting teams, Codification Commission at the Polish Ministry of Justice. Scientifically interested in European private law, consumer law, comparative law, legal education, judicial independence.

Harmonizing Digital Contract Law – an Introduction

A. Contract Law in Transition to the Digital Age 1
B. Innovative Features of the "Twin Directives" 8
  I. Conceptual Framework 8
  II. Data as Counter-Performance 9
  III. Supply of Digital Content 10
  IV. Adaptation of contractual obligation to digitization 11
  V. Objectification of the Concept of Contract 12
  VI. Remedies 14
C. Impact on the Law of Member States 16
  I. General Framework 16
  II. Definitions and Scope of Application 22
D. Conformity with the Contract 27
  I. The implementation of subjective and objective criteria for conformity .. 27
  II. Measures to Improve Sustainability and the Circular Economy 34
  III. Modification of Digital Content or Digital Service 35
  IV. The interruption of long-term supply of digital content or digital services ... 36
E. Liability of the Trader 37
F. Remedies 41
  I. Repair and replacement 41
  II. Right of withdrawal, right to termination and price reduction 48
  III. The restitutions 49
  IV. Hierarchy of Remedies and Environmental Sustainability 50
  V. Premature obsolescence of goods and the relationship with the internal rules on unfair commercial practices 51
  VI. Transfer of the rights against the initial seller from the initial consumer to a subsequent buyer 52
G. Commercial Guarantees 53
H. Time Limits 54
  I. The implementation of the provisions on time limits for the trader's liability 54
  II. Suspension and interruption 59
  III. The obligation to notify 63
I. Right of Redress 64
J. Relationship with other remedies and enforcement 65
  I. In particular: right to withhold the payment 65
  II. Enforcement and penalties 66
K. Conclusions 70
    Guidelines for Country Reports 75

A. Contract Law in Transition to the Digital Age

Digitalization has brought about a profound change in contractual practice. This change affects both the objects and the methods of concluding and implementing contracts. In particular, contracts for the supply of digital products and services – and more generally: trade with data[1] – has gained outstanding importance for many branches of the economy. Contracts are increasingly prepared and concluded online and with the help of artificial intelligence. The conclusion of a contract "machine to machine" in the Internet of Things is no longer an exception, but common practice in business

---

[1] Alberto De Franceschi and Reiner Schulze, 'Digital Revolution – New Challenges for Law: Introduction', in Alberto De Franceschi and Reiner Schulze (eds), *Digital Revolution – New Challenges for Law* (2019), 1 et seq.

dealings. Similarly, the use of artificial intelligence in the execution of contracts and in the enforcement of contractual claims, including the interruption or termination of contractual services, has become widespread (for example, through automated sanction mechanisms).[2] Even the resolution of conflicts between contracting parties has shifted significantly to online-based forms of communication using artificial intelligence.

2   In the European Union, legislation has for some time begun to respond to this far-reaching and profound change by adapting contract law to the new realities of the digital age.[3] In addition to legislative measures that some Member States have taken independently for their national law to varying degrees and with varying content, legal acts that the European Union has enacted in close succession in recent years have designed new contours of contract law with regard to the digital challenges.

3   The starting points for the emergence of this "digital law" of the Union were two documents presented by the European Commission after the failure of efforts to establish a "Common European Sales Law": the Communication on the "New Start" from 2014[4] and the "Digital Single Market Strategy"[5] that followed shortly thereafter. On their basis, addressing the challenges of the digital revolution has become the most powerful engine for the development of European Contract Law.[6]

4   Since then, the legislative development of contract law by the European Union has taken both paths: Regulations have created uniform law with regard to digital matters; and directives have harmonized Member States' law in this regard. Uniform law in the field of contract law has been created in particular by the regulations on geo-blocking, portability, online platforms and most recently by the private law parts of the Platform-to-Business Regulation[7], the Digital Markets Act[8] and the Digital Services Act.[9] The latter three have helped the EU to respond to one of the most important regulatory challenges posed by digitization with uniform law, namely the operation and use of internet platforms (as explained in more detail in the part of this volume on internet platform regulation).

5   At the same time, the harmonized law of the Member States has expanded considerably through a series of Directives, most of which provide for full harmonization. Among them, in addition to the Modernisation Directive[10], the "Twin Directives" from

---

[2] Sebastian Lohsse et al., *Liability for Artificial Intelligence and the Internet of Things* (2019); Mark A Geistfeld et al., *Civil Liability for Artificial Intelligence and Software* (2023).

[3] Alberto De Franceschi and Reiner Schulze, above fn. 1, 1 et seq.

[4] Communication from the Commission of 16.12.2014, Commission Work Program for 2015, A new start, COM (2014) 910 final.

[5] Communication from the Commission to the European Parliament, the Council, the European Economic and Social Committee and the Committee of the Regions "A Digital Single Market Strategy for Europe", COM(2015) 192 final.

[6] Reiner Schulze, 'European Private Law in the Digital Age – Developments, Challenges and Prospects', in André Janssen et al. (eds), *The Future of European Private Law* (forthcoming 2023).

[7] Regulation (EU) 2019/1150 of the European Parliament and of the Council of 20 June 2019 on promoting fairness and transparency for business users of online intermediation services [2019] OJ L 186. See Friedrich Graf von Westphalen, 'Some major issues of EU Regulation 2019/1150 on promoting fairness and transparency for business users of online intermediation services', in this volume.

[8] Regulation (EU) 2022/1925 of the European Parliament and of the Council of 14 September 2022 on contestable and fair markets in the digital sector and amending Directives (EU) 2019/1937 and (EU) 2020/1828 (Digital Markets Act) [2022] OJ L 265. See Philipp Fabbio, 'The Impact of the Digital Markets Act on Contract Law', in this volume.

[9] Proposal for a Regulation of the European Parliament and of the Council on a Single Market for Digital Services (Digital Services Act) and amending Directive 2000/31/EC [2022] OJ L 277. See Hans Schulte-Nölke, 'The EU Digital Services Act and EU Consumer Law', in this volume.

[10] Directive (EU) 2019/2161 of the European Parliament and of the Council of 27 November 2019 amending Council Directive 93/13/EEC and Directives 98/6/EC, 2005/29/EC and 2011/83/EU of the

2019 play a prominent role: the Digital Content and Digital Services Directive (DCD)[11] and the Sale of Goods Directive (SGD)[12].

These two Directives outline the contours for the harmonization of some of the most important areas of contract law in the age of digitization: the supply of digital content and digital services and the sale of goods including goods with digital elements. Their scope covers millions of contracts that consumers in the EU conclude every day, for example, to receive texts, films, music and all kinds of software on their computers and smartphones or to purchase goods of all kinds online or offline. In addition, the "Twin Directives" deserve special attention because they contain a number of innovative approaches that may become important for the future development of contract law at European and national level, also beyond their scope of application.

In the following, therefore, a brief insight into some of these innovative approaches is given first, before an overview of the impact of both Directives on the contract law of the Member States follows. This overview of the impact is limited to a concise synopsis of more detailed country reports from the Member States of the EU,[13] which examine the impact of the "Twin directives" on the respective national law for all 27 Member States from the same nine points of view.[14] The summary overview below is intended only as an introduction to these country reports that are published in the following part of the volume, and is structured according to the same nine aspects (see p. 35) as these.

B. Innovative Features of the "Twin Directives"

I. Conceptual Framework

It should not be underestimated that the "Twin Directives" make an innovative contribution to the adaptation of contract law to the changes brought about by digitization already through their definitions and their explanation of terms. For example, they contain the definitions of fundamental terms such as "digital content", "digital services", "goods with digital elements", "integration of digital content or digital environment" (Art. 2 DCD; Art. 2 SGD). The same applies to performance features for the supply of digital content and digital services and for the sale of goods with digital elements such as compatibility, functionality and interoperability (Art. 2 DCD; Art. 2 SGD). In addition, a number of terms are not explicitly defined in the Directives, but their factual content is determined, such as "supply of digital content or digital services" and "compliance with the obligation to supply" (Art. 5 DCD) or "continuous supply over a period of time", "single act of supply" and "series of individual acts of supply" (Art. 8 para. 2 DCD; Art. 7 para. 3 SGD). With regard to the relevance of such terms and definitions for the contracting, it must be taken into account that their potential scope of application is not necessarily limited to contracts currently covered by the "Twin Directives". Rather, the

---

European Parliament and of the Council as regards the better enforcement and modernisation of Union consumer protection rules [2019] OJ L 328/7.

[11] European Parliament and Council Directive (EU) 2019/770 of 20 May 2019 on certain aspects concerning contracts for the supply of digital content and digital services [2019] OJ L 136/1.

[12] European Parliament and Council Directive (EU) 2019/771 of 20 May 2019 on certain aspects concerning contracts for the sale of goods, amending Regulation (EU) 2017/2394 and Directive 2009/22/EC, and repealing Directive 1999/44/EC [2019] OJ L 136/28.

[13] The country reports refer to the national provisions transposing the DCD and the SGD.

[14] Within the framework of the uniform structure printed in the appendix to this paper, however, the country reports set their own priorities according to the respective circumstances of the legal system concerned.

"Twin Directives" provide a conceptual framework in this respect that may also be useful for the future development of contract law at European and national level.[15]

II. Data as Counter-Performance

9   A striking innovative approach is also evident in the provisions on the scope of application of the DCD: the recognition of the importance of data as subject of performance and of counter-performance for modern contract law.[16] The relevant rule of Art. 3 para. 1 subpara. 2 DCD is of a more technical nature in the sense that it defines the scope of the directive. But it is based on the assessment that the provision of personal data has a similar value as the payment of a price. It expresses the significant role of data not only as a performance owed by the trader according to the respective contract, but also as a counter-performance on the part of the recipient of such a performance. Although the provision only applies to consumer contracts on digital content and digital services, it could also be substantially extended to many contracts of a different kind.[17] Some Courts in EU Member States have already accepted that contracts between social networks operators and consumers are onerous consumer contracts, to which the rules on unfair contract terms must apply.[18]

III. Supply of Digital Content

10   The DCD combines the rules on conformity with the contract with the provisions on the obligation to supply the digital content in a single set of rules (whereas the SGD, like the Consumer Rights Directive before it, does not include the obligation to deliver the good, but leaves this matter to the Consumer Rights Directive). This integration of both elements into one legal text clarifies the connection between the obligation to perform and the requirement of conformity with the contract within the contractual obligation regime.[19] Within this framework, Art. 5 para. 2 specifies the criteria for the compliance with the obligation to supply the digital content or the digital services. This can be a starting point to adapt the concept of "compliance with the obligation to perform" to the changes caused by digitization.

---

[15] Reiner Schulze, 'European Private Law in the Digital Age – Developments, Challenges and Prospects', in André Janssen et al. (eds), *The Future of European Private Law* (forthcoming 2023), II. 2. c) bb); Hans-Wolfgang Micklitz, 'The Full Harmonization Dream' (2022) Journal of European Consumer and Market Law 117 et seq.

[16] Sebastian Lohsse et al., *Data as Counter-Performance – Contract Law 2.0?* (2020); Herbert Zech, 'Data as a Tradable Commodity', in Alberto De Franceschi (ed), *European Contract Law and the Digital Single Market* (2016), 51 et seq.; Andreas Sattler, 'Informationelle Privatautonomie' (2022) 205 ff.; Jan Trzaskowski, *Your Privacy Is Important to U$ – Restoring Human Dignity in Data-Driven Marketing* (Ex Tuto, Copenhagen, 2021) pp 208–209.

[17] Reiner Schulze, 'European Private Law in the Digital Age – Developments, Challenges and Prospects', in André Janssen et al. (eds), *The Future of European Private Law* (forthcoming 2023), II. 2. c) cc).

[18] CA Paris, pôle 2, ch. 2, 12.2.2016, n° 15/08624, *Sté Facebook Inc. c/ M.*, JurisData n° 2016-002888, (2016) *CCE*, comm 33, note Loiseau; TGI Paris, 7.8.2018, n° 14/07300, *UFC-Que choisir c/ Twitter*, JurisData n° 2018-014706, (2018) *CCE*, comm 74, note Grégoire Loiseau; Autorità Garante della Concorrenza e del Mercato, 29 November 2018, PS 11112 <https://www.agcm.it/dotcmsdoc/allegati-news/PS11112_scorr_sanz.pdf> accessed 15 January 2023; the decision was later partially repealed (by excluding the aggressive character of the above described commercial practice) by Tribunale Amministrativo Regionale Roma-Lazio, 10 January 2020, no 261 <https://giustizia-amministrativa.it> accessed 15 January 2023 and later on by Consiglio di Stato, 29 March 2021, no 2631 <https://giustizia-amministrativa.it> accessed 15 January 2023.

[19] Reiner Schulze and Fryderyk Zoll, *European Contract Law* (2021), ch. 6, mn. 26 et seq.

IV. Adaptation of contractual obligation to digitization

The central provisions of the "Twin Directives" on conformity with the contract adjust the design of contractual obligations to the requirements of the digital age in various respects. Among other things, they lay down a number of corresponding performance features (such as the already mentioned compatibility, functionality etc.; Art. 7 and 8 DCD; Art. 6 and 7 SGD) and deal with the integration into the consumer's digital environment (Art. 9 DCD). In particular, the introduction of updating obligations constitutes an outstanding response to the challenges of digitization (despite the dispute of the legal nature of these obligations in detail[20]). Compared to the traditional sales law, these new provisions lead to a "dynamization" of contractual obligations to enable consumers to use digital content or digital services and goods with digital elements in accordance with its reasonable expectations. In addition, the differentiation between the "continuous supply over a period of time" and the "single act of supply or a series of individual acts of supply" is relevant for the conformity with the contract as well as for other matters (such as the burden of proof, the obligations in the event of termination and the modification; Art. 7 para. 3; 11, para. 3 SGD; Art. 8 para. 2, 3 and 4; 12 para. 2 and 3; 16 para. 1; 19 para. 1 DCD). It therefore forms a new structural element within the European contract law.[21]

V. Objectification of the Concept of Contract

The orientation of the "Twin Directives" towards standardised objective criteria for the conformity with the contract – such as the "fit for purpose-test" and the reasonable expectations of the consumer – has relativised the individual-subjective understanding of the contract even further than the previous legal acts. The inclusion of the objective criteria in Art. 2 CSD and the consideration of public declarations of preceding links in the contractual chain (Art. 2 CSD; now Art. 8 para. 1, lett. b DCD; Art. 7 para. 1, let. d SGD) had previously limited the traditionally prevailing view that the content of the contract is essentially determined by the corresponding declarations of intent of the parties.[22] Even further, the "Twin Directives" now establish the same ranking of the objective with the subjective criteria (Art. 8, lett. 1 DCD; Art. 7, lett. 1 SGD) to protect the consumer if the (subjective) criteria provided for in the respective contract are less favorable for him than the objective requirements established by the directive. With this equating of the subjective and objective criteria, the relativization of the traditional view reaches a new level.[23]

In a way, this objectification of the requirements for conformity with the contract can be seen in the broader context of the standardization of contracting. The idea of the individually negotiated contract no longer reflects the reality of mass production, mass

---

[20] Hans Schulte-Nölke, 'Digital obligations of sellers of smart devices under the Sale of Goods Directive 771/2019' in Sebastian Lohsse et al. (eds) *Smart Products* (2022), 47 et seq; Christiane Wendehorst, 'The update obligation – how to make it work in the relationship between seller, producer, digital content or service provider and consumer' in Sebastian Lohsse et al. (eds) *Smart Products* (2022), 63 et seq; André Janssen, 'The Update Obligation for Smart Products – Time Period for the Update Obligation and Failure to Install the Update' in Sebastian Lohsse et al. (eds) *Smart Products* (2022), 91 et seq.
[21] Reiner Schulze, 'Die Digitale-Inhalte-Richtlinie – Innovation und Kontinuität im europäischen Vertragsrecht' (2019) 4 *ZEuP*, 695, 722.
[22] Reiner Schulze and Fryderyk Zoll, *European Contract Law* (2021), ch. 2 mn. 7 et seq., ch. 3 mn. 58.
[23] Reiner Schulze, 'European Private Law in the Digital Age – Developments, Challenges and Prospects', in André Janssen et al. (eds), *The Future of European Private Law* (forthcoming 2023), II. 2. b).

distribution and the corresponding mass contracting, which includes a "standardization" of both contract terms and customer expectations. This standardization was already well advanced in the 20th century. As a result of digitization, it can now be considered as the regular practice for concluding contracts on the internet, while the individual design of contract content and the process of concluding the contract became the exception. To this extent, the equality of subjective and objective criteria for conformity connects both: the concern to compensate for presumed structural asymmetries in the relationship between the contracting parties; and the adaptation of contract law to the considerably increased importance of mass contracting in contract practice.

VI. Remedies

14 Finally, only a few new accents can be highlighted here with regard to the remedies: According to Art. 14 para. 2 and 3 DCD, the trader now has the right to choose the means to bring digital products into conformity (whereas Art. 13 para. 2 SGD continues to retain the consumer's right of choice for the sale of goods, as did formerly Art. 3 para. 3 CSD). Moreover, unlike the former traditions in some Member States to bind the rescission from the contract to a judicial decision, it is now also explicitly stated that the right to terminate the contract is to be exercised by means of a statement to the trader (Art. 15 DCD; Art. 16 para. 1 SGD). It can therefore be assumed that the termination of the contract is conceived as a formative right ("*Gestaltungsrecht*") of the entitled party.[24]

15 However, the most important innovation in terms of contract termination is probably, that the DCD contains a comprehensive regime of the legal consequences of the termination of a contract including a number of new legal instruments. It sets out the mutual rights and obligations of trader and consumer (in contrast to most other provisions of the Directive which only deal with obligations of the trader and corresponding rights of the consumer). The new legal instruments of this regime take into account the importance of data as the subject of contractual obligations in the digital age with regard to the failure of contracts. For example, they provide the prohibition of the use of data, the right to retrieve data, the blocking of access to data and the obligation to delete data (Art. 16 and 17 DCD).

C. Impact on the Law of Member States

I. General Framework

16 The impact of these innovative approaches and the other provisions of the "Twin Directives" on the law of the Member States depends to a large extent on the general framework of implementation in the respective Member State. Above all, it can be crucial, in which code or legal act the Member State has transposed these Directives and whether their transposition has an impact on the structure of the existing general law of obligations and contracts and consumer law or other areas of law such as intellectual property law and data protection law.

17 As far as the general framework of implementation in the 27 Member States is concerned, however, a rather complex picture emerges. The approaches of the national legislators differ both in terms of "where" and "how" of implementation. With regard

---

[24] On rescission as a "formative right" see e.g. Renate Schaub, in: Gerhard Dannemann and Reiner Schulze (eds), German Civil Code I (2020), § 437, mn. 9.

C. Impact on the Law of Member States

to the "where" in the context of the national legislative acts, a large number of Member States have opted for the implementation of one or both of the Directives by new acts outside the existing codes (e.g. among many others Romania[25]; Croatia[26] and Malta[27] regarding the DCD). Some of them have transposed both directives together into one act (e.g. Bulgaria[28]; Hungary[29], combining an overarching general part with two separate chapters for sales of goods and for supply of digital content and digital services). However, a number of other Member States have preferred integration into an existing code for either or both of the Directives. Among these, most have chosen integration with the Consumer code (e.g. Bulgaria,[30] Finland,[31] France,[32] Italy[33] and Latvia[34]; Malta[35] only SGD), but some have incorporated the provision implementing both or one of the Directives into their Law of obligations Act (e.g. Estonia[36]; Croatia[37] only the SGD), into their Law on the Sale of goods (e.g. Denmark[38]) or into their Civil code (e.g. The Netherlands,[39] Germany,[40] and, to a large extent, Czech Republic[41]).

18 With regard to the "how" of implementation, there are considerable differences mainly from two points of view. Firstly, in contrast to the close adherence to the wording of the Directives in some Member States, other Member States have chosen a partial interweaving with some of their own national concepts (e.g. Germany by combining the criteria of the SGD for conformity with the contract with the traditional German concepts for material and legal defects in § 434 BGB).[42] Secondly, some Member States have strictly adhered to the scope of application of the Directives when transposing them (e.g. The Netherlands[43] and Hungary,[44] among others), while others have preferred an extended implementation of some of the provisions or principles of the Directives beyond the scope prescribed by European legislation (including France[45] and Germany[46]).

19 Against this background, a highly differentiated finding emerges with regard to framework conditions for the impact of the "Twin Directives" on the law of obligations in the respective jurisdiction. It suggests that favorable starting conditions for a relatively strong impact may exist as far as the implementation provisions are integrated into the overall framework of a Code of obligations or of a Civil code. Less favorable conditions for a significant influence on the national law of obligations beyond the scope of the Directives are likely to be assumed if the Directives are implemented in a separate legal act by almost verbatim reproduction, and the previously existing structure of the Code of

---

[25] See the country report on Romania, in this volume.
[26] See the country report on Croatia, in this volume.
[27] See the country report on Malta, in this volume.
[28] See the country report on Bulgaria, in this volume.
[29] See the country report on Hungary, in this volume.
[30] See the country report on Bulgaria, in this volume.
[31] See the country report on Finland, in this volume.
[32] See the country report on France, in this volume.
[33] See the country report on Italy, in this volume.
[34] See the country report on Latvia, in this volume.
[35] See the country report on Malta, in this volume.
[36] See the country report on Estonia, in this volume.
[37] See the country report on Croatia, in this volume.
[38] See the country report on Denmark, in this volume.
[39] See the country report on The Netherlands, in this volume.
[40] See the country report on Germany, in this volume.
[41] See the country report on Czech Republic, in this volume.
[42] See the country report on Germany, in this volume.
[43] See the country report on The Netherlands, in this volume.
[44] See the country report on Hungary, in this volume.
[45] See the country report on France, in this volume.
[46] See the country report on Germany, in this volume.

obligations or of the Civil code therefore remains unaffected. In addition to the transposition of the DCD in Estonia and some other countries, the German transposition offers a remarkable example of an obviously relatively far-reaching impact on the law of obligation in the case of integration into the Civil code. In particular, with this integration, the German legislature has adapted the systematics of the BGB to the changes of the digital age by inserting a new title on "Contracts on Digital Products" into the General Law of Obligations to implement the provisions of the DCD (§§ 327 et seq. BGB). Furthermore, it has not only changed the consumer sales law in the BGB in accordance with the SGD. Rather, it opted for extended implementation and revised some provisions of the General Sales Law according to the patterns provided in the Directive (in particular by adopting a large part of the criteria for conformity with the contract and the equation of these criteria with the subjective ones in General Sales Law to extend them to all sales contracts; § 434 para. 3 BGB).[47]

20   As for the impact of the "Twin Directives" on the structures of consumer law, this goes hand in hand with the impact on the law of obligations where the consumer law is incorporated into the Civil code. If in contrast the two directives or one of them has been incorporated into a consumer code (as in Finland,[48] Italy,[49] France[50] and Latvia,[51] among others), this incorporation should regularly lead to a corresponding extension of the national system of consumer law. However, the further impact on the conceptual structure of the national consumer law seems to differ in each Member State in these cases. It is likely to depend not least on the method of incorporation, particularly on the extent to which the incorporation into the consumer code is limited to a mere compilation or includes further interlocking.

21   Finally, as far as the references to legal areas other than the law of obligations and consumer law are concerned, based on the country reports, there do not appear to be any direct significant influences of the implementation of the "Twin Directives" on intellectual property law structures in the Member States. However, another aspect remains to be pointed out: In connection with the implementation of these Directives, some Member States have clarified the relationship between contract law and data protection with regard to the contractual consequences of a withdrawal of consent under data protection law (e.g. Estonia and Germany).[52]

II. Definitions and Scope of Application

22   As outlined with regard to the innovative feature of the "Twin Directives"[53] both Directives contain a considerable body of definitions and explanations of numerous terms that are fundamental to contracting in the digital age – from "digital content" to, for example, "continuous supply over a period of time". In the course of the implementation of the DCD and the SGD and according to the respective type of implementation, this body has passed into the Member States laws. It now forms a common pool of national contract laws in the EU. Certainly, it must be taken into account that some Member States have further developed individual definitions independently. But in doing so, they generally relied on the provisions of the Directives and have only created conceptual

---

[47] See the country report on Germany, in this volume.
[48] See the country report on Finland, in this volume.
[49] See the country report on Italy, in this volume.
[50] See the country report on France, in this volume.
[51] See the country report on Latvia, in this volume.
[52] See below V.2.
[53] Above II.1.

C. Impact on the Law of Member States

variations on a common European basis. For example, in German law the generic term "digital products" combines the terms "digital content" and "digital services" from the DCD. For the definition of this generic term, however, § 327 para. 1 and 2 BGB refers to the definitions of the two individual terms covered by it as designed in art. 2 para. 1 and 2 DCD.[54] A similar solution was chosen by the Austrian legislator, by introducing the generic term "digital performance".[55]

As regards the subjective scope of application it is noteworthy that Denmark has introduced a special intermediary rule,[56] which states that if two natural/private persons engage in a contract through an active professional intermediary, the contract between the two persons is regarded as a consumer contract and therefore the buyer profits of the consumer protection rules. Also other Member States (e.g. Italy[57] and Portugal[58]) introduced special rules regarding the contractual role and liability of online platforms. 23

Moreover, with regard to the impact of the "Twin Directives", it has already been addressed that the relevance of the definitions of these Directives is not necessarily limited to the scope of the national provisions transposing them. Rather, they can also serve as a model for future legislation in neighboring fields (for example, if a Member State wants to create rules for contracts between traders concerning data). Even if the legislator does not act, they can provide inspiration for case law and contractual practice on how to conceptualise the relevant situations in such neighboring fields. This potential impact of the terms and definitions of the Directives outside the current legislation of the Member States is difficult to assess in detail, but could reach far beyond the direct effect of the transposition provisions. 24

As regards the general scope of the provisions transposing the Directives, a number of Member States have limited this scope to the extent provided by Art. 3 DCD and Art. 3 SGD (for example, as mentioned, among many others The Netherlands[59]), while other Member States have opted for a broader transposition[60] (so-called "gold plating"). This extension may concern a single rule of the Directives, a set of their rules, or a principle underlying one of their rules. An outstanding example of such an extension – besides the application of a number of provisions of the SGD beyond consumer law in Germany – is the establishment of the principle arising from Art. 3 para. 1 subpara. 2 DCD regarding the provision of data by the consumer in France. Since the implementation of the Directive, the French Code de consommation contains provisions on such counter-performance in non-monetary form also for contracts outside the scope of Art. 3 DCD.[61] Another example is the broad Latvian reform of time limits, which extended the solutions provided in the "Twin Directives" also beyond business to consumers contracts.[62] This "gold plating" in some of the Member States indicates that in principle a considerable part of the provisions of the Directives can also be a model for future national legislation beyond the scope of application defined by the European legislator (provided that the relevant national legislature has the corresponding intention). Likewise, in the absence of national legislation, it can be considered as a source of inspiration for case law and 25

---

[54] See the country report on Germany, in this volume.
[55] See the country report on Austria, in this volume.
[56] See the country report on Denmark, in this volume. See also Marie Jull Sørensen, 'Digitale formidlingsplatforme – formidlingsreglen i dansk forbrugerret', *Ugeskrift for Retsvæsen*, U.2017B.119, 2017, pp. 119–127.
[57] See the country report on Italy, in this volume.
[58] See the country report on Portugal, in this volume.
[59] See the country report on The Netherlands, in this volume.
[60] Above III.1.
[61] See the country report on France, in this volume.
[62] See the country report on Latvia, in this volume.

contractual practice in such areas (similar to what has just been mentioned for the impact of the definitions in the Directives).

26 Furthermore, the country reports show that the transposition of the "Twin Directives" in some Member States – but by no means in all – has triggered or intensified a lively discussion on the further development of contract theory in the light of the changes caused by digitization, in particular on the patterns for the classification of contract types and on the understanding of the contractual synallagma with regard to the role of data as counterperformance. At present, however, the status of such considerations arising in the context of the transposition of the Directives seems to vary considerably between Member States. It therefore remains to be seen whether a Union-wide discourse on the new challenges for the theory of the Treaty will develop and which aspects will come to the fore.

D. Conformity with the Contract

I. The implementation of subjective and objective criteria for conformity

27 The provisions of the Twin Directives on conformity with the contract appear to have had considerable influence on the development of the law in the Member States, particularly with regard to the subjective and objective requirements of the conformity with the contract for the sale of goods and the supply of digital content and services. This influence may extend to the basic concepts in this area, as is particularly evident in Ireland. There, as a result of the implementation of the Directives, a displacement of traditional common law concepts in favour of the Directive's conceptualisation of conformity with the contract can be observed.[63]

28 But also in the other Member States a far-reaching impact of the Directive can be seen in particular through the establishment of two requirements in national contract law: the duty to inform and supply the consumer with updates, which is provided for in both Directives both as a subjective and as an objective requirement of conformity[64] (Art. 7 lett. d and Art. 8 para. 2 DCD; Art. 6 lett. d and Art. 7 para. 3 SGD); and durability, which is laid down as an objective requirement for goods in Art. 8 para. 1 lett. d SGD. Neither of these requirements was regulated, at least in this explicit form, in the contract law of most Member States, but were only introduced in the course of the transposition of the Directives. The only exceptions to this are the provisions contained in § 7 of the newly created Austrian Consumer Warranty Act (VGG) on the obligation to update digital services and goods with digital elements. Pursuant to § 1 para. 3 VGG, these also apply to B2B contracts. However, since this provision is unilaterally mandatory only in favour of consumers according to § 3 VGG, the provisions on the updating obligation can be waived in the case of a B2B transaction.[65] The Austrian Supreme Court of Justice has so far rejected an analogous application of consumer law provisions to B2B transac-

---

[63] See the country report on Ireland, in this volume.
[64] See above II.4.
[65] Explanatory Notes on the Government Draft of the GRUG (No. 949 of the Supplements to the Stenographic Protocols of the National Council of the XXVII Legislative Period), 15; Kristin Nemeth, in: Johannes W. Flume et al. (eds), *VGG* (2022), § 7, mn. 38; Christiane Wendehorst, 'Die Regelungen des VGG zu digitalen Leistungen unter besonderer Berücksichtigung der Aktualisierungspflichten' in Peter Bydlinski (ed), *Das neue Gewährleistungsrecht* (2022), 49 (69 et seqq).

D. Conformity with the Contract

tions as well – except for individual cases in which there was a pronounced imbalance between the contracting parties.[66]

This also applies to the provisions which were introduced into national law to supplement the provisions on the update duty with regard to the liability exemption for the case in which the consumer fails to install an update and with regard to the modification of the contract in the case of upgrades on the basis of Art. 8 para. 3 and Art. 19 DCD.[67] These provisions now form common core components of consumer contract law in the states in the European Union.

29

For the implementation of these two and further requirements, which the "Twin Directives" provide for conformity with the contract, and the supplementary provisions just mentioned, two basic forms can be recognised (in each case with variations in single Member States). On the one hand, a number of Member States have introduced these requirements into their national law within the framework of a literal or almost literal adoption of the relevant provisions of the Directives on conformity with the contract, for example France with regard to a large part of the provisions of the DCD and the SGD on conformity.[68] In this respect, they have directly transferred the structure and terminology used by the Directives with regard to conformity with the contract to national law (be it as a supplement to a corresponding structure and terminology already in use in the respective national law for other matters; be it as a new approach for the respective national law).[69] In this way, the model of the Directives for conformity with the contract, including its new components of update and durability requirements, has directly shaped the structure and terminology of national contract law in the scope of application of the transposition provisions in a number of Member States.

30

On the other hand, Member States have tried to adapt the provisions of the Directives on the requirements for conformity with the contract to already existing structures of national contract law and to integrate them into their own national terminology. This effort to combine the requirements of the Directives with their own national tradition is evident, for example, when the traditional concepts of "material defects" and "legal defects" are used in national sales law to determine conformity with the contract. The subjective and objective requirements of the Directives for conformity with the contract can be understood from this perspective as prerequisites for ensuring that the digital products or the goods are "free from material defects or from legal defects".

31

On this basis, German legislation in particular comes to a far-reaching integration of new requirements (such as the durability of the good) into an already existing structure and terminology of national sales law. These requirements are laid down in § 434 BGB as prerequisites for the good being "free from material defects". Accordingly, § 435 BGB adapts the implementation of Art. 9 SGD to the concept of "legal defects". However, this integration into a pre-existing structure may be accompanied by an extension of the scope of application of SGD requirements beyond consumer sales to contracts between other parties, if this corresponds to the pre-existing structure and terminology of na-

32

---

[66] RIS-Justiz RS0065288; RS0065327; OGH 11.08.2020 – 4 Ob 71/20z – *VbR* 2020, 213 (213 et seq.). For more details see the country report on Austria in this volume.

[67] Several criticisms have been raised in this regard. See e.g. the country reports on The Netherlands and Italy, in this volume.

[68] However with terminological modifications with regard to "subjective conformity" and "normal features", with an extended definition of updates etc.; for more details see the country report on France in this volume.

[69] The latter for example in Bulgaria, where, however, the close adherence to the Directives was combined with a few terminological accents of their own as the replacement of "subjective" criteria of conformity by "individual" criteria.

tional law (as shown in German law by § 434 BGB).[70] Also in Austria, the lack of durability of an item sometimes triggers warranty obligations under general law of obligations: Even before the implementation of the "Twin Directives", the Austrian Supreme Court of Justice ruled that it was generally expected in legal transactions that a brand-new motor vehicle engine would remain functional for more than two years.[71] Thus, the Austrian Supreme Court of Justice assumed that a certain functional life of an object can be considered as a usually presupposed characteristic within the meaning of § 922 para. 1 ABGB, for which liability is assumed under warranty law.[72]

33 The impact of the requirements laid down by the Directive on national law is thus veiled by the integration into the structures of national law; however, it can in fact affect national law far beyond the scope of application provided for by the Directive itself. Moreover, the combination of the traditional concept of "material defects" with the patterns of the Directive could lead to a further development of the conceptualisation of national law for the new matter of the supply of digital content and digital services, in that the new concept of "free of product defects" has been created for this matter to implement the provisions of the DCD on conformity with the contract.[73] In this conceptual respect, too, the most recent EU legislation has thus prompted an adaptation of national law to the changes brought about by digitisation, even if the Member State concerned has not fully adopted the conceptual structure of the Directives with regard to conformity with the contract.

II. Measures to Improve Sustainability and the Circular Economy

34 Measures to improve environmental sustainability and the circular economy were discussed in most Member States in the course of the implementation process of the Twin Directives, but in the end not taken. A positive exception in this regard is e.g. Spain, where the legislator has provided for generous after-sales services and availability of spare parts (Art. 127 *bis* TR-LGDCU). Discussions mainly focused on extending the warranty period beyond the minimum required by the SGD, on introducing an obligation to provide information on the minimum durability of goods and a direct consumer claim against the manufacturer or importer.[74] The reasons given for not implementing the other measures included the need to avoid excessive additional burdens for companies and expected initiatives of the EU in the area of sustainability in the future.[75]

III. Modification of Digital Content or Digital Service

35 While the DCD regulates in Art. 19 the modification of Digital Content or Digital Service, no specific provision in this regard is contained in the SGD and in the Member States' implementing provisions. This in regrettable, especially considered the circumstance that the modification of digital content may significantly affect the functioning of

---

[70] In German law, this extension concerns durability and a number of other performance features provided for in the SGD, but not the updating requirement; see the country report on Germany, in this volume.
[71] OGH 23.04.2015 – 1 Ob 71/15w – Zak 2015, 256 (256 et seq.).
[72] See for more details the country report on Austria, in this volume.
[73] See country report on Germany, in this volume, with regard to § 327 d BGB.
[74] See e.g. the country report on Austria, in this volume.
[75] See for the latest developments in this regard: EU Commission, 'Sustainable Product Policy and Ecodesign', at <https://single-market-economy.ec.europa.eu/industry/sustainability/sustainable-product-policy-ecodesign_en> accessed 15 January 2023.

goods with digital elements. It is desirable that the solutions contained in the DCD regarding the modification of Digital Content will be extended to the SGD. Though the abovementioned lack could theoretically be remedied by an intervention of the Member States' legislators, maximum harmonization may hinder that.

IV. The interruption of long-term supply of digital content or digital services

36 Regarding the case of interruption of a continuous supply of digital services, some Member States (e.g. Ireland and Lithuania), inspired by Recital 51 DCD, addressed the problem of short-term interruptions in relation to continuous supply contracts. Accordingly, the Irish legislator stated in s. 52 para. 4 Consumer Rights Act 2022 that where during such a continuous contract there is a short-term interruption of the supply which having regard to the type and purpose of the digital content or digital service and the circumstances and nature of the contract, is more than negligible, or which recurs, there is deemed to be a lack of conformity giving rise to remedies under the proposed legislation.[76]

E. Liability of the Trader

37 The impact of the provisions of the "Twin Directives" on the liability of the trader is essentially the same as has just been summarised for conformity with the contract. The implementation of these provisions has led to the fact that in the Member States there are now regulations for the liability of the trader which did not previously exist in such a specific way in most national laws. These rules concern consumer contracts for the supply of digital content and digital services and consumer sales contracts for goods and in particular for goods with digital elements; and in some Member States they also extend to contracts between other parties.

38 The Directives have thus had the effect that contractual liability in the law of the Member States has developed on a common basis in important areas in view of changes resulting from digitalization. This development has, however, taken quite different forms in the individual countries. The basic pattern is on the one hand the almost unbroken adoption of the terminology and structure of the Directives and on the other hand the extensive adaptation to the terminology and structures of the respective national law (similar to conformity with the contract). For example, some Member States have first laid down the liability of the trader in general terms in a basic standard along the lines of Art. 11 DCD and Art. 10 SGD, before the remedies of the consumer are laid down in subsequent provisions along the lines of Art. 13 et seq. DCD and Art. 13 ff. SGD. In contrast, other Member States have dispensed with such a separate regulation of liability in a separate standard. In these latter legal systems, the liability of the trader results implicitly from the provisions on the consumer's rights in the event of a lack of conformity with the contract (or in other terminology: in the event of a defect of the good or the digital product).[77] Unlike most other Member States, Portugal has used the possibility provided by Recitals 23 of SGD and 18 of DCD, stating that the online marketplace

---

[76] Recital 51 DCD: "[...] Short-term interruptions of the supply of digital content or a digital service should be treated as instances of lack of conformity where those interruptions are more than negligible or recur [...].
[77] E.g. in Germany §§ 327 i, 327 m; 437, 439 ff. BGB.

provider that, acting for purposes related to its activity, is a contractual partner of the trader that provides the good, the digital content or the digital service is jointly liable for the lack of conformity.[78] The decisive criterion for the liability of the online marketplace provider is the predominant influence on the contract concluded between consumer and trader. Such solution was significantly influenced by the ELI Model Rules on Online Platforms.[79]

39 However, much more than the different approaches to the transposition of the Directives' provisions on liability, the considerable differences in national provisions surrounding the transposition of the Directives could lead to problems with regard to the objective of European legislation "to achieve a genuine digital single market, increase legal certainty and reduce transaction costs, in particular for small and medium-sized enterprises".[80] In particular, the persisting differences in national laws regarding the consequences of a failure to deliver or to supply with respect to obstacles such as impossibility or *force majeure* and the effects of a serious change in circumstances could affect the willingness to engage in cross-border transactions. For example, for the change of circumstances in some Member States an adaptation of the contract and in special cases even the right to revoke the contract is provided for, but with different conditions in detail in the respective Countries,[81] while in other Member States there is no such regulation at all. The almost unlimited possibility for the Member States to determine the reasons for the exclusion of contractual obligations (e.g. change of circumstances or impossibility) in their own way relativises the duty to supply provided for in Art. 5 DCD.[82]

40 The lack of harmonisation of such neighbouring matters must therefore be taken into account as a factor that is likely to reduce the impact of the Directives on the harmonisation of contractual liability in sales law and in the supply of digital content and digital services in contractual practice.

F. Remedies

I. Repair and replacement

41 As already after the implementation of Directive 1999/44/EC, national legal systems provide the primacy of the creation of a defect-free condition through repair or replacement.

42 The exact role and competences of the judge in case a consumer invokes the 'wrong' remedy is disputed in some Member States.[83] In this regard it is necessary to consider, also concerning the implementing rules of DCD and SGD, the *CJEU Duarte* decision, according to which national legislation shall not preclude the national court hearing the dispute to grant of its own motion an appropriate reduction in the price of goods which are the subject of a contract of sale in the case where a consumer who is entitled to

---

[78] See the country report on Austria, in this volume. Cf. the country report on Italy, in this volume.
[79] European Law Institute, 'Model Rules on Online Platforms', <https://www.europeanlawinstitute.eu/projects-publications/completed-projects-old/online-platforms> accessed 15 January 2023. See Christoph Busch et al., "An Introduction to the ELI Model Rules on Online Platforms" (2020) 2 *EuCML*, 61.
[80] Recital 3 DCD.
[81] See for example in more detail for France and Germany Claude Witz, 'Störung des vertraglichen Gleichgewichts im neuen französischen Schuldrecht', in Florian Bien and Jean-Sébastien Borghetti, *Die Reform des französischen Vertragsrechts* (2018), p. 119 et seq.
[82] Reiner Schulze, 'Die Digitale-Inhalte-Richtlinie – Innovation und Kontinuität im europäischen Vertragsrecht' (2019) 4 *ZEuP*, 695, 707, 723.
[83] See in particular the country report on Belgium, in this volume.

such a reduction brings proceedings which are limited to seeking only rescission of that contract and such rescission cannot be granted because the lack of conformity in those goods is minor, even though that consumer is not entitled to refine his initial application or to bring a fresh action to that end.[84]

Most national legislators chose not to provide for fixed periods that could generally be considered reasonable for repair or replacement, although the Directives allow to do so. Therefore, it will be up to the national judge to determine the reasonableness of the period for repair or replacement. As for exceptions to that approach, some Member States (e.g. Portugal[85] and Slovenia[86]) provided that the period for repair or replacement shall not exceed 30 days. Furthermore, the Portuguese legislator expressly exempted from this regime situations where the nature and complexity of the goods, the seriousness of the lack of conformity and the effort necessary for the repair or replacement justify a longer period, while in Slovenia the reasonable time limit may be further extended by a maximum of 15 days if it is necessary for the completion of repair or replacement.[87] In other Countries (e.g. Sweden[88]) the consumer normally would be entitled to resort to the secondary remedies only after two failed attempts. 43

To the lists provided for in DCD and SGD, the Portuguese law adds as grounds for the possibility of exercising the remedies to price reduction and termination of the contract the manifestation of a new lack of conformity. In Romania the trader is obliged to bring the digital content or digital service into compliance, within a period not exceeding 15 calendar days from the moment the trader was informed of the non-compliance and which is expressly agreed upon with the consumer, without causing significant costs or significant inconveniences to the consumer.[89] 44

Repair and replacements have to be executed "without costs" for the consumer. In particular, the SGD "codified" the achievements of the Court of Justice of the European Union, in particular in the judgements *Quelle*,[90] regarding the normal use made of the replaced goods during the period prior to their replacement (Art. 14, para. 4 SGD) and *Putz/Weber*,[91] regarding the costs of installation and removal of the non-conforming goods (Art. 14, para. 3 SGD). This development has to be welcomed and marks a good example of a virtuous interplay between case law and legislation. The implementation provisions in some Member States (e.g. Austria) explicitly provide that the trader has to bear also shipping and transport costs,[92] others also including in this notion labour, materials which may be necessary to bring the good into conformity with the contract (e.g. Bulgaria).[93] Also the German legislator rightly provided that the seller must bear all expenses required for the purpose of cure, including transport (§ 439 para. 2 BGB). If the buyer has installed the defective good in another good in accordance with its nature and purpose of use or has affixed it to another good, the seller is also obliged within the scope of cure to reimburse the buyer for the expenses necessary for removing the defec- 45

---

[84] CJEU 3 October 2013, C-32/12, *Soledad Duarte Hueros v Autociba SA and Automóviles Citroën España SA*.
[85] See the country report on Portugal, in this volume.
[86] See the country report on Slovenia, in this volume.
[87] Art. 82 (2) CPA-1.
[88] See the country report on Sweden, in this volume.
[89] See the country report on Romania, in this volume.
[90] CJEU, 17 April 2008, C-404/06, *Quelle AG v Bundesverband der Verbraucherzentralen und Verbraucherverbände*.
[91] CJEU, 16 June 2011, C-65/09 and C-87/09, *Gebr. Weber GmbH v Jürgen Wittmer* and *Ingrid Putz v Medianess Electronics GmbH*. See also CJEU 23 May 2019, C-52/18, *Christian Fülla v Toolport GmbH*.
[92] See the country report on Austria, in this volume.
[93] See the country report on Bulgaria, in this volume.

tive thing and for the installation or affixing of the repaired or newly delivered thing free of defects (§ 439 para. 3 BGB). Specifically for consumer sales, it is also stipulated that in these two situations the consumer can demand advanced payment from the trader (§ 475 para. 4 BGB).[94]

46   By implementing the Twin Directives, some Member States entitled the buyer (or a third party on his behalf) to repair the defective good at the seller's expense if the seller abusively refuses to heed the consumer's choice (e.g. France)[95] or if the buyer has claimed repair from the seller but the seller has failed to do so within a reasonable period (see e.g. Estonia).[96]

EU Member States did not introduce specific rules on the place of repair and replacement nor on the transport costs: answers to these questions will therefore have to be found under the general law of obligations and contracts, taking into account the guidelines given by the CJEU in the *Fülla* case.[97]

47   The place of performance and subsequent performance continues to be determined according to the traditional rules of national law, which have not been changed in way of implementation. Even if the place of repair is therefore in principle to be determined according to the general rules on the place of performance, it must however be taken into account that the consumer must not suffer any "considerable inconvenience" (cf. Art. 14 para. 1 SGD). It must therefore be examined in each individual case whether this limit is exceeded, for example, if the way to the work takes unusually long when repairing a car.

II. Right of withdrawal, right to termination and price reduction

48   Both "Twin Directives" provide that the consumer shall exercise the right to terminate the contract by means of a statement to the trader expressing the decision to terminate the contract (Art. 15 DCD and Art. 16 SGD). This required some Member States (e.g. Austria) to adapt their warranty law, which previously stated that the right to price reduction or termination of the contract had to be asserted in Court.[98] In other Member States (e.g. France) this was already possible before the implementation of the twin Directives. Until the 2016 reform of the French general contract law, the *Code civil* did not accept termination by notice and termination normally had to be pronounced by the judge. The 2016 reform introduced termination by notice, however, so that there is now no discrepancy between the *Code de la consommation* and the *Code civil* in that respect.[99] In Germany, the consumer may terminate the contract if the trader does not immediately fulfil his due obligation to supply the digital product in response to a request by the consumer (§ 327 c, para. 1 *BGB*). In addition to this right of the consumer, which corresponds to Art. 13 DCD, § 327 c (2) *BGB* provides that the consumer may claim damages and compensation for futile expenses according to the general provisions of the German law of obligations.[100]

---

[94] See the country report on Germany, in this volume.
[95] Such regulation in national law is explicitly allowed under recital 54 SGD. See the country report on France, in this volume.
[96] See the country report on Estonia, in this volume.
[97] CJEU, Case C-52/18, 23 May 2019, *Christian Fülla v Toolport GmbH*.
[98] See e.g. the country report on Austria, in this volume.
[99] See the country report on France, in this volume.
[100] See the country report on Germany, in this volume.

III. The restitutions

After the cancellation of the contract or after the price reduction, the trader must refund the payments using the same means that were originally used (Art. 16 DCD and Art. 18, para. 2 SGD). Regarding the beginning of this 14-day period some Member States (e.g. Austria) do not refer to the day on which the trader is informed of the consumer's decision to terminate the contract, but to the time of receipt of the declaration of termination.[101]

Some EU Member States explicitly regulated the contractual consequences of consumer's withdrawal of consent to the processing of personal data. E.g. the Estonian legislator clarified that withdrawal of consent by the consumer should not be considered a breach of contract and does not entitle the trader to exercise any remedies against the consumer. The same provision excludes the trader's claim for damages in case of withdrawal of consent.[102] Worth mentioning is the solution provided by the Greek legislator, according to which, in case of termination the value of the data provided by the consumer should be calculated and reimbursed. The problem of calculation of the value of personal data will also arise when the recipient chooses to invoke the right to ask for a (proportionate) reduction of the price.[103] An attempt to regulate this issue was made – but in the end did not find concretization in the implementing rules of the DCD – by the Latvian legislator: the later withdrawn proposal provided that if after the consent's withdrawal the consumer still uses digital content (services) but no longer wants to remunerate the trader with personal data, he assumes duty to pay in money.[104] In any case, the calculation of the amount of money may be cumbersome.

IV. Hierarchy of Remedies and Environmental Sustainability

Stimulating consumers to require repair should encourage sustainable consumption and could contribute to greater durability of products (cf. Recital 48 SGD). While doctrinal and parliamentary[105] debate took place with regard to the opportunity to prioritize repair over replacement in way of implementation of the SGD, no Member State did adopt an explicit solution in this sense, although this has been subject to criticism in several Countries.[106] According to Art. 13 SGD, the consumer may choose between repair and replacement, unless the remedy chosen would be impossible or, compared to the other remedy, would impose costs on the seller that would be disproportionate. Some Member States provide the same rule for cases, which fall outside the scope of application of the SGD.[107] The French legislator did promote repair when implementing the SGD, by introducing an additional guarantee period in case the consumer opts for that remedy (see art. L-217-13 *Code de la Consommation*).[108] An interesting solution was chosen in Hungary, where – besides the contractual warranty regime – there is in place an additional extracontractual, statutory and mandatory remedy (for repair or replace-

---

[101] See the country report on Austria, in this volume.
[102] See more details in the country report on Estonia, in this volume.
[103] See the country report on Greece, in this volume.
[104] See the country report on Latvia, in this volume.
[105] See e.g. the country report on Belgium, and in particular the Belgian federal action plan for circular economy 2021–2024 <https://emis.vito.be/sites/emis/files/articles/91/2021/PAF%2016%20dec%202021_NL%20Clean%5B1%5D.docx> accessed 15 January 2023.
[106] See e.g. the country reports on Austria and Belgium, in this volume.
[107] See the country reports on Austria and Germany, in this volume.
[108] See the country report on France, in this volume.

ment) on the consumers' side directly against the producer, independent of any European law-making and harmonisation, according to which the consumer may demand – within two years after the latter placed the product on the market – that the producer repairs the product's defect, or, if repair is not possible within an appropriate time limit without causing harm to the consumer's interests, replace it.[109]

At the EU level there is also an ongoing lively discussion on the possibility of a 'circular replacement' (i.e. by a repaired, refurbished or remanufactured good) under the SGD.[110] Following the aforementioned developments, it is desirable and foreseeable that in the near future the EU legislator will amend the SGD in order to prioritize repair.[111]

V. Premature obsolescence of goods and the relationship with the internal rules on unfair commercial practices

51   In order to fight premature obsolescence of goods, no specific rules were adopted in way of implementation of the "Twin Directives".[112] Nevertheless, the consumer may have the right to damages according to tort law, challenge the validity of the contract because of error, complain non conformity because of lack of durability, or terminate the contract because of *laesio enormis*.[113]

Misleading actions or omissions regarding the expected lifespan of a product may also configure an unfair commercial practice,[114] an act of unfair competition or a breach of product safety rules.[115] National case law highlights fundamental criticisms concerning the effectiveness of current European consumer and market law. First of all, they raise serious doubts concerning the aptitude of the existing heterogeneous penalties laid down in way of implementation of the UCPD for effectively tackling the challenge of planned obsolescence, especially regarding goods with digital elements. And, furthermore, they raise the question of how consumer (contract) law could be

---

[109] See the country report on Hungary, in this volume.

[110] See Elias Van Gool and Anaïs Michel, 'The New Consumer Sales Directive 2019/771 and Sustainable Consumption: A Critical Analysis' (2021) *EuCML* 2021 (136) 145–146. See more in the country report on Belgium, in this volume.

[111] See European Commission, 22 March 2023, Proposal for a Directive of the European Parliament and of the Council on common rules promoting the repair of goods and amending Regulation (EU) 2017/2394, Directives (EU) 2019/771 and (EU) 2020/1828, COM(2023) 155 final; Evelyne Terryn, 'A Right to Repair? Towards Sustainable Remedies in Consumer Law' (2019) *European Review of Private Law* 851–873; Eva-Maria Kieninger, 'Recht auf Reparatur ("Right to Repair") und Europäisches Vertragsrecht' (2020) ZEuP 264–278. See also Susanne Augenhofer, 'ELI's Response to the European Commission's Public Consultation on Sustainable Consumption of Goods – Promoting Repair and Reuse' (2022) *European Law Institute*, 2022; BEUC, 'Sustainable Consumption of Goods – Promoting the Right to Repair and Reuse' <https://www.beuc.eu/sites/default/files/publications/beuc-x-2022-034_public_consultation_on_right_to_repair.pdf> accessed 15 January 2023; Elias Van Gool, Anaïs Michel, Bert Keirsbilck and Evelyne Terryn, 'Reply to the Public consultation as Regards the Sustainable Consumption of Goods – Promoting Repair and Reuse Initiative' <https://ec.europa.eu/info/law/better-regulation/have-your-say/initiatives/13150-Sustainable-consumption-of-goods-promoting-repair-and-reuse_en> accessed 15 January 2023.

[112] Elias Van Gool and Anais Michel, 'The New Consumer Sales Directive 2019/771 and Sustainable Consumption: A Critical Analysis' (2021) *EuCML* (136) 144–145; Bert Keirsbilck, Evelyne Terryn, Anaïs Michel and Ivano Alogna, 'Sustainable Consumption and Consumer Protection Legislation', available at < https://www.europarl.europa.eu/RegData/etudes/IDAN/2020/648769/IPOL_IDA(2020)648769_EN.pdf> accessed 15 January 2023.

[113] See the country report on Austria, in this volume.

[114] See e.g. the country reports on Italy and Latvia, in this volume.

[115] See the country report on Austria, in this volume.

improved in order to react to and prevent the above-mentioned phenomenon in the future.[116]

Facing the growing role of the servitized economy, suppliers are incentivized to build products for long-term durability, minimize maintenance needs, and reuse and recycle components.[117] The rules contained in the SGD about durability and the duty to update may stimulate the transition towards a "servitization of sales law". This gives the chance of a longer duration through maintenance through the Internet of Things and remote control. At the same time, it entails a risk of premature obsolescence through digital disruption, which requires the adoption of effective instruments to counteract such a negative phenomenon.

VI. Transfer of the rights against the initial seller from the initial consumer to a subsequent buyer

Member States did not provide the automatic transfer of the rights against the initial seller from the initial consumer to a subsequent buyer. Nevertheless, an assignment of warranty claims is in principle possible according to the national law of most Member States.[118] As regards business to consumer contracts, the provisions on unfair terms play an important role. When implementing the Twin Directives, e.g. the German legislator did not create additional standards to regulate the relationship between the initial seller and a subsequent buyer. However, irrespective of their implementation, a new provision came into force shortly before, which restricts the exclusion of assignments by general terms and conditions (§ 308 No. 9 *BGB*). This is mainly aimed at facilitating legal tech business models. It remains to be seen whether it will also have an impact on assignments from an initial consumer to a subsequent buyer in the case of the digital products under consideration here.[119] In any case, regarding the right of distribution of a copy of a computer program and in the event of the resale of a user license entailing the resale of a copy of a computer program downloaded from the copyright holder's website, the CJEU *UsedSoft*[120] will be relevant. 52

G. Commercial Guarantees

Regarding commercial guarantees, EU Member States did mainly choose to merely reproduce the wording of both Directives. A specific mention deserves the solution chosen by the Irish legislator, according to which where a commercial guarantee is provided to a consumer in relation to goods under a sales contract, and during the period of the guarantee the goods are acquired by another consumer, that other consumer is entitled to rely on the guarantee against the guarantor under s. 40 Consumer Rights Act or the trader (seller) under s. 41 Consumer Rights Act, as if they were the original consumer.[121] 53

---

[116] See the country report on Italy, in this volume.
[117] Arie Van Hoe and Guillaume Croisant (eds), 'Droit et durabilité – Recht en duurzaamheid' (Larcier, Bruxelles, 2022).
[118] See e.g. the country reports on Austria and Latvia, in this volume.
[119] See the country report on Germany, in this volume.
[120] CJEU, Case C-128/11, 3 July 2012, *UsedSoft*.
[121] See the country report on Ireland, in this volume.

H. Time Limits

I. The implementation of the provisions on time limits for the trader's liability

54 The "Twin Directives" attribute a wide discretionality to the Member States in determining the time limits.[122]

As in particular regards the sale of goods, longer liability periods and a longer period of reversed burden of proof could enhance durability and at the same time enhance sustainability and a circular economy. Most EU Countries did not choose for longer liability periods than the minimum periods provided for in the Twin Directives (for some exceptions, see e.g. Cyprus[123], Spain,[124] Portugal,[125] Romania[126] and Sweden[127]), mostly for the purpose of not causing extra burdens for traders and for the risk to fragment the internal market. Other Member States did not adopt a specific regulation in that regard, so the general rule of the law of obligations finds application (e.g. Finland, which provides a time limit of 10 years[128] or Ireland, where a time limit of 6 years applies[129]).

55 Some Member States provided that the prescription period shall not be completed until the expiry of a period of two months from the time when the lack of conformity was discovered (e.g. Greece[130], Italy[131]). Other countries (e.g. Italy) expressly stated that the consumer, who is defendant before a Court for the performance of the contract, may however always ask for repair or replacement, price reduction or termination.[132]

56 Discussions are still ongoing with regard to the opportunity to extend the legal guarantee period for specific categories of goods, which could have contributed to the promotion of goods with a longer lifespan, but such provision was finally not adopted.[133] On a general note, it would have been reasonable to make the provision of updates dependent on the durability foreseen for each type of good.[134]

57 Concerning second-hand goods, Art. 10 para. 6 SGD allows Member States to permit parties to contractually reduce the legal guarantee period to a minimum of one year. Some Member States (e.g. Belgium,[135] Czech Republic,[136] Hungary,[137] Italy,[138] Lithua-

---

[122] See e.g. Beate Gsell, 'Time limits of remedies under Directives (EU) 2019/770 and (EU) 2019/771 with particular regard to hidden defects' in Esther Arroyo Amayuelas and Sergio Cámara Lapuente, *El derecho privado en el nuevo paradigma digital* (Madrid 2020), 101 ff.
[123] See the country report in Cyprus, in this volume.
[124] See the country report on Spain, in this volume.
[125] See the country report on Portugal, in this volume.
[126] See the country report on Romania, in this volume.
[127] See the country report on Sweden, in this volume.
[128] See the country report on Finland, in this volume.
[129] See the country report on Ireland, in this volume.
[130] See the country report on Greece, in this volume.
[131] See the country report on Italy, in this volume.
[132] See the country report on Italy, in this volume.
[133] See the country report on Belgium, in this volume.
[134] See European Parliament Resolution of 25.11.2020 (P9 TA(2020)0318. 2020/2021(INI), paragraph 7(a): "corrective updates – i.e. security and conformity updates – must continue throughout the estimated lifespan of the device, according to product category".
[135] See the country report on Belgium, in this volume.
[136] See the country report on Czech Republic, in this volume.
[137] See the country report on Hungary, in this volume.
[138] See the country report on Italy, in this volume.

H. Time Limits

nia,[139] Luxembourg,[140] Romania[141] and Slovenia[142]) decided to use the SGD's option, allowing the parties for a reduction up to one year. In Portugal the period may be reduced to up to one and a half year, with exception of reconditioned goods, which are considered new goods.[143] Some others (e.g. France[144], Malta[145]) kept in that regard the legal guarantee period of two years.

Furthermore, some Member States extended the period of reversal of the burden of proof for goods (which is now e.g. of two years in Belgium,[146] Cyprus[147] and Spain[148]), going beyond the minimum of one year as provided for by the SGD, thereby bringing a significant enhancement in consumer protection.

58

II. Suspension and interruption

The SGD did not regulate the conditions under which the liability period or limitation period can be suspended or interrupted. Member States were, therefore, free to provide for the suspension or interruption of the liability period or limitation period, for example in the event of repair, replacement or negotiations between the seller and the consumer with a view to an amicable settlement.[149]

59

In way of implementation, some Member States (e.g. Belgium,[150] Croatia,[151] Malta[152] and Portugal[153]) expressly provided that the legal guarantee period shall be suspended during the period required for the repair or replacement of the good or in the event of negotiations between the seller and the consumer with a view to an amicable settlement. In particular, the Portuguese legislator provided that the deadline is suspended for the duration of the out-of-court settlement of the consumer dispute between the consumer and the trader or producer. This deserves to be welcomed also because of the educational nature of the reference, informing the consumer of the existence of faster, cheaper, and more effective ways of resolving the dispute compared to the courts. Particularly detailed is the provision introduced by the Spanish legislator, whereby, further to the aforementioned suspension, the seller/trader is liable within one year after the delivery of the good or the supply of the digital content or service if the same lack of conformity appears again.[154]

60

Other countries provide that in case of replacement or repair of the good, the 2-year time limit starts running again.[155]

61

In other Member States (e.g. France), liability is extended for six months when the good has been repaired pursuant to the legal guarantee of conformity. Besides that, if the consumer chooses to have the good repaired, but the seller does not do so, a new liability

62

---

[139] See the country report on Lithuania, in this volume.
[140] See the country report on Luxembourg, in this volume.
[141] See the country report on Romania, in this volume.
[142] See the country report on Slovenia, in this volume.
[143] See the country report on Portugal, in this volume.
[144] See the country report on France, in this volume.
[145] See the country report on Malta, in this volume.
[146] See the country report on Belgium, in this volume.
[147] See the country report on Cyprus, in this volume.
[148] See the country report on Spain, in this volume.
[149] Recital 44 SGD.
[150] See the country report on Belgium, in this volume.
[151] See the country report on Croatia, in this volume.
[152] See the country report on Malta, in this volume.
[153] See the country report on Portugal, in this volume.
[154] See the country report on Spain, in this volume.
[155] See the country report on Estonia, in this volume.

period attached to the replaced good shall begin to run for the consumer. This provision applies from the day the replaced good is delivered to the consumer.[156] Other countries (Portugal) provide that the repaired or replaced good shall benefit from an additional "guarantee" period of six months for each repair or replacement, up to a maximum of four repairs or replacements.[157] Such choices should be appreciated, as they are suitable to both better protect consumers, and to stimulate a longer lifespan for the purpose of sustainability and the circular economy.

III. The obligation to notify

63   According to Art. 12 SGD, Member States had the option to maintain or introduce provisions stipulating that, in order to benefit from the consumer's rights, the consumer has to inform the seller of a lack of conformity within a period of at least 2 months of the date on which the consumer detected such lack of conformity. Some Member States maintained (e.g. Estonia,[158] Hungary,[159] Malta,[160] The Netherlands,[161] Slovenia[162] and Sweden[163]) or introduced (e.g. Belgium[164] and Latvia[165]) such notification duty, while others refrained from doing so (e.g. Bulgaria,[166] Greece,[167] Germany,[168] Ireland,[169] Luxembourg[170] and Romania[171]) or even erased the previous "obligation" which was already contained in the implementing provisions of the CSD (e.g. Denmark,[172] Italy[173] and Spain[174]). Other Member States (e.g. Finland) simply provide that notification should be made within a reasonable time after the defect was discovered or ought to be discovered.[175]

I. Right of Redress

64   The rules on the right of redress contained in Art. 20 DCD and in Art. 18 SGD can be derogated by an agreement between the seller and the producer and/or other person or persons liable in the chain of commercial transactions. This may significantly reduce the chances of the final seller to be restored from the consequences of the lack of conformity.

---

[156] See the country report on France, in this volume.
[157] See the country report on Portugal, in this volume.
[158] See the country report on Estonia, in this volume, where nevertheless the Author underlines that "the different rules on notification obligation may lead to confusion in the case of a good with digital elements: depending upon whether sales rules or digital content rules are applicable in a given case, a consumer may or may not be obliged to notify the defect within two months".
[159] See the country report on Hungary, in this volume.
[160] See the country report on Malta, in this volume.
[161] See the country report on The Netherlands, in this volume.
[162] See the country report on Slovenia, in this volume.
[163] See the country report on Sweden, in this volume.
[164] See the country report on Belgium, in this volume.
[165] See the country report on Latvia, in this volume.
[166] See the country report on Bulgaria, in this volume.
[167] See the country report on Greece, in this volume.
[168] See the country report on Germany, in this volume.
[169] See the country report on Ireland, in this volume.
[170] See the country report on Luxembourg, in this volume.
[171] See the country report on Romania, in this volume.
[172] See the country report on Denmark, in this volume.
[173] See the country report on Italy, in this volume.
[174] See the country report on Spain, in this volume.
[175] See the country report on Finland, in this volume.

In order to reduce the risk of abuses in this regard, the Belgian legislator introduced an 'enhanced' right of redress, according to which where the seller is liable towards the consumer because of a lack of conformity, he shall be entitled to enforce remedies against the producer or any other contractual intermediary in the transfer of ownership of the consumer goods based on their contractual liability with regard to the goods, without any clause limiting or excluding liability being opposable to him.[176] A similar 'enhanced' right of redress is now also set out in the Belgian implementing provisions of the DCD.[177] Furthermore, the German legislator introduced a limitation period of six months for claims for reimbursement of expenses in the case of the sale of digital products and of two years in the case of the sale of goods (§§ 327 u para. 2 and 445 b BGB). The reversal of the burden of proof in the relationship of the last trader continues in the relationships of the previous links in the business chain to each other (§§ 327 u para. 3 and 478 para. 1 BGB). The preceding link in the business chain cannot rely on deviating agreements to the detriment of the following ones (§§ 327 u para. 4 and 478 para. 2 BGB with further specifications).[178] Recent Spanish case law on *Dieselgate*[179] has accepted that consumers can claim contractual damages from the manufacturer, on the understanding that this is a basic consumer right that could be frustrated by the difficulty of claiming them from a seller who could be insolvent.[180] Portuguese law grants a right of redress both to the trader vis-à-vis the producer or other "person at earlier stages of the contractual chain" and to the online marketplace provider *vis-à-vis* the trader.[181]

J. Relationship with other remedies and enforcement

I. In particular: right to withhold the payment

Some member States (e.g. Germany,[182] Ireland,[183] Italy,[184] Latvia,[185] Romania[186] and Spain[187]) explicitly introduced in way of implementation of the "Twin Directives" a dedicated right to withhold payment. For example, in Germany the consumer has a right to withhold payment according to § 273 BGB if the consumer has a due claim against the trader from the legal relationship from which he is obliged to pay (for example, the due claim for delivery of the good or for supply of the digital product). In addition, the consumer can refuse the payment on the basis of § 320 para. 1 BGB under the conditions that he owes the payment from a mutual contract and that he is not obliged to perform in advance.[188] Furthermore, the Irish legislator provided that the part of the price with-

---

[176] Article 1649sexies OCC, as implementing the SGD. See Bert Keirsbilck, 'Verhaalsrechten' (2022) DCCR (103) 118–127. See also Elias Van Gool and Anaïs Michel, 'The New Consumer Sales Directive 2019/771 and Sustainable Consumption: A Critical Analysis' (2021) *EuCML* (136) 143.
[177] Article 1701/16 OCC. See Bert Keirsbilck, 'Verhaalsrechten' (2022) DCCR (103) 118–127. See more on this in the country report on Belgium, in this volume.
[178] See the country report on Germany, in this volume.
[179] STS of 11.07.2021 (RJ 2020752); STS of 23.07.2021 (RJ 20213583).
[180] See the country report on Spain, in this volume.
[181] See the country report on Portugal, in this volume.
[182] See the country report on Germany, in this volume.
[183] See the country report on Ireland, in this volume.
[184] See the country report on Italy, in this volume.
[185] See the country report on Latvia, in this volume.
[186] See the country report on Romania, in this volume.
[187] See the country report on Spain, in this volume.
[188] See the country report on Germany, in this volume. In detail on the requirements of these provisions Reiner Schulze, in: Gerhard Dannemann and Reiner Schulze (eds), *German Civil Code I* (2020), § 273,

held by the consumer should be proportionate to the decrease in the value of the digital content or digital service received by the consumer that does not conform with the contract compared with the value the digital content or digital service would have if it were in conformity with the contract.[189] Furthermore, the Italian SGD implementing rules (Art 135-*bis*, para. 6 Consumer Code) provide then that the consumer shall have the right to withhold payment of any outstanding part of the price or a part thereof until the seller has fulfilled the seller's obligations under the SGD.[190]

II. Enforcement and penalties

66 In implementing Art. 19 SGD and Art. 21 DCD, some Member States (e.g. Belgium) did enable either public bodies, consumer organizations or professional organizations to take action, partly as a consequence of a broad implementation of the Directive 2019/2161/EU (so called Omnibus Directive).[191] In this regard, Art. 2 para. 6 of the Omnibus Directive provides that Member States shall ensure that when penalties are to be imposed in accordance with Article 21 of Regulation (EU) 2017/2394 (regarding coordinated actions for widespread infringements with a Union dimension), they include the possibility either to impose fines through administrative procedures or to initiate legal proceedings for the imposition of fines, or both, the maximum amount of such fines being at least 4 % of the trader's annual turnover in the Member State or Member States concerned, and this only for the directives amended by the Omnibus Directive.[192] There is no EU requirement to introduce such fines for infringements of the Twin Directives, nor for purely domestic infringements. The Belgian legislator has however chosen for a wider application of such fines to guarantee a coherent national sanctioning system.[193]

67 Also the French legislator introduced a fine, which may be imposed on the trader who obstructs in bad faith the implementation of the guarantee of conformity applying to contracts for the sale of goods or to contracts for the supply of digital content or services. The imposition of the fine can be requested before the court by the Ministry of Finance, consumer associations, the public prosecutor or the consumer himself. The amount of the fine 'can be no higher than 300,000€', but it can be increased, in proportion to the benefit derived from the illegal practices, to 10 % of the trader's average annual turnover, based on the last three annual turnovers known at the date of the decision. Another civil sanction provided by the French legislator consists in enhanced refunds.[194]

68 The solution chosen by the Belgian and the French legislator shall be welcomed. In order to enhance the effectivity of consumer rights, and, inter alia, to enforce the durability of goods and fight premature obsolescence, the abovementioned rule contained in Art. 2 para. 6 of Directive EU 2019/2161 should be extended beyond the scope of application of art 21 of Regulation EU 2017/2394, thereby including all unfair behaviours and not only the cases in which there is a reasonable suspicion that a widespread infringe-

---

mn. 6 et seq.; Max Oehm, in: Gerhard Dannemann and Reiner Schulze (eds), *German Civil Code I* (2020), § 270, mn. 6 et seq.

[189] Consumer Rights Act 2022, s. 32(2) and s. 69(2).
[190] See the country report on Italy, in this volume.
[191] Directive (EU) 2019/2161 of the European Parliament and of the Council of 27 November 2019 amending Council Directive 1993/13/EEC and Directives 1998/6/EC, 2005/29/EC and 2011/83/EU of the European Parliament and of the Council as regards the better enforcement and modernisation of Union consumer protection rules.
[192] Directives 98/6/EC, 2005/29/EC, 2011/83/EU and 1993/13/EEC.
[193] See the country report on Belgium, in this volume.
[194] See the country report on France, in this volume.

ment or a widespread infringement with a Union dimension is taking place. Rather than fixing an amount of money as the highest possible penalty, a link to the annual turnover would allow the trader's size, market power and – above all – market impact to be taken into account. This would avoid both "over"- and "undersanctioning".

On a general note, in many EU Member States limited access to justice is still a relevant problem in consumer contracts. In spite of the fact, that EU has tried to force Member States to develop alternative dispute settlement bodies for the settlement of consumer disputes, there is still much to do in this regard in order to improve consumer's rights in practice.

K. Conclusions

In a final overview of the implementation of the "Twin Directives", a considerable impact on the law of the Member States can already be seen. The effects on the structure, concepts and principles of Member States law range from the displacement of basic common law contract law concepts in favour of EU contract law concepts in Ireland to the expansion of the system of the law of obligations in a number of continental European countries and from the extended adoption of the understanding of personal data as consideration to the incorporation of the Directives' criteria for contractual conformity into the general law of sales in some Member States (to recall just a few of the examples).

However, the extent and forms of the impact differ significantly from one Country to another. For example, some Member States have introduced principles and terms from the Directive that were already in use in other national laws due to previous legislation. Some Member States have also limited themselves to taking over the provisions of the Directives mostly verbatim, while other Member States have further developed the terminology of the Directives and/or have adapted them and previously existing concepts of national law to each other, in particular in the context of an integration into the national Consumer code, the Law of obligation act or the Civil code.

Furthermore, the wide discretionality for the Member States to determine the reasons for the exclusion of contractual obligations (e.g. change of circumstances or impossibility) in their own way and to set the time limits reduces the harmonization effect.[195] The lack of harmonisation of such neighbouring matters must therefore be taken into account as a factor that is likely to reduce the impact of the Directives on the harmonisation of contractual liability in sales law and in the supply of digital content and digital services in contractual practice.

Finally, it should be borne in mind that an overview only of the Member States' legislation transposing the Directives can by no means give a complete picture of the impact of the Directives on the development of national law. Rather, in addition to the influence that can already be clearly identified, other components must also be taken into account. For example, the nature and extent of the influence in the respective Member State depends not least on the role the new provisions will play in contractual practice and in the judicial application of the law (the "law in action"). Furthermore, it remains questionable to what extent the objectives of the legislation (such as strengthening the internal market and reducing transaction costs in cross-border trade) can be achieved sufficiently in view of the regulatory deficits of harmonization, for example with regard to B-B contracts on the supply of digital content and digital services, or neighbouring

---

[195] Reiner Schulze, 'Die Digitale-Inhalte-Richtlinie – Innovation und Kontinuität im europäischen Vertragsrecht' (2019) 4 *ZEuP*, 695, 707, 723.

matters such as the impossibility of the supply of digital content and digital services and the change of circumstances.

74 Two other components of the impact on the national laws are also difficult to assess. However, they can indicate a greater influence than it appears at first glance if one only looks at the current implementation legislation. On the one hand, the Directives and the national transposition provisions contain numerous models that can also guide future legislation in the Member States in areas that have not been regulated so far. This concerns not only fundamental terms and definitions in the area of the distribution of goods with digital elements and the supply of digital content and services – or in general: trade with data. Rather, these provisions also contain a number of regulatory models that can be used beyond their scope of application, for example, for updating obligations and other requirements of contractual conformity or for the obligations of the parties after termination of the contract. This potential of the Directives and the transposition provisions for further legal development will come into play to the extent that the legislation of the Member States in the future will take into account the need to adapt further matters, in particular business to business legal relations, to the changes brought about by digitalization, and in doing so will strive for coherence with the provisions that have now emerged. On the other hand, it should not be overlooked that the Directives and their transposition provisions can also have effects beyond their scope of application independently of legislative measures. In particular, their conceptual and regulatory models can serve as a source of inspiration for the private shaping of law (for example, through contractual agreements, general terms and conditions or codes of conduct) and for the judicial resolution of conflicts in areas where no or no sufficiently detailed legislation on trade in data and related matters exists. Even if such "creeping effects" of implementation are difficult to detect, their importance for contractual practice should not be underestimated.

75 Such rather subtile components should be considered in addition to the effect that the "Twin directives" have already had immediately and clearly recognizable through the adoption of implementing legislation in the Member States to get a full picture of their impact. Therefore, if one takes them into account, despite the aforementioned regulatory shortcomings, there are good reasons to assume that the implementation of these Directives will prove to be a decisive step towards the harmonization of "Digital Law" in the EU.

Guidelines for Country Reports

Each Author of Country Reports was invited to consider the aspects listed in the following guidelines, with a focus on the questions and aspects considered more noteworthy for the respective Country.

I. Introduction. General Framework
   I.1. In which code / legal act did your Member State transpose the DCD and the SGD?
   I.2. Did the transposition of the Directives have an impact on the structure of the existing general law of obligation and contracts, consumer law, intellectual property law and data protection law? If so, what kind of impact?
II. Definitions and scope of application
   II.1. How did the notions contained in the DCD (see in particular Art. 2) and SGD (see in particular Art. 2) impact on the already existing rules and on the related doctrinal debate? In this regard, please consider in particular the

following notions of: digital content, digital service, goods with digital elements, integration, updates, price, digital environment, compatibility, functionality, interoperability, durable medium.

II.2. What is the impact on the general theory of contract / contract types of the figures of contracts for the supply of digital content / digital services and for the supply of goods with digital elements?

II.3. Which kind of impact did produce in your national legislation / doctrinal debate the introduction of a provision on data as a counter-performance? In this regard, did your Member State apply existing or did introduce new rules on contract formation / existence / validity?

II.4. Are the implementing provisions of the two Directives suitable to be applied to the B2B contracts?

III. Conformity of goods

III.1. How did your Member State implement the subjective and the objective requirements for conformity?
- Please consider in particular: i) the durability requirement; ii) the duty to inform and supply the consumer with updates which are necessary to keep the digital content or digital service in conformity; iii) the liability exemption for the case in which the consumer fails to install updates.

III.2. Did your Member State specify the provision regarding the exclusion of existence of a lack of conformity in the case provided by Art. 8, para. 5 DCD and Art. 7, para. 5 SGD (with particular regard to the concept of "particular characteristic")?

III.3. Did your Member State introduce measures to improve Sustainability and the Circular Economy?
- How did your Member State implement the "durability" requirement in Art. 7, para. 1, lett. d, SGD?
  - How did your Member State implement the requirements in product-specific Union legislation (see e.g. recital 32 SGD), especially the requirements relating to durability and repairability mentioned above?
  - What is the relationship, if any, between the two sets of provisions in national law?
  - Does your Member State have national rules on availability of spare parts and corresponding information obligations, and if so, what do they foresee?
  - Did your Member State coordinate the implementing provisions of the SGD with those of Directive 2009/125/EC establishing a framework for the setting of ecodesign requirements for energy-related products?
  - What penalties did your Member State implement according to Art. 20 directive 2009/125/EC? Are there for this any private law sanctions?
- Did your Member State adopt measures for enhancing environmental sustainability / circular economy in way of implementation of DCD and SGD (see e.g. recital 32 SGD)?

III.4. Please assess the consequences of the incorrect installation of the digital content or digital service.

III.5. How did your Member State handle the consumer's duty to provide personal data as a counter-performance in terms of its enforceability?

III.6. Did your Member State regulate the Modification of Digital Content or Digital Service in way of implementation of the SGD?

III.7. How did your Member State transpose Art. 10 DCD and Art. 9 SGD on third party rights in its national law? Did your Member State apply the DCD/SGD remedies for a lack of conformity to the situations covered by those provisions? If not, did your Member State apply rules on nullity or rescission and what would be their details?

III.8. Did your Member State regulate the relationship with Intellectual Property Law? Does the consumer have the right to "resell" digital contents?

IV. Liability of the Trader

IV.1. How did your Member State regulate the single act / long term supply of digital content / digital services?

IV.2. How did your Member State regulate the interruption of long-term supply of digital content / digital services?

IV.3. How does your national law regulate the consequences of a failure to deliver / supply with respect to obstacles like impossibility or force majeure? Does your national law provide for rules about change of circumstances?

IV.4. Did your Member State regulate early termination of Number-Independent Interpersonal Communication Service (NI-ICS)?

IV.5. How did your Member State coordinate Art. 107, para. 2 European Electronic Communications Code and Art. 3, para. 6, subpara. 3, dir. 2019/770/EU on bundles?

IV.6. What are in your Member State the consequences of the trader's non-compliance with the GDPR regarding contracts for the supply of digital content/digital services?

V. Remedies for the failure to supply and remedies for the lack of conformity

V.1. Did your Member State introduce / maintain a right to withhold payment for contracts under the DCD and what would be the conditions and modalities? What conditions and modalities apply for the exercise of the right to withhold payment for contracts under the SGD under national law?

V.2. Did your Member State adopt specific rules in order to define the place of delivery and the place of repair and replacement?

V.3. Does your Member State foresee rules about the costs of transport for the case of repair / replacement (e.g. being advanced or reimboursed)?

V.4. Is the provision of the right of withdrawal (regarding the consent for the processing of personal data) and the right of termination (see Art. 15 DCD) through declaration a deviation from the general structure of the right of withdrawal in your Member State or does it follow an already existing tendency in your Country?

V.5. Did your Member State introduce specific rules regarding the contractual consequences of withdrawal of consent for processing personal data, or do general contract law rules apply?

V.6. How did your Member State deal with restitution where the trader supplies digital content and/or digital services?

V.7. How did your Member State deal with restitution where the trader supplies digital content and / or digital services and the consumer provides personal data as a counterperformance?

V.8. Does your Member State prioritize repair over replacement in order to enhance environmental sustainability (see e.g. recital 48 SGD)? Is there doctrinal debate on this?

V.9. Which kind of sanctions does your Member State adopt for fighting premature / planned obsolescence of goods? What is in this regard the relationship with the internal rules on unfair commercial practices?

V.10. Does the law of your Member State provide an automatic transfer of the rights against the initial seller from the initial consumer to a subsequent buyer? If so, how is this transfer regulated?

V.11. If not, does the law of your Member State allow the initial consumer and a subsequent buyer to contractually agree that the rights against the initial seller are transferred to the subsequent buyer? If so, does your national law allow the initial seller to exclude the transferability of the rights under the legal guarantee or a commercial guarantee in his general terms and conditions?

Please explain whether your Member State provided express regulation for the cases in which:
i) the consumer bought goods and then moved to another Country;
ii) the seller delivered the goods in accordance with the Geo-Blocking Regulation and is now obliged to carry out repair or replacement in a country he does not offer delivery to.

VI. Commercial Guarantees

How did your national legislator regulate commercial guarantees? In particular: did your Member State use the option provided for in Art. 17 para. 4 SGD, laying down rules on other aspects concerning commercial guarantees which are not regulated in the SGD, including rules on the language or languages in which the commercial guarantee statement is to be made available to the consumer?

VII. Time Limits

VII.1. How did your Member State implement the provisions on time limits?

VII.2. In particular, how did your legislator made use of the concerning options provided by the Directives (Art. 10 SGD and Art. 11 DCD)?

VII.3. Did your Member State intend to maintain or introduce provisions on interruption or suspension of the liability period or limitation period? If so, what do these provisions foresee?

VII.4. Did your Member State maintain or introduce the "Obligation to notify" as allowed by Art. 12 SGD?

VIII. Right of Redress

How did your Member State implement the provision on the right of redress? How was it coordinated with the other remedies?

IX. Relationship with other remedies

What is the relationship between the implementing provisions of the DCD and SGD and the remedies otherwise provided by your national law of obligations and contracts (e.g. compensation, etc.)?

I.
THE IMPACT OF EU DIRECTIVES 2019/770 AND 2019/771

Austria

A. Introduction	1
I. Overview of Implementation Measures	2
II. Effects on the Structure of Austrian Private Law	6
B. Definitions and Scope of Application	7
I. Transposition of the Definitions Contained in the Directives	7
II. Implications for General Contract Doctrine and Contract Types for the Provision of Digital Services or Content	10
III. Effects of the Introduction of a Provision on Data as Counter-Performance	11
IV. Applicability of the Transposition Provisions to B2B Contracts	13
C. Contractuality	14
I. Subjective and Objective Requirements for Conformity with the Contract	14
1. Obligation to Update	16
2. Exceptions to the Obligation to Update	18
II. Deviation from Objective Requirements	19
III. Warranty and Sustainability	23
1. Durability	23
2. Product-Related Legislation	26
3. National Regulations on the Availability of Spare Parts	28
4. Relationship of the Transposition Measures to the Ecodesign Regulation 2007	30
5. Measures to Improve Sustainability as well as the Circular Economy	33
IV. Installation of Digital Services or Digital Content	35
V. Contractual Obligation of the Consumer to Provide Personal Data?	39
VI. Modification of the Digital Content or Digital Service	40
VII. Third-Party Rights	41
VIII. Relation to Copyright and the Right to Resell Digital Content	43
IX. Supply of Digital Content and Services	48
D. Remedies for Lack of Conformity	50
I. General	50
II. Individual Questions	53
1. Right of Retention	53
2. Place of Performance and Subsequent Performance	54
3. Transport Costs	57
4. Withdrawal and Termination of the Contract by Declaration	60
5. Reimbursement in Cases of the Provision of Digital Content or Digital Services	62
6. Reimbursement for the Provision of Digital Content or Digital Services in Exchange for the Provision of Personal Data	65
7. Relationship of Repair and Replacement	66
8. Obsolescence	68
9. Transferability of the Consumer's Rights Against the Seller	72
E. Contractual Guarantees	73
F. Time Limits	78
I. General Information	78
II. Material Defects	80
III. Legal Defects	83
IV. Obligation to Give Notice of Defects	86
G. Right of Redress	87
I. Previous Regulation	87
II. New Regulation	89
H. Relationship with Other Remedies	94
I. Default	94
II. Damages Instead of Warranty	95
III. Usury and Laesio Enormis	97
IV. Error	101
Bibliography	103

A. Introduction

1   Twenty years after the implementation of the Consumer Sales Directive (CSGD)[1] the Austrian legislator had to reform warranty law once again in order to meet its implementation obligations under the Digital Content Directive and the Sale of Goods Directive (DCD[2] and SGD[3], hereinafter referred to as the Directives). As was the case then,[4] an expert opinion of the Austrian Lawyer's Conference was prepared to examine the need for adaptation in national law and how the relevant directives could best be transposed into national law.[5] The article shows why a different way of transposing the two directives was chosen this time and what effects the transposition has on the general structure of Austrian private law.

I. Overview of Implementation Measures

2   The Warranty Directive Transposition Act (GRUG)[6] carried out the transposition of the DCD and the SGD in Austria. It contains selective changes to the Austrian Civil Code (ABGB)[7] and the Consumer Protection Act (KSchG)[8]. However, the vast majority of the Directive's provisions is implemented in the newly created Consumer Warranty Act (VGG).[9] In contrast to the CSGD, the legislator did not consider it desirable to incorporate the provisions into the general warranty law of the ABGB. This was mainly due to the scope and technical complexity of the SGD and the DCD, as well as the fact that both Directives are fully harmonising and therefore the Member States' scope for implementation is significantly smaller.[10]

---

[1] Directive 1999/44/EC of the European Parliament and of the Council of 25 May 1999 on certain aspects of the sale of consumer goods and associated guarantees.
[2] Directive (EU) 2019/770 of the European Parliament and of the Council of 20 May 2019 on certain aspects concerning contracts for the supply of digital content and digital services.
[3] Directive (EU) 2019/771 of the European Parliament and of the Council of 20 May 2019 on certain aspects concerning contracts for the sale of goods, amending Regulation (EU) 2017/2394 and Directive 2009/22/EC, and repealing Directive 1999/44/EC.
[4] Welser and Jud, 'Zur Reform des Gewährleistungsrechts' in *14. ÖJT* II/1 (2000).
[5] Forgó and Zöchling-Jud, 'Das Vertragsrecht des ABGB auf dem Prüfstand: Überlegungen im digitalen Zeitalter' in *20. ÖJT* II/1 (2018); cf. European Law Institute, *Statement of the European Law Institute on the European Commission's Proposed Directive on the Supply of Digital Content to Consumers* (2016).
[6] Bundesgesetz, mit dem ein Bundesgesetz über die Gewährleistung bei Verbraucherverträgen über Waren oder digitale Leistungen (Verbrauchergewährleistungsgesetz – VGG) erlassen wird sowie das allgemeine bürgerliche Gesetzbuch und das Konsumentenschutzgesetz geändert werden (Gewährleistungsrichtlinien-Umsetzungsgesetz – GRUG), BGBl I 2021/175.
[7] Allgemeines bürgerliches Gesetzbuch für die gesammten deutschen Erbländer der Oesterreichischen Monarchie, JGS 1811/946 idF BGBl I 2021/175.
[8] Bundesgesetz vom 8. März 1979, mit den Bestimmungen zum Schutz der Verbraucher getroffen werden (Konsumentenschutzgesetz), BGBl 1979/140 idF BGBl I 2021/175.
[9] Bundesgesetz über die Gewährleistung bei Verbraucherverträgen über Waren oder digitale Leistungen (Verbrauchergewährleistungsgesetz), BGBl I 2021/175; Artner and Vonkilch, 'GRUG: Zum objektiven Mangelbegriff des § 6 VGG' (2021) 10 *ecolex*, 890 (890); Stabentheiner, 'Grundzüge des neuen Verbrauchergewährleistungsrechts' (2022) 2a *ÖJZ*, 99 (100); Zöchling-Jud, 'Die Richtlinienvorschläge der Kommission über digitale Inhalte und Fernabsatzkaufverträge aus österreichischer Sicht' in Wendehorst and Zöchling-Jud (eds), *Ein neues Vertragsrecht für den digitalen Binnenmarkt?* (2016), 1 (11).
[10] Explanatory Notes on the Government Draft of the GRUG (No. 949 of the Supplements to the Stenographic Protocols of the National Council of the XXVII Legislative Period), 3 et seq; Zöchling-Jud, 'Die Richtlinienvorschläge der Kommission über digitale Inhalte und Fernabsatzkaufverträge aus österreichischer Sicht' in Wendehorst and Zöchling-Jud (eds), *Ein neues Vertragsrecht für den digitalen Binnenmarkt?* (2016), 1 (12 et seq).

A. Introduction

The VGG is divided into four sections.[11] The first of these sections contains general provisions that apply both to the purchase of goods and to contracts regarding digital services and content. These include, above all, the scope of application, the definitions, the mandatory character of the provisions, the definition of defects, the update obligation as well as the specifications regarding the installation of goods or the integration of the digital content. The two subsequent sections of the VGG contain the regulations that only apply to one of these areas.[12] Specifically, the second section applies to contracts regarding the sale of goods and regulates the seller's liability, the burden of proof, the warranty period and legal remedies. Section 3 applies (only) to contracts regarding digital services and, in parallel to Section 2, regulates the liability of the trader, the burden of proof, the warranty period and remedies. Finally, the fourth and last section contains limitation periods and final provisions, which in turn apply to all contracts subject to the VGG.[13]

At the same time, the warranty provisions of the ABGB were reformed and adapted to the new provisions of the VGG where the legislator deemed it appropriate. This led to both minor terminological adjustments and to an adjustment of the warranty and limitation provisions as well as of the provisions on the recourse of the transferor liable for the warranty.[14]

Finally, the warranty provisions of the KSchG were also adapted.[15] On the one hand, the warranty provisions of the ABGB were made mandatory for consumer contracts, which is of importance for consumer contracts that do not fall within the scope of application of the VGG. On the other hand, the new provisions on contractual guarantees and on the default of the transferor in B2C contracts were added to the KSchG.[16]

II. Effects on the Structure of Austrian Private Law

The VGG is – apart from an exception regarding the obligation to update[17] – only applicable to consumer contracts that involve the purchase of goods or the provision of digital services in return for payment or the provision of personal data.[18] The (personal and factual) scope of application of the VGG thus coincides with the scope of application of the SGD and the DCD. Compared to the previous Austrian warranty law, in which only §§ 8 et seq KSchG provided for special rules regarding warranties in consumer contracts,[19] this led to a far-reaching fragmentation of the law. B2B and C2C con-

---

[11] Stabentheiner, 'Was ist neu am neuen Gewährleistungsrecht?' (2021) 21 *ÖJZ*, 965 (966); Kodek, 'Vertragswidrigkeit und Mangelbegriff im neuen Gewährleistungsrecht' (2022) 2a *ÖJZ*, 103 (104).

[12] Kodek, 'Vertragswidrigkeit und Mangelbegriff im neuen Gewährleistungsrecht' (2022) 2a *ÖJZ*, 103 (104); Stabentheiner, 'Grundzüge des neuen Verbrauchergewährleistungsrechts' (2022) 2a *ÖJZ*, 99 (100).

[13] Neumayr, 'Das neue Verbrauchergewährleistungsrecht' (2021) 8 *RdW*, 536 (536); Kodek, 'Vertragswidrigkeit und Mangelbegriff im neuen Gewährleistungsrecht' (2022) 2a *ÖJZ*, 103 (104).

[14] Hafner-Thomic, 'Alles neu macht das GRUG?' (2022) 1 *ecolex*, 22 (22); Artner and Vonkilch, 'GRUG: Zum objektiven Mangelbegriff des § 6 VGG' (2021) 10 *ecolex*, 890 (890).

[15] Stabentheiner, 'Was ist neu am neuen Gewährleistungsrecht?' (2021) 21 *ÖJZ*, 965 (966); Neumayr, 'Das neue Verbrauchergewährleistungsrecht' (2021) 8 *RdW*, 536 (536).

[16] Cf. Art 3 GRUG.

[17] Cf. C.I.1.

[18] Dullinger, 'Das neue Gewährleistungsrecht' (2022) 1 *RFG*, 40 (40 et seq); Stabentheiner, 'Grundzüge des neuen Verbrauchergewährleistungsrechts' (2022) 2a *ÖJZ*, 99 (100 et seqq).

[19] According to § 9 KSchG, in contrast to general civil law, a contractual deviation from the statutory warranty law to the detriment of the consumer is invalid unless it is concluded after knowledge of the defect. Other special features only concern individual aspects of warranty law, such as the place of fulfilment of warranty obligations by the entrepreneur (§ 8 KSchG as amended by BGBl I 2021/175) or his liability for defects due to faulty instructions (§ 9a KSchG as amended by BGBl I 2001/48).

tracts are in principle subject to the warranty law of the ABGB, whereas now consumer transactions are either subject to the scope of application of the VGG or the ABGB with the special provisions of the KSchG. Excluded from the scope of application of the VGG are all those B2C transactions that do not involve the purchase of goods or the supply of digital services as well as, in particular, transactions for the purchase of immovable property or live animals.[20] Thus, in order to determine the applicable warranty rules, it must be examined whether the contract is a B2C transaction and whether the concrete object of performance falls within the scope of the VGG.[21]

B. Definitions and Scope of Application

I. Transposition of the Definitions Contained in the Directives

7   The definitions contained in Art. 2 SGD and Art. 2 DCD were predominantly implemented in the first section of the VGG, which applies equally to the purchase of goods and contracts regarding digital services. In principle, these provisions are a near verbatim adoption of the Directives. However, some definitions were adapted to national law and some simplifications were made. For example, "digital content" and "digital services" were combined under the umbrella term "digital performance", because according to Austrian terminology, "performance" refers to any contractual obligation.[22] The definitions new to Austrian law were included in § 2 VGG. This concerns the terms "goods with digital elements" (No. 4), "compatibility" (No. 5), "functionality" (No. 6), "interoperability" (No. 7), "digital environment" (No. 8), "integration" (No. 9), "durable medium" (No. 10), "durability" (No. 11) and "personal data" (No. 12).[23] The terms "producer" (Art. 2 para. 4 SGD) and "commercial guarantee" (Art. 2 para. 12 SGD) were not defined in the VGG, but were adopted in § 9a KSchG on contractual guarantees, which was created in implementation of Art. 17 SGD.[24]

8   The definition of "sales contract" in Art. 2 para. 1 SGD, which is central to the applicability of the SGD required some amendments. That is because it also covers contracts regarding movable tangible objects yet to be manufactured or produced as well as the assembly or installation of goods. Thus, it goes beyond the Austrian understanding of a sales contract according to § 1053 ABGB. Hence, the VGG explicitly includes the "purchase of goods [...] including those yet to be manufactured" in § 1 para. 1 subpara. 1.[25]

---

[20] Stabentheiner, 'Grundzüge des neuen Verbrauchergewährleistungsrechts' (2022) 2a *ÖJZ*, 99 (101 et seq); Schmitt, 'Das neue Gewährleistungsrecht ab 2022: Digitale Leistungen und mehr' (2021) 5 *jusIT*, 179 (182, 185).

[21] Schmitt, 'Das neue Gewährleistungsrecht ab 2022: Digitale Leistungen und mehr' (2021) 5 *jusIT*, 179 (179).

[22] Flume and Ziegler, in: Flume et al. (eds), *VGG* (2022), § 2, mn. 2; Wendehorst, 'Die Regelungen des VGG zu digitalen Leistungen unter besonderer Berücksichtigung der Aktualisierungspflichten' in Bydlinski (ed), *Das neue Gewährleistungsrecht* (2022), 49 (50 et seqq); Explanatory Notes on the Government Draft of the GRUG (No. 949 of the Supplements to the Stenographic Protocols of the National Council of the XXVII Legislative Period), 9.

[23] Flume and Ziegler, in: Flume et al. (eds), *VGG* (2022), § 2, mn. 6 et seqq; Explanatory Notes on the Government Draft of the GRUG (No. 949 of the Supplements to the Stenographic Protocols of the National Council of the XXVII Legislative Period), 17.

[24] Explanatory Notes on the Government Draft of the GRUG (No. 949 of the Supplements to the Stenographic Protocols of the National Council of the XXVII Legislative Period), 16.

[25] Kronthaler, in: Flume et al. (eds), *VGG* (2022), § 1, mn. 18; Wendehorst, 'Die Regelungen des VGG zu digitalen Leistungen unter besonderer Berücksichtigung der Aktualisierungspflichten' in Bydlinski (ed), *Das neue Gewährleistungsrecht* (2022), 49 (53 et seqq); Explanatory Notes on the Government Draft of the

B. Definitions and Scope of Application

For those terms that did not require a new definition or that could be adequately defined by references to other standards, no separate transposition took place.[26] This concerns the terms "goods" (Art. 2 para. 5 SGD) and "price" (Art. 2 para. 7 DCD), which already correspond to the current Austrian understanding of these terms.[27] The Austrian legislator also refers to the legal definitions already contained in § 1 KSchG for the terms "consumer" (Art. 2 para. 6 DCD and Art. 2 para. 2 SGD), "seller" (Art. 2 para. 3 SGD) or "trader" (Art. 2 para. 5 DCD).[28] The term "public auction" according to Art. 2 para. 15 SGD in the VGG was not defined, because the corresponding regulatory option of Art. 3 para. 5 lit. a DCD was not exercised.[29] Surprisingly, there is no definition of "free of charge" (Art. 2 para. 14 SGD) either. Instead the terms "free of costs" or "without costs" are used. Only the explanations clarify that free of charge also includes shipping, transport, labour and material costs.[30]

II. Implications for General Contract Doctrine and Contract Types for the Provision of Digital Services or Content

Austrian private law is characterised by the principle of freedom of contract, which in particular includes the freedom to enter and determine the contractual obligations.[31] While the ABGB regulates a large number of different types of contracts, it leaves the parties free to deviate from these legal requirements at will and to conclude atypical or mixed contracts.[32] Since contracts regarding digital content and digital services could already be freely concluded up to now,[33] the Austrian legislator refrained from introducing any special regulations for such contracts. Thus, no separate type of contract was implemented for contracts regarding digital performances, neither in the ABGB nor in the VGG. In this respect, the implementation of the DCD did not have any effects on the existing general contract doctrine and the statutory contract types in Austria.[34] The introduction of special statutory regulations would probably not have been appropriate in view of the different possibilities to design such contracts. At least the *essentialia negotii* of such a contract would have to be regulated by the law, which would not have

---

GRUG (No. 949 of the Supplements to the Stenographic Protocols of the National Council of the XXVII Legislative Period), 12; cf. Kogler, 'Digitale Leistungen und Waren gegen Zahlung mit Bitcoin – Anwendbarkeit des VGG?' (2022) 1 *ecolex*, 27 (28 et seq).

[26] Explanatory Notes on the Government Draft of the GRUG (No. 949 of the Supplements to the Stenographic Protocols of the National Council of the XXVII Legislative Period), 15.

[27] Explanatory Notes on the Government Draft of the GRUG (No. 949 of the Supplements to the Stenographic Protocols of the National Council of the XXVII Legislative Period), 15; another view is advocated by Flume and Ziegler, in: Flume et al. (eds), *VGG* (2022), § 2, mn. 27 et seqq.

[28] Explanatory Notes on the Government Draft of the GRUG (No. 949 of the Supplements to the Stenographic Protocols of the National Council of the XXVII Legislative Period), 15; Kronthaler, in: Flume et al. (eds), *VGG* (2022), § 1, mn. 2.

[29] Explanatory Notes on the Government Draft of the GRUG (No. 949 of the Supplements to the Stenographic Protocols of the National Council of the XXVII Legislative Period), 14.

[30] Explanatory Notes on the Government Draft of the GRUG (No. 949 of the Supplements to the Stenographic Protocols of the National Council of the XXVII Legislative Period), 17.

[31] Welser and Zöchling-Jud, *Grundriss des Bürgerlichen Rechts* II (2015), mn. 56; P. Bydlinski, *Bürgerliches Recht Allgemeiner Teil* (2018), 120 et seqq.

[32] P. Bydlinski, *Bürgerliches Recht Allgemeiner Teil* (2018), 121; Welser and Zöchling-Jud, *Grundriss des Bürgerlichen Rechts* II (2015), mn. 56 et seq.

[33] Forgó and Zöchling-Jud, 'Das Vertragsrecht des ABGB auf dem Prüfstand: Überlegungen im digitalen Zeitalter' in *20. ÖJT II/1* (2018), 168.

[34] Flume, 'Digitale Leistungen' (2022) 2a *ÖJZ*, 137 (140); Flume and Ziegler, in: Flume et al. (eds), *VGG* (2022), § 1, mn. 23.

been possible at all in view of the diversity of contracts regarding digital services.[35] Accordingly, legal transactions concerning the provision of digital services are, as before, often to be regarded as mixed contracts under Austrian law, to which, in the absence of a deviating agreement between the parties, the most appropriate legal provisions are to be applied.[36] Only non-performance and improper performance are now regulated for consumer contracts in the VGG.

III. Effects of the Introduction of a Provision on Data as Counter-Performance

11   According to § 1 para. 1 subpara. 2 lit. b VGG, the scope of application explicitly includes contracts regarding the provision of digital performance in exchange of the consumer's personal data. Thereby, the Austrian legislator adopted the corresponding provision of Art. 3 para. 1 subpara. 2 DCD.[37] Beyond that, the legislator refrained from creating new autonomous provisions that explicitly regulate the formation, existence or validity of contracts on the provision of personal data.

12   However, even before the new provisions came into force, it was the prevailing opinion in Austria that, if certain conditions are met, a contract for consideration[38] within the meaning of § 917 ABGB can be assumed if one contracting party promises the other personal data in return for a service.[39] According to this opinion, such agreements were already subject to Austrian warranty law, since the central criterion for its applicability is not the object of performance, but the existence of a contract for consideration.[40]

IV. Applicability of the Transposition Provisions to B2B Contracts

13   Pursuant to § 1 para. 1 VGG, the direct scope of application is limited to consumer transactions within the meaning of § 1 KSchG, i.e. to such transactions concluded by an entrepreneur for whom the transaction is part of the operation of his business with a person to whom this does not apply.[41] The only exceptions to this are the provisions contained in § 7 VGG on the obligation to update digital services and goods with digital ele-

---

[35] Forgó and Zöchling-Jud, 'Das Vertragsrecht des ABGB auf dem Prüfstand: Überlegungen im digitalen Zeitalter' in *20. ÖJT* II/1 (2018), 173 et seq.
[36] Schmitt, *Gewährleistung bei Verträgen über digitale Inhalte* (2017), 71 et seq; Flume and Ziegler, in: Flume et al. (eds), *VGG* (2022), § 1, mn. 26; Forgó and Zöchling-Jud, 'Das Vertragsrecht des ABGB auf dem Prüfstand: Überlegungen im digitalen Zeitalter' in *20. ÖJT* II/1 (2018), 173.
[37] Flume, in: Flume et al. (eds), *VGG* (2022), Vor § 16, mn. 13; European Law Institute, *Statement of the European Law Institute on the European Commission's Proposed Directive on the Supply of Digital Content to Consumers* (2016), 15 et seq; Wendehorst, 'Die Regelungen des VGG zu digitalen Leistungen unter besonderer Berücksichtigung der Aktualisierungspflichten' in Bydlinski (ed), *Das neue Gewährleistungsrecht* (2022), 49 (55 et seqq).
[38] "*Entgeltlicher Vertrag*" as defined in Kletečka and Welser, *Grundriss des Bürgerlichen Rechts* I (2018), mn. 376.
[39] Forgó and Zöchling-Jud, 'Das Vertragsrecht des ABGB auf dem Prüfstand: Überlegungen im digitalen Zeitalter' in *20. ÖJT* II/1 (2018), 241 et seqq; another view is advocated by Kern, 'Anwendungsbereich der Warenkauf- und der Digitale Inhalte-RL' in Stabentheiner et al. (eds), *Das neue europäische Gewährleistungsrecht* (2019), 33 (39); Zöchling-Jud, 'Die Richtlinienvorschläge der Kommission über digitale Inhalte und Fernabsatzverträge aus österreichischer Sicht' in Wendehorst and Zöchling-Jud (eds), *Ein neues Vertragsrecht für den digitalen Binnenmarkt?* (2016), 1 (11).
[40] Ofner, in: Schwimann and Kodek (eds), *ABGB: Praxiskommentar* (2021), § 922, mn. 4 et seqq; Zöchling-Jud, in: Kletečka and Schauer (eds), *ABGB-ON* (2016), vor §§ 922 – 933b, mn. 6.
[41] Hafner-Thomic, 'Alles neu macht das GRUG?' (2022) 1 *ecolex*, 22 (22); Neumayr, 'Zum Mangelbegriff des neuen VGG' (2021) 12 *RdW*, 833 (833); Kronthaler, in: Flume et al. (eds), *VGG* (2022), § 1, mn. 2.

ments. Pursuant to § 1 para. 3 VGG, these also apply to B2B contracts.[42] The Austrian legislator justified this gold-plating of the Directives by stating that the retailer should be provided with a "suitable basis" for fulfilling his obligation to update towards the consumer.[43] However, since this provision is unilaterally mandatory only in favour of consumers according to § 3 VGG, the provisions on the updating obligation can be waived in the case of a B2B transactions.[44] The Austrian Supreme Court of Justice has so far rejected an analogous application of consumer law provisions to B2B transactions as well – except for individual cases in which there was a pronounced imbalance between the contracting parties.[45]

C. Contractuality

I. Subjective and Objective Requirements for Conformity with the Contract

The requirements under EU law concerning the subjective and objective requirements for the conformity of goods and digital services to the contract were implemented in §§ 5 et seq VGG, closely following the corresponding provisions of the Directives.[46]

With regard to the relationship between the subjective and objective requirements of contractual compliance, it is to be assumed that they have equal priority.[47] This applies irrespective of whether one is of the opinion that § 6 VGG, which regulates the objectively required properties, standardises a duty of the trader that is detached from the content of the contract and already exists *ex lege*, or whether this provision merely objectifies the content of the contract.[48] In the event of a contradiction between the contractually agreed and the objectively necessary requirements, the prevailing opinion is that the higher standard shall be relevant.[49]

---

[42] Dullinger 'Das neue Gewährleistungsrecht' (2022) 1 *RFG*, 40 (43); Hafner-Thomic, 'Alles neu macht das GRUG?' (2022) 1 *ecolex*, 22 (23); Nemeth, in: Flume et al. (eds), *VGG* (2022), § 7, mn. 37; Wendehorst, 'Die Regelungen des VGG zu digitalen Leistungen unter besonderer Berücksichtigung der Aktualisierungspflichten' in Bydlinski (ed), *Das neue Gewährleistungsrecht* (2022), 49 (64 et seq).

[43] Explanatory Notes on the Government Draft of the GRUG (No. 949 of the Supplements to the Stenographic Protocols of the National Council of the XXVII Legislative Period), 15; Nemeth, in: Flume et al. (eds), *VGG* (2022), § 7, mn. 36.

[44] Explanatory Notes on the Government Draft of the GRUG (No. 949 of the Supplements to the Stenographic Protocols of the National Council of the XXVII Legislative Period), 15; Nemeth, in: Flume et al. (eds), *VGG* (2022), § 7, mn. 38; Wendehorst, 'Die Regelungen des VGG zu digitalen Leistungen unter besonderer Berücksichtigung der Aktualisierungspflichten' in Bydlinski (ed), *Das neue Gewährleistungsrecht* (2022), 49 (69 et seqq).

[45] RIS-Justiz RS0065288; RS0065327; OGH 11.08.2020 – 4 Ob 71/20z – *VbR* 2020, 213 (213 et seq).

[46] Stabentheiner, 'Ein Überblick über das Gewährleistungsrichtlinien-Umsetzungsgesetz' (2021) 6 *VbR*, 189.

[47] Kodek, 'Vertragswidrigkeit und Mangelbegriff im neuen Gewährleistungsrecht' (2022) 2a *ÖJZ*, 103 (106 et seq); Neumayr, 'Zum Mangelbegriff des neuen VGG' (2021) 12 *RdW*, 833 (834 et seq); Stabentheiner, 'Was ist neu am neuen Gewährleistungsrecht?' (2021) 21 *ÖJZ*, 965 (969); Laimer, in: Flume et al. (eds), *VGG* (2022), § 6, mn. 1.

[48] Stabentheiner, 'Was ist neu am neuen Gewährleistungsrecht?' (2021) 21 *ÖJZ*, 965 (970).

[49] Neumayr, 'Zum Mangelbegriff des neuen VGG' (2021) 12 *RdW*, 833 (835); Kodek, 'Vertragswidrigkeit und Mangelbegriff im neuen Gewährleistungsrecht' (2022) 2a *ÖJZ*, 103 (106); Laimer, in: Flume et al. (eds), *VGG* (2022), § 6, mn. 2.

1. Obligation to Update

16 The obligation of the trader to provide and inform about updates for digital services and contents as well as for goods with digital elements is regulated in § 7 VGG.[50] Pursuant to § 7 para. 1 VGG, in the case of contracts regarding goods with digital elements and digital services, the trader must provide the consumer, after prior information, with the updates that are necessary to ensure that the goods or the digital service continue to comply with the contract.[51] According to § 7 para. 1 VGG, an exception to this provision can only be made if the consumer expressly and separately agrees to a deviation from the updating obligation upon conclusion of the contract after being informed accordingly.[52] Pursuant to § 1 para. 3 VGG, the obligation to update also applies to B2B contracts.[53]

17 The period of time in which the trader has to provide necessary updates is defined in § 7 para. 2 VGG. A distinction is made between one-time and continuous provision: In the case of services that the trader has to provide continuously or over a certain or indefinite period of time, the updating obligation according to § 7 para. 2 subpara. 2 VGG exists for the entire provision period, but for goods with digital elements at least for two years.[54] If, on the other hand, the service is to be provided once or several times individually, the duration of the obligation to update is based on the "reasonable expectations" of the consumer pursuant to § 7 para. 2 subpara. 1 VGG.[55] This broad term creates legal

---

[50] Fida, 'Die neue Aktualisierungspflicht nach § 7 VGG' (2021) 12 *ecolex*, 1079 (1079); Stabentheiner, 'Ein Überblick über das Gewährleistungsrichtlinien-Umsetzungsgesetz' (2021) 6 *VbR*, 188 (189); Nemeth, in: Flume et al. (eds), *VGG* (2022), § 7, mn. 1.

[51] Neumayr, 'Das neue Verbrauchergewährleistungsrecht' (2021) 8 *RdW*, 536 (537); Fida, 'Die neue Aktualisierungspflicht nach § 7 VGG' (2021) 12 *ecolex*, 1079 (1079); Nemeth, in: Flume et al. (eds), *VGG* (2022), § 7, mn. 6; Wendehorst, 'Aktualisierungen und andere digitale Dauerleistungen' in Stabentheiner et al. (eds), *Das neue europäische Gewährleistungsrecht* (2019), 111 (122 et seqq); European Law Institute, *Statement of the European Law Institute on the European Commission's Proposed Directive on the Supply of Digital Content to Consumers* (2016), 23; Wendehorst, 'Die Regelungen des VGG zu digitalen Leistungen unter besonderer Berücksichtigung der Aktualisierungspflichten' in Bydlinski (ed), *Das neue Gewährleistungsrecht* (2022), 49 (71 et seqq).

[52] Hafner-Thomic, 'Alles neu macht das GRUG?' (2022) 1 *ecolex*, 22 (23); Fida, 'Die neue Aktualisierungspflicht nach § 7 VGG' (2021) 12 *ecolex*, 1079 (1082); Nemeth, in: Flume et al. (eds), *VGG* (2022), § 7, mn. 31; Wendehorst, 'Aktualisierungen und andere digitale Dauerleistungen' in Stabentheiner et al. (eds), *Das neue europäische Gewährleistungsrecht* (2019), 111 (134); Wendehorst, 'Die Regelungen des VGG zu digitalen Leistungen unter besonderer Berücksichtigung der Aktualisierungspflichten' in Bydlinski (ed), *Das neue Gewährleistungsrecht* (2022), 49 (63 et seq).

[53] Kogler, 'Der Ausschluss der Aktualisierungspflicht bei Waren mit digitalen Elementen und bei digitalen Leistungen' (2022) 2 *ecolex*, 118 (119); Dullinger, 'Das neue Gewährleistungsrecht' (2022) 1 *RFG*, 40 (43); Nemeth, in: Flume et al. (eds), *VGG* (2022), § 7, mn. 37; Wendehorst, 'Die Regelungen des VGG zu digitalen Leistungen unter besonderer Berücksichtigung der Aktualisierungspflichten' in Bydlinski (ed), *Das neue Gewährleistungsrecht* (2022), 49 (77 et seq).

[54] Kodek, 'Vertragswidrigkeit und Mangelbegriff im neuen Gewährleistungsrecht' (2022) 2a *ÖJZ*, 103 (112); Neumayr, 'Das neue Verbrauchergewährleistungsrecht' (2021) 8 *RdW*, 536 (538); Nemeth, in: Flume et al. (eds), *VGG* (2022), § 7, mn. 16; Wendehorst, 'Aktualisierungen und andere digitale Dauerleistungen' in Stabentheiner et al. (eds), *Das neue europäische Gewährleistungsrecht* (2019), 111 (130 et seq); Wendehorst, 'Die Regelungen des VGG zu digitalen Leistungen unter besonderer Berücksichtigung der Aktualisierungspflichten' in Bydlinski (ed), *Das neue Gewährleistungsrecht* (2022), 49 (50 et seqq); Wendehorst, 'Die Regelungen des VGG zu digitalen Leistungen unter besonderer Berücksichtigung der Aktualisierungspflichten' in Bydlinski (ed), *Das neue Gewährleistungsrecht* (2022), 49 (77).

[55] Dullinger, 'Das neue Gewährleistungsrecht' (2022) 1 *RFG*, 40 (43); Fida, 'Die neue Aktualisierungspflicht nach § 7 VGG' (2021) 12 *ecolex*, 1079 (1081); Nemeth, in: Flume et al. (eds), *VGG* (2022), § 7, mn. 11; Wendehorst, 'Aktualisierungen und andere digitale Dauerleistungen' in Stabentheiner et al. (eds), *Das neue europäische Gewährleistungsrecht* (2019), 111 (130); European Law Institute, *Statement of the European Law Institute on the European Commission's Proposed Directive on the Supply of Digital Content to Consumers* (2016), 22.

uncertainty, as it is difficult to adequately estimate the duration of the obligation period from the outset.[56]

2. Exceptions to the Obligation to Update

Pursuant to § 7 para. 3 VGG, the consumer is free to decide whether or not to install the update provided.[57] In the event that the consumer fails to install the update, the trader shall not be liable for any defects that are solely attributable to the omission to update.[58] However, such exclusion of liability shall only apply if the trader has informed the consumer about the availability of the update and about the consequences of failure to install it. The failure to install or the improper performance of the installation shall also not be attributable to defective installation instructions.[59]

II. Deviation from Objective Requirements

The provisions contained in Art. 8 para. 5 DCD and Art. 7 para. 5 SGD concerning deviations of certain characteristics of a good or digital service from the objective requirements of conformity with the contract were implemented in § 6 para. 1.[60] Accordingly, a trader is not liable for objectively required qualities within the meaning of § 6 VGG, if the consumer has expressly and separately consented to the deviation of a certain characteristic from these statutory requirements after having been specifically informed thereof.[61]

Both implied consent and consent to a trader's GTC are generally not sufficient for this purpose.[62] However, the consent to the deviation does not necessarily have to be

---

[56] Fida, 'Die neue Aktualisierungspflicht nach § 7 VGG' (2021) 12 *ecolex*, 1079 (1081); Stabentheiner, 'Was ist neu am neuen Gewährleistungsrecht?' (2021) 21 *ÖJZ*, 965 (971 et seq); Nemeth, in: Flume et al. (eds), *VGG* (2022), § 7, mn. 13; Wendehorst, 'Aktualisierungen und andere digitale Dauerleistungen' in Stabentheiner et al. (eds), *Das neue europäische Gewährleistungsrecht* (2019), 111 (130).

[57] Schmitt, 'Das neue Gewährleistungsrecht ab 2022: Digitale Leistungen und mehr' (2021) 6 *jusIT*, 221 (225); Fida, 'Die neue Aktualisierungspflicht nach § 7 VGG' (2021) 12 *ecolex*, 1079 (1081); Nemeth, in: Flume et al. (eds), *VGG* (2022), § 7, mn. 23; Wendehorst, 'Aktualisierungen und andere digitale Dauerleistungen' in Stabentheiner et al. (eds), *Das neue europäische Gewährleistungsrecht* (2019), 111 (133).

[58] Fida, 'Die neue Aktualisierungspflicht nach § 7 VGG' (2021) 12 *ecolex*, 1079 (1081 et seq); Schmitt, 'Das neue Gewährleistungsrecht ab 2022: Digitale Leistungen und mehr' (2021) 6 *jusIT*, 221 (226); Nemeth, in: Flume et al. (eds), *VGG* (2022), § 7, mn. 23; Wendehorst, 'Aktualisierungen und andere digitale Dauerleistungen' in Stabentheiner et al. (eds), *Das neue europäische Gewährleistungsrecht* (2019), 111 (133).

[59] Neumayr, 'Das neue Verbrauchergewährleistungsrecht' (2021) 8 *RdW*, 536 (538); Fida, 'Die neue Aktualisierungspflicht nach § 7 VGG' (2021) 12 *ecolex*, 1079 (1079 et seqq); Nemeth, in: Flume et al. (eds), *VGG* (2022), § 7, mn. 24; Wendehorst, 'Aktualisierungen und andere digitale Dauerleistungen' in Stabentheiner et al. (eds), *Das neue europäische Gewährleistungsrecht* (2019), 111 (133); Wendehorst, 'Die Regelungen des VGG zu digitalen Leistungen unter besonderer Berücksichtigung der Aktualisierungspflichten' in Bydlinski (ed), *Das neue Gewährleistungsrecht* (2022), 49 (63 et seq).

[60] Stabentheiner, 'Ein Überblick über das Gewährleistungsrichtlinien-Umsetzungsgesetz' (2021) 6 *VbR*, 189; Kodek, 'Vertragswidrigkeit und Mangelbegriff im neuen Gewährleistungsrecht' (2022) 2a *ÖJZ*, 103 (108); Laimer, in: Flume et al. (eds), *VGG* (2022), § 6, mn. 13.

[61] Kodek, 'Vertragswidrigkeit und Mangelbegriff im neuen Gewährleistungsrecht' (2022) 2a *ÖJZ*, 103 (108 et seq); Neumayr, 'Zum Mangelbegriff des neuen VGG' (2021) 12 *RdW*, 833 (836); Laimer, in: Flume et al. (eds), *VGG* (2022), § 6, mn. 13 et seqq; European Law Institute, *Statement of the European Law Institute on the European Commission's Proposed Directive on the Supply of Digital Content to Consumers* (2016), 19.

[62] Stabentheiner, 'Was ist neu am neuen Gewährleistungsrecht?' (2021) 21 *ÖJZ*, 965 (971); Kodek, 'Vertragswidrigkeit und Mangelbegriff im neuen Gewährleistungsrecht' (2022) 2a *ÖJZ*, 103 (108 et seq); Laimer, in: Flume et al. (eds), *VGG* (2022), § 6, mn. 18; European Law Institute, *Statement of the European*

in writing, even if this is expedient for the trader for reasons of proof, as the burden of proof for the consumer's consent lies with the trader.[63]

21 The consumer is only informed in a sufficient manner by specific information about a concrete deviation, whereas general information is not sufficient.[64] Moreover, there are good arguments for the fact that the consumer must be actively informed, i.e. it is not only a matter of positive knowledge, since this can also be obtained through other perceptions.[65]

22 In contrast to Art. 2 para. 3 CSGD, the Directives and thus the VGG do not provide for a blanket disclaimer of warranty for apparent defects.[66] § 928 ABGB, which restricts the warranty in case of apparent defects, therefore only applies outside the scope of application of the VGG.

III. Warranty and Sustainability

1. Durability

23 The term "durability" is defined in § 2 para. 11 VGG as the suitability of goods to retain their necessary functions and performance under normal use. It was adopted in § 6 para. 2 subpara. 5 VGG as an objectively required characteristic of a good or digital service in accordance with Art. 7 para. 1 lit. d SGD.[67] Therefore, the durability of a product must be warranted within the scope of application of the VGG. The contracting parties are only able to effectively deviate in the case of qualified consent of the consumer within the meaning of § 6 para. 1 VGG.[68]

24 Even outside the scope of application of the VGG, the lack of durability of an item sometimes triggers warranty obligations under Austrian law: Before the GRUG came into force, the Austrian Supreme Court of Justice ruled that it was generally expected in

---

Law Institute on the European Commission's Proposed Directive on the Supply of Digital Content to Consumers (2016), 19.

[63] Zöchling-Jud, 'Das neue Europäische Gewährleistungsrecht für den Warenhandel' (2019) 3 *GPR*, 115 (120); Dullinger, 'Das neue Gewährleistungsrecht' (2022) 1 *RFG*, 40 (42); Kodek, 'Vertragswidrigkeit und Mangelbegriff im neuen Gewährleistungsrecht' (2022) 2a *ÖJZ*, 103 (108); Laimer, in: Flume et al. (eds), *VGG* (2022), § 6, mn. 18, fn. 106; Wendehorst, 'Die Regelungen des VGG zu digitalen Leistungen unter besonderer Berücksichtigung der Aktualisierungspflichten' in Bydlinski (ed), *Das neue Gewährleistungsrecht* (2022), 49 (64).

[64] Kodek, 'Vertragswidrigkeit und Mangelbegriff im neuen Gewährleistungsrecht' (2022) 2a *ÖJZ*, 103 (109); Neumayr, 'Das neue Verbrauchergewährleistungsrecht' (2021) 8 *RdW*, 536 (537); Laimer, in: Flume et al. (eds), *VGG* (2022), § 6, mn. 15; Wendehorst, 'Die Regelungen des VGG zu digitalen Leistungen unter besonderer Berücksichtigung der Aktualisierungspflichten' in Bydlinski (ed), *Das neue Gewährleistungsrecht* (2022), 49 (63 et seq).

[65] Faber, 'Bereitstellung und Mangelbegriff' in Stabentheiner et al. (eds), *Das neue europäische Gewährleistungsrecht* (2019), 63 (82 et seq); Kodek, 'Vertragswidrigkeit und Mangelbegriff im neuen Gewährleistungsrecht' (2022) 2a *ÖJZ*, 103 (109); Laimer, in: Flume et al. (eds), *VGG* (2022), § 6, mn. 14; European Law Institute, *Statement of the European Law Institute on the European Commission's Proposed Directive on the Supply of Digital Content to Consumers* (2016), 19.

[66] Stabentheiner, 'Was ist neu am neuen Gewährleistungsrecht?' (2021) 21 *ÖJZ*, 965 (970); Neumayr, 'Zum Mangelbegriff des neuen VGG' (2021) 12 *RdW*, 833 (838).

[67] Stabentheiner, 'Ein Überblick über das Gewährleistungsrichtlinien-Umsetzungsgesetz' (2021) 6 VbR, 188 (189); Kodek, 'Vertragswidrigkeit und Mangelbegriff im neuen Gewährleistungsrecht' (2022) 2a *ÖJZ*, 103 (107 et seq); Flume/Ziegler, in: Flume et al. (eds), *VGG* (2022), § 2, mn. 14; Zöchling-Jud, 'Digital Consumer Contract Law And New Technologies – Implementation of The Digital Content Directive in Austria' (2021) 12 *JIPITEC*, 221 (221).

[68] Dullinger, 'Das neue Gewährleistungsrecht' (2022) 1 *RFG*, 40 (46); Stabentheiner, 'Ein Überblick über das Gewährleistungsrichtlinien-Umsetzungsgesetz' (2021) 6 *VbR*, 188 (189); Laimer, in: Flume et al. (eds), *VGG* (2022), § 6, mn. 8.

legal transactions that a brand-new motor vehicle engine would remain functional for more than two years.[69] Thus, the Austrian Supreme Court of Justice assumed that a certain functional life of an object can be considered as a usually presupposed characteristic within the meaning of § 922 para. 1 ABGB, for which liability is assumed under warranty law.[70]

In this context, it should be noted that the legislator considered creating special rules for durability defects in the course of implementing the new directives.[71] In particular, the introduction of a longer warranty period and an obligation of the seller to inform about the minimum durability of goods were discussed.[72] Ultimately, the legislator decided against such special norms and to wait for possible future developments at the European level.[73] As a consequence, an analogous application of the existing knowledge-dependent limitation period for legal defect can no longer be considered in the future. At most, an extension of the limitation period can be considered in individual cases by (implied) agreement of the parties.[74]

2. Product-Related Legislation

According to recital 32 SGD, ensuring a longer durability of goods is important for achieving more sustainable consumption patterns and a circular economy. *"For those purposes, product-specific Union legislation is the most appropriate means of introducing durability and other product-related requirements in relation to specific types or groups of products, using for this purpose adapted criteria"*. However, the warranty obligation for durability should only have a supplementary function since it is not suitable to improve sustainability standards.[75]

The Austrian legislator has refrained from introducing its own product-specific legislation. Therefore, the decisive factor in Austria is the durability the consumer can reasonably expect. All relevant circumstances are to be taken into account, such as public statements about the goods, the price, the intensity or frequency of use, but also the possible need for reasonable maintenance of the goods.[76]

3. National Regulations on the Availability of Spare Parts

The duration of the usability of a good is essentially determined by the availability of spare parts. Nevertheless, the SGD does not provide for an obligation of the seller to ensure the availability of spare parts during a certain period of time. At the same

---

[69] OGH 23.04.2015 – 1 Ob 71/15w – Zak 2015, 256 (256 et seq).
[70] Brenn and Karner, 'Verkäufer hat für die übliche Lebensdauer eines Motors einzustehen' (2016) 20 *EvBl*, 925 (927); Schoditsch, 'Gewöhnlich vorausgesetzte Eigenschaften eines Kfz-Motors' (2015) 11 *ecolex*, 946 (947).
[71] Explanatory Notes on the Government Draft of the GRUG (No. 949 of the Supplements to the Stenographic Protocols of the National Council of the XXVII Legislative Period), 7; Zöchling-Jud, 'Beweislast, Gewährleistungs- und Verjährungsfristen im neuen Gewährleistungsrecht' (2022) 2a *ÖJZ*, 113 (122).
[72] Zöchling-Jud, 'Beweislast, Gewährleistungs- und Verjährungsfristen im neuen Gewährleistungsrecht' (2022) 2a *ÖJZ*, 113 (122).
[73] Explanatory Notes on the Government Draft of the GRUG (No. 949 of the Supplements to the Stenographic Protocols of the National Council of the XXVII Legislative Period), 7.
[74] Zöchling-Jud, 'Beweislast, Gewährleistungs- und Verjährungsfristen im neuen Gewährleistungsrecht' (2022) 2a *ÖJZ*, 113 (122).
[75] Faber, 'Neues Gewährleistungsrecht und Nachhaltigkeit (Part I)' (2020) 1 *VbR*, 6 et seq; Zöchling-Jud, 'Das neue Europäische Gewährleistungsrecht für den Warenhandel' (2019) 3 *GPR*, 122 et seq.
[76] Recital 32 SGD; Maitz-Straßnig, 'Die neue Gewährleistung nach der Warenkauf-Richtlinie' (2020) 2 *RdW*, 79; Laimer, in: Flume et al. (eds), *VGG* (2022), § 6, mn. 8; Pollitzer et al, 'Privatrecht und Nachhaltigkeit: Gewährleistung für ESG-Verstöße im Wertschöpfungsprozess' (2022) 2 *NR*, 416.

29 time it is made clear that the Member States are free to provide for or maintain such an obligation on the part of the seller, manufacturer or other persons in preceding links in the chain of transactions.[77]

29 In Austria, no obligations of this kind have been imposed so far and corresponding provisions have not been introduced as part of the implementation of the Directives. In isolated cases, EU regulations issued on the basis of the Ecodesign Directive[78] provide for a public law obligation on the part of the manufacturer to ensure the availability of spare parts for a longer period of time.[79] However, there is no explicit link between these regulations and those of Austrian contract law.[80]

4. Relationship of the Transposition Measures to the Ecodesign Regulation 2007

30 Both the first[81] and the second Ecodesign Directive[82] were implemented in Austria by amending the Ecodesign Act (ODV 2007)[83]. The Ecodesign Act was not amended as part of the introduction of the GRUG, nor is it mentioned in its provisions or in the related explanatory notes.

31 Compliance with the provisions of this regulation is primarily secured by administrative penalty provisions. These can be found in the legal basis of the regulation, namely the Act against Unfair Competition (UWG)[84], the Act on Safety Measures, Normalisation and Typification in the Field of Electrical Engineering (ETG)[85] and the Business Regulation Act (GewO)[86].

32 Additionally, sanctions under private law are provided. Based on § 34 para. 3 UWG, an action for injunctive relief can be brought on the basis of a violation of the ODV 2007, as well as an action for damages in the event of fault. In order to secure claims for injunctive relief, preliminary injunctions may be obtained under facilitated conditions pursuant to § 24 UWG.

5. Measures to Improve Sustainability as well as the Circular Economy

33 Measures to improve environmental sustainability and the circular economy were only discussed in the course of implementing the Directives, but ultimately not taken.[87] Discussions included extending the presumption contained in Art. 11 para. 1 SGD and the warranty period beyond the minimum required by EU law, as well as introducing an

---

[77] Recital 33 SGD.
[78] Directive 2005/32/EC of the European Parliament and of the Council of 6 July 2005 establishing a framework for the setting of ecodesign requirements for energy-using products and amending Council Directive 92/42/EEC and Directives 96/57/EC and 2000/55/EC of the European Parliament and of the Council.
[79] Faber, 'Neues Gewährleistungsrecht und Nachhaltigkeit (Part I)' (2020) 1 VbR, 4 (9).
[80] Faber, 'Neues Gewährleistungsrecht und Nachhaltigkeit (Part I)' (2020) 1 VbR, 4 (9).
[81] Ecodesign Directive 2005/32/EC.
[82] Directive 2009/125/EC of the European Parliament and of the Council of 21 October 2009 establishing a framework for the setting of ecodesign requirements for energy-related products (recast).
[83] Verordnung des Bundesministers für Wirtschaft und Arbeit zur Schaffung eines Rahmens für die Festlegung von Anforderungen an die umweltgerechte Gestaltung energieverbrauchsrelevanter Produkte (Ökodesign-Verordnung 2007), BGBl II 2007/126 idF BGBl II 2011/187.
[84] Bundesgesetz gegen den unlauteren Wettbewerb 1984 – UWG, BGBl 1984/448 idF BGBl I 2019/104.
[85] Bundesgesetz über Sicherheitsmaßnahmen, Normalisierung und Typisierung auf dem Gebiete der Elektrotechnik (Elektrotechnikgesetz 1992 – ETG 1992), BGBl 1993/106 idF BGBl I 2017/27.
[86] Gewerbeordnung 1994 – GewO 1994, BGBl 1994/194 idF BGBl I 2020/65.
[87] Explanatory Notes on the Government Draft of the GRUG (No. 949 of the Supplements to the Stenographic Protocols of the National Council of the XXVII Legislative Period), 6 et seqq.

obligation to provide information on the minimum durability of goods and a direct consumer claim against the manufacturer or importer.[88]

The reasons given by the Austrian legislator for not implementing the other measures included the need to avoid *"excessive additional burdens for companies"* and expected initiatives of the EU in the area of sustainability in the future.[89]

IV. Installation of Digital Services or Digital Content

Under § 17 VGG, which was enacted in implementation of Art. 5 DCD, the trader is obligated to provide the digital services or content that is the subject of the contract.[90] Unless the parties agree otherwise, installation is not generally required for the fulfillment of this obligation; the consumer need only be given access.[91]

However, if the trader integrates the digital service into the consumer's digital environment or has it integrated under his responsibility and a defect is caused by improper conduct, § 8 para. 2 VGG stipulates that the trader is liable under warranty law in accordance with Art. 9 DCD.[92]

In certain cases, the trader is liable even though the digital service is to be integrated by the consumer. This is the case, if the integration is carried out improperly due to an error, incompleteness or lack of clarity in the instructions provided by the trader, resulting in a defect.[93]

The specific remedies available to a consumer in such cases under § 20 VGG depend on the circumstances of the specific case. In particular, the severity of the defect, the possibility of remedying the defect and the willingness of the trader to do so.[94]

V. Contractual Obligation of the Consumer to Provide Personal Data?

In the course of the implementation of the Directive, no national regulations were implemented that address the issue of the enforceability of a contractual obligation to

---

[88] Explanatory Notes on the Government Draft of the GRUG (No. 949 of the Supplements to the Stenographic Protocols of the National Council of the XXVII Legislative Period), 6 et seqq; cf. Wendehorst, 'Direkthaftung des Herstellers (Teil I)' (2020) 3 *VbR*, 94; Wendehorst, 'Direkthaftung des Herstellers (Teil II)' (2020) 4 *VbR*, 138.

[89] Explanatory Notes on the Government Draft of the GRUG (No. 949 of the Supplements to the Stenographic Protocols of the National Council of the XXVII Legislative Period), 6 et seqq.

[90] Dullinger, 'Das neue Gewährleistungsrecht' (2022) 1 *RFG*, 40 (42); Schmitt, 'Das neue Gewährleistungsrecht ab 2022: Digitale Leistungen und mehr' (2022) 1 *jusIT*, 1 (3); Klečetka and Neumayr, in: Flume et al. (eds), *VGG* (2022), § 17, mn. 3; Wendehorst, 'Die Regelungen des VGG zu digitalen Leistungen unter besonderer Berücksichtigung der Aktualisierungspflichten' in Bydlinski (ed), *Das neue Gewährleistungsrecht* (2022), 49 (79 et seq).

[91] Faber, 'Bereitstellung und Mangelbegriff' in Stabentheiner et al. (eds), *Das neue europäische Gewährleistungsrecht* (2019), 63 (70); Stabentheiner, 'Ein Überblick über das Gewährleistungsrichtlinien-Umsetzungsgesetz' (2021) 6 *VbR*, 188 (192); Klečetka and Neumayr, in: Flume et al. (eds), *VGG* (2022), § 17, mn. 5; Wendehorst, 'Die Regelungen des VGG zu digitalen Leistungen unter besonderer Berücksichtigung der Aktualisierungspflichten' in Bydlinski (ed), *Das neue Gewährleistungsrecht* (2022), 49 (79 et seq).

[92] Stabentheiner, 'Ein Überblick über das Gewährleistungsrichtlinien-Umsetzungsgesetz' (2021) 6 *VbR*, 190 (192); Hafner-Thomic, 'Alles neu macht das GRUG?' (2022) 1 *ecolex*, 22 (23); Kronthaler, in: Flume et al. (eds), *VGG* (2022), § 8, mn. 33 et seqq.

[93] Hafner-Thomic, 'Alles neu macht das GRUG?' (2022) 1 *ecolex*, 22 (23); Zöchling-Jud, 'Das neue Europäische Gewährleistungsrecht für den Warenhandel' (2019) 3 *GPR*, 124; Kronthaler, in: Flume et al. (eds), *VGG* (2022), § 8, mn. 38 et seqq.

[94] Stabentheiner, 'Ein Überblick über das Gewährleistungsrichtlinien-Umsetzungsgesetz' (2021) 6 *VbR*, 188 (192 et seq).

provide personal data. Accordingly, it is still necessary to refer to the provisions of the GDPR in this context, which, pursuant to Art. 3 para. 8 DCD, remains unaffected by the Directive's requirements.[95]

VI. Modification of the Digital Content or Digital Service

40   The requirements of Art. 19 DCD regarding the modification of digital services or content were implemented in § 27 VGG, which is principally mandatory in favour of the consumer. The modification of the digital service by the trader is tied to a contractual agreement in which a valid reason for the modification is provided for.[96] Further requirements are that the modification must be free of charge for the consumer and that clear and comprehensible information about the impending change is provided.[97] § 27 para. 2 VGG grants the consumer a right to terminate the contract in the event of a more than minor impediment of access to or use of the digital service, of which the consumer must be informed in advance by means of a durable data medium.[98] The period for exercising the right of termination of the contract starts at the date of the modification or at the date of receipt of the information if it was received later and lasts for 30 days.[99] There is no right to termination of the contract pursuant to § 27 para. 4 VGG if the trader enables the digital service to be retained in accordance with the contract without any additional costs.[100] Furthermore, § 27 para. 6 VGG exempts certain bundle contracts – in accordance with the DCD – from its scope of application.

---

[95] Flume, in: Flume et al. (eds), *VGG* (2022), Vor § 16, mn. 11; Wendehorst, 'Die Regelungen des VGG zu digitalen Leistungen unter besonderer Berücksichtigung der Aktualisierungspflichten' in Bydlinski (ed), *Das neue Gewährleistungsrecht* (2022), 49 (55 et seqq).

[96] Schmitt, 'Das neue Gewährleistungsrecht ab 2022: Digitale Leistungen und mehr' (2022) 1 *jusIT*, 1 (6 et seq); Stabentheiner, 'Ein Überblick über das Gewährleistungsrichtlinien-Umsetzungsgesetz' (2021) 6 *VbR*, 188 (193); Parzmayr, in: Flume et al. (eds), *VGG* (2022), § 27, mn. 10 et seq; Wendehorst, 'Hybride Produkte und hybrider Vertrieb' in Wendehorst and Zöchling-Jud (eds), *Ein neues Vertragsrecht für den digitalen Binnenmarkt?* (2016), 45 (68); Wendehorst, 'Die Regelungen des VGG zu digitalen Leistungen unter besonderer Berücksichtigung der Aktualisierungspflichten' in Bydlinski (ed), *Das neue Gewährleistungsrecht* (2022), 49 (82 et seq).

[97] Stabentheiner, 'Ein Überblick über das Gewährleistungsrichtlinien-Umsetzungsgesetz' (2021) 6 *VbR*, 188 (193); Schmitt, 'Das neue Gewährleistungsrecht ab 2022: Digitale Leistungen und mehr' (2022) 1 *jusIT*, 1 (6 et seq); Parzmayr, in: Flume et al. (eds), *VGG* (2022), § 8, mn. 14 and 16; Wendehorst, 'Die Regelungen des VGG zu digitalen Leistungen unter besonderer Berücksichtigung der Aktualisierungspflichten' in Bydlinski (ed), *Das neue Gewährleistungsrecht* (2022), 49 (83 et seqq).

[98] Dullinger, 'Das neue Gewährleistungsrecht' (2022) 1 *RFG*, 44; Kern, 'Das neue europäische Gewährleistungsrecht' (2019) 5 *VbR*, 168; Stabentheiner, 'Was ist neu am neuen Gewährleistungsrecht?' (2021) 21 *ÖJZ*, 975; Parzmayr, in: Flume et al. (eds), *VGG* (2022), § 27, mn. 19 et seq; Wendehorst, 'Hybride Produkte und hybrider Vertrieb' in Wendehorst and Zöchling-Jud (eds), *Ein neues Vertragsrecht für den digitalen Binnenmarkt?* (2016), 45 (68); European Law Institute, *Statement of the European Law Institute on the European Commission's Proposed Directive on the Supply of Digital Content to Consumers* (2016), 33 et seq; Wendehorst, 'Die Regelungen des VGG zu digitalen Leistungen unter besonderer Berücksichtigung der Aktualisierungspflichten' in Bydlinski (ed), *Das neue Gewährleistungsrecht* (2022), 49 (85 et seq).

[99] Kodek, 'Änderung digitaler Inhalte und digitaler Dienstleistungen (Art 19 DIRL)' in Stabentheiner et al. (eds), *Das neue europäische Gewährleistungsrecht* (2019), 141 (144); Schmitt, 'Das neue Gewährleistungsrecht ab 2022: Digitale Leistungen und mehr' (2022) 1 *jusIT*, 1 (7); Parzmayr, in: Flume et al. (eds), *VGG* (2022), § 27, mn. 21; European Law Institute, *Statement of the European Law Institute on the European Commission's Proposed Directive on the Supply of Digital Content to Consumers* (2016), 33 et seq; Wendehorst, 'Die Regelungen des VGG zu digitalen Leistungen unter besonderer Berücksichtigung der Aktualisierungspflichten' in Bydlinski (ed), *Das neue Gewährleistungsrecht* (2022), 49 (85 et seq).

[100] Schmitt, 'Das neue Gewährleistungsrecht ab 2022: Digitale Leistungen und mehr' (2022) 1 *jusIT*, 1 (7); Parzmayr, in: Flume et al. (eds), *VGG* (2022), § 27, mn. 21.

C. Contractuality

VII. Third-Party Rights

According to Austrian understanding, a legal defect exists if the transferor does not provide the transferee with the owed legal position.[101] A typical example of this is the sale of an object that is in the ownership of a third party or encumbered with other rights *in rem* of third parties.[102] Such defects have always been subject to the same rules as material defects according to Austrian law, and must therefore be warranted in the same way.[103] For this reason, the Austrian legislator considered a separate implementation of Art. 10 DCD and Art. 9 SGD to be unnecessary.[104]

However, this is not entirely unproblematic: according to the Austrian view up to this point, it is not necessary for a third party to interfere with the transferee's use in order for a legal defect to be enforceable, but it is sufficient that the owed legal position was undoubtedly not provided.[105] In contrast, the wording of both Art. 10 DCD and Art. 9 SGD requires for the existence of a legal defect that there is a "restriction" resulting from the infringement of third-party rights which prevents or restricts the use of goods or digital services.[106] Due to the fully harmonising character of the Directives, it is at least debatable whether this view can be upheld within the scope of application of the Directives. Considering the protective purpose of the provisions of EU law, one can assume that the concept of legal deficiency in the Directives also covers potential impairments and does not necessarily require an actual impairment of use.[107]

VIII. Relation to Copyright and the Right to Resell Digital Content

Art. 3 para. 9 DCD states that the Directive shall apply without prejudice to EU and national law on copyright and related rights. A more precise regulation of the relationship of copyright law with the implementation provisions of the DCD has not been issued in Austria. The consumer's right to resell digital content is thus governed by the pre-existing legal situation, which is determined in particular by the Copyright Act (UrhG),[108] dating back to 1936.[109]

According to the Austrian understanding, copyright is an "indivisible, indispensable and inalienable bundle of exclusive rights", which serve to protect the exploitation of

---

[101] Zöchling-Jud, in: Kletečka and Schauer (eds), *ABGB-ON* (2016), § 923, mn. 6; Reischauer, in: Rummel and Lukas (eds), *ABGB – Kommentar zum Allgemeinen bürgerlichen Gesetzbuch* (2018), § 923, mn. 143.
[102] Welser and Zöchling-Jud, *Grundriss des Bürgerlichen Rechts* II (2015), 76; Dullinger, *Schuldrecht Allgemeiner Teil* (2021), 75 et seq.
[103] Zöchling-Jud, in: Kletečka and Schauer (eds), *ABGB-ON* (2016), § 923, mn. 5 et seqq; Ofner, in: Schwimann and Kodek (eds), *ABGB: Praxiskommentar* (2021), § 922, mn. 3.
[104] Explanatory Notes on the Government Draft of the GRUG (No. 949 of the Supplements to the Stenographic Protocols of the National Council of the XXVII Legislative Period), 18; Kronthaler, in: Flume et al. (eds), *VGG* (2022), § 10, mn. 13.
[105] Welser and Zöchling-Jud, *Grundriss des Bürgerlichen Rechts* II (2015), 76; OGH 12.05.2009 – 10 Ob 21/08y – Zak 2009, 295 (295).
[106] Faber, 'Bereitstellung und Mangelbegriff' in Stabentheiner et al. (eds), *Das neue europäische Gewährleistungsrecht* (2019), 63 (102 et seqq); Kodek, 'Vertragswidrigkeit und Mangelbegriff im neuen Gewährleistungsrecht' (2022) 2a ÖJZ, 103 (110).
[107] Kodek and Leupold, *Gewährleistung NEU* (2019) 23; Faber, 'Bereitstellung und Mangelbegriff' in Stabentheiner et al. (eds), *Das neue europäische Gewährleistungsrecht* (2019), 63 (102 et seq); Kodek, 'Vertragswidrigkeit und Mangelbegriff im neuen Gewährleistungsrecht' (2022) 2a ÖJZ, 103 (110).
[108] Bundesgesetz über das Urheberrecht an Werken der Literatur und der Kunst und über verwandte Schutzrechte (Urheberrechtsgesetz), BGBl 1936/111 idF BGBl 2021/244.
[109] Appl, 'Urheberrecht' in Wiebe (ed), *Wettbewerbs- und Immaterialgüterrecht* (2018), 187 (190 et seq); Flume, in: Flume et al.(eds), *VGG* (2022), Vor § 16, mn. 12.

an intellectual creation, but also of the creative personality of the respective author.[110] The right to distribute a work protected by copyright, and to resell digital content, is generally granted only to its creator, unless the creator has consented to the distribution or another exception applies.[111]

45 The exclusive distribution right of the creator is limited above all by the principle of exhaustion. As a consequence the further distribution of a particular work is no longer bound to the consent of the author as soon as it has been put into circulation with the consent of the author in a Member State of the EU or a contracting state of the European Economic Area.[112]

46 According to the prevailing opinion, the distribution right and the principle of exhaustion are linked to physical works,[113] which is why it is questionable whether the latter is also applicable to digital content. Insofar as digital content is distributed in a medium-bound manner, this is mostly affirmed.[114] According to this understanding, there should at least be no obstacles to the resale of a physical data medium within the meaning of Art. 3 para. 3 DCD.

47 However, problems can arise with the carrierless sale of digital content online. In the *UsedSoft* case[115] the CJEU first clarified that the exhaustion principle also applies when computer programs as defined in the Computer Programs Directive (CPD)[116] are sold without a physical medium.[117] As a result, it had been unclear whether this case law could also be applied to digital content other than computer programs.[118] This was negated by the CJEU in the *Tom Kabinet* case,[119] in particular for e-books, but also for other digital content that does not fall within the scope of the CPD.[120] In light of this ruling, the carrierless resale of digital content that is not a computer program appears to be permissible in principle only with the consent of the author, unless the circumstances of the individual case lead to the conclusion that the public sphere is not entered by the sale.[121]

---

[110] Appl, 'Urheberrecht' in Wiebe (ed), *Wettbewerbs- und Immaterialgüterrecht* (2018), 187 (190 et seq).
[111] Anderl, in: Kucsko and Handig (eds), *urheber.recht* (2017), § 16, mn. 1, 11 et seqq; Appl, 'Urheberrecht' in Wiebe (ed), *Wettbewerbs- und Immaterialgüterrecht* (2018), 187 (219).
[112] Steinmayr, in: Ciresa (ed), *Österreichisches Urheberrecht* (2021), § 16, mn. 12 et seqq; Anderl, in: Kucsko and Handig (eds), *urheber.recht* (2017), § 16, mn. 11 et seqq.
[113] Anderl, in: Kucsko and Handig (eds), *urheber.recht* (2017), § 16, mn. 8 et seq; Appl, 'Urheberrecht' in Wiebe (ed), *Wettbewerbs- und Immaterialgüterrecht* (2018), 187 (226); Steinmayr, in: Ciresa (ed), *Österreichisches Urheberrecht* (2021), § 16, mn. 1 et seq.
[114] Appl, 'Urheberrecht' in Wiebe (ed), *Wettbewerbs- und Immaterialgüterrecht* (2018), 187 (226); Anderl, in: Kucsko and Handig (eds), *urheber.recht* (2017), § 16, mn. 26.
[115] CJEU, Case C-128/11, 03.07.2012, *UsedSoft GmbH v Oracle International Corp.*, ECLI:EU:C:2012:407.
[116] Directive 2009/24/EC of the European Parliament and of the Council of 23 April 2009 on the legal protection of computer programs.
[117] Steinmayr, in: Ciresa (ed), *Österreichisches Urheberrecht* (2021), § 16, mn. 16; Anderl, in: Kucsko and Handig (eds), *urheber.recht* (2017), § 16, mn. 28.
[118] Appl, 'Urheberrecht' in Wiebe (ed), *Wettbewerbs- und Immaterialgüterrecht* (2018), 187 (227).
[119] CJEU, Case C-263/18, 19.12.2019, *Tom Kabinet Internet BV*, ECLI:EU:C:2019:1111.
[120] Zemann, 'EuGH: E-Books entgehen Erschöpfung' (2020) 2 *ecolex*, 122 (123 et seq); Thiele, 'EuGH: Kein Verkauf "gebrauchter" E-Books ohne Zustimmung des Urhebers' (2020) 1 *ZIIR*, 89 (96 et seq); Homar, 'Unzulässigkeit der Weiterveräußerung von E-Books' (2020) 1 *Medien und Recht*, 27 (27 et seqq).
[121] Homar, 'Unzulässigkeit der Weiterveräußerung von E-Books' (2020) 1 *Medien und Recht*, 27 (27 et seqq); Zemann, 'EuGH: E-Books entgehen Erschöpfung' (2020) 2 *ecolex*, 122 (124).

IX. Supply of Digital Content and Services

In accordance with the requirements of Art. 5 and Art. 12 para. 1 DCD, the trader must supply the digital service pursuant to § 17 VGG immediately after conclusion of the contract, unless otherwise agreed, by making it available or accessible to the consumer or to a physical or virtual facility chosen by the consumer.[122] § 17 VGG does not differentiate between single acts of supply and continuous supply. Any differences in this respect with regard to warranty and presumption periods as well as with regard to the consequences of a reduction in the price or termination of the contract are governed by §§ 18, 19, 22 and 24 VGG. The possibility of a modification of performance provided for in Art. 19 DCD for cases of continuous supply was implemented in Austria by § 27 VGG.[123]

A national provision explicitly addressing the case of interruption of a continuous supply of digital services was not introduced by the GRUG. In cases of recurring or more than negligible interruptions, which are to be treated as a lack of conformity in accordance with recital 51 DCD, the general rule of § 18 VGG is applicable. Therefore, a contractor must warrant for any defect that occurs or becomes apparent during the period of the obligation to provide the service.[124] The specific consequences of such interruptions are governed, *inter alia*, by § 22 para. 3 VGG, which was adopted in implementation of Art. 14 para. 5 DCD. Accordingly, if a digital service to be provided on a continuous basis is defective, a reduction in the price can only be claimed for the period in which the service was defective.[125]

D. Remedies for Lack of Conformity

I. General

The basic concept of the ABGB has remained largely unaffected. § 932 ABGB as amended by the GRUG provides for a two-stage concept in the sense of the primacy of the creation of a defect-free condition through repair or replacement. The modalities of the primary remedies were not changed by the amendment. The remedies of price reduction and (in the case of a non-minor impediment) termination of the contract (previously: "redhibition", "*Wandlung*") are only subsidiary remedies (§ 932 para. 4 ABGB).

In §§ 12 and 20, the VGG essentially follows the concept presented in § 932 ABGB. Priority must be given to the primary remedies. While § 12 para. 2 VGG provides for a right to choose between repair or replacement, like the ABGB, such a right does not exist under § 20 VGG in the field of digital performances. The only primary remedy available is the entitlement of the consumer to "have the digital content or digital service

---

[122] Bischinger and Weber-Woisetschläger, 'Das neue Gewährleistungsrecht (Part II)' (2021/2022) 3 *JAP*, 181 (182 et seq); Zöchling-Jud, 'Das neue europäische Gewährleistungsrecht für den Warenhandel' (2019) 3 *GPR*, 115 (119); Kern, 'Das neue europäische Gewährleistungsrecht' (2019) 5 *VbR*, 164 (168).
[123] Cf. C.VI.
[124] Stabentheiner, 'Was ist neu am Gewährleistungsrecht?' (2021) 21 *ÖJZ*, 965 (972–973); Bischinger and Weber-Woisetschläger, 'Das neue Gewährleistungsrecht (Part II)' (2021/2022) 3 *JAP*, 181 (182); Kronthaler, in: Flume et al. (eds), *VGG* (2022), § 18, mn. 6.
[125] Schmitt, 'Das neue Gewährleistungsrecht ab 2022: Digitale Leistungen und mehr' (2022) 1 *jusIT*, 1 (3); Bischinger and Weber-Woisetschläger, 'Das neue Gewährleistungsrecht (Part II)' (2021/2022) 3 *JAP*, 181 (184); Kronthaler, in: Flume et al. (eds), *VGG* (2022), § 18, mn. 7.

brought into conformity".¹²⁶ The decision on how to establish this state, for example by transmitting an updated version or providing a new copy of the digital performance, is incumbent on the trader.

52 On a secondary level, the transferee has the subsidiary options of price reduction and (in the case of defects that are not minor) termination of the contract according to the ABGB and VGG (§ 932 para. 4 ABGB, § 12 para. 4 and 5, § 20 para. 4 et seqq VGG). According to § 20 para. 5 VGG, the possibility of price reduction does not exist if a digital service was not provided in exchange for payment.

II. Individual Questions

1. Right of Retention

53 Within the framework of the implementation of the Directives, no new regulations regarding rights of retention were introduced.¹²⁷ However, a similar principle (*Zug-um-Zug*; § 1052 ABGB) arises from general private law, which also applies to contracts that are subject to the scope of application of the SGD and the DCD.¹²⁸

2. Place of Performance and Subsequent Performance

54 The place of performance and subsequent performance continues to be determined according to § 905 ABGB, which was not changed by the GRUG. Accordingly, the transferor must fulfil his obligation to perform at his place of residence or, in case of business-related transactions, at his place of business, unless the contracting parties agree otherwise and nothing else arises from the nature or purpose of the transaction.¹²⁹ In general, the transferor must also fulfil his obligation to repair or replace at this place. However, something else may result from the nature and purpose of the contract.¹³⁰

55 In contrast, within the scope of § 1 KSchG, § 8 KSchG provides for unilaterally mandatory regulations only in favour of the consumer. This includes all contracts that fall within the scope of application of the VGG. In such transactions, the trader must in principle fulfil his obligation to repair or replace the goods at the place where the goods were handed over.¹³¹ If the trader has delivered the owed good to a domestic location in accordance with the contract, that location shall constitute the place of performance.¹³² Irrespective of such a delivery, the consumer may also demand that the trader fulfils his warranty obligations at the domestic place where the item is usually located. This pre-

---

¹²⁶ Wendehorst, 'Die Regelungen des VGG zu digitalen Leistungen unter besonderer Berücksichtigung der Aktualisierungspflichten' in Bydlinski (ed), *Das neue Gewährleistungsrecht* (2022), 49 (80 et seqq).

¹²⁷ Explanatory Notes on the Government Draft of the GRUG (No. 949 of the Supplements to the Stenographic Protocols of the National Council of the XXVII Legislative Period), 28.

¹²⁸ Koch and Kronthaler, in: Flume et al. (eds), *VGG* (2022), § 12, mn. 26; Dullinger, *Schuldrecht Allgemeiner Teil* (2021), 33 et seq; Verschraegen, in: Kletečka and Schauer (eds), *ABGB-ON* (2020), § 1052, mn. 1 et seqq; Spitzer and Kodek, in: Schwimann and Kodek (eds), *ABGB: Praxiskommentar* (2021), § 1052, mn. 23 et seqq.

¹²⁹ Dullinger, *Schuldrecht Allgemeiner Teil* (2021), 36 et seq; Kolmasch, in: Schwimann and Kodek (eds), *ABGB: Praxiskommentar* (2021), § 905, mn. 25 et seqq.

¹³⁰ Kolmasch, in: Schwimann and Kodek (eds), *ABGB: Praxiskommentar* (2021), § 905, mn. 30; Kietaibl, in: Kletečka and Schauer (eds), *ABGB-ON* (2020), § 905, mn. 18.

¹³¹ Zöchling-Jud, in: Kletečka and Schauer (eds), *ABGB-ON* (2016), § 932, mn. 16; Ofner, in: Schwimann and Kodek (eds), *ABGB: Praxiskommentar* (2021), § 932, mn. 11; Aichberger-Beig, in: Flume et al. (eds), *VGG* (2022), § 8 KSchG, mn. 7.

¹³² Dullinger, *Schuldrecht Allgemeiner Teil* (2021), 83 et seq; Zöchling-Jud, in: Kletečka and Schauer (eds), *ABGB-ON* (2016), § 932, mn. 16; Aichberger-Beig, in: Flume et al. (eds), *VGG* (2022), § 8 KSchG, mn. 7.

supposes that this place did not have to be unexpected for the trader and that transporting the item to the transferor would be impractical for the consumer.[133]

As compensation for these consumer-friendly regulations, the trader is granted the right to demand that the consumer sends the item to him, provided that this is feasible for him.[134] However, in contrast to the aforementioned transport, the term "consignment" ("*Übersendung*") does not refer to a delivery that the consumer carries out himself, but to a transport process for which external transport facilities are used.[135] If the transferor makes use of this right, he bears the risk of accidental loss of the item in transit in accordance with § 8 para. 2 KSchG.[136]

3. Transport Costs

Until the entry into force of the GRUG, § 8 para. 3 KSchG provided that in consumer transactions the transferor had to bear the costs necessary for repair or replacement.[137] This includes labour, material and shipping costs.[138]

§ 13 para. 1 VGG replaced § 8 para. 3 KSchG in the scope of application of the new EU law provisions. Accordingly, reparations and replacements are to be "without costs" for the consumer.[139] With reference to Art. 14 SGD, the explanatory notes clarify that this means "all costs that may arise in the course of remedying the defect" and, with reference to Art. 2 no. 14 SGD, also explicitly mention shipping and transport costs.[140]

Outside the scope of application of the VGG, § 932 para. 3 ABGB as amended stipulates that the transferor has to bear the costs of a repair or replacement.[141] The explanatory notes show that the legislator only wanted to reflect the general understanding that already existed in Austria. Accordingly, a party liable under a warranty is obligated to bear these costs outside the scope of application of the KSchG.[142] No modification of the general warranty law was intended in this respect. Therefore, the prevailing view in Austrian doctrine before the amendment still applies the scope of the transferor's obligation

---

[133] Ofner, in: Schwimann and Kodek (eds), *ABGB: Praxiskommentar* (2021), § 932, mn. 11; Zöchling-Jud, in: Kletečka and Schauer (eds), *ABGB-ON* (2016), § 932, mn. 16 et seq; Aichberger-Beig, in: Flume et al. (eds), *VGG* (2022), § 8 KSchG, mn. 8.

[134] Zöchling-Jud, in: Kletečka and Schauer (eds), *ABGB-ON* (2016), § 932, mn. 20; Dullinger, *Schuldrecht Allgemeiner Teil* (2021), 84; Aichberger-Beig, in: Flume et al. (eds), *VGG* (2022), § 8 KSchG, mn. 10.

[135] Krejci, in: Rummel (ed), *ABGB - Kommentar zum Allgemeinen bürgerlichen Gesetzbuch* (2002), § 8 KSchG, mn. 41; Zöchling-Jud, in: Kletečka and Schauer (eds), *ABGB-ON* (2016), § 932, mn. 20.

[136] Apathy, in: Schwimann and Kodek (eds), *ABGB: Praxiskommentar* (2015), § 8 KSchG, mn. 8; Reischauer, in: Rummel and Lukas (eds), *ABGB - Kommentar zum Allgemeinen bürgerlichen Gesetzbuch* (2018), § 932, mn. 262; Aichberger-Beig, in: Flume et al. (eds), *VGG* (2022), § 8 KSchG, mn. 10.

[137] Zöchling-Jud, in: Kletečka and Schauer (eds), *ABGB-ON* (2016), § 932, mn. 11 et seq; Apathy, in: Schwimann and Kodek (eds), *ABGB: Praxiskommentar* (2015), § 8 KSchG, mn. 10 et seqq; Aichberger-Beig, in: Flume et al. (eds), *VGG* (2022), § 8 KSchG, mn. 13.

[138] Apathy, in: Schwimann and Kodek (eds), *ABGB: Praxiskommentar* (2015), § 8 KSchG, mn. 10 et seqq; Zöchling-Jud, in: Kletečka and Schauer (eds), *ABGB-ON* (2016), § 932, mn. 10 et seqq; Aichberger-Beig, in: Flume et al. (eds), *VGG* (2022), § 8 KSchG, mn. 13.

[139] Faber, 'Rechtsbehelfe beim Warenkauf nach dem VGG' (2022) 2a *ÖJZ*, 123 (132); Stabentheiner, 'Ein Überblick über das Gewährleistungsrichtlinien-Umsetzungsgesetz' (2021) 6 *VbR*, 188 (191); Aichberger-Beig, in: Flume et al. (eds), *VGG* (2022), § 8 KSchG, mn. 15.

[140] Explanatory Notes on the Government Draft of the GRUG (No. 949 of the Supplements to the Stenographic Protocols of the National Council of the XXVII Legislative Period), 29; Aichberger-Beig, in: Flume et al. (eds), *VGG* (2022), § 8 KSchG, mn. 15.

[141] Art. 2 GRUG; § 932 para. 3 ABGB; Aichberger-Beig, in: Flume et al. (eds), *VGG* (2022), § 932 ABGB, mn. 6.

[142] Explanatory Notes on the Government Draft of the GRUG (No. 949 of the Supplements to the Stenographic Protocols of the National Council of the XXVII Legislative Period), 40; Aichberger-Beig, in: Flume et al. (eds), *VGG* (2022), § 932 ABGB, mn. 6.

to bear the costs outside the scope of application of the VGG. Depending on the place of subsequent performance, either the transferor (in the case an obligation to be fulfilled at the transferee's domicile) or the transferee (in the case of an obligation to collect or to deliver) has to bear any transport costs coinciding with the repair or replacement.[143]

4. Withdrawal and Termination of the Contract by Declaration

60   According to the previous legal situation in Austria, the right to price reduction or termination of the contract had to be asserted in court.[144] The extrajudicial notification of a defect within the warranty period led to a perpetuation of the defence of defectiveness. The transferee can invoke this defence if the transferor brings an action for payment after expiry of the warranty period.[145]

61   In this respect, Art. 15 DCD and Art. 16 SGD required the Austrian legislator to adapt Austrian warranty law: § 14 para. 1, § 15 para. 1, § 22 para. 1 and § 23 VGG now expressly provide that for the assertion of warranty rights no form is needed.[146] Due to the changed wording of § 932 para. 1 ABGB and the elimination of the requirement of judicial assertion in § 933 para. 1 ABGB, this also applies to general warranty law, although the freedom of form was not explicitly stipulated here as in the VGG.[147]

5. Reimbursement in Cases of the Provision of Digital Content or Digital Services

62   Art. 16–18 DCD on reimbursement in the event of termination of a contract regarding the supply of digital services were transposed in §§ 24–26 VGG in close accordance with the wording of the Directive. After termination, the trader must refund payments made on basis of the contract, while the consumer may no longer use the digital service.[148] In the case of continuous provision of the digital service over a definite or indefinite period, the trader must only refund the price on a pro rata basis, whereby the consumer shall not owe any remuneration for periods in which the service was defective.[149]

63   The trader may only use content provided or created by the consumer when using the digital service, which is not personal data, if it falls under the categories set forth in § 24 para. 5 subpara. 1–4 VGG. If such content does not fall under § 24 para. 5 subpara. 1–3

---

[143] Reischauer, in: Rummel and Lukas (eds), *ABGB – Kommentar zum Allgemeinen bürgerlichen Gesetzbuch* (2021), § 932, mn. 259 et seq; Klever and Schwamberger, 'Transportkostenvorschuss und Kosten der Mangelerhebung – Überlegungen aus Anlass der Neuerungen im deutschen Gewährleistungsrecht' (2018) 7 *wbl*, 357 (358 et seqq); I. Welser, 'Der Erfüllungsort für Verbesserungspflichten des Unternehmers nach § 8 KSchG' (2001) 20 *ÖJZ*, 745 (745); Aichberger-Beig, in: Flume et al. (eds), *VGG* (2022), § 932 ABGB, mn. 7.

[144] Aichberger-Beig, in: Flume et al. (eds), *VGG* (2022), § 932 ABGB, mn. 4; Welser and Zöchling-Jud, *Grundriss des Bürgerlichen Rechts* II (2015), 374–375; Dullinger, *Schuldrecht Allgemeiner Teil* (2021), 97.

[145] Zöchling-Jud, in: Kletečka and Schauer (eds), *ABGB-ON* (2016), § 933, mn. 21; Ofner, in: Schwimann and Kodek (eds), *ABGB: Praxiskommentar* (2021), § 933, mn. 26 et seq.

[146] Koch and Kronthaler, in: Flume et al. (eds), *VGG* (2022), § 14, mn. 1 and § 15, mn. 1.

[147] Explanatory Notes on the Government Draft of the GRUG (No. 949 of the Supplements to the Stenographic Protocols of the National Council of the XXVII Legislative Period), 40; Aichberger-Beig, in: Flume et al. (eds), *VGG* (2022), § 932 ABGB, mn. 4.

[148] Dullinger, 'Das neue Gewährleistungsrecht' (2022) 1 *RFG*, 40 (44); Flume, 'Digitale Leistungen' (2022) 2a *ÖJZ*, 137 (143 et seq); Flume, in: Flume et al. (eds), *VGG* (2022), § 24, mn. 3 and § 25, mn. 1.

[149] Neumayr, 'Das neue Verbrauchergewährleistungsrecht' (2021) 8 *RdW*, 536 (539); Stabentheiner, 'Ein Überblick über das Gewährleistungsrichtlinien-Umsetzungsgesetz' (2021) 6 *VbR*, 188 (193); Flume, in: Flume et al. (eds), *VGG* (2022), § 24, mn. 6.

D. Remedies for Lack of Conformity

VGG, the consumer has the right to regain the content from the trader in a commonly used and machine-readable format within a reasonable period.[150]

After the cancellation of the contract or after the price reduction, the trader must refund the payments within 14 days using the same means that were originally used.[151] After termination of the contract, the consumer must return the physical data medium on which the digital service was provided to the trader at the trader's expense if he is requested to do so within 14 days.[152] Regarding the beginning of this 14-day period, in contrast to Art. 17 and 18 DCD, §§ 25 and 26 VGG do not refer to the day on which the trader is informed of the consumer's decision to terminate the contract, but to the time of receipt of the declaration of termination.[153]

6. Reimbursement for the Provision of Digital Content or Digital Services in Exchange for the Provision of Personal Data

Apart from § 24 para. 4 VGG, which orders the trader to comply with the obligations under the GDPR with regard to the consumer's personal data, no specific refund rules have been created for cases where the consumer provides such data in return. In particular, the consumer will have the right to have his personal data deleted.[154] In order to avoid undue enrichment of the consumer, the trader will at least have claims to compensate this imbalance, the precise calculation of which could be difficult in practice.[155]

7. Relationship of Repair and Replacement

In accordance with Art. 13 SGD, Art. 12 VGG provides that the consumer may choose between repair and replacement, unless one of the remedies would be impossible or would impose disproportionately high costs on the seller compared to the other.[156] § 932 ABGB stipulates an identical rule for situations, which do not fall within the scope of application of the VGG.

In accordance with the provisions of the SGD, repair is in principle not given priority over replacement. However, the fact that the claim to repair can only not be invoked if it is associated with a disproportionately high costs or is impossible for the seller, can lead to a certain promotion of sustainability.[157]

---

[150] Schmitt, 'Das neue Gewährleistungsrecht ab 2022: Digitale Leistungen und mehr' (2022) 1 *jusIT*, 1 (5); Flume, 'Digitale Leistung' (2022) 2a *ÖJZ*, 137 (143 et seq); Flume, in: Flume et al. (eds), *VGG* (2022), § 24, mn. 11, 16.

[151] Stabentheiner, 'Ein Überblick über das Gewährleistungsrichtlinien-Umsetzungsgesetz' (2021) 6 *VbR*, 188 (193); Flume, 'Digitale Leistungen' (2022) 2a *ÖJZ*, 137 (143 et seq); Flume, in: Flume et al. (eds), *VGG* (2022), § 26, mn. 1 et seq.

[152] Schmitt, 'Das neue Gewährleistungsrecht ab 2022: Digitale Leistungen und mehr' (2022) 1 *jusIT*, 1 (3); Flume, 'Digitale Leistungen' (2022) 2a *ÖJZ*, 137 (143 et seq); Flume, in: Flume et al. (eds), *VGG* (2022), § 25, mn. 2.

[153] Neumayr, 'Das neue Verbrauchergewährleistungsrecht' (2021) 8 *RdW*, 536 (539); Stabentheiner, 'Ein Überblick über das Gewährleistungsrichtlinien-Umsetzungsgesetz' (2021) 6 *VbR*, 188 (193); Flume, in: Flume et al. (eds), *VGG* (2022), § 25, mn. 2 and § 26, mn. 1.

[154] Flume, in: Flume et al. (eds), *VGG* (2022), Vor § 16, mn. 25.

[155] Schmitt, *Gewährleistung bei Verträgen über digitale Inhalte* (2017), 233.

[156] Neumayr, 'Das neue Verbrauchergewährleistungsrecht' (2021) 8 *RdW*, 536 (538 et seq); Stabentheiner, 'Ein Überblick über das Gewährleistungsrichtlinien-Umsetzungsgesetz' (2021) 6 *VbR*, 188 (191); Koch and Kronthaler, in: Flume et al. (eds), *VGG* (2022), § 12, mn. 6.

[157] Neumayr, 'Das neue Verbrauchergewährleistungsrecht' (2021) 8 *RdW*, 536 (538 et seq); Stabentheiner, 'Ein Überblick über das Gewährleistungsrichtlinien-Umsetzungsgesetz' (2021) 6 *VbR*, 188 (191); Koch and Kronthaler, in: Flume et al. (eds), *VGG* (2022), § 12, mn. 6. Recital 48 SGD indicates that, according to the intention of the Directive's issuer, this provision should *inter alia* lead to the exclusion of the right to a

8. Obsolescence

68 In the course of transposing the Directives, the Austrian legislator has considered introducing an obligation for sellers to provide information on the minimum durability of goods in order to promote sustainability.[158] A longer warranty period for durability defects was also debated during the legislative process.[159]

69 However, such regulations were not adopted, which is justified in the explanatory notes *inter alia* by the fact that such an obligation to provide information could often lead to an undesirable, considerable extension of the transferor's warranty obligation. This would be associated with costs that the legislator did not want to burden the economy with during a pandemic. Finally, further EU legal requirements for the area of sustainability were expected.[160]

70 Nevertheless, it has been possible to counteract premature obsolescence with remedies under private law, especially tort law. In addition to warranty claims, the consumer may have claims for damages, rights under the law of error or the right to terminate a contract because of *laesio enormis*.[161]

71 If insufficient information is provided about the limited lifespan of a product, this may constitute a misleading commercial practice under § 2 UWG, which can be prosecuted under unfair competition law.[162] The Product Safety Act (PSG)[163] also provides the authorities with the possibility of ordering protective measures (§§ 11 et seqq PSG) and imposing fines (§§ 25 et seqq PSG) to protect against products that pose more than a minor risk to life and limb due to premature obsolescence.[164]

9. Transferability of the Consumer's Rights Against the Seller

72 The Austrian legal system does not provide for an automatic transfer of the consumer's rights against the trader to a subsequent consumer in the event of the resale of goods or digital services. However, an assignment of warranty claims is possible in principle. This applies in any case to the right to repair or replace, as their assignability is *inter alia* regulated in §§ 1392 et seq ABGB.[165]

---

replacement delivery if a repair is possible without problems and a replacement would cause considerable costs by comparison.

[158] Explanatory Notes on the Government Draft of the GRUG (No. 949 of the Supplements to the Stenographic Protocols of the National Council of the XXVII Legislative Period), 7; Stabentheiner, in: Flume et al. (eds), *VGG* (2022), 4.

[159] Zöchling-Jud, 'Beweislast, Gewährleistungs- und Verjährungsfristen im neuen Gewährleistungsrecht' (2022) 2a *ÖJZ*, 113 (122); Stabentheiner, in: Flume et al. (eds), *VGG* (2022), 4.

[160] Explanatory Notes on the Government Draft of the GRUG (No. 949 of the Supplements to the Stenographic Protocols of the National Council of the XXVII Legislative Period), 7; Stabentheiner, in: Flume et al. (eds), *VGG* (2022), 4.

[161] Koziol, *Obsoleszenzen im österreichischen Recht* (2016), 75 et seqq.

[162] Koziol, *Obsoleszenzen im österreichischen Recht* (2016), 30 et seq; Wrbka, *Geplante Obsoleszenz aus Sicht des Gewährleistungsrechts* (2015), 30 et seq; Commission staff working document, *Guidance on the implementation/application of directive 2005/29/EC on unfair commercial practices*, 25 June 2016, COM/2016/320 final, 75 et seq.

[163] Bundesgesetz zum Schutz vor gefährlichen Produkten (Produktsicherheitsgesetz 2004 – PSG 2004), BGBl I 2005/16 idF BGBl I 2018/32.

[164] Koziol, *Obsoleszenzen im österreichischen Recht* (2016), 104 et seq.

[165] Heidinger, in: Schwimann and Kodek (eds), *ABGB: Praxiskommentar* (2016), § 1393, mn. 19; Kepplinger, in: Schwimann and Neumayr, *ABGB: Taschenkommentar* (2020), § 1393, mn. 8.

E. Contractual Guarantees

The EU law provisions on contractual guarantees contained in Art. 6 CSGD had been transposed into national law by Art. 2 Warranty Amendment Act (GewRÄG)[166].[167] Said provision was adapted to the new requirements contained in Art. 2 no. 12 and Art. 17 SGD and moved to § 9a KSchG.[168] The implementation in the KSchG has the consequence that the rule continues to apply only to B2C and not to B2B or C2C contracts. 73

§ 9a para. 2 KSchG provides for an amended regulation on the manufacturer's durability guarantee. The consumer is granted a compulsory direct claim for repair or replacement of the goods against the manufacturer under the condition that the manufacturer has guaranteed their durability for a certain period of time.[169] Since Art. 17 para. 1 SGD and § 2 para. 2 KSchG allow for more favourable provisions for the consumer, the manufacturer may also grant him additional rights in the guarantee, such as, in particular, a claim for monetary compensation.[170] 74

According to § 9a para. 1 KSchG, the conditions stated in the advertising are binding if they are more advantageous than those contained in the guarantee statement and the advertising was not corrected with equal perceptibility before conclusion of the contract.[171] 75

Finally, the information obligations that must be fulfilled in the guarantee statement were also newly regulated. Additionally, the statements must be provided to the consumer on a durable medium at the latest when the goods are handed over. A violation of these regulations does not affect the validity of the guarantee, but can make the seller liable for damages in case of culpability.[172] 76

The Austrian legislator has not made use of the possibility provided for in Art. 17 para. 4 SGD to enact provisions concerning other aspects of contractual guarantees, such as the languages in which a guarantee statement must be made available to the consumer. 77

---

[166] Bundesgesetz, mit dem das Gewährleistungsrecht im Allgemeinen Bürgerlichen Gesetzbuch und im Konsumentenschutzgesetz sowie das Versicherungsvertragsgesetz geändert werden, BGBl I 2001/48.
[167] § 9b KSchG; Aichberger-Beig, in: Flume et al. (eds), *VGG* (2022), § 9a KSchG, mn. 2; Welser and Zöchling-Jud, *Die neue Gewährleistung* (2001), § 9b KSchG, mn. 1 et seqq.
[168] Art. 3 GRUG; Aichberger-Beig, in: Flume et al. (eds), *VGG* (2022), § 9a KSchG, mn. 2.
[169] Dullinger, 'Das neue Gewährleistungsrecht' (2022) 1 *RFG*, 40 (46); Kletečka and Neumayr, 'Rückgriff und Neuerungen im KSchG' (2022) 2a *ÖJZ*, 149 (156); Aichberger-Beig, in: Flume et al. (eds), *VGG* (2022), § 9a KSchG, mn. 21.
[170] Kletečka and Neumayr, 'Rückgriff und Neuerungen im KSchG' (2022) 2a *ÖJZ*, 149 (156); Kodek and Leupold, *Gewährleistung NEU* (2019) 40 et seq; Aichberger-Beig, in: Flume et al. (eds), *VGG* (2022), § 9a KSchG, mn. 21.
[171] Neumayr, 'Das neue Verbrauchergewährleistungsrecht' (2021) 8 *RdW*, 536 (541); Dullinger, *Schuldrecht Allgemeiner Teil* (2021), 114; Aichberger-Beig, in: Flume et al. (eds), *VGG* (2022), § 9a KSchG, mn. 9.
[172] Neumayr, 'Das neue Verbrauchergewährleistungsrecht' (2021) 8 *RdW*, 536 (541); Kletečka and Neumayr, 'Rückgriff und Neuerungen im KSchG' (2022) 2a *ÖJZ*, 149 (156); Aichberger-Beig, in: Flume et al. (eds), *VGG* (2022), § 9a KSchG, mn. 16.

F. Time Limits

I. General Information

78 Since the implementation of the CSGD, the warranty periods in Austria have been considered as limitation periods.[173] This system could have been retained in view of Art. 10 para. 5 SGD and Art. 11 para. 2 DCD, but was subjected to a change in the course of the transposition of the Directives.[174] Now, the term "warranty period" in the sense of the CJEU's decision in the *Ferenschild* case[175] refers to the period of time during which a lack of conformity must become apparent in order to trigger the transferor's liability under warranty law.[176] In contrast, the limitation period is the period within which the transferee can assert his warranty rights.[177]

79 According to § 3 VGG and § 9 KSchG, a shortening of the warranty or limitation period at the expense of a consumer is invalid.[178] Shortening the warranty or limitation periods in the context of B2B and C2C contracts is not subject to any explicit legal restriction, but may be *contra bonos mores* in the sense of § 879 para. 1 ABGB.[179]

II. Material Defects

80 The warranty period for material defects generally lasts for two years from delivery of the goods or provision of the digital performance (§§ 10, 18 VGG; § 933 ABGB).[180] According to § 18 para. 2 VGG, special rules apply for the continuous provision of digital services or digital content, where the warranty period in general corresponds to the duration of the obligation to provide the service.[181] If the digital services are to be provided on an ongoing basis and connected to movable tangible items which cannot fulfil their functions without the digital service (goods with digital elements), the warranty period

---

[173] Zöchling-Jud, in: Kletečka and Schauer (eds), *ABGB-ON* (2016), § 933, mn. 12; Welser and Zöchling-Jud, *Die neue Gewährleistung* (2001), § 933, mn. 10 et seqq; Reischauer, in: Rummel and Lukas (eds), *ABGB – Kommentar zum Allgemeinen bürgerlichen Gesetzbuch* (2018), § 933, mn. 6; Hafner-Thomic, 'Alles neu macht das GRUG?' (2022) 1 *ecolex*, 22 (23); S.-F. Kraus and Spendel, in: Flume et al. (eds), *VGG* (2022), § 28, mn. 1.

[174] §§ 10, 18, 28 VGG; § 933 ABGB.

[175] CJEU, Case C-133/16, 13.07.2017, *Ferenschild v JPC Motor SA*, ECLI:EU:C:2017:541.

[176] Explanatory Notes on the Government Draft of the GRUG (No. 949 of the Supplements to the Stenographic Protocols of the National Council of the XXVII Legislative Period), 37; S.-F. Kraus and Spendel, in: Flume et al. (eds), *VGG* (2022), § 28, mn. 2.

[177] Explanatory Notes on the Government Draft of the GRUG (No. 949 of the Supplements to the Stenographic Protocols of the National Council of the XXVII Legislative Period), 38; S.-F. Kraus and Spendel, in: Flume et al. (eds), *VGG* (2022), § 28, mn. 2.

[178] Bischinger and Weber-Woisetschläger, 'Das neue Gewährleistungsrecht (Part II)' (2021/2022) 3 *JAP*, 181 (187); Dullinger, *Schuldrecht Allgemeiner Teil* (2021), 70, 111; S.-F. Kraus and Spendel, in: Flume et al. (eds), *VGG* (2022), § 28, mn. 15.

[179] Welser and Zöchling-Jud, *Grundriss des Bürgerlichen Rechts* II (2015), 91; Dullinger, *Schuldrecht Allgemeiner Teil* (2021), 111; S.-F. Kraus and Spendel, in: Flume et al. (eds), *VGG* (2022), § 28, mn. 15.

[180] Zöchling-Jud, 'Beweislast, Gewährleistungs- und Verjährungsfristen im neuen Gewährleistungsrecht' (2022) 2a *ÖJZ*, 113 (119 et seq); Dullinger, *Schuldrecht Allgemeiner Teil* (2021), 102 et seqq; Kronthaler, in: Flume et al. (eds), *VGG* (2022), § 10, mn. 5 and § 18, mn. 4.

[181] Hafner-Thomic, 'Alles neu macht das GRUG?' (2022) 1 *ecolex*, 22 (22); Dullinger, *Schuldrecht Allgemeiner Teil* (2021), 105; Kronthaler, in: Flume et al. (eds), *VGG* (2022), § 18, mn. 6.

lasts for at least two years from the delivery of the goods pursuant to § 10 para. 2 VGG, even if the duration of the obligation to provide the digital service is shorter.[182]

In addition to the warranty periods, the Austrian legislator has also provided for a limitation period for material defects in § 28 VGG and § 933 ABGB, which ends three months after the expiry of the warranty period.[183] Since the enforcement of warranty remedies is already possible before the expiry of the warranty period, the limitation period already begins with the delivery of the goods.[184] In this sense, the explanatory notes[185] also speak of the "construction of the duration of the warranty right as a (real) warranty period, combined with a slightly longer limitation period".[186] This view can just as easily be reconciled with the wording of § 28 VGG and § 933 ABGB, which only determine the end, but not the beginning of the limitation period.

It is still possible for the consumer to oppose the seller's action for payment with a defence under § 28 para. 3 VGG and § 933 para. 3 ABGB without time limit, provided he notifies the transferor of the defect within the limitation period.[187] No use was made of the option provided for in Art. 10 para. 3 SGD and Art. 11 para. 2 DCD to provide for or maintain longer warranty periods. On the other hand, in accordance with Art. 10 para. 6 DCD, a reduction of the warranty period to one year is permissible for second-hand goods under § 10 para. 4 VGG if this has been individually negotiated.[188] In the case of motor vehicles, such a restriction is only valid if the vehicle has been registered for more than one year.[189]

---

[182] Dullinger, *Schuldrecht Allgemeiner Teil* (2021), 105; Zöchling-Jud, 'Beweislast, Gewährleistungs- und Verjährungsfristen im neuen Gewährleistungsrecht' (2022) 2a *ÖJZ*, 113 (120 et seq); Zöchling-Jud, 'Beweislast und Verjährung im neuen europäischen Gewährleistungsrecht' in Stabentheiner et al. (eds), Das neue europäische Gewährleistungsrecht (2019), 197 (211); Kronthaler, in: Flume et al. (eds), *VGG* (2022), § 10, mn. 8.

[183] Zöchling-Jud, 'Beweislast, Gewährleistungs- und Verjährungsfristen im neuen Gewährleistungsrecht' (2022) 2a *ÖJZ*, 113 (121); Dullinger, *Schuldrecht Allgemeiner Teil* (2021), 102, 105; S.-F. Kraus and Spendel, in: Flume et al. (eds), *VGG* (2022), § 28, mn. 4.

[184] Dullinger, 'Das neue Gewährleistungsrecht' (2022) 1 *RFG*, 40 (45); Zöchling-Jud, 'Beweislast, Gewährleistungs- und Verjährungsfristen im neuen Gewährleistungsrecht' (2022) 2a *ÖJZ*, 113 (120 et seq). S.-F. Kraus and Spendel, in: Flume et al. (eds), *VGG* (2022), § 933 ABGB, mn. 27 et seqq, advocate a limitation period of only three months, but ultimately arrive at the same result with the help of an analogy. Without explicit positioning Hafner-Thomic, 'Alles neu macht das GRUG?' (2022) 1 *ecolex*, 22 (23); Kodek, 'Vertragswidrigkeit und Mangelbegriff im neuen Gewährleistungsrecht' (2022) 2a *ÖJZ*, 103 (110).

[185] Explanatory Notes on the Government Draft of the GRUG (No. 949 of the Supplements to the Stenographic Protocols of the National Council of the XXVII Legislative Period), 40.

[186] The mere three-month "limitation period" mentioned elsewhere in the explanatory notes (Explanatory Notes on the Government Draft of the GRUG [No. 949 of the Supplements to the Stenographic Protocols of the National Council of the XXVII Legislative Period], 38 et seq) is accordingly to be understood merely as a period for calculating the point in time at which the limitation period ends.

[187] Dullinger, *Schuldrecht Allgemeiner Teil* (2021), 103; Zöchling-Jud, 'Beweislast, Gewährleistungs- und Verjährungsfristen im neuen Gewährleistungsrecht' (2022) 2a *ÖJZ*, 113 (119 et seq); S.-F. Kraus and Spendel, in: Flume et al. (eds), *VGG* (2022), § 28, mn. 5.

[188] This provision had already been inserted into the KSchG in the course of the GewRÄG and has now been moved to the VGG with a slight change in terminology, cf. § 9 KSchG as amended by BGBl I 2001/48; Kronthaler, in: Flume et al. (eds), *VGG* (2022), § 10, mn. 17.

[189] Zöchling-Jud, 'Beweislast, Gewährleistungs- und Verjährungsfristen im neuen Gewährleistungsrecht' (2022) 2a *ÖJZ*, 113 (120); Kronthaler, in: Flume et al. (eds), *VGG* (2022), § 10, mn. 21.

III. Legal Defects

83 Under Austrian law, a legal defect exists if the seller has not provided the consumer with the legal position owed.[190] In the case of legal defects, the consumer is entitled to remedies under warranty law if the defect was already present at the time of transfer of the goods or at the time of provision of the digital performance (§§ 10, 18 VGG; § 933 ABGB).[191] In contrast to the system of warranty and limitation periods for material defects, only a limitation period is provided for legal defects. Said period lasts for two years for movable and three years for immovable property and begins at the time the defect becomes known to the consumer (§ 28 para. 2 VGG, § 933 para. 3 ABGB).[192]

84 It should be noted that the limitation period for legal defects pursuant to § 28 para. 2 VGG does not begin before the delivery or provision.[193] The VGG also contains special rules for the continuous provision of digital performances. Here, according to § 10 para. 3, § 18 para. 2 VGG, the trader is not only liable for legal defects that exist at the time of the first provision, but for those that exist during the entire provision period.[194] The limitation period in these cases lasts for at least two years and ends three months after the end of the provision period, according to § 28 para. 2 VGG.[195]

85 This also applies to goods with digital elements that are to be provided on a continuous basis. For these, as with material defects, the seller is not only liable for defects that exist during the provision period, but also for those that exist within two years of delivery of the goods if the provision obligation is shorter than two years.[196]

IV. Obligation to Give Notice of Defects

86 The Austrian legislator has not made use of the option provided for in Art. 12 SGD to introduce or maintain an obligation of the consumer to give notice of defects. In principle, such an obligation does not exist in the area of application of the ABGB, but it does exist under § 377 Austrian Commercial Code (UGB)[197] for B2B transactions.[198]

---

[190] Reischauer, in: Rummel and Lukas (eds), *ABGB – Kommentar zum Allgemeinen bürgerlichen Gesetzbuch* (2018), § 923, mn. 143; Zöchling-Jud, in: Kletečka and Schauer (eds), *ABGB-ON* (2016), § 923, mn. 6; S.-F. Kraus and Spendel, in: Flume et al. (eds), *VGG* (2022), § 933 ABGB, mn. 11.

[191] Zöchling-Jud, 'Beweislast, Gewährleistungs- und Verjährungsfristen im neuen Gewährleistungsrecht' (2016) 2a *ÖJZ*, 113 (114 et seq); Dullinger, *Schuldrecht Allgemeiner Teil* (2021), 102,105; Kronthaler, in: Flume et al. (eds), *VGG* (2022), § 10, mn. 14.

[192] Dullinger, *Schuldrecht Allgemeiner Teil* (2021), 102,105; Zöchling-Jud, 'Beweislast, Gewährleistungs- und Verjährungsfristen im neuen Gewährleistungsrecht' (2016) 2a *ÖJZ*, 113 (119 et seq); S.-F. Kraus and Spendel, in: Flume et al. (eds), *VGG* (2022), § 28, mn. 6 and § 933 ABGB, mn. 22.

[193] Neumayr, 'Das neue Verbrauchergewährleistungsrecht' (2021) 8 *RdW*, 536 (539); Zöchling-Jud, 'Beweislast, Gewährleistungs- und Verjährungsfristen im neuen Gewährleistungsrecht' (2016) 2a *ÖJZ*, 113 (120 et seq); S.-F. Kraus and Spendel, in: Flume et al. (eds), *VGG* (2022), § 28, mn. 10.

[194] Zöchling-Jud, 'Beweislast, Gewährleistungs- und Verjährungsfristen im neuen Gewährleistungsrecht' (2016) 2a *ÖJZ*, 113 (120 et seq); Neumayr, 'Das neue Verbrauchergewährleistungsrecht' (2021) 8 *RdW*, 536 (538); Kronthaler, in: Flume et al. (eds), *VGG* (2022), § 10, mn. 15.

[195] Dullinger, *Schuldrecht Allgemeiner Teil* (2021), 105; Zöchling-Jud, 'Beweislast, Gewährleistungs- und Verjährungsfristen im neuen Gewährleistungsrecht' (2016) 2a *ÖJZ*, 113 (120 et seq); S.-F. Kraus and Spendel, in: Flume et al. (eds), *VGG* (2022), § 28, mn. 11.

[196] Kronthaler, in: Flume et al. (eds), *VGG* (2022), § 10, mn. 15.

[197] Bundesgesetz über besondere zivilrechtliche Vorschriften für Unternehmen (Unternehmensgesetzbuch), dRGBl. 219/1897 idF BGBl I 2021/86.

[198] Zöchling-Jud, in Torggler (ed), *UGB* (2016), § 378, mn. 4; Welser and Zöchling-Jud, *Grundriss des Bürgerlichen Rechts* II (2015), 91 et seq; Dullinger, *Schuldrecht Allgemeiner Teil* (2021), 111 et seq.

G. Right of Redress

I. Previous Regulation

87 Art. 4 CSGD was implemented in § 933b ABGB which regulates the right of redress.[199] It is available to an entrepreneur against his entrepreneurial predecessor, if a consumer was at the end of the chain of transactions.[200] In terms of content, § 933b ABGB in its old version did not standardise a full reimbursement[201] but "only" extended the assertion of warranty rights within the sales chain. Furthermore, the right of redress was limited in its amount to the own expenses of the party entitled to recourse.[202]

88 In addition, the right of redress was further limited. First, the party entitled to recourse had to assert its right in court within two months of the fulfilment of its own warranty obligation. Second, the liability of the party subject to the recourse would end within five years of the performance of its obligation.[203]

II. New Regulation

89 Although the new provisions under EU law on the right of redress in Art. 20 DCD and Art. 18 SGD do not differ from those in Art. 4 CSGD, the Austrian legislator decided to amend the previous national provision significantly.[204]

90 The new regulation is not limited to contracts that fall within the scope of the Directives, but is applicable to any contract for pecuniary consideration.[205] The previous personal scope of the regulation was not changed despite initial considerations.[206]

91 Contrary to the previous legal situation, the right of redress is not limited to the amount of the remuneration paid to the predecessor in cases where he provides warranty by repair or replacement.[207] If the seller requests his predecessor to remedy the defect immediately upon notification of the defect and he fails to do so within a reasonable period of time, the seller may claim compensation for all expenses incurred by him

---

[199] Art. 1 GewRÄG; § 933b ABGB idF BGBl I 2001/48; Welser and Zöchling-Jud, *Die neue Gewährleistung (2001)*, § 933b, mn. 1 et seqq.

[200] § 933b ABGB idF BGBl I 2001/48; Welser and Zöchling-Jud, *Die neue Gewährleistung (2001)*, § 933b, mn. 9.

[201] OGH 20.03.2019 – 3 Ob 243/18h – *Zak* 2019, 154 (154 et seq); Welser and Zöchling-Jud, *Die neue Gewährleistung (2001)*, § 933b, mn. 20 et seqq.

[202] Reischauer, in: Rummel and Lukas (eds), *ABGB – Kommentar zum Allgemeinen bürgerlichen Gesetzbuch* (2018), § 933b, mn. 45; Zöchling-Jud, in: Kletečka and Schauer (eds), *ABGB-ON* (2016), § 933b, mn. 22 et seq; Welser and Zöchling-Jud, *Die neue Gewährleistung (2001)*, § 933b, mn. 23.

[203] Zöchling-Jud, in: Kletečka and Schauer (eds), *ABGB-ON* (2016), § 933b, mn. 26 et seqq; Reischauer, in: Rummel and Lukas (eds), *ABGB – Kommentar zum Allgemeinen bürgerlichen Gesetzbuch* (2018), § 933b, mn. 131, 138; Welser and Zöchling-Jud, *Die neue Gewährleistung (2001)*, § 933b, mn. 26 et seqq.

[204] Kletečka and Neumayr, 'Rückgriff und Neuerungen im KSchG' (2022) 2a *ÖJZ*, 149 (149); Krenmayr and Moser, 'Der neue Händlerregress' (2021) 12 *ZVB*, 493 (493 et seq); Kletečka and Neumayr, in: Flume et al. (eds), *VGG* (2022), § 933b ABGB, mn. 3.

[205] Krenmayr and Moser, 'Der neue Händlerregress' (2021) 12 *ZVB*, 493 (494); Kletečka and Neumayr, in: Flume et al. (eds), *VGG* (2022), § 933b ABGB, mn. 6.

[206] Explanatory Notes on the Government Draft of the GRUG (No. 949 of the Supplements to the Stenographic Protocols of the National Council of the XXVII Legislative Period), 40; Kletečka and Neumayr, in: Flume et al. (eds), *VGG* (2022), § 933b ABGB, mn. 5.

[207] OGH 20.03.2019 – 3 Ob 243/18h – *Zak* 2019, 154 (154 et seq); Kletečka and Neumayr, in: Flume et al. (eds), *VGG* (2022), § 933b ABGB, mn. 8.

in remedying the defect.²⁰⁸ With this provision, the Austrian legislator reacted to the decision of the CJEU in the *Weber and Putz* cases²⁰⁹. It was considered inappropriate to limit the seller's right of redress by the contractual content of performance, while the consumers warranty claims are no longer limited in such a way in view of the ruling.²¹⁰

92   Another significant change concerns the validity of agreements that exclude or limit the right of redress under § 933b ABGB. Such agreements are only binding if they are individually negotiated and do not grossly disadvantage the seller, taking into account all circumstances.²¹¹ Under the old regulation, it was in principle possible to exclude claims under § 933b ABGB in GTCs, although such an agreement could be invalid under § 879 para. 3 ABGB if it was to be qualified as grossly disadvantageous.²¹²

93   The previous twofold time limit for exercising the right of recourse has been changed insofar as the period running from the fulfilment of the warranty obligations of the party entitled to recourse has been extended from two to three months.²¹³

H. Relationship with Other Remedies

I. Default

94   The creditor's right to terminate the contract in the event of default on the part of its contractual partner does not co-exist with the remedies under warranty,²¹⁴ as the rules on default generally only apply if the creditor has not yet accepted the performance without reservation.²¹⁵ The rules on default apply irrespective of whether the creditor justifiably refuses to accept a defective performance offered by the debtor, whether the performance has only been carried out with reservations or whether the debtor has not even attempted to complete the performance.²¹⁶ By contrast, in order to claim a warranty remedy, an unconditional acceptance must already have taken place, which

---

²⁰⁸ Krenmayr and Moser, 'Neuregelung des Händlerregresses in § 933b ABGB und (alte) Konkurrenzfragen' (2022) 10 *JBl*, 617 (617 seq); Klecetka and Neumayr, 'Rückgriff und Neuerungen im KSchG' (2022) 2a *ÖJZ*, 149 (151 et seq); Krenmayr and Moser, 'Der neue Händlerregress' (2021) 12 *ZVB*, 493 (496); Klecetka and Neumayr, in: Flume et al. (eds), *VGG* (2022), § 933b ABGB, mn. 9; Schoditsch, 'Der Händlerregress nach § 933b ABGB' in Bydlinski (ed), *Das neue Gewährleistungsrecht* (2022), 155 (172 et seqq).
²⁰⁹ CJEU, joined cases C-65/09 and C-87/09, 16.06.2011, *Gebr. Weber GmbH v Jürgen Wittmer and Ingrid Putz v Medianess Electronics GmbH*. ECLI:EU:C:2011:396.
²¹⁰ Explanatory Notes on the Government Draft of the GRUG (No. 949 of the Supplements to the Stenographic Protocols of the National Council of the XXVII Legislative Period), 8; Klecetka and Neumayr, in: Flume et al. (eds), *VGG* (2022), § 933b ABGB, mn. 9.
²¹¹ Krenmayr and Moser, 'Der neue Händlerregress' (2021) 12 *ZVB*, 493 (495 et seq); Klecetka and Neumayr, 'Rückgriff und Neuerungen im KSchG' (2022) 2a *ÖJZ*, 149 (153); Klecetka and Neumayr, in: Flume et al. (eds), *VGG* (2022), § 933b ABGB, mn. 16.
²¹² Zöchling-Jud, in: Klecetka and Schauer (eds), *ABGB-ON* (2016), § 933b, mn. 29 et seq; Ofner, in: Schwimann and Kodek (eds), *ABGB: Praxiskommentar* (2021), § 933b, mn. 19.
²¹³ Klecetka and Neumayr, 'Rückgriff und Neuerungen im KSchG' (2022) 2a *ÖJZ*, 149 (153); Krenmayr and Moser, 'Der neue Händlerregress' (2021) 12 *ZVB*, 493 (497); Klecetka and Neumayr, in: Flume et al. (eds), *VGG* (2022), § 933b ABGB, mn. 17.
²¹⁴ E.g. OGH 27.04.1999 – 1 Ob 60/99a – *RdW* 1999, 712 (712); OGH 03.08.2005 – 9 Ob 81/04h – *RdW* 2005, 687.
²¹⁵ P. Bydlinski, in: Koziol, Bydlinski and Bollenberger (eds), *ABGB: Kurzkommentar* (2020), § 922, mn. 5; Gruber, in: Klecetka and Schauer (eds), *ABGB-ON* (2019), § 918, mn. 8 et seqq.
²¹⁶ Reidinger and Mock, in: Schwimann and Kodek (eds), *ABGB: Praxiskommentar* (2021), § 918, mn. 10 et seq; Reischauer, in: Rummel and Lukas (eds), *ABGB – Kommentar zum Allgemeinen bürgerlichen Gesetzbuch* (2018), § 918, mn. 109 et seqq.

II. Damages Instead of Warranty

As an alternative to the warranty, claims for damages may be invoked if the seller is culpable.[218] Such fault is deemed to exist if the seller culpably caused the defect or at least culpably failed to remedy the defect by the time of transfer.[219]

In principle, the general rules of Austrian tort law in §§ 1293 et seqq ABGB apply to damages instead of warranty, but § 933a ABGB stipulates two distinctive features: First, the injured party can only demand monetary compensation under the conditions required for the assertion of the secondary warranty remedies (price reduction and termination of the contract).[220] Second, the presumption of fault of the contracting party provided for in § 1298 ABGB is limited to a period of ten years from the date of delivery.[221]

95

96

III. Usury and Laesio Enormis

Under certain circumstances, the transferee can also challenge the contract on the grounds of usury or *laesio enormis* instead of making use of a warranty remedy.[222] The common features of these remedies are that they each require a gross disproportion between the performance and the counter-performance and that they generally cannot be waived in advance.[223]

According to §§ 934, 935 ABGB, the prerequisite for a termination on grounds of *laesio enormis* is that a contracting party receives a performance which, at the time of the conclusion of the contract,[224] does not even reach half of the objective value of the counter-performance.[225] Thus, his remedy cannot be invoked if someone receives a performance that is worth less than half of the counter-performance due to a defect that only arose after the conclusion of the contract.[226] Apart from the objective disproportion of the contractually agreed performances there are no further requirements for the ter-

97

98

---

[217] P. Bydlinski, in: Koziol, Bydlinski and Bollenberger (eds), *ABGB: Kurzkommentar* (2020), § 922, mn. 5; Reidinger and Mock, in: Schwimann and Kodek (eds), *ABGB: Praxiskommentar* (2021) § 918, mn. 10 et seq.

[218] European Law Institute, *Statement of the European Law Institute on the European Commission's Proposed Directive on the Supply of Digital Content to Consumers* (2016), 32.

[219] Koch and Kronthaler, in: Flume et al. (eds), *VGG* (2022), § 13, mn. 27 and § 21, mn. 16; Ofner, in: Schwimann and Kodek (eds), *ABGB: Praxiskommentar* (2021), § 933a, mn. 2; Zöchling-Jud, in: Kletečka and Schauer (eds), *ABGB-ON* (2016), § 933a, mn. 2.

[220] Zöchling-Jud, in: Kletečka and Schauer (eds), *ABGB-ON* (2016), § 933a, mn. 5 et seqq; Ofner, in: Schwimann and Kodek (eds), *ABGB: Praxiskommentar* (2021), § 933a, mn. 4 et seqq.

[221] P. Bydlinski, in: Koziol, Bydlinski and Bollenberger (eds), *ABGB: Kurzkommentar* (2020), § 933a, mn. 14 et seq; Zöchling-Jud, in: Kletečka and Schauer (eds), *ABGB-ON* (2016), § 933a, mn. 51 et seqq.

[222] Koch and Kronthaler, in: Flume et al. (eds), *VGG* (2022), § 13, mn. 27 and § 21, mn. 16; Welser and Zöchling-Jud, *Grundriss des Bürgerlichen Rechts* II (2015), 101; Dullinger, *Schuldrecht Allgemeiner Teil* (2021), 115.

[223] Bollenberger and P. Bydlinski, in: Koziol, Bydlinski and Bollenberger (eds), *ABGB: Kurzkommentar* (2020), § 879, mn. 21; Gruber, in: Kletečka and Schauer (eds), *ABGB-ON* (2019), § 934, mn. 4; Perner, in: Schwimann and Kodek (eds), *ABGB: Praxiskommentar* (2021), § 935, mn. 1 et seqq.

[224] Perner, in: Schwimann and Kodek (eds), *ABGB: Praxiskommentar* (2021), § 934, mn. 9; P. Bydlinski, *Bürgerliches Recht Allgemeiner Teil* (2018), 214.

[225] Gruber, in: Kletečka and Schauer (eds), *ABGB-ON* (2019), § 934, mn. 5 et seqq; P. Bydlinski, *Bürgerliches Recht Allgemeiner Teil* (2018), 214 et seq.

[226] P. Bydlinski, *Bürgerliches Recht Allgemeiner Teil* (2018), 215.

mination of the contract pursuant to § 934 ABGB. However, a party to the contract can avert the termination by paying up to the objective value of the performance of the other party.[227] Pursuant to § 1487 ABGB, the remedy shall become time-barred within three years from the conclusion of the contract.[228]

99 Due to the similarities between *laesio enormis* and warranty remedies, it is questionable whether the Directives exclude the former, since they are fully harmonising. While there may be differences from the viewpoint of Austrian dogmatics, a functional approach would suggest that *laesio enormis* is barred within the scope of the Directives.[229]

100 A disproportion between performance and counter-performance at the time of conclusion of the contract is also required for a contract to be contested on grounds of usury pursuant to § 879 para. 2 no. 4 ABGB. However, in contrast to *laesio enormis*, this disproportion is not defined by a concrete value limit; it must merely be "conspicuous".[230] In addition, there must be an impairment of the freedom of decision of the party subject to usury, which the usurer exploits.[231] Unlike the termination of a contract due to *laesio enormis*, the invalidity of a usurious contract cannot be prevented by a payment of a surcharge. A challenge on grounds of usury is, according to some scholars, time-barred after 30 years from the conclusion of the contract, while according to others there is no time limit.[232]

IV. Error

101 According to the prevailing view in Austria, the right of error regulated in §§ 871 et seqq ABGB is a further alternative to the warranty remedies.[233] According to these provisions, a validly concluded contract can be amended or terminated if it was concluded erroneously.[234] The prerequisite for such a remedy is that the person who wishes to challenge or amend the contract had an erroneous perception of reality, which affects the content of the contract or his declaration, was causal for the conclusion of the contract and was either timely disclosed, induced by the other party or should have been noticed by the latter.[235] If these conditions are met, the mistaken person can amend the contract if both parties would have concluded it with different content or terminate the contract if it would not have been concluded at all if the mistake had not been made.[236]

---

[227] Gruber, in: Kletečka and Schauer (eds), *ABGB-ON* (2019), § 934, mn. 11 et seqq; P. Bydlinski, *Bürgerliches Recht Allgemeiner Teil* (2018), 214.

[228] P. Bydlinski, *Bürgerliches Recht Allgemeiner Teil* (2018), 215; Gruber, in: Kletečka and Schauer (eds), *ABGB-ON* (2019), § 934, mn. 8.

[229] Zöchling-Jud, 'Das neue Europäische Gewährleistungsrecht für den Warenhandel' (2019) 3 *GPR*, 115 (127).

[230] Riedler, in: Schwimann and Kodek (eds), *ABGB: Praxiskommentar* (2021), § 879 Part 2, mn. 21; P. Bydlinski, *Bürgerliches Recht Allgemeiner Teil* (2018), 184.

[231] P. Bydlinski, *Bürgerliches Recht Allgemeiner Teil* (2018), 37 et seq; Riedler, in: Schwimann and Kodek (eds), *ABGB: Praxiskommentar* (2021), § 879 Part 2, mn. 22 et seqq.

[232] Graf, in: Kletečka and Schauer (eds), *ABGB-ON* (2019), § 879, mn. 239; Krejci, in: Rummel and Lukas (eds), *ABGB – Kommentar zum Allgemeinen bürgerlichen Gesetzbuch* (2014), § 879, mn. 533.

[233] Koch and Kronthaler, in: Flume et al. (eds), *VGG* (2022), § 13, mn. 27 and § 21, mn. 16; Riedler, in: Schwimann and Kodek (eds), *ABGB: Praxiskommentar* (2021) § 871, mn. 46; Pletzer, in: Kletečka and Schauer (eds), *ABGB-ON* (2019), § 871, mn. 79. However, as with *laesio enormis*, concerns regarding the fully harmonising character of the Directives apply to error aswell.

[234] Pletzer, in: Kletečka and Schauer (eds), *ABGB-ON* (2019), § 871, mn. 60 et seqq; Pletzer, in: Kletečka and Schauer (eds), *ABGB-ON* (2019), § 872, mn. 8 et seqq.

[235] Riedler, in: Schwimann and Kodek (eds), *ABGB: Praxiskommentar* (2021), § 871, mn. 5 et seqq; P. Bydlinski, *Bürgerliches Recht Allgemeiner Teil* (2018), 193 et seqq.

[236] P. Bydlinski, *Bürgerliches Recht Allgemeiner Teil* (2018), 201 et seqq; Riedler, in: Schwimann and Kodek (eds), *ABGB: Praxiskommentar* (2021), § 871, mn. 33 et seqq.

These remedies can only be considered as alternatives to the warranty if the buyer is in error about the fact that the object of the contract is free of defects at the time of the conclusion of the contract.[237] They cannot be considered, however, if the contractual object only becomes defective between the conclusion of the contract and the delivery or if the buyer merely receives a defective item from a generally defect-free class of goods.[238]

Pursuant to § 1487 ABGB, the right of the erroneous party to terminate or amend the contract on the grounds of error becomes time-barred 3 years after the conclusion of the contract. The right to assert an error can in principle be effectively waived in advance, however, this does not apply to B2C transactions within the meaning of § 1 KSchG.[239] In addition, invoking such a waiver made in advance is invalid if the error was caused by gross negligence according to § 879 para. 1 ABGB.[240]

102

103

Bibliography

EU Legislation

Directive (EU) 2019/770 of the European Parliament and of the Council of 20 May 2019 on certain aspects concerning contracts for the supply of digital content and digital services.

Directive (EU) 2019/771 of the European Parliament and of the Council of 20 May 2019 on certain aspects concerning contracts for the sale of goods, amending Regulation (EU) 2017/2394 and Directive 2009/22/EC, and repealing Directive 1999/44/EC.

Directive 2009/125/EC of the European Parliament and of the Council of 21 October 2009 establishing a framework for the setting of ecodesign requirements for energy-related products (recast).

Directive 2009/24/EC of the European Parliament and of the Council of 23 April 2009 on the legal protection of computer programs.

Directive 2005/32/EC of the European Parliament and of the Council of 6 July 2005 establishing a framework for the setting of ecodesign requirements for energy-using products and amending Council Directive 92/42/EEC and Directives 96/57/EC and 2000/55/EC of the European Parliament and of the Council.

Commission staff working document, *Guidance on the implementation/application of directive 2005/29/EC on unfair commercial practices*, 25 June 2016, COM/2016/320 final.

Directive 1999/44/EC of the European Parliament and of the Council of 25 May 1999 on certain aspects of the sale of consumer goods and associated guarantees.

Austrian Legislation

Bundesgesetz, mit dem ein Bundesgesetz über die Gewährleistung bei Verbraucherverträgen über Waren oder digitale Leistungen (Verbrauchergewährleistungsgesetz – VGG) erlassen wird sowie das allgemeine bürgerliche Gesetzbuch und das Konsumentenschutzgesetz geändert werden (Gewährleistungsrichtlinien-Umsetzungsgesetz – GRUG), BGBl I 2021/175.

Allgemeines bürgerliches Gesetzbuch für die gesammten deutschen Erbländer der Oesterreichischen Monarchie, JGS 1811/946 idF BGBl I 2021/175.

---

[237] Welser and Zöchling-Jud, *Grundriss des Bürgerlichen Rechts* II (2015), 100.

[238] Pletzer, in: Kletečka and Schauer (eds), *ABGB-ON* (2019), § 871, mn. 33; P. Bydlinski, *Bürgerliches Recht Allgemeiner Teil* (2018), 194.

[239] Riedler, in: Schwimann and Kodek (eds), *ABGB: Praxiskommentar* (2021), § 871, mn. 42; Pletzer, in: Kletečka and Schauer (eds), *ABGB-ON* (2019), § 871, mn. 65.

[240] Pletzer, in: Kletečka and Schauer (eds), *ABGB-ON* (2019), § 871, mn. 65; Bollenberger and P. Bydlinski, in: Koziol, Bydlinski and Bollenberger (eds), *ABGB: Kurzkommentar* (2020), § 871, mn. 22.

Bundesgesetz vom 8. März 1979, mit dem Bestimmungen zum Schutz der Verbraucher getroffen werden (Konsumentenschutzgesetz), BGBl 1979/140 idF BGBl I 2021/175.

Bundesgesetz über die Gewährleistung bei Verbraucherverträgen über Waren oder digitale Leistungen (Verbrauchergewährleistungsgesetz), BGBl I 2021/175.

Explanatory Notes on the Government Draft of the GRUG (No. 949 of the Supplements to the Stenographic Protocols of the National Council of the XXVII Legislative Period).

Bundesgesetz über das Urheberrecht an Werken der Literatur und der Kunst und über verwandte Schutzrechte (Urheberrechtsgesetz), BGBl 1936/111 idF BGBl 2021/244.

Bundesgesetz über besondere zivilrechtliche Vorschriften für Unternehmen (Unternehmensgesetzbuch), dRGBl. 219/1897 idF BGBl I 2021/86.

Gewerbeordnung 1994 – GewO 1994, BGBl 1994/194 idF BGBl I 2020/65.

Bundesgesetz gegen den unlauteren Wettbewerb 1984 – UWG, BGBl 1984/448 idF BGBl I 2019/104.

Bundesgesetz zum Schutz vor gefährlichen Produkten (Produktsicherheitsgesetz 2004 – PSG 2004), BGBl I 2005/16 idF BGBl I 2018/32.

Bundesgesetz über Sicherheitsmaßnahmen, Normalisierung und Typisierung auf dem Gebiete der Elektrotechnik (Elektrotechnikgesetz 1992 – ETG 1992), BGBl 1993/106 idF BGBl I 2017/27.

Verordnung des Bundesministers für Wirtschaft und Arbeit zur Schaffung eines Rahmens für die Festlegung von Anforderungen an die umweltgerechte Gestaltung energieverbrauchsrelevanter Produkte (Ökodesign-Verordnung 2007), BGBl II 2007/126 idF BGBl II 2011/187.

Bundesgesetz, mit dem das Gewährleistungsrecht im Allgemeinen Bürgerlichen Gesetzbuch und im Konsumentenschutzgesetz sowie das Versicherungsvertragsgesetz geändert werden, BGBl I 2001/48.

EU Judicature

CJEU, Case C-263/18, 19.12.2019, *Tom Kabinet Internet BV*, ECLI:EU:C:2019:1111.

CJEU, Case C-133/16, 13.07.2017, *Ferenschild v JPC Motor SA*, ECLI:EU:C:2017:541.

CJEU, Case C-128/11, 03.07.2012, *UsedSoft GmbH v Oracle International Corp.*, ECLI:EU:C:2012:407.

CJEU, joined cases C-65/09 and C-87/09, 16.06.2011, *Gebr. Weber GmbH v Jürgen Wittmer and Ingrid Putz v Medianess Electronics GmbH*, ECLI:EU:C:2011:396.

Austrian Judicature

OGH 11.08.2020 – 4 Ob 71/20z – *VbR* 2020, 213 (213–214).

OGH 20.03.2019 – 3 Ob 243/18h – *Zak* 2019, 154 (154–155).

OGH 23.04.2015 – 1 Ob 71/15w – *Zak* 2015, 256 (256–257).

OGH 12.05.2009 – 10 Ob 21/08y – *Zak* 2009, 295 (295).

OGH 03.08.2005 – 9 Ob 81/04h – *RdW* 2005, 687.

OGH 27.04.1999 – 1 Ob 60/99a – *RdW* 1999, 712 (712).

Literature

Clemens Appl, 'Urheberrecht' in Andreas Wiebe (ed), *Wettbewerbs- und Immaterialgüterrecht* (4th edn, Facultas, Vienna 2018).

Bibliography

Felix Artner and Isabelle Vonkilch, 'GRUG: Zum objektiven Mangelbegriff des § 6 VGG' (2021) 10 *ecolex*, 890.

Alena Bischinger and Karl Maximilian Weber-Woisetschläger, 'Das neue Gewährleistungsrecht (Part II)' (2021/2022) 3 *JAP*, 181.

Christoph Brenn and Ernst Karner, 'Verkäufer hat für die übliche Lebensdauer eines Motors einzustehen' (2016) 20 *EvBl*, 925.

Peter Bydlinski, *Bürgerliches Recht Allgemeiner Teil* (8th edn, Verlag Österreich, Vienna 2018).

Meinhard Ciresa (ed), *Österreichisches Urheberrecht* (22nd edn, LexisNexis ARD ORAC, Vienna 2021).

Silvia Dullinger, 'Das neue Gewährleistungsrecht' (2022) 1 *RFG*, 40.

Silvia Dullinger, *Schuldrecht Allgemeiner Teil* (7th edn, Verlag Österreich, Vienna 2021).

European Law Institute, *Statement of the European Law Institute on the European Commission's Proposed Directive on the Supply of Digital Content to Consumers* (Vienna 2016).

Wolfgang Faber, 'Bereitstellung und Mangelbegriff' in Johannes Stabentheiner, Christiane Wendehorst and Brigitta Zöchling-Jud (eds), *Das neue europäische Gewährleistungsrecht* (Manz, Vienna 2019), 63.

Wolfgang Faber, 'Neues Gewährleistungsrecht und Nachhaltigkeit (Teil I)' (2020) 1 VbR, 6.

Wolfgang Faber, 'Rechtsbehelfe beim Warenkauf nach dem VGG' (2022) 2a ÖJZ, 123

Sophia Fida, 'Die neue Aktualisierungspflicht nach § 7 VGG' (2021) 12 *ecolex*, 1079.

Johannes W. Flume, 'Digitale Leistungen' (2022) 2a ÖJZ, 137.

Johannes W. Flume, Christoph Kronthaler and Simon Laimer (eds), *VGG* (Verlag Österreich, Vienna 2022).

Nikolaus Forgó and Brigitta Zöchling-Jud, 'Das Vertragsrecht des ABGB auf dem Prüfstand: Überlegungen im digitalen Zeitalter' in *20. ÖJT* II/1 (Manz, Vienna 2018).

Nina-Maria Hafner-Thomic, 'Alles neu macht das GRUG?' (2022) 1 *ecolex*, 22.

Philipp Homar, 'Unzulässigkeit der Weiterveräußerung von E-Books' (2020) 1 *Medien und Recht*, 27.

Cornelia Kern, 'Anwendungsbereich der Warenkauf- und der Digitale Inhalte-RL' in Johannes Stabentheiner, Christiane Wendehorst and Brigitta Zöchling-Jud (eds), *Das neue europäische Gewährleistungsrecht* (Manz, Vienna 2019), 33.

Cornelia Kern, 'Das neue europäische Gewährleistungsrecht' (2019) 5 *VbR*, 168.

Andreas Kletečka and Uwe Neumayr, 'Rückgriff und Neuerungen im KSchG' (2022) 2a ÖJZ, 149.

Andreas Kletečka and Martin Schauer (eds), *ABGB-ON* (Manz, Vienna 2016).

Andreas Kletečka and Rudolf Welser, *Grundriss des Bürgerlichen Rechts* I (15th edn, Manz, Vienna 2018).

Lukas Klever and Sebastian Schwamberger, 'Transportkostenvorschuss und Kosten der Mangelerhebung – Überlegungen aus Anlass der Neuerungen im deutschen Gewährleistungsrecht' (2018) 7 *wbl*, 357.

Georg Kodek, 'Änderung digitaler Inhalte und digitaler Dienstleistungen (Art 19 DIRL)' in Johannes Stabentheiner, Christiane Wendehorst and Brigitta Zöchling-Jud (eds), *Das neue europäische Gewährleistungsrecht* (Manz, Vienna 2019), 141.

Georg Kodek and Petra Leupold, *Gewährleistung NEU* (Manz, Vienna 2019).

Georg Kodek, 'Vertragswidrigkeit und Mangelbegriff im neuen Gewährleistungsrecht' (2022) 2a *ÖJZ*, 103.

Gabriel Kogler, 'Der Ausschluss der Aktualisierungspflicht bei Waren mit digitalen Elementen und bei digitalen Leistungen' (2022) 2 *ecolex*, 118.

Gabriel Kogler, 'Digitale Leistungen und Waren gegen Zahlung mit Bitcoin – Anwendbarkeit des VGG?' (2022) 1 *ecolex*, 27.

Helmut Koziol, *Obsoleszenzen im österreichischen Recht* (Jan Sramek Verlag, Vienna 2016).

Helmut Koziol, Peter Bydlinski, Raimund Bollenberger (eds), *ABGB: Kurzkommentar* (6th edn, Verlag Österreich, Vienna 2020).

Ulrich Krenmayr and Michael Moser, 'Der neue Händlerregress' (2021) 12 *ZVB*, 493.

Ulrich Krenmayr and Michael Moser, 'Neuregelung des Händlerregresses in § 933b ABGB und (alte) Konkurrenzfragen' (2022) 10 *JBl*, 617.

Guido Kucsko and Christian Handig (eds), *urheber.recht* (2nd edn, Manz, Vienna 2017).

Huberta Maitz-Straßnig, 'Die neue Gewährleistung nach der Warenkauf-Richtlinie' (2020) 2 *RdW*, 79.

Uwe Neumayr, 'Das neue Verbrauchergewährleistungsrecht' (2021) 8 *RdW*, 536.

Uwe Neumayr, 'Zum Mangelbegriff des neuen VGG' (2021) 12 *RdW*, 833.

Fabian Pollitzer, Chiara Schurich and Siba Auf, 'Privatrecht und Nachhaltigkeit: Gewährleistung für ESG-Verstöße im Wertschöpfungsprozess' (2022) 2 *NR*, 416.

Peter Rummel (ed), *ABGB – Kommentar zum Allgemeinen bürgerlichen Gesetzbuch* (3rd edn, Manz Vienna 2002).

Peter Rummel and Meinhard Lukas (eds), *ABGB – Kommentar zum Allgemeinen bürgerlichen Gesetzbuch* (4th edn, Manz, Vienna 2018).

Thomas Rainer Schmitt, 'Das neue Gewährleistungsrecht ab 2022: Digitale Leistungen und mehr' (2021) 5 *jusIT*, 179.

Thomas Rainer Schmitt, *Gewährleistung bei Verträgen über digitale Inhalte* (Verlag Österreich, Vienna 2017).

Thomas Schoditsch, 'Der Händlerregress nach § 933b ABGB' in Peter Bydlinski (ed), *Das neue Gewährleistungsrecht* (Verlag Österreich, Vienna 2022), 155.

Thomas Schoditsch, 'Gewöhnlich vorausgesetzte Eigenschaften eines Kfz-Motors' (2015) 11 *ecolex*, 946.

Michael Schwimann and Georg Kodek (eds), *ABGB: Praxiskommentar* (5th edn, LexisNexis ARD ORAC, Vienna 2021).

Michael Schwimann and Matthias Neumayr, *ABGB: Taschenkommentar* (5th edn, LexisNexis ARD ORAC, Vienna 2020).

Johannes Stabentheiner, 'Ein Überblick über das Gewährleistungsrichtlinien-Umsetzungsgesetz' (2021) 6 *VbR*, 189.

Johannes Stabentheiner, 'Grundzüge des neuen Verbrauchergewährleistungsrechts' (2022) 2a *ÖJZ*, 99.

Johannes Stabentheiner, 'Was ist neu am neuen Gewährleistungsrecht?' (2021) 21 *ÖJZ*, 965.

Clemens Thiele, 'EuGH: Kein Verkauf "gebrauchter" E-Books ohne Zustimmung des Urhebers' (2020)1 *ZIIR*, 89.

Bibliography

Ulrich Torggler (ed), *UGB* (2nd edn, Linde, Vienna 2016).

Irene Welser, 'Der Erfüllungsort für Verbesserungspflichten des Unternehmers nach § 8 KSchG' (2001) 20 *ÖJZ*, 745 (745).

Rudolf Welser and Brigitta Zöchling-Jud, *Grundriss des Bürgerlichen Rechts* II (14th edn, Manz, Vienna 2015).

Rudolf Welser and Brigitta Zöchling-Jud, 'Zur Reform des Gewährleistungsrechts' in *14. ÖJT* II/1 (Manz, Vienna 2000).

Rudolf Welser and Brigitta Zöchling-Jud, *Die neue Gewährleistung* (Manz, Vienna 2001).

Christiane Wendehorst, 'Aktualisierungen und andere digitale Dauerleistungen' in Johannes Stabentheiner, Christiane Wendehorst and Brigitta Zöchling-Jud (eds), *Das neue europäische Gewährleistungsrecht* (Manz, Vienna 2019), 111.

Christiane Wendehorst, 'Die Regelungen des VGG zu digitalen Leistungen unter besonderer Berücksichtigung der Aktualisierungspflichten' in Peter Bydlinski (ed), *Das neue Gewährleistungsrecht* (Verlag Österreich, Vienna 2022), 49.

Christiane Wendehorst, 'Direkthaftung des Herstellers (Teil I)' (2020) 3 *VbR*, 94.

Christiane Wendehorst, 'Direkthaftung des Herstellers (Teil II)' (2020) 4 *VbR*, 138.

Christiane Wendehorst, 'Hybride Produkte und hybrider Vertrieb' in Christiane Wendehorst and Brigitta Zöchling-Jud (eds), *Ein neues Vertragsrecht für den digitalen Binnenmarkt?* (Manz, Vienna 2016), 45.

Stefan Wrbka, *Geplante Obsoleszenz aus Sicht des Gewährleistungsrechts* (NWV, Vienna 2015).

Adolf Zemann, 'EuGH: E-Books entgehen Erschöpfung' (2020) 2 *ecolex*, 122.

Brigitta Zöchling-Jud, 'Beweislast, Gewährleistungs- und Verjährungsfristen im neuen Gewährleistungsrecht' (2022) 2a *ÖJZ*, 113 (122).

Brigitta Zöchling-Jud, 'Beweislast und Verjährung im neuen europäischen Gewährleistungsrecht' in Johannes Stabentheiner, Christiane Wendehorst and Brigitta Zöchling-Jud (eds), *Das neue österreichische Gewährleistungsrecht* (Manz, Vienna 2019), 197.

Brigitta Zöchling-Jud, 'Das neue Europäische Gewährleistungsrecht für den Warenhandel' (2019) 3 *GPR*, 115.

Brigitta Zöchling-Jud, 'Die Richtlinienvorschläge der Kommission über digitale Inhalte und Fernabsatzkaufverträge aus österreichischer Sicht' in Christiane Wendehorst and Brigitta Zöchling-Jud (eds), *Ein neues Vertragsrecht für den digitalen Binnenmarkt?* (Manz, Vienna 2016), 1.

Brigitta Zöchling-Jud, 'Digital Consumer Contract Law And New Technologies – Implementation Of The Digital Content Directive In Austria' (2021) 12 *JIPITEC*, 221.

Belgium

A. Legislative framework and temporal scope of application 1
B. Scope of application 4
C. Delivery and supply in conformity with the contract – obligation to supply updates 10
D. Liability of the seller / trader – time periods 20
E. Remedies 26
F. Commercial guarantees 36
G. Right of redress 37
H. Sanctions and enforcement 40
I. Conclusion 42
   Bibliography 44

A. Legislative framework and temporal scope of application

The Sales of Goods Directive (hereafter: "SGD")[1] and Digital Content and Digital Services Directive (hereafter: "DCD")[2] were implemented in Belgium by the *Act of 20 March 2022 amending the consumer sales provisions of the old Civil Code and inserting a new title VIbis in Book III old Civil Code and amending the Code of Economic Law*.[3] The new Belgian provisions apply to sales contracts concluded from 1 June 2022 and to digital content and digital services delivered from 1 June 2022.[4] It is well-known that both the SGD (replacing the Consumer Sales Directive (hereafter: "CSD"[5])) and the entirely novel DCD take a full harmonization approach with a number of exceptions and a number of regulatory options left to the Member States.[6] The Belgian legislator basically copied out the Directives' provisions in two parallel sets of rules in the Old Civil Code (hereafter: "OCC") – which essentially dates from 1804.

Hence, the state of play in July 2022 is as follows. The OCC contains general sales law, which establishes a regime on hidden defects (*vices cachés*)[7], as well as provisions on other specific contracts such as renting contracts or contract for works (which in some regards can be relevant in the context of supply of digital content or services[8]). General

---

[1] Directive (EU) 2019/771 of the European Parliament and of the Council of 20 May 2019 on certain aspects concerning contracts for the sale of goods, amending Regulation (EU) 2017/2394 and Directive 2009/22/EC, and repealing Directive 1999/44/EC, *OJ* L 136, 22.5.2019, p. 28–50.

[2] Directive (EU) 2019/770 of the European Parliament and of the Council of 20 May 2019 on certain aspects concerning contracts for the supply of digital content and digital services, *OJ* L 136, 22.5.2019, p. 1–27.

[3] Wet van 20 maart 2022 tot wijziging van de bepalingen van het oud Burgerlijk Wetboek met betrekking tot de verkopen aan consumenten, tot invoeging van een nieuwe titel VIbis in boek III van het oude Burgerlijk Wetboek en tot wijziging van het Wetboek van economisch recht, *BS* 31 maart 2022.

[4] Once again, Belgium failed to implement in time. However, directives lack horizontal direct effect.

[5] Directive 1999/44/EC of the European Parliament and of the Council of 25 May 1999 on certain aspects of the sale of consumer goods and associated guarantees, OJ L 171, 7.7.1999, p. 12–16.

[6] See D. Staudenmayer, "The Directives on Digital Contracts: First Steps Towards the Private Law of the Digital Economy", *ERCL* 2020, (219) 220–221; J. Vanherpe, "White Smoke, but Smoke Nonetheless: Some (Burning) Questions Regarding the Directives on Sale of Goods and Supply of Digital Content", *ERPL* 2020, (251) 258.

[7] Articles 1641–1649 OCC.

[8] See Explanatory Memorandum, *Doc. Parl.*, Ch. Repr., sess. Ord. 2021–2022, n° 2355/001, 7: "En effet, la directive n'a pas déterminé la nature juridique du contrat de fourniture de contenu numérique ou de service numérique, mais s'est focalisée sur l'objet du contrat pour édicter des règles concernant

contract law, which applies *inter alia* to business-to-business contracts, is now complemented with two specific regimes for business-to-consumer contracts: (i) the amended regime on business-to-consumer sales of goods (implementing the SGD)[9]; (ii) a new regime on business-to-consumer supply of digital content or services (implementing the DCD)[10].

3   In a bizarre 'non-relationship' with the OCC[11], the Code of Economic Law (hereafter: "CEL") implements most EU consumer (contract) law directives in its Book 6 "Market practices and consumer protection", which has its own set of relevant definitions.[12] Importantly, the CEL contains *inter alia* the provisions on delivery of goods[13] as well as on transfer of risk[14] in the context of business-to-consumer sales of goods, implementing relevant provisions of the Consumer Rights Directive (hereafter: "CRD").[15] Public enforcement of the provisions of the Civil Code implementing the SGD and the DCD is possible as well.[16] The recent "Omnibus Directive"[17] was implemented by the *Act of 8 May 2022 amending books I, VI and XV Code of Economic Law*[18], the provisions of which are applicable as of 28 May 2022.[19]

B. Scope of application

4   The scope of the two new Belgian regimes corresponds to the scope of the Directives' regimes on sale of goods and supply of digital content or services. The sales regime applies to the relation between sellers[20] and consumers[21] only. Likewise, the regime on

---

la conformité. Les modèles commerciaux qui sous-tendent l'offre de contenu numérique et de service numérique sont tellement variés, qu'aucune qualification juridique ne peut prévaloir (contrat de vente, contrat d'entreprise-service, contrat de location ou même contrat sui generis). L'approche qui a été suivie pour la transposition suit celle adoptée par la directive et se centre sur l'objet du contrat et sur l'obligation qui pèse sur le fournisseur de fournir une chose conforme au contrat." See also Art. I.8, 34° CEL for the definition of "service contract": "any contract other than a sales contract under which the trader supplies or undertakes to supply a service, including a digital service, to the consumer".

[9] Altered articles 1649bis-1649nonies OCC.

[10] New Articles 1701/1–1701/19 OCC.

[11] See B. Demarsin and B. Keirsbilck, 'Brave little Belgium? The new Code of Economic Law and its relationship with civil and commercial law' (2016) *Zeitschrift für Europäisches Privatrecht* 859–887.

[12] See Article I.8, 39° CEL for the definition of "business" ("any natural or legal person which pursues an economic goal in a sustainable way, including its associations"), Article I.8, 40° CEL for the definition of "product" ("goods, services, immovable goods, digital services, digital content, rights and obligations") and Article I.1, 2° CEL, for the definition of "consumer" ("any natural person who is acting for purposes which are outside his trade, business, craft or profession").

[13] Art. VI.43 CEL.

[14] Art. VI.44 CEL.

[15] See Articles 18 and 20 of Directive 2011/83/EU of the European Parliament and of the Council of 25 October 2011 on consumer rights, OJ L 304, 22.11.2011, p. 64–88.

[16] See Articles 1649nonies and 1701/19 OCC.

[17] Directive (EU) 2019/2161 of the European Parliament and of the Council of 27 November 2019 amending Council Directive 93/13/EEC and Directives 98/6/EC, 2005/29/EC and 2011/83/EU of the European Parliament and of the Council as regards the better enforcement and modernisation of Union consumer protection rules, OJ L 328, 18.12.2019, p. 7–28.

[18] Wet van 8 mei 2022 houdende wijziging van boeken I, VI en XV van het Wetboek van economisch recht, *BS* 2 June 2022.

[19] Although the Act was published only on 2 June 2022.

[20] Art. 1649bis, § 1, 2° OCC: "any natural person or any legal person, irrespective of whether privately or publicly owned, that is acting, including through any other person acting in that natural or legal person's name or on that person's behalf, for purposes relating to that person's trade, business, craft or profession".

[21] Art. 1649bis, § 1, 1° OCC: "any natural person who is acting for purposes which are outside his trade, business, craft or profession".

B. Scope of application

digital content or services applies to the relation between traders[22] and consumers[23] only. The re-introduction of the notion of trader (*"handelaar"* / *"professionnel"*), with a very similar definition as that of the concept of "seller", is to be regretted. For a natural person to qualify as a "consumer", the purposes at the time of the conclusion of the contract are decisive.[24] The Belgian legislator takes the view that the definition of "consumer" also covers natural persons who are acting for purposes that are partly within and partly outside the person's trade, where the private purpose is predominant in the overall context of the contract.[25]

The new sales regime applies specifically to contracts for the sale[26] of "consumer goods" (tangible movable goods, including so-called goods with digital elements)[27] concluded between consumers and sellers.[28] In line with the SGD, the new regime also applies to (i) digital content[29] or digital services[30] which are incorporated in or inter-connected with consumer goods, (ii) in such a way that the absence of that digital content or digital service would prevent the goods from performing their functions (so-called "goods with digital elements"), (iii) if the digital content or digital services are provided with such goods with digital elements under the sales contract, irrespective of whether such digital content or digital service is supplied by the seller or by a third party.[31] Contracts between a consumer and a seller for the supply of goods to

---

[22] Art. 1701/1, 5° OCC (same definition). See D. Staudenmayer, 'The Directives on Digital Contracts: First Steps Towards the Private Law of the Digital Economy' (2020) *ERCL* 2020, (219) 231-232.

[23] Art. 1701/1, 6° OCC (same definition).

[24] R. Steennot, 'Het toepassingsgebied van de nieuwe garantieregelingen voor goederen, digitale inhoud en digitale diensten' (2022) *DCCR* (3) 6.

[25] Explanatory Memorandum, *Doc. Parl.*, Ch. Repr., sess. Ord. 2021-2022, n° 2355/001, 9-10. See the option left to the Member States in recital 22 SGD and recital 17 DCD. See also D. Staudenmayer, 'The Directives on Digital Contracts: First Steps Towards the Private Law of the Digital Economy' (2020) *ERCL* (219) 232-233; R. Steennot, 'Het toepassingsgebied van de nieuwe garantieregelingen voor goederen, digitale inhoud en digitale diensten' (2022) *DCCR* (3) 6.

[26] See D. Staudenmayer, 'The Directives on Digital Contracts: First Steps Towards the Private Law of the Digital Economy' (2020) *ERCL* (219) 224, comparing the SGD with the CSD. See also R. Steennot, 'Het toepassingsgebied van de nieuwe garantieregelingen voor goederen, digitale inhoud en digitale diensten' (2022) *DCCR* (3) 13, rightly observing that the Belgian legislator did not copy the SGD's definition of "sales agreement": "any contract under which the seller transfers or undertakes to transfer ownership of goods to a consumer, and the consumer pays or undertakes to pay the price thereof".

[27] Art. 1649bis, § 1, 4° OCC: "a) any tangible movable items; water, gas and electricity are to be considered as goods within the meaning of this regime where they are put up for sale in a limited volume or a set quantity; b) any good with digital element, being any tangible movable items that incorporate or are inter-connected with digital content or a digital service in such a way that the absence of that digital content or digital service would prevent the goods from performing their functions". See R. Steennot, "Het toepassingsgebied van de nieuwe garantieregelingen voor goederen, digitale inhoud en digitale diensten", *DCCR* 2022, (3) 10.

[28] Art. 1649bis, § 2, first limb OCC.

[29] Art. 1649bis, § 1, 5° OCC.

[30] Art. 1649bis, § 1, 6° OCC.

[31] Art. 1649bis, § 2, second limb OCC. See also Article 1701/2, § 5 OCC. In the event of doubt as to whether the supply of incorporated or inter-connected digital content or an incorporated or inter-connected digital service forms part of the sales contract, the digital content or digital service shall be presumed to be covered by the sales contract. See also R. Steennot, 'Het toepassingsgebied van de nieuwe garantieregelingen voor goederen, digitale inhoud en digitale diensten' (2022) *DCCR* (3) 8-9 and 10-11; D. Staudenmayer, 'The Directives on Digital Contracts: First Steps Towards the Private Law of the Digital Economy' (2020) *ERCL* (219) 229-230; J. Vanherpe, 'White Smoke, but Smoke Nonetheless: Some (Burning) Questions Regarding the Directives on Sale of Goods and Supply of Digital Content' (2020) *ERPL* (251) 254, also claiming that it would have been better to these goods with digital elements entirely under the scope of the DCD. See K. Sein, 'The Applicability of the Digital Content Directive and Sales of Goods Directive to Goods with Digital Elements' (2021) *Juridica International* 23-31. https://doi.org/10.12697/JI.2021.30.04

be manufactured or produced are also deemed sales contracts for the purpose of this regime.[32]

6   However, the new Belgian consumer sales regime does not apply to 1° contracts for the supply of digital content or services (subject to the above-mentioned exception as regards goods with digital elements); 2° any tangible medium which serves exclusively as a carrier for digital content[33]; 3° any goods sold by way of execution or otherwise by authority of law; 4° contracts for the sale of living animals.[34] In relation to living animals, the pre-existing regime on business-to-consumer sales (implementing the CSD) continues to apply[35] until a new, more appropriate regime on business-to-consumer sales of living animals will have been adopted.[36] Importantly, the Belgian legislator decided not to use the SGD's option of excluding second-hand goods sold at a public auction from the scope of the consumer sales regime.[37]

7   In line with the DCD (which intentionally avoids qualifying the legal nature of contracts falling within its scope[38]), the new Belgian regime on digital content and digital services applies to any contract where the trader supplies or undertakes to supply digital content[39] or a digital service[40] to the consumer[41] and the consumer pays or undertakes to pay a price[42].[43] The regime also applies where the trader supplies or undertakes to supply digital content or a digital service to the consumer, and the consumer provides or undertakes to provide personal data[44] to the trader.[45] Comparable to the sales regime, the digital content / service regime also applies where the digital content or digital service is developed in accordance with the consumer's specifications.[46] With the exception

---

[32] Art. 1649bis, § 2, third limb OCC.

[33] See also R. Steennot, 'Het toepassingsgebied van de nieuwe garantieregelingen voor goederen, digitale inhoud en digitale diensten' (2022) *DCCR* (3) 12-13.

[34] Art. 1649bis, § 3 OCC.

[35] Old Articles 1649bis-1649nonies OCC.

[36] See also R. Steennot, 'Het toepassingsgebied van de nieuwe garantieregelingen voor goederen, digitale inhoud en digitale diensten' (2022) *DCCR* (3) 9-10, with references.

[37] Art. 3(5) SGD. See also R. Steennot, 'Het toepassingsgebied van de nieuwe garantieregelingen voor goederen, digitale inhoud en digitale diensten' (2022) *DCCR* 2022, (3) 10, with references.

[38] D. Staudenmayer, 'The Directives on Digital Contracts: First Steps Towards the Private Law of the Digital Economy' (2020) *ERCL* (219) 224.

[39] Art. 1701/1, 1° OCC: "data which are produced and supplied in digital form". See also Art. I.8, 35° CEL.

[40] Art. 1701/1, 2° OCC: "a) a service that allows the consumer to create, process, store or access data in digital form; or b) a service that allows the sharing of or any other interaction with data in digital form uploaded or created by the consumer or other users of that service". See also Art. I.8, 40° CEL.

[41] See also R. Steennot, 'Het toepassingsgebied van de nieuwe garantieregelingen voor goederen, digitale inhoud en digitale diensten' (2022) *DCCR* (3) 14-15.

[42] Art. 1701/1, 7° OCC: "money or a digital representation of value that is due in exchange for the supply of digital content or a digital service".

[43] Art. 1701/2, § 1 OCC. See also R. Steennot, "Het toepassingsgebied van de nieuwe garantieregelingen voor goederen, digitale inhoud en digitale diensten", *DCCR* 2022, (3) 15-17, with references.

[44] Art. 1701/1, 8° OCC: "personal data as defined in point (1) of Article 4 of Regulation (EU) 2016/679".

[45] Art. 1701/2, § 2 OCC (except where the personal data provided by the consumer are exclusively processed by the trader for the purpose of supplying the digital content or digital service or for allowing the trader to comply with legal requirements to which the trader is subject, and the trader does not process those data for any other purpose). See also R. Steennot, 'Het toepassingsgebied van de nieuwe garantieregelingen voor goederen, digitale inhoud en digitale diensten' (2022) *DCCR* (3) 17-18, with references; D. Staudenmayer, 'The Directives on Digital Contracts: First Steps Towards the Private Law of the Digital Economy' (2020) *ERCL* (219) 224-229; J. Vanherpe, 'White Smoke, but Smoke Nonetheless: Some (Burning) Questions Regarding the Directives on Sale of Goods and Supply of Digital Content' (2020) *ERPL* (251) 255-258.

[46] Art. 1701/2, § 3 OCC. See also R. Steennot, 'Het toepassingsgebied van de nieuwe garantieregelingen voor goederen, digitale inhoud en digitale diensten' (2022) *DCCR* (3) 15.

B. Scope of application

of Articles 1701/3 OCC (obligation to supply) and 1701/9 OCC (remedies for failure to supply), the DCD regime also applies to any tangible medium which serves exclusively as a carrier of digital content.[47]

Logically, the new Belgian regime on digital content or services does not apply to digital content or services which are incorporated in or inter-connected with goods with digital elements[48], and which are provided with the goods under a sales contract concerning those goods, irrespective of whether such digital content or digital service is supplied by the seller or by a third party[49], because then the sales regime applies. Where a single contract between the same trader and the same consumer includes in a bundle elements of supply of digital content or a digital service and elements of the provision of other services or goods, this regime applies only to the elements of the contract concerning the digital content or digital service.[50] In line with the DCD, there are quite a number of sectoral carve-outs from the scope of the new Belgian regime on digital content and digital services.[51]

As to the territorial scope of application of both new regimes, any clause which declares the law of a state which is not a member of the European Union applicable to a contract governed by any of the regimes, shall be null and void in respect of matters governed by these regimes if, in the absence of such clause, the law of a Member State of the European Union would be applicable and that law grants consumers a higher level of protection in these matters.[52]

8

9

---

[47] Art. 1701/2, § 4 OCC. See D. Staudenmayer, 'The Directives on Digital Contracts: First Steps Towards the Private Law of the Digital Economy' (2020) *ERCL* (219) 231.

[48] See Art. 1701/1, 3° OCC: "any tangible movable items that incorporate, or are inter-connected with, digital content or a digital service in such a way that the absence of that digital content or digital service would prevent the goods from performing their functions".

[49] Art. 1701/2, § 5 OCC.

[50] Art. 1701/2, § 6 OCC. See also D. Staudenmayer, 'The Directives on Digital Contracts: First Steps Towards the Private Law of the Digital Economy' (2020) *ERCL* (219) 235; R. Steennot, 'Het toepassingsgebied van de nieuwe garantieregelingen voor goederen, digitale inhoud en digitale diensten' (2022) *DCCR* (3) 20–21, with references.

[51] Art. 1701/2, § 7 OCC. The regime does not apply to contracts regarding: 1° the provision of services other than digital services, regardless of whether digital forms or means are used by the trader to produce the output of the service or to deliver or transmit it to the consumer; 2° electronic communications services, with the exception of number-independent interpersonal communications services; 3° health services provided by health professionals to patients to assess, maintain or restore their state of health, including the prescription, dispensation and provision of medicinal products and medical devices; 4° gambling services, namely, services that involve wagering a stake with pecuniary value in games of chance, including those with an element of skill, such as lotteries, casino games, poker games and betting transactions, by electronic means or any other technology for facilitating communication and at the individual request of a recipient of such services; 5° financial services as defined in Article I.8, 18°, CEL; 6° software offered by the trader under a free and open-source licence, where the consumer does not pay a price and the personal data provided by the consumer are exclusively processed by the trader for the purpose of improving the security, compatibility or interoperability of that specific software; 7° the supply of digital content where the digital content is made available to the general public other than by signal transmission as a part of a performance or event, such as digital cinematographic projections; 8° digital content provided by public sector bodies of the Member States. See also R. Steennot, "Het toepassingsgebied van de nieuwe garantieregelingen voor goederen, digitale inhoud en digitale diensten", *DCCR* 2022, (3) 18–21, with references.

[52] Art. 1649octies, second limb OCC and Art. 1701/18, second limb OCC. See also R. Steennot, 'Het toepassingsgebied van de nieuwe garantieregelingen voor goederen, digitale inhoud en digitale diensten', *DCCR* 2022, (3) 21–22.

C. Delivery and supply in conformity with the contract – obligation to supply updates

10 As mentioned, the CRD's rule on business-to-consumer delivery of goods – i.e. without undue delay, and no later than 30 days after the conclusion of the contract, unless otherwise agreed by the parties – was implemented in the CEL.[53] The implementation of the SGD did not lead to changes in this regard.[54] Implementing the DCD, Belgian law now copies out the trader's obligation to supply the digital content or digital service to the consumer. Unless the parties have agreed otherwise, the trader shall supply the digital content or digital service without undue delay after the conclusion of the contract.[55] The trader shall have complied with the obligation to supply when: 1° the digital content or any means suitable for accessing or downloading the digital content is made available or accessible to the consumer, or to a physical or virtual facility chosen by the consumer for that purpose; 2° the digital service is made accessible to the consumer or to a physical or virtual facility chosen by the consumer for that purpose.[56] The remedies in case of failure to deliver / supply reflect closely the provisions of the relevant directives.[57] In addition, Belgian law allows to invoke the *exceptio non adimpleti contractus* so that the consumer may withhold payment (if there was no obligation to pay prior to delivery / supply). This follows from the general law of obligations.[58] As mentioned, the CRD's rule on business-to-consumer transfer of risk in consumer sales – in principle at the moment of taking delivery – was implemented in the CEL.[59] The implementation of the SGD did not lead to changes in this regard.[60]

11 As in the twin directives, the seller or trader is obliged to deliver goods or supply digital content or services that meet the conformity requirements.[61] The subjective and objective conformity requirements set out in the SGD were copied out in the Belgian consumer sales regime. They put flesh to the bone to the general obligation to deliver goods in conformity with the contract.[62] Likewise, the new Belgian regime copies out the general obligation to supply digital content or services in conformity with the contract.[63]

---

[53] Article VI.43 CEL.

[54] See also H. Jacquemin, 'La conformité des biens, des contenus numériques et des services numériques, l'articulation des délais et la modification des éléments numériques' (2022) *DCCR* (25) 30.

[55] Art. 1701/3, § 1 OCC.

[56] Art. 1701/3, § 2 OCC. See also H. Jacquemin, 'La conformité des biens, des contenus numériques et des services numériques, l'articulation des délais et la modification des éléments numériques' (2022) *DCCR* (25) 28–29.

[57] For goods: Art. VI.43, § 2 CEL (implementation of Art. 18 CRD); for digital content / services: Art. 1701/9 OCC (implementation of Art. 13 DCD).

[58] Cf. Art. 5:98 CC. See also Art. 13(6) SGD and recital 15 DCD that mentions that Member States are free to regulate this. See F. Van Den Abeele and B. Tilleman, 'Remedies in het nieuwe consumenten(koop)recht: een (her)nieuw(d) getrapt system' (2022) *DCCR* (59) 60; J. Vanherpe, 'White Smoke, but Smoke Nonetheless: Some (Burning) Questions Regarding the Directives on Sale of Goods and Supply of Digital Content' (2020) *ERPL* (251) 265.

[59] Article VI.44 CEL.

[60] See also H. Jacquemin, 'La conformité des biens, des contenus numériques et des services numériques, l'articulation des délais et la modification des éléments numériques' (2022) *DCCR* (25) 30–31.

[61] See D. Staudenmayer, 'The Directives on Digital Contracts: First Steps Towards the Private Law of the Digital Economy' (2020) *ERCL* (219) 236, on the general approach and evolution of focus from subjective towards objective requirements.

[62] Art. 1649ter, § 1 OCC, which makes reference to Art. 1604 OCC (duty of delivery in general sales law).

[63] Art. 1701/4 OCC. See also H. Jacquemin, 'La conformité des biens, des contenus numériques et des services numériques, l'articulation des délais et la modification des éléments numériques' (2022) *DCCR* (25) 27–28.

C. Delivery and supply in conformity with the contract – obligation to supply updates

The DCD's subjective[64] and objective[65] conformity requirements were copied out as well and are quasi-identical to those set out in the consumer sales regime.

Hence, Belgian law now distinguishes between subjective and objective criteria for conformity. In order to conform with the contract, the goods / digital content or service must meet the following **subjective conformity requirements** as agreed between the parties (for digital content or services typically in a SLA).[66] First, they must be of the description, type[67], quantity and quality, and – relevant for digital goods / content / services – possess the functionality[68], compatibility[69], interoperability[70] and other features, as required by the contract.[71] Second, they must be fit for any particular purpose for which the consumer requires them and which the consumer made known to the seller / trader at the latest at the time of the conclusion of the contract, and in respect of which the seller / trader has given acceptance.[72] Third, they must be delivered with all accessories and instructions, including on installation, and customer assistance[73], as stipulated by the contract. Fourthly, they must be supplied with updates / updated as stipulated by the contract.[74] Furthermore, pre-contractual information as required by the CRD[75] also determines the contractual requirements.[76]

It should be noted that durability[77] is not explicitly mentioned in the above-mentioned non-exhaustive list of features, although it is admittedly related to the notion of functionality.[78] This has been regretted by some Belgian authors.[79] However, it is clear that the consumer should be able to also rely on durability information in pre-contractual statements as part of the subjective requirements for conformity.[80] It is also clear that

---

[64] Art. 1701/5 OCC.

[65] Art. 1701/6 OCC.

[66] Art. 1649ter, § 2 OCC and Art. 1701/5 OCC. See also recital 28 SGD and H. Jacquemin, 'La conformité des biens, des contenus numériques et des services numériques, l'articulation des délais et la modification des éléments numériques' (2022) *DCCR* (25) 31–34.

[67] This element is only mentioned in Art. 1649ter, § 2, 1° OCC, not in Art. 1701/5, 1° OCC.

[68] Art. 1649bis, § 1, 8° OCC and Article 1701/1, 11° OCC: "the ability of the goods / digital content or digital service to perform their functions having regard to their purpose". See also Art. I.8, 44° CEL.

[69] Art. 1649bis, § 1, 7° OCC and Article 1701/1, 10° OCC: "the ability of the goods / digital content or digital service to function with hardware or software with which goods / digital content or digital service of the same type are normally used, without the need to convert the goods, hardware or software / digital content or digital service". See also Art. I.8, 43° CEL.

[70] Art. 1649bis, § 1, 9° OCC and Article 1701/1, 12° OCC: "the ability of the goods / digital content or digital service to function with hardware or software different from those with which goods / digital content or digital service of the same type are normally used". See also Art. I.8, 45° CEL.

[71] D. Staudenmayer, 'The Directives on Digital Contracts: First Steps Towards the Private Law of the Digital Economy' (2020) *ERCL* (219) 237.

[72] Art. 1649ter, § 2, 2° OCC and Art. 1701/5, 2° OCC.

[73] This element is only mentioned in Art. 1701/5, 3° OCC, not in Art. 1649ter, § 2, 3° OCC. See also H. Jacquemin, 'La conformité des biens, des contenus numériques et des services numériques, l'articulation des délais et la modification des éléments numériques' (2022) *DCCR* (25) 33, rightly criticising this difference. See also D. Staudenmayer, 'The Directives on Digital Contracts: First Steps Towards the Private Law of the Digital Economy' (2020) *ERCL* (219) 236, on this "negligible difference in the wording".

[74] Art. 1649ter, § 2, 4° OCC and Art. 1701/5, 4° OCC. See also recital 28 SGD.

[75] Article 5 CRD (implemented in Art. VI.2 CEL) and Article 6 CRD (implemented in Art. VI.45 and Art. VI.64 CEL).

[76] Cf. Recital 26 SGD; recital 42 DCD. See also D. Staudenmayer, 'The Directives on Digital Contracts: First Steps Towards the Private Law of the Digital Economy' (2020) *ERCL* (219) 236.

[77] "Durability" is defined as "the ability of the goods to maintain their required functions and performance through normal use" (Art. 1649bis, § 1, 12° OCC).

[78] Art. 1649ter, § 2, 1° OCC and Art. 1701/5, 1° OCC.

[79] H. Jacquemin, 'La conformité des biens, des contenus numériques et des services numériques, l'articulation des délais et la modification des éléments numériques' (2022) *DCCR* (25) 32.

[80] Recital 32 SGD.

this is not a strong guarantee to ensure a high standard of durability:[81] if a trader is very straightforward in the pre-contractual information about the limitations in terms of durability of a good, this will affect the subjective requirements.

14 In addition to complying with any subjective requirement for conformity, the goods / digital content or digital services must also conform with a number of **objective conformity requirements**.[82] First of all, these must be fit for the purposes for which goods / digital content or digital services of the same type would normally be used, taking into account, where applicable, any existing Union and national law, technical standards or, in the absence of such technical standards, applicable sector-specific industry codes of conduct.[83] Second, where applicable, the goods must be of the quality and correspond to the description of a sample or model that the seller made available to the consumer before the conclusion of the contract.[84] Digital content or services must comply with any trial version or preview of the digital content or digital service, made available by the trader before the conclusion of the contract.[85] Thirdly, the goods / digital content or service must, where applicable, be delivered / supplied along with such accessories, including packaging[86], installation instructions[87] or other instructions, as the consumer may reasonably expect to receive.[88] Fourthly, they must be of the quantity and possess the qualities and other features[89], including in relation to durability[90], functionality, compatibility[91], accessibility[92], continuity[93] and security normal for goods / digital content or services of the same type and which the consumer may reasonably expect given the nature of the goods / digital content or services and taking into account any public statement made by or on behalf of the seller / trader, or other persons in previous links of the chain of transactions, including the producer[94], particularly in advertising or on labelling.[95]

---

[81] E. Van Gool, 'De nieuwe richtlijn consumentenkoop en duurzame consumptie', in I. Claeys and E. Terryn (eds.), *Nieuw recht inzake koop en digitale inhoud en diensten*' (Intersentia 2020) (303) 334, nr. 41.

[82] See also H. Jacquemin, 'La conformité des biens, des contenus numériques et des services numériques, l'articulation des délais et la modification des éléments numériques' (2022) *DCCR* (25) 35–43.

[83] Art. 1649ter, § 3, 1° OCC and Art. 1701/6, § 1, 1° OCC. See also D. Staudenmayer, 'The Directives on Digital Contracts: First Steps Towards the Private Law of the Digital Economy' (2020) *ERCL* (219) 238.

[84] Art. 1649ter, § 3, 2° OCC.

[85] Art. 1701/6, § 1, 4° OCC.

[86] This is only mentioned in Art. 1649ter, § 3, 3° OCC, not in Art. 1701/6, § 1, 3° OCC.

[87] This is only mentioned in Art. 1649ter, § 3, 3° OCC, not in Art. 1701/6, § 1, 3° OCC.

[88] Art. 1649ter, § 3, 3° OCC and Art. 1701/6, § 1, 3° OCC.

[89] Art. 1701/6, 2° OCC specifically mentions "performance features". See also H. Jacquemin, "La conformité des biens, des contenus numériques et des services numériques, l'articulation des délais et la modification des éléments numériques", *DCCR* 2022, (25) 38, rightly criticising this specific restriction to performance features only.

[90] This is only mentioned in Art. 1649ter, § 3, 4° OCC, not in Art. 1701/6, § 1, 2° OCC. "Durability" is defined as "the ability of the goods to maintain their required functions and performance through normal use" (Art. 1649bis, § 1, 12° OCC).

[91] See also H. Jacquemin, 'La conformité des biens, des contenus numériques et des services numériques, l'articulation des délais et la modification des éléments numériques' (2022) *DCCR* (25) 37, rightly criticising the lack of reference to interoperability. See in this regard also D. Staudenmayer, 'The Directives on Digital Contracts: First Steps Towards the Private Law of the Digital Economy' (2020) *ERCL* (219) 236.

[92] This is only mentioned in Art. 1701/6, § 1, 2° OCC, not in Art. 1649ter, § 3, 4° OCC.

[93] This is only mentioned in Art. 1701/6, § 1, 2° OCC, not in Art. 1649ter, § 3, 4° OCC.

[94] This is only mentioned in Art. 1649ter, § 3, 4° OCC, not in Art. 1701/6, § 1, 2° OCC. See also the definition of "producer" in Art. 1649bis, § 1, 3° OCC.

[95] Art. 1649ter, § 3, 4° OCC and Art. 1701/6, 2° OCC. However, pursuant to Art. 1649ter, § 4 OCC, the seller shall not be bound by public statements, as referred to in Art. 1649ter, § 3, 4° OCC, if the seller

C. Delivery and supply in conformity with the contract – obligation to supply updates

The explicit reference to "durability" in the objective conformity criteria for goods is a novelty also for Belgian law. Yet, given the extremely narrow definition of durability, little is expected of this addition in terms of effectively increasing sustainable consumption.[96] It has however been stressed rightfully in the literature that this new reference does definitely not exclude that other aspects of sustainability continue be taken into account to assess objective conformity.[97] Thus e.g. if a label is attached to a product that states the product was produced with no or limited impact on the environment, this can be taken into account to assess the qualities and thus the conformity of the good.

Conformity does not only cover material defects, but also legal defects.[98] The dedicated SGD and DCD provisions on third-party rights[99] were not explicitly implemented in Belgian law.

In line with the SGD, the amended Belgian consumer sales regime now also obliges the seller[100] of goods with digital elements to ensure that the consumer is informed of and supplied with **updates**, including security updates, that are necessary to keep those goods in conformity, for the period of time: 1° that the consumer may reasonably expect given the type and purpose of the goods and the digital elements, and taking into account the circumstances and nature of the contract, where the sales contract provides for a single act of supply of the digital content or digital service; or 2° indicated in Article 1649quater, § 1, second limb, where the sales contract provides for a continuous supply of the digital content or digital service over a period of time.[101] In line with the DCD, the new Belgian regime on digital content or services also imposes such an obligation on the trader of digital content or services.[102] This duty to supply updates applies either for the period of time during which the digital content or digital service is to be supplied under

---

shows that: 1° the seller was not, and could not reasonably have been, aware of the public statement in question; 2° by the time of conclusion of the contract, the public statement had been corrected in the same way as, or in a way comparable to how, it had been made; or 3° the decision to buy the goods could not have been influenced by the public statement. Art. 1701/6, § 1, 2° *in fine* OCC provides for a similar exception. See also D. Staudenmayer, 'The Directives on Digital Contracts: First Steps Towards the Private Law of the Digital Economy' (2020) *ERCL* (219) 238.

[96] See, critically, E. Van Gool, 'De nieuwe richtlijn consumentenkoop en duurzame consumptie', in I. Claeys and E. Terryn (eds), *Nieuw recht inzake koop en digitale inhoud en diensten* (Intersentia 2020) (303) 336-337, nr. 45.

[97] See E. Van Gool, 'De nieuwe richtlijn consumentenkoop en duurzame consumptie', in I. Claeys and E. Terryn (eds), *Nieuw recht inzake koop en digitale inhoud en diensten* (Intersentia 2020) (303) 336-337, nr. 45, and in the same sense: A. Beckers, 'Environmental Protection meets Consumer Sales: The Influence of Environmental Market Communication on Consumer Contracts and Remedies' (2018) *ERCL* 168; A. Michel, 'La directive 1999/44/CE sur la garantie des biens de consommation: un remède efficace contre l'obsolescence programmée?' (2016) *REDC* 219; K. Tonner, 'Sustainable Consumption, Consumer Policy and the Law' (2011) *REDC* 21.

[98] Recital 35 SGD and recital 54 DCD.

[99] Art. 9 SGD and Art. 13 DCD. See also D. Staudenmayer, 'The Directives on Digital Contracts: First Steps Towards the Private Law of the Digital Economy' (2020) *ERCL* (219) 241.

[100] See also H. Jacquemin, 'La conformité des biens, des contenus numériques et des services numériques, l'articulation des délais et la modification des éléments numériques' (2022) *DCCR* (25) 40, rightly pointing out that the enforcement of this obligation on the part of the seller might prove difficult in practice.

[101] Art. 1649ter, § 5 OCC. However, pursuant to Art. 1649ter, § 6 OCC, where the consumer fails to install the supplied updates within a reasonable time, the seller shall not be liable for any lack of conformity resulting solely from the lack of the relevant update, provided that: 1° the seller informed the consumer about the availability of the update and the consequences of the failure of the consumer to install it; and 2° the failure of the consumer to install or the incorrect installation by the consumer of the update was not due to shortcomings in the installation instructions provided to the consumer.

[102] See J. Vanherpe, 'White Smoke, but Smoke Nonetheless: Some (Burning) Questions Regarding the Directives on Sale of Goods and Supply of Digital Content' (2020) *ERPL* (251) 261, on the "subtle linguistic differences" between the SGD and the DCD in this regard. See also H. Jacquemin, 'La conformité des

the contract (continuous supply over a period of time) or for the period of time that the consumer may reasonably expect, given the type and purpose of the digital content or digital service and taking into account the circumstances and nature of the contract, where the contract provides for a single act of supply or a series of individual acts of supply.[103] Where the contract provides for a continuous supply of digital content or digital service over a period of time, the digital content or digital service must be in conformity throughout the duration of that period.[104] Unless the parties have agreed otherwise, digital content or a digital service shall be supplied in the most recent version available at the time of the conclusion of the contract.[105]

18 In line with the twin directives, the Belgian regimes provide that any lack of conformity resulting from the incorrect installation of the goods, or from the incorrect integration[106] of the digital content or digital service into the consumer's digital environment[107], shall be regarded as lack of conformity, if: 1° the installation / integration forms part of the contract and was carried out by the seller / trader or under the seller's / trader's responsibility; or 2° the installation of the goods, intended to be carried out by the consumer (colloquially known as the "IKEA-clause"), was done by the consumer and the incorrect installation / integration was due to shortcomings in the installation / integration instructions provided by the seller / trader or, in the case of goods with digital elements, provided by the seller or by the supplier of the digital content or digital service.[108]

19 In line with the SGD and the DCD, both new Belgian regimes clarify that there shall be no lack of conformity, if, at the time of the conclusion of the contract, the consumer was specifically informed that a particular characteristic of the goods / digital content or service was deviating from these objective conformity requirements and the consumer expressly and separately accepted that deviation when concluding the contract.[109]

D. Liability of the seller / trader – time periods

20 The seller shall be liable to the consumer for any lack of conformity which exists at the time when the goods were delivered and which becomes apparent **within two**

---

biens, des contenus numériques et des services numériques, l'articulation des délais et la modification des éléments numériques' (2022) *DCCR* (25) 41.

[103] Art. 1701/6, § 2 OCC. However, pursuant to Art. 1701/6, § 3 OCC, where the consumer fails to install, within a reasonable time, updates supplied by the trader in accordance with paragraph 2, the trader shall not be liable for any lack of conformity resulting solely from the lack of the relevant update, provided that: 1° the trader informed the consumer about the availability of the update and the consequences of the failure of the consumer to install it; and 2° the failure of the consumer to install or the incorrect installation by the consumer of the update was not due to shortcomings in the installation instructions provided by the trader.

[104] Art. 1701/6, § 4 OCC.

[105] Art. 1701/6, § 6 OCC. See also D. Staudenmayer, 'The Directives on Digital Contracts: First Steps Towards the Private Law of the Digital Economy' (2020) *ERCL* (219) 238; 240–241; J. Vanherpe, 'White Smoke, but Smoke Nonetheless: Some (Burning) Questions Regarding the Directives on Sale of Goods and Supply of Digital Content' (2020) ERPL (251) 261, noting that this obligation is not explicitly mentioned in the SGD.

[106] Art. 1701/1, 4° OCC: "the linking and incorporation of digital content or a digital service with the components of the consumer's digital environment in order for the digital content or digital service to be used in accordance with the requirements for conformity provided for by this Directive".

[107] Art. 1701/1, 9° OCC: "hardware, software and any network connection used by the consumer to access or make use of digital content or a digital service".

[108] Art. 1649ter, § 8 OCC and Article 1701/7 OCC. See also D. Staudenmayer, 'The Directives on Digital Contracts: First Steps Towards the Private Law of the Digital Economy' (2020) *ERCL* (219) 240.

[109] Art. 1649ter, § 7 OCC and Art. 1701/6, § 5 OCC.

D. Liability of the seller / trader – time periods

years of that time.[110] In the case of goods with digital elements, where the sales contract provides for a single act of supply of digital content or services, the seller shall be liable for any lack of conformity which exists at the time of supply and which becomes apparent within two years of that time.[111] Where the sales contract provides for a continuous supply of the digital content or digital service over a period of time, the seller shall also be liable for any lack of conformity of the digital content or digital service that occurs or becomes apparent within two years of the time when the goods with digital elements were delivered. Where the contract provides for a continuous supply for more than two years, the seller shall be liable for any lack of conformity of the digital content or digital service that occurs or becomes apparent **within the period of time during which the digital content or digital service is to be supplied under the sales contract**.[112] The Belgian (parliamentary) debate during the implementation process mainly focused on these legal guarantee periods.[113] The Belgian legislator finally did not choose for longer periods of liability than the minimum periods provided for in the directives.[114] A prior version of the draft implementation act provided for the possibility to extend the legal guarantee period by Royal Decree for specific categories of goods,[115] which could have contributed to the promotion of goods with a longer lifespan[116], but such provision was finally not adopted.[117] The legal guarantee period shall be suspended during the period required for the repair or replacement of the good or in the event of negotiations between the seller and the consumer with a view to an amicable settlement.[118] The Belgian legislator decided to use the SGD's option to permit parties to contractually reduce the legal guarantee period to a minimum of one year in the case of second-hand goods.[119] In line with the option left to the Member States in the SGD[120], Belgian law now also imposes an obligation on the consumer to inform the seller of a lack of conformity within a period of at least 2 months of the date on which the consumer detected such lack of conformity.[121]

---

[110] Art. 1649quater, § 1, first limb OCC.
[111] See H. Jacquemin, 'La conformité des biens, des contenus numériques et des services numériques, l'articulation des délais et la modification des éléments numériques' (2022) *DCCR* (25) 46, rightly noting that this hypothesis is not specifically envisaged by the legislator. See also D. Staudenmayer, 'The Directives on Digital Contracts: First Steps Towards the Private Law of the Digital Economy' (2020) *ERCL* (219) 247.
[112] Art. 1649quater, § 1, second limb OCC. See also D. Staudenmayer, 'The Directives on Digital Contracts: First Steps Towards the Private Law of the Digital Economy' (2020) *ERCL* (219) 247–248.
[113] A prior legislative proposal to extend the legal guarantee period was eventually not adopted, Wetsvoorstel houden de bescherming van de consumenten bij verkoop van consumptiegoederen, *Parl. St.* Kamer, doc. 55 693/001.
[114] As allowed by Art. 10(3) SGD.
[115] The explanatory memorandum still refers to such a possibility, MvT, *Parl. St.* Kamer, 2021–2022, doc 55, 2355/001, p. 56.
[116] See also E. Van Gool and A. Michel, 'The New Consumer Sales Directive 2019/771 and Sustainable Consumption: A Critical Analysis' (2021) *EuCML* (136) 141–142.
[117] See also H. Jacquemin, 'La conformité des biens, des contenus numériques et des services numériques, l'articulation des délais et la modification des éléments numériques' (2022) *DCCR* (25) 46–47.
[118] Art. 1649quater, § 1, third limb OCC.
[119] Art. 1649quater, § 1, fourth limb OCC. See Art. 10(6) SGD. See E. Van Gool and A. Michel, 'The New Consumer Sales Directive 2019/771 and Sustainable Consumption: A Critical Analysis' (2021) *EuCML* (136) 138, arguing convincingly that the Articles 3(5) and 10(6) SGD do not fit within the shift to a more circular economy.
[120] Art. 12 SGD.
[121] Art. 1649quater, § 2 OCC. See also H. Jacquemin, "La conformité des biens, des contenus numériques et des services numériques, l'articulation des délais et la modification des éléments numériques", *DCCR* 2022, (25) 49.

21   Turning to the DCD regime, where a contract provides for a single act of supply or a series of individual acts of supply, the trader shall be liable for any lack of conformity which exists at the time of supply and which becomes apparent **within two years of that time**.[122] Where the contract provides for continuous supply over a period of time, the trader shall be liable for a lack of conformity, that occurs or becomes apparent **within the period of time during which the digital content or digital service is to be supplied under the contract**.[123] The regime also provides for a similar suspension of the legal guarantee period as in the sales regime.[124] In line with the DCD, Belgian law does not impose an obligation on the consumer to inform the trader of a lack of conformity.[125]

22   The parliamentary debate also focused on the period during which the **burden of proof** (of the existence of a lack of conformity at the relevant time) is reversed; the consumer must of course still prove the lack of conformity itself.[126] The period of reversal of the burden of proof for goods was finally extended from 6 months (under the former consumer sales regime, reflecting the CSD) to two years (going beyond the minimum of one year as provided for by the SGD).[127] This definitely entails an important increase in consumer protection.[128] For goods with digital elements, an even more consumer friendly regime applies.[129] For digital content and digital services, Belgian law provides that the period of reversal of the burden of proof amounts to one year in case of a single act of supply (or a series of individual acts of supply) and to the whole contractual period of supply in case of continuous supply.[130]

23   Belgian law provides for rather short limitation periods for the consumer to invoke the remedies foreseen by the twin regimes: actions must be introduced within one year from the discovery of the defect.[131]

24   The rather peculiar system that the general sales law based on hidden defects (*vices cachés*) 'revives' when the period of liability under the specific provisions on consumer

---

[122] Art. 1701/8, § 2, first limb OCC.

[123] Art. 1701/8, § 3, first limb OCC. See also D. Staudenmayer, 'The Directives on Digital Contracts: First Steps Towards the Private Law of the Digital Economy' (2020) *ERCL* (219) 247.

[124] Art. 1701/8, § 2, third limb and Art. 1701/8, § 3, third limb OCC.

[125] See also H. Jacquemin, 'La conformité des biens, des contenus numériques et des services numériques, l'articulation des délais et la modification des éléments numériques' (2022) *DCCR* (25) 49. See also J. Vanherpe, 'White Smoke, but Smoke Nonetheless: Some (Burning) Questions Regarding the Directives on Sale of Goods and Supply of Digital Content' (2020) *ERPL* (251) 270, rightly criticizing the difference between the SGD and the DCD.

[126] See also D. Staudenmayer, 'The Directives on Digital Contracts: First Steps Towards the Private Law of the Digital Economy' (2020) *ERCL* (219) 248.

[127] Art. 1649quater, § 4 OCC. See the option left to the Member States in Art. 11(2) SGD: "Instead of the one-year period laid down in paragraph 1, Member States may maintain or introduce a period of two years from the time when the goods were delivered." See for a comparison with the CSD: J. Vanherpe, 'White Smoke, but Smoke Nonetheless: Some (Burning) Questions Regarding the Directives on Sale of Goods and Supply of Digital Content' (2020) *ERPL* (251) 264–265.

[128] See also H. Jacquemin, 'La conformité des biens, des contenus numériques et des services numériques, l'articulation des délais et la modification des éléments numériques' (2022) *DCCR* (25) 50–52. See also E. Van Gool and A. Michel, 'The New Consumer Sales Directive 2019/771 and Sustainable Consumption: A Critical Analysis' (2021) *EuCML* (136) 142.

[129] Art. 1649quater, § 4/1 OCC : where the contract of sale provides for the continuous supply of the digital content or service over a period of time, the burden of proof lies with the seller during that period.

[130] Art. 1701/8, § 2, second limb and Art. 1701/8, § 3, second limb OCC. The DCD does not allow any national deviations. See also H. Jacquemin, "La conformité des biens, des contenus numériques et des services numériques, l'articulation des délais et la modification des éléments numériques", *DCCR* 2022, (25) 52–53.

[131] For goods: Art. 1649quater § 3, OCC; for digital content and services: art. 1701/8, § 2, fourth limb and § 3, fourth limb OCC.

sales expires, as allowed by the SDG[132], was maintained.[133] Thus, when a defect becomes apparent more than two years after delivery, the consumer can (in theory) still invoke the remedies for hidden defects under the general sales law.[134] That possibility was also introduced, "if applicable", upon the expiry of the period of liability of the specific provisions for digital content and digital services.[135] In practice, the provisions of the general sales law are only rarely successfully invoked by consumers.[136]

The DCD provisions on modification of the digital content or digital service were implemented as well.[137]

E. Remedies

The Belgian provisions on remedies copy the provisions of the twin directives rather closely. The regulatory option to provide additional remedies for defects becoming apparent within 30 days was not used.[138] A 'right to reject' does not exist under Belgian law, and – fortunately, from a sustainability perspective[139] – no such remedy was introduced.

Like the former consumer sales law, the new provisions also provide for a hierarchy of remedies.[140] This hierarchy has caused some discussion in the Belgian legal literature and has given rise to diverging case law. More specifically the exact role and competences of the judge in case a consumer invokes the 'wrong' remedy is disputed.[141] Belgian procedural law in any event gives sufficient possibilities to a consumer to refine its initial action during the procedure[142] in order to be in conformity with the CJEU's decision in *Duarte*. The hierarchy has also been subject to criticism in the Belgian legal literature for its lack of attention to sustainability arguments.

Repair or replacement, or more generally "bringing into conformity", i.e. performance in kind, are the primary remedies under the twin directives and therefore also under Belgian law.[143] This is in line with the general law of obligations that also favours

---

[132] Art. 3(6) and recital 18 SGD; Art. 3(10) and recital 12 DCD. See D. Staudenmayer, 'The Directives on Digital Contracts: First Steps Towards the Private Law of the Digital Economy' (2020) *ERCL* (219) 235.

[133] Art. 1649quater, § 5 OCC, cf. Art. 3(7) SGD and recital 12 DCD. See J. Vanherpe, 'White Smoke, but Smoke Nonetheless: Some (Burning) Questions Regarding the Directives on Sale of Goods and Supply of Digital Content' (2020) *ERPL* (251) 263–264.

[134] The SGD explicitly allows Member States to have such rule, cf. Art. 3 (7) SGD.

[135] Art. 1701/8, § 5 OCC.

[136] See B. Tilleman, S. De Rey, N. Van Damme and F. Van Den Abeele, 'Overzicht van rechtspraak koop (2007–2020)' (2020) *TPR* 1506–1507. The onus of proof on the consumer that the defect existed at the time of conclusion of the contract and the need to introduce an action within a short period of time create important hurdles.

[137] Art. 1701/17 OCC.

[138] Art. 3 (7) SGD.

[139] See E. Van Gool and A. Michel, 'The New Consumer Sales Directive 2019/771 and Sustainable Consumption: A Critical Analysis' (2021) *EuCML* (136) 143.

[140] Art. 1649 quinquies OCC and Art. 1701/9 et seq. OCC.

[141] For a detailed discussion and overview of the (diverging) case law, see. F. Van den Abeele and B. Tilleman, 'Remedies in het nieuwe consumenten(koop)recht: een (her)nieuw(d) getrapt systeem' (2022) *DCCR* (59) 61–67.

[142] Art. 807 Procedural Code: "*A claim pending before the court may be extended or amended, if the new claim, …, is based on a fact or deed invoked in the summons, even if their legal qualification is different.*"

[143] Art. 1649 quinquies, § 2 OCC (unless the remedy chosen would be impossible or, compared to the other remedy, would impose costs on the seller that would be disproportionate, taking into account all circumstances, including: (a) the value the goods would have if there were no lack of conformity; (b) the significance of the lack of conformity; and (c) whether the alternative remedy could be provided without significant inconvenience to the consumer) and Art. 1701/11 OCC (unless this would be impossible or

performance in kind.¹⁴⁴ Repair or replacement, or bringing into conformity, shall be carried out free of charge, within a reasonable period of time from the moment the seller / trader was informed about the lack of conformity and without significant inconvenience.¹⁴⁵ The Belgian legislator chose not to provide for fixed periods that could generally be considered reasonable for repair or replacement, although the directives allow to do so.¹⁴⁶ It was considered more appropriate to leave some flexibility to take the concrete circumstances into account. The reasonableness of the period for repair or replacement therefore remains for the judge to determine.¹⁴⁷

29   Although **repair** is an inherently more sustainable remedy than replacement,¹⁴⁸ it is for the average consumer often less attractive than replacement.¹⁴⁹ No specific measures were however taken to promote repair when implementing the SGD, such as e.g. an additional guarantee period if the consumer chooses repair (as in France).¹⁵⁰ At federal level, the introduction of a reparability score is currently being considered.¹⁵¹

30   An aspect that is not regulated by the twin directives are the conditions under which the seller's obligation to repair can be performed by the consumer or a third party at the seller's expense. This issue is now explicitly regulated under Belgian law: the new Civil Code allows a consumer to replace the seller who fails to repair the good, in

---

would impose costs on the trader that would be disproportionate, taking into account all the circumstances of the case including: (a) the value the digital content or digital service would have if there were no lack of conformity; and (b) the significance of the lack of conformity). In addition, Art. 1649 quinquies, § 4 OCC provides that the seller may refuse to bring the goods into conformity if repair and replacement are impossible or would impose costs on the seller that would be disproportionate, taking into account all circumstances. See also D. Staudenmayer, 'The Directives on Digital Contracts: First Steps Towards the Private Law of the Digital Economy' (2020) *ERCL* (219) 242–244.

¹⁴⁴ Cf. Art. 5.234 Civil Code; F. Van Den Abeele and B. Tilleman, 'Remedies in het nieuwe consumenten(koop)recht: een (her)nieuw(d) getrapt systeem' (2022) *DCCR* (59) 67.

¹⁴⁵ Art. 1649 quinquies, § 3 OCC and Art. 1701/11, § 2 OCC. Art. 1649 quinquies, § 3 OCC further states that where the lack of conformity is to be remedied by repair or replacement of the goods, the consumer shall make the goods available to the seller. The seller shall take back the replaced goods at the seller's expense. Where a repair requires the removal of goods that had been installed in a manner consistent with their nature and purpose before the lack of conformity became apparent, or where such goods are to be replaced, the obligation to repair or replace the goods shall include the removal of the non-conforming goods, and the installation of replacement goods or repaired goods, or bearing the costs of that removal and installation. The consumer shall not be liable to pay for normal use made of the replaced goods during the period prior to their replacement. See also J. Vanherpe, 'White Smoke, but Smoke Nonetheless: Some (Burning) Questions Regarding the Directives on Sale of Goods and Supply of Digital Content' (2020) *ERPL* (251) 266–267.

¹⁴⁶ Cf. recital 50 and 55 SGD; recital 64 DCD.

¹⁴⁷ Explanatory memorandum, MvT, *Parl. St.* Kamer, 2021–2022, doc 55, 2355/001, 33–44.

¹⁴⁸ It avoids the environmental costs of the extraction, production, transportation and disposal processes resulting from replacement by a new good; it also offers social and economic benefits. See Deloitte, *Study on Socioeconomic impacts of increased reparability – Final Report* (European Commission 2016) 12–14 <https://data.europa.eu/doi/10.2779/463857> accessed 7/2/2021; see E. Van Gool and A. Michel, 'The New Consumer Sales Directive 2019/771 and Sustainable Consumption: A Critical Analysis' (2021) *EuCML* (136) 144–145.

¹⁴⁹ See E. Terryn, 'A Right to Repair? Towards Sustainable Remedies in Consumer Law' (2019) *European Review of Private Law* 851–873; E. Van Gool and A. Michel, 'The New Consumer Sales Directive 2019/771 and Sustainable Consumption: A Critical Analysis' (2021) *EuCML* (136) 144–145; E.M. Kieninger, 'Recht auf Reparatur („Right to Repair") und Europäisches Vertragsrecht' (2020) ZEuP 264–278.

¹⁵⁰ Although this was suggested during the parliamentary debate, *Parl. St.* Kamer, doc 55, 2355/007, p. 43. This is already the case in France, see art. L-217–13 Code de la Consommation, introduced by Act nr. 2020–105 of 10 February 2020.

¹⁵¹ See federal action plan for circular economy 2021–2024 <https://emis.vito.be/sites/emis/files/articles/91/2021/PAF%2016%20dec%202021_NL%20Clean%5B1%5D.docx> accessed 30 November 2022. In addition there are several proposals for legislations pending on reparability that would introduce additional information on reparability; availability of spare parts: see *Parl. Doc. Kamer* 55 0771/001 (Artt. 4–8); *Parl. Doc.* Kamer 55 0914/001 (Artt. 3–5).

E. Remedies

case of urgency or other exceptional circumstances and by written notification.[152] This provision codifies earlier case law of the *Cour de Cassation*.[153] If these conditions are however not met, the sanction will be that the consumer cannot recover the costs of repair nor claim additional damages.[154]

31 **Replacement** is the alternative primary remedy, also under Belgian law. There is an ongoing discussion on the possibility of a 'circular replacement' (i.e. by a repaired, refurbished or remanufactured good) under the current directives.[155] Michel and Van Gool have argued convincingly that this is not completely excluded under the SGD: the criterion is whether the replacement meets all contractually applicable conformity requirements. If a repaired, refurbished or remanufactured good meet these requirements and could initially have been delivered, it should be possible to offer it as a replacement remedy.[156] However, some uncertainty remains as certain national courts have already refused such replacements.[157] Hence, we have pleaded earlier for an amendment of the SGD by defining the replacement remedy in a way that allows 'circular replacement' except if this would not conform with the applicable conformity requirements.[158]

32 **Secondary remedies** for lack of conformity are price reduction or termination. As the twin directives, Belgian law sets out in detail when the consumer is entitled to opt for these secondary remedies.[159] The consumer shall be entitled to either a proportionate reduction of the price or the termination of the contract if: the seller / trader has not brought, or has refused to bring[160], into conformity; a lack of conformity appears despite the seller / trader having attempted to bring into conformity; the lack of conformity is of such a serious nature as to justify an immediate price reduction or termination of the contract; or the seller / trader has declared, or it is clear from the circumstances, that he will not bring into conformity within a reasonable time, or without significant inconvenience for the consumer.[161]

33 The **reduction of price** shall be proportionate to the decrease in the value of the goods / digital content or services compared to the value the goods / digital content or services would have if they were in conformity. Where the contract stipulates that the digital content or digital service shall be supplied over a period of time in exchange for

---

[152] Art. 5.85 (3) new Civil Code (entry into force on 1 January 2023).

[153] Cass. 18 juni 2020, *TBBR* 2020, 583, case note S. De Rey, see also F. Van Den Abeele and B. Tilleman, 'Remedies in het nieuwe consumenten(koop)recht: een (her)nieuw(d) getrapt systeem' (2022) *DCCR* (59) 79.

[154] See e.g. Court of appeal Ghent 6 May 2003, *NJW* 2003, 1005.

[155] See E. Van Gool and A. Michel, 'The New Consumer Sales Directive 2019/771 and Sustainable Consumption: A Critical Analysis' (2021) *EuCML* 2021 (136) 145–146.

[156] See E. Van Gool and A. Michel, 'The New Consumer Sales Directive 2019/771 and Sustainable Consumption: A Critical Analysis' (2021) *EuCML* (136) 145–146.

[157] See e.g. District Court Amsterdam 8 July 2016, ECLI:NL:RBAMS:2016:4197; District Court Amsterdam 18 April 2017, ECLI:NL:RBAMS:2017:2519. Tilleman and Van den Abeele are e.g. of the opinion that a 'circular' replacement would only be possible for second-hand goods, F. Van Den Abeele and B. Tilleman, 'Remedies in het nieuwe consumenten(koop)recht: een (her)nieuw(d) getrapt systeem' (2022) *DCCR* (59) 84.

[158] See E. Van Gool, A. Michel, B. Keirsbilck and E. Terryn, 'Reply to the Public consultation as Regards the Sustainable Consumption of Goods – Promoting Repair and Reuse Initiative' <https://ec.europa.eu/info/law/better-regulation/have-your-say/initiatives/13150-Sustainable-consumption-of-goods-promoting-repair-and-reuse_en>.

[159] See D. Staudenmayer, 'The Directives on Digital Contracts: First Steps Towards the Private Law of the Digital Economy' (2020) *ERCL* (219) 244–246; J. Vanherpe, 'White Smoke, but Smoke Nonetheless: Some (Burning) Questions Regarding the Directives on Sale of Goods and Supply of Digital Content' (2020) *ERPL* (251) 268–270.

[160] This is mentioned in Art. 1649 quinquies, § 5 OCC only, not in Art. 1701/12 OCC.

[161] Art. 1649 quinquies § 5 OCC and Art. 1701/12, § 1 OCC.

34 **Termination** is not possible when the lack of conformity is minor.[163] Under the former Belgian consumer sales regime, there was some discussion on the burden of proof with regard to whether the lack of conformity was minor.[164] In line with the twin directives, Belgian law now makes it explicit that the burden of proof lies with the seller / trader.[165] For digital content or services, however, it should be noted that the *de minimis* does not apply where the digital content or digital service is supplied in exchange for personal data.[166] As required by the twin directives, Belgian law allows termination both judicially and extra-judicially.[167] The latter possibility was confirmed by the *Cour de cassation* in 2019[168] and this is now also codified for the general law of obligations.[169] New for Belgian law – but merely an implementation of the twin directives – are the detailed provisions on the consequences of termination, especially in case data were provided or created by the consumer.[170]

35 In addition to the four mentioned remedies, the consumer is also entitled to claim compensation for damages.[171] Finally, the consumer will also be able to withhold performance if the conditions (determined by the general law of obligations) for the application of this remedy are met.[172]

F. Commercial guarantees

36 The implementation of the SGD also introduced the concept of a "commercial guarantee of durability" into Belgian law.[173] This new concept does however not add much in terms of durability or rather sustainability. Limited obligations are introduced if a producer provides such a guarantee of durability (on a voluntary basis), namely the liability for repair or replacement under the same conditions as the seller. Here again, repair and replacement are seen as substitutes although repair is preferable from a sustainability point of view. The Belgian information requirements furthermore reflect the provisions of the SGD. No specific rules on the language of the commercial guarantee were adopted. Whether the information requirements suffice to correctly inform

---

[162] Art. 1649 quinquies § 6 OCC and Art. 1701/12, § 2 OCC.

[163] Art. 1649quinquies, § 5, in fine OCC and Art. 1701/12, § 3 OCC. See D. Staudenmayer, 'The Directives on Digital Contracts: First Steps Towards the Private Law of the Digital Economy' (2020) *ERCL* (219) 246; J. Vanherpe, 'White Smoke, but Smoke Nonetheless: Some (Burning) Questions Regarding the Directives on Sale of Goods and Supply of Digital Content' (2020) *ERPL* 268–270.

[164] See e.g. C. Cauffman, 'De nieuwe wet op de consumentenkoop' (2005) *TPR* 871.

[165] Art. 1649quinquies, § 5, in fine OCC and Art. 1701/12, § 3, first limb OCC.

[166] Art. 1701/12, § 3 OCC.

[167] Art. 1649quinquies, § 7 OCC and Art. 1701/12, § 3, second limb OCC.

[168] Cass. 23 mei 2019, AR C.16.0254.F, www.cass.be, *TBBR* 2019, 474, case note S. Stijns en S. Jansen.

[169] Art. 5.93 CC.

[170] Art. 1649quinquies, § 7 OCC and Art. 1701/13–1701/15 OCC. See D. Staudenmayer, 'The Directives on Digital Contracts: First Steps Towards the Private Law of the Digital Economy' (2020) *ERCL* (219) 249.

[171] See explicitly for goods: Art. 1649 quinquies, § 1, al. 1 OCC for goods; the explanatory memorandum confirms that the general law of obligations applies. There is no explicit provision on additional damages for contracts for digital goods and content, but the general law of obligations can also be relied on to claim additional damages (see F. Van den Abeele and B. Tilleman, 'Remedies in het nieuwe consumenten(koop)recht: een (her)nieuw(d) getrapt systeem' (2022) *DCCR* (59) 100). See also J. Vanherpe, 'White Smoke, but Smoke Nonetheless: Some (Burning) Questions Regarding the Directives on Sale of Goods and Supply of Digital Content' (2020) *ERPL* (251) 270–271.

[172] Art. 5.239 CC; F. Van Den Abeele and B. Tilleman, 'Remedies in het nieuwe consumenten(koop)recht: een (her)nieuw(d) getrapt systeem' (2022) *DCCR* (59) 101.

[173] Article 1649septies OCC.

consumers and to enable them to distinguish the (free) legal guarantee from a (not necessarily) free commercial guarantee is questionable. Vandemaele suggested in her PhD on commercial guarantees to introduce a simplified model form with pictograms that traders could use to clearly set out the differences between the commercial and the legal guarantee.[174] The SGD does not seem to allow to introduce such a form at national level on a mandatory base anymore, but it could in our opinion still be introduced as a 'safe harbour' – allowing undertakings to use the form on a voluntary basis and confirming as a (national) legislator that the use of the form assures compliance with the information obligations concerning the commercial guarantee.

G. Right of redress

Where the seller is liable towards the consumer because of a lack of conformity, he shall be entitled to pursue remedies against the producer or any other contractual intermediary in the transfer of ownership of the consumer goods based on their contractual liability with regard to the goods, without any clause limiting or excluding liability being opposable to him.[175] A similar 'enhanced' right of redress is now also set out in the regime on digital content and services.[176] In addition, the consumer has a direct right of redress against the producer and other sellers in the contractual chain (based on the doctrine of 'qualitative rights'). Clauses limiting or excluding liability are not opposable to the consumer. However, since that *action directe* is based on the general regime of sale of goods, the consumer cannot claim repair or replacement and he must bring his claim before the court within a short period of time.[177] No such *action directe* by the consumer against the original designer of digital content or services is of avail under Belgian law.[178] **37**

Still it appears that the Belgian Government is planning to further reinforce the right of redress of the seller vis-à-vis the producer or any other contractual intermediary in the chain of transactions. New measures will be taken to ensure *"that the final seller (retailer) has an effective and effective right of redress against the producer when applying the legal guarantee scheme."*[179] **38**

In our view, there are plenty of good reasons why it would make sense to introduce direct producer liability at the EU level: (i) the internal market argument (decreasing 'transaction costs', increasing 'consumer confidence'); (ii) the 'consumer expectations' argument; (iii) the 'sustainable product incentive' argument; (iv) the 'product liability analogy' argument; (v) the 'fairness towards the seller' argument; (vi) the 'effective consumer protection' argument; (vi) the 'producer as cheapest cost-avoider' argument. Such a system of direct producer liability should be complementary to the liability of the seller and subject to strict conditions.[180] **39**

---

[174] S. Vandemaele, *Commerciële garanties in de verschillende koopregimes: naar een uniforme regeling?*, PhD KU Leuven 2019.

[175] Article 1649sexies OCC. See B. Keirsbilck, 'Verhaalsrechten' (2022) DCCR (103) 118–127. See also E. Van Gool and A. Michel, 'The New Consumer Sales Directive 2019/771 and Sustainable Consumption: A Critical Analysis' (2021) *EuCML* (136) 143.

[176] Article 1701/16 OCC. See B. Keirsbilck, 'Verhaalsrechten' (2022) DCCR (103) 118–127.

[177] See B. Keirsbilck, 'Verhaalsrechten' (2022) DCCR (103) 127–129.

[178] See B. Keirsbilck, 'Verhaalsrechten' (2022) DCCR (103) 129.

[179] Federal coalition agreement, 30 September 2020, 62–63.

[180] See in detail B. Keirsbilck, 'Verhaalsrechten' in I. Claeys and E. Terryn (eds.), *Nieuw recht inzake koop & digitale diensten*, (Intersentia 2020) 261–302.

H. Sanctions and enforcement

40 In terms of enforcement, Belgian law did undergo rather radical changes. This is partly a consequence of the implementation of the twin directives that demand Member States to enable either public bodies, consumer organizations or professional organizations to take action[181] and partly a consequence of a broad implementation of the Omnibus directive.[182] The private law remedies are to be found the OCC, the public enforcement system is regulated in the CEL. Explicit references to the enforcement system of CEL were now inserted in the OCC.[183]

41 New provisions in the CEL allow the Economic Inspection to take action in case of an infringement of the provisions implementing the twin directives if such infringement has caused, causes or may cause damage 'to the collective interests of consumers'. The concept of 'damage to the collective interests of consumers' was inspired by the CPC regulation[184] and is defined as actual or potential harm to the interests of a number of consumers affected by infringements.[185] Apart from actions for injunction,[186] the Economic Inspection also has the competence to impose an administrative fine. The (minimum and maximum) amount of such administrative fine equals the amount of the penal fines that can also be imposed.[187] For infringements of the implementing provisions of the twin directives (with actual or potential harm to the collective interests of consumers) a 'level 2 sanction' is foreseen.[188] That implies a fine of minimum 26 EUR and maximum of 10.000 EUR[189] or of up to 4 % of the total annual turnover in the last completed preceding business year, if this represents a higher amount. The Omnibus directive indeed required to introduce fines as a percentage of annual turnover, but it required this only for widespread infringements or widespread infringements with a Union dimension and only for the directives amended by the Omnibus directive.[190] There is no EU requirement to introduce such fines for infringements of the twin directives, nor for purely domestic infringements. The Belgian legislator has however chosen for a wider application of such fines to guarantee a coherent national sanctioning system.[191] Under Belgian law, these fines can also be imposed for purely domestic cases.

I. Conclusion

42 The choices made by Belgian legislator in implementing the SGD and the DCD in parallel in the OCC have exacerbated the lack of accessibility and coherence of current Belgian (consumer) contract law. For the time being, we have a legal patchwork of

---

[181] Art. 19 SGD; Art. 21 DCD.

[182] Implemented by the Act of 8 May 2022 amending books I, VI and XV of the CEL, *BS* 2 June 2022. See specifically on the new regime for sanctions and enforcement, C. Sammels, 'Quelles sanctions pour les infractions à la réglementation protégeant le consommateur? Voyage au cœur de la pratique de l'Inspection économique' (2022) *DCCR* 161-197.

[183] Art. 1649nonies OCC and Art. 1701/19 OCC.

[184] Regulation (EU) 2017/2394 of the European Parliament and of the Council of 12 December 2017 on cooperation between national authorities responsible for the enforcement of consumer protection laws and repealing Regulation (EC) No 2006/2004, OJ L 345, 27.12.2017.

[185] Art. I.20, 10° CEL.

[186] Art. XVII.2, 17° CEL.

[187] Art. XV.60/20 CEL.

[188] Art. XV.125/5 CEL.

[189] To be multiplied by the applicable surcharge rate ('opdeciemen') – currently by a factor of 8.

[190] Directives 98/6/EC, 2005/29/EC, 2011/83/EU and 93/13/EEC.

[191] CJEU 3 October 2013, C-32/12, *Soledad Duarte*, ECLI:EU:C:2013:637.

I. Conclusion

two parallel business-to-consumer regimes with similar list of concepts and definitions (twice in the OCC, once in the CEL) and similar provisions on conformity, somewhat isolated from general contract law in the OCC as well as from the vast amount of consumer contract law provisions included in the CEL (such as on unfair terms in business-to-consumer contracts[192], on distance contracts[193] and on contracts concluded outside of business premises[194]).

43 In our view, it is to be regretted that the Belgian legislator has not yet started the effort of trying to integrate the various conformity regimes into one single regime – going beyond the traditional divide between sales and service contracts – thereby taking the (mandatory) business-to-consumer rules on sales and supply of digital content or services as a starting point for the design of (default) business-to-business rules of general contract law.

44 The parallel implementation of both the SGD and the DCD in the OCC raises yet another fundamental problem. As the OCC is outdated, it currently undergoes a major overhaul and modernization.[195] This means that for the time being we have parallel application of the old and the new Civil Code ("NCC"). The NCC is gradually replacing the OCC.[196] The NCC will consist of 10 Books – three of which having a particular relevance for the topic of this paper. Book 1. "General Provisions"[197] entered into force on 1 January 2023[198], just like Book 5. "Obligations"[199] which applies to contracts concluded from 1 January 2023 onwards.[200] However, work on the new Book 7. "Specific contracts" is ongoing. The Expert Commission for the reform of specific contract law has not yet finished a draft and explanatory memorandum.[201] We can only express our hope that Book 7. "Specific contracts", in concert with Book 5. "Obligations", will lead to simplification and modernization of general contract law and consumer contract law (including rules implementing the SGD and the DCD), as the current state of play is needlessly complex.

---

[192] Art. I.8, 28°, Art. VI.37, Art. VI.82 e.s. CEL.
[193] Art. VI.44/1 e.s. CEL.
[194] Art. VI.63/1 e.s. CEL.
[195] The process is part of a broader process or 're-codification' which was launched by the former Minister of Justice Koen Geens in 2018. See <https://www.koengeens.be/policy/beleidsverklaringen/de-sprong-naar-het-recht-voor-morgen> accessed 30 November 2022.
[196] https://justitie.belgium.be/nl/bwcc.
[197] Wet van 28 april 2022 houdende boek 1 "Algemene bepalingen" van het Burgerlijk Wetboek, *BS* 1 July 2022.
[198] Book 2. Persons, family and relational property law (Act of 19 January 2022, BS 14 March 2022) partly entered into force on 1 July 2022. Book 3. Goods (Act of 4 February 2020, BS 17 March 2020) entered into force on 1 September 2021. Book 4. Inheritance, donations and wills (Act of 19 January 2022, BS 14 March 2022) entered into force on 1 July 2022.
[199] Wet van 28 april 2022 houdende boek 5 "Verbintenissen" van het Burgerlijk Wetboek, *BS* 1 July 2022.
[200] Book 6. Tort is still in the making. The Expert Commission for the reform of tort law has prepared a draft Act and an Explanatory Memorandum. However, the activities are ongoing. The Federal Government has not yet approved the Draft Act.
[201] Book 8. Proof (Act of 13 April 2019, BS 17 May 2019) entered into force on 1 November 2020. Proof 9. Securities is in the making. The Commission for the reform of the law concerning securities is working on a Draft Act. In addition, a dedicated Commission for reform of the law on mortgages was established. Book 10. Prescription is in the making. A Commission for the reform of the law on prescription was established.

Bibliography

A. Beckers, 'Environmental Protection meets Consumer Sales: The Influence of Environmental Market Communication on Consumer Contracts and Remedies' (2018) ERCL 157–189.

C. Cauffman, 'De nieuwe wet op de consumentenkoop' (2005) TPR 787–852.

B. Demarsin and B. Keirsbilck, 'Brave little Belgium? The new Code of Economic Law and its relationship with civil and commercial law' (2016) Zeitschrift für Europäisches Privatrecht 859–887.

H. Jacquemin, 'La conformité des biens, des contenus numériques et des services numériques, l'articulation des délais et la modification des éléments numériques' (2022) DCCR 25–57.

B. Keirsbilck, 'Verhaalsrechten' (2022) DCCR 103–131.

B. Keirsbilck, 'Verhaalsrechten' in I. Claeys and E. Terryn (eds.), Nieuw recht inzake koop & digitale diensten, (Intersentia 2020) 261–302.

A. Michel, 'La directive 1999/44/CE sur la garantie des biens de consommation: un remède efficace contre l'obsolescence programmée?' (2016) REDC 207–236.

C. Sammels, 'Quelles sanctions pour les infractions à la réglementation protégeant le consommateur? Voyage au cœur de la pratique de l'Inspection économique' (2022) DCCR 197–215.

K. Sein, 'The Applicability of the Digital Content Directive and Sales of Goods Directive to Goods with Digital Elements' (2021) Juridica International 23–31. https://doi.org/10.12697/JI.2021.30.04.

D. Staudenmayer, 'The Directives on Digital Contracts: First Steps Towards the Private Law of the Digital Economy' (2020) ERCL 219–250.

R. Steennot, 'Het toepassingsgebied van de nieuwe garantieregelingen voor goederen, digitale inhoud en digitale diensten' (2022) DCCR 3–24.

B. Tilleman, S. De Rey, N. Van Damme and F. Van Den Abeele, 'Overzicht van rechtspraak koop (2007–2020)' (2020) TPR 1007–1686.

K. Tonner, 'Sustainable Consumption, Consumer Policy and the Law' (2011) REDC 9–24.

S. Vandemaele, Commerciële garanties in de verschillende koopregimes: naar een uniforme regeling?, PhD KU Leuven 2019.

F. Van Den Abeele and B. Tilleman, 'Remedies in het nieuwe consumenten(koop)recht: een (her)nieuw(d) getrapt system' (2022) DCCR 59–102.

E. Van Gool, 'De nieuwe richtlijn consumentenkoop en duurzame consumptie', in I. Claeys and E. Terryn (eds.), Nieuw recht inzake koop en digitale inhoud en diensten' (Intersentia 2020) 303–386.

E. Van Gool and A. Michel, 'The New Consumer Sales Directive 2019/771 and Sustainable Consumption: A Critical Analysis' (2021) EuCML 136–148.

E. Van Gool, A. Michel, B. Keirsbilck and E. Terryn, 'Reply to the Public consultation as Regards the Sustainable Consumption of Goods – Promoting Repair and Reuse Initiative' <https://ec.europa.eu/info/law/better-regulation/have-your-say/initiatives/13150-Sustainable-consumption-of-goods-promoting-repair-and-reuse_en>.

J. Vanherpe, 'White Smoke, but Smoke Nonetheless: Some (Burning) Questions Regarding the Directives on Sale of Goods and Supply of Digital Content' (2020) ERPL 251–274.

Bulgaria[1]

A. Introduction: impact of digitalisation on the European and Bulgarian legal framework 1

B. General regulatory framework – national law transposition and impacts on the existing legal framework 5

C. Definitions and scope of application 17

D. Conformity requirements and beyond 23
  I. "Durability" requirement in Art. 7, para. 1, lett. d, SGD 24
  II. Supplying the consumer with updates and liability exemption 25
  III. The exclusion of existence of a lack of conformity in the case provided by Art. 8, para. 5 DCD and Art. 7, para. 5 SGD 27
  IV. Product specific Union legislation requirements – durability and repairability with views to Recital 32 SGD 28
  V. Ecodesign requirements – availability of spare parts and corresponding information obligations 29
  VI. Environmental sustainability and circular economy 34
  VII. Incorrect installation and/or integration of the goods and/or the digital content/digital service 36
  VIII. Third party rights in national law Art. 10 DCD and Art. 9 SGD 39

E. Liability of the Trader 42
  I. Single act/long-term supply of DC/DS and interruption of long-term supply 43
  II. Force majeure and change of circumstances 47
  III. Consequences of the trader's non-compliance with the GDPR regarding contracts for the supply of digital content/digital services 48

F. Remedies for the failure to supply and remedies for the lack of conformity .. 49
  I. The right to withhold payments 56
  II. Delivery, repair and replacement – specifics 57
  III. Right of withdrawal and right of termination 63

G. Legal and Commercial Guarantees & Time limits and limitation periods ... 67

H. Right of Redress & relationship with other remedies 75

I. Conclusion 83

  Bibliography 86

A. Introduction: impact of digitalisation on the European and Bulgarian legal framework

The past 15 years have been turbulent years for European Union (EU) consumer law, marked by several important Union projects, all with the goal of harmonising further EU law: revamp of the EU consumer *acquis*[2]; drafting of the optional Common European Sales Law (CESL) initiative[3] and launching the REFIT project (regulatory

---

[1] The opinions expressed in this country chapter shall represent the personal views of the author and not the official position of the European Parliament or its Members.
[2] European Parliament, *Towards new rules on sales and digital content*, March 2017, PE 599.359 (EP Study – rules on sales and digital content); see also: M.B.M. Loos, *Review of the European Consumer Acquis* (2008); Eidenmüller, Faust, Jansen, Wagner and Zimmermann 'Towards a revision of the consumer acquis' (2011) 48.4 *Common Mark. Law Rev.*, 1077–1123; European Commission, *Staff Working Document on a Digital Single Market Strategy for Europe – Analysis and Evidence*, 6 May 2015, COM(2015) 192 final, p 3 (EC, Staff Working Document on a Digital Single Market Strategy).
[3] Proposal for a Regulation of the European Parliament and of the Council on a Common European Sales Law, 11 October 2011, COM(2011) 635 final; EP Study – rules on sales and digital content (n 3); for further analysis on the topic, see Schulze, *Common European Sales Law: A Commentary* (Beck 2012).

fitness check of the legislation, incl. consumer law)[4]. The Twin Directives: Directive (EU) 2019/770 on certain aspects concerning contracts for the supply of digital content and digital services (DCD) and Directive (EU) 2019/771 on the sale of goods (SGD), introduced within this timeframe by the Juncker Commission, were pioneering pieces in the Digital Single Market (DSM) plan of the European Commission (EC), and key to the functioning of the single market in a time of emerging digitalisation.[5] Adopted nearly an year prior to the COVID-pandemic and covering extremely similar subject matter, these instruments tackle a big challenge of the digital age.[6] Namely, the barrier between digital and non-digital goods is becoming more blurry, as goods with integrated digital elements coexist with goods that are digitally interconnected.[7]

2 The rules stemming from these two Directives, together with several other legal texts reinforcing the DSM,[8] are expected to contribute to the resolution of a number of issues in the EU Single Market.[9] Principal among these is the lack of understanding regarding the application of different consumer protection rules among the EU Member States (MS).[10] Diverging national rules are often caused by difficulties in the implementation process. Therefore, it is essential to examine the way every MS has implemented the Directives in question, which leads to the case of Bulgaria.

3 Legal experts believe that the new rules have the potential to positively change the digital market in Bulgaria while fostering e-commerce practices by introducing a

---

[4] European Commission, *Evaluation and fitness check (FC) roadmap, REFIT Fitness Check of consumer law*, December 2015, COM (2015).

[5] Directive (EU) 2019/770 of the European Parliament and of the Council of 20 May 2019 on certain aspects concerning contracts for the supply of digital content and digital services (OJ L 136/1 22 May 2019) (DCD); Directive (EU) 2019/771 of the European Parliament and of the Council of 20 May 2019 on certain aspects concerning contracts for the sale of goods, amending Regulation (EU) 2017/2394 and Directive 2009/22/EC, and repealing Directive 1999/44/EC (OJ L 136/28 22 May 2019) (SGD); EC, Staff Working Document on a Digital Single Market Strategy (n 3); Zoll, 'The Remedies in the Proposals of the Online Sales Directive and the Directive on the Supply of Digital Content' (2016) 5 EuCML, 250; Vanherpe, 'White Smoke, but Smoke Nonetheless: Some (Burning) Questions Regarding the Directives on Sale of Goods and Supply of Digital Content', (2020) 2 Eur. Rev. Priv. Law, 251–274.

[6] European Parliament, *Debates*, 26 March 2019 – Strasbourg, 2015/0287(COD) – https://www.europarl.europa.eu/doceo/document/CRE-8-2019-03-26-ITM-004_EN.html accessed 15.03.2022; for a further overview of the legislative outcomes, see: European Parliament, *Contracts for online and other distance sale of goods*, February 2017, PE 599.286; European Parliament, *Contracts for supply of digital content to consumers*, March 2017, PE 599.310; European Commission, *Staff Working Document on the Impacts of fully harmonized rules on contracts for the sales of goods*, 31 October 2017, SWD(2017) 354 final.

[7] EP Study – rules on sales and digital content, (n 3) 4.

[8] Directive (EU) 2019/2161 of the European Parliament and of the Council of 27 November 2019 amending Council Directive 93/13/EEC and Directives 98/6/EC, 2005/29/EC and 2011/83/EU of the European Parliament and of the Council as regards the better enforcement and modernisation of Union consumer protection rules (OJ L 328/7 18 December 2019);

[9] European Commission, *A New Deal for Consumers*, 11 April 2018, COM(2018) 183 final; European Parliament, *Legal obstacles in Member States to Single Market rules*, November 2020, PE 658.189 (EP Study – Legal obstacles in Member States to Single Market rules) 138–140; European Commission, Directorate-General for the Information Society and Media, Flash Eurobarometer 413, *Companies Engaged in Online Activities*, May 2015, 10.2759/473539.

[10] For example, the diverging national rules in the area of contract law have led to expenses of small traders for the amount of EUR 4 bn, for more info: Republic of Bulgaria, Ministry of Economy, *Report on a comprehensive preliminary assessment of the impact of the draft law on the supply of digital content and digital services and on the sale of goods/Doklad ot izvarshena tsyalostna predvaritelna otsenka na vazdeystvieto na proekta na zakon za predostavyane na tsifrovo sadarzhanie i tsifrovi uslugi i za prodazhba na stoki* (September 2020) (Report on preliminary assessment of the impact of the draft Act on the supply of DC/DS and on the sale of goods) 4–6.

certain level of harmonisation of contractual rules among the EU MS.[11] The rules to be implemented represent a massive legislative reform as they are new and uncommon to the Bulgarian legal system.[12]

This country-specific chapter will look at how the Bulgarian legislator has transposed the DCD and SGD into national law, while also exploring some important aspects from the adoption of the Directives at EU level. It will discuss the national law transposition and impacts on the legal framework including some criticism on the manner and choice of transposition; definitions and scope of application; conformity requirements; trader liability and remedies; legal and commercial guarantees; time limits and limitation periods and right of redress.

B. General regulatory framework – national law transposition and impacts on the existing legal framework

The Parliament in Bulgaria has adopted the Act on the Supply of Digital Content and Digital Services and the Sale of Goods (the Act, the new Act or the Bulgarian Act) with the aim of transposing the DCD and SGD into national consumer law.[13] The Act represents a new piece of legislation with the goal of modernising the current legal framework in Bulgaria and preparing it for the new age of the Digital Market economy.[14] According to legal scholarship, this is the biggest reform of Bulgarian consumer law since the adoption of the Consumer Protection Act (CPA) in 2006.[15]

After entering into force, the law is applicable to any contract for the sale of goods after the transposition deadline has passed (from 1 January 2022) and to any contract for the supply of digital content and digital services, regardless of the date of signature (with the exception of Article 21 and 22 of the Act, which are applicable after 1 January 2022).[16] As expected by the subject matter of the legislation and its scope, the Act regulates both online and offline contracts.

Bulgarian legislator has singled out a few concrete aims of drafting the Act: to reach full conformity of the national legislation with the EU regulation (the Twin Directives); to establish a legal framework in the country for the protection of consumers when supplying digital content/digital services (DC/DS); to update the current Bulgarian framework with regards to the sale of goods; to overcome the differences in national contract law for the supply of DC/DS and for the sale of goods that appear as an obstacle

---

[11] Ivan Gergov, Maria Harizanova, 'Bulgaria enacts EU directives on regulated consumer digital environment' (CMS Law-Now™, 13 May 2021) https://www.cms-lawnow.com/ealerts/2021/05/bulgaria-enacts-eu-directives-on-regulated-consumer-digital-environment?cc_lang=en accessed 15.01.2022.

[12] Varadinov, 'Conformity of goods and consumer rights under the new Act on the provision of digital content, digital services and the sale of goods' (2022) 4/2022, *Commercial and contract law*, 1 (2).

[13] Act on the supply of digital content and digital services and on the sale of goods from 04 March 2021 (State Gazette/Durzhaven Vestnik, No. 23/2021, 19.03.2021) (Act on the supply of DC/DS and on the sale of goods).

[14] Republic of Bulgaria, Council of Ministers, Motives for the establishment of the draft Act on the provision of digital content and digital services and on the sale of goods/Motivi kam proekta na zakon za predostavyane na tsifrovo sadarzhanie i tsifrovi uslugi i za prodazhba na stoki (published 23 October 2020) (Motives for the establishment of the draft Act on the supply of DC/DS and on the sale of goods) 4.

[15] Varadinov (n13), 1.

[16] § 11, Transitional and Final provisions, Act on the supply of DC/DS and on the sale of goods; Art. 24 DCD and Art. 24 SGD.

8   for traders to conduct their businesses in other EU MS; and to increase the level of consumer trust when there is supply of DC/DS and sale of goods.[17]

8   Both Twin Directives impose maximum harmonisation, which means that the texts of national laws must mirror the Directives in their transposition unless otherwise provided for.[18] Moreover, if Member States previously provided for a higher level of protection, they would need to lower their standards following the transposition of these Directives.[19]

9   The right to consumer protection is a constitutional right, enshrined in Art. 19 para. 2 of the Bulgarian Constitution.[20] When it comes to consumer protection legislation in Bulgaria, the sources are subsidiary laws[21] and special laws[22], the CPA being part of the latter group. Prior to the adoption of the new Act, the CPA was the common source of regulation codifying consumer protection[23] as it contains general rules which govern consumer protection, but also specific rules related to the conclusion of different contracts.

10 Except for the repealing of some provisions of the CPA, no other law in Bulgaria is impacted by the Act.[24] To be specific, the provisions in the new Act, transposing the Twin Directives, repeal some of the provisions as stipulated by Directive 1999/44/EC[25] (transposed in Bulgarian law by the CPA) regulating some aspects of the sale of goods and related guarantees.[26]

11 An important difference is that the SGD as transposed in Bulgarian law (the Act) is a Directive of maximum harmonisation, whereas Directive 1999/44/EC that is transposed by the CPA imposes only some minimum standards. Moreover, the latter neither regulates the sale of goods containing digital elements, nor contains any objective requirements for conformity of the goods.[27] According to legal scholarship, this is a

---

[17] Motives for the establishment of the draft Act on the supply of DC/DS and on the sale of goods (n15) 4; Report on preliminary assessment of the impact of the draft Act on the supply of DC/DS and on the sale of goods, (n 11) 1–2.

[18] Art. 114 of the Treaty on the Functioning of the European Union (TFEU); EP Study – rules on sales and digital content (n 3)26- 27.

[19] EP Study – rules on sales and digital content, (n 3) 1.

[20] Constitution of the Republic of Bulgaria from 13 July 1991, (State Gazette/Durzhaven Vestnik, No. 56/1991, as amended SG, No.100/2015, 18 December 2015).

[21] Obligations and Contracts Act from 05 December 1950 (State Gazette/Durzhaven Vestnik, No. 2/1950, as amended SG, No. 35/2021, 27.04.2021) (Obligations and Contracts Act); Insurance Code from 29 December 2015, (State Gazette/Durzhaven Vestnik, No. 102/2015, as amended SG, No. 25/2022, 29.03.2022); Commercial Act from 18 June 1991, (State Gazette/Durzhaven Vestnik, No. 48/1991, as amended SG, No. 25/2022, 29.03.2022).

[22] Act on Consumer Protection from 09 December 2005, (State Gazette/Durzhaven Vestnik, No. 99/2005, as amended SG, No. 20/2022, 11.03.2022) (CPA); Consumer Credit Act from 05 March 2010 (State Gazette/Durzhaven Vestnik, No. 18/2010, as amended SG, No.104/2020, 8.12.2022); Tourism Act from 26 March 2013, (State Gazette/Durzhaven Vestnik, No. 30/2013, as amended SG, No. 21/2021, 12.03.2021); Act on the Provision of Financial Services from Distance from 22 December 2006, (State Gazette/Durzhaven Vestnik, No. 105/2006, as amended SG, No. 20/2018, 06.03.2018).

[23] Varadinov (n 13) 2.

[24] Report on preliminary assessment of the impact of the draft Act on the supply of DC/DS and on the sale of goods, (n 11).

[25] Directive 1999/44/EC of the European Parliament and of the Council of 25 May 1999 on certain aspects of the sale of consumer goods and associated guarantees (OJ L 171, 7 July 1999) (Directive 1999/44).

[26] Motives for the establishment of the draft Act on the supply of DC/DS and on the sale of goods, (n 15) 8.

[27] Report on preliminary assessment of the impact of the draft Act on the supply of DC/DS and on the sale of goods, (n 11) 17.

B. General regulatory framework

rather expected approach based on the reform of consumer sales contracts' regulation that provides for higher level of consumer protection.[28]

In fact, the minimum harmonisation approach that Directive 1999/44/EC imposed was said not to fulfil the goals of safeguarding a proper functioning of the internal market when Member States could go above the minimum rules, resulting in great fragmentation with regards to consumer sales.[29] This was considered to be one of the biggest obstacles impeding the development of cross-border trade in the EU Single Market, considerably affecting businesses, including SMEs and consumers.[30]

It is essential to mention that it is yet too early to make certain conclusions on the way the DCD and SGD operate, as most rules imposed by the two Directives took legal effect on 1 January 2022[31] and at the moment of writing there is therefore no jurisprudence in Bulgaria concerning the new legislation.[32] Furthermore, there is no formal analysis of the effects of the transposed laws by the European Commission.

In light of the study on the impacts of the draft law, the legislator reviewed the effects on the consumer market and regulatory framework with or without adopting a new piece of legislation and concluded that there would be more benefits both for the consumers and the Bulgarian market when the law is adopted and not when no action is taken.[33] Legal scholars believe that the Bulgarian legislator has reacted adequately with the draft proposal of the Act, arriving right on time to bridge some existent gaps in consumer law provisions.[34]

Furthermore, so far no legislative framework existed in the country that regulated specifically the supply of digital content and digital services, in contrast to the framework in other Member States such as the Netherlands or Ireland.[35] At the same time, the existent legislation regulating the sale of goods did not cover goods with digital elements such as e.g. a smart fridge, for example.[36] The similarities and complementarities between the contracts for the sale of goods that contain digital elements and of the contracts for the supply of digital content and digital services clearly necessitate the

---

[28] Maria João Pestana de Vasconcelos, 'New perspectives on sale of consumer goods – maximum harmonization and high protection of consumers as a condition for the further development of cross-border trade in single market' (UNIO EU Law Journal, 13 May 2019) (UNIO Journal, 'New perspectives on sale for consumer goods') <https://officialblogofunio.com/2019/05/13/new-perspectives-on-sale-of-consumer-goods-maximum-harmonization-and-high-protection-of-consumers-as-a-condition-for-the-further-development-of-cross-border-trade-in-single-market/#_edn1> accessed 30.03.2022.

[29] ibid.

[30] UNIO Journal, 'New perspectives on sale for consumer goods', (n 29); Reisenhuber, 'System and Principles of EC Contract Law', (2005) 3 Eur. Rev. Contract Law, 297, 306.

[31] § 11, Transitional and Final Provisions, Act on the supply of DC/DS and on the sale of goods; EP Study – Legal obstacles in Member States to Single Market rules (n 10) 139.

[32] Nevertheless please consider § 9 of the Transitional and Final Provisions of the Act on the supply of DC/DS and on the sale of goods – due to some provisions being directly transferred from the CPA, the text stipulates that ongoing court cases which have been opened on the basis of the CPA are to be treated and closed on the basis of the new law.

[33] Report on preliminary assessment of the impact of the draft Act on the supply of DC/DS and on the sale of goods, (n 11) 60–61.

[34] Aneliya Toroshanova, interview with Prof. Tanya Yosifova, 'The legislative changes in the civil law regulation are innovative and timely'/' Zakonodatelnite promeni v grazhdanskoto pravo sa novatorski i navremenni', (The Law and Themis/Zakonat i Temida, 12 February 2021) https://bnr.bg/post/101420643 accessed 16.02.2022.

[35] Nevertheless, prior to the adoption of the new Act some areas where covered by civil legislation regulating different types of services contracts, see further: Varadinov (n 13)1.;Report on preliminary assessment of the impact of the draft Act on the supply of DC/DS and on the sale of goods, (n 11) 9.

[36] Motives for the establishment of the draft Act on the supply of DC/DS and on the sale of goods, (n 15) 4.

16 Nevertheless, there are some critical remarks on the manner in which the Act will be applied together with the CPA and other pieces of legislation covering similar subject matters, such as the Act on contractual responsibilities, for example.[38] The necessity of creating a new normative Act instead of just transposing the Directives through the general CPA is also disputed.[39] Prior to the transposition of the Twin Directives, the CPA was the main act regulating the sale of goods and services, while specific matters such as consumer credit were covered by more specific legislation.[40] It remains to be seen how the different pieces of legislation will interplay. One thing is clear: the attempts of the legislator were justified by the desire to put the Bulgarian market on a level playing field with the European Union, where it would be easy for traders and consumers to interact with each other, also when carrying out their business/purchases abroad or coming from a different Member State. However, certain confusion on the choice of applicable legislation is not to be ruled out entirely, at least until there is jurisprudence.

C. Definitions and scope of application

17 The following elements are key points under the Act: definition of conformity of the digital content, digital services and goods; subjective and objective requirements that help determine the existence of conformity; legal and commercial guarantee; consumer protection when the provision of personal data is used as counter-performance for the supply of digital content and digital services; reverse burden of proof in case of lack of conformity of the digital content, digital services and goods in question; amending the digital content or digital service by the seller while complying with strict conditions.[41] When it comes to scope, some contracts for which special regulatory requirements exist, such as financial services, gambling and healthcare, are excluded from the scope of the Twin Directives and consequently, the scope of the Act.[42] The Act follows the structure of the Directives, drawing a distinction between the supply of digital content or digital services and the sale of goods, which are regulated by two separate sections therein.[43] The definitions of all notions are incorporated in the section "Additional Provisions" toward the end of the Act.[44]

---

[37] ibid 9.

[38] Obligations and Contracts Act; Varadinov (n 13) 3; Radoslava Makshutova, Nikola Stoychev, 'The most important on the new Act on consumer sales'/' Nay-vazhnoto za noviya zakon za potrebitelskite prodazhbi'? (*Capital*, 30 March 2021) (Capital commentary) <https://www.capital.bg/politika_i_ikonomika/pravo/2021/03/30/4190597_nai-vajnoto_za_noviia_zakon_za_potrebitelskite_prodajbi/> accessed 15.01.2022; Radoslava Makshutova, 'New moments in the Act on the supply of digital content and digital services and on the sale of goods'/' Kakvo novo v noviya Zakon za tsifrovite stoki i uslugi' (*Manager News*, 24 March 2021) (Manager comenntary), https://www.manager.bg/komentari/kakvo-novo-v-noviya-zakon-za-oblaganeto-na-cifrovite-stoki-i-uslugi> accessed 15.01.2022; LIBRe Foundation, *Opinion on the Draft Act on the supply of digital content and digital services and on the sale of goods*, (No. 143/23.11.2020) (LIBRe Foundation opinion).

[39] ibid.

[40] Varadinov (n 13); Capital commentary (n 39); Manager commentary (n 39).

[41] Motives for the establishment of the draft Act on the supply of DC/DS and on the sale of goods, (n 15) 5.

[42] Art. 3 para. 3, Art. 3 para.4 and Art. 3 para.5 SGD and Art. 3 para.4, Art. 3 para.5 DCD; Art. 6, Act on the supply of DC/DS and on the sale of goods; Motives for the establishment of the draft Act on the supply of DC/DS and on the sale of goods, (n 15) 4–5.

[43] Ch. 2 and ch. 3, Act on the supply of DC/DS and on the sale of goods.

[44] ibid, Additional provisions, § 6.

C. Definitions and scope of application

In general, it has been concluded in the impact assessment of the Ministry of Economy in Bulgaria that the current framework on the sale of goods on national level is completely different from what the new SGD provides for, and it is therefore necessary for it to be repealed.[45]

In Bulgarian law there was so far no existent regulation on the sale of goods containing digital elements.[46] The new law therefore defines the notion as "any movable material good containing digital content or digital service or is interconnected with digital content or digital service in such a manner that the lack of digital content or digital service would prevent the good from exercising its functions",[47] relying entirely on the wording as stipulated in Art. 2 para. 5 lett. b of the SGD. Similarly, the definition of digital content and digital service[48] is absolutely identical to the one as proposed by the texts of the DCD, pursuant to Art. 2 para. 1 and Art. 2 para. 2, where digital content is defined as "data which are produced and supplied in digital form"[49] and digital service is "a service that allows the consumer to create, process, store or access data in digital from; or a service that allows the sharing of or any other interaction with data in digital form uploaded or created by the consumer or other users of that service"[50]. Additionally, it is strictly defined that when it comes to the sale of such goods that contain digital elements, their sale will be entirely regulated by the provisions of the law that cover the sale of goods, regardless of whether the digital element/digital service is provided by the same supplier/seller or a third party.[51] In case of doubts as to whether the supply of digital content or a digital service is part of the initial contract of a sale, it is to be regarded as part of the contract.[52]

Even though the CPA contains certain rules when it comes to digital content (such as different information requirements to be provided prior contract signing or the right to withdraw from the contract)[53], it does not regulate the sale of goods that incorporate digital content, nor the supply of DC/DS which confirms the statement by the Bulgarian legislator that at the time of implementing the Directives, there was no legal framework regulating these concepts.[54]

The idea of personal data having a remuneratory characteristic is a particularly new concept for the Bulgarian consumer legal framework. This is yet another example of a premise very familiar for the Digital Age, namely that the new currency for consumers is called personal data, as suggested by EU Commissioner Vestager as early as 2014.[55] Naturally, special protection is envisaged in the Act in such cases when the consumers

---

[45] Report on preliminary assessment of the impact of the draft Act on the supply of DC/DS and on the sale of goods, (n 11) 10; see further: CPA.

[46] Motives for the establishment of the draft Act on the supply of DC/DS and on the sale of goods, (n 15) 4.

[47] § 6 para.3, Act on the supply of DC/DS and on the sale of goods.

[48] ibid, § 6 para. 1 and para. 2, Act on the supply of DC/DS and on the sale of goods.

[49] Art. 2 para. 1 DCD.

[50] ibid, Art. 2 para. 2.

[51] Art. 6 para. 1, Act on the supply of DC/DS and on the sale of goods; Art. 3 para. 3 SGD.

[52] ibid.

[53] see for example, Art. 48 para. 2, Art. 49 para. 8, Art. 55 para.7, Art. 61a, Art. 62 CPA among others;

[54] Report on preliminary assessment of the impact of the draft Act on the supply of DC/DS and on the sale of goods, (n 11) 9,10.

[55] Bakhoum, C. Gallego, Mackenrodt, Surblytė-Namavičienė, Personal Data in Competition, Consumer Protection and Intellectual Property Law, Towards A Holistic Approach (Springer, 2018), 157; European Parliament, Committee on Economic and Monetary Affairs, *Hearing of Commissioner-Designate for Competition, Margrethe Vestager*, (2 October 2014) 36 https://www.europarl.europa.eu/hearings-2014/resources/library/media/20141022RES75845/20141022RES75845.pdf accessed 03.03.2022 and <http://www.europarltv.europa.eu/en/player.aspx?pid=37678c4a-ab53-46d9-a874-a3b700ce4de8&epbox> accessed 03.03.2022.

who would be the recipients of digital content and digital services have provided their personal data, given the fact the contract is being terminated, for example.[56] Providing personal data bounds the trader in a very similar way, as if the consumer has paid utilising financial means. According to the Director General of the Consumer Protection Commission (CCP) in Bulgaria, this is an element of significant importance for the development both of consumer protection law and of the field of digital content as there are no "free digital services" or "free software" when consumers provide their personal data to use the given contents or services.[57] Therefore, they rightly deserve protection in case there would be lack of conformity.[58]

22 Legal scholarship defines the types of consumer contracts as stipulated in the Act to be contracts of remuneratory nature, i.e. contracts upon which a certain price is to be paid for the good/service/digital content to be provided, including personal data as remuneration.[59] The Act is suitable to be applied to business to consumer (B2C) relationships, following the definition of consumer as stipulated in the additional provisions of the Act, as a natural person acting outside their trade, business, craft or profession.[60]

D. Conformity requirements and beyond

23 The conformity requirements are of key importance for the DCD and SGD and consequently for the Bulgarian Act. In light of the text of the Act, the conformity requirements contain subjective and objective criteria that determine whether the supply of the DC/DS or the sale of the good in question is compliant with the contract.[61] The objective requirements for conformity are connected to the reasonable expectations of the consumer when it comes to the supply of DC/DS or the sale of goods, while the subjective ones are related to the contractual responsibilities of the trader/seller that are enlisted in the contract.[62] For the Bulgarian transposition, it is relevant to point out that in the Draft Act prior to the process of public consultations, the notion "subjective conformity requirements" was used instead of "individual" as it is currently in the Act.[63] Following the process of public consultations, the legislators accepted the use of the

---

[56] Motives for the establishment of the draft Act on the supply of DC/DS and on the sale of goods, (n 15) 6.

[57] Republic of Bulgaria, 44th National Assembly, Commission on Economic Policy and Tourism, *Presentation, discussion and voting of the draft Act on the supply of digital content/digital services and on the sell of goods*, 20.01.2021, Protocol No.101 (National Assembly, Protocol No.101) https://www.parliament.bg/bg/parliamentarycommittees/2578/steno/6338 accessed 28.03.22, see the statement of Dimitar Margaritov, Director General of the Commission on Consumer Protection.

[58] ibid; to analyse the relationship between the GDPR and the new Act please see section V.5 of this contribution.

[59] Aneliya Toroshanova, interview with Prof. Tanya Yosifova, 'New moments in the Act on the Supply of Digital Content and Digital Services and on the Sale of Goods'/'Novi momenti v Zakona za predostavyane na tsifrovo sadarzhanie i tsifrovi uslugi i za prodazhba na stoki', *(The Law and Themis/Zakonat i Temida*, 14 January 2022) (Prof. Yosifova New moments commentary) https://bnr.bg/hristobotev/post/101585903/novi-momenti-v-zakona-za-predostavane-na-cifrovo-sadarjanie-i-cifrovi-uslugi-i-za-prodajba-na-stoki accessed 22.01.2022;

[60] § 6 para. 6, Act on the supply of DC/DS and on the sale of goods.

[61] Report on preliminary assessment of the impact of the draft Act on the supply of DC/DS and on the sale of goods, (n 11) 8–9.

[62] ibid; Arts. 9–11 and Arts. 27–28 Act on the supply of DC/DS and on the sale of goods.

[63] Draft Act on the supply of digital content and digital services and on the sale of goods from 30 December 2020 (No. 002–01–76, Council of Ministers of the Republic of Bulgaria) (Draft Act on the supply of DC/DS and on the sale of goods), Art. 10 and Art. 27; Art. 10 and Art. 27, Act on the supply of DC/DS and on the sale of goods., – please see Art. 10 and Art. 27 of the Draft Act and compare with the New Act, in Bulgarian, the official translation of the term "subjective" in the text is actually "individual".

D. Conformity requirements and beyond

term "individual" replacing "subjective", as the latter would create confusion around the meaning of the text.[64] Other minor alterations were introduced following the process of consultations.[65] At the same time, the Bulgarian Chamber of Commerce and Industry expressed a positive opinion on the Draft Act.[66] The Bulgarian Act indicates both for the sale of goods but also for the supply of DC/DS that to comply with the conformity requirements certain criteria must be met, which are separately listed for both.[67] The following subsections of this chapter discuss the specifcs of some the conformity requirements in light of the new legislation.

I. "Durability" requirement in Art. 7, para. 1, lett. d, SGD

The "durability" requirement has been implemented as part of the other objective conformity requirements listed in Art. 7, para. 1, lett. d of the SGD. The wording of the Article in the Bulgarian Act mirrors the one in Art. 7, para. 1 lett. d, SGD. Important for the durability requirement is the significance of the notion "reasonable time", used a number of times throughout both Directives.[68] Before adopting the Bulgarian Act, the concept of "reasonable time" was discussed at length in the Bulgarian Parliament, with different Members of Parliament presenting opposing views on its significance and interpretation.[69] Regardless of the doubts expressed about the notion, the definition of "reasonable time" remained unchanged in the Act with its final adoption.[70] Throughout the discussion, the representatives from the Ministry of Economy and the CCP provided justifications stating that "when treating lack of conformity the context of the contract is instrumental to interpret the *reasonable time* requirement".[71] The notion can be applied as it is, also as this was the desired approach of the European legislator during the negotiations.[72]

24

---

[64] LIBRe Foundation opinion (n 39); Council of Ministers, Portal for public consultations, *Draft Act on the supply of digital content and digital services and on the sale of goods*, (Reference reflecting the proposals and opinions expressed, 23.10.2020), (Reference) <https://www.strategy.bg/PublicConsultations/View.aspx?@lang=bg-BG&Id=5553> accessed 18.03.2022 2–3;

[65] Reference (n 65), the text of Art. 9 para. 2 was brought in full conformity with the texts of the Directives – Art. 10 of the DCD and Art. 9 of the SGD; few changes were done with regards to writing style and punctuation.

[66] Bulgarian Chamber of Commerce and Industry, Opinion on the Draft Act on the supply of digital content and digital services and on the sale of goods, (No. 36/02.02.2021) (BCCI opinion).

[67] Art. 9 and Art. 26 of the Act on the supply of DC/DS and on the sale of goods.

[68] Recitals 50, 55 and Arts. 7 para. 4 and 13 para. 4 subpara. d SGD and Recitals 46, 64, 65, 71 and Arts. 8 para. 3, 14 para. 3 and para. 4 subpara. e, 16 para. 4 DCD.

[69] National Assembly, Protocol No.101 (n 58); Republic of Bulgaria, 44th National Assembly, Four Hundred and Forty-Seventh Plenary Session, 27.01.2021, Protocol, (National Assembly, Four Hundred and Forty-Seventh Plenary Session) https://www.parliament.bg/bg/plenaryst/ns/55/ID/10535, accessed 28.03.22;

[70] National Assembly, Four Hundred and Forty-Seventh Plenary Session (n 70); Act on the supply of DC/DS and on the sale of goods.

[71] National Assembly, Protocol No.101 (n 58); National Assembly, Four Hundred and Forty-Seventh Plenary Session (n 70).

[72] National Assembly, Protocol No.101 (n 58), see the interventions of Emil Aleksiev and Dimitar Margaritov.

II. Supplying the consumer with updates and liability exemption

25   An important element in the new Act when it comes to the conformity requirements is the duty to inform and supply the consumer with updates when necessary.[73] According to the new Act, this duty is to be respected when a long term supply of DC/DS is to be provided or when the content or service has to be completed within a specific deadline; or when the consumer can reasonably expect such an update when there is a single act supply or several single act supplies of the DC/DS.[74] If the consumer does not install the update in a reasonable time limit, when the trader has done everything required of them by the contract and by the applicable legislation to inform accordingly the consumer on the installation of updates, the trader is not to be held liable for the lack of conformity arising only from the absence of such an update and the consumer will not be able to challenge the contract with views to this provision.[75]

26   According to Bulgarian law, the digital content or digital service is not in conformity with the contract when this requirement is not complied with, i.e. when no information regarding any updates is presented according to the criteria set out in the Act.[76] In such cases, the consumer is given the possibility to terminate the contract, or to keep the digital content or digital service.[77] Alternatively, the consumer can use the option of immediate termination of the contract if specific conditions are met.[78]

III. The exclusion of existence of a lack of conformity in the case provided by Art. 8, para. 5 DCD and Art. 7, para. 5 SGD

27   The Bulgarian legislator has transposed identically both provisions of Art. 8, para. 5 DCD and Art. 7, para. 5 SGD, as the Directives suggest under the two separate sections regulating the conformity requirements for the supply of DC/DS and for the sale of goods in the Act, with particular regard also to the concept of "particular characteristic".[79] As a consequence, there is no lack of conformity if during the conclusion of the contract, the consumer has been informed regarding a particular characteristic of the DC/DS or the good/s that lacks conformity and has accepted this through an express and separate statement.[80]

IV. Product specific Union legislation requirements – durability and repairability with views to Recital 32 SGD

28   There is no reference to product specific Union legislation, neither in the provisions of the new Act, nor in the report from the comprehensive preliminary assessment of the impact of the Draft Act.[81] The report reflects, however, on the Union legislation

---

[73] Art. 11 para. 2, Act on the supply of DC/DS and on the sale of goods; Motives for the establishment of the draft Act on the supply of DC/DS and on the sale of goods, (n 15) 6.
[74] Art. 11 para. 2, Act on the supply of DC/DS and on the sale of goods.
[75] ibid Art. 11 para. 3.
[76] Arts. 11 and 12 Act on the supply of DC/DS and on the sale of goods; Motives for the establishment of the draft Act on the supply of DC/DS and on the sale of goods, (n 15) 6.
[77] ibid Art. 16 para. 1 and Art. 16 para. 2, Act on the supply of DC/DS and on the sale of goods.
[78] ibid, Art. 16 para. 3; for further analysis, please see Section VI.3 on the right to termination.
[79] ibid, Art. 11 para. 5 and Art. 28 para. 5.
[80] ibid.
[81] Act on the supply of DC/DSdc / ds and on the sale of goods; Report on preliminary assessment of the impact of the draft Act on the supply of DC/DS and on the sale of goods, (n 11) 17–18.

D. Conformity requirements and beyond

that is connected to the application of the Twin Directives which is the following: Directive (EU) 2018/1972 European Electronic Communications Code (Recast); GDPR Regulation 2016/679; Regulation (EU) 2017/2394 on cooperation between national authorities responsible for the enforcement of consumer protection laws; and Directive 2009/22/EC on injunctions for the protection of consumers' interests.[82] In the Act, durability is referred to when it comes to objective conformity requirements and commercial guarantees.[83] It is defined as the "ability of goods to maintain the requested from them functions and actions throughout their usual manner of usage".[84] When it comes to reparability, the notion is mentioned only when defining commercial guarantees.[85]

V. Ecodesign requirements – availability of spare parts and corresponding information obligations

In Bulgarian law, the availability and delivery of spare parts and corresponding information obligations is mainly linked to the Ecodesign Directive 2009/125/EC, implemented in Bulgarian law through the Technical Requirements to Products Act and the 10 ecodesign implementing regulations adopted under its framework.[86] The implementing regulations are the first to establish repair and maintenance provisions for the consumer goods in the Union, setting out requirements such as energy efficiency for some specific product groups.[87] In short, according to the rules stipulated in the ecodesign implementing regulations, spare parts for products must be available within a reasonable waiting period and at a price that is appropriate and attractive.[88]

The Bulgarian Act did not refer to the Ecodesign Directive 2009/125/EC in any specific manner, neither to any of the implementing regulations. All said provisions would be applicable simultaneously depending on the subject matter.

---

[82] ibid; Directive (EU) 2018/1972 of the European Parliament and of the Council of 11 December 2018 establishing the European Electronic Communications Code (Recast) (OJ L 321/36, 17 December 2018); Regulation (EU) 2016/679 of the European Parliament and of the Council of 27 April 2016 on the protection of natural persons with regard to the processing of personal data and on the free movement of such data, and repealing Directive 95/46/EC (General Data Protection Regulation)(OJ L 119/1, 4 May 2016) (GDPR); Regulation (EU) 2017/2394 of the European Parliament and of the Council of 12 December 2017 on cooperation between national authorities responsible for the enforcement of consumer protection laws and repealing Regulation (EC) No 2006/2004 (OJ L 345/1, 27 December 2017); Directive 2009/22/EC of the European Parliament and of the Council of 23 April 2009 on injunctions for the protection of consumers' interests (Codified version) (OJ L 110/30, 1 May 2009).

[83] Art. 28, para. 1, subpara. 4 and Art. 39, paras. 1 and 2, Act on the supply of DC/DS and on the sale of goods.

[84] ibid § 6 para. 23.

[85] ibid § 6 para. 22.

[86] Directive 2009/125/EC of the European Parliament and of the Council of 21 October 2009 establishing a framework for the setting of ecodesign requirements for energy-related products (OJ L 285/10, 31 October 2009) (Ecodesign Directive) and for example Commission Regulation (EU) 2019/2021 of 1 October 2019 laying down ecodesign requirements for electronic displays pursuant to Directive 2009/125/EC of the European Parliament and of the Council, amending Commission Regulation (EC) No 1275/2008 and repealing Commission Regulation (EC) No 642/2009 (OJ L 315/241, 5 December 2019).

[87] Helen Brown, Julia Hemmings, 'Sustainability Drives New "Right to Repair" Rules for Household Products in Latest Update to EU Ecodesign Legislation' (A blog by Baker McKenzie, 15 November 2019) https://www.globalcompliancenews.com/2019/11/15/sustainability-drives-new-right-to-repair-rules-household-products-eu-ecodesign-legislation-20191104/ accessed 10.01.22.

[88] ibid.

31   The Commission has already declared its intentions to put forward a legislative proposal on the right to repair, expected in the fourth quarter of 2022.[89] It is likely that this initiative will aim to impose targeted amendments to the SGD and create a new right to repair either within the text of the Directive or in a separate new instrument.[90]

32   The European Parliament has been openly supportive of consumers' right to repair for over a decade and has expressed this position in two recent resolutions, calling to make repairs "systematic, cost effective and attractive" and also "calling repairers and consumers to be given a free access to repair and necessary spare parts; standardisation of spare parts; mandatory minimum period for the provision of spare parts and reasonable delivery times; and ensuring that the price of spare parts is reasonable".[91] In the April 2022 plenary session of the EP, the Members debated the topic and adopted a resolution following an oral question procedure by the committee on Internal Market and Consumer Protection (IMCO).[92]

33   There is no specific coordination between the provisions of the SGD and those of the Ecodesign Directive 2009/125/EC on a national level. However, pursuant to the Technical Requirements to Products Act there are penalties to be applied (mainly penalty fees and confiscation of property) when violations arise.[93] Regulating the right to repair will have a significant impact on all Member States, including Bulgaria. According to available sources from the CCP, traders in Bulgaria prefer the practice of repairing the good to replacing it, therefore making repair more attractive and accessible to consumers is of extreme importance for the development of the Bulgarian market.[94] In light of recent data from Eurobarometer, 79% of EU citizens would require manufacturers to simplify repair conditions when it comes to digital devices and 77% would choose repair to purchasing a new device.[95]

VI. Environmental sustainability and circular economy

34   There are no specific measures within the provisions of the Act that would specifically cover enhancement of environmental sustainability. Nevertheless, prior to the adoption of the Act, the Bulgarian legislator analysed the potential effects of the transposition of the draft Act, also with regard to its environmental impacts. It concluded that the draft

---

[89] European Commission, *Work programme 2022 Making Europe stronger together*, 19 October 2021, COM(2021) 645 final; European Commission, *State of the Union 2021: Letter of intent*, 15 September 2021 <https://ec.europa.eu/info/sites/default/files/state_of_the_union_2021_letter_of_intent_en.pdf> accessed 12.01.2022

[90] European Parliament, *Right to repair*, January 2022, PE 698.869 (EP Study – Right to repair) 5.

[91] European Parliament, *European Parliament Resolution of 25 November 2020 on Towards a more sustainable single market for business and consumers*, 2020/2021(INI) (EP Resolution Sustainable single market); European Parliament, *European Parliament Resolution of 10 February on the New Circular Economy Action Plan*, 2020/2077(INI); EP Study – Right to repair (n 91).

[92] European Parliament, *European Parliament Resolution of 7 April 2022 on the right to repair*, 2022/2515(RSP);

[93] Technical Requirements to Products Act from 1 October 1999 (State Gazette/Durzhaven Vestnik, No. 86/1999, as amended SG, No. 105/2020, 11.12.2020) (Technical Requirements to Products Act).

[94] Hristo Nikolov interview with Konstantin Raykov (CCP) and Hristo Kapanarov (law firm), 'EU measures will stimulate online commerce between the Member States'/'Merki na ES shte stimulirat onlayn targoviyata mezhdu darzhavite chlenki', (Business Start/Biznes start, 04 February 2019) (Bloomberg EU measures interview) https://www.bloombergtv.bg/a/16-biznes-start/33541-merki-na-es-shte-stimulirat-onlayn-targoviyata-mezhdu-darzhavite-chlenki accessed 10.01.2022

[95] European Commission, Directorate-General for Environment, Flash Eurobarometer 388, *Attitudes of Europeans towards waste management and resource efficiency*, June 2014, 10.2779/14825; see also: EP Resolution Sustainable single market (n 92).

D. Conformity requirements and beyond

Act has the potential to foster competition and minimise expenses, resulting in a positive environmental impact optimal for the activities of SMEs.[96] It is not expected that the Act will negatively affect the fight against climate change or will have any influence over the use of energy and transport, biodiversity, purity of the atmospheric air, the quality of the soil and waters, water stocks, renewable or non-renewable resources, businesses and consumers on the environment when it comes to generating and recycling of waste and on animals with views to the relations regulated by the Act.[97]

As for the enhancement of the circular economy, even if no specific provisions are established under the Act, the transposition of the Twin Directives as part of the efforts of the EC for an improved Union digital strategy and a transformed consumer policy will certainly have a positive influence on improving the participation in circular economy.[98]

VII. Incorrect installation and/or integration of the goods and/or the digital content/digital service

The conditions differ slightly between the regulation of DC/DS and goods. According to the Act, when there is lack of conformity that originates from incorrect integration of the DC/DS in the digital environment of the consumer, it is to be regarded as a lack of conformity when the person responsible was the trader or another individual for whom the trader is responsible.[99] There is a lack of conformity also in the case when the consumer has to perform the integration given the instructions provided by the trader led to the lack of conformity.[100]

A detailed look at the wording of this section of the Act shows that when it comes to the supply of DC/DS, only the notion of "integration" is used, whereas when it comes to the sale of goods "installation" is used, mirroring precisely the wording of the Twin Directives[101] The Act mentions installation of DC/DS only when it comes to guidance on installing the DC/DS according to the individual (subjective) conformity requirements and when it comes to installing updates of the DC/DS.[102]

When this happens, the consumer has the right of redress according to Art. 17 of the Act. The specifics of the right of redress are discussed in more detail in section VI of this chapter. In brief, individuals who are in need of redress, can ask for a reclamation, to receive a proportionate price reduction, or terminate the contract.[103] The right to redress regarding the sale of goods is designed identically, providing consumers with the same list of redress options.[104]

---

[96] Report on preliminary assessment of the impact of the draft Act on the supply of DC/DS and on the sale of goods, (n 11) 53.
[97] ibid.
[98] European Commission Communication, *2030 Digital Compass: the European way for the Digital Decade*, 9 March 2021, COM(2021)118 final.
[99] Art. 12 para. 1, Act on the supply of DC/DS and on the sale of goods.
[100] ibid Art. 12 para. 2.
[101] ibid Art. 12 and Art. 29.
[102] ibid Art. 10 and Art. 11.
[103] ibid Art. 17.
[104] ibid Art. 33.

VIII. Third party rights in national law Art. 10 DCD and Art. 9 SGD

39   With regards to third party rights, the Bulgarian legislator has decided to apply the DCD/SGD remedies for a lack of conformity to the situations covered by those provisions. It is essential to note that lack of conformity caused by the violation of third-party rights includes violations of Intellectual Property rights.[105]

40   With views to the sale of goods, this matter is handled in the section on conformity of goods (in particular Art. 30), mirroring the wording of Art. 9 SGD and stating that consumers have the right to redress (according to Art. 33 of the Act), except in cases where the contract is void or voidable.

41   The legislator has transposed Art. 10 of the DCD in the same way (Arts. 9 and 13), this time referring to the right of redress as stipulated in Art. 17 of the Act, which covers redress when there is lack of conformity related to the supply of DC/DS.

E. Liability of the Trader

42   Following the texts of the Twin Directives, the new Act provides a high level of consumer protection in the cases where the duty to prove conformity with regards to the supply of DC/DS or goods lies within the obligations of the trader/seller.[106] Nevertheless, there are cases in which the trader would be exempt from such duty, for example, when the consumer was informed regarding an existent lack of conformity at the moment of concluding the contract.[107]

I. Single act/long-term supply of DC/DS and interruption of long-term supply

43   For the single act of supply of DC/DS, including when this is carried out through a sequence of separate single acts, the trader is liable for any lack of conformity of the digital content or services, be it an objective lack, an individual (subjective) lack or a lack of conformity with the integration of the content/service with the digital environment of the consumer.[108] The lack of conformity is either existent during the single act supply, or it arises or becomes apparent within two years of the supply.[109]

44   For the long-term supply of DC/DS, pursuant to the Act the trader is responsible for every lack of conformity of the contract, conformity requirements being individual (subjective), objective and the requirements connected to the integration of the DC/DS with the digital environment of the consumer.[110] The lack of conformity is either existent during the supply of the DC/DS or it arises or becomes apparent within the entire duration of the supply.[111]

---

[105] ibid Art. 9 para. 2; Art. 13; Art. 26; Art. 30; Report on preliminary assessment of the impact of the draft Act on the supply of DC/DS and on the sale of goods, (n 11) 9.
[106] Art. 15, Art. 32 and Art. 33 Act on the supply of DC/DS and on the sale of goods.
[107] ibid Art. 11 para. 5 and Art. 28 para. 5.
[108] ibid Art. 14 para. 2.
[109] ibid.
[110] ibid Art. 14 para. 4.
[111] ibid.

Regarding the long-term supply of DC/DS, the conformity requirements must be 45
met during the entire duration of the long-term supply, e.g. a subscription to an online
journal.[112]

Recital 51 of the DCD stipulates very explicitly that interruptions of long-term supply 46
of DC/DS are to be treated as instances of lack of conformity where they are more than
negligible or recur. The Bulgarian Act does not lay out such straightforward wording;
nevertheless, continuity/uninterruptedness is an integral part of the objective conformity
requirements pursuant to Art. 11 para. 1 subpara. 2 of the Act. Furthermore, according
to Art. 14 para. 4 of the Act, the trader is liable for any non-provision of the DC/DS
when the contract provides for an uninterrupted supply of DC/DS and there is a lack of
conformity with the individual (subjective) or objective requirements or the requirements for the integration of the DC/DS in the digital environment of the consumer.

II. Force majeure and change of circumstances

The legislator did not provide specific rules regarding force majeure or a sudden 47
change of circumstances pursuant to Recital 14 of the DCD in case of failure to deliver/supply. The sudden changes of circumstances are not covered by the Act at all in
any meaning, therefore in case of an emergency situation caused by force majeure
circumstances the general rules on failure to deliver/supply would be enforced unless
specifically agreed otherwise in the contract terms on an individual basis.[113]

III. Consequences of the trader's non-compliance with the GDPR regarding contracts for the supply of digital content/digital services

On several occasions[114] the Act refers to the requirements for the protection of 48
personal data as provided by the GDPR, stating that in cases where there is termination
of the contract for the supply of digital content/digitals services, the trader is obliged to
comply with the GDPR requirements for the protection of personal data of individuals.
Nevertheless, there is no specific provision that would treat the explicit consequences of
the trader's non-compliance with the GDPR rules in the Act. The Act explains, however,
that EU data protection law is to be applied in all cases where there is treatment of
personal data with regards to the contracts for the supply of DC/DS.[115] In cases where
there would be any conflicting interpretation between Heading 2 of the Act regulating
the supply of digital content/digital services and Union laws or between Bulgarian
legislation and Union laws, the Act stipulates that EU law is the one to be applied.[116]
Nevertheless, confusion may arise in some situations regarding the applicable law when
it comes to seeking redress regarding the protection of personal data and seeking redress
for violations under the new Act.

---

[112] ibid Art. 11 para. 4.
[113] Report on preliminary assessment of the impact of the draft Act on the supply of DC/DS and on the sale of goods, (n 11) 30–34.
[114] please see Art. 18 para. 4 in particular, but also § 3, § 6 para. 8.
[115] ibid § 3.
[116] ibid.

F. Remedies for the failure to supply and remedies for the lack of conformity

49   In general, the Bulgarian Act gives the following options when the consumer needs to protect their legal rights in case of failure to supply and for the lack of conformity: right to reclamation and accordingly repair of the goods or bringing the digital content and the digital services into conformity; proportionate price reduction; or, as a final remedy, terminating the contract.[117]

50   Nevertheless, one needs to make the following important distinction: the price reduction as a remedy may only be applied in the following cases: bringing the DC/DS into conformity is impossible or would lead to disproportionately high costs for the trader; the trader did not bring the DC/DS into conformity; there is a lack of conformity that is apparent regardless of the actions taken by the trader to bring the DC/DS into conformity; the lack of conformity is so immense that it justifies request for immediate price reduction; the trader has announced or circumstances show that he will not bring the DC/DS into conformity in a reasonable time period or without considerable inconveniences to the consumer.[118] In fact, the same conditions would apply in case the consumer would like to terminate the contract, so long as the lack of conformity is not insignificant.[119] However, contract termination is often seen as the final remedy step, unless specific circumstances cause immediate termination.[120] Section VI.3 will further examine this case.

51   Price reduction or contract termination may be applied to goods in the same situations, highlighting two essential differences.[121] Firstly, the consumer can choose between repair and replacement of the good and, secondly, the trader has the right to refuse bringing the good in conformity when this would be impossible or would lead to disproportionately large expenses for the trader.[122]

52   The European Consumer Centre Bulgaria (ECC Bulgaria), part of the European Consumer Centres Network (ECC-Net) and under the umbrella of the CCP in Bulgaria is the institution responsible for providing advice to consumers on contracts with a cross-border character.[123]

53   When it comes to the treatment of cross-border disputes through Alternative Dispute Resolution (ADR) mechanisms, the responsible authorities from one Member State handling such disputes are cooperating with the ones from the other Member States involved – to facilitate better information flow and exchange of positions.[124]

54   The Act does not regulate specific topics, such as the transfer of rights against the initial seller from the initial consumer to a subsequent buyer. Matters that are not regulated directly by the Act are likely to fall under the framework of the CPA. Nevertheless, jurisprudence is expected to clarify such situations in the near future.

55   The Act does not provide express regulation on cross-border cases and their implications; however, as mentioned, there are provisions on the authorities responsible for cross-border cases and ADR for cross-border matters.[125] If a consumer has moved to

---

[117] ibid Art. 17 and Art. 33.
[118] ibid Art. 17 para. 4.
[119] ibid Art. 17 para. 6.
[120] ibid Art. 16 para. 3; Prof. Yosifova New moments commentary (n 60).
[121] Art. 33 para. 4, Act on the supply of DC/DS and on the sale of goods.
[122] ibid Art. 33 para. 2 and art. 33 para. 3.
[123] ibid Art. 49 para. 3.
[124] ibid Art. 55.
[125] ibid.

another country after purchasing a good but at the moment of competing the purchase, both the consumer and the seller are in the same MS, then this is regarded a national dispute pursuant to the provisions of the CPA.[126]

I. The right to withhold payments

In light of the Act and both under the DCD and the SGD there are modalities related to withholding parts or the whole payment in case of failure to supply and lack of conformity[127]. Nevertheless, only the SGD explicitly gives the right to the consumer to withhold payment until the seller has fulfilled his obligations under the Directive.[128] Consequently, such right is regulated in the Act only when it comes to the sale of goods, which reads under Art. 33 para. 6 that "the consumer has the right to refuse the payment of the rest of the price or what is left from the price until the seller fulfils his duties to bring the good into conformity". When it comes to the supply of DC/DS, such right is not regulated in the text of the Act, despite Recital 15 of the DCD that leaves it in the hands of the MS to decide whether to introduce right to withhold the payment or not.

56

II. Delivery, repair and replacement – specifics

As discussed, 77 % of EU consumers report that they prefer to repair their broken goods before replacing them or discarding them.[129]

57

Place of delivery and place of repair and replacement are not specifically defined throughout the text of the Act. This aspect of the consumer regulation is still to be provided by the CPA.[130] Nevertheless, as already discussed, the EC is planning to come up with a legislative proposal on the right to repair by the end of 2022 to limit consumer costs and facilitate a circular economy in the Union, and it is likely to also cover specific regulatory measures regarding the place of delivery and place of repair and replacement.[131]

58

It is also essential to highlight that the SGD also provides rules on repair for products faulty at the moment of delivery, and during the first 12 months there is a reverse burden of proof on the seller to prove that the product was not faulty at delivery.[132] Only afterwards the consumer may be asked to provide evidence that the product is faulty at the moment of delivery.[133] Nevertheless, some experts argue that after the period of the reverse burden of proof lapses, it is often more onerous for consumers to make use of the legal guarantees.[134]

59

When it comes to returning all or some of the purchased goods when the consumer is using their right to terminate the contract, all expenses that the consumer has made for the return are for the seller to cover.[135] The additional provisions of the Act further re-

60

---

[126] Art. 181 CPA.
[127] Recital 15 DCD; Art. 13 para. 6 SGD.
[128] Art. 13 para. 6 SGD.
[129] European Parliament, *Consumers and repair of products*, September 2019, PE 640.158 2,8.
[130] Section II, CPA; Capital commentary (n 39).
[131] EP Study, Right to repair, (n 91) 1.
[132] Art. 15 para. 2, Art. 32 para.1,Act on the supply of DC/DS and on the sale of goods.
[133] EP Study, Right to repair (n 91) 1.
[134] European Parliament, *How an EU lifespan guarantee model could be implemented across the European Union*, January 2017, PE 583.121 (EP Study – EU Lifespan).
[135] Art 36 para. 3, Act on the supply of DC/DS and on the sale of goods.

flect on the meaning of the notion "free of charge" as used throughout the document.[136] It is provided that "free of charge" for the consumer would mean that no payment for any of the necessary expenses made to bring the goods into conformity with the contract, and especially the expenses related to the postal services, transport, labour or for materials would be required.[137] The legislators define further in Art. 34 of the Act that the repair/replacement of the goods is to be carried out free of charge throughout a reasonable period of time, as also defined in the Twin Directives.[138]

61 As mentioned above, it is often the case that Bulgarian traders prefer the practice of repairing the good to replacing it.[139] Legislative changes in 2019 gave the consumer the right to choose between the two, with some limitations related to proportionality rules.[140] The same right to choose and limitations have been recognised in the Act.[141]

62 Nevertheless, nowhere in the Act is the topic of environmental sustainability discussed, or its enhancement by prioritising repairs over replacement of the goods as foreseen in Recital 48 of the SGD. This has lately been a recurrent topic in the doctrinal debate on consumer rights in Bulgaria, therefore greater visibility in the consumer rights legislation is expected. Furthermore, a number of NGOs in the field of consumer protection have come up with initiatives to fight premature/planned obsolescence; however, to date there are no formal measures adopted at governmental level.[142]

III. Right of withdrawal and right of termination

63 When it comes to the supply of digital content and digital services in case the consumer is exercising his right to terminate the contract, the Act does not specify on the way this right is being expressed, but merely that the consumer exercises their right by informing the trader for his decision.[143] On the other hand, when it comes to the sale of goods, pursuant to Art. 36 of the Act, the consumer is compelled to submit a declaration to the seller to inform them on the decision to terminate the contract for the sale of the good.

64 Similarly to price reduction, as examined, the right to termination of the contract is possible when certain conditions are met and there are few differences when it comes to DC/DS and goods as provided in the beginning of this section.[144] According to Art. 16 para. 3 of the Act, the consumer has the right to immediately terminate the contract for the supply of DC/DS in two cases: the trader has announced or circumstances show that he will not supply with the DC/DS at all or not within the already agreed time period that is important for the consumer. Additionally, the consumer can also terminate the

---

[136] ibid Additional provisions § 6 para.24.
[137] ibid.
[138] Arts 8, 14, 16 DCD and Arts. 7, 13, 14 SGD.
[139] Bloomberg EU measures interview (n 95).
[140] ibid.
[141] Art. 33 para.2, Act on the supply of DC/DS and on the sale of goods.
[142] Active Consumers Association, 'Weekly newsletter'/'Sedmichen byuletin' (2021) 16 Active Consumers Association https://aktivnipotrebiteli.bg/%D0%BA%D0%B0%D0%BC%D0%BF%D0%B0%D0%BD%D0%B8%D1%8F/310/%D0%91%D1%8E%D0%BB%D0%B5%D1%82%D0%B8%D0%BD-%D0%90%D0%9A%D0%A2%D0%98%D0%92%D0%9D%D0%98-%D0%9F%D0%9E%D0%A2%D0%A0%D0%95%D0%91%D0%98%D0%A2%D0%95%D0%9B%D0%98,-%D0%B1%D1%80.-16,-23.04.2021# accessed 07.02.2022; for a detailed analysis of the topic, please see: European Environment Agency, European Topic Centre on Waste and Materials in a Green Economy, Electronic products and obsolescence in a circular economy, 18 June 2020, ETC/WMGE 2020/3 (EEA report); EP Study – Right to repair (n 91).
[143] Art. 18 among others (16, 17), Act on the supply of DC/DS and on the sale of goods.
[144] ibid, Art. 16, 17 and 33 among others; for differences between Art. 33 para. 2 and art. 33 para. 3, see the beginning of section VI.

contract when the trader does not provide the DC/DS without unreasonable delay or within an additional time period expressly agreed between the parties.[145] In comparison, the Act does not provide explicitly for an immediate contract termination in the case of sale of goods which is worthwhile analysing further when there is available jurisprudence on the topic.[146]

The right of withdrawal is not thoroughly assessed in the Act, but it is mainly covered by the CPA in Bulgaria, which transposes Directive 2011/83 on consumer rights. The right of withdrawal in the CPA resembles the right to termination, at least as stipulated in the Act on the supply of digital content/digital services and on the sale of goods. Pursuant to Annex 6 of the CPA, one can inform themselves on all the conditions of a withdrawal that is to be submitted through a declaration (in most of the cases).[147] Thus, looking at the currently available information stipulated from the legislation covering both the right of withdrawal and the right of termination, there is no deviation from the general structure and the two are rather similar. 65

Neither the new Act, nor the one on Consumer Protection introduce specific rules regarding the contractual consequences of withdrawal for the processing of personal data. Nevertheless, both do reflect on the necessary requirements to comply with the GDPR Regulation and the Personal Data Protection Act in Bulgaria. 66

G. Legal and Commercial Guarantees & Time limits and limitation periods

The Bulgarian legislator transferred the provisions regulating guarantees from the CPA to the framework of the new Act on the Supply of Digital Content and Digital Services and the Sale of Goods.[148] Nevertheless, the CPA still regulates legal and commercial guarantees, but only when for non-digital services.[149] 67

The DCD contains only one provision which provides for a lower level of harmonisation (minimum), as the Member States are allowed to establish the deadline for the legal guarantee to be longer than the two years provided for in Art. 11 para. 2 of the Directive. The Bulgarian legislator does not extend the period above two years, as doing this will create extra expenses for traders and fragment the internal market, making the Bulgarian rules differ compared to the other Member States.[150] Similarly, the legal guarantee in Art. 10 para. 3 of the SGD allows the Member States to impose a higher level of protection by extending the deadline above two years. Nevertheless, the Bulgarian legislator chooses the same approach also for the sale of goods with the aim of protecting sellers and creating a level playing field in the EU.[151] In addition, this rule will cover goods produced or manufactured in the future after the conclusion of the consumer contract.[152] 68

Applying the concept of legal guarantee to the contracts for the supply of DC/DS and to the contracts for the sale of goods with integrated digital elements is a new aspect for 69

---

[145] ibid, Art. 16 para. 2.
[146] ibid, Art. 33.
[147] Art. 47 CPA.
[148] Transitional and Final provisions, § 8 (see in particular para.13) para.13, § 9 Act on the supply of DC/DS and on the sale of goods; Motives for the establishment of the draft Act on the supply of DC/DS and on the sale of goods (n 15) 8.
[149] Capital commentary (n 39).
[150] Report on preliminary assessment of the impact of the draft Act on the supply of DC/DS and on the sale of goods (n 11) 29–30.
[151] Art. 44 and Art. 45, Act on the supply of DC/DS and on the sale of goods; Report on preliminary assessment of the impact of the draft Act on the supply of DC/DS and on the sale of goods (n 11) 31–32.
[152] ibid.

consumer regulation in Bulgaria.[153] The legal guarantee contains the following: a legal obligation upon the seller, meaning that the good will retain its qualities and will be in compliance with the conformity requirements; if this is not the case, then the seller can be held liable and in the worst-case scenario, the contract may be terminated.[154] The time limits when it comes to the functioning of the legal guarantees are important and depend on the type of contract and its duration.[155]

70   If the DC/DS is to be provided through a single act supply or several acts, then the trader is liable for any non-conformity that is proven within the time limit of two years from the commencement of the contract.[156] The same applies for the deadline for the contracts of sales of goods.[157] If however, the contract is for a longer duration than two years, both for the supply of DC/DS and for goods that have an integrated digital element, then the guarantee has a longer duration and covers the whole period of the duration of the contract.[158]

71   When it comes to limitations, this two-year guarantee will be extended throughout the period when the good is being repaired, as suggested by Recital 44 of the SGD.[159] According to the legislators, this is the preferred choice as it protects consumers' rights during the moment of repair/replacement where they cannot use their goods.[160]

72   Regarding the "obligation to notify" as laid down in Art. 12 of the SGD, the Bulgarian legislators chose not to introduce a provision in the Act, due to the concerns that the short time limit of only two months would limit their possibility to report a lack of conformity, thereby lowering the level of consumer protection and negatively impacting their rights.[161] Furthermore, the time period to bring the good in conformity will be extended if this obligation is utilised.[162]

73   As for the commercial guarantee, it is known to offer better guarantee conditions, such as longer duration of the guarantee outside the two-year period even when this requires additional payment.[163] This is carried out most often for domestic or kitchen appliances.[164] According to the rules, in case the seller provides for better conditions for commercial material than the ones given to the consumer, then the consumer has the right to request what has been provided for the commercial material.[165]

74   Pursuant to the Act, when providing a commercial guarantee for a good, the application for the guarantee will be provided also in the Bulgarian language, pursuant to

---

[153] Report on preliminary assessment of the impact of the draft Act on the supply of DC/DS and on the sale of goods (n 11) 8.
[154] Prof. Yosifova New moments commentary (n 60).
[155] ibid.
[156] Art. 14, Act on the supply of DC/DS and on the sale of goods.
[157] ibid, Art. 31.
[158] ibid Art. 31 para. 4 and Art. 14 para.4.
[159] Art. 45 para. 3, Act on the supply of DC/DS and on the sale of goods; Report on preliminary assessment of the impact of the draft Act on the supply of DC/DS and on the sale of goods (n 11) 37–38.
[160] Report on preliminary assessment of the impact of the draft Act on the supply of DC/DS and on the sale of goods (n 11) 37–38.
[161] ibid.
[162] ibid 33–34.
[163] Art. 39, Act on the supply of DC/DS and on the sale of goods; Prof. Yosifova New moments commentary (n 60).
[164] Denitsa Vateva, 'More rights for consumers: two years warranty and repair within a reasonable time'/'Oshte prava za potrebitelite: Dve godini garantsiya i remont v razumen srok' (Capital, 26 March 2021) (Capital commentary 2) https://www.capital.bg/moiat_capital/smart_spending/2021/03/26/4190278_oshte_prava_za_potrebitelite_dve_godini_garanciia_i/ accessed 09.01.2022.
[165] Art. 39 para.3, Act on the supply of DC/DS and on the sale of goods; Prof. Yosifova New moments commentary (n 60); Capital commentary (n 39).

Art. 17 para. 4 of the SGD.¹⁶⁶ Using this possibility would have a neutral effect on traders in Bulgaria and reduce costs from their side.¹⁶⁷ Moreover, this is very beneficial for Bulgarian consumers as they can familiarise themselves with the elements of the commercial guarantee in their own language, thus ensuring a higher level of consumer protection.¹⁶⁸

H. Right of Redress & relationship with other remedies

Recent data shows that Bulgarian consumers often suffer a certain level of confusion when it comes to which is the correct form of redress to use under the different legislative regulations, especially when it comes to ADR mechanisms or out of court disputes.¹⁶⁹

When it comes to the redress of the trader/seller, it is essential to highlight that both the Twin Directives (Art. 20 DCD and Art. 18 SGD) and the new Act (Art. 22 and Art. 38) provide with the right of redress for the supply of DC/DS and the sale of goods where the trader/seller is liable to the consumer because of a failure to supply the DC/DS or a lack of conformity resulting from an act or omission (incl. providing updates to goods with digital elements) committed by a person in previous links of the chain of transactions. In this case, the Twin Directives leave it to national law to determine the person against whom the trader/seller may pursue remedies and the relevant actions and conditions of such an exercise.¹⁷⁰

Pursuant to national law, for the right of redress to exist when supplying DC/DS, there needs to be a direct or indirect contractual relationship between the trader and the person/persons responsible for the failure or lack of conformity including the developer of the DC/DS.¹⁷¹ In light of such direct or indirect contractual relationship, the trader would be entitled to claim for compensation for any damages suffered.¹⁷² Any contract clause that limits or excludes this right is to be considered void.¹⁷³

When selling goods, the seller is also entitled to claim for compensation for damages suffered against the person/persons in previous links of the chain of transactions responsible for the failure or lack of conformity.¹⁷⁴ Nevertheless, this provision neither reflects on the existence of a direct/indirect contractual relationship between the seller and the person/persons responsible, nor provides that any contract clause limiting or excluding such right is to be considered void.¹⁷⁵

---

¹⁶⁶ Art. 40 para.3, Act on the supply of DC/DS and on the sale of goods; Report on preliminary assessment of the impact of the draft Act on the supply of DC/DS and on the sale of goods (n 11) 35.

¹⁶⁷ Report on preliminary assessment of the impact of the draft Act on the supply of DC/DS and on the sale of goods (n 11) 35.

¹⁶⁸ ibid.

¹⁶⁹ Aneliya Toroshanova, interview with Prof. Tanya Yosifova, 'Digital content and digital services – sellers and consumers'/'Digitalno sadarzhanie i digitalni uslugi – prodavachi i potrebiteli' (*The Law and Themis/Zakonat i Temida*, 26 November 2021) (Prof Yosifova Digital content and digital services commentary) https://bnr.bg/play/post/101562933/otnosheniata-mejdu-prodavachite-na-digitalno-sadarjanie-i-digitalni-uslugi-i-potrebitelite accessed 23.01.2022.

¹⁷⁰ Art. 20 DCD, Art 18 SGD.

¹⁷¹ Art. 22, Act on the supply of DC/DS and the sale of goods.

¹⁷² ibid.

¹⁷³ ibid.

¹⁷⁴ ibid, Art. 38.

¹⁷⁵ ibid.

79   The Act appoints the CCP as the main institution responsible for supervision when the consumer-seller contract is not respected.[176] Article 50 of the Act lists the requirements and specific conditions for submitting official claims and the signals that are to be used to demonstrate a breach of consumer rights.[177] Additionally, the Act stipulates the rights and obligations of experts from the CCP when it comes to conducting checks and collecting evidence pursuant to the claims received.[178]

80   When it comes to ADR, the Minister of Economy has approved a specific list of ADR institutions divided into sectors depending on the subject matter of the dispute and reflected in the CPA.[179] Thus, for utilising ADR consumers are to refer to the provisions stipulated in the CPA.[180]

81   Additionally, consumers always have the possibility to resort to the EU-wide platform on online dispute resolution administered by the EC, an easy-to-use digital platform that directs consumers to the competent authority for solving the consumer/seller dispute.[181] As already discussed, the ECC-Net is another institution that works under the regulation of the CCP and can assist consumers with advice on their disputes when it comes to cross-border matters.[182]

82   Applying the Act on the supply of digital content and digital services and on the sale of goods would not by any means require the creation of a new institutional framework in Bulgaria.[183] Checks on the execution of the law will be carried out solely by the CCP, the specialised state body responsible for the implementation of the legislation on consumer protection in Bulgaria. Nevertheless, there are mixed opinions when it comes to the *"ever-increasing"*[184] competences of the CCP in Bulgaria, including concerns that the new Act gives more competences to the institution.[185] However, experts have assured that this will not be the case as the competences will not be changed, increased or altered in any way following the transposition of the Twin Directives.[186] Similarly, positive feedback was also provided by the CCP itself.[187]

I. Conclusion

83   In light of this analysis, one can conclude that EU consumer protection legislation has been harmonised or at least there are major efforts going on to achieve this result. In the past few years, the EU has introduced a completely new layer of consumer protection for digital content, demonstrated by the adoption of the Twin Directives and other sources.

---

[176] ibid, Art. 49, Art. 50, Art. 56 (right to collective redress), Art. 57 Act on the supply of DC/DS and on the sale of goods; Motives for the establishment of the draft Act on the supply of DC/DS and on the sale of goods (n 15) 8-9.
[177] Art. 50, Act on the supply of DC/DS and on the sale of goods.
[178] ibid, Arts. 57-62;
[179] Art. 181p CPA; Prof Yosifova Digital content and digital services commentary (n 170).
[180] Art. 54 Act on the supply of DC/DS and on the sale of goods; Art. 181p CPA.
[181] European Commission, ODR Platform, <https://ec.europa.eu/consumers/odr/main/?event=main.complaints.screeningphase> accessed 25.02.2022; Regulation (EU) No 524/2013 of the European Parliament and of the Council of 21 May 2013 on online dispute resolution for consumer disputes and amending Regulation (EC) No 2006/2004 and Directive 2009/22/EC (Regulation on consumer ODR) (OJ L 165/1, 18 June 2013).
[182] Art. 49 para. 3, Act on the supply of DC/DS and on the sale of goods.
[183] Motives for the establishment of the draft Act on the supply of DC/DS and on the sale of goods (n 15) 9.
[184] Please note that the accent has been inserted by the author.
[185] National Assembly, Protocol No.101 (n 58).
[186] ibid.
[187] ibid.

New standards have been created that aim to boost the confidence of consumers in an ever-growing digital business-to-consumer market. Most important is that with the use of these measures fragmentation of the laws will be restricted, fostering trade practices in the Member States and making the supply chains more responsible.

As observed, the Bulgarian legislator has created a completely new legislative framework to regulate the supply of DC/DS and a semi-new one on the sale of goods, and this will certainly have a positive impact on consumers and traders in the country. Indeed, it is yet early to dissect the effects of the new Act, but as compared to the situation in other Member States, the transposition of the DCD and the SGD was carried out in a smooth and regular process in the country.[188]

There are some concerns expressed on the legal effects of the Act in combination with other pieces of consumer law.[189] However, legal scholars have expressed similar concerns at the EU stage with the arrival of the Twin Directives. Furthermore, it should also be acknowledged that other legislation on the implications of digital markets and services could also have an influence on the application of the DCD and the SGD.[190]

Both the Twin Directives and their Bulgarian transposition – the Act on the supply of digital content/digital services and on the sale of goods – have been designed to resolve a number of consumer issues and improve the functioning of the EU market. With nearly two years until the EC reviews the application of the Directives,[191] time will tell whether this regulatory exercise can be deemed a success.

Bibliography

I. Monographs

Mor Bakhoum, Beatriz Conde Gallego, Mark-Oliver Mackenrodt, Gintarė Surblytė-Namavičienė, *Personal Data in Competition, Consumer Protection and Intellectual Property Law, Towards A Holistic Approach* (Springer, 2018)

Marco B.M. Loos, *Review of the European Consumer Acquis* (Sellier European Law Publishers, 2008)

Reiner Schulze, *Common European Sales Law: A Commentary* (1st edn, Beck 2012)

II. Articles in Journals

Horst Eidenmüller, Florian Faust, Nils Jansen, Gerhard Wagner and Reinhard Zimmermann 'Towards a revision of the consumer acquis' (2011) 48.4 *Common Mark. Law Rev.,* 1077–1123

Karl Reisenhuber, 'System and Principles of EC Contract Law', (2005) 3 Eur. Rev. Contract Law, 297–322

Jozefien Vanherpe, "White Smoke, but Smoke Nonetheless: Some (Burning) Questions Regarding the Directives on Sale of Goods and Supply of Digital Content", European Review of Private Law 2–2020 [251–274], 2020 Kluwer Law International BV, The Netherlands

---

[188] Digital Europe Trade Association, *Digital industry's concerns with the Spanish transposition of the Sales of Goods Directive (2019/771)*, 01 June 2021 <https://www.digitaleurope.org/resources/digital-industrys-concerns-with-the-spanish-transposition-of-the-sales-of-goods-directive-2019-771/> accessed 16.03.2022.

[189] Varadinov (n13) 3.

[190] European Commission, Proposal for a Regulation of the European Parliament and of the Council on a Single Market For Digital Services (Digital Services Act) and amending Directive 2000/31/EC, 15 December 2020, COM(2020) 825 final, 2020/0361 (COD); European Commission, Proposal for a Regulation of the European Parliament and of the Council on contestable and fair markets in the digital sector (Digital Markets Act), 15 December 2020, COM(2020) 842 final, 2020/0374 (COD).

[191] Art. 25 DCD and SGD.

Ognyan Varadinov, 'Conformity of goods and consumer rights under the new Act on the provision of digital content, digital services and the sale of goods' (2022) 4/2022, *Commercial and contract law*, 1

Fryderyk Zoll, 'The Remedies in the Proposals of the Online Sales Directive and the Directive on the Supply of Digital Content' (2016) 5 *EuCML*, 250

III. EU Sources. Primary and Secondary Law

Amended Proposal for a Directive of the European Parliament and the Council on Certain Aspects Concerning Contracts for the Sales of Goods, Amending Regulation (EC) No. 2006/2004 of the European Parliament and of the Council and Repealing Directive 1999/44/EC of the European Parliament and of the Council, 31 October 2017, COM (2017) 637 final

Commission Regulation (EU) 2019/2021 of 1 October 2019 laying down ecodesign requirements for electronic displays pursuant to Directive 2009/125/EC of the European Parliament and of the Council, amending Commission Regulation (EC) No 1275/2008 and repealing Commission Regulation (EC) No 642/2009 (OJ L 315/241, 5 December 2019)

Consolidated Version of the Treaty on the Functioning of the European Union (OJ C 326/01 26 October 2012) (TFEU)

Directive (EU) 2019/771 of the European Parliament and of the Council of 20 May 2019 on certain aspects concerning contracts for the sale of goods, amending Regulation (EU) 2017/2394 and Directive 2009/22/EC, and repealing Directive 1999/44/EC (OJ L 136/28 22 May 2019) (SGD)

Directive (EU) 2019/770 of the European Parliament and of the Council of 20 May 2019 on certain aspects concerning contracts for the supply of digital content and digital services (OJ L 136/1, 22 May 2019) (DCD)

Directive (EU) 2019/2161 of the European Parliament and of the Council of 27 November 2019 amending Council Directive 93/13/EEC and Directives 98/6/EC, 2005/29/EC and 2011/83/EU of the European Parliament and of the Council as regards the better enforcement and modernisation of Union consumer protection rules (OJ L 328/7, 18 December 2019)

Directive 1999/44/EC of the European Parliament and of the Council of 25 May 1999 on certain aspects of the sale of consumer goods and associated guarantees (OJ L 171, 7 July 1999) (Directive 1999/44)

Directive 2009/22/EC of the European Parliament and of the Council of 23 April 2009 on injunctions for the protection of consumers' interests (Codified version) (OJ L 110/30, 1 May 2009)

Directive 2009/125/EC of the European Parliament and of the Council of 21 October 2009 establishing a framework for the setting of ecodesign requirements for energy-related products (OJ L 285/10, 31 October 2009) (Ecodesign Directive)

European Commission, Proposal for a Regulation of the European Parliament and of the Council on a Single Market For Digital Services (Digital Services Act) and amending Directive 2000/31/EC, 15 December 2020, COM(2020) 825 final, 2020/0361 (COD)

European Commission, Proposal for a Regulation of the European Parliament and of the Council on contestable and fair markets in the digital sector (Digital Markets Act), 15 December 2020, COM(2020) 842 final, 2020/0374 (COD)

Regulation (EU) 2016/679 of the European Parliament and of the Council of 27 April 2016 on the protection of natural persons with regard to the processing of personal data and on the free movement of such data, and repealing Directive 95/46/EC (General Data Protection Regulation) (OJ L 119/1, 4 May 2016) (GDPR)

Regulation (EU) 2017/2394 of the European Parliament and of the Council of 12 December 2017 on cooperation between national authorities responsible for the enforcement of consumer protection laws and repealing Regulation (EC) No 2006/2004 (OJ L 345/1, 27 December 2017)

Regulation (EU) No 524/2013 of the European Parliament and of the Council of 21 May 2013 on online dispute resolution for consumer disputes and amending Regulation (EC) No 2006/2004 and Directive 2009/22/EC (Regulation on consumer ODR) (OJ L 165/1, 18 June 2013)

IV. EU Sources. Documents of EU Organs

European Commission, *A New Deal for Consumers*, 11 April 2018, COM(2018) 183 final

European Commission Communication, 2030 Digital Compass: the European way for the Digital Decade, 9 March 2021, COM(2021)118 final

European Commission, Directorate-General for Environment, Flash Eurobarometer 388, *Attitudes of Europeans towards waste management and resource efficiency*, June 2014, 10.2779/14825

European Commission, Directorate-General for the Information Society and Media, Flash Eurobarometer 413, *Companies Engaged in Online Activities*, May 2015, 10.2759/473539

European Commission, *Evaluation and fitness check (FC) roadmap, REFIT Fitness Check of consumer law*, December 2015, COM (2015)

European Commission, ODR Platform, <https://ec.europa.eu/consumers/odr/main/?event=main.complaints.screeningphase> accessed 25.02.2022

European Commission, *Staff Working Document on a Digital Single Market Strategy for Europe – Analysis and Evidence*, 6 May 2015, COM(2015) 192 final

European Commission, *Staff Working Document on the Impacts of fully harmonized rules on contracts for the sales of goods*, 31 October 2017, SWD(2017) 354 final

European Commission, *State of the Union 2021: Letter of intent*, 15 September 2021 <https://ec.europa.eu/info/sites/default/files/state_of_the_union_2021_letter_of_intent_en.pdf> accessed 12.01.2022

European Commission, *Work programme 2022 Making Europe stronger together*, 19 October 2021, COM(2021) 645 final

European Environment Agency, European Topic Centre on Waste and Materials in a Green Economy, *Electronic products and obsolescence in a circular economy*, 18 June 2020, ETC/WMGE 2020/3 (EEA report)

European Parliament, *Consumers and repair of products*, September 2019, PE 640.158

European Parliament, *Contracts for online and other distance sale of goods*, February 2017, PE 599.286

European Parliament, *Contracts for supply of digital content to consumers*, March 2017, PE 599.310

European Parliament, *Debates*, 26 March 2019 – Strasbourg, 2015/0287(COD) https://www.europarl.europa.eu/doceo/document/CRE-8-2019-03-26-ITM-004_EN.html accessed 15.03.2022

European Parliament, *Hearing of Commissioner-Designate for Competition, Margrethe Vestager*, (October 2014) <http://www.europarltv.europa.eu/en/player.aspx?pid=37678c4a-ab53-46d9-a874-a3b700ce4de8&epbox> accessed 03.03.2022

European Parliament, *How an EU lifespan guarantee model could be implemented across the European Union*, January 2017, PE 583.121

European Parliament, *Legal obstacles in Member States to Single Market rules*, November 2020, PE 658.189

European Parliament, *European Parliament Resolution of 10 February on the New Circular Economy Action Plan*, 2020/2077(INI)

European Parliament, *European Parliament Resolution of 25 November 2020 on Towards a more sustainable single market for business and consumers*, 2020/2021(INI)

European Parliament, *European Parliament Resolution of 7 April 2022 on the right to repair*, 2022/2515(RSP)

European Parliament, *Right to repair*, January 2022, PE 698.869

European Parliament, *Towards new rules on sales and digital content*, March 2017, PE 599.359

V. Bulgarian Sources. Bulgarian Legislation

Act on Consumer Protection from 09 December 2005, (State Gazette/Durzhaven Vestnik, No. 99/2005, as amended SG, No. 20/2022, 11.03.2022)

Act on the Provision of Financial Services from Distance from 22 December 2006, (State Gazette/Durzhaven Vestnik, No. 105/2006, as amended SG, No. 20/2018, 06.03.2018)

Act on the supply of digital content and digital services and on the sale of goods from 04 March 2021 (State Gazette/Durzhaven Vestnik, No. 23/2021, 19.03.2021)

Commercial Act from 18 June 1991, (State Gazette/Durzhaven Vestnik, No. 48/1991, as amended SG, No. 25/2022, 29.03.2022)

Consumer Credit Act from 05 March 2010 (State Gazette/Durzhaven Vestnik, No. 18/2010, as amended SG, No.104/2020, 8.12.2022)

Draft Act on the supply of digital content and digital services and on the sale of goods from 30 December 2020 (No. 002-01-76, Council of Ministers of the Republic of Bulgaria)

Insurance Code from 29 December 2015, (State Gazette/Durzhaven Vestnik, No. 102/2015, as amended SG, No. 25/2022, 29.03.2022)

Obligations and Contracts Act from 05 December 1950 (State Gazette/Durzhaven Vestnik, No. 2/1950, as amended SG, No. 35/2021, 27.04.2021)

Technical Requirements to Products Act from 1 October 1999 (State Gazette/Durzhaven Vestnik, No. 86/1999, as amended SG, No. 105/2020, 11.12.2020)

Tourism Act from 26 March 2013, (State Gazette/Durzhaven Vestnik, No. 30/2013, as amended SG, No. 21/2021, 12.03.2021)

VI. Bulgarian Sources. Documents of Organs

Republic of Bulgaria, Council of Ministers, *Motives for the establishment of the draft Act on the provision of digital content and digital services and on the sale of goods/Motivi kam proekta na zakon za predostavyane na tsifrovo sadarzhanie i tsifrovi uslugi i za prodazhba na stoki* (published 23 October 2020)

Republic of Bulgaria, Ministry of Economy, *Report on a comprehensive preliminary assessment of the impact of the draft law on the supply of digital content and digital services and on the sale of goods/Doklad ot izvarshena tsyalostna predvaritelna otsenka na vazdeystvieto na proekta na zakon za predostavyane na tsifrovo sadarzhanie i tsifrovi uslugi i za prodazhba na stoki* (September 2020)

Council of Ministers, Portal for public consultations, *Draft Act on the supply of digital content and digital services and on the sale of goods*, (Reference reflecting the proposals and opinions expressed, 23.10.2020), <https://www.strategy.bg/PublicConsultations/View.aspx?@lang=bg-BG&Id=5553> accessed 18.06.2022

Republic of Bulgaria, 44th National Assembly, Commission on Economic Policy and Tourism, *Presentation, discussion and voting of the draft Act on the supply of digital content/digital services and on the sale of goods*, 20.01.2021, Protocol No.101, <https://www.parliament.bg/bg/parliamentarycommittees/2578/steno/6338> accessed 28.03.22

Republic of Bulgaria, 44th National Assembly, Four Hundred and Forty-Seventh Plenary Session, 27.01.2021, Protocol, <https://www.parliament.bg/bg/plenaryst/ns/55/ID/10535> accessed 28.03.22

Bibliography

Republic of Bulgaria, 44th National Assembly, Four Hundred and Sixty-Second Plenary Session, 04.03.2021, Protocol, <https://www.parliament.bg/bg/plenaryst/ns/55/ID/10550> accessed 20.02.22

VII. Bulgarian Sources. Opinions, commentaries, online blogs, online newspaper articles and interviews

Bulgarian Chamber of Commerce and Industry, *Opinion on the Draft Act on the supply of digital content and digital services and on the sale of goods*, (No. 36/02.02.2021) (BCCI opinion)

Active Consumers Association, 'Weekly newsletter'/'Sedmichen byuletin' (2021) 16 Active Consumers Association <https://aktivnipotrebiteli.bg/%D0%BA%D0%B0%D0%BC%D0%BF%D0%B0%D0%BD%D0%B8%D1%8F/310/%D0%91%D1%8E%D0%BB%D0%B5%D1%82%D0%B8%D0%BD-%D0%90%D0%9A%D0%A2%D0%98%D0%92%D0%9D%D0%98-%D0%9F%D0%9E%D0%A2%D0%A0%D0%95%D0%91%D0%98%D0%A2%D0%95%D0%9B%D0%98,-%D0%B1%D1%80.-16,-23.04.2021#> accessed 07.02.2022

LIBRe Foundation, *Opinion on the Draft Act on the supply of digital content and digital services and on the sale of goods*, (No. 143/23.11.2020) (LIBRe Foundation opinion)

Ivan Gergov, Maria Harizanova, 'Bulgaria enacts EU directives on regulated consumer digital environment' (CMS Law-Now™, 13 May 2021) <https://www.cms-lawnow.com/ealerts/2021/05/bulgaria-enacts-eu-directives-on-regulated-consumer-digital-environment?cc_lang=en> accessed 15.01.2022

Radoslava Makshutova, 'New moments in the Act on the supply of digital content and digital services and on the sale of goods'/' Kakvo novo v noviya Zakon za tsifrovite stoki i uslugi' (*Manager News*, 24 March 2021) <https://www.manager.bg/komentari/kakvo-novo-v-noviya-zakon-za-oblaganeto-na-cifrovite-stoki-i-uslugi> accessed 15.01.2022

Radoslava Makshutova, Nikola Stoychev, 'The most important on the new Act on consumer sales'/'Nay-vazhnoto za noviya zakon za potrebitelskite prodazhbi'? (*Capital*, 30 March 2021) <https://www.capital.bg/politika_i_ikonomika/pravo/2021/03/30/4190597_nai-vajnoto_za_noviia_zakon_za_potrebitelskite_prodajbi/> accessed 15.01.2022

Hristo Nikolov interview with Konstantin Raykov (CCP) and Hristo Kapanarov (law firm), 'EU measures will stimulate online commerce between the Member States'/'Merki na ES shte stimulirat onlayn targoviyata mezhdu darzhavite chlenki', (*Business Start/Biznes start*, 04 February 2019) <https://www.bloombergtv.bg/a/16-biznes-start/33541-merki-na-es-shte-stimulirat-onlayn-targoviyata-mezhdu-darzhavite-chlenki> accessed 10.01.2022

Aneliya Toroshanova, interview with Prof. Tanya Yosifova, 'New moments in the Act on the Supply of Digital Content and Digital Services and on the Sale of Goods'/'Novi momenti v Zakona za predostavyane na tsifrovo sadarzhanie I tsifrovi uslugi i za prodazhba na stoki', (*The Law and Themis/Zakonat i Temida*, 14 January 2022) <https://bnr.bg/hristobotev/post/101585903/novi-momenti-v-zakona-za-predostavane-na-cifrovo-sadarjanie-i-cifrovi-uslugi-i-za-prodajba-na-stoki> accessed 22.01.2022

Aneliya Toroshanova, interview with Prof. Tanya Yosifova, 'Digital content and digital services – sellers and consumers'/'Digitalno sadarzhanie i digitalni uslugi – prodavachi i potrebiteli' *(The Law and Themis/Zakonat i Temida*, 26 November 2021) <https://bnr.bg/play/post/101562933/otnosheniata-mejdu-prodavachite-na-digitalno-sadarjanie-i-digitalni-uslugi-i-potrebitelite> accessed 23.01.2022

Aneliya Toroshanova, interview with Prof. Tanya Yosifova, 'The legislative changes in the civil law regulation are innovative and timely'/' Zakonodatelnite promeni v grazhdanskoto pravo sa novatorski i navremenni', *(The Law and Themis/Zakonat i Temida*, 12 February 2021) <https://bnr.bg/post/101420643> accessed 16.02.2022

Denitsa Vateva, 'More rights for consumers: two years warranty and repair within a reasonable time'/'Oshte prava za potrebitelite: Dve godini garantsiya i remont v razumen srok' (*Capital*, 26 March 2021) <https://www.capital.bg/moiat_capital/smart_spending/2021/03/26/4190278_oshte_prava_za_potrebitelite_dve_godini_garanciia_i/> accessed 09.01.2022

VIII. Other Sources

Helen Brown, Julia Hemmings, 'Sustainability Drives New "Right to Repair" Rules for Household Products in Latest Update to EU Ecodesign Legislation' (A blog by Baker McKenzie, 15 November 2019) <https://www.globalcompliancenews.com/2019/11/15/sustainability-drives-new-right-to-repair-rules-household-products-eu-ecodesign-legislation-20191104/> accessed 10.01.22

Digital Europe Trade Association, Digital industry's concerns with the Spanish transposition of the Sales of Goods Directive (2019/771), 01 June 2021 <https://www.digitaleurope.org/resources/digital-industrys-concerns-with-the-spanish-transposition-of-the-sales-of-goods-directive-2019-771/> accessed 16.03.2022

Maria João Pestana de Vasconcelos, 'New perspectives on sale of consumer goods – maximum harmonization and high protection of consumers as a condition for the further development of cross-border trade in single market' (UNIO EU Law Journal, 13 May 2019) <https://officialblogofunio.com/2019/05/13/new-perspectives-on-sale-of-consumer-goods-maximum-harmonization-and-high-protection-of-consumers-as-a-condition-for-the-further-development-of-cross-border-trade-in-single-market/#_edn1> accessed 30.03.2022

Croatia

A. General Remarks 1
B. Definitions and Scope of Application 5
C. Conformity of Goods 8
   I. Subjective and Objective Requirements 9
   II. Durability Requirement 11
   III. Incorrect Installation and Integration and Modification of Digital Content or Digital Service 12
D. Trader's Liability 14
   I. Specific Rules on Single / Long-term Supply of Digital Content and Digital Services 16
   II. General Rules on Impossibility, Force Majeure and Change of Circumstances 20
   III. Right of Redress 21
E. Remedies 23
   I. Repair and Replacement 24
   II. Termination and Withdrawal 26
   III. Restitution in Contracts on Digital Content or Digital Services 27
   IV. Commercial Guarantees 29
F. Time Limits 30
   I. Interruption/Suspension of the Liability Period and Limitation Period 34
   II. Obligation to Notify 36
G. Sustainability and Premature Obsolescence of Goods 37
H. Third Party Rights and Personal Data Protection 41
I. Concluding Remarks 45
   Bibliography 45

A. General Remarks

This national report analysis the implementation of the so-called Twin Directives, namely of the Digital Content Directive[1] (hereinafter: DCD) and of the Sale of Goods Directive[2] (hereinafter: SGD) in Croatia. The Croatian legislator has decided to implement the SGD into the Obligations Act (hereinafter: OA)[3] as the general act on obligations relationships in the Croatian legal system. The DCD has been implemented into the newly adopted special legal Act on certain aspects concerning contracts for the supply of digital content and digital services (hereinafter: DCDA)[4]. It was the initial plan of the Croatian legislator to transpose the Twin Directives jointly into the special legal act on consumer protection,[5] most likely the Consumer Protection Act (hereinafter:

---

[1] Directive (EU) 2019/770 of the European Parliament and of the Council of 20 May 2019 on certain aspects concerning contracts for the supply of digital content and digital services, OJ L 136, 22.5.2019, pp. 1–27.

[2] Directive (EU) 2019/771 of the European Parliament and of the Council of 20 May 2019 on certain aspects concerning contracts for the sale of goods, amending Regulation (EU) 2017/2394 and Directive 2009/22/EC, and repealing Directive 1999/44/EC, OJ L 136, 22.5.2019, pp. 28–50.

[3] Obligations Act (Zakon o obveznim odnosima), OG Nos. 35/05, 41/08, 125/11, 78/15, 29/18 and 126/21.

[4] Act on certain aspects concerning contracts for the supply of digital content and digital services (Zakon o određenim aspektima ugovora o isporuci digitalnog sadržaja i digitalnih usluga), OG No. 110/21.

[5] The Proposal of Legislative Activities of the Ministry of Justice and Public Administration of the Republic of Croatia for 2021 (Prijedlog Plana zakonodavnih aktivnosti Ministarstva pravosuđa i uprave za 2021. godinu), available at: <https://esavjetovanja.gov.hr/Documents/Download?documentId=14870>.

CPA 2014)⁶ as *lex generalis* for consumer protection.⁷ The idea behind this proposal was to achieve more uniformity and to diminish the legal fragmentation of the consumer law in the Croatian legal system. However, the idea was abandoned and in June 2021, two separate legislative proposals for the implementation of the DCD and the SGD have been announced and opened to public discussion.⁸ This report is analysing the proposed and adopted legislative amendments to the OA and the DCDA, which entered in force on January 1, 2022. Where necessary, the report refers to the CPA 2014, which will be replaced by the new CPA 2022 due to alignment with the Omnibus Directive (EU) 2019/2161.⁹ The CPA 2022 enters into force on May 28, 2022 and is partially harmonized with some of the SGD and of the DCD provisions.¹⁰

2   The transposition of the SGD and the DCD did and will have an impact on the Croatian legal system and in particular on the enforcement of law. The legal fragmentation of the Croatian consumer law affects the legal certainty in B2C relationships and undermines the effectiveness of law enforcement. The legislative decision to transpose the SGD and the DCD separately and by introducing new legal acts will increase the level of fragmentation of the consumer law. This causes further issues related to hierarchy and relationships between the legal acts on consumer protection. Although their relationship is regulated by the CPA, the case-law shows issues in the interpretation and enforcement of provisions that are transposed separately and sporadically by different legal acts. In the Croatian legal system, the EU consumer law directives were transposed mainly by the CPA, but also by the OA and other special consumer protection acts.¹¹ According to Art. 4 CPA 2014 and Art. 3 CPA 2022, if not differently regulated by the CPA or special consumer protection acts, the rules of the OA prevail in B2C obligation-law relationships (para. 2). In case of the conflict between the CPA and provisions of special consumer protection acts, the latter prevail (para. 1).

3   Besides the legal fragmentation, there are issues in understanding and interpreting national rules in accordance with the *acquis*. The case-law confirms that judges often interpret and apply national provisions in the spirit and meaning of national civil law concepts rather than EU directives.¹² For instance, the Directive 99/44/EC was transposed into the OA and the scope of application of numerous rules was widened to all obligation-law relationships, including the commercial ones. On the other hand, some of the rules remained strictly applicable to B2C relationships.¹³ The choice of the

---

⁶ Consumer Protection Act (Zakon o zaštiti potrošača), OG Nos. 41/14, 110/15 and 14/19.
⁷ Mišćenić, 'Consumer Protection Law' in Josipović (ed), *Introduction to the Law of Croatia* (2014) 279 (279).
⁸ Proposal of the Act on Amendments of Obligations Act (Prijedlog Zakona o izmjenama i dopunama Zakona o obveznim odnosima), June 2021, available at: <https://www.sabor.hr/sites/default/files/uploads/sabor/2021-06-10/170202/PZE_148.pdf>. Proposal of the Act on certain aspects concerning contracts for the supply of digital content and digital services (Prijedlog Zakona o određenim aspektima ugovora o isporuci digitalnog sadržaja i digitalnih usluga), available at: <https://vlada.gov.hr/UserDocsImages/2016/Sjednice/2021/Lipanj/63%20sjednica%20VRH/63%20-%205.docx>.
⁹ Directive (EU) 2019/2161 of the European Parliament and of the Council of 27 November 2019 amending Council Directive 93/13/EEC and Directives 98/6/EC, 2005/29/EC and 2011/83/EU of the European Parliament and of the Council as regards the better enforcement and modernisation of Union consumer protection rules, OJ L 328, 18.12.2019, pp. 7–28.
¹⁰ Consumer Protection Act (Zakon o zaštiti potrošača), OG No. 19/22, in force from May 28, 2022.
¹¹ Mišćenić, 'Croatian Consumer Protection Law: From Legal Approximation to Legal Fragmentation (Part I)' (2018) 22 *Studia Iuridica Toruniensia*, 189 (189).
¹² Mišćenić, 'Uniform Interpretation of Article 4(2) of UCT Directive in the Context of Consumer Credit Agreements: Is it possible?' (2018) 3 *Revue du droit de l'Union européenne*, 127 (150).
¹³ Čikara, 'Die Angleichung des Verbraucherschutzrechts in der Europäischen Gemeinschaft, Unter besonderer Berücksichtigung des Verbraucherschutzrechtes in der Republik Kroatien' (2007) 28(2) *Zbornik Pravnog fakulteta Sveučilišta u Rijeci*, 1067 (1067 et seq).

legislator was justified by the fact that the OA was regulating the conformity of goods and guarantees even before the harmonization process. Moreover, the minimum level of harmonization enabled widening of the scope of application of Directives' provisions and made the transposition into the OA possible and easier. However, the regulation of conformity of goods was affected by the transposition of amendments to the Directive 99/44/EC introduced by the Consumer Rights Directive 2011/83/EU[14] (hereinafter: CRD). Due to the full targeted harmonization, the rules of the CRD related to the conformity of goods entered the CPA that is applicable only to B2C relationships. As a result, the Croatian civil law regulates the conformity of goods predominantly by the OA, while the rules on passing of risk, delivery of goods and definitions of consumer, consumer sale and guarantees are regulated by the CPA.[15] All in all, the transposition of the SGD mainly by the OA, and the separate transposition of the DCD by a special act, with some of the rules of both directives transposed by the CPA 2022, only contributes to the already existing legal fragmentation and affects adversely the enforcement of consumer law.

Besides of the described impact on the structure of the existing general law of obligation and contracts, as well as on the consumer law, the implemented rules do not affect the structure of already existing laws on the intellectual property and data protection. Unlike the European scholar doctrine that analyses such an impact,[16] there is no developed doctrinal debate on the impact of the Twin Directives on the general theory of contract or contract types. The literature on the Twin Directives is scarce and limited only to certain aspects and issues.[17] The Croatian legislator did not introduce new rules into the OA that would amend the existing rules on contract formation, existence or validity. Art. 5(12) and (13) DCDA emphasize that the DCDA provisions do not affect general consumer rights and the general legal act on obligations relationships related to conclusion, validity, nullity or legal consequences of contract termination, beyond the regulation in the DCDA. To the author's knowledge, there is no developed doctrinal debate on data as a counter-performance referring to relevant provisions of the Twin Directives. The issues related to data protection in consumer relationships are usually addressed in a more general manner, in the context of the GDPR or unfair commercial practices.[18]

B. Definitions and Scope of Application

When it comes to definitions arising under the *acquis*, the Croatian jurisprudence experienced difficulties in interpreting the main consumer-law notions, such as definitions

---

[14] Directive 2011/83/EU of the European Parliament and of the Council of 25 October 2011 on consumer rights, amending Council Directive 93/13/EEC and Directive 1999/44/EC of the European Parliament and of the Council and repealing Council Directive 85/577/EEC and Directive 97/7/EC of the European Parliament and of the Council (Text with EEA relevance) OJ L 304, 22.11.2011, p. 64–88.

[15] Mišćenić, 'Croatian Consumer Protection Law: From Legal Approximation to Legal Fragmentation (Part II)' (2018) 23 *Studia Iuridica Toruniensia*, 177 (185).

[16] Twigg-Flesner, 'Conformity of Goods and Digital Content/Digital Services' in Arroyo and Cámara Lapuente (eds), *El Derecho privado en el nuevo paradigma digital* (Marcial Pons, Barcelona-Madrid 2020); Morais Carvalho, 'Sale of Goods and Supply of Digital Content and Digital Services – Overview of Directives 2019/770 and 2019/771' (2019) 5 *EuCML* 194.

[17] General overview of the novelties introduced by the Twin directives was given by Petric, 'Ugovorna odgovornost prodavatelja' in Mišćenić (ed.), Europsko privatno pravo – Posebni dio (2021) 28 (28 *et seq*).

[18] Mišćenić, 'Protection of Consumers on the EU Digital Single Market: Virtual or Real One?' in Viglianisi Ferraro, Jagielska and Selucka (eds), *The Influence of the European Legislation on National Legal Systems in the Field of Consumer Protection* (2018) 219 (219 *et seq*).

of consumer and trader.[19] These are defined by the CPA, but also by other special legal acts implementing EU Directives, such as the Electronic Communications Act, Consumer Credit Act, Insurance Act etc.[20] All these acts transpose definitions literally by defining consumers as natural persons and traders as all persons (personal criterion), acting outside (consumers), i.e. within (traders) their trade, business, craft or professional activity (functional criterion).[21] Since the case-law shows misinterpretation of these definitions in practice, there might be difficulties in future interpretation of newly introduced concepts by the Twin Directives.[22] Despite of the full targeted harmonization, the newly introduced Art. 399.a OA transposing the main SGD concepts does not contain definitions of the seller, sales contract, goods, goods with digital elements, commercial guarantee etc. Some of these definitions, such as the sales contract and commercial guarantee can be found in Art. 5 CPA 2014 and Art. 4 CPA 2022.

6   The OA transposes definitions of the consumer, producer, digital content and digital service, as well as compatibility, functionality, interoperability, durability, durable medium and free of charge notions (Art. 399.a OA). However, the provisions of the relevant article refer to "things" instead of "goods" of EU directive definitions. It also introduces its own definition of the "consumer contract", as a contract between the consumer and every natural and legal person acting within its trade, business, craft or professional activity, including intermediaries (Art. 399.a(2) OA). When it comes to the "goods with digital elements", these can be found in amended Art. 400 and newly introduced Art. 401.a, 404.a and some other OA provisions, however redefined as the "thing(s) with digital elements". It confirms the legislator's intention to keep in line with the previous regulation, where the rules on conformity of goods and guarantees were applicable to "things".[23] From the onset, both the legislation and the case-law offered higher level of protection to consumers by guaranteeing their rights even in cases of non-conformity of services with the contract.[24] However, the CPA amendments in 2019 limited the protection in B2C relationships to cases of non-conformity of "goods" as tangible movable items.[25] The inconsistency continues in the CPA 2022 that aligns with some of the SGD provisions and refers to "goods" in articles on contract fulfilment and passing of risks

---

[19] Mišćenić and Tomljenović, 'National Report (Croatia)' in Hess and Law (eds), *Implementing EU Consumer Rights by National Procedural Law* (2019) 242 (242).

[20] Mišćenić (fn 11) 191.

[21] Mišćenić (fn 11) 198.

[22] In one of the cases, the competent authority and the court examining the decision of that authority widened the consumer protection to a craftswoman concluding a mobile phone contract within her professional activity. In another case, consumers were deprived of protection related to intermediary contracts. See judgement of the High Administrative Court of the Republic of Croatia of 28 February 2012, Us-3781/2011-4; IUS-INFO – Interpretation of the Ministry – Can a Real Estate Intermediation Agreement be Considered as a Consumer Contract (*Mišljenja ministarstva – Smatra li se ugovor o posredovanju nekretnina potrošačkim ugovorom*).

[23] The latter are understood in a broader sense following the definition of property law, which includes movables and immovables, things in and restricted in commerce, water, gas energy etc. See Art. 2 of the Act on Ownership and Other Real Rights (*Zakon o vlasništvu i drugim stvarnim pravima*) OG Nos. 91/96, 68/98, 137/99, 22/00, 73/00, 129/00, 114/01, 79/06, 141/06, 146/08, 38/09, 153/09, 143/12, and 152/14.

[24] Judgment of the Municipal Court in Varazdin of 18 April 2012, Gz. 339/12-2.

[25] Until amendments of the CPA in February 2019, the protection to consumers was offered in cases of non-conformity of "products", which are defined widely in Art. 5(20) CPA as every good or service, including immovable, rights and obligations. Under Article 4(30) CPA 2022 goods is tangible movable *thing*, with exception of those sold in enforcement or other mandatory proceeding, including water, gas and electricity, when they are sold in limited volume or in a limited quantity and the *thing* with incorporated digital content or digital service or connected to it in such a way that the *goods* would not be functional without the digital content or digital service (»goods with digital elements«). Even within the definition itself, there are noticeable inconsistencies related to the use of terms goods and things.

B. Definitions and Scope of Application

(Art. 47–49).[26] It remains to be seen, which approach is correct and whether the widening to "things" in the OA is consistent with the recital 12 of the SGD preamble.[27] Some of the newly introduced OA provisions suggest that there was no legislative intention to limit the protection of consumers only to cases of non-conformity of goods, but rather the opposite.[28] This can be confirmed by more general rule of Art. 357 OA, according to which the provisions on material and legal defects of things are applicable to all onerous contracts, if not otherwise provided for specific contracts. Differently, the notions contained in the DCD are transposed literally into Art. 3 DCDA, and some into Art. 4 CPA 2022 (e.g. digital content, digital service, functionality, interoperability, compatibility). Although there are no issues arising from the transposition of the main notions into the DCDA, the inconsistency caused by the use of different legal terms in the OA, the CPA and the DCDA will create difficulties in the interpretation and application of consumer-law rules in practice and possibly deprive consumers of their rights in cases of non-conformity.

The Croatian legislator opted to widen the scope of application of the SGD provisions, when transposing it into the national legal order. As explained, the relevant OA provisions are applicable also to other obligation relationships, including the commercial ones. The OA as *lex generalis* for obligation relationships follows the monistic approach and applies to all obligation relationships involving either natural or legal persons or both as parties, covering all types of contracts, both the civil law and the commercial contracts (Art. 14(1) OA). Still, as with the previous harmonization with the Directive 99/44/EC, some of the SGD provisions remain applicable only to B2C relationships.[29] For instance, the provision on duty of examining the thing for visible defects is limited to B2C relationships (Art. 403(4) OA). On the other hand, the rules on remedies in cases of non-conformity are (in principle) applicable to all obligation relationships (Art. 410 OA). Unlike the SGD, Art. 401 OA defines the list of situations in which the non-conformity exists. These are applicable also to B2B contracts, with the exception of para. 4. The latter is applicable only to B2C contracts and refers to consumer awareness or acceptance of the non-conformity in question. The OA provisions harmonized with the SGD and concerning the "thing(s) with digital elements" are restricted to B2C contracts (Arts. 401.a, 404.a OA). Due to literal transposition of the DCD into the DCDA, the latter act is applicable to B2C relationships as provided in Art. 1 on the subject matter and purpose of the DCDA. Finally, the scope of application of provisions of the CPA 2022 related to consumer contractual relationships applies to every contract concluded between a trader and consumer, including: "1. contracts for the supply of heating, water, gas and electric energy, whether or not they are not put up for sale in a limited volume or set quantity; 2. contracts where the trader supplies or undertakes to supply digital content that is not delivered on the tangible medium or a digital service to the consumer, and the consumer does not pay or oblige himself to pay the price, but provides or undertakes to provide personal data to the trader, except where the trader processes personal data provided by the consumer exclusively for the purpose of supplying the digital content that is not delivered on the tangible medium or digital service or for allowing the trader to

---

[26] Art. 47(2) CPA 2022 refers to application of OA provisions on material defects in cases of non-conformity of "goods".
[27] To the author's understanding of the recital 12 SGD, the notion is limited to goods as tangible movable items, with an existing option of the Member States to include also some immovable properties, such as residential buildings.
[28] Such as Art. 400(4) OA regulating the seller's liability in B2C contracts according to rules on sales contracts in case of things to be produced.
[29] Mišćenić (fn 11) 191.

comply with obligations to which the trader is subject, and the trader does not process those data for any other purpose" (Art. 43 CPA 2022).

C. Conformity of Goods

8   The Twin Directives introduced a variety of novelties in relation to the former regulation of the conformity of goods under the former Directive 99/44/EC. As provided by editors' guidelines, the chapter is addressing the subjective and objective requirements, the concept and requirement of durability and the novelties related to incorrect installation and integration and modification of digital content or digital service.

I. Subjective and Objective Requirements

9   Unlike the Directive 99/44/EC that was regulating complex relationship between the general request for conformity of goods and the presumption on conformity, the Twin Directives are distinguishing between subjective and objective requirements for conformity. The subjective requirements, which arise directly from the seller-consumer relationship are adequately transposed by the DCDA. For instance, Art. 8 DCDA transposes literally the subjective requirements from the DCD. On the other hand, Art. 401 OA was amended in order to adapt to subjective requirements of the SGD. However, the provision contains certain derogations. Firstly, the latter concerns the use of already discussed legal term "things" instead of the notion of "goods" from the SGD. Secondly, the provision contains the definition of non-conformity that is opposite to the formulation arising under the former Directive 99/44/EC and the SGD. Unlike directives, which both define when the goods are in conformity with the contract, Art. 401 OA transposes subjective requirements from the SGD by defining the existence of the lack of conformity. For example, under Art. 401(1)(4) OA there is a lack of conformity if "the thing is not supplied with updates as determined by the sales contract". The same approach was taken with respect to objective requirements, which rely on reasonable consumer expectations. These are defined negatively in Art. 401(2) OA. Consequently, the lack of conformity exists, if "the thing is not delivered with additional equipment including packaging, installation instructions or other instructions, as the consumer may reasonably expect to receive" (Art. 401(2)(3) OA). Such legislative regulation could work to the detriment of consumer rights, by limiting their protection only to situations of the non-conformity regulated by the law.

10 Due to literal transposition of the DCD into the DCDA, this did not repeat with respect to objective requirements transposed literally in Art. 9 DCDA. The traders' liability exemption in cases when the consumer failed to install the updates has been transposed literally from Art. 8(3) DCD into Art. 9(3) DCDA. Art 7(4) SGD is also literally transposed within the newly inserted paragraph 3 of Art. 401.a OA titled "Updates to things with digital elements in consumer contracts ". Both the DCDA and the OA regulate the exclusion of the lack of conformity in cases related to "particular characteristic" provided by Art. 8(5) DCD and Art. 7(5) SGD. This exception is literally transposed in Art. 9(5) DCDA and in the amended Art. 401(4) OA. The newly inserted provisions present an improvement with respect to the previous and more general exclusion according to which, the consumer "knew or reasonably should have known" about the lack of conformity. It is considered that the explicit and separate acceptance of the deviation

is a more consumer-friendly solution.³⁰ A similar exclusion of the seller's liability exists in Art. 401.a(4) OA related to "Updates to things with digital elements in consumer contracts ". It concerns cases, where the consumer was informed about "particular characteristic" of a thing deviating from requirements in Art. 401.a(1) and (2) OA and the consumer expressly and separately accepted that deviation when concluding the contract.

II. Durability Requirement

The definition of "durability" is transposed almost literally into the newly introduced Art. 399.a(10) OA as the "ability of things to maintain their functions and working performances through regular use". As explained *supra*, the main difference concerns the use of the notion „things ". Another difference concerns the way in which Art. 7(1)(d) SGD is transposed into Art. 401(2)(4) OA. The latter provision defines the existence of the lack of conformity, "if the thing does not correspond to the quantity or does not possess those features and other characteristics, including those related to durability...normal for the thing of the same type and which the buyer may reasonably expect ...". Such formulation that is opposite to the one arising from the SGD could adversely affect the use of consumer rights in cases of non-conformity of goods/things. In addition, differently than the SGD, the latter provision uses the term "features" instead of the "qualities", and mentions the "buyer" instead of the consumer. This seems to be in line with the recital 21 of the SGD preamble, according to which the Member States remain free to extend the protection afforded to consumers also to natural and legal persons that are not consumers within the meaning of the SGD. Although the definition and the requirement od "durability" is transposed by the OA provisions, there is a lack of awareness on the interaction of the requirement with the product-specific Union legislation (recital 32 SGD). The sustainability and circular economy are still not sufficiently recognized in the Croatian consumer law.³¹ In the Croatian legal system and society, they are still usually linked to other areas of law and policies, such as environment protection or waste management. There is no developed relationship between the product-specific Union legislation related to the achievement of the sustainable consumption and the rules on conformity of goods/things.

11

III. Incorrect Installation and Integration and Modification of Digital Content or Digital Service

Directive's provisions on incorrect installation and integration of the digital content or digital service are transposed almost literally by the OA and the DCDA. As regulated by the SGD and the DCD, incorrect installation results in lack of conformity of things, where the latter depends upon the installation duty. If the installation duty was on the seller or performed by a person under his control and the installation duty forms part of the sales contract, the incorrect installation will be regarded as a lack of conformity (Art. 401(2)(5) OA). The result will be the same, if the duty was on the consumer, but the incorrect installation resulted from poor installation instructions that are unclear to an average consumer. Under Art. 401(2)(6) OA incorrect installation is a lack of conformity even if the "buyer" was obliged to install the thing under the sales contract, but the in-

12

---

³⁰ Petrić (fn 17) 56.
³¹ Mišćenić, 'Sustainability, the Circular Economy and Consumer Law in Croatia' (2020) 4, *EuCML*, 172 (172–178).

correct installation resulted from shortcomings in installation instructions provided by the seller or supplier of the digital content or digital service. However, the trader will be exempted from liability in cases of consumer failure to install the updates (Art. 401.a(3) OA; Art 9(3) DCDA). Provisions concerning the incorrect integration of the digital content or digital service are transposed literally from Art. 9 DCD into Art. 10 DCDA. According to this article, the incorrect integration of the digital content or digital service will result in a lack of conformity if these were integrated by the trader or under his responsibility or they were intended to be integrated by the consumer, but there were shortcomings in the instructions provided by the trader.

13   Art. 19 DCD on modification of digital content or digital service is transposed literally into Art. 20 DCDA. However, these rules do not tackle the modification of things/goods, which cannot be found in the OA provisions transposing the SGD. When it comes to modification of the digital content or digital service, under Art. 20 DCDA the trader is allowed to modify them beyond what is necessary to maintain the digital content or digital service in conformity under certain conditions. According to these conditions the modification is allowed if the contract provides a valid reason for it (a), the modification is made without additional costs for the consumer (b), the consumer was informed about the modification in clear and comprehensive manner (c) and the consumer (in cases referred to in the following paragraphs 2 and 3) is informed in a reasonable time period before the modification of the features and the moment of modification and of the right to terminate the contract or of the possibility of keeping the digital content or digital service without such a modification (d). Under paragraph 2, the consumer has the right to terminate the contract if the modification affects negatively his access to or the use of the digital content or digital service, unless the negative impact is minor. In that case, paragraph 3 regulates the right of the consumer to termination of the contract free of charge within 30 days from receiving the information or from the moment of modification. These paragraphs are not applicable, if the trader has enabled the consumer to maintain, without additional costs, the digital content or digital service without modification and if these remain in conformity.

D. Trader's Liability

14   According to rules on the trader's liability, the seller is liable for material defects of things existing at the moment of passing of risk to the buyer (Art. 400(1) OA), and for those material defects that appeared after that moment, if they are the consequence of the cause existing prior to it (Art. 400(2) OA). The passing of risk in B2C relationships is regulated by the CPA as the moment in which the goods are transferred into consumer's possession or possession of the person determined by the consumer, such as the chosen delivery company (Art. 45 CPA 2014; Art. 49 CPA 2022). The trader's pre-contractual information duties include a transparent information on the existence of a legal guarantee of conformity of goods and digital content and digital services and on the existence of a commercial guarantee, where applicable, as well as information on functionality, interoperability and compatibility of goods with digital elements, digital content and digital services (Arts. 46 and 60 CPA 2022). It is presumed that every lack of conformity that demonstrated itself within one year from the moment of passing of risk, existed at that moment, unless the seller proves otherwise or it arises differently from the nature of the thing or of the defect (Art. 400(9) OA). As previously, there are several exceptions to the rules on seller's liability, such as the exclusion in case of public statements (Art. 401(3) OA), the newly introduced exclusion in case of the particular notice (Art. 401(4) OA;

D. Trader's Liability

Art. 9(5) DCDA), and the exclusion in case of buyer's unconsciousness that is not applicable to B2C relationships (Art. 402 OA). Of particular relevance is the provision of non-binding nature of contractual provisions limiting or excluding the liability of the trader in cases of non-conformity of things towards consumers (Art. 408(3) OA).

The following lines of the report are focused on specific novelties introduced by the Twin Directives related to a single or long-term supply of digital content and digital services and the right of redress. Moreover, the recital 14 DCD allows the Member States to regulate freely "the consequences of a failure to supply, or of a lack of conformity of, digital content or a digital service, where such failure to supply or lack of conformity is due to an impediment beyond the control of the trader and where the trader could not be expected to have avoided or overcome the impediment or its consequences, such as in the event of force majeure". Therefore, the report is also referring to general OA rules excluding trader's liability in cases of force majeure, impossibility and the change of circumstances.

I. Specific Rules on Single / Long-term Supply of Digital Content and Digital Services

Provisions on trader's liability related to a single or long-term supply of digital content and digital services are transposed literally from Art. 11 DCD into Art. 12 DCDA. The trader is liable for any failure of their supply in accordance with Art. 6 DCDA (Art. 12(1) DCDA). In cases of a single or a series of individual acts of supply, the trader is liable for any lack of conformity under Arts. 8, 9 and 10 DCDA, which exists at the time of supply (Art. 12(2) DCDA). The trader is liable for two years from the moment of delivery without prejudice to Art. 9(2)(b) DCDA (Art. 12(3) DCDA). The latter provision refers to trader's duty to inform the consumer on updates related to a single or a series acts of supply (Art. 9(2)(b) DCDA). In cases of continuous supply during a certain time period, the trader is liable for the lack of conformity under Arts. 8, 9, 10 DCDA that becomes apparent during the time period in which the digital content and digital service must be delivered in accordance with the contract (Art. 12(4) DCDA). The burden of proof related to the supply of digital content and digital services is on the trader (Art. 13(1) DCDA). The following paragraphs transpose literally the DCD rules on the burden of proof. As the DCD, Arts. 13(2) and (3) DCDA distinguish between two situations in which lack of conformity becomes apparent within a year or within the time period during which the digital content or digital service is to be supplied. The reversal of the burden of proof to consumer appears in situations, when the consumer fails to cooperate with respect to consumer's digital environment (Art. 13(7) DCDA).

Corresponding provisions of the SGD can be found in the OA rules on "thing(s) with digital elements". Under Art. 400(11) OA in consumer contracts on sale of thing(s) with digital elements in which there is a continuous supply of the digital content or digital service, the burden of proof that there is no lack of conformity is on the seller and lasts for two years from the moment of passing of risk. In cases in which the continuous supply lasts more than two years, the burden of proof is on the seller for the whole time of the agreed supply period. This provision corresponds to Art. 11(3) SGD on the burden of proof in sales contracts providing for continuous supply of the digital content or service over a period of time. Other specific provisions can be found in the newly inserted Art. 401.a OA on "Updates to things with digital elements in consumer contracts", which provides for rules related to duty on updates in contracts on continuous supply of digital content or digital service. Here, the seller's liability is excluded, if the consumer was informed about "particular characteristic" of the thing deviating from requirements set in Art. 401.a(1) and (2) OA and if the consumer expressly and separately accepted the deviation when concluding the contract (Art 401.a(4) OA).

18   Further on, the newly inserted Art. 404.a OA on "Lack of conformity in things with digital elements in continuous supply of digital content or digital service in consumer contracts" regulates the time limits of the seller's liability. In cases of contracts related to continuous supply for a time period longer than two years, the seller is liable for a lack of conformity that appeared during the time period agreed for the supply under the sales contract (Art. 404.a(1) OA). If the period is shorter, than the seller is liable for a lack of conformity that appears within two years from the moment of passing of risk (Art. 404.a(2) OA). The provisions correspond to the SGD's provisions on liability of the seller (Art. 10 SGD). Consequently, the SGD's provisions on goods with digital elements, where the sales contract provides for a continuous supply of the digital content or digital service (Arts. 10 and 11 SGD) can be found scattered across the OA in an unruly manner. While the burden of proof is regulated in Art. 400(11) OA on material defects for which the seller is liable, the seller's liability is regulated far more behind in the newly inserted Art. 404.a OA. This unfortunate choice of order of OA provisions transposing the SGD will render the understanding, interpretation and enforcement of these provisions difficult in practice.

19   There is no provision explicitly regulating the interruption of long-term supply of digital content or digital services. Therefore, the general rules on conformity apply to these types of contracts (Arts. 8 and 9 DCDA), including Art. 9(4) and (6) DCDA. Under Art. 9(4) DCDA, if a continuous supply of digital content or digital services is agreed for a specific time period, the digital content or digital services must be in conformity during the whole period. If contractual parties do not agree otherwise, the digital content or digital services are to be supplied in the latest version available at the moment of the contract conclusion (Art. 9(6) DCDA). Following the explanation from recital 51 DCD, the interruptions of supply should be treated as lack of conformity, if those are more than negligible or recur.

II. General Rules on Impossibility, Force Majeure and Change of Circumstances

20   The consequences of a failure to perform in cases of impossibility of performance or *force majeure* are regulated by general OA provisions applicable to obligation relationships. According to Art. 343 OA on *force majeure*, the debtor is free from damage liability, if he proves that he could not perform his obligation, i.e., if he was late in performance due to external, extraordinary and unpredictable circumstances that occurred after the contract conclusion, and which he was not able to prevent, remove or avoid. The rules on change of circumstances (lat. *rebus sic stantibus*) are regulated in Arts. 369 – 372 OA on "Alteration or Rescission of the Contract Due to the Changed Circumstances". If due to extraordinary circumstances, which occurred after the contract had been concluded and which were not foreseeable at the time of the contract conclusion, performance of obligation would become excessively onerous or inflict excessive loss to one contracting party, then this party can request alteration or even rescission of the contract (Art. 369(1) OA). The party cannot put forward such a request, if it was obliged to take these circumstances into account at the time of the contract conclusion, or could have avoided them or overcome them (Art. 369(2) OA). If one party demands rescission of the contract, the contract will not be rescinded, if the other party offers or accepts the

alteration of the relevant contractual term in a just manner (Art. 369(4) OA). Art. 370 OA regulates the duty of the entitled party to inform the other party about the intention to use the right to alter or to rescind the contract as soon as it finds out that such circumstances took effect. If the party omits to inform the other party of its intention, the party will be held liable for the damage caused to the other party by not informing it in time of the request (Art. 370 OA). The parties can agree in advance to waive the right to invoke certain changed circumstances, unless it is against the principle of consciousness and honesty (Art. 372 OA). The latter principle corresponds to the good faith principle.[32] When deciding on alteration or rescission of the contract, the court shall be guided by this principle and take into account the purpose of the contract, division of risks arising under the contract or law, duration and effects of extraordinary circumstances and interests of both parties (Art. 371 OA).[33] The rules on change of circumstances are followed by Arts. 373–374 OA regulating the impossibility of performance. When the performance of one party to the bilateral obligation contract became impossible due to extraordinary external events that occurred after conclusion of the contract and before the obligation is due, and the events were not foreseeable at the time of contract conclusion and neither party could have prevented, avoided or removed them, nor is responsible for them, the obligation of the other party also ceases to exist (Art. 373(1) OA). If the party has fulfilled some of its obligation, it can request the return by invoking the restitution rules in cases of unjust enrichment (Art. 373(1) OA). In case of a partial impossibility of performance due to events for which none of the parties is responsible, the other party can rescind the contract, if the partial performance does not correspond to its needs (Art. 373(2) OA). Otherwise, the contract stays in force and the other party has the right to request proportional reduction of its obligation (Art. 373(2) OA). Art. 374 OA regulates the impossibility to perform a contractual obligation due to an event for which the other party is responsible.

III. Right of Redress

Art. 20 DCD on the right of redress is transposed literally into Art. 21 DCDA regulating the right of the trader to a legal protection: "Where the trader is liable to the consumer because of any failure to supply the digital content or digital service, or because of a lack of conformity resulting from an act or omission by a person in previous links of the chain of transactions, the trader shall be entitled to pursue remedies against the person or persons liable in the chain of commercial transactions, in accordance with the general act on obligations law." The last part of the provision refers to the OA and legal remedies available under OA provisions, such as the right of reimbursement/regress, damage compensation etc.

The OA introduced Art. 422.a OA on "Liability for material defects in the chain of supply". The article regulates the relationship between the seller and the previous seller in the chain, the seller's liability in the case of non-conformity of things and sets time limit, within which the liability of the previous seller ceases to exist. Under Art 422.a(4) OA the previous seller is not liable for material defects for which the seller is liable to the buyer, if more than two years passed from the moment of passing of risk from the previ-

---

[32] Šarčević and Čikara, 'European vs. National Terminology in Croatian Legislation Transposing EU Directives' in Šarčević (ed), *Legal Language in Action: Translation, Terminology, Drafting and Procedural Issues*, (2009) 193 (193).

[33] Tomljenović, Mišćenić and Kunda, 'Croatia' in Baaij, Macgregor and Cabrelli (eds), *The Interpretation of Commercial Contracts in European Private Law* (2020) 87 (87).

ous seller to the seller. However, the previous seller and the seller can agree on other time limits, exclusions, limitations or extensions of liability (Art 422.a(5) OA). As opposed to Art. 18 SGD, Art. 422.a OA does not mention the lack of conformity resulting from an act or omission, including omitting to provide updates to goods with digital elements. It covers all these situations by referring to the buyer's rights resulting from the lack of conformity against the seller, who is entitled to enforce the rights against the previous seller on the ground of OA provisions on liability for material defects.

E. Remedies

23   Before transposing the current SGD, provisions of the OA and the CPA allowed the choice between the legal remedies available to the consumer in cases of non-conformity. According to *ex* Art. 410 OA, the buyer could choose among repair, replacement, price reduction and contract termination.[34] Additionally, the buyer could and still can require the damage compensation, according to general provisions on the compensation of damage, including the damage suffered on other goods due to the material defect of things (Art. 410(2) OA). The provisions made clear that the contract rescission is the last resort and can only be performed if the trader was previously given reasonable and additional time to fulfil the contractual obligations (Arts. 411–412 OA).[35] The introduction of provisions on the proportionality or disproportionality is a novelty, since these rules were not transposed by the directive 1999/44/EC and the judges were ruling by applying of the principle of consciousness and honesty (i.e., the good faith principle). Another novelty is a stricter division between the first and the second chain of remedies, which was not completely clear under the previous regulation.[36] Moreover, the OA transposed Art. 13(6) SGD on remedies, according to which the buyer has the right to withhold the payment of any of the unpaid parts of the price, until the seller does not fulfil his obligations on the ground of liability for material defects (Art. 410(6) OA). The provision does not foresee any further modalities or conditions for the exercise of the right to withhold a payment. The DCDA does not contain a rule according to which the consumer can withhold a payment of the price or part of it, until the digital content or digital service has been brought into conformity with the contract (recital 15 DCD). The OA provisions on other civil law remedies are adequately applicable to B2C obligation relationships. If not otherwise regulated by the CPA or special consumer protection acts, the OA rules prevail in B2C obligation relationships (Art. 4(2) CPA; Art. 3(2) CPA 2022).

I. Repair and Replacement

24   The current rules replicate the SGD and therefore prioritize the repair and replacement, but not the repair over the replacement.[37] Arts. 13–14 SGD are transposed literally into Arts. 410–410.a OA, including the conditions under which the remedies can be exercised. Consequently, the "buyer" can choose between the repair and replacement, unless the chosen remedy is impossible or disproportionate in costs (Art. 410(3) OA). The chosen remedy will be carried out free of charge, within a reasonable time period and

---

[34] Mišćenić (fn 15) 185 *et seq.*
[35] Petric (fn 17) 28 *et seq.*
[36] Čadjenović et al., *EU Consumer Contract Law, Civil Law Forum for South East Europe-Collection of studies and analyses* (2010) 529.
[37] Augenhofer, 'ELI's Response to the European Commission's Public Consultation on Sustainable Consumption of Goods – Promoting Repair and Reuse', *European Law Institute*, 2022, 16.

E. Remedies

without any significant inconvenience to the buyer (Art. 410.a(1) OA). Although the OA rules do not foresee specific provisions on the costs of transport in the case of repair or replacement of goods/things, the latter must be "free of charge". This is required both by general provision on remedies in cases of non-conformity (Art. 410(9) OA) and those addressing the repair and replacement (Art. 410a(1) OA). According to Art. 410(9) OA, the seller bears the costs of removing the defect and delivering the other thing without the defect, while the repair or replacement of the thing with the defect is free of charge under Art. 410a(1) OA. The latter notion is to be interpreted in accordance with the settled CJEU case-law,[38] as covering the costs incurred in order to bring the goods in conformity with the contract.[39]

The regulation of the place of delivery and the place of repair and replacement is left to the national law (recital 56 SGD). The more general provision of Art. 14(2) SGD on making things available to the seller is transposed literally into Art. 410.a(2) OA. The OA regulates the delivery of things in sales contracts in Arts. 389–399, irrespective of provisions transposing the SGD. According to these provisions, the seller is obliged to deliver the thing to the buyer in the place agreed in the contract, and if the place is not determined, in the place of seller's seat or residence existing when signing the contract. There are also general provisions on the place of fulfilment, i.e., performance in Arts. 178–179 OA. According to these rules the debtor of the performance is obliged to fulfil the obligation and the creditor to receive it in the place determined by the legal transaction or law (Art. 178(1) OA). If the place is not determined or determinable from the goal or the nature of the obligation, or other circumstances, in that case the obligation is to be fulfilled in the place where the debtor was seated or resided (place of domicile or residence) during the time when the obligation occurred (Art. 178(2) OA). Therefore, in cases in which the seller is the debtor of the performance, i.e., obligation under the sales contract, the general rules favour the seller rather than the consumer. This can further be supported by the CPA rules, which contain the corresponding provision on the fulfilment of the contract in B2C relationships. According to the latter, the trader is obliged to fulfil the contract in accordance with the contract provisions, the rules of the CPA and of the legal act regulating obligation relationships (Art. 43(1) CPA; Art. 47(1) CPA 2022).

II. Termination and Withdrawal

The provisions on the right of termination through declaration (Art. 15 DCD; Art 16(1) SGD) are both literally transposed into Art. 16(1) DCDA and Art. 413.a OA. According to Art. 413.a OA, if the seller does not fulfil the consumer contract in the additional reasonable period of time, the consumer is entitled to terminate the sales contract by means of a statement to the seller. Under Art. 16(1) DCDA, the consumer realizes the right to terminate the contract by a statement expressing the decision to terminate the contract. These newly introduced provisions do not deviate from general OA rules according to which, if one party does not fulfil its contract obligations, the other party has the right to terminate the contract by a simple statement, if the rescission does not occur by the law itself (Art. 360 OA). For instance, in cases where the fulfilment of the obligation is an essential element of the contract and the creditor requested fulfilment, that did not occur within a reasonable period of time, he can terminate the con-

---

[38] CJEU, Case C-404/06, 17.04.2008, *Quelle*, ECLI:EU:C:2008:231, paras. 31–34; CJEU, joined cases C-65/09 and C-87/09, 16.06.2011, *Gebr. Weber and Putz*, ECLI:EU:C:2011:396, para 46.

[39] On the interpretation of the "free of charge" notion see Miščenić, *Europsko privatno pravo: Opći dio* (Skolska knjiga, Zagreb 2019) 169 and 212.

tract by a statement (Art. 361(3) OA).⁴⁰ The provisions setting the conditions for the termination/rescission of the sales contract as a remedy are foreseen by Arts. 412–413 OA. According to these provisions the buyer can terminate the contract only if the seller was given additional and adequate time to fulfil the contract, with exception of situations in which the seller announced that he will not be able to fulfil the contract, or this is obvious under the given circumstances, and in cases when the buyer cannot realize the purpose of the sales contract (Arts. 412(2) OA). If the seller is unable to fulfil the sales contract within the additional time period, the termination/rescission occurs by the law, but the buyer may decide to keep it in force. The same is applicable to cases, where the fulfilment within the specific deadline is an essential element of the contract (Art. 413 OA). To some amount these provisions reflect solutions from Art. 18 CRD that has been partially implemented by Art. 44 CPA 2014 and Art. 48 CPA 2022.

The CPA 2022 provisions on the right of withdrawal, which are approximated with the CRD rules on the right of withdrawal for distance and off-premisses contracts were amended and to some extent are now harmonized with Arts. 16 and 17 DCD on obligations of the trader and of the consumer in the event of termination. Art. 83 (6)–(9) CPA 2022 repeat trader's obligations related to the use of any content other than personal data, which was provided or created by the consumer when using digital content or digital services that are discussed below under Art. 17(3) DCDA. Consequently, the newly introduced provisions are transposing the DCD rules on termination into the CPA articles on the legal consequences and traders and consumers obligations in case of the right of withdrawal. It seems to the author that the legislator confused the right to terminate the contract with the consumers' right of withdrawal. When it comes to the withdrawal of the consent for processing of personal data, there are no specific rules regulating the contractual consequences. The matter is regulated by the GDPR and the consumer's right to terminate the contract should be without prejudice to consumer's right to withdraw the consent for the processing of personal data (recital 39 DCD preamble). The latter consumer's right applies also to contracts covered by the DCDA (Art. 17(3) DCDA).

III. Restitution in Contracts on Digital Content or Digital Services

27   The provisions of the DCDA transpose Arts. 16–19 DCD literally, including the rules on the restitution. Under Art. 17(1) DCDA the trader must reimburse all the sums paid by the consumer on the ground of the contract. In cases where the supply is provided in exchange for a payment over a period of time and the digital content or digital service was in conformity for a period of time prior to contract termination, only a proportionate part of the price is due (Art. 17(2) DCDA). After the termination of the contract the consumer cannot use the digital content or digital service and make it available to third parties (Art. 18(1) DCDA). If the digital content was supplied on a tangible medium, the consumer shall return it to the trader without undue delay and at the expenses of the trader (Art. 18(2) DCDA). According to Art. 19 DCDA on trader's obligations and time limits, the trader is obliged to reimburse any amount owed to the consumer without undue delay or at latest within 14 days from being informed about the consumer's request for a price reduction or contract termination. The trader reimburses the paid amount by using the same means of payment that was used by the consumer to pay for the digital content or digital services (Art. 19(2) DCDA). The trader cannot calculate any fee for the return of the paid amount (Art. 19(3) DCDA).

---

⁴⁰ On different forms of termination of legal transactions in the Croatian law *see* Slakoper, Mihelcic, Belanic, Tot, Obvezno pravo, Opći dio s uvodom u privatno pravo (Informator, Zagreb 2022) 765–796.

There are no particular rules related to restitution in cases of supply of the digital 28
content or digital service in exchange for consumer's personal data as a counter performance. Provisions reflect the DCD rules and consequently refer to the trader's duty to comply with the obligations applicable under the GDPR in respect of the consumer's personal data (Art. 17(3) DCDA). There is a set of rules replicating the DCD provisions on the use of any content other than personal data, which was provided or created by the consumer in Art. 17(4) DCDA. The trader shall refrain from using that content, except where such content has no use outside the context of supplying digital content or digital service (a); only relates to consumer's activity when using the digital content or digital service (b); has been aggregated with other trader's data and cannot be disaggregated or only with disproportionate efforts (c); or has been generated jointly by the consumer and other persons, and other consumers may continue to use it (d) (Art. 17(4) DCDA). With exception of cases under (a), (b) and (c), the trader is obliged to make available to the consumer at his request any content other than personal data, which was provided or created by the consumer when using the digital content or digital service (Art. 17(5) DCDA). The consumer has the right to retrieve that content free of charge, without limitations imposed by the trader, within the reasonable time period and in the commonly used machine-readable format (Art. 17(6) DCDA). Corresponding provisions can be found in Art. 83 CPA 2022 on the right to unilaterally terminate the contract.

IV. Commercial Guarantees

The OA transposed literally the rules on commercial guarantees. Art. 423(1) OA de- 29
fines the commercial guarantee as "every obligation by which the seller or producer (guarantee offeror), in addition to seller's legal obligation on material defects of things, obliges to return the price paid to the buyer or to replace, fix or service the thing, if it does not satisfy the conditions from the guarantee statement or relevant advertising material available at the moment or before conclusion of the contract". The latter definition corresponds to definition of the commercial guarantee regulated in the CPA as the "guarantee of the rightness of the sold thing" (Art. 5(4) CPA 2014; Art. 4(8) CPA 2022). However, we still witness the inconsistent use of legal terms "goods" and "things" describing the object of the sales contract and commercial guarantee under the CPA. The SGD provisions on less advantageous conditions (Art. 423(7) OA), producer's liability during the entire period of the commercial guarantee of durability (Art. 423(3) OA), and more favourable conditions in the commercial guarantee of durability (Art. 423(4) OA) are adequately transposed. Art. 423(9) OA reproduces Art. 17(2) SGD on the content of the commercial guarantee statement and requires the use of plain and intelligible language. The option provided for in Art. 17(4) SGD was not used with respect to language requirements, but previous provisions on commercial guarantees are maintained. The latter concern the use of remedies (Arts. 424 and 426 OA), prolongation of the guarantee period (Art. 425 OA), expenses and risks (Art. 427 OA), several liability (Art. 428 OA) and the limitation period (Art. 429 OA). The only exception is the beginning of the guarantee period in case of replacement or essential repair of the thing from the moment of replacement or returning of the repaired thing regulated in Art. 425(2) OA.

F. Time Limits

Differently than other SGD provisions, the provisions on time limits are not literally 30
transposed. Instead, the legislator decided to keep the previous OA rules on time limits,

which suffer from certain inconsistencies. According to Art. 10(1) SGD the seller is liable for any lack of conformity which exists at the time of goods delivery and becomes apparent within two years from that time. These requirements can be found in four different provisions of the OA, thus rendering the rules difficult to follow and in turn apply and interpret in practice. Under Art. 400 OA the seller is liable for material defects of things existing at the moment of passing of risk to the buyer (Art. 400(1) OA), and for those material defects that appeared after that moment, if they are the consequence of the cause existing prior to it (Art. 400(2) OA). The moment of passing of risk in B2C relationships is regulated by the CPA, as the moment in which the "goods" were transferred into the possession of the consumer or the person determined by the consumer (Art. 45 CPA 2014; Art. 49 CPA 2022).

31   The second part of Art. 10 SGD can be found in Arts. 403 and 404 OA on visible and hidden material defects. Under Art. 403(4) OA in B2C contracts, the consumer as the buyer is not obliged to inspect the thing, but is obliged to inform the seller about the existence of visible defects within the two months from the day of discovery of the defect and at latest within two years from passing of risk to the consumer. With respect to hidden defects, the seller is not liable for defects that appear after two years from the moment of the thing's delivery (Art. 404(2) OA). The time period is shorter for second-hand things, where the parties can agree on the one-year period (Art. 404(3) OA) or prolong the agreed time period (Art. 404(4) OA).

32   The time limits in cases of continuous supply of digital content or digital service are transposed literally by the newly introduced OA provisions. Under Art. 404.a OA the seller is liable for the lack of conformity that appeared during the time period agreed for the supply under the sales contract (Art. 404.a(1) OA). If the period is shorter, than the seller is liable for the lack of conformity that appears within two years from the moment of passing of risk (Art. 404.a(2) OA). However, in case of repair, replacement or similar actions, the time limits from Art. 403 and 404 OA begin to run from the delivery of the repaired thing, replacement of parts and similar (Art. 405 OA). In accordance with the SGD, the period in which the burden of proof is on the seller that needs to demonstrate that the product is in conformity, is prolonged from six months to one year (Art. 400(9) OA), with the exception of commercial contracts (Art. 400(10) OA). Finally, Art. 422 OA prescribes the preclusion period of two years from timely informing the seller of the defect in which the buyer may enforce his rights.

33   As with other DCD provisions, the provisions on time limits are transposed literally. In case of a single or a series of individual acts of supply, the trader is liable for any lack of conformity under Arts. 8, 9 and 10 DCDA, which exists at the time of supply (Art. 12(2) DCDA). The trader is liable for two years from the moment of delivery without prejudice to Art. 9(2)(b) DCDA (Art. 12(3) DCDA). In cases of continuous supply during a certain time period, the trader is liable for the lack of conformity under Arts. 8, 9, 10 DCDA, that becomes apparent during the time period in which the digital content and digital service must be delivered in accordance with the contract (Art. 12(4) DCDA).

I. Interruption/Suspension of the Liability Period and Limitation Period

34   The Croatian legislator decided to keep in place the former OA provisions under Arts. 403 and 404 OA prescribing the time limits for invoking the visible and hidden material defects of thing against the seller. If due to the lack of conformity, the thing needs to be repaired, replaced in whole or just in parts or similar, the time limits start to

run from the moment of the delivery of the repaired thing, replacement of parts etc (Art. 405 OA). As allowed under Art. 10(4) and (5) SGD, the OA prescribes the preclusion period in Art. 422(1) OA, according to which the buyer's rights expire after two years from the day of notifying the seller of the detected defect. Since, according to the rules on time limits, the consumer as the buyer can inform the seller at latest within the objective time period of two years from passing of the risk to the consumer (Art. 403(4) OA), and the preclusion period is two years from informing the seller, it means that the consumer can reach up to four years within which he can exercise his rights.

The general OA rules on limitation period, interruption or suspension can be found in Arts. 214–246. The general limitation period is five years from the moment of the maturity of claims (Art. 225 OA) with the exception of one year period for certain services (e.g., electricity, gas, water etc) and different periods for insurance contracts (Art. 234 OA). The shorter period of three years is applicable to periodic claims that are due annually or in shorter periods (Art. 226 OA). The general limitation period is applicable to all obligation relationships, if not prescribed otherwise.[41]

35

II. Obligation to Notify

As allowed by Art. 12 SGD, the legislator decided to keep the rule on the time period within which the consumer is obliged to notify the seller about the existence of the material defect of the thing (Art. 403(4) OA). This OA provision is the result of harmonizing with the former Directive 99/44/EC. Differently than directives and the CJEU's interpretation in the *Faber* case,[42] Art. 403(4) OA prescribes two months within which the consumer is obliged to inform the seller about detected material defects.[43] Both directives prescribe the period "not shorter than two months" from the date when the consumer detected the lack of conformity. However, the obligation to notify can be exercised within the objective time period, i.e., at the latest within two years from passing of the risk to the consumer (Art. 403(4) OA). The same is repeated in provisions on the hidden material defects, where the buyer is obliged, "under the threat of losing his rights", to inform the seller of the defect within two months from the day of discovering the defect (Art. 404(1) OA).

36

G. Sustainability and Premature Obsolescence of Goods

In Croatia, there is no developed doctrinal debate on the relationship between the non-conformity, the sustainability and the circular economy.[44] The relevance of these valuable goals is still not recognized in the Croatian consumer law and policy. However, there are rulings in the existing case-law confirming that average consumers rather chose the repair over the replacement.[45] When implementing the Twin Directives, the legislator introduced new provisions on time limits that might eventually contribute to realization of the sustainability goals. According to Art. 405 OA, in case of repair and

37

---

[41] Slakoper, Mihelcic, Belanic, Tot (fn 40) 218.
[42] CJEU, Case C-497/13, 04.06.2015, *Faber*, ECLI:EU:C:2015:357, para. 65: "(...) provided that that consumer has a period of not less than two months from the date on which he detected that lack of conformity to give that notification."
[43] Mišćenić (fn 15) 185 *et seq.*
[44] Mišćenić (fn 31) 172. See also Kryla–Cudna, 'Sales Contracts and the Circular Economy' (2020) 6, *ERPL*, 1207 (1207).
[45] Judgement of the High Administrative Court of 15 March 2017, Usž 36372016–2.

replacement or similar actions, the time limits from Art. 403 and 404 OA begin to run from the delivery of the repaired thing, replacement of parts and similar actions. In case of commercial guarantees, the guarantee period is the starting over from the moment of replacement, i.e., returning of the repaired thing in case of replacement or essential repair of the thing (Art. 425(2) OA). These provisions might encourage consumers to choose the repair over the replacement of the goods, and producers to produce higher quality products in order to avoid the costs of constant repairing of things.

38 In relation to sustainability, one should also mention the rules on spare parts contained in the Act on Energy Efficiency (hereinafter: AEE)[46] and the relevant by-laws.[47] The rules are transposing the requirements of the Ecodesign Directive 2009/125/EC,[48] such as the information on availability of spare parts. The AEE provisions refer to consumer protection in several articles[49] and prescribe sanctions in form of financial penalties and supervision of the state inspectorate (Arts. 35–41.b AEE). Private-law remedies are not foreseen. Although there is no specific legislation on spare parts, the more general consumer protection rules on trader information duties can be found in the CPA. Articles transposing Art. 5 and 6 of the CRD on pre-contractual and contractual information regulate the trader's duty to inform the consumer about the main characteristics of goods, returning policy etc., without explicitly referring to spare parts. Other CPA provisions concern the transposition of the Directive 2005/29/EC[50] and its rules on misleading commercial practices related to service, spare parts, replacement or repair (Art. 33 CPA 2014; Art. 35 CPA 2022).

39 Although the premature or planned obsolescence of goods is not in the focus of national consumer law, the *acquis* introduced the rules addressing this important issue. Besides mentioned AEE provisions, the relevant provisions can be found both in the OA and the CPA. In transposing the SGD, the OA introduced provisions on durability (Art. 399.a(10) OA) and functionality of things (Art. 399.a(7) OA), including the objective requirements of conformity (Art. 401(2)(4) OA) and the rules on commercial guarantees (Art. 423 OA). Consequently, the material defect exists, if the thing does not have "features and other characteristics" related to durability, functionality, compatibility and security, which the buyer can reasonably expect with respect to the nature of things and public statements made by the seller or other persons in the transaction chain (Art. 401(2)(4) OA). The requirements of Art. 17 SGD on commercial guarantees of durability for certain things are adequately transposed by Art. 423(3) and (4) OA. Therefore, the violation of the objective requirement on durability due to premature obsolescence of goods may result in the non-conformity against which the consumer can invoke his/her rights.

40 The violation of these rules in B2C relationships is sanctioned by financial penalties and supervised by the state inspectorate (Art. 137(3)(4), (5) and (6), Art. 138(1)(48),

---

[46] Act on Energy Efficiency (Zakon o energetskoj učinkovitosti), OG Nos. 127/14, 116/18, 25/20, 32/21 and 41/21.

[47] Ordinance on setting of eco-design requirements for energy-related products (Pravilnik o utvrđivanju zahtjeva za eko-dizajn proizvoda povezanih s energijom), OG No. 50/15.

[48] Directive 2009/125/EC of the European Parliament and of the Council of 21 October 2009 establishing a framework for the setting of eco-design requirements for energy-related products, OJ L 285, 31.10.2009, pp. 10–35, as amended by Directive 2012/27/EU on energy efficiency.

[49] Arts. 1, 3, 13, 16, 18, 34 and 35 AEE.

[50] Directive 2005/29/EC of the European Parliament and of the Council of 11 May 2005 concerning unfair business-to-consumer commercial practices in the internal market and amending Council Directive 84/450/EEC, Directives 97/7/EC, 98/27/EC and 2002/65/EC of the European Parliament and of the Council and Regulation (EC) No 2006/2004 of the European Parliament and of the Council ('Unfair Commercial Practices Directive'), OJ L 149, 11.6.2005, pp. 22–39.

(49) and (50) CPA 2014; Art. 148(3)(5), (6) and (7) Art. 149(1)(50), (51) and (52) CPA 2022). While the financial penalties vary from 10.000,00 to 200.000,00 Croatian Kuna, the inspectors may order the removal of established violations within the set deadline. The relationship with rules on unfair commercial practices is rather weak, since the enforcement of these rules is not satisfactory in practice.[51] However, the rules transposing the Directive 2005/29/EC and the Omnibus Directive (EU) 2019/2161 regulate that misleading the consumer with respect to essential information about the product, such as basic characteristics and conditions related to contract fulfilment, can result in misleading commercial practices and be sanctioned (Arts. 33 and 34 CPA 2014; Arts. 35 and 36 CPA 2022). For instance, the misleading commercial practices may occur in relation to the existence or the nature of the product, its essential characteristics, the need for repair or replacement, spare parts or servicing, consumer rights on the ground of non-conformity. The sanctions include financial penalties and the state inspectorate supervision (Art. 137 and 138 CPA 2014; Art. 148 and 149 CPA 2022), as well as the damage liability introduced by the CPA 2022 (Art. 41 CPA 2022).

H. Third Party Rights and Personal Data Protection

41 The rules on third-party rights are transposed literally by the DCDA. The literal transposition of Art. 9 SGD into the OA was avoided, because of the general rule on liability in cases of material or legal defects related to contract performance. According to paragraphs 1 and 2 of Art. 357 OA in cases of onerous contracts, every contractor is liable for material and legal defects of the performance and is obliged to protect the other party from rights and demands of third parties that would limit or exclude the other party's right. According to paragraph 3, provisions of the OA on material and legal defects, i.e., on non-conformity adequately apply to these liabilities, if not otherwise provided for specific contracts. Art. 357 OA therefore seems to cover the content of Art. 9 SGD on third-party rights.

42 There are further and more specific rules on third-party rights and rights of the buyer (Arts. 430–434 OA). In these cases, the buyer is obliged to inform the seller about it, except in cases when the seller is aware of the third-party right, and to require the seller to free the thing from rights or demands of the third person within reasonable time period or to deliver another thing without legal defect (in case of things determined by the genus) (Art. 431 OA). If the seller does not fulfil the request and the thing is taken away from the buyer, the contract is terminated *ex lege*, while in cases of limitation of buyer's rights, the buyer can choose between termination of the contract or adequate price reduction (Art. 432(1) OA). If the purpose of the contract cannot be fulfilled because of third-party rights and the seller has not fulfilled the buyer's request within reasonable period of time, the buyer can terminate the contract (Art. 432(2) OA).

43 Art. 10 DCD is transposed almost literally into Art. 11 DCDA.[52] According to this provision, in cases of violations of third-party rights the consumer is entitled to legal remedies related to non-conformity from Art. 15 DCDA. The latter provision corresponds to Art. 14 DCD and prescribes the rights of consumer in cases of non-conformity, such as: bringing the digital content or digital service into conformity within a rea-

---

[51] Mišćenić and Mamilović, 'Nepoštena poslovna praksa u hrvatskome pravnom sustavu: uređenje i provedba' (2019) 10 *Godišnjak Akademije pravnih znanosti Hrvatske*, 273 (273).

[52] On issues related to Art. 10 DCD *see* Oprysk, 'Digital Consumer Contract Law without Prejudice to Copyright: EU Digital Content Directive, Reasonable Consumer Expectations and Competition', (2021) *GRUR International*, 1 (1–14).

sonable time, free of charge and without any significant inconvenience to the consumer; proportionate reduction of the price or termination of the contract in certain prescribed cases and if the lack of conformity is not minor. The last part of the sentence excluding consumer rights in cases of national rules on nullity or rescission of the contract for the supply of the digital content or digital services in such cases (Art. 10 DCD), was not transposed. To the author's knowledge, the OA amendments and the DCDA do not contain specific provisions on resale of digital content. This matter is to be addressed by application of the relevant rules on intellectual property rights in connection with the civil law rules of the OA. According to intellectual property law, there are limitations to the use of digital contents set by the licence agreement concluded with an end user (recital 53 DCD).[53] However, the DCDA does not refer to rules of the Act on Intellectual Property and Related Rights.[54]

44 The rules on consumer's personal data are transposed by provisions of the DCDA. Art. 3(h) DCDA defines the notion of personal data by referring to the GDPR. According to its Art. 5(2), the DCDA is applicable to contracts where the trader supplies or undertakes to supply digital content or digital service to the consumer, and the consumer provides or undertakes to provide personal data to the trader with the exception of trader processing the data for the purpose of supplying the digital content or digital service in accordance with this Act or in order to comply with legal requirements and is not processing the data for any other purpose. The provision can also be found in Art. 43(2) CPA 2022 regulating the scope of application of the chapter on consumer contractual relationships. Art. 5(11) DCDA replicates Art. 3(8) DCD and prescribes the application of the Union law on data protection for all data processed in relation to contracts for the supply of digital content or digital services. There is another relevant provision, which is transposed literally from Art. 16(2) DCD and which requires compliance with the GDPR (Art. 17(3) DCDA/Art. 83(5) CPA). Art. 17(3) DCDA requires traders to be compliant with the obligations applicable under Regulation (EU) 2016/679. The enforcement of these provisions is supervised by the competent state inspectorate authority (Arts. 23 and 24 DCDA). Due to the lack of other specific rules in the DCDA, the matter is to be addressed by the application of the relevant rules of the GDPR.[55] Additionally, Art. 11 CPA 2022 prohibits traders to give consumer's personal data to third parties without previous consumer's consent in accordance with the rules on data protection. In case of the conflict between provisions of the DCDA and the Union law on data protection, the latter prevails.

I. Concluding Remarks

45 In conclusion, it can be established that the implementation of the Twin Directives into the Croatian law is far from being optimal. The main issues concern the inconsistency and legal fragmentation of important institutes on the non-conformity that are regulated by the OA and partially by the CPA. Despite of the targeted full harmonisation

---

[53] See European Parliament, *Scope of Application and General Approach of the New Rules for Contracts in the Digital Environment*, Directorate-General for International Polices, Policy Department C: Citizens' Rights and Constitutional Affairs, 2016, p. 7; Geiregat, 'Copyright Meets Consumer Data Portability Rights: Inevitable Friction between IP and the Remedies in the Digital Content Directive' (2022) 71(6) *GRUR International* 495–515.

[54] Act on Intellectual Property and Related Rights (Zakon o autorskom i srodnim pravima) OG No. 111/21.

[55] Mišćenić and Hoffmann, 'The Role of Opening Clauses in Harmonisation of EU Law: Example of the EU's General Data Protection Regulation (GDPR)' (2020) 4 *ECLIC* 44–61.

approach, several of the SGD definitions were not transposed by the OA, while some concepts can be found in the CPA and regulated more thoroughly in the OA. The widening of the scope of application of the SGD provisions in the national regulation opened a serious question related to the scope of consumer rights in cases of the non-conformity. The separate implementation of the Twin Directives contributed to the legal fragmentation of the consumer law. While the DCD has been transposed literally into the newly adopted DCDA and partially into the CPA, the transposition of the SGD caused plenty of issues affecting the structure and the regulation of the non-conformity of goods/things in the Croatian legal system. The created mixture of national provisions on the non-conformity, some of which are applicable to all obligation relationships, while others are limited only to B2C relationships and their separate regulation within three different legal acts, namely the OA, the CPA, and the DCDA will certainly adversely affect the enforcement of consumer law in Croatia.[56]

Bibliography

Susanne Augenhofer, 'ELI's Response to the European Commission's Public Consultation on Sustainable Consumption of Goods – Promoting Repair and Reuse' (2022) *European Law Institute*, 2022, 1–20

Zvezdan Čadjenović, Emilia Čikara, Jadranka Dabović Anastasovska, Nada Dollani, Nenad Gavrilović, Marija Karanikić Mirić, Zlatan Meškić and Neda Zdraveva, *EU Consumer Contract Law, Civil Law Forum for South East Europe-Collection of studies and analyses* (Jugoslovenski pregled, Beograd 2010)

Emilia Čikara, 'Die Angleichung des Verbraucherschutzrechts in der Europäischen Gemeinschaft, Unter besonderer Berücksichtigung des Verbraucherschutzrechtes in der Republik Kroatien' (2007) 28(2) *Zbornik Pravnog fakulteta Sveučilišta u Rijeci*, 1067–1112

Katarzyna Kryla-Cudna, 'Sales Contracts and the Circular Economy' (2020) 6, *European Review of Private Law (EPRL)*, 1207–1230

Simon Geiregat, 'Copyright Meets Consumer Data Portability Rights: Inevitable Friction between IP and the Remedies in the Digital Content Directive' (2022) 71(6) *GRUR International* 495–515

Emilia Mišćenić, 'Consumer Protection Law' in: Tatjana Josipović (ed), *Introduction to the Law of Croatia* (Kluwer Law International/Alphen aan den Rijn 2014) 279–290

Emilia Mišćenić, 'Croatian Consumer Protection Law: From Legal Approximation to Legal Fragmentation (Part I)' (2018) 22 *Studia Iuridica Toruniensia*, 189–223 and (Part II)' (2018) 23 *Studia Iuridica Toruniensia*, 177–201

Emilia Mišćenić, 'Uniform Interpretation of Article 4(2) of UCT Directive in the Context of Consumer Credit Agreements: Is it possible?' (2018) 3 *Revue du droit de l'Union européenne*, 127–159

Emilia Mišćenić, 'Protection of Consumers on the EU Digital Single Market: Virtual or Real One?' in Angelo Viglianisi Ferraro, Monika Jagielska and Marketa Selucka (eds), *The Influence of the European Legislation on National Legal Systems in the Field of Consumer Protection* (Wolters Kluwer, Cedam 2018)

Emilia Mišćenić and Vesna Tomljenović, 'National Report (Croatia)' in Burkhard Hess and Stephanie Law (eds), *Implementing EU Consumer Rights by National Procedural Law* (Beck/Hart/Nomos, München 2019)

Emilia Mišćenić, *Europsko privatno pravo: Opći dio (European Private Law: General Part)* (Skolska knjiga, Zagreb 2019)

---

[56] Mišćenić, 'The Effectiveness of Judicial Enforcement of the EU Consumer Protection Law', in: Meškić et al. (eds.), *Balkan Yearbook of European and International Law* (Springer 2020), 129–153.

Emilia Mišćenić and Iva Mamilović, 'Nepoštena poslovna praksa u hrvatskome pravnom sustavu: uređenje i provedba' (Unfair Commercial Practices in the Croatian Legal System: Regulation and Enforcement) (2019) 10 *Godišnjak Akademije pravnih znanosti Hrvatske,* 273-299

Emilia Mišćenić, 'The Effectiveness of Judicial Enforcement of the EU Consumer Protection Law', in: Meškić Zlatan et al. (eds.), *Balkan Yearbook of European and International Law* (Springer 2020), 129-153

Emilia Mišćenić, 'Sustainability, the Circular Economy and Consumer Law in Croatia' (2020) 4, *Journal of European Consumer and Market Law (EuCML)* 172-178

Emilia Mišćenić and Anna-Lena Hoffmann, 'The Role of Opening Clauses in Harmonization of EU Law: Example of the EU's General Data Protection Regulation (GDPR)' (2020) 4 *EU and comparative law issues and challenges series (ECLIC),* 44-61

Jorge Morais Carvalho, 'Sale of Goods and Supply of Digital Content and Digital Services – Overview of Directives 2019/770 and 2019/771' (2019) 5, *Journal of European Consumer and Market Law* (*EuCML*) 194-201

Lilia Oprysk, 'Digital Consumer Contract Law without Prejudice to Copyright: EU Digital Content Directive, Reasonable Consumer Expectations and Competition', (2021) *GRUR International,* 1-14

Silvija Petric, 'Ugovorna odgovornost prodavatelja' (Seller's contractual liability) in Emilia Mišćenić (ed.), Europsko privatno pravo – Posebni dio (European Private Law – Special Part) (Skolska knjiga, Zagreb 2021)

Susan Šarčević and Emilia Čikara, 'European vs. National Terminology in Croatian Legislation Transposing EU Directives' in Susan Šarčević (ed), *Legal Language in Action: Translation, Terminology, Drafting and Procedural Issues,* (Globus, Zagreb 2009)

Zvonimir Slakoper, Gabrijela Mihelcic, Loris Belanic, Ivan Tot, Obvezno pravo, Opći dio s uvodom u privatno pravo (Obligations Law, General Part with the Introduction into the private Law) (Informator Zagreb 2022)

Vesna Tomljenović, Emilia Mišćenić and Ivana Kunda, 'Croatia' in Jaap Cornelius Baaij, Laura Macgregor and David Cabrelli (eds), *The Interpretation of Commercial Contracts in European Private Law* (Intersentia, Cambridge/Antwerp/Chicago 2020)

Christian Twigg-Flesner, 'Conformity of Goods and Digital Content/Digital Services' in Esther Arroyo Amayuelas and Sergio Cámara Lapuente (eds), *El Derecho privado en el nuevo paradigma digital* (Marcial Pons, Barcelona-Madrid 2020)

Cyprus

A.	Introduction. General Framework	1
B.	The Reach and Limits of the Twin Laws	15
C.	Definitions	27
D.	Conformity with the Contract	30
E.	Liability of the Trader, Burden of Proof and Time Limits	44
F.	Remedies for the Failure to Supply and Remedies for the Lack of Conformity	56
G.	Commercial Guarantees	68
H.	Right of Redress	69
I.	Enforcement	70
	Bibliography	70

A. Introduction. General Framework

The EU Directives 2019/770 (SGD) and 2019/771 (DCD) have been transposed into the Cypriot legal order by the Certain Aspects Concerning Contracts for the Sale of Goods Law of 2021 (Law 154(I)/2021) and the Certain Aspects Concerning Contracts for the Supply of Digital Content and Digital Services Law of 2021, (Law 155(I)/2021) respectively. Just like the Directives, the two Laws have passed on the same day and can be regarded as the dizygotic twin laws, which came to modernize and complement the law on consumer contracts. 1

Doubtless, this modernization and addition to the relevant legal landscape was warranted both at EU and at national level. The Consumer Sales Directive (CSD)[1] that had been regulating consumer sales dated back to 1999, whereas dramatic technological advancements of the last two decades have resulted in increased product sophistication, which in turn created new ways in which goods may fail, thereby frustrating consumer expectations. Said advancements, and more generally, the experience of the use of new and innovative products have also unearthed new needs to which goods have to be able to respond to; interoperability with other goods is one such example. The proliferation of goods with digital elements sums all these developments up and the rules on said goods are the main addition to the consumer *acquis* brought by the SGD. 2

On the other hand, the regulation of digital content (and digital service) contracts was notoriously absent from the EU consumer protection regime. The Consumer Rights Directive (CRD)[2] provides for information duties and the right of withdrawal, particularly in relation to distance and off-the-premises contracts among others of digital content and services, including digital services, but does not touch upon substantive contractual matters, such as contractual breaches and remedies.[3] The DCD came to 3

---

[1] Directive 1999/44/EC of the European Parliament and of the Council of 25 May 1999 on certain aspects of the sale of consumer goods and associated guarantees.

[2] Directive 2011/83/EU of the European Parliament and of the Council of 25 October 2011 on consumer rights, amending Council Directive 93/13/EEC and Directive 1999/44/EC of the European Parliament and of the Council and repealing Council Directive 85/577/EEC and Directive 97/7/EC of the European Parliament and of the Council Text with EEA relevance.

[3] For analysis of this legislative measure, see Markou, C., 2017. Directive 2011/83/EU of the European Parliament and of the Council of 25 October. In *EU Regulation of E-Commerce: a Commentary* (pp. 177–229). Edward Elgar Publishing and Markou, C., 2022. Directive 2011/83/EU of the European Parliament and of the Council of 25 October. In *EU Regulation of E-Commerce* (pp. 151–221). Edward Elgar Publishing.

fill in this regulatory gap and has wisely included within its scope the new breed of contracts, which have conquered the online world, namely the contracts in the context of which the consumer effectively 'pays' with personal data (instead of with money or other traditional monetary means, such as coupons). Though the rules in the DCD, particularly as far as digital services are concerned, have resulted in a paradox in the sense that EU contract law now contains substantive rules on *digital* services but not on services in general, i.e., non-digital services (or traditional) services, the twin Directives are most certainly very positive legal developments.

4   The benefit has not only been to the digital (internal) market, which has been the main aim behind their inception,[4] but also to consumer protection in individual Member States, especially those, such as Cyprus. Cyprus owes most, if not all of its consumer protection law to the consumer acquis. Unsurprisingly therefore, up until January 2022 when the rules transposing the SGD came into force, consumer contracts for the sale of goods were subject to the law implementing the Directive 99/44/EC, namely Law 7(I)/2000[5] with no amendments since its inception in 2000. By the same token, there were no contract law rules specifically governing digital content and/or digital services contracts, though as far as these are concerned, Cyprus does not seem to have been the exception;[6] most other Member States lacked relevant rules too.

5   Contract law rules covering *all* sales of goods, i.e., both consumer and business-to-business ones, also existed (and still exist) in the Sales of Goods Law of 1994, Law 10(I)/94, which is largely a reproduction of the (UK) Sale of Goods Act 1979. The relationship between Law 10(I)/94 and the aforementioned Law 7(I)/2000 governing consumer sales (now replaced by the Law 154(I)/2021 transposing the SGD), was somewhat complicated, though Law 7(I)/2000 was clearly *lex specialis*.[7] Law 10(I)/94 operates as *lex specialis* to the Contracts Law, Cap.149, a Colonial law, which up until to date is the general contract law in Cyprus acting as the *lex generalis*.[8] Neither Law 10(I)/94 nor Cap.149 contain any provisions specific to goods with digital elements, digital content or digital services. Such provisions now exist in the twin Laws, which together with Law 10(I)/94 and Cap.149 (in conjunction with common law[9]) largely comprise the law of contracts in Cyprus.

6   Both twin Laws make their relationship with Cap.149 explicit by stating that they apply without prejudice to the Contracts Law, especially its rules on the validity, conclusion or effect of a contract, including the consequences of termination, to the extent that said laws do not regulate general terms of the law of contracts.[10] Both Laws also explicitly

---

[4] Recitals 1–2 DCD and Recitals 1–4 SGD.

[5] The Law on Certain Aspects of the Sale of Consumer Goods and Related Guarantees Law of 2000 (7 (I) / 2000).

[6] Apart from the UK which is now not part of the EU anyway, prior to the DCD, most Member States lacked contract law rules on digital content and services, see Giliker P., 'Legislating on Contracts for the Supply of Digital Content and Services: An EU/UK/Irish Divide?' (2021) 2 *Journal of Business Law*, 143 (144–145), available at: https://research-information.bris.ac.uk/ws/portalfiles/portal/263625155/2021_JBL_2_Art_3_Giliker_Proof2amended.pdf.

[7] See below paras 8–9.

[8] This is stated clearly in Section 3 of Law 10(I)/94 according to which Cap.149 applies to the sale of goods, to the extent that is not inconsistent with the express provisions of the Law 10(I)/94.

[9] Common law constitutes part of the Cypriot legal order and is applicable in Cyprus when there is no other provision in Cyprus legislation, see Section 29 para. 3 subpara. c, Court Law of 1960, Law 14/60.

[10] Section 4 para. 2 Law 154(I)/2021 and Section 3 para. 7 Law 155(I)/2021. In fact, the wording above is utilized in Law 155(I)/2021. Law 154(I)/2021 utilizes a slightly different wording which conveys the meaning more accurately. More specifically, it finishes with the phrase "to the extent that no special provision is made in the present law" instead of the "to the extent that the present law does not regulate general terms of the law of contracts".

clarify that they apply without prejudice to the provisions of the Defective Products (Civil Liability) Law. Said Law copies the Product Liability Directive[11] and therefore, belongs in the area of non-contractual obligations (civil wrongs). The twin Laws do not thus in any way affect the particular law which performs a totally different purpose affording consumers and non-consumers the right to seek different remedies for totally types of harm largely against different parties, namely the producer and the importer.[12]

More necessary was for Law 154(I)/2021 to refer to its relationship with Law 10(I)/94 given that these two laws both regulate sales of goods and Law 10(I)/94 does not exclude from its scope consumer contracts. Just like Law 154(I)/2021, Law 10(I)/94 provides for certain implied contract terms, such as that the goods must be of acceptable quality and lays down remedies for when the goods do not comply with said terms. The question thus arises as to which of the two set of rules will apply to a consumer contract.

Law 7(I)/2000, based on the now repealed 1999 Consumer Sales Directive (CSD), did contain an explicit reference to Law 10(I)/94 stating that the latter continued to apply except to the extent that it was incompatible or in conflict with its own express provisions.[13] Yet, when two laws largely regulate the same thing in a very similar manner, it is difficult for them to co-apply. It is equally difficult to ascertain whether they are in conflict with one another. For example, there were differences in the remedies provided by said two laws.[14] Did that count as an incompatibility between the two or could the remedies laid down in Law 10(I)/94 be considered additional to those provided by Law 7(I)/2000? These questions were never explicitly answered by the Cyprus courts. In fact, the minimal case law on Law 7(I)/2000 seems to suggest that relevant cases were often examined under both Law 10(I)/94 and Law 7(I)/2000. One court expressly opined that the provisions of Law 10(I)/94 are not incompatible with those of Law 7(I)/2000 and therefore, both had to be considered as applicable.[15] In another case, the court applied both laws reaching the same outcome, namely that the plaintiff was entitled to terminate the contract; it happened in that case that the consumer unsuccessfully sought replacement first.[16] It would be interesting to see how the matter would have been dealt with if the consumer was entitled to terminate the contract under Law 10(I)/94 but not under Law 7(I)/2000.

Given that the 1999 Directive was a minimum harmonization one, a solution would be to apply Law 7(I)/2000, which was specific to consumer contracts together with all of the provisions of Law 10(I)/94 governing matters either not covered by Law 7(I)/2000 at all or going beyond them, thereby increasing the level of consumer protection. As already mentioned, this is not the approach followed by the courts and there were also cases in which certain provisions of the one law were examined in combination with some provisions of the other, such combinations often being difficult to explain; for example, in one case, the court opined that the question whether the goods were

---

[11] Council Directive 85/374/EEC of 25 July 1985 on the approximation of the laws, regulations and administrative provisions of the Member States concerning liability for defective products.

[12] The seller is liable only under specific limited circumstances, specifically as provided in Art. 3 para. 3 of the Product Liability Directive. The corresponding law in Cyprus has not been utilized often and there is little experience with its application, see Emilianides and Markou, *IEL Tort Law: Cyprus* (2021), paras 257–265.

[13] Section 15 Law 7(I)/2000.

[14] Law 10(I)/94 provided for a right to reject the goods and terminate the contract without first having to claim repair or replacement, a remedy that was unavailable under Law 7(I)/2000.

[15] *Gonergy Limited v. Michael Barrett*, civil action no. 399/08, 27.9.2013. Notably this is a case in which Law 7(I)/2000 was in reality inapplicable as it involved a business-to-business contract and not a consumer contract.

[16] *Mariou Dimitriou v. MTN Cyprus Limited*, civil action no. 5085/08, 24.11.2014.

defective (or not in conformity) was not answered by Law 7(I)/2000 and that therefore resort to Law 10(I)/94 was merited.[17]

10   Law 154(I)/2021 somewhat simplifies matters. As it transposes a maximum harmonization Directive, it should be considered exhaustively to govern all the matters it seeks to regulate in relation to consumer contracts, Law 10(I)/94 retaining a role in this context only with regard to matters which Law 154(I)/2021 does not touch at all, such as the rights of unpaid sellers, or which have explicitly been left to the Member States and have been addressed in Law 154(I)/2021 in a manner not incompatible with Law 10(I)/94 (in which case the two laws can apply together complementing one another). This in reality simplifies the legal regime relating to consumer sales and is expected to limit the confusion observed in previous case law, though it would be desirable that the relationship with Law 10(I)/94 was explicitly clarified in Law 154(I)/2021.

11   Importantly, Cyprus contract law was ready to accommodate the implicit recognition in Law 155(I)/2021 that contracts in the context of which the consumer offers personal data as counter-performance can be valid and binding. Indeed, 'consideration' under Cap.149 can be any action or abstinence from action as well as a promise for any action or abstinence,[18] which is lawful, that is, it is not legally prohibited, fraudulent or injurious to others and has not been deemed by a court to be immoral or contrary to public policy.[19] Any possibility of a court finding that personal data as contractual consideration is contrary to public policy has now been significantly reduced (despite the fact that said approach is at odds with the right to data protection as a human right in the European legal landscape[20]); such a finding would inevitably result in the contracts regulated by Law 155(I)/2021 being considered as void and Law 155(I)/2021 effectively a useless piece of legislation.[21] Though the DCD does not obligate Member States to accept these contracts as valid,[22] the existence of a law (Law 155(I)/2021), especially one coming from the EU, regulating such contracts in detail coupled with the absence of incomparable obstacles to contract validity under national contract law, make it highly unlikely that Cypriot courts will dare such a finding.

12   As Cyprus contract law was ready to absorb this important development, Law 155(I)/2021 does not (and did not have to) contain any new rules on contract formation or validity, the ones contained in Cap.149 being suitable to apply to this type of contracts too. Notably, Law 10(I)/94 does define price as "the monetary consideration for the sale of goods", yet said Law is clearly not applicable to (digital) services and as already hinted, it could not be considered as applicable to digital content either.[23] In this regard, a clash

---

[17] *Diexodos Ltd v. Dan-Form ApS*, civil action no. 7233/11, 14.4.2020. In reality, similar provisions regarding the need of goods to be of certain quality also existed in Law 7(I)/2000, the reference to "defectiveness" being fallible too, as Law 7(I)/2000 was not concerned with defective goods and did not utilize the relevant term at all.

[18] Section 2 para. 2 subpara. d. Cap.149.

[19] Section 23 Cap.149.

[20] The right to data protection is safeguarded by Article 8 of the Charter of Fundamental Rights of the European Union. See European Data Protection Supervisor, Opinion 4/2017 on the Proposal for a Directive on certain aspects concerning contracts for the supply of digital content, 7–10 who saw a friction between personal data as part of a contractual exchange and among others, the right to data protection. See also Morais Carvalho, 'Sale of Goods and Supply of Digital Content and Digital Services – Overview of Directives 2019/770 and 2019/771', (2019), 8(5), *Journal of European Consumer and Market Law*, 194, 197 who answers the relevant criticism and argues that contractual rights for consumer protection and compliance with data protection rules are not mutually exclusiv.

[21] By virtue of Section 23 Cap.149 when the consideration is unlawful, the relevant contract is void.

[22] Recital 24 of the DCD provides that "… Member States should however remain free to determine whether the requirements for the formation, existence and validity of a contract under national law are fulfilled".

[23] Supra at paras 4–5.

with Law 155(I)/2021 is avoided. Notably however, the absence of a definition of the term 'price' from the SGD is difficult to explain especially given that Recital 23 of the DCD recognizes that "Digital representations of value such as electronic vouchers or e-coupons are used by consumers to pay for different *goods or services* in the digital single market".[24] Moreover, the decision not include said definition in the SGD, unlike in the DCD, may unnecessarily cast doubt on whether electronic vouchers or e-coupons are recognized as methods of payment for the purposes of the SGD.

13 As already stated, the DCD and SGD have been introduced in Cyprus as two separate and independent pieces of legislation. Interestingly, in 2021, the Consumer Protection Law of 2021, Law 112(I)/2021 was introduced to bring several different consumer protection laws into one *multi-law* purporting to unifying, modernizing, and codifying them. Said laws, seven (7) in number, are all harmonizing laws except one[25] and include Law 7(I)/2000 implementing Directive 99/44/EC. The provisions of said law have, with certain relatively minor changes mostly relating to consumer remedies, been incorporated in Law 112(I)/2021, which has thus abolished Law 7(I)/2000. However, these provisions of Law 112(I)/2021, more specifically its Part V titled "Guarantees" will not get to be utilized, as those matters are now governed by Law 154(I)/2021 transposing the SGD. Unfortunately, both Law 112(I)/2021 and Law 154(I)/2021 are silent as to their relationship. It seems that this undesirable duplication of laws has most probably been unintended; Law 112(I)/2021 has been underway since 2017, i.e., before the inception of the SGD in 2019, so Part V must have been inserted in the draft Law 112(I)/2021 long before Law 154(I)/2021 transposing the SGD came into the picture (even in a draft form).

14 The result is that there are currently two sets of rules on consumer sales of goods causing uncertainty. Doubtless, Law 154(I)/2021, being more recent and implementing a positive harmonization EU Directive, prevails. Moreover, as these lines are being written, a draft amendment law removing Part V of Law 112(I)/2021 is pending before the Cypriot legislator so any confusion will be swept away. Of course, there may be other issues with Law 112(I)/2021. Though outside the scope of this report, one should mention the inclusion in said law of the rules transposing the Misleading and Comparative Advertising Directive[26] previously existing in separate legislation.[27] The result is that those rules which largely apply to business-to-business relationships[28] (with the exception of just one provision, namely the one on comparative advertising which extends to business-to-consumer ones[29]), now exist in Law 112(I)/2021, which is titled the Consumer Protection Law. At the same time, the same law does not include crucial consumer protection measures, such as those transposing the twin Directives. With this in mind, Law 112(I)/2021 does not really achieve its purpose of bringing together all main consumer protection measures.

---

[24] Emphasis added.
[25] The Conditions for the Sale of Goods at a Discount Law, Law 30(I)/90 as amended.
[26] Directive 2006/114/EC of the European Parliament and of the Council of 12 December 2006 concerning misleading and comparative advertising (codified version) (Text with EEA relevance).
[27] The Control of Misleading and Comparative Advertising Law, Law 92(I)/2000.
[28] Section 9 Law 112(I)/2021.
[29] Section 12 Law 112(I)/2021.

B. The Reach and Limits of the Twin Laws

15 Though Member States had the opportunity to extend the rules of the twin Laws to cover certain legal persons or natural persons acting in a professional capacity,[30] Cyprus has not taken up this opportunity. Accordingly, the term 'consumer' is defined restrictively along the lines of the corresponding definitions in Articles 2(6) and 2(2) of the DCD and SGD respectively. This achieves consistency with the rest of the consumer protection legislation in Cyprus including the aforementioned recent multi-law, which adopts the exact same definition. At the same time however, business-to-business contracts for the supply of digital content and services remain unregulated. By the same token, the regulation of non-consumer contracts for the sale of goods lacks the specific and technology-adapted provisions of the SGD and is left to the 'old and tired' sales of goods law incepted at a time when goods with digital elements were simply non-existent.

16 In fact, given the absence of regulation on digital content and services contracts,[31] the provisions of Law 155(I)/2021 could smoothly be made more widely applicable to cover all relevant contracts, including business-to-business ones. This is especially true given that said Law (and Law 154(I)/2021) allows the parties some escape route from the objective criteria of conformity.[32] A question could arise regarding whether certain modifications on the (reversal of the) burden of proof provisions should be made to avoid an overly paternalistic approach in a business context, though it could be argued that the providers of peculiar or sophisticated and technology-based products often stand in a stronger position *vis-à-vis* the other contracting party, whether said party is a consumer or another business.

17 Of course, given Law 10(I)/94 that applies to *all* sales of goods, including business-to-business ones, the extension of Law 154(I)/2021 to these contracts, would necessitate some work to bring it in line with the provisions of Law 10(I)/94, thereby avoiding inconsistencies and confusion. A solution would be to replace the provisions of Law 10(I)/94 on all matters regulated by Law 154(I)/2021 with the corresponding provisions of the latter law, leaving the rest of the provisions of Law 10(I)/94 intact. That would also correct the current issue of these two set of rules applying concurrently to consumer contracts.

18 Notably, neither the twin Laws nor any other piece of consumer protection legislation contains any specific reference to dual purpose contracts and the definition of 'consumer' in their context, so the matter has been left to the courts. The decision of the EU legislator to leave the matter to the Member States,[33] thereby deviating from the approach it has adopted in the context of the Consumer Rights Directive, where it is stated that a consumer acting partly for a professional or commercial purpose and partly for a personal one should be regarded as a 'consumer' if the non-personal purpose

---

[30] Recital 16 DCD and Recital 21 SGD.

[31] Law 10(I)/94 applies to 'goods' defined by Section 2 para. 1 as moveable property including shares and securities which does not automatically exclude digital content such as music or software. The definition is not confined to *tangible* moveable property. For a similar question that is being discussed by reference to the term 'product' in the Product Liability Directive, which is also defined as 'any moveable', see Markou, *Consumer Protection, Automated Shopping Platforms and EU Law* (2019), 93, 202. However, to date, there has been no application of Law 10(I)/94 to digital goods in Cyprus case law. Nor the question as to its applicable to relevant contracts has ever been raised or discussed. Moreover, according to English case law, the corresponding (UK) Sales of Goods Act 1979 does not apply to software not supplied on a durable medium. In this respect, it is safe to argue that contracts for the supply of digital content is not regulated in Cyprus.

[32] Section 7 para. 5 Law 154(I)/2021 and Law 155(I)/2021.

[33] Recital 17 DCD and Recital 22 SGD.

is not predominant,[34] may cause undesirable (and difficult to explain) outcomes. More specifically, the same person in the context of the same contract may be regarded a consumer for the purposes of the CRD but not for the purposes of the DCD and/or the SGD.[35] However, given the absence of an explicit provision regarding the concept of the 'consumer' in the context of dual use contracts in Cyprus law, the national consumer protection authority, namely the Consumer Protection Service of the Ministry of Energy, Commerce, Tourism and Industry and the courts are likely to take a uniform approach most probably adopting the only guidance provided on the matter, specifically the one contained in Recital 17, CRD.

It follows that that the scope of application of the twin Laws is confined to consumer contracts in a narrow sense resulting from the narrow definition of the term 'consumer' adopted in said Laws. However, responding to the possibility afforded by Recital 21 of the SGD, Cyprus has extended the scope of application of Law 154(I)/2021 to contracts for the sale of goods *and* the provision of services (mixed contracts), such as the case of a contract for the purchase of a computer and the provision of maintenance services. However, no provisions have been added to adjust said law to the particularities of services and therefore it is somewhat unclear how Law 154(I)/2021 is to apply when the problem concerns the 'service' part of the contract alone, particularly if there are cases in which the problem with the services does not have an impact on the fitness and/or quality of the goods.

With regard to the exceptions from the Law, Section 3(3) of Law 155(I)/2021 adopts all eight (8) exceptions of Article 3(3) of the DCD. Moreover, like the DCD,[36] Law 155(I)/2021 clarifies that in the case of contracts with multiple elements including both digital content/service elements and elements of other services or goods, it only applies to the former elements. However, quite unexplainably, the relevant provision has been included in Section 18 of the Law, which transposes Article 19 of the DCD on the modification of the digital content or digital service, rather than in Section 3 of the Law which defines the Law's scope of application.

Article 4(1) of Law 154(I)/2021 has introduced all five (5) exceptions provided for or permitted by the SGD, through its Articles 3(3), 3(4) and 3(5). Notably however said national provision seems to have gone beyond the SGD in a way not permissible by the measure's maximum harmonization nature. More specifically, though Article 3(5) of the SGD requires that consumers are clearly informed about the rights deriving from the Directive not applying in case of the potential exception in Article 3(5)(a) *only*, (which refers to the sale of second-hand goods in public auctions), Article 4(1) of Law 154(I)/2021 imposes the same information duty in relation to all five exceptions it lays down.

As regards the DCD, Law 155(I)/2021 has not taken up the possibility of extending its scope of application to the situations listed in Recital 25, such as the exposure of consumers to advertisements in exchange of digital content or a digital service. Right on the contrary, it seems that Cyprus has restricted the scope of application of Law 155(I)/2021, something that may pose problems relating to the compliance of Cyprus with its obligations to transpose the DCD. More specifically, the DCD applies to contracts for the supply of digital content and services both in exchange of monetary

---

[34] Recital 17 CRD.
[35] For a critique of this choice, see also Morais Carvalho, 'Sale of Goods and Supply of Digital Content and Digital Services – Overview of Directives 2019/770 and 2019/771', (2019) 8(5) *Journal of European Consumer and Market Law,* 194 196.
[36] Art. 3 para. 6 DCD.

consideration and the provision of personal data,[37] including contracts for the supply of customized or personalized digital content or service (developed in accordance with consumer specifications).[38] It does not arise from Article 3(2), DCD (or the relevant Recital 26) that the customized or personalized digital content or service falls within the Directive *only* if it is supplied in exchange of the payment of a price (and not if the counter-performance is the provision of personal data). Conversely, Law 155(I)/2021, through Section 3(1)(c) effectively states exactly this, namely that said law only applies to the supply of customized/personalized digital content or service in exchange of the payment of a price.

23 It is worth noting more generally that the options and freedoms allowed to Member States in the Recitals of the Directives (as opposed to their operative provisions) seem not to have been given enough consideration, as they have largely remained unexercised. Accordingly, one should not expect to see in the twin Laws any substantial provisions that do not exist in the Directives. Moreover, this limited consideration of the Recitals is unfortunate, as in several cases, Recitals contain valuable information that can prove very useful to national legislators regarding how to improve or shape national law both on the matters falling within the scope of the application of the EU measures and on matters that are left outside said scope.

24 The twin Laws, especially Law 155(I)/2021, could have an impact on other areas of law, namely data protection and intellectual property law. Such impact is not great however. More specifically, like the DCD, Law 155(I)/2021 explicitly states that the General Data Protection Regulation (GDPR) remains the measure to deal with all the matters relating to the processing of personal data including the processing involved in the context of contracts governed by the Law 155(I)/2021.[39] It further states that in case of a conflict between the two, the GDPR, the Law providing for the Protection of Natural Persons with regard to the Processing of Personal Data and for the Free Movement of such Data of 2018, Law 125(I)/2018 (the national GDPR-implementing law) and the Law on the Regulation of Electronic Communications and Postal Services of 2004, Law 112(I)/2004 (implementing, among others, the e-Privacy Directive[40]) shall prevail.[41] Section 15(2) of Law 155(I)/2021 reiterates that the provisions of the GDPR remain applicable and that the trader shall comply with the particular measure in the case of termination of the contract.

25 Still, there seems to be one potential conflict (or clash) between the two measures and this has to do with the validity of consent to the processing of personal data. The DCD explicitly states that it does not regulate the validity of consent, which shall continue to be governed by the GDPR.[42] It is true however that the DCD inherently recognizes that consent to the processing of personal data that is *not* necessary for the provision of the digital service or content may well be offered as counter-performance in the context of a (valid) digital service or content contract. The GDPR on the other hand, through Article 7(4),[43] hints that such consent may not be a valid consent meaning that the personal data processing based on such consent will be unlawful. A strict application

---

[37] Art. 3 para. 1 DCD.
[38] Art. 3 para. 2 DCD.
[39] Section 3 para. 5 Law 155(I)/2021.
[40] Directive 2002/58/EC of the European Parliament and of the Council of 12 July 2002 concerning the processing of personal data and the protection of privacy in the electronic communications sector (Directive on privacy and electronic communications).
[41] Section 3 para. 5 Law 155(I)/2021.
[42] Recital 38 DCD.
[43] Article 7 para. 4 GDPR: "When assessing whether consent is freely given, utmost account shall be taken of whether, *inter alia*, the performance of a contract, including the provision of a service, is

of Article 7(4) would effectively preclude the validity of the particular contracts, as according to Cyprus contract law, when the consideration is unlawful, the contract is void.[44] Thankfully, Article 7(4) of the GDPR states that said factor is just one, among others, which may be considered in assessing the validity of consent. It is true however that the DCD has inevitably weakened Article 7(4) of the GDPR and will probably prevent a strict application of said provision that would invalidate all digital content or service contracts in exchange of personal data.

Likewise, intellectual property law largely remains intact, as Law 155(I)/2021 expressly states that its application is without prejudice to said law. Copying corresponding provisions in the twin Directives,[45] Section 9 of the twin Laws clarify that if the lack of conformity arises from a violation of intellectual property rights of third parties, the consumer will still be entitled to the remedies for non-conformity with the contract. These provisions by no means interfere with intellectual property law, which remains the law responsible to determine whether there is any intellectual property infringement. Moreover, said provision state the obvious; digital content and services must conform with the contract. The reason behind any lack of conformity has never been relevant in a contractual context except from very limited cases, such as *force majeure*.

C. Definitions

The definitions in Section 2 of the twin Laws sit easily with existing general contract and consumer protection law and only have a desirable (and useful) enriching effect. This reinforces the above-expressed view that the rules of the twin Laws are largely suitable for application to business-to-business contracts too.[46] More specifically, Cyprus law lacked any definitions for the terms 'digital service', 'goods with digital elements', 'integration', 'updates' and 'digital environment' and it should be expected that the relevant definitions in the twin Laws (derived from the corresponding Directives) are to offer guidance to courts even outside the business-to-consumer context.

As for the terms 'digital content' and 'durable medium', the definitions of the Consumer Rights Directive exist in the Consumer Protection Law, Law 112(I)/2021 which largely copies the relevant definitions in the twin Directives (and the twin Laws). It has to be pointed out that in Law 154(I)/2021, digital content is defined as data, which is provided in digital form (as opposed to produced *and* provided in digital form). This must however have happened inadvertently, as Law 155(I)/2021 states said definition correctly and will most probably be corrected through a future amendment. Moreover, the 'durable medium' definition in said law refers to paper and email as examples of instruments that could comprise durable media. There is no problem with this extra help that the Law gives with regard to the relevant concept, yet care should be taken not to interpret this as stating that email is *de facto* a durable medium or that it will be considered as such under *all* circumstances. Indeed, courts should not overlook the fact that according to CJEU case law, an email seeking to provide information to the consumer may not satisfy the requirements of a 'durable medium' for example when said

---

conditional on consent to the processing of personal data that is not necessary for the performance of that contract".

[44] Section 24 Cap.149.
[45] Article 10 DCD and Article 9 SGD.
[46] Supra paras 15–17.

information is provided not in the body of the email but behind a link to a web page of the trader sent by email.[47]

29   The definition of the terms, 'compatibility', 'functionality' and 'interoperability' are new additions both at EU[48] and at national level and should certainly be welcomed given the central role these concepts play in relation to the qualities of goods with digital elements, digital content and services. Deviating from the SGD, Law 154(I)/2021 also included a definition of the term 'durability' copying the relevant reference in Recital 32 of the SGD which states that said term "should refer to the ability of the goods to maintain their required functions and performance through normal use". Durability already existed as an element of the quality of goods both in Law 7(I)/2000[49] (transposing the 1999 CSD) and Law 10(I)/94, though the latter contains a definition of said term which is different than the one included in Law 154(I)/2021. More specifically, in Law 10(I)/94, durability is defined as "the reasonable endurance in time and use including where necessary the availability of spare parts and specialized skills for ensuring such endurance".[50] Accordingly, albeit indirectly, Law 10(I)/94, which is applicable to all sales contracts including consumers ones, imposes an obligation on traders to ensure the availability of spare parts (when necessary to ensure durability). Despite the fact that the SGD (and Law 154(I)/2021) do not contain a similar obligation, the relevant provision of Law 10(I)/94 sits easily within the system of contract law as has been shaped by the SGD, as said Directive, through Recital 33, explicitly leaves relevant provisions in national law unaffected.[51]

D. Conformity with the Contract

30   Cyprus has implemented the conformity-related provisions of the twin Directives largely *verbatim* with many of the differences in the wording being mere linguistic variations with no effect on the meaning or intention of said provisions. Some of these variations are simply wrong and are expected to be corrected in the context of future amendments; for example, Section 7(4) of Law 155(I)/2021 transposing Article 8(4) of the DCD refers to a sales contract (as opposed to merely a contract), though said law does not regulate sales contracts but contracts for the supply of digital content and services. Other than those variations, Law 154(I)/2021 and Law 155(I)/2021 simply reproduce the subjective and objective requirements for conformity as laid down in the corresponding Directives without further specifying or expanding upon the vast majority of the provisions in Articles 6 and 7 of the SGD and Articles 7 and 8 of the DCD.

31   As a result, it is, for example, unclear how the courts are to interpret the reference to a 'particular characteristic' in Articles 7(5) and 8(5) of the SGD and the DCD respectively; does the liability exemption provided for therein only apply to the case where only a specific characteristic (as opposed to the goods, content or service in their entirety) deviates from the objective requirements of conformity? Nowhere in the Directives, the goods, content or services are broken down into their various 'characteristics', with each one of them being capable of being assessed against the requirements for conformity

---

[47] CJEU, Case C-49/11, 05.07.2012, *Content Services Ltd v Bundesarbeitskammer*, ECLI:EU:C:2012:419, paras 19, 20 and 51.
[48] The notions of functionality and interoperability were only explained in Recital 19 of the CRD but there were no definitions devoted to them.
[49] Section 4 para. 3 subpara. c. Law 7(I)/2000.
[50] Section 16 para. 4 Law 10(I)/94.
[51] See also infra para 30 however.

D. Conformity with the Contract

separately. Said provisions should perhaps have referred to a deviation from the objective requirements of the goods, content or services due to a particular characteristic of them, rather than to said characteristic itself deviating from those requirements. This is so provided that the intention has not been to limit said liability exemption to deviations of a specific characteristic rather than of the goods, content or services in their entirety, though this is unlikely; it is difficult to envisage a situation whereby a characteristic of the goods, but not the goods as such, deviates from conformity requirements.

32 Regarding 'durability', Law 154(I)/2021 does not in any away deviate from the SGD and no assistance is provided regarding the interpretation of said requirement. Thus, the courts as well as the Consumer Protection Service can resort to Recital 32 of the SGD which refers to "the nature of the specific goods, including the possible need for reasonable maintenance of the goods, such as the regular inspection or changing of filters in a car", public statements and "all other relevant circumstances, such as the price of the goods and the intensity or frequency of the use that the consumer makes of the goods" as factors to be taken into account in assessing durability.

33 However, as already stated, a 'durability' requirement also exists in Law 10(I)/94, said requirement also entailing a requirement relating to the availability of spare parts to the extent necessary to ensure durability; this obviously extends the durability requirement of Law 154(I)/2021. Importantly, in the light of the period of the trader's liability being only two years and given the fact that many products have a much longer expected lifetime, durability as an objective requirement for conformity would have little, if any, practical significance, in the absence of a requirement, even implicit, to ensure 'durability' by making available spare parts or specialized service at least when durability necessitates such spare parts or service.[52] 'Durability' in Law 10(I)/94 is an element of the implied term of acceptable quality but what is of utmost importance is that the liability of the seller under Law 10(I)/94 is only subject to the 6-year general limitation period for contract claims,[53] i.e., there is no shorter or any period of liability. Unfortunately, however, it is not clear whether a consumer who experiences a lack of conformity after the expiry of the 2-year period of liability of Law 154(I)/2021[54] and cannot therefore, successfully file an action under said law, will be able to bring his or her case under Law 10(I)/94. As already stated, the relationship between Law 154(I)/2021 and Law 10(I)/94 is not spelled out in Law 154(I)/2021. Moreover, the SGD is categorical that the conformity requirements and remedies shall be fully harmonized[55] and said aim would not be achieved if consumers remained free to choose between the system of the SGD transposition measure and any pre-existing or alternative relevant national regime.

34 This is bad news also when it comes to the fight against premature and/or planned obsolescence of goods. As commentators emphasize, "The issue of time is particularly crucial in the context of planned obsolescence because relevant defects are inherently latent and often become apparent only after the passage of a considerable amount of time".[56] Understandably, if the liability period is shorter than the amount of time needed for planned obsolescence to become apparent, legal warranties such as the ones provided by the SGD lose much of their strength as measures against this consumer-un-

---

[52] See also Morais Carvalho, 'Sale of Goods and Supply of Digital Content and Digital Services – Overview of Directives 2019/770 and 2019/771', (2019), 8(5), *Journal of European Consumer and Market Law*, 194 198.
[53] See infra para 45.
[54] Ibid.
[55] Recital 10 SGD.
[56] Wrbka and DiMatteo, 'Comparative Warranty Law: Case of Planned Obsolescence' (2019) 21 *J. Bus. L.*, 907 (939), available at: https://scholarship.law.upenn.edu/jbl/vol21/iss4/5.

friendly and inherently misleading practice.[57] Cyprus has not introduced any measures specifically targeting said practice, but the above-explained essentially indefinite liability period of Law 10(I)/94, if it remained applicable to consumer contracts, in conjunction with the 'durability' requirement in product-specific safety legislation[58] and the rules on unfair commercial practices[59] can work together towards reducing the problem[60].

35 Notably, durability requirements can also be found in the Cypriot regulations transposing the EU New Approach Directives,[61] to the extent that such Directives impose a 'durability' requirement. For example, one such requirement exists in Paragraph B.3 of Annex I of the Directive 2013/53/EU on recreational craft and personal watercraft, which is so detailed as to specify the normal life of relevant engines and which is adopted *verbatim* in the Cypriot transposition measure.[62] There is no direct relationship between this set of rules and the rules of Law 154(I)/2021 in the sense that they operate in different spheres of law. More specifically, while Law 154(I)/2021 operates in the private law sphere of contract law, the rules transposing the product-specific safety Directives mostly operate in the sphere of administrative and criminal law,[63] though a breach of an obligation they impose also gives rise to a right to private redress in tort, translating into a right to claim compensation for resulting death or personal injury.[64]

36 Nor Cyprus has in any way coordinated Law 154(I)/2021 with the provisions of the national measure transposing Directive 2009/125/EC establishing a framework for the setting of eco-design requirements for energy-related products, namely Law 17(I)/2011 (having the same title as that of the Directive). Law 154(I)/2021 makes no reference to said law, which similarly to the aforementioned Law 30(I)/2002[65] provides for criminal and administrative sanctions as well as for a private right to seek compensation for death or personal injury. Law 154(I)/2021 and Law 155(I)/2021 contain no specific provisions aimed at enhancing environmental sustainability or a circular economy. After all, Recital 32 of the SGD seems to suggest that this is mainly the job of other legislation (most probably, the aforementioned New-Approach Directives) and that the SGD should only

---

[57] On relevant concerns relating to warranty periods and planned obsolescence, see also ibid at p. 921.

[58] See infra at para 32.

[59] These are contained in Part B of Law 112(I)/2021, which transposes largely verbatim the Unfair Commercial Practices Directive 2005/29/EC.

[60] Planned obsolescence can, under certain circumstances, be considered an unfair commercial practice under the UCPD. On this matter, see Malinauskaite, J., & Erdem, F. B., 'Planned obsolescence in the context of a holistic legal sphere and the circular economy' (2021) 41(3) *Oxford Journal of Legal Studies*, 719 (733 and 734) and Koolhoven and Heerema, 'Fighting Planned Obsolescence or "The Lightbulb Conspiracy" as an Unfair Commercial Practice: For a Circular Economy' in Maria Miguel Carvalho (ed), *Law and Technology: E Tec Yearbook* (JustGov and University of Minho, 2018) 27

[61] See List of New Approach Directives, available at: https://www.cetest.nl/european-new-approach-directives.htm.

[62] Regulations (K.D.P.) 191/2017, The Basic Requirements (Pleasure Boats and Individual Boats) Regulations of 2017, which were issued by the Council of Ministers, according to article 59 of the Basic Requirements that must meet Specific Product Categories of Laws of 2002 to 2013, after being submitted to the Parliament of Representatives and approved by it, are published in the Official Gazette of the Republic in accordance with paragraph (3) of article 3 of the Submission to the House of Representatives of Regulations Issued by Authorization of Law, Law (L.99 of 1989 as amended by Laws 227 of 1990 to 3 (I) of 2010), available at: https://www.dms.gov.cy/dms/shipping.nsf/all/92DFAC5C342E1FB4C2258377003EE366/$file/K%CE%94%CE%A0%20191-2017.pdf?openelement (in Greek).

[63] Those rules are introduced in Cyprus as regulations issued on the basis of the Essential Requirements to be Met by Specified Categories of Products Law of 2002, Law 30(I)/2002, a law introduced to ensure the application of the EU Regulations 765/2008 and 1222/2009. The law, through Sections 52 and 53, provides for certain criminal offences and the imposition of administrative fines where there is a violation of provisions of said law and the regulations issued on its basis.

[64] Section 57 Law 30(I)/2002.

[65] See supra fn. 63.

perform a complementary role by including 'durability' in the list of the objective requirements for conformity.

Interestingly, what is stated in Recital 53 of the DCD perhaps deserved reference to an operative provision so that it is not missed by traders and also courts when applying Law 155(I)/2021. As is stated therein, a lack of conformity with the contract may even result from restrictions imposed on the use of the digital content or service through the end-user agreement between the consumer and the intellectual property right holder. This reference, though consistent with a high level of consumer protection, does not have the force of law and may thus create problems resulting in non-uniform application. Given the 'unread contract' principle of common law by virtue of which a party is bound by the terms of a concluded contract even if he has not read it[66] and provided that an end-user agreement term imposing a restriction is not unfair by reference to the Unfair Contract Terms Directive,[67] the consumer will be bound by it under general contract law. Finding that such a restriction leads to a lack of conformity with the contract necessitates not only to bypass the outcome which general contract law would lead to but also to accept that a consumer who has entered into an end-user contract explicitly restricting the use of some feature can nevertheless reasonably expect to be able to use said feature freely. According to the DCD, the trader can only avoid such a result and relevant liability by specifically bringing the relevant restriction to the attention of the consumer securing his explicit and separate agreement to it and this should ideally have been made clear in the provisions of Law 155(I)/2021, (which would be the case if the relevant clarification existed in the operative provisions of the DCD). 37

Regarding the provisions on the incorrect installation and integration of goods and digital content/services respectively, Law 154(I)/2021 and Law 155(I)/2021 refer to "incomplete, inaccurate or incorrect instructions" in the place of the phrase "shortcomings in the instructions" utilized by the Directives in Articles 8 and 9 respectively. What is notable is that Section 8 of Law 154(I)/2021 goes one step further, stating that instructions not provided in Greek are considered incomplete. The question may arise as to whether this addition is permissible by the maximum harmonization nature of the SGD, especially given that elsewhere, specifically in Article 17(4) on commercial guarantees, said Directive explicitly allows Member States to impose language requirements. Clearly, by automatically rendering instructions in any language other than Greek as incomplete and thus, any lack of conformity resulting from incorrect installation by the consumer as a lack of conformity of the goods for which the trader will be liable, Law 154(I)/2021, albeit indirectly, effectively imposes a language requirement relating to installation instructions. 38

It is submitted that the phrase 'shortcomings in the instructions' in Article 8 of the SGD is eligible to varying interpretations by the courts. The relevant provision in the Directive does not in any way preclude an interpretation to the effect that instructions in a foreign language are not sufficient (or are deficient). Therefore, it would make little sense to suggest that one such interpretation is impermissible when made by the legislature. Moreover, Recital 32 of the SGD explain 'shortcomings' by reference to "incompleteness or a lack of clarity making the installation instructions difficult to use for the average consumer"; instructions in a foreign language may very well be considered as *de facto* difficult to use by the average consumer. Notably, though Article 9 of the DCD is an analogous provision concerning the integration of digital content 39

---

[66] See for example, Ayres, 'The no-reading problem in consumer contract law' (2014) *Faculty Scholarship Series,* Paper 4872, 545 (548–549); available at: https://ianayres.yale.edu/sites/default/files/files/The%20No%20Reading%20Problem(2).pdf.

[67] Council Directive 93/13/EEC of 5 April 1993 on unfair terms in consumer contracts.

or service, Law 155(I)/2021 does not contain the aforementioned addition concerning instructions in a language other than Greek. This inconsistency between the twin Laws is difficult to explain and may cause unnecessary confusion.

40 Given that the twin Laws implement the twin Directives largely *verbatim*, one cannot find provisions on the modification of digital content or services in Law 154(I)/2021 (implementing the SGD). What arises clearly from the SGD is that the seller has no *obligation* to modify the content or service embedded in the goods by providing updates or upgrades beyond what is necessary to maintain said content or service in conformity. What is not equally clear is whether the seller has a *right* to modify embedded content or service for purposes unrelated to the conformity of the goods similar to the right recognized to suppliers by Article 19(1) of the DCD, when certain conditions are met.[68] The SGD (and Law 154(I)/2021) are silent on the particular matter but there seems to be nothing precluding traders contractually reserving a right to perform relevant modifications. In that case however, Law 154(I)/2021 lacks any provisions regulating the rights of consumers.

41 Article 9 of the SGD and Article 10 of the DCD on third party rights have also been transposed largely *verbatim*, though not in exactly the same way in the twin Laws. These provisions oblige Member States to secure to the consumer the remedies specified by the Directives in case of a lack of conformity, unless national law allows the consumer to nullify or rescind the contract right away. In relation to the sale of goods with digital elements, Cyprus, through Section 9 of Law 154(I)/2021, has opted to make available the lack of conformity remedies of the SGD. This has been a wise approach, as Cyprus contract law including Law 10(I)/94, lacks any specific provisions on goods with digital elements in general, let alone on a lack of conformity of such goods resulting from third party rights' violations. Accordingly, it is not entirely certain that a right to nullify or rescind (or terminate) the contract can be derived from Cyprus law in all cases of a deviation of the goods from the subjective and objective requirements of Law 154(I)/2021); relevant case law involving goods with digital elements does not seem to exist.[69] As the remedies under Law 154(I)/2021 also include a right to immediately terminate the contract when the lack of conformity is very serious or arises within 30 days,[70] the consumer benefits from the certainty achieved by provisions that clearly specify remedies in a such a case, without suffering any lowering of the level of consumer protection by totally being deprived of a remedy available under general contract law.

42 The wording of the corresponding Section 9 of Law 155(I)/2021 is somewhat different. More specifically, though it provides for the remedies that are available for a lack of conformity similarly to what Section 9 of Law 154(I)/2021 does, it states that this is "without prejudice of the provisions of any other law providing for the voidability and nullity of the contract in these cases". Consistency between the twin Laws should have been preferred. The wording of Section 9 of Law 155(I)/2021 will force the judge to explore whether general contract law in fact allows consumers immediately to avoid

---

[68] Clearly, the possibility cannot be excluded of the trader wishing to modify digital content or services embedded in goods. This arises clearly from the various purposes a trader may wish to do so as listed by way of examples by Farinha, 'Modifications on the digital content or digital service by the trader in the Directive (EU) 2019/770' (2021) 25 N.º 2, *RED – Revista Electrónica de Direito*, available at: https://cije.up.pt/client/files/0000000001/4-martim-farinha_1738.pdf, 85 (99), albeit by reference to digital content or services supplied independently, i.e., not embedded in goods and thus, governed by the DCD.

[69] See also Hadjinestoros and Charalambous, *Cyprus Law on the Sale of Goods and Consumer Protection* (2016), which does not refer to any relevant cases.

[70] Section 13 para. 4 subpara. c. and 13 para. 7 Law 154(I)/2021.

the contract, before proceeding with examining and applying the remedies for non-conformity in said Law.

43 The EU legislator did not obviously take up suggestions to cover in Section 9 restrictions not only to the use but also to the exploitation, including resale of goods with digital elements, digital content and/or digital services.[71] Accordingly, the right of the consumer to resell such goods, content and/or services has been left to the end-user agreements subject to the unfair contract terms laws of the Member States. At least with regard to goods with digital elements, the matter should have been regulated, as the consumer could not reasonably expect not to be free to sell his smart phone due to restrictions arising from third party rights in embedded digital content or services. Of course, such (restrictive) terms in end-user agreements may be deemed unfair by operation of the Unfair Contract Terms Directive (and corresponding national transposition measures). Still however, without a resale right being expressly provided for and regulated, there may be issues with providers preventing or restricting such resale indirectly, through technical and other practical measures, such as by preventing personalization of the device by the new owner, particularly due to usernames or other details being capable of being entered only once.[72] Given the absence of relevant provisions in the twin Directives, it is unsurprising that neither Law 154(I)/2021 nor Law 155(I)/2021 contain provisions regulating resale.

E. Liability of the Trader, Burden of Proof and Time Limits

44 Law 154(I)/2021, specifically Sections 10(1) and (2) reproduce the corresponding Articles 10(1) and (2) of the SGD regarding the liability of the trader except from the fact that Section 10(1) does not state that it also applies to goods with digital elements. This omission may at first seem to leave the period of liability for the case of goods with digital elements unspecified, yet this is not the case. In Law 154(I)/2021, references are made to 'goods', which can be taken to include goods with digital elements. Separate and specific references to 'goods with digital elements' are only made twice and it is only when the provision *only* concerns goods with digital elements and not goods without such elements.[73]

45 Moreover, responding to Article 10(6) of the SGD, Section 10(1) of Law 154(I)/2021 lays down a minimum of one-year period of liability that can be agreed between the parties in the case of sales of second-hand goods. Section 12(1) of Law 154(I)/2021 imposes on the consumer the obligation to notify the seller about a lack of conformity within two months, an option which has been expectable given that Cyprus has exercised said option also in the context of Law 7(I)/2000 transposing the now repealed CSD,

46 It is worth noting that though not a problem of the transposition measure, an issue may arise with the application of Sections 10(2)(a) and (b) with regard to contracts of an indefinite period (specifying no particular period for which the digital content or service is to be supplied). Do such contracts fall within Section 10(2)(a) or Section 10(2)(b)?

---

[71] European Parliament, Directorate-General for Internal Policies of the Union, Wenderhost, *Sale of goods and supply of digital content – two worlds apart?*, European Parliament 2016, 17, available at: https://www.europarl.europa.eu/cmsdata/98774/pe%20556%20928%20EN_final.pdf, arguing that it was essential for the third party rights provision in Proposal for a Directive of the European Parliament and of the Council on certain aspects concerning contracts for the online and other distance sales of goods COM/2015/0635 final – 2015/0288 (COD), "not only to focus on use, but equally on exploitation and re-sale, and to mention explicitly that the consumer must become owner of the goods".

[72] Ibid at pp. 9–10.

[73] Section 11 para. 2 and Section 18 Law 154(I)/2021.

Does Section 10(2)(b) apply only where the contract *explicitly* refers to a period longer than two years? The SGD does not shed any light on these questions.

47 As for Law 155(I)/2021, it reproduces Article 11(3) of the DCD governing the period of liability for the case of continuous supply of digital content or digital services but it seems that there has been some misunderstanding of Article 11(1). It arises from the first paragraph of Article 11(1) of the DCD that the EU legislator was prepared to allow an indefinite period of liability for a lack of conformity *existing at the time of single supply*,[74] something which is consistent with digital content or services not being subject to wear and tear.[75] The second paragraph of Article 11(1) just permitted Member States to limit said period to a lack of conformity that becomes apparent within a minimum of a 2-year period of time after supply. By no means, Article 11 of the DCD entailed an option for Member States between liability for a lack of conformity existing at the time of the supply and liability for *any* lack of conformity becoming apparent within a period of time after supply (i.e., regardless whether it existed at the time of the supply). The national legislator seems to have taken said provision to entail one such option, hence Section 10(2) of Law 155(I)/2021 effectively provides for a period of liability for any lack of conformity becoming apparent within a two-year period after supply without restricting liability to a lack of conformity existing at the time of supply. This is an extension of the liability of the trader beyond what is permitted by the DCD and also contradicts Section 11(2) transposing Article 12(2) of the DCD, which regulates the burden of proof by reference to a lack of conformity that *existed at the time of the supply* on the trader. This should be corrected. It is true that Section 11(3), which reproduces Article 10(3) of the DCD does not limit liability to a lack of conformity that exists at the time of supply either. However, this provision applies to the case of continuous supply and it thus makes sense to provide for liability for problems becoming apparent during the period of supply; in the vast majority of cases at least, said problems are bound to exist at the time of supply.

48 As for the provisions of the twin Directives on prescription periods, namely Article 10(5) of the SGD and Articles 11(2) and 11(3) of the DCD, the way they have been implemented in Law 154(I)/2021 and Law 155(I)/2021 is problematic. Those provisions of the Directives are relevant only to the extent that national law subjects the exercise of the remedies of the Directives to a prescription period; they provide that this must be a period that permits the consumer to exercise the remedies available to him under the Directives given the applicable periods of trader liability. Prescription periods in Cyprus are governed by Law 66(I)/2012 on the Limitation of Causes of Action except where specific laws provide for specific prescription periods. None of the twin Laws provide for a specific prescription period. Accordingly, given that an action by the consumer for the remedies for a lack of conformity will be an action relating to a contract, the applicable prescription period is provided for in Section 7(1) of Law 66(I)/2012, which states that actions concerning contracts should be brought within six (6) years from the time the basis of the action has been completed; that would be the time the lack of conformity has become apparent.

---

[74] This is confirmed by the last sentence of Recital 56 of the DCD.
[75] See Recital 43, Proposal for a Directive of the European Parliament and of the Council on certain aspects concerning contracts for the supply of digital content COM/2015/0634 final – 2015/0287 (COD): "Due to its nature the digital content is not subject to wear and tear while being used and it is often supplied over a period of time rather than as a one-off supply. It is, therefore, justified not to provide a period during which the supplier should be held liable for any lack of conformity which exists at the time of the supply of the digital content".

E. Liability of the Trader, Burden of Proof and Time Limits

Obviously, this long prescription period, being much longer than the period of trader liability, can pose no problems to the consumer with regard to the exercise of his or her rights under the twin Laws and therefore, meets the Directives' requirement for prescription periods allowing the consumer to exercise remedies. Accordingly, no additional provision was needed in the twin Laws, except perhaps from a provision explicitly confirming that the general prescription period for contracts applies to actions under said laws. However, Law 154(I)/2021 did not follow this approach. Instead, Section 10(3) states that regardless of any provisions of the Limitation of Causes of Action Law, the prescription period cannot expire less than two years from the time of delivery. This is a defective provision, as not only prescription periods cannot be provided in the form of minimum periods and need to be clearly specified but also said provision totally overlooks the case for which the trader's liability extends to the whole of the period during which digital content or services are supplied. Moreover, a two-year prescription period starting from the time of delivery would prevent consumers from bringing an action when the lack of conformity appears towards the end of the two-year period of liability or when the lack of conformity relates to digital content or services supplied on a continuous basis and arises after the lapse of two years. Equally problematic is Section 10(4) of Law 155(I)/2021, which also provides for a minimum of a 2-year prescription period starting from the time of the supply of the content or services.

There are no provisions in the twin Laws regarding interruption or suspension of the liability period or the limitation period, except from Section 13(8) of Law 154(I)/2021 which provides that the time during which the goods are being brought into conformity or the parties negotiate an amicable solution do not count in the trader's liability period. With regard to the limitation period however, the aforementioned Law 66(I)/2012 does not exclude from its scope legal actions based on the twin Laws and therefore, the provisions relating to interruption and suspension of the limitation period contained in Section 17 and Sections 12, 13, 15 of said Law respectively shall apply. These provisions are in no way specific to any particular causes of actions and for example, operate towards suspending the limitation period for a period during which due to *force majeure* the plaintiff has been unable to bring his legal action during the last six months of the limitation period[76] or interrupting and restarting the limitation period when the potential defendant has recognized in writing the right of action against him.[77]

The twin Laws also largely reproduce the provisions on the liability of the trader of the twin Directives, except from the fact that Section 11(1) of Law 154(I)/2021, relying on Article 11(2) of the Directive, imposes the relevant burden of proof on the seller during the whole of the two-year period of liability, thus increasing the level of consumer protection. Law 154(I)/2021 does not go as far as to increase the period of liability too, despite a relevant freedom being provided for in the SGD.[78] Just like the DCD, Law 155(I)/2021, which largely reproduces it, contains no provisions on the interruption of the supply of digital content or services and the courts are expected to deal with this issue assisted by the guidance contained in Recital 56 of the DCD.

Moreover, matters relating to a failure to deliver or supply due to factors outside the control of the trader are not regulated in the twin Laws, both of which refer to general contract law for contract-related matters not specifically regulated by them.[79] Section 56 of the Contracts Law, Cap.149 lays down the rules on frustration effectively rendering a contract void when performance becomes impossible or unlawful due to

---

[76] Section 13 para. a Law 66(I)/2012.
[77] Section 17 para. a Law 66(I)/2012.
[78] Article 10 para. 3 SGD.
[79] See supra at para 6.

an unpreventable event; these apply where there is a material change in circumstances which has rendered performance impossible.[80] When such a change causes hardship (as opposed to impossibility), there is no rule enabling a party to escape the contract but courts can achieve a fair solution through an interpretation of the contract, where this is possible from the wording of the contract and the circumstances of its conclusion.[81] *Force majeure* is also recognized under Cyprus law though it is not codified in Cap.149 (or elsewhere) and its operation heavily relies on the content of *force majeure* clauses in the contract; accordingly, it does not always lead to a right to immediately terminated the contract but may only suspend contractual obligations effectively giving the affected party some extension of time for fulfilling his or her obligations.[82] Like frustration however, *force majeure* can only be triggered if the event was totally outside the control of the affected contracting party and said party has made reasonable efforts to deal with the relevant event.[83]

53 As part of the reproduction of the provisions of the twin Directives, Section 3(3)(c) of Law 155(I)/2021 specifies that the provision of Number-Independent Interpersonal Communication Services as defined in Directive 2018/1972 on European Electronic Communications Code fall within its ambit, yet it contains no provisions specifically regulating relevant contracts. Similarly, Law 155(I)/2021 reproduces *verbatim* Article 3(6) of the DCD, albeit under Section 18, a provision regulating the modification of digital content and services. The first paragraph of Article 3(6) has been transposed as Section 18(5) but its placement under Section 19 is inappropriate; said paragraph relates to the scope of application of the Law as a whole and thus, belonged to Section 3. Having been made part of Section 18, which focuses on a totally irrelevant matter, it is likely to be missed by courts.

54 The second and third paragraphs of Article 3(6) have been transposed in Sections 18(6)(a) and (b) respectively. Section 18(6)(b) did not belong to Section 18 either and should have been placed within or right after the provisions on the obligations of the parties in case of termination. As Article 3(6)(b) of the DCD left the effects that the termination of one element of a bundle contract may have on the rest elements to Member States, Law 155(I)/2021, Article 18(6)9b) refers the matter to the Contracts Law, Cap.149. Interestingly, Cap.149 is very laconic on the effects of termination in general[84] and silent on the effects of termination of one element of a bundle contract. Common law rules relating to divisible or severable (as opposed to entire) contracts[85] can apply to give solutions however.

55 Finally, regarding the liability of the trader for violations of the GDPR, this is not a matter regulated by Law 155(I)/2021, and correctly so. As already explained,[86] said Law explicitly confirms that the application of the GDPR with regard to matters regulated by it remains totally unaffected. The GDPR and the Protection of Natural Persons with regard to the Processing of Personal Data and for the Free Movement of such Data Law of 2018, Law 125(I)/2018, the latter being the national implementing law, do not

---

[80] See also Polyviou, *The Law of Contracts (2014)*, Vol.2, 666.
[81] Ibid at pp. 717–723.
[82] Ibid at pp. 712–717.
[83] Ibid pp. 715–716.
[84] Section 64 Cap.149 provides that when a party rescinds a voidable contract, the other party does not have to fulfill his obligations and Section 75 Cap.149 provides for the right of the party who has lawfully terminated a contract to compensation.
[85] Polyviou, *The Law of Contracts (2014)*, Vol. 2, 648–651. Relevant provisions also exist in Law 10(I)/94, see Hadjinestoros and Charalambous, *Cyprus Law on the Sale of Goods and Consumer Protection* (2016), 231–232, 246–252.
[86] See supra at para 24.

of course specifically provide for the consequences of a violation of the GDPR on the part of digital content or service providers. Such traders, as data controllers within the meaning of Article 4(7) of the GDPR, are subject to the sanctions, mainly administrative fines provided for in Article 83 of the GDPR depending on the violation. Certain violations, such as the omission of a data controller to notify the Commissioner about a data breach in accordance with Article 33(1) of the GDPR, are rendered a criminal offence by virtue of Section 33 of Law 125(I)/2018. Moreover, where a violation of the GDPR on the part of a trader causes the consumer damage, the trader may be liable to pay compensation in accordance with Article 82 of the GDPR. Such trader may also be subjected to other judicial remedies, such as an injunction, pursuant to Article 79 of the GDPR.

F. Remedies for the Failure to Supply and Remedies for the Lack of Conformity

The twin Laws transpose the provisions of the twin Directives on remedies by deviating from them in some ways. Section 13(6) of Law 154(I)/2021 simply reproduces the corresponding *Article 13(8) of the SGD without specifying any conditions and modalities for the consumer to exercise the right to withhold the payment.* By the same token, as the DCD provides for no such right, Law 155(I)/2021 contains no relevant provision either.

Section 13(7) of Law 154(I)/2021 also provides for the right of the consumer to reject the goods and terminate the contract or claim immediate replacement if the lack of conformity has become apparent within thirty (30) days from delivery. This brings the law on consumer contracts more in line with Law 10(I)/94, which provides for a right to reject the goods and terminate the contract,[87] thereby preventing the anomalous situation whereby non-consumers would be better off than consumers in the case of a lack of conformity. Said freedom to Member States was afforded by Article 3(7) of the SGD and therefore, Section 13(7) of Law 154(I)/2021 is not inconsistent with the maximum harmonization nature of the SGD.

Section 13(9) of Law 154(I)/2021 provides that there shall be no lack of conformity if, at the time the contract was concluded, the consumer was aware, or could not reasonably be unaware of the lack of conformity, or if the lack of conformity is due to materials supplied by the consumer. Such provision existed in the repealed Consumer Sales Directive and thus in the Cypriot law transposing it but does not exist in the SGD. Moreover, the SGD does not seem to afford Member States a relevant freedom to go beyond Article 7(5) of the SGD, which refers to a deviation from the objective requirements specifically being made known to and agreed by the consumer.[88] Perhaps, the part of Section 13(9) of Law 154(I)/2021 referring to a lack of conformity due to consumer-provided materials may be seen as permitted by Article 13(7) of the SGD which allows Member States to regulate "whether and to what extent a contribution of the consumer to the lack of conformity affects the consumer's right to remedies" and in response to which Law 154(I)/2021 contains no other provision. Accordingly, Section 13(9) of Law 154(I)/2021 (at least part of it) seems to go beyond the SGD, thereby

---

[87] It should be clarified that the termination right under Law 10(I)/94 is not subject to a specific time frame but seems to be subject to a requirement of reasonable time by operation of Section 42(6), according to which, a buyer is considered to have accepted the goods if the buyer has not rejected them within reasonable time. Contract termination is not possible without a previous rejection of the goods, see Hadjinestoros and Charalambous, *Cyprus Law on the Sale of Goods and Consumer Protection* (2016) 230.

[88] Recital 20 of the SGD does not seem to go that far.

59 The same holds true of Section 14(2) of Law 154(I)/2021, which lays down seller obligations and consumer rights that do not exist in the Directive. More specifically, according to said provision, the seller shall provide the consumer with a receipt that the goods have been received or delivered for repair or replacement. Moreover, upon delivery of the replaced or repaired goods, the consumer has the right to be provided with the report of the technical inspection of the goods together with the findings of the technician who has performed said inspection.

60 Section 14(1)(b) of Law 154(I)/2021 deviates from the corresponding Article 14(1)(b) of the SGD also by placing a general cap of 25 days (from the time the seller has been informed about the lack of conformity) to the reasonable time within which the seller must bring the goods in conformity; if said period has to be extended, the consumer must explicitly consent to such extension.[89] Recital 55 permits Member States to interpret the notion of 'reasonable time' in the context of this provision and provide for specific time periods for specific categories of goods, yet the broad way in which Section 14(1)(b) of Law 154(I)/2021 is drafted ("…within reasonable time that shall not exceed 25 days…") may result in the notion of 'reasonable time' being interpreted as being equivalent to 25 days or in said timeframe becoming in practice the time that the seller is considered to have at his disposal for bringing the goods in conformity with the contract. Obviously, this period of time is particularly long and will in many cases be excessive. Therefore, the relevant provision in Law 154(I)/2021 risks to lower consumer protection in practice.

61 Finally, permitted by Recital 60 of the SGD, Section 16 of 154(I)/2021 on termination imposes a time limit within which the seller should reimburse the money to the consumer, this being 30 days from the date of receipt of the goods returned by the consumer (or of proof of return of the goods).[90] The seller shall also issue a receipt of receipt of the returned goods.[91] Other than that, Law 154(I)/2021 does not specifically regulate any other matter from those it could regulate by virtue of Recital 60 or which are not regulated by the SGD, such as the place of delivery or the place of repair/replacement or the costs of transport for the case of repair/replacement. Understandably, the latter are particularly important when the consumer and the trader are not based in the same country. Regarding the place of delivery however, there is a provision in the Sales of Goods Law, Law 10(I)/94 by virtue of which said place depends on the express or implied agreement of the parties.[92] In the absence of such agreement, the place of delivery of sold goods is the place where the goods are at the time of the sale.[93] In relation to goods agreed to be sold, the place of delivery is the place where the goods are at the time of the contract of sale.[94] As far as goods that do not exist at the time of the contract of sale (and are to be produced), the place of delivery is the place of the production of the goods.[95] As the place of delivery is not regulated by Law 154(I)/2021, this provision of Law 10(I)/94 shall apply.

62 Given the absence of a provision in national law on the place and costs of repair/replacement, Cyprus courts should be expected to consider the relevant guidance of the

---

[89] Section 14 para. 1 subpara. b. Law 154(I)/2021.
[90] Section 16 para. 3 subpara. b. Law 154(I)/2021.
[91] Ibid.
[92] Section 36 para. 1 Law 10(I)/94.
[93] Section 36 para. 1 Law 10(I)/94.
[94] Section 36 para. 1 Law 10(I)/94.
[95] Section 36 para. 1 Law 10(I)/94.

F. Remedies for the Failure to Supply and Remedies for the Lack of Conformity

CJEU given by reference to the now repealed CSD, the relevant provisions of which have been retained by the SGD. According to said guidance, the place at which the consumer shall make goods acquired in the context of a distant contract available for repair or replacement "must be appropriate for ensuring that they can be brought into conformity free of charge, within a reasonable time and without significant inconvenience to the consumer, taking into account the nature of the goods and the purpose for which the consumer required the goods".[96] Moreover, according to the Court, the seller is not obliged "to pay the cost of transporting those goods, for the purposes of bringing them into conformity, to the seller's place of business, unless the fact that the consumer must advance those costs constitutes such a burden as to deter him from asserting his rights…"[97] in which case this will be considered a 'significant inconvenience'.[98] This guidance is obviously quite general and does not address more specific situations, such as when the consumer has bought the goods in the Member State of the trader but subsequently moved to a different Member State, especially when the trader offers no delivery to said Member State. Such issues are not regulated at all by Cyprus law.

Law 155(I)/2021 on the other hand largely simply reproduces the provisions of the DCD on remedies, the differences between the two sets of provisions being minor ones relating to the words chosen rather than to the essence. As a result, apart from the provisions on the consequences of termination which largely reproduce Articles 16–18 of the DCD, Law 155(I)/2021 only contains a general provision, specifically Section 30, titled 'remedies', which provides for a private right of action for any violation of the provisions of the law and lists compensation, among other remedies including termination, price reduction and restitution of any damage suffered) that a consumer can claim against the seller. An identical provision, namely Section 29, is contained in Law 154(I)/2021. Obviously, the fully harmonized remedies for the case of a lack of conformity are clearly spelled out in the Directives (and the relevant transposition measures) and therefore, no additional provision on remedies reiterating that the consumer can claim price reduction for example, was necessary.

However, the national provisions titled 'remedies', namely Section 29(1) of Law 154(I)/2021 and Section 30(1) of Law 155(I)/2021, are broader and can prove useful. The twin Directives and consequently, the twin Laws contain certain additional or supplementary obligations, not all of which lead to a lack of conformity if violated. For example, Section 17(4) of Law 154(I)/2021 imposes obligations of content as well as clarity and language regarding commercial guarantees. Section 16 of the same Law and Section 15 of Law 155(I)/2021 impose specific obligations on the trader in the event of termination. Section 29(1) of Law 154(I)/2021 and Section 30(1) of Law 155(I)/2021 explicitly recognise a private right of action against the trader to consumers whose economic interests have been harmed because of "*any* violation of the provisions of the Law"[99]. Moreover, Section 29(3)(c) and (d) of Law 154(I)/2021 and Section 30(3)(c) and (d) of Law 155(I)/2021 confer on the court the power to order the trader to compensate the consumer or perform an action deemed reasonable by the court as a remedy or restitution of any damage caused.

It seems therefore that the consumer can through private action enforce all said additional or supplementary obligations imposed by the twin Laws. Moreover, the provisions on remedies in the twin Laws make it clear that the consumer will, in addition to the fully harmonized remedies in case of a lack of conformity, be entitled

---

[96] CJEU, Case C-52/18, 23.05.2019, *Christian Fülla v Toolport GmbH*, ECLI:EU:C:2019:447, para 56.
[97] Ibid.
[98] Ibid.
[99] Emphasis added.

to compensation.[100] Both Directives explicitly clarify that they are without prejudice to the freedom of the Member States to regulate, among others, the right to damages,[101] meaning that said provisions in the national transposition Laws create no issues with regard to the maximum harmonization nature of the Directives. There are however some imperfections in their wording which will have to be corrected. More specifically, they state that the court can order a trader among others to declare the contract as unlawful;[102] obviously, it is the court that will have to do so in an appropriate case, not the trader.

66 Importantly, Cyprus law does not provide for an automatic transfer of the rights against the initial seller from the initial consumer to a subsequent buyer. However, it adopts the position of common law and the law of equity, according to which assignment of choses in action is legally permissible; as a result, when there is a valid assignment, i.e., a clear intention to assign a right of action expressed in a relevant declaration signed by the assignor or an assignment agreement between the assignor and the assignee, the assignee can bring a legal action claiming what the assignor was entitled to prior to the assignment.[103] It follows that a consumer can expressly assign his or her rights under the twin Laws to another person, who can be the subsequent buyer. It is possible that the trader may seek to contractually exclude said right (via a term to that effect in the contract with the consumer). Cyprus law does not automatically regard such exclusion of rights clauses as void, however any relevant terms will be subject to the unfairness test of the rules on unfair contract terms contained in Part VII of Law 112(I)/2021, which implement the Unfair Contract Terms Directive 93/13/EC.

67 Interestingly, though Recital 40 explicitly leaves the consequences for the case where the consumer withdraws consent for the processing of personal data, to be regulated by national laws, Law 155(I)/2021 does not spell out any such consequences. Uncertainty may arise if the consumer withdraws consent but does not terminate the contract. Recital 39 clarifies that the right to termination under the DCD does not prejudice the right of consent withdrawal under the GDPR, which means that the consumer is free to exercise both rights under the conditions that each one of them is governed by the DCD and the GDPR respectively. This does not however touch upon the effects of the exercise of the consent withdrawal right only, on the contract. Such withdrawal will effectively disallow the trader to process the consumer's personal data as that would violate the GDPR. Consent withdrawal cannot be taken to amount to a breach of contract on the part of the consumer, as such an approach would effectively mean that the DCD prejudices the GDPR (by penalizing consent withdrawal which is an absolute right under the GDPR), whereas it is explicitly stated that this is by no means the intention.[104] Accordingly, it should probably be taken to amount to a termination of the contract, as the consumer will effectively stop counter-performing the contract, however, under Law 155(I)/2021 (and the DCD) termination is allowed in case of a lack of conformity with the contract (and not any time the consumer wishes to stop the processing of his personal data for example). The fact that the DCD states that

---

[100] General contract law principles are expected to apply to compensation under the twin Laws; these are largely contained in Section 73 of Cap.149, according to which the innocent party is entitled to compensation for any damage arising naturally and foreseeably from a breach of contract; compensation is not available for indirect or remote damage.

[101] Art. 3 para. 6 SGD and Art. 3 para. 10 DCD.

[102] Section 29 para. 3 subpara. a. Law 154(I)/2021 and Section 30 para. 3 subpara. a. Law 155(I)/2021.

[103] *PPF Services Ltd v. Kythraioti and others*, civil action no. 4907/2014, 12.10.2021; *Vassos Ayiomamitis Developments Ltd v. Artemi Thomaidi* (2000) 1 CLR 238; *Christodoulou Elena K v. Evrika Ltd* (2008) 1 CLR 1243.

[104] See Recital 37 DCD.

the consumer remains free to withdraw consent in accordance with the GDPR may be relied upon by courts inevitably to read in said freedom, a right to also terminate the contract (in case he would want to withdraw consent). Yet, it would be preferable if such a termination right was explicitly provided for in the DCD for the sake of avoiding uncertainty and non-uniform application. Indeed, an explicitly provided for termination right in this case would ensure that the consumer remains free to withdraw consent, thereby exercising data protection rights *without* risking being contractually penalized. At the same time, it would, when exercised by consumers, allow traders (lawfully) to cease providing the content and/or service, which is obviously fair.

G. Commercial Guarantees

68 Section 17 of Law 154(I)/2021 transposes largely *verbatim* the corresponding Article 17 of the SGD. The only differences between the two provisions are the language requirement introduced in Section 17 of Law 154(I)/2021 mentioned earlier in this Chapter[105] and a rather unnecessary addition relating to the requirement that the guarantee must be provided to consumers "*in writing or* on any other durable medium"[106] as opposed to merely "on a durable medium" as per the relevant provision in the SGD.

H. Right of Redress

69 Section 18 of Law 154(I)/2021 and Section 19 of Law 155(I)/2021 reproduce the corresponding provisions on the right of redress in the twin Directives and subject relevant legal actions by the final seller or trader by other traders in the same chain of transactions to the general law of contracts and torts. Accordingly, the seller or trader may bring an action in contract against the trader from whom he acquired the goods, content or service and with whom therefore he has a contractual relationship. A legal action against any other trader, such as the producer, if the final seller (or trader) has not purchased the goods directly from said party, will have to be based on general tort principles, in particular, on the law of negligence.[107]

I. Enforcement

70 Remedies under the twin Laws have been covered earlier in this Chapter.[108] It is worth adding that consumers as well as the Director of the Consumer Protection Service and associations protecting the collective interests of consumers can apply to the court of an injunction among others ordering a trader to cease a violation of the law or take corrective measures against the unlawful situation that has resulted from the violation.[109] Notably, apart from the remedies made available to aggrieved consumers through a private right of action, the twin Laws also contain quite detailed provisions on enforcement in general, specifically on the powers of the Consumer Protection Service relating to the investigation of a violation as well as its powers when a violation is found,

---

[105] See supra at para 35.
[106] Emphasis added.
[107] The main provision on negligence is Section 51 of the Torts Law, Cap.148 which codifies the common law on negligence, see Emilianides and Markou, *IEL Tort Law: Cyprus*, paras 70–85.
[108] Supra paras 61–62.
[109] Section 29 Law 155/2021 and Section 28 Law 154/2021.

this including the imposition administrative fines.[110] The failure or omission to comply with a decision of the Consumer Protection Service, the obstruction of an investigation and the supply to the Service of false or misleading information constitute a criminal offence.[111]

Bibliography

Literature

1. Ian Ayres, 'The no-reading problem in consumer contract law' (2014) *Faculty Scholarship Series* Paper 4872, 545, available at: https://ianayres.yale.edu/sites/default/files/files/The%20No%20Reading%20Problem(2).pdf.

2. Jorge Morais Carvalho, 'Sale of Goods and Supply of Digital Content and Digital Services – Overview of Directives 2019/770 and 2019/771', (2019) 8(5) *Journal of European Consumer and Market Law*, 194, available at: https://kluwerlawonline.com/journalarticle/Journal+of+European+Consumer+and+Market+Law/8.5/EuCML2019037.

3. C. Achilles Emilianides and Christiana Markou, *IEL Tort Law: Cyprus* (Britt Weyts (ed.), Kluwer Law International BV, Netherlands, 2021).

4. Martim Farinha, 'Modifications on the digital content or digital service by the trader in the Directive (EU) 2019/770' (2021) 25 N.º 2, RED – *Revista Electrónica de Direito*, available at: https://cije.up.pt/client/files/0000000001/4-martim-farinha_1738.pdf.

5. Paula Giliker, 'Legislating on Contracts for the Supply of Digital Content and Services: An EU/UK/Irish Divide?' (2021) 2 *Journal of Business Law*, 143, available at: https://research-information.bris.ac.uk/ws/portalfiles/portal/263625155/2021_JBL_2_Art_3_Giliker_Proof2amended.pdf.

6. Paula Giliker, 'Regulating Contracts for the Supply of Digital Content: The EU and UK Response.' in T. Synodinou, P. Jougleux, & C. Markou (Eds.), *EU Internet Law* (Springer International Publishing AG, Switzerland, 2017), 101.

7. Evripides Hadjinestoros, *Cyprus Law on the Sale of Goods and Consumer Protection* (Nomiki Bibliothiki, Greece, 2016).

8. Rosalie Koolhoven and Luc Heerema, 'Fighting Planned Obsolescence or "The Lightbulb Conspiracy" as an Unfair Commercial Practice: For a Circular Economy' in Maria Miguel Carvalho (ed), *Law and Technology: E Tec Yearbook* (JustGov and University of Minho 2018), 27.

9. Jurgita Malinauskaite and Fatih Buğra Erdem, 'Planned obsolescence in the context of a holistic legal sphere and the circular economy' (2021) 41(3) *Oxford Journal of Legal Studies*, 719.

10. Christiana Markou, 'Directive 2011/83/EU on Consumer Rights' in A.R. Lodder & A.D. Murray (eds.), *EU Regulation of E-Commerce: A Commentary* (Edward Elgar, 2017), 177.

11. Christiana Markou, *Consumer Protection, Automated Shopping Platforms and EU Law* (Routledge, 2019).

12. Christiana Markou, 'Directive 2011/83/EU of the European Parliament and of the Council of 25 October' in *EU Regulation of E-Commerce* (Edward Elgar 2022), 151–221.

13. G. Polyvios Polyviou, *The Law of Contracts* (Volume 2, Chrysafini and Polyviou, Nicosia, 2014).

14. Stefan Wrbka and Larry A. DiMatteo, 'Comparative Warranty Law: Case of Planned Obsolescence' (2019) 21(4) *Journal of Business Law (J. Bus. L.)*, 907.

---

[110] Sections 21–24 Law 155/2021 and Sections 20–23 Law 154/2021.
[111] Section 31 Law 155/2021 and Section 30 Law 154/2021.

Bibliography

Case law

European Court of Justice (CJEU).

CJEU, Case C-52/18, 23.05.2019, *Christian Fülla v Toolport GmbH*, ECLI:EU:C:2019:447.

CJEU, Case C 49/11, 05.07.2012, *Content Services Ltd v Bundesarbeitskammer*, ECLI:EU:C:2012:419.

Cyprus case law

Christodoulou Elena K v. Evrika Ltd (2008) 1 CLR 1243.

Diexodos Ltd v. Dan-Form ApS, civil action no. 7233/11, 14.4.2020.

Gonergy Limited v. Michael Barrett, civil action no. 399/08, 27.9.2013.

Mariou Dimitriou v. MTN Cyprus Limited, civil action no. 5085/08, 24.11.2014.

PPF Services Ltd v. Kythraioti and others, civil action no. 4907/2014, 12.10.2021.

Vassos Ayiomamitis Developments Ltd v. Artemi Thomaidi (2000) 1 CLR 238.

European Law

Charter of Fundamental Rights of the European Union.

Council Directive 85/374/EEC of 25 July 1985 on the approximation of the laws, regulations and administrative provisions of the Member States concerning liability for defective products (the Product Liability Directive (PLD).

Council Directive 93/13/EEC of 5 April 1993 on unfair terms in consumer contracts (the Unfair Contract Terms Directive).

Directive 1999/44/EC of the European Parliament and of the Council of 25 May 1999 on certain aspects of the sale of consumer goods and associated guarantees (The Consumer Sales Directive) (CSD).

Directive 2002/58/EC of the European Parliament and of the Council of 12 July 2002 concerning the processing of personal data and the protection of privacy in the electronic communications sector (Directive on privacy and electronic communications) (the e-Privacy Directive).

Directive 2005/29/EC of the European Parliament and of the Council of 11 May 2005 concerning unfair business-to-consumer commercial practices in the internal market and amending Council Directive 84/450/EEC, Directives 97/7/EC, 98/27/EC and 2002/65/EC of the European Parliament and of the Council and Regulation (EC) No 2006/2004 of the European Parliament and of the Council ('Unfair Commercial Practices Directive') (Text with EEA relevance) (the Unfair Commercial Practices Directive).

Directive 2006/114/EC of the European Parliament and of the Council of 12 December 2006 concerning misleading and comparative advertising (codified version) (Text with EEA relevance) (the Misleading and Comparative Advertising Directive).

Directive 2009/125/EC of the European Parliament and of the Council of 21 October 2009 establishing a framework for the setting of ecodesign requirements for energy-related products (Text with EEA relevance).

Directive 2011/83/EU of the European Parliament and of the Council of 25 October 2011 on consumer rights, amending Council Directive 93/13/EEC and Directive 1999/44/EC of the European Parliament and of the Council and repealing Council Directive 85/577/EEC and Directive 97/7/EC of the European Parliament and of the Council Text with EEA relevance (The Consumer Rights Directive (CRD).

Directive 2013/53/EU of the European Parliament and of the Council of 20 November 2013 on recreational craft and personal watercraft and repealing Directive 94/25/EC Text with EEA relevance (the Directive 2013/53/EU on recreational craft and personal watercraft).

Directive (EU) 2018/1972 of the European Parliament and of the Council of 11 December 2018 establishing the European Electronic Communications Code (Recast)Text with EEA relevance (Directive 2018/1972 on European Electronic Communications Code).

Directive (EU) 2019/770 of the European Parliament and of the Council of 20 May 2019 on certain aspects concerning contracts for the supply of digital content and digital services (Text with EEA relevance.) (SGD).

Directive (EU) 2019/771 of the European Parliament and of the Council of 20 May 2019 on certain aspects concerning contracts for the sale of goods, amending Regulation (EU) 2017/2394 and Directive 2009/22/EC, and repealing Directive 1999/44/EC (Text with EEA relevance.) (DCD).

Regulation (EU) 2016/679 of the European Parliament and of the Council of 27 April 2016 on the protection of natural persons with regard to the processing of personal data and on the free movement of such data, and repealing Directive 95/46/EC (Text with EEA relevance) (General Data Protection Regulation) (GDPR).

Documents of EU Organs

European Commission, *Proposal for a Directive of the European Parliament and of the Council on certain aspects concerning contracts for the supply of digital content*, 9.12.2015, COM/2015/0634 final – 2015/0287 (COD).

European Commission, *Proposal for a Directive of the European Parliament and of the Council on certain aspects concerning contracts for the online and other distance sales of goods*, 9.12.2015, COM/2015/0635 final – 2015/0288 (COD).

European Parliament, Directorate-General for Internal Policies of the Union, Wenderhost, *Sale of goods and supply of digital content – two worlds apart?*, European Parliament 2016, https://www.europarl.europa.eu/cmsdata/98774/pe%20556%20928%20EN_final.pdf.

Law of Cyprus

The Certain Aspects Concerning Contracts for the Sale of Goods Law of 2021 (Law 154(I)/2021).

The Certain Aspects Concerning Contracts for the Supply of Digital Content and Digital Services Law of 2021, (Law 155(I)/2021).

The Conditions for the Sale of Goods at a Discount Law (Law 30(I)/90).

The Contract Law, Chapter 149 (1959) (Cap.149).

The Control of Misleading and Comparative Advertising Law (Law 92(I)/2000).

The Consumer Protection Law of 2021 (Law 112(I)/2021).

The Essential Requirements to be Met by Specified Categories of Products Law of 2002 (Law 30(I)/2002).

The Law on Certain Aspects of the Sale of Consumer Goods and Related Guarantees Law of 2000 (Law 7 (I)/2000).

The Law providing for the Protection of Natural Persons with regard to the Processing of Personal Data and for the Free Movement of such Data of 2018 (Law 125(I)/2018).

The Law on the Regulation of Electronic Communications and Postal Services of 2004 (Law 112(I)/2004).

The Limitation of Actions Law (Law 66(I)/2012).

The Sales of Goods Law of 1994 (Law 10(I)/94).

The Torts Law (Civil Wrongs Law), Cap.148 (1959).

Bibliography

Regulations (K.D.P.) 191/2017, The Basic Requirements (Pleasure Boats and Individual Boats) Regulations of 2017, which were issued by the Council of Ministers, according to article 59 of the Basic Requirements that must meet Specific Product Categories of Laws of 2002 to 2013, after being submitted to the Parliament of Representatives and approved by it, are published in the Official Gazette of the Republic in accordance with paragraph (3) of article 3 of the Submission to the House of Representatives of Regulations Issued by Authorization of Law, Law (L.99 of 1989 as amended by Laws 227 of 1990 to 3 (I) of 2010), (The Basic Requirements (Pleasure Boats and Individual Boats) Regulations of 2017), https://www.dms.gov.cy/dms/shipping.nsf/all/92DFAC5C342E1FB4C2258377003EE366/$file/K%CE%94%CE%A0%20191-2017.pdf?openelement (in Greek).

Czech Republic

A. Introduction – General Framework 1
B. Definitions and Scope of Application 6
   I. Existing Legislatory Issues concerning Sales Law 7
   II. Inapplicable Rules and inconsistent Practice concerning Digital Contracts .. 9
   III. The new Regulation of Digital Content and Services 11
   IV. Data as Counter-Performance 16
C. Conformity of goods 19
   I. Implementation of the subjective and the objective Requirements for Conformity 19
   II. Exclusion of Existence of a Lack of Conformity 30
   III. "Durability" and repairability 33
   IV. Consequences of the incorrect Installation of the Digital Content 36
   V. Consumer's Duty to Provide personal Data as a Counter-Performance in Terms of its Enforceability 39
   VI. Modification of Digital Content or Digital Service 42
   VII. Art. 10 DCD and Art. 9 SGD on third Party Rights 44
   VIII. Relationship with Intellectual Property Law 47
D. Liability of the Trader 49
   I. Supply of digital content and digital services 49
   II. Interruption of long-term Supply of Digital Content 53
   III. Consequences of a Failure to Supply with Respect to Obstacles such as Impossibility 55
   IV. Early Termination of Number-Independent Interpersonal Communication Service 61
   V. Coordination with Art. 107, par. 2 European Electronic Communications Code 62
   VI. Consequences of the Trader's Non-Compliance with the GDPR regarding Contracts for the Supply of Digital Content 63
E. Remedies for the Failure to Supply and Remedies for the Lack of Conformity 64
   I. Right to Withhold Payment 64
   II. Specific Rules in Order to Define the Place of Delivery 69
   III. Rules on the Costs of Transport in the Event of Repair or Replacement 72
   IV. Right of Withdrawal 75
   V. Restitution where the Trader Supplies Digital Content 77
   VI. Environmental Sustainability and Repair over Replacement 81
   VII. Rights against the initial Seller from the initial Consumer to a subsequent Buyer 88
F. Commercial Guarantees 90
G. Time Limits 93
H. Right of Redress 99
I. Other Consumer Requests beyond Warranty and Guarantee in the Case of Non-Conformity 105
J. Conclusion 109
   Bibliography 111

A. Introduction – General Framework

The Twin Directives on Digital Content and Services (hereafter DCD) and on the Sale of Goods (SGD) were expected to be implemented by the European Member States to reshape their national Sales Law regulations by the end of 2021, so they could better tackle the challenges of our Digital Age. The Czech legislator was unable to comply with the implementation period; although the legislator sent the amending drafts[1] in due time – in September 2020 – to the Parliament, the legislator could not manage their transposition by the deadline. The reasons for the delay included the Covid pandemic, the Czech parliamentary elections in October 2021, and most recently the Russia – Ukraine crisis, which undoubtedly required more urgent action by the legislators. Fortunately, the new act entered into force on 6 January 2023 as Act no 374/2022 Coll[2]. Nevertheless, this delay clearly disadvantages Czech consumers, leaving them without concrete norms, for example on digital content. Furthermore, how the Czech jurisdiction interprets domestic law consistently with the consumer-friendly innovations in the Twin Directives, for example the one year long reversed burden of proof in contractual disputes, beginning in January 2022, remains a challenge. Due to the historical reluctance of Czech courts to interpret national rules in conformity with the EU Consumer Directives,[3] it can be presumed that Czech consumers cannot enjoy these innovations until their transposition.

2   The Act transposes the enforcement rules of Art 21 DCD and Art. 19 SGD into the Act on Consumer Protection[4]; together with the transposition of the Modernisation Directive (EU) 2019/2161[5], but the remaining majority of both Twin Directives is planned to be placed into the Czech Civil Code[6] (hereafter: CzCC). From the perspective of the legislator's technique, the Czech Republic follows the path of those countries (e.g. Germany and The Netherlands), which included their substantive consumer legislation in their Civil Code, despite the risk of making them a constant construction site[7] caused by the ever-changing EU consumer law. This transposition approach on one hand undoubtedly raises the gravity of the codification, expecting a smooth creation of further building blocks; however, on the other hand, it enables the Code to solve future challenges, and should be prized for its easier usability by practitioners. However, it is worth mentioning that not all amendments of the Civil Code deal with the transposition of the mentioned Twin-Directives. Several changes should fill the remaining gaps of earlier unsuccessful transposition, which were not resolved by the re-codification of the old Civil Code between 2000 and 2012. Nevertheless, academics and the legislator carefully reshaped the earlier post-communist Civil Code[8] but several inconsistencies concerning consumer law, especially regarding the Unfair Contract Terms Directive[9], the Consumer

---

[1] Sněmovní tisk 994/0, Novela z. – občanský zákoník (Parliamentary Press 994/0, Amendment to the Civil Code) available: https://www.psp.cz/sqw/historie.sqw?o=8&t=994.

[2] Zákon č. 374/2022 Sb.Zákon, kterým se mění zákon č. 634/1992 Sb., o ochraně spotřebitele, ve znění pozdějších předpisů, a zákon č. 89/2012 Sb., občanský zákoník (Act No. 374/2022 Coll.Act amending Act No. 634/1992 Coll., on Consumer Protection, and Act No. 89/2012 Coll., Civil Code) available: https://www.zakonyprolidi.cz/cs/2022-374.

[3] It was reported e.g. by European Commission, *Study for the Fitness Check of EU consumer and marketing law – Final report Part 3 – Country reporting*, May 2017, 255.

[4] Zákon 634/1992 Sb. ochrana spotřebitele (Act No. 634/1992 Coll. on Consumer Protection).

[5] Directive (EU) 2019/2161 of the European Parliament and of the Council of 27 November 2019 amending Council Directive 93/13/EEC and Directives 98/6/EC, 2005/29/EC and 2011/83/EU of the European Parliament and of the Council as regards the better enforcement and modernisation of Union consumer protection rules, OJ L 328, 18.12.2019, 7–28

[6] Zákon 89/2012 Sb. Občanský zákoník (Act No. 89/2012 Coll. Civil Code).

[7] From this reason the Czech recodification committee originally planned not to include consumer law into the new Civil Code see 1.2.3.1 of the Substantive intent of the Civil Code, available: http://obcanskyzakonik.justice.cz/images/pdf/vecny_zamer_OZ_2000.pdf and Dauner-Lieb et al., *Schuldrecht* (2002) 5.

[8] Zákon 40/1964 Sb. Občanský zákoník (Act No. 40/1964 Coll. Civil Code).

[9] Council Directive 93/13/EEC of 5 April 1993 on unfair terms in consumer contracts, OJ L 95, 31.4.1993 29–34.

Rights Directive[10], the Directive on late payment[11] and others[12] remained. The amendments aimed to solve these discrepancies as well.

The transposition of the Twin Directives impacts the structure of the existing law of obligations and contracts, but other fields of law, such as the law on intellectual property or data protection, did not change. 3

The changes due to the SGD impact the general law of obligations and contracts slightly, and all the new features of the SGD are incorporated to the existing special subdivision for purchase contracts with consumers. Not only general contract law, but also sales law gained their respective consumer part. New information obligations are stipulated in the implementing norms of the SGD, delivered in *Chapter 4 Provisions on obligations arising from contracts concluded with consumers* of *Title I. General provision of the obligations*, where all general information requirements on traders with regard to B2C contracts are included. Definitions of some terms, such as compatibility and interoperability, were also noted briefly here, but functionality, for example, was not defined. With regard to the conformity of goods and the liability of traders, the affected parts of the purchase contract section were amended and *Book IV. Relative Property Rights, II. Obligation arising from judicial Acts, - Chapter 1 Transfer of a thing into the ownership of another - Division 2 Purchase - and Subdivision 6 - Special provisions on the sale of consumer goods* were supplemented. New rules on the conformity of goods, liability of the trader and further remedies for the failure to supply were placed here, and also the lack of conformity was updated. However, neither the structure of the general law of obligations, nor special contract law was impacted. Only the hierarchy of rights derived from defective performance was modified slightly, partly because of the novel features of both Directives, partly because the legislator attempted, in parallel with the transposition, to combat confusing overlaps between the general rules on quality guarantees and special norms for purchase contracts[13]. However, all these novelties are only valid in B2C relations because the Ministry did not consider widening the scope of the SGD on businesses. 4

More significant structural changes should be noted concerning the transposition of the DCD, because the Ministry decided to create a new contract type, "*providing digital content*", which was placed at *Book IV. Relative Property Rights, II. Obligation arising from judicial Acts, - Chapter 2 Relinquishing a thing to be used by another*, in a new *Division 6, Providing Digital Content*. This follows the *Division 5 Licence*, where provisions on licence contracts, on items protected by the Copyright Act, on publishing and on the rights of database authors are collected. The new Division closed a long debate on the affiliation of digital contracts; and although the similarities to licence contracts should be expressed, the unique characteristics of providing digital content and services are also underlined. This placement could be useful for practitioners.[14] Some of the new rules 5

---

[10] Directive 2011/83/EU of the European Parliament and of the Council of 25 October 2011 on consumer rights, amending Council Directive 93/13/EEC and Directive 1999/44/EC of the European Parliament and of the Council and repealing Council Directive 85/577/EEC and Directive 97/7/EC, OJ L 304, 22.11.2011, 64-88.

[11] Directive 2011/7/EU of the European Parliament and of the Council of 16 February 2011 on combating late payment in commercial transactions, OJ L 48, 23.2.2011, 1-10.

[12] Further inconsistencies concerning Directive 2002/65/EC, Directive 2008/122/EC, Directive 2015/2302 and Directive 2000/31/EC.

[13] Sněmovní tisk 947/21, Návrh zákona, kterým se mění zákon č. 634/1992 Sb., o ochraně spotřebitele, ve znění pozdějších předpisů, a zákon č. 89/2012 Sb., občanský zákoník, ve znění pozdějších předpisů (Parliamentary Press 947/21 Draft to amend Act No. 634/1992 Coll., on Consumer Protection, and Act No. 89/2012 Coll., Civil Code) available: https://apps.odok.cz/veklep-detail?pid=ALBSBXVE6S65, 88.

[14] see Wendehorst, 'Die neuen Regelungen im BGB zu Verträgen über digitale Produkte' (2021) *NJW*, 2913 (2914).

concerning digital content and services, such as the undue performance of supply, the necessity for updates and the reversed burden of proof on conformity of items, are valid in both B2B and B2C relations, while the remedies for lack of conformity is different for the two kinds of buyer, enabling only consumers to enjoy more strict remedies.

B. Definitions and Scope of Application

6   Several institutions of the Twin Directives already existed in Czech contract law but, considering the transposition requirements, their scope was too narrow. In general, the impact of the proposed legislation on the related doctrinal debates was not significant, except for non-monetary counter-performance for digital content, which is definitely a novelty, although is still not widely debated in the Czech literature[15]. The main added value of the amendments is in establishing a new, advanced framework for the terminology of the digital environment. Defining the essence of digital content, and even more of digital services[16], was an urgent necessity in the Czech Republic, because neither the understanding of digital content, nor the classification of digital services was consistent. As such, clear definitions and concrete requirements for the supply of digital content seemed to be unavoidable tasks for the legislator.

I. Existing Legislatory Issues concerning Sales Law

7   With the amendments, the responsible Ministries[17] aimed to clarify the existing rules, fill the remaining implementation gaps, and comply with the SGD. First, overlapping national rules were to be abolished on remedies for lack of conformity with regard to existing contract law and sales contracts, which were not user-friendly in the existing Code[18] Uncertainties also surrounded the material scope of the Subdivision of CzCC "*sale of goods in business*". In particular, it was contested whether these rules were also applicable to purchases of immovable property[19], because the rules on immovables were regulated in a separate subsection. Furthermore, the current legislation did not take Articles 4 and 6 of the old Sales of Consumer Goods Directive[20] into sufficient account concerning the right of redress of the final seller against the persons liable in the contractual chain; leading to uncertainty for businesses in court procedures[21]. There was a similar situation concerning Art. 6 on commercial guarantee statements.

8   No significant changes in the Czech law occurred concerning the transposition issues of the SGD, which mainly focused on the hierarchy of the remedies. Only the strict Czech rules of notification of a defect, the so-called undue delay notification, needed to be softened to comply with the SGD. In addition, the amendments better differentiate

---

[15] Škorničková, 'Osobní údaje jako vzácný artikl' (2017) *gdpr.cz* available: https://www.gdpr.cz/blog/osobni-data-jako-vzacny-artikl/

[16] Richter, 'Směrnice EU 2019/770 o některých aspektech poskytování digitálního obsahu a digitálních služeb jako nástroj ochrany spotřebitele' (2020) 4 *Jurisprudence*, 9 (16)

[17] Responsible ministries: First draft – the Ministry of Justice, and second draft the Ministry of Industry and Trade.

[18] See Commentary to § 2169 CzCC in Švestka et al, *Občanský zákoník. Komentář. Svazek V (§ 1721–2520, relativní majetková práva 1. část)* (Wolters Kluwer, Praha, 2014).

[19] Concerning case law it was affirmed by Decision of the Supreme Court File No 33 Odo 1314/2005, from 27. 7. 2006.

[20] Directive 1999/44/EC of the European Parliament and of the Council of 25 May 1999 on certain aspects of the sale of consumer goods and associated guarantees, OJ L 171, 7.7.1999, 12–16.

[21] Explanatory Notes to Sněmovní tisk 947/21, (Parliamentary Press 947/21) 78.

between B2B and B2C remedies for lack of conformity. While the newly created requirements of *Subdivision 6 – Special provisions on the sale of consumer goods* follow the structure of Art 13 SGD, in B2B relations, businesses enjoy more discretion to agree which of the four main remedies they will prefer. However, consumer rights are more limited with regard to choosing the remedies, according to Art. 13 SGD.

II. Inapplicable Rules and inconsistent Practice concerning Digital Contracts

In the Czech Republic – similarly to most European countries, with exception of Ireland, the Netherlands and the UK – before the transposition of the DCD, a concrete definition of digital content was missing.[22] Although digital content fulfilled the definition of goods according to Section 489 CzCC, the responsible Ministries assumed that the existing intellectual property rights[23] were not sufficient to use them by analogy for digital content and digital services, because the two target different situations[24]. For instance, in the event of restricting the intellectual property rights of a third party, the rules on legal defect should be applied (§ 1920 CzCC), which would have hardly corresponded to the remedies for lack of conformity concerning the DCD.[25]

Turning to the understanding of digital content, it was contested in the Czech Republic whether data belong to digital content, if they are provided on a durable medium (e.g. DVD or pen drive). With regard to the national market surveillance carried out by the Czech Trade Inspectorate, if the digital content was delivered on a durable medium, then it was taken as a classic purchase of goods.[26] The problem was that this practice did not take into consideration whether or not it served exclusively as a carrier of digital content. Moreover, goods with digital elements which required digital content or a digital service in order to perform their functions were also not defined; not to mention how digital services were classified. These uncertainties should be solved by the new rules.

III. The new Regulation of Digital Content and Services

The Act established a new contract type on providing digital content and services; wherein all norms necessary for the transposition of the DCD were collected. For those aspects that were not regulated in the DCD, such as the formation, validity or nullity of digital contracts, no new rules were established and consequently, the existing general contract law is furthermore applicable. Regarding digital content, the Act makes a general distinction between obligations, the content of which is continuous performance for a certain period of time and those with the content of a one-off performance, or repeated one-time performance. As a basic rule, obligations with continuous performance for a certain period of time are deemed to be general regulation (Section 2389a CzCC), whereas the rules for one-off performance were set out explicitly. The definition of digital content was greatly widened to all relevant forms, and specific to both B2B and B2C relations. The amendment introduces a two-track solution for non-conformity. Whilst

---

[22] Rafel, "The Directive Proposals on Online Sales and Supply of Digital Content (Part I): will the new rules attain their objective of reducing legal complexity?' (2016) 23 *IDP UOC* 1.

[23] Zákon 121/2000 Sb. o právu autorském (Act No. 121/2000 Coll. on Copyright).

[24] Explanatory Notes to Sněmovní tisk 947/21, (Parliamentary Press 947/21) 79.

[25] See earlier court decisions, such as Decision of the Supreme Court File No. 29 Odo 1020/2003 from 23 March 2004.

[26] See Czech Trade Inspection, available: https://www.coi.cz/faq/a-co-je-vlastne-digitalni-obsah/.

the most significant rules ensuring the function of data (such as the time period of performance, updates and the reversed burden of proof on conformity of goods) are valid in both relations; the remedies for lack of conformity however differ depending on whether the buyer is a consumer or a trader. In B2B relations, the general contractual remedies are to apply, although the contractual partners can agree on them; in B2C relations the relevant rules of Art. 14 DCD are in force, which differ slightly from the usual contractual remedies.

12 Nevertheless, the amendment made an effort to underline the similarities and differences between "usual" contract law and contracts concerning digital content and the definition of digital content still only covers items, without mentioning any data. According to Section 2389a CzCC "By providing digital content, the provider undertakes to make an item in digital form (digital content) available to the user, for his own use and the user undertakes to pay a reward for it." The mentioned norm only names supply in digital form, but not production, although, in accordance with Art. 2 (a) DCD, data that are produced and supplied in digital form are also digital content. This version of the definition might generate interpretation issues, although the Ministry of Justice believes that the Czech version corresponds to the definition in the DCD and is – in the context of Czech law – more comprehensive.

13 Although digital services are not included at this definition, the amendments put a clarifying paragraph at the end of the *Digital Division* (Section 2389t CzCC); which concludes that the rules on digital content are also applicable to all types of digital services. This solution might not be assumed from the aspect of the legislator's construction, but fulfils the implementation requirements. In the future, the "supply-long" liability of traders for lack of conformity in continuous supply according to Art. 11 (3) DCD, which is applicable in the Czech Republic in both B2C and B2B situations (Section 2389c (1) CzCC), could be challenging. However, according to the Ministry of Justice, no practical difficulties in removing non-conformity of digital content are foreseeable, because a new installation of data can quickly solve the conformity problem.

14 *Goods with digital elements* and digital content provided on durable media share, according to the new rules, the destiny of goods. For *goods with digital elements*, e.g. cleaner robots, which are defined in Section 2158 CzCC, the special *Subdivision 6 – Special provisions on the sale of consumer good* are applicable, which means the transposed rules of SGD are in force. These provisions shall also apply to digital content or digital services, if they are provided by a third party. The only exception is when it is clear from the content of the contract and from the nature of the contract that the good and the content are provided separately. In that case, the *Digital Division* should apply to the digital content.

15 If the digital content is provided on a durable medium then, according to Section 1838 CzCC, it generally shares the destiny of goods. This rule seems to follow the former practice of Czech market surveillance, although the amendment finally distinguishes whether the durable medium serves only as a carrier. If a tangible movable serves only as a carrier of digital content, the *provisions on the sale of consumer goods* are not valid, with the exception of handover of the performance (Section 2159 CzCC) and the special withdrawal right after an unsuccessful additional reasonable period (Section 2159a CzCC). These bring the destiny of these types of content closer to real digital content.

B. Definitions and Scope of Application

IV. Data as Counter-Performance

The acknowledgement of personal data as counter-performance, is what Alex Metzger considers "one of the innovative elements" of the DCD, but "empirically, it is nothing more than the approval of a social practice"[27]. Changing the synallagmatic performance of users in this way was not only a doctrinal change, but it clearly intensifies the duties and rights of both the consumer and the supplier. On one hand, consumers are entitled to have the digital content or service brought into conformity (e.g. through updates), but, on the other hand, the consumer's duty to provide data is underlined. The new Czech wording, (Section 2389a CzCC), that "the *user* undertakes to pay a reward" is very broad. It can be immediate performance or a future one, and the rule is applicable to both B2B and B2C relations. The new rule does not further regulate whether the supplier and the user should clarify the submission of personal data as a separate contract. Neither the conclusion, nor the nullity nor the contractual obligation on data submission is specified; therefore, general contract law shall also apply to this type of counter-performance. Taking into consideration that the data are the main reward for a digital content or service (no further fees should be paid for the digital content), the supplier will have a justifiable interest in the contractual performance of the consumer. However, the Czech rules, similarly to the DCD, unfortunately miss the opportunity to go into more detail on which types of data could be counter-performance (e.g. only personal data in a narrow sense or data that are also sensitive[28]) or when the submission of data in the future is fulfilled. Those clarifying rules would protect consumers from contested "over-performance". The only clarification that is made in the new rules concerning contracts on digital content that are rewarded with data is that the remedies for the lack of conformity or failure to supply are only valid in B2C relations. This means that, for B2B contract relations, general contract law is applicable. Processing personal data only for the purpose of providing digital content or only to fulfill traders' legal obligations are both out of the scope of the reward.

16

How far the introduction of data as counter-performance will change the existing doctrine on synallagmatic performance has attracted little comment in the Czech literature; however, the Czech Authority for the Protection of Personal Data emphasized the immaterial values of personal data, which prevent them from being seen as counter-performance, which shows presumable practical problems in the future. Some of scholars criticize the legislator for not dealing conceptually with the contractual problem of data as counter-performance.[29] Štepán Richter warns further that the broad definition of data under Art. 4 No 1 of the GDPR, which is also applicable to the DCD[30], can be inappropriately broad in terms of contract law. The treatment of those data that are not *stricto sensu* personal data, but are used as such by traders because they have significant commercial value could also be problematic, because their position is not clarified by the DCD.[31] If they were to be taken as part of the reward, a disparity between the performances of the parties could occur.

17

---

[27] Metzger, 'Data as Counter-Performance: What Rights and Duties do Parties Have?' (2017) 8 *JIPITEC* 1.
[28] See clarification of Art. 4 and Art. 9 of GDPR.
[29] Richter, 'Ochrana osobních údajů v kontextu poskytování digitálních dat spotřebitelům' (2021) 9 *Právník*, 745 (750).
[30] See Art. 2 subpara 8 of DCD.
[31] Richter, 'Směrnice EU 2019/770 o některých aspektech poskytování digitálního obsahu a digitálních služeb jako nástroj ochrany spotřebitele' (2020) 4 *Jurisprudence*, 9 (11).

18   More contested in the Czech literature is how the application of the new DCD rules will collide with the principles of data protection.[32] The protection of persons and personal data are, according to Art. 8 of the Czech Constitution,[33] human rights, further specified by Art. 10 Sec. 3 of the Charter of Fundamental Right and Freedoms[34], which is part of the Constitution in broader sense where everyone is protected against unauthorized collection, disclosure or other misuse of personal data. These principles are also mirrored in the re-codified Civil Code, where the CzCC dedicates a *Division 6 Personality rights* for individuals in *Chapter II Persons*. The Czech jurisdiction gives very broad protection to personality rights. According to Section 87 CzCC, a person can anytime withdraw his or her consent for usage of personal data, also if it was given for a fixed period of time. However, the unlimited withdrawal right is also a principal idea of the GDPR, to which the DCD is without prejudice;[35] but the GDPR does not care about civil law. It can create practical problems when the consumer withdraws their consent, and how far the supplier's performance is disputed; not to mention that the consumer will hardly be able to check whether the trader has stopped using their personal data or not. The Explanatory Note of the Act itself comments that the personal data provided by the consumer may be misused for purposes other than those specified in the contract.[36] Nevertheless, this risk should be minimized, primarily using the GDPR with its mechanisms and sanctions provided for by national law, but the *Division 6 Personality rights* mentioned can also be beneficial as judicial protection in civil proceedings.

C. Conformity of goods

I. Implementation of the subjective and the objective Requirements for Conformity

19   At the beginning, an important note must be made vis-a-vis the terminology used. For the lack of conformity used both by the DCD and SGD, the Czech legislation uses the term *"vada"*. However, the same term *"vada"* is used in the case of regulating liability for damage caused by a defective product as laid down and defined by Directive No. 85/374/EEC and transposed to Section 2939 et seq. CzCC. The Czech Civil Code defines both concepts individually; however, the use of a single word *"vada"*, i.e. defect, is sometime confusing and, when applying the concept of lack of conformity or the defect under product liability, the person must be aware of the very fundamental difference between the two regulations.[37]

20   The current concept of lack of conformity of consumer goods is defined in Section 2161 CzCC, which sets the conditions for the goods under the headings *"quality at takeover"* (jakost při převzetí). A defect is then a deviation from the requirements set in this way. The provision requires that the goods be free from defects and thus *"perfect"*.

---

[32] Richter, 'Ochrana osobních údajů v kontextu poskytování digitálních dat spotřebitelům' (2021) 9 *Právnik*, 745 (749).
[33] Ústavní zákon č. 1/1993 Sb. (Act. No. 1/1993 Coll. Constitution).
[34] Listina základních práv a svobod zákon č. 2/1993 Sb. (Act. No. 2/193 Coll. Charter of Fundamental Right and Freedoms).
[35] See Reference 37 of DCD.
[36] Explanatory Notes to Sněmovní tisk 947/21, (Parliamentary Press 947/21) 98.
[37] Hrádek, 'Czech Republic' in Hajnal (ed), *Comparative Analysis of National Jurisdictions Regarding Consumer Sales and Unfair Commercial Practices* (2020), 7 (10).

C. Conformity of goods

Perfectness will always be measured against the agreement of the parties or with the legal requirement, if the required properties can be deduced from it.

The wording of Section 2161 CzCC now reflects both the subjective and objective requirements laid down in Art. 6 and 7 of the SGD.

As regards the subjective requirements, their existence depends on the ability of the buyer to agree upon them with the seller. This can be rather difficult, as a number of contracts will be deemed adhesive, which means that there is only a very limited possibility for the weaker party to specify the subjective requirements.

As to the objective requirements, strong emphasis is placed on the legal regulations and technical norms, which must be observed when assessing the item's suitability for purpose of use. However, when no objectively existing technical norms exist, a link should be made to codes of conduct established by the particular business branch, i.e. by the sellers. This last resort may endanger the situation of the buyer, since those codes of conduct will be established in favour of the seller. This is especially the case with digital content, where no technical norms exist in the Czech Republic.[38]

A positive development can be seen in the objective nature of the general purpose. Under current regulation, the purpose primarily results from the information made by the seller or from general usage of the item in general. Under the new regulation, the purpose shall be deemed and interpreted objectively based on the genaral use of the item.

If any of the required properties are missing, the item is considered defective. The defect will also be a defect of assembly, because assembly of the item is an integral part of the seller's obligations under the purchase contract.[39]'

The buyer does not have to prove the existence of the defect at the moment of takeover, but only the defectiveness, i.e. lack of conformity with the contract or the legal requirements. Moreover, the lack of conformity is established under the legal presumption.[40] As regards defences, the presumption must be completely rebutted by the seller. As regards the scope of evidence, only questioning the reasons for the defect does not suffice.

From the point of view of perfectness, it is necessary to mention that the regulation of the consumer purchase contract, pursuant to Section 2158 CzCC, applies to the sale of an item within the meaning of Section 489 CzCC, i.e. an item in a legal sense. However, unlike the previous wording, the item must be tangible (movable).

The same structure of subjective and objective requirements is laid down in Section 2389i CzCC, which reflects requirements laid down in Arts. 7, 8 and 9 of the DCD. The provision of Section 2389c requires that the goods are free from defects and the provider shall provide to the user the newest version of the digital content available at the moment of the conclusion of the contract. Under Section 2389d CzCC, the provider shall ensure that the user will get the agreed updates of the digital content as well as necessary updates which ensure that the digital content remains without defects during the term of the contract and he/she will be notified of them. Section 2389f regulates the provision of digital content that is provided at once.

Under Section 2389d para. 3 CzCC, if the user has not carried out the update pursuant to paragraph 2 within a reasonable time, he shall not be entitled to the rights of defect which arose only as a result of the non-performed update. This does not apply

---

[38] Richter, 'Směrnice EU 2019/770 o některých aspektech poskytování digitálního obsahu a digitálních služeb jako nástroj ochrany spotřebitele' (2020) 4 *Jurisprudence*, 9 (15).

[39] Hubková, '§ 2161' in Petrov et al., *Občanský zákoník, komentář* (C.H.Beck, Prague 2017), 2185.

[40] L. Tichý, § 2161 in Švestka et al., *Občanský zákoník. Komentář. Svazek V (§ 1721–2520, relativní majetková práva 1. část)* (Wolters Kluwer, Praha, 2014), (963).

if the user was not notified of the update or the consequences of not performing it, or did not perform the update or performed it incorrectly due to a deficiency in the instructions.

II. Exclusion of Existence of a Lack of Conformity

30   As regards the transposition of DCD, the provider shall not be responsible for objective requirements as stated in Section 2389i para 2 CzCC if the provider, prior to concluding the contract, has specifically warned the user that some features of the digital content are different and the user has explicitly agreed to this when concluding the contract (Section 2389i para. 4 CzCC). As Section 2389i para. 2 CzCC lays down objective requirements, it seems to be that the legislator correctly transposed the DCD in this regard.

31   The condition for such an exclusion is that the user explicitly agreed to such a feature of the item at the contract conclusion. As the consent of the user must be explicit, in the event of a dispute a content-control will be made of whether the user's consent was really granted and whether the user was aware of all outcomes of his/her consent.

32   The same clause excluding particular characteristics has been implemented to Section 2161 para. 4 CzCC with respect to SGD.

III. "Durability" and repairability

33   The issue of "durability" has been transposed into Section 2161 para. 2 CzCC, which explicitly states that the item shall correspond to quantity, quality and other characteristics, including durability, functionality, compatibility and safety, to the usual characteristics of the same kind that the buyer can reasonably expect, also with regard to public statements made by the seller or another person in the same contract chain, in particular by advertising or labelling.

34   Thus, durability is a general concept which will be interpreted as a general ability of the goods to maintain their required functions and performance through normal use, i.e. in conformity with the SGD.

35   The Czech Republic did not plan to create norms concerning the requirements of recital 32 SGD, nor on the availability of spare parts. No regulation is explicitly provided by the Czech amendments concerning provisions establishing a framework for setting eco-design requirements for energy-related products. However, Directive 2009/125/EC is transposed into Czech legal system by Act No. 406/2000 Coll. on Energy Management and the particular provisions on eco-design are laid down in Decree No. 319/2019 Coll., which establishes binding requirements for labelling for consumers as well. The sanctions according to Art. 20 Directive 2009/125/EC are laid down by Act No. 406/2000 Coll. on Energy Management, in particular by Section 12a para 2. This provision deals with sanction for breach of labelling duties and it prescribes fines of up to 5 mil. CZK (200,000 Euro). Whether such an amount is proportional in all cases is questionable but, due to the possibility to impose fines according to the facts of the case.it seems to be acceptable. Measures for enhancing environmental sustainability / circular economy by way of implementing the DCD and SGD are not planned.

IV. Consequences of the incorrect Installation of the Digital Content

The installation issue is regulated in two provisions. Under Section 2161a CzCC, the seller is liable to the buyer for a defect caused by incorrect assembly or installation, which was performed according to the contract by the seller or at his responsibility. This also applies if the assembly or installation was carried out by the buyer and the defect was due to a defect in the instructions provided by the seller or provider of the digital content or digital content service, if the item has digital properties. For the provision of digital content, Section 2189j CzCC states that the provider is liable to the user for a defect caused by the incorrect connection of digital content with the user's digital environment, which was carried out by the provider or under his responsibility according to the contract. This also applies if the connection was made by the user and the defect occurred as a result of a deficiency in the instructions supplied by the provider.

Thus, the consequences of the incorrect installation depend on the content of the contract or instruction provided by the seller. In cases when such a reason is not attributable to the seller, the consequence shall be borne by the buyer.

However, the provider/seller is liable for any incorrect integration to the user's environment and there is a reversal of the burden of proof, which improves the legal position of the user. Thus, it is not relevant whether the integration was carried out by the provider, on his behalf or by the user themself when he/she followed the instructions provided by the provider. In the case of incorrect instruction, the provider shall be held liable based on the provisions of Section 9 ad 10 of the Consumer Protection Act and general provisions of the CzCC (Section 1914).

V. Consumer's Duty to Provide personal Data as a Counter-Performance in Terms of its Enforceability

The specific provision on that issue is contained in Section 2389g para. 2 CzCC. It states that the regulation on the provision of digital content shall also apply if, instead of being remunerated to the provider, the user provides or undertakes to provide his personal data, unless the provider processes them only for the purpose of providing digital content or only to fulfil his legal obligations. In such a case, the user cannot claim a reasonable discount under Section 2389m para. 2 and 3 CzCC, and the Section on reimbursement by the trader in 2389p CzCC shall not apply.

The provision clearly states that the user may provide or undertake to provide his/her data as a counter-performance. As there are no other provisions that would establish any other procedure, the general provision on rules of counter-performance shall apply. This means in particular that if the user does not provide the data in accordance with the agreed scope, the performance of the user is deemed defective and the provider has rights arising from defective performance.

However, as regards the nature of the personal data, they do not enable the enforcement of the right by the other party. Personal rights are specific rights that cannot be abandoned by the holder.

VI. Modification of Digital Content or Digital Service

42 The modification is regulated solely in the new contract type established under Section 2389a et seq. CzCC, namely the contract on provision of digital content (*smlouva o poskytování digitálního obsahu*).

43 However, the situation is ambiguous with respect to items that are directly connected with digital content or a digital service. If the digital content is provided on a durable medium then, according to Section 1838 CzCC, it generally shares the destiny of the goods. This rule seems to follow the former practice of Czech market surveillance, although the amendment finally distinguishes whether the durable medium serves only as a carrier. However, under Section 2158 CzCC, if the object of purchase is a tangible movable item that is connected with digital content or a digital content service in such a way that it would not be able to perform its functions without them, the provisions on consumer purchase contract shall also apply to the provision of digital content or digital content services, even if provided by a third party. This does not apply if it is clear from the content of the contract and from the nature of the matter that they are provided separately.

VII. Art. 10 DCD and Art. 9 SGD on third Party Rights

44 The Czech law does not provide for a broad definition, but it states in Section 2389i para. 2 lett. a) CzCC that conformity is given if the digital content is suitable for the purpose for which digital content of this kind is normally used, also taking into account the rights of third parties, legislation, technical standards or codes of conduct in the sector, in the absence of technical standards.

45 An identical provision is contained in Section 2161 para. 2 lett. a) CzCC under which conformity is given if the item is suitable for the purpose for which the item is normally used, even with regard to third party rights, legislation, technical standards or codes of conduct in the sector, if there are no technical standards.

46 Therefore, in the event that conflicting rights of third parties exist, the user has rights to remedies for a lack of conformity.

VIII. Relationship with Intellectual Property Law

47 There is no explicit regulation of that relationship and general principles and regulations therefore apply. This is confirmed by Section 2389a para. 2 CzCC, which states that where the use of digital content requires an authorization to exercise intellectual property rights, the relevant provisions on license in Section 2358 et seq. of the CzCC shall apply.

48 With the contract on the provision of digital content, the provider undertakes to make the thing available to the user in digital form (digital content) for his own use and the user undertakes to pay a fee for it. Consequently, where a license was granted, no resale or sublicense of the digital content is possible without the consent of the holder of intellectual property rights. This results from Section 2364 CzCC, under which a licensee may assign the licence to a third party in whole or in part only with prior approval of the licensor, unless agreed otherwise in the contract, and from Section 2363 under which a licensee may grant the sublicence to a third party in whole or in part only if it was agreed in the license agreement.

D. Liability of the Trader

I. Supply of digital content and digital services

Czech law explicitly provides for a specific regime of a long-term supply of digital content as prescribed by Art. 19 DGD. This is subject to Section 2389q. CzCC.

If the digital content is to be provided for a certain period of time and the change is not necessary to keep the digital content flawless, the provider may change the digital content, a) if agreed in the contract, together with a fair reason for such a change, (b) if the user does not incur additional costs as a result of the change; and (c) if it notifies the user of the change in a clear and comprehensible manner. All three conditions must be met simultaneously.

However, if the change not only insignificantly worsens the user's access to digital content or its use, the provider shall further notify the user in text form of the nature of the change, time of its implementation and the right to terminate the obligation or the possibility to keep the digital content unchanged in a reasonable time before making the change.

The user may terminate the obligation without any penalty if the change impairs its access to or use of the digital content, but not only insignificantly, within 30 days of being notified of the change or of the time the digital content was changed. This again shall not apply if the provider allows the user to refuse the change and keep the digital content in its original form at no additional cost, without this being to the detriment of its flawless provision.

II. Interruption of long-term Supply of Digital Content

There is no significant regulation of the interruption of long-term supply. However, the differentiation between the long-term and one-time supply is very important for the notification of the defect.

Under Sec. 2389k CzCC, the user may notify the provider of a defect that makes apparent or occurs in the digital content during the term of the commitment. In the case of a one-time performance, it may complain about a defect that affects the digital content within twenty-four months of making it available. On the other hand, continuous performance assumes defectless performance throughout the duration of the obligation. As in the case of the purchase of goods, the assertion of the rights resulting from the defect is subject to a general three-year statutes of limitations.

III. Consequences of a Failure to Supply with Respect to Obstacles such as Impossibility

The Czech Civil Code provides for impossibility to perform in general, allowing the obligation to be cancelled only if impossibility to perform occurs. Change of circumstances or force majeure establish secondary rights to those parties who are involved.

The impossibility to perform is regulated under Section 2006 CzCC. If the performance becomes impossible after the obligation arises, the obligation ceases to exist due to the impossibility of performance. However, fulfilment is not impossible if the obligation can be settled under difficult conditions, at higher costs, with the help of another person or after a specified time. The impossibility of performance shall be proved by the obligee. Nevertheless, if impossibility exists from very beginning, such impossibility leads to the invalidity of the contractual relationship. In addition to this general regulation, the buyer or user under the commented regulation is entitled to withdrawal from contract or reduction in price if it becomes obvious that remedy of the defective performance is impossible.

57   As regards force majeure, the Civil Code acknowledges its importance only with respect to damages and the Czech legal theory uses the term "circumstances excluding liability" since liability under contract is deemed strict. This notion is set forth in Section 2913 para. 2 CzCC.

58   As regards the circumstances excluding liability, a person can exempt himself from the duty to compensate if he proves that he was prevented from fulfilling the contractual obligation, temporarily or permanently, by an extraordinary, unforeseeable and unavoidable obstacle that arose independently of his will. An obstacle that arose from the wrongdoer's personal circumstances, or that arose when the wrongdoer was in default in fulfilling his contractual obligation, or that the wrongdoer was obliged to overcome under the agreement shall not exempt him from liability.

59   Finally, Czech law also contains a provision on change of circumstances which is contained in Section 1764 et seq. CzCC. If, after the conclusion of the contract, the circumstances change to such an extent that performance under the contract becomes more difficult for one of the parties, this does not change its obligation to pay the debt. This does not apply in the cases provided for in Sections 1765[41] and 1766[42] CzCC.

60   The legal qualification of a change in circumstances has not been adjudicated by the higher Courts. So we can argue about which circumstances are qualified.

IV. Early Termination of Number-Independent Interpersonal Communication Service

61   Czech law does not provide for specific regulation. Section 2389q para 4 CzCC states that the provision on termination shall not apply to digital content that is provided together with an internet access service pursuant to Regulation (EU) 2015/2120 of the European Parliament and of the Council or an interpersonal number-based communication service.

---

[41] (1) If there is such a substantial change in circumstances that it creates a gross disproportion in the rights and duties of the parties by disadvantaging one of them either by disproportionately increasing the cost of the performance or disproportionately reducing the value of the subject of performance, the affected party has the right to claim the renegotiation of the contract with the other party if it is proved that it could neither have expected nor affected the change, and that the change occurred only after the conclusion of the contract or the party became aware thereof only after the conclusion of the contract. Asserting this right does not entitle the affected party to suspend the performance. (2) The affected party shall not acquire the right under Subsection (1) if it assumed the risk of a change in circumstances. Available: http://obcanskyzakonik.justice.cz.

[42] (1) Upon failure to reach agreement within a reasonable time limit, a court may, on the application of any of them, decide to change the contractual obligation by restoring the balance of rights and duties of the parties, or to extinguish it as of the date and under the conditions specified in the decision. The court is not bound by the applications of the parties. (2) A court shall dismiss an application to change an obligation if the affected party fails to assert the right to renew contract negotiations within a reasonable time after it must have ascertained the change in circumstances; this time limit is presumed to be two months. Available: http://obcanskyzakonik.justice.cz.

V. Coordination with Art. 107, par. 2 European Electronic Communications Code

Act No. 127/2005 Coll., on Electronic Communications, states in § 63c paragraph 2 that: "If a consumer has the right to terminate the obligation under the contract to any component of the package pursuant to paragraph 1 before the end of the agreed period due to defective performance or other breach of contract, he has the right to terminate the obligation under the contract for all components of the package."

VI. Consequences of the Trader's Non-Compliance with the GDPR regarding Contracts for the Supply of Digital Content

In respect of the consumer's personal data, the trader shall comply with the obligations applicable under Regulation (EU) 2016/679. The Czech Act No. 110/2019 Coll., on protection of personal data, regulates in Sections 61 ff. penalties and fines for breach of duties explicitly stipulated by the Act.

E. Remedies for the Failure to Supply and Remedies for the Lack of Conformity

I. Right to Withhold Payment

There is no special provision on withholding payments by the user under the DCD. However, the legislator adopted, in Section 2173 CzCC, the right of the buyer to withhold the so-far unpaid purchase price or its part unless the seller meets its obligations from defective performance. Such rights cannot be waived or limited prior to the notification of the defect.

Additional to this new provision, the CzCC also contains, in § 1912, general rules on withholding performance of a synallagmatic obligation under contract. Under such a provision, a party who shall perform under the contract may withhold such performance unless he/she receives performance from the other party or security is provided. The condition for such a procedure is, however, that the performance is threatened by circumstances that were not known at the conclusion of the contract nor relayed to the other party.

Moreover, under § 1911 CzCC, if the parties shall perform at the same time, performance can be demanded only by the party which has already fulfilled his/her debt or is ready to do so jointly with the other party.

Another provision which deals directly with a purchase contract is § 2108 CzCC, under which the seller does not need to pay the purchase price or its part corresponding to the right to discount it if the purchased performance was defective.

Based on the new special provision, all above-mentioned provisions will be deemed general and will apply only if the new Section 2173 CzCC does not apply.

II. Specific Rules in Order to Define the Place of Delivery

69 There is only a general regulation in the Consumer Protection Act. Pursuant to Section 13 of Act No. 634/1992 Coll.,[43] based on which the seller is obliged to duly inform on the scope, conditions and manner of exercising the right from defect ("complaint"), together with information on where the complaint can be lodged. When selling or providing services outside the announced branch, the seller is obliged to provide the consumer in writing with the name and address of the seller, where the complaint can be filed even after the end of that sale or provision of services.

70 The basic provisions on the place of asserting a claim are laid down in Section 2172 et seq. CzCC, which states that the rights resulting from a defect will be asserted with the seller from whom the item was purchased. However, if another person specified for the repair is mentioned in the proof of purchase or in the confirmation pursuant to Section 2166 CzCC, who is at the place of the seller or at a closer place for the buyer, the buyer will exercise the right to repair with the person who has to carry out the repair. The person so designated for repair will carry out the repair within the period agreed between the seller and the buyer when purchasing the item.

71 Except in cases where another person is designated to carry out the repair, the seller is obliged to accept the complaint at any establishment where the assertion of the complaint is possible with regard to the range of products or services provided, possibly also at the registered office or place of business. The seller is obliged to provide the consumer with a written confirmation of matters when the consumer exercised the right, the content of the complaint and the method of handling the complaint that the consumer requires.

III. Rules on the Costs of Transport in the Event of Repair or Replacement

72 As regards the costs connected with the assertion of rights, pursuant to Section 1924 CzCC, the consumer is entitled to reimbursement of the costs effectively incurred in exercising his rights. Typical costs associated with the complaint include postage or costs of other transportation of goods and the cost of an expert opinion obtained after the complaint was rejected.

73 However, it is the seller's right to assess the expediency of individual costs and, for example, to limit the claim of the injured party in the case of improper transport.

74 As regards the scope of the right to reimbursement, the law does not only refer to cases where the seller assesses the consumer's claims as justified, but cases where the consumer complains about an item that shows defects. Whether it also applies to cases in which the consumer abuses his right, is not clear or well-reasoned.[44] The literature states that, if the buyer is aware (or should have been aware) that the seller is not responsible for the defect (e.g. because the buyer himself caused it) and nevertheless asserts the rights arising from defective performance, such costs cannot be borne by the seller. In that case, such a conclusion cannot even be deemed a restriction on the consumer's right, since the consumer has no right and, moreover, is aware (or should have been aware) of this. In some cases, victimising the seller and the use of Section

---

[43] Zákon č. 634/1992 Sb., o ochraně spotřebitele (Act No. 634/1992 Coll. on Consumer Protection).

[44] The Supreme Administrative Court in File No. 3 As 60/2005 from 22.03.2006 considers any provision in the guarantee terms of the seller which make thes consumer aware of the costs of unreasoned complaints as "able to limit the consumer in his rights to assert his rights arising from defective performance".

2909 CzCC, which establishes liability for damage caused by breach of good morals, may be considered.[45]

IV. Right of Withdrawal

Withdrawal is an extraordinary legal action in Czech law, and the Civil Code sets forth that withdrawal is only possible if the law establishes such a right or if the parties agreed. Therefore, provided that the CzCC explicitly stipulates the right to withdraw, such a possibility is in line with the Czech approach. In the case of the DCD, the user may withdraw if the content is defective and repair is either impossible or disproportionate or when the provider is in delay with his performance. The particulars of the assertion of rights are in Section 2389h and 2389m CzCC. 75

There is no explicit provision that would lay down different regulation on consequences of withdrawal of consent for processing personal data. Therefore, the processor must comply with the rules and principles established by Regulation (EU) 2016/679. This means that, as soon as the user withdraws from the contract, the provider shall stop using the personal data of the user provided as counter performance. 76

V. Restitution where the Trader Supplies Digital Content

The restitution is explicitly regulated in 2389o CzCC. 77

If the user withdraws from the contract and if the tangible medium has been handed over to him in connection with the provision of digital content, he/she shall release it to the provider at his/her request and expense without undue delay. The provider may request the release of the tangible medium within fourteen days of the termination of the obligation. 78

Furthermore, if the user withdraws from the contract, he shall refrain from using the digital content, including its provision to a third party. 79

Unfortunately, there is no specific regulation adopted within the implementation of the DCD and SGD for restitution where the trader supplies digital content and/or digital services and the consumer provides personal data as counter- performance. 80

VI. Environmental Sustainability and Repair over Replacement

There is no specific provision and both options are covered under the concept of removal of defect. 81

Under Section 2169 CzCC, if the item has a defect, the buyer may request its removal. Analogous provision with respect to digital content and services is laid down in Section 2389l CzCC. At its option, the buyer or user may request the delivery of a new item without a defect or the repair of the item, unless the chosen method of eliminating the defect is impossible or unreasonably expensive compared to the other. This will be assessed by the seller/provider, in particular with regard to the significance of the defect, the value that the item would have without the defect, and whether the defect can be remedied in a second way without significant inconvenience to the buyer/user. The seller/provider may refuse to rectify the defect if it is impossible or unreasonably 82

---

[45] Bezouška, 'Neoprávněná reklamace' (2006) 12 *Právní rádce*, 15.

expensive, especially with regard to the significance of the defect and the value that the item would have without the defect.

83 The general provisions of Sections 1923, 2106 and 2107 on rights arising from defective performance shall not apply. Those provisions relate to general purchase contracts and do not follow the policies of the Twin Directives.

84 As regards the individual types of remedy, the right to removal of the defect is subject to consideration of the nature of the item, i.e. subject to assessment of the value of the item and the cost of replacing the part or repairing it. The replacement must be carried out for the same item (colour, type, etc.), but the law does not exclude the provision of a better-quality item. However, if the replaced item is of a higher quality, the seller is not entitled to demand additional payment. If only part of the item is defective then the right to replacement can be exercised only for that part.[46]

85 The consumer may exercise his right to removal of defect in form of either replacement or repair of the item. However, if despite the repair the defect occurs again, which according to the case law happens when the defect has been removed twice and occurs again, the buyer receives the right to withdraw from the contract or to adequate price reduction. The same applies if the seller did not remove the defect or refused to do so or if it is clear either from seller's statement or from circumstances that the defect will not be removed in an adequate time or without serious difficulties for the purchaser.

86 Consequently, the buyer has a choice between individual rights, but the individual rights do not have equal status and emphasis is placed on the seller's ability or competence. Thus, the buyer is rather limited in favour of the seller. Such an aspect is understood to be objective, having regard to the circumstances of the case. Nevertheless, the decisive aspect is the consumer's interest, which is expressed, for example, by the words "considerable difficulties for consumers".[47]

87 Furthermore, no specific regulation is adopted for fighting premature or planned obsolescence of goods within the implementation of DCD and SGD.

VII. Rights against the initial Seller from the initial Consumer to a subsequent Buyer

88 The rights arising from defective performance are not linked to the subject matter of the purchase but to the contracting parties to the purchase contract. If the original buyer wants to sell the thing to a new buyer, he/she can only transfer the rights from the defective performance to the buyer based on an assignment agreement, under which the particular receivables of the original buyer towards the original seller are assigned.

89 The receivable cannot be assigned if such assignment contradicts the prior agreement of the original buyer with the original seller. Therefore, if the general terms and conditions duly incorporated into the contract or other explicit contractual provisions prohibit assignment then such a legal act is not possible and the assignment is invalid. However, if not explicitly excluded, the receivable can be assigned without the consent of the debtor.

---

[46] Hrádek, 'Czech Republic' in Hajnal (ed), *Comparative Analysis of National Jurisdictions Regarding Consumer Sales and Unfair Commercial Practices* (2020), 7 (15).
[47] L. Tichý, § 2169 in Švestka et al., *Občanský zákoník. Komentář. Svazek V (§ 1721–2520), relativní majetková práva 1. část)* (Wolters Kluwer, Praha, 2014) 980.

F. Commercial Guarantees

Commercial guarantees are not new in Czech business practice, nor for the CzCC. Delivering commercial guarantees is very common for any consumer goods, such as electrical appliances, shoes or clothes; although they occur even more often in business practice, where the seller offers an immediate replacement of a defective good, for an extra fee, in the statutory guarantee period, without any investigation of whose fault was behind the malfunction, in the guarantee period ensured by the law, or by the given commercial guarantee.

The new amendment clarifies in more detail the existing norms of the voluntary quality guarantee, to comply fully with Article 17 of the SGD. The rules define first time commercial guarantees as a unilateral legal action by the guarantor – to make especially by the seller, manufacturer or other person – to undertake to provide a given performance beyond the guarantee provided by law, if the purchased good or service does not have certain requirements (lack of conformity) through Section 2113 CzCC. Due to the voluntary nature of this obligation, it is primarily up to the guarantor as to what obligations he undertakes, but the amendment underlines that this warranty can only be taken beyond the legal rights of the buyer for defective performance, not to deceive customers in this way.[48] Although the definition of commercial guarantees is placed in the general Purchase Contract, the necessary content of commercial guarantee is however located later, in *Subdivision 6 – Special provisions on the sale of a consumer good* (Section 2174a CzCC), which stresses that the stricter requirements are valid only for commercial guarantees in B2C relations. In particular, only consumers must be provided with details of how the rights under the guarantee are to be exercised (including details of the liable person).

The Czech Republic does not use the options provided for in Art. 17 (4) SGD to lay down national rules on further aspects – not included in the SGD – concerning commercial guarantees, such as the languages in which the guarantee statement should be provided. Actually the CzCC is very generous on entrepreneurs' communications with consumers, because B2C contract law does not specify Czech as the concluding language for contracts; Section1811 CzCC requires only that "all of an entrepreneur's communications with a consumer must be made clearly and understandably in the language in which the contract is concluded." Analogically, the same language requirements should apply to commercial guarantees. However, Section 11 of the Consumer Protection Act explicitly states that the seller shall secure that certain information, including information about rights resulting from defective performance, shall be provided in Czech language.

G. Time Limits

The implementation of the SGD Directive has not significantly changed the time limits of the liability periods, neither for new, nor for second hand goods; only the time limit for the reverse burden of proof regarding sold new products has doubled, from 6 months to one year. Concerning second hand consumer goods, the older rules of the CzCC required that the parties could limit by agreement the liability period to half of the statutory period, but a greater reduction was not allowed. These mostly corresponded with the one year liability limits according to Art. 10 (6) SGD. Although Art. 10 (3) SGD

---

[48] Explanatory Notes to Sněmovní tisk 947/21, (Parliamentary Press 947/21) 143.

allowed for Member States to extend the two year general liability period to increase the level of consumer protection or combat planned obsolescence in their national law but the Czech legislator, like many others, refrained from prolonging the already accepted in practice two-year liability period. For the Ministry of Justice, an extension could cause additional costs for sellers and manufacturers, and the danger of these costs being reflected in the end-prices of goods could not be ruled out.

94 In the case of digital content also concerning limitation periods, it is necessary to distinguish whether the obligation is a continuous performance or a one-off performance. In the first case, the provider is liable for the entire period for which it performs; in the second case there is a special regulation in § 2389f CzCC. In B2B relations, the time limits of the general contract law apply (Section 1921 CzCC), in B2C relations, the new rules of Section 2389k CzCC, which also deliver a two-year period. apply. Furthermore, the obligation to update according to Section 2389f CzCC must be taken into account – for a period that the user can "reasonably expect".

95 Interestingly, the suspension of the liability period has already been dealt with in earlier versions of the CzCC if the buyer's complaint against defects was successful. The rules of Section 1922 (2) CzCC required that if a buyer correctly claimed a defect against the trader, the time limit for asserting the right arising from defective performance shall be suspended for the time during which the acquirer cannot use the defective good. This rule was also beneficial enough for consumers in case the buyer had purchased digital content, therefore the legislator did not create new additional rules to be introduced in the Czech Republic.

96 Unlike Directive 1999/44/EC, the SGD required national law to allow consumers to seek redress in the event of a defect occurring at any time within two years of receipt. Thus, even in relation to a defect that only becomes apparent on the last day of a two-year period, the consumer must have sufficient time to make a complaint. The old Czech rules on the purchase contract for consumers did not require a special period for alleging a defect, therefore the general limitation period of three years was the maximum limit for seeking redresses, according to Section 629 CzCC. Nevertheless, in order not to encourage consumers to wait for reporting defects until the end of the prescription period, if the consumer complains only after the expiry of the two-year period, he or she will have to bear the burden of proof on whether the defect arose within that two-year period, which can be an uneasy task in practice.

97 Concerning the notification period of liability claims, the transposition of the Twin Directives brought minor changes, softening the notification requirements for consumers. The older CzCC did not explicitly stipulate any particular "objective" deadline, in which period the consumer must notify the identified defect to the seller, but Section 2112 CzCC included subjective deadlines for asserting rights from a defective performance towards the seller, which were applied by analogy also in B2C relations. This rule required that the buyer must assert right to have the defect repaired without undue delay after being able to identify it. Timely inspection and sufficient care were also expected in B2C relations, derived from the moral rules (good morals), since otherwise such a delay would be deemed *contra bonos mores*.[49] The transposition of the SGD seemingly softened these rules, because a new subsection of 2165 (3) states: "The court will grant the right of defect even if the defect was not claimed without undue delay after the buyer could have detected the defect upon the exercise of sufficient care."[50] However, some

---

[49] L. Tichý, *§ 2165*, in J. Švestka, J. Dvořák, J. Fiala *et al.*, Občanský zákoník, komentář (Civil Code, Commentary), Sv.V., Wolters Kluwer, Prague, 2014, p. 971.

[50] Draft amendment of the Civil Code No. 1170/19, available at: https://apps.odok.cz/veklep-detail?pid=KORNBFQGCDCT

academics argue that this new rule confirmed the applicability of the rules on general contractual liability[51]: the Explanatory Notes of the amending act underline that "unlike general contractual law, for a consumer purchase contract, there is no specific time limit for alleging a defect".[52] Therefore, the new subsection 2165 (3) CzCC should exclude possible negative consequences of a delayed notification of a defect. For similar reasons, the Czech legislator refrained from using the regulatory option of setting a so-called two months notification period (according to Article 12 SGD), because setting such period may lead to a reduction in consumers' rights, as disputes can arise as to whether the deadline has been met and whether the defect could not have been detected earlier if the necessary care had been taken.[53]

Concerning digital content, in B2B relations, due to the lack of special rules, the general contract law applies, which means that businesses must notify their claims within 6 months from the handover of the content or service. In B2C relations a new Section 2389k CzCC excludes the applicability of Section 1921, para. 2 CzCC of general contract law, and, similarly to the sale of goods, the court shall grant the right arising from a defect even if it was notified with a delay.

H. Right of Redress

For the right of redress, the legislator establishes a new provision of Section 2174b CzCC which transposes Art. 18 of the SGD and Art. 20 of the DCD. Under this provision, if the defect was caused by an act or omission of another person in the same contract chain, the final seller is entitled to compensation from the person who sold the thing to him in his business or who was obliged to provide digital content or a digital content service, including their updating. Reimbursement will be provided in the amount of the costs that the final seller expediently incurred to arrange a remedy. The right to compensation does not arise if the final seller knew of the defect of the thing at the time of its receipt or if the thing was not intended to be placed on the market for consumers.

The provisions of Section 2174b shall apply accordingly in the case of a defect in the digital content or a delay in making it available.

Based on the cited provision, the right to redress is based on supply chain liability and, in the past, there were number of cases when the particular persons in the supply chain denied their responsibility. The Czech law specifies that, as the person from whom the final seller (the last link in the chain) has the right to seek redress is the previous person in the chain, i.e. the entrepreneur who sold the item to the final seller, or who provided digital content or a digital content service according to the contract. This person in the chain will then have the right to seek redress from the entity that sold (provided) the defective item (defective digital content or service). This will be done in an ascending manner within the chain until the right to compensation is exercised against the entity that caused the defect by its actions or omissions, i.e. against the ultimate originator.

Compensation to the entitled person shall be provided in the amount of expediently incurred costs of arranging a remedy in relation to the consumer. Thus, for example, it may be a monetary amount corresponding to the cost of repairing the item, the discount

---

[51] Hrádek, 'Czech Republic' in Hajnal (ed), *Comparative Analysis of National Jurisdictions Regarding Consumer Sales and Unfair Commercial Practices* (2020), 7 (19).
[52] Explanatory Notes to Sněmovní tisk 947/21, (Parliamentary Press 947/21) 141.
[53] Ibid.

provided or the value of the goods, if the consumer withdrew from the contract or was replaced.[54]

103   The right to compensation does not arise if (in the sense of Section 4 para. 2 CzCC) the entrepreneur was aware of the defect at the time of its receipt from the previous supplier in the chain. The right to compensation also does not arise if the defective item or defective digital content or service was purchased from a previous supplier for purposes other than resale to consumers.

104   The provision is mandatory in nature. Neither the final seller nor other members of the supply chain who are subject to the right of redress may waive their right in advance.

I. Other Consumer Requests beyond Warranty and Guarantee in the Case of Non-Conformity

105   In connection with the provision of defective performance, which caused the occurrence of damage, liability for damage is possible. The damage is harm caused as a result of defective performance, i.e. property damage, not consisting of the defect of the object of purchase itself, but in the depreciation of this or another item as a result of defective performance. The concurrence of the two claims is based on the explicit provision of Section 1925 CzCC, according to which the right arising from defective performance does not exclude the right to damages; however, what can be achieved by exercising the right arising from defective performance cannot be claimed for another legal reason.

106   It is apparent from this regulation that liability for defects and liability for damage are different legal obligations, have a different purpose and are based on different principles and assumptions of liability. Liability for defects prosecutes deficiencies of the seller's own performance and ensures that the buyer receives the performance without any defects, so that the item he has purchased has the agreed features and does not suffer from defects. The purpose of liability for damages, on the other hand, is to compensate property damage incurred from a breach of a legal obligation or arising as a result of another legally recognized fact.[55]

107   In connection with the defective performance, which was the cause of damage, the liability for damage may occur pursuant to Section 2913 CzCC because of a breach of contractual obligation. Liability in contract must be divided between cases specifically regulated as particular types of contract, such as liability under purchase agreements, etc. and a general provision under Section 2913 CzCC. Pursuant to the general provision, if a contractually obligated party incurs damage due to a breach of contract, the victim is entitled to compensation regardless of the fault of the wrongdoer, and the liable party can only be exempted from liability if it proves that an extraordinary, unforeseeable burden arose independently of their will.[56]

108   The buyer may also seek compensation pursuant to Section 2939 et seq. CzCC which regulates liability for damage caused by a defective product and also for special types of liability resulting from the nature of the goods or contents as they are laid down in Sections 2924 et seq. CzCC. Moreover, those types of liability are deemed cases of strict liability and the buyer is entitled to compensation regardless of the fault of the wrongdoer and the exemption from liability is possible only in cases defined by law.

---

[54] Explanatory Notes to Sněmovní tisk 213/0, comments to Sec. 2165.
[55] Decision of the Supreme Court File No. 25 Cdo 1612/2004 from 30.08.2005.
[56] Hrádek and Bell, 'The New Civil Code and Compensation for Damage: Introductory Remarks' (2016) 3 *JETL*, 300 (303).

J. Conclusion

The transposition of the Twin Directives brought some slight structural changes for the Czech Civil Code, especially for contract law; but other fields of law, such as the law on intellectual property or data protection, were not changed.

In certain aspects, the existing legislation can be assessed as not very satisfactory in terms of clarity and comprehensibility. From the adoption of the Czech Civil Code, there has been a discussion of whether the legislator established a so-called legal warranty, which was already contained in the former Civil Code. Another problematic point is the form of the hierarchy of rights from defective performance, which is unclear due to the layering of general and special regulations. Third, the current legislation does not set forth clear limits of regulation applicable to consumers and a general regulation, and the material scope of the subsection on the sale of goods in a store is also unclear. Finally, the right of recourse of the final seller against the responsible entrepreneur and the requirements of the commercial guarantee are not sufficiently taken into account in the current legislation. In the amendments, the legislator focused not only on the transposition of the Twin Directives but also on repairing the above malfunctions.

However, beside these changes, the main added value of the amendments is in establishing a new, advanced framework for the terminology of the digital environment. The scope of the new contract type "providing digital content" was widened for both B2C and B2B relations; with a two-track solution in the case of non-conformity with digital content, enabling consumers to enjoy stricter remedies than businesses. Defining the digital content and services was an urgent necessity in the Czech Republic. However, the introduction of data as counter-performance deeply challenges the existing doctrine on synallagmatic performance, creating future practical problems, of how the consumer's duty to provide personal data as counter-performance can be enforced, considering the very broad protection of personality rights.

Bibliography

Petr Bezouška, 'Neoprávněná reklamace' (2006) 12 *Právní rádce*

Barbara Dauner-Lieb, Thomas Heidel, Manfred Lepa and Gerhard Ring, *Schuldrecht* (Deutscher Anwaltverlag, Bonn 2002)

European Commission, *Study for the Fitness Check of EU consumer and marketing law – Final report Part 3 – Country reporting*, May 2017, ISBN 978-92-79-68439-5

Jiří Hrádek, Andrew J. Bell, 'The New Civil Code and Compensation for Damage: Introductory Remarks' (2016) 3 *JETL*, 300–308

Jiří Hrádek, 'Czech Republic' in Zsolt Hajnal (ed), *Comparative Analysis of National Jurisdictions Regarding Consumer Sales and Unfair Commercial Practices* (C.H. Beck, Bucharest 2020), 7–35

Pavla Hubková, '§ 2161' in Jan Petrov, Michal Výtisk and Vladimir Beran et al., *Občanský zákoník, komentář* (C.H. Beck, Prague 2017)

Axel Metzger, 'Data as Counter-Performance: What Rights and Duties do Parties Have?' (2017) 8 *JIPITEC*

Štěpán Richter, 'Směrnice EU 2019/770 o některých aspektech poskytování digitálního obsahu a digitálních služeb jako nástroj ochrany spotřebitele' (2020) 4 *Jurisprudence*, 9–17

Rosa Milà Rafel, 'The Directive Proposals on Online Sales and Supply of Digital Content (Part I): will the new rules attain their objective of reducing legal complexity?' (2016) 23 *IDP UOC* 1–14

Štepan Richter, 'Ochrana osobních údajů v kontextu poskytování digitálních dat spotřebitelům' (2021) 9 *Právnik*, 745–758

Jiři Švestka, Jan Dvořák, Josef Fiala, *Občanský zákoník. Komentář. Svazek V (§ 1721–2520, relativní majetková práva 1. část)* (Wolters Kluwer, Praha, 2014)

Eva Škorničková, 'Osobní údaje jako vzácný artikl' *gdpr.cz* (2017) available: https://www.gdpr.cz/blog/osobni-data-jako-vzacny-artikl/

Christiane Wendehorst, 'Die neuen Regelungen im BGB zu Verträgen über digitale Produkte' (2021) *NJW*, 2913–2919

Denmark

A.	The Transposition	1
B.	Scope of Application	8
C.	Definitions	10
D.	Data as a Counter-Performance	14
E.	Application for B2B Contracts?	22
F.	Conformity of Goods	26
	I. Subjective and Objective Requirements for Conformity	26
	II. Concepts	28
	1. 'Particular characteristic'	28
	2. 'Durability' and sustainability	29
	III. Incorrect Installation of the Digital Content or Digital Service	33
	IV. Modification of Digital Content and Digital Services	34
	V. Third-Party Rights	35
G.	Liability of the Trader	36
	I. Time Limits	36
	II. Interruption of Long-Term Supply of Digital Content/Digital Services	39
	1. Force Majeure	40
	2. Change of Circumstances	41
	III. Early Termination of Number-Independent Interpersonal Communication Service (NI-ICS)?	43
	IV. Directive 2018/1972 Art. 107(2) European Electronic Communications Code and Art. 3(6) subpara. 3 DCD on Bundles	44
H.	Remedies	46
	I. DCD and SGD vs. National Law of Obligations and Contracts	46
	II. A Right to Withhold Payment	48
	III. Place of Delivery and Place of Repair and Replacement	50
	1. Place of Delivery	50
	2. Place of repair and replace	52
	IV. Costs of Transport for Repair/Replacement	53
	V. The Right of Withdrawal (regarding the Consent for the Processing of Personal Data) and the Right of Termination (see Art. 15 DCD) through Declaration vs. National Law	54
	VI. Restitution when Terminating Contracts for Supply of Digital Content and/or Digital Services	55
	VII. Repair over Replacement in Light of Environmental Sustainability	58
	VIII. Premature/Planned Obsolescence of Goods	59
	IX. The Right to Resell and the Rights of a Subsequent Buyer	60
	X. Cross Border Duties	63
I.	Commercial Guarantees	65
J.	Right of Redress	66
	Bibliography	66

A. The Transposition

In the Danish Sale of Goods Act[1], the DCD and SGD are mostly implemented in combination. The formal requirements for commercial guarantees and related sanctions in the SGD are implemented in the Danish Commercial Practices Act[2]. The Danish Sale of Goods Act regulates all sales (and swaps) of goods (traditionally defined as the transfer of ownership of an asset). This also includes financial products such as shares,

---

[1] Consolidated Act no 1853, 24 September, 2014, Sale of Goods Act with amendments.
[2] Act no 426, 3 May, 2017, on commercial practices with amendments.

currency and intellectual property, as well as the supply of gas, electricity, water, and heat. Included are also transfers of companies and estates, excluding immovable property. A specific section (article 72–87) of the Sale of Goods Act is dedicated exclusively to consumer sales, but parts of the rest of the Danish Sale of Goods Act also apply if the legal matter is not addressed by the specific section on consumer protection. Before implementing the twin directives, The Danish Sale of Goods Act also applied to digital content[3], but not to services. However, as the Danish Sale of Goods Act transposes much of the general law of obligations, the act serves as inspiration for services as well. After the implementation of the twin directives and as a rule, the consumer section now applies to both sale of goods and digital content and digital services. No other part of the Danish Sale of Goods Act applies to digital services. The implementation, especially with this expansion of the scope of application, has led to a more complex set of rules. As many rules apply to both goods (with and without digital content), digital content and digital services, the consumer section of the Danish Sale of Goods Act combines the two in the chapter. Where special rules apply to goods, digital content, and digital services, the Act contains rules of exemption or provisions specifically aimed at those areas, respectively.

2   The appointed committee charged with preparing a draft amendment to the Danish Sale of Goods Act implementing the DCD and the SGD only suggested amendments to the Sale of Goods Act and the Commercial Practices Act. Thus, no amendments were discussed or proposed regarding other legal areas. Consumer law is seen as a somewhat separate legal area, so at least for now, there is no visible impact on general law of obligations and contracts.

3   In the Danish Sale of Goods Act, consumer sales are now more thoroughly regulated in the specific consumer section, contrary to the former, more fractured structure where the holes in the regulation in the consumer chapter were filled by the rest of the Danish Sales of Goods Act. Most gaps in the consumer section have now been closed, mainly because of the new implementation but also because of additional suggestions from the implementation committee copying and reformulating some of the general provisions in the Sales of Goods Act and bringing them into the consumer section, e.g. regarding the right to terminate a contract in the case where an accidental loss of goods has occurred.[4] In addition, as mentioned, the section now also covers digital content and digital services following the DCD, which were previously not an expressed scope of application. Also, as a novelty, the rights and obligations regarding commercial guarantees are included in the consumer section of the Danish Sales of Good Act. Before the implementation, commercial guarantees were solely regulated by the Commercial Practices Act.

4   Apart from the overall changes, specific changes to the structure of the Danish Sale of Goods Act can be seen in the insertion of an article containing definitions. The definitions are: 'producer', 'digital content', 'digital service', 'goods with digital content', 'functionality', 'durability', 'compatibility', 'interoperability', 'digital environment', 'installation of digital content or a digital service', 'durable medium', 'public auction' and 'commercial guarantee'. Other structural changes can be identified in the lack of conformity, which is now divided into subjective and objective criteria in accordance with the twin directives. Previously, the Danish criteria were split into two somewhat mirrored articles of positive and negative presumption criteria, respectively. Regarding the interplay between the

---

[3] Henrik Udsen, *IT-ret* (5th edn, Ex Tuto, Copenhagen, 2021) p 587 with reference to other legal scholars discussing the issue.

[4] Preparatory work for the proposal of amendments to the Sale of Goods Act, no 223, 28 April, 2021, section 3.1.2.11.

remedies, the Danish Sale of Goods Act previously did not comply with the joined cases of C-65/09 and C-87/09 *Weber and Putz*, and thus presumably not with the directive.[5] In Denmark, lawmakers stated in the preparatory work to the previous Sale of Goods Act that the assessment of disproportionality can be made concerning *all* four remedies.[6] Thus, if e.g. replacement is impossible and the business can prove that repair is expensive, the solution would either be a reduction in price or a rescission of the contract. The explanatory notes in the former preparatory work can be seen as an attempt at a pragmatic solution to a potentially far-reaching principle of a right to a contractual good. This interpretation seems to be more in line with the SGD, which has *not* consolidated the far-reaching ruling of *Weber*. The Danish implementing committee suggested implementing the interplay between remedies very close to the wording of the SDG.

Previously – although subject of some discussion – digital content such as music and films delivered on physical mediums such as CDs were considered goods and therefore covered by the Danish Sale of Goods Act.[7] Now, the rules on supply of digital content in the consumer section of the Danish Sale of Goods Act apply to this type of sale.

Regarding mixed contracts where the contract includes sale of goods and a service, the previous Danish position cannot be upheld after the implementation. Previously, in mixed contracts, the predominant of the two would determine the type of contract. Thus now, if the service part of the contract is digital as prescribed by the DCD, this service will be covered by the provisions regarding services in the consumer section of the Danish Sale of Goods Act.

Even though some fundamental changes have been made when implementing the twin directives, regarding the categorisation of different types of contracts, there has been no doctrinal debate on this. The reason for this might be that, as mentioned before, though only sales of goods were previously regulated, the Danish Sale of Goods Act is a consolidation of general law of obligation and contracts and has also to some extent been applied to services.[8] Thus, it can be stated at the very general level that whether a contract concerns goods or services has not been decisive. However, specifically regarding mandatory consumer protection, there has been some doubt about whether these provisions applied to services.[9] Now, the DCD has clarified this for digital services.

B. Scope of Application

Denmark has chosen *not* to exclude living animals from the scope of application, except living horses. In general, there was little debate about the implementation of the twin directives in Denmark, but regarding living horses, opinions were strong on both sides.[10] The arguments for excluding living horses from the scope were that the parties in such trades are often semi-professionals, and the contract is often drawn up

---

[5] Marie Jull Sørensen, 'Forbrugerens ret til en kontraktmæssig vare – en relativ eller absolut uforholdsmæssighedsvurdering?' *Juristen*, no 5, 2012, p 281–289.

[6] Preparatory work to the amendment: Act no 213 of April 22, 2002 Amending the Sale of Goods Act, explanatory notes to article 78(2).

[7] Søren Sandfeld Jakobsen, *Opfyldelse af aftaler*, Chapter 8, in Jan Trzaskowski (ed), *Internetretten* (3rd edn, Ex Tutu Publishing, Copenhagen, 2017) p 451.

[8] Kim Frost, *Informationsydelsen* (Thomson, Copenhagen, 2002) p 69.

[9] Søren Sandfeld Jakobsen, *Opfyldelse af aftaler*, Chapter 8, in Jan Trzaskowski (ed), *Internetretten* (3rd edn, Ex Tutu Publishing, Copenhagen, 2017) p 451.

[10] See discussion of Danish Parliament on 7 May, 2021, regarding proposal L 223 amending the Sale of Goods Act.

from a standard contract. These arguments, however, were contradicted by organisations opposing the exclusion.[11]

9   According to Danish general contract law, a contract is a broad concept and encompasses all situations where it is possible to determine the rights and obligations of the parties.[12] The implementing committee foresees some practical issues related to identifying such obligations for the seller in cases where the seller collects *metadata* (when these are not personal data) as a 'payment for use' or where the consumer pays with their attention and accepts to be exposed to advertising. Thus, the Danish implementation does not expand the scope of application to these situations.

C. Definitions

10   In general, Denmark applies another definition of 'consumer' than the EU, including when implementing directives of total harmonisation. Thus, Denmark's concept of 'consumer' covers both *legal* and natural persons and persons acting *mainly* outside their trade or profession. The expansion of the scope of application of the EU consumer protection legislation to include legal persons is not contrary to EU consumer protection law as such. Still, it seems contrary to EU law to include them in the concept of 'consumer.' The only Danish Act where legal persons are added to the scope independently of the consumer concept is in the Danish Commercial Practices Act. This was done at the request of the EU Commission.[13] It seems as if the Danish including position on dual-purpose contracts is in line with the EU disregarding the concept 'consumer' applied in procedural EU consumer protection.[14] Thus, it is stated in SGD (preamble 22) and DCD (preamble 17) that a person acting for such dual purposes where the "trade purpose is so limited as not to be predominant in the overall context of the contract" can be included in the concept of a 'consumer'.[15] It should be noted here that the Danish translation of the SGD is not aligned with the English, French, German and Swedish texts. The Danish translation states that only a marginal part of the contract can be accepted as being inside a trade or business before a person is considered 'a consumer'. According to other translations, this part must not be 'predominant'. The Danish text must be a mistake which is supported by the fact that the Danish translation of the same wording in the DCD is in line with the rest of the translations, stating that the trade purpose cannot be predominant.[16]

11   Denmark also has a special intermediary rule[17] related to the scope of application of consumer protection. In brief, the intermediary rule states that if two natural/private

---

[11] E.g. The Danish Veterinary Association, cf. annex 3 to the consultation in Danish Parliament proposal L 223 amending the Sale of Goods Act, 2021.

[12] See Delbetænkning I, no 1576, p 91.

[13] Preparatory work for the proposal of amendments to the Commercial Practices Act, no 32 10 March, 2019, general remarks.

[14] E.g. Regulation (EU) No 1215/2012 of the European Parliament and of the Council of 12 December 2012 on jurisdiction and the recognition and enforcement of judgments in civil and commercial matters, Section 4. See also Marie Jull Sørensen, Forbrugerbegrebet – udvalgte problemstillinger – Procesretten vs. Civilretten, den danske udvidelse og synbarhedskravet, *Ugeskrift for Retsvæsen*, UfR 2022B.53, 2022, pp 53–63.

[15] In the Danish translation of preamble 22 in Directive 771/2019, the trade purpose can only be marginal. This seems to be an incorrect translation.

[16] Marie Jull Sørensen, Forbrugerbegrebet – udvalgte problemstillinger – Procesretten vs. Civilretten, den danske udvidelse og synbarhedskravet, *Ugeskrift for Retsvæsen*, 2022, UfR 2022B.53, pp 53–63.

[17] Marie Jull Sørensen, 'Digitale formidlingsplatforme – formidlingsreglen i dansk forbrugerret', *Ugeskrift for Retsvæsen*, U.2017B.119, 2017, pp 119–127.

persons (C2C) engage in a contract through an active professional intermediary, the contract between the two persons is regarded as a consumer contract. Consequently, the buyer is seen as a consumer and the seller as a business. All consumer protection regulations then protect the buyer. The intermediary (e.g. an online intermediary platform) is *not* liable for the contract between the platform users. Still, the intermediary can be sanctioned with fines for not complying with the information duties that it shares with the seller regarding pre-contractual information such as the right of withdrawal.[18] This intermediary rule, combined with the fact that the online platform will be regarded as the contracting party if it fails to inform correctly about its status as merely an intermediary, is the reason why Denmark has chosen *not* to make use of the opportunity in the SGD and DSD to automatically include online platforms into the concept of 'seller'. Doing so would be contrary to the principle of relativity in the general law of obligations and contracts.

There has been no doctrinal debate about either of the definitions of digital content, digital service, goods with digital elements, integration, updates, price, digital environment, compatibility, functionality, interoperability, durable medium, which have all been implemented word for word in the Danish Sale of Goods Act. Neither have the implementation committee given these concepts any attention in their commented draft proposal for the implementation of the twin directives, other than simply stating and explaining the definitions.

The striking lack of discussion of the twin directives in Danish legal doctrine not only relates to notions and definitions but could in general be explained by the fact that EU directives by some are perceived as stand-alone rules not linked to general law of obligations or reflecting (Danish) public policy.[19] Of course, the rules are to be followed, but they are sometimes considered strange elements in a legal doctrine mainly consisting of few and simple concepts.[20]

D. Data as a Counter-Performance

Previously, data has not explicitly been disqualified as counter-performance, and it seems as if data as counter-performance cannot in itself determine whether the parties have engaged in a contract.[21] Thus, the (diminutive) debate has been less about whether data can be a counter-performance and more about general (consumer) contract law regarding social media user contracts, e.g., unfair terms/balance, consent, minors as contracting parties, etc.[22] However, Professor Henrik Udsen from Copenhagen University has written an article about understanding personal data as counter-performance.[23] The following is based primarily on this article.

According to Udsen, data as counter-performance should not be regarded as a means of payment – rather it should be perceived as a performance in its own right. Therefore,

---

[18] See Sea and Trade Court SH2009.N.0001.07 from 18 June, 2009 (QXL), and Marie Jull Sørensen, 'Digitale formidlingsplatforme – formidlingsreglen i dansk forbrugerret', *Ugeskrift for Retsvæsen*, U.2017B.119, 2017, pp 119–127.
[19] Mads Bryde Andersen, *Lærebog i obligationsret I* (5th edn, Karnov, Copenhagen, 2020) p 55.
[20] Mads Bryde Andersen, *Lærebog i obligationsret I* (5th edn, Karnov, Copenhagen, 2020) p 55.
[21] Torsten Bjørn Larsen and Rasmus Kristian Feldthusen, 'De sociale mediers brugervilkår del I – aftalen', *Erhvervsjuridisk Tidsskrift* 2016.266 with references.
[22] Torsten Bjørn Larsen and Rasmus Kristian Feldthusen, 'De sociale mediers brugervilkår del I – aftalen', *Erhvervsjuridisk Tidsskrift* 2016.266 with references.
[23] Henrik Udsen, *Personoplysninger som en modydelse*, in Birgit Liin et al., *Festskrift til Palle Bo Madsen* (Djøf, Copenhagen, 2021) pp 481–495.

the contract where one party performs their duties by giving access to personal data against a service is a contract of exchange rather than a sales contract. However, Professor Udsen believes that personal data as counter-performance should be designated as 'counter performance' signalling that it is not a payment but that another performance (the digital service or digital content) defines the contract.[24]

16 Even though the contracts mentioned above are to be treated as regular sales contracts, some challenges arise because of the characteristics of personal data as counter-performance.[25] In the interplay with GDPR rules, the question is what the contractual consequences are if the consent to collect personal data is not considered voluntary and these are thus collected in violation of article 7(4) of the GDPR. First, it is not clear when consent is voluntary. A strict interpretation of article 7(4) is that consent can only be voluntary if there is a real alternative (e.g. an option to pay a fair and non-deterrent amount of money). This would mean that many digital services would be challenged. The ECJ will probably be the entity to decide on this matter. The Danish Data Protection Agency has ruled that it is ok to make consent to collect personal data a condition for certain benefits (such as membership discounts).[26]

17 If consent is *not* voluntary (or in case of other inconsistencies with GDPR rules), the question is whether this has contractual consequences. In Denmark, a contract can be deemed void under Danish Law 5-1-2 if it violates stated law, but this provision has been applied strictly and mainly in cases where essential social assets are threatened.[27] So, the contractual consequences must either depend on the contract under consideration of Directive 93/13/EEC on unfair terms or, in case the contract does not cover the matter, the consequences will depend on the general law of obligation and contract. Without a contract stating rights and obligations, the parties will thus both be entitled to terminate the contract.[28] The consumer can keep anything that might have been 'earned' (discounts, points, etc.) through the contract up until the time of termination. The GDPR regulates handling of the consumer's data received before and after such termination.

18 In the case of voluntary consent, which the consumer wishes to revoke with reference to GDPR article 7(3), the contractual consequences will be determined by the contract and/or the general law of obligations and contract.[29] Thus, the parties can agree that the business may terminate the contract. According to preamble 42 of the GDPR, this must be done without detriment to the consumer. According to Udsen, if there is no agreement regarding the contractual consequences of revoking consent, the result must be that the business can then terminate the contract, as they no longer receive the counter-performance that the contract is based on. However, as Udsen so honestly puts it: "The result seems more obvious than the arguments" – how this outcome should be argued is unclear. Udsen suggests three approaches: Failure of performance, failure

---

[24] Henrik Udsen, *Personoplysninger som en modydelse*, in Birgit Liin et al., *Festskrift til Palle Bo Madsen* (Djøf, Copenhagen, 2021) pp 482–485.

[25] Henrik Udsen, *Personoplysninger som en modydelse*, in Birgit Liin et al., *Festskrift til Palle Bo Madsen* (Djøf, Copenhagen, 2021) pp 485–491.

[26] Henrik Udsen, *Personoplysninger som en modydelse*, in Birgit Liin et al., *Festskrift til Palle Bo Madsen* (Djøf, Copenhagen, 2021) p 490.

[27] Henrik Udsen, *Personoplysninger som en modydelse*, in Birgit Liin et al., *Festskrift til Palle Bo Madsen* (Djøf, Copenhagen, 2021) p 490 with reference to Mads Bryde Andersen, '»Lov og ærbarhed« i nutidens aftaleret – med særligt fokus på løfter og aftaler i den menneskelige intimsfære', *Ugeskrift for Retsvæsen*, U2020B53, Karnov, 2020, p 53.

[28] Henrik Udsen, *Personoplysninger som en modydelse*, in Birgit Liin et al., *Festskrift til Palle Bo Madsen* (Djøf, Copenhagen, 2021) p 491.

[29] Henrik Udsen, *Personoplysninger som en modydelse*, in Birgit Liin et al., *Festskrift til Palle Bo Madsen* (Djøf, Copenhagen, 2021) pp 492–493.

of basic assumptions (the doctrine of fundamental breach), and the Danish Contracts Act article 36 (and article 38c) regarding unfair contracts. The two last arguments are most applicable, as it seems odd to state that the consumer has failed to perform when revoking their consent is based on a right stated in the protective GDPR. A revoked consent also constitutes a termination of the contract; the consumer can always terminate the contract. In connection to this, the business can hardly enforce any rights to the counter-performance.

Apart from the interplay with the GDPR, a contract where the counter-performance is personal data also challenges the applicable remedies. It makes no sense to claim a price reduction – a reduction of what?[30] In addition, a consumer can terminate the contract regardless of the extent of the lack of conformity. Denmark has not made specific provisions regarding other possibilities of restitution.

Another Danish professor, Jan Trzaskowski, challenges how we articulate the counter-performance of personal data.[31] He believes it might be misleading to say that we pay with our personal data as our personal data is not the actual price – it is the attention given to what our personal data is used for, e.g. advertising. Trzaskowski states that our attention and agency are scarcer and more precious than personal data, which can be given more than once and the value of which is quite abstract for the consumer.[32] Thus, the consumer must become aware that the price or counter-performance is really not their personal data but rather their attention.

The explicit provision regarding personal data as counter-performance is a novelty in Denmark. Still, the implementation has not caused extensive debate and was not discussed explicitly by the implementation committee.

E. Application for B2B Contracts?

Whether the new rules should or could also be applied to B2B has not been discussed in Denmark. A likely reason is that the Danish Sale of Goods Act is based on the very fundamental law of obligations, which is broadly respected. In addition, Denmark seems to embrace the more open and principle-based regulation of the area.

One must consider that the twin directives were made from the assumption that the system of consumer protection is based on the idea that the consumer is in a weak position vis-à-vis the seller or supplier in terms of both bargaining power and knowledge.[33] An ongoing discussion among consumer law stakeholders is whether this presumption is also valid in specific B2B contracts. For example, either one business is significantly smaller than the other, or a company buys goods/services unrelated to its primary production. In Denmark, this discussion has not led to an expansion of the scope of application of consumer protection legislation to businesses. The legal persons included in the Danish concept of 'consumer' are solely non-businesses such

---

[30] Henrik Udsen, *Personoplysninger som en modydelse*, in Birgit Liin et al., *Festskrift til Palle Bo Madsen* (Djøf, Copenhagen, 2021) pp 494–495.

[31] Jan Trzaskowski, *Your Privacy Is Important to U$ – Restoring Human Dignity in Data-Driven Marketing* (Ex Tuto, Copenhagen, 2021) pp 208–209.

[32] Jan Trzaskowski, *Your Privacy Is Important to U$ – Restoring Human Dignity in Data-Driven Marketing* (Ex Tuto, Copenhagen, 2021) pp 208–209.

[33] See Directive (EU) 2019/771 of the European Parliament and of the Council of 20 May 2019 on Certain Aspects Concerning Contracts for the Sale of Goods, amending Regulation (EU) 2017/2394 and Directive 2009/22/EC, and repealing Directive 1999/44/EC and Directive (EU) 2019/770 of the European Parliament and of the Council of 20 May, 2019, on certain aspects concerning contracts for the delivery of digital content and digital services. See also CJEU, C-618/10 14 June, 2012, Banco Español para de Crédito ECLI:EU:C:2012:349, para 39 and CJEU, C-415/11 14 March, 2013, Aziz ECLI:EU:C:2013:164, para 44.

as associations, unions, NGOs, etc., and these non-businesses are only included if the specific activity/contract in question is not to be regarded as a part of their trade (e.g. selling merchandise to make a profit).

24 That being said, it cannot be ruled out that the implemented provisions of the twin directives would be suitable for B2B contracts – at least where the same need for protection of the buyer is present – or where the consumer protection provisions merely codify main principles of law of obligations. The provisions on lack of conformity might be an example. In Denmark, the previous provisions on lack of conformity in the Consumer Sales Directive were simply considered to be a clarification of the existing provision in the Danish Sale of Goods Act. The new provisions regarding subjective and objective lack of conformity are, for the most part, not regarded as a change in the previous legal position on lack of conformity. And even though the concept of 'lack of conformity' is found in the consumer section of the Danish Sale of Goods Act, the concept is considered applicable for sale of goods contracts and service contracts regardless of whether these are consumer contracts or not.[34]

25 From a traditional Danish doctrinal perspective, applying the implemented provisions on B2B contracts would probably be considered too invasive to the freedom of contract. However, Danish law of obligations has moved away from the liberal starting point of *caveat emptor* (let the buyer beware) to a more paternalistic and buyer-protective *caveat venditor* (let the seller beware) perspective[35], which might make the extended application tolerable.

F. Conformity of Goods

I. Subjective and Objective Requirements for Conformity

26 Almost word for word, and compiled for both directives, the subjective and objective conformity requirements have been written into the Danish article 75 b and 75 c, respectively. The substance of the requirements is not so different from the former requirements in Danish law, but now the requirements also apply to digital services. The duty to supply future updates for contracts on digital content, digital services, and goods with digital content is regulated independently in article 75 d and is a novelty in Danish law. The liability exemption to this duty has been implemented word for word with no further considerations.

27 In article 76, the opportunity for Member States to add to the seller's duty to supply information expressed in preamble 20 of the SGD has been utilised. Thus, article 76 of the Danish Sale of Goods Act states that if a seller knew or should have known about matters relevant for the consumer's assessment of the goods (including goods with digital content) and the seller fails to give the consumer said information, the goods also lack conformity (the duty to disclose). This duty to disclose was also found in the previous Sale of Goods Act. As regards applying the duty to disclose to digital content and digital services as well, Denmark asked the EU-Commission, and they replied that such an obligation was *not* allowed under the DCD.[36]

---

[34] Joseph Lookofsky and Vibe Ulfbeck, *Køb – Dansk indenlandsk købsret* (5th edn, Djøf, Copenhagen, 2020) p 102 eq.

[35] Joseph Lookofsky and Vibe Ulfbeck, *Køb – Dansk indenlandsk købsret* (5th edn, Djøf, Copenhagen, 2020) p 102.

[36] Proposal L 223, 2021 amending the Sale of Goods Act, section 3.2.2.1.2.

F. Conformity of Goods

II. Concepts

1. 'Particular characteristic'

With no special attention made to the expression 'particular characteristic', Denmark has made an almost word-for-word implementation of the provisions regarding the exemptions to the lack of conformity both in article 75 c (objective requirements) and 75 d (update requirements). Such an exemption is not a novelty in Danish law. Aside from its value in itself, the rule is considered an indirect prohibition of *general* reservations made by the seller. In Denmark, both oral and written consent from the consumer is valid. The seller must prove that the consumer has consented to the specific reservation.

2. 'Durability' and sustainability

The Danish implementation committee was asked to consider if and how the options given to the Member States in the twin directives could/should be utilised to support the green transition.[37] For this work, the committee was assisted by the Ministry of Environment (Miljøministeriet) and the Ministry of Climate, Energy and Utilities (Klima-, Energi- og Forsyningsministeriet). The Ministries stated that extended durability and lifecycle-extending measures are key means to supporting the green transition. Measures such as extended time limits might work as incentives for sellers and producers to extend durability.[38] The implementation committee expressed that it is not for the committee to suggest product-specific requirements regarding durability and repair, because the impact of pointing to these means within their mandate would only be indirect. It was discussed whether a long(er) time limit for claims of lack of conformity would indirectly affect durability. Still, it was concluded that products with normal durability of 3 years would comply with the rules if they indeed worked for three years. A time limit of 5 years for claims of lack of conformity would not change this. Besides, in the contract, the seller can always make a specific deviation from the objective requirement of conformity regarding durability, if the criteria for the exemption from the lack of conformity provisions are met. Regarding the consumer choice between repair and replacement, the implementation committee stated that only repair that would prolong the durability *further* than the original (normal) durability period would have an effect benefitting the green transition. This statement can be contested as the lack of repair most likely would lead to the consumer obtaining other, similar goods earlier than if a repair had been made. Given that repair is greener than replacement (in most cases?), incentives to repair must then be preferred also in cases where the goods/services only achieve conformity with the contract. However, as stated by the committee based on various reports and statements by stakeholders, it is not always greener to produce spare parts and make repairs. This depends on the product in question. The committee discussed various pros and cons regarding repair and replacement and the potential indirect effect of extended time limits. Nevertheless, while it cannot be ruled out that extended time limits for claiming lack of conformity will affect the green transition, the committee did not suggest further extending the period for claiming lack of conformity or a longer time limit for the rule of presumption. A minority of the committee (1 of 13) stated that if durability is an objective criterion to be taken seriously, the time limit for claiming lack of conformity should be more than two years.

---

[37] Proposal L 223, 2021 amending the Sale of Goods Act, Section 2.
[38] Delbetænkning I, no 1576, section 1.3.2.6.

30   In general, the implementing committee referred to other initiatives from the EU, such as the Eco-design Directive[39] and the initiatives in the new plan for circular economy as better means to support the green transition. In addition, the committee believed that the balance between the seller and consumer is fair without extending the time limits.[40]

31   In Denmark, violations of the implementing provision of the Eco-Design Directive are solely sanctioned with fines, and there has been no coordination between the implementing provisions on the Eco-Design Directive and the implementing provisions on the SGD. There are no national rules on the availability of spare parts and corresponding information obligations.

32   Some stakeholders and researchers outside the legal branch of academia have discussed the topic of sustainability and remedies and time limits.[41] The debate shows the complexity of the topic as there are many parameters of consumer behaviour, producer behaviour, and product behaviour in addition to complex calculations of the environmental impact of different solutions. In Denmark, the twin directives did not result in either extended time limits or other sustainability initiatives, as the committee did not feel convinced of the impact on sustainability.

III. Incorrect Installation of the Digital Content or Digital Service

33   The provision regarding incorrect installation of the digital content or digital service combined with the similar provision regarding goods is implemented word for word in article 75 e in the Danish Sale of Goods Act. There has been no debate about the substance of the provision or its consequences. Although the provision is a novelty in Danish law, the legal position of incorrect installation has been known from determining lack of conformity regarding goods.[42] The author believes that this new provision will increase the seller's awareness on facilitating a successful installation, especially when the consumer performs installation themselves.

IV. Modification of Digital Content and Digital Services

34   As a rule, all provisions in the consumer section of the Danish Sale of Goods Act apply to goods as well as digital content and digital services, unless otherwise stated. Article 77 b of the Danish Sale of Goods Act has implemented Article 19 of the DCD verbatim, and the scope of application for this article states explicitly that it only applies to digital content and digital services. There has been no further discussion of the provisions on modification of digital content or digital services.

---

[39] Directive 2009/125/EC of the European Parliament and of the Council of 21 October 2009 establishing a framework for the setting of ecodesign requirements for energy-related products.

[40] Delbetænkning I, no 1576, section 1.3.2.7.

[41] For a presentation of views and statistics, see: Michael Søgaard Jørgensen, *Potentialet ved længere reklamationsperiode: Mange defekter indtræffer, når elektronik er 2-5 år gammelt*, 2021, Ingeniøren: https://ing.dk/blog/potentialet-ved-laengere-reklamationsperiode-mange-defekter-indtraeffer-naar-elektronik-2-5-11.

[42] See the old sale of goods directive, art. 2.5 and joined cases C-65/09 and C-87/09 Weber and Putz.

V. Third-Party Rights

Article 78(1) of the Danish Sale of Goods Act states that the consumer has a right to the four remedies: repair, replacement, price reduction, and to rescind the contract in accordance with the succeeding articles unfolding these articles and the interaction between them. In addition, article 78(2) simply states that article 78(1) also applies when the lack of conformity consists of a restriction caused by a violation of third-party rights. Article 78 applies to goods as well as digital content and digital services.

G. Liability of the Trader

I. Time Limits

The table below lists the time limits regarding claims for lack of conformity and the rule of presumption. The time limit for claiming lack of conformity for digital content and digital services supplied continuously is unique to Denmark. The implementation committee argued that it would be fair for both the consumer and the seller to have two months after the agreed delivery period to claim a lack of conformity. Such a 2-month period corresponds with the Danish 2-month relative time limit for the obligation to notify a lack of conformity for goods (and goods with digital content), stating that notifying the seller of a claim within two months from discovering the lack of conformity always falls within reasonable time. The obligation to notify continues to be stated in the Danish Sale of Goods Act, but only applies to goods.

Denmark did not decide to extend the general 1-year presumption period in the SGD.

	Lack of conformity – time limit			
	Goods	Goods with digital element (for the digital element)	Digital content	Digital services
Single act or series of individual acts	Two years (two months from discovery)	Two years (two months from discovery)	Expected time Min. two years	Expected time Min. two years
Continuous supply	Two years	The agreed period of delivery Min. 2 years	*Two months after the agreed period of delivery*	*Two months after the agreed period of delivery*

	Rule of presumption – time limit			
	Goods	Goods with digital element (for the digital element)	Digital content	Digital services
Single act or series of individual acts	One year (6 months for animals except for horses)	One year	One year	One year
Continuous supply	One year	The agreed period of delivery Min. two years	The agreed period of delivery	The agreed period of delivery

38   There are a few provisions stating exceptions to some of the time limits. Denmark has kept its exception in article 82 of the Danish Sale of Goods Act to the two-month relative time limit of the obligation to notify in article 81. Thus, according to article 82, there is no relative time limit if the seller has acted against due diligence or was grossly negligent. Also, there are exceptions to the two-year limit for claims of lack of conformity if the seller acts against due diligence, has agreed to extend the liability period, or the product has been called back because it is dangerous.

II. Interruption of Long-Term Supply of Digital Content/Digital Services

39   The Danish implementation has not addressed the interruption of long-term supply of digital content and services. Such interruption must be presumed to be covered by the general rules on lack of conformity – especially about the objective requirements for conformity.

1. Force Majeure

40   In the existing general provisions (articles 23 and 24) of the Danish Sale of Goods Act (also applicable to consumer contracts (both regarding goods, goods with digital content, digital content, and digital services), there are some approximated force majeure provisions. Article 23 states that, in the case of delay (including non-delivery) of specific goods, the seller must pay damages unless they can prove that the delay was not their fault. Article 24 concerns generic goods and is more restrictive. Here, the seller can only avoid paying damages if they made reservations in the contract or if the delay was caused by circumstances they could not have anticipated, such as war, embargo on imports, etc.

2. Change of Circumstances

41   There are no specific provisions on change of circumstance, but both written and unwritten rules embrace this issue. Thus, the general provision on unfairness in article 36 of the Danish Contracts Act can be, and has been, applied in cases where a change in circumstances has led to an unfair contract. Of course, this provision can only be applied

when the unfairness is more than just one party's business failure or poor judgement, etc.[43]

Denmark also has a doctrine of fundamental breach stating that if one party has a presupposed condition for entering into a contract and the seller is aware of this, then, if this condition fails, the contract can be deemed unenforceable under certain circumstances, which include an evaluation of risk allocation.[44]

III. Early Termination of Number-Independent Interpersonal Communication Service (NI-ICS)?

Denmark has not made special provisions to regulate early termination of Number-Independent Interpersonal Communication Service. Thus, such termination must be dealt with by examining the contract and applying the general law of obligation and contract.

IV. Directive 2018/1972 Art. 107(2) European Electronic Communications Code and Art. 3(6) subpara. 3 DCD on Bundles

Denmark has not coordinated article 107(2) of Directive 2018/1972 and article 3(6) subpara. 3 of the DCD. In article 10 of executive order number no 1887 of 12 August, 2020, on end-user rights in the area of telecommunication, article 107(2) of Directive 2018/1972 has been implemented verbatim, stating that if a bundle of services and goods entails at least an internet access service or a publicly available number-based interpersonal communication service, the consumer has a right to terminate the contract for all elements of the bundle if the right to terminate was granted to just one of the elements. When implementing the DCD, Denmark has exempted electronic communications services from the scope of the Danish Sale of Goods Act, except for number-independent interpersonal communications services as defined in the Danish Electronic Communication Network and Services Act. In addition, Denmark has made an exemption for the provisions regarding modification of digital content and digital services when the delivery of digital content or digital services also entails an element of an internet access service or a number-based interpersonal communication service.

Denmark has not made any other specific rules on the consequences of one element of a bundled contract being terminated. The topic is not discussed in the implementation committee report.

H. Remedies

I. DCD and SGD vs. National Law of Obligations and Contracts

With a few exceptions, the remedies of the twin directives are in line with the *general* provisions in the Danish Sale of Goods Act. Outside of consumer sales, the Danish Sale of Goods Act distinguishes between sales of specific goods (article 42) and sales of generic goods (article 43). If a *generic* good lacks conformity, the buyer can either claim replacement, price reduction, or rescission of the contract. Replacement and rescission

---

[43] Mads Bryde Andersen, *Grundlæggende Aftaleret* (5th edn, Gjellerup, Copenhagen, 2021) pp 447–456.
[44] Mads Bryde Andersen, *Grundlæggende Aftaleret* (5th edn, Gjellerup, Copenhagen, 2021) pp 447–456.

of the contract, however, can only be claimed if the lack of conformity is not minor, unless the seller has acted fraudulently or was aware of the lack of conformity in due time to provide non-faulty goods without unreasonable sacrifice. If *specific* goods lack conformity, the buyer can claim a price reduction or rescind the contract. The latter can only be claimed if the lack of conformity is not minor, unless the seller has acted fraudulently. In article 49, the seller has a right to try to repair under certain circumstances. A defective title will probably also give the buyer a right to terminate the contract, applying an analogy of articles 42 and 43.[45]

47   There are provisions giving the buyer a right to compensation/damages in specific cases for consumer contracts and other contracts. In the case of a defective title, the buyer can claim damages even if the seller was unaware of the defect, cf. article 59 of the Danish Sale of Goods Act (article 59 also applies to consumer contracts). In addition, the consumer can also, for example, claim damages according to article 80(2) if the seller has 1) acted against due diligence, 2) given misleading information that they could not have believed to be true, 3) failed to inform of a lack of conformity that they should have known about, or if 4) the goods lack qualities that have been guaranteed, or 5) the lack of conformity is caused by neglect on the part of the seller *after* the purchase. If the goods are generic, the buyer (consumer or other) will always have the right to damages – even if the seller is not to blame – unless the cause of the lack of conformity is a force majeure or unless the seller has disclaimed liability in the contract (cf. articles 43(3) and 24). Such an exemption, however, must undergo a fairness test.

II. A Right to Withhold Payment

48   With the implementation of the twin directives, Denmark has expanded the existing right to withhold payment. Thus, now this right exists for goods with digital elements, digital content, and digital services as well as (traditional) goods. Previously, the provision on the right to withhold payment covered only the consumer's repair or replacement claim. However, it was an unwritten rule of the general law of obligations that the right to withhold payment also existed in the case of a price reduction. Now, price reduction is specifically mentioned together with repair and replace in the implementing provision in the Danish Sale of Goods Act.

49   The consumer can only withhold payment of the price until the seller has fulfilled their obligations to repair or replace or has given the price reduction. If the lack of conformity is minor, the consumer cannot hold back an amount that would obviously exceed the cost to repair.

III. Place of Delivery and Place of Repair and Replacement

1. Place of Delivery

50   If goods are to be delivered to the consumer by the seller, the time of delivery is when the goods come into the possession of the consumer. Suppose the consumer has specifically asked that a specific carrier (not offered by the seller) delivers the goods – in such cases, the place of delivery is when the goods are handed over to the carrier. Regarding goods with digital elements, the digital elements are considered delivered when the digital part is made accessible. The 'possession' of the goods is defined as the consumer's

---

[45] Nis Jul Clausen et al., *Købsretten* (8th edn, Karnov, Copenhagen, 2021) p 205.

location (or a location agreed between the parties) and entails that the consumer has control over the goods.[46] For the consumer to have control, it is required that the *seller* no longer has control of the goods. It is not enough that the seller leaves the goods on the doorstep, unless the consumer requests this. If the seller sends the goods by post, the seller must prove that the goods reached the consumer. According to the Danish Consumer Ombudsman, delivery to the consumer's mail box, delivery to another agreed location (such as a shed), or delivery at the consumer's workplace counts as giving the consumer possession of the goods. In contrast, delivery to a package collection machine or a store will not constitute a location giving the consumer possession of the goods. In this case, *possession* will occur only when the consumer (or their representative) collects the goods from the machine or store.

Digital content not delivered on a physical medium and digital services are considered delivered when the consumer can access these or download them using the facility chosen by the consumer. Goods with digital elements are considered delivered when *both* the goods and the digital elements have been delivered correctly. 51

2. Place of repair and replace

The consumer must make the goods available to the seller to repair or replace. The seller must take back the goods at their own expense in case of replacement. If the goods need to be uninstalled, the seller has to do this (or pay for this to be done) as well as reinstall it. However, the provisions say nothing about the place of repair, if the goods need to be repaired and are not installed. No further provisions regulate this area. 52

IV. Costs of Transport for Repair/Replacement

This theme has not been discussed in connection with the implementation of the twin directives. However, according to existing case law, the interpretation of 'free of charge' is that the seller pays for the transportation unless they offer to collect the goods. If the consumer wishes to use a transportation service more expensive than regular transportation, e.g. express or otherwise, the seller will not be obligated to pay more than regular transportation cost.[47] It must be presumed that the ruling of the ECJ in C-52/18 *Fülla* will inspire cases where the cost of return is significant. 53

V. The Right of Withdrawal (regarding the Consent for the Processing of Personal Data) and the Right of Termination (see Art. 15 DCD) through Declaration vs. National Law

There is no general right of withdrawal in Denmark, and so, the only rights of withdrawal are the ones granted explicitly in e.g. Directive 2011/83 on Consumer Rights and the GDPR. It is well known that if a contracting party wishes to make use of their rights, be it the right of withdrawal or the right of cancellation, they will have to declare this to the other party. 54

---

[46] Forbrugerombudsmandens sag nr. 14/05433, see also the preparatory work to article 73 in the Sale of Goods Act, cf. Law no. 1460, 17 December, 2013 (Proposal L 40, 2013).

[47] See Judgement U2008.2283OE from the Eastern Regional Court.

VI. Restitution when Terminating Contracts for Supply of Digital Content and/or Digital Services

55   If a contract for the supply of digital content and/or digital services is terminated because of a lack of conformity, the seller must pay back 'all amounts' paid according to the agreement. The terms for repayment are stated in the Danish Sale of Goods Act articles 78c-e. If the digital content is delivered on a physical medium, the consumer must return the physical medium without undue delay at the request and expense of the seller. The seller has to make their request of returning the goods no later than 14 days after receiving notice of the wish to terminate. It is not entirely clear when the seller must pay back the amount. For goods, the seller must return the amount when receiving the returned goods, or when the consumer documents that the goods have been sent. Regarding digital content and digital services, the amount must be paid without undue delay no later than 14 days after the notice of the desire to terminate the contract has been given. In the case of termination, the physical (transporting) medium must be in the same condition as when it was sold, unless it has been destroyed or changed by either accidental event, its nature, or precautionary measures necessary to evaluate it, or if the measures were taken before the lack of conformity was or should have been discovered. It is not clear to what extend harmed goods where the harm is caused by careless use (dropping your phone) or even normal use will affect the right to terminate.

56   For long-term supply of digital content and/or digital services, the amount to be paid back to the consumer covers the period in which the content or service had a lack of conformity, plus amounts for future supply. Even if the consumer has had some use of the faulty content/service, the business cannot subtract the value of this use from the reimbursement.[48]

57   The amount to be returned must be paid back with the same means of payment as those used by the consumer to pay, unless the consumer expressly accepts other means of payment. There can be no fees for the repayment of the amount.

VII. Repair over Replacement in Light of Environmental Sustainability

58   According to the Danish implementation committee, the twin directives do not provide an opportunity for Member States to change the stated preferences of the remedies within the time limit for invoking lack of conformity. The implementation committee gathered and discussed information on the pros and cons for the environment regarding the possibility of extending the time limits. See the discussion under 'Durability' of this contribution. There has been no further doctrinal debate on the topic.

VIII. Premature/Planned Obsolescence of Goods

59   In Denmark, there are no specific rules sanctioning premature/planned obsolescence of goods. If goods show defects prematurely, it is thus up to the consumer to claim lack of conformity (e.g. regarding durability) and use the remedies provided in the Sale of Goods Act. If goods show signs of planned obsolescence, the Consumer Ombudsman can evaluate whether such practice falls under the scope of the Danish Commercial Practices Act. However, this has not been tried. Regarding the provisions implementing the Unfair Commercial Practices Directive, it might be relevant to apply the requirement

---

[48] Henrik Udsen, *IT-ret* (5th edn, Ex Tuto, Copenhagen, 2021) p 602.

H. Remedies

of due diligence. Still, it is not evident that this requirement encompasses the product's manufacturing as such. In Denmark, we have a broader standard, "Good (fair) commercial practice" ("god markedsføringsskik"), that applies when the special consumer protection rules do not. For something to go against good practice, it also must be considered whether a practice goes against the interest of society. Apart from the fact that a national ban on specific products might conflict with the freedom of movement principles of the EU, the Consumer Ombudsman may be able to use this standard of fair commercial practice first to issue a warning (or go into dialogue with) the sellers of the goods, and later apply their different sanctions such as injunctions. Recently, the standard has been applied to ban the sale of exam papers and targeted marketing of loans to people on an online platform showing interest in gambling. Both bans were made as a protection of (Danish) society.

IX. The Right to Resell and the Rights of a Subsequent Buyer

There are no specific provisions regulating resale. However, it is presumed that the buyer of goods where the ownership is transferred to the buyer can sell the goods to a subsequent buyer. This subsequent buyer has the same rights against the initial seller as the first buyer, as long as they hold documentation that this seller initially sold the goods. One would assume that digital content delivered on a physical medium might be sold to a subsequent buyer – at least as long as the digital content has not been uploaded or any user-specific code used. 60

The seller would not be able to exclude transferability of rights under the legal guarantee or a commercial guarantee in their general terms and conditions. According to article 38c of the Danish Contracts Act, this would be an unfair term. 61

Whether the rules for goods also apply to buying digital services or digital content is unclear and not addressed in the Sale of Goods Act. These products are more complex because the product is not sold for the buyer to own but rather to use. No specific Danish rules connect the provisions of the twin directives with intellectual property law. 62

X. Cross Border Duties

Denmark has made no specific rules where the consumer moves to another country. Despite the remedies being the same, the question is whether the cost of returning the goods should still fall on the seller. In a Danish court ruling,[49] the court found that the seller was to pay the normal transportation cost for a computer sent from the US, even though the computer was bought in Denmark. However, it seemed as if the court found that the seller *knew* about the move when agreeing to take the computer in for repair, and thus *accepted* that the computer would be sent from the US. The consumer had used an express postal service, but the seller was only obligated to pay for costs equivalent to the price of a normal postal service. Thus, the ruling does not state whether the seller is obligated to pay the cost for returning the goods when the consumer makes their claim from abroad. Presumably, such a case would be resolved by the seller paying the cost of transportation, as if the consumer had not travelled to another country. Any additional amounts would then be paid by the consumer. 63

The cost of returning the goods is not the only potential challenge. If the goods have been installed and now need to be taken out and reinstalled, and the business cannot do 64

---

[49] Eastern Regional Court, U2008.2388OE.

that themselves, this must be solved by reimbursing the consumer for the expenses they incur to pay someone else to do it. There is no case law on this, but one must presume that the consumer can claim reimbursement of reasonable expenses due to the repair and the removal and reinstall of the goods.

I. Commercial Guarantees

65   The implementation of the twin directives regarding commercial guarantees is split between the Danish Sale of Goods Act (the duties in SGD article 17(1) and the Danish Commercial Practices Act (the formal requirements in SGD article 17(2) and (3)). The Unfair Commercial Practices Act is also where we find a language requirement. Thus, if the advertisement has been conducted in Danish, the commercial guarantee must also be written in Danish.

J. Right of Redress

66   In Denmark, the question of the right of redress is not explicitly regulated. Still, in light of the principle of relativity, it is regarded as a matter between each party in the transactional chain. Thus, there is general access for a seller to claim damages from *their* seller and so on, as long as the conditions are met. This right of redress against the seller's seller is not based on the remedies of consumer sales but on general law of obligation and contracts and the contract of the parties. The implementation committee argued that the unwritten rules of the right of redress were sufficient. Also, they believed that the twin directives give the person or persons liable in the chain of commercial transactions a right to exempt themselves from their liability in the contract with the seller. According to the implementation committee, it would thus be misleading to have a provision granting the seller right of redress.

Bibliography

Mads Bryde Andersen, *Grundlæggende Aftaleret* (5th edn, Gjellerup, Copenhagen, 2021).

Mads Bryde Andersen, *Lærebog i obligationsret I* (5th edn, Karnov, Copenhagen, 2020).

Nis Jul Clausen et al., *Købsretten* (8th edn, Karnov, Copenhagen, 2021).

Kim Frost, *Informationsydelsen* (Thomson, Copenhagen, 2002).

Søren Sandfeld Jakobsen, *Opfyldelse af aftaler*, Chapter 8, in Jan Trzaskowski (ed), *Internetretten* (3rd edn, Ex Tutu Publishing, Copenhagen, 2017) 451.

Torsten Bjørn Larsen and Rasmus Kristian Feldthusen, 'De sociale mediers brugervilkår del I – aftalen', *Erhvervsjuridisk Tidsskrift* 2016.266 with references.

Joseph Lookofsky and Vibe Ulfbeck, *Køb – Dansk indenlandsk købsret* (5th edn, Djøf, Copenhagen, 2020).

Marie Jull Sørensen, 'Digitale formidlingsplatforme – formidlingsreglen i dansk forbrugerret', *Ugeskrift for Retsvæsen*, U.2017B.119, 2017, pp 119–127.

Marie Jull Sørensen, 'Forbrugerens ret til en kontraktmæssig vare – en relativ eller absolut uforholdsmæssighedsvurdering?' *Juristen*, no 5, 2012, 281–289.

Bibliography

Jan Trzaskowski, *Your Privacy Is Important to U$ – Restoring Human Dignity in Data-Driven Marketing* (Ex Tuto, Copenhagen, 2021) pp 208–209.

Henrik Udsen, *IT-ret* (5th edn, Ex Tuto, Copenhagen, 2021).

Henrik Udsen, *Personoplysninger som en modydelse*, in Birgit Liin et al., *Festskrift til Palle Bo Madsen* (Djøf, Copenhagen, 2021) pp 481–495.

Estonia

A. Introduction and General Framework 1
   I. Principal Transposition Choices 1
   II. Wider Impact of the Transposition 5

B. Extension of the Scope of Application of the Directives-based Rules 12

C. Data as Counter-Performance: Impact of the New Concept 14

D. Conformity Requirements 20

E. Liability of the Trader 24

F. Consequences of the Trader's Non-Compliance with the GDPR regarding Contracts for the Supply of Digital Content and Digital Services 28

G. Remedies for the Failure to Supply and Remedies for the Lack of Conformity 30
   I. General remarks 30
   II. Relationship with other remedies 33

H. Time Limits 39

I. Right of Redress 46

J. Conclusions 50

   Bibliography 52

A. Introduction and General Framework

I. Principal Transposition Choices

When explaining the choices of the transposition of the Digital Content Directive[1] and Sale of Goods Directive[2] in Estonia, one must start with the explanation of the general structure of the Estonian civil and consumer law. Similar to the German „*grosse Lösung*", Estonia has made a conscious choice to implement all consumer contract law directives in the Estonian Law of Obligations Act (LOA)[3], which is divided into a general part and a special part. Apart from non-contractual obligations, the special part of the LOA regulates all contract types with the exception of employment contract which is regulated in a separate act.[4] Consolidating all contract law rules into one legal act was considered vital to ensure regulatory uniformity and since 2002, all EU consumer contract law directives have been transposed in the LOA, the exact location depending upon whether the directives contain general rules applicable to all types of contract (such as rules on unfair terms) or provisions applicable only to a specific type of contract

1

---

[1] Directive (EU) 2019/770 of the European Parliament and of the Council of 20 May 2019 on certain aspects concerning contracts for the supply of digital content and digital services (DCD).

[2] Directive (EU) 2019/771 of the European Parliament and of the Council of 20 May 2019 on certain aspects concerning contracts for the sale of goods, amending Regulation (EU) 2017/2394 and Directive 2009/22/EC, and repealing Directive 1999/44/EC (SGD).

[3] RT I, 08.12.2021, 11.

[4] On the development and systematic choices of the Estonian Law of Obligations Act, see Varul, 'Legal Policy Decisions and Choices in the Creation of New Private Law in Estonia' (2001) *Juridica International*, 114-115; Käerdi, 'Westliche Rechtskonzepte in post-sozialistische Gesellschaft: Gesetzgeberische Erfahrungen in Estland' in Heiss (ed), *Brückenschlag zwischen den Rechtskulturen des Ostseeraums* (2001), 84; Sein, 'Estland – ein Versuchsfeld für das Europäische Privatrecht? Estnische Erfahrungen mit der Anwendung der Prinzipien des Vereinheitlichten Europäischen Privatrechts' (2013) *GPR*, 13–14.

(such as consumer sales or consumer credit contracts).⁵ Keeping in mind this historical decision, the transposition of the Directives in a separate legal act or a consumer code was never considered a serious alternative. True, Estonia has also adopted the Consumer Protection Act⁶; this act is, however, not a classical consumer code regulating consumer contracts but consists mainly of public law rules such as the organization and position of the consumer protection entity and its competence to impose sanctions for consumer law breaches. Hence, both the DCD as well as SGD have been transposed in the Estonian Law of Obligations Act but in different parts of the act.

2 The provisions of the SGD were implemented in the special part of the LOA by adding or changing certain provisions in the chapter on the sales contract. The transposition choices were more complicated due to the object-based approach of the DCD ie the fact that the Directive does not regulate the legal nature of contracts for the supply of digital content or digital service but applies in all cases where the object of the contract is a digital content or digital service. This is one of the biggest challenges for transposing it into civil-code type legislation and it would have been very difficult if not impossible to integrate the directive-based rules concerning digital content and services into the special part of the LOA, which is structured according to the type of contract.⁷ Whereas there were different options for the transposition of the DCD on the table, it is worth mentioning that there were no real public discussions on the topic, although the draft law from 23 March 2021 on the transposition of the directives was sent to ministries and interest groups for an opinion.⁸ Responses received from the Ministry of Economic Affairs and Communications, the University of Tartu, the Estonian Bar Association, the Estonian Chamber of Commerce and Industry, the Estonian Association of Information Technology and Telecommunications and the Consumer Protection and Technical Regulatory Authority mainly concentrated on certain topics, especially concerning the options of the Sale of Goods Directive and not on the general transposition alternatives – with the exception of the University of Tartu favoring the approach that was finally adopted.

3 As the directive-based rules must be co-applied with the national contract law rules regulating contract types such as sales rental or services contracts, one option would have been to foresee specific digital content rules for all contract types in the Law of Obligations Act. Creating a completely separate new type of contract⁹ would also have been an alternative – as well as the option chosen by the Dutch legislator to include the digital content provisions in the regulation of sales contracts and add references to the relevant provisions concerning digital content and services to other types of contracts.¹⁰ Finally, it was decided to transpose the directive-based provisions into the general part of the LOA¹¹ creating a new division 6 called 'Contract for the supply of digital content and digital services' in chapter 2. Using such a regulatory option will make the

---

⁵ Kull, 'Transposition of the Digital Content Directive (EU) 2019/770 into Estonian Legal System' (2021) 12 *JIPITEC*, 249–259.

⁶ RT I, 24.11.2021, 4.

⁷ Kull, 'Transposition of the Digital Content Directive (EU) 2019/770 Into Estonian legal system' (2021) 12 *JIPITEC*, 253.

⁸ Kull, 'Transposition of the Digital Content Directive (EU) 2019/770 Into Estonian legal system' (2021) 12 *JIPITEC*, 250.

⁹ As suggested eg by Axel Metzger for Germany. See Metzger, 'Verträge über digitale Inhalte und digitale Dienstleistungen: Neuer BGB-Vertragstypus oder punktuelle Reform?' (2019) JZ, 577–586.

¹⁰ See Loos, 'The (Proposed) Transposition of the Digital Content Directive in The Netherlands' (2021) 12 *JIPITEC*, 229 et seq.

¹¹ This option was also suggested by the scholars of Tartu University, Sein and Kalamees, Opinion to the Estonian Ministry of Justice on the transposition of the DCD. Opinion is not publicly available.

A. Introduction and General Framework

directive-based provisions applicable to all digital content contracts irrespective of their qualification.[12] At the same time, the newly added § 62^5(7) LOA clarifies that the digital content provisions will be applied together with the provisions of the general part of the LOA and provisions of the respective type of contract.

These developments show that the transposition of the Digital Content Directive has had a certain impact on the structure of the Law of Obligations Act. The changes induced by the transposition of the Sale of Goods Directive are significant as well but less so on the structural level as the existing consumer sales provisions are changed but no specific division or chapter has been added.

II. Wider Impact of the Transposition

It has been argued that the transposition of the DCD does not lead to significant changes in the Estonian private law system and only some discretionary possibilities left to the Member States have been used.[13] This is disputable to some extent as the transposition of the Directives has influenced not only the structure of the Law of Obligations Act as described above but also the understanding of the general law of obligations and contracts in Estonia – although to a limited extent. The influence is particularly visible in the following aspects: qualification of the contracts for the supply of digital content and digital services, the definition of the consumer sales contract, the hierarchy of remedies as well as the prerequisites of contract termination.

To start with, the proposal and the transposition of the DCD have accelerated the discussion about the legal qualification of digital content and digital services contracts: before the discussions on the Digital Content Directive started on the European level these issues were only scarcely debated in Estonia. When transposing the directive, Estonia did not regulate whether contracts for the supply of digital content or a digital service constitute a sale, service, rental or *sui generis* contract: the respective norms in the general part of the LOA will apply to all types of contracts if they meet the characteristics of a contract for the supply of digital content or a digital service. However, in order to understand how the pre-existing contract law rules function together with the rules based on the DCD, it is necessary to qualify the type of contract in question. In the legal literature, there seems to be a tendency to qualify one-off contracts for the supply of standard digital content mostly as sales contracts (§ 208(3) LOA)[14] or, in the case of tailor-made digital content, contracts for work (§ 635 LOA).[15] The question is more complicated in the case of long-term contracts such as cloud services, software-as-a-service contracts, or streaming subscriptions. It has been discussed recently whether these contracts should be qualified as rental contracts or rather some kind of contracts for services with the conclusion that in most cases such contracts should be considered service contracts, be it a contract for work (*Werkvertrag*) or a contract for services (*Auftrag/Geschäftsbesorgung*).[16]

---

[12] Explanatory memorandum of the proposal for amending the Law of Obligations Act, 32–33. The explanatory memorandum also refers to the similar transposition option in the German law.

[13] Kull, 'Transposition of the Digital Content Directive (EU) 2019/770 into Estonian legal system' (2021) 12 *JIPITEC*, 258.

[14] See Varul et al., *Võlaõigusseadus II. Kommenteeritud väljaanne* (2019), 42.

[15] Varul et al., *Võlaõigusseadus II. Kommenteeritud väljaanne* (2019), 42.

[16] See Koll, 'Qualification of Consumer Contracts for the Supply of Digital Services under Estonian Law' (2021) *Juridica International*, 40–48; Kalamees et al., *Lepinguõigus* (2017) 259.

7   The transposition of the DCD also started the debate about the inter-relationship between the provisions of sales/services contracts and the provisions of license contracts[17] in Estonia with the prevailing view that whereas these two contracts often are concluded simultaneously, in many cases the seller and the licensor are different persons and hence we should differentiate between these contracts. The sales/services contract on digital content/service regulates, *inter alia*, its conformity criteria whereas the license contract only entitles the buyer/licensee to use the intellectual property.[18] This is in conformity with the approach of the Digital Content Directive[19] and one can easily say that the development of this understanding was facilitated by the transposition of the DCD.

8   The transposition of the Directives has also had a minor influence on the Estonian hierarchy of remedies both for consumer contracts as well as for sales contracts in general. In the case of sales contracts as well as contracts for work price reduction used to be possible as a first-level remedy, although restricted by the debtor's right to cure and the good faith principle.[20] With the transposition of the directives, the so-called flexible hierarchy rules were extended also to B2B and C2C contracts: the reason for such a choice was the fact that the results under the new flexible hierarchy rules would often coincide with the ones already established under the somewhat restrictive case law on price reduction. Consequently, harmonizing the price reduction rules for all sales contracts seemed to be a reasonable option that would create more coherence. The real impact should not, however, be over-estimated as the flexible hierarchy rules under the Directives are very similar to the ones already established under the Estonian case law.[21]

9   Certain changes in the Estonian contract law were induced solely by the transposition of the Sale of Goods Directive. First, the definitions of the consumer sales contract (§ 208(4) LOA), as well as the definition of the contract for work (§ 635(4) LOA), were changed in order to apply the rules on goods with digital elements, including the obligation to update the digital element, also to the tailor-made consumer goods with digital elements. At the same time, it was made sure that certain services-specific provisions remain applicable to these situations.[22] Second, it was clearly established that termination of the contract due to the lack of conformity is only possible if the lack of conformity is not minor. This requirement was missing in the previous text of § 223 LOA regulating the prerequisites of termination of a sales contract. Hence, in theory, termination of the sales contract was previously also possible if minor defects were not repaired within a reasonable time. In practice, such results were corrected via the good faith principle: the Estonian Supreme Court ruled in 2017 that termination due to only minor defects could be violating the principle of good faith if the termination would be unjustified under the circumstances.[23] The new rule of § 223(5) LOA allowing termination only in case of not-minor defects applies to all sales contracts, be it B2C, C2B, C2C, or B2B contracts. How-

---

[17] Estonian contract law legislation is somewhat unique as it contains not only contract law provisions on the sales, rental and services contracts but also a separate chapter on license contracts. See §§ 368–374 LOA.

[18] Kalamees et al., *Lepinguõigus* (2017), 256–258; Varul et al., *Võlaõigusseadus II. Kommenteeritud väljaanne* (2019), 42, 472–473.

[19] See Rosenkrantz, in: Schulze and Staudenmayer (eds), EU Digital Law (2020), Art. 10 DCD mn 2–4.

[20] Varul et al., *Võlaõigusseadus II. Kommenteeritud väljaanne* (2019), 77; decision of the Estonian Supreme Court 3-2-1-156-11 para 20; Kalamees, 'Hierarchy of Buyer's Remedies in Case of Lack of Conformity of the Goods' (2011) *Juridica International*, 63–72.

[21] Sein, 'Tarbija õiguskaitsevahendid uues digisisu ja digiteenuste lepingute direktiivis' (2019) *Juridica*, 569.

[22] See the respective changes in § 208(5) and § 635(4) LOA.

[23] Estonian Supreme Court 19.4.2017 – 3-2-1-16-17.

ever, the presumption that the defect is not minor, applies only to consumer sales contracts.[24]

Finally, the transposition of the Sale of Goods Directive also enabled to clarify a certain issue about the conformity of the Estonian law with the EU consumer law. Namely, under the existing legislation, it was unclear whether termination of a consumer sales contract due to a lack of conformity was possible only during a reasonable time after the buyer had become aware of the lack of conformity as suggested by § 118(1) p. 1 LOA in the general part of the contract law. Of course, such an interpretation would have been contrary to the Sale of Goods Directive and therefore the legislator decided to rule out such interpretation possibility. The newly added § 223(6) LOA clarifies that § 118(1) LOA is not applicable to the termination of a consumer sales contract thereby ruling out an interpretation contrary to the directive. A similar clarification is added to § 62^{14}(6) for digital content contracts.

Whereas the transposition of the directives has had an impact on the general structure and certain issues of contract law, it had less or even close to no influence on the legal acts regulating consumer or data protection law, nor the rules governing intellectual property. The only notable change related to the data protection law is the addition of a specific provision regulating the contractual consequences of the withdrawal of consent.[25] The notions contained in the DCD such as interoperability, digital environment, or digital content have neither had an impact on the doctrinal debate but of course, the necessary notions have been transposed in the LOA.

B. Extension of the Scope of Application of the Directives-based Rules

Estonia has not used the opportunity to extend the application of the rules of the DCD to contracts that are excluded from the scope of the Directive, such as non-governmental organizations, start-ups, or SMEs. It should be noted that generally under Estonian law, the rules concerning consumer contracts have only been applied to B2C contracts, including dual-use contracts.[26] The stakeholders also did not favour changing this principle when transposing the Directives. The only exception to stretching the scope of application of the EU consumer contract rules to B2B contracts is the unfair terms provisions, which are also applicable – with certain modifications – to the contracts concluded between traders.[27]

Up to now, there has been no real discussion on whether it would be advisable to apply the rules of the directives, especially the provisions on the supply of digital content and digital services to B2B contracts. Yet, during the implementation process, the question was raised whether the conformity regulation of the Sale of Goods Directive would be suited to be applied to all sales contracts. The legislator did not opt for such a solution as then the consumer sales rules would then also apply to eg real estate sales and it raised two types of concerns. First, there has been no analysis of whether the new rules would fit such contracts, and it would be premature to extend the applicability to these relationships. Second, there is already an established case law, especially on the real estate contracts and it would have created considerable legal uncertainty to provide a new set of rules while it is unclear whether the previous case law could be resorted to also under the new regime. Therefore, the split solution was adopted: there are separate

---

[24] See § 223(5) second sentence LOA.
[25] This issue is dealt with below at C.
[26] Varul et al., *Võlaõigusseadus I. Kommenteeritud väljaanne* (2016), 9; Explanatory memorandum, 33.
[27] See §§ 35–45 LOA and Varul et al., *Võlaõigusseadus I. Kommenteeritud väljaanne* (2016), 189.

regimes for the conformity criteria for consumer sales and for all other sales contracts (including B2C real estate sales). As indicated above, certain consumer sales law provisions were still extended to all sales contracts: apart from the flexible hierarchy rules, this applies also to the *'Weber and Putz'* principle in Art. 14 para. 3 SGD.[28]

C. Data as Counter-Performance: Impact of the New Concept

14 The new concept of data as a counter-performance has not led Estonia to introduce new rules on contract formation/existence or its validity. Under Estonian law a contract is concluded by an offer and acceptance or by exchanging mutual declarations of will by another way, provided that it is clear that the parties have reached an agreement (§ 9(1) LOA). In the context of data as a counter-performance debate, it has been asked in the legal literature whether the consumer can give his declaration of will for concluding the contract also indirectly, et by registering as a user of a platform and starting to download the digital content. It is submitted that as the consent for using personal data must meet the requirements of the General Data Protection Regulation[29], such declaration of will for a contractual agreement is not to be considered consent for data processing. Moreover, the consent should not be considered valid if the contractual declaration of will does not contain a reference to the purposes of data processing and if the offer to conclude a contract did not allow a reasonable person to understand that his personal data is considered as a counter-performance. However, a breach of the data processing rules does not affect the validity of the contract.[30]

15 There has also been some debate as to whether the digital content rules should be applicable in the case of cookies. True: recital 25 DCD stresses that the Directive should not apply to situations where the trader only collects metadata, such as information concerning the consumer's device or browsing history, except where this situation is considered to be a contract under national law. However, Member States are free to extend the application of this Directive to such situations. Whereas no case law exists as to whether just browsing a website could be considered a contract under Estonian law, it is brought out in the explanatory memorandum of the transposition law that the inclusion of cookies should be seriously considered, as the Court of Justice of the European Union (CJEU) ruled that an active consent of the consumer is needed for using the cookies.[31] This raises the question of why personal data obtained through cookies and processed on the basis of consent should be excluded from the scope of the digital content provisions, whereas other personal data processed on the basis of consent would not.[32]

16 Whether or not personal data can be considered as counter-performance under Estonian law is open to debate and treated controversially even by the same experts. Whereas it is clear that data-paid contracts should not be considered 'free' contracts

---

[28] This rule is transposed in § 222 (4) second sentence LOA. The understanding that this rule is also applicable to other sales contracts is expressed in the legal literature. See Varul et al., *Võlaõigusseadus II. Kommenteeritud väljaanne* (2019), 124.

[29] Regulation (EU) 2016/679 of the European Parliament and of the Council of 27 April 2016 on the protection of natural persons with regard to the processing of personal data and on the free movement of such data, and repealing Directive 95/46/EC (General Data Protection Regulation).

[30] Kull, 'Digisisu üleandmine ja digiteenuste osutamine isikuandmete esitamise vastu' (2019) *Juridica*, 584.

[31] CJEU, Case C-673/17, 1.10.2019, Bundesverband der Verbraucherzentralen und Verbraucherverbände – Verbraucherzentrale Bundesverband e.V. versus Planet49 GmbH, ECLI:EU:C:2019:801, para 65.

[32] Explanatory memorandum, 36.

C. Data as Counter-Performance: Impact of the New Concept

under Estonian law[33], leading to the non-applicability of the lenient liability standards of eg donation contracts[34], it is less evident whether there is a reciprocal (synallagmatic) connection between the trader's obligation to supply digital content or service and the consumer's obligation to provide personal data.[35] Before the beginning of the transposition process, it was argued in the legal literature that there is a synallagmatic connection between these obligations with the result that in the case of eg a sales contract one should apply the provisions of the buyer's payment obligation. Hence, the trader can refuse to conclude a contract if the consumer is not ready to provide personal data necessary for the performance of the contract.[36] Moreover, according to this view, the trader should be entitled to use remedies against the consumer should the consumer withdraw his consent. Alternatively, the trader can conclude the contract under the condition that the consent is not withdrawn and foresee in its terms and conditions that in case of consent withdrawal the consumer may use services only to a limited extent.[37]

This position published before the transposition of the DCD might not be fully justified as during the implementation process a new provision of § 62[18] titled 'The contractual consequences of consumer's withdrawal of consent' was added to the Law of Obligations Act. Subsection 2 of this rule clarifies that withdrawal of consent by the consumer should not be considered a breach of contract and does not entitle the trader to exercise any remedies against the consumer. This provision excludes, *inter alia*, the trader's claim for damages in case of withdrawal of consent – although such a claim has been considered possible in the earlier literature.[38] Furthermore, the rule does not allow the trader to claim provision/transfer of personal data or a respective consent from the consumer as the claim for specific performance (ie provision of personal data/consent) is also a contractual remedy under Estonian law.[39] 17

Yet, this does not necessarily mean that the trader has no right to terminate the contract in cases where the consumer downloads a 'free' app, gives consent to process his data, and later withdraws the consent. The explanatory memorandum of the transposition law stresses the need for a balanced approach that takes into account both the trader's as well as the consumer's rights.[40] The newly added § 62[18](1) LOA provides that if in case of a contract for a supply of digital content or digital services continuously or by several individual acts of supply a consumer exercises his right to withdraw the consent for the processing of his personal data, the trader may terminate the contract under the conditions provided for in § 196(1) LOA. Under § 196(2) LOA, termination is possible for a valid reason, ie a situation where the terminating party cannot, taking into account all the circumstances and the mutual interest, reasonably be expected to continue the contract until the agreed date or the expiry of the notice period. It is already established 18

---

[33] Kull, 'Transposition of the Digital Content Directive (EU) 2019/770 Into Estonian legal system' (2021) 12 *JIPITEC*, 255; Varul et al., *Võlaõigusseadus II. Kommenteeritud väljaanne* (2019), 214.
[34] See § 264(2) LOA: liability only for intentional or gross negligent breach.
[35] Compare Kull, 'Transposition of the Digital Content Directive (EU) 2019/770 Into Estonian legal system' (2021) 12 *JIPITEC*, 255, stating that these obligations are not reciprocal and Kull, 'Digisisu üleandmine ja digiteenuste osutamine isikuandmete esitamise vastu' (2019) *Juridica*, 585 for the opposite view.
[36] Kull, 'Digisisu üleandmine ja digiteenuste osutamine isikuandmete esitamise vastu' (2019) *Juridica*, 585.
[37] Kull, 'Digisisu üleandmine ja digiteenuste osutamine isikuandmete esitamise vastu' (2019) *Juridica*, 587.
[38] Kull, 'Digisisu üleandmine ja digiteenuste osutamine isikuandmete esitamise vastu' (2019) *Juridica*, 587 stating that in principle the trader could claim damages in lieu of the performance from the consumer under § 115(1) LOA.
[39] See § 101(1) p. 1 and § 108 LOA.
[40] Explanatory memorandum, 81–82.

under the Estonian case law that a valid reason must not necessarily be the other party's breach of contract: termination of a contract for a valid reason may be possible in circumstances arising solely from the terminating party or even outside the sphere of the parties.[41]

19   Hence, a situation where a consumer withdraws his or her consent to the processing of personal data is not considered a breach of contract but may in certain cases be considered a valid reason to terminate the contract with the effect of *ex nunc*. Consequently, if the consumer's consent for processing his personal data is crucial for the trader, the trader may terminate the contract but not claim damages, a penalty payment – or the provision of the personal data from the consumer. In order to terminate the contract, the trader has to give notice to the consumer: the legislator intended to avoid a situation where the withdrawal of consent would lead to automatic termination of the contract as the consumer's will by consent withdrawal was not necessarily directed at the contract termination.[42]

D. Conformity Requirements

20   The rules on the conformity requirements of the Directives have been mostly transposed word-by-word and without any noteworthy additions or specifications. In particular, there are no specific rules in the Estonian Law of Obligations Act on the durability/repairability requirement or other sustainability-promoting provisions. There was also no coordination of the implementing provisions of the SGD with those of Directive 2009/125/EC establishing a framework for the setting of eco-design requirements for energy-related products. It seems that at least as far as the legislation is concerned, Estonia is not among the front-runners of the green transition: there is no doctrinal or other debate on whether to adopt any specific measures for fighting premature or planned obsolescence of goods.

21   Legal defects of digital content or a consumer good amount to a lack of conformity under Estonian law. Paragraph $62^7(5)$ LOA provides that digital content or digital service does not comply with the contract if its use is hindered or restricted by a restriction arising from infringement of the rights of any third parties, in particular intellectual property rights. A similar provision applies in the case of consumer sales contracts.[43] The rules on nullity or rescission are not applicable to such situations: § 12 LOA stresses that the validity of a contract is not affected by the fact that, at the time of entry into the contract, performance of the contract was impossible or one of the parties did not have the right to dispose of the object of the contract.

22   Estonia has not specifically regulated the relationship of the Directives-based rules with the intellectual property law. In particular, there is no legal regulation as to whether consumers have the right to eg resell digital content or transfer computer game accounts. These questions are left to be answered in the case law whereby the result should probably depend upon whether the consumer was entitled to reasonably expect the resale possibility taking into account the particular circumstances of the case.[44]

---

[41] See eg Estonian Supreme Court, 17.12.2007 – 3-2-1-114-07.
[42] Explanatory memorandum, 81.
[43] See § $217^1(6)$ LOA.
[44] Pro: Oprysk and Sein, 'Limitations in End-User Licensing Agreements: Is There a Lack of Conformity Under the New Digital Content Directive?' (2020) 51 *IIC*, 594–623; contra: Spindler, 'Digital Content Directive and Copyright-related Aspects' (2021) 12 *JIPITEC*, 111 et seq.

Finally, Estonia has not regulated the modification of the digital element when implementing the SGD as the legal consequences of the modification rules of the DCD are not fit for tangible goods, including goods with digital elements. Whereas under the DCD, the modification right is only foreseen for the continuous supply of digital content, consumer sales contracts are typical one-off contracts, and the consumer's termination right in case of detrimental modifications would not be suitable for them. Moreover, a national regulation could hinder the maximum harmonizing effect of the new Sale of Goods Directive.

E. Liability of the Trader

The liability for the one-off and long-term supply of digital content and digital services is regulated in § 62^{11} LOA. The Estonian legislator has transposed the digital content directive more or less word by word and has neither opted for a longer liability period than the two-year one foreseen by the directive nor added any specific regulation for the interruption of long-term supply of digital content or digital services. Further, § 62^{11}(3) LOA clarifies that the notification obligation generally foreseen for non-conforming sales, rental and work objects does not apply to the lack of conformity of digital content or digital services.

Recital 14 DCD states that the Member States remain free to regulate the consequences of a failure to supply, or of a lack of conformity of digital content or a digital service, where such failure to supply or lack of conformity is due to an impediment beyond the control of the trader and where the trader could not be expected to have avoided or overcome the impediment or its consequences, such as in the event of force majeure. Indeed, also under Estonian law, the liability of the debtor is excluded if his breach of contract was caused by *force majeure* (§ 103 LOA). The force majeure clause in the Estonian obligation law coincides with the classical definition of force majeure, found eg in Art. 79 CISG[45]: in order to qualify as *force majeure*, the circumstance has to be beyond the control of the debtor, be reasonably unforeseeable and unavoidable at the time of concluding the contract as well as not reasonably possible to overcome. In the legal literature, typical examples such as terror attacks, war, or natural catastrophes have been mentioned.[46] The transposition provisions have not precluded the applicability of the *force majeure* clause in § 103 LOA to the contracts on the supply of digital content or digital services. Hence, it could be imagined that if the delivery of a certain digital content fails due to an unexpected and unavoidable cyber-attack, the trader would not be liable for non-performance and the consumer could not claim damages. The situation is, however, different in the case of a lack of conformity of a sales object: the consumer can claim damages suffered due to a defect of a sold object even if the defect was caused by *force majeure*.[47] The same applies in the case of defective work[48], eg if a lack of conformi-

---

[45] Varul et al., *Võlaõigusseadus I. Kommenteeritud väljaanne* (2016), 481–482.

[46] Varul et al., *Võlaõigusseadus I. Kommenteeritud väljaanne* (2016), 484–485; Sein, 'Mis on vääramatu jõud?' (2004) *Juridica*, 518–519.

[47] This is the prevailing view in the case law and legal literature. See the Estonian Supreme Court, 14.03.2019 – 2-17-1937; the Estonian Supreme Court, 30.05.2017 – 3-2-1-46-17; the Estonian Supreme Court, 30.09.2015 – 3-2-1-100-15 and Varul et al., *Võlaõigusseadus II. Kommenteeritud väljaanne* (2019), 103; Kalamees et al., *Lepinguõigus* (2017), 72. For an opposing view, see Kalamees and Värv, 'The seller's liability in the event of lack of conformity of goods' (2009) *Juridica International*, 85–93. On the possibility and limits of contractually restricting seller's liability outside consumer sales, see Sein, 'Müüja vastutus lepingutingimustele mittevastava kinnisasja eest. Riigikohtu praktika ja vastutuse välistamise või piiramise võimalused' (2021) *Juridica*, 87–100.

[48] Estonian Supreme Court, 28.10.2008 – 3-2-1-80-08.

ty occurs in case of tailor-made software. Hence, the defence of *force majeure* applies in the case of non-supply but not in the case of lack of conformity.

26 *Force majeure*, however, doesn't prevent the consumer from terminating the contract, if the prerequisites for termination are met, ie a second chance fails as well.[49] The same applies to his right to withhold his performance under § 111 LOA and the remedy of price reduction under § 112 LOA: according to § 105 LOA the consumer is entitled to use these remedies even if the trader's liability is excluded due to *force majeure*.

27 In addition to the *force majure* provision, the Estonian law also contains a change in circumstances regulation in § 97 LOA which is very similar to the one in § 313 BGB or Art. 6:111 PECL.[50] Again, nothing in the transposition rules of the digital content directive prevents the application of this provision to the contracts on the supply of digital content or digital services. However, it is not to be expected to happen often, if at all: the Estonian Law of Obligations Act has been in force for 20 years and the doctrine of change in circumstances has been applied only in a couple of cases, mostly connected to the adaption of rental contracts after the economic crisis of 2008.[51] It is hard to imagine that this doctrine would play a central role in the digital consumer contracts which – at least according to the Estonian experience – rarely end up in judicial disputes anyway.

F. Consequences of the Trader's Non-Compliance with the GDPR regarding Contracts for the Supply of Digital Content and Digital Services

28 Estonian law does not provide for any specific remedies for breaching the rules of the GDPR. In the legal literature, it is submitted that whether or not a contract is concluded does not depend upon the provision of personal data or whether there is valid consent for their processing.[52] Hence, the breach of data protection rules does not render a contract void or invalid.

29 In case the data protection rules are breached, the consumer may resort to the remedies foreseen in the GDPR, most importantly the right to claim damages under Art. 82 GDPR. In line with recital 48 of the DCD, the breach of privacy by default or by design principle may constitute a lack of conformity of the digital content or digital service but there is no provision in the Estonian transposition law mentioning it explicitly.

G. Remedies for the Failure to Supply and Remedies for the Lack of Conformity

I. General remarks

30 The conditions and consequences of the consumer's remedies under the Directives are to a great extent similar to the ones that existed in Estonian law before the transposi-

---

[49] Varul et al., *Võlaõigusseadus I. Kommenteeritud väljaanne* (2016), 497.

[50] Principles of European Contract Law, available at http://translex.uni-koeln.de/400200/_/pecl/.

[51] Sein, 'Eriolukorra mõju üürilepingutele Eesti ja Saksa õiguse kohaselt' (2020) *Juridica*, 186; Sein, 'The Principle of Change in Circumstances in Estonian Contract Law – "Much Ado About Nothing?"' in *Jurisprudence and Culture: Past Lessons and Future Challenges* (2014), 586–594.

[52] Kull, 'Digisisu üleandmine ja digiteenuste osutamine isikuandmete esitamise vastu' (2019) *Juridica*, 585.

tion. The differences concern certain nuances and not the underlying principles.[53] For example, both the right of withdrawal as well as the right of termination of a contract are exercised by a unilateral declaration (notice) under Estonian law.[54] When drafting and adopting the Estonian Law of Obligations Act in the late 1990s a conscious decision was taken to design termination as a *Gestaltungsrecht*[55] and this principle has been followed in the case law ever since.[56] Therefore, the Directives' approach follows the already well-established practice in Estonia.

Estonia has not used an option to set forth specific regulations for the sale of goods, neither concerning the place of delivery or the place of repair and replacement nor on the nuances of the transport costs: these questions continue to be answered under the general contract law principles and corrected, if necessary, via the guidelines given by the CJEU in the *Fülla* case.[57] Estonia has also refrained from addressing the cross-border sales and the problems that may arise for the sellers from their obligations under the Geoblocking Regulation. It can generally be argued that Estonia has not grabbed the opportunity to make use of the discretion left to the Member States: in many cases, the directives have been transposed word-by-word and without raising the consumer protection level even if the directive is minimum harmonizing. The rare exception to this general tendency of "no additional rules" is § 218(3^1) LOA stipulating that in case of replacement or repair of the good, the 2-year time limit starts running again. Another specific regulation is found in § 222(5) LOA which entitles the buyer (or a third party on his behalf) to repair the defective good at the seller's expense if the buyer has claimed repair from the seller but the seller has failed to do so within a reasonable period.[58] However, this provision was not induced by the transposition of the SGD but has been in place already since the adoption of the Law of Obligation Act. 31

Finally, it should be mentioned that Estonian law does not provide for an automatic transfer of the rights against the initial seller from the initial consumer to a subsequent buyer. At the same time, there is no provision prohibiting the initial consumer and a subsequent buyer from contractually agreeing that the rights against the initial seller are transferred to the subsequent buyer. Should the initial seller exclude the transferability of the rights under the legal guarantee or a commercial guarantee in his general terms and conditions, such a standard term would not render the transfer of claims[59] invalid: § 166(2) LOA stresses that agreements concluded between an obligor and an obligee whereby assignment of the claim is precluded or the right to assign the claim is restricted have no effect against third parties. Whereas this does not preclude or restrict the liability of the obligor for violation of the contractual prohibition to assign the claim (§ 166(3) LOA), such a contractual prohibition in standard terms would most probably be found unfair and thus void by the courts. Namely, § 42(3) p. 26 blacklists standard terms that 'preclude or unreasonably restrict the right of the other party to assign claims'. Such standard terms are considered void, ie not binding to the consumer. 32

---

[53] Sein, 'Tarbija õiguskaitsevahendid uues digisisu ja digiteenuste lepingute direktiivis' (2019) Juridica, 577.
[54] See § 188(1) and § 112(3) LOA.
[55] See eg Varul, 'Performance and Remedies for Non-performance: Comparative Analysis of the PECL and DCFR' (2008) *Juridica International*, 109.
[56] Varul et al., *Võlaõigusseadus I. Kommenteeritud väljaanne* (2016), 925–926.
[57] CJEU, Case C-52/18, 23.05.2019 – Fülla, ECLI:EU:C:2019:447.
[58] Such regulation in national law is explicitly allowed under recital 54 SGD.
[59] The situation is somewhat different for the so-called *Gestaltungsrechte*, such as termination and price reduction: it is not possible to transfer these rights independent from the whole contractual relationship. However, it is possible to give an authorization to use these rights. Varul et al., *Võlaõigusseadus I. Kommenteeritud väljaanne* (2016), 835 with references to the case law.

II. Relationship with other remedies

33 The rules on other contract law remedies such as the right to damages or to withhold performance remain applicable under the conditions set forth in the Law of Obligations Act.[60] The Estonian law proceeds from the principle of cumulation of remedies, meaning that eg damages can usually be claimed together with other remedies unless it would be contrary to the nature of the other remedy (§ 101(2) LOA).[61]

34 Estonian contract law contains a general remedy of the right to withhold one's performance, differentiating between this right for reciprocal (§ 111 LOA) and non-reciprocal obligations (§ 110 LOA). Payment obligation is considered a reciprocal obligation: it is in a reciprocal relationship with the trader's obligations to supply as well as to deliver an object which is in conformity with the contract.[62] Consequently, in the case of contracts for the supply of digital content or digital services the consumer would be entitled to withhold payment under § 111 LOA under the following conditions. First, the trader's obligation must be due, for example, the deadline for supply must have been passed. Second, according to the contract, the consumer must pay simultaneously with or after the trader's supply. The right to withhold is excluded under § 111(3) LOA, if its exercise would be unreasonable or against good faith, particularly if the trader has performed his obligations in most parts or without significant deficiencies. In the case of a contract for work, the Estonian Supreme Court has ruled that it would be against good faith to refuse the whole payment in cases where the work delivered by the debtor has only minor defects: here the creditor is only entitled to withhold the amount necessary for repairing the defects and compensating other expenses or losses incurred by the defects.[63] It is to be expected that the same argumentation would also be applied in the case of contracts for the supply of digital content or digital services. Finally, the consumer may use his right to withhold performance even in cases where he reasonably believes that there will be non-performance by the trader, especially due to his potential insolvency. The trader may, in turn, avert this right by giving an adequate assurance of due performance.[64]

35 For the consumer sales contract, the same principles apply in the case of non-delivery as well as for the lack of conformity of the good. In the latter case, one must of course consider the *lex specialis* provision of Art. 16 para. 3 subpara. b SGD which is transposed in § 223(7) LOA.

36 In case of damages, it was discussed whether to allow for some contractual flexibility for the digital content contracts as especially in the case of data-paid contracts we are moving in 'new waters' which could justify more party autonomy than it is possible under Estonian consumer sales law. Currently, § 237(1) LOA forbids all contractual restrictions or limitations of trader's liability and consumer's remedies, including the right to damages. Hence, the seller is not entitled to contractually limit the amount of the damages or lower his liability standard; this is only possible after the consumer has notified the defect.[65]

---

[60] For digital content contracts, the right to use other remedies foreseen in the LOA is expressly set forth in § 62^{14}(8) LOA.

[61] In depth, see Varul et al., *Võlaõigusseadus I. Kommenteeritud väljaanne* (2016), 477–479.

[62] Varul et al., *Võlaõigusseadus I. Kommenteeritud väljaanne* (2016), 533–534. For sales contract, see the Estonian Supreme Court, 12.06.2006 – 3-2-1-50-06.

[63] Decisions of the Estonian Supreme Court, 28.10.2008 – 3-2-1-80-08; the Estonian Supreme Court, 2.03.2015 – 3-2-1-145-14.

[64] See the nuances in § 111(4)-(6) LOA.

[65] Of course, an express and separate agreement deviating from the objective conformity standards remains possible as well (§ 237(3) LOA).

In the case of digital content contracts, § 62²²(2) LOA allows more contractual flexibility and legitimizes contractual restrictions for damages claims. These contractual restrictions are, however, only allowed within the limits already set by the unfair term rules as well as by § 106(2) LOA[66] forbidding contractual liability restrictions for intentional non-performance or allowing the debtor to perform an obligation in a manner materially different from that which could be reasonably expected by the creditor, or which unreasonably exclude or restrict liability.

Although it was not expressly addressed by the legislator during the transposition process, the directive-based rules on consumer's remedies should also have some impact on the so-called damages in lieu of performance under § 115(1) second alternative of the LOA. Namely, claiming damages in lieu of performance is regarded as a functional equivalent to termination in Estonian law: the Estonian Supreme Court has repeatedly expressed the view that claiming damages in lieu of performance can mean implicit termination of the contract.[67] Consequently, claiming damages in lieu of performance should be possible only under the same conditions that are set forth in the Directives: otherwise the aim of maximum harmonizing the remedy of termination would be compromised.

H. Time Limits

One of the most difficult decisions during the transposition process was the question of regulating the time limits. When describing the difficult choices, one has to start by explaining that the general prescription period under Estonian law is three years.[68] When transposing the 1999 Consumer Sales Directive[69] the legislator chose to apply additionally the absolute time limit of two years.[70] Hence, the consumer can file a claim for three years, provided that the defect became apparent during the first two years after delivery.[71] The three-year prescription period also starts to run from the delivery of the good.[72] A similar regulatory technique was suggested as one option also for the transposition of the rules on time limits under the DCD.[73] This would have meant keeping the existing system valid for consumer sales and extending it to digital content and digital services.

Alternatively, it was suggested to waive the 2-year time limit and apply only the prescription rules with the result that consumer's claims could be filed for three years since the delivery of the good or digital content. The rationale behind that suggestion was the argument that otherwise, consumers would be in a worse position concerning time limits than businesses to whom the general three-year prescription period applies.[74] However, during the transposition process, a number of stakeholders expressed the

---

[66] Explanatory memorandum, 88.

[67] See eg the Estonian Supreme Court, 12.06.2006 – 3-2-1-50-06; the Estonian Supreme Court, 9.02.2011 – 3-2-1-138-10; the Estonian Supreme Court, 5.06.2012 – 3-2-1-42-12. Critical on this view Pavelts, *Kahju hüvitamine täitmise asemel ostja õiguste näitel* (2017), 295–296.

[68] See § 146 of the General Part of Civil Law Act.

[69] Directive 1999/44/EC of the European Parliament and of the Council of 25 May 1999 on certain aspects of the sale of consumer goods and associated guarantees.

[70] See § 218(2) LOA.

[71] Varul et al., *Võlaõigusseadus II. Kommenteeritud väljaanne* (2019), 138.

[72] See § 227(1) LOA for sales contracts and § 651(1) LOA for contracts for work.

[73] Urgas and Koll, 'Nõuetele vastavus ning ettevõtja vastutus uues digitaalse sisu ja teenuste lepingute direktiivis' (2019) 8 *Juridica*, 563.

[74] Sein and Kalamees, Opinion to the Estonian Ministry of Justice on the transposition of the DCD. Opinion is not publicly available.

view that replacing the current two-year limitation period with a general three-year prescription period would put traders into an overly difficult position, as already a two-year period is considered too long to prove the existence of a lack of conformity of certain types of goods at the time of delivery.[75] Therefore, the Estonian legislator opted for the solution under *de lege lata* with the result that the transposition law provides both the time limit of 2 years as well as a prescription period of three years, starting from the delivery of the good.

41   In the case of goods with digital elements, this solution leads to some difficulties as the provision of digital services (as a digital element of a smart good) may last for more than three years. Application of § 227 LOA would lead to the result where claims arising out of the defects in digital service would also prescribe in three years from the delivery of the good: hence, if the 5-year subscription of a digital service shows a defect on the fourth year, the consumer would not be able to use any remedies as the claims would have already been prescribed. The legislator intended to prevent such outcomes and consider the specifics of goods with digital elements by regulating the starting point of the prescription period[76]: thus, a new section was added to § 227 LOA. This provision stipulates that if a sales contract of a good with digital elements foresees a continuous supply of digital elements over a period of time, the limitation period for the claim arising from the non-conformity of the digital elements begins upon the occurrence of the non-conformity. The same applies to the non-conformity caused by the breach of the updating obligation.[77]

42   Estonia also has a specific consumer-friendly prescription regulation foreseeing the restart of the prescription period in case of repair and replacement. Namely, under § 227(1) LOA, in case of replacement, a new prescription period starts to run from the delivery of the replaced good. The same principle applies in the case of repairment. These provisions, however, have already been in place since the implementation of the 1999 Consumer Sales Directive and the legislator has made no attempt to change them during the recent transposition process. True, Estonia was aware of the possibility of the national legislator foreseeing longer time limits/prescription periods[78] but the existing and already familiar 2-year limit did not put the legislator under political pressure to go beyond the minimum time limits foreseen in the Directives. The consumer-friendly solution of § 227(1) LOA foreseeing the restart of the prescription period in case of repair or replacement is allowed under recital 44 DCD and it could also be considered a sustainability-promoting solution. In case of repair or replacement, the 2-year time limit starts running again as well (§ 218(3^1) LOA), aligning the rules for time limit with the ones for the prescription (§ 227(1) LOA).

43   While the rules on prescription are rather detailed in the case of consumer sales, the Estonian legislator decided not to foresee any specific provisions regulating prescription in case of contracts on supply of the digital content or digital services. The specific time limits of the DCD, however, have been transposed: the 2-year time limit for one-off contracts is regulated in § 62^{11}(1) LOA, and the liability for the whole contract time in case of a continuous supply in § 62^{11}(2) LOA. In addition to these time limits, the general

---

[75] Kull, 'Transposition of the Digital Content Directive (EU) 2019/770 Into Estonian legal system' (2021) 12 *JIPITEC*, 257; Explanatory memorandum, 63–64. According to a view in the legal literature the 2-year time limit for consumer goods is justified as in most cases the defects of such goods should become visible during this period, at the latest. Varul et al., *Võlaõigusseadus II. Kommenteeritud väljaanne* (2019), 106.

[76] According to recital 42 DCD this is left within the competence of the Member States.

[77] Explanatory memorandum, 124.

[78] Urgas and Koll, 'Nõuetele vastavus ning ettevõtja vastutus uues digitaalse sisu ja teenuste lepingute direktiivis' (2019) 8 *Juridica*, 561.

prescription rules apply, depending upon the qualification of the particular contract. For example, if a one-off contract can be qualified as a sales contract, the rules of § 227 LOA on consumer sales described above will be applicable: although digital content is not a consumer good, under § 208(3) LOA the rules on the sale of goods will be applied *mutatis mutandis* also to other objects of the sales contract.[79]

Application of the general prescription rules is a bit more complicated in the case of digital services contracts such as cloud computing or streaming services but according to the Explanatory Memorandum of the transposition act, these rules should not be interpreted as to start the general three-year prescription period from the first supply of the service. Rather, any moment of the services should be considered the moment of supply with the consequence that the three-year period starts running from the moment the defect occurred. With such an interpretation the legislator found that there is no need for additional national regulation.[80]

Finally, one must emphasize that Estonia belongs to the countries with the consumer's notification obligation. This obligation was already introduced with the transposition of the 1999 Consumer Sales Directive and has not been causing any difficulties in practice. On the contrary, it ensures that the communication between the seller and the consumer on the solving of the dispute starts relatively soon after the defect has occurred.[81] Therefore the consumer's obligation to notify the trader of the lack of conformity within two months (§ 220 (1) LOA) was upheld. Understandably, the consumer's notification obligation cannot be applied to digital content contracts[82]: a provision clarifying this is found in § 62[11](3) LOA. Yet, the different rules on notification obligation may lead to confusion in the case of a good with digital elements: depending upon whether sales rules or digital content rules are applicable in a given case, a consumer may or may not be obliged to notify the defect within two months.[83] Therefore it would be advisable for him always to notify of the defect as otherwise he might risk losing the remedies under § 220(3) LOA.

I. Right of Redress

Before putting together the draft law transposing the Directives, the Ministry of Justice asked different stakeholders for an opinion on several transposition options. Inter alia, they inquired whether the existing rules on right to redress are deemed to be satisfactory or whether certain changes would be necessary. The stakeholders expressed the opinion that the existing regulatory framework on right to redress in consumer sales was adequate and therefore the Estonian Ministry of Justice decided not to plan any major changes or extensive new rules in this area.[84] The rules for the right of redress follow the same principles both for the digital content as well as for consumer sales contracts and allow redress against any party in the supply chain.[85]

Most importantly, the legislator decided not to change the existing principle of private autonomy although it was considered in the first place. On the one hand, the Ger-

---

[79] Explanatory memorandum, 65.
[80] Explanatory memorandum, 65–66.
[81] Varul et al., *Võlaõigusseadus II. Kommenteeritud väljaanne* (2019), 113.
[82] Recital 11 DCD.
[83] Sein, 'Tarbija õiguskaitsevahendid uues digisisu ja digiteenuste lepingute direktiivis' (2019) *Juridica*, 569.
[84] Explanatory memorandum, 125.
[85] In cases where there is no contractual relationship between the seller and the person in previous links of the chain of transactions, a delictual claim is considered possible in the legal literature. Varul et al., *Võlaõigusseadus II. Kommenteeritud väljaanne* (2019), 139–140.

man transposition draft that was used as a blueprint when designing the Estonian rules lays down a mandatory right of redress[86] and a similar suggestion can be found in the legal writing.[87] On the other hand, the existing regulation of the right of redress was a dispositive one[88] and stakeholders did not indicate any need for a fundamental change. Moreover, recital 63 of the SGD stresses that the directive should not affect the principle of freedom of contract between the seller and other parties in the chain of transactions. As there was no indication of the need for change from the stakeholders and because a mandatory right of redress can be undermined in cross-border cases by choosing a foreign law allowing for contractual freedom, the Estonian legislator decided to keep the existing non-mandatory right of redress. Hence, the first section of § 228 LOA clarifies that the seller may use legal remedies against the person concerned, including claiming damages, 'in accordance with the relationship between them'. This includes the possibility of contractual restrictions.

48   Some changes were, however, made to the prescription rules to allow for redress within the contractual chain also in cases where the primary claims are already prescribed under the general prescription rules. The explanatory memorandum brings an example where the consumer has filed his claim against the seller only at the end of the three-year prescription period making it very likely that the seller's claim against his contractual partner is already prescribed. The problem becomes more urgent as the consumer might be able to file claims because of the breach of the updating obligation even longer.[89] Hence, the newly added § 228(2) LOA stipulates that claims of a seller (who sold the good to the consumer) against his contractual partner do not prescribe before the expiry of two months after the satisfaction of the consumer's claim. This rule should enable the seller to use his remedies against his contractual party at least for a rather short time after compensating the consumer's claim.

49   Another specific rule was added to § 228(3) LOA with the aim to apply the same principles also to the redress claims within the supply chain. It ensures that also redress claims against the contractual partner do not prescribe before two months have elapsed since the trader has compensated his contractual partner. The seller or another person in the supply chain may also be liable for defects that were not existent at the time of delivery, but which occurred after that point in time due to the breach of the updating obligation.[90]

J. Conclusions

50   Estonian contract law was designed in the late 1990s and the beginning of the 2000s, using the most modern European contract law instruments, the CISG as well as the 1999 Consumer Sales Directive as a blueprint. Consequently, the general principles, as well as the system of remedies in the Estonian Law of Obligations Act, are in line with the latest developments in European contract law. Transposition of the Directives, therefore, did not create a need for a major change in the general understanding of contract law in Estonia. Most importantly, the conditions and consequences of the consumer's remedies under the directives are to a great extent similar to the ones that existed in the

---

[86] See § 327u (4) BGB for contracts on digital products.
[87] Kalamees, 'Goods with Digital Elements And The Seller's Updating Obligation' (2021) 12 *JIPITEC*, 142.
[88] Varul et al., *Võlaõigusseadus II. Kommenteeritud väljaanne* (2019), 140.
[89] Explanatory memorandum, 126.
[90] Explanatory memorandum, 126.

Estonian law before the transposition: the differences concern certain nuances and not the underlying principles.

Yet, the transposition process has enabled clarification of some existing uncertainties and ambiguities as to the prerequisites of the contractual remedies in the Estonian law, especially for the right of repair and replacement regulation in the sales contract rules. Hence one can argue that in addition to raising the consumer protection level the Directives have proved to constitute a certain incentive to create more coherence in the national contract law. On the other side, the transposition has also induced a change in the structure of the Law of Obligations Act as a new division on the digital content contracts was added to its general part and difficult questions about its co-application with the provisions of the particular contract types are likely to arise in the future. Moreover, the updating obligation has changed the nature of the classical sales contract and turned it partially into a service-like contract. Finally, it should be stressed that Estonia has joined the group of countries regulating the contractual consequences of the withdrawal of consent by the data subject and prohibited sanctioning the non-transfer of personal data.

Estonia has made only modest use of the options and discretion left to the Member States. In many aspects, Directives have been transposed word-by-word and it can be argued that even where the directives are only of minimum harmonizing nature, Estonian legislator has not raised the consumer protection level set forth by the directives. One should also not overestimate the practical importance of the new rules: consumer disputes are rare in the Estonian courts, and it is not to be expected that they will gain considerably more importance in the future.

Bibliography

Explanatory memorandum of the proposal for amending the Law of Obligations Act.

Piia Kalamees, 'Goods with Digital Elements And The Seller's Updating Obligation' (2021) 12 *JIPITEC*, 131.

Piia Kalamees, 'Hierarchy of Buyer's Remedies in Case of Lack of Conformity of the Goods' (2011) *Juridica International*, 63.

Piia Kalamees and Age Värv, 'The seller's liability in the event of lack of conformity of goods' (2009) *Juridica International*, 85.

Piia Kalamees, Martin Käerdi, Sander Kärson and Karin Sein, *Lepinguõigus* (Juura, Tallinn 2017).

Kristiina Koll, 'Qualification of Consumer Contracts for the Supply of Digital Services under Estonian Law' (2021) *Juridica International*, 40.

Irene Kull, 'Digisisu üleandmine ja digiteenuste osutamine isikuandmete esitamise vastu' (2019) *Juridica*, 578.

Irene Kull, 'Transposition of the Digital Content Directive (EU) 2019/770 Into Estonian legal system' (2021) 12 *JIPITEC*, 249.

Martin Käerdi, 'Westliche Rechtskonzepte in post-sozialistische Gesellschaft: Gesetzgeberische Erfahrungen in Estland' in Helmut Heiss (ed.), *Brückenschlag zwischen den Rechtskulturen des Ostseeraums* (Mohr-Siebeck, 2001).

Marco Loos, 'The (Proposed) Transposition Of The Digital Content Directive In The Netherlands' (2021) 12 *JIPITEC*, 229.

Axel Metzger, 'Verträge über digitale Inhalte und digitale Dienstleistungen: Neuer BGB-Vertragstypus oder punktuelle Reform?' (2019) *JZ*, 577.

Liliia Oprysk and Karin Sein, 'Limitations in End-User Licensing Agreements: Is There a Lack of Conformity Under the New Digital Content Directive?' (2020) 51 *IIC*, 594.

Arsi Pavelts, Kahju hüvitamine täitmise asemel ostja õiguste näitel (Tartu Ülikooli Kirjastus 2017).

Reiner Schulze and Dirk Staudenmayer (eds.), *EU Digital Law* (Nomos, Baden-Baden 2020),

Karin Sein, 'Müüja vastutus lepingutingimustele mittevastava kinnisasja eest. Riigikohtu praktika ja vastutuse välistamise või piiramise võimalused' (2021) *Juridica*, 87.

Karin Sein, 'Eriolukorra mõju üürilepingutele Eesti ja Saksa õiguse kohaselt' (2020) *Juridica*, 180.

Karin Sein, 'Tarbija õiguskaitsevahendid uues digisisu ja digiteenuste lepingute direktiivis' (2019) *Juridica*, 568.

Karin Sein, 'Estland – ein Versuchsfeld für das Europäische Privatrecht? Estnische Erfahrungen mit der Anwendung der Prinzipien des Vereinheitlichten Europäischen Privatrechts' (2013) GPR, 13.

Karin Sein, 'The Principle of Change in Circumstances in Estonian Contract Law – "Much Ado About Nothing?"' in *Jurisprudence and Culture: Past Lessons and Future Challenges* (University of Latvia Press, Riga 2014).

Karin Sein, 'Mis on vääramatu jõud?' (2004) *Juridica*, 511.

Gerald Spindler, 'Digital Content Directive and Copyright-related Aspects' (2021) 12 *JIPITEC*, 111.

Kaidi Urgas and Kristiina Koll, 'Nõuetele vastavus ning ettevõtja vastutus uues digitaalse sisu ja teenuste lepingute direktiivis' (2019) *Juridica*, 551.

Paul Varul, 'Legal Policy Decisions and Choices in the Creation of New Private Law in Estonia' (2001) *Juridica International*, 114.

Paul Varul, 'Performance and Remedies for Non-performance: Comparative Analysis of the PECL and DCFR' (2008) *Juridica International*, 109.

Paul Varul, Irene Kull, Villu Kõve, Martin Käerdi and Karin Sein, Võlaõigusseadus I. Kommenteeritud väljaanne (2nd edn, Juura, Tallinn 2016).

Paul Varul, Irene Kull, Villu Kõve, Martin Käerdi and Karin Sein, *Võlaõigusseadus II. Kommenteeritud väljaanne* (Juura, Tallinn 2019).

Finland

A. Introduction	1
I. Regulatory basis	1
II. Enforcement agencies	5
III. Later reforms	9
B. Implementation of EU directives 2019/770 and 2019/771	12
I. The implementation procedure and structure	12
II. Earlier regulation of digital contents and services	14
III. Seller's delay and buyer's obligation	19
C. Conformity of goods	20
I. Earlier regulation and reforms	20
II. Implementation in year 2021	27
D. Liable Persons	31
I. The main rule	31
II. Commercial guarantee	32
III. Liability of the previous sellers	35
E. Time limits	37
I. Notice of defect	37
II. Limitation period for seller's liability	43
F. Remedies	49
I. The original remedy system	49
II. The later reforms	55
III. The implementation of the SGD	59
IV. The implementation of the DCD	62
V. Compensation of damages	64
G. Conclusions	71
I. Problems in harmonization	71
II. Effects in Finland	75
III. Further harmonization needed?	78
IV. From consumer protection to client protection?	81
V. Better access to justice	84
Bibliography	84

A. Introduction

I. Regulatory basis

In spite of the fact that Finland and the other Nordic countries are regarded as civil law countries, these countries have never adopted large civil codes, which would regulate the central areas of civil law. In these countries, civil law issues have always been regulated by separate acts. In Sweden the sale of goods was regulated in year 1734 by the Commercial Book (in Swedish *Handelsbalken*, in Finnish *Kauppakaari*). This act was still valid in 19th century when Finland was attached as a part of the Russian Empire, and kept its own former legislation. Even now some parts of this book are still in force. However, these parts do not regulate sale of goods. 1

The other Nordic countries adopted rather similar sale of goods acts in the beginning of the 20th century. Finland was not able to follow this development due to the existing political problems with the Russian government. As the Commercial Code had become outdated in questions concerning sale of goods, the Finnish courts started to use the 2 principles expressed in the new sale of goods acts which had been adopted in the other Nordic countries.¹

3   The Finnish Contract Act (*oikeustoimilaki* (228/1929)) was adopted in year 1929, but it regulates only the general questions concerning the formation of contracts and their validity. It does not contain any provisions directly targeting sale of goods. So, until the end of 1970's the sale of good was not properly regulated in Finland. Finally, the Consumer Protection Act (*kuluttajansuojalaki* (38/1978)), hereinafter CPA) came into force in September 1, 1978. Its chapter 5 regulates sale of tangible movable items from traders to consumers.

4   The Finnish Sale of Goods Act (*kauppalaki* (355/1987), hereinafter SGA) was adopted in 1987. This act regulates sale of movable property between enterprises but also between individual private persons. So, it is applicable in all situations where the seller may not be regarded as a trader and the buyer may not be regarded as a consumer. The SGA was based on long lasting co-operation between Nordic countries, which lead that also other Nordic countries updated their legislation on sale of goods. In this co-operation also the content of new UN Convention on Contracts for International Sale of Goods (CISG) from year 1980 was taken into account as much as it was possible.²

II. Enforcement agencies

5   At the same time when the new CPA entered into force, certain authorities and dispute settlement bodies were established in order to ensure consumers' access to justice also in practice. The Consumer Ombudsman (*kuluttaja-asiamies*) – as in the other Nordic countries – has the task to protect consumers' collective interests, which means in practice mainly supervision of marketing and supervision of unfair standard contract terms.³ The original sanction system was rather slow and toothless, and that is why it was reformed in year 2020 at the same time when the EU Cooperation Regulation (2017/2394) was implemented.

6   Nowadays, if the trader does not stop his illegal activities in a voluntary way, the Consumer Ombudsman may issue an injunction order against him strengthen with conditional fines. Before this reform, the Ombudsman had in most cases to take the case to the Market Court, which then was entitled to issue the injunction order. The 2020 reform introduced also new economic sanctions which may be used against unscrupulous traders.⁴ It is important to remember, that, unlike many Central European countries, the Nordic Consumer Ombudsmen are public bodies and do not have very much to do with the settlement of normal individual consumer disputes.

7   In Finland, two State financed bodies were established in 1978 for the settlement of individual consumer disputes. Firstly, at local level consumer advisers (*kuluttajaneuvoja*) consult and try to achieve an agreement in disputes between a consumer and a trader. Secondly, if an agreement is not reached, the consumer may take his case to the Consumer Dispute Board (*kuluttajariitalauta*), which gives a recommendation on how the dispute should be solved. So, its decisions are not enforceable. This Board

---

[1] See, e.g., Pohjoismaiset kauppalait (1984), I.
[2] See, e.g., Pohjoismaiset kauppalait (1984:5), 29–35.
[3] For more information of the Nordic consumer ombudsmen, see, e.g., Viitanen (2007), 85–93.
[4] For more details, see Villa et al (2020), pp. 1050–1056.

solves thousands of individual consumer disputes every year. The procedure is totally in writing and free of charge.[5]

Naturally, a consumer may also take his case to a court, but at this moment this alternative is not very tempting. In Finland there are no small claims procedure available for consumer and for other similar kind of disputes where legal expenses normally prevent the use of courts. The loser pays all expenses – cost rule is applied in most civil cases, which means that legal expenses of the losing party may nowadays easily rise to tens of thousands of euros.

III. Later reforms

In 1994 the contract law parts of the Finnish CPA faced a fundamental reform (Act 16/1994). For example, the whole chapter 5 was rewritten so that many articles concerning sale of goods in the CPA and the SGA became more or less identical to each other. However, one central difference remained. The provisions in chapter 5 of the CPA are mandatory in consumer contracts, but the articles of the SGA, which are applicable in other sale of goods contracts, are still always non-mandatory. Parties may always agree otherwise.

The non-mandatory nature of the articles of the SGA is not a problem in contracts between large enterprises with equal bargaining power, but the situation can be rather problematic, when the other party is in a clearly weaker negotiation position, but cannot, however, regarded as a consumer. For example, most small and medium size enterprises and small non-governmental organizations need in practice protection against large enterprises. At this moment neither SGA nor CPA is protecting them. In principle, since 1982 it has been possible to adjust unfair contract terms also outside consumer contracts. This is based on article 36 (956/1982) of the Contract Act, but the Supreme Court has been in practice very reluctant to adjust terms in these contracts. Adjustments have normally been possible only in situations where there has been an essential change of circumstances after the contract was concluded.[6]

The following reform of chapter 5 of the CPA took place in 2001, when the Sale of Goods Directive (1999/44/EC) was implemented (Act 1258/2001). As this directive was a minimum harmonization directive, its implementation did not cause any significant changes to the Finnish legislation. The biggest change was the adoption of so called six months legal guarantee. It meant that even in cases where commercial guarantee had not been granted, a trader had to show that a good, which had been bought less than six months earlier, was not defective at the time of delivery. Before this amendment, a consumer had the burden of proof.

B. Implementation of EU directives 2019/770 and 2019/771

I. The implementation procedure and structure

The twin EU directives 2019/770 and 2019/771 were adopted in May 2019, and Member States had to implement them to their national legislation before July 1, 2021. In Finland, the Ministry of Justice set a working group for the implementation of these

---

[5] Similar Consumer Dispute Boards exists also in the other Nordic countries. For more details, see, e.g., Viitanen (1996).
[6] See, e.g., Finnish Supreme Court judgements KKO 1990:138 and KKO 1996:27.

directives in February 2020, and its report was published in May 2021.[7] It contained a draft for government's proposal and was send for consultations to a wide range of different interest groups. The government's proposal concerning the implementation of the twin directives was published in October 2021,[8] and it was adopted by the Parliament in December 2021. The Act (1242/2021), which contained changes and amendment to the Finnish CPA, entered into force in January 1, 2022. The implementation did not cause amendments to other legislation.

13   The new Sale of Goods Directive (hereinafter SGD) was implemented by amending the already existing chapter 5 of the CPA, and the Digital Content Directive (hereinafter DCD) was implemented by adding to the CPA a totally new chapter 5a. From the viewpoint of the implementation, this was naturally the clearest solution. However, one may with good reasons ask whether also the DCD could have been implemented into the already existing chapter 5. Now there are two chapters which scope of application is different, but which contain a lot of very similar or totally identical articles.

II. Earlier regulation of digital contents and services

14   Before the implementation of the twin directives the legal situation concerning the supply of digital contents and digital services was rather unclear in Finland. As long as computer programs and games were still sold in CD- and DVD diskettes, the articles of the existing chapter 5 of the CPA could be used, as there were clear tangible movables available. The diskettes were treated as tangible goods as meant in chapter 5 in spite of the fact that the diskette served only as a carrier of its digital content.[9]

15   The situation became more unclear when diskettes turned to be outdated and the speedier internet connections made it possible to download even large programs directly from trader's server to consumer's computer. The articles of chapter 5 were no applicable to the cases we just mentioned. This meant that there were no mandatory rules available for consumer disputes concerning sale of digital contents. The articles of the SGA were available, as the scope of application of the SGA is larger than the scope of application in chapter 5 of the CPA. The SGA covers the sale of movable property (art. 1) and not only the sale of tangible movable items as chapter 5 of the CPA.

16   However, the SGA provided only non-mandatory rules, and the trader had a full freedom to use his own standard contract terms. In these cases, a consumer could only try to argue that these contract terms were unfair on the basis of chapter 4 in CPA, and they should be adjusted. Unfortunately, in practice this is always a rather uncertain way when comparing to the possibility to use substantial mandatory rules which main purpose is to protect the weaker party.

17   After traders started to submit to consumers only fixed-term licenses instead of ownership of the digital content, even the SGA became inapplicable. These disputes could only be solved by using general contract law principles, the same principles which were used in the sale of goods before CPA or SGA were adopted. According to these principles the product or service should conform to the contract terms and consumer's general expectations; if they did not, there was a breach of contract. In that case the other party had a right to remedies which varied on the basis of the seriousness of the breach. Traditionally, the right to rescind the contract is given only when the breach of contract is an essential one. However, also here the freedom of contract is playing a huge

---

[7] See Työryhmän mietintö 2021:17.
[8] See Hallituksen esitys n:o 180/2021.
[9] See, e.g., Hallituksen esitys n:o 180/2021, 17 and 28.

role, and due to the lack of mandatory legislation, mistreated consumers may only argue that trader's standard contract terms are unfair.

So, the Act 1242/2021 clarified the situation clearly regarding the sale and supply of digital contents. The new chapter 5a is applicable in all modern time digital contents, and a consumer is provided protection by its mandatory articles. This protection is available not only in the sale of digital contents, but also in fixed-time licenses of digital contents.

III. Seller's delay and buyer's obligation

For some reasons, the SGD does not cover situations where seller is in delay concerning the delivery of the good. Neither the SGD nor the DCD regulate buyer's obligations. The remedy provisions concerning compensation of damages all also missing in both directives. So, these questions have been left totally to the national legislators in spite of the fact that they form central parts of national sale of goods regulation. In Finland when the twin directives were implemented, the articles concerning seller's delay were left untouched in chapter 5 of the CPA. Some reforms were made for national reasons to articles concerning buyer's obligations. However, the totally new chapter 5a concerning digital contents and digital services got also articles regulating seller's delay (CPA ch. 5a, art. 5–9). These articles are rather identical to similar articles in chapter 5 concerning seller's delay in the traditional sale of goods.

C. Conformity of goods

I. Earlier regulation and reforms

Also in Finnish sales law the requirements for the conformity of goods have been traditionally divided between subjective requirements ("*what has been agreed*") and objective requirements ("*buyer's general expectations*"). The sold good may be regarded as defective if it does not fulfil these requirements.[10]

Conformity of goods was regulated in article 1 of chapter 5 in the original CPA since 1978 (38/1978). Subjective requirements were not at all mentioned in that text. The clear emphasis had been put on the objective requirements ("*is not such as buyers in general have cause to expect*"). According to the same article, goods might also be deemed defective if false or misleading information had been given and this information might be presumed to have a bearing on the transaction.

The original chapter 5 in CPA contained also a separate article concerning sale of second-hand goods. According to article 6 of chapter 5, in spite of the fact that goods was sold in condition "*as it is*", it might be deemed defective, if it did not conform the given information or if the seller did not give information which had essential significance to the conclusion of contract. A good might be deemed defective also if it was substantially poorer in quality than what the buyer had grounds to expect when taking into account the price and the other circumstances. This article has been widely used by the Consumer Dispute Board, especially in disputes concerning the sale of second-hand cars.[11]

---

[10] See, e.g., Aaltonen (1978), 100.
[11] See, e.g., Simonen (1982), 515–522.

23   In 1994, the chapter 5 in the CPA faced a total reform (Act 16/1994). The whole chapter was rewritten and made much more detail and systematic comparing to the original one. Inspiration was taken from the new SGA which had been adopted in year 1987, and after the reform many articles in both acts were rather identical. However, the main difference of these both acts remained clear. The mandatory articles of the CPA were applied only in consumer contracts. Meanwhile the SGA was applied in other sale contracts and the nature of its articles remain non-mandatory.

24   Conformity of goods were regulated in articles 12, 13 and 14 (16/1994) of the chapter 5 in the CPA. Article 12 defined the subjective and objective requirements for conformity. Especially interesting in this article was the durability-requirement. Durability of good should have corresponded to what a consumer may ordinarily expect in the purchase of such goods. Article 13 regulated situations where the goods did not conform to the information given by the seller or by a person in a previous level of supply chain or on behalf of the seller. Article 14 regulated the use of "*as it is*" clause, and was rather identical than in the original version of chapter 5 adopted in year 1978.

25   When the Sale of Goods Directive from year 1999 (1999/44/EC) was implemented into Finnish legislation in year 2001, it had some influence on the articles which regulated conformity of goods. A new article 12a (1258/2001) concerning defects arising from installation or lack of instructions was added to chapter 5. According to it, if the installation or assembly was included into the contract, and if the seller or someone else on the behalf of the seller had made the installation, the goods may be deemed defective if installation did not correspond to what had been agreed or what the buyer might have generally expected.

26   In article 14, which regulated the use of "*as it is*"-clause, the word "*substantially*" was dropped away, so that it was enough if a goods was of poorer quality than what the buyer had grounds to expect. So, it was no more necessary that the good was substantially poorer comparing to consumer's expectations. However, it is unclear whether this change had any practical influence. It has never been studied whether or not the threshold to deem, e.g., a second-hand car defective, dropped lower in the practice of Consumer Dispute Board after the reform. The presumption is, however, that no relevant changes took place.

II. Implementation in year 2021

27   When the twin directives were implemented into Finnish CPA, the articles concerning conformity of goods in chapter 5 were once again reformed. The new article 12 (1242/2021) contains the subjective and objective requirements for the conformity of goods. It corresponds almost word by word to the articles 6 and 7.1–7.2 of the SGD. Also the durability-requirement is still mentioned in the legal text, but it is no more emphasized in the same way than earlier. The new article 13 is regulating incorrect installation and it is based on article 8 of the SGD. It is rather similar to the former article, but covers now also situations where a consumer installed the goods, but the problems was incorrect installation instructions provided by the seller. New article 13a in chapter 5 of the CPA covers situations where the seller has neglected to inform consumer on safety and other program updates. It is based on par. 3 and 5 of article 7 SGD.

28   The former article 14 concerning the use of "*as it is*"-clause was dropped away. This article had been widely used in disputes concerning sale of second-hand cars even in cases where this clause had not been expressly used. According to the Ministry of Justice

there was no reason to apply different rules in the sale of second-hand goods.[12] So, now the defects in the sale of second-hand goods are to be assessed by using the same rules existing for the sale of new goods. It is too early to say whether this will have consequences also in the practice of Consumer Dispute Board. The problem is, that now the use of "*as it is*"-clause means that the subjective requirements are met, and the only way to deem the goods defective is to use objective requirements.

The former article 12 concerning misleading information was dropped away, but it has been integrated to new articles 12 and 13. According to article 12.2.4., when assessing the fulfilment of consumer's general expectations, one should also take into account any public statement made by or on behalf of the seller particularly in advertising or on labelling. However, article 13.3. provides certain restrictions of this liability. By these articles, Finland implemented articles 7.1.d and article 7.2. of the SGD. 29

The conformity requirements of digital contents and services set by the DCD were implemented in Finland by articles 10–14 in the brand-new chapter 5a of the CPA (1242/2021). These articles are based almost word by word on articles 7–9 of the DCD. Article 10 in chapter 5a sets the subjective and objective requirements for the conformity. Article 12 regulates updates, article 13 incorrect integration and article 14 so called legal defects, situations where a right of a third party prevents or limits the use of digital content or digital service. These articles are almost identical to corresponding conformity requirements in chapter 5 on the CPA. 30

D. Liable Persons

I. The main rule

In the sale of goods, the seller has been traditionally regarded as the liable person in spite of fact that he has not produced the defective goods. Whether he has a right to demand compensation for the expenses caused by remedies given to the consumer, it depends on the contract between him and those who belong to the earlier stages of the supply chain, usually the importer or producer. According to article 4 in the Sale of Goods Directive 1999/44/EC, Member States had an obligation to provide to the final seller an opportunity to pursue remedies against a previous seller in the same chain of contracts. However, in Finland this article was never implemented to the Finnish legislation, and the liability between final and previous sellers were left to be settled by their mutual contracts. The present directive 2019/771 does no longer contain a similar article on liability between the final and previous sellers. 31

II. Commercial guarantee

In certain situations, a consumer may target his demands also against liable persons other than the seller. A most typical case concerns commercial guarantee. The use of commercial guarantees has become the main rule in the sale of durable goods, such as new cars, home appliances and different electronic goods (televisions, mobile phones etc.). Commercial guarantees are regulated in article 17 of the SGD. This article has been implemented into the Finnish legislation by articles 15a and 15b of chapter 5 in the CPA (1242/2021). According to article 15a, a commercial guarantee is binding on the 32

---

[12] See Arviomuistio kuluttajansuojan muutostarpeista (2012), 16.

guarantor under the conditions laid down in the commercial guarantee statement or in the associated advertising. On the basis of article 15b a consumer has the right to receive the guarantee statement in written form or by another durable medium, and it should contain certain basic information.

33   Article 17.4. of the SGD is providing to the Member States an opportunity to give more detailed rules concerning commercial guarantees. This has been used in Finland. According to article 15a, the guarantor has the burden of proof of whether the good was defective at the time of delivery. So, during the guarantee period the reversed burden of proof is applied. That is why during the guarantee period it is more profitable to a consumer to demand remedy on the basis of the given commercial guarantee instead of seller's liability based on law.

34   However, on the basis of article 11 of the SGD, during the first twelve months the seller's normal liability is based on the reversed burden of proof. This burden of proof-rule, which has sometimes been called as a legal guarantee, was first time introduced in Sale of Goods Directive 1999/44/EC, according to which the reversed burden of proof was applied only during the first six months. This period has now been prolonged in the new directive to twelve months. In addition, the Member States may prolong by their national legislation this period up to two years. However, Finland did not use this option, and implemented only the one year term (CPA ch. 5, art. 15.3 (1242/2021)).

III. Liability of the previous sellers

35   So, in case a commercial guarantee has been granted by a producer or an importer, a buyer may also demand remedies from them and a reversed burden of proof is applied during the guarantee period. However, the Finnish CPA provides to a consumer another opportunity to present his claims against a previous seller. This liability of the previous level of the supply chain was first time introduced in year 1994. According to article 31 of chapter 5 in the CPA (16/1994) the buyer had the right to direct his claims based on a defect in the goods also to a business who at an earlier level of supply chain had supplied the goods for resale. Originally, the purpose of this rule was to protect a consumer in situation where the final seller went to bankrupt and was unable to provide remedy. However, the right to direct the claims at the previous sellers was not restricted to bankrupt situations. The buyer had no obligation to try first to get remedy from the final seller. He could always direct his claims to the importer or the producer.[13]

36   However, there were certain restrictions in the liability of the previous sellers. First of all, they were not liable for defects, which were arisen after they have delivered the goods, or claims which were based on promised given by somebody else. Secondly, in monetary claims their liability was restricted to the amount that the contracting party vis-a-vis the said business could have claimed on the same ground (CPA ch. 5, art. 31.2. (16/1994)). In the case law a vital restriction has also been set. This liability form is available only for the first buyer. If he sells the goods, the new owner has no right to direct claims at the previous sellers. So, this right is available only in the sale of new goods, e.g., new cars, but not in the sale of second-hand goods.[14] In the latest reform of the CPA in year 2021, this liability form was maintained, and it can be found in article 31 of the chapter 5 in the CPA (1242/2021).

---

[13] See Hallituksen esitys n:o 360/1992, 74–77.
[14] See, e.g., Helsinki Court of Appeal Judgement n:o 1495, S 18/1936, 26.11.2019.

E. Time limits

I. Notice of defect

In Finland, on the contrary to many other European countries, there have never been any exact time limits for buyer's reactions. Neither the CPA nor the SGA contain any articles which would define in which exact time period buyer should contact the seller in order to get redress for the defective goods. According to article 13 in chapter 5 of the original CPA (38/1978), the buyer had an obligation to notify the seller *within a reasonable time* (1) after he discovered or (2) ought to have discovered the defect. The SGA contains a similar regulation (32§).[15]

The reason not to adopt an obligation to notify the defect within a fixed time limit, is simply the fact that, especially in consumer contracts, the buyer is often unfamiliar with his legal rights and how to exercise them. A consumer may also have problems to identify whether a good is attached with a technical defect or not. In the practice of Consumer Dispute Board the accepted reasonable time is usually varied between 3–6 months.[16]

The Sale of Goods Directive 1999/44/EC provided to the Member States an option to impose to the buyers an obligation to notify the seller not later than within two months after the consumer had discovered the defect. This option was never used in Finland. However, the chapter 5 of the CPA was amended in a way that gave to the buyer the right to notify always within two months of his discovery of the defect (art. 16.1 (1258/2001)). In theory, this amendment expanded buyer's rights in cases where he ought to have discovered the defect earlier, but he did not. However, it is difficult to assess whether this reform had any practical effects at all, as the Consumer Dispute Board have stated that the beginning of the notice time should always be counted from the moment a consumer ought to have discovered the defect.[17]

The first proposals of the directive 2019/771 did not contain any obligation to the buyer to complain in a certain exact time limit.[18] However, in the final version this obligation returned. As the new directive is a maximum harmonization directive, this would have caused problems to the Finnish system where the buyer had an obligation to notify within reasonable time instead a certain fixed time limit. The problem was solved in the directive by leaving to the discretionality the Member States' the regulation of this obligation. So, Member States may decide whether to adopt any obligation to notify or not. If the obligation is adopted, the time limit for notification should be at least of two months. So, a Member State may, e.g., adopt a six month time limit (art. 12).

Finland did not adopt any kind fixed time limit for buyer's notification. It decided to maintain the system where the notification should be made within a reasonable time after the defect was discovered or ought to be discovered (CPA ch. 5, art. 16a (1242/2021)). According to the same article, the buyer has still the right to always notify within two months after he actually discovered the defect. However, as mentioned earlier, the Consumer Dispute Board had not paid attention on this amendment. So, it is presumable that in Finland the notice time will be also in future counted from the moment when a consumer ought to have discovered the defect. This means that

---

[15] Also Sweden has adopted the same rule in their general sales law and in consumer contract law. See, e.g., Ramberg (1995), 386–391 and Eriksson et al (2011), 171–175.
[16] See, e.g., Peltonen-Määttä (2015), 317–325.
[17] See, e.g., Consumer Dispute Board drno 03/33/578, 15.3.2005.
[18] See COM(2015) 635 final, 23 and COM(2017) 637 final, 17.

differences between Finland and other Member States which have implemented fixed time limits for buyer's notification are in practice not so big, especially if the time in the latter countries is counted only from the moment when a consumer have discovered the defect.

42   The DCD does not contain any provisions on buyer's duty to notify. This meant that new chapter 5a in the Finnish CPA does not either contain these provisions, and a consumer do not have any obligation to notify in a reasonable time after he ought to have discovered the defect. So, there is a clear difference between buyer's duty to notify between chapter 5 and chapter 5a in the CPA. However, according to the preparatory works, this difference should not have an essential significance as the notice of defect does not play similar role in the supply of digital contents and serviced than in the sale of traditional goods.[19]

II. Limitation period for seller's liability

43   Many European countries have also adopted fixed time limitation periods for seller's liability. In Finland there have never been any short limitation periods, which would have been based on fixed time limits. In this question the Finnish system differs also from Sweden, where the limitation period in the general sales law is two years and in consumer contract law three years.[20] Neither there has been any serious discussion on whether Finland should adopt a limitation period. That is why, also the arguments pro and contra of these limitation periods have not been presented. One may argue that there should be a certain fixed time limit for seller's liability. One the other hand, everybody knows that when the buyer has the burden of proof concerning the facts whether the good was defective at the time of delivery, in practice the seller's liability may not last very many years. So, the discussion on whether Finland should adopt fixed time limitation period, e.g., 4 years is rather theoretical.

44   Sustainable consumption has become a very topical issue in the international environmental discussion. The quality of consumer goods has weakened as a consequence of hard price competition between producers. Durable goods, which used to last normally at least a decade, may be broken already after a couple of years use. Poor quality products means more burden to the environment in the form of growing waste problem and increasing consumption of limited raw materials. That is why there is a growing need that producers should start to fabricate more durable goods especially from the viewpoint of environmental protection. Rather short limitation periods for seller's liability do not support the achievement of this goal. If the European Union or national legislators clearly state, that it is enough from the viewpoint of consumer protection to produce durable goods, such as cars, home appliances and electrical appliances which last only two years, this does not encourage them to the production of better quality – and more environmental-friendly – consumer goods.

45   In theory, also in Finland there is a time limit for seller's liability. That is the general limitation period for debts and obligations. According to article 7 of the Act on the Statute of Limitations on Debt (in Finnish *laki velan vanhentumisesta* (728/2003)) this time limit is ten years.[21] However, in practice seller's liability does not last so long. The Consumer Dispute Board have had cases where the seller has been held liable for defect which have been discovered 3–4 years after the delivery. In these cases, it has been a

---

[19] See Hallituksen esitys n:o 180/2021, 29–30.
[20] See, e.g., Ramberg (1995), 391–392 and Herre-Ramberg (2009), 274–278.
[21] For more details, see, e.g., Saarnilehto et al., 289–295.

question of sale of durable goods, which has been broken after the granted commercial guarantee period has expired.[22]

According to Sale of Goods Directive 1999/44/EC, this limitation period should have been at least two years (art. 5.1.). As this directive was only a minimum harmonisation directive, there was no need to make any changes to the Finnish legislation as the directive was implemented in year 2001. However, the proposal of the new, full harmonization SGD contained also the same two years limitation period. As this would have caused a need to make substantial changes to the former Finnish system, the Finnish government opposed this proposal.[23]

The problem was solved, once again, by making this two years limitation period in SGD optional. The Member States are entitled to maintain or introduce longer time limits (art. 10.3.). It is not totally clear, whether this article in SGD means that the Member States have an obligation to adopt at least some limitation period based on fixed time, e.g. five years, or may they left this question fully open. In DCD it is clearly stated that the Member States may freely decide, whether to adopt any kind of limitation period or not. In case they adopt one, it has to be at least 2 years (art. 11.2). Finland added a reference rule to chapters 5 and 5a. According to article 22a in chapter 5 and article 29 in chapter 5a, limitation period for liability is regulated by the Act on the Statute of Limitations on Debt. This means that it is still 10 years.

The SGD entitles the Member States to adopt shorter limitation periods for the sale of second-hand goods. However, this limitation period should not be shorter than one year (article 10.6.). When taking into account the general reluctance to adopt any kind of fixed limitation periods in Finland, it is not surprising that this option was not used when the SGD was implemented in year 2021.

F. Remedies

I. The original remedy system

In case goods have been deemed defective, the Finnish contract law has traditionally provided to the buyer several remedies. The buyer has a right to claim replacement of the defective good or reduction of the price. The right to rescind the contract is available only if the defect could be regarded as essential. In addition, the buyer may have a right to require compensation of his other economic damages. In order to receive compensation, negligence on seller's side is normally needed, but the burden of proof concerning its existence is reversed. So, in order to avoid pay compensation for buyers' damages, the seller has an obligation to proof that he had not acted in a negligent way.[24]

This solution was mainly adopted in the original version of the CPA in year 1978. According to article 2 in chapter 5 (38/1978), the buyer was entitled to require a new good free from defects or price reduction. The buyer had the right to rescind the contract only if no other remedy was considered fair from his point of view. So, the threshold to ask for the rescission of the contract was clearly higher compared to the use of the other remedies.

However, according to the same article, the seller had a right to reject all other remedies if he offered to repair the defective goods at his own expense and without

---

[22] See, e.g., Consumer Dispute Board recommendations n:o 3793/32/2012, 26.2.2015 and n:o 4292/32/2019, 3.6.2020.

[23] See, e.g., U 25/2015, 10.

[24] See, e.g., Aaltonen (1978), 129–154.

delay. Repair might not reduce the value of the goods and should take place without substantial inconvenience to the buyer. Seller's right to repair at least once the defective goods was an important remedy especially in the sale of durable goods. The buyer could not repair the defective goods elsewhere, and then afterwards require the expenses from the seller. The seller had a right to try to repair the goods. Otherwise, he could reject other remedies.[25]

52   However, later on in the practice of Consumer Dispute Board a more consumer friendly interpretation of this right was adopted. In cases where the seller had not been able to use his right to repair the defect, he was obliged to compensate to the buyer the amount of money he would have to spend if the right to repair would have been offered to him.[26]

53   Article 12 in chapter 5 contained a temporary remedy. If the buyer had not paid the goods at the time of delivery, he was entitled to withhold the payment until the defect was abolished. There was no limitation concerning this remedy. It meant that the buyer had the right to withhold even the whole sale price in case the goods was defective.

54   Buyer's right to compensation of damages was regulated in article 9 in chapter 5. The seller was liable to pay compensation for expenses incurred by the buyer due to measures that have become necessary because of a defect as well as for expenses incurred due to necessary measures that have become useless because of the defect (direct damages). So, on the contrary to the former contract law principles, the liability for these damages did not depend on seller's negligent behavior. However, in case the buyer had suffered other damages than those mentioned in the article (indirect damages), seller's liability was based on negligence with reversed burden of proof.

II. The later reforms

55   In 1994 the earlier remedy system was modified by introducing a two-step system, which resembled greatly the system which was later on adopted in Sale of Goods Directive (1999/44/EC). Firstly, there were the rights to require repair or replacement. So, the earlier seller's right to repair the defective goods was enlarged to buyer's right to require repair as an alternative to replacement (CPA ch. 5, art. 18 (16/1994)). In case repair or replacement were not possible, the buyer was entitled to require price reduction or to rescind the contract. The latter remedy was available only if defect was of major significance (CPA ch. 5, art. 19 (16/1994). So, the right to rescind the contract still remained as a final remedy which was available only in most serious cases.

56   The buyer's right to withhold the payment was restricted to an amount that evidently corresponded the claims he was entitled to on the basis of the defect (CPA ch. 5, art. 17 (16/1994)). So, after this amendment the buyer, who is using this remedy, takes not only the risk that goods is not later on regarded as defective, but also that he has withhold a sum of money which exceeded the size of the defect. In both cases the seller may use remedies which are available when the buyer's defaults of payment has occurred.

57   The regulation concerning compensation of damages was reformed too. According to articles 10 and 20 in chapter 5 (16/1994), the buyer is entitled to compensation for loss that he suffered because of a defect in the goods (direct damages). This liability is still strict. In indirect damages, such as loss of income and essential loss of the use of the product, the liability is still based on seller's negligence. Unfortunately, it is no more

---

[25] See Hallituksen esitys n:o 8/1977, 46–47 and Kivivuori et al. (1978), 147–149.
[26] See, e.g., Villa et al. (2020), 1164.

mentioned in the legal text, who has the burden of proof concerning the existence of seller's negligence. This means that it will be decided separately in each case.

In year 2001, when the Sale of Goods directive (1999/44/EC) was implemented into the chapter 5 of the CPA, also the remedy system was slightly changed. The threshold for the buyer's right to rescind the contract was lowered. It was no more necessary that the defect was of major significance, it was enough that it was not of minor significance (CPA ch. 5, art. 19 (1258/2001)). This reform was based on the directive, which was more consumer friendly than the former Finnish legislation. After this reform there have been a clear difference between CPA and SGA, as in the latter, rescind of the contract is still possible only if defect is of major significance (article 39 in SGA).

III. The implementation of the SGD

The articles 13–16 of the SGD from year 2019 regulates buyer's remedies in the sale of goods. These articles were implemented into Finnish legislation by amending to chapter 5 new articles 16, 18, 18a, 19 and 19a (1242/2021). Article 16 is simply listing buyer's remedies. According to article 18, a consumer may choose between repair and replacement. However, the seller may refuse to repair or to replace in case chosen remedy would be impossible or would impose disproportionate costs for the seller when taking into account, e.g., the value of the goods and the significance of the defect. In the preparatory works an example is given. In case the defect is of minor importance and may be easily repaired, the seller may refuse to replace and offer to repair the defect.[27]

This means that in spite of the fact that the seller's right to repair has lost its former strong position to reject other remedies, it has not disappeared. The practical consequences of this reform, e.g., to the sale of new and second-hand cars in Finland, are still unfamiliar. In these fields of business, the repair – and especially seller's right to repair – has been the dominant remedy during the last four decades.

Article 3.7. of the SGD entitles Member States to give to a consumer a right to choose freely between all potential remedies in case the defect is discovered not later than within 30 days after delivery. As this kind of rule has been unfamiliar in the former Finnish contract law, this option was not used when the SGD was implemented into CPA.

IV. The implementation of the DCD

The rules on remedies contained in articles 13–19 of the DCD were implemented into articles 6–8 and 18–26 of chapter 5a of the Finnish CPA (1242/2021). Articles 6–8 regulate remedies for the failure to supply. Article 6 consists of consumer's right to withhold payment until the digital content or service has been supplied and it is similar to article 17 (16/1994) in chapter 5. According to article 7 the consumer may insist that the trader supplies the digital content or service unless this would cause to the trader unreasonable expenses or would be impossible. Article 8 provides to the consumer the right to rescind the contract in case the trader fails to supply the digital content or service without undue delay or within expressly agreed additional period of time. Article 9 regulates compensation of damages when the trader has failed to supply in agreed time.

---

[27] See Hallituksen esitys n:o 180/2021, 54.

63   Articles 18–26 regulate consumer's rights when a digital content or digital service is deemed defective. As the first step, the consumer may withhold the part of the payment which is corresponding to the size of the defect (article 18). He has also the right to insist asking repair or replacement. The trader may reject to repair or replace in case the expenses would be unreasonable high or such a remedy would be impossible (article 19). In case the trader has not eliminated the defect or replaced the defective digital content or service, the consumer may as the second step insist asking price reduction or ask to rescind the contract. The latter remedy is available only if the defect is not of minor importance (article 20). The article 21 regulates how the size of price reduction should be calculated. Articles 22–23 concern compensation of damages and articles 24–26 the legal effects of the termination of the contract.

V. Compensation of damages

64   One striking feature was already contained in the Sale of Goods Directive 1999/44/EC. One remedy had been left totally outside of harmonization. That was compensation of damages. The same observation may also be found in twin EU directives 770/2019 and 771/2019. This is rather odd as both of these directives are full harmonization directives. So, the regulation of these questions has been left totally to the Member States. They may freely decide according to which conditions and under what circumstances the compensation of damages may be given.

65   According to recital 61 SGD and recital 73 DCD compensation of damages is a central part of the remedy system, but these questions have been left outside the harmonization as all Member States have already rules in this regard. This explanation is not very convincing, especially when it is question of full harmonization. The Member States have had also regulation of other remedies, but this has not been used as a reason to leave them outside of harmonization. The reason for harmonization of the remedy system has not been lack of certain remedies, but the fact that remedy systems are different between the Member States.

66   The main problem here is that compensation of damages is rather near to another remedy, namely price reduction. In both cases it is a question of monetary remedy: the seller or supplier of a service is paying to the buyer a certain sum of money without the termination of the contract. In practice these remedies are easily overlapping each other. For example, in UK the price reduction was unknown as a remedy before the implementation of the Sale of Goods Directive 1999/44/EC. Instead of price reduction, compensation of damages was used as a corresponding remedy.[28]

67   In Finland it has been noticed that the concepts of price reduction and compensation of damages have often been confused in the practice of Consumer Dispute Board. In cases where the seller was unwilling to use his right to repair, the seller was often recommended to pay price reduction in case the buyer had not yet repaired the defect by a third party, but compensation of damages for the repair expenses if it had been already done.[29] Naturally, from the viewpoint of the buyer it is not relevant by which name the monetary remedy is called, but these examples show clearly the close connection between these two remedies. That is why it may be regarded rather problematic that compensation of damages in consumer contracts have been left totally outside of harmonization especially when the purpose of the twin directives is full harmonization.

---

[28] See, e.g., Weatherill-Howells (2005), 201.
[29] See, e.g., Sisula-Tulokas (1992), 45–59.

In Finland the compensation of damages in the contract law has been traditionally divided between direct and indirect damages. Direct damages are damages which have been directly caused by the breach of contract. Indirect damages are, e.g., loss of income and essential loss of the use of the undelivered or defective goods. The seller's liability has always been harder in direct damages. In the Finnish Sale of Goods Act from year 1987, the seller is liable for direct damages always unless the damages have been caused by force majeure. In indirect damages the liability is based on negligence (art. 27 and 40). The burden of proof concerning the existence of negligence have been left unregulated, so it will be decided separately in each individual case.[30]

In direct damages seller's liability is a little bit harder in consumer contracts than according to the SGA. In direct damages the seller may use force majeure-argument only when the delivery of the goods has been delayed, but not when the goods are deemed defective. However, in indirect damages the situation is similar than in the SGA. A consumer may receive compensation for indirect damages only if the seller has been negligent. Burden of proof have been left also here to be decided in casu.[31] However, in practice it often means that seller has to prove that he has not acted in a negligent way.

When the twin directives were implemented, there was no need to reform the Finnish rules concerning compensation of damages. However, the new chapter 5a concerning digital contents and services got also provisions on compensation of damages (articles 22–23). There are rather similar than articles in chapter 5.

G. Conclusions

I. Problems in harmonization

Contract law belongs clearly to the hard core of national civil law legislation in every European country. All nations have long traditions in this regard and the roots have been dig deep into their legal culture. This is the main reason why is has been so difficult to harmonize general contract law at the level of European Union. In many other fields of law, where the EU has succeeded to harmonize Member States legislation, it has been a question of legislation, which has been rather new in most countries without long lasting legal traditions.

However, clear progress in harmonization has been made in the field of consumer contract law where Unfair Contract Terms Directive (93/13/EEC) was adopted in year 1993 and the Sale of Goods Directive (1999/44/EC) in year 1999. However, these both directives were still minimum harmonization directives, so that Member States were entitled to give better protection to their citizen than what was provided by these directives. Unfair Contract Term Directive was integrated in year 2011 to the widely discussed Consumer Rights Directive (2011/83/EU), which was already a full harmonization directive. The sale of consumer goods got its new full harmonization directive in year 2019, when the SGD was adopted. At the same time, the regulation was widened also to the so-called digital contents and digital services by the DCD.

The legal nature of EU consumer law directives has changed during the last 20 years from minimum harmonization to maximum harmonization directives. Unfortunately, this has often happened without significant improvements of the level of consumer protection. Minimum protection has simply become also maximum protection which

---

[30] See, e.g., Wilhelmsson et al.(2006), 88.
[31] See, e.g., Villa et al. (2020), 1152 and 1167.

the Member States may not exceed in their national legislation. This development has naturally caused a lot of resistance among those Member States where the maximum harmonization has forced to weaken the substantial rules of their consumer protection legislation. In the SGD and DCD these political conflicts have often been solved in a way which is very typical to EU legislation: by giving several options to the Members States. However, these options, together with the questions which have been left totally outside of the harmonization, e.g., compensation of damages, mean that instead of the planned full harmonization only partial harmonization will be achieved.

74 The new SGD is basically rather similar to the former Sale of Goods Directive from year 1999. However, one clear reform is the prolonged legal guarantee. The reversed burden of proof is now twelve months instead of the earlier six months. The practical significance of this reform is diminished by the fact that in the sale of durable goods consumers normally already have this benefit on the basis of granted commercial guarantee.

II. Effects in Finland

75 In Finland the implementation of the SGD in year 2021 did not cause any fundamental changes to the former legislation. The reason was partly based on the several options provided by the directive, e.g., concerning time limits for the notice of defect and limitation period for seller's liability. Maybe the biggest reform compared to the earlier stage was the weaken position of seller's right to repair. Already the original CPA from year 1978 had contained seller's right to repair as a way to reject buyer's other remedies, and to diminish his own expenses. In Finland, this right have had an important role especially in the sale of new and second-hand cars.

76 According to the SGD, a consumer has the exclusively the right to choose between repair and replacement. Trader may use his right to repair in case replacement would be impossible or would impose disproportionate costs to the seller when taking account, e.g., the value of the goods and the significance of the defect. Time will show whether this reform will be implemented also at the practical level, in everyday life in the car shops where business is made and most disputes solved. It is possible that buyers will face in most cases an offer which is very hard to resist. The defect is promised to be repaired instantly. Another alternative would be some other remedy "much more later on". It is obvious that most consumers will choose the repair.

77 The regulation of digital contents and digital services is a rather new phenomenon in most Member States, included Finland. This kind of regulation, which filled a clear gap, is naturally more than welcome. The legislative technique used was an adoption of a separate directive. The same idea of separate regulation was used also in Finland. The DCD was implemented by adding to the CPA a totally new chapter 5a. As mentioned already earlier in this article, this solution was certainly clear, but not the only possibility. Another solution would have been to integrate the articles based on the new DCD to the already existing chapter 5 of the CPA. The chosen solution means that there are now two chapters, chapters 5 and 5a, which contain a lot of rather similar or even identical articles.

III. Further harmonization needed?

78 The DCD regulates the most essential questions on the supply of digital content and digital services: conformity and remedies. However, a huge number of relevant questions

G. Conclusions

have been left outside, and they are in practice regulated by standard contract terms written by the provider of the digital content or services. It is obvious, that they are clearly in favor of the trader, who is nowadays often a large multi-national company. The only choice which has been left to a consumer is to decide, whether to read tens of pages more or less non-understandable legal text or not, and whether to click "*I agree*"-button or not.

Should the EU try to fix this contractual imbalance? In fact the same problems exist also in other consumer contracts. The mandatory regulation covers in practice only partially the questions parties may agree with in their contracts. One solution could be more detailed mandatory EU regulation. However, large scale efforts to harmonize European contract law have so far failed, and there are no indications that future attempts would be more successful. 79

Another way would to leave more space for the freedom of contract, but limit it in certain situations. The *doctrine of surprising and hard contract terms* has long traditions also in the Finnish contract law, where it has been applied in all kinds of contracts. According to this doctrine, a contract term which is exceptionally surprising and hard for the other contracting party, will not became a part of the contract unless the other party, who has written the contract terms, expressly draws other party's attention on it and on its significance. This means that the trader may not simply give to a consumer a long list of contracts terms. He has to clearly introduce the most significant contract terms. These terms would otherwise not be void.[32] So far this doctrine has had its biggest practical relevance in insurance and banking sector. 80

IV. From consumer protection to client protection?

Another central question is, should we widen the protection outside of consumer contracts? So far, the border line between consumer contracts and other contract has been rather strict at least in Finland. Mandatory rules cover only consumer contracts, and in all other contracts parties have full freedom of contract. For example in Finland, other than consumers may not benefit from the implementation of the DCD, as the scope of application of the brand new chapter 5a in the CPA does not cover other than consumer contracts. 81

Freedom of contract is based on a presumption of parties who have equal negotiation power. However, in practice the parties are often far from equal. Small enterprises and corporations, such as housing cooperatives and non-governmental organizations have to face in their contractual relations large companies, which are willing to use only their own standard contract terms. So, in practice these small entities are confronted with exactly the same problems as consumers in their relations with traders, the non-existing freedom of contract. Freedom of contract has been limited to the stronger party's right to write the contract terms. 82

In case we want to provide better protection also to small enterprises and corporations, the next question is naturally whether we should proceed at the EU level or leave it totally to the Member States. The earlier attempts to harmonize European Contract Law have so far demonstrated to be rather unsuccessful. At the national level the results might be also considered as disappointing. For example, in Finland the problem has not been clearly identified yet. Certain preventive and repressive protection against unfair contract terms is already available, but in practice the system is rather toothless. Organizations which represent small enterprises or corporations may take legal action 83

---

[32] See, e.g. Hemmo (2003), pp. 162–170.

in a court against large companies and claim for an injunction order against the use of unfair contract terms. Secondly, an individual enterprise or corporation may insist adjustment of unfair contract terms in already concluded contracts.[33] Both methods are rather uncertain and consist of huge economic risks for the plaintiffs, in practice tens of thousands of euros.

V. Better access to justice

84 However, poor access to justice is still a great problem in consumer contracts. In spite of the fact, that EU has tried to force Member States to develop alternative dispute settlement bodies for the settlement of consumer disputes, there is still much to do in this field. For example, in Finland the Consumer Dispute Board receives nowadays more than 6 000 new written complaints every year. The average handling time of these cases is more than a year, and the result is still only a recommendation, which too many traders neglect to comply with. Access to courts is in principle possible, but in practice out of question due to high legal expenses.[34] The present situation is far from satisfactory. This is very sad as there is a clear relation between substantial rules and access to justice. Without effective or at least functioning systems for consumer's access to justice the improvement in the substantial rules will have very little influence on consumer's life in practice.

Bibliography

Aaltonen Aimo, *Irtaimen kauppa* (1st edn, Lainopillisen ylioppilastiedekunnan kustannustoimikunta, Vammala 1978).

Amended proposal for a Directive of the European Parliament and of the Council on certain aspects concerning contracts for the sales of goods. COM(2017) 637 final, Brussels 31.10.2017.

Arviomuistio kuluttajansuojan muutostarpeista. Oikeusministeriön mietintöjä ja lausuntoja 9/2012. Helsinki 2012.

Digisopimusdirektiivin ja tavarakauppadirektiivin täytäntöönpano. Työryhmän mietintö 2021:17. Oikeusministeriö. Helsinki 2021.

Eriksson Anders, Nordling Lotty and Palm Torsten, *Konsumentköp* (Karnov Group, Stockholm 2011).

Hallituksen esitys Eduskunnalle kuluttajansuojalainsäädännöksi n:o 8/1977.

Hallituksen esitys Eduskunnalle laiksi kuluttajansuojalain muuttamisesta ja eräiksi siihen liittyviksi laeiksi n:o 360/1992.

Hallituksen esitys eduskunnalle laiksi kuluttajansuojalain muuttamisesta n:o 180/2021.

Hemmo Mika, *Sopimusoikeus I* (2nd edn, Talentum, Helsinki 2003).

Herre Johnny and Ramberg Jan, *Konsumentköplagen* (3rd edn, Norstedts Juridik, Stockholm 2009).

Kivivuori Antti, Schulten Jerry, Sevon Leif and Tala Jyrki, *Kuluttajansuoja* (Kustannusosakeyhtiö Tammi, Helsinki 1978).

---

[33] See, e.g., Wilhelmsson (2008), 200–205.
[34] See, e.g., Viitanen (2003), 424–465 and Viitanen (2011), 125–181.

Bibliography

Peltonen Anja and Määttä Kalle, *Kuluttajansuojaoikeus* (Talentum Pro, Helsinki 2015).

Pohjoismaiset kauppalait. Pohjoismaisen kauppalakityöryhmän ehdotus. NU 1984:5. Helsinki 1984.

Proposal for a Directive of the European Parliament and of the Council on certain aspects concerning contracts for the online and other distance sales of goods. COM(2015) 635 final, Brussels 9.12.2015.

Ramberg Jan, *Köplagen* (Fritzes, Stockholm 1995).

Saarnilehto Ari, Annola Vesa, Hemmo Mika, Kartio Leena, Tammi-Salminen Eva, Tolonen Juha, Tuomisto Jarmo and Viljanen Mika, *Varallisuusoikeus* (2nd edn, Sanoma Pro Oy, Helsinki 2012).

Simonen Irja, *Käytetyn auton kauppaa koskevista valituksista kuluttajavalituslautakunnassa* (Defensor Legis 1982) 515–522.

Sisula-Tulokas Lena, *Hinnanalennus* (Lakimiesliiton kustannus, Helsinki 1992).

Valtioneuvoston kirjelmä eduskunnalle ehdotuksista Euroopan parlamentin ja neuvoston direktiiveiksi (digitaaliset sopimukset), U 25/2015.

Viitanen Klaus, 'The Scandinavian Public Complaint Boards' (1996) 4 *Consumer Law Journal* 118–126.

Viitanen Klaus, 'Enforcement of consumers' collective interests by regulatory agencies in the Nordic countries' in van Boom Wilhelm – Loos Marco (eds), *Collective Enforcement of Consumer Law* (European Law Publishing, Groningen 2007).

Viitanen Klaus, *Lautakuntamenettely kuluttajariitojen ratkaisukeinona* (Suomalainen Lakimiesyhdistys, Helsinki 2003).

Viitanen Klaus, *Asianajopalkkiot – kilpailu vai sääntely?* (Edita, Helsinki 2011).

Villa Seppo, Airaksinen Manne, Jauhiainen Jyrki, Kaisanlahti Timo, Mähönen Jukka, Raitio Juha and Viitanen Klaus, *Yritysoikeus* (4th edn, Alma Talent, Helsinki 2020).

Weatherill Stephen and Howells Geraint, *Consumer Protection Law* (2nd edn, Ashgate, Aldershot 2005).

Wilhelmsson Thomas, Sevon Leif and Koskelo Pauliine, *Kauppalain pääkohdat* (Talentum, Helsinki 2006).

Wilhelmsson Thomas, *Vakiosopimus ja kohtuuttomat sopimusehdot* (Talentum, Helsinki 2008).

France

A. Introduction	1
B. Definitions and Scope of Application	11
C. The Trader's Obligations	21
I. The Obligation to Deliver	22
II. The Guarantee of Conformity	26
1. Durability	30
2. Updates	33
3. Contractual Adaptations	38
4. Third Parties' Rights	40
D. Remedies	44
I. Remedies for Failure to Supply	45
II. Remedies for Lack of Conformity	49
1. Withholding of Payment	52
2. Bringing into Conformity	53
3. Price Reduction and Termination	59
III. Time Limits	63
IV. Other remedies	69
1. General Rule on the Combination of Remedies	70
2. Damages	75
3. Combination with the GDPR	76
V. Commercial Guarantee	77
VI. Transfer of Rights, International Settings, and Right of Redress	80
E. Other Sanctions	83
I. Criminal Sanctions	84
II. Civil Sanctions	85
III. Administrative Sanctions	89
Bibliography	89

A. Introduction

French law belongs to those legal systems which have chosen to deal with consumer law separately from "common" law, i.e., in a civil law country like France, from civil law. This choice has been embodied in the creation of a *code de la consommation* (CCons), distinct from the *code civil* (CC). While the CC dates back to 1804, the CCons is obviously much younger and entered into force in 1993. Its creation was a mixed blessing for consumer law. On the one hand, consumer law was recognised as a branch of the law in its own right, with its own code, something not negligible in a country where codification has long been regarded as very important. On the other hand, the clear distinction between civil law and consumer law has resulted in the latter being rather disregarded, in both senses of the term. While civil law has always been held as a noble matter, the very heart of (private) law,[1] consumer law is often viewed as a rather ancillary subject, not as worthy of attention. Consumer law is indeed comparatively understudied in France. This is true both in teaching and in research. Students in French law faculties typically do not study consumer law as part of their bachelor degree[2] and consumer law is generally only offered as an optional course in some masters degrees. Many French lawyers have therefore never studied consumer law as such during their time at university and know very little about the rules in that field. The relative disregard

---

[1] As is well known, there is a sharp divide in French law between private law and public law. This results in civil law having limited relevance in the field of public law.

[2] Except those on unfair contract terms, which are mentioned in the course on general contract law, a basic second-year course at university.

for consumer law also explains why comparatively few academics specialise in this branch of the law, and almost never so on an exclusive basis. Things are starting to change, however, as is shown by the increasing number of textbooks on consumer law and the greater place given to the subject in legal journals.[3]

2 The twin EU Directives on digital content (DCD)[4] and on Sale of Goods (SGD)[5], and their implementation in French law, offer a good illustration both of this relative disregard for consumer law and of this change of tide. The DCD and the SGD have attracted comparatively little attention, at least in the academic world, but there seems to be a growing awareness of the importance of the matters they deal with, and the rules they set may have an influence on future French legislation, even outside the field of application of the Directives.

3 To fully understand how French law approached the implementation of the Directives, it is worth going back shortly to the current structure of the law of sales in France and to the transposition of Directive 1999/44/EC of the European Parliament and of the Council of 25 May 1999 on certain aspects of the sale of consumer goods and associated guarantees (1999 SGD). The contract of sale has been regulated in the CC since 1804 and the provisions that deal with it have remained practically unchanged since that time. Through Pothier, one of the Code's great inspirators, the CC inherited from Roman law the warranty for hidden defects (*garantie des vices cachés*). To this day, Art. 1641 CC provides: "The seller is bound to a warranty against hidden defects in the thing sold that render it unfit for its intended use, or that so impair its use that the buyer would not have bought it, or would only have given a lesser price for it, if he had known of the defects." As time went by, however, the courts emphasised the specificity of the warranty vis-à-vis "ordinary" contractual liability (then regulated at Arts. 1146 ff. CC). This is problematic since, as is apparent from the definition in Art. 1641 CC, the *garantie des vices cachés* only covers what can be termed the "objective conformity" of the good sold, i.e., the conformity to what could reasonably be expected by an ordinary buyer, as opposed to the "subjective conformity", i.e., the conformity to what had been specifically agreed between the parties. If the good sold is not "subjectively conform", then the buyer cannot rely on the *garantie des vices cachés* but must ground his claim on the rules of ordinary contractual liability, which can lead to very different outcomes. This situation can hardly be regarded as satisfactory, especially as the distinction between objective and subjective conformity is rather elusive in practice.

4 After the adoption of the 1999 SGD, the French Ministry of Justice (also called *Chancellerie*) created a commission, chaired by Professor Geneviève Viney, France's leading tort scholar, to draft the transposition bill that was to be submitted to Parliament. In its proposed bill, published in 2001,[6] the commission took the position that the transposition of the Directive should be the occasion to modernise the whole law of sales, along the lines of the Directive and of the Convention on the International Sale of Goods (CISG), and to create a single action in case of lack of conformity, which would cover both objective and subjective conformity. Under this approach, the rules contained in the 1999 SGD would have become the common rules for sales contracts under French law, thus in effect broadening the scope of application of consumer law

---

[3] See, e.g., *Revue des contrats*, a prominent civil law journal, which devotes a section to consumer law.
[4] Directive (EU) 2019/770 of the European Parliament and the Council of 20 May 2019 on certain aspects concerning contracts for the supply of digital content and digital services.
[5] Directive (EU) 2019/771 of the European Parliament and the Council of 20 May 2019 on certain aspects concerning contracts for the sale of goods.
[6] The text of the proposal is available at http://www.justice.gouv.fr/art_pix/0000.pdf (last accessed 24 March 2022).

A. Introduction

rules and bringing them into the CC – which is more or less what happened in Germany through the *Schuldrechtsreform* of 2001. However, the proposals made by the Viney Commission met with fierce criticism by some authors, who were radically hostile to the CC being revised along the lines of European law.[7] This criticism led the *Chancellerie* to backtrack. The bill drafted by the Viney Commission was abandoned and never brought before Parliament. The Directive was eventually transposed a few years later, by way of an *ordonnance*, i.e., delegated legislation.[8] Besides, the new provisions were inserted into the CCons, without any modification of the CC. The warranty created by the 1999 SGD therefore effectively came on top of the remedies already existing under French law, but it only applied to the sale of consumer goods. This added a layer of complexity to the French law of sales.

The adoption of the DCD and of the SGD, and the obligation to transpose them, could have reignited the debate on the necessity or opportunity to reform the whole French law of sales. This has indeed become inevitable since the general rules of French contract law where reformed in 2016,[9] while the rules on specific contracts have remained unchanged, thus creating new articulation problems between the new and the old rules, which are particularly acute as far as the *garantie des vices cachés* is concerned. On the other hand, it is not only the law of sales that needs to be reformed and updated, but all the rules applicable to specific contracts contained in the CC (and elsewhere). The *Chancellerie* therefore created in 2021 a new commission, chaired by Professor Philippe Stoffel-Munck, in charge of drafting a bill on the reform of specific contracts, which published a first proposal in the Spring of 2022.[10] However, the *Chancellerie* did not want to re-enact the controversy that had occurred in 2001. Accordingly, it was decided that the transposition of the SGD was not to be transformed into an occasion to reform the whole law of sales, or any other part of the CC. Such broader reform should take place at a later stage and be based only on the proposals of the Stoffel-Munck Commission. Rather, even before a short public consultation was organised on the transposition of the twin Directives,[11] the choice was made to transpose the SGD into the CCons, by way of an *ordonnance*.

5

---

[7] See esp. Paisant and Leveneur, 'Quelle transposition pour la directive du 25 mai 1999 sur les garanties dans la vente de biens de consommation?' (2002), *JCP* 135; O. Tournafond, 'Remarques critiques sur la directive européenne du 25 mai 1999, relative à certains aspects de la vente et des garanties des biens de consommation' (2000) *D Cah. Dr. aff.*, 159; Tournafond, 'De la transposition de la directive du 25 mai 1999 à la réforme du code civil' (2002) *D*, 2883.

[8] An *ordonnance* is an act whereby the Government, upon special authorisation by Parliament, enacts rules which should normally have been adopted by the latter. The Government used to resort to ordonnances to enact more speedily rules that were regarded as very technical, or not so important. This was still the case in 2005 and the choice to transpose the 1999 SGD by way of an ordonnance could therefore be seen as reflecting the lesser importance of consumer law. An additional reason was that the Government found itself in a hurry after France had been condemned for breaching the transposition delay: CJEC, Case C-311/03, 1.7.2004, *Commission v France*, ECLI:EU:C:2004:405. Over the last decade, however, the Government has resorted increasingly to ordonnances, to speed up legislation, and/or to avoid difficult debates in Parliament, so that important pieces of legislation have been adopted in that way, such as the recent reform of general contract law, on which see *infra* fn. 9.

[9] Ordonnance n° 2016-131 du 10 février 2016 portant réforme du droit des contrats, du régime général et de la preuve des obligations (the 2016 ordonnance).

[10] The text of the proposal is available at http://www.textes.justice.gouv.fr/textes-soumis-a-concertation-10179/consultation-sur-lavant-projet-de-reforme-du-droit-des-contrats-34548.html (last accessed 13 January 2023).

[11] Berheim-Desvaux, 'Réflexion autour de l'ordonnance n° 2021-1247 du 29 septembre 2021 relative à la garantie légale de conformité pour les biens, les contenus numériques et les services numériques' (2021) 11 *CCC*, comm 174 (0).

6   This choice was never seriously challenged by authors. The DCD, the SGD and their transposition have in fact attracted limited attention. This is slightly disappointing, especially as the European proposals that eventually led to the adoption of the DCD and the SGD were the subject of many analyses in France.[12] But this this was probably because these proposals were replacing the aborted project of a Common European sales law, which had been strongly debated in France.[13] When the DCD and the SGD were eventually adopted, the interest in the subject had declined,[14] and the fact that the new Directives focused on consumer law did not help to rouse it.[15]

7   In theory, the transposition of the DCD could have been dissociated from that of the SGD. One might have argued that, while a general reform of the law of sales through the transposition of the SGD was not advisable on technical and political grounds, the transposition of the DCD, which is 'contract-neutral' (in the sense that it does not apply to a specific type of contract, such as the contract of sale), was an occasion to modernise the CC by bringing into it the notion of digital content and services. However, that, too, would have been very delicate. Contracts for the supply of digital content or services are not necessarily contracts of sale, but their regime, as defined by the DCD, is extremely close to the one which applies to such contracts under the SGD. Besides, there was still the risk that some French lawyers would oppose a modernisation of the CC based too openly on EU legislation.[16] It was therefore much safer, and easier, to transpose the DCD along with the SGD into the CCons.

8   This is precisely what has been done by *ordonnance* n° 2021-1247 of 29 September 2021 *relative à la garantie légale de conformité pour les biens, les contenus numériques et les services numériques* (the 2021 *ordonnance*).[17] It was adopted by the French Gov-

---

[12] See, e.g., Douville, 'Marché unique numérique et droit des contrats' (2016) *JCP*, 382; Loiseau, 'Vers une harmonisation totale des règles nationales de protection des consommateurs dans les ventes en ligne?' (2016) 3 *CCE*, comm 23; Sénéchal, 'La diversité des services fournis par les plates-formes en ligne et la spécificité de leur rémunération, un double-défi pour le droit des contrats' (2016) *AJ Contrats d'affaires*, 141; Usunier, 'Du droit commun européen de la vente aux propositions de directives sur les contrats de vente en ligne et de fourniture de contenu numérique : la montagne accouche d'une souris' (2016) *RTD civ*, 304.

[13] See, e.g., Deshayes (ed), *Le Droit commun européen de la vente. Examen de la proposition de règlement du 11 octobre 2011* (2012).

[14] Génicon, 'Nouvelle garantie de conformité dans la vente au consommateur : l'heure des choix' (2021) *D*, 534 (534).

[15] See, however, Aubert de Vincelles, 'Nouvelle directive sur la conformité dans la vente entre professionnel et consommateur. À propos de la directive 2019/771/UE du 20 mai 2019' (2019) *JCP*, 758; Berheim-Desvaux, 'De nouvelles règles contractuelles en matière de conformité seront applicables à compter du 1ᵉʳ janvier 2022!' (2019) 7 *CCC*, comm 130; Huet, 'Directives de 2019 : d'une part, sur les biens de consommation, d'autre part, sur les contenus et services numériques' (2020) 4 *RDC*, 46; Julien, 'Garantie de conformité : la directive 1999/44/CE du 25 mai 1999 est abrogée et remplacée par la directive 2019/771/UE du 20 mai 2019' (2019) 3 *RDC*, 85; Pellier, 'Le droit de la consommation à l'ère du numérique' (2019) 4 *RDC*, 86; Staudenmayer, 'Les directives européennes sur les contrats numériques' (2019) 4 *RDC*, 125; Zolynski, 'Contrats de fourniture de contenus de services numériques. À propos de la directive (UE) 2019/770/UE du 20 mai 2019' (2019) *JCP*, 1181.

[16] As I have argued elsewhere, the contract law reform of 2016 resulted in a Europeanisation of French contract law, which is now probably the national contract law (along with the recently reformed Belgian contract law) that stands closest to the European model embodied by the Principles of European Contract Law (PECL) or other similar instruments: see Borghetti, 'Le nouveau droit français des contrats, entre continuité et européanisation' (2017) *Annuario del contratto*, 3 (9). However, the 2016 reform was not connected to the need to transpose EU legislation and the European influence on it, though significant, was often indirect, and not always clearly perceived by French lawyers.

[17] On which see Berheim-Desvaux, 'Réflexion autour de l'ordonnance n° 2021-1247 du 29 septembre 2021 relative à la garantie légale de conformité pour les biens, les contenus numériques et les services numériques' (2021) 11 *CCC*, comm 174; Lasbordes-de Virville, 'Nouveautés en matière de garantie légale de conformité dans la vente de biens de consommation. À propos de la transposition des directives (UE)

A. Introduction

ernment following a legislative authorisation granted by *loi* n° 2020–1508 of 3 December 2020 *portant diverses dispositions d'adaptation au droit de l'Union européenne en matière économique et financière* (LDDAU). The new provisions entered into force on 1st January 2022 and apply to contracts concluded as of that date.[18] All new provisions are public policy ones, meaning that the parties are not free to set them aside, even when they go beyond what was required by the SGD or the DCD.

Even though the two Directives contain provisions that are to a large extent similar, the 2021 *ordonnance* has transposed them in separate sections of the CCons, the structure of which must be briefly explained.[19] The first book of the Code deals with information to consumers and commercial practices. Book II deals with the conclusion and performance of contracts. Title I of book II is devoted to the general terms of contracts, and title II to the rules on the formation and performance of certain contracts. Most of the provisions of the SGD have been transposed into chapter VII of title I, the heading of which is 'Obligation of Conformity in Contracts for the Sale of Goods' (Arts. L 217–1 to L 217–32 CCons).[20] Most of the provisions of the DCD, on the other hand, have been transposed into chapter IV of title II, which deals with 'Specific Rules for Contracts with a Particular Purpose', where they constitute a new section 2bis called 'Contracts for the Provision of Digital Content and Services' (Arts. L 224–25–1 to L 224–25–31 CCons). In truly consumer-law fashion,[21] the provisions in this chapter go beyond transposing the DCD and include rules on the elements of information which must be provided to the consumer when entering such contracts.[22]

9

The twin Directives have therefore had no impact on the structure of the existing general law of obligations and contracts, which is regulated in the CC. Likewise, the existing provisions on intellectual property law or data protection law have not been modified by the 2021 *ordonnance*. At first sight, the transposition is thus a purely consumer law matter. It is likely, however, that it will have an impact on other branches of the law, if only on the long run.

10

2019/770 et 2019/771 du 20 mai 2019 par l'ordonnance n° 2021–1247 du 29 septembre 2021' (2021) 11 *CCC*, étude 11; Loiseau, 'L'ordonnance du 29 septembre 2021 : un texte fondateur d'un droit des contrats portant sur les biens et services numériques' (2021) 12 *CCC* étude 12; Pellier, 'La nouvelle garantie légale de conformité est arrivée!' (2022) *RDC*, 71.

[18] A few provisions also apply as of 1st January 2022 to the supply of digital content and digital services, even if the contract in application of which that supply is made was concluded before that date: article 21(2) 2021 *ordonnance*.

[19] The CCons has two parts: a legislative one (*partie legislative*), which contains provisions having legislative value (numbered L XX), and a regulatory one (*partie réglementaire*), which contains provisions having an infra-legislative value (numbered R XX). The provisions of the 2021 *ordonnance*, which have been adopted by the Government based on a lesgislative authorisation, have been inserted into the legislative part.

[20] It would have been more logical in my view to transpose these provisions into title II.

[21] Loiseau, 'L'ordonnance du 29 septembre 2021 : un texte fondateur d'un droit des contrats portant sur les biens et services numériques' (2021) 12 *CCC* étude 12 (4).

[22] Namely: the identity and contact details of the trader, the nature of the benefit granted by the consumer instead of or in addition to the price the duration of the contract, the conditions for renewal and interruption of the service, any charges for early termination of the contract, the personal data necessary for the provision of digital content or services or collected in the context of such provision, the type of action a trader may take to respond to a security incident or to deal with threats or vulnerabilities, products and services designed for people with disabilities.

B. Definitions and Scope of Application

11   In 2014, an Introductory Art. (*article liminaire*) was added to the CCons, defining the notion of 'consumer' (*consommateur*). In 2016, that definition was slightly modified and the definitions of 'trader' (*professionnel*) and 'non-trader' (*non-professionnel*) were added into the article. This made perfect sense, as these three definitions help delineate the scope of application of the whole code.

12   Somewhat surprisingly, the 2021 *ordonnance* has added into the CCons' Introductory Art. many of the definitions contained in Art. 2 DCD and Art. 2 SGD: those of 'producer' (*producteur*), 'good with digital elements' (*bien comportant des éléments numériques*), 'digital content' (*contenu numérique*), 'digital service' (*service numérique*), 'durable medium' (*support durable*), 'functionality' (*fonctionnalité*), 'compatibility' (*compatibilité*), 'interoperability' (*interopérabilité*), 'durability' (*durabilité*), but also of 'personal data' (*données personnelles*), which is defined by reference to Art. 4, 1 of the General Data Protection Regulation (GDPR).[23]

13   This has changed the nature of the Introductory Art. The definitions it contains are not any more intended only to define the scope of application of consumer law. Rather, the article has become a definitions article, like those contained in many EU instruments. It is also noteworthy that these definitions have been put at the very beginning of the CCons, and not at the beginning of the sections dealing with the sale of consumer goods or with digital contents or services.[24] While this has been criticised,[25] it could be interpreted as expressing the Government's implicit intention to start to set up a common law of digital goods and services, the basis of which would be found in the CCons.[26]

14   The 2021 *ordonnance* has also addressed the hypothesis where a digital content or services is provided in exchange, not of a price, but of personal data, more broadly than was required by the DCD. It has modified Art. L 111-1 CCons, which sets a general duty to inform in consumer contracts. This provision used to apply only to contracts for the supply of goods or services, but the new version is applicable to all 'onerous contracts' entered by a consumer. Art. 1107 para. 1 CC defines an onerous contract as a contract 'where each of the parties receives a benefit from the other in return for what he provides.'[27] There is therefore a clear acknowledgment that the benefit received by the trader in exchange for the good or service he provides can be something else than a monetary

---

[23] Regulation (EU) 2016/679 of the European Parliament and of the Council of 27 April 2016 on the protection of natural persons with regard to the processing of personal data and on the free movement of such data.

[24] The definitions of 'digital environment' (*environnement numérique*) and 'integration' (*intégration*) have been inserted not in the preliminary article, but at the beginning of the new section on contracts for the supply of digital content and services. Why these two definitions have been set apart from the others is something of a mystery.

[25] See, e.g., Berheim-Desvaux, 'Réflexion autour de l'ordonnance n° 2021-1247 du 29 septembre 2021 relative à la garantie légale de conformité pour les biens, les contenus numériques et les services numériques' (2021) 11 *CCC*, comm 174 para. 1; Loiseau, 'L'ordonnance du 29 septembre 2021 : un texte fondateur d'un droit des contrats portant sur les biens et services numériques' (2021) 12 *CCC* étude 12 (2); Pellier, 'La dénaturation de l'article liminaire du code de la consommation' (2021) *D*, 1873.

[26] Pointing out that the CCons has adapted to digital contracts better than the CC, see Loiseau, 'L'ordonnance du 29 septembre 2021 : un texte fondateur d'un droit des contrats portant sur les biens et services numériques' (2021) 12 *CCC*, étude 12 (1).

[27] The English version of the CC provisions on general contract law are borrowed from the translation of the 2016 *ordonnance* by Cartwright et al., available at http://www.textes.justice.gouv.fr/dossiers-thematiques-10083/loi-du-170215-sur-la-simplification-du-droit-12766/traduction-de-lordonnance-du-10-fevrier-2016-en-langue-anglaise-28998.html (last accessed 25 March 2022).

price, and this something else will very often be personal data. This can be seen as an anticipation[28] of the transposition of Directive 2019/2161 on the better enforcement and modernisation of Union consumer protection rules.[29] Interestingly, some French courts have already accepted that contracts between social networks operators and consumers are onerous consumer contract, to which the rules on unfair contract terms must apply.[30] Accordingly, Art. L 217–1 para. I CCons, which defines the scope of application of the conformity guarantee in consumer sales contracts, provides in its second paragraph: 'For the purposes of this Chapter, contracts under which the trader delivers a good and transfers the ownership thereof to a consumer and the consumer provides any other benefit, instead of or in addition to the payment of a price, shall be deemed to be sales contracts.'[31] The 2021 *ordonnance* has also created a new Art. L 112–4–1 CCons, which sets a specific duty to inform where a contract for the sale of goods or for the supply of digital content or services is offered in exchange for something else than a price. And Art. L 211–2 para. I CCons, dealing with general terms and conditions in consumer contracts, now requires the mention of the nature of the advantage provided by the consumer within the meaning of Arts. L 217–1 and L 224–25–2 instead of or in addition to a price.[32]

The elements of information that must be provided by the trader in a consumer contract have also been updated. Art. L 111–1 para. 1(1) CCons used to state that the trader must provide the consumer with certain elements of information in a legible and comprehensible manner, starting with the essential characteristics of the good or service offered. Now, the trader must also provide the essential characteristics 'of the digital service or digital content, taking into account their nature and the communication medium used, and in particular the functionalities, compatibility and interoperability of the digitally-enhanced good, digital content or digital service, as well as the existence of any software installation restrictions'. This change in Art. L 111–1, which was not required by the DCD nor the SGD, expresses the Government's intention to address the issue of digital content and digital service comprehensively and to go beyond the formal scope of application of the 2019 Directives.

This is also illustrated by the creation of Art. L 111–6 CCons, which sets a duty for the producer of goods with digital components to inform the professional seller of the period of time during which software updates, provided by the producer, will remain compatible with the functionality of the goods. Correlatively, the seller has a duty to make these elements of information available to the consumer. The producer must also inform the consumer, in a legible and comprehensible manner, of the essential characteristics of each update of the digital components of the good, in particular the

---

[28] Berheim-Desvaux, 'Réflexion autour de l'ordonnance n° 2021–1247 du 29 septembre 2021 relative à la garantie légale de conformité pour les biens, les contenus numériques et les services numériques' (2021) 11 *CCC*, comm 174 (2).

[29] Directive (EU) 2019/2161 of the European Parliament and of the Council of 27 November 2019 amending Council Directive 93/13/EEC and Directives 98/6/EC, 2005/29/EC and 2011/83/EU of the European Parliament and of the Council as regards the better enforcement and modernisation of Union consumer protection rules.

[30] CA Paris, pôle 2, ch. 2, 12.2.2016, n° 15/08624, *Sté Facebook Inc. c/ M.*, JurisData n° 2016–002888, (2016) *CCE*, comm 33, note Loiseau; TGI Paris, 7.8.2018, n° 14/07300, *UFC-Que choisir c/ Twitter*, JurisData n° 2018–014706, (2018) *CCE*, comm 74, note Loiseau.

[31] Under Art. 1582 CC, there is a contract of sale only where ownership of a thing is transferred in exchange for a price.

[32] As an author points out, however, these provisions do not specify how precise the information given in that respect must be: Loiseau, 'L'ordonnance du 29 septembre 2021 : un texte fondateur d'un droit des contrats portant sur les biens et services numériques' (2021) 12 *CCC*, étude 12 (3).

storage space it requires, its impact on the performance of the good and the changes in functionality it entails.

17 As is obvious from the location of these new provisions, the intention to broaden the scope of the new rules and mechanisms connected to digital contents and services stops at the border of consumer law, at least for the time being. This is confirmed by the scope of application *rationae personae* of the new rules introduced by the 2021 *ordonnance*. They are not to be applied to B2B contracts. The 2021 *ordonnance* has also not made use of the possibility, explicitly mentioned in Recital 18 DCD and Recital 23 SGD, to extend the application of the new regime to platform providers that do not fulfil the requirements for being considered a trader or a seller under these Directives. This can easily be understood, as this would have been a rather radical move, anticipating the Digital Services Act that was then being discussed in Brussels. However, under Art. L 217–1(I)(1) and L 224–25–2(I)(1) CCons, it is not only the seller or the trader, but also 'any person presenting themselves or acting as such', who may be liable in case of lack of conformity. This extension was probably inspired by the 1985 Product Liability Directive,[33] whose Art. 3 para. 1 imposes liability upon the manufacturer 'and any person who, by putting his name, trademark or other distinguishing feature on the product presents himself as its producer'.[34] Although Art. L 217–1 para. I subpara. 1 and L 224–25–2 para. I subpara. 1 CCons are unlikely to apply very often in practice, they may nevertheless result in platforms having to answer for a good, digital content or digital service's lack of conformity, when they have not made it clear enough that they acted only as an intermediary.

18 In another slight departure from their original scope of application, the rules of the twin Directives have been made applicable to contracts concluded between traders and 'non-traders'.[35] A non-trader is defined in the Introductory Art. of the CCons as 'any legal person who is not acting for business purposes'. The category includes for example non-profit organisations. French courts started a long time ago to apply some of the protective consumer law rules to non-traders and this has been confirmed by the French Government and Legislator on many occasions,[36] including in the 2021 *ordonnance*.[37]

19 The Government's clear intention, when transposing the 2019 Directives, was therefore to broaden their scope of application, but also to stop short of 'intruding' into general contract law. There was a technical reason for that, namely that the LDDAU clearly stated that this transposition was intended to enhance consumer protection,[38] thus implicitly forbidding a modification of the CC (which would have meant going beyond consumer protection). But this was also intended to avoid the re-enactment of the debates stirred by the transposition of the 1999 SGD.

20 However, the new provisions may have spill-over effects on general contract law. First, consumer contract law in France is not totally separated from general contract

---

[33] Council Directive 85/374/EEC of 25 July 1985 on the approximation of the laws, regulations and administrative provisions of the Member States concerning liability for defective products.

[34] Pellier, 'La nouvelle garantie légale de conformité est arrivée!' (2022) *RDC*, 71 (74).

[35] See, e.g., Arts. L 216–8, L 217–32 and L 224–24–31 CCons.

[36] Berheim-Desvaux, 'Réflexion autour de l'ordonnance n° 2021–1247 du 29 septembre 2021 relative à la garantie légale de conformité pour les biens, les contenus numériques et les services numériques' (2021) 11 *CCC*, comm 174 (2).

[37] On the other hand, the 2021 *ordonnance* has chosen not to apply the rules of the SGD to second-hand goods sold at public auctions where consumers can participate in person as well as to domestic animals (Art. L 217–2 CCons). The latter are the subject of special rules, whose combination with the rules of the CCons proved rather complicated in the past: Lasbordes-de Virville, 'Nouveautés en matière de garantie légale de conformité dans la vente de biens de consommation. À propos de la transposition des directives (UE) 2019/770 et 2019/771 du 20 mai 2019 par l'ordonnance n° 2021–1247 du 29 septembre 2021' (2021) 11 *CCC*, étude 11 (5).

[38] See LDDAU, chapter 1.

law. All issues that are not governed by specific consumer law rules are governed by the general rules in the CC. This includes for example the rules on the conclusion and validity of contracts.[39] Second, there is no reason why the concepts now defined in the CCons could not be used in the context of general contract law. For example, durability should certainly be a general factor to assess the conformity of some goods to the contract in application of which they were transferred, regardless of whether it is a consumer contract. Likewise, data as counter-performance, which is not the subject of a definition but is obviously a central feature of the DCD, can be found in contracts that have nothing to do with consumer law.

C. The Trader's Obligations

The SGD and the DCD set an obligation to deliver and a guarantee of conformity, which are better considered separately. 21

I. The Obligation to Deliver

The trader's first obligation is to deliver the good or content or services he has promised. This obligation is addressed by the CCons in a chapter devoted to 'delivery, supply, and transfer of risk', the rules of which apply to all consumer contracts. The content of this chapter has been slightly modified by the 2021 *ordonnance*, mostly to include the hypothesis where the contract provides for the supply of digital content, and to incorporate references to the new provisions of the CC on general contract law remedies. The rules in this chapter apply to contracts for the sale of goods and to contracts for the supply of digital content or services. 22

According to Art. L 216-1 para. 3 CCons, where the contract does not set a delivery date, the good or service must be delivered 'without undue delay' and no later than 30 days after the conclusion of the contract. On the other hand, there is no provision on the place of delivery, meaning that the general rule of Art. 1342-6 CC must apply: 'Unless legislation, the contract or the court otherwise provide, satisfaction [ie, performance] must be rendered at the place of domicile of the debtor.' 23

Art. L 216-5 para. 1 CCons further provides: 'The trader shall indicate in writing to the consumer at the time of purchase, if applicable, the cost of delivery and of putting the goods into service. The consumer shall be given the opportunity to express reservations, particularly in the event of a defect in the goods or failure to provide the instructions for use or installation instructions.' Very importantly, however, Art. L 216-5 para. 2 adds on: 'The absence of reservations formulated by the consumer upon receipt of the goods does not exempt the trader from the guarantee of conformity of the goods which he owes the consumer.' This means that the consumer cannot be deprived of her right to invoke a lack of conformity, even if that lack of conformity was apparent or obvious at the time of delivery.[40] 24

The CCons also regulates the passing of risk. Under the general rule, 'as regards contracts whose object is the alienation of ownership or the assignment of some other right, 25

---

[39] Subject to the special information duties that may exist in consumer law, some of which have been mentioned above.
[40] From a strictly technical point of view, however, one can doubt if this provision is applicable to contracts for the supply of digital content or services, since it speaks of 'purchase' (*achat*), and such contracts are not contracts of sale; see Pellier, 'Retour sur la liberté du consommateur dans la mise en œuvre de la garantie légale de conformité' (2022) D, 563 (4).

transfer takes place at the time of the conclusion of the contract' (Art. 1196 para. 1 CC). This means that, unless otherwise stated in the contract, the passing of risk also takes place on conclusion of the contract, even if delivery is postponed to a later date. This rule, which can be quite harsh on buyers, is set aside in consumer contracts. Art. L 216-2 CCons provides: 'Any risk of loss of or damage to the goods shall pass to the consumer at the time when the consumer or a third party designated by the consumer takes physical possession of the goods.'

II. The Guarantee of Conformity

26 The 2021 *ordonnance* has stuck closely both to the SGD and the DCD as far as the definition of conformity is concerned.

27 Arts. 5 to 7 SGD have been transposed almost literally at Arts. L 217-3 to L 217-5 CCons. The Code does not speak of 'subjective requirements for conformity', however, but of 'conformity to the contract' (Art. L 217-4), whereas objective requirements for conformity are described rather surprisingly as conformity requirements 'in addition to requirements for conformity to the contract' (Art. L 217-5). The explanation seems to be that, under the system of the CC, subjective conformity is described simply as 'conformity', whereas objective conformity is sanctioned using the *garantie des vices cachés* and is therefore not understood as part of conformity. Likewise, Arts. 6 to 8 DCD have been transposed almost literally at Arts. L 224-25-12 to L 224-25-14 CCons.

28 The provisions on the installation of goods or on the integration of the digital content or the digital service have also been faithfully transposed, though not into a separate article.[41] The 2021 *ordonnance* has also introduced general provisions stressing the importance of providing the consumer with installation information where the contract is for the delivery of a good. Art. L 216-4 CCons now provides: 'The delivery or commissioning of the goods shall be accompanied by the handing over of the operating and installation instructions and, if applicable, the commercial guarantee contract.' Art. L 216-5 para. 1 adds on: 'The trader shall indicate in writing to the consumer at the time of purchase, if applicable, the cost of delivery and of putting the goods into service. The consumer shall be left with a written record when he takes possession of the goods, indicating the possibility for the consumer to express reservations, particularly in the event of a defect in the goods or failure to provide the instructions for use or installation.'

29 Several elements, which help define more precisely the conformity obligation, must be considered more closely: durability, updates, contractual adaptations and third parties' rights.

1. Durability

30 The 2021 *ordonnance* does not elaborate on the durability requirement set at Art. 7 para. 1 subpara. d SGD, the text of which has been carried over almost literally at article L 217-5 para. I subpara. 6° CCons. The only difference is that the French Code speaks of the quantity, quality and other features, including durability, that the consumer 'can legitimately expect', whereas the SGD refers to 'normal features'. However, this is only intended as a reformulation, and not as a modification, of the rule in the SGD.

---

[41] Art. 8 SGD has been transposed at Art. L 217-3 para. 5 CCons (the introductory provision on the conformity obligation in consumer sales contracts) and Art. 9 DCD at Art. L 224-25-12 para. 5 CCons (the introductory provision on the conformity obligation in contracts for digital contents or services).

C. The Trader's Obligations

31 No explicit connection has been made in the 2021 *ordonnance* or in the CCons between that requirement and product-specific legislation, as suggested in Recital 32 SGD. Likewise, the implementing provisions of the SGD have not been coordinated with those of Directive 2009/125/EC establishing a framework for the setting of ecodesign requirements for energy-related products, which are to be found in *décret* n° 2011-764 of 28 June 2011 *relatif à la procédure de surveillance du marché national des produits ayant un impact sur la consommation d'énergie* and have been inserted into the Environment Code (*code de l'environnement*). More generally, the 2021 *ordonnance* does not adopt measures for enhancing environmental sustainability / circular economy by way of implementation of the SGD and DCD.[42]

32 Besides, there is no general requirement on the availability of spare parts under French law. Art. L 111-4 CCons only sets a general requirement to inform consumers about their availability or non-availability, and the time during which they will be available.

2. Updates

33 The 2021 *ordonnance* stresses the importance of updates. The chapter on the 'Obligation of Conformity in Contracts for the Sale of Goods' contains a special subsection on updates (Arts. L 217-18 to L 217-20 CCons) and the section on 'Contracts for the Provision of Digital Content and Services' contains a special paragraph on the subject (Arts. L 224-25-24 to L 224-25-26 CCons).

34 Art. L 217-18 para. 2 CCons defines updates, in relation with the sale of goods with digital elements, as 'updates or modifications to maintain, adapt or enhance the functionality of the good, including security updates, whether or not such updates are necessary to maintain the conformity of the good.' The article thus retains a broad conception of updates, which is not limited to safety updates nor to updates necessary to maintain the conformity of the good with digital elements, but also includes any modification of these elements.

35 Art. L 217-19 transposes Art. 7 para. 3-4 SGD and deals with updates necessary to maintain the conformity of the good, while Art. L 217-20 deals with updates that are not necessary to maintain that conformity. Art. L 217-20 is apparently an addition to the SGD, but in effect transposes and adapts the rule in Art. 19 DCD on modification of the digital content or services. It provides that, for updates that are not necessary to maintain the conformity of the goods, the contract must allow for the principle of such updates and provide a valid reason for them; the seller must inform the consumer, in a clear and comprehensible manner, reasonably in advance and on a durable medium, of the planned update, specifying the date on which it will take place, and; the update must be carried out at no additional cost to the consumer. The seller must also inform the consumer that she has the right to refuse the update or, where appropriate, to uninstall it, if the update has a negative impact on her access to or use of the digital content or services. In the latter case, the consumer may terminate the contract at no cost, within a maximum period of thirty days, unless the update has only a minor impact on her. However, the consumer may not terminate the contract if the seller has offered to keep the digital content or services unchanged, including by uninstalling the update, and if the digital content or services remains in conformity with the conditions set out in the Code.

---

[42] An author has pointed out the contradiction between the concern for environmental sustainability (Recital 32 SGD) and the goal of developing cross-border B2C sales of goods (Recital 1 SGD): Génicon, 'Nouvelle garantie de conformité dans la vente au consommateur : l'heure des choix' (2021) *D*, 534 (6).

36 Art. L 217-20 clearly expresses the intention of the French Government to take a broader approach to digital content, and to its update, than the SGD. The requirement that the update that is not necessary to maintain conformity should be carried out at no additional cost to the consumer may sound surprising, especially as Art. L 217-20 is a public policy provision, meaning that the parties are not allowed to set aside this rule. However, the rule implicitly applies only during the duration of the contract, so that once the initial contract has come to an end, the professional can ask for a price in exchange for the update of the content.

37 Arts. L 224-25-24 to L 224-25-26 CCons, which deal with updates in contracts for provision of digital content or services, mirror very closely Arts. L 217-18 to L 217-20. Art. L 224-25-25 is almost the exact equivalent of Art. 8 para. 2-3 DCD, while Art. L 224-25-26 is an equivalent of Art. L 217-20 and transposes Art. 19 DCD.

3. Contractual Adaptations

38 The 2021 *ordonnance* has not specified how the parties can agree on a deviation from objective conformity, as provided by Art. 7 para. 5 SGD and Art. 8 para. 5 DCD. These provisions have been transposed literally at Arts. L 217-5 para. III and L 224-25-14 para. III CCons.

39 This possibility to 'contract out of conformity' has been criticised in France, on the ground that it is normally not possible, under the CC, for the seller to limit the *garantie des vices cachés*, which reflects the 'objective conformity' requirement.[43] On the other hand, it can be argued that Art. 7 para. 5 SGD and Art. 8 para. 5 DCD reflect the traditional rule whereby a buyer cannot complain about a defect which existed and of which he was aware at the time of the sale. There is therefore nothing shocking about this rule, even if the 2021 *ordonnance* would have been an occasion to specify it.

4. Third Parties' Rights

40 When third parties' rights, including intellectual property rights, prevent or limit the use of the good or of the digital content or service, and lead to a lack of conformity, the 2021 *ordonnance* has chosen to refer to the CC. According to Art. L 217-30 para. 2 CCons (sale of goods) and Art. L 224-25-29 para. 2 CCons (supply of digital content or services), 'the nullity of the contract or any other action of a contractual or extra-contractual nature may be incurred by application of the provisions of the Civil Code'. In practice, in contracts for the sale of goods, the consumer will be able to rely on the so-called *garantie d'éviction* (Arts. 1626 ff. CC), which allows the buyer to rescind the contract when a third party's right on the thing sold, of which the buyer had not been informed, restricts her prerogatives on the good as an owner.

41 However, contracts for the supply of digital contents or services cannot be regarded as contracts of sale if they do not provide for a transfer of ownership. *Garantie d'éviction*, which is a remedy specific to the contract of sale, will therefore not apply. But the general contractual remedies, including damages, will be applicable – as is the case for any other lack of conformity.[44]

42 The new CCons provisions do not indicate if the specific remedies for lack of conformity derived from the DCD and the SGD should apply when the lack of conformity stems from the existence of a third party's right. This silence could be interpreted as an exclusion of those remedies. On the other hand, there appears to be no reason why the

---

[43] Génicon, 'Nouvelle garantie de conformité dans la vente au consommateur : l'heure des choix' (2021) D, 534 (9).
[44] See *infra* D, IV.

consumer should be deprived of these remedies only in this case. Besides, the logic of the 2021 *ordonnance*, as far as the combination of remedies is concerned, is one of addition and not of mutual exclusion.[45] The most sensible interpretation of Arts. L 217-30 para. 2 and L 224-25-29 para. 2 CCons is therefore that, while additional civil law remedies, including those of *garantie d'éviction*, may be applicable when third parties' rights result in a lack of conformity of the good sold or of the digital content or services provided, the consumer law remedies for lack of conformity remain applicable.

The new provisions are also silent on the possibility for the consumer to 'resell' the digital content she has been provided with under the contract. Intellectual property law rules should apply in that respect, subject to any valid term of the contract entered by the consumer excluding or restricting her right to 'resell'. 43

D. Remedies

The general rules on contractual remedies have been thoroughly modernised by the 2016 reform of contract law. They are now quite close to those suggested by the various international harmonisation instruments, such as the Principles of European Contract Law or the aborted Common European Sales Law. They therefore combine quite well with the remedies set out by the SGD and the DCD. 44

I. Remedies for Failure to Supply

Under Arts. L 216-6 para. I subpara. 1° and L 224-25-11 para. I subpara. 1° CCons, if the trader fails to deliver the good or service, or the digital content or service, the consumer can withhold payment in accordance with the general rule in Art. 1219 CC, which provides: 'A party may refuse to perform his obligation, even where it is enforceable, if the other party does not perform his own and if this non-performance is sufficiently serious.' An anticipatory suspension is also possible under Art. 1220 CC, whereby: 'A party may suspend the performance of his obligation as soon as it becomes evident that his contracting partner will not perform his obligation when it becomes due and that the consequences of this non-performance are sufficiently serious for him. Notice of this suspension must be given as quickly as possible.' 45

The consumer can also terminate the contract if, after having given notice to the trader to make the delivery or provide the service within a reasonable additional period, the trader has not done so within that period (Arts. L 216-6 para. I subpara. 2° and L 224-25-11 para. I subpara. 2° CCons).[46] Immediate termination is possible 'where the trader refuses to deliver the goods or provide the service or where it is obvious that he will not deliver the goods or provide the service', or 'where the trader fails to perform his obligation to deliver the goods or provide the service on the date or at the end of the period provided for in Art. L 216-1 and this date or period constitutes an essential condition of the contract for the consumer' (Art. L 216-6 para. II). Termination takes place on receipt by the trader of the letter or written document informing him of such termination unless the trader has performed in the meantime. Until the 2016 reform 46

---

[45] See *infra* D, IV.
[46] Art. L 224-25-11 para. 1 subpara. 2° states that the consumer can terminate the contract if the trader has failed to perform without undue delay or within an additional period expressly agreed between the parties, thus indicating that the parties can agree to extend the delay within which the trader must deliver the digital content or services Although this is not explicitly mentioned, there is no reason why such agreement could not also take place in a contract of sale.

of general contract law, the CC did not accept termination by notice and termination normally had to be pronounced by the judge. The 2016 reform introduced termination by notice, however, so that there is now no discrepancy between the CCons and the CC in that respect.

47 Art. 216-7 CCons requires that, in case of termination, the trader reimburse the consumer for all sums paid, at the latest within fourteen days of the date on which the contract was terminated.

48 These rules also apply when the trader is prevented from performing by force majeure, even though this is not mentioned explicitly by the CCons. The recent reform of French contract law introduced the possibility for a party to ask for a judicial modification of the contract when an unforeseen change of circumstances has rendered performance excessively onerous for him (Art. 1195 CC), but it is unlikely that this general rule, though theoretically applicable to consumer contracts, will often be relied on in that context.

II. Remedies for Lack of Conformity

49 In contracts for the sale of goods, the 2021 *ordonnance* has made use of the option granted by Art. 11 para. 2 SGD: any lack of conformity which becomes apparent within twenty-four months of delivery of the goods, including goods with digital elements, shall, in the absence of proof to the contrary, be presumed to have existed at the time of delivery, unless this presumption is incompatible with the nature of the goods or of the defect claimed (Art. L217-7 para. 1). For second-hand goods, however, the presumption that the lack of conformity existed at the time of delivery only applies if that lack of conformity appears within one year of delivery (Art. L 217-7 para. 2).[47]

50 Likewise, the 2021 *ordonnance* has chosen not to establish a special rule to 'regulate whether and to what extent a contribution of the consumer to the lack of conformity affects the consumer's right to remedies', as was possible under Art. 13 para. 7 SGD. The words used by the SGD are not totally clear but have been interpreted by French authors as referring to the possibility to impose on the consumer a duty to mitigate her losses.[48] Save in very specific circumstances, French law does not recognise such a duty and the *Cour de cassation*, France's highest court in civil matters, is very hostile to it.[49] It is therefore not surprising that the *ordonnance* does not to recognise such a duty. However, there can be no doubt that, in application of general contract law principles, if the consumer contributed to the lack of conformity in the first place (and did not simply abstain from mitigating the loss flowing from that lack of conformity), her behaviour will reduce the extent of the trader's liability.

51 For the sake of clarity, the various remedies available in case of lack of conformity will be considered in turn.

1. Withholding of Payment

52 The 2021 *ordonnance* extends the right to withhold payment until the lack of conformity has been corrected to contracts for the supply of digital content or services.

---

[47] The one-year delay was initially established by Art. 22 of *loi n° 2020-105 du 10 février 2020 relative à la lutte contre le gaspillage et à l'économie circulaire*.

[48] Aubert de Vincelles, 'Nouvelle directive sur la conformité dans la vente entre professionnel et consommateur. À propos de la directive 2019/771/UE du 20 mai 2019' (2019) *JCP*, 758; Pellier, 'La nouvelle garantie légale de conformité est arrivée!' (2022) *RDC*, 71 (78).

[49] See, e.g., Cass. 2ᵉ civ., 19 June 2003, n° 00–22.302, Bull. civ. II, n° 203.

D. Remedies

Whether in contracts of sale (Art. L 217–8 para. 2 CCons) or in contracts for the supply of digital content or services (Art. L 224–25–17 para. 2 CCons), this right must be exercised in accordance with Arts. 1219 and 1220 CC.[50]

2. Bringing into Conformity

The CCons's provisions on the bringing into conformity of the good sold or of the digital content or services are very close to those of the SGD and DCD. A few points are worth mentioning, however.

Art. L 217–10 para. 1 CCons provides that, when the consumer chooses to have the good sold brought into conformity, the trader must repair or replace the good within a reasonable period which may not exceed thirty days following the consumer's request. In contracts for the supply of digital content or services, the Code only refers to a reasonable period, and sets no maximal length to it (Art. L 224–15–18 CCons).

The *ordonnance* does not say explicitly that the costs of transport are to be borne by the trader in case of repair or replacement. However, the CCons only speaks of removing the defective good (Art. L 217–10), and not of removing it or bearing the costs of the removal, as does Art. 13 para. 3 SGD. This suggests that the trader must organise the removal and pay for it. It is confirmed by Art. L 217–14 para. 1 subpara. 3°, which provides that the consumer is entitled to a price reduction or to terminate the contract when she must bear the final cost of taking back or removing the non-conforming goods, or the cost of installing the repaired or replacement goods. Further specification may also be provided in the future, as Art. L 217–10 para. 3 provides that a governmental order (*décret*), which is yet to come, shall specify the modalities for bringing the good into conformity.

The CCons does not prioritise repair over replacement, but it is doubtful if that would be authorised under the SGD, despite its Recital 48 stressing that repair enhances the durability of products and environmental sustainability. The absence of such a prioritisation has been a ground for criticism of the SGD by some French authors, as it creates no incentive for traders to produce and sell truly durable goods.[51]

The many cases in which the trader can refuse to heed the consumer's choice have also been criticised.[52] This might be a reason why the CCons requires that any refusal by the seller to proceed according to the consumer's choice or to bring the goods, content or services into conformity shall be justified in writing or on a durable medium (Arts. L 217–12 para. 4 and L 224–25–19 para. 3 CCons).

The Code also provides that, where the trader abusively refuses to heed the consumer's choice, the consumer may, after having given formal notice to the trader, seek performance in kind of the solution initially requested, in accordance with Arts. 1221 ff. CC (Arts. L 217–12 para. 3 and L 224–25–19 para. 2 CCons). Under Art. 1221 CC: 'A creditor of an obligation may, having given notice to perform, seek performance in kind unless performance is impossible or if there is a manifest disproportion between its cost to the debtor in good faith and its interest for the creditor.' Art. 1222 further allows performance by a third parties, under certain conditions: 'Having given notice to perform, a creditor may also himself, within a reasonable time and at a reasonable cost, have an obligation performed or, with the prior authorisation of the court, may have something

---

[50] See *supra* D, I.
[51] See esp Génicon, 'Nouvelle garantie de conformité dans la vente au consommateur : l'heure des choix' (2021) *D*, 534 (10).
[52] Pellier, 'Retour sur la liberté du consommateur dans la mise en œuvre de la garantie légale de conformité' (2022) *D*, 563.

3. Price Reduction and Termination

59 The CCons marginally specifies the hypotheses in which the consumer can ask for a price reduction or termination of the contract in contracts for the sale of goods. Under Art. L 217-14 para. 1, she can make such a request, inter alia, where conformity is achieved after a period of thirty days following the consumer's request, or where the consumer must bear the final cost of taking back or removing the non-conforming goods, or where she bears the costs of installing the repaired or replacement goods.

60 As has been explained above,[53] termination by notice has become a general contract law remedy in 2016, so that there is no discrepancy in that respect between the CCons and the CC. Likewise, the 2016 reform of general contract law has introduced price reduction as a general remedy, and the provisions of the SGD and DCD on the subject, which have been closely followed by the CCons, are very similar to that of Art. 1223 CC.

61 The new provisions on restitution faithfully mirror those of the Directives (Arts. L 217-16 and L 224-25-22 CCons). However, Art. L 217-17 para. 2 extends to contracts for the sale of goods the rule of Art. 18 DCD, whereby the trader must reimburse the money paid by the consumer within 14 days of the day on which the trader is informed of the consumer's decision to terminate the contract, by using the same means of payment as the one used by the consumer at the time of the conclusion of the contract, unless the consumer expressly agrees otherwise and in any event at no additional cost. The 2021 *ordonnance* does not otherwise specify the modalities for return and reimbursement, and no special rules have been created for the case where the consumer provided personal data as counterperformance. Arts. L 224-25-22 and L 224-25-23 only allude to it by saying that the trader must reimburse the price paid by the consumer or 'any other benefits received under the contract', but it gives no further detail as to how such 'reimbursement' can take place.

62 When the contract that the consumer chooses to terminate is part of a bundle including elements of an internet access service, the consumer is entitled to terminate simultaneously all bundled contracts (Art. L 224-25-22 para. I subpara. 2 CCons).

III. Time Limits

63 The drafters of the 2021 *ordonnance* have made almost no use of the options granted by the SGD and the DCD as far as time limits are concerned. No shorter time limit has been set for the sale of second hand goods (Art. 10 para. 6 SGD) and no obligation has been imposed on the consumer to inform the seller of a lack of conformity within a certain period if she wishes to exercise her rights (Art. 12 SGD). More importantly, the 2021 *ordonnance* has made almost no use of the freedom granted by Art. 11 para. 2 SGD and Art. 10 para. 3 DCD to extend the delay within which a consumer can complain of a lack of conformity.[54]

64 In the context of both contracts for the supply of goods and contracts for the supply of digital content or services, the trader is liable for a lack of conformity only if it appears within two years of the date of delivery (Arts. 217-3 para. 2 and 224-25-12 para. 2

---

[53] See *supra* D, I.
[54] Even though they had been strongly incited to do so: Génicon, 'Nouvelle garantie de conformité dans la vente au consommateur : l'heure des choix' (2021) *D*, 534 (18).

D. Remedies

CCons). Where the contract provides for the continuous supply of digital content or services for a period of more than two years, the trader is liable for any lack of conformity arising during the period where the content or services are supplied under the contract (Arts. 217-3 para. 3 subpara. 2° and 224-25-12 para. 3 CCons).[55] However, under Art. 217-13 para. 1 CCons, liability is extended for six months when the good has been repaired pursuant to the legal guarantee of conformity. Besides, under Art. L 217-13 para. 2, if the consumer chooses to have the good repaired, but the seller does not do so, a new liability period attached to the replaced good shall begin to run for the consumer from the day the replacement good is delivered to the consumer.[56]

Even taking into account the rules set by Art. L 217-13, the fact that the period during which the trader can be made liable for a lack of conformity normally starts to run with the delivery of the good, content or service, contrasts with the rule applicable to *garantie des vices cachés* in the CC, where the action must be brought by the purchaser within two years of the discovery of the defect (Art. 1648 CC). The consumer's claim will therefore be time-barred under the CCons if the lack of conformity appears more than two years after delivery (and if there has been no repair or replacement), whereas it would not be under the CC.[57] The solution already applied under former Art. 217-12 CCons, which transposed the 1999 SGD, but is open to criticism. In practice, it strongly limits the usefulness for consumers of the CCons remedies and contributes to keeping consumer law in the shadow of civil law. In many cases of non-conformity, the consumer will turn to the CC instead of the CCons to avoid being time-barred. As an author has pointed out, the starting point of the two-year delay in the SGD also questions the official goal of that instrument to promote durability, since traders know that, under the SGD and the CCons, they cannot be made liable more than two years after the product has been sold.[58] 65

It is indeed hard to understand why the 2021 *ordonnance* has not set the discovery of the lack of conformity as the starting point of the two-year period, as is the case under Art. 1648 CC and also under the general rule on prescription of Art. 2224 CC, according to which: 'Personal actions or movable rights of action prescribe in five years from the day the holder of a right knew or should have known the facts enabling him to exercise his right.' Admittedly, the *ordonnance* analyses the two-year delay it sets not as a real prescription period, but rather as a 'guarantee period' (*délai de garantie*) that must be combined with the normal prescription period of Art. 2224 CC. This is made clear by Arts. 217-3 para. 6 and 224-25-12 para. 6 CCons, which both provide: 'This guarantee period shall apply without prejudice to Arts. 2224 et seq. of the Civil Code. The starting point of the prescription period for the consumer's action is the day on which the consumer becomes aware of the lack of conformity.'[59] This is not very helpful for consumers, however, since, whatever the length or starting point of that prescription period, they will not be 66

---

[55] However, when the digital content or services are supplied as an accessory to a good, and where the contract provides for the continuous supply of that digital content or services for a period of two years or less, or where the contract does not specify the period of supply, the seller is liable for any lack of conformity of the digital content or digital service which becomes apparent within two years from the date of delivery of the goods: Art. 217-3 para. 3 subpara. 1° CCons.

[56] These two rules were initially established by Art. 22 of *loi n° 2020-105 du 10 février 2020 relative à la lutte contre le gaspillage et à l'économie circulaire*.

[57] Or at least not necessarily, as a 20-year long-stop period, running as of the date of the contract, also applies to *garantie des vices cachés* under Art. 2232 CC.

[58] Génicon, 'Nouvelle garantie de conformité dans la vente au consommateur : l'heure des choix' (2021) D, 534 (10).

[59] In theory, the 20-year long-stop period of Art. 2232 CC, which runs as of the conclusion of the contract, also applies, but it is hard to figure how it co play any role in practice.

able to sue if the lack of conformity appears more than two years after delivery (or after the supply of the digital content or services has ceased, when that supply lasted more than two years).

67   Since the guarantee period is not a regular prescription period, the ordinary rules on suspension or interruption of prescription do not apply to it. In particular, the consumer cannot rely on Art. 2234 CC, which provides for the suspension of prescription when force majeure makes it impossible for the claimant to sue. Admittedly, the 2021 *ordonnance* has introduced two causes of suspension of the guarantee period, based on the freedom granted by Recital 44 SGD. Under Arts. L 217–28 paras. 1–2 and L 224–25–28 paras. 1–2 CCons, where the consumer asks the trader to bring the good or content into conformity, the guarantee period is suspended between the moment when the consumer formulates her claim and the moment when the good or content becomes available again to her. The guarantee period is also suspended when the consumer and the trader enter negotiations towards an amicable settlement (Arts. L 217-28 para. 3 and L 224–25–28 para. 3 CCons) This is not really helpful, however, as this suspension can only take place after the consumer has discovered the initial lack of conformity; and if discovery takes place more than two years after delivery, the consumer will have no remedy under the CCons.

68   It is possible that the drafters of the 2021 *ordonnance* did not pay much attention to the issue of time limits and thought that they had made a good job by expressly combining the guarantee period, which already applied under the transposition of the 1999 SGD, with the regular prescription period of Art. 2224 CC. However, as has been explained above, the transposition of the 1999 SGD was conceived as a mere addition to existing remedies, and the effectivity of the new remedies was not seen as very important. The remedies created by the new SGD and the DCD also come on top of existing remedies,[60] but the context is now different. Consumer law has developed in France over the last 20 years and the drafters of the *ordonnance* should have been more concerned with the effectivity of the remedies granted to consumers. Besides, the *ordonnance* is not just a servile transposition of the SGD and DCD, which makes it even more disappointing that the drafters did not pay closer attention to the issue of time limits.

IV. Other remedies

69   The 2021 *ordonnance* sets general rules as far as the combination of the SGD and DCD remedies with other remedies is concerned, but the availability of damages and the combination with the GDPR deserve special attention.

1. General Rule on the Combination of Remedies

70   The new general French contract law provides for five types of remedies (which the CC calls sanctions) in case of breach of contract: withholding performance, performance in kind, price reduction, termination, and damages (Art. 1217 CC). The first four remedies are also available under the SGD and DCD and their regime is very close in the CC and the CCons. One significant difference, however, is the delay during which the consumer can invoke the remedy. As indicated above, the normal prescription period in French law is five years and starts to run 'from the day the holder of a right knew or should have known the facts enabling him to exercise his right' (Art. 2224 CC). Even when general contract law and the 2021 *ordonnance* in essence provide for the same

---

[60] See *infra* IV.

D. Remedies

remedy, a consumer may therefore have an interest to rely on the former if the remedy under the *ordonnance* is time-barred. Likewise, in the case of a contract for the sale of goods, the buyer may want to rely on the *garantie des vices cachés*, which does not offer substantially different remedies from those in the SGD, but whose time limits are less strict, since the buyer can terminate the contract, reduce the price or claim damages within two years of her discovering the defect (Art. 1648 CC).

The 2021 *ordonnance* adopts a very liberal position on the issue of cumulation of remedies. In relation both to contracts for the sale of goods and to contracts for the supply of digital content or services, the CCons provisions on lack of conformity 'shall not deprive the consumer of the right to bring an action under the guarantee for latent defects as provided for in Arts 1641 to 1649 of the Civil Code or any other action of a contractual or extra-contractual nature available to him under the law' (Arts. L 217–30 para. 1 and L 224–25–29 para. 1). 71

This liberal rule may significantly limit the impact of the SGD and the DCD in French law. If all the remedies available under the CCons are also available under the CC, and under less stringent time limits, why should consumers bother to rely on the CCons, with its complicated and not always very user-friendly provisions, instead of relying on the CC? 72

The risk that the CCons remedies will be neglected by consumers is all the greater as the 2016 reform of general contract law has thoroughly modernised the rules on remedies and made them clearer and more creditor-friendly. They are more favourable than the consumer law remedies not only in terms of delay, but also because they grant plaintiffs greater discretion. The SGD and the DCD seriously limit the consumer's freedom to choose between repair and replacement, and the trader can very often impose replacement, instead of repair, to the consumer.[61] On the other hand, under general French contract law, the buyer or client can demand repair, unless there is a manifest disproportion between its cost to the debtor in good faith and its interest for the creditor (Art. 1221 CC).[62] Besides, in contracts of sale, the *garantie des vices cachés* allows the buyer to terminate the contract or reduce its price without the seller being given a chance to mend the lack of conformity in the first place (Art. 1644 CC). Consumers who are not satisfied with the hierarchy of remedies set out by the SGD or the DCD may therefore prefer to rely on the CC rules. 73

Adding remedies on top of each other instead of imposing certain redress routes on plaintiffs is typical of the French law of sales, and of French consumer law generally. It is good news for consumers, at least on the face of it, but it makes the law much more complex and undermines the impact of consumer law in the long run, especially if consumer law remedies are no better that general contract law remedies. If consumer law offers nothing to consumers in addition to the general law of contract, then why bother with consumer law? The habit of regarding consumer law remedies as additional ones for consumers, instead of having distinct sets of remedies for consumers and non-consumers, illustrates the French tendency to see consumer law as a non-essential supplement to the law, and not as a branch of the law in its own right. This could be interpreted as a lack of confidence in consumer law, and also reflects the reluctance of many French lawyers to have European rules supersede the CC. 74

---

[61] Pellier, 'Retour sur la liberté du consommateur dans la mise en œuvre de la garantie légale de conformité' 2022) *D*, 563 (564).

[62] The law on this issue is not very clear, however: see Borghetti, 'À la recherche d'une sanction méconnue de l'inexécution contractuelle : la correction de la mauvaise exécution', *Mélanges en l'honneur de François Collart Dutilleul* (2017) 131 (25).

2. Damages

75 The CCons makes it clear that the specific remedies it sets in case of failure to supply or of lack of conformity apply without prejudice to the award of damages (Arts. L 216–6 para. 3, L 217–8 para. 3, L 224-25-11 para. 5 and L 224-25-17 para. 3 CCons). The consumer can therefore claim damages from the trader under Art. 1231-1 CC: 'A debtor is condemned, where appropriate, to the payment of damages either on the ground of the non-performance or a delay in performance of an obligation, unless he justifies this on the ground that performance was prevented by force majeure.' As is usual in contract, only losses that were foreseeable at the time of the conclusion of the contract can be compensated (Art. 1231-3 CC). However, there is some uncertainty under French law on whether damages in case of termination must compensate the reliance or the expectation interest, i.e., put the creditor in the situation in which she would have been if there had been no contract at all, or the situation she would have been in if the contract had been correctly performed. The CCons offers no answer to that question.

3. Combination with the GDPR

76 Arts. L. 217–6 and L 224-25-15 CCons provide that where, in the course of a contract for the sale of goods or for the supply of digital content or services, personal data are processed by the trader, a failure on his part to comply with his obligations under the GDPR or the French statute on data protection,[63] if such failure results in non-compliance with one or more of the conformity criteria set out in the code, shall be treated as a failure to comply, without prejudice to the other remedies provided for in these texts. Here again, the articulation of remedies is in fact an addition.

V. Commercial Guarantee

77 The provisions on commercial guarantee (Arts. L 217–21 to 217–24 CCons) slightly differ from those in the SGD.[64] Art. L 217–21 para. 1 defines the commercial guarantee as 'any contractual undertaking by a trader, whether the seller or the producer, including through any other person acting in their name or on their behalf (hereinafter referred to as "guarantor"), towards the consumer. The purpose of this commitment is to reimburse the purchase price, replace the goods, repair them or provide any other service in relation to the goods, or to meet any other requirements not related to conformity and set out in the commercial guarantee, in addition to the seller's legal obligations to ensure the conformity of the goods.' Art. L 217–22 goes on to set the formal requirements of such a guarantee, in accordance with Art. 17 paras. 1–2 SGD.

78 Art. L 217–23 para. 1 regulates a special type of commercial guarantee, not expressly foreseen by the SGD: the commercial guarantee of durability. This guarantee can be offered by the producer and must be for two years at least: 'The producer may grant the consumer a commercial guarantee binding him for a given period of time, longer than two years, known as a "commercial guarantee of durability". If he offers such a commercial guarantee of durability, the producer is directly obliged, with respect to the consumer, to repair or replace the good, during the period indicated in the offer

---

[63] *Loi n° 78–17 du 6 janvier 1978 relative à l'informatique, aux fichiers et aux libertés.*
[64] Art. L 217–24 enables the trader offering the commercial guarantee to request the administrative authority in charge of competition and consumer law to take a position as to whether that guarantee conforms to the conditions set out at Arts. L 217–21 to L 217–23. Arts. L 217–25 to L 217–27 CCons deal with after-sales services and impose information duties on traders in that respect.

for the commercial guarantee of durability; he is also obliged to implement it under the same conditions as the legal guarantee.'[65] In essence, the commercial guarantee of durability is therefore an extension beyond the two-year period of the legal guarantee of conformity offered by the producer. The necessity of Art. L 217–23 is not obvious, since the producer would have been free to offer such a commercial guarantee of durability on the basis of Art. L 217–21 alone, but this additional article does signal the Government's concern for durability and hopefully creates an incentive for producers to offer such a guarantee.

There are no provisions in the section on commercial guarantees on the language or languages in which the commercial guarantee statement is to be made available to consumers. However, Art. 2 of the Statute of 4 August 1994 on the use of the French language applies:[66] 'The use of the French language is compulsory in the description, offer, presentation, instructions for use, description of the scope and conditions of guarantee of a good, product or service, as well as in invoices and receipts.'

VI. Transfer of Rights, International Settings, and Right of Redress

French law has long accepted that the remedies associated with a contract of sale are transferred with the thing that was the subject-matter of that contract when that thing is re-sold. The solution is not in the CC but has been adopted by the courts as early as the 19th century.[67] Accordingly, Art. L 217–29 CCons provides: 'In the event of transfer of ownership of the goods between consumers in exchange for consideration or free of charge, the sub-purchaser shall benefit from the rights acquired by the original purchaser in respect of the legal guarantee of conformity vis-à-vis the professional seller and, where applicable, the commercial guarantee vis-à-vis the guarantor, in accordance with the provisions of this Chapter.' Given the preexisting rules of French law on this issue, the same solution would probably have applied even if there had been no express rule to that effect. Art. L 217–29 is in fact rather restrictive, since it excludes the transfer of rights when the good is transferred to someone who is not a consumer. Such a hypothesis should be rather uncommon in practice, however, except maybe when a consumer re-sells her car to a professional.[68]

On the other hand, the 2021 *ordonnance* does not contain any rule for the cases in which the consumer bought the good and moved to another country, nor for those where the seller delivered the goods in accordance with the Geo-Blocking Regulation[69] and is now obliged to carry out repair or replacement in a country he does not offer delivery to.

The provisions on the right of redress are rather uncompromising. Under Arts. L 217–31 and L 224–25–30 CCons, a recourse action may be brought by the seller or the trader who provided the digital content or services against any person upstream

---

[65] Art. 217–23 paras. 2–3 provides that the producer may offer to the consumer more favorable conditions than those described in the first paragraph and that the requirements set forth in Art. L 217–22 are applicable to the commercial guarantee of durability.

[66] Loi n° 94–665 du 4 août 1994 relative à l'emploi de la langue française.

[67] Borghetti, 'Breach of contract and liability to third parties in French law: how to break deadlock?' (2010) 2 *ZEuP*, 279 (284).

[68] But, in such a case, the time limit would often prevent the sub-purchaser to rely on the consumer law remedies anyhow.

[69] Regulation (EU) 2018/302 of the European Parliament and of the Council of 28 February 2018 on addressing unjustified geo-blocking and other forms of discrimination based on customers' nationality, place of residence or place of establishment within the internal market and amending Regulations (EC) No 2006/2004 and (EU) 2017/2394 and Directive 2009/22/EC.

in the chain of commercial transactions, including the producer, in accordance with the provisions of the CC.

E. Other Sanctions

83 French consumer law often takes a criminal or quasi-criminal flavour. There are many cases where illegal behaviours by traders give rise to criminal, civil or administrative sanctions. New cases have been added by the 2021 *ordonnance*.

I. Criminal Sanctions

84 The 2021 *ordonnance* has not introduced new criminal sanctions into consumer law. However, there already existed a specific offence under French law which has special relevance in relation with the conformity requirement set by the SGD. Art. L 441-2 CCons provides: 'The practice of planned obsolescence, which is defined as the use of techniques, including software, by which the person responsible for placing a product on the market deliberately aims to reduce its lifespan, is prohibited.' Under Art. L 454-6 CCons, this offence is punishable by two years' imprisonment and a fine of 300,000€; and the amount of the fine may be increased, in proportion to the benefit derived from the offence, up to 5 % of the average annual turnover, based on the last three annual turnovers known at the time of the offence. This may sound very dissuasive, but it seems that no trader has been condemned on the basis of these provisions so far.[70]

II. Civil Sanctions

85 The 2021 *ordonnance* has created two types of civil sanctions in relation with the implementation of the SGD and the DCD: civil fines, and enhanced refunds.

86 A civil fine is a fine which is provided for in a civil statute (as opposed to a criminal one) and to which one can be sentenced by a civil court (as opposed to a criminal one). Civil fines are paid to the Treasury. They were initially intended mostly as a sanction for trying to avoid a public or civic duty or for abusing one's right to sue, but they are now increasingly common in other contexts, including consumer law.

87 Under Arts. L 241-5 and L 242-18-1 CCons, which have been introduced by the 2021 *ordonnance*, a civil fine may be imposed on the trader who obstructs in bad faith the implementation of the guarantee of conformity applying to contracts for the sale of goods or to contracts for the supply of digital content or services. The imposition of the fine can be requested before the court by the Ministry of Finance (which oversees fighting against unfair commercial practices), consumer associations, the public prosecutor[71] or the consumer herself. The amount of the fine 'can be no higher than 300,000€', but it can be increased, in proportion to the benefit derived from the illegal practices, up to 10 % of the trader's average annual turnover, based on the last three annual turnovers known at the date of the decision. This civil sanction can therefore be very harsh for the trader, and it undoubtedly constitutes a much greater incentive to correctly implement

---

[70] On the issue of planned obsolescence in French law more generally, see Dupont, 'Peut-on en finir avec l'obsolescence programmée?' (2014) 10 *CCC*, étude 10.

[71] Under French law, the public prosecutor (*ministère public*) can choose to intervene in civil cases, but he seldom does so in practice.

the new guarantee, than the remedies which the consumer may seek (and which can be implemented, including damages, regardless of the imposition of a civil fine).

Another civil sanction, not so common, consists in enhanced refunds. Under Art. 241-6 CCons, the trader who charged the consumer for the cost of delivery to bring the goods into conformity shall reimburse that cost within fourteen days from the day on which the consumer is informed that the goods have been taken over. The amount due shall automatically be increased by 10 % if the reimbursement is made no later than fourteen days after this deadline, by 20 % if it is made up to thirty days after the deadline, and by 50 % thereafter. The same applies where the contract is for the supply of digital content and this content is supplied on a tangible medium (Art. L 242-18-2 CCons). Likewise, where, in case of termination of the contract, the trader has not reimbursed the sums paid by the consumer within the period prescribed by the Code, the total amount outstanding shall automatically be increased by 10 % if the reimbursement is made no later than fourteen days after this deadline, by 20 % if it is made up to thirty days after this deadline, and by 50 % thereafter (Arts. L 241-7 and L 242-18-3 CCons).

III. Administrative Sanctions

Administrative fines are provided for in various statutes and are imposed by an administrative authority, without prior judicial review. In the context of consumer law, it is the *Direction générale de la concurrence, de la consommation et de la répression des fraudes* (DGCCRF), a service of the Ministry of Finance, which is competent to impose these administrative fines. No fewer than 14 new administrative fines have been created, which apply in case of breach of the various civil obligations imposed on the trader by the 2021 *ordonnance* (Arts. L 241-8 to L 241-15 and L 242-18-4 to L 242-18-8 CCons). Depending on the cases, the amount of these administrative fines is either 3,000€ for a natural person and 15,000€ for a legal person, or 15,000€ for a natural person and 75,000€ for a legal person. Every single breach may give rise to a distinct administrative fine, which means that if, for example, a company violated its obligation to speedily refund the consumer in case of termination in 80 cases, it may have to pay 80 fines of 75,000€ each. This can be highly dissuasive, but gives the impression that, in the end, consumer law is not so much intended to improve the consumer's remedies as to punish naughty traders.

Bibliography

Carole Aubert de Vincelles, 'Nouvelle directive sur la conformité dans la vente entre professionnel et consommateur. À propos de la directive 2019/771/UE du 20 mai 2019' (2019) *JCP*, 758

Sabine Berheim-Desvaux, 'De nouvelles règles contractuelles en matière de conformité seront applicables à compter du 1er janvier 2022!' (2019) 7 *CCC*, comm 130

Sabine Berheim-Desvaux, 'Réflexion autour de l'ordonnance n° 2021-1247 du 29 septembre 2021 relative à la garantie légale de conformité pour les biens, les contenus numériques et les services numériques' (2021) 11 *CCC*, comm 174

Jean-Sébastien Borghetti, 'Breach of contract and liability to third parties in French law: how to break deadlock?' (2010) 2 *ZEuP*, 279

Jean-Sébastien Borghetti, 'Le nouveau droit français des contrats, entre continuité et européanisation' (2017) *Annuario del contratto*, 3

Jean-Sébastien Borghetti, 'À la recherche d'une sanction méconnue de l'inexécution contractuelle : la correction de la mauvaise exécution', *Mélanges en l'honneur de François Collart Dutilleul* (Dalloz, Paris, 2017) 131

Olivier Deshayes (ed), *Le Droit commun européen de la vente. Examen de la proposition de règlement du 11 octobre 2011* (Société de législation comparée, Paris 2012)

Thibaut Douville, 'Marché unique numérique et droit des contrats' (2016) *JCP*, 382

Nicolas Dupont, 'Peut-on en finir avec l'obsolescence programmée?' (2014) 10 *CCC*, étude 10

Thomas Génicon, 'Nouvelle garantie de conformité dans la vente au consommateur : l'heure des choix' (2021) *D*, 534

Jérôme Huet, 'Directives de 2019 : d'une part, sur les biens de consommation, d'autre part, sur les contenus et services numériques' (2020) 4 *RDC*, 46

Jérôme Julien, 'Garantie de conformité : la directive 1999/44/CE du 25 mai 1999 est abrogée et remplacée par la directive 2019/771/UE du 20 mai 2019' (2019) 3 *RDC*, 85

Victoire Lasbordes-de Virville, 'Nouveautés en matière de garantie légale de conformité dans la vente de biens de consommation. À propos de la transposition des directives (UE) 2019/770 et 2019/771 du 20 mai 2019 par l'ordonnance n° 2021-1247 du 29 septembre 2021' (2021) 11 *CCC*, étude 11

Grégoire Loiseau, 'Vers une harmonisation totale des règles nationales de protection des consommateurs dans les ventes en ligne?' (2016) 3 *CCE*, comm 23

Grégoire Loiseau, 'L'ordonnance du 29 septembre 2021 : un texte fondateur d'un droit des contrats portant sur les biens et services numériques' (2021) 12 *CCC*, étude 12

Gilles Paisant and Laurent Leveneur, 'Quelle transposition pour la directive du 25 mai 1999 sur les garanties dans la vente de biens de consommation?' (2002) *JCP* 135

Jean-Denis Pellier, 'Le droit de la consommation à l'ère du numérique' (2019) 4 *RDC*, 86

Jean-Denis Pellier, 'La dénaturation de l'article liminaire du code de la consommation' (2021) *D*, 1873

Jean-Denis Pellier, 'La nouvelle garantie légale de conformité est arrivée!' (2022) *RDC*, 71

Jean-Denis Pellier, 'Retour sur la liberté du consommateur dans la mise en œuvre de la garantie légale de conformité' (2022) *D*, 563

Juliette Sénéchal, 'La diversité des services fournis par les plates-formes en ligne et la spécificité de leur rémunération, un double-défi pour le droit des contrats' (2016) *AJ Contrats d'affaires*, 141

Dirk Staudenmayer, 'Les directives européennes sur les contrats numériques' (2019) 4 *RDC*, 125

Philippe Stoffel-Munck, 'La préparation d'une réforme des contrats spéciaux' (2020) 4 *RDC*, 1

Olivier Tournafond, 'Remarques critiques sur la directive européenne du 25 mai 1999, relative à certains aspects de la vente et des garanties des biens de consommation' (2000) *D Cah Dr aff*, 159

Olivier Tournafond, 'De la transposition de la directive du 25 mai 1999 à la réforme du code civil' (2002) *D*, 2883.

Laurence Usunier, 'Du droit commun européen de la vente aux propositions de directives sur les contrats de vente en ligne et de fourniture de contenu numérique : la montagne accouche d'une souris' (2016) *RTD civ*, 304

Célia Zolynski, 'Contrats de fourniture de contenus de services numériques. À propos de la directive (UE) 2019/770/UE du 20 mai 2019' (2019) *JCP*, 1181

Germany

A. Introduction. General Framework	1
I. Transpostion in the German Civil Code	1
1. Incorporation into the Civil Code	1
2. Integration into the System	3
II. Impact on legal Structures	7
1. Overview	7
2. Expansion of the General Law of Obligations	8
3. Generalisation beyond Consumer Law	10
4. Structuring Concepts and Principles	14
B. Definitions and Scope of Application	15
I. Definitions	15
II. Application across Contract Types	20
III. Data as a Counter-Performance	22
IV. Application to B – B-Contracts	24
C. Conformity with the Contract	26
I. Implementation of the subjective and objective Requirements	26
1. Implementation for digital Products	26
2. Implementation for Sale of Goods	27
3. Equal Ranking of subjective and objective Criteria	29
4. Updating Obligations	30
II. Negative Quality Agreements	32
III. The "Durability" Requirement	33
IV. Incorrect Installation	36
V. Duty to provide Personal Data	37
VI. Modification of Digital Content or Digital Service	38
VII. Third Party Rights	40
VIII. Relationship with Intellectual Property Law	42
D. Liability of the Trader	43
I. Supply in a Single Act and Long-Term Supply	43
II. Interruption of Long-Term Supply	45
III. Impossibility and Change of Circumstances	46
1. Impossibility	46
2. Change of Circumstances	49
IV. Number-independent interpersonal Communication Services	52
V. Package Contracts	53
VI. Non-compliance with the GDPR	54
E. Remedies for the Failure to Supply and Remedies for the Lack of Conformity	55
I. Overview: Remedies with Regard to Contracts for Digital Products and with Regard to the Sale of Goods; Right to Withhold	55
1. Contracts for Digital Products	55
2. Sale of Goods	57
3. Right to Withhold	59
II. Place of Delivery and Place of Repair and Replacement	60
III. Cost of Transport in the Event of a Repair	61
IV. Right of Termination	62
1. Declaration	62
2. Uniform Requirements	63
3. Restitution	64
V. Contractual Consequences of Withdrawal of Consent for Processing Data	65
VI. Price Reduction	67
VII. Items not covered by the Implementation of the Directives	68
1. Environmental Sustainability	68
2. Subsequent Buyer	69
F. Commercial Guarantees	70
G. Time Limits	71
I. Sale of Goods	71

Reiner Schulze

II. Supply of digital products 73
III. Notification 74
H. Right of Redress 75
I. Relationship with other remedies 77
J. Conclusion 78
   Bibliography.. 81

A. Introduction. General Framework

I. Transpostion in the German Civil Code

1. Incorporation into the Civil Code

1   Germany has transposed the "twin directives" on Digital Content and Digital Services (DCD) and on Sale of Goods (SGD) into its Civil Code (Bürgerliches Gesetzbuch; BGB). The German legislation thus follows the path it took with the "Modernisation of the Law of Obligations" in 2002: it integrates the provisions transposing the European consumer contract law into the Civil Code. This "integration model" was directed at a recodification in the 2002 reform, which was intended to secure the importance of the Civil Code also for the everyday transactions of citizens and at the same time to use suggestions from European legislation for the modernisation of the German Civil Code.[1] With regard to modernisation, German legislation combined the integration of consumer law with the "extended" adoption of a number of terms and principles from the European directives beyond their scope of application as provided for in Union law (such as conformity with the contract, right to repair or replacement, priority of cure, etc.). Such terms and principles from the consumer protection directives served as patterns for general provisions applicable not only to consumer contracts, but in principle also to contracts between all other parties.[2]

2   The integration of consumer law in this way promoted a far-reaching "Europeanisation" of the German law of obligations, which is now continuing with the implementation of the provisions from the "twin directives" on digital content and services and on the sale of goods. Just as with the 2002 reform, the German legislator is using the provisions of these directives to modernise the German Civil Code – in particular with regard to new challenges resulting from digitalisation. The provisions transposing the two European directives thus constitute both further steps on the path of "Europeanisation" of the German Civil Code and starting points for its adaptation to the "digital age".

2. Integration into the System

3   The implementation of the "twin directives" also followed the model of the modernisation of the law of obligations of 2002 in that the integration of the European requirements into the German Civil Code was not limited to a mere external "addition" (for example, in the way that a new book with the provisions implementing the European directives would be appended to the BGB). Rather, the new contents that the BGB

---

[1] Dannemann and Schulze, in: Dannemann and Schulze (eds), *German Civil Code I* (2020), Introduction, mn. 52, 53; Lorenz, 'Schuldrechtsreform 2002: Problemschwerpunkte drei Jahre danach (2005)', *NJW*, 1889; Schulze and Schulte-Nölke, 'Schuldrechtsreform und Gemeinschaftsrecht' in Schulze and Schulte-Nölke (eds), *Die Schuldrechtsreform vor dem Hintergrund des Gemeinschaftsrechts* (2001) 3 et seq.

[2] Huber and Faust, *Schuldrechtsmodernisierung* (2002); Schulze, 'Recent Influences of the European Acquis – Communautaire on German Contract Law' (2022) 17 *NTBR*, 132 (132).

received due to the European directives were fitted into the systematics of this code; and in part, this systematics was further developed due to the new contents.

Due to this approach, the implementation of the European directives was combined in particular with the adaptation to the pandectist tradition (characteristic of the BGB) of proceeding "from the general to the particular".[3] In the systematics of the law of obligations within the BGB, this concerns in particular the relationship between the General Law of Obligations (which in its third section contains the general provisions for "obligations arising out of contracts") and the subsequently regulated Special Part of the Law of Obligations, which in a series of specific titles regulates individual types of contracts such as sale, lease, services, etc. The provisions implementing directives that cover several types of contracts (e.g., sale and lease) are to be inserted into the General Law of Obligations in this system (in particular in its third section with the general provisions for "Obligations arising out of contracts"). On the other hand, provisions dealing with only one type of contract (e.g., sale) are placed under the relevant title of the Special Law of Obligations.

In the "modernisation of the law of obligations", the German legislator therefore implemented, for example, the information duties and the rights of withdrawal in distance contracts and in contracts concluded away from business premises by means of provisions in the General Law of Obligations of the German Civil Code (§§ 312 et seq. and 355 et seq. of the German Civil Code), because these provisions – in accordance with the provisions of the Directives on which they are based – cover several types of contracts (sales contracts and service contracts). In implementing the DCD, German legislation has proceeded accordingly: For the most part, it has also inserted the provisions transposing this Directive into the General Law of Obligations, since the scope of application of the DCD also extends to several types of contracts. In the section of the General Law of Obligations on "Obligations arising out of Contracts", most of the provisions transposing the Directive are now contained in a new Title 2a "contracts for Digital Products" (§§ 327 et seq.).

In contrast, the provisions of the SGD essentially only concern the specific contract type of sale. They are therefore – just as the provisions implementing the previous Directive, the Consumer Sales Directive (CSD) – not assigned to the General Law of Obligations in the systematics of German civil law. Rather, they have been given their place within the Special Part of the Law of Obligations in the title on sales (§§ 433 et seq. BGB). In this title, numerous provisions that were newly created or reorganised on the basis of the CSD during the modernisation of the law of obligations in 2002 have now been supplemented or amended again in accordance with the SGD.

II. Impact on legal Structures

1. Overview

The implementation of the DCD and the SGD has not only continued the integration of consumer law into the BGB through the inclusion of further matters but has also brought about further structural developments. They mainly affect the law of obligations of the Civil Code, while the relationship to other areas of private law (such as "Intellectual Property Law") is hardly affected by the implementation of these Directives, at least

---

[3] Dannemann and Schulze, in: Dannemann and Schulze (eds), *German Civil Code I* (2020), Introduction, mn. 11, 33; Schulze, 'Die Verletzung vertraglicher Pflichten im System des chinesischen und des deutschen Zivilrechts' in Möllers and Hao Li (eds), *Der Besondere Teil des chinesischen Zivilgestzbuchs. Zwischen Tradition und Moderne* (2022), 155 (155, 174 et seq.).

directly. However, in connection with the implementation of the DCD, the German legislature has independently added a new provision which serves to clarify the relationship between the provisions of contract law and the (primarily public law) provisions of data protection law (§ 327 q BGB).[4]

2. Expansion of the General Law of Obligations

8   As far as the implementation of the DCD is concerned, the structural further development of the law of obligations can be seen above all in the expansion of the General Law of Obligations through a new title specifically dedicated to contracts on digital products and thus specifically responding to a challenge of the "digital age". Outside of this new title, a number of individual provisions also serve to implement this directive (in particular § 312 (1a) BGB with regard to the principles for consumer contracts and some provisions for individual contract types such as § 516a BGB for donations; §§ 548a and 578b BGB for lease; § 650 BGB for contracts to produce digital content). However, the emphasis of the implementation is clearly on the new Title 2a of the section on "Obligations arising out of contracts" in the General Law of Obligations with its 21 paragraphs (§§ 320 to 327u BGB). This is based on the fact that Art. 3 (1) DCD provides for the application of the provisions of this Directive irrespective of the traditional classification of contract types; and accordingly, the German provisions are assigned to the General Law of Obligations in the systematics of the BGB. The new provisions on digital products thereby significantly reinforce a tendency to expand the General Law of Obligations[5], which had already become apparent before under the influence of European directives (inter alia with the expansion of the General Law of Obligations to implement the E-Commerce Directive, the Consumer Rights Directive and its predecessors, the Directives on Doorstep Selling and on Distance Selling).

9   The new title within the General Law of Obligations also combines provisions for contracts between traders and consumers with provisions for B – B contracts, in that the first subtitle "Consumer Contracts on Digital Products" is followed by a second subtitle "Special Provisions for Contracts on Digital Products between traders". This second subtitle concerns the redress of the trader against a previous trader in the business chain in the event of liability for the non-delivery or non-contractual delivery of digital products. It serves to implement Art. 20 DCD and is accordingly limited to claims between traders resulting from the existence of a consumer contract at the end of the business chain. Ultimately, the German legislator did not decide on a more far-reaching regulation for B – B contracts on digital products that goes beyond the scope of the Directive, although the European legislature's express reference to the admissibility of such an extension[6] gave reason to consider this possibility for Germany as well. Nevertheless, the inclusion of this subtitle with provisions for contracts on digital products between traders in the General Law of Obligations can form a starting point for future considerations on a more general regulation of this matter.[7]

---

[4] See below, E V.

[5] Schulze, 'Recent Influences of the European Acquis – Communautaire on German Contract Law' (2022) 17 *NTBR*, 132 (136).

[6] See recital 16 DCD.

[7] Schulze, 'Die Digitale-Inhalte-Richtlinie – Innovation und Kontinuität im europäischen Vertragsrecht' (2019) 4 *ZEuP*, 695 (702 s.); Metzger, 'Verträge über digitale Inhalte und digitale Dienstleistungen: Neuer BGB-Vertragstypus oder punktuelle Reform?' (2019), *JZ*, 577 (584).

A. Introduction. General Framework

3. Generalisation beyond Consumer Law

What the German legislator has not yet dared to do for contracts on digital products, it has done to a large extent in the implementation of the SGD in sales law: In contrast to the implementation of the DCD, it has clearly reached beyond consumer law here. A considerable part of the provisions of this Directive forms the basis for regulations that do not only apply to sales contracts with consumers but constitute general sales law. This concerns both pre-existing provisions that previously implemented provisions of the CSD and now serve to implement identical provisions of the SGD,[8] as well as additions and amendments to the previous German sales law to implement new provisions of the SGD.

For the sales law, the method of "extended" transposition (or "gold plating"), which the German legislator already used in the modernisation of 2002, is thus continued. The structure created at that time continues the pandectist tradition by distinguishing between a General Part of the Sales Law and a Special Part, which includes the specific provisions for consumer contracts. The former precedes the latter in Subtitle 1 of the Sales Law ("General Provisions"; §§ 433 et seq. BGB), while the specific provisions for consumer contracts (including the special provisions for the trader's redress in such contracts) follow in a later subtitle ("Sale of Consumer Goods"; §§ 474 et seq. BGB).

The transposition of the SGD now fits into this structure: Insofar as the German legislator wants to extend the transposition provisions and cover sales contracts in general, the relevant provisions are contained in Subtitle 1 on "General Provisions". In so far as their application is to be limited to sales contracts between traders and consumers, they are assigned to the subtitle on the "sale of consumer goods". Within this structure, however, the German legislator has regularly implemented the new provisions of the SGD that were not yet included in the CSD by amending or supplementing numerous already existing provisions in both subtitles. This has had the effect of making the wording of the many provisions more complicated and the law of sales less clear overall.[9]

The "gold plated" part of the Directive's provisions, which have become General Sales Law in Germany, include, inter alia, the equality of objective and subjective requirements of conformity and most of the criteria of conformity under Art. 6 and 7 SGD. However, for example, one of the central elements of these requirements of conformity with the contract, namely the obligation to update pursuant to Art. 6 lit. d and Art. 7 (3) and 4 SGD, has not been included in the General Sales Law, but only in the subtitle on the "Sale of Consumer Goods" with §§ 475 a and 475 b BGB.[10]

4. Structuring Concepts and Principles

In summary, the implementation of the "twin directives" has had a considerable impact on the structure of the German law of obligation – from the enrichment of the continuing pandectist basic pattern with new elements related to digitization to the "generalisation" of European provisions for consumer contracts into general rules of sales law. If one looks more closely beyond the system of German law of obligations to the overarching concepts and principles that are decisive as "internal" structures for the coherence of this area of law, a considerably wider spectrum of already clearly

---

[8] On the relationship of the SGD to the CSD and to other preceding set of rules Ferrante, 'The Amended Proposal COM (2017) 637: a „New" European Sales Law?', in Janssen and Schulte-Nölke (eds), *Researches in European Private Law and Beyond* (2020), 43 (43 et seq.).
[9] Güster and Booke, 'Umsetzung der Warenkaufrichtlinie'(2022), *MMR*, 92; Lorenz, 'Die Umsetzung der EU-Warenkaufrichtlinie in deutsches Recht (2021)', *NJW*, 2065.
[10] For more detail see below B IV and C.

recognisable and possible future impacts of the new directives comes into view. It extends to all the individual areas to be considered in the following, from the definitions of fundamental terms to conformity with the contract to remedies and their relationship to other areas of law and will be addressed in each of the relevant chapters.

B. Definitions and Scope of Application

I. Definitions

15   In German law, it is not customary to precede the substantive provisions with a catalogue of definitions as found in Art. 2 DCD and Art. 2 SGD in accordance with the practice of EU legislation. Instead, German legislation has proceeded in four different ways with regard to the definitions contained in these catalogues of directives.

16   (1) Adapting the German legislative technique, a large part of the definitions from the "twin directives" have been inserted into the substantive provisions at the point where the term in question is used for the first time. For example, the term "goods with digital elements" is defined in the context of the rules limiting the application of the provisions implementing the DCD (§ 327 (3) BGB). Similarly, the clarification that the term "price" includes the digital representation of value (Art. 2 No. 7 DCD) is found in the context of the rules on the scope of application of these transposition provisions (albeit with the express stipulation that this definition only concerns the provisions on contracts for digital products; § 327 (1) p. 2 BGB). The terms "functionality", "compatibility" and "interoperability" (Art. 8 No. 10 to 12 DCD; Art. 2 No. 8 to 10 SGD) are used for the first time in the context of the provision on the defect of a digital product to indicate the requirements for the digital product (§ 327 e (1) BGB); the following paragraph of this provision then contains the definitions of these terms. The requirements for "integration of the digital product" are set out in the first sentence of § 327 (4) BGB; the second sentence of this section contains the definitions of "integration" and "digital environment".

17   (2) With regard to some terms, German legislation has modified and supplemented the model of the Directives with its own definitions, but without aiming at substantial changes. In particular, it has introduced the term "digital product" as a generic term for the terms "digital content" and "digital services" (§ 327 (1) p. 1 BGB). However, it has taken the definitions for these two forms of digital product substantially unchanged from the Directives (§ 327 (2) BGB). For the concept of updates, German law – like the Directives – does not contain a definition but limits itself to a description of the obligations of the trader in this respect and the relevant period of time (§ 327 f BGB). With regard to this period, however, it introduces the definitions of "continuous supply over a period" and "period of supply" (§ 327 e (1) BGB).

18   (3) For the concept of durability the German legislator has refrained from explicitly adopting the definition of Art. 2 No. 13 SGD when defining this requirement in § 434 (2) BGB. Doctrine and case law will have to refer to this definition in the Directive and the explanations in recital 32 SGD to interpret this provision.[11]

19   (4) On the other hand, the definitions of a number of terms which not only concern the provisions transposing the "twin directives", but have also been used previously for other matters within the Civil Code, are to be found in the General Part of the Civil Code (due to the method of "bracketing" the general terms and rules). This applies in particular to the terms "trader" and "consumer" (cf. Art. 2 No. 5 and 6 DCD), which are

---

[11] See, e.g., Saenger, in: Schulze et al., *Handkommentar BGB* (2022), § 434, mn. 27.

defined by §§ 13 and 14 BGB.[12] The term "durable medium" is also defined in the General Part of the BGB (§ 126 b (1) S. 2 BGB).

II. Application across Contract Types

§ 327 (1) of the Civil Code transposes into German law the provision of Art. 3 (1) DCD that the scope of application of the provisions of this Directive generally extends to contracts concluded by traders with consumers for the distribution of digital content and services. The provisions transposing the Directive are therefore applicable to numerous types of contracts governed by the Special Law of Obligations (including contracts of sale, §§ 433 et seq. BGB; lease, §§ 535 et seq. BGB; service contracts, §§ 611 et seq. BGB; contracts to produce a work, §§ 631 et seq. BGB). 20

The questions of classification of the new provisions within the doctrine of types of contracts are not to be answered uniformly at European level on the basis of the Directive, but are left to the respective national law.[13] They have also led to a lively discussion in Germany.[14] Regardless of the different opinions in the doctrine, however, it must be taken into account that the classification of the transposition provisions in §§ 327 et seq. BGB in the general law of obligations is not based on a completely new approach from a systematic point of view. Rather, it corresponds to the approach of German legislation also with regard to other provisions for contracts that are characterised by a similar subject matter or other common features, but may belong to different contract types of the Special Law of Obligations (for example, contracts relating to standard business terms pursuant to §§ 305 et seq. BGB; contracts on particular types of distribution pursuant to 312 et seq. BGB; contracts on continuing obligations under § 314 BGB). In all these cases, provisions of the General Law of Obligations covering several types of contracts in the Special Law of Obligations may be applicable alongside specific provisions of the Special Law of Obligations for the type of contract in question. In this respect, the implementation of the DCD does not pose a completely new challenge to German contract theory. However, it makes it particularly necessary to coordinate the application of both groups of norms in a specific case and, in particular, to distinguish the regulatory areas of the overarching provisions in the General Law of Obligations and the respective specific provisions for the relevant contract type in the Special Law of Obligations. 21

III. Data as a Counter-Performance

New questions for the German doctrine of contract law may arise, above all, from the applicability of the new provisions to the supply of digital products where the consumer provides or undertakes to provide personal data (Art. 3 (1) p. 2 DCD; § 327 (3) BGB). This concerns, on the one hand, the doctrines on contractual synallagma and, on the other hand, the conclusion of the contract. In the former respect, these provisions reflect the increased importance of data in the "digital age" not only as a contractually owed 22

---

[12] On these regulations and their peculiarities compared to the corresponding European terms Beurskens, in: Dannemann and Schulze (eds), *German Civil Code I* (2020), I, § 13 mn. 4, § 14 mn. 4 mn. 52, 53.

[13] See recital 12 DCD.

[14] See, for example, Metzger, 'Dienst gegen Daten: Ein synallagmatischen Vertrag' (2016), 216 *AcP*, 817 (817 et seq.); Specht, 'Daten als Gegenleistung – verlangt die Digitalisierung nach einem neuen Vertragstypus?' (2017), *JZ*, 763 (763 et seq.); Rosenkranz, 'Spezifische Vorschriften zu Verträgen über die Bereitstellung digitaler Produkte im BGB' (2021) *ZUM*, 195 (196 et seq.).

performance but also as counter- performance for consideration. With regard to personal data, however, the assessment as counter-performance is controversial at both German and European level.[15] The concerns from the perspective of data protection are based primarily on the fact that personal data are to be attributed to the sphere of the right of personality and its protection.[16] On the other hand, it is rightly argued that this in no way precludes classification as counter-performance under civil law, given the actual significance of such data as an object of trade.[17] Nevertheless, the German legislator wanted to avoid a decision on this question and left it open whether the provision of personal data by the consumer stands in a reciprocal relationship with the provision of the digital product by the trader and is to be regarded as counter-performance.[18] Accordingly, it did not assign the provisions for contracts on digital products within the General Law of Obligations to Title 2 on reciprocal contracts, but to a new separate Title 2a.

23 With regard to the conclusion of the contract, a direct influence of the new provisions on personal data provided by the consumer on this matter is out of the question due to Art. 3 (10) DCD and also due to the separation of the matters in the Civil Code. However, corresponding evaluations can exist insofar as the economic interest of the trader in the value of the consumer's data is decisive both in the evaluation of this data within the framework of Art. 3 (1) DCD and § 327 (3) BGB and with regard to the conclusion of the contract, insofar as the intention by the parties to be legally bound ("*Rechtsbindungswille*") is to be examined.[19]

IV. Application to B – B-Contracts

24 As far as the application to B – B – contracts are concerned, the German legislator – as explained[20] – has partly extended the provisions of the SGD for the law of sales and also included B – B – contracts by incorporating them into the general law of sales. However, the provisions implementing the SGD are only mandatory for consumer contracts (§ 476 BGB), whereas they are generally default law for other contracts.

25 The German legislature's refusal to implement also the provisions of the DCD extended to B – B contracts[21] has been criticised, among other things, because smaller businesses are also in need of protection and, moreover, in the case of multifunctional software, for example, it is often not even recognisable in practice whether the customer is a consumer or an entrepreneur.[22] It remains to be seen whether this deficit will be overcome in a future reform. Irrespective of this, it can be assumed that in the German practice of contracting and also in the German case law relating to it, numerous terms and definitions which are contained in the new §§ 327 et seq. BGB on the basis of the Direc-

---

[15] On the spectrum of opinions Lohsse et al., *Data as Counter-Performance – Contract Law 2.0?* (2020).

[16] See, e.g., Lohsse et al., 'Trading Data in the Digital Economy' in Lohsse et al. (eds), *Trading Data in the Digital Economy* (2017), 13, 14.

[17] Schulze and Zoll, *European Contract Law* (2021), § 1 mn. 61.

[18] Government draft BT-Drs. 19/27653, p. 38.

[19] In more detail government draft BT-Drs. 19/27653, p. 38; Schulze and Zoll, *European Contract Law* (2021), § 1 mn. 61, § 3 mn. 78–79 and § 5 mn. 34–35.

[20] Above A II 3.

[21] For some reasons for the European legislator's reluctance, however Martin Fries, 'Data as Counter-Performance in B2B Contracts'. in Lohsse et al., *Data as Counter-Performance – Contract Law 2.0?* (2020), 253 (253 et seq.).

[22] Spindler and Sein, 'Die endgültige Richtlinie über Verträge über digitale Inhalte und Dienstleistungen' (2019), *MMR*, 415 (416); Schulze, 'Die Digitale-Inhalte-Richtlinie – Innovation und Kontinuität im europäischen Vertragsrecht' (2019) 4 *ZEuP*, 695 (702 et seq.).

C. Conformity with the Contract

I. Implementation of the subjective and objective Requirements

1. Implementation for digital Products

The criteria of conformity with the contract form a core area of the new provisions for contracts for digital products in German law as in the DCD. They are regulated in 327 d et seq. BGB following the provisions on the supply of digital products (§§ 327 b and 327 c BGB). In substance, they essentially correspond to the provisions of the Directive. However, the structure deviates in several respects from the model of the Directive. In particular, the consequences of a failure to supply directly follow the requirements for the supply and the consequences of a non-conformity directly follow the requirements for the conformity (whereas the DCD first specifies the requirements for the supply and the conformity and then the consequences for failure to supply and the non-conformity). Moreover, the conformity requirements are spread over several paragraphs. The introductory § 327 d BGB combines the Directive concept of Conformity with the Contract with the traditional German terminology by introducing the terms "product defect" and "legal defect". The following §§ 327 e et seq. BGB then deal separately with the product defect, the updates ("*Aktualisierungen*") as a special form of product defect and the legal defect.

2. Implementation for Sale of Goods

For the law of sales, the provisions of the SGD on conformity with the contract have been integrated into the general provision on material defects, insofar as their application is to be extended to all sales contracts. According to § 434 (1) of the German Civil Code (BGB), an object is free from material defects if it complies with the subjective requirements, the objective requirements and the assembly requirements according to the following paragraphs of the provision at the time of passing of the risk. The second paragraph of this provision then regulates the subjective requirements, the third paragraph the objective requirements and the fourth paragraph the requirements regarding assembly. For the objective requirements, the provision refers, *inter alia*, to the suitability for customary use and to the quality that is usual in goods of the same kind and that can be expected by the buyer. As criteria of usual quality, in accordance with the SGD, are expressly stated, inter alia, durability, functionality, compatibility and safety. § 434 (5) BGB clarifies that the delivery of an *aliud* is equivalent to a material defect.

In the subtitle on the sale of consumer goods, § 475 b BGB regulates the requirements for conformity with the contract, insofar as the provisions of the Directive are to be implemented only for consumer sales. This provision with the heading "Material defect of a good with digital elements" also adapts the terminology to the conventional German terminology of "material defect". In accordance with the SGD's requirements for consumer sales, it supplements the subjective and objective requirements in relation to consumer sales, above all by the trader's duty to update (not provided for in § 434 BGB generally for sales contracts) and by stipulations on installation when purchasing a good with digital elements. In addition, § 475 c BGB specifies the trader's liability for the consumer purchase if, in the case of goods with digital elements, a permanent supply of the digital elements is agreed.

3. Equal Ranking of subjective and objective Criteria

29 As a new core element of German sales law based on the SGD, it should be emphasized that now §§ 327 e (1), 434 (1) and 475 b BGB stipulate that the subjective and objective criteria of conformity with the contract have equal rank (unlike the previous German sales law based on the CSD). They thus aim to protect the buyer from agreements with the seller undermining the protection provided by objective criteria. This change of perspective towards the equal ranking of objective and subjective criteria has even more far-reaching consequences in Germany than in some other EU member states, because the German legislator did not limit it to consumer law regarding sales but transferred it to the General Sales Law (§ 434 (1) BGB). In this respect, the "extended" implementation has made German law not only more consumer-friendly, but generally more buyer-friendly. However, the practical effect is less than the theoretical relevance of this generalisation: only in the case of consumer contracts do the increased requirements provided for by the Directives apply in order to counteract the conclusion of a "negative quality agreement" by the parties (Art. 7 (5) SGD; § 476 (1) p. 2 BGB).

4. Updating Obligations

30 Furthermore, the introduction of the updating obligations provided by the "twin directives" means a profound innovation for German sales law. In contrast to conventional understanding, the seller's liability for conformity with the contract does not generally end with the "passage of risk", which is regularly linked to the delivery of the item. Rather, the contract law of the BGB now recognises that in the "digital age" there are continuing obligations beyond this point.[23] Connected with this "dynamisation" of contractual obligations is the differentiation between the "permanent supply of a digital product" and the "other cases" (§§ 327 f (1) p. 2 nos. 1 and 2; 475 c BGB in correspondence to the "continuous supply over a period of time" and the "single act of supply or a series of individual acts of supply" in the terminology of Art. 8(2) DCD and Art. 7 (3) SGD). It also has relevance to the burden of proof, the rescission of terminated contracts and modifications to digital products (§§ 327 k (2), 327 o (3), 327 q (2), 327 r) and is thus now one of the structural elements of contract law.

31 In addition, the new provisions on updates expand the significance of information duties in modern German contract law by combining continuing duties to perform with regard to the supply of updates with (likewise continuing) duties to inform (§§ 327 f (1) p. 1, 475 b (4) no. 2 BGB; "two-track" duties of the trader with regard to updates).[24] These information duties are also particularly relevant for practice insofar as the trader's liability in the case of an installation omitted by the consumer is only excluded if the trader has informed the consumer about the availability of the update and the conse-

---

[23] The legal nature of this obligation is disputed in detail. According to the explanatory statement in the government draft (BT-Drs. 19/27653) it is an "independent obligation of the trader" ("unabhängige Verpflichtung des Unternehmers"); for discussions in the doctrine see Schulte-Nölke, 'Digital obligations of sellers of smart devices under the Sale of Goods Directive 771/2019' in Lohsee et al. (eds) *Smart Products* (2022), 47 et seq; Wendehorst, 'The update obligation – how to make it work in the relationship between seller, producer, digital content or service provider and consumer' in Lohsee et al. (eds) *Smart Products* (2022), 63 et seq; André Janssen,'The Update Obligation for Smart Products – Time Period for the Update Obligation and Failure to Install the Update' in Lohsee et al. (eds) *Smart Products* (2022), 91 et seq.

[24] Schulze and Zoll, *European Contract Law* (2021), ch. 5, mn. 47.

quences of omitted information (§§ 327 f (2) no. 1, 475 b (5) no. 1 BGB). However, this adaptation of the BGB to the changes brought about by digitalisation is again limited to consumer contracts (§§ 327 (1), 327 f; 474, 475 b BGB). The German legislator has so far shied away from a generalisation beyond the scope of application of the directives – although in principle a similar situation and a similar need for regulation exist for B – B contracts on digital products and on goods with digital elements.

II. Negative Quality Agreements

The provisions in Art. 8 (5) DCD and Art. 7 (5) SGD on the "negative quality agreements" just mentioned,[25] which form the basis of §§ 327 h and 476 (1) p. 2 BGB,[26] are problematic with regard to consumer protection because they allow the consumer to waive objective requirements for conformity with the contract, including the trader's updating obligations, with a simple "click" on a trader's form on the internet.[27] Deviations in favour of the consumer were nevertheless out of the question when transposing into German law because of the full harmonisation according to Art. 4 DCD and Art. 4 SGD. However, the purposes of the relevant European directives and their German transposition provisions, as well as the systematics of the BGB, argue that the provisions transposing the "twin directives" do not exclude consumer protection on the basis of §§ 305 et seq. BGB that implement the Directive on Unfair Terms.[28] The rules on "negative quality agreements" in §§ 327 h and 476 b BGB therefore allow deviations from the objective requirements of conformity with the contract only within the framework defined by the content control and the transparency control according to 305 et seq. BGB.

III. The "Durability" Requirement

With the implementation of the "durability" requirement from Art. 7 (1) lett. d SGD in § 434 (3) p. 2 BGB, the idea of durability has found its way into German sales law. In the context of the objective requirements, durability is in a series with functionality, compatibility and safety, which as "other characteristics" (*"sonstige Merkmale"*) of the good belong to its "usual quality" in addition to quantity and quality. In the legislative process, the explanatory statement in the government draft pointed out that the introduction of this criterion is not intended to establish a legal guarantee of durability with the content that the good actually retains all its necessary functions and its performance under normal use.[29] Rather, this criterion refers only to the expectation that the good has the capacity to retain its necessary functions and performance under normal use at the time of the passing of risk (as the doctrine clarifies with reference to the definition in Art. 2 No. 13 SGD).[30]

A specification of the requirements resulting from the criterion of "durability" in detail or additional provisions on the "reparability" of goods and the stocking of spare parts

---

[25] Above B I 3.
[26] In detail to this provision Lorenz, 'Die Umsetzung der EU-Warenkaufrichtlinie in deutsches Recht' (2021), *NJW*, 2065.
[27] Schulze, in: Schulze et al., *Handkommentar BGB* (2022), § 327 h mn. 5, 6.
[28] Spindler, 'Umsetzung der Richtlinie über digitale Inhalte in das BGB' (2021), *MMR*, 451 (456 et seq.); Schulze, in: Schulze et al., *Handkommentar BGB* (2022), § 327 h mn. 5, 6.
[29] BT-Drs. 19/27424, 24.
[30] Saenger, in: Schulze et al., *Handkommentar BGB* (2022), § 434 mn. 27.

are not contained in the German legal text,[31] although the full harmonisation character of the SGD would not have ruled this out[32] and the issue was already under consideration before the implementation of the SGD.[33] In practice, however, the recourse to the public statements of the seller or another link in the contractual chain (including the manufacturer), which is provided for in § 434 (3) p.1 no. 2 BGB, will be of considerable importance for the concretisation of the requirement in individual cases. A content filling and concretisation of "durability" in § 434 (3) BGB by sector-specific or product-specific requirements also seems appropriate and possible by referring to corresponding specific provisions for goods of the relevant kind in EU legislation, German law and technical standards, where they exist, and otherwise also by taking into account sector-specific codes of conduct (as the explanatory statement in the government draft for the implementation of SGD[34] and doctrine[35] of the interpretation of "customary quality" under § 434 (3) BGB recognise).

35 Finally, as far as the purposes and terminology of the new criterion of "durability" are concerned, it remains to be pointed out that they are not only in the context of European-inspired legislation with an ecological orientation, such as the provisions implementing Directive 2009/125/EC[36] (without, however, the implementation of these different directives having been directly interlocked in German law). Rather German law has already taken the ecological aspects of sustainability and saving energy into account, within the framework of the BGB in tenancy law (among other things, with regard to energy saving and climate protection in the modernisation of housing; § 555 b no. 2 BGB). With the "durability" requirement, a further starting point for the orientation of contract law towards ecological concerns – and insofar for the "greening" of German private law – has now been added. Due to the adoption of this requirement into the General Sales Law – and thus its relevance for all sales contracts – the impact of the European model on German law in this respect reaches far beyond the scope of the SGD. However, it is not currently apparent whether and how an overarching framework of concepts and rules directed at the sustainability of goods and services, or similar ecological goals will emerge in German private law from such approaches, including provisions of the German Civil Code.

IV. Incorrect Installation

36 The incorrect installation or integration by the trader and the defective installation instructions are regulated in §§ 327 e (4) and 434 (4) BGB according to the model of Art. 9 DCD and Art. 8 SGD. If a digital product does not comply with these integration requirements, this is considered a product defect (§ 327 e (1) BGB); and the general provisions on the trader's liability and the consumer's rights in the event of defects in a digital product apply, as set out in §§ 327 i et seq. BGB. If a good does not meet the installation requirements of § 434 (4), this is considered a material defect under § 434 (1) BGB;

---

[31] Critically Kieninger, 'Recht auf Reparatur („Right to Repair") und europäisches Vertragsrecht' (2020), 2 ZEuP, 274 (274 et seq.).
[32] Schulze and Zoll, *European Contract Law* (2021), ch. 5, mn. 45, compare there fn. 111.
[33] See the (however ultimately negative) judgement e.g., OLG Frankfurt 18.2.2019 – 13 U 186/17.
[34] BT-Drs. 19/27424, 24.
[35] Saenger, in: Schulze et al., *Handkommentar BGB* (2022), § 434 mn. 26.
[36] Transposed into German law by the "Energieverbrauchsrelevante -Produkte -Gesetz" (EVPG) of 7.2.2008; as sanctions, § 13 EVPG primarily provides for fines.

and the general provisions on the buyer's rights in case of defects under § 437 (with the references therein) apply.[37]

V. Duty to provide Personal Data

The BGB takes into account the consumer's duty to provide personal data when defining the scope of application of the new provisions for contracts on digital products (§ 327 (3) BGB). From this explicit inclusion in the scope of application, it can be inferred that contracts that provide for such an obligation should in principle be permissible and effective. However, § 327 does not contain a rule that specifically determines the enforceability of the duty of the consumer to provide personal data in favour of the trader. If in the case in question a contract has been concluded according to the general rules on the conclusion of contracts (§§ 145 et seq. BGB), the general principles on the binding effect of contracts ("*pacta sunt servanda*") and the right of the obligor to claim performance owed under the contract (cf. § 241 (1) BGB) must rather be taken into account. However, these principles of contract law are in a much-discussed area of tension with data protection law.[38]

VI. Modification of Digital Content or Digital Service

The German legislator has implemented the provisions of Art. 19 DCD on the modification of digital content or digital service within the framework of the provisions for contracts on digital products in § 327 r BGB. However, a corresponding provision for the law of sale has not been introduced in the way of implementation of the SGD within the framework of §§ 433 et seq. or 474 et seq. BGB.

As far as § 327 r BGB is concerned, it is noteworthy that the content of this provision substantially corresponds to the provisions of Art. 19 DCD, but its structure and wording partly deviate considerably from the underlying European model. In this respect, § 327 r BGB is a significant example of the German legislator's effort to implement Directive provisions unchanged in terms of content but improved in terms of the technique of the regulation. § 327 r (1) of the German Civil Code (BGB) contains the basic rule for the trader's power to modify digital products in contracts for permanent provision, based on Art. 19 (1) of the DCD but with different wording. It restricts the power to modifications that go beyond what is necessary to maintain conformity with the contract ("upgrades" as distinct from "updates") and binds it to three further conditions (which correspond to Art. 19 (1) nos. 1 – 3 DCD). § 327 r (2) BGB sets out the content and time limit for the trader's information obligations (including the requirements of Art. 19 (1) no. 4 DCD) and excludes the power of modification in the case of insignificant impairments. Para. 3 of the provision grants the consumer the right to terminate the contract free of charge and sets the relevant time limits; para. 4 excludes this right of termination in the cases provided for in Art. 19(4) DCD. For the declaration of termination of the contract and its legal consequences, according to para. 5, the provisions

---

[37] See D. below for the rules on these consumer rights.
[38] See, e.g., Schmidt-Kessel/Grimm, 'Unentgeltlich oder entgeltlich? – Der vertragliche Austausch von digitalen Inhalten gegen personenbezogene Daten' (2017), *ZfPW*, 84 (84 et seq.); Schmidt-Kessel, Right to Withdraw Consent to Data Processing – The Effect on the Contract, Lohsse et al. (eds), *Trading Data in the Digital Economy* (2017), 129 (129 et seq.); Dix, 'Daten als Bezahlung – Zum Verhältnis zwischen Zivilrecht und Datenschutzrecht' (2017), *ZEuP*, 1 (1 et seq.); Schulze, 'Haftung auf Schadensersatz im Vergleich' (2022), in Kindl et al. (eds), *Die Schadensersatzhaftung* (2022), 123 (123 et seq.).

which §§ 327 o and 327 p BGB contain for the termination of the contract in case of nonconformity with the contract are to be applied accordingly. Finally, para. 6 excludes the application of these provisions for certain package contracts in favour of the special provisions of the German Telecommunications Act (TKG).

VII. Third Party Rights

40   The provisions of Art. 10 DCD on third party rights are implemented by the concise § 327 g BGB, adapted to the terminology and style of the German legislation. According to this provision, the digital product is free from "legal defects" if the consumer can use it in accordance with the subjective or objective requirements previously set out in § 327 (2) and (3) without infringing third party rights. The basic rule on consumer rights in § 327 i BGB covers "product defects" and "defects of title" in the same way (in line with the German tradition that the term "defect" includes both "material defect" and "legal defect"). The provisions implementing the DCD's rules on remedies for a lack of conformity are therefore equally applicable to legal defects arising from the existence of third-party rights as to the material defects of the product itself. The consumer can therefore demand cure, terminate the contract or reduce the price (subject to the specific conditions laid down for each remedy). In addition to these remedies under the Directive, a claim for damages (§§ 280 (1) or 327 m (3) BGB) or for reimbursement of futile expenses (§ 284 BGB) may be considered under German law.

41   For the implementation of the SGD in the law of sales, the corresponding results from §§ 435, 437 BGB.

VIII. Relationship with Intellectual Property Law

42   Within the framework of the implementation of the "twin directives", no new provisions have been created concerning the relationship with intellectual property law beyond the provisions on third party rights mentioned above. In this respect, the legal situation that already existed before and the resulting problems essentially remain (including the dependence of the consumer's rights to "resell" digital contents on contractual stipulations over which he regularly has no influence).[39]

D. Liability of the Trader

I. Supply in a Single Act and Long-Term Supply

43   In the system of German provisions on contracts for digital products and also in the system of German sales law, there are no provisions along the lines of Art. 11 DCD and Art. 10 SGD that deal specifically with the liability of the trader. Rather, after the provisions on conformity with the contract, a basic rule on the rights of the consumer in case of defects leads over to the remedies of the consumer in case of a defect of the digital product or the good (§§ 327 i and 437 BGB).

---

[39] Schulze et al., 'Contracts for the Supply of Digital Content: Regulatory Challenges and Gaps – An Introduction', in Schulze et al., *Contracts for the Supply of Digital Content: Regulatory Challenges and Gaps* (2017), 11 (11, 22 et seq.); Spindler, 'Contract Law and Copyright – Regulatory Challenges and Gaps', in Schulze et al., *Contracts for the Supply of Digital Content: Regulatory Challenges and Gaps* (2017), 211 (211 et 0seq.).

Specific provisions for the supply of digital products in a single act on the one hand, 44
and for long term supply on the other hand, are found in this system at the points where
differentiation is required in each case. Accordingly, the "continuous supply over a period of time" is first addressed in connection with the relevant time for conformity with
the contract – or more precisely: the absence of defects of the product – and with the
time of supply (§ 327 e in conjunction with § 327 b BGB). In this context, the terms "permanent supply" and "period of supply" are also introduced. These terms – and as
counter terms the "single act of supply" and the "series of single acts" – are used in the
following provisions on conformity with the contract and on remedies, respectively, if
the distinction in this respect is important (e.g. for updates § 327 f (1) BGB; for the reversal of the burden of proof § 327 k BGB; for price reduction § 327 n (2)).[40]

II. Interruption of Long-Term Supply

Interruptions of the supply period during the contractually agreed provision period 45
are not expressly regulated in German law (nor in the DCD). However, § 327 e BGB –
especially with regard to the requirement of continuity in its para. 3 no. 1 and taking into
account recital 51 p. 3 DCD – is to be interpreted in such a way that even short-term
interruptions of the provision are to be regarded as a lack of conformity.[41] This does not
apply only in the case of one-off (non-recurring) interruptions which impair the supply
owed so slightly that they can be neglected. For the delimitation, the type, purpose and
duration of the provision owed in each case must be taken into account. For example, a
one-minute interruption in the context of a one-month music streaming subscription is
negligible, but an interruption of the same duration in a streaming contract for a single
football match is not.[42]

III. Impossibility and Change of Circumstances

1. Impossibility

A failure to supply digital products or to deliver goods because of impossibility is 46
not covered by the provisions of the Civil Code, which in the title for contracts for
digital products and in the law of sales specifically serve to implement the DCD and the
SGD. This is in line with the clarification in Recital 14 DCD that the regulation of such
impediments to performance should be left to the law of the Member States.[43] In these
cases, the general provisions of the German law of obligations on impossibility are rather
to be applied.

Impossibility in the narrower sense ("genuine impossibility") leads *ipso iure* ("automa- 47
tically") to the exclusion of the obligation to perform according to § 275 (1) BGB. This
applies irrespective of whether the performance is impossible only for the debtor or for
everyone (subjective or objective impossibility), and also irrespective of whether it cannot be performed for legal or factual reasons and whether the impediment to performance already existed at the time of conclusion of the contract or only arose afterwards
(initial or subsequent impossibility). If, on the other hand, performance is theoretically

---

[40] See above C I 4 and below E.I.
[41] Schulze, in: Schulze et al., *Handkommentar BGB* (2022), § 327 e, mn. 28.
[42] Staudenmayer, in Schulze and Staudenmayer, *EU Digital Law*, DCD Art. 8, mn. 102.
[43] Schulze, 'Die Digitale-Inhalte-Richtlinie – Innovation und Kontinuität im europäischen Vertragsrecht' (2019) 4 *ZEuP*, 695 (707 et seq.).

possible but disproportionate according to § 275 (2) ("factual impossibility") or unreasonable according to para. 3 of this provision ("personal impossibility"), the debtor has a right to refuse performance. He can therefore decide whether he wants to perform despite the extraordinary burden or refuse performance.

48 The legal consequence in all these cases of impossibility is not an invalidity of the contract itself, but merely the exclusion of the debtor's obligation to perform as originally contractually owed. Accordingly, the debtor loses his claim to counter-performance (§ 326 (1) p. 1 BGB). However, the exclusion of the duty to perform only relates to the original ("primary") performance obligations under the contract. On the other hand, it does not in principle affect the creditor's "secondary" rights regarding compensation for damages and revocation of the contract (§ 275 (4) BGB).[44] The consumer therefore retains these rights ("remedies") provided for in §§ 327 c and 280, 283 to 285, 311 a and 326 BGB, even if the trader's obligation to supply the digital content or to deliver the good is excluded due to impossibility.

2. Change of Circumstances

49 The provisions on the "interference with the basis of the contract" (313 BGB) may give rise to a party's claim under German law for adjustment of the contract to changed circumstances (and thus for a change in the obligations under the contract compared to the originally stipulated content). However, an adjustment of the contract according to this provision is not possible if performance is excluded due to impossibility according to § 275 BGB[45] (priority of § 275 over § 313 BGB). § 313 (1) BGB provides for an adjustment of the contract if circumstances which became the basis of a contract have significantly changed since the contract was entered into. As further prerequisites for the adjustment of the contract in addition to this "factual element", the provision stipulates that the parties would not have entered into the contract or would have entered into it with different contents if they had foreseen this change ("hypothetical element") and that, taking account of all circumstances of the specific case, in particular the contractual or statutory distribution of risk, one of the parties cannot reasonably be expected to uphold the contract without alteration ("normative element"). § 313 (2) of the Civil Code also allows for the adjustment of the contract in cases of mutual mistake by equating a change of circumstances with the fact that material conceptions which have become the basis of the contract are found to be incorrect.

50 The legal consequence of an interference of the basis of the contract under § 313 (1) or (2) is the affected party's right to adjust the contract[46] (for example, by reducing or increasing the amount owed, extending the period for performance, allowing partial performance, etc.). If the adjustment of the contract is not possible in a specific case or is not reasonable for one of the parties, 313 (3) provides as a last resort for the possibility of dissolving the contract through a right to revoke the contract or, in the case of continuing obligations, through a right to terminate the contract.

51 It is not clear from the wording of Art. 3 (10) DCD and from the formulations of recitals 12 and 14 whether provisions on the adaptation of contracts such as § 313 BGB are not affected by the scope of application of the Directive. Under the assumption that § 313 BGB is applicable to contracts on digital products despite the full harmonisation character of the DCD, an adaptation of such contracts is also permissible under the conditions of this provision. In the special cases of § 313 (3) BGB, a trader could, for exam-

---

[44] Schulze, in: Dannemann and Schulze (eds), *German Civil Code I* (2020), § 275, mn. 1, 2.
[45] Oehm, in: Dannemann and Schulze (eds), *German Civil Code I* (2020), § 313, mn. 12.
[46] Oehm, in: Dannemann and Schulze (eds), *German Civil Code I* (2020), § 313, mn. 21.

ple, even eliminate his obligation to supply digital products (§ 327 b BGB) by declaring the revocation or termination of the contract due to the interference of the basis of the business. A binding clarification of this question will ultimately require a decision by the ECJ.

IV. Number-independent interpersonal Communication Services

Contracts for electronic communication services (as defined in § 3 No. 61 German Telecommunications Act; TKG[47]) are excluded from the scope of the German rules on contracts for digital products under § 327 (6) No. 2 BGB. As a counter-exception, however, this provision stipulates (on the basis of Art. 3 (5) lit. b DCD) that number-independent interpersonal communication services (in the sense of § 3 No. 40 TKG) are included in the scope of application (for example, e-mail services and instant messaging services[48]). For such services, the provisions of §§ 327 ff. BGB are therefore also generally applicable to such services with regard to remedies in the event of a breach of the trader's obligations. 52

V. Package Contracts

The application of §§ 327 et seq. BGB to package contracts is regulated in 327 a (1) BGB in order to implement Art. 3 (6) DCD. Sentence 1 of the provision adopts the concept of a package contract from the Directive. Sentence 2 restricts the application to those elements of the package contract that concern digital products. A reference to Art. 107 (2) European Electronic Communication Code is neither contained in this provision nor in the explanatory memorandum of the government draft. However, the German legislator has used the design option provided by Art. 3 (6) subpara. 3 DCD to break through the before mentioned restriction to the components of the package contract that concern digital products by means of §§ 327 c (6) and 327 m (4) BGB. Provided that a consumer is entitled to terminate the contract, he may, according to these provisions, withdraw from the contract with regard to all components of the package contract if he has no interest in the other part of the package contract without the non-supplied or defective digital product. However, this does not apply to package contracts where the other component is a telecommunications service (within the meaning of Art. 3 No. 61 TKG). 53

VI. Non-compliance with the GDPR

If a trader who has concluded a contract with a consumer for the supply of digital products violates provisions of the GDPR, the sanctions provided for in the GDPR are fully applicable. The consumer concerned can therefore, for example, claim damages under Art. 82 of the GDPR and invoke the judicial remedies available under under Art. 79 GDPR. The provisions for contracts for digital products in the BGB do not affect these rights under the GDPR. This also applies to § 327 q BGB. Rather, this provision clarifies that the exercise of rights of the affected consumer due to data protection has no effect on the existence of the contract on digital products and cannot result in any claims 54

---

[47] Dated 23.6.2021,BGBl (Federal Law Gazette) I p. 1858.
[48] See explanatory statement in the government draft BT-Drs.19 27653 with reference to recital 28 DCD.

against the consumer.[49] Furthermore, it entitles the trader in these cases to terminate the contract under narrow conditions if a continuation can no longer be expected of him from an economic point of view.[50] However, it in no way relieves him of sanctions provided for in the GDPR.

E. Remedies for the Failure to Supply and Remedies for the Lack of Conformity

I. Overview: Remedies with Regard to Contracts for Digital Products and with Regard to the Sale of Goods; Right to Withhold

1. Contracts for Digital Products

55   In the context of the new German provisions on contracts for digital products, § 327 c BGB sets out the consumer's remedies for the failure of supply. According to para. 1 of this provision, the consumer may terminate the contract if the trader does not immediately fulfil his due obligation to supply the digital product in response to a request by the consumer. In addition to this right of the consumer, which corresponds to Art. 13 DCD, § 327 c (2) BGB provides that the consumer may claim damages and compensation for futile expenses according to the general provisions of the German law of obligations.

56   For the lack of conformity, the basic rule in § 327 i BGB contains a catalogue of the consumer's rights, which is concretised and supplemented by the following provisions. According to the model of the DCD, this catalogue includes the cure according to § 327 l BGB, the termination of the contract according to § 327 m BGB and the reduction of the price according to § 327 n BGB. In addition to the remedies provided for in the DCD, it also stipulates by reference to the general provisions of the law of obligations that the consumer may also claim damages and compensation for futile expenses.

2. Sale of Goods

57   For the sale of goods, the German legislator has not enacted any specific provisions when transposing the SGD, for the cases of failure of supply (which are not covered by this Directive). Rather, the general provisions of the law of obligations apply (including the general provisions for consumer contracts), which provide in particular for revocation (after expiry of an additional period), damages and compensation for futile expenses (§§ 323; 280,281; 284 BGB).

58   For the lack of conformity, the implementation of the SGD has led to a rather complex regulation. § 437 BGB, which served as a model for § 327 i BGB[51], contains – similar to this for digital products – a catalogue of the buyer's rights with references to the following provisions in the law of sales and to provisions in the general law of obligations. On this basis, the buyer can also demand cure, rescission from the contract or price reduction and demand damages or compensation for futile expenses. However, a number of the provisions of the General Sales Law and the General Law of Obligations referred to in § 437 BGB are specifically applied to consumer sales contracts (in the sense of the definition of "sale of consumer goods" in § 474 BGB) with modifications and additions that §§ 475 and 475 d et seq. BGB set out. These deviations from the general

---

[49] See explanatory statement in the government draft BT-Drs. 19/27653, p. 23.
[50] See below E V.
[51] See explanatory statement in the government draft BT Drs. 19/27653, 60.

provisions concern, among other things, the time for the respective performance, the risk of accidental deterioration, substitution for the value of benefits, advance payment for expenses, the time limit and modalities of cure, the costs of return (§ 475 (1) to (6) BGB), the setting of a time limit for rescission or damages (§ 475 d BGB) and the limitation of claims (§ 475 e BGB). In addition, § 475 a BGB provides for further deviations from the general provisions on an even more specific level (under the heading "consumer goods sales contract for digital products") in order to fully implement the SGD provisions for physical data carriers that serve exclusively as carriers of digital content (§ 475 d (1) BGB) and for contracts for goods with digital elements (§ 475 d (2) BGB). For the latter, it is stipulated, among other things, that the provisions of the new title on digital products (§§ 327 et seq. BGB) replace provisions of the law on sales concerning the time of performance and the rights of the buyer in case of defects.

3. Right to Withhold

The German legislator has not regulated the right to withhold in the context of the implementation of the "twin directives". According to Recital 15 DCD, the Member States should still be free to regulate the rights to withhold. This suggests that the previously existing provisions remain applicable in principle to contracts within the scope of application of the directives. Therefore, the consumer has a right to withhold payment according to § 273 BGB if he has a due claim against the trader from the legal relationship from which he is obliged to pay (for example, the due claim for delivery of the good or for supply of the digital product). In addition, the consumer can refuse the payment on the basis of § 320 (1) BGB under the conditions that he owes the payment from a mutual contract and that he is not obliged to perform in advance.[52]

II. Place of Delivery and Place of Repair and Replacement

No special provisions have been created for the place of delivery in the implementation of the "twin directives". Rather, the general provisions are to be applied (in particular § 269 BGB). This also applies in principle to cure by repair or replacement.[53] This has not changed due to the new § 439 (5) BGB. This provision merely stipulates the buyer's duty to make the item available to the seller so that he can examine the item for defects and carry out the cure.[54] It does not, however, specify the place where the obligation to cure is to be fulfilled. Even if the place of repair is therefore in principle to be determined according to the general rules on the place of performance, it must however be taken into account that the consumer must not suffer any "considerable inconvenience" (cf. Art. 14 (1) SGD). It must therefore be examined in each individual case whether this limit is exceeded, for example, if the way to the workshop is unusually long when repairing a car.[55]

---

[52] In detail on the requirements of these provisions Schulze, in: Dannemann and Schulze (eds), *German Civil Code I* (2020), § 273, mn. 6 et seq.; Oehm, in: Dannemann and Schulze (eds), *German Civil Code I* (2020), § 270, mn. 6 et seq.

[53] Bundesgerichtshof (Federal Court of Justice) (BGH) 13.04.2011 – VIII ZR 220/10 – NJW 11, 2278, 2280.

[54] BR- Drs. 146/21, 24.

[55] In detail Schulze, in: Schulze et al., *Handkommentar BGB* (2022), § 269, mn. 5; Saenger, in: Schulze et al., *Handkommentar BGB* (2022), § 439, mn. 11; Schaub, in: Dannemann and Schulze (eds), *German Civil Code I* (2020), § 439, mn. 8.

III. Cost of Transport in the Event of a Repair

61 For the cost of repair or replacement the General Sales Law contains the rule that the seller must bear all expenses required for the purpose of cure, including transport (§ 439 (2) BGB). If the buyer has installed the defective thing in another thing in accordance with its nature and purpose of use or has affixed it to another thing, the seller is also obliged within the scope of cure to reimburse the buyer for the expenses necessary for removing the defective thing and for the installation or affixing of the repaired or newly delivered thing free of defects (§ 439 (3) BGB). Specifically for consumer sales, it is also stipulated that in these two situations the consumer can demand advanced payment from the trader (§ 475 (4) BGB).

IV. Right of Termination

1. Declaration

62 The right to terminate a contract for the supply of digital products due to failure to supply or lack of conformity with the contract is exercised by declaration (§ 327 o in conjunction with §§ 327 c, 327 m BGB). This corresponds not only to the provision of Art. 15 DCD, but also to the German tradition. In this tradition, especially two core terms of the law of obligations functionally correspond to the "termination" of the contract in the European Directives: on the one hand the revocation of the contract or "recission"[56] ("*Rücktritt vom Vertrag*"; §§ 323 et seq. BGB) and on the other hand the termination, for a compelling reason, of contracts for the performance of a continuing obligation ("*Kündigung eines Dauerschuldverhältnisses aus wichtigem Grund*"; § 314 BGB). These two rights are exercised by a declaration of the entitled party to the other party. The same applies to a number of other rights that enable a release from the contract (such as the avoidance for mistake or on the ground of deceit or duress according to §§ 119, 123, 143 BGB and the rights of withdrawal in consumer contacts according to §§ 355 et seq. BGB). The right of withdrawal regarding the consent to the processing of personal data is also exercised through declaration. An overarching theoretical basis for these different rights is the doctrine of "formative rights".[57]

2. Uniform Requirements

63 Although the declaration as an instrument of the entitled party to release from the contract has long been familiar to German lawyers, the implementation of the provisions of the DCD on the termination of the contract has led to an important innovation for German law. With the term "termination of the contract", the German legislator adopts a term from the EU legislation that is new to the law of obligations in the BGB. This term is now used in §§ 327 c and 327 m BGB as a generic term for factual situations that were previously designated and regulated separately[58] (as just mentioned): on the one hand revocation or recission ("*Rücktritt*"); on the other hand, termination of contracts with continuing obligations ("*Kündigung*"). The former used to be the basic model

---

[56] Both English terms are commonly used as translation of "Rücktritt"; see e.g., Schaub, in: Dannemann and Schulze (eds), *German Civil Code I* (2020), § 437, mn. 9.

[57] Schulze and Zoll, *European Contract Law* (2021), ch. 5, mn. 58; Schaub, in: Dannemann and Schulze (eds), *German Civil Code I* (2020), § 437, mn. 9.

[58] Schulze, 'Recent Influences of the European Acquis – Communautaire on German Contract Law' (2022) 17 *NTBR*, 138 (138 et seq.).

E. Remedies for the Failure to Supply and Remedies for the Lack of Conformity

of resolution of mutual contracts; the latter was the specific form of resolution of contracts with continuing obligations (such as leasing, company and insurance contracts and similar types of "long-term contracts"). Art. 13, 14 (2) and 15 DCD have now served as a model for the German legislator to establish uniform requirements for termination of the contract in §§ 327 c and 327 o (1) BGB for these two factual situations. Although according to these provisions the uniform concept of termination of the contract is only applicable to contracts on digital products, the sectoral introduction could raise the question of whether in future such an approach should acquire more general significance in German law (especially since the current conceptual structure is under discussion[59]).

3. Restitution

Where the trader supplies digital products to a consumer, the legal consequences of a termination of the contract including matters of restitution are regulated in the 327 o (2) to (5) and 327 p BGB. These provisions contain a new regime of restitution and return after termination of contracts. Although it is in principle compatible with the traditional German doctrine of the statutory restitutionary relationship ("*gesetzliches Rückgewährschuldverhältnis*")[60], it deviates in part from the traditional German regime of the consequences of a revocation of the contract in §§ 346 et seq. BGB and, on the basis of Art. 16 to 18 DCD, leads to an innovative adaptation of this area of German law of obligations to requirements of the digital age and in particular of trade with data. Among other things, it stipulates that the trader must reimburse the consumer for payments made by the consumer to fulfil the contract and that the trader's claim to payment of the agreed price expires for services that the trader is no longer required to provide due to the termination of the contract (§ 327 o (2) BGB). The consumer is obliged to return tangible media which he has received from the trader (§ 327 o (5) BGB). In addition, such new items and legal instruments are regulated as the prohibition of use and the blocking of use of data and the recovery of data (§ 327 p BGB). These provisions are directly applicable only to consumer contracts on digital products. But they contain terms and principles that can also be applied to the termination of many other types of contracts involving data. It seems likely that contractual practice will make use of this conceptual stock beyond consumer law. In this respect, the provisions transposing the Directive may form the nucleus for future general rules in the law of obligations on the termination of contracts concerning data. 64

V. Contractual Consequences of Withdrawal of Consent for Processing Data

One of the open questions after the enactment of the DCD was, in particular, what the consequences under contract law are if the consumer provides personal data on the basis of a contract and initially gives his consent under data protection law to the processing of this data, but then withdraws this consent pursuant to Art. 7 (3) of the General Data Protection Regulation. The German legislator has now regulated the consequences of this withdrawal under data protection law and of other declarations of the consumer under data protection law in § 327 q BGB. With this provision, it has au- 65

---

[59] Doralt, *Langzeitverträge* (2018).
[60] Wendland, in: Dannemann and Schulze (eds), *German Civil Code I* (2020), § 346, mn. 8.

tonomously created an additional regulation within the subtitle on contracts for digital products beyond the implementation of the provisions of the DCD.

66 The main purpose of this provision is to clarify that no sanctions under contract law should occur if the consumer exercises his rights under data protection law. According to § 327 q (1) BGB, therefore, the validity of his contract with the trader remains unaffected when exercising rights under data protection law; and according to para. 3 of this provision, claims for compensation by the trader due to restrictions on his data processing are excluded. This is to ensure that the consumer can exercise his data protection rights without hindrance and without having to fear legal disadvantages.[61] However, according to § 327 (2) BGB, the trader should have the right to terminate the contract without a notice period if it obliges him to provide a number of individual digital products or to provide a digital product on a permanent basis. Though, this right of termination is limited by further conditions: The continuation of the contract until the agreed end of the contract or until the expiry of a notice period must be unreasonable for the trader. In order to assess this, the interests of both parties must be weighed; and the extent to which data processing is still permissible in the specific case despite the consumer's withdrawal must also be taken into account. As these latter provisions show particularly clearly, with § 337 q BGB the German legislator is aiming overall for an appropriate balance of interests between consumer and trader with regard to the consequences under contract law associated with the exercise of rights based on data protection.

VI. Price Reduction

67 The implementation of Art. 14 (4) and (5) DCD on price reduction has also led to a remarkable structural innovation for the German law of obligations. On this basis, §§ 327 i No. 2 and § 327 n BGB now provide for the consumer's right to reduce the price in contracts for digital products, irrespective of the type of contract. The price reduction has thus found its way into the General Law of Obligations. Previously, it had only specifically regulated for a number of individual contract types in the Special Law of Obligations (e.g., for sale; lease and services; § 437 No. 2 in conjunction with § 441; § 536; § 638 BGB). Although this innovation only applies within the scope of application of the rules for contracts on digital products, it could have an influence on the discussion as to whether price reduction in German law deserves recognition in principle as a creditor's right not specifically bound to certain types of contracts and should therefore be assigned to general contract law (as is also the case in the drafts for European contract law).[62]

VII. Items not covered by the Implementation of the Directives

1. Environmental Sustainability

68 In order to enhance environmental sustainability, the German legislator has limited itself in the implementation of the "twin directives" to introducing the provision on

---

[61] See explanatory statement in the government draft BT Drs. 19/27653, 75.
[62] Art. 9:401 PECL; following it, Art. III.-3:601 DCFR. Art. 120 and 155 CESL accordingly provide for price reduction both for sales contracts and for contracts on digital content as well as for related service contracts. See Schulze and Zoll, *European Contract Law* (2021), ch. 6, mn. 100 et seq. and for example in the new French law of obligations Art. 1223 Code civil.

the durability of the goods into the law of sale.[63] However, within this framework it has not created any further-reaching regulations in ecological terms, such as a priority of repair over replacement or additional specific measures against premature planned obsolescence of goods.

2. Subsequent Buyer

When implementing the twin Directives, the German legislator did not create additional standards to regulate the relationship between the initial seller and a subsequent buyer. However, irrespective of their implementation, a new provision came into force shortly before, which restricts the exclusion of assignments by general terms and conditions (§ 308 No. 9 BGB). It is mainly aimed at facilitating legal tech business models.[64] It remains to be seen whether it will also have an impact on assignments from an initial consumer to a subsequent buyer in the case of the digital products under consideration here.

F. Commercial Guarantees

The warranty of the seller and also of the manufacturer and any other third party is regulated within the framework of the General Sales Law in § 443 BGB. Specifically, for guarantees in a consumer purchase, § 476 (1) BGB sets out the mandatory character of these provisions and § 479 BGB provides for special provisions in terms of form and content based on Art. 17 SGD. In particular, according to para. 1 and 2 of this provision, the commercial guarantee statement shall be expressed in plain, intelligible language, must contain information in accordance with the requirements of Art. 17 (2) SGD and shall be provided to the consumer on a durable medium at the latest at the time of the delivery of the goods. Para. 3 provides for minimum requirements for guarantees of durability according to the model of Art. 17 (1) p. 2 and 3 SGD; and para. 4 specifies the binding effect according to Art. 17 (3) SGD. However, when the German legislator implemented the directive, in the BGB it has not made use of the option provided for in Art. 17 (4) SGD by supplementing this provision with additional rules on the language or languages in which the commercial guarantee statement is to be made available to the consumer.

G. Time Limits

I. Sale of Goods

The provisions of Art. 10 SGD on time limits are implemented by § 438 BGB in the General Sales Law and § 475 e BGB in the Consumer Sales Law. According to these provisions the limitation period for defects of the goods is in principle two years (§ 438 (2) no. 3). However, if a defect has become apparent within this period, the limitation period does not start to run before the expiry of four months (§ 475 e (3) BGB). A period of one year from the transfer of risk is provided for the reversal of the burden of proof in favour of the consumer (§ 477 BGB). The German legislator has not made use of the options in Art. 10 (2) and 11 (2) SGD.

---

[63] See above C III.
[64] Schulte-Nölke, in: Schulze et al., *Handkommentar BGB* (2022), § 308, mn. 28.

72 For material defects of goods with digital elements § 475 e (1) and (2) BGB contain special provisions if the trader owes a permanent provision or if an updating obligation is breached. In these cases, the limitation period does not end before the expiry of twelve months after the period of supply or of the period of obligation to update. For special situations in which the consumer has handed over the good to a third party at the trader's instigation, the limitation period also does not start before two months after the return of the goods to the consumer in accordance with § 475 e (4) BGB, in order to ensure that the consumer has sufficient time to inspect the goods.[65]

II. Supply of digital products

73 The provisions of Art. 11 (2) and (3) DCD on time limits are implemented in § 327 j BGB. Accordingly, claims for product defects and defects of title generally become statute-barred two years after the supply of the digital product. This is modified by a corresponding suspension period of four months as provided for in § 475 e (3) BGB. For the permanent supply and the breach of updating obligations, corresponding special rules are also laid down as in § 437 e (1) and (2). The government draft for the new provisions has argued against an extension of the regular limitation period beyond two years with two arguments: The special features of digital products do not require such a deviation from the previous law for sales contracts and contracts for work and services; and of greater importance for consumers was the reversal of the burden of proof.[66] For this reversal of the burden of proof, § 327 k BGB (corresponding to Art. 12 DCD) provides for a period of one year since supply and, in the case of permanent supply, the period of supply.

III. Notification

74 The German legislator has not made use of the possibility under Art. 12 DCD to introduce a duty to notify. In Germany, such a notification is neither provided for in the General Sales Law nor in the Consumer Sales Law, but only concerns sales contracts between merchants (§ 377 German Commercial Code).

H. Right of Redress

75 The rights of redress according to Art. 20 DCD and Art. 18 SGD are implemented in Germany in such a way that the traders are not entitled to a direct claim against the manufacturer or a choice among the preceding links in the business chain, but that they are limited to a claim against their respective contractual partner. According to § 327 u BGB (for the supply of digital products) and §§ 445 a ff., 478 BGB (for the sale of goods), the last trader in the business chain may recover its expenses from the preceding link in the business chain if this preceding link has caused the expenses by a failure to supply or by the breach of an updating obligation according to § 327 f BGB or if the defect was already present at the time of supply/delivery by it. Accordingly, this previous link and all other previous links in the business chain can take action against the respective previous link.

---

[65] See explanatory statement in the government draft BT Drs. 19/27424, 41.
[66] See explanatory statement in the government draft BT Drs. 19/27653, 60.

In addition, these provisions on redress also take into account the further effects of the provisions on the relationship between the last trader and the consumer on the preceding contractual relationships in the business chain. Among other things, a limitation period of six months is provided for claims for reimbursement of expenses in the case of the sale of digital products and of two years in the case of the sale of goods (§§ 327 u (2) and 445 b BGB with more detailed provisions on the beginning of the period). The reversal of the burden of proof in the relationship of the last trader continues in the relationships of the previous links in the business chain to each other (§§ 327 u (3) and 478 (1) BGB). The preceding link in the business chain cannot rely on deviating agreements to the detriment of the following ones (§§ 327 u (4) and 478 (2) BGB with further specifications).

I. Relationship with other remedies

The implementation of the "twin directives" within the framework of the Civil Code has enabled the German legislator to integrate the remedies provided for by the directive into the system of creditors' rights in the German law of obligations and to develop this system further through the requirements of the directives.[67] For example, the references in §§ 327 c (2), 327 (3), 437 no. 3 BGB to the general provisions on damages have built bridges from the transposition of these Directives to core provisions of the German law of obligations, which were essentially created by the 2002 reform on the basis of the CSD. In the law of sales, moreover, the new provisions on remedies as a whole have been inserted into a structure that has essentially emerged from this reform by modifying or supplementing a number of already existing provisions.[68] The new provisions for digital products in particular contribute to the further development of the system of remedies in the German law of obligations. They integrate price reduction for their area of application into the General law of obligations (§§ 327 c (1), 327 m (1), 327 o BGB); and in this respect they replace the dualism of "revocation" (or "recission") and "termination" (termination of contracts that provide for a continuing obligation) (§§ 327 n BGB) with the termination of the contract as an overarching regulation.[69]

J. Conclusion

Taken as a whole, the implementation of the "twin directives" has brought about both: considerably deepened the "Europeanisation" of the German law of obligations on the basis of the 2002 reforms and considerably advanced its adaptation to the changes in the digital age after the preceding smaller steps. The integration of consumer law into the German Civil Code has made it much easier for the two Directives to gain such influence on the development of German law of obligations. Based on this integration, the German Civil Code now contains a separate set of rules for contracts on digital products in a subtitle within the General Law of Obligations (§§ 327 et seq. BGB) and numerous new provisions in the Sales Law, some of which (as a result of "extended" transposition) concern all sales contracts, others specifically consumer sales.

One of the most important consequences of the transposition is the further development of the systematics of the Civil Code through the inclusion of the new subtitle and

---

[67] See above A II.
[68] See above E I 2.
[69] See above E IV and VI.

the provisions for consumer sales contracts for digital products and for goods with digital elements (§§ 475 a et seq. BGB). This is associated with a considerable expansion of the legal conceptualisation and terminology of German civil law, especially with regard to the new objects that are included as a result of digitalisation. In part, this terminology has been taken over directly from the Directives into German civil law – from "goods with digital elements" to elements of conformity with the contract such as "functionality", "compatibility", "interoperability", etc. In part, however, the German legislator has also developed the European models independently. This concerns, for example, the terms "digital products" as a generic term for digital contents and digital services (§ 327 (1) BGB), "things with digital elements" as an extension of "goods with digital elements" to include immovables (§ 327 a BGB) and "period of supply" (§ 327 e (1) BGB). This conceptual arsenal can be used far beyond the scope of application of the " twin directives" in the practice of contracting and the related case law for other areas of the supply of digital products (also in B – B relationships) and of trade with data. In this respect, the provisions transposing the Directives contain starting points for the development of a general terminology (not limited to consumer law) with which German civil law can adapt to the new requirements of the digital age based on European models.

80   The transposition provisions also contain a number of other innovations that will concern German jurisprudence and legal doctrine in the near future, and which may also have an impact on German law beyond the scope of the Directives. In particular, the new rules on the provision of data by the consumer take into account the immense economic and legal importance of personal data for the first time under German law of obligations. With the "termination of contract", a new approach has also found its way into German contract law (deviating from the previous dualism of revocation or recission on the one hand and the "termination" of continuing obligations on the other). At the same time, new concepts have been developed for the legal consequences of contract termination, which take into account the peculiarities of the supply of digital products and trade in data (including specific prohibitions of use and claims for recovery of digital content). Price reduction has been given a place in the General Law of Obligations for the first time (whereas it was previously only provided for in the Special Law of Obligations for individual types of contracts). Furthermore, the provisions on updating have relativised the traditional model of the "transfer of risk" and led to a dynamisation of contractual obligations in the law of sales. In addition to these legal responses to the challenges of digitalisation, one of the new contours that sales law has acquired in the course of the implementation of the Directives is that the durability of the good has become an objective criterion of conformity with the contract and thus the idea of sustainability has found its way into this area of law.

81   The example of all these approaches shows that the implementation of the "twin directives" has not only had a considerable impact on the recent development of the German law of obligations and can be regarded as its most important reform since the modernisation of 2002. Rather, the new provisions also offer numerous starting points for future developments in this area of law far beyond the matters now regulated. The tendency towards the development of a German law of obligations with European features, which had become apparent in the modernisation of 2002, therefore seems to continue and intensify in view of the new challenges of the digital age.

Bibliography

Beurskens, in: Dannemann and Schulze (eds), *German Civil Code I* (2020), I, § 13 mn. 4, § 14 mn. 4 mn. 52, 53.

Dannemann and Schulze, in: Dannemann and Schulze (eds), *German Civil Code I* (2020), Introduction, mn. 52, 53.

Dix, 'Daten als Bezahlung – Zum Verhältnis zwischen Zivilrecht und Datenschutzrecht' (2017), *ZEuP*, 1 (1 et seq.).

Doralt, *Langzeitverträge* (2018).

Ferrante, 'The Amended Proposal COM (2017) 637: a „New" European Sales Law?', in Janssen and Schulte-Nölke (eds), *Researches in European Private Law and Beyond* (2020), 43 (43 et seq.).

Fries, 'Data as Counter-Performance in B2B Contracts' in Lohsse et al., *Data as Counter-Performance – Contract Law 2.0?* (2020), 253 (253 et seq.).

Güster and Booke, 'Umsetzung der Warenkaufrichtlinie'(2022), *MMR*, 92.

Huber and Faust, *Schuldrechtsmodernisierung* (2002).

Janssen, 'The Update Obligation for Smart Products – Time Period for the Update Obligation and Failure to Install the Update' in Lohsee et al. (eds) *Smart Products* (2022), 91 et seq.

Kieninger, 'Recht auf Reparatur („Right to Repair") und europäisches Vertragsrecht' (2020), 2 *ZEuP*, 274 (274 et seq.).

Lohsse et al., *Data as Counter-Performance – Contract Law 2.0?* (2020).

Lohsse et al., 'Trading Data in the Digital Economy' in Lohsse et al. (eds), *Trading Data in the Digital Economy* (2017), 13, 14.

Lorenz, 'Die Umsetzung der EU-Warenkaufrichtlinie in deutsches Recht (2021)', *NJW*, 2065.

Lorenz, 'Schuldrechtsreform 2002: Problemschwerpunkte drei Jahre danach' (2005) *NJW*, 1889.

Metzger, 'Dienst gegen Daten: Ein synallagmatischen Vertrag' (2016), 216 *AcP*, 817 (817 et seq.).

Metzger, 'Verträge über digitale Inhalte und digitale Dienstleistungen: Neuer BGB-Vertragstypus oder punktuelle Reform?' (2019), *JZ*, 577 (584).

Oehm, in: Dannemann and Schulze (eds), *German Civil Code I* (2020), § 313, mn. 12.

Rosenkranz, 'Spezifische Vorschriften zu Verträgen über die Bereitstellung digitaler Produkte im BGB' (2021) *ZUM*, 195 (196 et seq.).

Specht, 'Daten als Gegenleistung – verlangt die Digitalisierung nach einem neuen Vertragstypus?' (2017), *JZ*, 763 (763 et seq.).

Saenger, in: Schulze et al., *Handkommentar BGB* (2022), § 434, mn. 27.

Schaub, in: Dannemann and Schulze (eds), *German Civil Code I* (2020), § 437, mn. 9.

Schmidt-Kessel, Right to Withdraw Consent to Data Processing – The Effect on the Contract, Lohsse et al. (eds), *Trading Data in the Digital Economy* (2017), 129 (129 et seq.).

Schmidt-Kessel/Grimm, 'Unentgeltlich oder entgeltlich? – Der vertragliche Austausch von digitalen Inhalten gegen personenbezogene Daten' (2017), *ZfPW*, 84 (84 et seq.).

Schulte-Nölke, 'Digital obligations of sellers of smart devices under the Sale of Goods Directive 771/2019' in Lohsee et al. (eds) *Smart Products* (2022), 47 et seq.

Schulze et al., 'Contracts for the Supply of Digital Content: Regulatory Challenges and Gaps – An Introduction', in Schulze et al., *Contracts for the Supply of Digital Content: Regulatory Challenges and Gaps* (2017), 11 (11, 22 et seq.).

Schulze, 'Die Digitale-Inhalte-Richtlinie – Innovation und Kontinuität im europäischen Vertragsrecht' (2019) 4 *ZEuP*, 695 (702 s.).

Schulze, 'Die Verletzung vertraglicher Pflichten im System des chinesischen und des deutschen Zivilrechts' in Möllers and Hao Li (eds), *Der Besondere Teil des chinesischen Zivilgestzbuchs. Zwischen Tradition und Moderne* (2022), 155 (155, 174 et seq.).

Schulze, 'Haftung auf Schadensersatz im Vergleich' (2022), in Kindl et al. (eds), *Die Schadensersatzhaftung* (2022), 123 (123 et seq.).

Schulze, 'Recent Influences of the European Acquis – Communautaire on German Contract Law' (2022) 17 *NTBR*, 132 (132).

Schulze and Schulte-Nölke, 'Schuldrechtsreform und Gemeinschaftsrecht' in Schulze and Schulte-Nölke (eds), *Die Schuldrechtsreform vor dem Hintergrund des Gemeinschaftsrechts* (2001) 3 et seq.

Schulze and Zoll, *European Contract Law* (2021).

Spindler, 'Contract Law and Copyright – Regulatory Challenges and Gaps', in Schulze et al., *Contracts for the Supply of Digital Content: Regulatory Challenges and Gaps* (2017), 211 (211 et seq.).

Spindler, 'Umsetzung der Richtlinie über digitale Inhalte in das BGB' (2021), *MMR*, 451 (456 et seq.); Schulze, in: Schulze et al., *Handkommentar BGB* (2022), § 327 h mn. 5, 6.

Spindler and Sein, 'Die endgültige Richtlinie über Verträge über digitale Inhalte und Dienstleistungen' (2019), *MMR*, 415 (416).

Wendehorst, 'The update obligation – how to make it work in the relationship between seller, producer, digital content or service provider and consumer' in Lohsee et al. (eds) *Smart Products* (2022), 63 et seq.

Wendland, in: Dannemann and Schulze (eds), *German Civil Code I* (2020), § 346, mn. 8.

Greece

A. Introduction ... 1
  I. L. 4967/2022: structure and main regulatory choices ... 1
    1. State act for the transposition ... 1
    2. Contract for the provision of digital content or digital service ... 3
    3. Sale of Goods ... 7
  II. Notions and definitions ... 9
  III. Personal data as counter-performance ... 13

B. Conformity of Goods-Main obligations of the supplier ... 14
  I. Sale of Goods ... 14
  II. Provision of digital content or digital service ... 20
    1. Initial non-performance of the supplier's obligations ... 20
    2. Non conformity of the digital content or the digital service ... 24
    3. Non performance of the recipient's obligations ... 29
  III. Goods with digital elements ... 31

C. Liability of the supplier-remedies ... 34
  I. Sale of Goods ... 34
  II. Digital Content-Digital Service ... 43
    1. Remedies of the recipient ... 43
    2. The case of personal data as counter-performance ... 48

D. Commercial guarantees ... 50

E. Time limits ... 54
  1. Sale of Goods ... 54
  2. Digital content and digital service ... 58

F. Right of Redress ... 60

G. Epilogue ... 61

  Bibliography ... 63

A. Introduction

I. L. 4967/2022: structure and main regulatory choices

1. State act for the transposition

L. 4967/2022 (*"Transposition of the Directive (EU) 2019/770 of the European Parliament and of the Council of 20 May 2019 on certain aspects concerning contracts for the supply of digital content and digital services (L. 136), as well as the Directive (EU) 2019/771 of the European Parliament and of the Council of 20 May 2019 on certain aspects concerning contracts for the sale of goods, amending Regulation (EU) 2017/2394 and Directive 2009/22/EC, and repealing Directive 1999/44/EC (L. 136) and other provisions"*) was approved by the Greek Parliament on the 7th of September 2022, and published in the Official Gazette (FEK) on the 9th of September, 2022 (A-171/09.07.2022). As per the provision of art. 70, the law was put into effect on the 9th of September 2022 (date of publication in the Official Gazette). 1

The Greek Legislator adopted a mixed approach for the implementation of the "Twin Directives". The DCD (EU 2019/770) was implemented through the introduction of a new contract form, the "Contract for the provision of digital content or digital service" in a separate regulation system (art. 3–32 L. 4967/2022). On the contrary, the SGD (EU 2019/771) was implemented through the amendment of the provisions of the Greek Civ- 2 il Code on Sale (art. 534–561 GrCC) and of L. 2251/1994 (On Consumer protection)[1]. It is, however, to be noted that the Greek Law expanded the scope of application *of both directives*, since the new Law shall not only apply in supplier-consumer (B2C) relationships, but in all contracts. As a result, the rules which will be adopted, both on the new contractual form and on the amendment of the Civil Code, will govern the provision of digital content and digital service and the sale of goods, irrespectively of the status of the parties.

2. Contract for the provision of digital content or digital service

3   Part B of the Law (Titled *"Transposition of the Directive (EU) 2019/770"*) contains 30 articles and provides regulation for the "Contract for the provision of digital content or digital service". The Legislator chose to introduce a new form of contract[2] and provide for the regulation of its main aspects. However, the regulation does not cover all issues (formation, conditions of validity, termination etc), but mainly emphasises on the aspects regulated by directive 2019/770. This should not be seen as a weak point of the legislator, as this type of regulation is in harmony with the Greek Civil Law system. Like its model, the German BGB[3], the Greek Civil Code consists of five books, the first one with the title "General Principles". In this first book, basic institutions common to the whole of private law are examined, among which the "juridical act" (art. 127–200 GrCC). This regulation (formation, validity, nullity etc) governs all specific juridical acts that are regulated in the other books (Law of Obligations, Property Law etc)[4]. Furthermore, the Greek Law of Obligations is traditionally divided into a General Part and a Special Part. The General Part (art. 287–495 GrCC) provides general rules for all types of obligations (performance, termination, fault, breach etc)[5]. As a result, the regulation of specific forms of contracts (in the Special Part of the Law of Obligations, or in special laws) only needs to contain regulation on matters that are regulated in a different way than the provisions of the General Principles and the General Part of the Law of Obligations (specific types of breach, such as liability for defects, special ways of termination etc). In this sense, the rules governing the "Contract for the provision of digital content or digital service" consists of the provisions of the above-mentioned rules of the Greek Civil Code (General Principles and General Part of the Law of Obligations), and the specific provisions of art. 3 ff L. 4967/2022.

4   As per the provision of art. 3 L. 4967/2022 *"A contract for the provision of digital content or a digital service is a contract where the supplier undertakes[6] to supply digital content or a digital service to the recipient and the recipient undertakes to pay the price"*. Art. 5

---

[1] In favour of this approach see Valtoudis, *Directive 2019/771 on Consumer Sales and its implementation in Greek Law*, Greek Justice 2020, 1616-1617.

[2] For the division between regulated and non-regulated specific obligations in Greek Law see, among others, Georgiades, *Law of Obligations, Special Part, Manual* (2014), § 2 mn. 1 ff.; Kornilakis, *Law of Obligations, Special Part, Handbook* (2020), § 2 mn. 1 ff.

[3] On the structure of BGB see, among others, Zweigert and Kötz (transl. Weir), *An Introduction to Comparative Law* (1998), 144 ff; Larenz and Wolf, *General part of the BGB (in German)* (2004), § 1 mn. 47 ff.

[4] See, among others, Georgiades, *General Principles of Civil Law* (2019), § 7 mn. 3–4; Ladas, *General Principles of Civil Law I* (2007), § 2 mn. 30; Papasteriou, *General Principles of Civil Law* (2009), § 1 mn. 49 ff.

[5] Stathopoulos, *Law of Obligations, General Part* (2018), § 1 mn. 6; Georgiades, *Law of Obligations, General Part* (2015), § 1 mn. 5; Kornilakis, *Law of Obligations, Special Part, Handbook* (2020), § 1 mn. 2.

[6] Greek Law did not adopt the wording "supplies or undertakes to supply" of the directive, since, according to the Greek legal system, transactions whose ultimate aim is the transfer of a right require two contracts: with the first one, obligations are undertaken, and with the second one obligations are fulfilled. In other words, the promissory contract is distinguished from the contract which transfers the right. See Stathopoulos, *Law of Obligations, General Part* (2018), § 4 mn. 11 ff.

par.1a reads that the provisions of the law also apply when through the contract the recipient undertakes the obligation to provide personal data to the supplier as a price[7]. The legislator chose to provide for a new, special form of contract, describing the main obligations of the parties, rather than attempting to regulate the rights and duties of the parties in existing contractual types (sale, work, services etc.) which could have the supply of digital content or digital service as their object.

According to art. 5 par. 6 of L. 4967/2022, the provisions of the law shall not affect the provisions of the EU and national legislation on intellectual property and related rights. L. 4967/2022 does not regulate whether, through the conclusion of a contract for the provision of digital content and digital service, the recipient obtains any intellectual property rights on the digital element. As a result, the rights and obligations of the recipient of the digital elements regarding intellectual property rights, both towards the supplier and towards third parties (allowed use of the elements, specific rights, protection etc) shall be governed by the applicable legislation and the relevant terms of the contract for the provision of digital content or digital service.

While the Directive (EU) 2019/770 applies only to relationships between suppliers and consumers (any natural person who, in relation to contracts covered by the Directive, is acting for purposes which are outside that person's trade, business, craft, or profession), L. 4967/2022 regulates the contract for the provision of digital elements in general, i.e. without limiting its scope to B2C relationships. As already mentioned, art. 3 reads that the contract for the provision of digital content or digital service may be concluded between a "supplier" and a "recipient" (any natural or legal person which is supplied with digital content or digital service). However, art. 30 of the law reads that (only) if the recipient is a consumer, the provisions of the law are considered *ius cogens*. Agreements which deviate from the provisions of the law to the detriment of the consumer are null, while deviation in favour of the consumer is valid. On the contrary, if the recipient is not a consumer, i.e. acts for purposes which fall within that person's trade, business, craft, or profession, the supplier and the recipient may freely adopt agreements contrary to the provisions of the L. 4967/2022[8].

3. Sale of Goods

Part C of the Law (Titled *"Transposition of the Directive (EU) 2019/771"*) contains 31 articles and amends existing Greek legislation, the Greek Civil Code (Chapter A of the Part) and L. 2251/1994, on *"Consumer Protection"* (Chapter B of the Part).

The Greek legislator chose to implement the Sale of Goods Directive in the Greek Civil Code, expanding the scope of application in all contracts of sale. This solution was also adopted in the implementation of the Directive 99/44/EC: L. 3043/2002 had also amended the Greek Civil Code, expanding the regulation of the directive to all types of sale, including B2B contracts. According to the explanatory memorandum of L. 4967/2022, the expansion of the scope of application serves the coherence and

---

[7] Except where the personal data provided by the recipient are exclusively processed by the supplier for the purpose of supplying the digital content or digital service or for allowing the supplier to comply with legal requirements to which he/she is subject, and the supplier does not process those data for any other purpose (art. 5 par. 2 of L. 4967/2022).

[8] In any case, taking into account that, according to art. 332 GrCC, any agreement limiting liability for wilful conduct or gross negligence is null. Furthermore, if the exoneration clause is contained in a term of the contract which was not an object of individual negotiation (especially if it is contained in standard terms), limitation of liability even for slight negligence is also null. See indicatively Stathopoulos, *Law of Obligations, General Part* (2018), § 6 mn. 124 ff; Georgiades, *Law of Obligations, General Part* (2015), § 23 mn. 56 ff; Spyridakis, *Law of Obligations, General Part* (2018), 96 ff.

integrity of the system of contract law and strengthens its evaluative unity, as every sale is regulated in a uniform manner, regardless of the status of the parties as traders or consumers. Moreover, the occasion of implementation of Directive (EU) 2019/771 was considered an opportunity to update the provisions of GrCC on sale, so that they fit the needs of modern digital economy.

II. Notions and definitions

9   As far as the definitions contained in the DCD (Art. 2) and the SGD (Art. 2) are concerned, L. 4967/2022 adopted different solutions.

10 Art. 3 of the Law (titled *"Definitions"*) contains 14 definitions which apply for the regulation of the contract of provision of digital content or digital service. Most of the definitions correspond to the definitions of Art. 2 of the DCD (digital content, digital service, thing with digital elements, integration, compatibility, functionality, interoperability, durable medium, consumer, digital environment), while others define notions chosen by the Greek Law (supplier, recipient).

11 Regarding the SGD, and taking into account that it was transposed into the Greek Civil Code, the legislator limited the definitions to minimum and chose different ways of providing a definition. Some of the definitions were included *into the text of the law*, not in a specific article, but in the way that is used in the GrCC, i.e. including the word defined in parentheses just after its definition[9]; the notions "thing with digital elements" "digital content" and "digital service" are defined in a separate subparagraph of art. 513A, which regulates the extension of the scope of contracts for sale[10]; other notions (sales contract, goods, seller, free of charge) were not defined, as were considered to describe notions whose meaning is widely accepted in Greek Law.

12 As is obvious, most notions that are to be considered crucial for the application of the directives and, in any case, were not previously defined in Greek Law (digital content, digital service, goods with digital elements, integration, compatibility, functionality, interoperability, durable medium) were specifically defined, following more or less the exact wording of the directives.

III. Personal data as counter-performance

13 Regarding the provision of personal data as counter-performance, the Greek legislator adopted a rather minimalistic approach as far as the provision of specific rules is concerned. L. 4967/2022 only contains rules on the possibility to provide personal data

---

[9] For example (art. 535A GrCC): *"The seller fulfills the obligation of art. 535, when the thing has the qualities which the parts have agreed upon and especially: 4. possesses the ability to function with hardware or software with which things of the same type are normally used, without the need to convert the things, hardware or software (compatibility), and the ability to function with hardware or software different from those with which things of the same type are normally used (interoperability), as stipulated by the contract ..."*.

[10] Art. 513A GrCC: *"The rules on sale also apply in the sale of a thing with digital elements, if the digital elements are part of the contract for sale, irrespective of whether they are supplied by the seller or by a third party. A thing with digital elements is any movable thing which incorporates or is interconnected with digital content or a digital service in such a way that the absence of that digital content or digital service would prevent the thing from performing its function. Digital content means data which are produced and supplied in digital form; Digital service is the service which provides to the user the ability to create, process, store, share access or interact with data in digital form; A contract for the sale of a thing with digital elements covers, in the event of doubt, the provision of digital content or digital service"*.

as exchange for digital elements (art. 5 par. 1) and on the obligation of the supplier to comply with the provisions of Regulation (EU) 2016/679 after the termination of the contract (art. 23 par. 3), which basically repeat the provisions of the DCD. The specification of the rules on formation, performance and breach of the contract in this case have been left to science and jurisprudence, which are to apply the general provisions of the law of obligations (see also infra nr 48-49). In particular, the legislative committee did not adopt the proposal to set out a rule which would provide the supplier *the right to terminate the contract* if the recipient withdraws his/her consent to the processing of his/her personal data without the supplier being in breach of any of his/her duties. On this issue, the explanatory memorandum reads as follows: *"The exercise of rights and the invocation of principles based on the legislation on the protection of personal data are regulated by ius cogens rules, which are not affected or amended by this Law. Moreover, the exercise of such a right alone could not, in particular in consumer contracts, have an adverse effect on the operation of a contract (e.g. compensation). However, it cannot be precluded, that the exercise of such rights by the recipient (e.g. the right to withdraw the consent to the processing of the data or the right to object to their processing) may have an effect on the contractual relationship between him (the recipient) and the supplier, especially in continuous contracts. An important criterion in assessing the extent of the above impact on the functioning of the contract is the possible imbalance between supply and consideration. However, the diversity and complexity of the cases that may occur and the early stage of the relevant scientific discussion make it premature to adopt a special provision. As a result, the addressing of these issues is left to the interpreters of the Law and the Courts, which, where appropriate, will weigh the respective interests based on the system and the teleology of the existing rules, in combination with the general provisions and clauses of the Law of Obligations".*

B. Conformity of Goods-Main obligations of the supplier

I. Sale of Goods

As already mentioned, the provisions of the SGD were transposed in the Greek Civil Code, and the Chapter on Seller's Liability for defects of the thing and lack of agreed qualities (art. 534–562) was extensively amended. The amended provisions had been adopted through L. 3043/2002, which implemented the Directive 1999/44/EC and replaced the initial provisions of the Greek Civil Code (1946), which mainly expressed the principles of Roman Law tradition (on "warranty liability" of the vendor)[11].

As per the new amendment, the Greek Civil Code explicitly adopts the notion of "conformity of the thing with the sales contract". Art. 534 GrCC reads that the seller is obliged to deliver a thing that conforms with the contract *"within the meaning of art. 535 to 538"*. In other words, a thing conforms with the contract when it fulfills all conditions set out in art. 535–538. Art. 535 GrCC rules that the thing is in conformity when it is delivered without a defect; art. 535A states that the thing lacks a defect when it possesses the qualities the parties have agreed upon, and especially meets the subjective requirements for conformity[12], while art. 535B states that, in order for a thing to be considered

14

15

---

[11] On the amendment of GrCC by L. 3043/2002 see, indicatively, Papanikolaou, "Main features of the new regulation" in Papanikolaou (ed), *The new Law of the Seller's Liability* (2003), 142; Pouliadis, *The seller's responsibility in the system of breach of contract* (2005), 1 ff.

[12] *"Art. 535A. Subjective requirements for conformity."*

to lack a defect it should also meet the objective requirements for conformity[13]. As is obvious already from the wording, the subjective requirements are listed indicatively and the contracting parties may agree on additional requirements. When the parties agree to deviate from an objective requirement for conformity, their agreement shall be valid, unless there is a consumer contract, regulated by L. 2251/1994[14]. Art. 536 states that the thing *is not in conformity* in case of an incorrect installation, if the installation *formed part of the sales contract* and was carried out by the seller or if it was carried out by the buyer but the incorrect installation was due to shortcomings in the installation instructions provided by the seller or, in the case of goods with digital elements, provided by the supplier of the digital element. In all the above-mentioned cases, the seller is in breach of one of his/her primary obligations.

16 Art. 537 reads that a movable thing is not in conformity when, because of a violation of any right of a third party, in particular intellectual property rights, its use in accordance with art. 535A-535B GrCC is prevented fully or partly. The restriction in the use of the thing because of a violation of a right of a third party has been treated as a violation of a primary obligation of the seller, which provides the purchaser with the remedies for lack of conformity (see infra nr 34 ff). This case should not be confused with the case of legal defects (art. 514 GrCC), which are *rights of a third party over the thing, or the right being sold*, which may be opposed to the purchaser (mortgage, pledge, lease etc.). Supplying a thing with legal defects also constitutes a violation of a primary obligation of the seller and his/her liability is also objective. However, in this case GrCC provides the purchaser with the remedies provided for breach of reciprocal contract (mutual release, compensation, rescission, art. 380 ff GrCC)[15].

17 Finally, it has to be noted that in art. 547 par. 2 GrCC the seller is also held liable for lack of agreed qualities of the thing, i.e. qualities the seller promised the thing would possess and he/she undertook the responsibility for their lack, irrespective of fault. In

---

The Seller fulfills the obligation of art. 535, when the thing possesses the qualities upon which the parties have agreed, and especially: 1. fits the description, type, quantity and quality, and possess the functionality and other features as stipulated by the contract, 2. is fit for the particular use that has been agreed in the contract, 3. is delivered with all accessories, packaging and instructions, as stipulated by the contract, 4. possesses the ability to function with hardware or software with which things of the same type are normally used, without the need to convert the things, hardware or software (compatibility), and the ability to function with hardware or software different from those with which things of the same type are normally used (interoperability), as stipulated by the contract, 5. is supplied with updates as stipulated by the contract".

[13] "Art. 535B. Objective requirements for conformity
The seller fulfills the obligation of art. 535 when the thing: 1. is fit for the purposes for which goods of the same type would normally be used, 2. is of the quality and corresponds to the description of a sample or model that the seller made available to the purchaser, 3. is delivered along with accessories, packaging, and instructions, which the purchaser may reasonably expect to receive, 4. possesses the ability to maintain its required functions and performance through normal use (durability) which the purchaser may reasonably expect, 5. is of the quantity and possesses the qualities and other features, given its nature, especially in relation to functionality, compatibility and security, which are normal for goods of the same type and which the purchaser may reasonably expect. For the identification of the purchaser's reasonable expectation, are taken into account any public statement made by the seller or his representative, or by other persons, including the producer, particularly in advertising or on labelling. The seller shall not be bound by public statements, if he proves that he was not, and could not reasonably have been, aware of the public statement in question or that by the time of conclusion of the contract, the public statement had been corrected in the same way as, or in a way comparable to how, it had been made or that the decision of the purchaser to buy the things could not have been influenced by the public statement."

[14] See Kosmides, *The New Sales' Law of the Civil Code after L. 4967/2022, Applications of Civil Law 2022*, 1284; Karampatzos/Titsias, in: Georgiades (ed), *Short Commentary of the Civil Code I²* (2022), Art. 535 mn. 27.

[15] See Georgiades, *Law of Obligations, Special Part, Manual* (2014), § 8 mn. 9-10; Kornilakis, *Law of Obligations, Special Part, Handbook* (2020), § 29 mn. 8 ff.

this case, apart from the remedies for lack of conformity, the purchaser is also entitled to seek compensation.

As is obvious, the conditions for non-conformity practically correspond to the regulation of art. 5–9 of the SGD. The notion of "defect of the thing" which was one of the main conditions for liability in earlier law, in the new version of the GrCC mainly[16] corresponds to the lack of the subjective and objective requirements for conformity, while the description of those requirements (in art. 535A-535B GrCC) implements the provisions of art. 6–7 SGD respectively.

According to art. 539 GrCC *"The seller is liable, irrespectively of his/her fault, if the thing, at the time when the risk passes to the purchaser, does not conform with the contract, unless the purchaser, at the conclusion of the contract, was aware of the lack of conformity or if the lack is a result of material provided by the purchaser"*. The exclusion of the seller's liability is much wider than that of the provision of art. 7 par. 5 SGD (*"There shall be no lack of conformity within the meaning of paragraph 1 or 3 if, at the time of the conclusion of the sales contract, the consumer was specifically informed that a particular characteristic of the goods was deviating from the objective requirements for conformity laid down in paragraph 1 or 3 and the consumer expressly and separately accepted that deviation when concluding the sales contract."*). The Greek legislator adopted the above-mentioned provision of the directive only in consumer contracts. Par. 3 of art. 5 of L. 2251/1994 (on consumer protection) has been amended, and states: *"Knowledge of the consumer, which excludes the liability of the seller in the sense of art. 539 par. 1 GrCC exists when the consumer, at the time of the conclusion of the contract, was specifically informed that a particular characteristic of the thing was deviating from the objective requirements for conformity and he/she expressly accepted"*. As a result of this provision, in B2C relationships, knowledge of the consumer would not be enough for the exoneration of the supplier, but an explicit declaration of acceptance of the lack of conformity is required.

II. Provision of digital content or digital service

1. Initial non-performance of the supplier's obligations

The supplier is obliged to provide digital content or digital service to the recipient, who is obliged to pay the price (which may consist in personal data).

Unless the parties have agreed otherwise, the supplier shall supply the digital content or digital service without undue delay after the conclusion of the contract (art. 6 par. 1 L. 4967/2022). If the supplier fails to supply the digital element, he/she is liable objectively, i.e. it is indifferent whether he/she is at fault for his failure to perform (art. 7 par. 1). The burden of proof with regard to whether the digital content or digital service was supplied in accordance is on the supplier (art. 7 par. 2).

If the supplier fails to perform, the recipient is entitled to ask for the initial, specific performance (art. 8 par. 1). The Greek legislator transposed the provision of art. 13 par. 1 of the DCD (*"the consumer shall call upon the trader to supply the digital content or digital service"*) without causing systemic irregularities in the civil law system, since in Greek civil law it is accepted that, in cases of breach, the creditor may enforce specific

---

[16] Art. 535 GrCC reads that *"The thing conforms with the contract when it is delivered without defects"*; Art. 535A and 535B states that the seller *"fulfills the obligation of art. 535"* when it meets the subjective and objective requirements. However, it cannot be precluded that the thing has a defect, even if it meets all the above-mentioned requirements. This should especially be the case with immovables, for instance when the building infringes urban planning regulation.

performance[17]. If the supplier fails to supply the digital content or digital service without undue delay, or within the additional period of time, which has expressly been agreed to by the parties, the recipient is entitled to terminate the contract (art. 8 par. 1 subp. 2). Par. 1 does not apply, and the recipient is entitled to terminate the contract immediately (without requesting specific performance) when the supplier has declared, or it is equally clear from the circumstances, that the supplier will not supply the digital content or digital service or when the recipient and the supplier have agreed, or it is clear from the circumstances, that the provision shall be executed in a specific time or within a specific term (art. 8 par. 2). In case of termination, art. 22–25 apply (see infra nr. 45-46).

23   The regulation of art. 8 transposes art. 13 of the DCD and slightly deviates from the general provisions of Greek Law of obligations. According to those, if the debtor fails to supply his/her performance (which is still possible), he is in default only when the delay may be attributed to his/her fault (art. 342 GrCC) and the creditor gives him/her a warning (art. 341 GrCC). When the debtor is in default in a reciprocal contract, the creditor may set for him/her a reasonable time limit for performance declaring at the same time that if the time limit passes, he/she rejects the performance (art. 383 GrCC)[18]. The creditor may serve the warning and issue the time limit in the same declaration. After the time limit passes, the creditor may either seek compensation or rescind the contract. It is not necessary for a time limit to be set if it can be seen from the attitude of the debtor that this would be pointless, or if, due to the delay, the creditor no longer has an interest in the execution of the contract (art. 385 GrCC). As is apparent, the regulation of art. 8 differs in several points, of which two are to be pointed out: In the case of the contract for the provision of digital content or digital service, the recipient may terminate the contract even when the supplier is not in default (especially when he/she is not at fault, since art. 7 par. 1 subp. 1 sets out an objective liability[19]). Furthermore, the recipient is entitled to terminate without requesting specific performance when the recipient and the supplier have agreed, or it is clear from the circumstances, that the provision shall be executed *in a specific time or within a specific term*, i.e. in all cases when a fixed date has been agreed for the performance[20].

2. Non conformity of the digital content or the digital service

24   The structure of the regulation for the conformity of the digital content or the digital service to the contract is similar to the structure of the regulation of the seller's liability, that has been outlined above (B, I). Art. 9 of L. 4967/2022 sets out the primary rule (*"The Supplier is obliged to supply to the recipient digital content or digital service which conforms to the contract within the meaning of art. 10–14"*). Conformity to the contract is a main obligation of the supplier, and should he/she fail, he/she is held liable for non-performance irrespectively of his/her fault. The general provisions of the Greek Civil Code on breach are set aside by the special regulation of L. 4967/2022. To conform with the contract, the digital content or digital service shall: meet the subjective requirements

---

[17] Stathopoulos, *Law of Obligations, General Part* (2018), § 19 mn. 12 ff.
[18] Stathopoulos, *Law of Obligations, General Part* (2018), § 21 mn. 56 ff; Georgiades, *Law of Obligations, General Part* (2015), § 30 mn. 1 ff; Spyridakis, *Law of Obligations, General Part* (2018), 487 ff.
[19] However, according to art. 8 par. 4 of L. 4967/2022, if the supplier's failure to supply is attributed to his/her fault, the recipient is entitled to accumulate the rights of termination and compensation, for the damage he/she suffered and is not covered by termination (e.g. for paying a higher price to another supplier for the provision of the digital service, or for loss of profit).
[20] According to the general provisions (art. 342 GrCC), when a fixed date has been agreed, it is not necessary for the creditor to serve a warning, for the debtor to be in default. Nevertheless, art. 383 GrCC also applies in this case, and an issue of a time limit to perform would be necessary before rescission.

B. Conformity of Goods-Main obligations of the supplier

(art. 10)[21]; meet the objective requirements (art. 11)[22]; be correctly integrated into the recipient's digital environment if integration were part of the contract and performed by the supplier or under his/her responsibility or performed by the recipient and the incorrect integration was due to shortcomings in the integration instructions provided by the supplier (art. 12); not be prevented or limited in its use, because of a violation of any right of a third party, in particular intellectual property rights (art. 13). As in the case of sale of goods, incorrect installation of the digital content or the digital service is considered a breach of one of the supplier's main obligations. Even if art. 11 was not adopted, installation would probably be treated as a collateral duty, grounded on good faith (art. 288 GrCC)[23]. However, its provision as a main obligation supplies the recipient with all the remedies for non-performance. Similarly, the restriction of the use of the digital element because of the violation of a right of a third party constitutes a breach of a main obligation of the supplier, even if he/she is not at fault (objective responsibility (art. 13 and 15 par. 1 of L. 4967/2022). The recipient is entitled to invoke the remedies provided for in art. 18 (see infra nr. 43 ff).

Furthermore, according to art. 14, the supplier is obliged to ensure that the consumer is informed of and supplied with updates, including security updates, that are necessary to keep the digital content or digital service in conformity. If the contract is to be performed in one or more successive acts of supply, the supplier is obliged to supply updates for the period, during which the recipient may reasonably expect to be provided with updates, given the type and purpose of the digital content or digital service and taking into account the circumstances and nature of the contract. If the contract is to be performed with a continuous provision, the supplier is obliged to provide updates for the complete period of provision of digital content or digital service.

---

[21] *"Art. 10. Subjective requirements for conformity.*
The digital content or digital service conforms to the contract when it possesses the qualities upon which the parts have agreed, and especially:
a) is of the description, quantity and quality, and possesses the functionality, compatibility, interoperability and other features, as required by the contract,
b) is fit for any particular purpose that was agreed upon in the contract,
c) is supplied with all accessories, instructions, including on installation, and support service, as required by the contract,
d) is updated, as stipulated by the contract".
[22] *"Art. 10. Objective requirements for conformity*
1. The digital content or digital service conforms to the contract when:
a) it is fit for the purposes for which digital content or digital services of the same type would normally be used, taking into account, where applicable, any existing Union and national law, technical standards or, in the absence of such technical standards, applicable sector-specific industry codes of conduct,
b) complies with any trial version or preview of the digital content or digital service, made available by the supplier to the recipient,
c) is supplied along with any accessories and instructions which the recipient may reasonably expect to receive,
d) is of the quantity and possesses the qualities and performance features, including in relation to functionality, compatibility, accessibility, continuity and security, normal for digital content or digital services of the same type and which the recipient may reasonably expect.
2. For the identification of the recipient's reasonable expectation, are taken into account the nature of the digital content or digital service, as well as any public statement made by the supplier, or his/her representative, or other persons in previous links of the chain of transactions, particularly in advertising or on labelling. The supplier shall not be bound by public statements, if he proves that he/she was not, and could not reasonably have been, aware of the public statement in question or that by the time of conclusion of the contract, the public statement had been corrected in the same way as, or in a way comparable to how, it had been made, or that the decision of the recipient could not have been influenced by the public statement."
[23] Stathopoulos, *Law of Obligations, General Part* (2018), § 5 mn. 59 ff; Georgiades, *Law of Obligations, General Part* (2015), § 14 mn. 24 ff.

26 Regarding the necessary updates, the Greek legislator has provided for the responsibility of the supplier to supply all updates which are necessary to keep the digital content or digital service in conformity, regardless of whether the contract is a continuous one or not. The recipient has the burden of installing these updates properly: As per art. 16 par. 2, the supplier shall not be deemed liable for lack of conformity resulting solely from the lack of a specific update, which the recipient failed to install within a reasonable time after its provision, if: a) the supplier informed the recipient about the availability of the update and the consequences of the failure to install it and b) the failure of the recipient to install or the incorrect installation by the recipient of the update was not due to shortcomings in the installation instructions provided to him/her.

27 Knowledge of the recipient of the lack of conformity also excludes the supplier's liability. However, the Law did not choose the wording of the GrCC which transposed the SGD (*"unless the purchaser, at the conclusion of the contract, was aware of the lack of conformity"* see supra, nr. 18) but adopted the wording of art. 8 par. 5 DCD, in this case even for non-consumer contracts. Specifically, art. 16 par. 1 reads: *"The supplier shall not be liable if the recipient, at the time of the conclusion of the contract, was specifically informed that a particular characteristic of the digital content or digital service was deviating from the objective requirements for conformity and expressly accepted that deviation"*. It is obvious that knowledge of the recipient is not enough, but an explicit acceptance of the lack of conformity is necessary.

28 The Supplier's liability for breach of his/her obligation to provide digital content or digital service conforming with the contract is objective. Art. 15 expressly reads: *"1. The supplier is liable, irrespective of his/her fault, if at the time of supply the digital content or the digital service does not conform with the contract. 2. If the contract is to be executed with a continuous provision, the supplier is liable for lack of conformity of the digital content or the digital service for the complete period of the obligation to provide"*. It is irrelevant whether the lack shall be attributed to the supplier, to third parties, or to chance events. Fault of the supplier is only required if the recipient seeks compensation.

3. Non performance of the recipient's obligations

29 The recipient is obliged to pay the agreed price. If the price is agreed as a monetary counter-performance, his/her delay shall lead him in default (art. 340 ff, 383 ff GrCC). The supplier will be entitled to seek specific performance (the amount of the price), as well as interest (art. 345 GrCC), and any other *damnum emergens* (actual loss) he/she will be able to prove. In case of a continuous contract, the supplier will also be entitled to oppose the plea of "unperformed contract" (art. 374 GrCC) and deny (further) performance until the recipient provides his/her counter-performance. Finally, if the conditions (mainly issuing time limit for performance) are met, the supplier shall be entitled to rescind the contract (or terminate a continuous contract).

30 If the recipient undertakes to provide personal data as a price, the recipient shall also be in default if he fails to provide the personal data. Such failure should also exist if the recipient withdraws his/her consent to the processing of his/her personal data (art. 7 par. 3 of Regulation (EU) 2016/679). In case of a default, the supplier shall be entitled to oppose the plea of "unperformed contract" and may also seek compensation because of the default (art. 343, 383 GrCC). However, it is not certain that a claim for specific performance would be considered valid by Courts, or could be enforced. In most cases, the supplier shall be entitled to rescind the contract (or terminate a continuous contract), unless it is judged that the personal data already provided (e.g. before the withdrawal) constitute a fair price for the remaining of the supplier's provision.

III. Goods with digital elements

As mentioned above, the rules of the GrCC on sale also apply in the sale of a thing with digital elements, i.e. of any movable thing which incorporates or is interconnected with digital content or a digital service in such a way that the absence of that digital content or digital service would prevent the thing from performing its function (art. 513A GrCC).

According to art. 538 GrCC, the seller of a thing with digital elements shall ensure that the purchaser is informed of and supplied with updates, including security updates, that are necessary to keep the thing in conformity. If the contract is to be performed in one or more successive acts of supply, the seller is obliged to supply updates for the period, during which the purchaser may reasonably expect to be provided with updates, given the type and purpose of the thing and taking into account the circumstances and nature of the contract. If the contract is to be performed with a continuous provision of the digital elements, the seller is obliged to provide updates for the complete period of provision of the digital elements.

The seller is liable if the thing is not in conformity at the time of the provision of the digital elements. If the contract is to be performed with a continuous provision of the digital elements, the seller is liable for non-conformity for the complete period during which he/she is obliged to provide the digital elements (art. 539 subp. 2–3 GrCC). However, the seller shall not be liable for lack of conformity resulting solely from the lack of a specific update, which the purchaser failed to install within a reasonable time from its provision, provided that the seller informed the purchaser about the availability of the update and the consequences of the failure to install it and the failure of the purchaser to install or the incorrect installation by him/her was not due to shortcomings in the installation instructions provided to him/her (art. 540 GrCC).

C. Liability of the supplier-remedies

I. Sale of Goods

Art. 539 GrCC reads that *"The seller is liable, irrespectively of his/her fault, if the thing, at the time when the risk passes to the purchaser, does not conform with the contract, unless the purchaser, at the conclusion of the contract, was aware of the lack of conformity or if the lack is a result of material provided by the purchaser"*. Any lack of conformity which becomes apparent within one year of the time when the thing was delivered shall be presumed to have existed at the time when the thing was delivered, unless this presumption is incompatible with the nature of the thing or with the nature of the lack of conformity. The liability of the seller was and remains objective, i.e. it does not presuppose fault on the part of the seller.

In earlier law, the purchaser was entitled to seek (alternatively, not cumulatively) repair of the thing, replacement, reduction of the purchase price and rescission of the contract (in the existence of a major defect). Furthermore, in the case of lack of agreed qualities or in the case of defect which could be attributed to the seller's fault, the purchaser was entitled to seek compensation, even in accumulation with other rights. According to the new art. 542 GrCC, the purchaser is entitled to have the thing brought into conformity, to receive a reduction in the price, to rescind the contract and to seek compensation. However, he/she is no longer entitled to choose one of the remedies at his discretion; the new regulation *offers protection in two distinct stages*, as per the regulative choice of the SGD[24].

36 In the first stage, the purchaser may choose repair and replacement (art 543 GrCC), unless the remedy chosen would be impossible or, compared to the other remedy, would impose costs on the seller that would be disproportionate, taking into account the value of the thing, the significance of the lack of conformity and the possibility of a provision of the alternative remedy without significant inconvenience to the purchaser. On the other hand, the seller may refuse to bring the goods into conformity if repair and replacement are impossible or would impose costs on him/her that would be disproportionate, taking into account especially the value of the thing and the significance of the lack of conformity. The law does not, as a principle, prioritise repair over replacement.

37 According to art. 544 subp. 2 GrCC, when the thing is brought into conformity *the purchaser shall end up, at no cost, in the situation he/she would be if the lack of conformity never existed*". This provision burdens the seller with the costs of transport for the case of repair or replacement and excludes the possibility that the purchaser is burdened for normal use made of the replaced thing during the period prior to their replacement (see art. 13 par. 2, 4 SGD).

38 The remedies of reduction of the purchase price and rescission of the contract are available to the purchaser only when: 1. The seller either has justifiably refused to bring the goods into conformity or he/she has declared or it is clear from the circumstances, that the seller will not bring the goods into conformity fully and duly, 2. the seller does not complete the restoration of lack of conformity fully and duly, 3. despite the seller having attempted to bring the goods into conformity the same or another lack of conformity appears, 4. the lack of conformity is of such a serious nature as to justify an immediate price reduction or rescission of the contract, 5. The lack of conformity has become apparent within 30 days after the delivery of the thing and the purchaser has notified the seller on the lack of conformity without culpable delay (art. 545 GrCC)[25]. The burden of proof regarding whether the lack of conformity is minor shall be on the seller.

39 After the rescission, the purchaser is obliged to return the thing free from any burden added to it, as well as the benefits obtained, while the seller is obliged, upon receipt of the thing or proof of dispatch, to return the price with interest, the costs of the sale and of the return of the thing, as well as what the purchaser has spent for it (i.e. expenses for the maintenance or the storage of the thing).

40 Finally (art. 547 GrCC), if, at the time when the risk passes to the purchaser, the thing lacks conformity because of the seller's fault, the purchaser is entitled to claim compensation cumulatively with the other rights of art. 542, for the damage not covered by their exercise (loss of profit, damage which the defective thing caused to other property of the purchaser etc.), or, instead of inducing any other remedy, to seek compensation for non performance of the contract. In the latter case, the purchaser shall seek all damage incurred, including damage owed to the diminishment of the value of the thing because of the lack of conformity. A right to compensation shall also be provided when the thing lacks a quality, which was agreed upon by the parties, if the seller undertook the responsibility for its lack irrespectively of his/her fault (agreed quality).

---

[24] Karampatzos/Titsias, in: Georgiades (ed), *Short Commentary of the Civil Code* I² (2022), Art. 542 mn. 10; Kosmides, *Applications of Civil Law 2022*, 1286.

[25] The Greek Legislator chose to adopt the solution left at the discretion of Member States by art. 3 par. 7 of the SGD (*"This Directive shall not affect the freedom of Member States to allow consumers to choose a specific remedy, if the lack of conformity of the goods becomes apparent within a period after delivery, not exceeding 30 days."*).

C. Liability of the supplier-remedies

It has been a matter of debate in theory and jurisprudence, whether the purchaser, apart from the specific rights for non-conformity, can claim the general rights of the creditor in case of non-performance. What is of particular interest is whether the purchaser, when he/she discovers the lack of conformity upon delivery of the thing, may oppose the plea of "unperformed contract" (art. 374 GrCC) and withhold payment[26]. If the view that the purchaser has this right is adapted, he/she will be able to withhold payment, and when the seller files a claim for the price, the purchaser shall invoke his rights based on the seller's non-performance (provision of the thing non-conforming with the contract). 41

The remedies of the purchaser are governed by the principle of the relativity of obligations: the effect of the contractual relationship is developed only between the contracting parties. As a result, if the purchaser sells the thing to another person, the rights against the initial seller are not transferred to the subsequent buyer. The latter shall have rights against his/her counterparty, since they would have also concluded a sales contract. However, the purchaser may transfer his/her claims[27] against the initial seller to the subsequent buyer (art. 455 ff GrCC), by a contract between the purchaser and the subsequent buyer, which must be followed by a notification of the assignment to the debtor (the initial seller). The initial seller may exclude the transferability of these rights in an agreement with the purchaser (art. 466 GrCC). 42

II. Digital Content-Digital Service

1. Remedies of the recipient

According to art. 15 of L. 4967/2022, the supplier is liable, irrespectively of his/her fault, if, at the time of the supply, the digital content or the digital service does not conform with the contract. Where the contract provides for a continuous supply of digital content or digital service over a period of time, the digital content or digital service shall be in conformity throughout the duration of that period. According to art. 18, in the case of a lack of conformity, the recipient shall be entitled to have the digital content or digital service brought into conformity, receive a reduction in the price, terminate the contract or, if the lack may attributed to the supplier's fault, to seek compensation. 43

As in the case of sale of goods, the new regulation offers protection in two distinct stages. In the first place, the recipient shall be entitled to have the digital content or digital service brought into conformity (art. 19). This right shall be excluded if this would be impossible or would impose costs on the supplier that would be disproportionate, taking into account all the circumstances of the case and especially the value the digital content or digital service would have if there were no lack of conformity and the significance of the lack of conformity. The recipient is entitled to ask for a reduction in the price, or to terminate the contract only when: 1. The supplier either has justifiably refused to bring the digital content or digital service into conformity or he/she has declared or it is clear from the circumstances, that the supplier will not bring the digital content or digital service into conformity fully and duly, 2. the supplier does not complete the restoration 44

---

[26] Georgiades, *Law of Obligations, Special Part, Manual* (2014), § 10 mn. 149; Karampatzos, in: Georgiades (ed), *Short Commentary of the Civil Code* I (2010), Art. 540, mn. 13.

[27] It is, however, debated whether and to what extent *formative rights*, which alter or abolish a legal relationship (such as the right for rescission) may be transferred by an assignment. See Stathopoulos, *Law of Obligations, General Part* (2018), § 27 mn. 143 ff; Georgiades, *Law of Obligations, General Part* (2015), § 42 mn. 92.

of lack of conformity fully and duly, 3. despite the supplier having attempted to bring the digital content or digital service into conformity the same or another lack of conformity appears, 4. the lack of conformity is of such a serious nature as to justify an immediate price reduction or termination of the contract (art. 20 par. 1 of L. 4967/2022).

45 The right of the recipient to terminate the contract is not regulated in a different way than the general rights of the creditor to end the contract with a unilateral declaration (rescission or termination[28]) in case of a breach. Therefore, the general provisions regarding the form of the declaration, its dispatch etc., shall apply.

46 Contrary to the rescission, which has a retroactive effect, the termination of the contract acts *ex nunc* and will not affect the period during which the digital content or the digital service was properly supplied. If the contract provides for the supply of the digital content or digital service over a period of time, and the digital content or digital service had been in conformity for a period of time prior to the termination of the contract, the supplier shall return only the part of the price which corresponds to the period of time during which the digital content or digital service was not in conformity, and any part of the price paid by the recipient in advance for any period of the contract that would have remained had the contract not been terminated. The supplier may prevent any further use of the digital content or digital service by the recipient, in particular by making the digital content or digital service inaccessible to the recipient or disabling the user account of the recipient (art. 23 par. 6).

47 According to art. 26 of L. 4697/2022, if at the time of the supply the digital content or the digital service is not in conformity with the contract, *because of the supplier's fault*, the recipient is entitled to claim compensation cumulatively with other rights, *for the damage not covered by their exercise*. The same shall apply when the digital content or the digital service lacks a quality, which was agreed upon by the parties, if the seller undertook the responsibility for its lack irrespectively of his/her fault. In the case of the provision of digital content or digital service, the creditor is not entitled to seek the so-called "large" compensation (compensation for non- performance), as in the case of sale of goods (art. 547 GrCC), but only compensation for the damage which is not covered by the exercise of other rights, for instance loss of profit because of the inability to use the digital content or digital service, damages incurred for the provision of digital content by another supplier in a higher price etc.

2. The case of personal data as counter-performance

48 Particular issues are raised regarding the case when the recipient has agreed to provide personal data as a price for the digital content or digital service. The law has not adopted specific rules for the results of the termination or the calculation of the compensation. As a result, the interpreter has to apply the general provisions of the law of personal data and the law of obligations.

49 According to art 23 par. 3 of L. 4967/2022, in case of termination *"the supplier shall comply with the duties applicable under Regulation (EU) 2016/679"*. Since the consent of the recipient to the processing of his/her personal data shall be considered to have ended (to have been withdrawn) through the notice of termination, the processing of data shall no longer be lawful (art. 6 par. 1 of the Regulation (EU) 2016/679). The lawfulness of processing based on consent before the termination shall not be affected (art. 7 par. 3 of the Regulation). As a result, no mutual claims shall arise for the period

---

[28] Both rescission and termination end the contractual relationship. However, rescission has a retroactive effect, and what has already been performed may be recovered by means of the provisions on unjust enrichment (art. 904 ff GrCC).

when the supplier provided digital content or digital service in exchange for personal data. Nevertheless, as has already been noted, in case of termination, the supplier shall return the part of the price which corresponds to the period of time during which the digital content or digital service was not in conformity. In this case, *the value of the data provided should be calculated and reimbursed.* The problem of calculation of the value of personal data will also arise when the recipient chooses to invoke the right to ask for a (proportionate) reduction of the price, as the calculation of the reduction presupposes the calculation of the value of the personal data and the estimation of the decrease in the value of the digital content or digital service which was supplied to the recipient compared to the value that the digital content or digital service would have if it were in conformity. In both cases (termination or reduction of the price), return of the personal data *in natura* would not be possible. As a result, the supplier should return an amount of money corresponding to the value of the data. The difficulty of calculating that value is obvious, and may result in the Courts awarding a sum *ex aequo et bono*.

D. Commercial guarantees

50 The Greek legislator transposed art. 17 of the SGD in L. 2251/1994, limiting the scope of the provision only in B2C relationships. Specifically, art. 643 of L. 4967/2022 amended the provisions of art. 5a of L. 2251/1994 on commercial guarantees: par. 1a and 1b were added, and par. 2 of the article was amended. The new provisions read as follows:

51 *"1a: When a producer offers to the consumer a commercial guarantee of durability for certain goods for a certain period of time, the producer shall be liable directly to the consumer, during the entire period of the commercial guarantee of durability for repair or replacement of the goods in accordance with art. 542 of the GrCC. The producer may offer to the consumer more favourable conditions in the commercial guarantee of durability statement.*

52 *1b: If the conditions laid out in the commercial guarantee statement are less advantageous to the consumer than those laid down in the associated advertising, the commercial guarantee shall be binding under the conditions laid down in the advertising relating to the commercial guarantee, unless, before the conclusion of the contract, the associated advertising was corrected in the same way or in a comparable way to that in which it was made.*

53 *2. The seller or producer shall provide the guarantee referred to in the preceding paragraph in writing or on another durable medium which is available and accessible to the consumer. The guarantee shall include, in plain, legible and intelligible language in Greek, at least the name and address of the guarantor, the good to which the guarantee refers, the precise content of the guarantee, the duration and extent of its territorial validity, and the procedure to be followed by the consumer in order to achieve the application of the commercial guarantee. The guarantee clearly and comprehensively states the rights of the consumer and clarifies that these rights are not affected by the commercial guarantee. The guarantee must comply with the rules of good faith and must not be cancelled by excessive exemption clauses."*

E. Time limits

1. Sale of Goods

54 According to art. 554 GrCC, the rights of the purchaser due to non-conformity of the things with the contract are barred after five years regarding immovable things and two years regarding mobile things. The prescription begins from the delivery of the thing to the purchaser, even if the purchaser discovered the lack of conformity at a later time. However, the prescription period shall not be completed until the expiry of a period of two months from the time when the lack of conformity was discovered. The "obligation to notify" (art. 12 of the SGD) was not adopted.

55 In case of a contract which is to be executed with continuous provision of digital elements, the rights of the purchaser arising exclusively from the non conformity of the digital elements are barred after six months from the expiration of the contractual period.

56 The rights of the purchaser arising exclusively from a breach of the duty to provide updates are barred after six months from the time when the update was to be provided.

57 Art. 255 ff and 260 ff GrCC provide for suspension and interruption of prescription[29]. These rules shall also apply in the prescription under examination. For instance, prescription is suspended (and continues when the reason of suspension ceases to apply) in case of cessation of administration of justice or force majeure within the last six months of the period of prescription, or if the debtor with a willful act averted the creditor from invoking his/her claim. Prescription is interrupted (and a new full period of prescription begins) if the debtor acknowledges the claim, or if the creditor files a claim or undertakes other legal proceedings.

2. Digital content and digital service

58 According to art. 28 of L. 4967/2002, the rights of the recipient due to non-conformity with the contract are barred after two years from the provision of the digital content or the digital service, even if the recipient discovered the lack of conformity at a later time. However, the prescription period shall not be completed until the expiry of a period of two months from the time when the lack of conformity was discovered.

59 In case of a contract which is to be executed with continuous provision of digital content or digital service, the rights of the recipient are barred after six months from the end of the contract. The rights of the purchaser arising exclusively from a breach of the duty to provide updates are barred after six months from the time when the update was to be provided.

F. Right of Redress

60 The Greek Legislator chose not to establish a right of redress in a specific rule and left the answer to the question whether there is a right of the seller (or the supplier) against a person in previous links of the chain of transactions in the provisions of their contractual relationship. However, the law provides (art. 29 and art. 560 GrCC) that the

---

[29] Georgiades, *General Principles of Civil Law* (2019), § 25 nr. 36 ff; Ladas, *General Principles of Civil Law I* (2007), § 29 nr. 42 ff; Papasteriou, *General Principles of Civil Law* (2009), § 46 nr. 1 ff.; § 47 nr. 1 ff.

prescription of the rights of the seller/supplier against a person in previous links of the chain for non-conformity with the contract (i.e. with the contract they have concluded) shall begin to run when the purchaser/ recipient was satisfied, unless a final judgment has been taken against the final supplier, in which case the limitation period shall begin to run from the date on which that decision is final. With these provisions, the Greek Law shall prevent the case in which, when the supplier satisfies the purchaser's claims and decides to file his/her claims against his/her counterparty (the previous supplier), based on their contractual relationship, these claims have already been barred.

G. Epilogue

In the transposition of EU Directives 2019/770 and 2019/771 the Greek Legislator did not follow the usual pattern of Greek Legislation, i.e. to transpose the directive texts mostly mot à mot in a special legislative act. As regards the DCD, a new form of regulated contract, the contract for the provision of digital content and digital service, was introduced; As regards the SGD, the provisions on sale of goods were transposed into the Greek Civil Code. While not deviating from the text of the directives, L. 4967/2022 attempts to follow the main regulatory choices of the European Legislator, without causing systemic irregularities or contradictions in the system of civil law. 61

Facing the dilemma of transposition, the Greek Legislator chose the middle path, attempting to implement the regulation of the twin directives into existing forms of national Law. The obvious advantage is systemic unity and harmony. However, one can also see disadvantages[30]. On the one hand, extending a maximum harmonisation regulation *planned for consumers* to everyone, from international sales to real estate, may prove that *one size does not fit all*. On the other hand, attempting to keep the style of the Greek Civil Code intact may lead to problems in the transposition and uncertainties regarding the results of the implementation. For instance, most of the content of art. 14 of the SGD is transposed in a single phrase of art. 544 GrCC (*"the purchaser shall end up, at no cost, in the situation he/she would be if the lack of conformity never existed"*). 62

In any case, as is obvious in most interventions in traditional codifications, a great part of the success of the reformation depends on the evolution of the scientifical discussion and the interpretation adopted by jurisprudence in the implementation of new provisions in real cases. As a result, the influence of the transposition of the twin directives in Greek Law cannot be predicted and is to be examined in the future. 63

Bibliography

Apostolos Georgiades, *General Principles of Civil Law,* 5th ed., PN Sakkoulas, Athens, 2019.

Apostolos Georgiades, *Law of Obligations, General Part,* 2nd ed., PN Sakkoulas, Athens, 2015.

Apostolos Georgiades, *Law of Obligations, Special Part (Manual),* PN Sakkoulas, Athens, 2014.

Antonios Karampatzos in Georgiades (ed), Short Commentary of the Civil Code I, PN Sakkoulas, Athens 2010.

Antonios Karampatzos/Dimitrios Titsias in Georgiades (ed), Short Commentary of the Civil Code I, PN Sakkoulas, 2nd ed., Athens 2022.

---

[30] Kosmides, *Applications of Civil Law 2022,* 1281-1282.

Panos Kornilakis, *Law of Obligations, Special Part (Handbook)*, 4th ed., Sakkoulas edition, Athens-Thessaloniki, 2020.

Timoleon Kosmides, *The New Sales' Law of the Civil Code after L. 4967/2022, Applications of Civil Law (Journal) 2022*, 1280–1287.

Panagiotis Ladas, *General Principles of Civil Law I,* Sakkoulas edition, Athens-Thessaloniki, 2007.

Karl Larenz, Manfred Wolf, *General part of the BGB (in German)*, 9th ed., Beck, München, 2004.

Panagiotis Papanikolaou, "Main features of the new regulation", in Papanikolaou (ed), *The new Law of the Seller's liability,* Ant. Sakkoulas, Athens-Komotini, 2003, 142–187.

Dimitrios Papasteriou, *General Principles of Civil Law,* 2nd ed., Sakkoulas edition, Athens-Thessaloniki, 2009.

Athanassios Pouliadis, *The seller's responsibility in the system of breach of contract,* Ant. Sakkoulas, Athens-Komotini, 2005.

Ioannis Spyridakis, *Law of Obligations, General Part,* 2th ed., Sakkoulas edition, Athens-Thessaloniki, 2018.

Michael Stathopoulos, *Law of Obligations, General Part,* 5th ed., Sakkoulas edition, Athens-Thessaloniki, 2018.

Anastassios Valtoudis, *Directive 2019/771 on Consumer Sales and its implementation in Greek Law, Greek Justice (Journal) 2020,* 1607–1617.

Konrad Zweigert, Hein Kötz (transl. Weir), *An Introduction to Comparative Law, (in English)* (3d ed.), Clarendon Press, Oxford, 1998.

Hungary

A. Introduction, General Framework	1
I. The *Status quo ante:* Implementation of the Consumer Sales Directive of 1999	1
II. Suggestions on the Implementation of the Twin Directives in the Hungarian Legal Scholarship	5
III. Implementation of the Twin Directives into Hungarian Civil Law – an Overview	8
IV. Some Reflections on the Implementation	11
1. Hungarian Reflections on some Original Sins	12
2. (Lack of) Relationship of the Implemented Rules with other Legal Provisions	17
a) Private Law	17
b) Other Branches of Law	21
B. Some Details of the Implementation, Variabilities	23
I. Definitions	23
II. Scope of Application	24
1. Sales Contract on Goods to be Manufactured v. Service Contract	28
2. Personal Data as Counter-performance – Retuning Reciprocity?	31
a) A Contract for Consideration? Some Basic Questions	31
b) First Steps; Hints from other Fields of Law	38
c) Withdrawal of Consent according to the GDPR: Impact on the Contract	40
III. Conformity	45
IV. Liability of the Trader, Burden of Proof, Remedies	51
1. Liability of the Trader	51
2. Burden of Proof	55
3. Remedies	56
a) Sale of Goods	56
b) Supply of Digital Content and Services	69
V. Other Provisions	75
1. Commercial Guarantees (Art. 17 SGD)	75
2. Modification of the Digital Content or Digital Service (Art. 19 DCD)	78
3. Right of Redress (Art. 18 SGD, Art. 20 DCD)	81
C. Some Conclusions	82
Bibliography	86

A. Introduction, General Framework

I. The *Status quo ante:* Implementation of the Consumer Sales Directive of 1999

In order to gain a better understanding on the recent implementation,[1] reference needs to be made to the implementation of the earlier Consumer Sales Directive (CSD).[2] The Hungarian legislator took the implementation back then as an opportunity to reform the general rules on contracts and extended the provisions far beyond the scope

---

[1] Directive (EU) 2019/770 of the European Parliament and of the Council of 20 May 2019 on certain aspects concerning contracts for the supply of digital content and digital services, hereinafter referred to as DCD and Directive (EU) 2019/771 of the European Parliament and of the Council of 20 May 2019 on certain aspects concerning contracts for the sale of goods, amending Regulation (EU) 2017/2394 and Directive 2009/22/EC, and repealing Directive 1999/44/EC, hereinafter referred to as SGD.

[2] Directive 1999/44/EC of the European Parliament and of the Council of 25 May 1999 on certain aspects of the sale of consumer goods and associated guarantees. Hereinafter referred to as above: Consumer Sales Directive or CSD.

of consumer sales contracts. This extension applied in two ways. Since the provisions to be implemented were inserted organically into the general part of contract law, first they applied beyond consumer contract law to C2C and B2B contracts as well and, second, to all kinds and types of agreements (for valuable consideration, i.e. all contracts except gratuitous ones) beyond sales law.³ This approach was and is called the organic insertion (implementation) of EU law; the "big solution" (*große Lösung*) or "substantial integration" that was characteristic not only of the CSD but also for the implementation of other consumer contract law-related directives, such as the Unfair Contract Terms Directive and the Late Payment Directive.⁴

2 Since the CSD did not provide for maximum harmonisation, the legislator took advantage of providing more favourable remedies to the benefit of consumers (or buyers and obligees in general), among whom special attention should be paid to the buyer's self-help (*Selbstvornahme*). It means that if the obligor did not undertake to repair or replace, or was unable to comply with this obligation under the conditions set out in the law, or if the obligee's interest in repair or replacement no longer existed, the obligee (in the event of a sales contract, the buyer) may – as an alternative to price reduction or cancelling the contract – also repair the defect himself or have it repaired by somebody else at the obligor's (seller's) expense.⁵

3 The legislator – when reforming civil law in 2013 and enacting a new Civil Code (Act V/2013, hereinafter referred to as the HCC or the Civil Code) – opted for drafting in a high level of abstraction, therefore no particular verbatim reference was made in the wording of the relevant provisions either to the incorrect installation or to the shortcomings of installation instructions, nor to statements made in advertising and labelling. According to the prevailing view in the commentaries, these details could be deduced without any difficulty from the general rules on quality requirements of the performance and from the broad notion of defective performance, and this and only this extensive interpretation was and is in compliance with the primacy of EU law.⁶

4 There were no particular rules on contracts on digital content or digital services before the implementation of the Digital Content Directive (DCD), either in the Civil Code or in any other laws. According to the prevailing views in scholarship, these agreements qualify either as contracts to produce a work (service contracts, *Werkvertrag*), lease (rental) contracts or mixed contracts.⁷

---

³ Fuglinszky, 'Verbrauchsgüterkauf im ungarischen Privatrecht' (2016) 24 *ZEuP*, 121 (123–24). In the judicial practice, remedies for defective performance were also applied to the breach of secondary obligations (*Nebenpflichten*) accordingly (such as duty to inform the other party, handing over the user manual and other documents needed to operate the contractual object, appropriate packaging and labelling, etc). Cf. Opinion No. 1/2012 (VI.21.) of the Civil Law Division of the Supreme Court of Hungary, Part 1. This practice has been maintained also after the new Civil Code's entering into force. Cf. Kemenes, in Vékás and Gárdos (eds), *Nagykommentár a Polgári Törvénykönyvhöz* I (2020), Section 6:157, 1744–45.
⁴ Szilágyi, 'The Implementation of Directives 2019/770 and 2019/771 in Hungary' (2021) 10 *EuCML*, 267 (268).
⁵ Cf. Section 306 Para 1 lit. b of the former Civil Code of Hungary (i.e. Act No. IV/1959), hereinafter referred to as former Civil Code or old Civil Code (fCC or oCC) and also Section 6:159 Para 2 lit. b of the Civil Code (in force) of Hungary.
⁶ For further reading see fn. 15–17 in Fuglinszky, 'Verbrauchsgüterkauf im ungarischen Privatrecht' (2016) 24 *ZEuP*, 121 (126).
⁷ Vékás 'Az uniós fogyasztói szerződési jog megújítása és az új irányelvek átültetése' (2021) 68 *Magyar Jog*, 65 (70). The lease component is somewhat more apparent if the consumer does not download the digital content, but uses it (and receives the digital service) through the website/server of the provider (such as via cloud computing), similarly Wilhelmi, in: Gsell, Krüger, Lorenz and Reymann (eds), *Beck-online Grosskommentar BGB* (Update: 01. 01. 2022) § 453 BGB, mn. 190.

II. Suggestions on the Implementation of the Twin Directives in the Hungarian Legal Scholarship

The most appropriate way of implementing the directives had already been on legal scholars' mind well before the legislator took action. The former head of the Codification Committee for the new Civil Code, Lajos Vékás, published a detailed paper in early 2021 on the critical analysis of the directives and made a suggestion on how to implement them smoothly into Hungarian law. He advocated the extension of the provisions of the Sale of Goods Directive (SGD) beyond B2C contracts in order to avoid double-track regulation of the same subject matter and unnecessary repetition of norms. The implemented rules should be mandatory in B2C contracts and serve as default and backup rules behind other (i.e. non-consumer) contracts.[8]

According to him, the implementation of the SGD did not require fundamental changes and amendments in the Civil Code in order to achieve an appropriate and effective transposition of the EU sale of goods regime. Many of the provisions to be implemented would be still deducible from the general rules already within the Civil Code (having been drafted at a high level of abstraction); and only a couple of the SGD's provisions required explicit new norms to be added to the code (such as the burden of proof as far as goods with digital elements are concerned; the burden of proof with regard to whether the lack of conformity is minor; the right of termination if the lack of conformity relates only to some goods, nevertheless the consumer cannot be reasonably expected to accept and to keep those goods conforming either). According to him the self-help remedy referred to above should be repealed according to the maximum harmonization requirement, since it is not in line with the remedies provided for in the SGD (there is no such remedy specified in the SGD).[9] To summarise, Vékás supported the substantial (also substantive) implementation of the SGD within the Civil Code. However, this was not what finally happened.

In contrast, the DCD could not be included into the Civil Code – continued Vékás, since it covers a new branch of contract law, sets up a new and so far unknown methodology and contains meticulously fragmented and technically influenced provisions. Therefore, he suggested to implement the DCD into Government Decree No. 45/2014 (II.26.) on Certain Particular Provisions of Consumer Contracts (hereinafter GDCC) which is nothing else but the implementing law of the Consumer Rights Directive.[10] Having this in mind, a new "little code" on consumer contract law could have come into being, with the Civil Code as a background regime.[11]

---

[8] Vékás 'Az uniós fogyasztói szerződési jog megújítása és az új irányelvek átültetése' (2021) 68 *Magyar Jog*, 65 (66–67).

[9] Vékás 'Az uniós fogyasztói szerződési jog megújítása és az új irányelvek átültetése' (2021) 68 *Magyar Jog*, 65 (74). This is however a misundersanding, cf. Recital No. 54 SGD: "Member States should be able to regulate the conditions under which the performance of the debtor can be fulfilled by another person, for example the conditions under which the seller's obligation to repair a good can be performed by the consumer or a third party at the seller's expense." Thus, the self-help remedy could have been kept insofar, since it seems to be just a modality of repair.

[10] Directive 2011/83/EU of the European Parliament and of the Council of 25 October 2011 on consumer rights, amending Council Directive 93/13/EEC and Directive 1999/44/EC of the European Parliament and of the Council and repealing Council Directive 85/577/EEC and Directive 97/7/EC of the European Parliament and of the Council.

[11] Vékás 'Az uniós fogyasztói szerződési jog megújítása és az új irányelvek átültetése' (2021) 68 *Magyar Jog*, 65 (74).

III. Implementation of the Twin Directives into Hungarian Civil Law – an Overview

8   The legislator decided to enact a separate law to implement the two directives. This is Government Decree No. 373/2021 (VI.30.) on the Detailed Rules of Contracts between Consumers and Undertakings on the Sale of Goods and on the Performance of Digital Content and Digital Services (hereinafter the implementing decree or ID). The Civil Code was amended only insofar as the self-help remedy has been repealed provided that the contract is covered by the scope of the ID.[12] Of course, if the contract is not a B2C contract, or even if it is, but it is not a sales contract or a contract on the supply of digital content or services (thus not within the scope of the ID and herewith of the directives, for example a pure construction contract), then this remedy is still at the party's disposal as well.[13] Section 6 of the Implementing Decree serves as a bridge between the ID and Civil Code, as it is stated therein that the provisions of the ID on the undertaking's defective performance apply together with the respective rules on the same subject matter in the Civil Code.

9   The official reasons for implementing the directives in this particular way were published by the Government itself. As was first summarised in English by Szilágyi, the more general provisions of the two directives "are based on the same principles, regulatory logic and, to some extent, content." He then continues: "The set of definitions provided in both directives overlap to some extent, and the general requirements for the conformity of the performance with the contract can be defined consistently for both directives."[14] The Implementing Decree is therefore structured into 3 parts. Chapter I (General Provisions) covers the scope (Section 1–2), the mandatory nature of its provisions (Section 3), the set of definitions from both directives (Section 4) and finally the general requirements of conformity, both from a subjective and objective point of view (Section 5)[15] are implemented here together in a consolidated and combined manner that is in compliance with the directives both textually and on the substance. Chapter II (Section 8–16) contains the special provisions on contracts for the sale of goods, while Chapter III (Section 17–27) those on the supply of digital content and the performance of digital services.

10   In Hungarian legal scholarship, Szilágyi attempted to find out why the Hungarian legislator distanced itself from the opportunity of a substantial implementation of the directive, i.e. from inserting and including their provisions into the Civil Code, though they "touch upon the core issues of contract law". He identified various reasons for that. First, he is of the view that the legislator considered the two directives – with special regard to the DCD – as a kind of work in progress, and he adds that even the terminology is somewhat strange in comparison with traditional civil law vocabulary in Hungary.[16] Second, he emphasizes the directive's scope as "more specific and narrower" than that of

---

[12] Cf. Section 6:159 Para 2 lit. b and the new Para (2a) HCC. As referred to above in fn. 9, the repeal was in fact unnecessary, since the self-help remedy can be kept, as it is explicitly stated in Recital No. 54 SGD.

[13] Cf. the official reasoning on Sections 52–54 of Act No. LI/2021 on the Amendment of Certain Acts in Connection with the Postal Delivery of Official Documents and with the Regulation of the Judicative Branch.

[14] For the details cf. Szilágyi, 'The Implementation of Directives 2019/770 and 2019/771 in Hungary' (2021) 10 *EuCML*, 267 (269).

[15] That is both Art. 6–7 SGD and Art. 7–8 DCD (apart from Art. 7 Para 3–5 SGD and Art. 8 Para 2–5 DCD, i.e. the provisions on updates and on the express acceptance of non-conformity).

[16] Szilágyi, 'The Implementation of Directives 2019/770 and 2019/771 in Hungary' (2021) 10 *EuCML*, 267 (268). He refers to the word "good" as an example, which appears hardly ever in the Civil Code, wherein the other term "thing" is for crucial importance.

the Civil Code.[17] In the end he welcomes the legislator's approach in both aspects. The DCD does not create an overwhelming European digital contract law, but rather lays their foundations (herewith Szilágyi seems to confirm the work-in-progress-approach). According to him, it is not worthwhile to "go into the system" of the Civil Code designed originally for analogue, not digital relations, to the depth "that the integration of digital contract law would require". He presumes that the legislator intended to "preserve the system and internal coherence" of the Civil Code. The legislator may regard digital consumer contract law as a separate regulatory regime outside the code, "with the latter that operates as the background and backup regime." Szilágyi emphasises the legislator's presumed good intention to release anyone from dealing with "thorny doctrinal issues" and from possibly rethinking conceptual categories (as a side effect of substantive implementation?). He means further that the different levels of abstraction, of the directives on the one hand and of the Civil Code on the other hand, could not have been adjusted and tuned appropriately. Moreover, he underlines the specific purpose and nature of the rules to be implemented, namely consumer protection. This very characteristic is – besides the selectivity of the scope of the directives and the rapidly changing nature of regulatory approaches in the digital world – what justifies the non-integrative way of implementation. Finally, he admits that at least a partly integrative transposition would have been more in line with the Hungarian private law traditions and implementation techniques having been preferred so far. The legislator is presumed not to have followed this track in order to avoid "any risk arising from the immaturity of digital contract law." The way the directives have been implemented can be seen also as a "step towards a consumer contract law code."[18] Indeed enacting special laws might seem to be more appropriate (and less risky) than bringing already existing codes and (general) norms under the X-ray of EU-conform interpretation.[19] However, if the terminology is not adjusted with and therefore alien to the implementing (private) law, there is a risk that the implementing rules will become empty formulae, a bubble not really operating. At this point the snake swallows its tail: in order to achieve efficient implementation, the legislator sticks to a verbatim transposition in a special norm, but may create an inoperative shop window instead.[20]

IV. Some Reflections on the Implementation

Within the frame of any assessment of the implementation, the following issues need to be considered here: first, the "original sins" – i.e. inconsistencies, immanent contradictions, lacunae, ambiguities and bad compromises – of the directives themselves, since they will certainly (re)appear at the level of national laws of the Member States as well; second, additional issues that can be traced back to the rigidity (low adaptability) of the implementing legal systems and also to implementation mistakes (if any).

11

---

[17] Szilágyi, 'The Implementation of Directives 2019/770 and 2019/771 in Hungary' (2021) 10 *EuCML*, 267 (269).
[18] Szilágyi, 'The Implementation of Directives 2019/770 and 2019/771 in Hungary' (2021) 10 *EuCML*, 267 (272).
[19] Józon, 'Az európai uniós jogharmonizáció mint állandó viszonyítási-értékelési-igazodási folyamat' (2020) 16 *IAS*, 29 (37).
[20] Józon, 'Az európai uniós jogharmonizáció mint állandó viszonyítási-értékelési-igazodási folyamat' (2020) 16 *IAS*, 29 (38–39, 45).

1. Hungarian Reflections on some Original Sins

12 As will be referred to, a couple of "original sins" also awoke some Hungarian legal scholars' interests. For instance, Vékás considers the flexibility regarding the deadlines within which the remedies can be exercised as a bad compromise that undermines the goals of maximum harmonization.[21]

13 Additionally, the many exceptions and the fragmentation reflected as a result in Art. 3 Para 5 DCD and the overall casuistic regulatory approach displays the general weaknesses of EU legislative activities that make substantive and organic implementation very difficult, especially in those legal systems wherein private law is organized around a central statute, namely the civil code.[22]

14 To make matters worse, the directives use terms with uncertain and ambiguous content but at the same time contain confusingly meticulous casuistic provisions; this is why the rules are going to be quite incomprehensible for those whom they aim to protect: for consumers.[23]

15 The distinction of the scopes of the two directives (as a kind of legislative crossover, as if the two directives bit a piece out of each other) has also been criticized already, with special regard to Art. 3 Para 3 DCD that subsumes those tangible media under the scope of the DCD that serve exclusively as a carrier of digital content, because this approach completely overlooks "classic principles of terminology," serving also as a base for contract typology;[24] while tearing a classical transaction on transfer of ownership (of a thing) out of the scope of the SGD.

16 Another theoretical patch with significant practical consequences can be identified in Art. 3 Para 3 SGD that extends its scope to digital content or digital services which are incorporated in or interconnected with goods and are provided with the goods under the sales contract, irrespective of whether such digital content or digital service is supplied by the seller or by a third party. As a result, some of the respective digital content and services underlie the SGD and not the DCD, while some very relevant provisions are missing in the former, such as retrieval rights for user-generated content upon termination and the trader's right to make modifications.[25] The trader has to provide the consumer with the most recent version of the digital content or service under the DCD, but there is no such explicit provision in the SGD.[26] Both directives include the trader's obligation to provide the consumer with necessary updates, but there are some not insignificant differences in the details on continuous supply.[27] If the consumer's digital environ-

---

[21] Vékás 'Az uniós fogyasztói szerződési jog megújítása és az új irányelvek átültetése' (2021) 68 *Magyar Jog*, 65 (66, 74).

[22] Vékás 'Az uniós fogyasztói szerződési jog megújítása és az új irányelvek átültetése' (2021) 68 *Magyar Jog*, 65 (69, 74).

[23] Vékás 'Az uniós fogyasztói szerződési jog megújítása és az új irányelvek átültetése' (2021) 68 *Magyar Jog*, 65 (69, 74). With reference to the broad concepts that will certainly need interpretation (normal, reasonable, durability, etc.) cf. Vanherpe, 'White Smoke but Smoke Nonetheless: Some (Burning) Questions Regarding the Directives on Sale of Goods and Supply of Digital Content' (2020) 28 *ERPL*, 251 (262, 272).

[24] Vékás 'Az uniós fogyasztói szerződési jog megújítása és az új irányelvek átültetése' (2021) 68 *Magyar Jog*, 65 (68, 69–70, 74). However he seems to understand the logic behind this legislative miscarriage: the real subject matter of the contract is the digital content or service, even if those are carried on and by a tangible medium.

[25] Sein and Spindler, 'The new Directive on Contracts for the Supply of Digital Content and Digital Services – Scope of Application and Trader's Obligation to Supply – Part 1' (2019) 15 *ERCL*, 257 (276).

[26] Vanherpe, 'White Smoke but Smoke Nonetheless: Some (Burning) Questions Regarding the Directives on Sale of Goods and Supply of Digital Content' (2020) 28 *ERPL*, 251 (261).

[27] Vanherpe, 'White Smoke but Smoke Nonetheless: Some (Burning) Questions Regarding the Directives on Sale of Goods and Supply of Digital Content' (2020) 28 *ERPL*, 251 (261). Updates must be provided during the whole period of supply under Art. 7 Para 3 and Art. 8 Para 4 DCD, but only during the two-

ment is not compatible with the technical requirements of the digital content or service, the burden of proof gets shifted back to the consumer if all preconditions specified in Art. 12 Para 4–5 DCD are met. However, there is no counterpart of these provisions in the SGD; therefore they do not apply to digital content or services included in or connected with smart goods that underlie the SGD.[28]

2. (Lack of) Relationship of the Implemented Rules with other Legal Provisions

a) Private Law

As it is explicitly referred to in Art. 3 Para 6 SGD and Art. 3 Para 10 DCD, rules on the formation, validity, nullity or effects of contracts (including the consequences of its termination), insofar as they are not regulated in the respective directive, and the right to damages still remain in the legislative competence of the Member States. *Prima facie*, no structural or systemic impact on the existing rules of contract law (or consumer law) can be envisaged in Hungary. Nevertheless, some question marks appear. 17

First it is beyond all reason that the Hungarian legislator did not extend the special digital content and digital services-related provisions of the DCD beyond consumer contracts to B2B relations, at least as default rules. 18

Second, the implementation of the DCD and the allowance to maintain national legislative competence for issues not covered by the DCD place special emphasis on the classification of contracts on digital content and digital services in order to know which particular rules apply as backup rules. As referred to above, these agreements can qualify either as contracts to produce a work (service contracts, *Werkvertrag*) or lease (rental) contracts or mixed contracts. Some authors here identify a risk of divergence in the absence of a uniform and autonomous European concept of the objective criteria (of expectations) related to digital content and services. The classification of the respective contracts – which is left to the Member States – as a service, rental, etc. contract can influence the standards to be expected as far as the objective criteria are concerned.[29] 19

Third, difficulties can arise with regard to the everyday application of some legal terms provided for in the directives. A spectacular example is that of the right of "termination." There is no mature dogmatic content behind this EU law-related term, which nevertheless requires autonomous interpretation. Even so, it must be transposed into the private laws of the Member States, where there systemized and crystallized notions of and institutions for dissolving contracts exist. Two implementation-related expectations seem to clash here. On the one hand, the national legislator cannot provide more rights to the consumers than are provided for in the directive, otherwise the principle of maximum harmonization is infringed. But, on other hand, how is it possible to draw the line between "identical" or "equivalent" and "more favourable" if the point of reference, the origo (here: the meaning of termination under the directive) is without clarified content (within the autonomous European law)? The Hungarian legislator decided on a neutral term "*megszüntetés*", thus not taking a position on whether it is about an *ex tunc* remedy ("*elállás*" generally translated into English as cancellation), which dissolves the contract retroactively, projected to the time of being entered into; or about an *ex nunc* right to dissolve the contract for the future ("*felmondás*" basically translated – to make it more 20

---

years liability period unless the supply period goes beyond two years, cf. Art. 10 Para 2 SGD in this respect.

[28] Vanherpe, 'White Smoke but Smoke Nonetheless: Some (Burning) Questions Regarding the Directives on Sale of Goods and Supply of Digital Content' (2020) 28 *ERPL*, 251 (265).

[29] Sein and Spindler, 'The new Directive on Contracts for the Supply of Digital Content and Digital Services – Conformity Criteria, Remedies and Modification – Part 2' (2019) 15 *ERCL*, 365 (368).

confusing – as termination in English). Vékás fears that even departing from the neutral and unclear terminology of the directives might qualify as an inappropriate implementation, contrary to the maximum harmonization principle. Nevertheless, he dares to convert that term into *ex tunc* cancellation with reference to sale of goods and into *ex nunc* termination with reference to digital content and services.[30] This distinction is probably in compliance with the directives, since Art. 16 Para 3 SGD (and also Section 15 Para 3 ID) requires the consumer to return the good(s) and the seller to reimburse the whole contract price. This equals the meaning of *ex tunc* "*elállás*" (cancellation) according to Section 6:213 Para 1 and 6:212 Para 3 HCC.[31] More or less the same way, termination in the context of digital content and services seems to be closer to the *ex nunc* "*felmondás*" (termination) according to Section 6:213 Para 1 and Section 6:212 Para 2 HCC. In this case, "the parties shall owe no further services and shall be required to settle with each other for the services already performed prior to the dissolution." The consumer shall basically be reimbursed for all sums paid under the contract according to Art. 16 Para 1 DCD and Section 24 Para 1 ID, but not for the part pro rata to the period when the content or service was in conformity. This confirms also the *ex nunc* approach. The prohibition of the trader's using the consumer's content (other than personal data) applies also *ex nunc* according to Art. 16 Para 3 DCD and Section 25 Para 2 ID; the same way as the consumer's duty to refrain from using the digital content or service or to make it available to third parties – according to Art. 17 DCD and Section 26 ID – can only be interpreted as an *ex nunc* obligation (the use under the contract exercised in the past cannot be erased retroactively). In that very moment, one again confronts the inconsistency regarding the scope of the directives. Since goods with digital elements fall under the scope of the SGD according to its Art. 3 Para 3, in the event of termination Section 15 Para 3 ID (based on Art. 16 Para 3 SGD) – which reminds much more of *ex tunc* cancellation as the returning of the good and the reimbursement of the whole price is required – therefore prevails (also related to the digital elements integrated in the goods) over the provisions of the Civil Code on *ex nunc* termination (according to the maximum harmonization principle), though *ex nunc* termination fits better as far as digital content and services (integrated in the goods) are concerned.

b) Other Branches of Law

21   The implementation of the directives did not have any (legislative) impact on intellectual property law in Hungary. Therefore, the answer to the question, for example, of whether the consumer has the right to resell digital content depends on the "state of the art" of IP law (profoundly influenced by European law). As far as software is concerned, the UsedSoft GmbH v Oracle International Corp. judgment of the CJEU (C-128/11) is

---

[30] Vékás 'Az uniós fogyasztói szerződési jog megújítása és az új irányelvek átültetése' (2021) 68 *Magyar Jog*, 65 (74). With reference to digital content and services similarly Sein and Spindler, 'The new Directive on Contracts for the Supply of Digital Content and Digital Services – Conformity Criteria, Remedies and Modification – Part 2' (2019) 15 *ERCL*, 365 (380).

[31] According to Section 6:213 Para 1 sentence 2: "in the event of cancellation, the rules on the rescission of the contract shall apply, with the proviso that the party shall only be entitled to cancel the contract if he offers the simultaneous return of the service he received". This refers to Section 6:212 Para 3 "In the event of the rescission of the contract, the services already performed shall be returned. If the original situation cannot be restored in kind then the contract shall not be rescinded." It is left to the national legislator's competence to provide for what happens, if the good cannot be returned any more for any reason. With reference to Hungarian law cf. Fuglinszky, *Fogyasztói adásvétel* (2016), 89–123. (Translation of the Hungarian Civil Code and other Hungarian statutes – as far as available – are provided by the Hungarian Ministry of Justice and are accessible at https://njt.hu after indicating the number of the respective statute.)

binding under Hungarian law, too, according to which "the right of distribution of a copy of a computer program is exhausted if the copyright holder who has authorised, even free of charge, the downloading of that copy from the internet onto a data carrier has also conferred, in return for payment of a fee intended to enable him to obtain a remuneration corresponding to the economic value of the copy of the work of which he is the proprietor, a right to use that copy for an unlimited period" (Para 89). With this, the exhaustion of copyright – as provided for in Section 23 Para 5 of Act No. LXXVI/1999 on Copyright[32] – has been extended to the download of software. However – as it is discussed in Hungarian legal scholarship – this CJEU judgment cannot be applied extensively and projected to intellectual property rights on digital content or services other than software (streamed, downloaded or provided via cloud-based opportunities).[33] The CJEU came to the same conclusions in its judgment Nederlands Uitgeversverbond and Groep Algemene Uitgevers v Tom Kabinet Internet BV and Others (C-263/18), according to which "[t]he supply to the public by downloading, for permanent use, of an e-book is covered by the concept of 'communication to the public' and, more specifically, by that of 'making available to the public of [authors'] works in such a way that members of the public may access them from a place and at a time individually chosen by them' […]" therefore it does not constitute an act of distribution and as such is not subject to the rule on exhaustion of the distribution right. This is why the licensor's consent to resell the digital content (other than software) is needed. Even if the digital content is included (incorporated would not be an appropriate expression, since digital content is *per se* not corporal) in corporal goods, it is doubtful whether it can be considered a component (sharing the fate of the principal thing), because, as it follows from Section 5:15 HCC, the component too must be generally corporal. Therefore, intellectual property (other than software) included in goods (in the terms of the SGD, goods with digital elements) needed – at least in a strict approach – a particular provision according to which IP rights underlie the principle of exhaustion. Though the enactment and later on the implementation of the SGD and DCD were good occasions to adjust (digital) contract law and IP law, this did not happen.

Interesting is the adjustment of the DCD with Directive (EU) 2018/1972 of the European Parliament and of the Council of 11 December 2018 establishing the European Electronic Communications Code (hereinafter the ECC Directive). The DCD applies to number-independent interpersonal communication services (NI-ICS) according to Art. 3 Para 5 lit. b, and so does the Implementing Decree (Section 2 Para 2 lit. b). However, Art. 3 Para 6 Subpara 3 states that "[w]ithout prejudice to Article 107(2) of Directive (EU) 2018/1972, the effects that the termination of one element of a bundle contract may have on the other elements of the bundle contract shall be governed by national law." According to the respective Art. 107 Para 2 of the ECC Directive referred to here, the consumer is entitled to terminate the contract with respect to all elements of the bundle (provided the bundle comprises at least an internet access service or a publicly available number-based interpersonal communications service), if the consumer can terminate any element of the bundle because of lack of conformity (or a failure to supply). This provision is implemented in Section 134 Para 15b of Act No. C/2003 on Electronic Communication, which is the almost verbatim translation of the ECC Directive (though

---

[32] "If an entitled person or other duly authorized person places copies of works into circulation in the territory of the European Economic Area by selling them or in any manner transferring ownership of them, the distribution right – with the exception of renting, lending, and import rights – can no longer be exercised with regard to the copies of works thus placed on the market."

[33] In the Hungarian scholarship, reference is made to the judgments of German courts on e-books and audiobooks, cf. Mezei, *Jogkimerülés a szerzői jogban* (2016), 130–132, and 155 on cloud-based services.

the Hungarian legislator added that the detailed conditions for the termination of a fixed term contract shall be defined by the service provider in their standard contract conditions). However – as in the ECC Directive itself – numerous provisions do not apply to number-independent interpersonal communication services; the non-applicable provisions are enumerated in Section 126/A Para 2 of the same statute. Section 134 Para 15b is not among them. This means that even the non-conformity of the NI-ICS enables the consumer to terminate the whole bundle, provided he or she is entitled to terminate the contract related to the NI-ICS according to the applicable rules of the Implementation Decree based on the DCD. Some detailed rules supplementing the Act on electronic communication can be found in Decree of the National Authority of Media and Electronic Communication No. 22/2020. (XII. 21.) on Particular Provisions of Subscription Contracts on Electronic Communication Services. Section 26 Para 3 thereof refers to Section 134 Para 15b of the Electronic Communication Act and regulates the alternative prerequisites of termination (of the whole bundle), such as if the provider cannot remedy the failure within 15 days after the expiry of a reasonable deadline; the subscriber experienced and announced more than ten failures (that really existed) within ninety days before their notice of termination; or the provider does not provide the services throughout thirty days. To our understanding, if the termination of the whole bundle is based on the non-conformity of the NI-ICS, then it is not these alternative prerequisites, but only the respective provisions of the Implementing Decree (based on the DCD) that apply, which supersede the provisions quoted here as being *lex specialis* related to them.

B. Some Details of the Implementation, Variabilities

I. Definitions

23   As Szilágyi correctly records, the Hungarian legislator systemized and merged the list of definitions of both directives into one consolidated list (Section 4 ID).[34] The definitions seem to be the verbatim translations of the directive, sometimes with small (and insignificant) deviations in the wording without any impact on the meaning or content.[35] In some cases, the wording is different from those of the directives just because the legislator consolidated the two lists, therefore some definitions contain the respective references to both directives.[36] Finally, if the respective notion already exists and is codified in Hungarian law (for example is included in the Civil Code itself) then the ID does not repeat that definition but only refers to the one included in the Civil Code (since there is no difference regarding the content), or the ID does not contain the respective notion at all, since that can clearly be found in the Civil Code.[37] The ID did

---

[34] Szilágyi, 'The Implementation of Directives 2019/770 and 2019/771 in Hungary' (2021) 10 *EuCML*, 267 (270).

[35] Cf. producer, goods, goods with digital elements, digital content, digital service, durable medium, integration, durability, personal data and digital environment (verbatim translations). "Price" in Art. 2 No. 7 DCD is transposed with a slight difference, since the term in the DCD refers explicitly to "digital representation of value" besides money, but Section 3 No. 18 ID provides for a very general wording such as *"fizetendő ellenszolgáltatás"* (can be translated as "consideration to be paid"). Apparently, there is no issue with this kind of transposition, since consideration is a broad legal term in Hungarian; it covers any kind of value given in exchange; and even if that were not enough, euro-conform interpretation requires anyway to understand the term as including "digital representation of money" as well.

[36] Cf. "compatibility", "functionality", "interoperability" and "free of charge".

[37] See for example the notion of "sales contract" in Section 6:215 Para 1 HCC. For "consumer," reference is made to the HCC as such. The respective definition is in Section 8:1 Para 1 no. 3 HCC. For "seller,"

B. Some Details of the Implementation, Variabilities

not transpose the term "public auction", but there is no need to do so either, since the Hungarian legislator did not make use of the possibility to exclude the public auction of second-hand goods from the scope of the SGD regime.

II. Scope of Application

The implementing decree reflects the scope of the directives accordingly and, besides the common provisions (on the scope, on the set of definitions and on the general requirements of conformity), invokes the application of chapter two for the contracts on sale of goods as covered by the SGD and that of chapter three for contracts on the supply of digital content and digital services. According to Art. 3 Para 4 lit. a SGD, Art. 3 Para 3 DCD and Section 1 Para 3 ID, chapter three (i.e. that on digital content and services) applies to any tangible medium which serves exclusively as a carrier of digital content, apart from Section 17 Para 1–2 (supply of digital content and the time of supply) and Section 23 (remedy for the failure to supply) ID. The rules of the Civil Code on consumer sales contracts apply for the latter.

Hungary did not make use of the opportunity to exclude either living animals or second hand goods sold at public auctions (specified in Art. 3 Para 5 SGD) from the scope, nor to allow a specific remedy "if the lack of conformity of the goods becomes apparent within a period after delivery, not exceeding 30 days" nor to introduce any specific rule (not specific to consumer contracts) "providing for specific remedies for certain types of defects that were not apparent at the time of conclusion of the sales contract" (Art. 3 Para 7 SGD). The explanation can be that the deadlines to claim a remedy related to defective goods and services underlie the statute of limitation, which means that they can be suspended and interrupted and therefore no special rules, as referred to in Art. 3 Para 7 SGD, are needed.[38]

None of the implemented provisions applies to B2B contracts as already touched upon; the Hungarian legislator missed the opportunity to set up a default regime for contracts on the supply of digital content or service beyond consumer contracts.

The inconsistencies inherent in the directives already referred to are of course present in the implementing law as well. The criticisms on the scope (and the inconsequent crossovers) already emphasized above shall not be repeated here, except one. There is a

---

reference is made to the notion of "undertaking" within the HCC (cf. Section 8:1 Para 1 no. 4) with a particular mention of acting on behalf or in the name of that person in the ID. Somewhat more complex is the implementation of the term "commercial guarantee". Section 4 No. 11 ID refers to the HCC and uses the same term, which is used there for guarantee (*jótállás*) in general. The wording underlines that guarantee under the ID is a duty taken voluntarily beyond statutory duties (imposed by law), but does not explicitly transpose the second part of the term as drafted in Art. 2 No. 12 SGD. This means that there is no explicit reference to the "relevant advertising", and the remedies are not enumerated here either as they are enumerated in the SGD. However Section 16 Para 1 in Chapter II ID contains the missing reference to advertisements. The general reference to the HCC points to Sections 6:171–6:173 HCC wherein the rules on guarantees – taken over voluntarily but also those imposed by law – can be found. Reference is made here to the guarantee statement and it is clarified that guarantee has the legal effect of reversal of the burden of proof (cf. Section 6:171 Para 1 sentence 2: "He shall be exempted from the obligation of guarantee if he proves that the reason of the defect occurred after the performance.") Section 6:173 Para 2 provides for that "[t]he rules applicable to exercising remedies for breach of warranty for material defects shall otherwise apply accordingly to the enforcement of the guarantee claim." This reference is to be understood as a kind of *renvoi* within the substantive law, it refers back to the remedies specified in the SGD and therefore in the ID. The connection with the missing second part of Art. 2 No. 12 SGD is constructed via this somewhat confusing detour.

[38] For the general provisions on statute of limitation cf. Sections 6:21–6:25 HCC. For the statute of limitations with respect to a claim of warranty for material defects cf. Section 6:163 HCC.

quite dangerous combination of flaws in the two directives that also (re)appear in the implementing decree. Goods with digital elements underlie the scope of the SGD and not of the DCD (flaw no. 1), but the SGD does not cover (sales) contracts wherein the consumer provides their personal data in exchange (flaw no. 2), though it can happen. As a result, the consumer falls between two stools: neither of the respective regimes applies to this occurrence.[39]

1. Sales Contract on Goods to be Manufactured v. Service Contract

28 Since the scope also covers contracts on the supply of goods to be manufactured or produced, the classification of the contract as a sales contract or as a contract for the provision of services can be crucial. This should be left to national law according to recital no. 17 SGD. Whether or not the respective contract is within the scope of the joint rules and of Chapter two of the Implementing Decree depends on the result of the classification.

29 According to Vékás, the nature and subject matter of the contract determine the classification. If the installation or assembly is dominant then the contract qualifies as a service contract and does not fall within the scope of the consumer sales contract regime.[40]

30 If the obligee acquires the material to be worked with and provides it to the obligor then no transfer of ownership takes place; the agreement qualifies as a service contract or contract to produce a work (*Werkvertrag*), and is therefore not within the scope of the consumer sales contract regime. If the obligor acquires the material (or intermediate or semi-finished good, etc.), there is a transfer of ownership upon performance and the agreement can qualify both as a sales contract and a service contract (to produce a work) and further criteria are needed to decide whether the transfer of ownership was dominant or, on the contrary, the assembly or installation. Such ancillary criteria are *inter alia* the added value of the processing and workmanship in proportion to the value of the material (intermediate good) and whether the contractual item is a serial product (even if it is assembled for the obligee) or a unique service is offered adjusted to the special needs and requests of the obligee (regarding size or other parameters according to the particular demand of the contracting party).[41]

2. Personal Data as Counter-performance – Retuning Reciprocity?

a) A Contract for Consideration? Some Basic Questions

31 According to Art. 3 Para 1 DCD and its verbatim translation in Section 1 Para 3 lit. a ID, the special regime (for contracts on the supply of digital content and services) also applies if the consumer provides or undertakes to provide personal data to the trader (with some exceptions). Just as the European legislator did, so did the Hungarian, and followed the bashful approach of the former: there is no clear statement in the imple-

---

[39] Mischau, 'Daten als "Gegenleistung" im neuen Verbrauchervertragsrecht' (2020) 28 ZEuP, 335 (353).

[40] Vékás refers to the so-called absorption-theory, Vékás 'Az uniós fogyasztói szerződési jog megújítása és az új irányelvek átültetése' (2021) 68 *Magyar Jog*, 65 (68).

[41] See in this respect Fuglinszky and Tőkey, *Szerződési jog* (2018), 142–43. For example, if the buyer buys wood in a DIY market but he or she gets it cut to size, it is still a sales contract, since the cutting does not represent a high added value and is not a sophisticated and long lasting operation. However, if a wealthy family orders a special Toscana glass roof to be installed in their villa's bathroom in order to see the night sky with the stars while having a bath, however pricy the special glass is, the preparation, transport and installation prevails from both the added value's and from the time investment's point of view. As such, this is a service and not a sales contract.

B. Some Details of the Implementation, Variabilities

menting decree whether the provision of personal data qualifies as a valid counter-performance (consideration) or not and therefore whether these contracts are gratuitous contracts or qualify as contracts for valuable consideration (i.e. in return for payment in a wider sense).[42]

According to Vékás, the content of the DCD as such allows one already to draw the conclusion in this respect that the European legislator at least tolerates the approach to consider the provision of personal data as a kind of counter-performance. The discussion reminds him of the debates back in socialist-era Hungary, on whether a workforce can be seen as a good or not.[43] In fact, the European legislator takes care not to take a clear stand on this issue, since it wishes to serve two masters at the same time: "[w]hile fully recognising that the protection of personal data is a fundamental right and that therefore personal data cannot be considered as a commodity, this Directive should ensure that consumers are, in the context of such business models, entitled to contractual remedies."[44] No doubt personal data is a Janus-faced phenomenon, since, besides being able to be monetized and obviously to serve as payment, it is a fundamental right protected by the constitution of Hungary as well. According to Art. VI Para 3 of the Fundamental Law: "[e]veryone shall have the right to the protection of his or her personal data, as well as to access and disseminate data of public interest." Moreover, the right to protection of personal data is a personality right named in Section 2:43 lit. e HCC.

Though it is possible to make Delphic statements and extend the scope of the DCD to contracts wherein the consumer provides personal data "in return" without qualifying these transactions, it is still hardly avoidable to make a clear decision on this issue in the private laws of the Member States. Sticking to the fundamental rights approach (along the lines of "you cannot put a price tag on a fundamental right"[45]) and denying the use of well-known contract law tools in this respect can be counterproductive in leaving the consumers without appropriate support, while regarding personal data as of value and as a kind of consideration is already factually present.[46] This crucial question has highest significance, since the application of many rules inside and outside of the Civil Code turns upon whether the respective contract was a gratuitous one or, on the contrary, an agreement with due consideration (counter-performance, or in return for payment). Just to mention a couple, the preconditions for contesting the contract and claiming for invalidity with reference to mistake are different;[47] and liability for losses caused by the

---

[42] Vanherpe takes the view that the DCD's scope should have been extended to all contracts, irrespective of whether there is a consideration or not (i.e. including those whereby the supply of digital content or service is free of charge). Vanherpe, 'White Smoke but Smoke Nonetheless: Some (Burning) Questions Regarding the Directives on Sale of Goods and Supply of Digital Content' (2020) 28 *ERPL*, 251 (257).

[43] Vékás 'Az uniós fogyasztói szerződési jog megújítása és az új irányelvek átültetése' (2021) 68 *Magyar Jog*, 65 (69).

[44] Recital No. 24 DCD. For its recapitulation in the Hungarian legal scholarship cf. Czapári, 'A személyes adatok felhasználására vonatkozó szerződés lényeges kérdései' (2021) 6 *Polgári jog*, mn. 34. According to Sattler, 'Autonomy or Heteronomy – Proposal for a Two-Tier Interpretation of Art 6 GDPR' in Lohsse, Schulze and Staudenmayer (eds), *Data as Counter-Performance – Contract Law 2.0?* (2020) 225. (250) this wording was the "lowest common denominator."

[45] Lohsse, Schulze and Staudenmayer, 'Data as Counter-Performance – Contract Law 2.0? An introduction' in Lohsse, Schulze and Staudenmayer (eds), *Data as Counter-Performance – Contract Law 2.0?* (2020) 9. (16).

[46] Ződi, 'A jog és a kód' in Polyák (ed), *Algoritmusok, keresők, közösségi oldalak és a jog – A forgalomirányító szolgáltatások szabályozása* (2020) 15 (30). He uses the word "hypocritical".

[47] See in this respect Section 6:90 [Mistake], Para 1 sentence 1: "[a]nybody mistaken upon the conclusion of the contract with regard to a substantial circumstance may contest his contractual juridical act if his mistake was caused or could be recognised by the other party" and Section 6:93 [Error of intention in gratuitous contracts]: "[a] gratuitous contract shall be open to contest on the grounds of a mistake, […] if the other party was unable to recognise these circumstances."

breach of contract is a strict one if the contract is for due consideration but fault-based (even restricted to intentional breach in some cases) if the contract was gratuitous.[48] Though qualification problems do not arise as long as it is about those very aspects of the contract that fall within the scope of the special regime on (consumer) contracts aimed at the supply of digital content or digital services; difficulties however emerge if other questions arise, depending on the nature of the contract as gratuitous or not. Additionally, since the Hungarian legislator missed the opportunity to extend the digital contract regime to B2B relations, if (for example) a natural person in his capacity as a sole trader provides personal data for digital services then, first, the remedies related to digital contracts do not apply, since the contract is not a B2C contract, and, second, general remedies (warranty, etc.) of the Civil Code apply only as far as the contract is considered to be one for consideration and not as gratuitous.

34 We share the view of those authors according to whom the DCD's approach opens the way to consider the respective contracts as non-gratuitous from the national contract law's point of view, too.[49] The indeterminate nature of the economic value of personal data by no means indicates that there is no value at all.[50] As far as uncertainties regarding the gratuitous or reciprocal nature of contracts wherein personal data is provided by the one party are concerned, the economic-financial gain on the service provider's side cannot be denied; therefore, those privileges connected to the altruistic approach present in services offered and performed free of charge shall not apply.[51] A general principle of the Hungarian law of obligations might be of assistance, namely the presumption of reciprocity in Section 6:61 HCC: "[a] consideration shall be due for a service stipulated in a contract, unless it follows otherwise from the contract or the circumstances." From the circumstances specified above follows the opposite (i.e. the rule and not the exception): the reciprocal characteristic of the agreement, whereby digital content and/or services are offered in exchange for personal data.

35 With this, however, only some of the issues are resolved. Since it is difficult to monetize, i.e. assess the (exact) financial value of personal data, further analyses are ahead of us regarding those provisions within the Civil Code that also reflect and protect, beyond the general principle of reciprocity, the *synallagma*, namely the app. value-equivalence of the service (performance of the primary contractual duty) and the consideration (counterperformance basically in money). Section 6:97 HCC prohibits so-called usurious contracts as follows: "[i]f, by exploiting the other party's situation, the contracting party has stipulated clearly disproportionate benefits upon the conclusion of the contract, the contract shall be null and void." Similarly, Section 6:98 Para 1 – following the Roman law approach on *laesio enormis* – entitles the aggrieved party to contest the contract if "upon the conclusion of the contract, there is an obvious disproportionality between the value of the service and the consideration, and there is no intention by one of the parties to grant benefits free of charge". How can and shall be these invalidity provisions apply if although we know for sure that the counter-performance (providing personal data) definitely has a monetary value, we however do not know – for the lack of a transparent market comparison – how much worth this value is in terms of money?

---

[48] Cf. the general rule in Section 6:142 [Liability for damage caused by breach of contract] and Section 6:147 [Liability in damages in the event of gratuitous contracts].

[49] Sein and Spindler, 'The new Directive on Contracts for the Supply of Digital Content and Digital Services – Scope of Application and Trader's Obligation to Supply – Part 1' (2019) 15 *ERCL*, 257 (265).

[50] Hacker, 'Regulating the Economic Impact of Data as Counter-Performance: From the Illegality Doctrine to the Unfair Contract Terms Directive' in Lohsse, Schulze and Staudenmayer (eds), *Data as Counter-Performance – Contract Law 2.0?* (2020) 47. (54).

[51] Schmidt-Kessel and Grimm, 'Unentgeltlich oder entgeltlich?' (2017) 3 *ZfPW*, 84 (100–101).

B. Some Details of the Implementation, Variabilities

This can however result in two different approaches. First, there are several types 36
of contracts and cases related to which it is not possible to check the contractual synallagma in traditional private law, though there is no doubt of their onerous nature (i.e. the contractual service is provided in exchange for consideration). This applies obviously to contracts having the immanent characteristic of being based on luck, such as maintenance and life annuity contracts according to Sections 6:491–6:497 HCC. The maintenance is to be provided (or the life annuity is to be paid) lifelong, therefore the exact amount (value) cannot be established in advance; while the value of the counter-performance (most frequently the transfer of ownership of assets – predominantly immovables) is fixed.[52] The same stands true if the respective good or service does not belong in a (competitive) market, therefore the price cannot be compared with an appropriate market value.[53]

Another approach might be to set up a data-specific variant of synallagma, a kind of 37
"data-based *laesio enormis*", i.e. to weigh up the complexity of and advantages provided by the good (service) on the one hand and the volume, number and identification-level of the personal data requested in exchange.[54] This latter analysis has however not yet begun in Hungary.

b) First Steps; Hints from other Fields of Law

The lack of systematized analyses on this issue in the private law-related legal 38
scholarship does not mean that the question of reciprocity has not been raised at all. The issue was tackled for example in the context of Act No. XLVII/2008 on Unfair Business-to-Consumer Commercial Practices (UCPA) based on Directive 2005/29/EC (the UCP Directive).[55] The Hungarian Competition Authority fined Facebook because

---

[52] Vékás, in Vékás and Gárdos (eds), *Nagykommentár a Polgári Törvénykönyvhöz* I (2020), Section 6:98, 1607.

[53] But again, not being able to measure the synallagmatic relationship between the contractual goods (service) and the counter-performance does not mean that the contract is gratuitous. Similarly in the recent French case law, cf. Sénéchal, 'Article 16(2) of the 'Digital Content and Digital Services' Directive on the Consequences of Termination of Contract, or the Difficult Articulation between Union Law on Consumer Contract and Union Law on the Protection of Personal Data' in Lohsse, Schulze and Staudenmayer (eds), *Data as Counter-Performance – Contract Law 2.0?* (2020) 147. (158). The Paris Court of first instance applied Art. 1107 of the (reformed) Code Civil: "[a] contract is onerous where each of the parties receives a benefit from the other in return for what he provides", but did not go so far to recognize the synallagmatic nature of the contract and to apply Art. 1106 Code Civil. ("A contract is synallagmatic where the parties undertake reciprocal obligations in favour of each other.")

[54] Hacker, 'Regulating the Economic Impact of Data as Counter-Performance: From the Illegality Doctrine to the Unfair Contract Terms Directive' in Lohsse, Schulze and Staudenmayer (eds), *Data as Counter-Performance – Contract Law 2.0?* (2020) 47. (72–73). Researches, analyses and results emphasized in other legal systems with similar statutory provisions might be seen as valuable sources. Cf. for example in this respect Hacker, 'Daten als Gegenleistung' (2019) 5 *ZfPW*, 148 (193–194). He is of the view that sometimes information on the value can be drawn from professional data-trade; and, in general, the higher the grade of identification of the users, the more valuable the acquired personal data are. Moreover he suggests a qualitative assessment based on the principles of data protection law, such as data minimisation and privacy-by-design. According to him, the control of synallagma shall be understood as a kind of Dataexcess-control (*Datenexzesskontrolle*) in some case groups. Attention shall be given to particular factors such as the wide range of personal data required (even more so if sensible data is involved), the manifold destinations whereto the data are intended to be forwarded, complication and hardening of exercising the right of withdrawal, etc. But even he admits that this qualitative overview does not help if there is no hint at all on the value of the digital content or services offered in return, such as joining a social media platform.

[55] Directive 2005/29/EC of the European Parliament and of the Council of 11 May 2005 concerning unfair business-to-consumer commercial practices in the internal market and amending Council Directive 84/450/EEC, Directives 97/7/EC, 98/27/EC and 2002/65/EC of the European Parliament and of the

of its infringement of Section 6 Para 1 UCPA. Facebook made a statement that the use of its services is free of charge, this will stay so and anyone can join. According to the Authority, this was misleading, since the consumers provided their personal data as consideration (counter-performance) for the use of the social platform, whereby a kind of barter agreement was entered into. For the service provider, not only the personal data provided but also the possibility of monitoring the users' activities was a source of value, since both enable the provider to obtain a profit from the advertisers who can place targeted advertisements on the platform. Compliance with data protection rules does not release the provider from the consequences of the infringement (making a false statement on the gratuitous nature of its services). Consumers might have decided differently if they had been aware of the value of their personal data and of users' activity to the benefit of the provider. The court of first instance – which was the Metropolitan Tribunal of Budapest – overturned the decision of the competition authority and interpreted the term "price" (in the respective section of UCPA) in a restrictive manner, meaning that only monetary consideration (a value in return in terms of money) is covered by that particular law and the UCP directive. Therefore, Facebook's statement was not untrue or misleading in this respect. The Curia (the highest court in Hungary) confirmed this decision. Nevertheless, both courts highlighted that they did nothing else but had interpreted the term "price" in the light of that particular law (and directive), which did not mean that data cannot theoretically be subsumed under the term of "price" in the future, but this required legislative action and cannot be achieved by interpretation *de lege lata*. In principle, the courts did not deny that personal data have a (monetary) value.[56] The outcome of this case shall not be overestimated for various reasons. First, the judgment is restricted to the general term "price" in the light of the UCPA, therefore cannot necessarily be transposed into private law in order to answer the question whether contracts wherein personal data is provided in exchange are reciprocal (i.e. for consideration) or not. Second, the term "price" is in fact – even from a linguistic point of view – narrower than consideration, counter-performance or similar.[57]

39   GDPR-related publications also tend to address this issue. Some of them conclude that it is just an illusion that these contracts are free of charge, since personal data nevertheless have a (financial) value, even if it is difficult to assess their (exact) monetary amount.[58] They highlight – correctly – that lengthy and complicated privacy policies do

---

Council and Regulation (EC) No 2006/2004 of the European Parliament and of the Council ('Unfair Commercial Practices Directive').

[56] Cf. the decision of the Hungarian Competition Authority No. Vj-85/2016/189, available here: https://www.gvh.hu/dontesek/versenyhivatali_dontesek/dontesek_2016/vj-852016189 in particular Paras 234–259. For the final and binding judgment cf. Curia, II.Kfv.37.243/2021/11/3, in particular Paras 22–27 (summarizing the judgment of the first instance court) and Paras 57–71 (reasoning of the Curia).

[57] Cf. the very critical analysis of Szoboszlai and Tóth, 'A Kúria Facebook-ügyben hozott ítéletének margójára' (2022) 1 *Fogyasztóvédelmi jog*, mn. 25 with reference to the opposite judgments of Italian courts on the same subject matter and to the Guidance on the interpretation and application of Directive 2005/29/EC of the European Parliament and of the Council concerning unfair business-to-consumer commercial practices in the internal market, (2021/C 526/01), section 3.4. ("There is an increasing awareness of the economic value of information related to consumers' preferences, personal data and other user-generated content. The marketing of such products as 'free' without adequately explaining to consumers how their preferences, personal data and user-generated content are going to be used could be considered a misleading practice in addition to possible breaches of data protection legislation.")

[58] Tóth, 'A tisztességes adatkereskedelmet biztosító szabályozás szükségességéről' (2021) 62 *Állam- és Jogtudomány*, 100 (104, 107–108, 116). Hacker, 'Daten als Gegenleistung' (2019) 5 *ZfPW*, 148 (151–152). Schmidt-Kessel and Grimm, 'Unentgeltlich oder entgeltlich?' (2017) 3 *ZfPW*, 84 (94). On the overview of the various techniques of measuring the economic value of personal data (market valuation methods – such as financial results per data record, valuation based on market prices of professional data brokers,

B. Some Details of the Implementation, Variabilities

not provide consumers with appropriate protection of their interests.[59] These findings upvalue the private law's pathfinding attempts. Elsewhere, it is established correctly that personal data cannot be subject to ownership; personal data are not things in the sense of the Civil Code.[60] Therefore, those contracts wherein the one party (in practice the consumer) provides their personal data should qualify as a kind of license agreement in order to ensure that the party can exercise their right provided for in the GDPR to withdraw consent any time.[61] Some scholars emphasise convincingly that the qualification of (protection of) personal data as a personality right does not necessarily stand in the way of commercialization, since, according to Section 2:43 Para 3 HCC "[a] conduct to which the person concerned has given his consent shall not violate personality rights." Giving consent can happen of course, both free of charge but also in exchange for something. In the event of the latter – no doubt – a contract has been entered into.[62]

c) Withdrawal of Consent according to the GDPR: Impact on the Contract

Another important private law-related question – beyond whether the respective agreements are gratuitous or not – is on the contractual consequences of the consumer's withdrawal of their consent to data processing, provided this was the legal basis of the data processing.[63] According to recital no. 40 DCD "[s]uch consequences should remain

---

differences between the prices platforms charge for personalised and non-personalised advertisements, economic costs of a data breach for data record; individuals' valuation – such as surveys and experiments) cf. Hacker, 'Regulating the Economic Impact of Data as Counter-Performance: From the Illegality Doctrine to the Unfair Contract Terms Directive' in Lohsse, Schulze and Staudenmayer (eds), *Data as Counter-Performance – Contract Law 2.0?* (2020) 47. (49–53).

[59] Tóth, 'A tisztességes adatkereskedelmet biztosító szabályozás szükségességéről' (2021) 62 *Állam- és Jogtudomány*, 100 (109).

[60] Czapári, 'A személyes adatok felhasználására vonatkozó szerződés lényeges kérdései' (2021) 6 *Polgári jog*, mn. 40, 42.

[61] Czapári, 'A személyes adatok felhasználására vonatkozó szerződés lényeges kérdései' (2021) 6 *Polgári jog*, mn. 56. Similarly in German law Specht, 'Daten als Gegenleistung' (2017) 72 *JZ*, 763 (764).

[62] Menyhárd, 'Forgalomképes személyiség?' in Menyhárd and Gárdos-Orosz (eds), *Személy és személyiség a jogban* (2016) 57 (80–81).

[63] However, it is noted in legal scholarship that not only consent but also other legal bases of data processing can apply within the framework of contractual relationships of these kinds, such as performance of a contract (Section 6 Para 1 lit. b GDPR) or legitimate interest (Section 6 Para 1 lit f GDPR). Hacker, 'Daten als Gegenleistung' (2019) 5 *ZfPW*, 148 (162, 178). See however the different view of Schmidt-Kessel and Grimm, 'Unentgeltlich oder entgeltlich?' (2017) 3 *ZfPW*, 84 (90). In the Hungarian scholarship on data protection, it is also emphasised that the Hungarian approach was very much (even too much) consent-oriented before the GDPR's entering into force and this is why the practice does not yet make full use of the flexibility and variability of (other) legal bases of data processing specified in Art. 6 GDPR. See in this respect Domokos, 'Gyakorlati tapasztalatok a GDPR-megfelelés során' in Szabó (ed), *Az Infotörvénytől a GDPR-ig* (2021) 209 (214). Other authors highlight however that Art. 6 Para 1 lit. b GDPR (processing is necessary for the performance of a contract to which the data subject is party or in order to take steps at the request of the data subject prior to entering into a contract) shall be interpreted restrictively, cf. Osztopáni, in: Péterfalvi, Révész and Buzás (eds), *Magyarázat a GDPR-ról* (2021), Art. 6 GDPR, 135, 137. And most personal data requested by the provider are not necessary for the performance of the contract. Moreover, if Art. 6 Para 1 lit. b GDPR applies, DCD very probably does not, because there is an exception from the scope in Art. 3 Para 1 DCD according to which "where the personal data provided by the consumer are exclusively processed by the trader for the purpose of supplying the digital content or digital service." Similarly Metzger, 'A Market Model for Personal Data: State of Play under the New Directive on Digital Content and Digital Services' in Lohsse, Schulze and Staudenmayer (eds), *Data as Counter-Performance – Contract Law 2.0?* (2020) 25. (35). Sattler, 'Autonomy or Heteronomy – Proposal for a Two-Tier Interpretation of Art 6 GDPR' in Sebastian Lohsse, Reiner Schulze and Dirk Staudenmayer (eds), *Data as Counter-Performance – Contract Law 2.0?* (2020) 225. (241). Performance of a contract as a legal basis for data processing (GDPR) on the one hand and the exception from the scope of the DCD if personal data is processed only for the purpose of supplying the digital content or service on the other hand may frequently overlap. Art. 6 Para 1 lit. f GDPR (legitimate interest) as a legal basis of data processing also involves some

a matter for national law." However, the Hungarian contract law is not prepared to cover this situation, namely if the consumer committed themselves contractually to provide personal data, but then exercised their right of withdrawal according to the GDPR. GDPR seems to have been drafted and enacted without having its relationship with and impacts on contract law in mind.[64]

41 The starting point is certainly that any contracts of this kind can only be enforced within the limits of data protection law.[65] Scholars are right in noting that the data subjects' right to withdraw their consent freely anytime precludes indirectly the enforcement of the obligation in kind, but on the other hand, including data as *de facto* counter-performance in the DCD, allows at least *in abstracto* the conclusion that such a contract can have binding effect (certainly until the withdrawal).[66] Hence, the contract-law qualification of withdrawal cannot be spared. Though there seem to be several conceivable solutions, none of them fits perfectly.

42 One of them is the concept of "impossibility for a legal reason." According to Section 6:179 Para 1 HCC, if performance has become impossible, the contract shall terminate. The legal consequences are distributed according to Section 6:180 whether one of the parties or both of them are liable for the performance having become impossible. Exercising a right provided for among the mandatory rules of the GDPR is highly likely not to trigger liability,[67] therefore Section 6:180 Para 1 applies: "[m]onetary reimbursement shall be provided for the service provided prior to the termination of the contract." The provision of personal data substitutes the monetary payment in this respect. Since the service providers make the launch of the digital services usually conditional on the provision of personal data, the service provider already has access to the personal data before the other party's withdrawal. Therefore, the data processing before the withdrawal/termination is considered to have been lawful; it cannot be made to unhappen, but the service provider shall refrain from the data processing in the future, and is entitled not

---

challenges. Though it can be referred to also in the event of direct marketing (direct marketing purposes constitute legitimate interest according to Recital No. 47 GDPR), Section 6 Para 1 of Act No. XLVIII/2008 on the Preconditions and Certain Restrictions of Economic Advertising requires nevertheless explicit, clear prior consent in order to be provided with advertisements via direct marketing with special regard to e-mail and other equivalent personal communication tools, cf. Osztopáni, in: Péterfalvi, Révész and Buzás (eds), *Magyarázat a GDPR-ról* (Wolters Kluwer, Budapest, 2021), Art. 6 GDPR, 152. But even if this clash of the two acts is disregarded, the Hungarian data protection authority requires the data controller to perform and document a substantial (and individual) weighing of interests prior to the data processing and if this is omitted, the data processing cannot qualify as lawful with reference to the controller's legitimate interest. Beyond the content and quantity of the respective data and the range of use of the data, it is also to be taken into consideration that the processing does not serve the exercise of fundamental rights or public interest, but only the third (i.e. weakest) category, i.e. other legitimate interest. Jóri in Jóri (ed), *A GDPR magyarázata* (2018) Art. 6 GDPR, 174–175, 177. Having all these factors in mind, consent still seems to be the most relevant legal basis of data processing further on.

[64] Lohsse, Schulze and Staudenmayer, 'Data as Counter-Performance – Contract Law 2.0? An introduction' in Lohsse, Schulze and Staudenmayer (eds), *Data as Counter-Performance – Contract Law 2.0?* (2020) 9. (19).

[65] Metzger, 'A Market Model for Personal Data: State of Play under the New Directive on Digital Content and Digital Services' in Lohsse, Schulze and Staudenmayer (eds), *Data as Counter-Performance – Contract Law 2.0?* (2020) 25. (45).

[66] Schmidt-Kessel, 'Right to Withdraw Consent to Data Processing – The Effect on the Contract' in Lohsse, Schulze and Staudenmayer (eds), *Data as Counter-Performance – Contract Law 2.0?* (2020) 129. (140).

[67] Similarly regarding German law Schmidt-Kessel and Grimm, 'Unentgeltlich oder entgeltlich?' (2017) 3 *ZfPW*, 84 (106–107). Specht, 'Daten als Gegenleistung' (2017) 72 *JZ*, 763 (767). We share this view; nevertheless, the contractual liability regime in Hungarian law is based on strict liability and not on fault based liability (with presumed fault) as in German law. Since GDPR must prevail in this respect, this characteristic feature of Hungarian contract law does not make a difference. Cf. Section 6:142 HCC.

B. Some Details of the Implementation, Variabilities

to provide the digital content or service any longer according to the termination of the contract as specified in Section 6:179 Para 1 HCC.[68] According to Art. 7 Para 3 GDPR: "[t]he withdrawal of consent shall not affect the lawfulness of processing based on consent before its withdrawal." Therefore, the conclusion that withdrawal deprives the controller of the legal basis of data processing with an *ex nunc* effect only is confirmed by the GDPR too. Due to the mandatory nature of the GDPR, contractual clauses excluding the right of withdrawal, or even imposing penalties on the party in order not to withdraw their consent, shall be null and void for violating or circumventing mandatory laws according to Section 6:95 HCC.[69] This is again in line with the GDPR, since consent is not deemed to have been given freely, if – according to Recital No. 42 GDPR – "the data subject [...] is unable to [...] withdraw consent without detriment." Imposing any kind of payment in the event of withdrawal would definitely be such a detriment.[70] In the practice of the Hungarian National Authority for Data Protection and Freedom of Information and of the competent courts, it was clarified well before the GDPR's enactment that it is unlawful to request consent irrevocably.[71]

An alternative solution besides impossibility can be that the withdrawal of consent is interpreted as withdrawal of the consumer contract under Directive 2011/83/EU (Consumer Rights Directive)[72] that has been implemented as Section 20 GDCC. However, attention shall be paid to the temporal restriction of exercising this right, which is basically 14 days from the conclusion of the contract (services) or from taking the good(s) into possession (sale of goods). While this approach provides only a short-term solution, the general (i.e. not contract type related) rules on termination (by the law) are the other way around: they offer a solution, according to Section 6:213 Para 3 HCC, only if the respective contract is a permanent one and was entered into for an indefinite

---

[68] Similarly Czapári, 'A személyes adatok felhasználására vonatkozó szerződés lényeges kérdései' (2021) 6 *Polgári jog*, mn. 75–79. According to Hacker, data processing is not only lawful until the withdrawal, but also enforceable as a contractual duty, therefore – in the light of German contract law – the agreement is to qualify as a long-term contract with an extraordinary right of termination, cf. Hacker, 'Daten als Gegenleistung' (2019) 5 *ZfPW*, 148 (170). Similarly Specht, 'Daten als Gegenleistung' (2017) 72 *JZ*, 763 (768). This is however downgraded by the right of withdrawal that can be exercised anytime and therefore the enforceability can be deactivated immediately.

[69] For the mandatory nature of the respective GDPR-provisions see also Schmidt-Kessel, 'Right to Withdraw Consent to Data Processing – The Effect on the Contract' in Lohsse, Schulze and Staudenmayer (eds), *Data as Counter-Performance – Contract Law 2.0?* (2020) 129. (138, 139–40). Otherwise the policy goals of the GDPR could be circumvented.

[70] The data-protection focused interpretation of the term "detriment" is extremely extensive, however. For example, as stated in Guidelines 05/2020 on consent under Regulation 2016/679 published by the European Data Protection Board (EDPB) Paras 46–47 and 114, it is also a detriment if the service provider lowers service levels after the withdrawal. This conclusion is in irreconcilable conflict with one of the basic principles of contract law, i.e. contractual freedom, but also cuts the ground from under the feet of many social media providers' business models. From a contractual point of view, no-one is expected (and even less forced) to provide any service for free. Therefore we plead for reciprocity to be taken into account and for the application of Section 6:179 HCC accordingly as described above. Art. 7 Para 4 GDPR seems to be *prima facie* even more dangerous to this business model, since it is stated therein that "[w]hen assessing whether consent is freely given, utmost account shall be taken of whether, inter alia, the performance of a contract, including the provision of a service, is conditional on consent to the processing of personal data that is not necessary for the performance of that contract." Appearances – prohibition of bundling of consent and contract performance – are however deceitful, since there is a degree of flexibility, see Metzger, 'A Market Model for Personal Data: State of Play under the New Directive on Digital Content and Digital Services' in Lohsse, Schulze and Staudenmayer (eds), *Data as Counter-Performance – Contract Law 2.0?* (2020) 25. (34).

[71] Dudás, 'A magyar rendes bíróságok adatvédelmet érintő döntései' in Szabó (ed), *Az Infotörvénytől a GDPR-ig* (2021) 57 (61).

[72] Durovic and Lech, 'A Consumer Law Perspective on the Commercialization of Data' (2021) 29 *ERPL*, 701 (713).

period of time, because if (and only if) these preconditions are met, the party can unilaterally terminate the contract with an appropriate notice period. This is a mandatory provision that cannot be deferred. Besides the restriction of the scope to long-term contracts concluded for an indefinite period of time, the other incompatibility with the respective situation is that there is a notice period, while consent can be withdrawn with immediate effect according to the GDPR. Finally, it is doubtful whether a standalone and *sui generis* termination right (related to the contract) can be deducted from the GDPR itself.

44 A third approach could be to consider the contract as entered into under a resolutive condition according to Section 6:116 Para 2 HCC: "[i]f the parties have made the termination of the contract's effectiveness conditional upon an uncertain future event, the contract shall become ineffective upon the occurrence of that condition." The exercise of the right of withdrawal can qualify as the occurrence of the resolutive condition; moreover, since the right of withdrawal is based on mandatory law (the GDPR), it can be argued that the withdrawal of consent as a resolutive condition automatically forms part of the contract since according to 6:63 Para 4 HCC. "[t]he parties do not need to agree on issues that are provided by law." The first difficulty related to this approach is that it is strongly debated in legal scholarship whether the decision of one of the contracting parties can serve as an "uncertain future event" at all.[73] The second challenge is that, according to Section 6:117 Para 1 HCC, "[a]s long as the occurrence of the condition is pending, neither party shall do anything that would impair or frustrate the right of the other party in the event of the occurrence or frustration of that condition." In Para 2 it is added that the party cannot "base any right" on the frustration of the condition if he or she was at fault in causing it. This objection can however be refuted with reference to the GDPR itself: exercising a right guaranteed by (mandatory) law cannot be excluded by any contract law provision or be evaluated as fault. Apart from that, this solution seems also fit to the respective scenario, since if the contract becomes ineffective with the occurrence of the resolutive condition (i.e. the withdrawal of consent according to the GDPR) then – according to Section 6:119 Para 2 HCC – the legal consequences of invalid contracts shall apply accordingly. Without going into the details, one of the legal consequences is that the performance of the contract cannot be demanded any longer, and, apart from that, there is nothing else to do or to restitute (account for), because, due to the characteristic of the contract (reciprocal performance of the digital content or service on the one hand and of the provision of personal data on the other hand), there are no services that remained without consideration.[74]

III. Conformity

45 As already referred to above, the Hungarian legislator merged and consolidated the rules on conformity from both directives as far as it was possible. Therefore Art. 6, Art. 7 Para 1–2 SGD and Art. 7, Art. 8 Para 1 DCD are implemented together: Section 5 Para 1 ID covers the subjective, while Para 2 the objective requirements regarding both types of the respective (consumer) contracts. Minor deviations from the wording of the directives can be identified, but these either do not touch upon the content or can be seen as the implementation-relicts of the earlier Consumer Sales Directive. As an example of the

---

[73] In the affirmative Vékás, in Vékás and Gárdos (eds), *Nagykommentár a Polgári Törvénykönyvhöz* I (2020), Section 6:116, 1654.
[74] Wellmann in Wellmann (ed), *A Ptk. magyarázata V/VI. Kötelmi jog első és második rész* (2021), Section 6:113, 284.

B. Some Details of the Implementation, Variabilities

latter, public statements must be related to a particular feature of the good (Section 5 Para 3 lit. a ID), while this specific term is not included in the wording of Art. 7 Para 1 lit. a SGD. Conversely, while Art. 7 Para 1 lit. a SGD refers to normal use, there is no such restriction included in the implementing provision. These minor deviations shall be dissolved – if needed – by means of euroconform interpretation; legislative action does not seem to be necessary.

Accordingly, specific requirements characteristic either of sales contracts or contracts on the supply of digital content (or services) are implemented in the respective chapter of the implementing decree accommodating the specific rules (Chapter II on sales contracts and Chapter III on digital content and services). This means that the rules on updates (with regard to goods with digital elements) in Art. 7 Para 3–4 SGD are implemented in Section 8 Para 1–3 ID. The same way, the rules on updates in Art. 8 Para 2–3 DCD are implemented in Section 17 Para 3–4 and Section 18 Para 1 ID. As far as goods with digital elements are concerned, imposing the duty to update on the seller was the conscious consumer-friendly decision of the European legislator in order to spare the consumer from exercising any remedies directly against the producer or a third party (responsible in fact for the updates). This approach has been heavily criticized and called as a sword of Damocles above sellers.[75] We share the view that a failure to install the updates can also qualify as contributory fault as far as the consumer's damage claims are concerned (covered by the national laws of the Member States).[76] The consumer's failure to install the update (Art. 8 Para 3 DCD, Art. 7 Para 4 SGD) might have been seen as already covered by Section 6:150 HCC on interim breach of contract;[77] but the directives contain more specific and detailed provisions on this issue; therefore the way chosen by the legislator to insert specific provisions into the ID are more in line with the requirement to be on the safe side regarding appropriate and effective implementation. According to Vékás, as far as goods with digital elements are concerned, a kind of mixed contract is entered into, combining sale of goods (transfer of ownership) with a *praestare* element (updates). He underlines that the temporal extension of liability for conformity (as provided for in Art. 7 Para 3 SGD and in Section 8 Para 2 and Section 10 ID regarding updates of the digital element) is not alien to the Hungarian contract law either, since this reminds him of Section 6:178 Para 1 HCC[78] on "[d]efective performance with regard to contracts for use or exploitation", according to which: "[i]f the obligee is entitled to the temporary use or exploitation of the thing of another person or the protected subject matter of a property right of another person, the obligor shall be liable, throughout the entire duration of the contract […] for the thing or the protected subject matter to be fit for use or exploitation in conformity with the contract." Article 8 Para 4 DCD (conformity throughout the whole duration of the contract) is implemented in Section 17 Para 5 ID. Art. 8 Para 6 DCD, requiring performing with the most recent version of digital content or service, is also a verbatim translation that can be found in Section 17 Para 1 ID.

---

[75] Janssen, 'Die Aktualisierungspflicht des Letztverkäufers für Smart Products: Ein neues haftungsrechtliches Damoklesschwert?' (2021) 29 *ERPL*, 557 (557–58).

[76] Sein and Spindler, 'The new Directive on Contracts for the Supply of Digital Content and Digital Services – Conformity Criteria, Remedies and Modification – Part 2' (2019) 15 *ERCL*, 365 (370).

[77] Section 6:150: "[Interim breach of contract] (1) A party commits a breach of contract if he fails to take the measures or make the statements necessary for the appropriate fulfilment of the other party's obligations arising from the contract. (2) Failure to take a measure or make a statement required from one of the parties shall exclude the breach of such an obligation of the other party, the performance of which is prevented by the failure to take that measure or make that statement."

[78] Vékás 'Az uniós fogyasztói szerződési jog megújítása és az új irányelvek átültetése' (2021) 68 *Magyar Jog*, 65 (70).

47 Art 8 SGD and Art 9 DCD on incorrect installation are transposed as Section 9 and 19 ID and reflect the verbatim translation of the respective texts of the directives.

48 Art. 8 Para 5 DCD and Art. 7 Para 5 SGD release the trader from liability if the consumer was specifically informed of the good's (digital content's, digital service's) deviation from the objective requirements for conformity and the consumer expressly and separately accepted that when concluding the contract. The Hungarian legislator provided the verbatim translation of these provisions in Section 18 Para 2 ID (digital content and service) and Section 8 Para 4 ID (sale of goods). The explicit transposition of these provisions was necessary since Section 6:157 Para 1 sentence 2 HCC reflects still the approach of the former Consumer Sales Directive, according to which not only the party's positive awareness of the non-conformity at the time of the conclusion of the contract, but also the (reasonably) expectable awareness thereof deprives the party of remedies. (This rule still applies to contracts outside the scope of the ID.) According to Vékás, this was the only provision related to sales contracts that really needed an explicit transposition into Hungarian contract law, since the rest was already covered by Section 6:123–6:124 HCC (based on the implementation of the former Consumer Sales Directive); he criticizes the European legislator on the fragmentation of the conformity requirements.[79]

49 Both Art. 10 DCD and Art. 9 SGD allow Member States to maintain their national laws on restrictions resulting from a violation of third party rights (in particular intellectual property rights), provided that these regimes provide for the nullity or rescission of the contract. This issue is very relevant, since digital content and digital services in particular can generally be protected by intellectual property rights.[80] The Hungarian legislator made use of this opportunity. Sections 6:175–6:176 HCC on "[w]arranty for legal defects" (located among the general rules on contracts) are referred to correctly in Hungarian legal scholarship[81] as the provisions that fulfil that requirement and cover the respective situations. This regime includes both, if the respective party cannot acquire the good or right because of a third party right and also if the "acquisition" is possible, but the exercise of any rights related to the goods is limited or decreased in value due to third party rights. The regime consists of double-stage remedies (similarly to the system of the directives); rescission (to be precise: cancellation according to the English translation of the Hungarian text) is conceived somewhat as a last resort remedy in the event the seller (provider) does not "resolve the obstacle" within reasonable time; or (if the use is limited) resolving the obstacle is "impossible or would incur disproportionate costs."

50 At structural level, an additional question arises, namely the relationship between product-specific EU legislation in order to ensure longer durability for the sake of policy reasons such as sustainability and circular economy, as it is explicitly referred to in Recital No. 32 SGD on the one hand and (private law) conformity (plus remedies in the event of non-conformity) on the other hand. The European legislator regards these two regimes as being complementary to each other. The same way as Art. 7 Para 1 lit. a SGD and Art. 8 Para 1 lit. a DCD refer now explicitly to existing Union and national law as part of the objective requirements of conformity (and as it is implemented as Section 5 Para 3 lit. a ID), the Hungarian legislator constructed this bridge between public law provisions on requirements (as minimum standards) regarding some sort of products

---

[79] Vékás 'Az uniós fogyasztói szerződési jog megújítása és az új irányelvek átültetése' (2021) 68 *Magyar Jog*, 65 (70–71).
[80] Vékás 'Az uniós fogyasztói szerződési jog megújítása és az új irányelvek átültetése' (2021) 68 *Magyar Jog*, 65 (71).
[81] Vékás 'Az uniós fogyasztói szerződési jog megújítása és az új irányelvek átültetése' (2021) 68 *Magyar Jog*, 65 (71). Szilágyi, 'The Implementation of Directives 2019/770 and 2019/771 in Hungary' (2021) 10 *EuCML*, 267 (270).

B. Some Details of the Implementation, Variabilities

and the private law regime of (non-)conformity already earlier. According to Section 6:123 Para 1 lit. e HCC, the contractual performance "shall comply with the quality requirements set out by law." Therefore, compliance with public law provisions on products automatically forms part of the contractual expectations, also in line with Section 6:63 Para 4 HCC, according to which "[t]he parties do not need to agree on issues that are provided by law." This is why it is extremely important how – for example – the policy goals, such as sustainability and circular economy, are reflected in product-related public (administrative) laws, since the Hungarian legislator did not make any specific reference to these goals in the implementation of SGD and DCD. Of course, mandatory product-related expectations provided for by law do not apply to all types of products and sometimes they have only an indirect impact on national law, because the European legislator willingly left room to the Member States to design their respective laws partly on their own. For example, Art. 20 on penalties of Directive 2009/125/EC establishing the framework for the setting of ecodesign requirements for energy-related products allows the Member States to enact their own sanction for the event of infringement of the national rules pursuant to the Directive. The Hungarian legislator seems to have restricted those particular "penalties" to public law ones, namely to withdrawal from circulation (recall of the products) and prohibition to put the product into circulation for the future (as last resort after an appropriate warning to remedy the non-compliance; fines can be imposed too).[82] Nevertheless, these requirements can be channelled into the concept of private law non-conformity indirectly through the respective provisions of the HCC referred to above. However, such published judgment cannot yet be identified.

IV. Liability of the Trader, Burden of Proof, Remedies

1. Liability of the Trader

In this respect, the provisions of the Implementing Decree and of the Civil Code are more interwoven. First, the liability of traders (Art. 11 Para 1 DCD; Art. 10 Para 1 SGD) does not necessarily need to be expressly stated in the ID, since it is covered by Section 6:137 Para 1 sentence 1 HCC, according to which "[t]he obligor performs defectively if, at the time of performance, the service does not comply with the quality requirements laid down in the contract or by law." The relevant (period) of time when (within which) the goods (goods with digital elements, digital content, digital service; and then single acts or series of individual acts of supply, continuous supply over a period of time) must be in conformity with the subjective and objective requirements (Art. 11 Para 2–3 DCD, Art. 10 Para 2 SGD) is reflected accordingly and literally in the ID (Section 20 and 10 ID). 51

The Hungarian legislator made use of the opportunity provided for in Art. 11 Para 2 DCD and Art. 10 Para 5 SGD to maintain their limitation-only-period for the remedies, provided that the national limitation period allows the consumer to exercise the remedies within the (two years) period indicated by the directives. Similarly, the legislator kept the possibility to agree upon a shorter limitation period regarding second-hand goods (allowed by Art. 10 Para 6 SGD), which cannot however be shorter than one year. The respective provision is provided for in Section 6:163 Para 2 HCC, according to which: "[f]or contracts between consumers and undertakings, the consumer's claim of 52

---

[82] Section 9 Paras 1–2 of Government Decree No. 65/2011 (IV.15.) on Ecodesign Requirements of Energy-related Products and on General Requirements of their Putting into Circulation and of their Compliance Evaluation.

warranty for material defects shall lapse after two years from the time of performance. If the subject matter of a contract between a consumer and an undertaking is a thing that has been used previously, the parties may agree on a shorter limitation period; however, setting forth a limitation period shorter than one year in such cases shall not be valid either." However, since this is a limitation period, it is suspended according to Section 6:24 Para 1 HCC if "the obligee is unable to enforce the claim for an excusable reason" with the effect that "the claim may be enforced within a time limit of one year […] after the obstacle ceases to exist if the limitation period has already expired or only a period of less than one year […] remained of it" (Para 2 of the same Section). Limitation can also be interrupted for the reasons exclusively specified in Section 6:25 Para 1 HCC.[83] In this case, the limitation period restarts. This legislative choice can have the result that the consumer can exercise the remedies even a long time after performance of the contract (for example, due to the suspension of the limitation period if the defect appeared much later). But first, the European legislator must surely have taken this into account when it allowed the Member States to make this choice. Second, it is represented in Hungarian legal scholarship that this advantage is counterbalanced on the one hand by the burden of proof: the more time lapses (and the applicable presumptions expired), the more difficult it is for the consumer (or any contracting party) to prove that the defect was already present at the time of performance; on the other hand, the natural useful lifespan of the good limits the enforceability of any remedy anyway.[84] Needless to say that longer deadlines are more in line with the idea of durability and sustainable consumption.

53   Art. 12 SGD allows Member States to maintain their rules on the consumer's notification duty towards the seller, provided the consumer has at least two months to do so from the date he or she detected the lack of conformity. The HCC contains such a provision, which continues to apply. Section 6:162 Para 1 HCC requires the obligee "to communicate the defect to the obligor without delay" following the detection of the defect. Para 2 makes this provision EU-compatible in stating that: "[f]or contracts between consumers and undertakings, a defect communicated within two months following the detection shall be considered communicated without delay." If the consumer does not fulfil this duty, he or she is not deprived of the remedies, but – according to Para 3 – he or she "shall be liable for the damage arising from delayed communication." Losses suffered due to meanwhile deterioration, for example increased costs of repair due to the time lapse (price increase, extension of the defect)[85] thus cannot be claimed from the seller provided there is a close causal connection between the consumer's omission (to notify) and the respective losses, inasmuch as they could have been prevented by timely notification. Sein and Spindler are right in noting that there is no such approval in the DCD, therefore reference to Section 6:162 Para 1 HCC can be barred by the maximum harmonisation principle as far as digital content or services are concerned in a consumer contract,[86] unless it is about digital content included in or digital service related to goods with digital elements that underlie the SGD and not the DCD. Vanherpe confirms this

---

[83] Cf. Section 25 Para 1 HCC: "(1) The limitation period shall be interrupted a) by the obligor's acknowledgement of the debt; b) by the amendment of the obligation by agreement, and a settlement agreement; c) by the enforcement of the claim against the obligor in court procedures, if the court adopted a final and binding decision on the merits that concluded the procedure; or d) by the notification of the claim in bankruptcy proceedings."

[84] Cf. Kemenes, in Vékás and Gárdos (eds), *Nagykommentár a Polgári Törvénykönyvhöz* I (2020), Section 6:163, 1765.

[85] Cf. Kemenes, in Vékás and Gárdos (eds), *Nagykommentár a Polgári Törvénykönyvhöz* I (2020), Section 6:162, 1760.

[86] Sein and Spindler, 'The new Directive on Contracts for the Supply of Digital Content and Digital Services – Conformity Criteria, Remedies and Modification – Part 2' (2019) 15 *ERCL*, 365 (375).

B. Some Details of the Implementation, Variabilities

with reference to Recital 11 DCD, wherein imposing a duty to notify on the consumer is explicitly prohibited.[87]

Since Art. 3 Para 6 SGD and Art. 3 Para 10 DCD leave the regulation of general contract law to the Member States in so far as not covered by the directives (in particular but not limited to formation, validity, nullity, consequences of termination and damages), a brief reference is made here to two significant aspects. The HCC includes a change of circumstance clause (Section 6:192) that enables the court to amend (only) long term contracts if, due to a circumstance that occurred after the conclusion of the contract, the performance of the contract with unchanged conditions would harm one of the parties' substantial legal interest, and "a) the possibility of a change in the circumstances was not foreseeable at the time when the contract was concluded; b) the change in circumstances was not caused by him; and c) the change in circumstances falls outside his normal business risk." This might be more relevant for the continuous supply of digital content or digital services or if the sale of goods is combined with such services. The other important background regime to be highlighted is that of contractual liability for losses caused by the breach of contract (including but not limited to impossibility). According to Section 6:142 HCC this liability is a strict one that has been transplanted from Art. 79 of the Convention on International Sale of Goods and the party in breach shall be exempted from liability only if he proves "that the breach of contract was caused by a circumstance that was outside of his control and was not foreseeable at the time of concluding the contract, and he could not be expected to have avoided that circumstance or averted the damage."[88]

2. Burden of Proof

Art. 11 SGD is transposed as a verbatim translation into Section 11 ID. The same stands true for Art. 12 Paras 1–4 DCD, which are implemented as Section 21 Paras 2–5 ID. There are minor textual differences regarding the implementation of the consumer's duty to cooperate in finding out whether the digital environment is responsible for the lack of conformity (Art. 12 Para 5 DCD). This is implemented in Section 21 Para 6–7 ID. For example, the part "to the extent reasonably possible and necessary" is missing in Para 6. Thus, if applied, this kind of proportionality in favour of the consumer must be kept in mind in compliance with the euroconform interpretation principle.

3. Remedies

a) Sale of Goods

As far as the remedies in (consumer) sales contracts are concerned, the Hungarian legislator seems to rely more on the already existing rules of the HCC and tries to complete them with some specific provisions taken from the SGD into the Implementing Decree. The double-stage character of the remedies did not change.

Art. 13 Para 2 SGD on repair or replacement is implemented as Section 6:159 Para 2 lit. a HCC. Since the legislator kept the former rule (reflecting the former Consumer Sales Directive), some minor and insignificant differences can be recognised in the

---

[87] Vanherpe, 'White Smoke but Smoke Nonetheless: Some (Burning) Questions Regarding the Directives on Sale of Goods and Supply of Digital Content' (2020) 28 *ERPL*, 251 (270).

[88] For the details see Fuglinszky, 'The Reform of Contractual Liability in the New Hungarian Civil Code: Strict Liability and Foreseeability Clause as Legal Transplants' (2015) 79 *RabelsZ*, 72 and Fuglinszky, 'Legal Transplants: Snapshots of the State of the Art and a Case Study from Central Europe: Post Transplantation-adjustment of Contractual Liability in the New Hungarian Civil Code' (2020) 16 *ERCL*, 267.

wording in comparison with the respective SGD provision; for example the HCC refers explicitly to the infringement of the consumer's interest as one of the factors to be taken into account when deciding between repair or replacement. According to Section 6:159 Para 2 lit. b HCC, the consumer's interest, to be more precise, if the consumer's interest in repair or replacement becomes lost, is one of the circumstances that justifies the consumer's switch to secondary remedies such as price reduction and cancellation of the contract. Those authors might be right when they underline that the "loss of interest in repair or replacement" does not fit to any of the justifications specified in Art. 13 Para 4 SGD to switch to price reduction or termination, therefore it should be rescinded, at least regarding those contracts that underlie the scope of the SGD.[89] It is puzzling why the Hungarian legislator did not insert such an appropriate restriction into the HCC.

58   Though Recital No. 48 explicitly refers to the consumers' right of choice for repair as an opportunity to encourage sustainable consumption (in connection with a greater durability of products), there is no sign of prioritizing repair over replacement in order to enhance environmental sustainability either in the SGD or in the implementing law. There are no doctrinal debates known to the author on this issue in Hungary. However, the more these aspects will be considered in (public law) legislation (inspired and instructed also by European law), the more they can be taken into consideration by the courts in interpreting and evaluating factors such as the "significance of lack of conformity" or the significance of the inconvenience combined with repair compared with replacement, etc. There are recently some promising signs. Act No. II/2021 amended Act. No. CLV/1997 on Consumer Protection. According to the new provision in Section 16 Para 6, the manufacturer and the distributor of products shall make efforts in order to switch to the circular economy, to exclude and refrain from premature or planned obsolescence, and to ensure the same lifespan for units and components of the product; moreover, to ensure the product's developability, supplementability and the modular character of their units. The same way, manufacturers are expected to ensure the supply of components (spare parts) and to maintain a repair network during the whole lifespan of the product; to ensure the use of recycled materials and recyclability of the product itself; to assume duties regarding the lifespan of digital tools and the obsolescence of software and to minimize risks related to the obsolescence of the software and operating system provided simultaneously with the product. The details shall be regulated by a specific government decree that has not yet been enacted at the time of composing this report. As will be referred to below, there is – besides the contractual warranty regime – an additional extracontractual, statutory and mandatory remedy (for repair or replacement) on the consumers' side directly against the producer, the so-called product warranty (Sections 6:178–6:170 HCC), independent of any European law-making and harmonisation. According to Section 6:168 Para 1 sentence 1: "[i]n the event of a defect in movable thing sold by an undertaking to a consumer [...], the consumer may demand that the producer repairs the defect in the product, or, if repair is not possible within an appropriate time limit without causing harm to the consumer's interests, replace the product." In this wording, preference seems to be given to repair over replacement, even if this is watered down in the second part of the provision. There is no sign in the official reasons of the HCC whether this can be seen as a result of sustainability considerations.

59   Art. 13 Para 3 SGD needed an explicit implementation and that is what happens in Section 12 Para 1 ID, because this very rule extends the proportionality requirement beyond the horizontal relation (i.e. between repair and replacement) to the vertical dimen-

---

[89] Schubel, 'Die zweite Andienung des Verkäufers nach der Umsetzung der Warenkaufrichtlinie' (2022) 77 JZ, 73 (79).

B. Some Details of the Implementation, Variabilities

sion (change for price reduction or termination), clarifying this so far highly debated aspect.[90] The alternative preconditions of switching to price reduction or termination in Art. 13 Para 4 SGD are almost literally translated and located into Section 12 Para 2 ID.

Art. 13 Para 5 SGD – no termination if lack of conformity is only minor, but the burden of proof lies with the seller – is partly transposed as Section 12 Para 3 ID (burden of proof) and the other half is placed (and was already in force) in Section 6:159 Para 3 HCC, according to which: "[a]n insignificant defect shall not give rise to cancellation." (The same interplay is present regarding Art. 14 Para 6 DCD: besides the respective provision in the HCC, Section 22 Para 6 ID is relevant on the burden of proof.)

The consumer's right to withhold payment is again transposed in an explicit provision (Section 12 Para 4 ID); no further conditions and modalities are provided for (though this would be possible according to the SGD). This particular rule might be seen as the unnecessary duplication of Section 6:139 HCC on the general right to retain, according to which "the obligee may retain the pro rata part of his own due services until performance by the obligor or until the provision of adequate financial security." The only difference is that under the SGD and the ID the right to withhold is not restricted *pro rata*. Since the right to withhold payment is not explicitly mentioned in the DCD, it is again up to the borders of maximum harmonization whether such right to withhold can be exercised in (consumer) contracts on the supply of digital content or services.[91] Section 6:139 HCC could serve as the legal basis, at least for a *pro rata* retention due to its general formulation, so it really depends on the contours of maximum harmonization.

The Hungarian legislator makes use of the opportunity (Art. 13 Para 7 SGD) to take the consumer's contribution to the lack of conformity into account. According to Section 6:166 Para 2 HCC "[i]f the failure of the obligation to perform maintenance activities by the obligee has also contributed to the defect of the thing, the costs related to the performance of the obligation to perform maintenance activities shall be borne by the obligee pro rata to his contribution, if he had the knowledge required for the maintenance of the thing, or if the obligor fulfilled his obligation to provide information in this regard." (There is no such approval in the DCD, thus it is up to the borders of maximum harmonization whether the cited HCC provision may apply regarding consumer contracts on the supply of digital content or services.)[92]

The ways and means of repair and replacement can be found partly in the Implementing Decree itself and partly the already existing rules not contradictory to the SGD have been maintained. Art. 14 Para 1 SGD for example has been divided among three different provisions. First Section 13 Para 1 ID refers to the deadline within which the repair or replacement shall be performed; second, the requirement to perform it without any significant inconvenience is resonated in Section 6:159 Para 4 HCC as follows: "[r]epair or replacement shall be completed within an appropriate time limit, by appro-

---

[90] Hajnal, 'A fogyasztási cikkek adásvételének szabályozási kísérlete és legújabb módosításai az Európai Unióban és a magyar jogban' (2020) 28/7–8 *Gazdaság és jog*, 6 (9). Vékás was of the view that this was obvious even without an explicit provision, cf. Vékás 'Az uniós fogyasztói szerződési jog megújítása és az új irányelvek átültetése' (2021) 68 *Magyar Jog*, 65 (71). This view was reflected in the reasoning of the law implementing the former Consumer Sales Directive (Act. no. XXXVI/2012) and was also accepted by the Curia (i.e. the highest court of Hungary) in its Opinion No. 1/2012 Chapter 4 on Certain Issues of Defective Performance. See Fuglinszky, 'Verbrauchsgüterkauf im ungarischen Privatrecht' (2016) 24 *ZEuP*, 121 (132–33).

[91] Vanherpe, 'White Smoke but Smoke Nonetheless: Some (Burning) Questions Regarding the Directives on Sale of Goods and Supply of Digital Content' (2020) 28 *ERPL*, 251 (267–68).

[92] Vanherpe, 'White Smoke but Smoke Nonetheless: Some (Burning) Questions Regarding the Directives on Sale of Goods and Supply of Digital Content' (2020) 28 *ERPL*, 251 (267).

priately considering the interests of the obligee and taking the characteristics of the thing and its designated purpose that can be expected from the obligee into account." And third Section 6:166 Para 1 HCC makes and made it clear already before that all costs shall be borne by the seller.[93] Nevertheless Art. 14 Para 2–3 SGD (removal and installation costs) are literally transposed as Section 13 Para 2–3 ID. According to Vékás, it was clear enough due to the very generally drafted Section 6:166 Para 1 HCC that also the removal and (re)installation costs were and are to be covered by the seller,[94] while other authors welcome this legislative clarification.[95] Again others emphasized that though there was no clear reference to this issue in the former Consumer Sales Directive, but that one reflected the minimum harmonization principle, therefore it did not infringe EU law to read these costs into the consumer's remedies (to be covered by the seller). Since the SGD is based on maximum harmonization, the explicit clarification on the removal and installation costs makes sense. There is no specific reference to transport costs or to the place of repair and replacement either in the HCC or in the Implementing Decree. According to the very general wording of Section 6:166 Para 1 HCC, transport costs shall be also borne by the seller if the defective good needs to be transported somewhere else in order to be repaired. In our understanding, not even maximum harmonization stands in the way of the interpretation that the transport costs are to be borne by the seller in the event of repair and replacement, despite these costs not being explicitly mentioned in Art. 14 Para 3 SGD. As far as delivering the good to be repaired or replaced to a different place is necessary, the costs thereof must then be able to be interpreted as part of the costs of removal and installation. In the absence of any specific rule, the venue of repair depends basically on the technical circumstances; however, the commentaries highlight that the consumer's interests shall be preferred and safeguarded. If there is no specific technical necessity, the good shall be repaired at the consumer's residence or where the good is placed.[96] If this is so, no transportation costs arise.

64 There is no explicit implementation norm on Art. 14 Para 4 SGD (no payment duty for the normal use before replacement); according to Vékás, this requirement is appropriately reflected in Section 6:167 Para 2 HCC: "[i]n the event of replacement or cancellation, the obligee shall not be required to compensate the part of depreciation of the thing that resulted from it having been used in accordance with its designated use."[97] We do not share this view, since "depreciation" (loss of value) is not equal to the "payment for normal use". Therefore Art. 14 Para 4 SGD is not correctly implemented.

---

[93] Vékás denied the necessity to draft a particular rule on that; according to him, Section 6:159 Para 4 and Section 6:166 Para 1 HCC suffice. Cf. Vékás 'Az uniós fogyasztói szerződési jog megújítása és az új irányelvek átültetése' (2021) 68 *Magyar Jog*, 65 (71, 72).
[94] Cf. Vékás 'Az uniós fogyasztói szerződési jog megújítása és az új irányelvek átültetése' (2021) 68 *Magyar Jog*, 65 (72).
[95] Hajnal, 'A fogyasztási cikkek adásvételének szabályozási kísérlete és legújabb módosításai az Európai Unióban és a magyar jogban' (2020) 28/7–8 *Gazdaság és jog*, 6 (9).
[96] Cf. Farkas in Wellmann (ed), *A Ptk. magyarázata V/VI. Kötelmi jog első és második rész* (2021), Section 6:159, 493.
[97] Cf. Vékás 'Az uniós fogyasztói szerződési jog megújítása és az új irányelvek átültetése' (2021) 68 *Magyar Jog*, 65 (72). The same way Kemenes, in Vékás and Gárdos (eds), *Nagykommentár a Polgári Törvénykönyvhöz* I (2020), Section 6:167, 1770 without any explanations. In another commentary on the HCC, reference is made in that sense to the former court practice, cf. Farkas in Wellmann (ed), *A Ptk. magyarázata V/VI. Kötelmi jog első és második rész* (2021), Section 6:167, 510–11. Görög and Kaufmann-Mohi explain this statement in a way that the depreciation is caused – at least in part – by the use of the good before repair or replacement, therefore if there is no claim for depreciation, there can be no such claim for any payment for the use being included in the depreciation either, but this is not convincing. Cf. Görög and Kaufmann-Mohi, 'A fogyasztási cikkek adásvételének szabályozási kísérlete és legújabb módosításai az Európai Unióban és a magyar jogban' (2020) 28/7–8 *Gazdaság és jog*, 23 (27).

B. Some Details of the Implementation, Variabilities

Art. 15 SGD on price reduction has been taken over as a verbatim translation in Section 14 ID. The provisions on termination (statement; terminating the contract in part or regarding all goods having been acquired together with those lacking conformity; returning the good and reimbursing the payment) in Art. 16 SGD have also been implemented as literal translations and can be found in Section 15 ID. Since SGD entitles the Member States to determine the modalities for return and reimbursement, Decree No. 19/2014 of the Minister of National Economics on Handling of Warranty and Guarantee Claims regarding Things Sold in Consumer Contracts deserves mention. Though this decree does not contain explicit provisions on return and reimbursement in a narrow sense, it nevertheless provides for many details on handling the consumers' respective claims, such as best-effort (maximum) deadline to perform the repair (15 days, Section 5); mandatory content of the receipt given in exchange for the defective product (Section 6), etc. Since Art. 14 Para 1 lit b. SGD provides for the repair or replacement to be performed within a "reasonable period of time", certainly in many events this deadline shall be considered as shorter than the best effort deadline of 15 days. The latter does not exclude the application of a shorter deadline according to the circumstances of the case (in compliance with the SGD), if a shorter one is reasonable, since it is just the maximum duration of the respective (best effort) deadline.

65

Unlike the remedies based on (commercial) guarantees, the statutory remedies described here are not accessory to the goods, therefore they do not get transferred automatically (by law) if the goods are (re)sold under Hungarian law. To the contrary: the buyer as the new owner has its own remedies based on the law against his or her contracting party, the (last or direct) seller. Of course, it is not prohibited to assign the remedies in the sales contract;[98] this is quite common practice among consumers in C2C relations: the seller assigns the remedies to the buyer and the same time the parties exclude by mutual agreement the seller's liability for defects.[99]

66

It deserves mention that the Hungarian legislator introduced (with the general recodification of civil law in 2013) a new extracontractual, statutory and mandatory remedy (for repair or replacement) on the consumers' side directly against the producer, the so-called product warranty (Sections 6:178–6:170 HCC),[100] which is a kind of legal hybrid, a Satyr. In the front it looks like the contractual remedy for repair or replacement (but lacks the second stage, i.e. price reduction and rescission, which is understandable, since the consumer and the producer generally do not have a direct contractual relationship with each other), but in the back some defences that can be referred to by the producer have been imported from the classic product liability law (first, it has not produced or distributed the product within its business activities; second, the defect was not recognisable given the state of scientific or technical knowledge when the product was placed on the market; and third, the product's defect was caused by the application of a law or a mandatory authority provision). The consumer can exercise these direct remedies against the manufacturer within two years after the latter placed the product

67

---

[98] Cf. Farkas in Wellmann (ed), *A Ptk. magyarázata V/VI. Kötelmi jog első és második rész* (2021), Section 6:159, 487.

[99] In this respect, Section 6:195 deserves attention. According to Para 1: "[c]lauses excluding the assignment of claims shall be ineffective towards third parties." This means that the consumer can validly assign their warranty right despite such kind of contractual prohibition. If there was such a prohibition in the contract then the breach thereof triggers the contractual liability of the party. However, as provided for in Para 2: "[c]ontract clauses ensuring the right of unilateral termination or setting forth a contractual penalty payment obligation for such a breach of contract shall be null and void."

[100] For a critical analysis with a comparative approach cf. Fuglinszky, 'The Conceivable Ways and Means of the Further Harmonization of European Product Liability Law – Mandatory Direct Claim against the Producer for Repair or Replacement?' (2018) 26 *ZEuP*, 590.

on the market. The expiry of this time limit shall cause the forfeiture of rights. If the product is (re)sold, the product warranty rights can be enforced by the new owner (if also a consumer), but only within the original deadline. According to Section 6:168 Para 2 HCC, besides the manufacturer, the "distributor" can also be the addressee of the remedy and the notion "distributor" is not restricted to intermediary traders upwards in the contractual chain, but the last (direct) seller is included, too. Our understanding, regarding the maximum harmonisation principle, is that any direct remedy against the direct seller is governed only, i.e. solely and exclusively, by the new rules implementing the SGD's provisions. Nevertheless, the direct remedy described above against the producer and all (indirect) sellers upwards in the contractual chain is not superseded by the SGD and the mandatory rules of the implementing decree (since this subject matter and the respective remedies are not covered by the SGD).

68 As already referred to above, the directives do not cover damages; this remedy remains in the autonomous legislative competence of the Member States. The relevant provision is Section 6:174 HCC (that applies to the defective performance of all types of contracts, thus also to those on digital content and services), according to Para 1: "[t]he obligor shall be required to compensate for the obligee's damage arising from defective performance, unless he provides an excuse for his defective performance." This refers to the strict liability in Section 6:142 HCC. However – in order not to evade the deadlines for warranty claims – if the harm (loss) occurred in the object of the contract itself (contractual service, such as loss of value or costs of repair); in other words, if the performance interest (*Leistungsinteresse*) is infringed, i.e. it is about a loss that could be remedied (also) by repair or replacement, then – according to Para 2 – the right to damages can be exercised only within the very same deadlines as warranty claims can, and only if the switch to the second stage remedies (price reduction or rescission) were allowed, because "repair or replacement is not possible, or if the obligor did not undertake to provide repair or replacement, or was unable to perform this obligation, or if the obligee's interest in the repair or replacement has ceased to exist."[101] In contrast, if damages are claimed for losses beyond the contractual performance (loss of profit, personal injuries, property damage to other assets or pure economic loss caused by the defective performance; in other words, not the performance interest, but the protectional interest *Schutzinteresse* is infringed), since these losses cannot be automatically remedied by specific performance (repair or replacement of the contractual goods or service), the above mentioned precondition does not apply, damages can be claimed directly and within the regular prescription period of five years. Another difference is that, for loss of profit and other consequential losses, the foreseeability limitation in Section 6:143 HCC (transplanted from Art. 74 CISG) applies.

b) Supply of Digital Content and Services

69 The legislator obviously stayed on the safe side and opted mostly for the verbatim translation of the DCD. This applies for example to Art. 13 (Remedy for the failure to supply, which can be found in Section 23 ID); to Art. 15 (Exercise of the right of termination, Section 22 Para 8 ID) and with some minor textual (but not substantive) differences to Art. 17 (Obligations of the consumer in the event of termination, Sec-

---

[101] This is why damages is seen as a secondary remedy in this respect, since the same losses can be remedied much easier by warranty claims for repair and replacement, or if this is not possible, etc. then by price reduction or rescission. (Warranty claims are even stricter than the strict liability in contract: there is no possibility to be exempted at all.) See in this respect Farkas in Wellmann (ed), *A Ptk. magyarázata V/VI. Kötelmi jog első és második rész* (2021), Section 6:174, 526.

B. Some Details of the Implementation, Variabilities

tion 26 ID). Section 24 Paras 2–4 ID is equivalent to Art. 18 (Time limits and means of reimbursement by the trader), but with one not insignificant difference. While Art. 18 Para 3 DCD forbids the trader to impose any "fee" on the consumer in respect of the reimbursement, according to Section 24 Para 4 ID the costs of reimbursements shall be borne by the undertaking. From this legislative allocation of costs, it does not necessarily follow that the undertaking is prohibited from imposing any fee on the consumer. Either the ID should be amended, or at least the prohibition set forth in the DCD shall be complied with via euroconform interpretation.

The Implementing Decree and the Civil Code seem to supplement each other in some respect and a peculiar amalgam comes into being. Though the legislator transposed Art. 14 DCD (Remedies for lack of conformity) basically the same way as Art. 13,[102] the content of Art. 14 Para 2 DCD can be identified in two different components. First, Art. 6:159 Para 2 lit. a HCC seems to be relevant, which (as a general rule on the remedies) is stating that "the obligee, subject to his choice, a) may claim repair or replacement, unless the performance of the chosen remedy for breach of warranty for material defects is impossible, or if it would result in disproportionate additional costs to the obligor compared to satisfying a different claim for warranty for material defects, taking into account the value that the service would have in flawless condition, the gravity of the breach of contract and the harm to interests caused to the obligee by satisfying the right of warranty for material defects". However, since first it does not make sense to identify separately and to differentiate between repair and replacement as far as digital content or digital service are concerned; and second, since the consumer is generally not in a position to decide upon the modality and way of rectifying the non-conformity, Section 22 Para 3 ID adds that it is up to the undertaking to choose the manner and modality to bring the content or service into conformity with the subjective and objective requirements. The rest of Art. 14 DCD has been implemented more or less literally in Section 22 ID.

Though it follows *a contrario* from Art. 14 Para 6 DCD and accordingly from Section 6:159 Para 3 HCC and Section 22 Para 6 ID, nevertheless the Hungarian legislator considered the importance of inserting a particular provision into the ID (as its Section 22 Para 7), stating that if personal data is provided in exchange, the consumer is entitled to terminate the contract even if the lack of conformity is minor but he or she cannot request price reduction. Thus, the legislator did nothing else but enacted the first half of recital no. 67 DCD as part of the Implementing Decree.

Art. 16 DCD (Obligation of the trader in the event of termination) has also been literally translated and enacted as Section 24 Para 1 and Section 25 ID. However, the Hungarian legislator made the interpretation thereof a bit complicated, since it supplemented the text with some additional requirements which focus on data protection. Though Art. 16 Para 3 DCD refers to "content other than personal data", the legislator supplemented the text implementing lit b (being placed in Section 25 Para 2 lit. b ID: the content only relates to the consumer's activity when using the digital content or digital service supplied by the trader) with the additional alternative requirements that either that data processing is necessary to perform the services[103] or the consumer provided their consent according to the GDPR or the undertaking automatically and immediately anonymised those data related to the consumer's activity in an irreversible manner. It is

---

[102] It is certainly just an error that, in Section 22 Para 1 lit. c ID transposing Art. 14 Para 4 lit. c DCD, there is "good" in the text instead of digital content and service.

[103] If this is the case, i.e. the personal data provided by the consumer are exclusively processed by the trader for the purpose of supplying the digital content or digital service, then DCD (and ID) does not apply at all. Cf. Art. 3 Para 1 Subpara 2 DCD.

confusing, why these GDPR-conform actions are imposed on the trader although the respective provision of the DCD is *expressis verbis* not on personal data, but on any content other than personal data. Maybe the European legislator confused its national counterpart with this provision, the necessity of which is not unambiguously comprehensible. As is emphasised in legal scholarship: since the notion and scope of personal data under the GDPR is conceived very broadly, the content and substance of the term "content other than personal data", which is thus not personal data, but can nevertheless be projected and assigned to a particular person, is highly likely to be nothing more than an empty set.[104] Art 16 Para 5 DCD refers to the trader's right to make the content or service inaccessible or to disable the consumer's user account. The Hungarian legislator – while it implements this provision literally in Section 25 Para 5 ID – adds that disabling the user account does not deprive the consumer of exercising their right to request a copy of the personal data (undergoing processing) according to Art. 15 Para 3 GDPR. Since the GDPR applies anyway, it is not clear why the legislator felt tempted to insert this *addendum*.

73   Sein and Spindler are right in noting that Art 16 DCD does not apply if the trader, not the consumer, terminates the contract and the same stands true if it is not this particular termination right but another termination right based on the applicable contract law that is exercised. Nevertheless, maximum harmonization does not hold back the national legislator to extend the respective special rules on reimbursement, compliance with the GDPR and non-use of consumer generated content other than personal data to other options of termination provided for in the contract or by law.[105] The Hungarian legislator did not embrace this opportunity.

74   The trader's non-compliance with the GDPR triggers the consequences specified in the GDPR itself, i.e. administrative fines (Art. 83) and penalties (damages, Art. 84). However, Section 2 Para 2 of Act No. CXII/2011 on the Right to Informational Self-determination and on the Freedom of Information renders some more sanctions applicable, such as Section 61 Para 2, according to which the National Authority for Data Protection and Freedom of Information may order the publication of its decision (on the non-compliance) so as to include the identification data of the controller or processor as well if "a) the decision concerns a wide range of persons, b) the decision was adopted in connection with the activities of an organ performing public duties, or c) the gravity of the infringement justifies publication." Remarkable is that the Authority can publish the decision even if the data controller brings an action to challenge the decision in front of (administrative) court, hence the authority does not have to wait with the publication until the court's final judgment. Moreover, as referred to in Recital No. 48 of the DCD, lack of compliance with the GDPR may also be considered "to constitute a lack of conformity of the digital content or digital service with subjective or objective requirements for conformity".

---

[104] Similarly Sein and Spindler, 'The new Directive on Contracts for the Supply of Digital Content and Digital Services – Conformity Criteria, Remedies and Modification – Part 2' (2019) 15 *ERCL*, 365 (382). An uploaded photo for example definitely constitutes personal data. See also Vanherpe, 'White Smoke but Smoke Nonetheless: Some (Burning) Questions Regarding the Directives on Sale of Goods and Supply of Digital Content' (2020) 28 *ERPL*, 251 (269). Mischau, 'Daten als "Gegenleistung" im neuen Verbrauchervertragsrecht' (2020) 28 *ZEuP*, 335 (351). Moreover data initially non-personal may become personal later by virtue of analytics. Cf. Durovic and Lech, 'A Consumer Law Perspective on the Commercialization of Data' (2021) 29 *ERPL*, 701 (728, 731).

[105] Sein and Spindler, 'The new Directive on Contracts for the Supply of Digital Content and Digital Services – Conformity Criteria, Remedies and Modification – Part 2' (2019) 15 *ERCL*, 365 (379).

B. *Some Details of the Implementation, Variabilities*

V. Other Provisions

1. Commercial Guarantees (Art. 17 SGD)

Guarantees are not new in the Hungarian law of obligations. They are provided for in Sections 6:171–6:173 HCC. There are even some mandatory guarantees covered by special legislative acts.[106] The main legal effect of a guarantee – be it imposed by law or assumed voluntarily – is the reversal of burden of proof. The obligor under the guarantee has to rectify the defect (non-conformity with the requirements specified in the guarantee statement or in the legislative act that provides for the guarantee) unless it proves that the reason for the defect occurred after the performance (Section 6:171 Para 1). This duty applies during the whole guarantee period. The guarantee period is a strict limitation deadline: the right itself ceases with the expiry (not only the judicial enforceability, Section 6:173 Para 1). The guarantee claim (in contrast with the contractual remedies for repair and replacement based on the law) is reminiscent of the French concept of *action directe*, since if the good's ownership changes, the guarantee right becomes automatically transferred to the new owner just as an accessory to the good (Section 6:172). However, the deadline does not restart, therefore the new owner can exercise its right only within the original strict deadline (that cannot be suspended or interrupted).

It is therefore questionable why the Hungarian legislator felt the need to transpose Art. 17 SGD as an almost verbatim translation into Section 16 ID. There are two elements in the wording of Art. 17 that are missing from the HCC. First, an explicit reference to the associated advertising (though can be understood as covered by Section 6:173 Para 2 HCC referring to remedies provided for in the HCC in the event of defective performance, i.e. non-conformity, wherein public statements are included). It was and is clear even before (without) the SGD (and in compliance with the former Consumer Sales Directive) that the statements made in the associated advertising are binding on the guarantor (now in Art 17 Para 1 SGD and Section16 Para 3 ID). Second, the respective HCC provisions do not explicitly mention the producer as the direct addressee of the remedies, but Art. 17 SGD does. However, the SGD itself does not impose any specific duty on producers either; it "just" establishes a legal framework undertaken by the guarantor, be it the producer or someone else (practically upwards in the contractual chain or a third party on their behalf). It was possible even before the implementation of the SGD for producers to undertake direct guarantees under Hungarian law.

As far as the opportunity to lay down rules on other aspects of guarantees (especially the language) is concerned, the Hungarian legislator requires the guarantor to provide the consumer with the guarantee statements also in Hungarian (Section 16 Para 5 ID). Some other aspects are already covered in the HCC (see above), and they do not need to be reshaped.

2. Modification of the Digital Content or Digital Service (Art. 19 DCD)

Art. 19 DCD has also been implemented as an almost literal translation (Section 27 ID). The only minor implementation bug is that the specific reference in the wording of DCD "whichever is later" (of the two points in time that can trigger the 30 days deadline within which the consumer can exercise their termination right) is miss-

---

[106] Cf. Government Decree No. 151/2003 (IX.22.) on Mandatory Guarantee for Certain Durable Consumer Goods; Government Decree No. 249/2004 (VIII.27.) on Mandatory Guarantee for Certain Repair and Maintenance Services; Government Decree No. 181/2003. (XI. 5.) on Mandatory Guarantee for Construction of Flats.

ing in the Hungarian text, i.e. the two options are simply drafted as alternatives. The DCD's text however provides sufficient support for a euroconform interpretation.

79 The modification of the digital content or service is – no doubt – an amendment of the contract from the legal point of view. According to the general provision in Section 6:191 Para 4 HCC, the unilateral amendment of the contract by one of the parties is possible "if this is provided for in the contract, or if the law authorises the party to do so." Section 27 ID is that particular law on which the right to modification is based (The mandatory rules provided for in the DCD and now in the Implementing Decree cannot be set aside by mutual agreement.)

80 The European legislator overlooked that the same issue can arise also with regard to goods with digital elements and omitted to include a similar provision in the SGD. Though this could theoretically be remedied by an appropriate legislative intervention of the Member States' legislators, maximum harmonization may stand in the way.

3. Right of Redress (Art. 18 SGD, Art. 20 DCD)

81 The right of redress is referred to in the first (general) chapter of the implementing decree, in Section 7, according to which the undertaking (liable to the consumer) can pursue remedies against a person in previous links of the chain of transactions based on the contract between them (if there is a contractual relationship between them, i.e. they are a kind of direct neighbours in the contractual chain). According to Vékás, Section 6:148 Para 3 HCC is referred to here: "[t]he obligor may enforce his rights against the vicarious agent arising from the vicarious agent's breach of contract for as long as he is required to stand liable towards the obligee." If the undertaking (liable to the consumer) and defendant upwards in the contractual chain are not direct neighbours, i.e. are not in contractual relationship with each other then extracontractual liability applies.[107]

C. Some Conclusions

82 The Hungarian legislator likely intended to stay on the safe side, without a willingness to scrutinize the respective provisions of the HCC, to filter and recompose them in the light of the directives and to consider which provisions fit easily into the code in order to avoid overlaps and parallelisms; therefore the directives have been implemented in a separate law outside the HCC. Within this law however, the legislator's pursuit was to set up a general part for those provisions of the directives that can be generalized and merged and then to implement the specific contents in two separate chapters (sale of goods; digital content and services). The implementation is in compliance with the directive, both at a structural level and also regarding the details. Different formulations in the wording basically do not change the content. There are only a few obvious implementation flaws, but euroconform interpretation can help to rectify them in practice, until the legislator intervenes. Nevertheless, it can be confusing if provisions or parts of provisions that belong together are divided between the HCC (where already existing rules fit on the merits) and the implementing decree (such as Art. 14 Para 2 DCD on the modalities of bringing the content into conformity and Art. 13 Para 5 SGD, Art. 14

---

[107] Vékás 'Az uniós fogyasztói szerződési jog megújítása és az új irányelvek átültetése' (2021) 68 *Magyar Jog*, 65 (66–73). Janssen is right in noting that the United Nations Convention on Contracts for the International Sale of Goods (CISG) may be applicable to the B2B contracts before the consumer contract in the supply chain, wherein there is no explicit duty to update. Appropriate drafting (of the respective contract) is therefore essential. Cf. Janssen, 'Die Aktualisierungspflicht des Letztverkäufers für Smart Products: Ein neues haftungsrechtliches Damoklesschwert?' (2021) 29 *ERPL*, 557 (559).

C. Some Conclusions

Para 6 DCD on minor defects and the burden of proof, etc.). The Hungarian legislator embraced the opportunity to opt in or to opt out (allowed explicitly by the directives in some respect), for example to take the consumer's contribution to the non-conformity into account; to maintain the consumer's notification duty and to uphold the applicable provisions on limitation periods (that can be suspended or interrupted); but did not make use of the opportunity to exclude living animals and second hand goods sold at public auctions from the scope.

Of course, all the "original sins" of the directives are reflected in the laws of the Member States, too. Especially "dangerous" is the encounter and liaison of more structural challenges "offered" by the directives themselves. For example, if the inconsistency regarding the scope of the directives (cf. the goods with digital elements: digital elements underlie the SGD) meets inconsistencies in the content: it was forgotten to include provisions present in the DCD into the SGD and they therefore cannot apply to the digital content included in the goods. The practical effect of these *lacunae* is increased by the harsh approach of maximum harmonization: the loopholes in the law cannot be remedied by case law, since this would be equal to extending the regime provided for in the respective directive (cf. for example the consumer's notification duty is present in the SGD but is missing in the DCD; or the other way round: modification of the digital content is covered by the DCD but not so by the SGD, though goods with digital elements underlie the SGD). The same stands true for notions and terms with uncertain content, such as termination. Is the maximum harmonisation still complied with if the Member State's legislator specifies the latter directive-specific and neutral term either as *ex tunc* or *ex nunc* rescission? How can the Member States adjust their laws to the autonomous concepts of EU law if many of them are still just empty boxes, or at least require meticulous analysis based on the particular rules of the directives and on some connecting provisions of the GDPR? 83

Unsurprisingly, the maximum harmonization has manifold impacts on the respective field of law. As far as the self-help remedy (*Selbstvornahme*) is concerned, the Hungarian legislator exaggerated and performed a kind of unnecessary (legal) self-mutilation and repealed the opportunity that the consumer can also repair the defect himself or have it repaired by somebody else at the seller's expense (Though it is explicitly allowed to keep this remedy according to Recital No. 54 SGD). Elsewhere the legislator simply did not take note of the maximum harmonization requirement and allowed such options that are not in line with the respective directive to survive (for example: switching to the second stage remedies in consumer sales law if the consumer-buyer's interest in repair or replacement is lost). 84

The advantage is the almost flawless implementation of the directives. However, the particular (Hungarian) way of implementation can also be evaluated as a bundle of missed opportunities. First, the opportunity to review sales law as such and contract law in general (as it happened with the implementation of the CSD back then) was not taken. Second, with a bit more careful and diligent drafting the overlaps and repetitions between the Civil Code and the implementing decree could have been avoided. Third, the digital contract regime has not been extended beyond B2C transactions to B2B contracts, not even as default rules. Fourth, the implementation was unfortunately not seen as an occasion to harmonise the respective parts of contract law with intellectual property and electronic communication law, though this cannot be attributed to the Member States' legislators only, since the adjustment could have been performed at EU level in some respects. Fifth, the (European) legislator also forewent channelling the requirements of sustainability and circular economy in a more tangible way into the directives. As far as the Hungarian legislative environment is concerned, there is never- 85 theless a bridge to link these and other policy goals with the contract law provisions on remedies, provided that these goals find their way at least into public (administrative) laws either at EU or at national level. Minimum standards provided for by (administrative, such as product safety) law automatically form part of the objective requirements of conformity. The first promising signs appeared with the recent amendment of the (Hungarian) consumer protection act. Nevertheless, the overall priority of repair over replacement has not yet been declared.

86 The biggest achievement of the directives and their implementation is no doubt that they trigger the re-evaluation and critical overview of general contract law due to unstoppable digitalization processes. This is more than timely and necessary, otherwise those who are the most vulnerable (consumers) end up in a legal vacuum regarding some rights and positions. Disregarding reality can be very counterproductive. An emblematic issue is thus personal data as contractual consideration, including but not limited to issues whether such contractual assumptions are enforceable or not; whether the respective contracts are gratuitous (they are not, according to the prevailing view) and, last but not least, how the contractual reflection of withdrawal of consent shall be conceived. Though strictly private law-related analyses have hardly begun in Hungary, some preliminary results can nevertheless be identified. First, the withdrawal-situation does not fit perfectly to any of the recent existing contract law concepts (such as impossibility or resolutive condition), but can be reconciled with them by a slight *praeter legem* interpretation. Second, the reciprocity of contractual services (performance of the primary duty in exchange for consideration) does not necessarily mean that they are also in a synallagmatic relationship with each other. As if the respective concepts were concentric circles, all synallagmatic transactions are reciprocal, but not all reciprocal transactions are synallagmatic. It is exciting to follow up whether contracts with personal data as counterperformance – which are no doubt reciprocal – will qualify as a kind of contract regarding which the synallagma cannot be examined and judged upon at all, or to the contrary: a data-specific synallagma-concept will come into being.

Bibliography

Dóra Czapári, 'A személyes adatok felhasználására vonatkozó szerződés lényeges kérdései' (2021) 6 *Polgári jog*, electronic journal, paper available at: https://uj.jogtar.hu/#doc/db/193/id/A2100601.POJ/.

Márton Domokos, 'Gyakorlati tapasztalatok a GDPR-megfelelés során' in Endre Győző Szabó (ed), *Az Infotörvénytől a GDPR-ig* (Ludovika Egyetemi Kiadó, Budapest, 2021) 209.

Gábor Dudás, 'A magyar rendes bíróságok adatvédelmet érintő döntései' in Endre Győző Szabó (ed), *Az Infotörvénytől a GDPR-ig* (Ludovika Egyetemi Kiadó, Budapest, 2021) 57.

Mateja Durovic and Franciszek Lech, 'A Consumer Law Perspective on the Commercialization of Data' (2021) 29 *ERPL*, 701.

Ádám Fuglinszky, 'The Reform of Contractual Liability in the New Hungarian Civil Code: Strict Liability and Foreseeability Clause as Legal Transplants' (2015) 79 *RabelsZ*, 72.

Ádám Fuglinszky, 'Verbrauchsgüterkauf im ungarischen Privatrecht – Vom verwaisten "Weber" und "Putz" zu einem Satyr des Verbraucherprovatrechts' (2016) 24 *ZEuP*, 121.

Ádám Fuglinszky, *Fogyasztói adásvétel, kellék- és termékszavatosság – Elemzések az uniós jog és az új Ptk. kapcsolatához* (Wolters Kluwer, Budapest, 2016).

Bibliography

Ádám Fuglinszky, 'The Conceivable Ways and Means of the Further Harmonization of European Product Liability Law – Mandatory Direct Claim against the Producer for Repair or Replacement?' (2018) 26 *ZEuP*, 590.

Ádám Fuglinszky and Balázs Tőkey, *Szerződési jog – Különös rész* (ELTE Eötvös Kiadó, Budapest, 2018).

Ádám Fuglinszky, 'Legal Transplants: Snapshots of the State of the Art and a Case Study from Central Europe: Post Transplantation-adjustment of Contractual Liability in the New Hungarian Civil Code' (2020) 16 *ERCL*, 267.

Márta Görög and Emese Kaufmann-Mohi, 'A hibás fogyasztási cikk kicserlése az európai magánjogban' (2010) 18/9–10 *Gazdaság és jog*, 23.

Beate Gsell, Wolfgang Krüger, Stephan Lorenz and Christoph Reymann (eds), *Beck-online Grosskommentar BGB* (Stand: 01. 01. 2022).

Phillip Hacker, 'Daten als Gegenleistung: Rechtsgeschäfte im Spannungsfeld von DS-GVO und allgemeinen Vertragsrecht' (2019) 5 *ZfPW*, 148.

Phillip Hacker, 'Regulating the Economic Impact of Data as Counter-Performance: From the Illegality Doctrine to the Unfair Contract Terms Directive' in Sebastian Lohsse, Reiner Schulze and Dirk Staudenmayer (eds), *Data as Counter-Performance – Contract Law 2.0?* (Nomos, Baden-Baden, 2020) 47.

Zsolt Hajnal, 'A fogyasztási cikkek adásvételének szabályozási kísérlete és legújabb módosításai az Európai Unióban és a magyar jogban' (2020) 28/7–8 *Gazdaság és jog*, 6.

André Janssen, 'Die Aktualisierungspflicht des Letztverkäufers für Smart Products: Ein neues haftungsrechtliches Damoklesschwert?' (2021) 29 *ERPL*, 557.

András Jóri (ed), *A GDPR magyarázata* (hvgorac, Budapest 2018).

Mónika Józon, 'Az európai uniós jogharmonizáció mint állandó viszonyítási-értékelési-igazodási folyamat tagállami szinten: módszertani elemzés' (2020) 16 *IAS*, 29.

Attila Menyhárd, 'Forgalomképes személyiség?' in Attila Menyhárd and Fruzsina Gárdos-Orosz (eds), *Személy és személyiség a jogban* (Wolters Kluwer, Budapest, 2016) 57.

Axel Metzger, 'A Market Model for Personal Data: State of Play under the New Directive on Digital Content and Digital Services' in Sebastian Lohsse, Reiner Schulze and Dirk Staudenmayer (eds), *Data as Counter-Performance – Contract Law 2.0?* (Nomos, Baden-Baden, 2020) 25.

Péter Mezei, *Jogkimerülés a szerzői jogban* (NMHH Médiaturományi Intézet, Budapest, 2016).

Lena Mischau, 'Daten als "Gegenleistung" im neuen Verbrauchervertragsrecht' (2020) 28 *ZEuP*, 335.

Sebastian Lohsse, Reiner Schulze and Dirk Staudenmayer, 'Data as Counter-Performance – Contract Law 2.0? An introduction' in Sebastian Lohsse, Reiner Schulze and Dirk Staudenmayer (eds), *Data as Counter-Performance – Contract Law 2.0?* (Nomos, Baden-Baden, 2020) 9.

Attila Péterfalvi, Balázs Révész and Péter Buzás (eds), *Magyarázat a GDPR-ról* (Wolters Kluwer, Budapest, 2021).

Andreas Sattler, 'Autonomy or Heteronomy – Proposal for a Two-Tier Interpretation of Art 6 GDPR' in Sebastian Lohsse, Reiner Schulze and Dirk Staudenmayer (eds), *Data as Counter-Performance – Contract Law 2.0?* (Nomos, Baden-Baden, 2020) 225.

Martin Schmidt-Kessel and Anna Grimm, 'Unentgeltlich oder entgeltlich? – Der vertragliche Austausch von digitalen Inhalten gegen personenbezogene Daten' (2017) 3 *ZfPW*, 84.

Martin Schmidt-Kessel, 'Right to Withdraw Consent to Data Processing – The Effect on the Contract' in Sebastian Lohsse, Reiner Schulze and Dirk Staudenmayer (eds), *Data as Counter-Performance – Contract Law 2.0?* (Nomos, Baden-Baden, 2020) 129.

Christian Schubel, 'Die zweite Andienung des Verkäufers nach der Umsetzung der Warenkaufrichtlinie' (2022) 77 *JZ*, 73.

Karin Sein and Gerald Spindler, 'The new Directive on Contracts for the Supply of Digital Content and Digital Services – Scope of Application and Trader's Obligaton to Supply – Part 1' (2019) 15 *ERCL*, 257.

Karin Sein and Gerald Spindler, 'The new Directive on Contracts for the Supply of Digital Content and Digital Services – Conformity Criteria, Remedies and Modification – Part 2' (2019) 15 *ERCL*, 365.

Juliette Sénéchal, 'Article 16(2) of the 'Digital Content and Digital Services' Directive on the Consequences of Termination of Contract, or the Difficult Articulation between Union Law on Consumer Contract and Union Law on the Protection of Personal Data' in Lohsse, Schulze and Staudenmayer (eds), *Data as Counter-Performance – Contract Law 2.0?* (Nomos, Baden-Baden, 2020) 147.

Louisa Specht, 'Daten als Gegenleistung – Verlangt die Digitalisierung nach einem neuen Vertragstypus' (2017) 72 *JZ*, 763.

Ferenc Szilágyi, 'The Implementation of Directives 2019/770 and 2019/771 in Hungary' (2021) 10 *EuCML*, 267.

Izabella Szoboszlai and András Tóth, 'A Kúria Facebook-ügyben hozott ítéletének margójára' (2022) 1 *Fogyasztóvédelmi jog*, electronic journal, paper available at: https://uj.jogtar.hu/#doc/db/557/id/A2200103.FVO/.

András Tóth, 'A tisztességes adatkereskedelmet biztosító szabályozás szükségességéről' (2021) 62 *Állam- és Jogtudomány*, 100.

Jozefien Vanherpe, 'White Smoke but Smoke Nonetheless: Some (Burning) Questions Regarding the Directives on Sale of Goods and Supply of Digital Content' (2020) 28 *ERPL*, 251.

Lajos Vékás and Péter Gárdos (eds), *Nagykommentár a Polgári Törvénykönyvhöz* I (Wolters Kluwer, Budapest 2020).

Lajos Vékás 'Az uniós fogyasztói szerződési jog megújítása és az új irányelvek átültetése' (2021) 68 *Magyar Jog*, 65.

György Wellmann (ed), *A Ptk. magyarázata V/VI. Kötelmi jog első és második rész* (hvgorac, Budapest 2021).

Zsolt Ződi, 'A jog és a kód' in Gábor Polyák (ed), *Algoritmusok, keresők, közösségi oldalak és a jog – A forgalomirányító szolgáltatások szabályozása* (hvgorac, Budapest, 2020) 15.

Ireland

A.	Introduction	1
B.	Definitions and Scope of Application	8
	I. Definitions	8
	II. Types of Contracts and Scope of Application	12
	III. Data as Counter-Performance and the Doctrine of Consideration	15
	IV. Business to Business (B2B) Contracts	18
C.	Conformity of Goods	19
	I. Information Requirements in Distance and Off-Premises Contracts	21
	II. Spare Parts and After-Sale Services	22
	III. Right to Sell/Supply & Terminate; Freedom from Charges or other Encumbrances	23
	IV. Implied Contract Terms	25
	V. Exclusion or Limitation of Liability	26
	VI. Recipients of a Gift and Users of Motor Vehicles	27
	VII. The Durability Requirement	30
	VIII. The Duty to Inform and Supply Updates	34
	IX. Exclusion of Conformity	38
	X. Third Party Rights	39
D.	Liability of the Trader	45
E.	Remedies for the failure to supply and remedies for the lack of conformity	52
F.	Commercial Guarantees	65
G.	Time Limits	72
H.	Right of Redress	76
I.	Relationship with other Remedies	77
J.	Concluding Remarks	79
	Bibliography	79

A. Introduction

The Digital Content Directive[1] (DCD) and Sale of Goods Directive[2] (SGD) have been transposed into Irish law by the Consumer Rights Act 2022. In May 2021, the Government published a Scheme (legislative outline) for a Consumer Rights Bill 2021, which sought to transpose the SGD in Part 2, and the DCD in Part 3, and a Consultation on the Scheme for a Consumer Rights Bill, was commenced at the same time.[3] Following a lengthy consultation and drafting process, proposed legislation in the form of the Consumer Rights Bill 2022 was introduced to Parliament (the Oireachtas) on 22 April 2022 and the Consumer Rights Act 2022 completed its passage through the Oireachtas and was enacted on 7 November 2022. The whole Act, bar one provision[4], came into effect from 29 November 2022.

The transposition of the DCD and the SGD is part of a wider consolidation and reform process of Irish consumer law which started over a decade ago. Initially, reform

---

[1] Directive (EU) 2019/770 of the European Parliament and of the Council of 20 May 2019 on certain aspects concerning contracts for the supply of digital content and digital services, [2019] OJ L 136/1.

[2] Directive (EU) 2019/771 of the European Parliament and of the Council of 20 May 2019 on certain aspects concerning contracts for the sale of goods, amending Regulation (EU) 2017/2394 and Directive 2009/22/EC, and repealing Directive 1999/44/EC, [2019] OJ L136/28.

[3] See https://enterprise.gov.ie/en/Consultations/Consultation-on-Scheme-of-Consumer-Rights-Bill-20 21.html (last accessed 5 July 2022).

[4] Section 161 had not been commenced, at the time of writing.

of consumer sale of goods law was recommended by a Government appointed expert group, the Sales Law Review Group, in its final Report on the Legislation governing the Sale of Goods and Supply of Services in 2011.[5] While the majority of the Report's recommendations addressed B2B transactions, important changes were also recommended in relation to consumer sales and related transactions. In broad terms, the recommendations involved a further 'Europeanisation' of Irish consumer sales law; while certain distinct aspects of the domestic legal framework were to be retained. For example, in relation to definitions, the definition of 'consumer goods' in Directive 1999/44 was to be adopted as the basis of the general definition of 'goods' in future legislation[6]; as was the EU definition of 'consumer'[7], leading to a narrowing of the existing definition which is not expressly limited to natural persons or individuals. At the same time, the common law concepts of conditions, warranties and implied terms as a vehicle for delivering the 'quality standard' of goods, as well as a short-term right to reject defective goods, even for a minor defect, were to be retained but integrated with the EU remedies from Directive 1999/44.[8] More importantly perhaps, the Group recommended that a separate Consumer Contract Rights Act should be enacted that would incorporate the main statutory provisions applicable to consumer contracts, thereby simplifying and consolidating consumer law.[9]

3   Following a period of time, a consultation process was launched, and a Scheme for a Consumer Rights Bill implementing the above recommendations was published in 2015.[10] However, within a short number of months the EU Commission published its proposals for the two new directives, whose implementation is being considered here: one on contracts for the supply of digital content, and a second concerning online sales and distant sales.[11] In light of these developments at EU level, it was decided to pause the domestic reform agenda until the EU legislative process was completed.

4   The adoption of the DCD and the SGD in 2019 clearly delayed completion of the domestic reform agenda; but at the same time, the pursuit of an ambitious consolidation and reform process of consumer contractual rights has also delayed the transposition of the DCD and the SGD into Irish law.

5   The above delays and developments have resulted in some significant changes in policy and to the legislative framework for the protection of consumer contract rights in Ireland. The transposition of these two directives has dove-tailed with and influenced the wider reform agenda. Changes in policy include a jettisoning of the traditional common law concepts of conditions, warranties and implied terms, in favour of the requirements of subjective and objective conformity; and an acceptance of data as a form of counter performance in relation to contracts for digital content and digital services, something which did not feature in the earlier Consumer Rights Bill 2015. At the same time there has been a degree of cross fertilisation between the two directives and between the other provisions of the Consumer Rights Act 2022. For example, while Part 2 of the 2022 Act deals with sale of goods, and Part 3 with digital content and

---

[5] Sales Law Review Group, *Final Report on the Legislation Governing Sale of Goods and Supply of Services* (July 2011) (available at https://enterprise.gov.ie/en/Publications/Report-on-the-Legislation-Governing-the-Sale-of-Goods-and-Supply-of-Services.html last accessed 5 July 2022).
[6] *Ibid.* para. 2.4
[7] *Ibid.* para. 5.22
[8] *Ibid.* Ch. 4.
[9] *Ibid.* para.14.4.
[10] See https://enterprise.gov.ie/en/Consultations/Consultation-on-the-Scheme-of-a-proposed-Consumer-Rights-Bill.html (last accessed 5 July 2022).
[11] COM (2015) 634 final and COM (2015) 635 final. The former proposal was later extended to cover digital services and the latter proposal was subsequently generalised to cover all consumer sales.

services, Part 4 seeks to reform the rules on contracts for the supply of services, and the concepts of subjective and objective conformity have been adopted and tailored to apply to the service contract, along with a similar tailored remedial scheme.[12] In addition, while the proposed rules on sale of goods require payment of a price, the Consumer Rights Act also includes a provision that this requirements may be extended by ministerial order to include data as counter performance in relation to smart goods, in certain circumstances in the future.

It is notable that other related areas, such as intellectual property law and data protection law remain untouched by the transposition of the two Directives. 6

Having set the transposition of the DCD and the SGD in its wider context, the remainder of this Chapter focuses on *how* the DCD and the SGD have been implemented in Irish law with reference to certain key issues, namely, definitions and scope of application; conformity; liability of the trader; remedies; commercial guarantees; time limits; rights of redress, and other remedies. 7

B. Definitions and Scope of Application

I. Definitions

The notions or terms defined in the DCD (in particular Art. 2) and the SGD (in particular Art. 2) are transposed faithfully in the Interpretation sections of the Consumer Rights Act 2022, namely in s.2 (in general); s.10 (in relation to the SGD in particular); and s.48 (in relation to the DCD in particular). For instance, 8

> 'goods' means any tangible moveable items (other than money and any item sold by way of execution or otherwise by authority of law) and includes
> (a) any tangible movable items that incorporate, or are inter-connected with, digital content or a digital service in such a way that the absence of that digital content or digital service would prevent the goods from performing their functions, and
> (b) water, gas and electricity where they are supplied in a limited volume or set quantity;

but in keeping with the pre-existing legal position, the option was not taken to exclude second hand goods sold at public auction or living animals.

The vast majority of the definitions relevant to digital contracts (e.g. digital content, digital service, goods with digital elements, integration, updates, price, digital environment, compatibility, functionality, and interoperability, bar durable medium) are novel to Irish consumer legislation, but have not given rise to any significant doctrinal debate.[13] Given the novelty of these terms, the definitions of 'digital content' and 'digital service' have been expanded to include non-exhaustive illustrative examples from Recital 19 DCD, giving national legal effect to Recital 19, such that 9

---

[12] Part 5 of the Act transposes the consumer rights directive; and Part 6 unfair terms. The remaining Parts deal with enforcement and consequential amendments.

[13] Kelly, "Consumer Reform in Ireland and the UK: Regulatory Divergence before, after and without Brexit", (2018) 47 *Common Law World Review* 53; "The Digital Single Market for Consumers: Mapping Reforms of European Union Consumer Law", (2018) 25 *Commercial Law Practitioner,* 148; Gardiner, "Scheme of Consumer Rights Bill 2015: Paving the Way for Digital Consumers", (2015) 22 *Commercial Law Practitioner,* 222.

"digital content" means data which are produced and supplied in digital form, *including in particular computer programs, applications, video files, audio files, music files, digital games, e-books and other e-publication*; [authors' italics]

"digital service" means
(a) a service that allows a consumer to create, process, store or access data in digital forms, or
(b) a service that allows the sharing of or any other interaction with data in digital form uploaded or created by the consumer or other user of that service,
and includes in particular video and audio sharing and other file hosting, social media, and word processing and games offered in the cloud computing environment; [authors' italics]

10 More generally, and in a similar vein with reference to the relevant recitals (e.g. SGD, Recital 22), the definition of consumer is transposed faithfully, with an additional qualification in relation to dual purpose contracts such that:

"consumer" means an individual acting for purposes that are *wholly or mainly* outside that individual's trade, business, craft or profession;

11 Lastly in relation to definitions, the Consumer Rights Act 2002 uses the term 'trader' throughout, to encompass 'seller' in the SGD, given the fact that the 2022 Act is a consolidating Act dealing with a variety of transactions and regulatory measures, including the DCD and the SGD, as well as service contracts in Part 4; the consumer rights directive in Part 5; and the unfair contract terms directive in Part 6.

II. Types of Contracts and Scope of Application

12 In relation to the different types of contracts within the scope of application of the Consumer Rights Act 2022, the legislation applies to sales contracts, including for the supply of goods with digital elements in Part 2; to digital content contracts (including any tangible medium which serves exclusively as a carrier of digital content) and digital service contracts in Part 3; and to service contracts in Part 4.

13 Prior to the Consumer Rights Act 2022, there was no legislative provision for the supply of goods with digital elements, digital content contracts and digital service contracts in Ireland. At common law, there was no direct legal authority on these types of contracts but based on legal doctrine from other common law jurisdictions with a similar legal framework (namely, the UK and Australia) it seems highly likely that;

- contracts for the supply of goods with digital elements (such as a smart TV or laptop with software pre-installed) would have come within the statutory definition of a sale of goods contract pursuant to the Sale of Goods Acts 1893 and 1980;
- contracts for the supply of digital content on a carrier (such software saved on a CD or a memory stick) would have also come within the statutory definition of a sale of goods contract pursuant to the Sale of Goods Acts 1893 and 1980;
- contracts for the supply of digital content/services alone (e.g. downloaded or otherwise copied) would have not come within the definition of a sale of goods contract

pursuant to the Sale of Goods Act 1893 and 1980, but could have been classified as a contract of services or sui generis.[14]

Thus, the impact of the transposition of the DCD and the SGD appears to be as follow:

- contracts for the supply of goods with digital elements are treated the same under pre-existing legislation and the Consumer Rights Act 2022;
- contracts for the supply of digital content on a carrier are treated differently, and will no longer be classified as sale of goods contracts, but instead will be regulated by the DCD and Part 3 of the Consumer Rights Act 2022;[15]
- contracts for the supply of digital services are excluded from the scope of Part 4 on service contracts, and instead will be regulated by the DCD and Part 3 of the Consumer Rights Act 2022.

While this involves some re-classification of certain contracts, the transposition of the SGD and the DCD brings clarity in terms of the classification of transactions and the application of the different rules, as well as enhancing consumer protection by filling a legislative gap in relation to digital contracts.

III. Data as Counter-Performance and the Doctrine of Consideration

Irish law has no problem is accepting data as counter-performance. The common law doctrine of consideration, with its complicated rules and voluminous jurisprudence, is flexible in recognizing a wide range of forms of counter performance as good consideration for a valid enforceable contract. Thus, in doctrinal terms, the introduction of a provision on data as a counter performance fits neatly with existing contract law doctrine and has not given rise to any doctrinal debate.[16]

Section 2 of the Consumer Rights Act 2022 expressly defines 'digital content contract' and 'digital services contract' to make clear that data as counter performance is good consideration. Accordingly,

'digital content contract' means a contract under which
(a) a trader supplies or undertakes to supply digital content to a consumer, and
(b) the consumer either or both:
  (i) pays or undertakes to pay the price of the digital content;
  (ii) provides or undertakes to provide personal data to the trader, other than where the personal data are processed by the trader only for the purpose of supplying the digital content in accordance with this Act or complying with any other legal requirement to which the trader is subject;

'digital service contract' means a contract under which
(a) a trader supplies or undertakes to supply a digital service to a consumer, and
(b) the consumer either or both:

---

[14] See e.g. Sales Law Review Group, *Final Report on the Legislation Governing Sale of Goods and Supply of Services* (July 2011) paras 2.5 – 2.29 (available at https://enterprise.gov.ie/en/Publications/Report-on-the-Legislation-Governing-the-Sale-of-Goods-and-Supply-of-Services.html last accessed 5 July 2022).

[15] Consumer Rights Act 2022, s.12(6) and s.49(3).

[16] See generally, McDermott and McDermott, *Contract Law*, 2nd edn (London: Bloomsbury Professional, 2017) Ch3 and Clark, *Contract Law in Ireland*, 8th edn (Dublin: Round Hall, 2016, Ch2).

(i) pays or undertakes to pay the price of the digital service;
(ii) provides or undertakes to provide personal data to the trader, other than where the personal data are processed by the trader only for the purpose of supplying the digital service in accordance with this Act or complying with any other legal requirement to which the trader is subject;

While legal doctrine posed no obstacle to data as counter performance, the policy approach to this issue has vacillated in recent years. In 2014, the Department of Jobs, Enterprise and Innovation published a Consultation Paper on Reform of the Law on Consumer Contract Rights[17] which considered the issue of digital content supplied other than for a price. While noting that legislative initiatives in the EU and the UK, at that time, had taken somewhat different approaches, the Consultation Paper, which sought views on this issue, also noted that transactions of this kind appeared to constitute an important part of the business model and revenue generating capacity of some digital content providers. In 2015, a Scheme of a Consumer Rights Bill[18] was published, and Part 3 on contracts for the supply of digital content was drafted to apply only where digital content was supplied for a price. This position would appear to have been influenced by the UK position in their Consumer Rights Act 2015 and a recognition of the important role of tech companies as vehicles for direct foreign investment in the Irish economy.

17 In relation to the sale of goods, s.13 of the Consumer Rights Act 2022 gives the relevant Minister of State the power to extend the application of Part 2 (on sale of goods) to contracts for the sale of goods with digital elements where the consumer

(a) does not pay or undertake to pay the price of the goods, and
(b) provides or undertakes to provide personal data to the trader, other than where the personal data are processed by the trader for the purpose only of supplying the goods with digital elements in accordance with this Part or complying with any other legal requirement to which the trader is subject.

This power can only be exercised where the Minister is satisfied, after consultation with such persons as the Minister considers appropriate, that (a) such contracts are being concluded on a significant scale, and (b) the regulation of such contracts would be in the interests of consumer protection and fair competition.

IV. Business to Business (B2B) Contracts

18 It might be wondered whether the provisions of the two Directives could apply to B2B contracts. In principle, the provisions of the two Directives would appear suitable for B2B contracts, with some modifications. Traditionally, pursuant to the Sale of Goods Acts 1893 and 1980, in relation to the sale of smart goods, and goods which act as a carrier for digital content, as well as in relation to service contracts for the supply of digital content, the same quality/conformity requirements apply to B2B and B2C transactions, subject to modifications. In particular, different rules regulating the use of limitation of liability and exclusion clauses apply, whereby in B2B transactions, parties are given freedom to limit or exclude their liability, in certain circumstances. Any future

---

[17] August 2014, available at https://enterprise.gov.ie/en/Consultations/Consultations-files/Consultation-Paper-Reform-of-the-Law-on-Consumer-Contract-Rights.pdf (last accessed 5 July 2022).
[18] May 2015, available at https://enterprise.gov.ie/en/Consultations/Consultations-files/Scheme-of-a-proposed-Consumer-Rights-Bill-May-2015.pdf (last accessed 5 July 2022).

B2B legislation would need to take account of the needs of businesses to be able to regulate their own risks and liability, via such clauses.

C. Conformity of Goods

19 Subject to some minor textual amendments and the re-ordering of some provisions, the Consumer Rights Act 2022, Part 2 (s.17(1) and s.18) and Part 3 (ss.53(1) and s.54) faithfully transposes the subjective and objective requirements of conformity in the SGD and the DCD, respectively. One potentially significant amendment, by way of the insertion of an additional word, was made in relation to para. (a) of the objective conformity requirements whereby goods must "be fit for *all* the purposes for which goods of the same type would be normally used, …". This refinement derives from Irish legal doctrine of the definition of 'merchantable quality' under the Sale of Goods Act 1893 and clarifies that where goods have more than one normal purpose, they must be fit for all their normal purposes.[19] The faithful transposition of the directives also extends to incorrect installation which in relation to smart goods, is dealt with in s.19 of the Consumer Rights Act 2022; in relation to digital content and digital services, s.55 is the relevant provision. Both sections transpose faithfully, with minor textual amendments, Art. 8 SGD and Art. 9 DCD.

20 In addition, the Consumer Rights Act 2022 takes advantage of a number of the options made available to member states, and also legislates outside the areas within the scope of the DCD and the SGD, to regulate certain matters, namely in relation to:

– information requirements in distance and off-premises contracts;
– spare parts and after-sale services;
– the right to sell/supply & terminate;
– implied contract terms;
– exclusion or limitation of liability; and
– recipients of a gift and users of motor vehicles.

These distinct features of the Irish Consumer Rights Act 2022 are considered further below, as well as matters of durability, updates, exclusion of conformity, and third party rights.

I. Information Requirements in Distance and Off-Premises Contracts

21 In relation the sales contracts in Part 2, s.17 addresses further matters under the heading of subjective conformity. First, s.17(2) provides that the information that a trader is required to provide in relation to distance and off-premises contracts forms part of the sales contract, and s.17(3) states that goods sold in these circumstances must comply with any terms of the contract which derive from these information requirements that are additional to the subjective requirements in s.17(1).[20] In relation to digital content and digital service contracts, similar information provisions apply in s.53(2) and (3).[21] The express inclusion of these information requirements as subjective conformity requirements brings a degree of coherency between the consumer rights

---

[19] *James Elliot Construction Ltd v Irish Asphalt Ltd* [2011] IEHC 269, approved in [2014] IESC 74; see further White, "The meaning of 'merchantable quality'", (2012) 47 *The Irish Jurist*, 225.
[20] See Recital 26 SGD.
[21] See Recital 42 DCD.

II. Spare Parts and After-Sale Services

22 A second subjective conformity requirement addressed in Part 2, s.17 relates to spare parts and after-sales services.[22] Section 17(4) provides that spare parts and an adequate after-sales service must be made available by the trader

(a) in such circumstances as are stated in an offer, description or advertisement by the trader on behalf of the producer or on the trader's own behalf, and
(b) for such period as is so stated or, if no period is so stated, for a reasonable period.

A similar provision exists in the Sale of Goods and Supply of Services Act 1980, s.12. Importantly, this provision does not require a trader to provide spare parts or an after-sales service. Instead, it is only where spare-parts and an after-sales service are offered, described or advertised by the trader, that the trader is legally obliged to make the spare-parts and after-sales service available. Moreover, this obligation applies to all goods, including smart goods, and is not limited to any particular class of goods, but it has no application in relation to digital content and digital service contracts.

III. Right to Sell/Supply & Terminate; Freedom from Charges or other Encumbrances

23 As a preliminary to the subjective and objective requirements of conformity, and further to Recitals 18 and 35 SGD and Recital 12 DCD, Part 2 on sales contracts and Part 3 on digital content and digital service contracts, also include an obligation on the trader to have the right to sell the goods/supply the digital content or digital service, and where the trader does not have the right to sell/supply, the consumer has the right to terminate the contract.[23]

24 In addition, Part 2 on sales contracts also includes a requirement that the goods are free from any charge or other encumbrance not disclosed to the consumer and that the consumer will enjoy quiet possession of the goods.[24] There is also provision for the sale of a limited title to the goods.[25] These provisions are reminiscent of s.12 of the Sale of Goods Act 1893.

IV. Implied Contract Terms

25 Part 2 on smart goods and Part 3 on digital content and digital services both include a provision which states that the traders' obligations, including the subjective and objective conformity requirements, shall operate as implied terms in the relevant contracts.[26] This is of particular importance where consumers wish to seek additional remedies, such as damages, for a trader's failure to comply with their obligations.

---

[22] See Recital 33 SGD.
[23] Consumer Rights Act 2022, s.14 re smart goods and s.50 re digital content and digital services.
[24] Consumer Rights Act 2022, s.16(1).
[25] Consumer Rights Act 2022, s.16(2).
[26] Consumer Rights Act 2022, s.20 re goods and s.56 re digital content and digital services.

C. Conformity of Goods

V. Exclusion or Limitation of Liability

Further to Art. 21, Part 2 on smart goods and Part 3 on digital content and digital services both include a provision which states that a term of a contract between a consumer and a trader shall not exclude or restrict the trader's liability, in relation to the various trader obligations in the legislation, and any such term is not binding on the consumer.[27] Further, the provisions elaborate on what is meant by the exclusion or restriction of the trader's liability, and the legislation also provides that an agreement to submit differences to ADR within the scope of the European Union (Alternative Dispute Resolution for Consumer Disputes) Regulations 2015[28] is not to be regarded as such an exclusion. A similar provision can be found at s.31 of the UK Consumer Rights Act 2015.

VI. Recipients of a Gift and Users of Motor Vehicles

Chapter 6, in two provisions, extends the rights and remedies of consumers to third parties in certain circumstances. These provisions should be considered in the context of a lack of general legislation on third party contract rights in Irish law. Accordingly, a subsequent buyer does not contractually have rights against the initial seller. The initial buyer would have had to have assigned those rights.[29] As a matter of contractual freedom the initial seller is able to exclude the transferability of the rights under the legal guarantee or a commercial guarantee in his general terms and conditions.

First, inspired by a provision from the Australian Competition and Consumer Act 2010[30], Part 2 on sales contracts addresses the common scenario where a consumer buys goods to give as a gift to another, such as a family member or a friend. Because of the doctrine of privity of contract in Irish law, the recipients of such gifts do not have rights or remedies against the trader under the sales contract. Accordingly, s.46 provides that where a consumer who is a party to a sales contract gives goods acquired under the contract to another consumer as a gift, that other consumer shall be entitled to exercise all rights and remedies under Part 2 on the same terms as the consumer who is a party to the sales contract.

Second, inspired by s.13 of the Sale of Goods and Supply of Services Act 1980 on the sale of motor vehicles, where a consumer purchases a motor vehicle under a sales contract, and the motor vehicle is not in conformity with the sales contract, and the lack of conformity would render the motor vehicle a danger to the public (including any person travelling in the motor vehicle) any person who uses the motor vehicle with the consent of the consumer and suffers loss as a result of that lack of conformity may maintain an action for damages in respect of that lack of conformity against the trader who sold the motor vehicle as if he or she were the consumer.[31]

---

[27] Consumer Rights Act 2022, s.39 re goods and s.71 re digital content and digital services.
[28] S.I. No. 343 of 2015.
[29] Supreme Court of Judicature (Ireland) Act 1877, s.28(6).
[30] Australian Competition and Consumer Act 2010, s.266 of Schedule 2.
[31] Consumer Rights Act 2022, s.47.

VII. The Durability Requirement

30 As well as durability being identified as an objective conformity requirement, s.18(2) drawing on Recital 32 SGD provides an elucidation of the requirement of durability such that

> "… the reference to the durability of the goods is a reference to the ability of the goods to maintain their functions and performance through normal use and to possess the ability to do so which is normal for goods of the same type and which the consumer can reasonably expect having regard to
> (a) the specific nature of the goods,
> (b) the possible need for reasonable maintenance of the goods,
> (c) any public statement on the durability of the goods made by or on behalf of any person constituting a link in the chain of transactions, and
> (d) all other relevant circumstances, including the price of the goods and the intensity or frequency of the use made of the goods by the consumer."

31 Durability was an express feature of the pre-existing 'merchantable quality' requirement pursuant to the Sale of Goods Acts 1893 and 1980, however, there is no case law exploring this statutory requirement of durability, in practice. Product-specific Union legislation relevant to durability, such as the EcoDesign Directive 2009/125, has been transposed in domestic law by Regulation. In general, these transposing measures go no further than what is necessary to comply with EU law. The measures transposing product-specific Union legislation operate as stand-alone measures with no direct relationship to provisions transposing SGD in national law.

32 Directive 2009/125/EC is transposed in the European Union (Ecodesign Requirements for Certain Energy-related Products) (Amendment) Regulations 2013.[32] The Regulations provide for a range of enforcement options (including investigation powers; warning measures; compliance directions; withdrawal from the market directions; court orders directing withdrawal; and criminal sanctions and penalties for breach of the Regulations). In terms of penalties, a person guilty of an offence under these Regulations is liable

- on summary conviction, to a class A fine (currently up to maximum of €5,000), or
- on conviction on indictment, to a fine not exceeding €250,000.

The Regulations do not make provision for any private law sanctions.

33 As regards durability and links to sustainability the provisions on spare parts and after-sales services in s.17(4) of the Consumer Rights Act, should be noted. It is also arguable that the six-year limitation period (see further below), even in relation to second-hand goods, is relevant in pursuing sustainability and a circular economy, although somewhat worryingly recent research from the Competition and Consumer Protection Commission suggests that the majority of consumers are not familiar with the operation of the limitation period.[33]

---

[32] S.I. No. 454 of 2013.
[33] See https://www.ccpc.ie/consumers/2022/01/11/a-guide-to-january-returns-faulty-goods/ (last accessed 5 July 2022).

C. *Conformity of Goods*

VIII. The Duty to Inform and Supply Updates

While Art. 7(3) of the SGD deals in a single provision with the supply of updates in sales contracts for goods with digital elements that involve a *single act of supply* of the digital content or digital service and contracts that provide for *a continuous supply* of the digital content or digital service, it was considered simpler and clearer to deal with the two types of contracts in separate provisions in the Consumer Rights Act 2022.[34] In addition, Art. 7(3) of the SGD states that where a contract for the sale of goods with digital elements provides for the continuous supply of the digital content or digital service over a period of time, the seller shall ensure that the consumer is informed of and supplied with the necessary updates for the period of time 'indicated in Article 10(2) or (5) as applicable'. Article 10(2) provides that where such a contract provides for the continuous supply of the digital content or digital service for more than two years, the seller shall be liable for any lack of conformity of the digital content or digital service that occurs or becomes apparent within the period of time during which the digital content or digital service is to be supplied under the sales contract. Article 10(2) further provides that where a contract for the sale of goods with digital elements provides for a continuous supply of digital content or a digital service over a period of time (i.e less than two years), the seller shall be liable for any lack of conformity that occurs or becomes apparent within two years of the time when the goods with digital elements were delivered. The Consumer Rights Act 2022 addresses both these scenarios in separate provisions for clarity. Accordingly, where a sales contract for the sale of goods with digital elements provides for

- a single act of supply of the digital content or digital service, the trader shall ensure that the consumer is
  (a) informed of the availability of, and
  (b) supplied with,
  any update (including a security update) that is necessary for the goods to be in conformity with the sales contract for the period of time that the consumer may reasonably expect given the type and purpose of the goods and the digital elements, and taking into account the circumstances and nature of the sales contract[35];
- a continuous act of supply of the digital content or digital service for a period exceeding two years, the trader shall ensure that the consumer is informed of the availability of, and supplied with, any update (including a security update) that is necessary for the goods to be in conformity with the sales contract during that period[36];
- a continuous act of supply of the digital content or digital service for a period not exceeding two years, the trader shall ensure that the consumer is informed of the availability of, and supplied with, any update (including a security update) that is necessary for the goods to be in conformity with the sales contract for the period of two years beginning with the relevant time.[37]

Similarly, while Article 8(2) of the DCD deals in a single provision with the supply of updates in digital content and digital service contracts that involve a continuous supply over a period of time and contracts that involve a single act of supply or a series of

---

[34] See Scheme of Consumer Rights Bill 2021, pp.53 – 54, available at https://enterprise.gov.ie/en/Consultations/Consultation-on-Scheme-of-Consumer-Rights-Bill-2021.html (last accessed 5 July 2022).
[35] Consumer Rights Act 2022, s.18(4).
[36] Consumer Rights Act 2022, s.18(5).
[37] Consumer Rights Act 2022, s.18(6).

individual acts of supply, the Consumer Rights Act 2022 transposes this in s.54(4) in relation to the duty to inform and supply, and in s.54(9) where the different 'relevant period' is defined.

36   The liability exemption where the consumer fails to install updates is transposed in s.18(7) for smart goods and s.54(5) for digital content and digital services, as per the Directives.

37   Part 3 on digital content and digital service contracts transposes rules on modification beyond what is necessary to maintain the digital content/service in conformity[38], but the transposition in Ireland has no further rules on the modification in Part 2 on smart goods beyond what may be necessary to provide updates.

IX. Exclusion of Conformity

38   The exclusion of the existence of a lack of conformity in the case provided by Art. 8(5) DCD and Art. 7(5) SGD where the consumer is specifically informed that a particular characteristic of the goods, digital content or digital service was deviating from the objective requirements was transposed in s.18(8) for smart goods and s.54(7) for digital content and digital services. Both these provisions expressly extend the exclusion beyond a "particular characteristic" to include a disclosed lack of conformity with the contract 'caused by a restriction resulting from a violation of an intellectual property right or any other third party right'. Moreover, s.18(9) for smart goods and s.54(8) for digital content and digital services provide that in case of dispute, it shall be for the trader to show that the consumer (a) was specifically informed about a particular characteristic which deviated from the legislative requirements, and (b) expressly and separately accepted that deviation when concluding the sales contract. It seems appropriate that this burden should be placed on the trader, in these circumstances.

X. Third Party Rights

39   Art. 10 DCD on third party rights is transposed faithfully in s.57 of the Consumer Rights Act 2022. In addition, s.50 requires that the trader has a right to supply the digital content or digital service at the time at which it is to be supplied (inspired by a similar provision in relation to goods in the Sale of Goods Acts 1893 and 1980, s.12).

40   The transposition of Art. 9 SGD concerning third party rights is a little more complicated, as Art. 9 SGD is integrated into domestic provisions on the trader's right to sell and freedom from charges or other encumbrances, which derive from the Sale of Goods Act 1893 and 1980, s.12.

41   First, s.14 provides that the trader must ensure that, at the time ownership of the goods is to be transferred, the trader has the right to sell the goods.[39] Where the trader does not have the right to sell goods, the consumer has the right to terminate the sales contract[40] (this right must be exercised in accordance with s.28 on consumers'

---

[38] Consumer Rights Act 2022, s.64.

[39] Consumer Rights Act 2022, s.14(1). It has been held, for example, that where an owner of goods can be stopped by process of the law from selling the goods (by a trademark owner alleging infringement of their IP rights), that the seller does not have the right to sell: *Niblett v Confectioners' Materials Co Ltd*, [1921] 3 K.B. 387. See also, *The Irish Digest 1939–1948*, Col.107; and *O'Reilly v Fineman* [1942] Ir. Jur. Rep. 36.

[40] Consumer Rights Act 2022, s.14(2).

obligations on termination, and s.30 on traders' obligations on termination[41]). Moreover, the burden of proof is on the trader to show that the trader has the right to sell the goods.[42]

Second, s.16 provides that trader must ensure that (a) at the time when the ownership of goods is to be transferred under a sales contract, the goods are free from any undisclosed charge or other encumbrance, and (b) the consumer will enjoy quiet possession of the goods.[43]

Importantly, the consumer has the right to the remedies specified in the legislation (short term right to terminate or repair/replace, followed by price reduction and final right of termination) where the above obligations are breached and including where:

(d) a restriction resulting from a violation of any right of a third person, in particular an intellectual property right, prevents or limits the use of the goods in accordance with section 17 or 18.

In case of dispute, it is for the trader to show that

(a) the goods complied with the requirements of s.16;
(b) the trader disclosed all known charges or encumbrances;
(c) the consumer enjoyed quiet possession of the goods.

The DCD/SGD remedies apply to these provisions, subject to a right to terminate where the trader has no right to sell under s.14, and a short-term right to terminate (as an alternative to repair/replace) otherwise under s.16.

Ireland has not adopted specific rules in order to define the place of delivery. Under the general law of sale of goods it is a matter for contract, express or implied, whether it is for the buyer to take possession of the goods or for the seller to send them to the buyer. If the contract is silent the place of delivery is the seller's place of business, if he has one, and if not, his residence. However, if the contract is for the sale of specific goods, which to the knowledge of the parties when the contract is made are in some other place, then that place is the place of delivery.[44]

D. Liability of the Trader

In terms of trader liability, the DCD distinguishes between the one-off supply of digital content and services; a series of individual acts of supply; and a contract for the continuous supply of such content or services over a period. The Consumer Rights Act 2022 adopts these distinctions around the modality of supply in relation to the duty to supply (s.51) and the liability of the trader (s.58). Accordingly Irish law provides where a digital content contract or digital service contract is concluded between a trader and a consumer, that the trader shall normally supply the digital content or the digital service to the consumer without undue delay after the conclusion of the contract.[45] However, where a digital content contract or digital service contract provides for a continuous supply of the digital content or digital service for a period specified in the contract, the trader is obliged to supply the digital content or digital service to the consumer for

---

[41] Consumer Rights Act 2022, s.14(3).
[42] Consumer Rights Act 2022, s.14(4).
[43] Consumer Rights Act 2022, s.16(1). Section 16(2) makes provision for the sale of a limited title in goods, i.e. subject to disclosed charges or encumbrances).
[44] Sale of Goods Act 1893, s.29.
[45] Consumer Rights Act 2022, s.51(2).

that period.[46] Where a digital content contract or digital service contract provides for the supply of the digital content or digital service on more than one occasion during the period for which the contract subsists, the trader must supply the digital content or digital service to the consumer on each of those occasions.[47]

46 In addition, s. 53(4) provides that where the digital content contract or digital service contract provides for a continuous supply of digital content or a digital service for a period specified in the contract, the digital content or digital service shall comply with the requirements of subjective conformity during that period; while in relation to objective conformity, s. 54(6) specifies that where the contract provides for a continuous supply of digital content or a digital service for a period specified in the contract, the trader shall ensure that the digital content or digital service is in conformity with the contract during that period.

47 In term of liability of the trader, the Consumer Rights Act 2022 states that where a digital content contract or a digital service contract is concluded between a trader and a consumer, the trader shall be liable to the consumer for any failure to supply the digital content or digital service in accordance with s. 51.[48] More particularly, where a digital content contract or digital service contract provides for a single act of supply, or a series of individual acts of supply, the trader is liable for any lack of conformity, including any lack of conformity resulting from a violation of an intellectual property right or any other right of a third person, which exists at the time of supply of the digital content or digital service.[49] Whereas, where a digital content contract or digital service contract provides for a continuous supply of digital content or a digital service for a period specified in the contract, the trader is liable for a lack of conformity that occurs or becomes apparent during that period.[50]

48 Inspired by Recital 51 DCD, s. 52(4) addresses the problem of short-term interruptions in relation to continuous supply contracts. Accordingly, where during such a continuous contract there is a short-term interruption of the supply which having regard to the type and purpose of the digital content or digital service and the circumstances and nature of the contract, is more than negligible, or which recurs, there is deemed to be a lack of conformity giving rise to remedies under the legislation.

49 There are no special rules in the Irish implementing law on impossibility, force majeure or change of circumstances. The contract will be subject to the general law of contract and in particular the frustration doctrine though this is restrictively interpreted. Force majeure clauses may be included in the supply contract and will be enforced so long as they do not infringe unfair terms legislation.

50 As regards the rules on bundling contracts and coordination with Art. 107(2) European Electronic Communications Code, the Irish solution is that the consumer shall have the right to terminate where digital content or a digital service is supplied to a consumer under a contract that provides also for the sale of goods, or the supply of a service so long as the consumer would be entitled to terminate if it were a digital content contract or a digital service contract only, and the value of the goods or service to the consumer would be materially reduced in the absence of the digital content or digital service.[51] However, this right to terminate does not apply to a bundle within the scope European Electronic Communications Code which includes elements of an internet ac-

---

[46] Consumer Rights Act 2022, s.51(3).
[47] Consumer Rights Act 2022, s.51(4).
[48] Consumer Rights Act 2022, s.58(1).
[49] Consumer Rights Act 2022, s.58(2).
[50] Consumer Rights Act 2022, s.58(4).
[51] Consumer Rights Act 2022, s.65(1).

cess service or a number-based interpersonal communications service together with digital content or a digital service.[52]

Where non-compliance with the GDPR regarding contracts for the supply of digital content and digital services constitutes non-conformity then the Acts scheme of remedies will be available.[53] The Act does not specify which failures to comply will amount to non-conformity, but it must be presumed that any such breach of the GDPR will be a non-conformity as they will be the background expectations of the contract.

E. Remedies for the failure to supply and remedies for the lack of conformity

Chapter 4 of Part 2 deals with 'other rules in sales contracts' and in s.36 addresses issues around the delivery (or supply) of the goods (including smart goods). Section 36 transposes Art. 18 of the Consumer Rights Directive, Directive 2011/83 in relation to the time of delivery and more. Art. 18 does not directly state the trader's obligations to deliver the goods. As this is the trader's primary obligation under the sales contract, and in line with s.27 of the Sale of Goods Act 1893, this primary duty to deliver is re-stated in s.36(1). Moreover, where a trader refuses to deliver (or supply) the goods or where the time of delivery is essential and no delivery is made on time, the consumer has an immediate right to terminate.[54] Otherwise, where goods are not delivered on time (as agreed or within 30 days after the conclusion of the contract) the consumer must call upon the trader to make delivery within an additional period of time. Further failure to deliver on time, gives the consumer the right to terminate.

In relation to remedies for lack of conformity of goods, Ireland has followed the UK's lead in introducing a 30 day short term right to reject.[55] The consumer also has the choice of repair or replacement.[56] As regards the remedies of repair and replacement the law says the consumer should make the goods available to the trader to enable him to cure.[57] Where they should be made available is not stated though the requirement that the remedy should be carried out free of charge[58] and should not cause significant inconvenience to the consumer may limit where repair and replacement can reasonably be carried out.[59] The Consumer Rights Act 2022 provides that the trader must take back the replaced goods and the goods are to be repaired his own expense.[60] Ireland does not prioritize repair over replacement in order to enhance environmental sustainability. We are unaware of any Irish doctrinal debate on this. There are no regulatory sanctions adopted for fighting premature/planned obsolescence of goods.

If the problem is not remedied the consumer may be able to go on to seek price reduction or final termination.[61] If the right of final termination is invoked there may be a deduction for any depreciation in the value of the goods in excess of the depreciation that could reasonably be expected to result from their normal use.[62] In some

---

[52] Consumer Rights Act 2022, s.65(6).
[53] Consumer Rights Act 2022, s.52(5).
[54] Consumer Rights Act 2022, s.36(4).
[55] Consumer Rights Act 2022, s.24.
[56] Consumer Rights Act 2022, s.25.
[57] Consumer Rights Act 2022, s.25(4).
[58] Consumer Rights Act 2022, s.25(2)(a).
[59] Consumer Rights Act 2022, s.25(2)(c).
[60] Consumer Rights Act 2022, s.25(5).
[61] Consumer Rights Act 2022, s.26.
[62] Consumer Rights Act 2022, s.30(3).

circumstances the consumer may need to allow the trader another attempt to cure.[63] The consumer remains free to seek other remedies such as damages.[64]

55 In Part 3 on digital content and digital service contracts, similar remedies for failure to supply[65] and for lack of conformity (including a right to have the digital content/service brought into conformity, price reduction and termination) are provided for.[66] The consumer remains free to seek other remedies such as damages.[67]

56 Ireland has introduced a specific right to withhold payment in consumer contracts under the DCD.[68] The Consumer Rights Act 2022 provides that the consumer has the right to withhold payment of any outstanding part of the price until the trader has fulfilled the trader's obligations under the legislation.[69] The part of the price withheld by the consumer should be proportionate to the decrease in the value of the digital content or digital service received by the consumer that does not conform with the contract compared with the value the digital content or digital service would have if it were in conformity with the contract.[70] It is assumed that this would be calculated in the same way as price reduction. In addition, the consumer shall exercise the right to withhold payment by means of a statement to the trader expressing the consumer's decision to withhold payment until the trader has fulfilled his trader's obligations under this legislation.[71]

57 Ireland has also introduced a specific right to withhold payment in consumer contracts under the SGD, along the same lines as with the DCD.[72] Thus, consumers are allowed to withhold payment until the trader has fulfilled his obligations to deliver goods in conformity with the contracts, at the relevant time.[73] The amount withheld should be proportionate to the decrease in value of the goods received compared to the value the goods would have if they had been in conformity.[74] Again, it is assumed that this would be calculated in the same way as price reduction. The right to withhold payment will be exercised by the consumer making a statement to the trader expressing the consumer's decision to withhold payment until the trader has fulfilled their obligation to deliver goods that are in conformity with the sales contract.[75]

58 Previously the position was governed by the Irish Sale of Goods Acts 1893 and 1980. The buyer would have to decide whether to accept or reject the tender of goods. If goods were accepted a breach of condition would be treated as a breach of warranty. A breach of warranty alone did not entitle the buyer to reject the goods; but he may set up against the seller the breach of warranty in diminution or extinction of the price or maintain an action against the seller for damages for the breach of warranty.[76]

59 The requirement in Art. 15 DCD that the termination be through a statement to the trader is more prescriptive that the norm in Irish law whereby termination could be inferred by conduct though in the digital context conduct may be harder to show.

---

[63] Consumer Rights Act 2022, s.26(5).
[64] Consumer Rights Act 2022, s.34.
[65] Consumer Rights Act 2022, s.60.
[66] Consumer Rights Act 2022, ss.61 – 63.
[67] Consumer Rights Act 2022, s.73.
[68] Consumer Rights Act 2022, s.69.
[69] Consumer Rights Act 2022, s.69(1).
[70] Consumer Rights Act 2022, s.69(2).
[71] Consumer Rights Act 2022, s.69(3).
[72] Consumer Rights Act 2022, s.32.
[73] Consumer Rights Act 2022, s.32(1).
[74] Consumer Rights Act 2022, s.32(2).
[75] Consumer Rights Act 2022, s.32(3).
[76] Sale of Goods Act 1893, s.53(1).

E. Remedies for the failure to supply and remedies for the lack of conformity

The position regarding the rules on the right of terminate possibly affecting the right to withdraw consent for the processing of personal data and the contractual consequences thereof has not been addressed in Irish law. Consideration had been given to the inclusion of such a provision, but the Data Protection Commission's view, prevailed that "the inclusion of such a provision risked creating a prescriptive rule that went beyond what was foreseen in the GDPR."[77] It was felt that this could result in a situation where new and potentially different data protection rules introduced in Member States could undermine a harmonised approach, but of course that is the very risk if left to national law where there is uncertainty over what the legal consequences are when this is left to the general law of contract.

In Ireland where the trader supplies digital content and/or digital services restitution is achieved on termination by the consumer not using the digital content or digital service or making it available to any third person.[78] Where the digital content was supplied on a tangible medium, the consumer shall, upon request return the tangible medium to the trader without undue delay.[79] Failure to fulfil these criteria will lead to the requirement to pay damages.[80]

Where the consumer provides personal data as a counter performance, the trader after termination shall not normally use any content that was provided or created by the consumer when using the digital content or digital service.[81] However, the trader may use such content so long as the content is not personal data and the content

(a) has no utility outside the context of the digital content or digital service supplied by the trader,
(b) relates only to the consumer's activity when using the digital content or digital service supplied by the trader,
(c) has been aggregated with other data by the trader and cannot be disaggregated or can be disaggregated only with disproportionate effort, or
(d) has been generated jointly by the consumer and others, and other consumers are able to continue to make use of the content.[82]

When requested the trader shall, at the request of the consumer, make available to the consumer any digital content (other than personal data), which was provided or created by the consumer when using the digital content or digital service.[83] This obligation does not apply to data under (a)-(c) above.

Consumers should be able to retrieve the digital content free of charge, without hindrance from the trader, within a reasonable time, and in a commonly used and machine-readable format.[84] Notwithstanding the obligation to return data the trader may prevent any further use of the digital content or digital service by the consumer, in particular by making the digital content or digital service inaccessible to the consumer or disabling the user account of the consumer.[85]

---

[77] Department of Enterprise, Trade and Employment, *Consultation on Scheme of Consumer Rights Bill 2021*, para. 3.18.
[78] Consumer Rights Act 2022, s.66(3).
[79] Consumer Rights Act 2022, s.66(4).
[80] Consumer Rights Act 2022, s.66(6) – (7).
[81] Consumer Rights Act 2022, s.67(5).
[82] Consumer Rights Act 2022, s.67(6).
[83] Consumer Rights Act 2022, s.66(7).
[84] Consumer Rights Act 2022, s.67(9).
[85] Consumer Rights Act 2022, s.67(10).

64 Ireland provides no express regulation for the cases in which:
- the consumer bought goods and then moved to another country;
- the seller delivered the goods in accordance with the Geo-Blocking Regulation and is now obliged to carry our repair or replacement in a country he does not offer delivery to.

F. Commercial Guarantees

65 The Consumer Rights Act 2022 seeks to regulate commercial guarantees in Chapter 5 (ss.40 – 45) of Part 2 of the 2022 Act. In doing so, Chapter 5 seeks to transpose Art. 17 SGD and more, thereby relying on the option provided in Art. 17(4).

66 In general, the Consumer Rights Act 2022 seeks to transpose Art. 17 by following closely the wording of the Directive, subject to a number of minor textual changes. Accordingly,
- s.40 transposes Art. 17(1) on the liability of guarantors and producers for their commercial guarantees, and the relationship between guarantee statements and associated advertising; and
- s.44 transposes Art. 17(2) and (3) on the provision and content of the guarantee statement.

A couple of minor points of textual divergence may be of note. First, the rules on commercial guarantees are expressly made applicable 'to goods sold under a sales contract' (see e.g. s.2 definition of 'commercial guarantee'; and s.44(1) on provision of commercial guarantee to consumer). Second, Part 5 utilises the word 'trader', and not 'seller' (in line with broader context of whole Act).

67 The remaining provisions of Part 5 (ss.41 – 43 and s.45) make use of the option to lay down rules on other aspects concerning commercial guarantees which are not regulated by the SGD. These additional rules are both inspired and shaped by pre-existing rules on guarantees found in the Sale of Goods and Supply of Services Act 1980 (ss.15 – 19). In brief, the additional rules in ss.41 – 43 and s.45 seek to provide additional trader liability; protection to subsequent consumers; along with a right of action; and rules on the exclusion or limitation of rights in commercial guarantees.

68 More particularly, s.41 provides that where a trader (seller) gives a consumer a commercial guarantee provided by another guarantor, the trader (seller) shall be liable for the observance of the guarantee as if the trader (seller) were the guarantor.[86] Thus, for example, in the typical situation where goods are sold to a consumer in a retail outlet and the goods are sold with a guarantee statement from a producer/manufacturer, (i) the producer/manufacturer will be liable as guarantor under s.40 (transposing Art 17(1)), and (ii) in addition, the retailer/trader/seller will be liable for the observance of *that guarantee also*. The consumer thus has a choice of two persons who are equally liable under the guarantee and against whom the consumer can choose to enforce the one guarantee. Importantly, the trader (seller) can avoid this type of *dual liability* in two different circumstances. First, where the trader (seller) expressly indicates that they will not be liable under the guarantee given by another person (e.g. producer/manufacturer) when the guarantee is given to the consumer.[87] And second, where the trader (seller) gives the consumer the *trader's own guarantee*, it is presumed, unless the contrary is

---

[86] Consumer Rights Act 2022, s.41(1).
[87] Consumer Rights Act 2022, s.41(1).

F. Commercial Guarantees

proven, that the trader (seller) is not liable under any guarantee from another guarantor which the trader has given to the consumer.[88]

Section 42 expressly addresses the position of the rights of subsequent consumers in relation to guarantees. This provision operates in the broader context of a lack of legislation on third party rights in Irish contract law, and the doctrine of privity of contract at common law.[89] Accordingly, where a commercial guarantee is provided to a consumer in relation to goods under a sales contract, and during the period of the guarantee the goods are acquired by another consumer, that other consumer is entitled to rely on the guarantee against the guarantor under s.40 or the trader (seller) under s.41, as if they were the original consumer. In other words, the guarantee attaches to the goods, for its duration, and is not personal or limited to the original consumer. Moreover, these rights can be passed along a chain of subsequent consumers, so long as the guarantee period remains operative. Arguably, similar rights for subsequent consumers could be implied in Art. 17 SGD, but are not explicit. **69**

Drawing on the common law distinction between conditions and warranties in Irish contract law (whereby a condition is an important term of the contract, breach of which allows the innocent party to repudiate – or terminate – the contract and sue for damages; and a warranty is a less important or minor term of the contract, breach of which does not allow the innocent party to repudiate – or terminate – the contract but they may sue for damages), s.43 provides that a consumer may maintain an action against a guarantor, or other person liable under s.41, who fails to comply with the terms of the guarantee, as if the guarantor or other person has sold the goods and had committed a breach of warranty.[90] Where such an action is taken, a court may order the guarantor or other person to pay damages to the consumer.[91] Moreover, where a guarantor or other person is liable for damages, the court may, at its discretion, afford the guarantor or other person the opportunity of performing the obligations under the guarantee to the satisfaction of the court.[92] Importantly, this remedy of *specific performance* is at the court's discretion and not a right of the guarantor or the consumer. **70**

Lastly, s.45 prohibits certain terms in commercial guarantees and the criminal law is utilised to enforce this provision. Three particular features of guarantees are identified in this provision: **71**

1. a commercial guarantee must not exclude or limit the rights of consumers under any enactment or rule of law;
2. a commercial guarantee must not impose obligations on the consumer that are additional to their obligations under the sales contract;
3. a commercial guarantee must not purport to make the guarantor the sole authority to decide whether goods are in conformity with the sales contract or whether the consumer is entitled to make a claim under the guarantee.

---

[88] Consumer Rights Act 2022, s.41(2). Section 40(3) makes clear that the liability of a trader (seller) under s.41 is without prejudice to the rights conferred on a consumer under s.40.

[89] This common law position persists in Ireland, despite a recommendation from the Law Reform Commission in 2008 that legislation should be introduced allowing for third party rights in certain circumstance (Law Reform Commission, *Report on Privity of Contract and Third Party Rights* (LRC 88–2008).

[90] Consumer Rights Act 2022, s.43(1).
[91] Consumer Rights Act 2022, s.43(2).
[92] Consumer Rights Act 2022, s.43(3).

In terms of sanctions, any provision in a guarantee contrary to the above is not binding on the consumer[93], and a guarantor who gives a guarantee in contravention of the above commits an offence.[94]

G. Time Limits

72   Ireland has not introduced a two year liability period and instead the general six year limitation period for contractual claims applies for goods and digital content and digital services as permitted by Art. 10 SGD and Art. 11 DCD. This is in keeping with an earlier measure which transposed Directive 1999/44 on consumer sales.[95] In a consultation paper, the Department of Enterprise, Trade and Employment did not consider that there was any reason for having a restricted two year period 'regardless of the type, cost and durability of the goods concerned or the nature of the lack of conformity'.[96] The Department has taken a similar approach in relation to digital content and digital services, offering consistency on the matter for consumers and business alike.[97] On consultation, different views were expressed about the limitation period, with some respondents seeking a shorter limitation period[98], although consumer organisations favoured maintaining the current 6 year period.[99] This latter view has prevailed in the Consumer Rights Act 2022, although there is some evidence that consumers are not generally aware of the 6 year limitation period.[100]

73   The general rule on the limitation period is found in s.11 of the Statute of Limitations, 1957 which provides that an action founded on contract cannot be brought after the expiration of six years from the date on which the cause of action accrued. Further relevant rules on digital content and digital services can be found in the Consumer Rights Act 2022. Accordingly, the consumer's right to a remedy in respect of a lack of conformity for which the trader is liable applies for 6 years from

(a) the time of the supply of the digital content or digital service, in the case of a digital content contract or digital service contract which provides for a single act of supply, or a series of individual acts of supply, and
(b) the time at which the lack of conformity occurs or becomes apparent, in the case of a contract which provides for a continuous supply of the digital content or digital service.[101]

---

[93] Consumer Rights Act 2022, s.45(2).
[94] Consumer Rights Act 2022, s.45(3). For penalties, see 2022 Act, s.142.
[95] See European Community (Certain Aspects of the Sale of Consumer Goods and Associated Guarantees) Regulations 2003, S.I. No.11 of 2003.
[96] Department of Enterprise, Trade and Employment, *Consultation on Scheme of Consumer Rights Bill 2021*, para 2.21.
[97] Department of Enterprise, Trade and Employment, *Consultation on Scheme of Consumer Rights Bill 2021*, para 3.10.
[98] See e.g. Law Society Submission, where a three-year limitation period was proposed to counter-balance the improved position of consumers: para. 3.8, available at https://enterprise.gov.ie/en/Consultations/Consultations-files/Law-Society-submission-submission-consumer-rights-bill-2021-consultation.pdf (last accessed 26 May 2022).
[99] See e.g. CCPC Submission, p.4, available at https://enterprise.gov.ie/en/Consultations/Consultations-files/CCPC-submission-consumer-rights-bill-2021-consultation.pdf (last accessed 5 July 2022).
[100] See https://www.ccpc.ie/consumers/2022/01/11/a-guide-to-january-returns-faulty-goods/ (last accessed 5 July 2022).
[101] Consumer Right Act 2022, s.58(5).

The consumer's right to a remedy in respect of a failure to supply for which the trader is liable applies for 6 years from the time at which the trader was required to supply the digital content or digital service in accordance with s.51.[102]

In the consultation paper, the Department of Enterprise, Trade and Employment stated that it saw no need for having rules on interruption or suspension of the limitation period given that they adopted a six rather than two-year period.[103] On a related point, the Department had given serious consideration to providing for the suspension of the thirty day period for the short term right to terminate the contract as it considered this would be of benefit to consumers. However, the European Commission advised the Department that the discretionary provision for this right was not intended to be extended by a facility for its suspension.[104] With respect, this seems more a political statement to keep the exception within limited bounds. If the short term right is permissible it seems entirely appropriate that it should not be made less effective by the period not being suspended if the consumer allows the trader to cure. This is indeed the position as regards the short term right to reject under the UK Consumer Rights Act 2015.[105]

In relation to an obligation to notify, there is no tradition of imposing a notification requirement on the consumer as a condition for seeking redress for non-conformity in Irish law. Therefore, the option of requiring notification of non-conformity within two months was not taken up. This is in keeping with an earlier measure which transposed Directive 1999/44 on consumer sales.[106] In the consultation paper, the Department considered such an obligation to be unfair and unreasonable and would give rise to obvious issues and difficulties that were not justified absent a convincing policy rationale for an obligation of this kind.[107] It was noted that delay in seeking redress for a significant length of time would have the practical effect of making it more difficult for the consumer to obtain redress. This in itself would provide an incentive for the consumer to act promptly. Consumers have complex busy lives at times and providing a technical defence to a substantively merited claim seems unnecessary. Most consumer claims are for relatively small amounts and there is not the same need for contracting parties to be put on notice as there might be in large commercial claims.

H. Right of Redress

Where there is a lack of conformity in goods or digital services or content, or failure to supply digital services and content, then the trader is entitled to pursue remedies against the party in the chain of transactions who is liable for the failure or non-conformity.[108] This is a rather curious provision for it seems merely to restate the ordinary rule that a contracting party can seek to pass liability up the value chain. The ability to do so is dependent on the rights the parties have under those contracts. As these contracts are most likely commercial in nature they may have clauses that extensively

---

[102] Consumer Rights Act 2022, s.58(6).
[103] Department of Enterprise, Trade and Employment, *Consultation on Scheme of Consumer Rights Bill 2021*, para 2.22.
[104] Department of Enterprise, Trade and Employment, *Consultation on Scheme of Consumer Rights Bill 2021*, para 2.22
[105] UK Consumer Rights Act 2015, s.22(6).
[106] See European Community (Certain Aspects of the Sale of Consumer Goods and Associated Guarantees) Regulations 2003, S.I. No.11 of 2003.
[107] Department of Enterprise, Trade and Employment, *Consultation on Scheme of Consumer Rights Bill 2021*, para 2.39.
[108] Consumer Rights Act 2022, s.38 (goods) and s.72 (digital content and digital services).

exclude or restrict liability. This provision does not provide any restriction on the normal commercial freedom of a party to negotiate contracts and restrict their obligations to the extent permitted by the law. In other words, it adds no new rights of redress. An earlier measure transposing a similar requirement in Directive 1999/44 on consumer sales was silent on this issue of right of redress for the trader for this very reason.[109] However, the approach to transposition would appear to have changed in the meantime with this rather obvious provision being expressly transposed in the Consumer Rights Act 2022. This right to redress for the trader is transposed in stand-alone provisions and is not coordinated with the consumer remedies in any way.

I. Relationship with other Remedies

77   The remedies implementing the SGD and the DCD do not affect the right of the consumer to pursue other remedies where goods or digital content and digital services are not in conformity with the contract. However, the legislation makes clear that the consumer is not allowed to recover twice for the same loss.[110] These other remedies are said to include:

- claiming damages,
- relying on the lack of conformity against a claim by the trader for payment of the price,
- seeking to recover money paid to the trader if there is non-conformity,
- having a lack of conformity remedied elsewhere and recovering reasonable costs from the trader[111]

In the case of goods, an order can also be sought for specific performance under s.52 of the Sale of Goods Act,1893 in an action for breach of contract to deliver specific or ascertained goods. While comprehensive, this is not intended to operate as an exhaustive list of other remedies.

78   In order to facilitate an action for damages (and the application of the relevant common law rules on damages) following a breach of contract, s.20 on goods and s.56 on digital content and digital services provide that the various trader obligations in s.14 and ss.16 – 19 on goods (the right to sell; freedom from charges or other encumbrances; requirements of subjective and objective conformity and rules around incorrect installation) and s.50 and ss.53 – 55 (the right to supply; requirements of subjective and objective conformity and rules around incorrect integration of digital content or digital service) are implied in every contract and have the effect as if they were terms of the contract.

J. Concluding Remarks

79   The transposition of the DCD and the SGD, in relation to smart goods, and digital content and services has been broadly welcomed as it fills a major gap in Irish consumer protection, providing a detailed and coherent legislative framework of consumer rights and remedies in relation to digital contracts, while at the same time forming part of a

---

[109] See European Community (Certain Aspects of the Sale of Consumer Goods and Associated Guarantees) Regulations 2003, S.I. No.11 of 2003.
[110] Consumer Rights Act 2022, s.34(1) (goods), and s.73(1) (digital content and services).
[111] Consumer Rights Act 2022, s.34(2) (goods), and s.73(2) (digital content and services).

wider agenda of reform in the form of the Consumer Rights Act 2022. Transposition of the DCD and the SGD represents a significant further 'Europeanisation' of Irish consumer law. And yet, despite the maximum harmonising nature of these two Directives, a review of the Consumer Rights Act 2022 shows that many examples of the common law and legislative tradition have been maintained, including the very generous 6 year limitation period and the use of implied terms in relation to the subjective and objective conformity requirements as a vehicle to deliver other remedies, such as damages. This hybrid approach, marrying European concepts and norms with our common law and legislative tradition is most evident in relation to the SGD and Parts 2 of the Consumer Rights Act 2022 in relation to the short term right to reject, the rules on spare parts and services, and commercial guarantees, for example, ensuring the highest levels of protection for Irish consumers. Now that the Consumer Rights Act 2022 has been enacted, further major challenges lie ahead, in informing and educating consumers and traders alike about this new consumer protection regime, which is vast, with many novel features, and largely depend on private enforcement to be a success.

Bibliography

Clark, *Contract Law in Ireland*, 8th edn (Dublin: Round Hall, 2016).

Department of Enterprise, Trade and Employment, *Consultation on Scheme of Consumer Rights Bill 2021*.

Gardiner, "Scheme of Consumer Rights Bill 2015: Paving the Way for Digital Consumers", (2015) 22 *Commercial Law Practitioner*, 222.

Kelly, "Consumer Reform in Ireland and the UK: Regulatory Divergence before, after and without Brexit", (2018) 47 *Common Law World Review,* 53.

Kelly "The Digital Single Market for Consumers: Mapping Reforms of European Union Consumer Law", (2018) 25 *Commercial Law Practitioner,* 148.

Law Reform Commission, *Report on Privity of Contract and Third Party Rights* (LRC 88–2008).

McDermott and McDermott, *Contract Law*, 2nd edn (London: Bloomsbury Professional, 2017).

Sales Law Review Group, *Final Report on the Legislation Governing Sale of Goods and Supply of Services* (July 2011) (available at https://enterprise.gov.ie/en/Publications/Report-on-the-Legislation-Governing-the-Sale-of-Goods-and-Supply-of-Services.html last accessed 5 July 2022).

Italy

A. Introduction	1
B. Relationship between consumer law and general civil law	8
C. Definitions and scope of application	14
I. Definitions	14
1. The notions of "consumer" and "trader"	15
2. The contractual role of online platforms	16
II. Dual purpose contracts	18
III. Data as a consideration	19
IV. Bundles	22
V. Second-hand goods, second-hand goods sold at public auction and living animals	23
D. Conformity of goods	26
I. The conformity criteria	26
II. The implementation of the durability requirement contained in Art. 7, para 1, lett. d SGD, the coordination with the EC Eco-Design Directive and the forthcoming EU Eco-Design Regulation	29
E. The Modification of Digital Content or Digital Service in the implementation provisions of the SGD	31
F. Third party rights and the relationship with Intellectual Property Law	33
G. Liability of the Trader	34
I. Liability Requirements	34
II. Remedies for the Failure to Supply and Remedies for the Lack of Conformity	37
H. Sustainability, premature and planned obsolescence and the relationship with the internal rules on unfair commercial practices	47
I. The transfer of the rights against the initial seller from the initial consumer to a subsequent buyer	62
J. Commercial Guarantees	65
K. Time limits	66
I. Prescription	66
II. Notification	71
L. Right of Redress	72
M. Mandatory nature	73
N. Concluding Remarks	76
Bibliography	79

A. Introduction

In the implementation of Directive EU 2019/770 on the supply of Digital Content and Digital Services (hereinafter: DCD) and Directive EU 2019/771 on the Sale of Goods (hereinafter: SGD) the Italian legislator did choose to deal with consumer law outside the Civil Code. DCD and SGD were implemented, by, respectively, Legislative Decree (hereinafter: LD) no 173[1] and LD no 170[2] of 4 November 2021. The new provisions resulting from the transposition are: Art. 128 to 135-*septies* («*Capo I – Della vendita di beni*») Consumer Code, implementing the SGD;[3] Art. 135-*octies* to 135-*vicies ter* («*Capo I-bis – Dei Contratti di fornitura di contenuto digitale e di servizi digitali*») Consumer Code, implementing the DCD. While the new provisions reproduce to a large extent the wording of DCD and SGD, they also contain some innovative solutions, which ensure a better coordination with the Civil Code.

2 Nevertheless, the coordination of the two normative "clusters", introduced by way of the implementation of the two Directives, with the general private law remains problematic, although the new formulation of the coordination provisions seems more helpful in this regard (see below para. B.). This also in light of the circumstance that the phenomena regulated by the implementing provisions equally regard and affect also the business-to-business environment, which did not provide an adequate coordination of the new rules with those on intellectual property law and data protection law.

3 The Italian "general private law" remains still untouched by the digitalization. The legislator missed indeed again the opportunity to provide a "modernization" of the law of obligations, by integrating the provisions transposing the EU consumer contract law into the Civil Code. This perpetuates a fundamental criticism: the Italian Civil Code,

---

[1] Legislative Decree 4 November 2021, no 173 <https://www.normattiva.it/atto/caricaDettaglioAtto?atto.dataPubblicazioneGazzetta=2021-11-25&atto.codiceRedazionale=21G00185&atto.articolo.numero=0&atto.articolo.sottoArticolo=1&atto.articolo.sottoArticolo1=10&qId=30298f4e-04b2-46ad-9c88-de537773aae3&tabID=0.06454540653602281&title=lbl.dettaglioAtto> accessed 15 December 2022. On the potential impact of the DCD on the Italian legal system, see e.g. Carmelita Camardi, 'Prime osservazioni sulla direttiva (UE) 2019/770 sui contratti per la fornitura di contenuti e servizi digitali. Operazioni di consumo e circolazione di dati personali' (2019) Giustizia civile 499 ff.; Alberto De Franceschi, 'La circolazione dei dati personali tra privacy e contratto' (ESI, Napoli, 2017); Claudia Irti, 'Consenso "negoziato" e circolazione dei dati personali' (Giappichelli, Torino, 2021); Giuseppe Versaci, 'La contrattualizzazione dei dati personali dei consumatori' (ESI, Napoli, 2020).

[2] Legislative Decree 4 November 2021, no 170 <https://www.normattiva.it/atto/caricaDettaglioAtto?atto.dataPubblicazioneGazzetta=2021-11-26&atto.codiceRedazionale=21G00186&atto.articolo.numero=0&atto.articolo.sottoArticolo=1&atto.articolo.sottoArticolo1=10&qId=&tabID=0.06454540653602281&title=lbl.dettaglioAtto> accessed 15 December 2022. See e.g. Giovanni De Cristofaro (ed), *La nuova disciplina delle vendite mobiliari nel codice del consumo* (Giappichelli, Torino, 2022); Alberto De Franceschi, 'Italian Consumer Law after the Transposition of Directives (EU) 2019/770 and 2019/771' (2022) Journal of European Consumer and Market Law 72 ff.; Angelo Luminoso, 'La nuova disciplina delle garanzie nella vendita al consumatore (una prima lettura del d.lgs. n. 170/2021)' (2022) Europa e Diritto privato 483 ff.; Angelo Luminoso, 'La vendita', in Roppo and Anelli (eds), Trattato di Diritto civile e commerciale Cicu-Messineo, 2nd ed. (Giuffrè, Milano, 2022) 578 ff. See on the SGD e.g. Guido Alpa, 'Aspetti della nuova disciplina delle vendite nell'Unione europea' (2019) Contratto e impresa/Europa 825 ff.; Federico Azzarri, 'Consegna e passaggio del rischio nelle vendite di beni mobili ai consumatori: considerazioni in vista dell'attuazione della direttiva (UE) 2019/771' (2021) Responsabilità civile e previdenza, 1095 ff.; Andrea Barenghi, 'Osservazioni sulla nuova disciplina delle garanzie nella vendita di beni di consumo' (2020) Contratto e impresa 806 ff.; Alberto De Franceschi, 'La vendita di beni con elementi digitali' (ESI, Napoli, 2019); Mirko Faccioli, 'La nuova disciplina europea della vendita di beni ai consumatori (dir. (UE) 2019/771): prospettive di attuazione delle disposizioni sui termini' (2020) Le nuove leggi civili commentate 250 ff.; Edoardo Ferrante, 'La Direttiva 19/771/UE in materia di vendita al consumo: primi appunti' in D'Angelo and Roppo (eds), *Annuario del contratto 2018* (Giappichelli, Torino, 2020) 23 ff.; Fabio Addis, 'Spunti esegetici sugli aspetti dei contratti di vendita di beni regolati nella nuova direttiva (UE) 2019/771' (2020) Nuovo diritto civile, 5 ff.; Stefano Pagliantini, 'A partire dalla dir. 2019/771 (UE): riflessioni sul concetto di armonizzazione massima' (2020) Nuovo diritto civile 11 f.; Chiara Sartoris, 'La risoluzione della vendita di beni di consumo nella dir. n. 771/2019 UE' (2020) La nuova giurisprudenza civile e commentata, II, 720 ff.

[3] They replace the former Art 128-135 Consumer Code, which – as mentioned above – contained the implementation provisions of Directive EC 1999/44: See e.g. Alberto De Franceschi, 'La vendita di beni di consumo: difetti di conformità e responsabilità del professionista', in Roppo (ed), *Trattato dei contratti*, V (Giuffrè, Milano, 2014), 209 ff.

A. Introduction

which in 2022 turned 80 years old, is – at least in its wording – impermeable to the developments of European Private Law.

Actually, two (bland) attempts were made in order to "integrate" consumer contract law into the Civil Code.

In 1996, Directive EEC 1993/13 on unfair contract terms was implemented into Art 1469-*bis* to 1469-*sexies* Civil Code, also in the "General Part" of Contract Law (Libro IV, Titolo II of the Civil Code). The scope of application of those provisions remained limited to business to consumer contracts without an adequate coordination with the already existing rules on obligations and contracts.[4]

In 2002, Directive EC 1999/44 on consumer sales was implemented into Art. 1519-*bis* to 1519-*novies* Civil Code, in the framework of the provisions on sales law (Libro IV, Titolo III, Capo I of the Civil Code). Also those provisions had a scope of application limited to business to consumer contracts. Furthermore, they were not adequately coordinated with the already existing rules on obligations and contracts, as it remained in particular unclear whether the newly introduced rules – and in particular those providing the hierarchy of remedies – could be derogated by the more favourable ones contained in other provisions of the Italian legal system.[5] In 2005, as the Consumer Code was published,[6] the transposition provisions of Directive EEC 1993/13 on unfair contract terms and of Directive EC 1999/44 on consumer sales were inserted into that Code (respectively at Art. 33-38 and Art. 128-135 Consumer Code).

Furthermore, while implementing DCD and SGD, the Italian legislator did not adopt specific rules in order to enhance environmental sustainability. In particular, it did not take the chance to prioritize repair over replacement in order to enhance environmental sustainability (see e.g. recital 48 SGD).[7] Planned and premature obsolescence increasingly impacts everyday life, undermining the performances of "analogue" goods, and now especially of goods with digital elements, from mobile phones to personal computers, connected cars and smart homes. Addressing the legal implications of such phenomenon has thus become a necessity.[8] Current sanctions and the approach of the

---

[4] See e.g. Giorgio Cian, 'Il nuovo capo XIV bis sulla disciplina dei contratti coi consumatori' (1996) Studium Iuris 425 ff.; Andrea Zoppini, 'Sul rapporto di specialità tra norme appartenenti ai "Codici di Settore" (Lo *ius variandi* nei codici del consumo e delle comunicazioni elettroniche)' (2016) Rivista di Diritto civile, I, 136 ff.; Vincenzo Roppo, 'Il contratto asimmetrico tra parte generale, contratti di impresa e disciplina della concorrenza' (2008) Europa e Diritto privato I, 529 ff.

[5] On that debate see e.g. Alberto De Franceschi, 'I rimedi del consumatore nelle vendite di beni di consumo', in Roppo (ed), *Trattato dei contratti* (Giuffrè 2014) 257 f.

[6] Legislative Decree 6 September 2005, no 206 <https://www.normattiva.it/atto/caricaDettaglioAtto?atto.dataPubblicazioneGazzetta=2005-10-08&atto.codiceRedazionale=005G0232&atto.articolo.numero=0&atto.articolo.sottoArticolo=1&atto.articolo.sottoArticolo1=10&qId=&tabID=0.8177761124770271&title=lbl.dettaglioAtto> accessed 15 December 2022. See e.g. Carlo Castronovo, 'Diritto privato generale e diritti secondi. La ripresa di un tema' (2008) Europa e Diritto privato 397 ff.; Giuseppe Vettori, 'Il diritto dei contratti fra Costituzione, codice civile e codici di settore' (2008) Rivista trimestrale di Diritto e procedura civile 751 ff.; Vincenzo Roppo, 'Parte generale del contratto, contratti del consumatore e contratti asimmetrici (con postilla sul terzo contratto)' in Roppo (ed), *Il contratto del duemila* (Giappichelli 2020) 91 ff.

[7] See Hans-Wolfgang Micklitz, Victor Mehnert, Louisa Specht-Riemenschneider, Christa Liedtke and Peter Kenning, 'The Right to Repair' (2022) available at <https://www.svr-verbraucherfragen.de/wp-content/uploads/2022_SVRV_PB_Rigtht_to_Repair.pdf> accessed 15 December 2022. Cf. Francesca Bertelli, '«Dichiarazioni pubbliche fatte dal o per conto del venditore», conformità oggettiva ed economia circolare', in De Cristofaro (ed), *La nuova disciplina delle vendite mobiliari nel codice del consumo* (Giappichelli, Torino, 2022) 242 ff.

[8] See e.g. Christian Hess, 'Geplante Obsoleszenz' (Nomos, Baden-Baden, 2018) 29 ff.; cf. Tobias Brönnecke and Andrea Wechsler (eds), 'Obsoleszenz Interdisziplinär' (Nomos, Baden-Baden, 2015); Alberto De Franceschi, 'Planned obsolescence challenging the effectiveness of consumer law and the achievement of a sustainable economy' (2018) Journal of European Consumer and Market Law 217 ff. Cf. Elias Van

EU and national legislator in this regard show so far a lack of effectiveness, leaving open some fundamental questions (see below, H.).

B. Relationship between consumer law and general civil law

8   The relationship between consumer law and general private law is regulated, in the implementation provisions of the SGD, by Art. 135-*septies* Consumer Code[9] and, in the implementation provisions of the DCD, by Art. 135-*vicies ter* Consumer Code. Both articles have the same formulation and provide that, as far as not regulated by the implementing provisions of the twin Directives, the rules of the Civil Code regarding formation, validity and effects of contracts, including the consequences of contract termination and compensation, shall apply (Art. 135-*septies*, para. 1 and 135-*vicies ter*, para. 1 Consumer Code).

9   Furthermore, in order to solve the question regarding the possible concurring application of the "general" provisions on the law of obligations, contracts – and specifically those on sales law contained in the Civil Code (respectively, Art. 1176-1320, Art. 1321-1469-*bis*, Art. 1470-1547 Civil Code) – as well as other rules, both Art. 135-*septies*, para. 2 and Art. 135-*vicies ter* para. 2 Consumer Code provide that for the aspects regulated by the implementing provisions of both Directives "do not find application any other rules which have the effect to ensure to the consumer a different level of protection".[10]

10 This should bring to an end[11] a long dispute which originated from the formulation of the now repealed Art. 135 Consumer Code, which provided that the implementing provisions of Directive EC 1999/44 did "not exclude or limit the rights attributed to the consumer by other rules of the legal system" (Art. 135 para. 1 Consumer Code), and that for those aspects not regulated by the implementing provisions of Directive EC 1999/44, the rules of the Civil Code regarding sales contract had to be applied (Art. 135 para. 2 Consumer Code).[12]

11 This gave rise to the opinion according to which the consumer should have been left free to choose between the enforcement of the implementing rules of Directive EC 1999/44 or of those of the "general sales law" contained in the Civil Code (CC), having in this second option direct access to termination or price reduction and thereby avoiding the hierarchy of remedies.[13] This opinion was strongly opposed by those who highlighted that this solution would have given rise to an unjustified derogation and disruption of the system contained in the 1999 Sale of Goods Directive, which indeed prioritized both repair and replacement.[14] In any case, such derogation should not be accepted

---

Gool and Anaïs Michel, 'The New Consumer Sales Directive 2019/771 and Sustainable Consumption: a Critical Analysis' (2021) Journal of European Consumer and Market Law 89 ff.

[9] See e.g. Angelo Luminoso, Angelo Luminoso, 'La nuova disciplina delle garanzie nella vendita al consumatore (una prima lettura del d.lgs. n. 170/2021)' (2022) Europa e Diritto privato 483 ff.

[10] See more below G.II.

[11] In this sense also Angelo Luminoso, 'La nuova disciplina delle garanzie nella vendita al consumatore (una prima lettura del d.lgs. n. 170/2021)' (2022) Europa e Diritto privato 483 ff., who praises the new solution.

[12] See above fn. 5.

[13] See e.g. Pietro Sirena, 'Art. 135 Codice del consumo' in Bianca (ed), *La vendita di beni di consumo. Commentario* (CEDAM, Padova, 2016) 390 ff.; Tommaso Dalla Massara, 'Art. 135 c. cons.: per una sistematica dei rimedi in tema di vendita di beni di consumo' (2007) Rivista di Diritto civile II, 123 ff.

[14] See e.g. Alberto De Franceschi, 'La sostituzione del bene non conforme al contratto di vendita' (2009) Rivista di Diritto civile II, 559 ff. Cf. CJEU, Case C-404/06, *Quelle AG v Bundesverband der Verbraucherzentralen und Verbraucherverbände* (2008) ECLI:EU:C:2008:231, para 27; CJEU, C-65/09 and

B. Relationship between consumer law and general civil law

in the legal framework resulting from the SGD, where consumer remedies for lack of conformity are fully harmonized (Recital 47 SGD). Nevertheless, if the defect is of a serious nature, the buyer can directly terminate the contract (Art. 13 para. 4, lett. c SGD and Art. 135-*bis* para. 4, lett. c Consumer Code), thereby derogating from the hierarchy of remedies.

Therefore Art. 135-*septies* Consumer Code (for the sale of goods)[15] and art 135-*vicies ter* Consumer Code (for the supply of digital content and digital services) exclude the application of other provisions which have the effect to ensure to the consumer a level of protection, which is different from that ensured by the implementing rules of both Directives. Focusing on the sale of goods, this excludes in particular the application of Art. 1477 para. 1 CC (delivery of the goods), 1490 CC (guarantees for material defects), 1491 CC (exclusion of the guarantee), 1492 para. 1 and 2 CC (effects of the guarantee), 1493 CC (effects of contract termination), 1494 CC (special rule on compensation of damages in sales contracts; instead of it, the general tort law rule' of 2043 will apply), 1495 CC (time limits), 1496 CC (sale of animals) and 1497 CC (lack of qualities in the good goods) Civil code. It seems to be excluded also the applicability of art 1492 para. 3 CC, which provides that if the thing delivered has perished as a consequence of the defects, the buyer is entitled to rescission of the contract; if, on the other hand, it has perished by accident or through the buyer's fault, or if the buyer has alienated or transformed it, the buyer can only claim a price reduction.

Digitalization makes it necessary to harmonize consumer contract law with other matters, such as data protection and intellectual property. Regarding the DCD, Art. 135-*terdecies* Consumer Code (implementing art 10 DCD) provides that the remedies mentioned in Art. 135-*octiesdecies* Consumer Code (implementing Art. 14 DCD) shall be extended to the case of impediment or limitation of the use of the digital content or digital services according to what provided by Art. 135-*decies*, para. 4 and 5, Consumer Code (implementing Art. 6 and 7 DCD) as a consequence of a restriction deriving from the violation of third parties' rights, in particular of intellectual property rights, with exception of the other provisions regarding voidness, voidability and other cases of rescission of the contract.[16] The same solution was adopted in way of transposition of the SGD (see Art. 132 Consumer Code, which implements Art. 9 SGD). Therefore, no implementing provision contains rules for the license contract, nor a mention of consumer rights to make copies, use the digital content on different devices, share it among other persons, or transfer it against a counterperformance. This increases the problem of delimiting the consumer's expectations for the purpose of establishing objective conformity.[17]

C-87/09, *Weber GmbH v Wittmer* and *Putz v Medianess Electronics GmbH* (2011) ECLI:EU:C:2011:396, paras 44, 66.

[15] Cf. Angelo Luminoso, 'La nuova disciplina delle garanzie nella vendita al consumatore (una prima lettura del d.lgs. n. 170/2021)' (2022) Europa e Diritto privato 483 ff.; Tommaso dalla Massara, 'Art. 135 *septies* cod. cons.: il coordinamento tra codice del consumo e codice civile in tempi di armonizzazione massima', in De Cristofaro (ed), *La nuova disciplina delle vendite mobiliari nel codice del consumo* (Giappichelli, Torino, 2022) 485 ff.

[16] See the Explanatory Report to the Implementation of the DCD, Art. 135-*terdecies* para. 6 Consumer Code, available at <https://www.governo.it/sites/governo.it/files/DLGS_DIRETTIVA_2019_770_RI.pdf> accessed 15 December 2022.

[17] See Liliia Oprysk and Karin Sein, 'Limitations in End-User Licensing Agreements: Is There A Lack of Conformity Under the New Digital Content Directive?' (2020) 51 IIC 594-623; Gerald Spindler, 'Digital Content Directive and Copyright-related Aspects' (2021) 2 JIPITEC 111, 118 ff.

C. Definitions and scope of application

I. Definitions

14   While the new rules introduced in way of implementation of the "Twin Directives" cover contracts for supply of digital content and digital services and contracts for sale of goods with or without embedded digital elements, recital 12 DCD states, *inter alia*, that the Directive should not determine the legal nature of contracts for the supply of digital content or digital service, and the question of whether such contracts constitute, for instance, a sales, service, rental or *sui generis* contract, should be left to national law. Against this background, the Italian legislator did not state anything in that regard.

1. The notions of "consumer" and "trader"

15   As concerns the notions of "consumer" and "trader", the Italian implementation provisions tendentially (but see, on the contractual role of online platforms, below para. 2.) reproduce the scope of application of the twin Directives. In particular, regarding the notion of "consumer", both Art. 128, para. 2 lett. b Consumer Code (implementing Art. 2, para. 1, n. 2 SGD) and Art. 135-*octies*, para. 2, lett. f Consumer Code (implementing Art. 2, para. 1, n. 6 DCD) refer to what stated in Art. 3, para. 1, lett. a) Consumer Code: The new rules shall therefore apply only to natural persons, who, in relation to contracts covered by the implementing provisions, are acting for purposes which are outside that persons' trade, business, craft or profession. Nevertheless, according to the case law of the CJEU, the above mentioned definition seems not to preclude that the Directive's implementing rules also apply to a contract between a seller or supplier and a subject of the law (such as the *condominium*), notwithstanding that such a subject of the law does not fall within the scope of that Directive.[18]

2. The contractual role of online platforms

16   Recitals 18 DCD and 23 SGD allowed national legislators to clarify the role of platform operators. According to those recitals, online platform providers could be considered to be traders or sellers under this Directive if they act for purposes relating to their own business and as the direct contractual partner of the consumer for the sale of goods. Member States are therefore free to extend the application of the twin Directives' implementing rules to platform providers that do not fulfil the requirements for being considered a trader or a seller under those Directives.

17   Both in way of implementation of DCD and the SGD, the Italian legislation has in this vein enlarged the notion of "trader" and "seller", by including in them also "the supplier of platforms that is acting for purposes relating to that person's activity and as a contractual counterparty of the consumer for the supply of digital content or digital services".[19] The Italian legislator adopted exactly the same formulation in the implementa-

---

[18] CJEU, Case C-329/19, 2 April 2020, *Condominio di Milano v Eurothermo SpA*. See in this regard e.g. Giovanni De Cristofaro, 'Diritto dei consumatori e rapporti contrattuali di condominio: la soluzione della Corte di Giustizia UE' (2020) La nuova giurisprudenza civile commentata, I, 842 ff.

[19] See e.g. Christoph Busch, Gerhard Dannemann, Hans Schulte-Nölke, Aneta Wiewiórowska-Domagalska and Fryderyk Zoll, 'The ELI Model Rules on Online Platforms' (2020) Journal of European Consumer and Market Law 61 ff.; Alberto De Franceschi, '*Uber Spain* and the "Identity Crisis" of Online Platforms' (2018) Journal of European Consumer and Market Law 1 ff. See *in primis* CJEU Case C-434/15, *Asociación Profesional Elite Taxi v Uber Systems Spain SL*, ECLI:EU:C:2017:981; for similar conclusions, see Consiglio di Stato (Italian Supreme Administrative Court), 23 December 2015, Section I,

tion of both Directives (see, respectively, Art. 128, para. 2, lett. c and Art. 135-*octies*, para. 2, lett. e Consumer Code), even if it is clear that the implementing provision of the SGD would have required the explicit mention not only of traders who supply digital content or digital services, but also of those who act for purposes relating to their own business and as the direct contractual partner of the consumer for the sale of goods. The abovementioned omission can be integrated by way of interpretation.

II. Dual purpose contracts

According to recital 17 DCD and 22 SGD, the definition of consumer should cover natural persons who are acting outside their trade, business, craft or profession. However, Member States were left free to determine in the case of dual purpose contracts – where the contract is concluded for purposes that are partly within and partly outside the person's trade, and where the trade purpose is so limited as not to be predominant in the overall context of the contract – whether, and under which conditions, that person should also be considered a consumer. Given the circumstance that the Italian legislator did not take position in this regard, it seems that the natural person which concludes a contract for dual purposes can never be qualified as a consumer according to the Italian Law. **18**

III. Data as a consideration

Art 135-*octies*, para. 4 Consumer Code provides, following Art. 3, para. 1, subpara. 2 DCD, that the implementation provisions of the DCD should apply to contracts where the trader supplies or undertakes to supply digital content or a digital service to the consumer, and the consumer provides or undertakes to provide personal data to the trader, except where the personal data provided by the consumer are exclusively processed by the trader for the purpose of supplying the digital content or digital service in accordance with the DCD or for allowing the trader to comply with legal requirements to which the trader is subject, and the trader does not process those data for any other purpose. According to Art. 2, para. 1, no. 8 DCD "personal data" means "personal data as defined in Art. 4 of Regulation 2016/679/EU" (hereinafter: GDPR). However, the DCD does not provide any rule which clarifies whether consent to conclude the contract must be given in accordance with the GDPR.[20] The Italian implementing provisions do not address payment through other non-personal data or metadata (e.g. information about the device, browsing history, etc.), but the silence of the legislator is not sufficient indication that there could not be a contract in such a case. The introduction of this provision did not produce an impact on national legislation which goes beyond the scope of application of the DCD implementing provisions in the business to consumer contracts. In this regard, the Italian legislator did not take the opportunity to explicitly declare as applicable existing rules on contract formation, validity or existence or to introduce new ones on the same aspects (see Art. 3, para. 10 DCD). **19**

Nevertheless, some interesting Italian case law should be considered regarding the issue of data as a counterperformance. On 29 November 2018 the Italian Autorità Garante **20**

---

no 3586/2015 <https://giustizia-amministrativa.it> accessed 15 December 2022; Alberto De Franceschi, La vendita di beni con elementi digitali (ESI, Napoli, 2019) 67 ff.

[20] See on the DCD proposal, cf. Alberto De Franceschi, 'La circolazione dei dati personali tra *privacy* e contratto' (ESI, Napoli, 2017); cf. Sebastian Lohsse, Reiner Schulze and Dirk Staudenmayer (eds), 'Data as Counter-Performance – Contract Law 2.0?' (Hart – Nomos, Oxford – Baden-Baden, 2020).

della Concorrenza e del Mercato (hereinafter: AGCM), closed an investigation for alleged violations of the Consumer Code by Facebook Ireland Ltd. and its parent company Facebook Inc., imposing two fines for a total of 10 million Euros. The Authority assessed that Facebook, in violation of art 21 and 22 of the Consumer Code (implementing, respectively, art 6 and 7 of Directive EC 2005/29 on unfair commercial practices (hereinafter: UCPD)) misled consumers into registering in the Facebook platform, while not immediately and adequately informing them during the creation of the account that the data they provide would be used for commercial purposes. More generally, Facebook emphasized the free nature of the service but not the commercial objectives that underlie the provision of the social network service, thus inducing users into making a transactional decision that they would not have taken otherwise (i.e., to register in the social network and to continue using it).[21] The information provided was assessed as in fact general and incomplete and not adequately making a distinction between the utilization of data for the purpose of the personalization of the service (in order to connect "consumer" users with each other) and data used in order to carry out advertising campaigns aimed at specific targets. In the same proceeding, the AGCM also found that Facebook, in violation of Art. 24 and 25 of the Consumer Code (implementing, respectively, Art. 8 and 9 UCPD), carried out an aggressive practice, as it exerted undue influence on registered consumers, who suffered, without express and prior consent and therefore unconsciously and automatically, the transmission of their data from Facebook to third-party websites/apps for commercial purposes, and vice versa. According to the AGCM, the undue influence was caused by the pre-selection by Facebook of the broadest consent to data sharing. In particular, the Authority assessed that when users decided to limit the extent of their consent, they were faced with significant restrictions on the use of the social network and third-party websites / apps, which induced users to maintain the pre-selected choice. In particular, through the pre-selection of the "Active Platform" function, Facebook did pre-set the ability of its users to access websites and external apps using their Facebook accounts, thus enabling the transmission of their data to the single websites or apps, without any explicit consent. Facebook then reiterated the opt-out pre-selection mechanism, with respect to data sharing, whenever users access third-party websites or apps, including games, using their Facebook accounts. In this case also, users could in fact only deselect the pre-setting operated by Facebook, without being able to make a free, informed choice. In consideration of the relevant effects of the practice on consumers, the AGCM also requested Facebook to publish – pursuant to art 27, para 8, Consumer Code – an amending declaration on its website and App.[22]

Then, Facebook Ireland Ltd. and Facebook Inc. failed to comply with the order requiring to remove the unfair practice on the use of user data and to publish the amending declaration requested by the Authority. As a consequence, the AGCM sanctioned Facebook Ireland Ltd. and its parent company Facebook Inc. for a total of 7 million

---

[21] This solution had been already suggested, regarding the DCD proposal, by Alberto De Franceschi, 'La circolazione dei dati personali tra privacy e contratto' (ESI, Napoli, 2017) 101 ff. In this regard, see also Giorgio Resta and Vincenzo Zeno-Zencovich, 'Volontà e consenso nella fruizione dei servizi in rete' (2018) Rivista trimestrale di diritto e procedura civile 411 ff.; Vincenzo Ricciuto, 'La patrimonializzazione dei dati personali. Contratto e mercato nella ricostruzione del fenomeno' (2018) Il diritto dell'informazione e dell'informatica 689 ff.

[22] Autorità Garante della Concorrenza e del Mercato, 29 November 2018, PS 11112 <https://www.agcm.it/dotcmsdoc/allegati-news/PS11112_scorr_sanz.pdf> accessed 15 December 2022; the decision was later partially repealed (by excluding the aggressive character of the above described commercial practice) by Tribunale Amministrativo Regionale Roma-Lazio, 10 January 2020, no 261 <https://giustizia-amministrativa.it> accessed 15 December 2022 and later on by Consiglio di Stato, 29 March 2021, no 2631 <https://giustizia-amministrativa.it> accessed 15 December 2022.

Euros for failing to comply with the order issued against them in November 2018. This second investigation showed that the two companies had not published the amending declaration and had not ceased the misleading practice: despite having eliminated the claim of the free of charge nature of the service when registering with the platform, they still did not provide an immediate and clear information on the collection and use of user data for commercial purposes. The Authority highlighted that consumers need such information in order to decide whether to subscribe to the service, considering the economic value that the data transferred assume for Facebook, which constitutes the same consideration for using the service.[23]

IV. Bundles

According to Art. 3, Para. 6 DCD, where a single contract between the same trader and the same consumer includes in a bundle elements of supply of digital content or a digital service and elements of the provision of other goods or services, the DCD shall only apply to the elements of the contract concerning the digital content or digital service. Art. 19 DCD shall not apply where a bundle within the meaning of Directive EU 2018/1972 includes elements of an internet access service as defined in point 2 of Art. 2 of Regulation EU 2015/2120 or a number-based interpersonal communications service as defined in point 6 of Art. 2 of Directive EU 2018/1972. In particular, Art. 3, para. 6, subpara. 3 states that without prejudice to Art. 107, para. 2 of Directive EU 2018/1972, the effects that the termination of one element of a bundle contract may have on the other elements of the bundle contract shall be governed by national law. In this regard the Italian legislator merely reproduced in Art 135-*novies*, para. 4 Consumer Code the content of Art. 107, para. 2 Directive EU 2018/1972.[24]

V. Second-hand goods, second-hand goods sold at public auction and living animals

In transposing Art. 3, para. 5, lett. a SGD, the Italian legislator decided to include in the scope of application of the implementing provisions of the SGD[25] also contracts for the sale of second-hand goods (Art. 128, para 5, Consumer Code). The same applies also in the case in which second-hand goods are sold at public auction and no clear and comprehensive information about the inapplicability of the rights deriving from the implementing provisions of SGD was made easily available to consumers.

Furthermore, in way of transposition of Art. 3, para 5, lit b SGD, the Italian legislator decided also to explicitly include in the notion of "good" also "living animals" (Art. 128, para 2, lit e Consumer Code).[26]

---

[23] Autorità Garante della Concorrenza e del Mercato, 9 February 2021, IP330, *Facebook* <https://en.agcm.it/en/media/press-releases/2021/2/IP330> accessed 15 December 2022. In the same vein, see also more recently Autorità Garante della Concorrenza e del Mercato, 9 November 2021, *Apple* <https://en.agcm.it/en/media/press-releases/2021/2/IP330> accessed 15 December 2022; Autorità Garante della Concorrenza e del Mercato, 16 November 2021, *Google* <https://en.agcm.it/en/media/press-releases/2021/2/IP330> accessed 15 December 2022.

[24] See Dirk Staudenmayer, 'Article 3. Scope', in Schulze and Staudenmayer (eds), *EU Digital Law* (Beck – Hart – Nomos, München – Oxford – Baden-Baden, 2020) 84 ff.

[25] With regard to Art. 3 para. 5 lett. a SGD see e.g. Alberto De Franceschi, 'La vendita di beni con elementi digitali' (ESI, Napoli, 2019) 26 ff.

[26] For the application to living animals of the repealed art 128-135 Consumer Code (implementing provisions of Directive EC 1999/44) see Corte di Cassazione, sec. II, 25 September 2018, no. 22728. See e.g.

25   Following the solution provided by Art. 3, para 4, lit. a SGD, the implementing provisions of that Directive do not apply to the tangible medium which acts solely as a carrier of the digital content, and to goods subject to forced sale or otherwise sold by judicial authorities, also by delegation to notaries, or in accordance with other modalities provided for by law (Art. 128, par 4 Consumer code).

D. Conformity of goods

I. The conformity criteria

26   In the implementation of both Directives, the Italian legislator merely reproduced the subjective and the objective requirements for conformity contained in the EU provisions.[27] As specifically regards the objective requirements for conformity, the Italian legislator clarified – even if it was already clear from the context –, as to the relevance of the public statements made by or on behalf of the trader, or other persons in previous links of the chain of transactions, particularly in advertising or on labelling, that the exemption cases indicated in Art. 8, para. 1, lett. b (i-iii) DCD (the trader was not, and could not reasonably have been, aware of the public statement in question; by the time of conclusion of the contract, the public statement had been corrected in the same way as, or in a way comparable to how, it had been made; or the decision to acquire the digital content or digital service could not have been influenced by the public statement) apply "alternatively" and not cumulatively (Art. 135-*decies*, para. 5, lett b, no. 1-3 Consumer code).

27   No specific criteria were introduced with regard to the durability requirement (but see below para II.). With regard to the duty to inform and supply the consumer with updates which are necessary to keep the digital content or digital service or the smart good in conformity or the liability exemption for the case in which the consumer fails to install updates (Art. 8, para. 2 DCD and Art. 7, para. 3 SGD: the trader or the seller "shall ensure that the consumer is informed of and supplied with updates"), the Italian legislator put on the professional side the duty to "keep the consumer informed about the available updates": if we stick to this formulation, the rule sounds quite contradictory in particular as regards the implementation provisions of the SGD, as it puts on the final seller the duty to provide information they in the most cases actually do not have access to or control on.[28] Actually, the final seller will be just liable for the lack of the relevant information, and will have the right of redress and therefore to pursue remedies against the person or the persons liable in the chain of commercial transactions (Art. 20 DCD and Art. 18 SGD, implemented respectively into Art. 135-*quindecies* and Art. 134 Consumer Code).

28   Furthermore, the Italian legislator did not specify the provision regarding the exclusion of existence of a lack of conformity in the case provided by Art. 8, para. 5 DCD with regard to the situation in which the consumer, at the time of the conclusion of the con-

---

Roberto Senigaglia, 'Riflessioni sullo stato giuridico degli animali di affezione e sue ricadute in materia di vendita e responsabilità civile' (2021) Il diritto di famiglia e delle persone 1772 ff.

[27] See e.g. Matilde Girolami, 'La conformità del bene al contratto di vendita: criteri "soggettivi" e criteri "oggettivi", in De Cristofaro (ed), *La nuova disciplina delle vendite mobiliari nel codice del consumo* (Giappichelli, Torino, 2022), 65 ff.

[28] See Gabriele Perfetti, 'Beni con elementi digitali e aggiornamenti nella novellata disciplina dei contratti di vendita B2C', in De Cristofaro (ed), *La nuova disciplina delle vendite mobiliari nel codice del consumo* (Giappichelli, Torino, 2022) 264 ff.

tract, was specifically informed that a particular characteristic of the digital content or the digital service was deviating from the objective requirements for conformity laid down in paras 1 or 2 and the consumer expressly and separately accepted that deviation when concluding the contract.

II. The implementation of the durability requirement contained in Art. 7, para 1, lett. d SGD, the coordination with the EC Eco-Design Directive and the forthcoming EU Eco-Design Regulation

The Italian legislator did not adopt specific measures for enhancing environmental sustainability or circular economy in way of implementation of DCD and SGD. In particular, as previously mentioned, it did not further specify the implementation of the "durability" requirement in Art. 7, para. 1, lett. d SGD nor implemented the requirements in product-specific Union legislation (cf. recital 32 SGD), especially the requirements relating to durability and repairability. Therefore, according to Italian Law, there is no explicit coordination between the two sets of provisions.

In particular, the Italian legal system has no specific rules on availability of spare parts and corresponding information obligations. Furthermore, the Italian legislator did not coordinate the implementing provisions of the SGD with those of Directive 2009/125/EC establishing a framework for the setting of ecodesign requirements for energy-related products. Regarding sanctions, Art. 20 of Directive EC 2009/125 was implemented into Art. 17 of the Legislative Decree 16 February 2011, no. 15, which provides only for administrative sanctions.[29] According to the abovementioned provision, whoever places on the market or puts into service products without the "CE" marking or the EC declaration of conformity or with a forged counterfeit marking or declaration shall be punished, unless the fact is provided for as a criminal offence, with a pecuniary administrative sanction of the payment of a sum from twenty thousand euro to one hundred and fifty thousand euro. The manufacturer, its authorised representative or the importer, who does not comply with the marketing prohibition imposed pursuant to Art. 10, para. 2 Legislative Decree 16 February 2011 no. 15[30] (implementing Art. 8 para. 2 subpara 2 dir. EC 2009/125), shall be punished with a pecuniary sanction consisting of the payment of a sum from ten thousand euro to fifty thousand euro. The manufacturer, his authorised representative or the importer, who does not comply with the prohibition or restriction referred to in Art. 10 para. 3 second sentence of the abovementioned Legislative Decree,[31] shall be punished with a pecuniary sanction from forty thousand euro

---

[29] Legislative Decree 16 February 2011, no 15 <https://www.normattiva.it/atto/caricaDettaglioAtto?atto.dataPubblicazioneGazzetta=2011-03-08&atto.codiceRedazionale=011G0055&atto.articolo.numero=0&atto.articolo.sottoArticolo=1&atto.articolo.sottoArticolo1=10&qId=&tabID=0.953508470616611&title=lbl.dettaglioAtto> accessed 15 December 2022.

[30] Art. 10, para 2 Legislative Decree 16 February 2011, no. 15: "Where there is evidence to suggest that a product, although bearing the CE marking, may be non-compliant, or where the manufacturer or his authorised representative or, in the absence of the latter, the importer, does not allow samples, the declaration of conformity and the related technical documentation to be obtained in time for the necessary verifications, the competent authority shall, following a warning, prohibit the placing on the market of the product for the time strictly necessary to ascertain its conformity and, in any case, for a period not exceeding 60 days".

[31] Art 10, para 3 Legislative Decree 16 February 2011, no. 15: "Where, as a result of the monitoring and verification procedures referred to in Article 7, it is established that although the product bears the CE marking and the declaration of conformity, it does not comply with the applicable implementing measure or with the measure implementing that measure, the competent authority shall require the manufacturer or its authorised representative or, where this is not possible, the importer, to bring the product into

to one hundred and fifty thousand euro. Whoever violates the provisions set forth in Art. 11, para. 3 Legislative Decree 16 February 2011 no. 15[32] shall be punished, unless the act has been established as a criminal offence, with the pecuniary administrative sanction of the payment of a sum from five thousand euro to thirty thousand euro. The sanctions referred to in the same provision shall be imposed by the Chamber of Commerce, Industry, Crafts and Agriculture territorially competent and to the extent compatible with the aforementioned Decree the provisions of Law no. 689 of 24 November 1981. The sums deriving from such sanctions shall be paid to the State budget.

E. The Modification of Digital Content or Digital Service in the implementation provisions of the SGD

31   Art. 19 DCD on the modification of digital content or digital service was implemented, without any modifications, into Art. 135 *vicies-semel* Consumer Code.

32   Regrettably the SGD does not contain a similar provision. This is probably due to the hurry which characterised the adoption of the Directive. Following that solution, the Italian legislator did not regulate the modification of digital content or digital service in way of implementation of the SGD. Therefore, as an explicit regulation is missing, it seems reasonable to apply, via interpretation, the rule contained in art 19 DCD:[33] in particular, the application of this rule also to the sale of goods with digital elements would be appropriate to provide adequate and effective protection of consumers' interests. Otherwise Art. 33, para. 1 lett. m Consumer Code can apply.

F. Third party rights and the relationship with Intellectual Property Law

33   Art. 10 DCD and Art. 9 SGD on third party rights were implemented, respectively, into Art. 135-*terdecies* and Art. 132 Consumer Code, which apply the remedies provided by the for a lack of conformity to the situations covered by those provisions. Nevertheless, the abovementioned provisions explicitly do not affect the applicability of the rules provided by the legal system with regard to voidness (Art. 1418 ff. CC), annullability (Art. 1441 ff. CC) and other cases of termination (Art. 1453 ff. CC) of a contract. Furthermore, the Italian legislator did not regulate neither the relationship with Intellectual Property Law nor the right to "resell" digital contents.

---

conformity with the applicable implementing measure. Where the non-conformity of the product cannot be remedied or persists beyond the deadline set, the competent authority shall, by means of a reasoned measure, prohibit or restrict its placing on the market or putting into service by the manufacturer or its authorised representative or, failing that, the importer. In case of prohibition of placing on or withdrawal from the market, the authority shall immediately inform the European Commission and the other Member States."

[32] Art 11, para 3 Legislative Decree 16 February 2011, no. 15: "After placing on the market or putting into service a product subject to the enforcement measures, the manufacturer or its authorised representative shall keep relevant documents relating to the conformity assessment performed and declarations of conformity issued available for inspection by the authority for a period of 10 years after the last of such products has been manufactured. The relevant documents shall be made available within 10 days after receipt of the request by the competent authority."

[33] For this solution, see Alberto De Franceschi, 'La vendita di beni con elementi digitali' (ESI, Napoli, 2019) 98 ff.

G. Liability of the Trader

I. Liability Requirements

Art. 11 DCD and Art. 10 SGD were implemented into Art. 135-*quaterdecies* and Art. 133 Consumer Code without any modifications regarding the liability requirements, but only with regard to the time limits (see below para. M.).

The Italian legislator did not adopt specific regulation on the interruption of long-term supply of digital content or digital services. As regards the consequences of a failure to deliver or supply with respect to obstacles like impossibility or force majeure, Italian law provides general instruments in the law of contracts at, respectively, Art. 1463 (impossibility of performance) ff. CC and Art. 1467 (excessive onerousness) CC.

Concerning the relationship with the GDPR, the Italian legislator merely stated that, as regards consumer's personal data, the trader shall comply with the duties arising from EU Regulation 2016/679 and from Legislative Decree 10 August 2018, no. 101, which implemented the GDPR.[34]

II. Remedies for the Failure to Supply and Remedies for the Lack of Conformity

The Italian legislator introduced a specific right to withhold payment for contracts under the DCD. Implementing Art. 13, para. 6 SGD, Art. 135-*bis*, para. 6 Consumer Code provides that the consumer shall have the right to withhold payment of any outstanding part of the price or a part thereof until the seller has fulfilled the seller's obligations under the SGD (see more on this below under D.). In particular, in implementing the last sentence of Art. 13, para. 6 SGD, the aforementioned provision of the Consumer Code states that "The provisions of the Civil Code governing the exception of non-performance [...] remain unaffected". As regards the exception of non-performance, Art. 1460 Codice civile provides that "in contracts for pecuniary interest, either party may refuse to perform its obligation if the other does not perform *or does not offer to perform* at the same time, unless different terms for performance have been agreed upon by the parties or result from the nature of the contract". In any case, the consumer should have the right to refuse the delivery of the good not in conformity with the contract, according to Art. 1181 CC.[35]

---

[34] Law Decree 10 August 2018, no. 101, "Disposizioni per l'adeguamento della normativa nazionale alle disposizioni del regolamento (UE) 2016/679 del Parlamento europeo e del Consiglio, del 27 aprile 2016, relativo alla protezione delle persone fisiche con riguardo al trattamento dei dati personali, nonché alla libera circolazione di tali dati e che abroga la direttiva 95/46/CE (regolamento generale sulla protezione dei dati)".

[35] Art. 1181 CC: "The creditor may refuse partial performance even if the performance is divisible, unless the law or customs provide otherwise". See the Explanatory Report to the Implementation of the SGD, Art. 135-*bis* para. 6 Consumer Code, available at <https://www.giustizia.it/giustizia/it/mg_1_2_1.page?facetNode_1=1_8%282021%29&facetNode_2=0_17&contentId=SAN345568&previsiousPage=mg_1_2#rel> accessed 15 December 2022: "It was deemed appropriate to exercise the option provided for in [Art. 13] paragraph 6, second sentence [SGD], by referring to the general provisions of Article 1460 of the Civil Code, as the reference made to the national provisions by Article 135-septies [Consumer Code] was not deemed sufficient. It was also considered appropriate to exercise the option provided for in [Art. 13] paragraph 7 [SGD] and refer to the national rules [i.e. Art. 1227 of the Civil Code] on the concurrence of the behaviour of the consumer, so as to clarify their applicability in these cases." See, in favour of the solution chosen by the Italian legislator, Angelo Luminoso, 'La vendita', in Roppo and Anelli (eds), Trattato di Diritto civile e commerciale Cicu-Messineo, 2nd ed. (Giuffrè, Milano, 2022) 668.

No specific rules were adopted in order to define the place of delivery and the place of repair and replacement or to define the costs of transport for the case of repair/replacement (e.g. being advanced or reimbursed).

38   Furthermore, no specific rules were introduced regarding the contractual consequences of withdrawal of consent for processing personal data or with regard to restitution where the trader supplies digital content and/or digital services. Therefore, general contract law rules apply in these cases.

39   Art. 135-*quater*, par 1 Consumer Code (implementing Art. 15 SGD) does not specify the modalities for enforcing the right to price reduction. In particular, it does not clarify whether the consumer is allowed – similar to what Art. 16 SGD provides for the termination of the contract – to reduce the price by means of a statement to the seller. On this point there is uncertainty in the Italian literature.[36] At first glance, the relevant difference between the two formulations may support a negative solution. Nevertheless, it seems reasonable to pledge for a positive answer, given that the consumer has, according to Art. 135-*bis*, para 6 Consumer Code the right to refuse to pay any part of the price until the seller has fulfilled its obligations under the implementing provisions of the SGD.[37]

40   As regards termination, Art. 135-*quater*, para 3 Consumer Code (implementing Art. 16, para 2 SGD) provides that if the lack of conformity concerns only some of the goods delivered under the contract of sale and there is a cause for termination of the sales contract under Art. 135-*bis* Consumer Code, the consumer may terminate the contract only with respect of the non-conforming goods and those purchased together with the non-conforming goods, if it is not reasonably foreseeable that there exists an interest consumer's interest in retaining at his disposal the goods that are not defective. This formulation should be interpreted according to Art. 1464 CC regarding the partial supervening impossibility of the performance,[38] so that the consumer is entitled to terminate the entire contract in case he has no appreciable interest to the partial performance.

41   Art. 16 para 3 SGD provides that where the consumer terminates a sales contract as a whole or, in accordance with para 2, in relation to some of the goods delivered under the sales contract, the consumer shall return to the seller, at the seller's expense, the goods; and the seller shall reimburse to the consumer the price paid for the goods upon receipt of the goods or of evidence provided by the consumer of having sent back the goods.

42   For the purposes of this paragraph, Member States were left free to determine the modalities for return and reimbursement. In this regard Art. 135-*quater* Consumer Code refers not only to the consumer having "returned" but also to the consumer having "sent back"[39] the good not in conformity with the contract.

43   The Italian legislator did not provide anything specific with regard to the modalities for return, send back and reimbursement, thereby not making use of the option contained in Art. 16, para. 3 last sentence SGD.

---

[36] See e.g. Fabio Addis, 'Spunti esegetici sugli aspetti dei contratti di vendita di beni regolati nella nuova direttiva (UE) 2019/771' (2020) 23 f.

[37] See Francesco Oliviero, 'La nuova disciplina dei c.d. rimedi "secondari": riduzione del prezzo e risoluzione del contratto', in De Cristofaro (ed), *La nuova disciplina delle vendite mobiliari nel codice del consumo* (Giappichelli, Torino, 2022) 340 ff.

[38] Art. 1464 CC: "When one party's performance has become only partially impossible, the other party is entitled to a corresponding reduction of the performance owed by it, and may also withdraw from the contract if it has no appreciable interest in partial performance."

[39] See the Explanatory Report to the Implementation of the SGD, Art. 135-*quater* para. 6 Consumer Code, available at <https://www.giustizia.it/giustizia/it/mg_1_2_1.page?facetNode_1=1_8%282021%29&facetNode_2=0_17&contentId=SAN345568&previsiousPage=mg_1_2#rel> accessed 15 December 2022: "It should be noted that, in [Art. 135-*quater*] paragraph 3(b) [Consumer Code] it was decided to insert the word "or sent back", in order to align the Italian formulation with the English text (having sent back the goods) and the French text (*leur renvoi fournie*) [of the SGD]"

The compensation for damages is not regulated by the new rules, but is expressly permitted in Art. 135-*septies* para 1, referred to repeatedly in the SGD (see recitals 18 and 61 and Art. 3 para. 6). The questions that arise in this regard are substantially similar to those examined by literature and case law under Directive EC 1999/44.[40] Since the new rules generically refer to the provisions of the Civil Code, Art. 1218 ff. (non-performance) and Art. 2043 ff. (extra-contractual liability) CC and any other relevant rule on compensation for damages (such as, for example, those on penalties and down payments) and extra-contractual damage (such as, for example, Art. 114 ff. Consumer Code on defective products) should apply. It seems reasonable not to allow the consumer to ask for the pecuniary equivalent of the loss corresponding to the lower value of the thing in cases when the rules implementing the SGD allow the consumer only to require the replacement or repair of the good. In such cases, it seems reasonable that the consumer may only claim compensation for "supplementary" damage, i.e. damage that remains despite the repair or replacement of the good. In the event that the restoration of conformity is not possible or would entail disproportionate costs on the seller or is not executed within a reasonable period time from the moment the seller has been informed by the consumer about the lack of conformity or is executed causing significant inconvenience to the consumer, it seems reasonable that the consumer may autonomously claim compensation for so-called "substitutive damages".[41]

Implementing Art. 13 para. 7 SGD, Art. 135-*bis*, para. 6 Consumer Code states that "The rules of the Civil Code governing [...] the concurrence of the consumer's behaviour remain unaffected". Here Art. 1227 (Contributory negligence of the creditor) CC should find application. In particular Art. 1227 para. 1 CC provides that if the negligent act of the creditor has contributed to the damage, compensation shall be reduced in accordance with the gravity of the fault and the extent of the consequences resulting therefrom; Para. 2 of the same article provides that compensation is not due for damages that the creditor could have avoided by using ordinary diligence.

Finally, according to Article 135-*septies* para. 1 Consumer code, the consumer should be entitled to bring an action for annulment of the contract for vices of will, especially in cases in which the deception put in place by the seller, with regard to the qualities of the goods, induced the consumer to purchase them.

H. Sustainability, premature and planned obsolescence and the relationship with the internal rules on unfair commercial practices

Italian legislator did not adopt specific rules in order to enhance environmental sustainability of the Twin Directives implementing provisions. In particular, as regards the sale of goods, it did not take the chance to prioritize repair over replacement in order to enhance environmental sustainability (see e.g. recital 48 SGD).[42]

Planned and premature obsolescence increasingly impacts everyday life, undermining the performances of "analogue" goods and smart devices, from mobile phones to personal computers, connected cars and smart homes. Addressing the legal implications

---

[40] See e.g. Alberto De Franceschi, La vendita di beni di consumo: difetti di conformità e responsabilità del professionista, in Roppo (ed) *Trattato dei contratti* V (Giuffrè, Milano, 2014), 209 ff.

[41] See Angelo Luminoso, 'La vendita', in Roppo and Anelli (eds), Trattato di Diritto civile e commerciale Cicu-Messineo, 2nd ed. (Giuffrè, Milano, 2022) 641 f.

[42] See Hans-Wolfgang Micklitz, Victor Mehnert, Louisa Specht-Riemenschneider, Christa Liedtke and Peter Kenning, 'The Right to Repair' (2022) available at <https://www.svr-verbraucherfragen.de/wp-content/uploads/2022_SVRV_PB_Rigtht_to_Repair.pdf> accessed 15 December 2022.

of such phenomenon has thus become a necessity.⁴³ In 2018 the Italian legislator made an attempt to regulate planned obsolescence, but that proposal did not find further concretisation so far.⁴⁴ Current sanctions and the approach of the national and EU legislator on this point show a lack of effectiveness until today, leaving open several fundamental questions. Ensuring longer durability of consumer goods is indeed crucial for achieving more sustainable consumption behaviour, waste reduction and environmental protection.⁴⁵

49   Various attempts to tackle this have been started at both national and EU level. In some European Member States, discussions are under way concerning possible solutions.⁴⁶

50   The SGD delivers a contribution in this direction: indeed, among the objective criteria of conformity, the EU legislator expressly lists durability (Art. 7, para. 1, lett. d SGD).⁴⁷ Nevertheless, the SGD contains provisions which leave the door open to abuses by the trader, in particular regarding the rules on updates of digital contents and on the liability exemption laid down in its Art. 7 para. 4: the possible consumer's decision not to install the updates may indeed lead to the exclusion of the trader's liability for lack of conformity.⁴⁸ Such rules should be therefore considered as complementary to those of the UCPD (especially those on misleading commercial practices) and to those of Directive EU 2011/83 on consumer rights. In particular, European rules on unfair commercial practices play a crucial role in ensuring the effectiveness also of the SGD, and specifically in tackling the phenomenon of planned obsolescence, as they cover traders' behaviour before, during and after a commercial transaction in relation to a product.⁴⁹ Indeed, with specific regard to the practices of the major players in the global market, it seems that private law rules are not effective enough in influencing traders' behaviour to solve the above-mentioned problem.

---

⁴³ See e.g. Christian Hess, 'Geplante Obsoleszenz' (Nomos, Baden-Baden, 2018) 29 ff.; cf. Tobias Brönnecke and Andrea Wechsler (eds), 'Obsoleszenz Interdisziplinär' (Nomos Baden-Baden, 2015); Alberto De Franceschi, 'Planned obsolescence challenging the effectiveness of consumer law and the achievement of a sustainable economy' (2018) Journal of European Consumer and Market Law 217 ff. Cf. Elias Van Gool and Anaïs Michel, 'The New Consumer Sales Directive 2019/771 and Sustainable Consumption: a Critical Analysis' (2021) Journal of European Consumer and Market Law 89 ff.

⁴⁴ Legislative Draft of 9 July 2018 on 'Modifiche al codice di cui al decreto legislativo 6 settembre 2005, n. 206, e altre disposizioni per il contrasto dell'obsolescenza programmata dei beni di consumo', available at <https://www.senato.it/japp/bgt/showdoc/18/DDLPRES/0/1105851/index.html?part=ddlpres_ddlpres1> accessed 15 December 2022.

⁴⁵ See <http://ec.europa.eu/environment/circular-economy/index_en.htm> accessed 15 December 2022. Elias Van Gool and Anais Michel, 'The New Consumer Sales Directive 2019/771 and Sustainable Consumption: A Critical Analysis' (2021) *EuCML* (136) 144–145; Bert Keirsbilck, Evelyne Terryn, Anaïs Michel and Ivano Alogna, 'Sustainable Consumption and Consumer Protection Legislation', available at <https://www.europarl.europa.eu/RegData/etudes/IDAN/2020/648769/IPOL_IDA(2020)648769_EN.pdf> accessed 15 December 2022.

⁴⁶ See the country reports on the implementation of DCD and SGD, in this volume.

⁴⁷ Matthias Wendland, 'Sonderprivatrecht für digitale Güter' (2019) Zeitschrift für die vergleichende Rechtswissenschaft 191 ff.

⁴⁸ See in this regard Alberto De Franceschi, 'La vendita di beni con elementi digitali' (ESI, Napoli, 2019) 119 ff.

⁴⁹ See European Commission, 'Guidance on the interpretation and application of Directive 2005/29/EC of the European Parliament and of the Council concerning unfair business-to-consumer commercial practices in the internal market' of 29.12.2021' 84 ff., available at <https://eur-lex.europa.eu/legal-content/EN/TXT/PDF/?uri=CELEX:52021XC1229(05)> accessed 15 December 2022.

H. Sustainability, premature and planned obsolescence

On this point, it is useful to analyse Italian case law. In 2018, the Italian Competition Authority (AGCM) fined *Apple*[50] and *Samsung*[51], under two separate decisions – both confirmed in 2020 by the second instance Administrative Court of Rome-Lazio,[52] but later repealed in 2023 by the third instance Consiglio di Stato[53] –, for unfair commercial practices concerning software updates which seriously impaired the functioning of certain models of mobile phones. The two big firms were fined 10m (for two commercial practices: each 5m Euros) and 5m Euros respectively. Such decisions immediately gained worldwide resonance. In particular, the AGCM ascertained that the two companies had carried out misleading and aggressive commercial practices, thereby breaching the implementing provisions of Art. 5, 6, 7 and 8 UCPD regarding the release of firmware updates for their mobile phones. These had caused serious malfunctions, significantly reducing the performances of the smart devices and, as a consequence, had accelerated their replacement with more recent products.

In the *Apple* case, the AGCM ascertained the unfairness of two commercial practices. The first one concerned the situation, in which consumers who purchased iPhone 6, 6Plus, 6s and 6sPlus, were insistently asked to update their operating system to iOS 10 and, subsequently, to iOS 10.2.1, which modified functional characteristics and significantly reduced the performances of the above-mentioned phones. This was done without customers being adequately informed in advance about the inconvenience that the installation of these updates might cause and giving only limited and belated advice about how to remedy these shortcomings, for example by means of a downgrading or battery substitution. In addition, it was ascertained that *Apple* used undue influence over consumers as, on the one hand, it induced them to install a firmware update by means of insistent request to download and install updates, as well as by not providing adequate assistance to consumers who wished to restore the previous functionality of their devices. This speeded up the replacement of such devices with new iPhone's models. This practice was fined under Art. 5, 6, 7 and 8 UCPD.[54] Furthermore, the AGCM fined *Apple* according to the implementing provision of Art. 7 UCPD for misleading omissions concerning the lack of information relating to duration, handling and costs for substitution of the mobile phone's batteries, with specific reference to the case in which, after the above mentioned updates, the performance significantly decreased and, as a consequence, consumers were induced to purchase a new phone instead of being appropriately informed about the opportunity to replace the battery. In the *Samsung* case, the AGCM ascertained an unfair commercial practice according to the implementing provisions of Art. 5, 6, 7 and 8 UCPD, as the trader developed and insistently suggested to customers of the Samsung Galaxy Note 4 to proceed to firmware updates, which modified the phone's functionalities, by sensibly reducing performances and preventing consumers from assuming a conscious decision as to whether or not to install new updates to their device. Additionally, it was ascertained that *Samsung* deliberately decided not to

---

[50] See Italian Competition Authority, 25 September 2018, PS11039, *Apple* <http://www.agcm.it/dotcmsdoc/allegati-news/PS11039_scorr_sanzDich_rett_va.pdf> accessed 15 December 2022.

[51] See Italian Competition Authority, 25 September 2018, PS11039, *Samsung* <http://www.agcm.it/dotcmsdoc/allegati-news/PS11009_scorr_sanz_omi_dichrett.pdf> accessed 15 December 2022.

[52] Tribunale Amministrativo Regionale Roma-Lazio, 18 January 2021, no. 656, available at <https://www.giustizia-amministrativa.it/> accessed 15 December 2022; Tribunale Amministrativo Regionale Roma-Lazio, 29 May 2020, Section I, no. 5736 <https://www.giustizia-amministrativa.it/> accessed 15 December 2022.

[53] Consiglio di Stato, 13 January 2023, no. 448 <https://www.giustizia-amministrativa.it/> accessed 31 January 2023, where the Court assessed inter alia a lack of preliminary investigation.

[54] See on those provisions Mateja Durovic, 'European Law on Unfair Commercial Practices and Contract Law' (Hart, Oxford, 2016) 10 ff.

provide assistance for the products, which were no longer under warranty, requiring high costs for repair and not providing the downgrade to the precedent firmware version, thereby intentionally accelerating the products' substitution. Both Apple and Samsung were also required, according to Art. 27 para 8 of the Consumer code, to publish an amending declaration on the Italian homepage of their websites, with a link to the respective AGCM decision.

53   The AGCM's *Apple* and *Samsung* cases highlight fundamental criticisms concerning the effectiveness of current European consumer and market law. First of all, the decisions raise serious doubts concerning the aptitude of the existing penalties laid down in way of implementation of the UCPD for effectively tackling the challenge of planned obsolescence, especially in the digital economy. And, furthermore, they raise the question of how consumer (contract) law could be improved in order to react to and ideally prevent the above-mentioned phenomenon in the future.

54   As concerns the first point, it is in particular questionable whether a penalty up to 5m Euros (that was the maximum amount provided for by Art. 27 para 9 of the Italian Consumer Code until the implementation of EU Directive 2019/2161: now it is 10m Eur) or 10m Eur) is sufficient to effectively dissuade big traders from adopting the above outlined and other kinds of unfair practices. In this regard, Art. 13 UCPD provides that Member States shall lay down penalties for infringements of national provisions adopted in application of this Directive, and that "these penalties must be effective, proportionate and dissuasive". First of all, from a systematic point of view, the fact that the European legislator did not provide clear harmonised penalties for the case of breach of the prohibition of unfair commercial practices opened the door to a fragmentation of the national solutions resulting from the implementation of UCPD: that fragmentation impairs consistency and the realisation of an efficient EU-wide strategy against unfair practices.[55] Secondly, but not less important, effectiveness and dissuasiveness can be actually achieved mainly through proportionality of penalties. In order to better substantiate the concept of proportionality, the penalty shall be linked to the annual turnover of the trader being sanctioned for an unfair commercial practice. Rather than fixing an amount of money as the highest possible penalty, a link to the annual turnover would allow the trader's size, market power and – above all – market impact to be taken into account. This would avoid both "over"- and "undersanctioning".

55   With particular regard to the practices of the major players in the global market, it seems that private law remedies and enforcement are not effective enough for influencing traders' behaviour to solve the above-mentioned problem.[56] Therefore, as shown below, a consistent and effective EU-harmonized set of sanctions would be needed. This would also ensure the effectiveness of private consumer law and encourage fair trading behaviour. It is not by chance that *Apple* significantly modified its practices in a virtuous way after the lodgement of the abovementioned Italian case, in order to comply with the provisional requirements of the AGCM.[57] While the average consumer is often

---

[55] Cf. the reports on the implementation of the UCPD in the EU Member States published in issues 5/2015, 6/2015 and 2/2016 of the Journal of European Consumer and Market Law.

[56] See e.g. Rupprecht Podszun, Christoph Busch and Frauke Henning-Bodewig, 'Behördliche Durchsetzung des Verbraucherrechts?' (2018) available at <https://www.bmwi.de/Redaktion/DE/Publikationen/Studien/behoerdliche-durchsetzung-des-verbraucherrechts.pdf?__blob=publicationFile&v=10> accessed 15 December 2022; cf. Andreas Mundt, 'Verbraucherschutz braucht eine stärkere behördliche Komponente' (2018) Wettbewerb in Recht und Praxis, Issue 9, Editorial.

[57] Cf. the example of art L213-4-1 Code de la Consommation: "L'obsolescence programmée se définit par l'ensemble des techniques par lesquelles un metteur sur le marché vise à réduire délibérément la durée de vie d'un produit pour en augmenter le taux de remplacement. L'obsolescence programmée est punie d'une peine de deux ans d'emprisonnement et de 300.000 € d'amende. Le montant de l'amende peut être

H. Sustainability, premature and planned obsolescence

dissuaded from bringing a matter before a civil court, the compelling pressure generated by prospective or actual proceedings before a competition authority like the AGCM (which has the power to impose public law penalties) is often sufficient to ensure a better enforcement of consumer private law rights.

A good example of this is represented by the results of the enforcement of Art. 6 para. 2 lett. g UCPD, which qualifies as misleading a commercial practice deceiving or being likely to deceive the average consumer in relation to their rights to replacement or reimbursement under the Consumer Sales Directive, or the risks they may face. Such rule is proving to be key in compelling businesses to acknowledge consumer rights. If the perspective of being brought before a civil court is frequently not enough for dissuading the trader from misleading the consumer about their contractual rights, the parallel "risk" to undergo an investigation by the market and competition authority (with the risk of a pecuniary sanction, and especially – as this has an impact on the traders' image – of the publication of the decision or a corresponding corrective statement, according to Art. 27 para. 7 Consumer Code, so that the practices cease their negative effects) creates more deterrence against unfair commercial practices. This synergy should be improved by the EU legislator. 56

A useful example in this direction can be found in Art. 2, para. 6 of Directive EU 2019/2161, regarding the amendments to Art. 13 UCPD, where it provides that Member States shall ensure that when penalties are to be imposed in accordance with Art. 21 of Regulation EU 2017/2394, they include the possibility either to impose fines through administrative procedures or to initiate legal proceedings for the imposition of fines, or both, the maximum amount of such fines being at least 4% of the trader's annual turnover in the Member State or Member States concerned. Without prejudice to that Regulation, Member States may, for national constitutional reasons, restrict the imposition of fines to: (a) infringements of Art. 6, 7, 8, 9 and of Annex I to the same Directive EU 2019/2161; and (b) a trader's continued use of a commercial practice that has been found to be unfair by the competent national authority or court, when that commercial practice is not an infringement referred to in point (a). 57

In order to strengthen the effectivity of consumer rights and to fight planned and premature obsolescence and, inter alia, to enhance the durability of goods with digital elements, the abovementioned rule contained in Art. 2, para. 6 of Directive EU 2019/2161 should be extended beyond the scope of application of Art. 21 of Regulation EU 2017/2394, thereby including all unfair commercial practices and not only the cases in which there is a reasonable suspicion that a widespread infringement or widespread infringement with a Union dimension is taking place. 58

More detailed consumer contract law rules can indeed have a straight-jacket effect, especially if done on a fully harmonised basis. Also, from a consumer's perspective, additional rights may be of little use if enforcement is going to be difficult and/or slow. The amendment to the UCPD and its implementing provisions might be a better and more effective solution. 59

As mentioned above, the SGD contains provisions which leave the door open to abuses by the trader, in particular regarding the rules on updates of digital contents and on the liability exemption laid down in its Art. 7, para. 4: the possible consumer's decision not to install the updates may indeed lead to the exclusion of the trader's liability for lack of conformity. Given this experience in the business-to-consumer relationships, it seems 60

---

porté, de manière proportionnée aux avantages tirés du manquement, à 5 % du chiffre d'affaires moyen annuel, calculé sur les trois derniers chiffres d'affaires annuels connus à la date des faits" (see <https://www.legifrance.gouv.fr> accessed 15 December 2022). Such article – in force from 19 August 2015 to 1 July 2016 – was later repealed by Ordonnance n° 2016-301 of 14 March 2016, Art. 34(V).

adequate to extend such reasonings and rules also to the business-to-business sector. It will be important to progress from incentives for resource efficiency and recycling towards mandatory standards, e.g. by imposing a minimum duration of goods which shall be linked to their economic value. Looking at the future recast of the SGD, this shall lead to insert environmental standards into production and sales law.

61   In the current increasingly servitized economy, suppliers are incentivized to build products for long-term durability, minimize maintenance needs and reuse and recycle components.[58] The new EU rules on the sale of goods with digital elements contained in the SGD about durability and the duty to update may stimulate the transition towards a "servitization of sales law". This gives the chance of a longer duration through maintenance through the Internet of Things and remote control. At the same time, there is a risk of premature obsolescence through digital disruption, which requires the adoption of effective instruments to counteract that negative phenomenon.

I. The transfer of the rights against the initial seller from the initial consumer to a subsequent buyer

62   In way of implementation of both Directives, the Italian legislator did not provide an automatic transfer of the rights against the initial seller from the initial consumer to a subsequent buyer.

63   Nevertheless, Italian law allows the initial consumer and a subsequent buyer to contractually agree that the rights against the initial seller are transferred to the subsequent buyer. In particular, Italian law does not allow the initial seller to exclude the transferability of the rights under the legal guarantee. This would indeed represent a breach of Art. 135-*sexies* and Art. 135-*vicies bis* Consumer Code (implementing, respectively, Art. 21 SGD and Art. 22 DCD: such agreement should therefore be considered void. Differently, there is no prohibition to exclude the transferability of the rights under the commercial guarantee (see below, para. L.) in the general terms and conditions.

64   Furthermore, the Italian legislator did not provide express regulation for the cases in which the consumer bought goods and then moved to another country or when the seller delivered the goods in accordance with the Geo-Blocking Regulation and is now obliged to carry our repair or replacement in a Country he does not offer delivery to.

J. Commercial Guarantees

65   Art. 17 SGD was implemented into 135-*quinquies* Consumer code, which fundamentally reproduces the wording of the Directive. The Italian legislator adopted a rather vague provision and thereby missed the opportunity to draft more precisely the structure of commercial guarantees.[59] In particular, following Art. 17 para. 2 and 4 SGD, Art. 135-*quinquies* para. 3 Consumer Code provides that the guarantee shall be formulated in Italian with characters, which are no less evident that those in other languages. Reproducing Art. 17 para. 3 SGD, Art. 135-*quinquies* para. 4 Consumer Code states that the failure to comply with the provisions contained in Art. 135-*quinquies* para. 2[60] shall

---

[58] Arie Van Hoe and Guillaume Croisant (eds), 'Droit et durabilité – Recht en duurzaamheid' (Larcier, Bruxelles, 2022).

[59] See e.g. Stefano Cherti, 'Le garanzie commerciali', in De Cristofaro (ed), *La nuova disciplina delle vendite mobiliari nel codice del consumo* (Giappichelli, Torino, 2022), 417 ff.

[60] Art. 135-*quinquies* para. 2 Consumer Code: "The conventional guarantee statement shall be provided to the consumer on a durable medium at the latest at the time of delivery of the goods. The statement of

not prejudice the binding effect of the contractual guarantee for the guarantor. Therefore, the consumer will be entitled to enforce the commercial guarantee. Nevertheless, the consumer may claim compensation of damages for breach of information duties and the consumer associations may ask an injunction relief.[61]

K. Time limits

I. Prescription

Regarding time limits, the EU legislator gave space to the discretionality of Member States' legislators. Implementing Art. 11, para. 2 DCD, Art. 135-*quaterdecies*, para. 2-3 Consumer Code provides that, where a contract provides for a single act of supply or a series of individual acts of supply, the trader is only liable for defects of conformity that become apparent within two years from the time of delivery, subject to Article 135-*undecies* para. 1, lett. b Consumer code.[62] Furthermore, the right to action directed to enforce a lack of conformity existent at the moment of the supply and not deliberately hidden by the trader expires, in any case, 26 months from that moment, if the lack of conformity becomes apparent by that time limit (Art. 135-*quaterdecies*, para. 4 Consumer Code).[63] Implementing Art. 11 para. 3 DCD, Art. 135-*quaterdecies* para. 5 Consumer Code states that if the contract provides that for continuous delivery over a period of time, the trader shall be liable for a lack of conformity if the defect manifests itself or becomes apparent during the period of time during which the digital content or the digital service is to be provided in accordance with the contract. An action for defects which become apparent in the course of the delivery and are not maliciously concealed by the trader shall in any event expire within twenty-six months from the last act of supply (Art. 135-*quaterdecies*, para. 6 Consumer Code). It seems reasonable that in case the defects have been maliciously concealed by the trader, the prescription does not run.[64]

Implementing Art. 10 SGD, Art. 133 para. 1 Consumer Code provides that the seller shall be liable to the consumer for any lack of conformity which exists at the time of the delivery (according to Art. 61 Consumer Code[65]) of the goods and which becomes ap-

66

67

---

the contractual guarantee shall be written in plain and intelligible language. It shall include the following elements: (a) a clear statement that the consumer has by law free of charge, remedies for lack of conformity against the seller and that such remedies are not affected by the conventional warranty; (b) the name and address of the guarantor; (c) the procedure to be followed by the consumer to enforce the contractual warranty; (d) the designation of the goods to which the contractual warranty applies; (e) the terms of the contractual guarantee".

[61] See Angelo Luminoso, 'La vendita', in Roppo and Anelli (eds), Trattato di Diritto civile e commerciale Cicu-Messineo, 2nd ed. (Giuffrè, Milano, 2022) 659.

[62] Art. 135-*undecies*, para. 1 Consumer Code: "The trader is obliged to keep the consumer informed of available updates, including security updates, which are necessary in order to maintain the conformity of the digital content or the digital service, and to provide them to the consumer during the period of time (a) during which the digital content or digital service is to be provided in accordance with the contract, where the contract provides for continuous supply over a specified period of time; or (b) which the consumer can reasonably expect, given the type and purpose of the digital content or digital service and taking into account the circumstances and the nature of the contract, if the contract provides for a single act of supply or a series of individual acts of supply."

[63] On Art. 11 DCD see e.g. Fryderyk Zoll, 'Article 11. Liability of the trader', in Schulze and Staudenmayer (eds) (above fn. 24) 199 ff.

[64] See Angelo Luminoso, 'La vendita', in Roppo and Anelli (eds), Trattato di Diritto civile e commerciale Cicu-Messineo, 2nd ed. (Giuffrè, Milano, 2022) 654 f.

[65] Art. 61, para 1 and 2 Consumer Code: "1. Unless otherwise agreed upon by the parties to the contract of sale, the trader is obliged to deliver the goods to the consumer without undue delay and at the latest

parent within two years from that time. Notwithstanding the provisions of Art. 130 para. 2 Consumer Code,[66] this also applies to goods with digital elements. In the case of goods with digital elements, when the contract of sale contract provides for the continuous supply of the digital content or of the digital content or service for a period of time, the seller is also liable for any lack of conformity of the digital content or digital service that occurs or becomes apparent within two years from the time of delivery of the goods with digital elements. If the contract provides for continuous supply for more than two years, the seller shall be liable for any lack of conformity of the digital content or digital service that occurs or becomes apparent during the period of time during which the digital content or digital service is to be provided under the sale contract (Art. 133 para. 2 Consumer Code). An action for defects which have not been fraudulently concealed by the seller shall in any event be time-barred within twenty-six months after delivery of the goods; the consumer, who is sued for the performance of the contract, may however always assert the rights under Art. 135-*bis* Consumer Code (repair, replacement, termination and price reduction) (Art. 133 para. 3 Consumer Code).[67]

68 The abovementioned time limits apply only to the remedies of repair, replacement, termination and price reduction.

69 As it was already the case in the implementation of Directive 1999/44/EC, also in the implementation of the SGD the Italian legislator did not regulate the duration of the warranty to which the buyer is entitled for defects from which the goods repaired or replaced by the seller are affected.[68]

70 The Twin Directives did not regulate the conditions under which the liability period or a limitation period can be suspended or interrupted. Member States were, therefore, be able to provide for the suspension or interruption of the liability period or limitation period, for example in the event of repair, replacement or negotiations between the seller and the consumer with a view to an amicable settlement.[69] The Italian legislator did not take position in this regard.

---

within thirty days from the date of the conclusion of the contract. 2. The obligation to deliver is fulfilled by the transfer of the physical possession or control of the goods to the consumer".

[66] Art. 130, para. 2 Consumer Code: "In the case of goods with digital elements, the seller is obliged to keep the consumer informed of the updates available, including security updates, necessary to maintain the conformity of those goods, and to provide him with such updates in the period of time: (a) that the consumer can reasonably expect, given the type and purpose of the goods and digital elements, and taking into account the circumstances and the nature of the contract, if the contract of sale provides for a single act of supply of the digital content digital content or digital service; or (b) referred to in Article 133(2) or (3), as the case may be where the contract of sale provides for a continuing supply of the digital content or digital service over a period of time".

[67] With regard to the implementing provisions of Directive EC 1999/44, see, in favour of the interruption of prescription through an out-of-court injunction: Corte di Cassazione, Sezioni Unite, 11 July 2019, no. 18672 (2019) Foro italiano 2019, I, 3116 ff. In this regard cf. e.g. Stefano Pagliantini, 'Tra equivoci dogmatici e miraggi: l'interruzione della prescrizione edilizia secondo cass. 18672/2019' (2020) Nuova giurisprudenza civile commentata II, 146 ff.

[68] For a critic in this regard see Angelo Luminoso, Angelo Luminoso, 'La nuova disciplina delle garanzie nella vendita al consumatore (una prima lettura del d.lgs. n. 170/2021)' (2022) Europa e Diritto privato 506. See also Fabrizio Piraino, 'La violazione della vendita di beni al consumatore per difetto di conformità: i presupposti della c.d. responsabilità del venditore e la distribuzione degli oneri probatori', in De Cristofaro (ed), *La nuova disciplina delle vendite mobiliari nel codice del consumo* (Giappichelli, Torino, 2022), 168.

[69] Recital 44 SGD.

II. Notification

The Italian legislator did not use the option (Art 12 SGD) to maintain the notification obligation contained in Art. 132 para. 2 Consumer Code, which stipulated that, in order to benefit from the consumer's rights, the consumer had to inform the seller of a lack of conformity within a period of at least two months of the date on which the consumer detected such lack of conformity.[70] Such solution was heavily debated during the legislative process. In particular, business associations pledged for maintaining it. In my opinion the current solution has to be welcomed as it provides a higher level of protection for consumers.[71]

L. Right of Redress

Art. 20, para. 1 DCD provides that where the trader is liable to the consumer because of any failure to supply the digital content or digital service, or because of a lack of conformity resulting from an act or omission by a person in previous links of the chain of transactions, the trader shall be entitled to pursue remedies against the person or persons liable in the chain of commercial transactions. Such provision is merely reproduced in Art. 135-*quindecies*, para 1 Consumer Code. As regards the implementation of Art. 20 para. 2 DCD – according to which the person against whom the trader may pursue remedies, and the relevant actions and conditions of exercise, shall be determined by national law – Art. 135-*quindecies* para. 2 Consumer Code provides that the trader who executed the remedies enforced by the consumer may pursue remedies, within one year from the execution of the performance, against the person or the persons who are responsible and ask for reintegration to what he performed to the consumer.[72] The aforementioned rule does impose neither a notification obligation on the seller within a certain time limit nor any procedural requirements for the person or the persons who are responsible to be sued. The same solutions were chosen by the Italian legislator when implementing Art. 18 SGD into Art. 135-*quindecies* Consumer Code.

M. Mandatory nature

According to Art. 22 para. 1 DCD, Art. 135-*vicies bis* para. 1 Consumer Code provides that except as otherwise provided in the DCD implementing rules, any agreement, prior to the communication to the trader of the lack of conformity, or the consumer's information by the trader about the modification of the digital content or the digital service, intended to exclude or limit to the detriment of the consumer, even indirectly, the rights granted by the DCD implementing provisions shall be void. In this regard, the leg-

---

[70] See e.g. Alberto De Franceschi, 'I rimedi del consumatore nelle vendite di beni di consumo', in Roppo (ed) *Trattato dei contratti* (Giuffrè, Milano, 2014) 257 f.

[71] In favour of this solution see: with regard to the SGD Alberto De Franceschi, La vendita di beni con elementi digitali (ESI, Napoli, 2019) 123 ff.; concerning the implementing provisions see Angelo Luminoso, 'La nuova disciplina delle garanzie nella vendita al consumatore (una prima lettura del d.lgs. n. 170/2021)' (2022) Europa e Diritto privato 501. In favour of maintaining the obligation to notify: Fabrizio Piraino, above fn. 68, 162 ff.; Mirko Faccioli, 'La violazione della vendita di beni al consumatore per difetto di conformità', in De Cristofaro (ed), *La nuova disciplina delle vendite mobiliari nel codice del consumo* (Giappichelli, Torino, 2022), 413.

[72] See e.g. Gabriele Salvi, 'Il regresso del venditore finale e la disciplina delle vendite b-to-b', in De Cristofaro (ed), *La nuova disciplina delle vendite mobiliari nel codice del consumo* (Giappichelli, Torino, 2022), 445 ff.

islator explicitly provided that the voidness can be enforced only by the consumer and can be detected *ex officio*, thereby following the same solution provided by Art. 36 para. 3 Consumer Code for unfair terms in consumer contracts.[73]

74 The same solution was chosen when implementing the SGD. According to Art. 21 para. 1 SGD, Art. 135-*sexies* para. 1 Consumer Code provides that save as otherwise explicitly provided in the SGD implementing provisions, any agreement, prior to the communication to the seller of the lack of conformity, intended to exclude or limit even indirectly to the detriment of the consumer, the rights conferred by the same SGD implementing provisions, shall be void.[74] Furthermore, the Italian legislator explicitly provided that the voidness can be enforced only by the consumer and can be detected *ex officio*, thereby following the same solution provided by Art. 36 para. 3 Consumer Code with regard to unfair contract terms.[75]

Therefore, the prohibitions contained in Art. 135-*vicies bis* para. 1 and Art. 135-*sexies* para. 1 Consumer Code do not include domestic law remedies available to the consumer under Art. 135-*septies* para. 1 Consumer Code, and in particular the right to compensation for damages.

75 As regards the burden of proof (Art. 11 SGD), the Italian legislator did not make use of the option granted by Art. 11 para. 2 SGD – according to which instead of the one-year period laid down in Art. 11 para. 1 SGD Member States may maintain or introduce a period of two years from the time when the goods were delivered – and kept the one-year period in Art. 135 Consumer Code. The same choice was made in Art. 135-*sexiesdecies* Consumer Code, implementing Art. 12 DCD.

N. Concluding Remarks

76 The Italian "general private law" remains still untouched by the digitalization, as the legislator missed indeed again the opportunity to provide a "modernization" of the law of obligations, by integrating the provisions transposing the consumer contract law into the Civil Code. This perpetuates a fundamental criticism: the Italian Civil Code, which in 2022 turned 80 years old, remains – at least literally – impermeable to the developments of European Private Law.

77 This leaves to scholars and judges the delicate task clarify of the relationship between the general law of obligations and contracts and the implementing provisions of the Twin Directives. In the same vein, the Italian legislator did not provide an explicit coordination of the new rules with those on intellectual property law and data protection law.

78 Both in way of implementation of DCD and the SGD, the Italian legislator has – following what allowed by Recitals 18 DCD and 23 SGD – explicitly enlarged the notion of "trader" and "seller", by including in them also "the supplier of platforms that is acting for purposes relating to that person's activity and as a contractual counterparty of the

---

[73] See on Art. 36 para. 3 Consumer Code e.g. Aurelio Gentili, 'La "nullità di protezione' (2011) Europa e diritto privato 79 ff.; Giovanni D'Amico, 'Nullità virtuale-nullità di protezione, variazioni sulla nullità' (2008) Contratti 732 ff.; Vincenzo Scalisi, 'Contratto e regolamento nel piano d'azione delle nullità di protezione' (2005) Rivista di Diritto civile, I, 459 ff.

[74] See e.g. Arturo Maniaci, 'Grado di imperatività della disciplina italiana della vendita di beni di consumo, alla luce del nuovo art. 135 *sexies* cod. cons.', in De Cristofaro (ed), *La nuova disciplina delle vendite mobiliari nel codice del consumo* (Giappichelli, Torino, 2022), 469 ff.

[75] See e.g. Aurelio Gentili (above fn. 88) 79 ff.; Giovanni D'Amico (above fn. 88) 732 ff.

consumer for the supply of digital content or digital services".[76] The Italian legislator adopted exactly the same formulation in the implementation of both Directives (see, respectively, Art. 128 para. 2 lett. c and Art. 135-*octies* para. 2 lett. e Consumer Code), even if it is clear that the implementing provision of the SGD would have required the explicit mention not only of traders who supply of digital content or digital services, but also of those who act for purposes relating to their own business and as the direct contractual partners of the consumer for the sale of goods. The abovementioned omission can be integrated by way of interpretation.

Furthermore, while implementing DCD and SGD, the Italian legislator did not adopt any rules for enhancing environmental sustainability. In particular, it did not take the chance to prioritize repair over replacement in order to enhance environmental sustainability (see e.g. recital 48 SGD).[77] Planned and premature obsolescence increasingly impacts everyday life, undermining the performances of physical goods and smart devices, from mobile phones to personal computers, connected cars and smart homes. Addressing the legal implications of such phenomenon has thus become a necessity.[78] Current sanctions and the approach of the EU legislator on this point so far show a lack of effectiveness, leaving open some fundamental questions, which need to be timely addressed.

Bibliography

Fabio Addis, 'Spunti esegetici sugli aspetti dei contratti di vendita di beni regolati nella nuova direttiva (UE) 2019/771' (2020) Nuovo diritto civile, 5 ff.

Giorgio Afferni, 'La nozione di "difetto di conformità": il problema del vizio giuridico e dell'*aliud pro alio*', in De Cristofaro (ed), *La nuova disciplina delle vendite mobiliari nel codice del consumo* (Giappichelli, Torino, 2022), 121 ff.

Guido Alpa, 'Aspetti della nuova disciplina delle vendite nell'Unione europea' (2019) Contratto e impresa/Europa 825 f.

Andrea Barenghi, 'Osservazioni sulla nuova disciplina delle garanzie nella vendita di beni di consumo' (2020) Contratto e impresa 806 ff.

Francesca Bertelli, '«Dichiarazioni pubbliche fatte dal o per conto del venditore», conformità oggettiva ed economia circolare', in De Cristofaro (ed), *La nuova disciplina delle vendite mobiliari nel codice del consumo* (Giappichelli, Torino, 2022) 219 ff.

---

[76] See e.g. Christoph Busch, Gerhard Dannemann, Hans Schulte-Nölke, Aneta Wiewiórowska-Domagalska and Fryderyk Zoll, 'The ELI Model Rules on Online Platforms' (2020) Journal of European Consumer and Market Law 61 ff.; Alberto De Franceschi, '*Uber Spain* and the "Identity Crisis" of Online Platforms' (2018) Journal of European Consumer and Market Law 1 ff. See *in primis* CJEU Case C-434/15, *Asociación Profesional Elite Taxi v Uber Systems Spain SL*, ECLI:EU:C:2017:981; for similar conclusions, see previously Consiglio di Stato (Italian Supreme Administrative Court), 23 December 2015, Section I, no. 3586/2015 <https://giustizia-amministrativa.it> accessed 15 December 2022; Alberto De Franceschi, La vendita di beni con elementi digitali (ESI, Napoli, 2019) 67 ff.

[77] See Hans-Wolfgang Micklitz, Victor Mehnert, Louisa Specht-Riemenschneider, Christa Liedtke and Peter Kenning, 'The Right to Repair' (2022) available at <https://www.svr-verbraucherfragen.de/wp-content/uploads/2022_SVRV_PB_Rigtht_to_Repair.pdf> accessed 15 December 2022.

[78] See e.g. Christian Hess, 'Geplante Obsoleszenz' (Nomos, Baden-Baden, 2018) 29 ff.; cf. Tobias Brönnecke and Andrea Wechsler (eds), 'Obsoleszenz Interdisziplinär' (Nomos, Baden-Baden, 2015); Alberto De Franceschi, 'Planned obsolescence challenging the effectiveness of consumer law and the achievement of a sustainable economy' (2018) Journal of European Consumer and Market Law 217 ff. Cf. Elias Van Gool and Anaïs Michel, 'The New Consumer Sales Directive 2019/771 and Sustainable Consumption: a Critical Analysis' (2021) Journal of European Consumer and Market Law 89 ff.

Tobias Brönnecke and Andrea Wechsler (eds), 'Obsoleszenz Interdisziplinär' (Nomos, Baden-Baden, 2015).

Christoph Busch, Gerhard Dannemann, Hans Schulte-Nölke, Aneta Wiewiórowska-Domagalska and Fryderyk Zoll, 'The ELI Model Rules on Online Platforms' (2020) Journal of European Consumer and Market Law 61 ff.

Carmelita Camardi, 'Prime osservazioni sulla direttiva (UE) 2019/770 sui contratti per la fornitura di contenuti e servizi digitali. Operazioni di consumo e circolazione di dati personali' (2019) Giustizia civile 499 f.

Stefano Cherti, 'Le garanzie commerciali', in De Cristofaro (ed), *La nuova disciplina delle vendite mobiliari nel codice del consumo* (Giappichelli, Torino, 2022), 417 ff.

Carlo Castronovo, 'Diritto privato generale e diritti secondi. La ripresa di un tema' (2008) Europa e Diritto privato 397 ff.

Giorgio Cian, 'Il nuovo capo XIV bis sulla disciplina dei contratti coi consumatori' (1996) Studium Iuris 425 ff.

Tommaso Dalla Massara, 'Art. 135 c. cons.: per una sistematica dei rimedi in tema di vendita di beni di consumo' (2007) Rivista di Diritto civile II, 123 ff.

Tommaso dalla Massara, 'Art. 135 *septies* cod. cons.: il coordinamento tra codice del consumo e codice civile in tempi di armonizzazione massima', in De Cristofaro (ed), *La nuova disciplina delle vendite mobiliari nel codice del consumo* (Giappichelli, Torino, 2022) 485 ff.

Luciana D'Acunto, 'L'ambito di applicazione degli artt. 128-135 *septies* cod. cons.: le fattispecie contrattuali', in De Cristofaro (ed), *La nuova disciplina delle vendite mobiliari nel codice del consumo* (Giappichelli, Torino, 2022) 51 ff.

Giovanni D'Amico, 'Nullità virtuale-nullità di protezione, variazioni sulla nullità' (2008) Contratti 732 ff.

Giovanni De Cristofaro (ed), 'La nuova disciplina della vendita mobiliare nel codice del consumo' (Giappichelli, Torino, 2022).

Giovanni De Cristofaro, 'Diritto dei consumatori e rapporti contrattuali di condominio: la soluzione della Corte di Giustizia UE' (2020) La nuova giurisprudenza civile commentata, I, 842 ff.

Alberto De Franceschi, 'I rimedi del consumatore nelle vendite di beni di consumo', in Roppo (ed) *Trattato dei contratti* (Giuffrè 2014) 257 f.

Alberto De Franceschi, 'Italian Consumer Law after the Transposition of Directives (EU) 2019/770 and 2019/771' (2022) Journal of European Consumer and Market Law 72 ff.

Alberto De Franceschi, 'La circolazione dei dati personali tra privacy e contratto' (ESI, Napoli, 2017).

Alberto De Franceschi, 'La sostituzione del bene non conforme al contratto di vendita' (2009) Rivista di Diritto civile II, 559 ff.

Alberto De Franceschi, La vendita di beni con elementi digitali (ESI, Napoli, 2019).

Alberto De Franceschi, 'La vendita di beni di consumo: difetti di conformità e responsabilità del professionista', in Roppo (ed), *Trattato dei contratti*, V (Giuffrè, Milano, 2014), 209 ff.

Alberto De Franceschi, 'Planned obsolescence challenging the effectiveness of consumer law and the achievement of a sustainable economy' (2018) Journal of European Consumer and Market Law 217 ff.

Alberto De Franceschi, '*Uber Spain* and the "Identity Crisis" of Online Platforms' (2018) Journal of European Consumer and Market Law 1 ff.

Mateja Durovic, 'European Law on Unfair Commercial Practices and Contract Law' (Hart, Oxford, 2016).

Bibliography

Mirko Faccioli, 'La nuova disciplina europea della vendita di beni ai consumatori (dir. (UE) 2019/771): prospettive di attuazione delle disposizioni sui termini' (2020) Le nuove leggi civili commentate 250 ff.

Mirko Faccioli, 'La violazione della vendita di beni al consumatore per difetto di conformità', in De Cristofaro (ed), *La nuova disciplina delle vendite mobiliari nel codice del consumo* (Giappichelli, Torino, 2022), 383 ff.

Edoardo Ferrante, 'La Direttiva 19/771/UE in materia di vendita al consumo: primi appunti' in D'Angelo and Roppo (eds), *Annuario del contratto 2018* (Giappichelli, Torino, 2020) 23 f.

Aurelio Gentili, 'La "nullità di protezione"' (2011) Europa e diritto privato 79 ff.

Matilde Girolami, 'La conformità del bene al contratto di vendita: criteri "soggettivi" e criteri "oggettivi", in De Cristofaro (ed), *La nuova disciplina delle vendite mobiliari nel codice del consumo* (Giappichelli, Torino, 2022), 65 ff.

Beate Gsell, 'Article 14. Remedies for lack of conformity', in Reiner Schulze and Dirk Staudenmayer (eds) EU Digital Law (Beck – Hart – Nomos, München – Oxford – Baden-Baden, 2020) 241 ff.

Christian Hess, 'Geplante Obsoleszenz' (Nomos 2018) 29 ff.; cf. Tobias Brönnecke and Andrea Wechsler (eds), 'Obsoleszenz Interdisziplinär' (Nomos, Baden-Baden, 2015).

Claudia Irti, 'Consenso «negoziato» e circolazione dei dati personali' (Giappichelli, Torino, 2021).

Bert Keirsbilck, Evelyne Terryn, Anaïs Michel and Ivano Alogna, 'Sustainable Consumption and Consumer Protection Legislation', available at <https://www.europarl.europa.eu/RegData/etudes/IDAN/2020/648769/IPOL_IDA(2020)648769_EN.pdf> accessed 15 December 2022.

Sebastian Lohsse, Reiner Schulze and Dirk Staudenmayer (eds), 'Data as Counter-Performance – Contract Law 2.0?' (Hart – Nomos, Oxford – Baden-Baden, 2020).

Angelo Luminoso, 'La nuova disciplina delle garanzie nella vendita al consumatore (una prima lettura del d.lgs. n. 170/2021)' (2022) Europa e Diritto privato 483 ff.

Angelo Luminoso, 'La vendita', in Roppo and Anelli (eds), Trattato di Diritto civile e commerciale Cicu-Messineo, 2nd ed. (Giuffrè, Milano, 2022) 578 ff.

Hans-Wolfgang Micklitz, Victor Mehnert, Louisa Specht-Riemenschneider, Christa Liedtke and Peter Kenning, 'The Right to Repair' (2022) available at <https://www.svr-verbraucherfragen.de/wp-content/uploads/2022_SVRV_PB_Rigtht_to_Repair.pdf> accessed 15 December 2022.

Andreas Mundt, 'Verbraucherschutz braucht eine stärkere behördliche Komponente' (2018) Wettbewerb in Recht und Praxis, Issue 9, Editorial.

Francesco Oliviero, 'La nuova disciplina dei c.d. rimedi «secondari»: riduzione del prezzo e risoluzione del contratto', in De Cristofaro (ed), *La nuova disciplina delle vendite mobiliari nel codice del consumo* (Giappichelli, Torino, 2022), 340 ff.

Liliia Oprysk and Karin Sein, 'Limitations in End-User Licensing Agreements: Is There A Lack of Conformity Under the New Digital Content Directive?' (2020) 51 IIC 594-623.

Stefano Pagliantini, 'A partire dalla dir. 2019/771 (UE): riflessioni sul concetto di armonizzazione massima' (2020) Nuovo diritto civile 11 f.

Stefano Pagliantini, 'Tra equivoci dogmatici e miraggi: l'interruzione della prescrizione edilizia secondo cass. 18672/2019' (2020) Nuova giurisprudenza civile commentata II, 146 ff.

Fabrizio Piraino, 'La violazione della vendita di beni al consumatore per difetto di conformità: i presupposti della c.d. responsabilità del venditore e la distribuzione degli oneri probatori", in De Cristofaro (ed), *La nuova disciplina delle vendite mobiliari nel codice del consumo* (Giappichelli, Torino, 2022) 162 ff.

Rupprecht Podszun, Christoph Busch and Frauke Henning-Bodewig, 'Behördliche Durchsetzung des Verbraucherrechts?' (2018) available at <https://www.bmwi.de/Redaktion/DE/Publikationen/Studien/behoerdliche-durchsetzung-des-verbraucherrechts.pdf?__blob=publicationFile&v=10> accessed 15 December 2022.

Giorgio Resta and Vincenzo Zeno-Zencovich, 'Volontà e consenso nella fruizione dei servizi in rete' (2018) Rivista trimestrale di diritto e procedura civile 411 ff.

Vincenzo Ricciuto, 'La patrimonializzazione dei dati personali. Contratto e mercato nella ricostruzione del fenomeno' (2018) Il diritto dell'informazione e dell'informatica 689 ff.

Vincenzo Roppo, 'Il contratto asimmetrico tra parte generale, contratti di impresa e disciplina della concorrenza' (2008) Europa e Diritto privato, I, 529 ff.

Vincenzo Roppo (ed), *Il contratto del duemila* (Giappichelli 2020).

Gabriele Salvi, 'Il regresso del venditore finale e la disciplina delle vendite b-to-b', in De Cristofaro (ed), *La nuova disciplina delle vendite mobiliari nel codice del consumo* (Giappichelli, Torino, 2022), 445 ff.

Chiara Sartoris, 'La risoluzione della vendita di beni di consumo nella dir. n. 771/2019 UE' (2020) La nuova giurisprudenza civile e commentata, II, 720 ff.

Vincenzo Scalisi, 'Contratto e regolamento nel piano d'azione delle nullità di protezione' (2005) Rivista di Diritto civile, I, 459 ff.

Roberto Senigaglia, 'Riflessioni sullo stato giuridico degli animali di affezione e sue ricadute in materia di vendita e responsabilità civile' (2021) Il diritto di famiglia e delle persone 1772 ff.

Pietro Sirena, 'Art. 135 Codice del consumo' in Cesare Massimo Bianca (ed), *La vendita di beni di consumo. Commentario* (CEDAM, Padova, 2016) 390 ff.

Gerald Spindler, 'Digital Content Directive and Copyright-related Aspects' (2021) 2 JIPITEC 111, 118 ff.

Dirk Staudenmayer, 'Article 3. Scope', in Reiner Schulze and Dirk Staudenmayer (eds), *EU Digital Law* (Beck – Hart – Nomos, München – Oxford – Baden-Baden, 2020) 84 ff.

Elias Van Gool and Anaïs Michel, 'The New Consumer Sales Directive 2019/771 and Sustainable Consumption: a Critical Analysis' (2021) Journal of European Consumer and Market Law 89 ff.

Arie Van Hoe and Guillaume Croisant (eds), Droit et durabilité - Recht en duurzaamheid (Larcier, Bruxelles, 2022).

Giuseppe Versaci, 'La contrattualizzazione dei dati personali dei consumatori' (ESI, Napoli, 2020).

Giuseppe Vettori, 'Il diritto dei contratti fra Costituzione, codice civile e codici di settore' (2008) Rivista trimestrale di Diritto e procedura civile 751 ff.

Matthias Wendland, 'Sonderprivatrecht für digitale Güter' (2019) Zeitschrift für die vergleichende Rechtswissenschaft 191 ff.

Stefan Wrbka, 'Warranty Law in Cases of Planned Obsolescence' (2017) Journal of European Consumer and Market Law 67 ff.

Fryderyk Zoll, 'Article 11. Liability of the trader', in Reiner Schulze and Dirk Staudenmayer (eds) EU Digital Law (Beck – Hart – Nomos, München – Oxford – Baden-Baden, 2020) 199 ff.

Andrea Zoppini, 'Sul rapporto di specialità tra norme appartenenti ai "Codici di Settore" (Lo *ius variandi* nei codici del consumo e delle comunicazioni elettroniche)' (2016) Rivista di Diritto civile, I, 136 ff.

Latvia

A. Introduction and General Framework 1
B. Definitions and Scope of Application 8
C. Conformity of Goods, Digital Content and Digital Services 15
D. Liability of the seller or service provider 20
E. Remedies for the Failure to Supply and Remedies for the Lack of Conformity 24
F. Commercial Guarantees 42
G. Time Limits 45
H. Right of Redress 51
I. Relationship with Other Remedies 53
J. Conclusions 56
   Bibliography 57

A. Introduction and General Framework

In order to explain the transposition of the Sale of Goods Directive[1] and Digital Content Directive[2] in Latvia, the general structure of Latvian system of civil law (private law) shall be described first. According to Latvian legal tradition, civil law of the country is split into two parts: general civil law and special civil law. The provisions of general civil law apply to everyone and are codified in the Civil Law (*Civillikums*, hereinafter also: CL). This basic legal act of Latvian civil law was adopted on 28 January 1937 and restored 1991–1993, shortly after the country regained its independence after almost fifty years of Soviet occupation. Since then, the Civil Law has been substantially modernized, although the structure remained the same. The law consists of an Introduction and four books: Family Law, Inheritance Law, Property Law and Law of Obligations. As far as contracts are concerned, Law of Obligations part plays the most important role. The law of Obligations of the Civil Law contains general provisions on obligations as well as provisions on specific contracts including the contract of sale. 1

Special rules of civil law apply in cases, where a so-called "special subject" is involved, e.g. consumer, merchant, employee. In general, special norms of civil law are usually included in separate specific laws that supplement and modify the regulation of the Civil Law. The Consumer Rights Protection Law[3] (*Patērētāju tiesību aizsardzības likums*, hereinafter also: PTAL) of 18 March 1999 is one of those numerous laws. According to Art. 2 PTAL the aim of this law is to ensure the opportunities for consumers to fulfill and defend their lawful rights, as well as defending their collective interests. It has to be remarked, that in one instance the rights of a consumer are regulated in the Civil Law despite the general character of the provisions of this law. Namely, the statutory interest rate in contractual relationships in which the consumer is a participant amounts to six per cent from a hundred in a year (Art. 1765 para. 2 CL). 2

A consumer according to the recently adopted version of Art. 1 Item 3 PTAL is a natural person who expresses an intent to acquire, acquires or could acquire goods, service, digital content or digital service for a purpose not connected with his or her business or professional trade. The PTAL is a comprehensive consumer protection act that mainly 3

---

[1] Directive (EU) 2019/771, OJ 2019, L 136/28 (Sale of Goods Directive, SGD).
[2] Directive (EU) 2019/770, OJ 2019, L 136/1 (Digital Content Directive, DCD).
[3] Patērētāju tiesību aizsardzības likums, Latvijas Vēstnesis, Nr. 104/105, 01.04.1999.

includes rules on contracts between a consumer and a seller, a service provider or a manufacturer. Moreover, the PTAL includes regulations on the state consumer protection entity (*Patērētāju tiesību aizsardzības centrs*, the Centre of Protection of Consumers' Rights) and a number of procedural provisions on protection of consumer's rights.

4   Latvia transposed the DCD and the SGD into the Consumer Rights Protection Law. The Latvian Parliament (*Saeima*) did so by adopting amendments to the PTAL on 17 February 2022.[4] The amendments came into force on 15 March 2022. Thus, the Latvian lawmakers failed to meet the deadline of transposition (1 July 2021) and the deadline of the application the necessary measures (1 January 2022).

5   According to the Transitional Provisions of the PTAL, the new provisions of the law shall apply to the supply of digital content or digital services which occurs from 15 March 2022, with the exception of Art. 16[5] and Art. 33 PTAL that shall apply only to contracts concluded from that date. The new Art. 16[5] PTAL (modification of the digital content or digital service) introduces the requirements of the Art. 19 SGD. The pre-existing Art. 33 of the PTAL (the liability of a manufacturer, seller or service provider) was accordingly amended in order to transpose the rules of Art. 20 of the SGD (right of redress). As far as the period from 1 January to 15 March 2022 is concerned, the pre-existing norms of the PTAL should be interpreted, as far as possible, in line with both Directives.[5] The necessity of interpretation of Latvian consumer law in line with EU consumer law directives was stressed by the Supreme Court (Senate) of Latvia already before the incorporation of the DCD and SGD into national law of the country.[6]

6   The transposition of the DCD and SGD has not changed the structure of Latvian laws. Only the Consumer Rights Protection Law was directly affected. As stated in the annotation to the Draft Amendments to the PTAL, prepared by the Ministry of Economics, the transposition was aimed at 1) defining consumer's rights in case of a lack of conformity of digital content or digital service acquired or supplied, thus contributing to a higher level of consumer protection in the digital field, and 2) clarifying and strengthening the provisions on protection of consumers' rights when non-conforming goods have been purchased.[7] The transposition of both Directives required the most elaborate and extensive amendments to the PTAL in years.

7   The impact of the Directives (notably the DCD) on existing Latvian intellectual property law (copyright law) and data protection law has been so far discussed in Latvia only in general terms. The Latvian legislator has not specifically regulated the relationship of the Directive-based rules with the intellectual property law. It has been noted in Latvia that goods with digital elements may contain objects of copyright protection and under the existing copyright regulations the purchaser of these goods would be entitled to resell them without a consent of the author.[8] As to the data protection, there had been a suggestion already in 2021 to amend Latvian national law with a clear rule that would

---

[4] Grozījumi Patērētāju tiesību aizsardzības likumā, Latvijas Vēstnesis, Nr. 43, 02.03.2022, available at: https://www.vestnesis.lv/op/2022/43.3.

[5] Vadims Mantrovs (ed), Digitālais pirkuma objekts: Patērētāju tiesību aizsardzības likumā ietvertais regulējums saistībā ar 2019. gada patērētāja pirkuma direktīvu ieviešanu, Rīga, 2022, p. 15.

[6] See: Judgment of the Civil Department of the Supreme Court (Senate) of the Republic of Latvia from 15 December 2020 (Nr. SKC-693/2020), available at: https://www.at.gov.lv/lv/tiesu-prakse/judikaturas-nolemumu-arhivs/civillietu-departaments/hronologiska-seciba?year=2020.

[7] The Report (Annotation) on Assessment of the Preliminary Impact of the Draft Law „Amendments to the Consumer Rights Protection Law", p. 1, available at: https://titania.saeima.lv/LIVS13/SaeimaLIVS13.nsf/0/946D649B5CF1D56CC22587680040405B?OpenDocument.

[8] Kristaps Silionovs, Autortiesības Direktīvas 770/2019 gaismā, Jurista Vārds, 23.11.2021, Nr. 47, p. 35.

give data protection law a priority over consumer protection rules.[9] Such a priority rule, if enacted, could enable the consumers to invoke their rights stipulated in the DCD in case their data is illegally processed by a trader.[10] The priority of data protection law is now stipulated in Art. 2¹ para. 6 PTAL: provisions of the PTACL apply to personal data in consumer contracts for supply of digital content or digital services except as otherwise provided in the special norms on personal data processing (i.e. the General Data Protection Regulation (GDPR)[11] and the Latvian Law on Personal Data Processing[12]).

B. Definitions and Scope of Application

Art. 1 PTAL includes an extensive list with definitions of legal notions used in this law. Goods generally means any item offered or sold to a consumer, including water, gas and electricity where they are put up for sale in a limited volume or a set quantity (see Art 1 item 6 PTAL). The renewed list of Art 1 PTAL includes, inter alia, the concepts mentioned in Art. 2 DCD and Art. 2 SGD: digital content, digital service, goods with digital elements (defined in the PTAL as a subtype of goods), integration, digital environment, compatibility, functionality, interoperability and durable medium. Most of these concepts are new in Latvian law. Some of them, however, have been known in Latvia before. For example, the notion of digital content was implemented in the PTAL in 2014.[13] The Latvian legislator included this concept into law in order to transpose the EU Directive 2011/83 on consumer rights.[14] According to Art. 1 item 8 PTAL, digital content means data which are produced and supplied in digital form. This short definition has been retained in the current version of the Consumer Rights Protection Law. 8

It should be mentioned that there is slight difference between the term "trader" used in the DCD and the corresponding Latvian terminology of the PTAL. The notion of a trader (in Latvian: *tirgotājs*) is used also in Latvian version of the DCD. The PTAL since its adoption in 1999 uses the notions of "a seller or service provider" (in Latvian: *pārdevējs vai pakalpojuma sniedzējs*). According to Art. 1 item 5 PTAL, the seller is a natural or legal person (also an importer) who within the scope of his or her economic or professional activity offers or sells goods to consumers, in his or her own name or by means of using intermediaries acting in the name or at instruction of the seller. As defined in Art. 1 item 4 PTAL, the service provider is a natural or legal person who within the scope of his or her economic or professional activity provides a service to a consumer. 9

In Latvia, the transposition of the DCD has had certain impact on the concept of a price (in Latvian: *cena* or *maksa*) in local private law. There is no definition of the notion of a price in the PTAL or in any other Latvian legislative act. Generally, price means a market price of goods measured in terms of money. According to Art. 2012 CL, a purchase price (in a contract of sale) shall be expressed in money. Until the transposition of the DCD a common understanding in Latvia was that the price in consumer contracts should be always measured in money including the cases where a trader accepted second 10

---

[9] Irēna Ņesterova, Zanda Dāvida, Patērētāju personas dati kā pamattiesības, nevis tirgojama prece: ES digitālā satura regulējuma izaicinājumi, Jurista Vārds, 23.11.2021, Nr. 47, p. 15.
[10] Ibid.
[11] Regulation (EU) 2016/679, OJ 2016, L 119/1.
[12] Fizisko personu datu apstrādes likums. Latvijas Vēstnesis, 04.07.2018, Nr. 132, available at: https://likumi.lv/ta/id/300099-fizisko-personu-datu-apstrades-likums.
[13] Grozījumi Patērētāju tiesību aizsardzības likumā, Latvijas Vēstnesis, 14.05.2014, Nr. 92, available at: https://www.vestnesis.lv/op/2014/92.6.
[14] Directive (EU) 2011/83, OJ 2011, L 304.

hand goods as a partial equivalent of the price.[15] Now, Art. 2¹ para. 4 PTAL stipulates that the PTAL shall also apply where the seller or service provider supplies or undertakes to supply digital content or a digital service to the consumer, and the consumer provides or undertakes to provide personal data to the seller or service provider, except where the personal data provided by the consumer are exclusively processed by the seller or service provider for the purpose of supplying the digital content or digital service in accordance with this law or for allowing the seller or service provider to comply with legal requirements to which the seller or service provider is subject, and the seller or service provider does not process those data for any other purpose.

11 According to one Latvian legal publication, the aforementioned Art. 2¹ para. 4 PTAL means that purchase price for digital content or digital service can be expressed in form of personal data.[16] Such conclusion is not entirely true because personal data is no commodity and neither the DCD nor the PTAL call providing personal data a price. As follows from Recital 24 DCD, providing personal data is not the same as paying a price. From the point of view of Latvian law, providing personal data to a trader could be characterised as a counter-performance in form of remuneration (in Latvian: *atlīdzība*), but not as a payment of price.

12 From the point of view of general theory of contract, the figures of contracts for the supply of digital content or digital services and for the supply of goods with digital elements, fit quite well into the existing system of Latvian contract law. The general rules on legal transactions including the provision on formation, existence and validity of contracts are found in the law of obligations part of the Civil Law. The law of obligations part of the CL also contains provisions on the main types of contracts. Among them are the contract of sale, the contract of supply (in fact a subtype of the contract of sale) and the contracts for services. As mentioned above, other legislative acts of Latvian private law, for example, the Consumer Protection Law, the Commercial Law, the Labour Law rarely create fully independent types of contracts. The function of the legal norms contained in these special laws is to modify and supplement the regulation of the Civil Law as far as necessary for the needs of the specific sub-branch of Latvian civil (private) law. According to Art. 2¹ para 2 PTAL, the provisions of this law, unless otherwise provided, do not impact contractual relationships, especially validity, conclusion and legal consequences of a contract. Therefore, contracts for the supply of digital content or digital services and for the supply of goods with digital elements, depending of the subject-matter of the respective contract, can be considered either contracts of sale or contracts for services, albeit heavily modified by provisions of consumer law and therefore largely independent.

13 The Latvian legislator made a limited use of the opportunity provided in Rec. 16 DCD and Rec. 21 SGD, extending the application of the rules of the DCD and the SGD to contracts with certain non-consumers. As a general principle, the norms of the PTAL apply to B2C (business-to-consumer) contracts. However, there is a modification according to Art. 4.¹ para. 1 PTAL: the provisions of the Chapters III and IV of the PTAL shall apply not only to legal relations between a seller or service provider and consumer, but also to legal relations between a seller or service provider and any other legal subject that expresses an intent to acquire, acquires or could acquire goods, service, digital content or digital services for a purpose not connected with its business or professional trade.

---

[15] Vadims Mantrovs (ed), Digitālais pirkuma objekts: Patērētāju tiesību aizsardzības likumā ietvertais regulējums saistībā ar 2019. gada patērētāja pirkuma direktīvu ieviešanu, Rīga, 2022, p. 42.
[16] Ibid., p. 43.

It should be noted that the initial version of Art. 4¹ was added to the PTAL in 2005, when transposition of the provisions of diverse EU consumer law directives took place in Latvia.[17] The notions of digital content and digital service were added to Art. 4.¹ para. 1 PTAL in the course of transposition of the DCD and SGD. Chapter III of the PTAL regulates conformity of goods and services whereas Chapter IV includes provisions on information about goods, services, digital content and digital services. The notion "any other legal subject that expresses an intent to acquire, acquires or could acquire goods, service, digital content or digital services for a purpose not connected with its business or professional trade" relates, in theory, to any legal entity recognized by Latvian law except commercial companies. The Commercial Law of Latvia (*Komerclikums* or KCL)[18] includes an extended regulation of commercial transactions, namely transactions entered into by merchants. Commercial companies do not have any "private life". Thus, any contract entered by a commercial company will be a commercial transaction and as such connected with the business of the respective company. Contrary to commercial companies, individual merchants (i.e. natural persons registered with the commercial register) can act as consumers outside their business activities. Thus, Art. 4.¹ para. 1 and the provisions of the PTAL can be applied to non-commercial entities, e.g. associations or foundations (endowments) under the Law on Associations and Foundations (*Biedrību un nodibinājumu likums*[19]).

14

C. Conformity of Goods, Digital Content and Digital Services

In the PTAL, the conformity requirements of digital content and digital services have been separated from the general regulation on conformity of goods and services. The requirements of the SGB concerning conformity of goods have been introduced to the existing Chapter III on "Conformity of goods and services with contractual terms". Article 14 PTAL that already regulated conformity of goods was amended accordingly. The rules on conformity of digital content and digital services are now to be found in an entirely new Chapter III¹ on "Conformity of digital goods and digital services with contractual terms". In transposing the subjective and objective requirements for conformity of the DCD and SGD, the Latvian legislator has closely followed the wording of the respective Directives. For example, the provisions regarding the durability requirement for goods (Art. 7 para. 1 letter d SDG) or the exclusion of existence of a lack of conformity (Art. 8 para. 5 DCD, Art. 7 para 5 SGD) are transposed almost precisely word-by-word.

15

In Latvia, there has been not any co-ordination of implementing provisions of the SGD with those of Directive 2009/125/EC establishing a framework for the setting of ecodesign requirements for energy-related products[20]. Nor has the country in the course of transposition of DCD and SGD adopted any specific measures for enhancing environmental sustainability and circular economy. There is only a brief mention in the annotation to the Draft Amendments of the PTAL that ensuring durability of goods is necessary for achieving sustainable consumption patterns and circular economy.[21] The

16

---

[17] Grozījumi Patērētāju tiesību aizsardzības likumā, Latvijas Vēstnesis, 11.11.2005, Nr. 181, available at: https://likumi.lv/ta/id/121231-grozijumi-pateretaju-tiesibu-aizsardzibas-likuma.

[18] Komerclikums, Latvijas Vēstnesis, 04.05.2000, Nr. 158/160.

[19] Biedrību un nodibinājumu likums, Latvijas Vēstnesis, 17.10.2002, Nr. 150.

[20] Directive 2009/125/EC of the European Parliament and of the Council of 21 October 2009 establishing a framework for the setting of ecodesign requirements for energy-related products, OJ 2009 L 285/10.

[21] The Report on Assessment of the Preliminary Impact of the Draft Law 'Amendments to the Consumer Rights Protection Law', p. 6, available at: https://titania.saeima.lv/LIVS13/SaeimaLIVS13.nsf/0/946D649B5CF1D56CC22587680040405B?OpenDocument.

impact of the concept of sustainable consumption on consumer law has yet to be discussed by Latvian legal scholars. It is worth mentioning, however, that on 4 September 2020 the Cabinet of Ministers (the Government) of Latvia adopted the Action Plan on Transition to Circular Economy in 2020–2027.[22] This Action Plan declares the intended policies of the Latvian government and does not contain any specific references to desirable changes in the Consumer Rights Protection Law or other laws. The Action Plan is a mid-term policy planning document that includes, amongst others, a sub-chapter on promoting a sustainable consumption and another sub-chapter on policy actions concerning sustainable products.

17 An incorrect installation (Art. 9 DCD, Art. 16[4] PTAL) causes seller's or service provider's liability only if it results in a lack of conformity of the digital content or digital service. It has been stressed in a legal publication that incorrect installation as a notion of consumer law is closely connected with the general preconditions for civil liability in Latvian law.[23] This means that there must be causality between an incorrect installation and a lack of conformity. In order to ascertain whether this is the case, the *condition sine qua non* test should apply.[24]

18 Latvia has not extended the rules of the PTAL on modification of digital content or digital service to goods with digital elements. As mentioned above, conformity of digital content and digital services is regulated separately from the provisions of conformity of goods and services. As stressed in the Annotation to the Draft Amendments of the PTAL, digital content and digital services are independent objects of this law and the conformity requirements for them are therefore separated from the conformity requirements for goods.[25]

19 The significance of Art. 10 DCD for the rights of a consumer to submit claims against the seller or service provider has been noted in Latvian legal literature already before the transposition of the DCD and SGD.[26] However, the requirements of Art. 10 DCD and Art. 9 SGD have not been specifically implemented in the PTAL. It is not known why the Latvian legislator omitted the transposition of these provisions of both Directives. It means that a lack of conformity has to be ascertained according to the general criteria, when the use of goods, digital content or digital services is hindered or limited by restriction arising from infringement of the rights of third parties, in particular intellectual property rights. In any case, the respective general provisions of the PTAL should be interpreted in line with Art 10 DCD and Art. 9 SGD to ensure that the consumer is entitled to the remedies for the lack of conformity.

D. Liability of the seller or service provider

20 In regulating liability of the seller or service provider, the Latvian legislator has not made any difference between single act and long-term supply of digital content and digi-

---

[22] Ministru kabineta rīkojums Nr. 489 'Par rīcības plānu pārejai uz aprites ekonomiku 2020.–2027. gadam', Latvijas Vēstnesis, 09.09.2020, Nr. 174, available at: https://likumi.lv/ta/id/317168-par-ricibas-planu-parejai-uz-aprites-ekonomiku-20202027-gadam.

[23] Vadims Mantrovs (ed), Digitālais pirkuma objekts: Patērētāju tiesību aizsardzības likumā ietvertais regulējums saistībā ar 2019. gada patērētāja pirkuma direktīvu ieviešanu, Rīga, 2022, p. 60.

[24] Ibid.

[25] The Report on Assessment of the Preliminary Impact of the Draft Law „Amendments to the Consumer Rights Protection Law", p. 5, available at: https://titania.saeima.lv/LIVS13/SaeimaLIVS13.nsf/0/946D649B5CF1D56CC22587680040405B?OpenDocument.

[26] See: Kristaps Silionovs, Autortiesības Direktīvas 770/2019 gaismā, Jurista Vārds, 23.11.2021, Nr. 47, p. 31.

D. Liability of the seller or service provider

tal services. There is no specific regulation for the interruption of long-term supply of digital content or digital services. According to Art. 27 para. 1 PTAL, in case of non-conformity, a consumer is entitled to submit his or her claims against the seller or service provider within a time period of two years since the day when digital content or digital service was delivered. This provision also applies to goods and non-digital services.

As stated in Recital 14 DCD, Member States shall remain free to regulate the consequences of a failure to supply, or of a lack of conformity of digital content or digital service, where such failure to supply or lack of conformity is due to an impediment beyond the control of the trader and where the trader could not be expected to have avoided or overcome the impediment or its consequences, such as in the event of force majeure. The legal consequences of force majeure are an issue of general civil law. In Art. 1773 of the Civil Law (CL) force majeure is named as a cause for accidental loss. According to Art. 1774 CL accidental loss is not required to be compensated by anyone. Thus, force majeure would release from liability a seller of digital content or a provider of digital service. According to the jurisprudence of the Supreme Court (Senate) of Latvia, there are four preconditions for force majeure: 1) the circumstances were not known to the parties at the time of conclusion of the contract, 2) performance is altogether impossible, and not only for one party, 3) the circumstances are not a fault of the debtor and 4) the circumstances are unavoidable or they could not be prevented despite all efforts of the debtor.[27]

The Civil Law of Latvia does not provide for rules on change of circumstances. Draft amendments to the Civil Law in order to regulate change of circumstances were prepared by the Ministry of Justice in 2007 but were not adopted by the Parliament (*Saeima*).[28] The legislator feared that a regulation of change of circumstances would create an opportunity for dishonest debtors to withdraw from contracts. Interestingly, a change of circumstances regulation was introduced few years later in the Art. 478 of the Commercial Law of Latvia as one of the possibilities of modifying or cancelling a franchise contract. As noted in Latvian legal literature, the concept of change in circumstances, at least to certain extent, can be derived from the principle of good faith defined in Art. 1 CL. In case of change of circumstances, the principle of good faith may justify an adjustment of a contract, but definitely not a termination of it.[29]

Regarding contracts for the supply of digital content or digital services, there are no specific rules about the consequences of seller's or service provider's non-compliance with personal data processing provisions. In case the data protection rules are breached by a seller or service provider, the consumer may resort to the general regulation of personal data processing and invoke the remedies of the GDPR, notably the right to compensation and liability according to Art. 82 GDPR.

---

[27] Judgment of the Civil Department of the Supreme Court (Senate) of the Republic of Latvia from 26 January 2011 (Nr. SKC-11/2011), available at: https://www.at.gov.lv/lv/judikaturas-nolemumu-arhivs-old/senata-civillietu-departaments/hronologiska-seciba_1/2011.

[28] Grozījumi Civillikumā, likumprojekts, available at: https://www.saeima.lv/Likumdosana/9S_DK/lasadd=LP0528_0-1.htm.

[29] Kaspars Balodis, Apstākļu izmaiņu ietekme uz līguma saistošo spēku un labas ticības princips (Impact of Change in Circumstances on Binding Force of Contract and Principle of Good Faith), in: Tiesības un tiesiskā vide mainīgos apstākļos, Latvijas Universitātes 79. starptautiskās zinātniskās konferences rakstu krājums. Rīga, 2021, p. 133, available at: https://www.apgads.lu.lv/fileadmin/user_upload/lu_portal/apgads/PDF/Juridiskas-konferences/JUZK-79-2021/juzk.79.13_Balodis.pdf.

E. Remedies for the Failure to Supply and Remedies for the Lack of Conformity

24 To regulate consumer's remedies in case of a failure to supply the digital content or digital service, the Latvian legislator has transposed the provisions of Art. 13 DCD word-by word. Art. 30² para. 1 PTAL says: where the seller or service provider has failed to supply the digital content or digital service in accordance with this law, the consumer shall call upon the seller or service provider to supply the digital content or digital service; if the seller or service provider then fails to supply the digital content or digital service without undue delay, or within an additional period of time, as expressly agreed to by the parties, the consumer shall be entitled to terminate the contract. Art. 30² para 2 PTAL, by repeating the wording of Art. 13 para. 2 DCD, regulates preconditions for consumer's right to immediately terminate the contract. In case of a lack of conformity of digital content or digital service a consumer can claim: 1) bringing the digital content or digital service into conformity; 2) receiving a proportionate reduction in the price; 3) termination of the contract and restitution of price paid for the digital content or digital service (Art. 29¹ para. 1 PTAL, Art. 14 para 1 DCD).

25 It should be noted that the Latvian wording of the PTAL on execution of the right to terminate the contract is somewhat inaccurate. Art. 30³ para. 1 PTAL literally says that "the consumer is entitled to request termination of the contract by stating this to the seller or service provider". In Latvian civil law there are quite many provisions where a unilateral withdrawal from a contract is possible only by claiming the termination of the contract in the court. For example, when rules of the Civil Law apply to delivery of defective goods, the buyer can unilaterally withdraw from the contract only by claiming the termination in the court (see Art. 1620 CL). However, this is definitely not the case with the aforementioned provision of the PTAL. Art. 30³ para. 1 PTAL has to be correctly interpreted in line with Article 15 DCD, so that the consumer could exercise his or her right to terminate a contract by means of a mere statement to the seller or service provider.

26 In Latvia, the execution of the right of withdrawal by unilateral declaration is an exemption from general civil law rules, although widely known. Outside consumer law, a number of legal provisions allow termination of a contract in such manner. Under the Civil Law any party of a lease or a rental contract regarding immovable property, entered into for an indefinite period of time, can terminate the contract, unless otherwise agreed, after six months prior notice to the counterpart (Art. 2166 CL). Usually though, a right to cancel the contract unilaterally merely by notice is reserved for the "weaker" contractual party. E.g. an employee under the Labour Law[30] of Latvia or a tenant under the Law of Residential Tenancy[31] are entitled to termination of the respective contract by unilateral notice.

27 The remedies provided in the PTAL for the failure to supply goods and for the lack of conformity of goods have largely remained the same as before the transposition of the SGD. In the event of a lack of conformity, the consumer who has purchased goods or received them for the purposes of use is entitled to have them brought into conformity, to have them replaced by conforming goods or to receive a proportionate reduction in the price, or to terminate the contract and request the reimbursement of the purchase price (Art. 28 para. 1 PTAL). According to Art. 28 para. 2 PTAL the consumer is entitled, in first instance, to request bringing the goods into conformity or replacing them with

---

[30] Darba likums, Latvijas Vēstnesis, 06.07.2001, Nr. 105.
[31] Dzīvojamo telpu īres likums, Latvijas Vēstnesis, 06.04.2021, Nr. 65A.

E. Remedies for the Failure to Supply and Remedies for the Lack of Conformity

conforming goods free of charge, unless the remedy chosen would be impossible or disproportionate.

Consumer's right to withhold payment (Art. 13 para. 6 SGD) has been introduced to Art. 28 para. 12 PTAL. If the consumer chooses to withhold payment, he or she shall notify the seller or service provider in writing and without undue delay. The Latvian legislator has not granted to a consumer similar right with regard to digital content or digital services. **28**

It should be noted that the Civil Law contains the so-called objection to non-performance of a bilateral contract. According to Art. 1591 CL, if an action is brought concerning the performance of a bilateral contract, the plaintiff shall either promise appropriate performance, or prove that he or she has already performed the contract on his or her part; otherwise an objection may be raised against him or her for not performing the contract, unless it arises from the nature of the contractual relationship that the defendant shall perform first. **29**

A contract for supply of digital content or digital services is a bilateral (reciprocal) contract. It would be correct to say that a consumer could rise an objection to non-performance by withholding a payment only in case the seller or service provider failed to supply digital content or digital service. In case of non-conformity, the consumer would be entitled to the above-mentioned remedies under Art. 29^1 para. 1 PTAL. As follows from the wording of Art. 1591 CL, this provision does not apply in case a party shall perform first, for example, a consumer shall pay before receiving digital content or digital service. Therefore, it is quite unlikely for a consumer who bought digital content or digital service to withhold payment by invoking Art. 1591 CL. **30**

Latvia has not adopted specific rules in order to define the place of delivery of goods. The Latvian legislator introduced few rules about the costs of bringing the goods for repair or replacement. According to Art. 28 para. 9 PTAL, the seller or service provider has to take non-conforming goods for correction of non-conformity (i.e. repair) or replacement on his or her own expense. If the seller or service provider refuses to take the goods, the consumer is entitled to bring the goods himself (herself) or with an assistance of a third person on seller's or service provider's expense. **31**

If the goods are brought in by the consumer, the seller or service provider has to reimburse the consumer within three days after the latter presented a cost supporting document (Art. 28 para. 10 PTAL). If dismantling of already installed goods is required for taking them for repair or replacement, the seller bears the costs of dismantling and reinstalling of the goods in accordance with Art. 28 para 11 PTAL. Thus, the aforementioned provisions of Art. 28 PTAL require the seller or service provider to take the goods from the consumer but they do not explicitly regulate the place of repair and replacement. **32**

Regarding the restitution where the seller or service provider supplies digital content or digital services, the Latvian legislator has almost word-by-word transposed the respective provisions of Art. 14, 16, 17 and 18 DCD. As mentioned above, one of consumer's remedies in case of non-conforming digital content or digital services is to terminate the contract and request a reimbursement of the price paid (Art. 29^1 para 1 item 3 PTAL). After the termination of contract, the consumer on his on her part shall: 1) refrain from using the digital content or digital service and from making it available to third parties, and 2) where the digital content was supplied on a tangible medium, at the request and the expense of the seller or service provider, return the tangible medium to the seller or service provider without undue delay (Art. $30,^3$ para. 2, 3 PTAL). **33**

According to Art. 30^3 para. 5 PTAL, in the event of termination of a contract for the supply of digital content or digital services, the seller or service provider shall reimburse **34** the consumer for all sums paid under the contract. In cases where the contract provides for the supply of the digital content or digital service in exchange for a payment of price and the digital content or digital service had been in conformity for a period of time prior to the termination of the contract, the seller or service provider shall reimburses the consumer only the proportionate part of the price paid corresponding to the period of time during which the digital content or digital service was not in conformity, and the sum paid by the consumer in advance for any period of the contract that would have remained had the contract not been terminated. As stated in Art. 30^3 para. 9 PTAL, in case of price reduction or termination of the contract, the seller or service provider shall reimburse the consumer without undue delay but not later than 14 days from the day when the consumer informed the seller or service provider about the decision to invoke his or her right to reduce price or to terminate the contract. The seller or service provider shall carry out the reimbursement using the same means of payment as the consumer used to pay for the digital content or digital service, unless the consumer expressly agrees otherwise, and provided that the consumer does not incur any fees as a result of such means of reimbursement (Art. 30^3 para. 10 PTAL). Moreover, the seller or service provider in not entitled to impose any fee on the consumer in respect of the reimbursement (Art. 30^3 para. 11 PTAL).

35 It should be remarked that the aforementioned reimbursement rules of the DCD introduced to the PTAL are one of the few special restitution mechanisms governing the consequences of termination of a contract in Latvian private law. In comparison, the law of obligations of the Civil Law of Latvia lacks general reimbursement and return rules that would specifically apply in case of termination of a contract. In case of terminated non-consumer contracts, the claims arising from unjust enrichment (Art. 2369–2392 CL) are usually invoked for the purposes of restitution, unless a specific regulation with regard certain types of contracts can be found in the law. The restitution rules of the PTAL, however, are typical consumer law provisions aimed at protecting and benefiting the consumer. Therefore, the restitution rules of Latvian consumer law cannot be a universal model for possible improvements to the law of obligations provisions of the Civil Law.

36 Latvia has not introduced any specific rules regarding the contractual consequences of withdrawal of consent for personal data with regard to contract for the supply of digital content or digital services. Nor has the Latvian legislator explicitly prioritized repair of goods over their replacement in order to enhance environmental sustainability. The respective provisions of the law, i.e. Art. 28 PTAL, mention "correction of non-conformity of goods" and "replacement of goods" as equal alternatives. There also has not been a doctrinal debate on this issue. In consumer law literature no difference is made between repair and replacement.[32] It must be noted, however, that according to Art. 28 para. 2 PTAL repair applies instead of replacement if the latter is impossible or disproportionate.

37 To some extent, the goal of sustainability is facilitated, at least indirectly, by the provisions of Art. 28 para. 6 PTAL. The consumer shall not be entitled to terminate the contract and ask for a reimbursement of the price, if the lack of conformity is only minor and cannot substantially influence the use of the goods by consumer. The lack of conformity is considered minor, if it does not significantly decrease the quality of performance of basic functions of the goods or characteristics of the use and can be removed without creating visual changes in appearance of the goods. These provisions on the consequences of a minor lack of conformity existed in the PTAL already before the transposi-

---

[32] See: Baiba Vītoliņa, Patērētāju tiesību aizsardzības pamati, Rīga, 2015, p. 73.

tion of the SDG. In the course of transposition, a sentence was added to Art. 28 para. 6 PTAL, according to which the burden of proof with regard to whether the lack of conformity is minor shall be on the seller.

The Latvian legislator has not adopted or even considered any specific measures for fighting premature planned obsolescence of goods. The Law on Prohibition of Unfair Commercial Practice[33] (*Negodīgas komercprakses aizlieguma likums*, hereinafter: NKAL) was amended in 2015 for the last time and is not specifically aimed at dealing with the issue. However, in certain circumstances selling prematurely obsolescent goods could be considered a misleading commercial practice under the NKAL. Under Art. 10 NKAL misleading omission can amount to unfair (misleading) commercial practice. A commercial practice is misleading, for example, in cases where a business hides substantial information that an average consumer needs, according to the context, to take an informed decision, and as a result a transactional decision is taken by the consumer which otherwise would not have been taken (Art. 10 para. 1 item 1 NKAL). Accordingly, a business applying misleading commercial practice can be sanctioned under the NKAL including imposing of a monetary fine or even suspending the business enterprise until the cessation of the violation (see Art. 15^2, 17 NKAL).

The Consumer Protection Law of Latvia does not provide for an automatic transfer of the rights against the initial seller from the initial consumer to a subsequent buyer. Under the PTAL, contracts can be concluded in which a consumer does not initially participate but acquires his or her rights as a third person. Namely, Art. 7 PTAL regulates contracts where a manufacturer or seller promises to deliver goods or a service provider promises to provide digital content or digital service to a consumer as a third person and where the consumer, by joining the contract, acquires a right to independently claim a performance of the contract (or compensation for loss in case of non-performance or delay) from the manufacturer, seller or service provider. Art. 7 PTAL existed already before, by the transposition of the DCD and SGD only the notions of the digital content and digital service were added to this provision.

Under the rules of the Civil Law governing the cession of claims it should be generally possible for a consumer to cede his or her claims against the seller to another consumer. According to Art. 1793 CL, claims may be transferred from a former creditor to a new one by cession that also can be executed by means of legal transaction. Art. 1798 CL says: all claims may be the subject-matter of a cession, irrespective of whether they arise from a contract, or from wrongful acts, including also such claims as to which their term has not come into effect, as well as conditional and even future and uncertain claims. However, according to Art. 1799 CL exempted from the provisions of Art 1798 CL are: 1) all claims the exercise whereof is associated with the person of the creditor, whether pursuant to an agreement of the contracting parties or pursuant to law; 2) claims the substance whereof would alter completely if they were performed for another person, rather than the actual creditor.

Thus, under Art. 1798 item 1 CL it would be possible for contractual parties to exclude the transferability of claims arising from a contract. The consumer law regulation on commercial guarantee (Art. 16 PTAL) does not explicitly foresee any restrictions for the initial seller to exclude the transferability of consumer's rights in his or her general terms and conditions. Therefore, the provisions of the PTAL on unfair terms in consumer contracts apply. If a restriction on ceding consumer's contractual rights appeared in seller's general terms and conditions, it could be under the specific circumstances of a case considered unfair and declared void by the court. Namely, contractual terms re-

---

[33] Negodīgas komercprakses aizlieguma likums, Latvijas Vēstnesis, 12.12.2007, Nr. 199.

stricting the rights of the consumer to enter contracts with third parties are contrary to the principle of legal equality of the parties and therefore shall be deemed unfair and void (Art. 5 para 2 item 2, Art. 6 para. 3 item 1 PTAL).

F. Commercial Guarantees

42 By transposing the SGD, the Latvian legislator replaced the previous rules of Art. 16 PTAL on a guarantee with more elaborate provisions on the commercial guarantee. Before the transposition of the SGD, a remark was made in Latvian consumer law literature that Art. 16 PTAL could remain unchanged because of its conformity with requirements of Art. 17 SGD.[34] However, the provisions of aforementioned article of the PTAL were substantially amended by the legislator to ensure full conformity with the requirements of the SGD.

43 According to the legal definition provided for in Art. 16 para. 1 PTAL, commercial guarantee is a promise made by the manufacturer, seller or service provider to the consumer to reimburse the price paid for the goods, to replace the goods with conforming goods, to correct non-conformity without asking for remuneration, to maintain functionality of goods by any means in case the goods do not conform with specifications, or to undertake other actions, if the goods do not conform with their description in advertisements or in the commercial guarantee at the moment of the conclusion of the contract or before the conclusion of contract.

44 The criteria for a commercial guarantee under Art. 16 para. 2 PTAL repeat those stated in Art. 17 SGD. By transposing the SGD, the legislator has not adopted any specific rules on the language in which the commercial guarantee statement has to be made available to the consumer. However, practically important rules concerning the language used in documentation of goods can be found in the language laws, notably the State Language Law (SLL).[35] If markings, manuals, guarantee documents or technical passports of imported goods are in foreign language, a translation into state language (Latvian) shall be added (Art. 21 para. 3 SLL). If goods are produced in Latvia, labels, markings, manuals, inscriptions on the produce, on the packaging and containers according Art. 21 para. 2 SSL shall be in state language. If foreign language is used besides the state language, the Latvian text shall fill dominant space and it cannot be smaller or narrower as the text in foreign language. These provisions do not apply to Latvian produced goods destined for export. Art. 21 para. 2 SSL, for unknown reasons, does not explicitly mention guarantee documents of goods produced in Latvia. It can be implied, however, that these must be made available in Latvian language.

G. Time Limits

45 As mentioned above (chapter IV), in case of a lack conformity, a consumer is entitled to file claims against the seller or service provider within a time period of two years since the day when goods, service, digital content or digital service were delivered or received

---

[34] Vadims Mantrovs. Jaunā patērētāja pirkuma direktīva (Direktīva 2017/771): izaicinājumi un iespējas Latvijas likumdevējam (New Consumer Sales Directive (Directive 2019/771): challenges and possibilities for Latvian legislator), in: Starptautisko un Eiropas Savienības tiesību piemērošana nacionālajās tiesās, Latvijas Universitātes 78. starptautiskās zinātniskās konferences rakstu krājums, Rīga, 2020, p. 325, available at: https://www.apgads.lu.lv/fileadmin/user_upload/lu_portal/apgads/PDF/Juridiskas-konferences/JUZK-78-2020/juzk.78-Book.pdf.

[35] Valsts valodas likums, Latvijas Vēstnesis, 21.12.1999, 428/433.

G. Time Limits

(Art. 27 para. 1 sentence 1 PTAL). According to Art. 27 para. 1 sentence 2 PTAL the claim shall be submitted to the seller or service provider within two months after the consumer detected non-conformity of goods or service with the terms of the contract. The latter provision applies only to goods, including goods with digital elements, and non-digital services. Thus, regarding the digital content or digital service the consumer can submit the claims arising for a lack of conformity in two years-time, but is not required to file them within two months after non-conformity was discovered.[36]

It should be noted that according to the previous version of Art 27 para. 1 sentence 1 PTAL introduced in 2001[37] the consumer could submit claims arising from a lack conformity within a time period of two years from the day of purchase of goods. As allowed by Art. 12 SGD, the Latvian legislator has maintained the regulation of Art. 27 para. 1 sentence 2 PTAL introduced in 2014[38] that a claim arising from a lack of conformity of goods or service has to be submitted within a period of two months on the date on which the lack of conformity was detected.

In order to clarify and amend the aforementioned provisions of Art. 27 PTAL concerning a single act of supply or a series of individual acts of supply of digital content or digital services (Art. 11 para. 2 DCD), the Latvian lawmakers introduced several special rules. According to Art. 16^1 para. 3 sentence 1 PTAL, if a contract for the supply of digital content or digital services foresees a single supply or a number of individual acts of supply, the seller or service provider is liable for non-conformity discovered within two years from the day of delivery of digital content or digital services. If the lack of conformity of digital content or digital service is discovered within a year from the day of delivery, the seller or service provider bears the burden of proof that the digital content or digital service was in conformity during the delivery period (Art. 16^1 para. 3 sentence 1 PTAL). If according to the contract the digital content or digital service shall be supplied over a certain period of time, the seller or service provider is liable for non-conformity discovered within this period of time (Art. 16^1 para. 4 sentence 1 PTAL). If the lack of conformity of digital content or digital service is discovered within this period of time, the seller or service provider bears the burden of proof that the digital content or digital service was in conformity during that period of time ((Art. 16^1 para. 2 sentence 1 PTAL).

According to the PTAL, time limits do not impact the term of a commercial guarantee. In case the manufacturer, seller or service provider gave a commercial guarantee for goods, the consumer is entitled to file claims according to the terms of the commercial guarantee, if the time limit of the commercial guarantee exceeds the aforementioned term of two years (Art. 27 para. 2 PTAL).

The Latvian legislator chose not to extend the two-year time limit, although it was possible under Art. 11 para. 2 DCD. According to the Annotation to the Draft Amendments to the PTAL, two years from the day of delivery is an adequate time limit that ensures balance between the interests of consumers and the possibilities available for merchants.[39] At the same time this Annotation which is prepared by the Latvian Ministry of Justice envisions a possible extension of the two year limit in future in line with the EU strategy of promoting product sustainability.[40]

---

[36] Vadims Mantrovs (Editor), Digitālais pirkuma objekts: Patērētāju tiesību aizsardzības likumā ietvertais regulējums saistībā ar 2019. gada patērētāja pirkuma direktīvu ieviešanu, Rīga, 2022, p. 56.

[37] Grozījumi Patērētāju tiesību aizsardzības likumā, Latvijas Vēstnesis, 12.12.2001, Nr. 180.

[38] Grozījumi Patērētāju tiesību aizsardzības likumā, Latvijas Vēstnesis, 14.05.2014, Nr. 92.

[39] The Report (Annotation) on Assessment of the Preliminary Impact of the Draft Law "Amendments to the Consumer Rights Protection Law", p. 5.

[40] Ibid., p. 6.

50   The time limits for consumer's claims in the PTAL are exhaustive. They cannot be prolonged by applying any general prescription terms of the Civil Law. According to Article 1895 CL all obligation rights which have not been expressly exempted from the impact of prescription and the use of which is not by law subject to shorter terms, shall terminate if the party entitled to them does not use them within a ten year time period. Ten years is the general prescription term in Latvian civil law. However, even the Civil Law foresees shorter prescription terms for some claims (see chapter IX of this report). As mentioned above, Latvian private law is precisely split between the general regulation of the Civil Law and special provisions included in the PTAL and other laws. The PTAL is aimed at maximum protection for a consumer. Therefore, the rules of general civil law do not foresee any additional time limits extending the enforcement of consumer's rights.

H. Right of Redress

51   As stipulated in Art. 20 DCD and Art. 18 SGD, the person against whom the trader or seller may pursue remedies, and the relevant actions and conditions of exercise, shall be determined by national law. The first provision regulating the right of redress as a remedy available to a seller or service provider was introduced to PTAL already in 1999, when the law was enacted by the Latvian legislator. The right of redress is regulated in Art. 33 PTAL under the broad and somewhat imprecise title "The liability of the manufacturer, seller or service provider". Redress provided for in Art. 33 PTAL is not explicitly coordinated with other remedies. Art. 33 para. 2 PTAL in the initial version of this law from the year 1999 said that the seller or service provider who had compensated the consumer for loss or reimbursed the price the latter paid for goods or service, had a redress claim against the person from whom the goods or materials were purchased. By transposition of the DCD the notions of digital content and digital service were added to the range of products (goods and services) already mentioned Art. 33 para 2 PTAL.

52   In case the lack of conformity of goods, service, digital content or digital service is caused by actions or an inaction of the manufacturer, seller, distributor or another person, the seller or service provider is entitled to file a redress claim against the respective persons (Art. 33 para. 4 PTAL). Thus, the provisions of PTAL allow the seller or service provider to pursue redress claims against a wide range of persons in the previous link of transactions. In addition, under Art. 33 para. 3 PTAL the manufacturer, seller or service provider is free to conclude an agreement with a third person to remove defects from goods, service, digital content or digital service. However, such an agreement does not release the manufacturer, seller or service provider from the direct liability towards the consumer.

I. Relationship with Other Remedies

53   Since consumer law in Latvia is understood as a special branch of civil (private) law and there is a clear line between the general regulation of the Civil Law and the special provisions of other law, the remedies available to a consumer under the implementing provisions of the DCD and SGD only indirectly relate to comparable remedies known in the law of obligations of the Civil Law of Latvia. In case of a lack of conformity of goods or in case of failure to supply, there are differences in buyer's remedies depending on whether or not the buyer is a consumer. Of course, there are similarities because a number of remedies available to a consumer have their roots in general law of obligations.

Interestingly, there is only one example in the PTAL where the consumer is explicitly redirected to remedies available under the Civil Law. If the consumer has appointed a carrier for delivery of goods and if the seller or service provider has not offered such option to the consumer, the risk of destruction or damage regarding the goods is transferred to the consumer at the moment, when the goods are handed over to the consumer; in this case the consumer can bring an action against the carrier under the Civil Law (Art. 30¹ para. 2 PTAL).

The best known contractual remedies of general civil law are included in a subchapter of law of obligations of the Civil Law under the title "Liability for defects and characteristics" (Art. 1612–1634 CL). These are remedies of the acquirer against the alienor in the so-called alienation contracts that most notably include the contract of sale, contract of supply and contract of barter. Under Art. 1620 para. 1 CL the alienor who has failed to disclose or concealed, in bad faith, certain defects of the item he or she was aware of, or has expressly declared that it has certain characteristics, shall compensate the acquirer for all losses. In all other cases, the acquirer shall only have the right to request pursuant to his or her own choice either the setting aside of the contract, or a reduction in the price of the item (Art. 1620 para. 2 CL). The right to bring an action to set aside the contract shall be extinguished through prescription six months from the day of entering into the contract, or from the day of any special guarantee (Art. 1633 CL). According to Art. 1634 CL the right to bring an action for price reduction shall lapse a year from the day of entering into the contract, or from the day of any special guarantee.

Such remedies as bringing goods into conformity by repairing them or replacement of goods are unknown to the Civil Law. Few years ago it was proposed in Latvian consumer law literature to take the awaited transposition of the SGD as an opportunity for unifying buyer's remedies by extending the respective PTAL rules to all buyers.[41] The author of the publication noted that contemporary private law makes no difference between a consumer or non-consumer when a contractual remedy is made available to a person.[42] It should be remarked, however, that such far-reaching modernization of the system of contractual remedies would have required substantial systemic amendments to the Civil Law. In general, the Latvian legislator is very cautious to change fundamental laws such as the Civil Law because these form the base of the legal system. The legislator obviously wanted to avoid complications in the transposition of the SGD and DCD and did not even consider a broader reform of contractual remedies.

J. Conclusions

The development of the contemporary consumer protection law in Latvia started in 1999 when the Parliament (*Saeima*) adopted a new Consumer Rights Protection Law (*Patērētāju tiesību aizsardzības likums*, PTAL). One of the reasons to introduce this law was the anticipation of Latvia's accession to the European Union. In more than twenty years, the PTAL was permanently amended keeping it in line with the EU consumer law directives. The PTAL is a law that includes special civil law provisions with the aim of protecting the interests of a special legal subject – the consumer. The „basic law" of

---

[41] Vadims Mantrovs. Jaunā patērētāja pirkuma direktīva (Direktīva 2017/771): izaicinājumi un iespējas Latvijas likumdevējam (New Consumer Sales Directive (Directive 2019/771): challenges and possibilities for Latvian legislator), in: Starptautisko un Eiropas Savienības tiesību piemērošana nacionālajās tiesās, Latvijas Universitātes 78. starptautiskās zinātniskās konferences rakstu krājums, Rīga, 2020, p. 324, available at: https://www.apgads.lu.lv/fileadmin/user_upload/lu_portal/apgads/PDF/Juridiskas-konferences/JUZK-78-2020/juzk.78-Book.pdf.

[42] Ibid.

Latvian civil (private) law is the Civil Law of Latvia that contains general rules applying to everybody. Therefore, the rules of the Civil Law apply also to the contractual relations of a consumer, as far as there are no special provisions that regulate a particular situation in which a consumer participates. The PTAL includes a detailed regulation of consumer's rights including remedies available to a consumer. Therefore, the impact of the rules of the Civil Law on the contractual relations between the seller or service provider, on one side, and a consumer, on the other side, is somewhat limited.

57   The Digital Content Directive and Sale of Goods Directive were transposed by the Saeima by amending the PTAL. The lawmakers abstained from making changes or amendments in any other laws. The respective amendments to the PTAL were adopted on 17 February 2022 and came into force on 15 March 2022, thus exceeding the deadline for adoption by seven and a half months and the deadline for application – by two and a half months. The Latvian legislator chose a minimalist approach by amending the pre-existing regulation of the PTAL as little as possible. Many of the requirements of the DCD and SGD were incorporated into PTAL word-by-word. The options offered and discretion left by the Directives to Member States were hardly used by the legislator. On the other hand, the transposition of the DCD and SGD amounted to the most extensive reform of the Latvian Consumer Rights Protection Law in years, substantially modernizing this law and significantly enhancing consumer rights as a result.

Bibliography

Kaspars Balodis, Apstākļu izmaiņu ietekme uz līguma saistošo spēku un labas ticības princips (Impact of Change in Circumstances on Binding Force of Contract and Principle of Good Faith), in: Tiesības un tiesiskā vide mainīgos apstākļos, Latvijas Universitātes 79. starptautiskās zinātniskās konferences rakstu krājums (Rīga 2021), available at: https://www.apgads.lu.lv/fileadmin/user_upload/lu_portal/apgads/PDF/Juridiskas-konferences/JUZK-79-2021/juzk.79.13_Balodis.pdf.

Vadims Mantrovs (ed), Digitālais pirkuma objekts: Patērētāju tiesību aizsardzības likumā ietvertais regulējums saistībā ar 2019. gada patērētāja pirkuma direktīvu ieviešanu (Rīga 2022), available at: https://www.apgads.lu.lv/fileadmin/user_upload/lu_portal/apgads/PDF/Monografijas/Digitalais_pirkuma_objekts-Mantrovs.pdf.

Vadims Mantrovs, Jaunā patērētāja pirkuma direktīva (Direktīva 2017/771): izaicinājumi un iespējas Latvijas likumdevējam (New Consumer Sales Directive (Directive 2019/771): challenges and possibilities for Latvian legislator), in: Starptautisko un Eiropas Savienības tiesību piemērošana nacionālajās tiesās, Latvijas Universitātes 78. starptautiskās zinātniskās konferences rakstu krājums (Rīga 2020) 325, available at: https://www.apgads.lu.lv/fileadmin/user_upload/lu_portal/apgads/PDF/Juridiskas-konferences/JUZK-78-2020/juzk.78.34-Mantrovs.pdf.

Irēna Ņesterova and Zanda Dāvida, Patērētāju personas dati kā pamattiesības, nevis tirgojama prece: ES digitālā satura regulējuma izaicinājumi, Jurista Vārds, 23.11.2021, Nr. 47.

Kristaps Silionovs, Autortiesības Direktīvas 770/2019 gaismā, Jurista Vārds, 23.11.2021, Nr. 47.

Baiba Vītoliņa, Patērētāju tiesību aizsardzības pamati' (Riga 2015).

Lithuania

A.	Introduction	1
B.	Definitions and scope of application	12
C.	Some legal requirements for the performance of contract	27
	I. Conformity	27
	II. Special issues	33
	1. 'Green' economy	33
	2. Personal data	37
	3. Copyright	38
D.	Liability of the Trader	39
E.	Remedies for the failure to supply and remedies for the lack of conformity	47
F.	Commercial Guarantees	60
G.	Time Limits	62
H.	Right of Redress	68
I.	Relationship with other remedies	71
J.	Conclusions	73
	Bibliography	77

A. Introduction

The focus on comprehensive consumer protection in Lithuania has been brought from the very beginning of Lithuanian independence in the early 1990's. Undisputable evidence of such ambitious attitude is the clause on consumer protection included directly in the Art. 46 of the Lithuanian Constitution of 1992, which declares that the State shall defend the interests of the consumer. For some time, this was mostly a constitutional declaration, as substantive and institutional system on consumer protection in Lithuania, during transition period from command economy to market economy, had only been in the stage of early development. 1

Gradually, consumer protection in Lithuania became a significantly more important policy of the State. Several years before the formal accession in 2004 to the European Union, some important European directives, such as The Unfair Terms in Consumer Contracts Directive 93/13/EEC, were already implemented into Lithuanian law. After accession, EU law started to shape Lithuanian law even more intensively, especially in the field of consumer law. 2

Although consumer law in Lithuanian legal doctrine is characterized as encompassing both private law and public law aspects, prevailing one is the aspect of private law. This is because the relations between traders and consumers are private legal relations in substance, whereas public law regulates only ancillary – procedural and institutional – aspects of consumer protection. 3

More precisely – consumer relations in Lithuania are called civil legal relations (lit. *civiliniai teisiniai santykiai*) to connote their belonging to the subject matter of *ius civile*. This clarification is used because civil law in Lithuania is a basic branch of private law, although not the only one as there are also other branches – labour law and private international law. Thus, to attribute legal relation simply to the realm of private law may be too abstract. 4

Within the internal structure of Lithuanian civil law, consumer relations belong to the subject matter of law of obligations, as most often consumer legal relations arise from the contract, but also may arise from the tort in case of defective production. 5

6   Civil legal nature of consumer contracts was so self-evident for Lithuanian society and legal community that drafters of Lithuanian Civil Code (hereinafter – LCC)[1] implemented consumer contract law directly into the draft LCC without any noticeable public opposition or fierce discussions. Into LCC were directly included the definition of consumer contract, rules on conflict of consumer contract laws, prohibition of unfair consumer contract terms, tort liability for defective production, peculiarities of nominate contracts in cases of consumer sales, lease, work (processing) and credit. As consumer relations are relations *in personam*, they were mostly included in Book 6 of LCC on law of obligations.

7   The same trend was maintained with Consumer Rights Directive, which for the first time in Lithuanian law has introduced concept of the digital content (transposed in 2013), as well as with conceptually similar DCD and SGD directives (transposed in 2021). All of them were transposed in Book 6 of LCC on law of obligations and now forms constitutive part of Lithuanian consumer contract law.

8   Another noticeable trend of implementation of EU directives into Lithuanian law is a technique of copy-paste from original source into national act, only with linguistic improvements of minor importance. Such overly cautious approach of national legislator is especially evident in cases of maximum harmonisation directives, such as SGD and DCD. Nevertheless, even in the light of maximum harmonisation there is a space for optimisation of transposed consumer law rules within the overall framework and concepts of national contract law. Moreover, such optimisation is necessary for a more coherent and efficient application of same transposed rules. However, legislative technique adopted for the transposition is far from satisfactory. To show it, I will present two examples here.

9   First of all, although DCD and SGD are both derived from the same legislative package, share common logic and equal functional level, they were transposed differently from the structural point of view. DCD was transposed in the separate (second) section in the chapter XVIII[1] titled "Consumer contracts for supply of digital content and digital services", i. e. in the general part of contract law. SGD, in contrast, was transposed in the section on consumer sales, i. e. in the special part of contract law dealing with nominate contracts. In my opinion, this is not only incongruent, but also a conceptually wrong choice, because contracts of supply of digital content by their nature are new type of *contractus nominatus*. Instead, rules on digital content from Consumer Rights Directive and DCD should have been aligned and codified in the special part of contract law next to rules on consumer sales of movables based on SGD. This would have brought more clarity and logic within the whole structure of LCC and better reflect the equivalence between two types of consumer contracts – supply of digital content and sales of tangible movables.

10   Secondly, rules from separate directives on digital consumer contracts in LCC were not systemised and as a result – chaotically dispersed even within the same chapter XVIII[1] in the general part of contract law. For instance, LCC Art. 6.228^{12} regulates the withdrawal from digital content contracts, i.e. the end of the contract, whereas after several articles in LCC Art. 6.228^{17} and further there is a definition of such contracts and scope of application for related rules. In other words, in the same chapter one may at first find rules on the end of the contract and only later the definition of that type of contract.

---

[1] LCC (*Official Gazette*, 2000, No 74–2262) was adopted in 18th of July 2000 and came in force year after – 1st of July 2001.

The impact of DCD and SGD in Lithuanian legal doctrine was mostly analysed within the context of contract law, consumer law and the ordinary property law.[2] Much less (if at all) attention was paid in Lithuanian legal scholarship to this topic from the perspective of intellectual property law and data protection law, because those branches of Lithuanian law had no immediate impact due to DCD and SGD implementation.

B. Definitions and scope of application

The notions contained in the DCD (see in particular Art. 2) and SGD (see in particular Art. 2), had a significant, although not dramatic, impact on the evolution of Lithuanian private law. From one side, the immediate conceptual effect of legislative package on national law was reduced because the concept of contracts for a digital content was already known to Lithuanian legal system since its introduction in 2013 after the transposition of Consumer Rights Directive. The same was with the concept of durable medium which has already been extensively used in financial market regulation, first and foremost in the Law on Financial Market Instruments[3] transposing MiFID II directive.[4]

From the other side, transposition of DCD and SGD has brought further elaboration and development of statutory rules on digital content together with some contract law innovations into Lithuanian legal system, i.e. rules on digital services, goods with digital elements, integration, updates, payment by personal data, digital environment, compatibility, functionality, interoperability, etc. DCD and SGD rules are far more developed and detailed than former LCC rules on consumer sales. For example, whereas former consumer contract law (LCC Art. 6.363) regulated only problems of installation, new rules have also touched upon issues of functionality, compatibility, interoperability and integration. The same is with most other newly introduced rules, namely on supply, conformity and remedies. Express calibration and division of conformity rules in two separate blocks (subjective conformity and objective conformity) is a legal innovation for both – EU law and national contract law. Another interesting example is a reversal of burden of proof against consumer who does not cooperate with the trader (DCD Art. 12). From the perspective of fairness, which is the cornerstone of a contract law, this rule looks very sound and welcome.

Doctrinal analysis in consumer contract law during the last decade mostly focused on formal aspects of implementation of the recent consumer law directives and place of consumer law in general, such as where to implement Consumer Rights Directive in national law[5] and what brings maximum harmonisation of the SGD.[6] Next to it, the substance of DCD rules was also explored, firstly, by analysing the notion of digital

---

[2] Bublienė, 'Vartotojų teisių direktyvos perkėlimas į Lietuvos teisę – tolesnis vartotojų apsaugos teisės dekodifikavimas ar kodifikavimas?' *Teisė: mokslo darbai* (2012) 83, 37–60; Selvestravičiūtė, 'Naujoji Europos Parlamento ir Tarybos direktyva (ES) 2019/771 dėl tam tikrų prekių pirkimo-pardavimo sutarčių aspektų – maksimalaus harmonizavimo pasirinkimas ir reikšmė'. *Teisė* (2021) 119, 118–130; Didžiulis, 'EU Digital Content Directive and Evolution of Lithuanian Contract Law', 12 *Journal of Intellectual Property, Information Technology and E-Commerce Law* (2021), 260–270.

[3] Law on Markets in Financial Instruments of the Republic of Lithuania (*Official Gazette*), 2007, No 17-627.

[4] Directive 2014/65/EU of the European Parliament and of the Council of 15 May 2014 on markets in financial instruments, OJ L 173, 12.6.2014, 349–496.

[5] Bublienė, 'Vartotojų teisių direktyvos perkėlimas į Lietuvos teisę – tolesnis vartotojų apsaugos teisės dekodifikavimas ar kodifikavimas?' *Teisė: mokslo darbai* (2012) 83, 37–60.

[6] Selvestravičiūtė, 'Naujoji Europos Parlamento ir Tarybos direktyva (ES) 2019/771 dėl tam tikrų prekių pirkimo-pardavimo sutarčių aspektų – maksimalaus harmonizavimo pasirinkimas ir reikšmė', *Teisė* (2021) 119, 118–130.

15   Legal characterisation of contracts regulated by SGD raises no major questions and obviously falls under the well-known category of consumer sales contract (LCC Art. 6.350), irrespective whether goods contain some digital elements or not. Such characterisation, relating to sale of goods with digital element, namely smart TVs, even before the implementation of SGD was affirmed by the Supreme Court of Lithuania.[8]

16   In contrast, the characterisation of contracts with digital content is a much more challenging and complex issue. For instance, it may be said that where consumer gets data files against payment of money, such transaction, from functional perspective, should point to sales contract. From the other side, according to LCC Art. 6.307, 6.383, 6.402, 6.428, eligible objects of sales contract may be only things (including various sorts of energy and even business enterprise), financial assets (foreign currency and securities) and patrimonial rights, including intellectual property rights. Since digital assets are not (at least expressly) listed in possible objects of sales contract, sale of digital content could not be characterised as sale. Of course, this narrow scope of sales contracts seems to be obsolete. However, there are still two ways to apply sales rules for supply of digital content: first, sales rules may be applicable by analogy (LCC Art. 1.8); second, where supply of digital content equals sale of copyright, as is in case of unlimited licence against payment covering the market price of computer programs which was characterised as a sale in *UsedSoft* case.[9] In instances where digital content is transferred against personal data as consideration, the contract should be characterised as a barter. However, barter rules here may be applicable only by the analogy as LCC Art. 6.432 restricts barter to corporeal things. Where digital content is developed in accordance with the consumer's specifications (situation mentioned in DCD Art. 3(2)), the contract should be characterised as a work contract (LCC Art. 6.644).

17   Streaming, storage of data, file hosting, data sharing, access to the online games or use of social media and all other forms of digital content supply and services, which do not involve permanent transfer of digital records to consumer, should fall in the scope of services contracts *lato sensu*. Most contracts in this respect will be contracts of remunerative services (services contract *stricto sensu*, LCC Art. 6.716) as well as work contracts where trader has assumed duty to create or repair digital content (LCC Art. 6.644). Rules on some other specific types of services, such as lease, loan for use, deposit may be applicable only by analogy because they are limited to tangible items (LCC Art. 6.477, 6.629, 6.830). In cases where digital content is facilitated for use against personal data as consideration, the contract cannot be even characterised as a service contract, because remunerative service contracts must be paid by money, not data. Once again, this does not preclude the application of rules regulating service contracts by analogy for express contracts for unregulated types of services.

18   Legal analysis above shows how complicated is the issue of characterisation of digital content contracts in national civil law. Although LCC is relatively a new code (adopted in 2000), its classical rules on nominate contracts currently are not adapted to accommodate new types of goods, for example, digital content. Oddly, an even usually more conservative and inflexible branch of law – property law – acknowledges wider spectrum of legal objects than special part of Lithuanian contract law dealing with nominate contracts. Application of existing rules on nominate contracts by analogy may

---

[7] Didžiulis, 'EU Digital Content Directive and Evolution of Lithuanian Contract Law', *12 Journal of Intellectual Property, Information Technology and E-Commerce Law* (2021), 260–270.
[8] Judgment of the Lithuanian Supreme Court of 10 June 2020 in the civil case No 3K-3-186-1075/2020.
[9] CJEU, Case C-128/11, 3 July 2012, *UsedSoft*, ECLI:EU:C:2012:407.

B. Definitions and scope of application

be a formal solution, however, not an efficient one, since supply of digital content is a multifaceted phenomenon which may attract various rules and create uncertain and volatile case law.

It should be added that difficulties described above are inevitable, where rules on digital content contracts are located in the general part of contract law, since such legislative technique says nothing about the characterisation of digital content contract and presupposes search for additional rules in special part of Lithuanian contract law, dealing with nominate contracts. This situation could probably be justified where just few rules on digital content contracts had existed (as formerly was with LCC Art. 6.228[12] and several other rules transposed from Consumer Rights Directive), but not anymore in case of more comprehensive regulation presented by DCD.

This leads us to the conclusion that contracts for supply of digital content deserve to be named *sui generis* by their nature and should be classified separately from other nominate contracts. Such solution would enable legal system to overcome full set of problems related to complex characterisation and cross-application of various rules regulating other types of contracts. Furthermore, this conclusion corresponds with the logic of Consumer Rights Directive, according to which contracts for digital content which is not supplied on a tangible medium should be classified, for the purpose of the Directive, neither as sales contracts, nor as service contracts (Recital 19). From the other side, it is hard to deny its conceptual similarity to the sales contract, due to the fact that in both cases valuable objects are exchanged for a price.[10] Therefore, in my opinion, DCD should have been transposed in Lithuanian law by introducing digital content contracts as new specific type of nominate contract in LCC chapter close to sales contracts, instead of awkwardly putting DCD rules in general part of contract law.

Obvious innovation in European contract law was the introduction of provision on data as a counter-performance in contracts for digital content. In fact, it was recognition of market reality and subsequent regulation has provided novel form of consideration within whole system of Lithuanian private law. Such innovation (so far) did neither receive any opposition from legal doctrine, nor provoked discussions about the need to change conceptual framework of payments within the Lithuanian contract law or reshape general rules on contract formation and validity. However, this discussion likely will take place as soon as more difficult and conceptual legal issues will reach courts.

Interestingly, Lithuanian drafters even attempted to further develop European rules on digital content, although this initiative was later withdrawn. More concretely, DCD does not regulate the consequences for the contracts where the consumer withdraws the consent for the processing of the consumer's personal data. Such consequences should remain a matter for national law (Recital 40 of the Directive). On this point Pre-draft on LCC Art. 6.228[18] had prescribed that if the consumer withdraws the consent, the trader is not entitled to payment for digital content (services) supplied until the moment of withdrawal. Such national rule, in my opinion, is sound and coherent with the DCD Art. 17 (3) according to which, the consumer shall not be liable to pay for any use made of the digital content or digital service in the period, prior to the termination of the contract, during which the digital content or the digital service was not in conformity. Therefore, if consumer still uses digital content (services) but no longer wants to remunerate trader with special consideration – personal data – he assumes duty to pay mon-

---

[10] This is also evidenced by sources of soft law – Draft Common Frame of Reference and CESL, where supply of digital content is regulated within or closely with the sales contract. See Von Bar et al. (eds), *Principles, Definitions and Model Rules of European Private Law. Draft Common Frame of Reference (DCFR)*. Full ed., Sellier (2009); Proposal for a Regulation on a Common European Sales Law. COM/2011/0635 final – 2011/0284 (COD).

ey. Of course, traders should warn about such consequences in advance to avoid any misunderstandings that digital content was supplied free of charge. However, during last stages of legislation this rule was abandoned and not included in LCC.

23 Regarding the scope of application, Lithuanian legislator faced several choices and in fact exploited them by reducing the scope of SGD rules application. First, it had and effectively used the possibility to exclude contracts for the sale of second-hand goods at public auctions and possibility to exclude contracts for the sale of living animals (Art. 3(5)) from the scope of SGD implementing act. Secondly, during the implementation of both directives, there was a possibility to extend an application of their rules to dual-purpose contracts (DCD recital 17, SGD recital 22). This was important for Lithuania, because rules in general section of Lithuanian consumer contract law are already applicable for dual-purpose contracts and this did not change (LCC Art. 6.228³). Since, as it was stressed above, DCD and SGD were transposed in different parts of LCC sixth book (DCD in general part, SGD in special part of contract law), there is now an awkward situation where DCD rules are applicable on dual-purpose contracts and SGD are not.

24 Also, several words should be said about the impact of directives beyond the B2C contracts. The starting point is that SGD and DCD are consumer protection directives focused on the B2C relations and not designed having in mind commercial (B2B) contracts. Complexity and unavoidable rigidity of consumer protection rules are rarely welcome in commercial agreements, where party autonomy prevails. For example, before the implementation of SGD and DCD buyer could, on his own judgment, elect civil remedies, which were most suitable for her.[11] However, after the implementation of directives, such possibility in consumer contracts was restricted by prearranged hierarchy or remedies. Obviously, parties in commercial contracts will not be barred and will avoid this statutory limitation, unless they will write it in the contract itself. Despite this, SGD and especially DCD rules are slightly relevant even to commercial contracts.

25 Firstly, by 'gold-plating' European rules on remedial time limits, national implementing act went beyond consumer contracts and set unified for all contracts prescription term on claims for defective goods, digital content and services. Before the implementation of SGD and DCD, the prescription term on claims for defective goods was 6 months, whereas claims for defective services are limited by a general ten-year prescription term (LCC Art. 1.125). Only in consumer sales of tangible movables for most claims the limitation was two years (LCC Art. 6.363). Now limitation on all those claims and claims for defective digital content is barred by two-year prescription period. This rule is included in LCC Art. 1.125 and applicable for consumer, commercial and general civil contracts of sale and services. Although such broad change is not obligatory under directives, it is apparently aimed to bring more legal clarity and unity for contract law remedies. All in all, six months was obviously too short prescription period for a sales claim, especially in cases of defective real estate.

26 Secondly, both consumer protection directives have introduced in Lithuanian contract law several important innovations, such as the division of conformity conditions into subjective and objective, as well as the set of tailored for digital markets concepts, like goods with digital elements, digital environment, integration, compatibility, functionality, interoperability, durability, payment by data (SGD Art. 2, DCD Art. 2–3). Those concepts, although not directly applicable to commercial contracts, may serve as

---

[11] Before the implementation of directives, Lithuanian Supreme Court has confirmed that Lithuanian law prescribes more protective rules for consumers than those Consumer Sales Directive 1999/44/EC, namely that Lithuanian law has no hierarchy of consumers' remedies. See judgment of the Lithuanian Supreme Court of 10 June 2020 in the civil case No 3K-3-186-1075/2020.

useful examples and conceptual basis for courts which are deciding B2B cases, especially involving supply of digital content and services.

C. Some legal requirements for the performance of contract

I. Conformity

27 The concept of conformity used in directives was transposed into Lithuanian law under the label of 'quality',[12] although neither in directives, nor in Lithuanian contract law those concepts are synonymous. Conformity is a much broader concept, which includes not only quality, but also quantity, completeness, fitness, packing and other requirements. Quality is a major requirement of conformity, which is further distinguished into factual and legal quality.

28 After transposition of both directives, LCC Art. 6.228[19] and 6.363 now enlists the subjective and the objective requirements and other conformity rules for consumer contracts of sales, supply of digital content and services, which simply repeat their counterparts in SGD and DCD. For instance, regarding the installation issues, the general rule set in LCC Art. 6.228[19] is that the trader is responsible for defects caused by incorrect integration of the digital content or digital service into the consumer's digital environment in those cases: (a) the digital content or digital service was integrated by the trader or under the trader's responsibility; (b) the digital content or digital service was intended to be integrated by the consumer and the incorrect integration was due to shortcomings in the integration instructions provided by the trader. Consequently, as in directives, the same LCC 6.228[19] provides that where the consumer fails to install updates in time, the trader is not liable for any lack of conformity resulting solely from the lack of the relevant update, provided that the trader informed the consumer about the availability of the update and the consequences of the failure of the consumer to install it; and the failure of the consumer to install or the incorrect installation by the consumer of the update was not due to shortcomings in the installation instructions provided by the trader.

29 However, textual analysis explains that there are some deviations, which may not necessarily be explained by rational reasoning. For example, one of the objective conformity requirements in the directives is the compliance of goods with any public statement made by or on behalf of the trader, or other persons in previous links of the chain of transactions, particularly in advertising or on labelling. However, this rule in LCC is transposed differently for digital content and sale of goods. Only the conformity of digital content is tied with statements of persons in previous links of the chain of transactions, whereas conformity of goods is tied with statements of any persons, i.e. not necessarily from previous links of the chain of transactions. Not only such distinction lacks rationale, but hypothetically it may even lead to unexpected and even unfair situations where conformity of trader's goods is defined by, for example, consumer associations or even politicians who may have their own populistic interest to heighten up quality requirements to the maximum. Therefore, LCC Art. 6.363 should be changed or at least applied in the court in strict compliance with SGD Art. 7.

30 Another deviation is a warning by the trader that goods, content or services do not conform the objective requirements, which, if done properly, effectively denies possibility to find non-conformity in that case. It should be noted that wording of LCC slightly differs from that in directives: whereas directives require to *specifically* inform (DCD

---

[12] See wording in LCC Art. 6.228[19] and 6.363.

Art. 8, SGD Art. 7), LCC Art. 6.228[19] and 6.363 require to *clearly* inform the consumer about deviations. However, as both words require the same result – proper information to the consumer about deviations, this should not be seen as the significant difference or failed implementation.

31 Lithuanian law in LCC Art. 6.228[24] (based on DCD Art. 19) regulates the modification of digital content or digital service on the initiative of the trader only with respect to contracts of digital content or services. The possible extension of those rules by systemic application (as rules in the general part of contract law which may be applicable to specific contracts) and even by analogy (LCC Art. 1.8) to sale of goods is expressly precluded by LCC Art. 6.228[24](4). Therefore, no tailored rules exist on this point in LCC. However, it is still possible to agree on modification of digital content or services embedded in tangible goods on basis of general freedom of contract subject to general control of unfair terms of consumer contract under LCC Art. 6.228⁴. Without doubt it would be permitted where such modification facilitates conformity requirements and probably where it is objectively justified, for instance, on basis of general migration to the new software generation, and at least does not reduce level of conformity of goods.

32 According to the general rule in LCC Art. 6.321, the seller has duty to provide goods free of any burdens, including third party rights. This is so called the requirement of legal quality, i.e. the 'clean' legal title to the property. It means that not only claims but even the sole existence of unknown third-party rights is a breach of conformity requirements and automatically – a breach of contract. This 'legal quality' logic has been maintained in transposition of SGD and DCD rules in LCC Art. 6.228[19] and 6.363, both of which in cases of restrictions based on third-party rights refer to the remedies on non-conformity.

II. Special issues

1. 'Green' economy

33 Lithuanian legislator has transposed both directives into national law without additional special measures for environmental sustainability, circular economy, durability or eco-design. However, it does not mean that those issues in connection with consumer contracts were not mitigated in Lithuanian legal system at all, since LCC Art. 6.228[13] even before the implementation of SGD has prescribed that consumer goods and services should be safe and of proper quality under requirements set by laws and other legal acts.

34 Regarding the SGD's durability requirement, i.e. ability of the goods to maintain their required functions and performance through normal use, it constitutes part of objective requirements of goods set in LCC Art. 6.363(3). Thus, durability in light of Lithuanian contract law now forms part of quality requirements for compliance of which the trader is responsible.

35 The same is with product-specific legislation, which also falls under objective requirements for quality and mitigated by new LCC rules. Let's take for example, eco-design requirements for energy-related products. Lithuanian legislator implemented SGD conformity rules in LCC without making any direct reference to the Eco-design directive or its implementing act (Eco-design technical regulation adopted by the Ministry of Economy).[13] Now, eco-design technical standards obviously fall under objective conformity requirements, set in LCC Art. 6.363(3), which requires the goods to comply with legal

---

[13] *Official Gazette*, 2007, No 111–4555.

C. Some legal requirements for the performance of contract

norms, technical standards and codes of conduct. Even before the implementation of SGD, LCC rules on quality of goods were fully sufficient to enforce those requirements. For instance, the consumer has sued the trader in the State Consumer Rights Protection Authority for alleged non-conformity of heat pump system against to EC regulation No 813/2013 implementing the Eco-design directive. The claim was dismissed because the dispute resolution body found that this system does conform technical standard setting 8 kW power requirement for such equipment.[14]

The Eco-design technical regulation in Art. 28 states that persons who did violation of this Regulation are liable under Lithuanian laws. According to the Code of Administrative Offences Art. 139, it is an administrative offence to sell and supply in the chain of transactions goods which do not conform technical standards and quality requirements set by law. Currently such violations may attract fine up to EUR 140 for trader's employees or unincorporated traders and up to EUR 560 for trader's directors and other responsible persons. For the latter group of persons in case of repeated offence a fine may be extended up to EUR 1200. As it may be seen, administrative fines are applicable only for natural persons and are clearly inadequate to dissuade corporate entities from breaching technical standards. That's why in extreme cases criminal liability may be applicable, most likely where misselling of eco-design non-compliant goods was done with scienter to defraud consumers and get financial benefit from this. Persons liable for criminal fraud may obliged, under Criminal Code Art. 182, to pay fine or even face up to 8 years of imprisonment (for gross fraud). Fraud also attracts corporate criminal liability up to EUR 4 200 000. Regarding private law sanctions, most dissuading for the trader most likely is collective claim of defrauded consumers for award of economic and non-economic damages in group civil action (Code of Civil Procedure section XXIV^1), whereas civil remedies in individual cases may have less significant impact on the trader's behaviour.

2. Personal data

Lithuanian legislator fully transposed DCD and its novelty – personal data as counter-performance into LCC Art. 6.228^{17} and 6.228^{23}. Consequently, consumer protection rules on digital content contracts are applicable also for contracts where the trader supplies or undertakes to supply digital content or a digital service to the consumer, and the consumer provides or undertakes to provide personal data to the trader, except where the personal data provided by the consumer are exclusively processed by the trader for the purpose of supplying the digital content or digital service or for allowing the trader to comply with legal requirements to which the trader is subject, and the trader does not process those data for any other purpose. As the DCD is focused only on trader's duties, enforceability of the consumer's duty to provide personal data as a counter-performance in terms of its enforceability it is left for the national contract law. In this respect, pursuant to LCC Art. 6.213 (based on UNIDROIT Principles of International Commercial Contracts) if a party fails to perform its non-monetary obligation, the other party may demand specific performance, except in some prescribed cases, including (1) where ordering the specific performance of a contractual obligation is impossible in law or in fact, or (2) the non-performed obligation is of exclusively personal character. In case of duty to provide personal data as consideration, both those exceptions are applicable. Firstly, according to Art. 7 of the GDPR, which has priority over the DCD rules (Recitals para 37), the data subject has the right to withdraw his or her consent at any time. It means, that after the consent to processing of personal data is withdrawn, it is

---

[14] Resolution of State Consumer Rights Protection Service No 10E-100, January 14, 2021.

not legally possible to still force person to provide his (her) personal data. Secondly, without doubt personal data is inalienable part or product of human personality, therefore obligation to provide personal data is of exclusively personal character and may not be specifically enforced in court. However, where withdrawal to give consent or reluctance to provide personal data as counter-performance is in breach of the contract, other remedies, primarily compensatory, may be applicable instead.

3. Copyright

38   DCD Art. 3(9) provides priority of copyright law over its rules. Lithuanian Law on author and related rights Art. 15 provides that the author has the exclusive rights to *inter alia* authorise or to prohibit distribution of the original or copies of a work to the public by sale, rental, lending, or by any other transfer of ownership or possession, as well as by communication to the public of a work in any way, including the making available to the public of a work via computer networks (on the Internet), etc. Consequently, any mode of the use of the of a work without the permission of the author, his successor in title or the person duly authorised by him is considered illegal. As regards to the digital content, its resale should fall under the concept of the right to communicate to the public, not under the distribution right which is reserved only to tangible items and subject to exhaustion after the first sale or other voluntary transfer (Law on author and related rights Art. 16).[15] Today the only exception to this delineation is the transfer of copies of computer software programs which according to ECJ, on the occasion of their first sale, have been downloaded from the internet onto the first acquirer's computer. Those copies are subject to the exhaustion of the distribution right.[16] In sum, the consumer under Lithuanian law cannot resell the digital content, except copies of computer software programs.

D. Liability of the Trader

39   Lithuanian Constitution Art. 30 prescribes that compensation for economic and non-economic damage inflicted upon a person shall be established by law. This is so called constitutional principle of 'reparation of damage' stemming from person's civil liability for wrongs.[17] In concert with this, SGD Recital 61 and DCD Recital 73 provides that the principle of the liability of the trader for damages is an essential element of contracts for the sale of goods, supply of digital content or digital services. Consequently, SGD Art. 10 and DCD Art. 11 establishes the general principle of trader's liability for a breach of contract. However, the articles are implemented in LCC Art. 6.228[20] and 6.364 under the title 'guarantee by law', thus narrowing its focus on legal guarantee periods to discover defects of subject-matter of contract after delivery.

40   Liability of the trader, according to the DCD and even SGD scheme, differs depending on whether digital content or digital services are supplied by the single act on continuously, i.e. as long term supply. Where a contract provides for a single act of supply or a series of individual acts of supply, e.g. in case of the offline game, the trader is liable for any lack of conformity which exists at the time of supply and becomes apparent within a period of two years from the time when the digital content or digital service was sup-

---

[15] About the requirement of tangibility for the effective exhaustion of distribution right see. Mizaras, *Autorių teisė. Tomas I* (2009), 412–43; CJEU, Case C-263/18, 19 December 2019, *Tom Kabinet*, ECLI:EU:C:2019:1111.

[16] CJEU, Case C-128/11, 3 July 2012, *UsedSoft*, ECLI:EU:C:2012:407.

[17] Ruling of The Constitutional Court of the Republic of Lithuania of December 13, 2004, August 19, 2006, January 6, 2011.

plied (LCC Art. 6.228[20] (2)). In case of a dispute, the burden of proof with regard to whether the supplied digital content or digital service was in conformity at the time of supply is on the trader for a lack of conformity which becomes apparent within a period of one year from the time when the digital content or digital service was supplied (LCC Art. 6.228[21] (2)). However, where a contract provides for a continuous supply over a period of time, e.g. in case of the online game, the trader is liable for a lack of conformity that occurs or becomes apparent within the period of that continuous supply under the contract (LCC Art. 6.228[20] (3)). Pursuant to recital 51 of the DCD, short-term interruptions of the continuous supply of digital content or digital service should be treated as instances of lack of conformity where those interruptions are more than negligible or recur. Where interruptions are negligible and do not repeat, they should not be treated as non-conformity and breach of contract. If those interruptions are not justified, they breach the 'continuity' element of objective conformity pursuant to DCD Art. 8 (1)(b) and LCC Art. 6.228[19] (2). In case of a dispute, the burden of proof regarding whether the digital content or digital service was in conformity within the period of continuous supply rests on the trader if a lack of conformity becomes apparent within that period (LCC Art. 6.228[21] (3)).

DCD does not regulate the impossibility to perform leaving it for the national law. In Lithuanian contract law, *ex post* impossibility to perform the contract is divided into two cases: impossibility due to the *force majeure* (justified impossibility) and impossibility imputable to the debtor (culpable impossibility). In a latter case the debtor is not relieved from liability. The rule on justified *ex post* impossibility in Lithuanian contract law, following the Romanic tradition,[18] is called irresistible force or *force majeure*. Rules on *force majeure* at large are based on UNIDROIT Principles of International Commercial Contracts. According to the LCC Art. 6.212, a party is exempted from liability for breach of a contract if it proves that the breach was due to the circumstances which were beyond its control and could not have been reasonably expected by it at the time of the conclusion of the contract, and the arising of such circumstances or consequences thereof could not be prevented. For example, State action prohibiting the supply of online content, which is used for hostile propaganda, may amount to *force majeure*. To establish the *force majeure* as an affirmative defence in Lithuanian contract law, the defendant should prove three classic criteria of the fortuitous events which prevented performance: externality, unforeseeability and irresistibility. An irresistible force (*force majeure*) does not include such circumstances as absence of goods in the market needed for the performance of the obligation, or lack of the necessary financial resources on the part of the party, or violation of their own obligations committed by the counterparties of the debtor. **41**

Change of circumstances (hardship) in Lithuanian contract law is regulated by LCC Art. 6.204, which is also based on UNIDROIT Principles of International Commercial Contracts. Hence, where the performance of a contract becomes more difficult for one of the parties, for example, the royalty fee payable by the trader for a provision of digital content has risen dramatically, this party is bound to perform the contract in accordance with the procedure set in the LCC Art. 6.204. Under this article, the performance of a contract is considered obstructed under such circumstances which fundamentally alter the balance of the contractual obligations, i.e. either the cost of performance has essentially increased or the value thereof has essentially diminished if: these circumstances occur or become known to the aggrieved party after the conclusion of the contract; these circumstances could not reasonably have been foreseen by the aggrieved party at the **42**

---

[18] About the influences of main legal traditions on Lithuanian contract law, see Laurynas Didžiulis. *Contract law in Lithuania* (Wolters Kluwer, 2019), p. 22.

time of the conclusion of the contract; these circumstances are beyond the control of the aggrieved party; and the risk of occurrence of these circumstances was not assumed by the aggrieved party. The practical effect of hardship rule is that in the event where the performance of a contract becomes obstructed, the aggrieved party shall have the right to make a request to the other party for the modification of the contract. Such request shall have to be made immediately after the occurrence of obstructions and the grounds on which the request is based indicated therein. The request for modification of the contract shall not in itself entitle the aggrieved party with the right to suspend performance of the contract. Where within a reasonable time the parties fail to reach an agreement on the modification of the contractual obligations, any of them may bring an action into a court. The court may: (1) terminate the contract and establish the date and terms of its dissolution; and (2) modify the conditions of the contract with a view to restoring the balance of the contractual obligations of the parties, for instance change the price for a digital content.

43   Next to LCC, there are additional sources for liability of the trader. For example, type of digital services is so called 'number-independent interpersonal communication service' (NI-ICS), regulated by DCD and European Electronic Communications Code (hereinafter – EECC).[19] In Lithuania next to the LCC it is covered by the Electronic Communications Act (framework law) and Rules for the Provision of Electronic Communications Services (lower regulation, which transposes EECC). However, since NI-ICS are regulated by DCD and therefore by LCC rules on digital services, sector specific legislation is not applicable to the early termination of NI-ICS contracts by the consumer. This comes not only from DCD and LCC rules on scope of application[20], but also from Rules for the Provision of Electronic Communications Services themselves, which consistently carve-out from NI-ICS the application of its early termination rules. However, where the consumer fundamentally breaches the contract, it may be terminated at the initiative of the trader in the manner specified in the contract and notifying the consumer not later than 5 working days in advance (Rules for the Provision of Electronic Communications Services Art. 28).

44   The scope of DCD application for bundle contracts is defined in Art. 3(6). The general principle here is *dépeçage*, according to which the bundle contract should be broken down in separate pieces and regulated by relevant rules. However, in respect of termination of bundle contract encompassing number-based interpersonal communications services, the EECC Art. 107(2) is applicable for the whole bundle contract, including digital content and services. According to this rule, where the consumer has a right to terminate any element of the bundle before the end of the agreed contract term because of a lack of conformity with the contract or a failure to supply, the consumer should also have the right to terminate the contract with respect to all elements of the bundle. Therefore, DCD Art. 3(6)3 gives priority for EECC Art. 107(2). In cases outside the bundle contract encompassing number-based interpersonal communications services, the effects that the termination of one element of a bundle contract may have on the other elements of the bundle contract shall be governed by national law.

45   On a national level situation seems more complicated, because while DCD is implemented in LCC, which is adopted in the Lithuanian Parliament (Seimas) and is the main legal act for the private law after the Constitution. In contrast, EECC is implemented in a lower regulation – Rules for the Provision of Electronic Communications Services,

---

[19] Directive (EU) 2018/1972 of the European Parliament and of the Council of 11 December 2018 establishing the European Electronic Communications Code (Recast)Text with EEA relevance. OJ L 321, 17.12.2018, 36–214.

[20] DCD Art. 3(5)b), LCC Art. 6.228^{17}(5)2).

adopted by the Director of Communications Regulatory Authority of the Republic of Lithuania (RRT). This creates legal problem, since according to LCC Art. 3(4), civil relationships may be regulated by the legal acts of executive state institutions only in the cases and to the extent expressly indicated by laws. Where legal acts of executive state institutions contradict the provisions of the LCC, the provisions of the LCC shall prevail. The priority against LCC by its Art. 3(3) is given for EU implementing instruments, however in a form of laws (parliamentary acts), not lower legislation. Therefore, at least by the letter of law, Rules for the Provision of Electronic Communications Services are not sufficient to give priority for EECC Art. 107(2) rule and override the general rule in DCD Art. 3(6)3. In effect, even with respect of termination of bundle contract encompassing number-based interpersonal communications services, the effect of the termination of one part of the contract should be decided by national law. In Lithuanian contract law the *favor contractus* principle favours survival of the contract wherever it is possible.[21] LCC Art. 6.221(3) provides that termination of the contract should not affect its terms which, taking in regard to their nature, may remain in force even after termination. Hence, the termination of the part of contract may lead to the end of the whole contract only where the remaining part of the contract will make no sense for the consumer and (or) the contractual obligations are not divisible (LCC Art. 6.25).

In addition, rules on personal data protection are fully applicable to the processing of personal data in connection with analysed consumer contracts. Consequences of the trader's non-compliance with the data protection requirements are stated in the GDPR itself, also in Law on legal protection of personal data and LCC. Firstly, the trader may incur administrative liability. Pursuant to GDPR Art. 83 supervisory authority shall impose administrative fines under procedure detailed in the Law on legal protection of personal data. Secondly, trader may incur civil consequences, including liability to compensate loss. According to GDPR Art. 82, the consumer who has suffered economic or non-economic damage due to an infringement of GDPR has right to claim compensation from the trader for the damage suffered. Particular rules on the application of civil liability and award of compensatory damages are regulated by LCC. However, breach of the GDPR may attract also other civil consequences, for instance, serious failure to protect consumer's data in a digital content contract may amount to fundamental breach under LCC Art. 6.228[22] and invoke right to terminate the contract or reduce price.

E. Remedies for the failure to supply and remedies for the lack of conformity

Overreaching principle applicable for whole system of civil remedies in Lithuanian is the principle of comprehensive judicial protection of civil law rights (LCC Art. 1.2). This substantive principle, backed by procedural right of access to court, means that injured person should have available in her disposition all necessary remedies to cure the breach. For this purpose, LCC Art. 1.138 provides for open list of civil remedies, which the claimant is free to elect subject to conditions and restrictions in substantive law. Before the implementation of DCD and SGD, freedom to elect remedies was also characteristic to consumer sales law.[22] However, now remedial disposition is restricted since the introduction of new rules. For instance, according to previous legislation, consumer as a primary remedy had a right to claim price reduction, whereas now under the LCC

---

[21] Judgment of the Lithuanian Supreme Court of June 26, 2012 in the civil case No 3K-7-306/2012.
[22] Judgment of the Lithuanian Supreme Court of 10 June 2020 in the civil case No 3K-3-186-1075/2020.

Art. 6.228²² and 6.364¹ price reduction is only a subsidiary remedy, applicable to cure ordinary breaches of contract where repair or replacement is not possible. However, the fact that both directives have introduced into Lithuanian law more structured and restrictive approach on election of remedies, should not be taken dramatically. All in all, European remedial structure, which is now mandatory for Lithuania as well, is focused on proportionality and is time tested. It is important that all this should provide legal certainty on rights and duties of both – trader and consumer.

48 According to SGD Art. 13(6), the consumer shall have the right to withhold payment of any outstanding part of the price or a part thereof until the seller has fulfilled the seller's obligations under this directive. This rule is transposed in LCC Art. 6.364¹(6). DCD does not even provide a right to withhold performance, i.e. payment for contracts, leaving this question to national law, however LCC Art. 6.228²²(10) in concert with Art. 6.364¹(6), is also giving right for consumer to withhold payment until non-conformity of digital content or service will be cured. Regarding the basic rules of the remedy in national law, under LCC, actual or anticipatory failure to properly supply digital content gives right to consumer to withhold (suspend) the payment as a form of self-help. In such a case, the consumer should issue notice to the trader about suspension of payment and may even claim damages. No right to withhold (suspend) payment exists where trader cannot perform its obligations due to circumstances beyond its control or due to the fault of the consumer, e. g. where consumer does not timely connect to trader services. The right of suspension of performance of an obligation must be used by the parties in good faith, reasonably and proportionally. For instance, if the part of digital services is delivered the payment may be suspended only in part, i.e. with regard to undelivered part of services (LCC Art. 6.58, 6.65, 6.207).

49 Within the cross-border EU internal market it is also important to determine the place where contractual subject-matter should be delivered and remedied. DCD provides for place of performance rules in Art. 5, transposed in LCC Art. 6.228¹⁸(2), according to which the trader shall have complied with the obligation to supply when: (a) the digital content or any means suitable for accessing or downloading the digital content is made available or accessible to the consumer, or to a physical or virtual facility chosen by the consumer for that purpose; (b) the digital service is made accessible to the consumer or to a physical or virtual facility chosen by the consumer for that purpose. However, as no similar rules exist in SGD, the issue of default place of delivery and the place of repair and replacement of goods is reserved for national law. According to the LCC, default rule for all obligations in general and seller's obligation of delivery in particular is that obligation should be performed at place of the debtor (seller) (LCC Art. 6.52(2)5, 6.318(2)3). If, however, consumer sales contract provides that the goods must be delivered to the buyer, pursuant to LCC Art. 6.359(1), the seller is bound to deliver the goods in timely manner to the place stated by the buyer and where there is no statement of the place of delivery – to the buyer's place of residence. Since contractual right to claim performance, according to LCC Art. 6.214, includes right to demand a repair or replacement of a defective performance, all those actions should be carried out at the same place. In conclusion, if the contract does not provide otherwise, goods should be delivered, repaired and replaced at the same place of a trader. In any case, according to LCC Art. 6.364²(1)1, repair and replacement should be free of charge for the consumer; therefore, the trader has no right to compensation of the costs for transporting, mailing, workforce or materials.

50 Those plain LCC rules also offer simple answers for cross-border cases, for instance where (1) the consumer has bought goods and then moved to another country or (2) the seller delivered the goods and now is demanded to carry out repair or replacement in a

country he does not offer delivery to. In the first case, consumer's movement into another country should not change the contract, including the place of performance, which in default cases should remain the place of the trader. Even if consumer sales contract provides that the goods must be delivered to the buyer, after initial delivery, change of consumer's seat should not change the place of further performance (repair, replacement). As regards to the second case, it should be stressed in advance that Geo-blocking regulation[23] does not impose an obligation to deliver goods cross-border to another Member State where the trader would not otherwise offer the possibility of such delivery to its customers (Recital 28). Therefore, goods should be repaired or replaced at the original place of delivery, since all those actions, according to LCC Art. 6.214, are specific manifestations of the same contractual performance and should be done at the same initial place.

51 DCD does not regulate the consequences for the digital content contracts where the consumer withdraws the consent for the processing of the consumer's personal data but establishes the right to terminate the contract by means of a statement to the trader expressing the decision to terminate the contract (DCD Recital 40, Art. 15). It flows from this that DCD treats withdrawal of consent and termination of contract as two independent juridical acts. However, under Lithuanian contract law, which is highly based on the theory of will, withdrawal of consent may still be equalised to termination of contract where, according to circumstances, it is clear that the consumer has no interest for the performance of the contract and the performance without her consent is impossible. In such case one may say that the consumer's apparent will is to terminate the contract and withdrawal of consent at the same time is a notice of termination. From the other side, according to LCC Art. 6.64(1)1, an unjustified withdrawal of consumer's consent, while the contract is still in force and binding, may be characterised as non-cooperation and the breach of contract by the consumer (*mora creditoris*).

52 According to both directives, the consumer shall exercise the right to terminate the contract by means of a statement to the trader expressing the decision to terminate the contract (DCD Art. 15, SGD Art. 16). This rule, transposed in LCC Art. 6.228^{23} and 6.364^3, provides for a simple termination without any additional requirements and changes the law for relevant consumer contracts, because the general national rule requires notice to be sent at agreed time or least 30 days before the termination will come in force (LCC Art. 6.218).

53 Harmonised rules on consequences of termination and related restitutionary obligations of parties are directly set in DCD Art. 16–18 and SGD Art. 16. In Lithuanian law they are transposed in LCC Art. 6.228^3 and 6.364^3 respectively. Those rules are applicable following the consumer's decision to exercise the right to terminate the contract. Where trader terminates the contract, national rules on restitution are applicable. Thus, according to LCC Art. 6.222, upon termination of the contract, each party has the right to claim the restitution of whatever it has supplied the other party under the contract. If restitution in kind is not possible or appropriate to the parties due to modification of the subject matter of the contract, a compensation of value of what has been received must be made in money, provided that such compensation does not contradict the criteria of reasonableness, good faith and justice. If the performance of a contract is successive and divisible, the party may claim restitution only of what has been received after the termination of the contract.

---

[23] Regulation (EU) 2018/302 of the European Parliament and of the Council of 28 February 2018 on addressing unjustified geo-blocking and other forms of discrimination based on customers' nationality, place of residence or place of establishment within the internal market and amending Regulations (EC) No 2006/2004 and (EU) 2017/2394 and Directive 2009/22/EC. OJ L 60I, 2.3.2018, 1–15.

54 In comparison with a complete system of national contract law, one may notice apparent imbalance and insufficiency in the DCD scheme of contractual restitution. Namely, in case where the trader failed to supply the digital content (services) against personal data and consumer subsequently terminated the contract, DCD Art. 16–18 and LCC Art. 6.228³ give no possibility to compensate the consumer for temporary use of her personal data. In contrast, where consumer has failed to provide personal data as a counter-performance and trader subsequently terminated the contract, the consumer according to LCC Art. 6.222 must return the monetary value of supplied digital content (services), which in practical terms may equal to the payment of price. Therefore, DCD should be improved on this point and equalise restitution of benefits for both parties not depending on who terminated the contract.

55 SGD does not provide for non-contractual remedies for the consumer, in the event of lack of conformity of goods, against persons in previous links of the chain of transactions, for example manufacturers, or other persons that fulfil the obligations of such persons. Under Lithuanian contract law this issue is solved in LCC Art. 6.333, according to which the manufacturer, distributor, supplier, importer or any other person distributing the goods in its own name is bound under a statutory warranty of the quality of the goods. Warranty is not applicable against any latent defect known to the buyer or any apparent defect that can be perceived by a prudent and diligent buyer without any need of expert inspection. Therefore, defects of goods may be remedied not only by the action of the consumer against trader but also by the direct action against the manufacturer or other person in the chain of transactions. In such context, contractual assignment of remedial rights from primary to subsequent buyers is relevant only where contractual warranty is broader in scope. In any case contract may not limit the scope of statutory warranty.

56 SGD recital 48 reveals that by giving consumers a choice in Art. 13(2) between repair or replacement for bringing goods into conformity, the European legislator is trying to encourage sustainable consumption and could contribute to greater durability of products. SGD Art. 13(2) is transposed in LCC Art. 6.364¹ and in principle should prevent unreasonable and costly replacement of goods where they may be efficiently repaired. Indeed, Lithuanian contract law establishes principles of economy and reasonableness (LCC Art. 1.5, 6.38, 6.200), which, in concert with environmental protection principles set in Lithuanian public law,²⁴ could, in theory, prioritise repair over replacement in order to enhance environmental sustainability. However, no such Lithuanian case law currently exists at this point. Moreover – text of SGD Art. 13 casts doubts whether it is even possible to prioritise repair over replacement in order to enhance environmental sustainability where repair and replacement are equally appropriate solutions for both parties even if at much higher social costs. Reference on sustainable consumption in SGD recital 48 is presented as a goal which should motivate consumer to pick more sustainable remedy, but it does not seem mandatory for him to do it, since remedial constraints are focused only on the private costs of parties, first of all, costs for a trader. Therefore, judicial reasoning, which would block remedy of replacement solely in order to enhance envi-

---

²⁴ Law on environmental protection Art. 4 provides that, in the Republic of Lithuania, environmental protection shall be the concern and duty of the State and each resident thereof. The policy and practice of the administration of environmental protection must direct public and private interests towards the improvement of the quality of the environment, encourage the users of natural resources to seek the ways and means to avoid or reduce adverse effects on the environment, and to make production ecologically safe. Natural resources must be utilised in a rational and complex way, taking into consideration the feasibility of preservation and rehabilitation of nature, as well as the specific natural and economic features of the Republic of Lithuania. Environmental protection shall be based on comprehensive, accurate and timely pooled environmental information.

ronmental sustainability, where for the trader both remedies produce similar costs, may go in conflict with SGD itself, which is a measure of maximum harmonisation and not subject for flexible and as a result – divergent interpretation in national courts. The possible solution would be to modify SGD or wait for ECJ ruling.

From the other side, actual possibilities of repair may closely depend on the availability of spare parts. Although there is no express general rule in Lithuanian law requiring the trader to ensure availability of spare parts or to inform consumers about such availability, as referenced in SGD recital 33, general contractual mechanism may be used to mitigate this issue. According to LCC Art. 6.38, the obligations must be performed in good faith, properly and without delay, pursuant to the requirements indicated in laws or the contract, and in case of absence of relevant requirements, obligations must be performed in accordance with the criteria of reasonableness. LCC Art. 6.200 prescribes that in performing a contract, each party shall be bound to contribute to and to cooperate with the other party. Those general principles imply duty of the trader to take all necessary steps in advance in order to perform the contract properly, otherwise the contract may be terminated or its performance may be withhold on basis of anticipatory breach (LCC Art. 6.58, 6.219). It means that during the demand for repair the trader must either have spare parts by itself or have availability to effectively get those parts in the market or by its suppliers. Therefore, according to LCC Art. 6.220, where consumer has the objective ground or evidence to believe that it is not the case and the contract will be fundamentally breached by failing to repair defective goods, she may demand the trader to present an assurance of due performance. The consumer may suspend performance of her obligations under the contract until the trader will provide the assurance that it has sufficient capabilities to properly repair goods. Where the assurance is not received within a reasonable time, the consumer may terminate the contract. Next to this general contractual reasoning, one may even find fragmentary regulation in Lithuanian public law of doubtless importance. For instance, there is a requirement in a lower regulation for persons providing services of technical maintenance and repair of vehicles to have instruments and equipment necessary to provide their services.[25] Thus, if the trader is selling cars and providing repair by itself, he may be bound by such rule. However, the rule is obviously too abstract and uncertain for public supervision.

Another issue related to the sustainability is the practice of premature (planned) obsolescence of goods. In light of Lithuanian law, such practice clearly compromises principles of fairness, reasonableness and economy (LCC Art. 1.5, 6.200), therefore is wrongful and even deceitful. Premature (planned) obsolescence of goods is a factual defect (non-conformity) which may invoke not only SGD based special remedies of the buyer (LCC Art. 6.364[1]), but also general civil remedies, including avoidance of the contract due to fraud and award of damages (LCC Ar. 1.91). In addition, practice of covert premature (planned) obsolescence of goods may be characterised as unfair commercial practice, namely, misleading omission of information and subject to administrative fines under the Law on the Prohibition of Unfair Business-to-Consumer Commercial Practices Art. 13. Even in cases, where the premature (planned) obsolescence of goods is disclosed in consumer contract, it may nevertheless be characterised as unfair consumer contract term under the LCC Art. 6.228[4].

There was legislative option for Member States to provide for or maintain specific remedies on hidden defects (SGD Art. 3(7), DCD Recital 12). Such remedies, mainly right to terminate contract in cases where hidden defect destroys goods, exist in general

---

[25] February 1, 2016 Description of the procedure for the provision of vehicle maintenance and repair services. The Head of the State Road Transport Inspectorate under the Ministry of Transport and Communications. Order No 2BE-45.

sales law (LCC Art. 6.334 (2–3)), however until legal nature of digital content contracts is settled, the possibility to rely on those norms is uncertain. From the other side, application of latter rules should not create real problems, because if contractual subject-matter is destroyed, for instance, where software became unusable due to programming error, transposed DCD rules on conformity (LCC Art. 6.228^{19}) will be applicable. Also, according to the SGD Article 3(7), there was a possibility to provide for specific remedies if the lack of conformity becomes apparent within a maximum of 30 days after delivery, however this option was left unused, most probably because such short-term remedies are not characteristic to Lithuanian contract law.

F. Commercial Guarantees

60   With respect to rules on commercial guarantees Lithuanian legislator has adopted an interesting choice. Despite that new SGD has repealed former Directive 1999/44/EC with effect from 1 January 2022 and changed regulation on commercial guarantees, Lithuanian legislator decided to transpose new rules of SGD at the same time retaining national rules based on those of Directive 1999/44/EC. Therefore, LCC now contains an interesting mix of rules of both chronologically concurrent directives at once: LCC Art. 6.364^4 (article included in the special part of contract law, applicable for consumer sales contracts) fully transposed rules of SGD Art. 17, whereas LCC Art. 6.228^{14} (article included in the general part of contract law, applicable for consumer contracts in general) is based on Directive 1999/44/EC Art. 6 and definition of commercial guarantees taken from Consumer Rights Directive. However, it seems that rules are not conflicting in substance, because LCC Art. 6.364^4 is *lex specialis* with respect to Art. 6.228^{14} and the latter article provides rule on language, which is directly omitted from scope of SGD. LCC Art. 6.228^{14} provides that commercial guarantee should be provided in State language, which according to Constitution Art. 14 is Lithuanian. Also, the article states that commercial guarantee should state that it does not restrict rights of the consumer who acquired defective goods or services and it should in plain intelligible language set out the contents of the guarantee and the essential particulars necessary for making claims under the guarantee, notably the duration and territorial scope of the guarantee as well as the name, address and e-mail of the guarantor.

61   Although, LCC Art. 6.228^{14} is included in the general part of contract law, applicable for consumer contracts in general, its application for digital content and services is complicated. The problem is that according to LCC Art. 6.228^1, LCC Art. 6.228^{14} is applicable only for tangible goods and services (including digital services, as there are no exceptions for them). It means that commercial guarantees for intangibles, such as digital content, are left for operation of general contract law principles of freedom of contract (LCC Art. 6.156) and *pacta sund servanda* (LCC Art. 6.189). This leads to unreasonable legal fragmentation, because, with respect to contractual guarantees, digital services and digital content fall under different rules. However, this is not formal failure to transpose DCD, because it does not provide rules on commercial guarantees for digital content and services.

G. Time Limits

62   Regarding remedial time limits, European legislator has left to Member States the legislative option to choose from either (1) the legal guarantee (time limit to discover defects after delivery), or (2) prescription period (time limit to sue trader in court), or

G. Time Limits

(3) combine both concepts at once for purposes of remedying non-conformity. Lithuanian drafters, following general pattern in Lithuanian contract law, opted to maintain both those time periods in tandem.

Firstly, the trader is liable for any lack of conformity which exists at the time of supply and becomes apparent within a period of two years from the time when the digital content or digital service (standalone or included in goods) was supplied by a single act of supply or a series of individual acts of supply. Only in the case of second-hand goods, such as the used car, the seller and the consumer can agree with a shorter liability period but not less than one year. Where a contract provides for a continuous supply of a digital content or digital service (standalone or included in goods) over a period of time the trader is liable for a lack of conformity that occurs or becomes apparent within the period of that continuous supply under the contract (LCC Art. 6.228^{20}, 6.364). It should also be noted that Lithuanian legislator, under the discretion given by SGD Art. 12, opted in LCC Art. 6.364^1 for a provision that establishes the consumer's obligation to notify the seller about non-conformity within two months (Article 12). Such obligation is applicable only for sale of goods and not allowed for contracts on digital content (DCD Recital 11).

Secondly, in addition to legal guarantee period, after discovery of defects there is additional abridged two-year limitation (prescription) period applicable for claims due to defects of goods, services and digital content under LCC Art. 1.125(8).[26] It means that consumer has one time limit to discover defects and the additional time limit to sue trader in court after the discovery of defects and refusal by the trader to cure them. This coexistence, in my opinion, is positive as it facilitates for better consumer protection and reflects situation already existing in Lithuanian contract law (LCC Art. 1.125, 6.338).

Neither directive regulates conditions under which the liability period or a limitation period can be suspended or interrupted, leaving this to national law. Lithuanian law also does not provide special rules for suspension or interruption of time limits for consumer contracts, thus general rules are applicable. Even when no rules for suspension or interruption of legal warranty period exist, the consumer should be fully aware of remaining time limits and respond accordingly. This is especially important because according to the Supreme Court of Lithuania expiry of warranty term means loss of relevant remedial rights,[27] which, in turn, pursuant to LCC Art. 1.117(6) should preclude possibility to restore it in court even if expiry was caused by important obstacle.

According to Lithuanian case law, limitation period to sue seller in the court begins to count only after seller ignores or expressly refuses to satisfy buyer's claim to remedy defects which were detected during warranty period.[28] Following this reasoning, if consumer has notified in time the trader about the particular defects and latter ignored or refused to satisfy consumer's demands, then two-year limitation period begins, which in contrast to legal warranty period, may be interrupted and suspended for various statutory prescribed reasons. Most relevant reason for consumer contracts which suspends prescription is the participation in dispute resolution by mediation (Law on Mediation Art. 18)[29], whereas most relevant reason which interrupts limitation period, is behaviour of a trader by which it acknowledges its obligation to the consumer, for instance, promises to repair goods or proceeds with it. Practical difference between those two no-

---

[26] LCC Art. 1.125(13) prescribes that limitation periods are imperative and not subject to alteration by agreement.
[27] Judgment of the Lithuanian Supreme Court of February 13, 2007 in civil case No 3K-3-43/2007; judgement of Lithuania court of appeal of January 18, 2022 in civil case No e2A-129-881/2022.
[28] Judgment of the Lithuanian Supreme Court of March 12, 2015 in civil case No 3K-3-137-706/2015.
[29] *Official Gazette*, July 31, 2008, No 87-3462.

tions is that prescription still proceeds counting after the end of suspension (LCC Art. 1.129), whereas after interruption it starts counting again from the beginning (LCC Art. 1.130). Finally, even if the prescription was not suspended or interrupted and its term has expired, it may nevertheless be restored by the court if claimant can prove important reasons which led to expiration of such term (LCC Art. 1.131), for instance illness, misleading behaviour of the trader, etc.

67   Another class of time limits concerns the burden of proof. Before the implementation of SGD and DCD, a time period for the trader's burden of proof in consumer sales contracts was 6 months (LCC Art. 6.363). This period is now extended up to one year, therefore the burden of proof regarding whether the supplied subject-matter of the contract was in conformity at the time of supply is on the trader for a lack of conformity which becomes apparent within a period of one year from the time when the supply has taken place (LCC Art. 6.228[21], 6.364).

H. Right of Redress

68   Both directives establish a trader's right to redress. Hence, pursuant to SGD Art. 18 and DCD Art. 20, where the trader is liable to the consumer due to actions of a person in previous links of the chain of transactions, the trader shall be entitled to pursue remedies against the person or persons liable in the chain of commercial transactions. The person against whom the trader may pursue remedies, and the relevant actions and conditions of exercise, shall be determined by national law.

69   *Travaux préparatoires* of national implementing legislation reveals that SGD Art. 18 and DCD Art. 20 were not specifically transposed in LCC on the premise that this situation is already addressed in Lithuanian law by LCC Art. 6.280.[30] This article provides that a person who has compensated the damage caused by another person shall have the right of recourse against the person by whom the damage was caused in the amount equal to the paid compensation unless a different amount is established by the law. This is, indeed, true – Lithuanian law effectively provides for a right of recourse, however not by LCC Art. 6.280, because latter article belongs to the tort law and regulates right of redress after damages were paid in response of the tort and not the breach of contract.

70   In Lithuanian law, as in other Romanic (from the perspective of patrimonial law) jurisdictions, there is strict delimitation between tort law and contract law, in favour of contract law (the principle of *non-cumul*). Consequently, the trader's right of redress should be addressed by contractual, rather than tortious, liability against contractual counterparties which failed to supply the trader with proper materials or other elements required to deliver proper goods, digital content or services to consumers. Right of redress is apparently stemming from the breach of commercial contracts and normally will take form of a strict liability to pay damages or penalty (LCC Art. 6.256). In addition to this, other persons may be liable in a chain of transactions by direct action under LCC Art. 6.333, according to which the manufacturer, distributor, supplier, importer or any other person distributing the goods in its own name is bound under a statutory warranty of the quality of the goods. However, due to the privity of a contract, liability of other persons in chain of supply transactions should be subsidiary to liability of direct counterparty, which should remain primary liability.

---

[30] Correlation table of national legislation and the Directive (EU) 2019/771. Access from the internet: https://e-seimas.lrs.lt/rs/lasupplement/TAP/6e6feb90a8ce11eb98ccba226c8a14d7/af881eaba9f411eba6328c92adabc234/format/ISO_PDF/.

I. Relationship with other remedies

The relationship between the implementing provisions of the DCD and SGD and the remedies provided in Lithuanian law of obligations may be described as the relative autonomy. Autonomy, because directives do not directly regulate such civil remedies as avoidance of contracts or damages. Relative because implementing provisions of the DCD and SGD still make impact on the application of purely national remedies. Such impact may be barely visible even for the remedy of contract avoidance. For instance, in order to avoid contract due to mistake about the functionality of goods, consumer may need to rely on conformity rules (LCC Art. 6.363) in order to prove that his subjective understanding on functionality differs from that which was formally agreed.

More extensive impact implementing provisions of the DCD and SGD have on civil liability for damages. Both directives state that the principle of the liability of the trader for damages is an essential element of respective consumer contracts. The consumer, thus, should be entitled to claim compensation for detriment caused by a lack of conformity or a failure to supply the subject-matter of the contract. The compensation should put the consumer as much as possible into the position in which the consumer would have been had the subject-matter of the contract been duly supplied and been in conformity (SGD Recital 61 and DCD Recital 73). Leaving aside obvious elements of civil liability which are mentioned in those sentences (breach, loss, causation, quantum of damages), implementing provisions of the DCD and SGD even more important because they provide for so called 'special remedies'. According to Lithuanian case law, general contractual remedies, including award of compensatory damages, are subsidiary to special remedies stemming from sales law.[31] It means that compensatory damages available only to the extent where specific remedies, including specific performance, repair of defects or price reduction, are not available. Application of special remedies automatically narrows residual scope for compensatory damages. For instance, if consumer has demanded to bring the digital content or digital service into conformity or claimed price reduction, after successful application of such remedy there is correspondingly less (if still is) loss, which may be compensated by damages.

J. Conclusions

Efficient consumer protection in Lithuania is a constitutional obligation of the State, which implies duty to adapt legislation for changes in economic relations. In the course of ongoing digital revolution, harmonised and tailored European consumer law on digital content, digital services and goods with digital elements should strongly contribute for fulfilment of this duty. Paradoxically, European legislator by adopting SGD and especially DCD has helped national legislator to perform its duties under Constitution.

So far, we have faced only immediate impact of those two directives in Lithuanian law, namely on the introduction of new statutory rules of consumer protection in LCC. Lithuanian experience of implementation mostly reflects cautious and conservative approach for implementation of the DCD within Lithuanian private law. Hesitation to develop more coherent national law around transposed rules most probably may be explained by the lack institutional competencies and uncertainty on further development and content of EU rules on subject matter. The analysis has shown that there are some failures of transposition – mostly minor and technical, but one is clearly fundamental –

---

[31] Judgment of the Lithuanian Supreme Court of May 5, 2017 in civil case No e3K-7-63-969/2017.

the DCD was transposed in the general part of contract law, instead of the special part dealing with nominate contracts next to rules of SGD. Such legislative technique says nothing about the characterisation of digital content contract and presupposes search for additional rules in special part of Lithuanian contract law dealing with nominate contracts. In my opinion, contracts for supply of digital content deserve to be named *sui generis* by their nature and should be classified separately from other nominate contracts. Such solution would enable legal system to overcome full set of problems related to complex characterisation and cross-application of various rules regulating other types of contracts. Conservative copy-paste approach has also precluded Lithuanian legislator from designing the additional measures for 'greener' consumer contracts, dealing with environmental sustainability, circular economy, durability or eco-design.

75   At the same time, we may legitimately expect for more deeper and long-term effect of European rules on national contract laws. Inclusion of new set of rules into LCC – one of the key legal acts in whole Lithuanian legal system – should begin to stimulate doctrinal discussion and judicial development of digital contract law in Lithuania. Although it is not realised in Lithuania so far but in the developed European society is unavoidable. The impact of new rules should not be confined to simply consumer protection, but in addition elevate the conceptual understanding of contract law in general and through it – even property law, thus aligning them to the market realities. The straightforward product of this conceptual evolution will be correction of implementation failures, in particular putting DCD rules in the right place and optimisation of digital consumer contract law.

76   From the other side, rules of both directives, are far from complete. There is set of issues, which were left for divergent national law of Member States. Of course, it is naïve to expect to have complete regulation in SGD and DCD, for this one should adopt whole European Civil Code or at least DCFR. However, some issues could have been already addressed in the directives, such as conditions for withholding of performance, place of performance, complete restitution in case of payment by personal data, etc. Having in mind the character of maximum harmonisation, which dramatically limits national initiatives, European legislator should also consider direct adoption of 'green' criteria for selection of remedies, in particular between repair and replacement.

77   Finally, seeing two similar directives with partly coinciding rules, suggests that European bodies should think again how to systemise and substantially codify European consumer contract law in, for example, the European Consumer Code. Because in case of every new consumer law directive it becomes more and more difficult for a national legislator to avoid further fragmentation and distortion of national contract laws. All in all, despite the internal quality of new rules, their effect is dramatically reduced by such side-effects.

Bibliography

Monographs

Vytautas Mizaras, *Autorių teisė. Tomas I* (Justitia, Vilnius, 2009).

Laurynas Didžiulis, *Contract law in Lithuania* (Wolters Kluwer, 2019).

Edited books

Christian von Bar, Eric Clive, Hans Schulte-Nölke, Hugh Beale, Johnny Herre, Jérôme Huet, Matthias Storme, Stephen Swann, Paul Varul, Anna Veneziano and Fryderyk Zoll (eds), *Principles, Definitions and Model Rules of European Private Law Draft Common Frame of Reference (DCFR)* (Full ed. Edition, Sellier, Munich, 2009).

Bibliography

Journal Articles

Danguolė Bublienė, 'Vartotojų teisių direktyvos perkėlimas į Lietuvos teisę – tolesnis vartotojų apsaugos teisės dekodifikavimas ar kodifikavimas?' (2012) 83, *Teisė: mokslo darbai*, 37–60.

Laurynas Didžiulis, 'EU Digital Content Directive And Evolution Of Lithuanian Contract Law' (2021), *12 Journal of Intellectual Property, Information Technology and E-Commerce Law*, 260–270.

Agnė Selvestravičiūtė, 'Naujoji Europos Parlamento ir Tarybos direktyva (ES) 2019/771 dėl tam tikrų prekių pirkimo-pardavimo sutarčių aspektų – maksimalaus harmonizavimo pasirinkimas ir reikšmė' (2021) 119, *Teisė*, 118–130.

Case Law

CJEU, Case C-128/11, 3.7.2012, *UsedSoft*, ECLI:EU:C:2012:407.

CJEU, Case C-263/18, 19.12.2019, *Tom Kabinet*, ECLI:EU:C:2019:1111.

Constitutional Court of the Republic of Lithuania, 13.12.2004, Ruling 51/01–26/02–19/03–22/03–26/03–27/03, Official Gazette 181–6708.

Constitutional Court of the Republic of Lithuania, 19.8.2006, Ruling 23/04, Official Gazette 90–3529.

Constitutional Court of the Republic of Lithuania, 6.1.2011, Ruling 13/2008, Official Gazette 3–93.

Supreme Court of Lithuania, 13.2.2007, Civil Case 3K-3-43/2007.

Supreme Court of Lithuania, 26.6.2012, Civil Case 3K-7-306/2012.

Supreme Court of Lithuania 12.5.2015, Civil Case 3K-3-137-706/2015.

Supreme Court of Lithuania, 5.5.2017, Civil Case e3K-7-63-969/2017.

Supreme Court of Lithuania, 10.6.2020, Civil Case 3K-3-186-1075/2020.

Court of appeals of Lithuania, 18.1.2022, Civil Case e2A-129-881/2022.

State Consumer Rights Protection Service, 14.1.2021, Resolution 10E-100.

Luxembourg*

A. Method of Transposition of the Twin Directives	2
B. Integration of the New Legislation into the Existing Legal Framework	4
C. Conformity of Goods, Digital Content and Services	13
D. Remedies for the Failure to Supply and Remedies for the Lack of Conformity	24
E. Enhancing a Sustainable Regime of Conformity in Goods	31
F. Coordination of the Transposed Regimes with other Disciplines	34
I. Law of Contracts and Obligations	34
II. Intellectual Property Law	47
III. Law of Communications	49
IV. Data Protection	51
V. Geo-Blocking Regulation	56
G. Time Limits	57
Bibliography	67

1 The text below reflects the answers given to a questionnaire sent by the editors of this book and focusing on issues raised by the transposition into national legislations of the so-called twin directives: Directive 2019/770 on certain aspects concerning contracts for the supply of digital content and digital services and Directive 2019/771 on certain aspects concerning contracts for the sale of goods. With the objective of offering a smoother reading of the answers provided, the text was redrafted and split into sections. It introduces the general features of the transposition (Section I and II), emphasises the main changes to Luxembourg legislation due to the transposition of the two directives (Section III, Section IV, and Section VII) as well as the challenges faced by the national legislature by reason of the novelties introduced by the two directives (Section V and Section VI).

A. Method of Transposition of the Twin Directives

2 **Consumer protection belongs to the consumer code.** The Law of 8 December 2021[1] transposes the provisions of DCD[2] and SGD[3] into the consumer code. This law entered into force on 1 January 2022. It only governs B2C relationships. The provisions contained in this Law were transposed into Article L.010 – 1 regarding the general definitions (Code I. Legislative Part), into Article L.113 – 1(1)(e) concerning consumer information relating to contracts other than distance or off-premises contracts (Book 1. Title 1. Chapter 3), Articles L.212 – 1 to L.212 – 11 related to contracts for the sale of tangible personal property (Book 2. Title 1. Chapter 2. Section 1.1), Articles L.212 – 12

---

* Section I, Section III (para. 2, 3, 4, 6), Section VI (para. 3, 4, 5), Section V, Section VI(e) were tackled by Laura Aade while Section II, Section III (para. 1, 5, 7, 8), Section IV (para. 1, 2, 6), Section 6(a), (b), (c), (d) and Section VII were tackled by Elise Poillot. Section III (para. 9) was tackled by the two authors.
[1] Loi du 8 décembre 2021 portant modification du code de la consommation aux fins de transposition de la directive (UE) 2019/770 du Parlement européen et du Conseil du 20 mai 2019 et de la directive (UE) 2019/771 du Parlement européen et du Conseil du 20 mai 2019 relative à certains aspects concernant les contrats de vente de biens (hereafter Law of 8 December 2021).
[2] Directive (EU) 2019/770 of the European Parliament and of the Council of 20 May 2019 on certain aspects concerning contracts for the supply of digital content and digital services (hereafter DCD).
[3] Directive (EU) 2019/771 of the European Parliament and of the Council of 20 May 2019 concerning contracts for the sale of goods, amending Regulation (EU) 2017/2394 and Directive 2009/22/EC, and repealing Directive 1999/44/EC (hereafter SGD).

to L.212 – 29 on contracts for the supply of digital content and services (Book 2. Title 1. Chapter 2. Section 1.2), Articles L.212 – 30 to L.212 – 31 respectively dealing with legal guarantees and commercial guarantees (Book 2. Chapter 2. Section 2), Articles L. 212–32 to L.212 – 33 regarding repair (Book 2. Title 1. Chapter 2. Section 3) and Article L.320 – 7 dealing with injunctive and prohibitory actions (Book 3. Title 2).

3   The transposition of the two Directives inevitably impacted Luxembourg consumer law as it finally established a regime for digital content and digital services since no reflection at the national level on the impact of digitalisation on consumer contracts had been conducted before.

B. Integration of the New Legislation into the Existing Legal Framework

4   **General context.** *Verbatim* transposition is typical in the Grand-Duchy since Luxembourg legislative and executive powers deal with the same number of norms as bigger countries. Yet, human resources are relatively limited compared to those of other countries. The ever-increasing complexity of legislation is also something difficult to deal with given the short lapse of time imposed on Member States to transpose EU legislation. *Verbatim* transpositions facilitate the work of both the legislature and the executive. They also guarantee a certain foreseeability of legislative policies, and, in the specific field of consumer law, they keep the level of consumer protection at an acceptable level for important actors of the EU economy settled in Luxembourg, as full targeted harmonisation allows for a more protective approach for certain subjects.

5   **Transposition of the twin directives.** No exception to the "*verbatim* approach" was made when transposing the twin directives. Consequently, the concepts of goods with digital elements, integration, updates, digital environment, compatibility, functionality, interoperability, durable medium, digital content, and service were not (or ever – for those already inserted into domestic legislation by transposition of EU law) discussed at the national level.

6   A consequence of the servile transposition of DCD was the introduction of the concept of "pseudo-contract"[4] into Luxembourg law (the relationships based on the provision of personal data by the consumer as a counter performance are not treated as contracts). By doing so, it excluded the possibility of having personal data treated as "the price paid by the consumer". Article L.212 – 12 of the consumer code provides that rules applying to contracts for the supply of digital content or digital services shall apply "where the trader supplies or undertakes to supply digital content or a digital service to the consumer, and the consumer provides or undertakes to provide personal data to the trader, except where the personal data provided by the consumer are exclusively processed by the trader for the purpose of supplying the digital content or digital service in accordance with this sub-section or for allowing the trader to comply with legal requirements to which the trader is subject, and the trader does not process those data for any other purpose."[5] Accordingly, there was no need to introduce new rules on contract formation/existence/validity. Following the approach of the Directive, such agreements are treated, by analogy, as contractual by the Law of 8 December 2021.

7   Another characteristic of Luxembourg consumer law is its "compartmented feature". Even before the promulgation of the consumer code, all legislation regarding consumer

---

[4] See *infra*, answer to Section III.5.
[5] Art. 3 of DGD.

B. Integration of the New Legislation into the Existing Legal Framework

rights was passed through the channel of specific acts, not enshrined in the civil code.[6] It is therefore not surprising that the types of contracts for the supply of digital content/digital services and for the supply of goods with digital elements had no impact on general contract law. That said, a reform of contract law is being considered by the Ministry of Justice.[7] The core question currently discussed concerns the model to be followed, as France and Belgium, the two reference countries in the field of civil law, just revised their contract law. If any impact of supply of digital content or digital service contracts on general contract law was to be observed, it would be similar to that provoked by the transposition of the directive in the legal system to be taken as a reference by Luxembourg for reforming its law of contracts.

In the same vein, as of yet, the introduction of contracts for the supply of digital content / digital services and for the supply of goods with digital elements had no significant impact on the general theory of contract / contract types. 8

Expansion of the legal regimes to B2B contracts. The suitability of the Directives' provisions for B2B contracts raises two issues: (1) are there obstacles, at the national level, for expanding the scope of application of the provisions at stake? and (2) would it be conceivable, from a policy standpoint, to transpose the B2C contract regime to B2B relationships? 9

(1) Technically, there is no obstacle for applying the conformity regime established by the directives to B2B contracts. The lack of a general regulation of the contract figures is not desirable and a reflection on adopting general rules for this type of contract should be conducted. Such a choice would have an impact on the structure of the legal system and should be thoroughly thought through. The low number of claims brought in front of the courts also impact the functioning of the legal system. Luxembourg case law follows the trend of Belgian or French legislations and the interpretation made by these Member States' Courts. Therefore, it is rather unlikely that the Luxembourg legislature would adopt any legislation on these figures of contracts if Belgium or France abstain from doing it. 10

(2) The choice to adopt a consumer code partly relies on the willingness to strictly distinguish the regime of B2C contracts from that of all other contracts.[8] The persistence of a general regime of non-conformity ("*garantie des vices cachés*")[9] in Luxembourg civil code is a clear indication that, following the French model,[10] consumer law is to be considered as a specific branch of law. Yet, no consumer-oriented legislation has been a source of inspiration for regulating B2B or other relationships. Such option would require some adaptations. 11

Consumer law is based on the assumption that consumers are in a weak position vis-à-vis sellers or suppliers, as regards both their bargaining power and level of knowledge. Traders are supposed to be more aware of the consequences possibly deriving from the 12

---

[6] The code was promulgated in 2011 by the Law of 8 April 2011 portant sur l'introduction d'un Code de la consommation.

[7] See Ministère de la Justice, 'Assises du Code civil : Quelles réformes pour moderniser le Code civil?' (Press Release 15 October 2021
<https://gouvernement.lu/fr/actualites/toutes_actualites/communiques/2021/10-octobre/15-assises-code-civil.html#:~:text=Le%2015%20octobre%202021%20s,appui%20du%20groupe%20de%20r%C3%A9flexion> accessed 1 June 2022.

[8] See Poillot, 'Codification of French and Luxembourg Consumer Law: are French and Luxembourg consumer codes going the same Road?' (2018) 17 *RBDCivil*, 125(135); Poillot, 'Le Code luxembourgeois de la consommation : étude de droit interne et comparé' (2013) *Journal des Tribunaux Luxembourg*, 1.

[9] Art. 1641 to 1649 of the Luxembourg civil code.

[10] See Poillot, *Droit européen de la consommation et uniformisation du droit des contrats* (2006), 368; Poillot, 'Les codes de l'intégration du droit de la consommation dans le système juridique. Regards franco-allemands' in *Mélanges en l'honneur du Professeur Claude Witz* (2018), 671.

non-performance of a contract. They are also expected to act according to professional diligence. The protection granted to the buyer should therefore be tailored to the B2B context.

C. Conformity of Goods, Digital Content and Services

13 **Servile transpositions.** The Luxembourg legislature has again chosen to transpose mostly in a servile manner the legal regime established by the SGD, mainly keeping its provisions distinct from those of the DCD. Many articles of the consumer code transpose the provisions of the two directives *verbatim*.

14 **Conformity requirements.** Article L.212 – 3 of the consumer code enshrines the subjective requirements for the sale of goods with or without embedded digital elements, while Article L.212 – 4 sets out the objective criteria. In the context of contracts for the supply of digital content and services, the subjective and objective requirements related to conformity are respectively contained in Articles L.212 – 15 and L.212 – 16 of the consumer code. Provisions excluding the existence of a lack of conformity in case of "particular characteristics deviating from the objective requirements for conformity" of which consumers where informed (Articles 8(5) of DCD and Article 7(5) of SGD) were respectively transposed into Article L.212 – 16(5) and Article L.212 – 4(5) of the consumer code. Consequences of the incorrect installation of the digital content or digital service (Article 8 of DCD) are to be found in Article L.212 – 16(3) of the consumer code. The liability exemptions (Article 7(4) of SGD and Article 8(3) of DCD) are enshrined in Articles L.212 – 4(4) and L.212 – 16(3). Those provisions are also *verbatim* transpositions of the directives' regimes.

15 **Duty to inform and supply the consumer with updates.** Article 8(2) of DCD and Article 7(3) of SGD established a duty to inform and supply the consumer with updates which are necessary to keep the digital content or digital service in conformity. To transpose such duty into national law, the Luxembourg legislature has introduced two distinct articles in the consumer code, using the same wording as the Twin Directives (Article 8 DCD was transposed in Article L.212 – 16(2) and Article 7(3) of SGD in Article L.212 – 4(3) of the consumer code). Articles L.212 – 4(4) and L.212 – 16(3) of the consumer code also literally reproduce the provisions of Article 8(3) DCD and Article 7(4) SGD regarding the liability exemption for cases in which the consumer fails to install updates.

16 **Immediate and continuous supply of digital content and services.** Article L.212 – 18 of the consumer code, transposing Article 11 of DCD, establishes the rules for the liability of the trader in the context of contracts for the supply of digital content and services for a lack of conformity resulting from an act or omission, including the failure to provide updates. This article makes a distinction between, on the one hand, contracts providing for a single act of supply or a series of individual acts of supply, and on the other hand, contracts providing for continuous supply over a period of time. In the context of the former, Article L.212 – 18(2) of the consumer code establishes that the trader of digital content and services is liable for any lack of conformity existing at the time of the supply for a period of two years. Any lack of conformity that appears within one year from the supply is presumed to have existed at the time of the delivery, as stated in Article 212–19(2) of the consumer code transposing Article 12(2) of DCD, not using the possibility to extend the delay of one year as allowed by the Directive. For the case of continuous supply of digital content and services over a period of time, the liability period corresponds to the duration of the contract pursuant Article L.212 – 18(3) of the

consumer code. In this type of contract, any lack of conformity that appears within the entire period of the contract is presumed to have existed at the time of the delivery, as stated in Article 212-19(3) of the consumer code transposing Article 12(3) of DCD.

Interruption of long-term supply of digital content and services. No provisions 17 regulating such situation were implemented by the Luxembourg legislature in way of transposition of DCD. Subsequently, such non-performance will be handled under general contract law.

Modification of Digital Content or Digital Service in way of implementation of 18 **the SGD.** The Luxembourg legislature transposed *verbatim* Article 19 DCD in Article L.212 – 26 of the consumer code. The only difference to be noted is that Article L.212-reproduces in its (5) the content of Article 3 (6) second paragraph, excluding from its scope of application the bundle within the meaning of Directive (EU) 2018/1972 including elements of an internet access service as defined in point (2) of Article 2 of Regulation (EU) 2015/2120 of the European Parliament and of the Council (22) or a number-based interpersonal communications service as defined in point (6) of Article 2 of Directive (EU) 2018/1972. (See also *infra* VI. (b)).

Third parties' rights and lack of conformity due to the violation of third parties' 19 **rights.** Article 9 SGD and 10 DCD were respectively transposed in Articles L.212 – 10 and L.212 – 28 Consumer code in a servile way. When third parties' rights are violated, two alternatives are offered to consumers by Article L.212 – 28 of the consumer code. They can seek for the nullity of the contract or claim that they are deprived of the possibility to exercise their property rights and invoke the "*garantie légale d'éviction*" ("legal guarantee on eviction") as per Article 1626 of the civil code.[11] In this case consumers may ask for price restitution as well as the restitution of any benefit produced by the good and expenses related to the claim. They may be compensated for the damages suffered.[12]

Nullity seems to be adequate to the context since, under Luxembourg law, the *cause* 20 of the contract (Article 1131 of the civil code) would be unlawful (*illicite* – Article 1133 of the civil code) and as such endangering to the right to property, a fundamental principle of society. In this case, nullity would be "absolute", meaning that it could be invoked by the consumer and the trader and not only by the consumer as is usually the case for nullities sanctioning a violation of a provision of the consumer code – the nullity then qualifying as "relative" being of protective essence. Instead, when the "*cause*" of an agreement is held unlawful, nullity can be invoked by all parties because the respect of public interest must be fully achieved. In this precise case, the company could indeed seek for nullity to demonstrate its willingness to stop the unlawful situation and not to violate the property right of the third party.

While there is no reason to question nullity of contracts or "pseudo-contracts" violat- 21 ing rights of third parties, since such situation can be considered as contrary to public interest order ("*ordre public*"), the choice to offer to consumers the possibility to claim for the application of Article 1626 is, in our view, highly disputable when it comes to a lack of conformity of digital services. The remedy provided by Article 1626 is based

---

[11] "*Quoique lors de la vente il n'ait été fait aucune stipulation sur la garantie, le vendeur est obligé de droit à garantir l'acquéreur de l'éviction qu'il souffre dans la totalité ou partie de l'objet vendu, ou des charges prétendues sur cet objet, et non déclarées lors de la vente.*"

[12] Article 1630 of the Luxembourg civil code: "*Lorsque la garantie a été promise, ou qu'il n'a rien été stipulé à ce sujet, si l'acquéreur est évincé, il a droit de demander contre le vendeur: 1) la restitution du prix; 2) celle des fruits, lorsqu'il est obligé de les rendre au propriétaire qui l'évince; 3) les frais faits sur la demande en garantie de l'acheteur, et ceux faits par le demandeur originaire; 4) enfin les dommages et intérêts, ainsi que les frais et loyaux coûts du contrat.*"

on the existence of a property right transferred in the frame of a sales contract. It was tailored for this type of contract. As we will see, an extensive application of the guarantee could however be admitted for the supply of digital content. But in many cases of supply of digital services, there will be no transfer of property. Let's think about the context whereby the consumer chooses a subscription plan and pays a fixed sum of money to a company, operating through a digital platform, to watch licensed videos on demand. If the company offers to consumers videos in breach of intellectual property law, this situation qualifies as a contractual lack of conformity according to the DCD. Yet, there is no sale contract between the company and the consumer, and the consumer is not deprived of a property right. Therefore, we support the view that Article L.212 – 28 only offers an alternative to consumers. The legal guarantee on eviction can only apply where a property right exists. This may not be excluded in the case of the supply of digital content where consumers have a property right that comes with the supply of the digital content. In certain contexts, invoking the legal guarantee of eviction could be strategically more adapted. NFT (standing for Non-Fungible Token) Art could be an example of such possibility. We can imagine a scenario in which an artist author of an animation claims that her/his asset has been traded by a virtual art gallery in violation of her/his property right. The author seeks for an injunction. The court holds that the piece of art should not have been sold. In this specific case, the "buyer" could claim to have been "evicted" from exercising his/her property right. He/she could ask for, beyond the restitution of the price, compensation of the damages related to the "eviction". The buyer would probably ask for the nullity of the contract, which, in this precise case, would probably be based on Article 6 of the civil code prohibiting agreements considered as deviating from public policy ("*ordre public*") and good morals[13] and/or on the unlawful cause of the contract (Article 1133 of the Civil code). The contract being void because the piece of art was traded in violation of a property right – the buyer could probably also claim damages on an extracontractual basis if he/she succeeds in demonstrating that she/he suffered a loss or a damage. Since one of the remedies provided by the legal guarantee on eviction is the compensation of the damage caused, it would strategically be more adapted to bring a lawsuit on this ground. As a matter of fact, the legal guarantee's eviction regime allows for a strict liability. This would not require the author to demonstrate the existence of a wrong and a causal link to the damage.

22 **Interruption of long-term supply of digital content or services.** No provisions regulating the interruption of long-term supply of digital content / digital services were implemented by the Luxembourg legislature in way of transposition of DCD. Subsequently, such non-performance will be handled under general contract law.

23 **Commercial guarantees.** Article L.212 – 31(2) transposes in a literal way Article 17(1) of SGD. However, Luxembourg used the option granted in Article 17(4). The latter allows Member States to establish rules on other aspects related to commercial guarantees which were not covered in that article, such as the language(s) in which the guarantee must be made available to the consumer. Article 212–31(2) provides that commercial guarantees should be written in simple and intelligible terms, in French or German, depending on the consumer's choice. Considering the choice of the consumer is somehow illusory. This would mean that the guarantee should be made available once the contract has been concluded. How can the trader in fact guess the language to be chosen by the consumer? Our practical advice to traders operating on the Luxembourg

---

[13] According to Article 6 of the Luxembourg Civil code: *"On ne peut déroger, par des conventions particulières, aux lois qui intéressent l'ordre public et les bonnes mœurs."*

market would be to propose such guarantees in the two languages. However, this certainly has an economic cost and could be an extra burden for small entrepreneurs.

D. Remedies for the Failure to Supply and Remedies for the Lack of Conformity

Obligation to notify the seller of a lack of conformity. The obligation to notify had not been introduced when the non-conformity regime established by EC Directive 99/44 was implemented in Luxembourg law. Luxembourg legislature sticked to this approach when transposing the SGD.

Non-performance of the contract by the trader. Under Luxembourg law, the consumer is entitled to withhold payment of the price, or part of it, for the contracts covered by DCD and SGD until the trader/seller has fulfilled her/his obligations. While such right is provided by Article L. 212-21(7) of the consumer code in the context of contracts for the supply of digital content and services, Article L. 212-6(6) grants this right for contracts regarding the sale of goods with or without embedded digital elements. As stated in these two Articles, the conditions for consumers to withhold payment are laid down in Articles 1134-1 and 1134-2 of the civil code. According to the former, an agreement giving rise to reciprocal obligations obliges each party to perform its obligation so that it coincides with the correlative obligation of the other party, unless otherwise intended or used. Article 1134-2 of the civil code specifies that if one party fails to perform any of its obligations, the other party may suspend performance of its obligation as the direct counterpart of that which the first party fails to perform, unless the agreement has provided for deferred performance in favour of that party. In other words, consumers are entitled to exercise the right to withhold payment provided that the latter is the direct counterpart of the obligation which the seller failed to perform. That is to say that a consumer cannot withhold payment on the grounds that the seller did not carry out the repairs to which he/she is bound, as the obligation to pay the good is counterbalanced by the seller's obligation to provide the good.[14] This requirement is well-established in the Luxembourg legal regime and has been confirmed several times in previous judgments issued by national courts.[15] However, the question arises whether it would not be possible to bring into play the exception where the unfulfilled obligation – without constituting strictly speaking the direct counterpart of that obligation – prevents the achievement of the contractual aim: for instance, is the consumer entitled to withhold payment if the seller has promised to install the good in the consumer's house and delivers the good without installing it? This would only be possible if the sale and the installation were the subject of the same contract: Article 1134-2 of the civil code seems to exclude that the exception can be brought into play between obligations arising from two distinct contracts even if they are interdependent, as also suggested by the Belgian Court of Cassation.[16] It should also be mentioned that Article 1134-2 of the civil code does not allow the consumer to withhold payment if the agreement has provided for deferred performance in favour of the seller. It would be contradictory to grant the seller a time limit to perform and then refuse to pay on the grounds that the seller has not yet fulfilled his/her obligations.[17]

---

[14] See Ancel, *Contrats et obligations conventionnelles en droit luxembourgeois* (2015), 726.

[15] Trib. Luxembourg, 3 June 2005, n° 94465, *BIJ*, 2005, p. 167; Trib. Luxembourg, 27 June 2008, n° 115138, *BIJ*, 2008, p. 131.

[16] Cass. Be., 8 September 1995, Pas. Be., 1995, I, p. 785.

[17] See Ancel, *Contrats et obligations conventionnelles en droit luxembourgeois* (2015), 727.

26 **Choice of remedy.** Luxembourg has chosen not to prioritise repair over replacement in its legal regime. Pursuant to Article L.212 – 6(2) of the consumer code, the consumer is entitled to choose between repair or replacement of the goods where there is a lack of conformity. This option, however, does not apply if the remedy chosen is impossible or if, compared to the other remedy, it would impose costs on the seller which would be disproportionate considering the following circumstances: (i) the value the goods would have had in the absence of the lack of conformity, (ii) the significance of the lack of conformity and, (iii) whether the other remedy could be chosen without significant inconvenience to the consumer. Article L.212 – 6(3) further states that the seller can refuse to bring the goods into conformity if replacement and repair are impracticable or would impose disproportionate costs on the seller, considering all the circumstances, including those referred to above. Nevertheless, a hierarchy of remedies can still be identified in the event of a lack of conformity in the national legal regime. Unlike previously, only after an attempt has been made to bring the goods into conformity by repair or replacement will it be possible to terminate the contract or reduce the price, according to Article L.212 – 6(4) of the consumer code. Two exceptions are made if (i) the lack of conformity is so serious that it justifies an immediate reduction of the price or the termination of the contract, or (ii) the seller has stated, or it is clear from the circumstances, that the seller will not bring the goods into conformity within a reasonable time or without causing significant inconvenience to the consumer. For the moment, it seems to appear that no doctrinal debate took place at the national level regarding the prioritisation of repair over replacement in order to enhance environmental sustainability.

27 **Place of delivery, repair, and replacement.** Article L.212 – 7 of the consumer code, following Article 14 of SGD, specifies the rules under which the seller must remedy a lack of conformity by repairing or replacing the goods. Articles 3(6) and 16(3) of DCD, together with Recitals 18, 56, 60 and 61, allow Member States to specify certain aspects regarding repair and replacement, such as the place where it should take place and where the obligations of a debtor must be performed. In the case of Luxembourg, the legislator has decided not to use this opportunity by implementing Article 14 of DCD into national law *ad verbum*.

28 **Costs of transport for the case of repair or replacement.** Following Article 2(14) of DCD, Article L. 212–7(1)(a) of the consumer code defines free of charge as "free of the necessary costs incurred in order to bring the goods into conformity, particularly the cost of postage, carriage, labour or materials". No additional rules were introduced, except that the consumer should not pay for the costs of transport in case of repair or replacement.

29 **Right of redress.** Such right is provided by article L.212 – 29 that does not specifically determine the person against whom the trader may pursue remedies, and the relevant actions and conditions. It states that "principles of the civil code"[18] will apply. The broad reference made to the application of "principles of the civil code" probably implies that the right of redress is enshrined in Article 1251–3 of Luxembourg civil code dealing with legal subrogation.[19] In other words, the seller held liable for an infringement of

---

[18] According to Art. L.212 – 29 : "Lorsque la responsabilité du professionnel est engagée à l'égard du consommateur du fait d'un défaut de fourniture du contenu numérique ou du service numérique ou d'un défaut de conformité résultant d'un acte ou d'une omission imputable à une personne située en amont dans la chaîne de transactions, le professionnel a le droit d'exercer un recours contre la ou les personnes responsables intervenant dans la chaîne de transactions commerciales, *selon les principes du Code civil*".

[19] It must be stressed that we could not identify any court decision rendered on this specific issue – subrogation to the consumer's rights by the seller and therefore that such interpretation does not reflect

the conformity requirements is automatically subrogated to the rights of the consumer under the condition that he/she did not know the defect in the thing.[20]

One interesting point under Luxembourg law is that while the direct liability of the producer towards the consumer is not regulated,[21] the Luxembourg legislature introduced in the consumer code a specific provision on that matter. Article L.212 - 11 states that a recourse action can be filed by the seller against successive sellers or intermediaries, and the producer of the goods according to the principles of the civil code.

E. Enhancing a Sustainable Regime of Conformity in Goods

Durability. The concept of "durability" was transposed *ad verbum* in Article L.010 - 1(13) of the Consumer code, as "the ability of the goods to maintain their required functions and performance through normal use", as was the requirement regarding this concept in Article L.212 - 4(1)(d). The Luxembourg legislature did not take the opportunity of the transposition of SGD to enhance environmental protection. The requirement of durability and repairability was not extended to other products and no national rules were identified regarding the availability of spare parts and corresponding information obligations. Coordination of the SGD provisions with those of EC Directive 2009/125 establishing a framework for the setting of eco-design requirements for energy-related products was not considered.[22] That said, Article L.212 - 32 of the Consumer code already provided that the person carrying out repairs on a good must indicate on the invoice the nature of the work, specifying, if necessary, the replaced or added elements and the duration of the work. Article L.212 - 13 further provides that a person who repairs a good or who makes improvements to it may not retain the item as a guarantee for the payment of such repairs or improvements where there is a clear disproportion between the value of the good and the amount due. The government also released a circular economy strategy in February 2021[23] aiming to establish a framework combining regulatory, financial, and information management methods and instruments to improve circular activities in a variety of key economic sectors.

Penalties sanctioning the breach of requirement by Directive 2009/125/EC establishing a framework for setting eco-design requirements for energy-using products. Directive 2009/125 was transposed by the Law of 15 December 2010,[24] amending the Law of 19 December 2008 establishing a framework for setting eco-design requirements

---

the state of art of case law. That said, Article L1251–3 Civil code has been repeatedly interpreted as offering the possibility to the *solvens* to be subrogated to the right of the *accipiens*. See Ancel, *Contrats et obligations conventionnelles en droit luxembourgeois* (2015), 985.

[20] See Sauphanor et al., *Les contrats de consommation. Règles communes* (2018), 1014.

[21] Recital 63 of SGD states that "whenever the consumer can also raise a direct claim against a person in previous links of the chain of transactions should not be regulated in this Directive, except in cases where a producer offers the consumer a commercial guarantee for the goods". Recital 12 of DCD also points in the same direction, meaning that Member States are free to regulate this matter.

[22] Directive 2009/125/EC of the European Parliament and of the Council of 21 October 2009 establishing a framework for setting eco-design requirements for energy-related products (recast) (hereafter Directive 2009/125).

[23] See Schosseler, Tock and Rasqué, 'Circular Economy Strategy Luxembourg' (February 2021) <https://gouvernement.lu/dam-assets/documents/actualites/2021/02-fevrier/08-strategie-economie-circulaire/Strategy-circular-economy-Luxembourg-022021.pdf> accessed 25 May 2022.

[24] Loi du 15 décembre 2010 établissant un cadre pour la fixation d'exigences en matière d'écoconception applicables aux produits liés à l'énergie et modifiant la loi du 19 décembre 2008 établissant un cadre pour la fixation d'exigences en matière d'écoconception applicables aux produits consommateurs d'énergie (hereafter Law of 15 December 2010).

for energy-using products.[25] Article 14 of Law of 19 December 2008, transposing Directive 2005/32[26] into national law and amended by Law of 15 December 2010, only provides for criminal sanctions in three situations. First, any person who has placed or made available on the market an energy-related product or a batch of energy-related products that he/she knows, or should have known, does not comply with the requirements of the Law should be punished with a fine of €251 to €25 000, or by imprisonment for a term of eight days to one year. Second, any person who fails to comply with the decisions taken under Article 3 of Law of 19 December 2010 regarding the placing on the market or putting into service of an energy-related product should be liable to the same penalties, with a maximum fine of €125 000. Third, a distributor who has made available on the market an energy-related product or a batch of energy-related products that does not comply with the requirements of Law of 19 December 2010 should be punished by a fine of €25 to €250. According to Article 14 *bis* introduced by the Law of 15 December 2010, the latter infringement can also lead to a so-called tax warning: an administrative fine imposed on the offender when the payment of a sum equal or less than €250 is considered a sufficient sanction.[27] There are therefore no private law sanctions as the penalties implemented according to Article 20 of Directive 2009/125 are either criminal or administrative sanctions (tax warnings).

33 **Planned obsolescence of goods.** The concept of planned obsolescence is unknown from Luxembourg law. Subsequently, no specific sanctions for planned obsolescence are provided However, there are several national provisions in the field of consumer protection that can play a role in limiting this practice, such as unfair commercial practices. One could argue for instance that this practice falls within the scope of misleading actions enshrined in Article L.122 – 2 of the consumer code. It should also be mentioned that the Luxembourg legal regime provides for a guaranty in the repair of goods as established in Articles L.212 – 12 and L.212 – 13. As already mentioned (see *infra* II), Article L.212 – 12 states that the person who repairs the good must indicate on the invoice the nature of the work carried out specifying, if necessary, the replaced or added elements, as well as the duration of the work. With respect to this work and the new parts, this person assumes the same guarantees as a seller. Article L.212 – 13 further specifies that a person who repairs a good entrusted to him/her for this purpose or who makes improvements to it may not retain the good as security for the payment of such repairs or improvements where there is a clear disproportion between the value of the good and the amount due.

---

[25] Loi du 19 décembre 2008 établissant un cadre pour la fixation d'exigences en matière d'écoconception applicables aux produits consommateurs d'énergie (hereafter Law of 19 December 2008).

[26] Directive 2005/32/EC of the European Parliament and of the Council of 6 July 2005 establishing a framework for the setting of eco-design requirements for energy-using products and amending Council Directive 92/42/EEC and Directives 96/57/EC and 2000/55/EC of the European Parliament and of the Council (hereafter Directive 2005/32).

[27] See Pitzalis, 'La sanction de l'obligation légale d'information en droit des contrats de consommation : étude du droit français et luxembourgeois' (2016) available on open access at : <http://docnum.univ-lorraine.fr/public/DDOC_T_2016_0239_PITZALIS.pdf> accessed 1 June 2022.

F. Coordination of the Transposed Regimes with other Disciplines

I. Law of Contracts and Obligations

Other remedies for non-conformity. The Luxembourg legislature did not specifically regulate the possible interaction between the remedies offered by the directives and those provided by the law of obligations. Theoretically, all remedies provided by the law of obligations could apply, unless they conflict with or are excluded by those set by the directives.[28] For example, SGD leaves room for the application of national rules not specific to consumer contracts providing for specific remedies for certain types of defects that were not apparent at the time of conclusion of the sales contract.[29] The Luxembourg legislature interpreted it as permitting consumers to choose to sue a seller for a non-apparent defect in a good on the grounds of the provisions of the civil code related to the "*garantie des vices cachés*" (Articles 161 ff.), as had already been the case when Article 8 of Directive EC 99/44 was transposed.[30] In France, where the same approach was taken, Aubert de Vincelles argued that this may not be fully in line with the spirit of the Directive and that other Members States such as Belgium, Germany, and Spain chose to apply a unique regime.[31] The argument, developed on the grounds of a restrictive reading of Article 8 of EC Directive 99/44, relies on the wording of the article that would not allow for the parallel application of other regimes covering non-conformity in sales contracts. The author's opinion was founded on the fact that the "*garantie des vices cachés*" should be treated as a remedy and not as a principle governing "contractual liability" as per the wording of Article 8. Article 3(6) SGD refers to remedies and not anymore to liability, which probably makes Aubert de Vincelles' argument non-operational. Some questions however remain open. What if consumers do not clearly refer in their claim to the legal provisions on which they ground their legal actions? Which regime should apply? The Court of Justice of the European Union held, in case C-497/13 (*Faber*),[32] that "a national court before which an action relating to a contract which may be covered by that directive has been brought, is required to determine whether the purchaser may be classified as a consumer within the meaning of that directive, even if the purchaser has not relied on that status, as soon as that court has at its disposal the matters of law and of fact that are necessary for that purpose or may have them at its disposal simply by making a request for clarification."

This consequently implies, in our opinion, that the conformity regime derived from EC Directive 99/44 must always be considered in consumer cases. The French Cour de

---

[28] See the wording of Article 3 (6) of SGD. This Directive shall not affect the freedom of Member States to regulate aspects of general contract law, such as rules on the formation, validity, nullity or effects of contracts, including the consequences of the termination of a contract, in so far as they are not regulated in this Directive, or the right to damages and Article 3 (7): "this Directive shall not affect national rules not specific to consumer contracts providing for specific remedies for certain types of defects that were not apparent at the time of conclusion of the sales contract."

[29] See Article 3 (7): "this Directive shall not affect national rules not specific to consumer contracts providing for specific remedies for certain types of defects that were not apparent at the time of conclusion of the sales contract."

[30] As per Article L.212 – 10 (1) of consumer code: "Les dispositions de la présente sous-section ne privent pas le consommateur du droit d'exercer les actions résultant des vices rédhibitoires et de la garantie des vices cachés telles qu'elles résultent des Articles 1641 à 1649 du Code civil, ou toute autre action de nature contractuelle ou extra-contractuelle qui lui est reconnue par la loi."

[31] See Sauphanor et al., *Les contrats de consommation. Règles communes* (2018), 1024.

[32] CJEU, Case C-497/13, 4 June 2015, *Froukje Faber v Autobedrijf Hazet Ochten BV*, ECLI:EU:C:2015:357, para. 48.

cassation probably acknowledged such requirement, without referring to the *Faber* case, holding in a case dated to 2020, that the two regimes can be invoked by the consumer in her/his claim.[33] There is no evidence of a similar question brought in front of a Luxembourg court. Courts seem however not to reject such possibility.[34] A different interpretation would however be difficult to justify in the light of the *Faber* case.

36   Another important issue will be that of understanding how to integrate "pseudo-contracts" in Luxembourg law. Courts are certainly used to deal with the interaction of general contract law and the legislation related to "specific contracts". With the transposition of these two directives, they will face the new challenges of regulating "pseudo-contractual relationships" and of coordinating data protection law with contract law.

37   **Enforceability of the consumer's duty to provide personal data as a counter-performance.** No specific provisions were established as to the enforceability of such duty. This question will be handled by the courts. Contract law will probably apply by analogy GDPR provisions prevailing when necessary.

38   The sensitive issue will be to decide whether specific performance will apply. Following Article 1142 of the Luxembourg civil code, such remedy is theoretically available when the "obligation" that one party failed to perform qualifies as an "*obligation de donner*" (to transfer property).[35] As "pseudo-contracts"[36] are treated like contracts as to their regime by DCD, national courts would probably follow this trend.

39   In this type of agreement, the "duty" at issue would be that of "doing something" ("*obligation de faire*"), in other words, the duty to transfer his/her personal data to the trader. In this case, the trader has the right to be compensated for the breach of (pseudo-)contract but is not offered the possibility to seek for specific performance. On a practical level, it must be stressed that this distinction, based on a literal interpretation of the provisions of the French civil code, was not implemented by French courts.[37] A consolidated case law, followed by the Luxembourg courts,[38] admitted that the breach of an "obligation to do something" could lead to specific performance.[39] This approach was further confirmed by the French reform on contract law (Article 1221 of the French civil code). It may be assumed that the Luxembourg courts would not overrule this doctrine. Besides, French law now allows for a specific performance, whatever the nature of the obligation, under the conditions that the performance is possible and does not cause a significant imbalance in the parties' interests (cost for the debtor acting in good faith and interest in having the contract performed for the creditor). Obviously, this interpretation of Luxembourg civil code will find its limits in GDPR provisions. Is it possible to force a consumer to provide personal data? Would this not lead to breach GDPR provisions if consent is the only legal basis for the processing of data? Practically speaking, data transfer is immediately performed by AI. Consequently, the question remains highly theoretical with the exception of the case in which consumers would have provided incorrect data. In this context however, consumers would always have the right, under

---

[33] Civ. 1ᵉ 1 July 2020, n° 19–11.119, see Poillot, 'Panorama de droit de la consommation' (2021) *Recueil Dalloz*, 594 (599).

[34] Cour d'appel, 5 octobre 2016, n° 42867 du rôle and Cour d'appel, 6 novembre 2019, n° CAL-2018-00218 du rôle, available on <https://justice.public.lu/fr/jurisprudence/juridictions-judiciaires.html> accessed 1 June 2022.

[35] See Ancel, *Contrats et obligations conventionnelles en droit luxembourgeois* (2015), 752.

[36] The servile transposition in Luxembourg law of the periphrasis used to describe this type of agreement leads to the conclusion that the figure at stake is not a contractual one.

[37] See Ancel, *Contrats et obligations conventionnelles en droit luxembourgeois* (2015), 753.

[38] Cour d'appel, 11 January 1984, *Pas.*, 26 (139); see Ancel, *Contrats et obligations conventionnelles en droit luxembourgeois* (2015), 756 ff.

[39] See Terré et al., *Les obligations* (2019), 1597 ff.

F. Coordination of the Transposed Regimes with other Disciplines

GDPR, to be forgotten and therefore to ask for the erasure of her/his personal data. This practically leads to a "reversibility of specific performance", making it devoid of interest. In this specific context, and in the interest of the creditor, we would therefore suggest to only allow for compensation.

"Restitution" of digital content and/or digital services. Luxembourg law imposes obligations relating to restitution on both the trader and the consumer in case of the termination of a contract. One the one hand, Article L.212 – 23(4) of the consumer code establishes that the trader must make available to the consumer, at his/her request, any content other than personal data which was provided or created by the consumer when using the digital content or digital service supplied by the trader. It further states that consumers should have the right to retrieve such digital content free of charge, without any interference from the trader, within a reasonable timeframe as well as in a commonly used and machine-readable format. On the other hand, consumers must refrain from using said digital content or digital services, and from making it available to third parties after the termination of the contract pursuant to Article L.212 – 24 of the consumer code. If digital content was provided on a tangible medium, the consumer shall return the tangible medium to the trader, at the trader's request and expense, without undue delay. If the trader requests the return of the physical medium, this request must be made within fourteen days from the date on which the trader is informed of the consumer's decision to terminate the contract.

"Restitution" where consumers provided personal data as counter-performance. This matter was not dealt with by the Luxembourg legislature. If the consumer withdraws consent for the processing of personal data and where digital content or services were provided by the trader, the question as to whether the consumer will owe payment to the trader will be dealt with by courts. It could reasonably be assumed that the trader will have to erase the data of the consumer and demonstrate evidence of such action.[40] The question will of course be that of the extent of her/his obligation to erase data in case it had been processed and traded. If data were further processed to "data brokers", depending on the context (and mainly on whom the first recipient of data is: a multinational company like Google or a small business), the consequences of data trading will differ. The trader should be required to adopt "reasonable means" (based on the technology available and the costs involved) to inform third parties about the data subject's requests (art. 17(2) GDPR).

Failure to deliver the good or supply digital content or service in the context of force majeure. There is no *verbatim* definition of force majeure in French and Luxembourg law.[41] The concept was traditionally intended by scholars as "*an unforeseeable and irresistible event which, arising out of a cause external to the debtor of an obligation or the perpetrator of harm, releases him from his obligation or exonerates him from his liability.*"[42] The Luxembourg courts, like the French courts, first interpreted the concept in a narrower manner as to its effects, imposing a condition of "externality" for the doctrine to apply. This approach was further abandoned in contract law and since a decision of the French cour de cassation, "unforeseeability" and "irresistibility" are the two criteria

40
41
42

---

[40] Unless there is another legitimate basis for the processing, different from consent (Art. 17(1)(b) of GDPR).

[41] Luxembourg civil code is a quasi-replica of French civil code. Contract law in Luxembourg has been mostly inspired by French Law. The code, as did the French one, refers to the impossibility to perform in different ways "*cause étrangère*" (Article 1147), "*force majeure et cas fortuit*", (Article 1148), "*cas fortuit ou force majeure*" (Article 1348). But the expression "force majeure" is the one commonly used and "can be treated as a synonymous of all others"; See Ancel, *Contrats et obligations conventionnelles en droit luxembourgeois* (2015), 828.

[42] See Cornu, *Vocabulaire juridique*. Association Henri Capitant (2022), verbo 'Force Majeure'.

to be met in order to excuse contractual performance, assuming that the debtor acted in good faith (Article 117 of the Civil code), and have the contract terminated.[43] Besides, the duty to compensate the damage will be set aside. French reform on contract law confirmed this approach.[44] As emphasised by Ancel, this however happens only when the "obligation" to be performed qualifies as an *"obligation de résultat"* (i.e., an obligation directed at guaranteeing the attainment of a specific result),[45] which is the case for both the delivery of the goods and the supply of digital content or digital services.

43   In sale contracts, the impossibility to perform is governed by another doctrine: the *"théorie des risques"*. This doctrine derives from the *solo consensu* principle and the immediate transfer of the good once the offer has met an acceptation. The burden of risks (e.g., to see the good destroyed) is on the buyer, who will still has to pay the price and will not be able to claim damages (*res perit debitori*).[46] Derogatory clauses are however permitted.

44   In our opinion, the most challenging aspects in the digital context will be for courts to deal with the role of intermediaries, a crucial issue since digital platforms play an extremely important role in the supply chain. For instance, if I need to retrieve results of an ADN test available on a platform not managed by the supplier of the result and cannot because the platform was hacked, will this be held as force majeure? Would such event qualify as unforeseeable and irresistible, given the many cases of hospitals having their systems hacked? There is yet no courts' decision on this issue in Luxembourg. Such scenario however plays in favour of the establishment, at the EU level, of a special liability for platforms.

45   **Change of circumstances.** It is not yet clear whether, under Luxembourg law, a change of circumstances could loosen the binding nature of contracts. For a long time, Luxembourg law followed French case law, more precisely the case law decided by courts dealing with civil law. The Canal de Craponne case[47] is world famous for its strict approach. Overruling a judgement by the cour d'appel d'Aix-en-Provence, the French Cour de cassation did not allow the adaptation of the contract terms to the change of circumstances. The case is said to have notably influenced the laws of Belgium and Luxembourg.[48] However, the only case dealing with this question decided by the Luxembourg cour de cassation appears to possibly depart from this approach[49] taking its distance from the rigid appraisal of the principle *pacta sunt servanda*. The judgement considered that under the circumstances at issue, the conditions to take into account a change of circumstances were not met. But the case was decided according to the rules on temporal applicability of the law. Therefore, there is still some uncertainty as to whether the Court would have accepted to give legal effects to the change of circumstances. Still, such possibility cannot be excluded. The answer will probably come from the legislature since Luxembourg contract law should be reformed in a near future. As a new doctrine on change of circumstances found its way into the Belgian and French civil codes[50] it is probable that this doctrine will be implemented in Luxembourg law.

---

[43] French cour de cassation, Assemblée plénière, 14 avril 2006, pourvoi n° 02.11.168; See Ancel, *Contrats et obligations conventionnelles en droit luxembourgeois* (2015), 830.
[44] Art. 1218 of the French civil code.
[45] See Ancel, *Contrats et obligations conventionnelles en droit luxembourgeois* (2015), 830.
[46] See Ancel, *Contrats et obligations conventionnelles en droit luxembourgeois* (2015), 770.
[47] Cass. civ. 18 mars 1876.
[48] Kadner Graziano, *Comparative Contract Law. Cases, Materials and Exercises* (2019), 385. Luxembourg scholars argue in this sense, see Spielmann and Dupong, 'Quelques réflexions sur la théorie de l'imprévision' in *Le bicentenaire du Code civil : une contribution luxembourgeoise* (2008), 150.
[49] Cass. 24 October 2013, n° 64/13, *Pas.* 36, (393).
[50] Art. 5.77 of the Belgian Civil code and 1195 of the French Civil code.

F. Coordination of the Transposed Regimes with other Disciplines

Transfer of rights against the initial seller from the initial consumer to a subsequent buyer. Luxembourg courts follow an established doctrine in French case law allowing for the transferability of rights against different actors in the chain of transactions on the doctrinal grounds of *action directe*. In a decision of the French cour de cassation dating from 1820, the final buyer of a good was allowed to file a warranty claim for latent defects and ask compensation for damages against a previous seller. The scope of this direct claim has been broadly extended to a variety of contexts.[51] Non-conformity in B2C sales contracts is certainly one of them.[52] Luxembourg and Belgian courts implemented such doctrine in their case law. More specifically, a decision of the Luxembourg Court of Appeal acknowledged that the warranty provided by Articles 1641 ff. of the civil code ("*vice cachés*") was transferred to subsequent buyers. The Court of Appeal, following the French cour de cassation's doctrine, justified the "*action directe*" with the accessory character of the rights flowing from the defects in the goods.[53] As observed, in this case the liability is "an obligation *propter rem* i.e., an obligation that runs with the product sold."[54] The consequence of such reasoning is that the initial seller can oppose to any subsequent buyer all terms agreed upon in the initial contract. This has a limited effect for subsequent buyers since the initial contract is a B2C contract as exemption clauses regarding non-conformity are prohibited, jurisdiction and arbitration agreements can be challenged, if unfair, on the grounds of unfair terms' legislation.

46

II. Intellectual Property Law

Right to resell digital content. As per Article L.212 – 12(9), the application of the transposed provisions of Article 3(9) of the directive are "without prejudice to Union and Luxembourg law on copyright and related rights, including the Act of 18 April 2001 on copyright, related rights and databases transposing Directive 2001/29/EC of the European Parliament and of the Council." Here again, the transposition of DCD was made in a servile way. No specific provisions coordinating the new conformity regime introduced in the consumer code with the law on copyright and related rights were adopted. The process of full integration into the legal system of the new legislation will once more be left to the judiciary.

47

National law is however framed by the EU acquis and its interpretation by the Court of Justice. On the question of whether there is a right to re-distribute digital content, Oprysk observed that "Article 10 (DCD) presupposes that it is a task for a trader to obtain a licence honouring reasonable consumer expectations from the right holder, potentially granting broader user freedoms than those guaranteed under copyright."[55] She however also stressed that "the reasonable consumer expectations on which the DCD relies are difficult to define in practice. (…) Just recently, the CJEU denied the

48

---

[51] In this specific case an "action en garantie des vices cachés". On the French doctrine of "action directe", see Cannarsa and Moréteau, "The French "Action Directe": The Justification for Going Beyond Privity' in Eberds, Janssen and Meyer (eds), *European Perspectives on Producers' Liability: Direct Producers' Liability for Non-conformity and the Sellers' Right of Redress* (Otto Schmidt/De Gruyter European law publishers, Cologne 2009), 311.

[52] See Seubé, 'Conformité' in Fenouillet (ed.), *Droit de la consommation 2021–2022. Droit interne et européen* (Dalloz Action, Paris 2020), 527.

[53] Court of Appeal, 12 July 1996, *Pas.* 30 (129) and 27 October 1999, *Pas.* 31 (185).

[54] Beale et al., *Cases, Material and Text on Contract Law* (2019), 1330.

[55] See Oprysk, 'Digital Consumer Contract Law without Prejudice to Copyright: EU Digital Content Directive, reasonable Consumer Expectations and Competition' (2021) 70 *GRUR International,* 943 (956).

application of the exhaustion principle to digital copies in the *Tom Kabinet* case,[56] eliminating one of the most powerful tools under copyright, yet the court did not clarify the reasonableness of the consumer expectation to transfer their content."[57] The judgement concerns e-books and its scope of impact is probably to be limited to such content. For the rest, Luxembourg law is aligned with EU law. The Law of 18 April 2001 on copyrights, related rights and databases[58] transposing Directive 2001/29/EC of the European Parliament and of the Council of 22 May 2001 on the harmonisation of certain aspects of copyright and related rights in the information society introduced the principle that the first sale in the Community of the original of a work or copies thereof by the right holder or with his consent exhausts the right to control resale of that object in the Community.

III. Law of Communications

49 **Early termination of Number-Independent Interpersonal Communication Services (NI-ICS).** The general legal framework for NI-ICS Luxembourg is the act transposing Directive (EU) 2018/1972 of the European Parliament and of the Council of 11 December 2018 establishing the European Electronic Communications Code.[59] This act is a servile transposition of the Directive and does not regulate the termination of NI-ICS services. Consequently, there is no specific regulation of such services under Luxembourg law.

50 **Bundles.** Such contracts are also regulated by Article 107(2) of the European Electronic Code. There was therefore a need for coordination of the two provisions. Luxembourg coordinated its provisions with those of Article 3(6) subpara 3 DCD by excluding bundles from the scope of application of principles that apply when the digital content or the digital service is modified in the context of a contract, providing that the digital content or digital service is to be supplied or made accessible to the consumer over a period of time (see supra III. § 6).

IV. Data Protection

51 **Consequences of the trader's non-compliance with the GDPR regarding contracts for the supply of digital content or services.** There is no specific regulation of this situation under Luxembourg law. In this case, non-compliance could certainly be regarded as a lack of conformity on the grounds of Article 8(1)(a) DCD[60] transposed *ad verbum* in Article L.212 – 16 (1) (a). However, such infringement should also be treated

---

[56] CJEU, Case C-263/18, 19 December 2019, *Nederlands Uitgeversverbond and Groep Algemene Uitgevers v Tom Kabinet Internet BV and Others*, ECLI:EU:C:2019:1111.

[57] See Oprysk, 'Digital Consumer Contract Law without Prejudice to Copyright: EU Digital Content Directive, reasonable Consumer Expectations and Competition' (2021) 70 *GRUR International*, 943 (956).

[58] Loi du 18 avril 2001 sur les droits d'auteur, les droits voisins et les bases de données.

[59] Loi du 17 décembre 2021 portant transposition de la directive (UE) 2018/1972 du Parlement européen et du Conseil du 11 décembre 2018 établissant le code des communications électroniques européen et portant modification de la loi modifiée du 30 mai 2005 portant : 1) organisation de l'Institut Luxembourgeois de Régulation; 2) modification de la loi modifiée du 22 juin 1963 fixant le régime des traitements des fonctionnaires de l'État.

[60] The good must "be fit for the purposes for which digital content or digital services of the same type would normally be used, taking into account, where applicable, any existing Union and national law, technical standards or, in the absence of such technical standards, applicable sector-specific industry codes of conduct ...".

F. Coordination of the Transposed Regimes with other Disciplines

as a violation of the GDPR provisions and sanctioned according to Article 83 of the Act establishing the Data Protection authority (*Commission Nationale de protection des Données*).[61] The sanction would probably be the nullity of the agreement. Depending on the context, the possibility of applying the non-conformity regime could be excluded because the agreement would be void for public interest reasons. Two situations need to be considered: (1) that of the infringement of a contract and (2) that of the infringement of a "pseudo-contract". In this specific case, since the consumer's counter-performance will be materialised by the supply of personal data, the existence of the "pseudo-contract" may be questioned.

(1) In this situation non-compliance has no impact on the contract validity and can be interpreted as a lack of conformity and treated as such. Besides, sanctions provided by Article 83 of the GDPR will apply.

(2) When the counter-performance of the consumer consists in providing personal data to the trader, the non-compliance with GDPR provisions, more specifically with its Article 7 – in this context the processing of data is based on consent – would lead to the application of general contract law. The effect of the lack of consent would be the illegality of the contract. This results from a combined application of the provisions of GDPR and EU Directive 2011/83.

Most "pseudo-contracts" are concluded remotely. Thus, and as per Article 4 (2)(b) of EU Directive 2019/2161 amending EU Directive 2011/83, they fall under the scope of application of the latter. Consequently, the information to be disclosed to the consumer shall be made "available in a way appropriate to the means of distance communication" (Article 8 of the EU 2011/83 Directive). When contracts are concluded online, this means that the information will be disclosed in a written manner. In this context, the offer should be presented in a way that clearly distinguishes the general terms and conditions of the agreement from the consent to be given for having the personal data processed (Article 7 GDPR). Should it not be the case, and according to Article 7 of the GDPR, "any part of such a declaration which constitutes an infringement of this Regulation shall not be binding". This would probably lead to the "nullity" of the agreement considered as deviating from public policy (*"ordre public"*) and good morals (Article 6 of the civil code) and as having an "unlawful cause" (Article 1133 of the civil code). By excluding the contractual nature of agreements based on the provision of data as counter-performance by the consumer,[62] the Luxembourg legislature – implicitly – acknowledged the view of the European Data Protection Supervisor on the non-commodification of personal data and the importance of protecting them as fundamental rights.[63] The emphasis put on the necessity to protect data as a fundamental right and

---

[61] As per Article 48 of the Loi du 1 août 2018 portant organisation de la Commission nationale pour la protection des données et mise en œuvre du règlement (UE) 2016/679 du Parlement européen et du Conseil du 27 avril 2016 relatif à la protection des personnes physiques à l'égard du traitement des données à caractère personnel et à la libre circulation de ces données, et abrogeant la directive 95/46/CE (règlement général sur la protection des données), portant modification du Code du travail et de la loi modifiée du 25 mars 2015 fixant le régime des traitements et les conditions et modalités d'avancements des fonctionnaires de l'Etat (hereafter Law of 1 August 2018).

[62] "Where the trader supplies or undertakes to supply digital content or a digital service to the consumer, and the consumer provides or undertakes to provide personal data to the trader, except where the personal data provided by the consumer are exclusively processed by the trader for the purpose of supplying the digital content or digital service in accordance with this sub-section or for allowing the trader to comply with legal requirements to which the trader is subject, and the trader does not process those data for any other purpose."

[63] European Data Protection Supervisor, *Opinion 4/2017 on the Proposal for a Directive on certain aspects concerning contracts for the supply of digital content*, 14 March 2017. Available at: <https://edps.europa.eu/sites/default/files/publication/17-03-14_opinion_digital_content_en.pdf> Accessed 1 June 2022.

to not – only – reduce them to simple consumer interests would, as a matter of fact, bring, under Luxembourg law, the question of the infringement of "*ordre public*". The contractual regime would of course apply by analogy, following the trend of the DCD. Given the public-interest-based nature of the sanction, the nullity would be of "absolute nature", meaning that it could be invoked by the two parties and raised on its own motion by a court.[64]

55   **Right of withdrawal/termination in the context of a relationship based on the supplying of personal data by the consumer.** The provision of personal of data by consumers as a counter-performance does not lead to a contractual relation. However, such "pseudo-contractual" situation is treated as a contract. Concretely speaking, the withdrawal of consent for processing data would lead to the "termination of the relationship" based on this processing. Article L.212 – 22 of the consumer code, transposes *ad verbum* Article 15 of DCD. Comparably to the principle already enshrined in Article L.221 – 3 of the consumer code, its provisions entitle the consumer to withdraw in writing or orally, depending on the type of "contract". It is to be noted that no specific rules were introduced regarding the consequences of the withdrawal of consent for processing personal data. Article L.212 – 12 of the consumer code is a servile transposition of Article 3 DCD. Following this approach, it is highly probable that in this case, the Luxembourg courts will apply general contract law and ask for restitution.[65]

V. Geo-Blocking Regulation

56   **Repairing or replacing goods delivered in accordance with the Geo-Blocking Regulation.** While this specific matter does not seem to be regulated by the Luxembourg legislature, it should however be mentioned that Article L.212 – 6(3) of the consumer code allows the seller to refuse to bring the good into conformity if repair and replacement are impossible or would impose costs on the seller that would be disproportionate taking into account all the circumstances, including the value that the goods would have if there were no lack of conformity and the significance of the lack of conformity. Provided that these requirements are met, this would therefore imply that the seller is no longer under the obligation to repair or replace the good. Nevertheless, the consumer would be entitled to either a proportional reduction in price or to terminate the contract pursuant to Article L.212 – 6(4).

G. Time Limits

57   **General framework.** Not surprisingly, the Luxembourg legislature mostly stuck to the provisions of DCD and SGD, transposing their content in a servile way. The intro-

---

In this opinion, the EDPS stated that "fundamental rights such as the right to the protection of personal data cannot be reduced to simple consumer interests, and personal data cannot be considered as a mere commodity."

[64] Article 61 of the Nouveau Code de Procédure Civile. Luxembourg Courts seems to rather go for a faculty and not an obligation to raise legal arguments on their own motion. See Bolard, 'La Cour de cassation consacre l'obligation de requalifier. A propos de l'arrêt de la Cour de cassation du 10 mars 2011' (2012) *Journal des Tribunaux Luxembourg*, 8 (23). That said, such context would probably materialise if the trader were to be imposed a fine by the Commission Nationale de Protection des Données and the case be brought in front of an administrative court where no case law regarding such issue could be identified.

[65] On the consequences of restitution see *supra,* Section VI.(a).

G. Time Limits

duction of longer time limits than those referred to and suggested by the directive was not favoured.

Time limits for the sale of goods. The period of the liability of the seller is the same as that imposed by SGD. If the goods include continuously supplied digital elements, following the Directive, Article L.212 – 5(2) of the consumer code also draws distinction depending on the duration of the contract. Article L.212 – 5(4) of the consumer code deals with the rules concerning the presumption regarding the existence of the defect in the good and reproduces in a servile manner the provisions of the directive.

Time limits for the supply of digital content or digital services. The time limits regarding the liability of service providers for the content or the service supplied do not deviate from those stated (and proposed) by the directive (Article L.212 – 18 (1) and Article L.212 – 18 (2), if the delivery is continuous.

Article L.212 – 19 of the consumer code transposed *ad verbum* the provisions of Article 12 DCD regarding the presumption regarding the non-conformity in the content or of the service, of the consumer code.

Second-hand goods. The Luxembourg legislature took the opportunity offered by the directive (Art. 10 SGD) to provide for a shorter period of time – a one-year-period – regarding the liability of the seller for second-hand goods (Article L.212 – 5(3) of the consumer code).

Specific rules on prescription. The specific rules on prescription existing under the law transposing Directive 99/44/EC have been maintained.[66] The action of the consumer against the seller can be time-barred ("*déchue*"). The forfeiture delay is of two years, starting from the notification to the seller of the lack of conformity. One derogation is however considered: the situation in which the consumer would have been barred from bringing her/his action due to a fraudulent behaviour of the trader. The rule applies to contracts of sale of goods (Article L.212 – 9 consumer code) and for the supply of digital content and services (Article L.212 – 27). The two-year delay is the minimum tolerated by the two directives. By adopting such delay, the Luxembourg legislature did not rule in favour of the consumer. In our opinion, a two-year delay is not adapted to the weak bargaining position of the consumer vis-à-vis the trader. Neither is it adapted to its "procedural weakness" due to the complexity of procedural rules.

For the Luxembourg legislature, the justification for such regime certainly lays in the current regime of prescription that can be perceived as unfair to the trader. Luxembourg law on prescription is "outdated" with regard to the legislation of its neighbours.[67] Article 2262 of the civil code refers to a delay of thirty years for "*actions personnelles*" i.e., actions related to a contract. If it is not disputable that such delay is far too long, a compromise could have been adopted, especially considering the existing derogatory regimes. Article 2277 of the civil code for example, provides a prescription delay of five years for the payment of a specific rent. Such delay, which is also today the delay of prescription of actions for a dispute regarding a contract in France,[68] seems to be reasonable and sufficiently protective of the interests of both traders and consumers.

---

[66] Loi du 21/4/2004 relative à la garantie de conformité due par le vendeur de biens meubles corporels portant transposition de la Directive 1999/44/CE sur certains aspects de la vente et des garanties des biens de consommation et modifiant la loi modifiée du 25/8/1983 relative à la protection juridique du consommateur; further integrated in the consumer code (see more specifically Article L.212 – 6 of the consumer code before the Law of 8 December 2021).

[67] For a comparative overview, see the Report of the French Senate drafted in view of the reform of the law of prescription in France available at <https://www.senat.fr/rap/r06-338/r06-33831.html> accessed 4 June 2022.

[68] Art. 2224 of the French civil code.

64 **Interruption of the limitation period.** Articles L.212 – 9 and L.212 – 27 consumer code have maintained the existing provisions on the interruption of the limitation period.

65 First, the two-year forfeiture delay is interrupted by any negotiation (*pourparlers*) related to the conformity problem brought to the attention of the trader. The concept of negotiations is rather broad. There is no case law on this issue. As the term "negotiations" implies a discussion, we tend to believe that judges would not consider that the notification of the lack of conformity by the consumer would interrupt the delay. This situation is rather unsatisfactory since, as already observed, traders are not always very reactive when consumers invoke a lack of conformity. Another risk would be that of a too restrictive interpretation of the concept. Negotiations could also be understood as a discussion leading to a compromise and not a mere exchange of views. What if, besides, the discussion was only conducted in an oral manner? How would the consumer prove it?

66 Second, the delay is interrupted by an interim action, or an action brought in front of a court on the grounds of the presumed lack of conformity.

67 Eventually, it is to be noted that both Articles L.212 – 9 and L.212 – 27 consumer code provide that a new forfeiture delay of one year will run starting from the notification to the consumer by the trader that he/she breaks off the negotiations. This new delay also runs when the consumer has been informed of the closing of the judiciary investigations on the case (*"clôture de l'instruction"*).

Bibliography

Articles

Élise Poillot, 'Le Code luxembourgeois de la consommation : étude de droit interne et comparé' (2013) *Journal des Tribunaux Luxembourg*, 1.

Élise Poillot, 'Codification of French and Luxembourg Consumer Law: are French and Luxembourg Consumer Codes going the Same Road?' (2018) 17 *RBDCivil*, 125.

Élise Poillot, 'Panorama de droit de la consommation 2020' (2021) *Recueil Dalloz*, 594.

Liliia Oprysk, 'Digital Consumer Contract Law without Prejudice to Copyright: EU Digital Content Directive, reasonable Consumer Expectations and Competition' (2021) 70 *GRUR International*, 943.

Vincent Bolard, 'La Cour de cassation consacre l'obligation de requalifier. A propos de l'arrêt de la Cour de cassation du 10 mars 2011,' (2012) *Journal des Tribunaux Luxembourg*, 8.

Books

Élise Poillot, *Droit européen de la consommation et uniformisation du droit des contrats*. (LDGJ, Paris 2006).

François Terré, Philippe Simler, Yves Lequette and François Chénédé, *Les obligations* (12th edn, Dalloz, Paris 2019).

Gérard Cornu, *Vocabulaire juridique : Association Henri Capitant* (14th edn, Presses Universitaires de France, Paris 2022).

Hugh Beale, Bénédicte Fauvarque-Cosson, Jacobien Rutgers and Stefan Vogenauer, *Cases, Material and Text on Contract Law* (3rd edn, Hart, Oxford, London, New York, New Delhi, Sydney 2019).

Bibliography

Natacha Sauphanor, Carole Aubert de Vincelles, Geoffray Brunaux, Laurence Usunier, *Les contrats de consommation. Règles communes,* (2nd edn, LGDJ, Paris 2018).

Pascel Ancel, *Contrats et obligations conventionnelles en droit luxembourgeois* (1st edn, Larcier, Brussels 2015).

Thomas Kadner Graziano, *Comparative Contract Law. Cases, Materials and Exercises*, (2nd edn, Edward Elgar Publishing, Cheltenham/Northampton 2019)

Contributions in Books

Dean Spielmann and Henri Dupong, 'Quelques réflexions sur la théorie de l'imprévision' *in Le bicentenaire du Code civil : une contribution luxembourgeoise* (Portalis, Luxembourg 2008), 150.

Élise Poillot, 'Les codes de l'intégration du droit de la consommation dans le système juridique. Regards franco-allemands' in *Mélanges en l'honneur du Professeur Claude Witz* (LexisNexis, New York 2018), 671.

Jean-Baptiste Seube, 'Conformité' in Dominique Fenouillet (ed), *Droit de la consommation 2021-2022. Droit interne et européen* (Dalloz Action, Paris 2020), 527.

Michel Cannarsa and Olivier Moréteau, 'The French "Action Directe": The Justification for Going beyond Privity' in Martin Ebers, André Janssen and Olaf Meyer (eds), *European Perspective on Producers' Liability: Direct Producers' Liability for Non-Conformity anf the Sellers' Right of Redress* (Otto Schmidt/De Gruyter European law publishers, Cologne 2009), 311.

Online Sources

Ministère de la Justice, 'Assises du Code civil : Quelles réformes pour moderniser le Code civil' (Press Release 15 October 2021) <https://gouvernement.lu/fr/actualites/toutes_actualites/communiques/2021/10-octobre/15-assises-code-civil.html> accessed 1 June 2022.

Paul Schosseler, Christian Tock and Paul Rasqué, 'Circular Economy Strategy Luxembourg' (February 2021) <https://gouvernement.lu/dam-assets/documents/actualites/2021/02-fevrier/08-strategie-economie-circulaire/Strategy-circular-economy-Luxembourg-022021.pdf> accessed 25 May 2022.

Thesis

Cécile Pitzalis, 'La sanction de l'obligation l'égale d'information en droit des contrats de consommation. Étude de droit français et luxembourgeois' (2016) <http://docnum.univ-lorraine.fr/public/DDOC_T_2016_0239_PITZALIS.pdf> accessed 1 June 2022.

Malta*

A. Introduction. General Framework 1
   I. The Maltese Legal System: A Very Brief Overview 1
   II. A Very Brief History of Consumer Law in Malta 3
   III. Civil, Commercial and Consumer Protection Law 7

B. The Civil Law of Obligations 12
   I. The Contract of Sale 17
      1. Where the thing sold is not of 'quality promised' 21
      2. Warranty in respect of Latent Defects of the Thing Sold 24

C. Transposition of the DCD and the SGD 29
   I. Definitions and scope of application 30
   II. Conformity of goods 34
      1. Subjective and objective requirements for conformity 34
      2. "Durability" and Environmental Sustainability 36
      3. Incorrect Installation of Digital Content or Digital Service 39
      4. Third party rights 41
   III. Liability of the Trader 45
   IV. Remedies for the failure to supply and remedies for the lack of conformity .. 54
   V. Commercial Guarantees 61
   VI. Time Limits 69
   VII. Right of Redress 77
   VIII. Conclusion 79
      Bibliography 79

A. Introduction. General Framework

I. The Maltese Legal System: A Very Brief Overview

The Maltese legal system is a mixed legal system.[1] The main sources of the general principles of Maltese Law are the civil law for private law and the common law for public law. As Aquilina observes, 'it is primarily the civil law and the common law legal traditions which have made up the Maltese mixed legal system.'[2] However, Maltese law is also influenced by international law and, more recently, European Union law. Generally, public law prevails on private law in so far as human rights and fundamental freedoms are concerned,[3] while European Union law also prevails on Maltese ordinary primary (and subsidiary) law.[4]

1

---

* I would like to thank Ms Odette Vella and others at the Malta Competition and Consumer Affairs Authority for helpful exchanges.

[1] For an in-depth analysis, see Aquilina, K. (2013) 'The nature and sources of the Maltese mixed legal system: strange case of Dr. Jekyll and Mr. Hyde?' *Comparative Law Review*, 4(1), 1–38.

[2] Ibid. p.1.

[3] See the Constitution of Malta, Article 6: '... if any other law is inconsistent with this Constitution, this Constitution shall prevail and the other law shall, to the extent of the inconsistency, be void.'; cf. also Article 65(1): 'Subject to the provisions of this Constitution, Parliament may make laws for the peace, order and good government of Malta in conformity with full respect for human rights, generally accepted principles of international law and Malta's international and regional obligations in particular those assumed by the treaty of accession to the European Union signed in Athens on the 16 April, 2003'; and the European Convention Act, Cap. 319 of the Laws of Malta, Article 3(2): 'Where any ordinary law is inconsistent with the Human Rights and Fundamental Freedoms, the said Human Rights and Fundamental Freedoms shall prevail, and such ordinary law, shall, to the extent of the inconsistency, be void.'

[4] See the European Union Act, Cap. 460 of the Laws of Malta, Article 3(2): 'Any provision of any law which from the said date [of accession to the European Union] is incompatible with Malta's obligations under the Treaty or which derogates from any right given to any person by or under the Treaty shall to

2   Historically in Malta, during the time of the Knights of St. John and in the early period of British rule, legislative drafting was characterised by the promulgation of Codes of law. As a result of the British influence, over time this style of legislative drafting common in the civil law tradition was abandoned in favour of British style statutory law-making, consisting of Acts of Parliament regulating specific subject-matters. In fact, no Codes of law have been enacted since Malta obtained its independence from the British in 1964; the drafting style became inspired by English Law, a situation that prevails. Consumer protection law in Malta fits within this general pattern: it is enacted not as part of the Civil Code, but in British legislative drafting style as a separate and distinct law. As time goes by, Maltese law is becoming more autochthonous in nature, and following Union accession in 2004 is being increasingly influenced by international and especially European Union law.

II. A Very Brief History of Consumer Law in Malta

3   Consumer Protection Law in Malta has a relatively short history. It developed significantly as a direct result of Malta's EU accession programme and requirements.[5] However, Malta did not wait and borrow the entire Community Consumer law policy off the shelf and include it lock stock and barrel in Maltese law. A strategy for a comprehensive domestic consumer law programme had been launched in 1991,[6] years before and independently of the screening and negotiation stages of accession.[7] Nevertheless, in the consumer law field, in those years leading up to membership, Malta as a candidate country was pushed to introduce significant new laws in favour of consumers.

4   A new Consumer Affairs Act[8] was enacted in 1994 and brought into force in January 1996. Fabri explains that 'The Consumer Affairs Act, a product and the principal accomplishment of a process begun in 1990, marked a conceptual and legislative turning point. It later absorbed various Community Directives and greatly benefitted from the alignment programme.'[9] It is as a result inspired by various laws: certain definitions such as those of 'consumer' and 'trader' are based on European Union law, whilst other aspects of the Act are diversely inspired.[10]

---

the extent that such law is incompatible with such obligations or to the extent that it derogates from such rights be without effect and unenforceable.'

[5] Malta's formal application to join the European Community was submitted in July 1990. Formal accession negotiations started in 2000 and were completed by the end of 2002. At the time the question of EU membership was a hot political issue in Malta, which was only settled following a referendum held on 8 March 2003, followed by a general election on 12 April 2003, which paved the way for EU membership. Following the signature of the Treaty of Accession in April 2003, Malta joined the EU a year later, on 1st May 2004.

[6] Department of Information, *Rights for the Consumer* (White Paper, 1991). A second White Paper followed in 1993: Department of Information, *Fair Trading...the next step forward. Proposals for Legislative Reforms* (White Paper, 1993).

[7] For an account of the transposition of the EU consumer legislative *aquis* within the context of the evolution of Maltese consumer law and policy and of Maltese party politics, see Fabri D. (2015) From application to accession: the interplay between the EC Consumer Directives and selected areas of national consumer law and policy – a case study from Malta (1990–2004), PhD thesis (Faculty of Laws, University of Malta). Note that, save for this doctoral thesis, a complete coherent history of consumer law in Malta has not been written and no textbook on Maltese consumer law is yet available.

[8] Cap. 378 of the Laws of Malta.

[9] Fabri (2015), p.19.

[10] For a full account see Micallef P. E. (2008) 'The Impact of the European Union on Consumer Policy in Malta: A Mixed Blessing?', *The Yearbook of Consumer Law* 2009, 109–146.

Act XXVI of 2000 introduced EU consumer Directives to the Maltese legal system. Fabri reports that

> 'With very few exceptions, the method and the style of the transpositions were very faithful to the respective Directives. This approach served to assure the Commission enlargement experts and accelerated the completion of the accession procedures. This largely verbatim approach frequently adopted was unfortunate but probably inevitable in the circumstances of haste that conditioned the transposition exercise.'[11]

The Consumer Affairs Act of 1994, as amended in 2000,[12] included *inter alia* Part VIII, 'Sale of Good to Consumers', Articles 72 – 92, which (previously) transposed Directive 1999/44/EC on certain aspects of the sale of consumer goods and associated guarantees. Prior to these amendments the sale of goods to consumers was regulated in accordance with the general rules on sale found in the Civil Code. The Consumer Affairs (Amendment) Act 2022[13] further amended the said Act with the declared purpose being 'to implement the provisions of Directive (EU) 2019/771 of the European Parliament and of the Council of 20 May 2019 on certain aspects concerning contracts for the sale of goods, amending Regulation (EU) 2017/2394 and Directive 2009/22/EC, and repealing Directive 1999/44/EC (Text with EEA relevance) and the provisions of [Part X 'Sale of goods to consumers'] shall be applied and interpreted accordingly.'[14]

III. Civil, Commercial and Consumer Protection Law

Both the Civil and the Commercial Codes have remained unaffected by the introduction of consumer protection laws, and in particular the Consumer Affairs Act. The latter have been introduced in a silo and have not affected changes to the Codes. On their part, the Codes do not acknowledge, and therefore do not build upon, the various significant consumer rights introduced as a result of Malta's commitments to transpose the EU Consumer Protection law acquis. Therefore, consumer protection in Maltese law has been achieved through special legislation, in particular the Consumer Affairs Act and subsidiary legislation passed thereunder. Neither the Civil, nor the Commercial Code makes reference to consumers or consumer transactions, with some minimal exceptions.[15]

One may debate whether consumer law should be incorporated within a Civil Code or in a separate Consumer Code on the Italian and French models. Hondius expresses his preference for the former option as it 'keeps an important part of civil law in the Civil Code', thereby giving consumer law a sense of 'permanence', adding that: 'since consumer contracts have to do with everyday relations between citizens, a Civil Code

---

[11] Fabri (2015), p.168.
[12] Consumer Affairs (Amendment) Act, 2000, Act XXVI of 2000 <https://legislation.mt/eli/act/2000/26/eng/pdf> accessed 4 May 2022.
[13] Consumer Affairs (Amendment) Act, 2022, Act I of 2022, enacted 14 January 2022, in force 1 January 2022 <https://legislation.mt/eli/act/2022/1/eng> accessed 4 May 2022.
[14] Consumer Affairs Act, Article 93B.
[15] In the Civil Code, Article 2125 (e) concerning the suspension of prescription in cases where a consumer who has a dispute with a trader, has recourse to an ADR procedure in accordance with the Consumer Affairs Act. In the Commercial Code, Article 26B concerning the inapplicability of the provisions of the Commercial Code on late payments made as remuneration for commercial transactions, which do not regulate transactions between consumers; Article 32A concerning permitted comparative advertising.

seems the natural place to regulate it.'[16] Nevertheless, as Fabri notes, in Malta 'the Civil Code played no part at all in the implementation of important Community rules which directly affect and alter the provisions on contract, sale and responsibility for defective products.'[17]

9   In Maltese legislation there is a hierarchy of norms: the Civil Code lays down the general law, while the Commercial Code may be considered a special law which specifies the provisions of the Civil Code. This is evidenced in Article 3 of the Commercial Code which provides that "In commercial matters, the commercial law shall apply: Provided that where no provision is made in such law, the usages of trade or, in the absence of such usages, the civil law shall apply."

10 For its part, Consumer Protection law is considered a subset of Commercial law, and hence a further specification of the legal provisions on commercial obligations. Thus, in Malta Consumer law operates as a *lex specialis* or overriding law over the Civil and Commercial Codes. This is evidenced in Article 47B of the Consumer Affairs Act which provides that the provisions of Part VII of the Act on Unfair contract terms 'shall prevail over anything to the contrary contained in the Civil Code and the Commercial Code.' Moreover, with regard to 'unfair commercial practices and illicit schemes' (Part VIII of the Consumer Affairs Act) it is provided in Article 55 that the provisions in that Part 'shall prevail over anything to the contrary contained in the Commercial Code.'

11 Article 92 of the Consumer Affairs Act provides that the provisions of the Part of the Act on 'Sale of goods to consumers', that is those provisions which transpose to Maltese law the Sale of Goods Directive, 'where they are more favourable to the consumer, shall prevail over the provisions of any other law.' Therefore, the rights arising under the Consumer Affairs Act operate in addition to the rights under the Civil Code and prevail to the extent that they are more favourable to the consumer.

B. The Civil Law of Obligations

12 Article 959 of the Civil Code[18] provides that obligations which are not created by the mere operation of law, arise from contracts, quasi-contracts, torts, or quasi-torts. The following provision, Article 960, defines a contract as 'an agreement or an accord between two or more persons by which an obligation is created, regulated, or dissolved.'

13 Furthermore, Civil Code, Article 966 lays down the conditions deemed essential to the validity of a contract. These are:

(a) the capacity of the parties to contract;
(b) the consent of the party who binds himself;
(c) a certain thing which constitutes the subject-matter of the contract;
(d) a lawful consideration.

The consent of the party who binds him or herself may be vitiated by error, violence or fraud; according to Article 974 of the Civil Code, 'Where consent has been given by error, or extorted by violence or procured by fraud, it shall not be valid.'

14 As regards the 'Subject-matter of contracts', Article 982 of the Civil Code provides that every contract has for its subject-matter 'a thing which one of the contracting

---

[16] Ewoud Hondius, The Notion of Consumer: European Union versus Member States (2006) 28(1):89 Sydney Law Review <http://classic.austlii.edu.au/au/journals/SydLawRw/2006/5.html> accessed 4 May 2022, pp 97–98.
[17] Fabri (2015), p.156.
[18] Title IV, 'Of Obligations in General'.

parties binds himself to give, or to do, or not to do.' Furthermore, only things that are not *extra commercium*[19] can be the subject of an agreement. This provision could be interpreted broadly to include digital content and services, but certainly does not explicitly contemplate them.

Under Article 987 of the Civil Code, 'an obligation without a consideration, or founded on a false or an unlawful consideration, shall have no effect.' Furthermore Article 988 provides that nevertheless the agreement is valid 'if it is made to appear that such agreement was founded on a sufficient consideration, even though such consideration was not stated.' In onerous contracts *causa* is the consideration in view of which the parties bind themselves.[20] This begs the question as to whether personal data can be a 'lawful consideration' under Maltese law. This author posits that both a textual as well as a teleological interpretation of the law would lead to the conclusion that 'a lawful consideration' may encompass personal data. This has however not yet been the subject of any court judgement in Malta.

Contracts that are legally entered into have the force of law between the parties and may only be revoked by mutual consent of the parties, or on grounds allowed by law.[21] Moreover, contracts must be carried out in good faith and are binding not only with regard to their terms and conditions, but also 'in regard to any consequence which, by equity, custom, or law, is incidental to the obligation, according to its nature.'[22]

I. The Contract of Sale

The Civil Code provides a definition of a contract of sale, as follows: 'A sale is a contract whereby one of the contracting parties binds himself to transfer to the other a *thing* for a *price* which the latter binds himself to pay to the former.'[23] (my emphasis). Immediately one notices that under our Civil Code a contract of sale does not also cover a contract of services. However, a 'thing' can be corporeal (goods) or incorporeal.[24] In this author's opinion 'incorporeal things' could legitimately be interpreted to encompass digital content, although of course it was not originally intended to do so.

The Civil Code further provides that the price 'must be in money'. Nevertheless, the contract does not cease to be a contract of sale if, *in addition to the sum of money agreed upon*, the buyer binds himself to give something in kind by way of a supplement to the price."[25] [author's emphasis.] Our Civil law of sale does not contemplate other forms of counter-performance.

However one should also note the provisions of the Civil Code on exchange[26] whereby 'the parties mutually bind themselves to give to one another a thing, not being

---

[19] A doctrine originating in Roman law, holding that certain things may not be the object of private rights, and therefore cannot be traded.

[20] The standard read for Maltese third year law students are the 'Notes on Civil Law' Revised Edition, by Professor V. Caruana Galizia, and reprinted by The Law Students' Society (*Ghaqda Studenti tal Liġi*). In gratuitous contracts, the consideration is satisfied by the intention of liberality.

[21] Civil Code, Title IV, 'Of Obligations in General', Sub-title I, 'Of contracts', §II'Of the Effects of Contracts, Article 992.

[22] Above n.21, Article 993.

[23] Civil Code, Title VI 'Of Sale', Sub-title 1 'Of the Contract of Sale', Article 1346.

[24] See Civil Code Article 1382: 'The delivery of incorporeal things takes place either by the use which the buyer makes of such things with the consent of the seller, or by handing over the documents of title in the case of any right the title to which is transferable by endorsement or delivery.'

[25] Civil Code Article 1352.

[26] Civil Code, Title VII 'Of Exchange', Articles 1485–1493.

money.'[27] A final provision of this Title provides that 'Any other rule relating to the contract of sale shall also apply to a contract of exchange.' Although one may stop to consider whether a supply of digital content or digital service in return for the provision of personal data could be considered an exchange under the Civil law of Malta, this author would not consider personal data to be 'a thing' and thus such an extension of these rules would appear to be unwarranted and incorrect at law.

20 Under the Civil Code the seller has two principal obligations: to deliver, and to warrant the thing sold.[28]

1. Where the thing sold is not of 'quality promised'

21 The Civil Code provides that if the thing which the seller offers to deliver is not of the quality promised, or is not according to the sample on which the sale was made, the buyer may elect either (1) to reject the thing and demand damages, or (2) to accept the thing with a diminution of the price upon a valuation by experts.[29] The action of the buyer for a diminution of the price or for repudiation of the contract is barred by the lapse of two years from the day of the contract.[30]

22 Therefore the Civil Code gives a two year period of warranty where the seller supplies goods to a buyer which are not of the agreed quality. As Fabri notes, this remedy is available to the purchaser and is restricted to disputes on quality, which is conceptually different from the notion of latent defect. Roman law clearly distinguished disputes on the agreed quality from disputes on defective products.[31] However it would appear that both these disputes would, in the language of the 'twin' Directives, be considered to be disputes for 'lack of conformity'.

23 The Civil Code does not provide for the first in the hierarchy of remedies of the 'twin' Directives, that is the right to have goods brought into conformity by repair or replacement, where goods are supplied which are not of the agreed quality. It does however envisage similar remedies to those provided for in the 'twin' Directives in case of more serious or persistent lack of conformity, that is reduction of the price or termination of the contract. Under Consumer Protection legislation transposing the DCD and the SGD, the first remedy is that of having the goods brought into conformity, and the consumer may choose between repair and replacement, under the conditions stated in the relevant provisions. In this context it is important to recall Article 92 of the Consumer Affairs Act by virtue of which the rights arising under the Consumer Affairs Act operate in addition to the rights under the Civil Code. Therefore, if it is more advantageous to him or her, a consumer may opt to bring an action according to these provisions of the Civil Code, rather than under the Consumer Affairs Act.

2. Warranty in respect of Latent Defects of the Thing Sold

24 Under the Maltese Civil Code the seller owes the buyer warranty in respect of the quiet possession of the thing sold and of any latent defect therein.[32] The Civil Code remedy in the law of sale for defective products applies to all contracts of sale entered between sellers and buyers. In other words, it applies even in a B2B (or C2C) context.

---

[27] Civil Code Article 1485(1).
[28] Civil Code, Sub-title IV 'Of the Obligations of the Seller', Article 1378.
[29] Civil Code Article 1390.
[30] Civil Code Article 1407(1).
[31] Fabri (2015), p.151.
[32] Civil Code, Article 1408.

B. The Civil Law of Obligations

The seller is obliged by law to warrant the thing sold against 'any latent defects which render it unfit for the use for which it is intended, or which diminish its value to such an extent that the buyer would not have bought it or would have tendered a smaller price, if he had been aware of them.'[33] However, the seller is not answerable for any apparent defects which the buyer might have discovered for himself.[34] Nevertheless, 'he is answerable for latent defects, even though they were not known to him, *unless he has stipulated that he shall not in any such case be bound to any warranty*.'[35] (my emphasis) Therefore as Fabri observes 'the legal warranty in the Civil Code still suffers from this fundamental weakness: it can be restricted, limited or even totally excluded by agreement between the parties.'[36] On the contrary, Consumer Protection law restricts such 'freedom to contract' of the parties, in view of the power imbalance assumed to exist between a trader and a consumer. In fact, Article 81 of the Consumer Affairs Act provides for the mandatory nature of the provisions implementing the Sale of Goods Directive, as follows: 25

> Unless otherwise provided for in this Part, any contractual agreement which, to the detriment of the consumer, excludes the application of this Part [Part X Sale of goods to consumers], derogates from them, or varies their effect, before the lack of conformity of the goods is brought to the seller's attention by the consumer, shall not be binding on the consumer.

In an action for latent defects 'the buyer may elect either, by instituting the *actio redhibitoria*, to restore the thing and have the price repaid to him, or, by instituting the *actio aestimatoria*, to retain the thing and have a part of the price repaid to him which shall be determined by the court.'[37] If the defects of the thing sold were known to the seller, he may be liable in damages towards the buyer over and above the obligation to repay the price. If on the contrary the defects were not known to the seller, he will only be obliged to repay the price and to refund to the buyer the expenses incurred in connection with the sale.[38] 26

In regard to movables, these actions have to be availed of by the buyer within six months[39] from the day of the delivery of the thing sold or, if it was not possible for the buyer to discover the latent defect of the thing, from when it was possible for him to discover such defect.[40] By comparison, under Article 78 of the Consumer Affairs Act, the seller is liable to the consumer for any lack of conformity which exists at the time when the goods were delivered, and which becomes apparent within two years of that time. 27

Therefore, by comparison, the limitation period for the Civil Code action for latent defects does not run before it is possible for the buyer to discover the latent defect of the thing, while the liability/limitation period under the Consumer Affairs Act (discussed further below) runs from when the goods were delivered. Moreover, under the Civil Code the buyer is not obliged to give the seller notice within a stipulated period of time, while a notification obligation was maintained in the Consumer Affairs Act (discussed further below), thus missing out on the opportunity to introduce a higher level of 28

---

[33] Civil Code, Article 1424.
[34] Civil Code, Article 1425.
[35] Civil Code, Article 1426.
[36] Fabri (2015), p.149.
[37] Civil Code Article 1427.
[38] Civil Code Article 1429.
[39] Among the changes proposed in the 1991 White Paper was an amendment to the Civil Code to lengthen the prescriptive period within which the buyer of a product with a latent defect could initiate court proceedings from one to six months. This amendment was enacted in 1994 together with the Consumer Affairs Act (Act XXVIII of 1994, Article 45) and came into force on 23 January 1996.
[40] Civil Code, Article 1431.

protection by removing such obligation. Furthermore, the Civil Code warranty extends to both movable and immovable property, whereas immovable goods are outside the scope of the SGD.[41] However, the Civil Code does not create any presumption similar to that envisaged in Article 80 of the Consumer Affairs Act ('any lack of conformity which becomes apparent within one year of the time when the goods were delivered shall be presumed to have existed at the time when the goods were delivered (...)'); nor does it have any specific provisions on commercial guarantees. Nevertheless, the Civil Code remedies for products with hidden defects remain available to consumers.[42]

C. Transposition of the DCD and the SGD

29   Malta transposed the SGD through amendments to the Consumer Affairs Act (Cap. 378), Part X Sale of Goods to consumers,[43] and the DCD in Subsidiary Legislation 378.20 Digital Content and Digital Services Contracts Regulations (S.L. 378.20).[44] The transposition of the Directives had no impact whatsoever on the structure of the existing general law of obligations and contracts, consumer protection law, intellectual property law and data protection law.

I. Definitions and scope of application

30   The definitions contained in the DCD, in particular in Article 2, and the SGD, in particular in Article 2, are transposed verbatim to Maltese law. They have not impacted already existing rules or doctrinal debate in Malta. Thus, the notions of 'digital content', 'digital service', 'goods with digital elements', 'integration', 'updates', 'price', 'digital environment', 'compatibility', 'functionality', 'interoperability', and 'durable medium' all have the same precise definition as under the Directives.

31   The sale of second-hand goods sold at public auction have been excluded from the scope of the national transposing legislation, an option allowed by the SGD Article 3(5), provided that 'clear and comprehensive information that the rights deriving from this Part do not apply shall be made easily available to consumers by auctioneers as defined in the Auctioneers Act.'[45]

32   Furthermore, the transposing provisions of the two Directives are not applied to B2B contracts.

33   The introduction in Consumer legislation of a provision on data as a 'counter-performance' has not yet produced any impact on our national legislation or doctrinal debate. No new rules on contract formation/existence/validity were introduced in the Civil Code. Rather, regulation 3(2) SL 378.20 replicates the wording of the Directive, provid-

---

[41] "Goods" are defined in Article 72 of the Consumer Affairs Act (mirroring the equivalent provision in the SGD) as: (a) any tangible movable items of property (...); (b) tangible movable items that incorporate or are inter-connected with digital content or a digital service in such a way that the absence of that digital content or digital service would prevent the goods from performing their functions, hereinafter referred to as "goods with digital elements".

[42] Cf. SGD recital (18) 'This Directive should also not affect national rules that do not specifically concern consumer contracts and provide for specific remedies for certain types of defects that were not apparent at the time of conclusion of the sales contract, namely national provisions which may lay down specific rules for the seller's liability for hidden defects.'

[43] Act No. I of 2022, <https://legislation.mt/eli/act/2022/1/eng> accessed 4 May 2022.

[44] Subsidiary Legislation 378.20 Digital Content and Digital Services Contracts Regulations, Legal Notice 406 of 2021, <https://legislation.mt/eli/sl/378.20/eng> accessed 4 May 2022.

[45] Consumer Affairs Act, Article 72(5)(c).

II. Conformity of goods

1. Subjective and objective requirements for conformity

34 As regards the subjective and the objective requirements for conformity, our law merely reproduces the provisions of the Directives: S.L.378.20 regulations 5 ('conformity of the digital content or digital service'), 6 ('subjective requirements for conformity'), 7 ('objective requirements for conformity') and 8 ('incorrect integration of the digital content or digital service') are a word for word reproduction of DCD Articles 6, 7, 8 and 9. The Consumer Affairs Act Article 73 is a word for word transposition of SGD Articles 5 – 8.

35 As regards the exclusion of the existence of a lack of conformity in the case provided by Article 8(5) DCD and Article 7(5) SGD, Maltese national law merely reproduces the relevant Directive articles verbatim. Thus, S.L.378.20 regulation 7(5) provides that if at the time of the conclusion of the contract the consumer was specifically informed that a particular characteristic of the digital content or service was deviating from the objective requirements for conformity, and the consumer expressly and separately accepted that deviation when concluding the contract, then there shall not be considered to be a lack of conformity with the said requirements. The same applies to Article 73(6) of the Consumer Affairs Act.

2. "Durability" and Environmental Sustainability

36 As regards the "durability" requirement in Article 7(1)(d) SGD, the transposition in Maltese legislation follows closely the wording of the Directive, and provides that, in addition to complying with the subjective requirements for conformity, the goods must also possess the qualities and other features, including in relation to durability, normal for goods of the same type and which the consumer may reasonably expect.[46]

37 Regarding national rules on availability of spare parts, the Consumer Affairs Act Article 93 provides that if the goods being the object of a sales contract between a trader and a consumer are of a nature that may require maintenance, or possible replacement of parts, 'replacement parts and appropriate repair service must be made available for a reasonable time from the date of the delivery of the goods by the seller to the consumer.'[47] Previously a seller could release himself from this requirement if he expressly warned the consumer in writing before the contract to purchase the goods was entered into that he does not supply replacement parts or provide repair services.[48] This 'opt-out' clause for the seller has been repealed, thus strengthening consumer rights. Nevertheless, it is a weakness of the law that no indication is given regarding what may constitute a "reasonable time". As noted by Micallef, 'In Malta, perhaps even more than

---

[46] Consumer Affairs Act, Article 73(2)(d).
[47] As amended when transposing the SGD.
[48] Act XXVI of 2000, Article 15, introducing a new Article 93(2) 'The trader or the producer may release himself from this obligation by specifically and expressly warning the consumer in writing, before the contract is entered into, that he does not supply replacement parts or repair service.'

in most other Member States, the issue of having in place measures regulating after-sales services is of paramount importance given that many goods are imported from abroad and that time and again many consumers have to go to considerable lengths in order to rectify matters at times even communicating directly with the producers abroad.'[49]

38 Malta did not adopt further measures for enhancing environmental sustainability / the circular economy in way of implementation of DCD and SGD. Moreover, no evidence has been found that Malta has coordinated the implementing provisions of the SGD with those of Directive 2009/125/EC, transposed to Maltese law by virtue of S.L. 427.64 Framework for the Setting of Ecodesign Requirements for Energy-Related Products Regulations. This is a subsidiary law under Cap. 427 of the Laws of Malta, the Product Safety Act. S.L. 427.64 regulation 12 provides that the penalties as provided by the Product Safety Act shall apply in respect of the infringement of the Regulations. The penalties (fines) are stipulated in Article 32; they consist of public law fines (*multa*) and/or imprisonment terms.

3. Incorrect Installation of Digital Content or Digital Service

39 S.L. 378.20 regulation 8 provides that if the lack of conformity results from the incorrect integration of the digital content or service into the consumer's digital environment and the integration was carried out by the trader or under his/her responsibility, or the incorrect integration by the consumer was due to shortcomings in the integration instructions provided by the trader, then this shall be regarded as a lack of conformity of the digital content or service. The wording of the national law is practically a word-for-word transposition of DCD Article 9.

40 Similarly, the Consumer Affairs Act Article 73(7) provides that if the lack of conformity results from the incorrect installation of the goods and the installation was either included within the sales contract and was carried out by the seller or under his/her responsibility, or was done by the consumer and the incorrect installation was due to shortcomings in the installation instructions provided by the seller (or, in the case of goods with digital elements, provided by the seller or by the supplier of the digital content or service), then this shall be regarded as a lack of conformity of the goods. Once again this provision in the national law is a word-for-word transposition of the equivalent provision in the SGD (Article 8).

4. Third party rights

41 Where a restriction resulting from a violation of any right of a third party, in particular intellectual property rights, prevents or limits the use of the digital content or service in accordance with the requirements for conformity, the consumer is entitled to the remedies for lack of conformity.[50] This provision is also a word-for-word transposition of the equivalent Article of the DCD (Article 10).

42 Similarly, where a restriction resulting from a violation of any right of a third party, in particular intellectual property rights, prevents, or limits the use of the goods in accordance with the requirements for conformity, the consumer is entitled to the remedies established for lack of conformity, unless the law provides for the nullity or rescission of the sales contract in such cases.[51] Once again the wording of the national transposition reflects a word-for-word adoption of the language of the SGD.

---

[49] Micallef (2008), at p.125.
[50] S.L. 378.20, regulation 9.
[51] Consumer Affairs Act, Article 73A.

Malta applied the DCD/SGD remedies for a lack of conformity to the situations covered by those provisions.[52]

Malta has not further regulated the relationship with Intellectual Property law and there is no local jurisprudence on the matter of whether the consumer has the right to "resell" digital content.

III. Liability of the Trader

S.L. 378.20 provides that the trader shall be liable for any failure to supply the digital content or digital service in accordance with regulation 4.[53] Where a contract provides for a single act of supply or a series of individual acts of supply, the trader is liable for any lack of conformity which exists at the time of supply and that becomes apparent within two years from that time, without prejudice to regulation 7(2)(b) (on the provision of updates that the consumer may 'reasonably expect').[54] This provision is a specification of DCD Article 11(2) subpara 2. Therefore, in Malta the trader is only liable for lack of conformity that becomes apparent within two years from the time of supply, which is the minimum period as per the Directive. Where the contract provides for continuous supply over a period of time, the trader shall be liable for a lack of conformity that occurs or becomes apparent within the period of time during which the digital content or digital service is to be supplied under the contract.[55]

Similarly, under the Consumer Affairs Act, the seller is liable to the consumer for any lack of conformity which exists at the time when the goods were delivered and which becomes apparent within two years of that time.[56] This also applies to goods with digital elements, provided that where the contract provides for a continuous supply over a period of time, the seller is liable for any lack of conformity of the digital content or digital service that occurs or becomes apparent within two years of the time of delivery; and where the contract provides for a continuous supply of more than two years, the seller is liable for any lack of conformity that occurs or becomes apparent within the period of time during which the digital content or digital service is to be supplied under the sales contract.[57] Therefore, the Maltese legislator exercised the option provided for in SGD Article 10(3) by not introducing longer time limits for the trader's liability. Furthermore, the national rule that the said two-year period is suspended for the duration of negotiations carried on between the seller and the consumer with a view to an amicable settlement was maintained.[58]

As regards burden of proof, SGD Article 11(2) provides that instead of the one-year period from delivery of the goods within which any lack of conformity is presumed to have existed at the time the goods were delivered and it is therefore incumbent upon the trader to prove otherwise, Member States may maintain or introduce a period of two years from the time when the goods were delivered. The Maltese legislator did not exercise this option and the Consumer Affairs Act provides that the period of time within which any lack of conformity which becomes apparent shall be presumed to have existed at the time when the goods were delivered shall be that of one year of the time

---

[52] S.L.378.20 regulation 13 is a close transposition of DCD Article 14; Consumer Affairs Act Article 74(1), (2), (3), (4), Article 75(1) and Article 76(2) are close transpositions of SGD Article 13.
[53] S.L.378.20, Article 10(1); Close transposition of DCD Article 11(1).
[54] S.L.378.20, Article 10(2).
[55] S.L.378.20, Article 10(3).
[56] Consumer Affairs Act, Article 78(1).
[57] Consumer Affairs Act, Article 78(1) proviso.
[58] Consumer Affairs Act, Article 78(2).

when the goods were delivered, unless proved otherwise or unless this presumption is incompatible with the nature of the goods or with the nature of the lack of conformity. This also applies to goods with digital elements.[59]

48 Even though the SGD provides, in Article 10(6), that Member States have the option of providing that, in the case of second-hand goods, the seller and the consumer can agree to contractual terms or agreements with a shorter liability or limitation period than those referred to in the preceding paragraphs (provided that such shorter periods shall not be less than one year), Malta did not introduce a shorter liability period for second-hand goods.

49 Malta did not further regulate the interruption of long-term supply of digital content / digital services.

50 S.L. 378.20, regulation 3(6)(b) provides that the regulations do not apply to contracts regarding electronic communications services, as defined in Directive 2018/1972[60] Article 2(4),[61] with the exception of number-independent interpersonal communications services, as defined in Directive 2018/1972 Article 2(7).[62] This regulation transposes DCD Art. 3(5)(b).

51 Furthermore, S.L.378.20 regulation 3(8) provides that regulation 18 (on modification of the digital content or digital service) does not apply where a bundle (within the meaning of Directive 2018/1972) includes elements of an internet access service (as defined in Regulation 2015/2120, Article 2(2)) or a number-based interpersonal communications service (as defined in Directive 2018/1972 Article 2(6)), provided that, without prejudice to Directive 2018/1972 Article 107(2),[63] the effects that the termination of one element of a bundle contract may have on the other elements of the bundle contract shall be governed by national law.' Once again the Maltese legislator has merely transposed the DCD (Article 3(6)(2) – (3)) verbatim.

52 As regards the consequences of the trader's non-compliance with the General Data Protection Regulation (GDPR)[64] regarding contracts for the supply of digital con-

---

[59] Consumer Affairs Act, Article 80(1).
[60] Directive (EU) 2018/1972 establishing the European Electronic Communications Code (Recast) OJ L 321/36.
[61] Directive 2018/1972, Article 2(4) "electronic communications service' means a service normally provided for remuneration via electronic communications networks, which encompasses, with the exception of services providing, or exercising editorial control over, content transmitted using electronic communications networks and services, the following types of services:
(a) 'internet access service' as defined in point (2) of the second paragraph of Article 2 of Regulation (EU) 2015/2120;
(b) interpersonal communications service; and
(c) services consisting wholly or mainly in the conveyance of signals such as transmission services used for the provision of machine-to-machine services and for broadcasting. '
[62] Directive 2018/1972, Article 2(7) "number-independent interpersonal communications service' means an interpersonal communications service which does not connect with publicly assigned numbering resources, namely, a number or numbers in national or international numbering plans, or which does not enable communication with a number or numbers in national or international numbering plans.'
[63] Directive 2018/1972, Article 107(2) 'Where the consumer has, under Union law, or national law in accordance with Union law, a right to terminate any element of the bundle as referred to in paragraph 1 before the end of the agreed contract term because of a lack of conformity with the contract or a failure to supply, Member States shall provide that the consumer has the right to terminate the contract with respect to all elements of the bundle.'
(paragraph 1 'If a bundle of services or a bundle of services and terminal equipment offered to a consumer comprises at least an internet access service or a publicly available number-based interpersonal communications service ...')
[64] Regulation (EU) 2016/679 on the protection of natural persons with regard to the processing of personal data and on the free movement of such data, and repealing Directive 95/46/EC (General Data Protection Regulation) OJ L 119/1.

C. Transposition of the DCD and the SGD

tent/digital services, S.L.378.20 regulation 3(10) provides that EU law on the protection of personal data shall apply to any personal data processed in connection with contracts where the trader supplies digital content or a digital service and the consumer provides personal data to the trader. In particular, the regulations found in S.L.378.20 are without prejudice to the GDPR, the Data Protection Act[65] and the Processing of Personal Data (Electronic Communications Sector) Regulations.[66] In the event of conflict between the provisions of the regulations of S.L.378.20 and EU data protection law, the latter prevails. This sub-regulation is a faithful transposition of DCD Article 4(8).

Furthermore, S.L. 378.20, regulation 15(2) on the obligations of the trader provides that in respect of personal data of the consumer in the event of termination, the trader must comply with the obligations applicable in terms of the GDPR and the Data Protection Act. This is a faithful transposition of DCD Article 16(2). 53

IV. Remedies for the failure to supply and remedies for the lack of conformity

Malta did not introduce a right to withhold payment in cases of a lack of conformity for contracts under the DCD. As regards the SGD, Article 74(4) of the Consumer Affairs Act provides that the consumer 'shall have the right to withhold payment of any outstanding part of the price or a part thereof until the seller has fulfilled the seller's obligations under this Part.' No further conditions or modalities regarding the withholding of payment of the price by the consumer are specified in our local legislation. 54

Furthermore, Malta has adopted no specific rules in order to specify the place of delivery and the place of repair and replacement.[67] Instead, SGD Article 14(1)-(4) on repair or replacement of the goods is transposed verbatim at Article 75(2)-(5) of the Consumer Affairs Act. Neither does Maltese legislation foresee rules about the costs of transport for the case of repair/replacement. 55

The Maltese legislation did not consider the interaction between the right to withdraw consent for the processing of personal data under data protection law, and the right of termination through a statement to the trader. S.L.378.20 regulation 14 merely transposes DCD Article 15 verbatim, as follows: "The consumer shall exercise the right to terminate the contract by means of a statement to the trader expressing the decision to terminate the contract." Neither did Malta introduce specific rules regarding the contractual consequences of withdrawal of consent for processing personal data. Possibly general contract law rules would apply. 56

As regards restitution where the trader supplies digital content and/or digital services, DCD Articles 16 and 17 on the obligations of the trader and of the consumer respectively in the event of termination are transposed practically verbatim to S.L.378.20 regulations 15 and 16. Regarding personal data of the consumer, the law merely provides that the trader must comply with the obligations applicable in terms of the GDPR and the Data Protection Act. 57

With regard to the matter of prioritising repair over replacement in order to enhance environmental sustainability (e.g. recital 48 SGD), the law in Malta does not go beyond what is provided in the SGD, and there is no doctrinal debate on the matter either. 58

Malta has not adopted sanctions for fighting premature / planned obsolescence of goods. S.L. 378.20 regulation 7(2) is effectively a verbatim transposition of DCD Article 59

---

[65] Cap. 586 of the Laws of Malta.
[66] S.L. 586.01.
[67] SGD recital (56).

8(2) providing *inter alia* that the trader must ensure that the consumer is informed of and supplied with updates, including security updates, necessary to keep the digital content/service in conformity. Regarding goods with digital elements, the Consumer Affairs Act, Article 73(2)(4), similarly provides *inter alia* that the seller must ensure that the consumer is informed of and supplied with updates, including security updates, necessary to keep those goods in conformity. The Consumer Affairs Act Article 73(2)(4) also constitutes a close transposition of Article 7(3) SGD.

60 The law in Malta does not contain any provision concerning the automatic or contractual transfer of the rights against the initial seller from the initial consumer to a subsequent buyer. Neither does the law clarify whether the initial seller may exclude the transferability of the rights under the legal guarantee in his general terms and conditions. Malta also did not provide express regulation for the cases in which the consumer bought goods and then moved to another country; or the seller delivered the goods in accordance with the Geo-Blocking Regulation and is subsequently obliged to carry out repair or replacement in a country he does not offer delivery to.

V. Commercial Guarantees

61 The Consumer Affairs Act provides that a commercial guarantee is an additional guarantee which places the beneficiary of such a guarantee in a more advantageous position than that established at law. Moreover, a commercial guarantee shall not adversely affect other available remedies under any other law governing contractual or tort liability.[68]

62 SGD Article 17(4) provides that Member States may lay down rules on other aspects concerning commercial guarantees which are not regulated in that Article. Malta has used this option as follows:

63 The Consumer Affairs Act Article 83(1) provides that a commercial guarantee statement must be provided to the consumer on a durable medium, at the latest at the time of the delivery of the goods. The commercial guarantee statement must be expressed in plain, intelligible language and it must:

(a) be formulated in at least one of the official languages of Malta;
(b) specify the name and address of the guarantor,[69] and clearly state the permanent address of the place of trade or business and the name of the person who is supplying the consumer with the commercial guarantee;
(c) clearly state the contents of the guarantee including its territorial scope if this is limited, as well as the duration of the guarantee from the date of purchase; different periods may be stipulated for different components of any goods;
(d) clearly specify the procedure to be followed by the consumer to obtain the implementation of the commercial guarantee. If a person who, in supplying a commercial guarantee, fails to provide the consumer with the information required under this paragraph, he shall then be responsible for the execution of the commercial guarantee at his expense;
(e) clearly state whether the commercial guarantee may be transferred to others. Unless otherwise stipulated the commercial guarantee may also be availed of by any subsequent owners of the goods to which the commercial guarantee refers:

---

[68] Consumer Affairs Act, Article 82.
[69] The Consumer Affairs Act provides a definition of the term "guarantor" as meaning 'the person who is responsible to the consumer for the execution of a commercial guarantee and includes any other person acting for or on behalf of the guarantor.'

C. Transposition of the DCD and the SGD

Provided that unless the commercial guarantee specifically states otherwise, it shall be assumed that in the case of goods, the commercial guarantee covers any defects that may result during the period of guarantee;
(f) the designation of the goods to which the commercial guarantee applies;
(g) a clear statement that the consumer is entitled by law to remedies from the seller free of charge in the event of a lack of conformity of the goods and that those remedies are not affected by the commercial guarantee; and
(h) the terms of the commercial guarantee.

Article 83(1) is the local transposition of SGD Article 17(2) and (4), while Article 83(2) which provides that non-compliance with the first sub-article shall not affect the binding nature of the commercial guarantee for the guarantor is the local transposition of SGD Article 17(3). Other relevant national provisions are found in the Consumer Affairs Act Articles 84–91.

The law, as amended when transposing the SGD, provides that 'Where a seller or any other person gives a commercial guarantee to a consumer, irrespective of when or how it is given, then that seller or other person shall be liable to the consumer for the observance of the terms and execution of the commercial guarantee as if he were the guarantor'.[70] Furthermore, a commercial guarantee and any rights granted to a consumer in terms of that guarantee shall not in any way, directly or indirectly, exclude or limit the rights of a consumer under the Consumer Affairs Act or under any other law; any such exclusion or limitation stipulated in violation of this prohibition shall be null and ineffective.[71] The latter provision pre-dates the 2022 amendments, i.e. the amendments introduced to transpose the SGD.

The law further provides that unless expressly and clearly stipulated in the commercial guarantee, a guarantor may not, when performing or executing a commercial guarantee, request a consumer to pay any fee or any charge however designated.[72] Moreover, unless otherwise stipulated in the commercial guarantee, the guarantor shall assume the cost of any carriage incurred in respect of the performance of a commercial guarantee.[73] These provisions also pre-date the 2022 amendments.

Another provision that pre-dates the 2022 amendments provides that the duration of a commercial guarantee shall be automatically extended for a period equal to the time during which the guarantor had the goods (or part thereof) in his possession in order to perform or execute the commercial guarantee, or as a result of the recall of the goods (or part thereof) by the manufacturer.[74] The designation by the guarantor of a third person to execute a commercial guarantee does not free the guarantor from the obligation towards the consumer pursuant to the commercial guarantee given to the consumer.[75]

Article 90 of the Consumer Affairs Act is a close transposition of Article 17(1) SGD providing (in part) that a commercial guarantee shall be binding on the guarantor under the conditions laid down in the commercial guarantee statement and associated advertising available at the time, or before the conclusion, of the contract. If the former are less advantageous to the consumer than the latter, the commercial guarantee shall be binding under the conditions laid down in the advertising relating to the commercial

---

[70] Consumer Affairs Act, Article 84.
[71] Consumer Affairs Act, Article 85.
[72] Consumer Affairs Act, Article 86.
[73] Consumer Affairs Act, Article 87.
[74] Consumer Affairs Act, Article 88.
[75] Consumer Affairs Act, Article 89.

guarantee, unless, before the conclusion of the contract, the said advertising was corrected in the same or in a comparable way to that in which it was made.

68   Maltese law further provides that (without prejudice to any other remedies at law) a consumer may institute civil proceedings against a guarantor who fails to observe any of the terms or undertakings stipulated in a commercial guarantee. If civil proceedings are instituted, the court may (a) order the guarantor to take such remedial action as may be necessary to observe the terms of the guarantee, or (b) order the guarantor to perform his obligations under the commercial guarantee to its satisfaction within such period as the court may establish. Furthermore, the court may order the guarantor to pay to the consumer a sum not exceeding one hundred and twenty euro (€120) for each day of default in case of non-compliance after the lapse of the period established by the court.[76] This provision pre-dates the 2022 amendments.

VI. Time Limits

69   SGD Article 10(1) and (2) are transposed practically verbatim in the Consumer Affairs Act Article 78(1). SGD Article 10(3) provides that Member States may maintain or introduce longer time limits than the two (2) year liability period laid down in paragraphs 1 and 2. The Consumer Affairs Act did not introduce longer time limits for the trader's liability, providing that the seller 'shall be liable to the consumer for any lack of conformity which exists at the time when the goods were delivered and which becomes apparent within two years of that time.'[77] Furthermore, our legislator maintained the suspension of the said period for the duration of negotiations with view to an amicable settlement: the two-year period is suspended for the duration of negotiations carried on between the seller and the consumer with a view to an amicable settlement.[78]

70   SGD Article 10(6) gives Member States the option to allow traders and consumers to agree to a shorter liability or limitation period in the case of second-hand goods, provided that such shorter period shall not be less than one year. Malta did not however introduce a shorter liability period for second-hand goods.

71   The understanding of the Office for Consumer Affairs in Malta is that under Maltese law the remedies provided under SGD Article 13 / Consumer Affairs Act Article 74 are subject to a limitation period that is also the liability period; thus, 2 years from when the goods were delivered. This author has communicated with the said Office and they have confirmed that they understand that the time-barring with regard to Article 74 of the Consumer Affairs Act (remedies for lack of conformity), in consumer redress cases, is established in Article 78 of the Act (the liability of the seller). Furthermore, under Maltese law, in order to benefit from the available remedies, the consumer has an obligation to notify the seller of any such lack of conformity on a durable medium 'within a period of at least two months from the date on which the consumer detected such lack of conformity.'[79]

---

[76] Consumer Affairs Act, Article 91.

[77] Consumer Affairs Act, Article 78(1).

[78] Consumer Affairs Act, Article 78(2). Cf. recital (44): "This Directive should not regulate the conditions under which the liability period, as provided for in this Directive, or a limitation period can be suspended or interrupted. Member States should, therefore, be able to provide for the suspension or interruption of the liability period or limitation period, for example in the event of repair, replacement or negotiations between the seller and the consumer with a view to an amicable settlement."

[79] Consumer Affairs Act, Article 79.

C. Transposition of the DCD and the SGD

However, this author submits that Article 78 establishes a liability period, and not a limitation (or prescription) period. The liability period is the legal basis on which a court action can be brought (in other words, it gives the consumer a cause of action). However, in this author's view, a liability period is not synonymous with a limitation period; the limitation period being a period of time within which the consumer may bring an action before the courts, provided the lack of conformity is detected within the two year liability period. Importantly, SGD Article 10(4) provides that: 'If, under national law, the remedies provided for in Article 13 are also subject to a limitation period, Member States shall ensure that such limitation period allows the consumer to exercise the remedies laid down in Article 13 for any lack of conformity for which the seller is liable pursuant to paragraphs 1 and 2 of this Article, and which becomes apparent within the period of time referred to in those paragraphs.'[80] If the lack of conformity becomes apparent towards the end of the two (2) year liability period, there should be a limitation period that goes beyond the liability period, allowing the consumer the time necessary within which to bring an action. So it is a weakness of the local transposing legislation that the limitation period is deemed to coincide with the liability period.

Nevertheless, the Office for Consumer Affairs confirmed as follows:

> Article 78 of the Consumer Affairs Act (the Act) establishes the prescriptive term within which to proceed that may be suspended in terms of sub-article (2) thereof, that states:
> "The two-year period mentioned in sub-article (1) shall be suspended for the duration of negotiations carried on between the seller and the consumer with a view to an amicable settlement."
> Coming to the obligation to notify established in article 79 of the Act, this has to be exercised within the said two year term. What counts is that the notice is sent prior to the expiration of the said two year term, and even if the two months term will continue to run after the two year term there is no extension thereof, since the action will have to be instituted within the said two years (except where there has been a suspension according to article 78(2).[81]

However, this author submits that the law is quite unsatisfactory, and that the limitation period should extend beyond the liability period in order to satisfy the requirement that 'such limitation period allows the consumer to exercise the remedies (...) for any lack of conformity for which the seller is liable'.

Regarding the DCD, Article 11 is transposed in S.L.378.20 regulation 10. Under our national law, where a contract provides for a single act of supply, or a series of individual acts of supply, 'the trader shall only be liable for any lack of conformity that becomes apparent within two years from the time of supply, without prejudice to point (b) of regulation 7(2).'[82] The other provisions of DCD Article 11 are faithfully transposed in S.L.378.20 regulation 10.

SGD Article 12 allows Member States to maintain or introduce provisions stipulating that, in order to benefit from the consumer's rights, the consumer has to inform the seller of a lack of conformity within a period not shorter than 2 months from the date on

---

[80] See also SGD recital (42), providing in part 'For reasons of coherence with the existing national legal systems, Member States should be free to provide either that sellers are liable for a lack of conformity that becomes apparent within a specific period of time, possibly coupled with a limitation period, or that consumers' remedies are only subject to a limitation period. In the former case, Member States should ensure that the period for the seller's liability is not circumvented by the limitation period for the consumer's remedies. While this Directive should, therefore, not harmonise the starting point of national limitation periods, it should ensure that such limitation periods do not curtail the consumers' right to exercise their remedies for any lack of conformity which becomes apparent in the period during which the seller is liable for a lack of conformity.'

[81] E-mail correspondence with a Senior Legal Officer at the Office for Consumer Affairs, 10 June 2022, on file with the author.

[82] S.L.378.20 Article 10(2) proviso.

which the consumer detected such lack of conformity. As aforementioned, in accordance with Article 79 of the Consumer Affairs Act, in order to benefit from the remedies available under the Act that transpose the remedies provided for in the SGD, a consumer must notify the seller on a durable medium of any lack of conformity 'within a period of at least two months from the date on which the consumer detected such lack of conformity.' The phraseology 'within a period of at least two months' is evidence of the literal copying engaged in by the Maltese legislator, as it reflects the precise wording of the Directive rather than sets the period of time within which such notification needs to be made. While Malta has maintained the obligation to notify, Article 79 has actually been amended to make it easier for consumers to notify the trader, as previously the law specified that this notification was to be given by registered mail.

VII. Right of Redress

77   Article 77 of the Maltese Consumer Affairs Act provides that where the seller is liable to the consumer because of a lack of conformity resulting from an act or omission (including omitting to provide updates to goods with digital elements) by a person in previous links of the chain of transactions, the final seller shall be entitled to pursue remedies against the person or persons liable in the chain of transactions. This is a verbatim transposition of the SGD Article 18 (omitting the final sentence which states that: 'The person against whom the seller may pursue remedies and the relevant actions and conditions of exercise, shall be determined by national law.'). There is no specific coordination with other remedies.

78   Similarly, S.L.378.20 regulation 19 provides that where the trader is liable to the consumer because of any failure to supply the digital content/service, or because of a lack of conformity resulting from an act or omission by a person in previous links of the chain of transactions, the trader shall be entitled to pursue remedies against the persons liable in the chain of commercial transactions. Once again, this is a verbatim transposition of the DCD Article 20, save for omitting the final sentence which states that: 'The person against whom the trader may pursue remedies, and the relevant actions and conditions of exercise, shall be determined by national law.' Once again too, there is no specific coordination with other remedies.

VIII. Conclusion

79   As regards the interaction and interplay between civil law rules on the one hand, and consumer protection rules on the other, Malta has maintained a silo approach, meaning that the two sets of rules remain separate and distinct. Neither the Civil, nor the Commercial Code have been adapted and updated to reflect contemporary private law issues and disputes. Rather, all consumer protection measures have been implemented outside the Civil Code, through special legislation.[83] Indeed, this report provides some indication that at this stage Malta is closely following the developments in EU secondary law, without much debate and/or initiative at national level. The content of the Digital Content and Sale of Goods Directives has been superimposed on the civil law rules, without any real inter-connectedness between the two. This begs the question regarding the extent to which the transposition of EU laws and concepts into the Maltese legal system is occurring in an integral manner, and more generally whether there is still

---

[83] For a critique of this strategy, see Fabri (2015), in particular pp.152 – 157.

scope for a home-grown consumer policy. Bearing in mind the Digital Single Market target, and the move towards full rather than minimum harmonisation Directives as the instrument of choice to achieve such target, certainly the scope for national variance in consumer policy is reduced. Nevertheless, the implementation of consumer law remains a challenging area with significant diversity among EU Member States in view of the impact and interplay with the principles and provisions of Civil law, as well as national law choices.[84] The co-existence of remedies provided under Consumer legislation (and in particular the Consumer Affairs Act and subsidiary legislation passed thereunder) with those provided under the Civil Code may yet throw up challenges of application and interpretation, which will fall to the Courts to resolve. While many issues will have to be decided by courts, from a consumer's perspective one may need to compare the alternative remedies available to determine which is more advantageous. As a result, legal practitioners need to navigate the terrain carefully when considering which rules and which remedies apply and are most advantageous to their clients.

Bibliography

Kevin Aquilina, 'The nature and sources of the Maltese mixed legal system: strange case of Dr. Jekyll and Mr. Hyde?' (2013) 4(1) *Comparative Law Review*, 1–38.

David Fabri, *From application to accession: the interplay between the EC Consumer Directives and selected areas of national consumer law and policy – a case study from Malta (1990–2004)* (unpublished PhD thesis, Faculty of Laws, University of Malta 2015).

Ewould Hondius, 'The Notion of Consumer: European Union versus Member States' (2006) 28(1) *Sydney Law Review* 89 <http://classic.austlii.edu.au/au/journals/SydLawRw/2006/5.html> accessed 4 May 2022.

Paul Edgar Micallef, 'The Impact of the European Union on Consumer Policy in Malta: A Mixed Blessing?' (2008) in Deborah Parry, Annette Nordhausen and Geraint Howells (eds), *The Yearbook of Consumer Law 2009* (1st Edition, Routledge, London, 2008), 109–146.

Official documentation from the Government of Malta.

---

[84] For example, the 'Declaration of Principles' at Article 43 of the Consumer Affairs Act 1994, added in 2000, which 'shall not be directly enforceable in any court or tribunal, but shall be adhered to in the interpretation and implementation of this Act and any regulations made thereunder.'

Department of Information, *Rights for the Consumer* (White Paper, 1991).

Department of Information, *Fair Trading ... the next step forward: Proposals for Legislative Reforms* (White Paper, 1993).

The Netherlands*

A. Introduction and General Framework	1
I. Layered System	1
II. Digital Content Contracts before Transposition of the Digital Content Directive	4
B. Scope of application	7
I. Consumer Contracts or beyond?	7
II. Sale of Second-hand Goods	13
III. Sale of Animals	15
C. Contracts in exchange for Payment of a Price	21
D. Contracts in exchange for the Provision of Personal Data	24
I. Personal Data as Counter-performance	24
II. Consent to Processing of Personal Data and Withdrawal of Consent	26
III. No Liability for the Failure to Provide (correct) Personal Data and Processing thereof	29
IV. The Poor Pay More – with their Privacy	31
E. Conformity and remedies for lack of conformity	32
I. Mixing Conformity Period, Reversal of the Burden of Proof, and Duty to Notify	32
II. Updates	37
III. Durability and Sustainability with regard to Updates of Goods with Digital Elements	42
IV. Producer's Liability?	44
V. Durability and Sustainability with regard to 'Ordinary' Goods	46
F. Conclusion	49
Bibliography	51

A. Introduction and General Framework

I. Layered System

1 The Dutch Civil Code (*Burgerlijk Wetboek*, hereinafter: BW) consists of several books. The law of obligations is codified in book 3 (Patrimonial law in general) and book 6 (General part of the Law of Obligations), whereas specific contracts are codified in books 7, 7A, and 8. In accordance with current Dutch legal tradition, directives nowadays are transposed almost *ad verbatim*, typically without making use of the options offered by the European legislator to expand or limit the scope of a directive or to derogate from it to the benefit of either the consumer or the trader, in order to speed up the process of transposition.

2 As Dutch law does not have a separate Consumer Code, European consumer law Directives are normally implemented in the Civil Code, either in a separate title (as is the case for timeshare contracts and package travel contracts) or in an existing title applicable to consumer contracts and commercial contracts alike. The latter is, for instance, the case with the transposition of the 1999 Consumer Sales Directive (hereafter also: CSD),[1] which has led to substantial changes of Title 7.1 BW on sales contracts. As the Sale of Goods Directive (hereafter also: SGD)[2] is more or less an update of the 1999

---

* This paper is to a large extent based on an earlier paper: Marco Loos, 'The (proposed) transposition of the Digital Content Directive in The Netherlands' (2021) 2 *Jipitec* 229.
[1] Directive 1999/44/EC, OJ 1999, L 171/12 (Consumer Sales Directive, CSD).
[2] Directive (EU) 2019/771, OJ 2019, L 136/28 (Sale of Goods Directive, SGD).

Consumer Sales Directive, the legislator decided to transpose this Directive by amending Title 7.1 BW on sales contracts. The Digital Content Directive (hereafter also: DCD)[3] is transposed in a new Title 7.1AA BW placed directly after Title 7.1 BW, signifying the close relationship between the two sets of provisions. In accordance with the Civil Code's layered structure, and in line with art. 3 (7) SGD and art. 3 (10) DCD, where the provisions of Title 7.1 on sales or of Title 7.1AA on digital content and digital services do not contain a specific provision, general contract law applies.[4]

3   Both Directives have been transposed by the same act, which was adopted only on 20 April 2022 and formally published on 26 April 2022.[5] The Dutch legislator, therefore, has failed to meet not only the deadline for transposition of the Directives[6] but also the date by which the transposed provisions should be applied.[7] As the act is directly applicable to digital content contracts[8] this is mostly problematic with regard to consumer sales contracts, as the act is applicable for such contracts only as of 27 April 2022.[9] Where possible, courts will have to interpret the pre-existing legislation in line with the Sale of Goods Directive. Where this is not possible and a party sustains damage as a result of the failure to timely transpose the Sale of Goods Directive, that party is entitled to damages under the *Francovich* doctrine[10] for state liability.

II. Digital Content Contracts before Transposition of the Digital Content Directive

4   Obviously, prior to the transposition of the Digital Content Directive, courts have already had to deal with matters pertaining to 'digital content'. In Dutch law, contracts whereby the digital content is supplied to a consumer on a durable medium, such as a memory stick, a CD, or a DVD have since long been classified as consumer sales contracts. In 2012, in a business-to-business case, the Dutch Supreme Court confirmed that sales law could be applied by analogy to the supply of standardized software, irrespective whether that software was supplied on a durable medium.[11]

5   That state of affairs was explicitly acknowledged by the legislator in 2013 when a bill transposing the Consumer Rights Directive (hereafter also: CRD)[12] was submitted to parliament.[13] On that occasion, the government proposed to amend the definition of a consumer sales contract and to provide for explicit analogous application of consumer sales rules to digital content contracts in order to codify the 2012 decision of the

---

[3] Directive (EU) 2019/770, *OJ* 2019, L 136/1 (Digital Content Directive, DCD).
[4] Cf. *Kamerstukken II* 2021/22, 35 734, no. 3, p. 25 and 38.
[5] *Implementatiewet richtlijnen verkoop goederen en levering digitale inhoud*, Act of 20 April 2022, *Staatsblad* 2022, 164.
[6] Both directives should have been transposed before 1 July 2021, see art. 24 (1) DCD and art. 24 (1) SGD. A formal notice of infringement of the transposition requirements was received already on 30 September 2021, *Kamerstukken II* 2021/22, 21 109, no. 252.
[7] The same provisions indicate that the provisions transposing the SGD are to be applied to contracts that are *concluded* after 1 January 2022, whereas the DCD is (with two exceptions) to be applied to contracts that are to be *performed* as of 1 January 2022 (the two exceptions pertain to the right of redress and the right to modify the digital content, which are to be applied only to contracts concluded after 1 January 2022).
[8] Cf. art. 197a Overgangswet Nieuw Burgerlijk Wetboek.
[9] Cf. art. 196a Overgangswet Nieuw Burgerlijk Wetboek.
[10] Named after CJEU 19 November 1991, joined cases C-6/90 and C-9/90, *Francovich et al./Italian Republic*, ECLI:EU:C:1991:428.
[11] Hoge Raad 27 April 2012, ECLI:NL:HR:2012:BV1301 (Beeldbrigade).
[12] Directive 2011/83/EU, *OJ* 2011, L 304/64 (Consumer Rights Directive, CRD).
[13] *Kamerstukken II* 2012/13, 33 520, no. 3, p. 19.

Supreme Court for consumer contracts.[14] The Act transposing the Consumer Rights Directive and expanding the application of consumer sales law to all digital content contracts was adopted on 12 March 2014[15] and applied to contracts concluded as of 13 June 2014.[16] Upon request by the senate, streaming contracts – that accidentally had not been excluded from this bill – were excluded from the scope of this act by a new act that was adopted without controversy and applied as of 19 June 2015.[17] The government insisted, however, that this restriction of the scope of consumer sales law would not leave consumers of streaming services out in the cold as consumer protection would be provided through, in particular, the provisions of Section 6.5.2B BW (the provisions transposing the CRD) and of Section 6.5.3 BW (the provisions transposing the Unfair Contract Terms Directive[18]).[19] Moreover, additional protection was offered by general contract law, for instance with regard to the consequences of non-performance.[20]

The provisions on consumer sales did not apply to the supply of 'free' digital content as a sales contract presupposes the payment of a price *in money*.[21] The same is true for the provisions transposing the CRD, as the notion of a consumer sales contract, again, requires payment of a price in money,[22] and so does the definition of a services contract, which expressly refers to a contract, whereby the trader undertakes to provide a service and the consumer to pay a price.[23] The bill transposing the Modernization Directive[24] expressly extends the scope of this section to include contracts whereby the trader provides or undertakes to provide digital content or digital services and the consumer provides or undertakes to provide personal data.[25] Until this bill and the bill transposing the Digital Content Directive have been adopted, only general contract law applies to 'free' digital content and 'free' digital services.

B. Scope of application

I. Consumer Contracts or beyond?

Art. 3 (1) SGD and 3 (1) DCD both indicate that the Directive applies if a seller or trader concludes a contract with a *consumer*. Member States are, of course, free to extend the application of rules intended for consumer contracts beyond that scope: as non-consumer contracts do not fall within the scope of the Directives, Member States may regulate such contracts as they see fit. This includes the possibility to apply the provisions transposing a directive also to contracts that do not fall within the scope of the Directives. The recitals to the preamble of both Directives even expressly suggest such extension of the scope to other contracts. So what has become of this under Dutch law?

---

[14] *Kamerstukken II* 2012/13, 33 520, no. 3, p. 57.
[15] Wet van 12 maart 2014, *Stb.* 2014, 140.
[16] See art. X of this Act.
[17] Act of 4 June 2015, *Stb. 2015,* 220.
[18] Directive 1993/13/EEC, *OJ* 1993, L 95/29.
[19] *Kamerstukken II* 2014/15, 34 071, no. 3, p. 3.
[20] *Kamerstukken II* 2014/15, 34 071, no. 5, p. 4–5.
[21] See art. 7:1 BW; see also Asser/Hijma 7-I (2019) no. 393.
[22] See art. 6:230g under (c) BW.
[23] See art. 6:230g under (d) BW.
[24] Directive (EU) 2019/2161, *OJ* 2019, L 328/7.
[25] See art. I under F of the bill transposing the Modernization Directive, amending art. 6:230h (1) BW, *Kamerstukken II* 2021/22, 35 940, no. 2.

8   Before delving into this question, one must first determine what, under EU law and under Dutch law, is understood by the notion of 'consumer'. This notion is defined in Art. 2 under (2) SGD and 2 under (6) DCD as meaning 'any natural person who, in relation to contracts covered by this Directive, is acting for purposes which are outside that person's trade, business, craft, or profession'. From this definition, which is in line with the definition in other European directives, it follows that a consumer can only be a natural person, and that natural person may not be acting for a purpose related to that person's trade or profession. Art. 7:5 (1)(a) and 7:50aa (e) BW contain the same definition.

9   This definition causes problems when a natural person acts for both private and professional purposes. For instance, imagine I want to purchase antivirus software for the desktop computer on which I write this paper. Clearly, this means that I use the desktop computer, and thus also the antivirus software installed, for professional purposes. Still, it is *my* desktop computer, which I bought from my own money, and which I choose to use for my personal reasons (instead of the laptop computer my employer has made available to me). Moreover, I have also stored music files, photos and other digital content on my desktop computer, and the antivirus software is also meant to protect such files from becoming infected by a computer virus. So am I acting for purposes *outside* my profession when purchasing either the desktop computer or the antivirus software or not? The definitions of the notion of consumer do not in any way reflect whether a person purchasing goods or digital content for mixed purposes may be regarded as consumers. It is therefore up to the courts to determine whether contracts concluded for such mixed purposes are governed by consumer law or should be excluded therefrom.

10   At EU level, the Court of Justice has established, in a case pertaining to international jurisdiction, that the notion of consumer – at least in such cases – should be interpreted restrictively. The reason for this may be that in the law governing international jurisdiction, two protective provisions may be in conflict with one another. Under art. 17-19 of (currently) the Brussels I Regulation (recast),[26] a consumer may sue a trader in the country where the consumer lives. This provision deviates from the main rule in the law governing international jurisdiction: art. 4 Brussels I Regulation (recast) provides that a party may be sued in the country where that party lives. That provision aims at protecting a party from having to defend itself in another country. This conflict of competing protective instruments justifies a restrictive approach to the notion of consumer in this area. In that respective it is not surprising that the Court in *Gruber*[27] decided that in mixed purpose cases, a party can only be considered to be a consumer if the trade or professional purpose is so limited as to be negligible in the overall context of the contract. Outside the area of private international law, such competing protective instruments are rare – normally, the only party potentially worthy of protection is the natural person who is acting for mixed purposes. Even if at EU level contracts concluded between a trader and such person would not be considered to be consumer contracts, there are good reasons why such contracts could be considered as consumer contracts under national law. Such an extensive interpretation of the definition of the notion of 'consumer' would be in line with the prevailing interpretation of that notion in Germany[28] and Belgium[29] and recital 17 of the Consumer Rights Directive, and is

---

[26] Regulation (EU) 1215/2012, *OJ* 2012, L 351/1 (Brussels I Regulation (recast)).
[27] CJEU 20 January 2005, case C-464/01, *Gruber*, ECLI:EU:C:2005:32).
[28] Cf. BGH 30.09.2009 – VIII ZR 7/09, *NJW* 2009, 3780.
[29] Ilse Samoy, 'Het toepassingsgebied van de verschillende koopregelingen in kaart gebracht (gemeenrechtelijke koop, consumentenkoop en internationale koop), met bijzondere aandacht voor gemengd gebruik en gemengde overeenkomsten', 2009 *TBBR* 71 (75-76). See also Court of Appeal Antwerp

B. Scope of application

supported in The Netherlands by *Schaub*.[30] I concur with her view: when purchasing the computer or the antivirus software installed on it, my bargaining power is not in any way different from that of any other natural person purchasing these products. For this reason, in my view a natural person should be regarded as a consumer unless there are clear indications that this person has primarily acted for professional purposes, e.g. because that person requires a VAT invoice (which is of relevance only to traders for tax purposes) or because delivery is to be made at a place which clearly has an office function only.[31] Unfortunately, the explanatory memorandum of the bill transposing the Directives is silent on this matter.

It should be noted that even if one would not extend the notion of consumer to such mixed purpose contracts, there is a chance that the provisions transposing the DCD (and the SGD) could be applied nonetheless. General contract law offers the possibility to set aside otherwise applicable rules of a contract or of contract law if application of such rules would be unacceptable in the circumstances of the case (Art. 6:248 (2) BW), and also provides that courts may apply rules to a contract which follow from the requirements of good faith and fair dealing (Art. 6:248 (1) BW). Both provisions allow for, what is called in Dutch *reflexwerking* ('mirror application', in German: *Indizwirkung*). Whether courts will indeed extend the scope of the provisions transposing the Digital Content Directive (and the Sale of Goods Directive) to such 'non-consumers' is of course uncertain. **11**

The explanatory memorandum is also silent regarding another potential extension of the scope of the provisions transposing the Directives: nothing is said about the possibility to apply these provisions to NGOs, start-ups or SMEs, as was suggested by recital 16 DCD and recital 21 SGD. Of course this does not mean that courts cannot find inspiration in these rules when deciding a case where a natural person acts for mixed purposes when purchasing digital content and that person is, in the circumstances of that case, not seen as a consumer, or where an SME concludes a digital content contract with a professional supplier thereof: again, mirror application of the rules on digital content and digital services, or those on consumer sales, is in theory possible. Courts tend to be rather restrictive to award mirror application of consumer rules to non-consumers, though. An extension of the scope of application, even by way of mirror application, to businesses who are not SMEs is even rather unlikely. Unless, of course, new developments at the European level force the Dutch legislator to develop such rules or such provisions are adopted by way of a European regulation. **12**

II. Sale of Second-hand Goods

The Sale of Goods Directive also offers Member States options to *exclude* certain sales contracts from the scope of application of the transposing act. This applies in the first place to the purchase of second-hand goods sold at public auctions.[32] A similar option already existed under the old Consumer Sales Directive,[33] but was not used by the legislator at the time. The legislator saw no reason to reconsider this choice now.[34] **13**

---

[30] June 2009, *NjW* 2010, 504, with case-note by Reinhard Steennot; Court of Appeal Ghent 19 October 2012, *NjW* 2014, 32, with case-note by Reinhard Steennot.
[30] Martien Schaub, 'Wie is consument?', (2017) 1 *TvC* 30 (37).
[31] Marco Loos, 'De (voorgestelde) omzetting van de Richtlijnen verkoop goederen en digitale inhoud', (2021) 4 *TvC* 216 (219–220).
[32] Cf. art. 3 (5)(a) SGD.
[33] Cf. art. 1 (3) CSD.
[34] *Kamerstukken II*, 2020/21, 35 734, no. 3, p. 9.

The separate option to offer parties the possibility of agreeing on a shorter liability or limitation period in the case of the purchase of second-hand goods was not used either.[35] This option was also already included in the Consumer Sales Directive,[36] and on this point, too, the government saw no reason to reconsider the earlier choice not to make use of the option.[37] The government's choice proved to be uncontroversial as these choices have not been debated at all in parliament.

14 Although sustainability does not seem to have played a role in the choices made by the legislator, both choices seem to me to be justifiable from that point of view: if, in the context of sustainability, we want to encourage the industry and consumers to use goods as long as possible before they are finally consigned to the dump, it seems insufficient to 'only' ensure that goods can be reused. An additional condition would seem to be that consumers have the confidence that previously used goods, whether or not refurbished, meet the reasonable expectations that consumers may have of such second-hand goods. When the professional seller cannot live up to these expectations (which are possibly lower than what a consumer could expect from new goods), the consumer should, in my opinion, have the same rights and remedies as she would have had with regard to non-conforming new goods.

III. Sale of Animals

15 Another option was much more controversial. According to Article 3 (5) (b) of the Sale of Goods Directive, Member States may exclude the application of the Directive to the purchase of animals. This option did not exist under the Consumer Sales Directive, which meant that pleas to have the presumption of proof of (then) art. 7:18 (2) BW not applied to the sale of animals[38] were simply directed at the wrong legislator: such pleas should have been made to the European legislator adopting the directive and not at the Dutch legislator transposing it. As a result, the B2C-sale of animals simply fell under consumer sales law. Of course, where relevant, use could be made of the exceptions to the reversal of the burden of proof if the ensuing presumption of non-conformity is incompatible with the nature of the goods or of the lack of conformity. In many cases it will be immediately clear that the reversal of the burden of proof should not be applied. For example, the nature of the goods stands in the way of the application of the reversal of the burden of proof when the average life expectancy of an animal species is only a few months and that period has expired: in such case, the consumer simply could not expect the animal to grow older. For example, some species of octopuses have an average life expectancy of around 6 months.[39] The mere fact that such an octopus turns out to have died after five months, then does not justify the presumption that the octopus already had a hidden defect upon delivery: if the *average* life expectancy of the octopus is around 6 months, the consumer must take into account the possibility that the specimen she is buying may live somewhat longer but also that it may die a bit earlier. On the other hand, a broken neck in a guinea pig will indicate that the animal fell *after* delivery (otherwise the consumer would not have taken it home with her),[40] so that in this

---

[35] Cf. art. 10 (6) SGD.
[36] Cf. art. 7 (1) CSD.
[37] See *Kamerstukken II*, 2020/21, 35 734, no. 3, p. 62–63.
[38] *Kamerstukken I* 2002/03, 27 809, no. 32, p. 2.
[39] Cf. <https://en.wikipedia.org/wiki/Octopus#Lifespan> accessed on 1 February 2022.
[40] The example is borrowed from *Kamerstukken I* 2002/03, 27 809, no. 32, p. 2.

B. Scope of application

case, the presumption of non-conformity is incompatible with the nature of the lack of conformity.

When transposing the Sale of Goods Directive, the government decided not to make use of the option to exclude the sale of animals from the scope of the act transposing the Directive arguing that this would decrease consumer protection.[41] According to the government, the extension of the reversal of the burden of proof (from six to twelve months) would not lead to substantially higher burdens for the pet industry, because the most common problems with frequently sold pets do not often manifest themselves in the period from six to twelve months after delivery.[42] Moreover, excluding the sale of animals from the scope of the act would mean that no reversal of the burden of proof applies at all.[43] Finally, a stricter liability regime could contribute to professional breeders taking more precautions to prevent diseases and defects in animals, so that animal welfare also argues against making use of this option, the government argued.[44]

16

However, in parliament, several political parties questioned the government's choice on this point. The government was asked to consider excluding the sale of animals altogether, excluding these sales contracts from the extension of the period for which the reversal of proof applies, or excluding the sale of some types of animals (e.g. horses and farm animals).[45] The government replied, first of all, that it had chosen to apply a uniform period of time for the reversal of the burden of proof for all products – goods including living animals, digital content and digital services – as such a uniform period offers clarity and legal certainty for both consumers and traders.[46] Moreover, according to the government, the Sale of Goods Directive only offers Member States the possibility to exclude animals from the scope of the directive, but not to shorten the reversal of the burden of proof from one year to half a year.[47] A distinction between types of animals – with some species that would be governed by the act transposing the Directive and some not – also was seen to be in conflict with the Directive.[48] In addition, the government repeated its remarks on the absence of any rule on the reversal of the burden of proof if the sale of animals would be excluded[49] and on animal welfare and the need for a stricter liability regime in order to stimulate professional breeders to take more precautionary measures.[50]

17

Whereas the latter argument may have been correct, the former arguments certainly are not. The Sale of Goods Directive indeed only allows Member States to determine whether or not to apply the act transposing the Directive to the sale of animals. However, when a Member State makes use of this option, the sale of animals does not fall within the harmonised area for that Member State, just as the sale of goods sold to consumers by way of execution does not fall within the scope of the Directive by virtue of Article 3(4)(b) of the Sale of Goods Directive. This then means that that Member State is free to determine which rules apply to such sales contracts. The national legislator may then choose to declare the rules of the consumer purchase to apply *mutatis mutandis* to the purchase of animals with the adaptations that that Member State considers desirable – such as a shorter or longer reversal of the burden of proof, a different period of

18

---

[41] *Kamerstukken II*, 2020/21, 35 734, no. 3, p. 24.
[42] *Kamerstukken II*, 2020/21, 35 734, no. 3, p. 9.
[43] *Kamerstukken II* 2020/21, 35 734, no. 3, p. 24.
[44] *Kamerstukken II*, 2020/21, 35 734, no. 3, p. 24.
[45] *Kamerstukken II* 2020/21, 35 734, no. 6, p. 5–6 and 9–10.
[46] *Kamerstukken II* 2020/21, 35 734, no. 7, p. 6 and 11–12.
[47] *Kamerstukken II* 2020/21, 35 734, no. 7, p. 11 and 19.
[48] *Kamerstukken II* 2020/21, 35 734, no. 7, p. 19.
[49] *Kamerstukken II* 2020/21, 35 734, no. 7, p. 11–12 and 19.
[50] *Kamerstukken II* 2020/21, 35 734, no. 7, p. 12.

liability or a different regulation for the duty to notify. Even the choice to apply the act transposing the Directive to some species of animals and not to apply to other species (e.g. horses or farm animals) would be within the legislator's discretion. In order to do so, the legislator could make use of the same legislative technique as that by which, under art. 7:5 (5) BW, the rules of on consumer sales have been declared applicable by analogy to the supply of energy (with some amendments), or by providing that some provisions of consumer sales law do not apply or are modified, as the legislator has done in art. 7:19 BW with regard to goods sold to consumers by way of execution. European law would not oppose such choice, precisely because Member States have been given the possibility to retain their authority on this matter.

19 Whether this possibility should be used is ultimately a political decision. In this respect it is not surprising that in parliament two amendments were suggested to limit the reversal of the burden of proof to three or six months.[51] Both amendments were rejected,[52] but in the senate the question was raised again.[53] In turn, the government insisted that a uniform period for the reversal of the burden of proof for all consumer sales contracts was preferable from the point of view of clarity, legal unity and legal equality, as well in the interest of good animal welfare and a better legal position for consumers. The government urged the senate to continue its deliberations as the time for transposition of the directives has already elapsed.[54] The senate then accepted a motion calling for a bill reintroducing the six months period for the sale of animals, arguing that the pre-existing legislation contained a good balance between the interests of consumers and sellers of living animals, and that it provided ample incentive for professional breeders to take precautionary measures to prevent diseases and defects in animals. Moreover, it was argued that since the government pursues an international level playing field, it was considered relevant that several countries had made use of the option provided by the directive to exclude the sale of live animals from its scope altogether.[55] The government then gave in, and accepted to submit a bill in accordance with the senate's wishes as soon as possible. With that promise, the senate then accepted the bill as proposed.[56] The bill to amend the law accordingly is currently pending in parliament.[57]

20 The sale of animals is therefore currently governed by the same rules as for the sale of other consumer goods, but it looks like that, at a later moment, the period for the reversal of the burden of proof will be restricted to six months after delivery. Personally I do not consider the arguments in favour of a different treatment for the sale of animals to be valid. But that sentiment is personal indeed – I can imagine that a professional seller of, for instance, horses would argue that the sale of horses is in fact special, given the fact that an animal needs care and attention and that a lot may happen to the animal after its delivery to the consumer to which the seller is not privy.[58]

---

[51] *Kamerstukken II* 2020/21, 35 734, nos. 11 (three months) and 10 (six months).
[52] *Handelingen II* 2021/22, no. 44, item 10, p. 1.
[53] *Kamerstukken I* 2021/22, 35 734, no. B, p. 2.
[54] *Kamerstukken I* 2021/22, 35 734, no. C, p. 2.
[55] *Kamerstukken I* 2021/22, 35 734, no. F, p. 1–2.
[56] As mentioned above, the act was formally published on 26 April 2022 and is applicable to consumer sales contracts concluded as of 27 April 2022.
[57] *Kamerstukken I* 2021/22, 36 163, no. 2.
[58] See the explanation of the amendment to restrict the reversal of the burden of proof to three months: *Kamerstukken II* 2020/21, 35 734, no. 11.

C. Contracts in exchange for Payment of a Price

For the SGD to apply, the consumer must have agreed to pay a price. The DCD may also apply where the consumer undertakes to provide or provides personal data in exchange for the supply of the digital content or the digital service. These notions will be discussed below in this section and the next.

Dutch law does not expressly indicate what is meant by 'price'. This notion is not explained in the SGD either, but art. 2 under (7) DCD defines 'price' as 'money or a digital representation of value that is due in exchange for the supply of digital content or a digital service'. Whereas price as such is not defined, art. 7:50aa (f) BW does define the notion of 'digital representation of value' with a somewhat circular definition as 'a digital representation of value other than a price in money, that is due in exchange for the supply of digital content or a digital service'. This includes both crypto-coins and e-coupons.[59] This suggests that the notion of 'price' is restricted for an amount in money. This is implicitly confirmed in the explanatory memorandum, which first indicates that the Sale of Goods Direct pertains to sales contract by which goods are delivered to a consumer in exchange for the payment of a price *in money*.[60] The Digital Content Directive, by contrast, is said to pertain to aspects of contracts under which digital content or a digital service is supplied against payment of a) a price, b) a digital representation of value, or c) in exchange for the supply of personal data.[61] This seems to confirm that 'price' does not relate to a digital representation of value.

When looking more closely, a peculiarity in both recital 23 of the preamble to the DCD, and the explanatory memorandum of the Dutch government[62] is revealed. Both the recital and the explanatory memorandum indicate that crypto-coins can only be considered as 'digital representation of value' if and in so far as these crypto-coins have been recognized as such under national law – which so far is not the case under Dutch law. Such a restrictive approach to the notion of 'digital representation of value' does not follow from the text of art. 2 (7) DCD or of art. 7:50aa (f) BW. Moreover, I also think this is wrong. Obviously, whether or not crypto-coins can be regarded as *money*, is something that the legislator has a say in. But if it is not money, it should be seen as an alternative means of payment (just as e-vouchers are regarded as such) – provided of course that both the consumer and the trader agree that such payment discharges the consumer's obligation to pay. Moreover, if the parties would agree to such payment *and* payment by crypto-currency would not be seen as payment within the meaning of a price (in the sense of art. 2 (7) DCD) or of 'digital representation of value' (in the sense of art. 7:50aa (f) BW), this would mean that contracts by which goods, digital content or a digital service is provided in exchange of a payment in a crypto currency would not be within the scope of consumer sales, digital content or digital services law. This would then mean that such contracts are simply unregulated and that the consumer may not rely on the protection of mandatory law applicable to the sale of goods or the supply of digital content and digital services.

---

[59] *Kamerstukken II* 2021/22, 35 734, no. 3, p. 5 and 40, and recital 23 of the preamble to the DCD.

[60] *Kamerstukken II* 2021/22, 35 734, no. 3, p. 3: 'De richtlijn verkoop goederen heeft betrekking op koopovereenkomsten waarbij tastbare goederen tegen betaling van een prijs *in geld* worden geleverd aan de consument' (emphasis added, MBML). See also *Kamerstukken II* 2021/22, 35 940, no. 3, p. 40.

[61] *Kamerstukken II* 2021/22, 35 734, no. 3, p. 5: 'De richtlijn heeft betrekking op aspecten van overeenkomsten waarbij digitale inhoud of een digitale dienst tegen betaling van a) een prijs, b) een digitale weergave van waarde, of c) in ruil voor persoonsgegevens wordt geleverd aan de consument'.

[62] *Kamerstukken II* 2021/22, 35 734, no. 3, p. 40.

D. Contracts in exchange for the Provision of Personal Data

I. Personal Data as Counter-performance

24   The Digital Content Directive does not regulate whether the provision of personal data is to be seen as a real counter-performance for the supply of the digital content or the digital service and whether the consumer could be held liable or whether the trader may terminate the contract in case the consumer does not provide the personal data or provides incorrect personal data, e.g. by giving a false address. Similarly, the Directive does not regulate whether withdrawing consent to processing of personal data is to be seen as a unilateral termination of the digital content contract by the consumer or entitles the trader to terminate for non-performance: this is left to the Member States.[63] In practice, of course the consumer offers the trader something which is of value to that trader, in order to receive the digital content or digital service. In economic terms, this implies that the personal data is indeed to be seen as the counter-performance for the digital content or digital service that is provided to the consumer. This is also how the Dutch legislator sees the consumer's obligation to provide the trader with personal data.[64]

25   Although the matter has not been regulated before, this does not appear to be a new position for Dutch law. Already in 2017, the Minister of Economic Affairs, in answer to questions from parliament,[65] stated that the possibility for consumers to pay with personal data should be welcomed in order to stimulate innovation and economic growth, subject, however, to the consumer being fully informed prior to her acceptance of the exchange, and to the application of the rules on privacy protection, nowadays governed by the General Data Protection Regulation (hereafter: GDPR).[66] Moreover, in literature it has been observed that contracts under which the consumer 'pays' with personal data are not a novelty: such contracts can also be within the scope of the Services Directive,[67] the E-commerce Directive[68] and the Telecomcode,[69] as long as the consumer's counterpart has a commercial interest in the personal data that is provided in exchange.[70] Indeed, in the parliamentary proceedings the government indicated that it is already customary for a consumers to be supplied with digital content or digital services in exchange for consenting to the processing of her personal data, and that the consumer thus is entitled to a properly functioning product. In the view of the government, the act transposing the Digital Content Directive (merely) ensures that with regard to the legal remedies for lack of conformity it is irrelevant whether the consumer has paid for the digital content or the digital service in money, by way of 'digital representation of value', or by providing personal data.[71] In this respect it is hardly surprising that the introduction of art. 7:50ab (1)(b) BW, which provides for the extension of the scope of the provisions on digital content to contracts under which the

---

[63] Cf. Karin Sein and Gerald Spindler, 'The new Directive on Contracts for the Supply of Digital Content and Digital Services – Scope of Application and Trader's Obligation to Supply – Part 1', (2019) 3 ERCL 257 (265).

[64] *Kamerstukken II*, 2020/21, 35 734, no. 3, p. 10.

[65] *Aanhangsel van Handelingen II* 2016/17, 2669.

[66] Regulation (EU) 2016/679, OJ 2016, L 119/1.

[67] Directive 2006/123/EC, OJ 2006, L 376/36.

[68] Directive 2000/31/EC, OJ 2000, L 178/1.

[69] Directive (EU) 2018/1972, OJ 2018, L 321/36.

[70] Esther van Schagen, 'De kwalificatie van de overeenkomst tot levering van digitale diensten en inhoud in het Europese recht', (2021) 3 *TvC* 137 (145).

[71] *Kamerstukken II*, 2020/21, 35 734, no. 3, p. 10.

D. Contracts in exchange for the Provision of Personal Data

consumer 'pays' for the digital content or the digital service by providing personal data to the provider, has not spiked much attention in Dutch literature and in parliamentary proceedings.

II. Consent to Processing of Personal Data and Withdrawal of Consent

Notwithstanding the relatively unequivocal acceptance of the applicability of the legislation to contracts under which the consumer 'pays' for the digital content or the digital service by providing personal data to the trader, some critical remarks have been made, in particular by the Dutch Data Protection Authority (AP). The regulator advised the government to express in the wording of art. 7:50ab (1)(b) BW that payment with personal data should be seen as consent to process the personal data.[72] The government responded that this is not required by the Directive and that it is not in accordance with government policy to introduce additional rules in the act transposing a directive.[73] In my view, it seems doubtful whether an express legal provision is necessary here. Application of general contract law in this case will lead to the conclusion that such consent is indeed provided as obtaining the consumer's consent to process her personal data is the reason for requesting the personal data in the first place – and the consumer cannot reasonably be unaware of that. The mere fact that the consumer cannot conclude the contract unless she has consented to the processing of her personal data, e.g. by ticking a box, need not stand in the way of the consent having been given freely as she can decide not to conclude the contract[74] – which in the case of digital content or digital services is not illusionary as both this trader and its competitors may offer the same or similar content or services under different conditions, e.g. for payment of a modest price in money.

The consumer remains, however, entitled to withdraw her consent for the processing of her personal data under Art. 7 (3) GDPR. Moreover, the trader is required to inform the consumer thereof before she gives her consent.[75] In the context of a contract for the supply of digital content or digital services in exchange for the provision of personal data, this implies that the consumer must be informed of her right to withdraw her consent before the contract is concluded. Art. 7:50ab(5) BW indicates that for a digital content contract where the consumer does not (also) undertake to pay a price, the consumer's withdrawal of consent is to be understood as implying that the consumer is no longer bound to the contract. The withdrawal of consent thus implies unilateral termination of the digital content contract.[76] The consumer is not required to return any performances already received from the trader. The government justifies this by explaining that the GDPR's provisions on the giving and withdrawing of consent aim for the protection of the person whose personal data are processed, and an obligation to return any performances already received from the trader would undermine the protection offered to the consumer by the GDPR.[77]

---

[72] AP, Advice of 16 April 2020, *Kamerstukken II*, 2020/21, 35 734, annex to no. 3, p. 9.

[73] *Kamerstukken II*, 2020/21, 35 734, no. 3, p. 4.

[74] Cf Hans Graux, 'Privacybescherming op sociale netwerken: heeft u nog een privéleven', in Peggy Valcke et al. (eds.), *Sociale media. Actuele juridische aspecten* (2013), 1 (10–11).

[75] Art. 7(3) and 13(2)(c) GDPR.

[76] *Kamerstukken II*, 2020/21, 35 734, no. 3, p. 11. See in this sense also AP, Advice of 16 April 2020, *Kamerstukken II*, 2020/21, 35 734, annex to no. 3, p. 4.

[77] *Kamerstukken II*, 2020/21, 35 734, no. 3, p. 12.

28   The question then is whether the opposite is true as well: should the consumer's statement to the trader expressing her decision to terminate the contract[78] be interpreted as to *also* include a statement expressing her decision to withdraw consent to the processing of the personal data she provided? It should be noted that neither the GDPR nor the Digital Content Directive specify how the consumer is to withdraw her consent to the processing of the personal data: art. 7(3) GDPR merely indicates that withdrawing consent must be as easy as giving it, and its wording suggest that the consumer is required to take action towards the trader. The question of how to withdraw consent is left to national law. Dutch data protection law does not contain an explicit provision to this extent, but general patrimonial law does: art. 3:37 (1) BW provides that statements may be made in any form. In other words: no formal requirements exist as regards the manner in which the consumer may withdraw her consent for the processing of information.[79] The explanatory memorandum confirms that no formal requirement applies to the withdrawal of consent[80] and adds that the consumer needs not separately withdraw her consent to the processing of her personal data when terminating the contract.[81] From this it follows that a consumer's notice of termination should be interpreted as implying also withdrawal of that consumer's consent to processing her personal data.

III. No Liability for the Failure to Provide (correct) Personal Data and Processing thereof

29   The Dutch legislator confirmed that since, according to the GDPR, the consumer is entitled to withdraw consent at any time, she cannot be held liable for breach of contract if she withdraws consent.[82] In such a case, however, the trader cannot be expected to continue to perform its obligations under the contract and is entitled to block the consumer's access to the digital content or the digital service.[83]

30   If the consumer neither withdraws consent to the processing of her personal data nor terminates the digital content contract, she is of course required to honour her obligations under the contract. The question arises whether the trader is entitled to a remedy if she does not – either by not providing the promised personal data or by

---

[78] There are free situations where the consumer may terminate the digital content contract:
(1) as a remedy for non-performance for the trader's failure to supply the digital content even after having received a notice allowing the trader a final period to perform her obligation within a reasonable time after having received the notice (art. 7:50ah(1) BW;
(2) as a remedy for lack of conformity, if the consumer is not entitled to demand that the trader brings the digital content or the digital service into conformity, the trader is not able or willing to cure the lack of conformity within a reasonable period and without causing significant inconvenience to the consumer, or the lack of conformity is such as to justify immediate termination (art. 7:50ai(4) BW); or
(3) in case of a digital content contract that is to be performed over a period of time, when the trader changes the digital content or the digital service to a larger extent than is necessary to keep the digital content or service in conformity with the contract, and the change bears negative and non-negligible consequences for the consumer's access to or use of the digital content or the digital service (art. 7:50al (2) BW).

[79] According to Art. 3:59 BW, Art. 3:37(1) BW applies also outside the field of patrimonial law since such application is neither incompatible with the nature of the juridical act of withdrawing consent nor with the nature of the relation between the trader and the consumer.

[80] *Kamerstukken II*, 2020/21, 35 734, no. 3, p. 11–12. The website of the Dutch regulator for data protection, the AP, contains model letters showing consumers how to actually withdraw consent, https://autoriteitpersoonsgegevens.nl/nl/zelf-doen/voorbeeldbrieven-privacyrechten (last accessed on 1 February 2022).

[81] Cf. *Kamerstukken II*, 2020/21, 35 734, no. 3, p. 14. See in this sense also AP, Advice of 16 April 2020, *Kamerstukken II*, 2020/21, 35 734, annex to no. 3, p. 4.

[82] *Kamerstukken II*, 2020/21, 35 734, no. 3, p. 12 and 46.

[83] *Kamerstukken II*, 2020/21, 35 734, no. 3, p. 12.

providing false data. In my view, the fact that the consumer can withdraw consent and thus terminate the digital content contract at any time without being liable for damages suggests that a non-performance by the consumer to provide the (correct) personal data does not lead to liability either.[84] This does not mean that the trader in such a case is required to perform its obligations under the contract nonetheless. It may be that data protection law stands in the way of liability of the consumer, but the specific nature of the consumer's non-performance does not justify that the trader would also be deprived from its right to invoke termination of the contract for non-performance.

IV. The Poor Pay More – with their Privacy

In its advice to the government, the AP also pointed to the risk that people who have less money to spend are put under undue influence to permit the infringement of their fundamental rights[85] and that unequal bargaining positions and too wide a scope for consent could seriously erode the protection of personal data.[86] The AP therefore recommended that the bill should designate forms of consent that are to constitute counter-performance for the supply of digital content and digital services that are presumed to be unacceptable and therefore lead to the possibility for the consumer to invoke avoidance of the contract. Since the rules on validity of contracts have not been harmonized, the Member States have retained the possibility to maintain or introduce rules in this area, the AP argues.[87] The government, however, did not consider it expedient to only regulate the possible avoidance of contracts for the supply of digital content and digital services, as similar cases exist where personal data are supplied 'in exchange' for the supply of 'free' toy cars, tennis balls and pregnancy boxes. According to the government, this matter should be solved more generically, and not within the course of this bill, as that would go beyond what is necessary for the proper implementation of the Directives.[88] That the frequency of 'free' digital content and digital service being offered in exchange for personal data is considerably higher than that of the supply of 'free' toy cars, tennis balls and pregnancy boxes, and that the risks of abuse of personal data are considerably higher in the former case, is as such ignored by the government. Yet, the government did announce that it will consider 'possible directions for solutions at the national and European level' and to inform parliament thereof.[89]

E. Conformity and remedies for lack of conformity

I. Mixing Conformity Period, Reversal of the Burden of Proof, and Duty to Notify

With regard to conformity, the reversal of the burden of proof and the duty to notify, the legislator has chosen to change the existing rules on consumer sales as little as

---

[84] Cf. Carmen Langhanke and Martin Schmidt-Kessel, 'Consumer Data as Consideration' (2015) 6 *EuCML* 218 (221–222).
[85] AP, Advice of 16 April 2020, *Kamerstukken II*, 2020/21, 35 734, annex to no. 3, p. 15.
[86] Ibidem, p. 7.
[87] Ibidem, p. 6.
[88] *Kamerstukken II*, 2020/21, 35 734, no. 3, p. 14.
[89] *Kamerstukken II* 2020/21, 35 734, no. 7, p. 14 and 15. The report was said to be sent to parliament in the autumn of 2021. However, enquiries with the Ministry of Justice and Security revealed that the report will not be sent to parliament until around the summer of 2022.

possible and to follow the text of the Directives closely. This implies that the conformity period is not capped at two years after delivery of the goods; remedies, therefore, remain available throughout the economic lifespan of the goods. In exchange, the consumer's duty to notify a lack of conformity continues to apply, and the reversal of the burden is not (further) extended than is required by the Sale of Goods Directive.

33 The conformity period is thus not capped at two years after delivery of the goods; remedies, therefore, remain available throughout the economic lifespan of the goods. Limiting liability to two years after delivery, the government argued, would be in stark contrast to the call from parliament during the discussions on the Directives for a high level of consumer protection. Moreover, it argued, this decision is in line with the ordinary approach to not further amend the law than is required for the proper transposition of the Directives.[90]

34 In exchange, the legislator made use of the option to maintain the consumer's duty to notify the defect within a reasonable period of time after the consumer has discovered the lack of conformity.[91] The Authority for Consumers and Markets (ACM), in its advice to the government, had suggested to reconsider the decision to maintain the duty to notify. In recent case-law the Supreme Court held that if the seller did not sustain any disadvantage as a consequence of the breach of the duty to notify, the mere breach would not automatically lead to the conclusion that the consumer would have lost all remedies for the lack of conformity. Instead, the Supreme Court called for a weighing of the mutual interests of seller and buyer. The ACM stated that in light of this case-law the duty to notify should either be abolished for consumer sales contracts or retained only when certain (unspecified) conditions were met.[92] The government merely repeated its earlier argument that the duty to notify is an important pillar in the Dutch system of conformity and that it is necessary to strike a good balance between the interests of consumers and sellers and a proper functioning of the open period for lack of conformity for goods with differing economic life spans.[93]

35 The legislator has also chosen not to (further) extend the reversal of the burden of proof from one to two years after delivery.[94] The ACM in its advice to the government had advised the government to make use of this option because, according to the Authority, consumers, in particular vulnerable consumers, find it difficult to assert their rights in the event of a lack of conformity and the ACM itself, when enforcing the Consumer Protection Enforcement Act, also encounters the difficulty of proving that a product is not in conformity upon delivery. An extension of the reversal of the burden of proof to two years would make application of the Consumer Protection Enforcement Act by the ACM easier.[95] By contrast, the government took the view that a uniform period for reversing the burden of proof for defective goods, digital content and digital services would offer clarity and legal certainty for both consumers and traders – as was mentioned above with regard to the inclusion of contracts for the sale of animals.[96] In this respect, the government argued, it is relevant that for digital content and services, art. 12 (1) DCD, codified in art. 7:50a (3)(b) BW, restricts the reversal of the burden of proof to one year after delivery without the possibility for Member States to introduce

---

[90] *Kamerstukken II* 2020/21, 35 734, no. 3, p. 21.
[91] Cf. art. 12 SGD.
[92] Advice ACM, p. 3, published as attachment to *Kamerstukken II* 2020/21, 35 734, no. 3.
[93] *Kamerstukken II* 2020/21, 35 734, no. 3, p. 20.
[94] Cf. art. 11 (1) and (2) SGD.
[95] Advice ACM, p. 2-3, published as attachment to *Kamerstukken II* 2020/21, 35 734, no. 3. In the report of parliament's standing committee on Justice and Security, some political parties supported this suggestion whereas other parties opposed it, cf. *Kamerstukken II*, 2020/21, 35 734, no. 6, p. 4-6.
[96] *Kamerstukken II* 2020/21, 35 734, no. 7, p. 6 and 11-12.

or maintain a longer period. In addition, an extension of the presumption of the reversal of the burden of proof to two years was considered disproportionate for sellers. It would thus disturb the balance between the protection of the consumer and the obligations of sellers.[97] In this particular case I have sympathy for the government's choice for a uniform period for reversing the burden of proof. In this respect, it should be noted that DVDs, USB sticks, memory cards and other tangible durable media that serve exclusively as a carrier of digital content do not fall under the regulation of consumer sales but under that of digital content and digital services. It seems difficult to explain to consumers and sellers alike why the burden of proof would be reversed for only one year if a consumer purchased music on a CD or downloaded a music file from a website, but for two years of the consumer had purchased an 'old-fashioned' album on vinyl.

36 For digital content and digital services, a slightly different regime had to be construed as the Digital Content Directive does not allow for the introduction or maintenance of a duty to notify. Art. 7:50ap (2) BW therefore provides that the duty to notify under general contract law (art. 6:89 BW) is not applicable in the case of a contract for the supply of digital content or digital services. For this reason, the legislator introduced a prescription period for all claims and defences based on a lack of conformity of two years after delivery, unless the consumer did not know and need not have known of the lack of conformity, taking into account in any case the price or digital representation of value and the reasonable expectations of the consumer as to the duration of use of the digital content or digital service (art. 7:50ag (2) BW).[98] Effectively, this means that liability for defective digital content or defective digital services is not capped to two years either. Moreover, this provision is also intended to transpose art. 11 (3) DCD with regard to a contract which provides for continuous supply over a period of time in case the lack of conformity manifests within the contract period.[99] Finally, it also deals with a lack of conformity which is in fact caused by a defective update or upgrade that was provided by the trader in order to keep the digital content or the digital service in conformity with the contract or to improve its functionality, interoperability or compatibility, as any such defect could not have been discovered by the consumer before the update or upgrade was supplied. The legislator did not indicate when the prescription period commences when such a hidden defect manifests, but it would seem logical that this period would then start at the moment when the hidden defect is or should have been discovered by the consumer.

II. Updates

37 Art. 7:18 (4) BW, with regard to goods with digital elements, and art. 7:50ae (4) BW, with regard to digital content and digital services, provide that the trader is required to provide the updates, including security updates, that are necessary to ensure that the goods, the digital content or the digital services remain in conformity as long as the consumer may reasonably expect them to be provided, and to inform the consumer of their availability. The explanatory memorandum indicates that these provisions, which transpose art. 7 (3) SGD and art. 8 (2) DCD, make clear that an update is to be seen as the supply of additional digital content, which is necessary to ensure that the goods, the digital content or the digital service at least continue to function at the level they functioned at the moment of the original delivery or supply of that good, that digital content or that digital service. Unless contractually agreed, the trader is not required to supply an up-

---

[97] *Kamerstukken II*, 2020/21, 35 734, no. 3, p. 7–8 and 20.
[98] See *Kamerstukken II* 2020/21, 35 734, no. 3, p. 51 and 69.
[99] See *Kamerstukken II* 2020/21, 35 734, no. 3, p. 69.

date to *improve* the functionality of the good, the digital content or the digital service beyond the requirements of conformity, e.g. by offering an upgrade to a newer version of the operating system.[100]

38   Before the bill transposing the SGD and the DCD was submitted to parliament, an (almost identical) draft was published for consultation on the Internet.[101] The response from the business side to the draft-version of art. 7:18 (4) BW was unanimously negative. Business organizations (as well as one individual) all emphasized that imposing such an obligation on the *seller* (or, as the case may be, on the provider of the digital content) – instead of on the developer of the digital content is the wrong idea: the seller does not play a role in practice in the development and provision of updates; is not capable of successfully demanding updates from the developer of the digital content; is not informed by them of updates; and – in particular with regard to contracts concluded on business premises – often does not even have the correct contact details of the consumer and therefore could not comply with this obligation even if it wanted to. One business organization expressly argued that insofar as the seller is accountable for the provision of updates, an obligation should be imposed on developers of digital content to inform sellers when an update is available.[102]

39   The legislator acknowledged that the obligation of the seller or the provider of digital content to update the digital content in practice requires the trader to conclude a contract with a third party, such as the producer of the goods or of the digital content or a third party to provide such updates. The government, however, also pointed in another direction: the traders could also make use of the possibility under art. 7:18 (6) and the corresponding provision under art. 7:50a (6) BW, to exclude their obligation to provide an update altogether, provided that they inform the consumer thereof expressly and the consumer accepts the exclusion expressly and separately. In such case, the government stated expressly, there is not a lack of conformity if no updates are provided and as a consequence the goods, the digital content or the digital service no longer functions properly.[103] In its advice to the government, the Dutch Advisory Board on Regulatory Burden (*Adviescollege toetsing regeldruk*, ATR)[104] argued that if traders would extensively make use of this option, for example because producers do not want to make any promises about updates, and consumers would agree to the exclusion, this would have major consequences for consumers. According to the ATR, the update obligation could become a 'paper reality'.[105]

40   In fact, it could be worse. If the possibility to escape from the obligation to send updates is used, the trader might not even be liable for lack of conformity if a security update would be necessary in order to be able to continue using the goods or the digital content or service without running the risk of damage thereto or to other goods or digital content that belong to the consumer, in particular if the lack of conformity manifests after one year has passed since delivery, as the consumer is then required to prove that the security risk existed already at the original moment of delivery – which is pretty much impossible for a consumer to prove.

---

[100] *Kamerstukken II* 2021/22, 35 734, no. 3, p. 7.
[101] The consultation draft, as well as the consultation memorandum and the responses thereto are available (in Dutch), <https://www.internetconsultatie.nl/verkoop_goederen_levering_digitale_inhoud>, accessed on 3 February 2022.
[102] See the response by Techniek Nederland.
[103] *Kamerstukken II* 2021/22, 35 734, no. 3, p. 7.
[104] The ATR is is an independent and external advisory body that advises government and parliament on how to minimize regulatory burdens.
[105] Advice ATR, p. 3, published as attachment to *Kamerstukken II* 2020/21, 35 734, no. 3.

Moreover, this offers online traders – over the back of consumers – a competitive advantage vis-à-vis traders that operate through traditional shops (and that in many cases are SMEs). Traders dealing via a web shop can develop a script whereby the consumer purchasing goods with digital elements, digital content or digital services online may be faced with a warning that no updates will be provided and be required to expressly and separately accept the exclusion before being able to continue ordering the product they want to purchase. The procedure would be more or less the same as what is already in place with regard to the acceptance of the applicability of standard terms – and everyone is aware that consumers effectively have no alternative but to tick the box expressing their acceptance. Traders dealing on business premises – i.e. electronics companies offering their products in a brick-and-mortar shop – are far less likely to be able to exclude the update obligation in such manner or to obtain and keep proof of the consumer's express acceptance.

III. Durability and Sustainability with regard to Updates of Goods with Digital Elements

The European legislator's choice to impose the update obligation on that trader, and to even allow the seller or provider to exclude this obligation altogether, is regrettable also with a view to sustainability, in particular with regard to goods with digital elements. First, the update obligation aims at prolonging the economic lifespan of the goods by requiring the trader to update the digital content in order to remedy any bugs that have been discovered and thus to allow the consumer to safely continue using them. When updates are (no longer) provided, consumers may find themselves forced to purchase new goods, even though technically there is nothing wrong with the older goods (yet). That is a waste of valuable resources that could easily have been prevented.

Moreover, as the seller typically cannot provide the updates themselves, it will have to rely on the developer of the digital content or a third party to provide the update (whether the seller is aware of the update being provided or not and whether or not the seller has concluded an express contract for such updates). As the seller of the goods is under an obligation of result to provide the update, it will be liable for lack of conformity if the developer of the digital content fails to provide the updates. The consumer may then have a claim for replacement, termination, price reduction or damages, but repair – which is the most sustainable remedy in case of the sale of goods – cannot be offered without the help of a knowledgeable third party as the seller of the goods with digital elements is typically not able to provide the updates itself. If the consumer chooses repair over replacement, in accordance with art. 7:21 (4) BW and art. 13 (2) SGD, the seller may block that choice if this would impose disproportionate costs on the seller, taking into account all circumstances, including whether replacement could be provided without significant inconvenience to the consumer. Moreover, even if the consumer would be entitled to repair as the costs may be high but not disproportionate for the seller, enforcing that right where the seller *refuses* to offer an update is illusionary: it would effectively force the consumer to go to court. In such case it is more likely that the consumer would either accept the seller's offer for replacement or simply terminate the contract and obtain a replacing good from another seller – and if need be take the first seller to court for reimbursement of the sales price: that, at least, would save the consumer time before being able to make use of the goods again. But, again, that would mean that goods that possibly could easily have been 'repaired' through an update will simply be thrown away or, at best, be returned to the original seller.

IV. Producer's Liability?

44 The European legislator has chosen not to implement an alternative scenario: that of a producer's liability for defective digital content. Of course, since the matter is not regulated in either the Sale of Goods Directive or the Digital Content Directive, Member States are free to impose an obligation to provide updates also on the developer of the digital content. In fact, recital (13) of the preamble to the Digital Content Directive even invites Member States to regulate liability claims against the developer if that developer is not the supplier of the digital content to the consumer. The introduction of such an obligation would bring about a system, which would be more or less in line with the 1985 Product Liability Directive.[106] Unfortunately, the Dutch legislator has not introduced such solution.

45 Such liability may, however, have been introduced through the backdoor, as it is not always clear whether and to what extent the Digital Content Directive applies. For instance, what happens if the consumer purchases goods with digital elements, but can only make use thereof if she subsequently agrees to the terms of an End User's Licence Agreement (EULA), which is provided by either the producer of the goods or the producer of the digital content? Obviously, the contract with the seller is a consumer sales contract, but how about the EULA? I have previously argued[107] that the DCD should apply to such a contract if in addition to or in the process of concluding the EULA the consumer is required to provide personal data, such as her email address. The producer forcing the consumer to conclude the EULA would then by virtue of art. 7:50ae (4) BW be required vis-à-vis the consumer to provide updates instead of the consumer having to rely on the seller of the goods with digital elements or the supplier of the digital content or service to succeed in concluding a contract with the producer to supply them with such updates. If the producer would then fail to provide updates where these could be expected in order to keep the goods or the digital content or service in conformity, the consumer could invoke contract law remedies against the producer.

V. Durability and Sustainability with regard to 'Ordinary' Goods

46 Even though it was challenged to do so by *Pavillon* in her response to the draft-bill that was circulated on the Internet,[108] the government refrained from a thorough consideration on the matter of sustainability 'as the bill transposing the Directive does not lean itself to dealing with sustainability extensively'.[109] The government merely stated that within the context of art. 7:18 (2) BW, durability pertains to the ability of the goods to continue to be fit for use and therefore as such does not relate to a contribution to a sustainable environment. Nevertheless, the government argued, assuring that goods are more sustainable within the meaning of art. 7:18 (2) BW is important in order to come to more sustainable consumption patterns and to a circular economy. The government stated, however, that durability in the sense of striving for an extension of the life span of a product is as such not an objective of the Sale of Goods Directive.[110]

---

[106] Council Directive 85/374/EEC, OJ 1985, L 210/29.

[107] Marco Loos, 'Not good but certainly content. The proposals for European harmonisation of online and distance selling of goods and the supply of digital content', in: Ignace Claeys et al. Terryn (eds.), *Digital contents & Distance sales. New developments at EU level* (2017), 3 (32).

[108] Charlotte Pavillon, *Reactie op de internetconsultatie* (2020).

[109] *Kamerstukken II* 2020/21, 35 734, no. 3, p. 24: 'De implementatiewet leent zich er niet voor om uitgebreid op het aspect duurzaamheid in zijn algemeenheid in te gaan'.

[110] Ibidem.

The government's reluctant reaction to *Pavillon's* response is regrettable, as the points 47
she makes regarding durability deserve more substantive consideration. *Pavillon* states
that the government should pay attention to its Government-wide Circular Economy
Programme[111] and that in the light of this, the government should critically ascertain
whether the existing scheme of remedies for lack of conformity is in line with sustainability goals. She acknowledges that durability (or sustainability, if you prefer) is not in
itself an objective of the Directives, but argues that they have an important impact on
and could offer a contribution to a shift from a linear towards a circular economy. In
this respect, she points to the question to what extent consumer protection goals and
sustainability goals are reconciled in the provisions on (consumer) sales. In particular,
she argues that the government should elaborate on whether the current Dutch system
of a long period for liability, a duty to notify defects within a short period after the
discovery of a lack of conformity, and the reversal of the burden of proof if a lack
of conformity manifests itself within a year from delivery, provides for the optimal
alignment of consumer protection and sustainability goals.[112]

The argument *Pavillon* makes falls squarely within the leeway that is offered to the 48
Member States when determining the optimal balance between liability of the seller and
the limitations thereof. Moreover, the balance that is struck by the government, in fact,
is not at all too bad from the perspective of sustainability. That may be different with
regard to the *remedies* for lack of conformity, as the Sale of Goods Directive does not
favour repair over replacement, and allows consumers to directly resort to termination
in more cases than the Consumer Sales Directive did. However, the national legislator
was bound by these choices made at the European level, and therefore sustainability
considerations could not have led to a different outcome as to the provisions transposing
these rules into Dutch law.

F. Conclusion

The transposition of the Sale of Goods Directive and the Digital Content Directive 49
into Dutch law has taken an awful long time. The reason for this is not easily discernible:
the bill that was finally submitted to parliament is almost a carbon-copy of the consultation draft that was published on the Internet a year earlier. Moreover, the legislator
has chosen to amend the pre-existing legislation as little as possible, and not to make
use of any options the directives offered unless making use of them was necessary to
prevent having to amend pre-existing legislation nor to expand the scope of application
to non-consumers purchasing goods, digital content or digital services. Regrettably, the
Dutch legislator also did not pick up on recital (13) of the preamble to the Digital
Content Directive, which invites Member States to regulate liability claims against the
developer if that developer is not the supplier of the digital content to the consumer.
In so far as no EULA is concluded or the EULA would not lead to the conclusion of a
separate contract for the supply of digital content, the consumer is left with the seller's or
digital content or service provider's ineffective update obligation.

From a European perspective, the outcome of the transposition process in The 50
Netherlands may appear somewhat surprising. The consumer sales rules apply in full to
the sale of second-hand goods and of animals, and the seller cannot benefit from the two

---

[111] The report *Nederland circulair in 2050. Rijksbreed programma Circulaire Economie* was published on 14 September 2016 and is available at https://www.rijksoverheid.nl/documenten/rapporten/2016/09/14/bijlage-1-nederland-circulair-in-2050 (accessed on 18 January 2022).
[112] Charlotte Pavillon, *Reactie op de internetconsultatie* (2020).

year cut-off period after delivery for limitation of liability. On the other hand, the seller may invoke the consumer's breach of the duty to notify a lack of conformity, and the reversal of the burden of proof is restricted to one year after delivery. It is a pity that the Dutch legislator missed the opportunity to discuss these matters from the perspective of sustainability, but especially the choice to allow conformity claims throughout the economic lifespan of the goods would seem to fit will with sustainability considerations. Such considerations could also have supported the introduction of a regime for liability of the producer of digital content next to that of the seller of goods with digital elements. The application of the consumer sales rules to the sale of animals proved to be the most controversial. Ultimately, parliament accepted that such sales contracts would be governed by the transposing act, under the condition that the government would submit a bill restricting the reversal of the burden of proof again to six month after delivery in case of the sale of living animals.

51 The provisions on digital content and digital services have been placed in a new title of the Civil Code but largely mirror those on consumer sales. The exception to the rule is the duty to notify, as the Digital Content Directive does not allow for the maintenance of the duty with regard to digital content and digital services. Instead, the two-year prescription period for invoking a remedy for lack of conformity starts at delivery *with the exception* of defects that could not have been discovered at delivery. Presumably, prescription then only starts at the moment when the defect is or should have been discovered. That rule will also apply with regard to contracts for the continuous supply of digital content or digital services, and for defects in updates or updates supplied to the consumer. The legislator also seems to have found a way to incorporate the concept of 'payment with personal data' into the scope of application, albeit that the proof of the pudding, as always, is in the eating. That is certainly true with regard to the update obligation under both Directives. I am afraid that this particular pudding will taste rather bland.

Bibliography

Hans Graux, 'Privacybescherming op sociale netwerken: heeft u nog een privéleven', in Peggy Valcke et al. (eds.), *Sociale media. Actuele juridische aspecten* (Intersentia, Antwerp/Cambridge 2013), 1

Jac. Hijma, *Mr. C. Assers Handleiding tot de beoefening van het Nederlands Burgerlijk Recht, Deel 7-I, Bijzondere overeenkomsten. Koop en ruil* (9th edition, Wolters Kluwer, Deventer 2019)

Carmen Langhanke and Martin Schmidt-Kessel, 'Consumer Data as Consideration' (2015) 6 *Journal of European Consumer and Market Law* 218

Marco Loos, 'De (voorgestelde) omzetting van de Richtlijnen verkoop goederen en digitale inhoud', (2021) 4 *Tijdschrift voor Consumentenrecht & handelspraktijken* 216

Marco Loos, 'The (proposed) transposition of the Digital Content Directive in The Netherlands' (2021) 2 *Journal of Intellectual Property, Information Technology and Electronic Commerce Law* 229

Ilse Samoy, 'Het toepassingsgebied van de verschillende koopregelingen in kaart gebracht (gemeenrechtelijke koop, consumentenkoop en internationale koop), met bijzondere aandacht voor gemengd gebruik en gemengde overeenkomsten', 2009 *Tijdschrift voor Belgisch Burgerlijk Recht* 71

Esther van Schagen, 'De kwalificatie van de overeenkomst tot levering van digitale diensten en inhoud in het Europese recht', (2021) 3 *Tijdschrift voor Consumentenrecht & handelspraktijken* 137

Martien Schaub, 'Wie is consument?', (2017) 1 *Tijdschrift voor Consumentenrecht & handelspraktijken* 30

Bibliography

Karin Sein and Gerald Spindler, 'The new Directive on Contracts for the Supply of Digital Content and Digital Services – Scope of Application and Trader's Obligation to Supply – Part 1', (2019) 3 *European Review of Contract Law* 257

Poland[1]

A. Introduction – does it make sense to write this article? 1
B. The brief story on the Polish implementations of the sales directives 8
C. The interpretation of the civil code after the lapse of the period for implementation of the Sales Directive 15
D. Conclusion 26
   Bibliography 26

A. Introduction – does it make sense to write this article?

The initial plan was to write an article on the way in which the new consumer sales directive (2019/771/EU)[2] has been implemented into the Polish legal system. The previous consumer sales directive (1999/44/EC)[3] after a very long process has been successfully implemented into the Polish legal system[4] and a framework has been established for further development of the sales law,[5] inspired by the European law. As a result, it was expected that at least the directive 2019/771/EU (SGD) would be implemented smoothly by amending the existing provisions on seller's liability in the Polish civil code (PCC). In contrast, PCC lacked the framework for the easy implementation of the directive 2019/770/EU (DCD).[6]

The implementation of the SGD was not necessarily an easy task, especially given the full harmonization requirement, but it was manageable within the time given for the implementation to adopt necessary revisions to the PCC. Alternatively, a transposition outside of the PCC could have been prepared, which, however, was not advised for a number of reasons.[7]

---

[1] This article presents part of the research within the project "Homo consumens, Homo ecologicus — ecological efficiency test of the new directive on certain aspects concerning contracts for the sale of goods" financed by Narodowe Centrum Nauki (NCN, National Science Centre) in Kraków, Poland, with the number of 2019/34/A/HS5/00124.

[2] Directive (EU) 2019/771 of the European Parliament and of the Council of 20 May 2019 on certain aspects concerning contracts for the sale of goods, OJ L 136, 22.5.2019, 28–50.

[3] Directive 1999/44/EC of the European Parliament and of the Council of 25 May 1999 on certain aspects of the sale of consumer goods and associated guarantees, OJ L 171, 7.7.1999, 12–16.

[4] On the difficulties during the transposition process, especially in regard to the first transposition of the directive 1999/44 in the Act of 27 July 2002 on special conditions of consumer sales (Journal of Laws 2002 No. 141 pos. 1176) see: Kurowska, 'Implementacja dyrektywy o sprzedaży konsumenckiej do porządków prawnych wybranych państw członkowskich' (2008) 6 *Problemy Współczesnego Prawa Międzynarodowego, Europejskiego i Porównawczego* 96–97; and the subsequent retransposition into the PCC by the Act 30 May 2014 on Consumer Rights (Journal of Laws 2020, pos. 287); Zoll, *Rękojmia. Odpowiedzialność sprzedawcy* (2018) 20–21; Wiewiórowska-Domagalska, 'O celu i metodzie transpozycji dyrektyw unijnych – na przykładzie projektu ustawy o prawach konsumenta' (2014) 1 *Kwartalnik Prawa Prywatnego* 128, 130.

[5] Wiewiórowska-Domagalska, Zoll, Południak-Gierz, Bańczyk, 'Transpozycja dyrektywy Parlamentu Europejskiego i Rady UE 2019/771 z dnia 20 maja 2019 w sprawie niektórych aspektów umów sprzedaży towarów' (2021) 4 *Kwartalnik Prawa Prywatnego* 919, 929.

[6] Pecyna, 'Implementacja dyrektywy o umowach o dostarczanie treści cyfrowych lub usługi cyfrowej — wyzwania dla ustawodawcy krajowego' (2021) 3 *Kwartalnik Prawa Prywatnego* 611–614.

[7] Habryn-Chojnacka, 'Art. 556' in Gutowski, *Kodeks cywilny. Komentarz*, Legalis 2022, No. 8; Wiewiórowska-Domagalska, Zoll, Południak-Gierz, Bańczyk, 'Transpozycja dyrektywy Parlamentu Europejskiego i Rady UE 2019/771 z dnia 20 maja 2019 w sprawie niektórych aspektów umów sprzedaży towarów' (2021) 4 *Kwartalnik Prawa Prywatnego* 917–928.

3   The Polish authorities have not shown sufficient interest in a timely implementation.[8] The process of implementation of the SGD in Poland was hindered by the recent lack of interest in the European integration in general[9] and in the private law as a whole (though there have been a few uncoordinated interventions in the private law recently). Consequently, it is over a year after the deadline for the transposition of the SGD (1.07.2021), the measures necessary to comply with the SGD should have been applied since 1.01.2022, and yet, Poland did not fulfil its implementation duties until 1.01.2023.

4   Polish legislator was not idle during that time. The draft prepared by the Ministry of Justice[10] was submitted to the Parliament on 29th June 2022, and the first reading took place on 16th September 2022.[11] Finally, the Ministry's proposal, with minor changes, was adopted as the Act of 4 November 2022 amending the Act on Consumer Rights, the Act – Civil Code and the Act – Private International Law.[12] The Act entered into force on 1.01.2023.

5   As to the merits, the easiest way of proceeding has been chosen. Instead of considering whether the law derived from the SGD can be integrated into the sales law of the PCC, the drafters opted for the copy-paste approach. They decided to prepare a transposition within an already existing act on the consumer protection (being a statute implementing the directive 2011/83), adding to this (as a new chapter) a set of rules – together with provisions transposing the DCD[13]. The simplistic approach of the governmental drafters has a potential, once adopted, to create chaos in the operation of the system of sales.[14] This Act brings completely different terminology, ignoring that the terms and concepts used in the PCC and by the EU legislator (despite different wording) express the same underpinning ideas, since the differences in understanding of terminology used by PCC and in the directive 1999/44/EC have been already removed in 2014, and the SGD follows the core assumptions of the directive 1999/44/EC.[15]

6   Many of Polish private law academics were surprised as the floor for consultations regarding the government draft was open only for a very limited period of time. In the face of the above, an academic working group[16] was founded to prepare an alternative draft

---

[8] Zoll, Południak-Gierz, Bańczyk, 'The Struggle on Implementation of the Acquis Communautaire into Polish Civil Code' (2022) 20 Nederlands *Tijdschrift voor Burgerlijk Recht* 158.

[9] See on varied issues in which activities of Polish authorities were contrary to the European Union values, including primacy of EU law and independence of justice – Zoll, Południak-Gierz, Bańczyk, *Primacy of EU law and jurisprudence of Polish Constitutional Tribunal*, 8–9; Zoll, Wortham, 'Judicial Independence and Accountability: Withstanding Political Stress in Poland' (2019) 42 *Fordham Int'l L.J.* 889-906; Zoll, Wortham, 'Weaponizing judicial discipline: Poland', in Devlin, Wildeman (ed), *Disciplining judges: Contemporary challenges and controversies* (2021) 284-285.

[10] 'Projekt ustawy o zmianie ustawy o prawach konsumenta i kodeksu cywilnego (2021) 1 Kwartalnik Prawa Prywatnego' 139–156.

[11] https://www.sejm.gov.pl/sejm9.nsf/PrzebiegProc.xsp?nr=2425 (accessed 1.10.2022)

[12] Journal of Laws 2022 pos. 2337.

[13] Directive (EU) 2019/770 of the European Parliament and of the Council of 20 May 2019 on certain aspects concerning contracts for the supply of digital content and digital services, OJ L 136, 22.5.2019, 1–27.

[14] Habryn-Chojnacka, 'Art. 556' in Gutowski, *Kodeks cywilny. Komentarz*, Legalis 2022, No. 8; Wiewiórowska-Domagalska, Zoll, Południak-Gierz, Bańczyk, 'Transpozycja dyrektywy Parlamentu Europejskiego i Rady UE 2019/771 z dnia 20 maja 2019 w sprawie niektórych aspektów umów sprzedaży towarów' (2021) 4 *Kwartalnik Prawa Prywatnego* 916.

[15] Wiewiórowska-Domagalska, Zoll, Południak-Gierz, Bańczyk, 'Transpozycja dyrektywy Parlamentu Europejskiego i Rady UE 2019/771 z dnia 20 maja 2019 w sprawie niektórych aspektów umów sprzedaży towarów' (2021) 4 *Kwartalnik Prawa Prywatnego* 929.

[16] Project reporters: Aneta Wiewiórowska, Fryderyk Zoll, Marlena Pecyna, project team: Wojciech Bańczyk, Aneta Biały, Michał Brożyna, Weronika Herbet, Monika Jagielska, Anastazja Kołodziej, Elwira Macierzyńska-Franaszczyk, Magdalena Marucha-Jaworska, Jerzy Pisuliński, Katarzyna Południak-Gierz, Anna Rachwał, Ludmiła Savanets, Katarzyna Wiśniewska, Joanna Wolska, Michał Wyrwiński.

A. Introduction – does it make sense to write this article?

of transposition of both SGD and DCD. This proposal was discussed during a series of open conferences, organized by the Jagiellonian University in Kraków in the framework of Academic Draft of the Civil Code (Akademicki Projekt Kodeksu Cywilnego) that emerged among academics after dissolution of the Codification Commission under the Ministry of Justice headed by Prof. Zbigniew Radwański[17], resolved in 2015 (that Codification Commission prepared the drafts implementing the directive 1999/44/EC into the PCC)[18]. The implementation into the PCC was chosen as the most adequate manner of transposing said directives into the Polish legal system. The draft with the motives has been published in a well-recognised legal journal Kwartalnik Prawa Prywatnego.[19] The main function of this so-called "academic draft" was to prove that that the main assumption of the governmental drafters, expressed in their motives, stating that it is almost impossible to transpose these new directives into the PCC, is unfounded.[20] The easiest way to present such a proof was to prepare an alternative transposition draft. Though the academic draft was completed, and is well-received by the jurisprudence,[21] it was not adequately considered by the authorities. The academic draft was, nevertheless, sent to some senators (in the Senate the opposition has a fragile majority) and to some politicians from the opposition. It is difficult to assess whether the existence of such an alternative draft had impact on the delay in the proceeding of the governmental draft. At least, one may hope that after the elections, it will be possible to reopen the discussion on the implementation and to repair damages to Polish private law, caused by the adoption of the governmental draft.

When the article was being prepared, the situation in Poland was still unclear: the ministerial draft had not yet been submitted to the Senate at that time. Therefore, the authors, who had been asked to comment on the Polish implementation of the SGD, wondered whether it was reasonable to write an article in such moment. The transposition road seemed uncertain at that stage, the development of the process of implementation could not be predicted yet. From the scientific point of view, it was, however, worthy to look at this period of transition, because it gave quite a unique opportunity to look at the legal system, when the duty to implement these two important private law directives had not been fulfilled. It allowed to pose the question about the limits of the European-friendly interpretation. It was also quite a specific situation because the provisions under interpretation (namely the rules on seller's liability transposing the directive 1999/44/EC which were and still are functioning within the PCC) already had an EU-background. It showed the challenges of the transition from a minimum harmonization directive to the maximum harmonization one.[22] Hence the text maintains its usefulness, even though the transitional situation changed. Also, it should be noted that the new rules apply to contracts concluded after 31.12.2022 (Article 4.1 of the Act).

---

[17] https://www.gov.pl/web/sprawiedliwosc/komisja-kodyfikacyjna-prawa-cywilnego (accessed 3.10.2022).

[18] Zoll, 'Akademicki Projekt Kodeksu Cywilnego – O nowym sposobie prac kodyfikacyjnych – rozwiązanie doraźne czy stały element architektury stanowienia prawa?' (2017) 3 *Krajowa Rada Sądownictwa* 77.

[19] 'Akademicki projekt zmiany kodeksu cywilnego' (2021) 2 *Kwartalnik Prawa Prywatnego* 309–338.

[20] Wiewiórowska-Domagalska, Zoll, Południak-Gierz, Bańczyk, 'Transpozycja dyrektywy Parlamentu Europejskiego i Rady UE 2019/771 z dnia 20 maja 2019 w sprawie niektórych aspektów umów sprzedaży towarów' (2021) 4 *Kwartalnik Prawa Prywatnego* 920–928.

[21] E. Habryn-Chojnacka, 'Art. 556' in Commentary to PCC, ed. M. Gutowski, Legalis 2022, No. 9.

[22] Kołodziej, 'Wpływ zastosowania metody harmonizacji pełnej w zakresie uprawnień konsumenta w dyrektywie 2019/771 na przyszłą zmianę kodeksowego poziomu ochrony konsumenta z rękojmi (część I)' (2021) 127 *Przegląd Prawa i Administracji* passim.

B. The brief story on the Polish implementations of the sales directives

8   The reasoning of the drafters of the copy-paste implementation, presented in the brief motives attached to the draft, was unfortunately guided by the deep misunderstanding of the existing provisions of the PCC.[23] Such misunderstanding concerned most of all the central notion of the defect (in Polish: *wada*) which is used in the PCC. In the draft the notion of the lack of conformity is used. The drafters have completely missed that the term "defect" has been used in the PCC as meaning the lack of conformity under the directive 1999/44/EC (it is explicitly stated in Article 556^1 § 1 sentence 1). The PCC no longer uses the notion of defect in its old sense[24] – as the objectively perceived defect (actually such objective understanding was not seen even under the old redaction of the PCC).[25]

9   The first implementation of the directive 1999/44/EC was completed in a separated statute: the Act of 27 July 2002 on special conditions of consumer sales. It caused paradoxes, since in many cases a non-consumer, to whom provisions of the PCC applied, was better protected than a consumer.[26] The well-considered implementation would have made the use of the minimum-harmonization clause of the consumer sales directive and at least try to reconcile the PCC's rules on the liability for defective goods with the system which has been provided by the special consumer sales law statute. This Act on special conditions of consumer sales was, though, treated as a temporary solution,[27]

---

[23] Wiewiórowska-Domagalska, Zoll, Południak-Gierz, Bańczyk, 'Transpozycja dyrektywy Parlamentu Europejskiego i Rady UE 2019/771 z dnia 20 maja 2019 w sprawie niektórych aspektów umów sprzedaży towarów' (2021) 4 *Kwartalnik Prawa Prywatnego* 927.

[24] Following the demand on autonomous interpretation of European-originated terms, see e.g. Riesenhuber, 'Die Auslegung' in Riesenhuber (ed), *Europäische Methodenlehre Handbuch für Ausbildung und Praxis* (2010) 320.

[25] Wiewiórowska-Domagalska, Zoll, Południak-Gierz, Bańczyk, 'Transpozycja dyrektywy Parlamentu Europejskiego i Rady UE 2019/771 z dnia 20 maja 2019 w sprawie niektórych aspektów umów sprzedaży towarów'(2021) 4 *Kwartalnik Prawa Prywatnego* 927. On the change of notion of defect – e.g. Bańczyk, 'Zmiany przesłanek odpowiedzialności sprzedawcy w prawie polskim (od wady rzeczy sprzedanej do jej niezgodności z umową)' (2018) 3 *Acta Iuris Stetinensis* 9–10; Habryn-Chojnacka, 'Art. 556' in Gutowski, *Kodeks cywilny. Komentarz*, Legalis 2022, No. 6; Jagielska, 'Nowelizacja przepisów o odpowiedzialności za wady fizyczne rzeczy', in Skoczny, Karczewska, Namysłowska (ed), *Ustawa o prawach konsumenta. Komentarz*, (2015), point 3; Siemaszkiewicz, 'Zmiany w regulacji odpowiedzialności za jakość rzeczy sprzedanej dotyczące sprzedaży między profesjonalistami' (2016) 1 *Acta Iuris Stetinensis* 94; Widło, 'Rękojmia za wady fizyczne w świetle nowelizacji Kodeksu cywilnego' (2015) 4 *Monitor Prawniczy* 177; Zoll, *Rękojmia. Odpowiedzialność sprzedawcy* (2018) 68, 103.

[26] Południak-Gierz, *Wpływ regulacji dyrektyw 2019/770 oraz 2019/771 z zakresu rękojmi na poziom ochrony polskich konsumentów względem rozwiązań w tym zakresie obowiązujących w Kodeksie cywilnym. Implementacja do polskiego porządku prawnego dyrektyw konsumenckich na przykładzie dyrektyw 2019/770 i 2019/771*, Report for Instytut Wymiaru Sprawiedliwości 2022, passim; Zoll, *Rękojmia. Odpowiedzialność sprzedawcy* (2018) 1; Łętowska, *Europejskie prawo umów konsumenckich* (2004) 294–295; Wiewiórowska-Domagalska, 'Refleksje na tle orzecznictwa sądów powszechnych w zakresie sprzedaży konsumenckiej' (2014) 20 *Prawo w działaniu. Sprawy cywilne* 216, 267–268.

[27] Uzasadnienie rządowego projektu ustawy o szczególnych warunkach sprzedaży konsumenckiej, druk nr 465 Sejmu IV kadencji, https://orka.sejm.gov.pl/Druki4ka.nsf/wgdruku/465/$file/465.pdf (accessed: 3.10.2022), p. 12–13; Bagińska, 'Prawo umów konsumenckich w strukturze kodeksu cywilnego' (2017) 2 *Transformacje Prawa Prywatnego* 14; Brzozowski, 'Art. 556' in Krzysztof Pietrzykowski (ed), *Kodeks cywilny. Komentarz*, Edn 10, Legalis 2021, No 7; Habryn-Chojnacka, Art. 556 in Gutowski, *Kodeks cywilny. Komentarz*, Legalis 2022, No. 3; Kurowska, 'Implementacja dyrektywy o sprzedaży konsumenckiej do porządków prawnych wybranych państw członkowskich' (2008) 6 Problemy Współczesnego Prawa Międzynarodowego, Europejskiego i Porównawczego 93–94; Łętowska, *Prawo umów konsumenckich* (2002) 393; Pecyna, 'Wprowadzenie' in Pecyna (ed), *Szczególne warunki sprzedaży konsumenckiej oraz zmiana Kodeksu cywilnego. Komentarz*, LEX 2003, point 3; Pisuliński, 'Sprzedaż konsumencka' in Rajski (ed), *Prawo zobowiązań. – część szczegółowa. System Prawa Prywatnego, Tom 7* (2011) 173; Radwański (ed), *Zielona księga. Optymalna wizja Kodeksu cywilnego w Polsce* (2006) 110; Wiewiórowska-Domagalska,

B. The brief story on the Polish implementations of the sales directives

adopted shortly before the accession of Poland to the European Union, to be able to produce an easy proof that Poland fulfilled its obligation to adopt the *acquis communautaire* on this field, as well as to simplify the difficult duty of this adoption.[28] From the beginning the Codification Commission had an intention to integrate the European consumer sales law into the PCC. An opportunity to do so emerged with the obligation to implement the directive 2011/83/EU (CRD).[29] The Codification Commission submitted a draft integrating the provisions on sales from the directive 1999/44/EC and the CRD into the PCC (albeit the core of the provisions of the CRD has been put into the separated statute on consumer rights). The Polish law maker has used the minimum harmonization clause. *Inter alias* the EU law-based hierarchy of remedies has been rejected. Under the Article 560 § 1 PCC the buyer can terminate the contract or declare the price reduction without demanding earlier repair or replacement of the good (the issues arising from this regulatory choice will be further discussed in this article). Naturally, the buyer can also exercise the remedy of the replacement or repair. In case of contract termination or the price reduction the seller may still cure the sale by offering repair and replacement (the consumer may, however, still choose between these two).

The implementation of the CRD into the PCC allowed to unify terminology and to resolve the paradoxes in the protection scheme.[30]

The obligation to transpose the SGD appeared when Polish legal and justice system was already in a deep crisis. One of the main issues was that the authorities lacked professional group of academics supporting the lawmaking process. The liquidation of the Codification Commission was one of the first decisions of the new Minister of Justice in 2015[31]. As a result, the ministry lost the independent body of experts, working i.a. on the implementation of the *acquis communautaire* into the Polish law. Hence the group of academics was not available any more, the draft of the implementation was probably prepared by the officials working at the Ministry of Justice. For rather bizarre reasons the drafters decided to proceed in the easiest way – to copy the directive into the statute on consumer rights and to remove provisions on the consumer sales from the PCC.

Consequently, the consistent terminology of the Polish sales law is lost again. The reasoning presented in the draft's justification shows that this regulatory decision was taken due to the lack of proper understanding of the meaning of current PCC provisions at the side of the ministerial drafters. The most fundamental misunderstanding concerns the notion of the "defect". The ministerial drafters have written in their motives that the transposing the directive into the PCC was impossible at present – eventually, in the

---

'O celu i metodzie transpozycji dyrektyw unijnych – na przykładzie projektu ustawy o prawach konsumenta' (2014) 1 *Kwartalnik Prawa Prywatnego* 128; Zoll, *Rękojmia. Odpowiedzialność sprzedawcy* (2018) 5–6.

[28] Ernst, 'Polen' in Riesenhuber (ed), *Europäische Methodenlehre Handbuch für Ausbildung und Praxis* (2010) 836.

[29] Directive 2011/83/EU of the European Parliament and of the Council of 25 October 2011 on consumer rights, OJ L 304, 22.11.2011, 64–88.

[30] The retransposition of directive 1999/44 was generally well-received by legal scholars. Bagińska, 'Prawo umów konsumenckich w strukturze kodeksu cywilnego' (2017) 2 *Transformacje Prawa Prywatnego* 15; Habryn-Chojnacka, 'Art. 556' in Gutowski, *Kodeks cywilny. Komentarz*, Legalis 2022, No. 4; Jagielska, 'Nowelizacja przepisów o odpowiedzialności za wady fizyczne rzeczy', in Skoczny, Karczewska, Namysłowska (ed), *Ustawa o prawach konsumenta. Komentarz*, (2015), point 6; Widło, 'Rękojmia za wady fizyczne w świetle nowelizacji Kodeksu cywilnego' (2015) 4 *Monitor Prawniczy* 178; Wiewiórowska-Domagalska, 'O celu i metodzie transpozycji dyrektyw unijnych – na przykładzie projektu ustawy o prawach konsumenta' (2014) 1 *Kwartalnik Prawa Prywatnego* 128; Zoll, *Rękojmia. Odpowiedzialność sprzedawcy* (2018) 1.

[31] Zoll, 'Akademicki Projekt Kodeksu Cywilnego – O nowym sposobie prac kodyfikacyjnych – rozwiązanie doraźne czy stały element architektury stanowienia prawa?' (2017) 3 *Krajowa Rada Sądownictwa* 77.

13 far future, it might become possible. It was argued that it would also be unreasonable to lower the standard of the protection provided by the PCC (which means that the drafters have accepted – again – the situation that a consumer will be less protected than a non-consumer).

13   In the second redaction of the draft, which, in principle, was subject only to some cosmetic changes, a new paradox appeared.[32] Previously, one of the amendments to the PCC[33] has extended (partially) the consumer protection to some small businesses (individual entrepreneurs being physical persons).[34] This extension was copied in the revised draft and is being introduced into the act on consumer rights.[35]

14   The counter-draft prepared by the academic community as a reaction to the planned destruction of the PCC, was drafted not necessarily with hope to be adopted by the present authorities but at least to rebut the assumption of the governmental draft that the proper integration of the implementation within the PCC is "impossible". Also, now, when the governmental draft has already been adopted in the Act, the academic draft may help reverse the damage caused to the Polish private law system by this unfortunate legal intervention.

C. The interpretation of the civil code after the lapse of the period for implementation of the Sales Directive

15   In the period between 1.01.2022 and 1.01.2023, the SGD was not transposed yet and, in consequence, there was no national law, adopting measures necessary to comply with the SGD, to be applied. This raised the question of the directive-friendly interpretation of the existing legal provisions.[36] This question had several dimensions. Firstly, there were matters directly covered by the scope of the directive. Secondly, there were matters in which the Polish law-maker extended the application of the consumer law to other personal configurations (small businesses). Finally, there were matters that arose

---

[32] Wiewiórowska-Domagalska, Zoll, Południak-Gierz, Bańczyk, 'Transpozycja dyrektywy Parlamentu Europejskiego i Rady UE 2019/771 z dnia 20 maja 2019 w sprawie niektórych aspektów umów sprzedaży towarów' (2021) 4 *Kwartalnik Prawa Prywatnego* 917.

[33] Act of 31 July 2019 Act amending certain acts to reduce regulatory burdens (Journal of Laws 2019, pos. 1495)

[34] Namely, a natural person concluding a contract directly related to his economic activity, where the contents of this contract indicate that it has not professional nature for this person, resulting in particular from the object of the economic activity conducted by said person, made available under the provisions on the Central Records and Information on Economic Activity. Critically: Gnela, 'Uwagi na temat wybiórczego rozszerzania ochrony konsumenckiej na niektórych przedsiębiorców będących osobami fizycznymi' (2022) 334 *Acta Universitatis Wroclaviesis* 607.

[35] New Article 7aa of the Act on consumer rights. Critically: Kołodziej, 'Wpływ zastosowania metody harmonizacji pełnej w zakresie uprawnień konsumenta w dyrektywie 2019/771 na przyszłą zmianę kodeksowego poziomu ochrony konsumenta z rękojmi (część I)' (2021) 127 *Przegląd Prawa i Administracji* 222–223.

[36] On the obligation to interpret the national law in accordance with the wording and the aim of the directive see the judgments of the European Court of April 10, 1984, 14/83, Sabine von Colson and Elisabeth Kamann v. Land Nordrhein-Westfalen, ECLI: EU: C: 1984: 153, paragraph 28; of 5 October 2004, joined cases C-397/01 to C-403/01. Bernhard Pfeiffer (C-397/01), Wilhelm Roith (C-398/01), Albert Süß (C-399/01), Michael Winter (C-400/01), Klaus Nestvogel (C-401/01), Roswitha Zeller (C-402/01) and Matthias Döbele (C-403/01) v Deutsches Rotes Kreuz, Kreisverband Waldshut eV., ECLI: EU: C: 2004: 584, paragraphs 114 to 118; of 4 July 2006, C-212/04, Konstantinos Adeneler et al. v. Ellinikos Organismos Galaktos (ELOG), ECLI: EU: C: 2006: 443.

from the fact that Polish legislator opted for extended implementation of the directive 1999/44, by including into the general scheme the B2B and P2P relationships.[37]

Within the scope of the directive a member state is obliged to interpret the national law in the directive-friendly way[38] and this duty arises directly from the European law.[39] The main structure of the Polish law does not differ from the one found in the SGD. It made the process of the interpretation easier due to the fact that the general concept of the liability for the defective goods in the SGD and in PCC was based upon similar foundations. Nevertheless, there were some essential differences. Hence, in this paper we will focus on them, discussing a few most evident cases in which the limits of the European-friendly interpretation may be examined in the most illustrative way.

The definition of the lack of conformity, also traditionally called defect (in Polish *wada*),[40] used in the PCC, does not distinguish explicitly between the subjective and objective requirements of conformity, but provides a mixed list of various requirements (Article 556^1). The main purpose of the clear distinction between subjective and objective requirements of conformity is to facilitate solving the problem of so-called "negative agreement on the good's feature"[41]. Concluding such a negative agreement can be seen as a way to circumvent the mandatory nature of provisions governing the liability of the seller for the lack of conformity towards consumers.[42] The SGD requires a qualified consent of the consumer to accept features of the sold goods which deviate to the detriment of the consumers from the standard set by the objective requirements of conformity (Article 7.5). The definition of the lack of conformity as provided in Articles 556 and 556^1 PCC allows to distinguish between objective and subjective requirements of conformity (although it does not explicitly name them as such). The more complicated question is whether the qualified consent of the consumer could be required even though there was no explicit provision on this issue in the PCC. Even before the adoption of the SGD this problem, albeit scarcely seen in the literature,[43] needed to be solved in the way preventing the circumvention of the mandatory nature of the rules on consumer protection. It could be argued that the general rules on consent and declaration of intent should be then interpreted in accordance with the European law and also in a way that observes the need to avoid a threat of the circumvention of the mandatory law. The requirement of the clear consent to such deviation from the standard of the objective requirements of conformity could be also achieved in the way of the directive-friendly interpretation of the Article 65 PCC. This provision is a general norm, governing the interpretation of the declaration of intent. It refers in its § 1 to the justified perspective of the addressee of the

---

[37] Wiewiórowska-Domagalska, Zoll, Południak-Gierz, Bańczyk, 'Transpozycja dyrektywy Parlamentu Europejskiego i Rady UE 2019/771 z dnia 20 maja 2019 w sprawie niektórych aspektów umów sprzedaży towarów' (2021) 4 *Kwartalnik Prawa Prywatnego* 924–925.

[38] Baran, 'Dyrektywa', in Biernat (ed), *Podstawy i źródła prawa Unii Europejskiej. System Prawa Unii Europejskiej. Tom 1* (2020) 1043.

[39] Article 4(3) Treaty on European Union and Article 288 Treaty on the Functioning of the European Union, as clearly indicated in judgment of the European Court of 10 April 1984, Case 14/83, Sabine von Colson and Elisabeth Kamannv. Land Nordrhein-Westfalen, European Court Reports (ECR) 1984, p. 01891.

[40] Habryn-Chojnacka, 'Art. 556(1)' in Gutowski, *Kodeks cywilny. Komentarz*, Legalis 2022, No. 7.

[41] Schulze, Zoll, *European Contract Law* (2021) 49. On the negative description of goods see: Zoll, Problem negatywnego uzgodnienia cech rzeczy sprzedanej — w oczekiwaniu na wspólne europejskie prawo sprzedaży' (2012) 2 *Transformacje Prawa Prywatnego* 169–170; Zoll, *Rękojmia. Odpowiedzialność sprzedawcy* (2018) 109.

[42] Zoll, *Rękojmia. Odpowiedzialność sprzedawcy* (2018) 119.

[43] Zoll, *Rękojmia. Odpowiedzialność sprzedawcy* (2018) 119; F. Zoll, 'Problem negatywnego uzgodnienia cech rzeczy sprzedanej — w oczekiwaniu na wspólne europejskie prawo sprzedaży', *Transformacje Prawa Prywatnego* 2012/2, p. 170.

declaration of intent. This perspective must be reconstructed also in the light of the European law, which means taking into account the requirement of the qualified consent of the consumer. This way of interpretation does not go against the rule of the PCC itself, it is not a *contra legem* interpretation.[44] Therefore, a result identical with the directive could be achieved.

18 SGD's rules on the negative agreement on the features of the goods made an old provision of the Roman law provenience, stating that there is no liability if at the time of the conclusion of the contract the buyer knew the defect, obsolete. The PCC contains such provision in Article 557 § 1. Since in the light of the directive consumer's knowledge does not suffice to exclude seller's liability, but the qualified consent is required to accept goods of objectively lowered quality, the respective provision had to be teleologically reduced following the standards of the directive. As a result, it could not apply within the scope of the directive.[45]

19 The second doubtful area, where the limits of the European-friendly interpretation needed to be examined, was the problem of seller's liability in case of the goods with digital elements. Goods with digital elements were not anyhow mentioned in the PCC.[46] The issue is even more serious, since also the directive 2019/770 on supply of digital content and services was not implemented in time (both directives 2019/770 and 2019/771 were transposed by the Act of 4 November 2022 amending the Act on Consumer Rights, the Act – Civil Code and the Act – Private International Law into the Act on Consumer Rights; said amendments came into force on 1.01.2023). This situation caused several problems on various levels.

20 First, the lack of specific rules on sales of goods with digital elements and the rules governing the supply of digital content and service created a real gap in the private law system. In case of goods with digital elements the qualification of the contract as a contract of sales could be achieved by adopting an approach which is usually used when examining mixed contracts. If rights and duties typical for the contract of sales prevailed in a contract, the theorem of absorption should apply and said contract should be subordinated to this dominating type of contract, namely sales. The fine distinctions between the scopes of application of the SGD and DCD have to be then taken into consideration in the process of classifying the analyzed contract to the respective category.[47]

21 There are also some other difficulties, *inter alias* related to the duty of update,[48] to the consequences of defective update of goods and to the question of the transfer of the risk (the latter is relevant for determining at which moment defect has to exist to be legally

---

[44] The obligation of a directive-friendly interpretation ceases if it leads to a contra legem result – e.g. Wulf-Hemming, 'Die richtlinien-konforme Auslegung' in Riesenhuber (ed), *Europäische Methodenlehre Handbuch für Ausbildung und Praxis* (2010) 414, i.e. contradicting the literal meaning of the national provision. Baran, 'Dyrektywa', in Biernat (ed), *Podstawy i źródła prawa Unii Europejskiej. System Prawa Unii Europejskiej. Tom 1* (2020) 1046; Rowiński, 'Nakaz dokonywania wykładni prounijnej jako dyrektywa wykładni systemowej' (2016) 1 Ruch Prawniczy, Ekonomiczny i Socjologiczny 101; Sołtys, *Obowiązek wykładni prawa krajowego zgodnie z prawem unijnym jako instrument zapewniania efektywności prawa Unii Europejskiej* (2015) 530.

[45] Sołtys, *Obowiązek wykładni prawa krajowego zgodnie z prawem unijnym jako instrument zapewniania efektywności prawa Unii Europejskiej* (2015) 137–138.

[46] If there are no national provisions on the matter governed by the directive, then a directive friendly interpretation may very difficult or even impossible – the national law norms that could be subject to such an interpretation are lacking. Baran, 'Dyrektywa', in Biernat (ed), *Podstawy i źródła prawa Unii Europejskiej. System Prawa Unii Europejskiej. Tom 1* (2020) 1046.

[47] Recital 20 and Article 3 sec. 1 and 4 of Directive 2019/770, recital 13 and Article 3 sec. 3 of Directive 2019/771.

[48] Sein, 'Spindler, The new Directive on Contracts for Supply of Digital Content and Digital Services – Conformity Criteria, Remedies and Modifications – Part 2' (2019) 15.4 *European Review of Contract Law* 369–371.

C. The interpretation of the civil code

relevant). The PCC contains only a traditional rule that a defect in good must exist at the moment of the transfer of risk at the latest to justify seller's liability (Article 559). The transfer of risk is generally associated with handing over the good to the buyer (Article 548 § 1, 3 PCC). It is, in general, a non-mandatory provision but in the consumer law it gained a semi-mandatory character.[49] The parties could deviate from it to advantage of the consumer. In case of e.g. the sales of a car with the digital elements which needed to be updated or such kind of the update was a part of the promises of the seller, it should be accepted that the parties also deviated from the rule on the transfer of the risk and assume that in their contract they prolonged the liability of the seller for the defects resulting from lack of actualization. According to the Article 56 PCC a legal transaction shall have not only the effects expressed in it but also those which follow from statutory law, the principles of community life (this latter is a good-faith principle expressed by the language of the year 1964 in Poland[50]), and the established customs. This provision plays within the Polish legal system a role similar to the concept of the implied terms or of the completing interpretation (*ergänzende Willensauslegung*). The theoretical explanation is different, since the Article 56 PCC does not refer to the hypothetical intention of the parties, but rather to the power of the law as such[51]. It opens the path to the indirect effect[52] of the directive into the Polish law. In such case a sale of the goods with a digital element had to produce similar effects to those envisaged in the directive. A professional seller of the goods with the digital elements had to consider that contract concerning such category of goods is a long-term relationship[53] and the following contractual obligations encompassed also the duties related to the actualization. This impacted the whole transaction[54], which meant that a consumer could exercise then the remedies in relation to the whole object of sales.

The most apparent difficulty with the directive-friendly interpretation concerned the system of the remedies. As already explained, during the transposition of directive 1999/44/EC the Polish law-maker made in this case a use of the minimum harmonization clause.[55] A buyer could terminate the contract or declare the price reduction without a necessity to resort first to the remedies of repair or replacement. The seller could however cure the contract by offering immediately a repair or replacement (Article 560 § 1). In such case, a consumer remained entitled to choose which way of cure should be applied (Article 560 § 2). This system generally went beyond the maximum standard of the fully harmonized SGD. There was a possibility to try to reduce teleologically the respective norms of the PCC to achieve the result conforming with the directive. Such way of interpretation would however go relatively quickly beyond the *contra legem* limits,

22

---

[49] Art. 548 § 3 states: "If the thing sold is to be sent by the seller to the buyer who is a consumer, risk of accidental loss or damage to the thing shall pass to the buyer at the time of its release to the buyer. The thing shall be deemed released once entrusted with the carrier by the seller if the seller did not have an influence on the selection of the carrier by the buyer. The provisions less favourable to the buyer shall be null and void." See Habryn-Chojnacka, 'Art. 548' in Gutowski, *Kodeks cywilny. Komentarz*, Legalis 2022, No. 2; Jezioro, 'Art. 558' in Gniewek, Machnikowski, *Kodeks cywilny. Komentarz*, Legalis 2021, No 1; Zoll, *Rękojmia. Odpowiedzialność sprzedawcy* (2018) 51.

[50] Rott-Pietrzyk, 'Art. 65', in Machnikowski (ed), *Kodeks cywilny. Komentarz*, Legalis 2022, No 12.

[51] Grochowski, 'Art. 56' in Machnikowski (ed), *Kodeks cywilny. Komentarz*, Legalis 2022, No 40.

[52] See e.g. Schmidt-Kessel, 'Europäisches Vertragsrecht', in Riesenhuber (ed), *Europäische Methodenlehre Handbuch für Ausbildung und Praxis* (2010) 496.

[53] About specificity of long-term contracts see e.g. Bańczyk, *Alokacja ryzyka zmiany okoliczności w czasie wykonywania długoterminowej umowy o dzieło i o roboty budowlane* (2017) 17.

[54] Zoll, *Rękojmia. Odpowiedzialność sprzedawcy* (2018) 153.

[55] Wiewiórowska-Domagalska, Zoll, Południak-Gierz, Bańczyk, ‚Transpozycja dyrektywy Parlamentu Europejskiego i Rady UE 2019/771 z dnia 20 maja 2019 w sprawie niektórych aspektów umów sprzedaży towarów' (2021) 4 *Kwartalnik Prawa Prywatnego* 930.

23 Recital 19 SGD allows the national law-maker to provide a right to immediate termination of the contract, if the period to exercise this right does not exceed 30 days (see also Article 3(7)). This exception serves to allow for maintaining an equivalent of the English right to reject[56]. One could argue that at least within this period of 30 days a consumer would be entitled to the immediate termination of the contract. The remaining part of the national provision would have to be again teleologically reduced to the maximum standard arising from the directive. This interpretation of the Article 560 § 1 PCC would definitely cause some controversies. Such European-friendly interpretation would lead to the differences between the consumer and non-consumer law. It would open the question, whether the directive would allow an *ab maiori ad minus*-argument, that also a price reduction could be exercised within the 30-days period immediate after the delivery of the goods. This result would, however, be doubtful. The recital 19 *in fine*, providing the possibility to modify the sequence of the remedies, refers only to the termination and replacement, but not to the other remedies. The directive-friendly interpretation of the Article 560 PCC would therefore be close to the *contra legem* interpretation – only a small und uncertain path for some kind of partial and provisionary adjustment would be left.

24 This state of law was only partly corrected by the possibility of understanding the PCC provisions in light of Article 13.4.c of the SGD. Under Art 13.4.c immediate price reduction or termination is possible if it is justified by serious nature of the lack of conformity. According to the SGD (Article 13.5 sentence 1) and Polish law (Article 560 § 4) termination, as a rule, is only available if the lack of conformity (defect) is "not minor". "Not minor" could be interpreted[57] as meaning the same as being "of serious nature" under Article 13.4.c of the directive, thus, allowing to reach a result similar to the one demanded by the SGD at least in consumer cases regulated by the directive. Still, this would undermine either the coherence of the system (when alike premise is understood differently in different types of cases) or make it more difficult to terminate the contract for other cases than regulated by the directive. The directive-friendly interpretation of Article 560 could (but it is again very close to *contra legem* interpretation) be understood that also price reduction is available only to such defects that are "of serious nature".

25 A similar problem concerns the objection of the absolute disproportionality of the repair or replacement chosen by the buyer. The Polish law reflected explicitly[58] the *Weber/Putz* case[59] and therefore in consumer cases the objection of the absolute disproportionality (which means the excessive relation of the chosen remedy's cost in relation to the price of the acquired sale's object) was excluded. The absolute disproportionality could be, however, raised in B2B relations – Article 561 § 3 sentence 2 PCC explicitly states that *if the buyer is an entrepreneur, the seller may refuse to replace the thing for one free from defects or to remove defects when the costs of discharging of that duty exceed the price*

---

[56] On the right to reject and its function see: Watson, *Das Right to Reject In Consumer Rights Act 2015 (Europaisches Privatrecht)* (2019) passim.

[57] On interpretation of general clauses to effectuate European law – e.g. Röthel, 'Die Konkretisierung von Generalklauseln' in Riesenhuber (ed), *Europäische Methodenlehre Handbuch für Ausbildung und Praxis* (2010) 364

[58] Zoll, *Rękojmia. Odpowiedzialność sprzedawcy* (2018) 305. Only about conformity of the PCC with the Weber/Putz judgment Tulibacka, 'Art. 556(1)', in Osajda (ed), Borysiak (ed. of the volume), *Kodeks cywilny. Komentarz*, Legalis 2022, Edn 30, No 2.

[59] Judgment of the CJEU of 16 June, 2011, joined cases C-65/09 and C-87/09, Gebr. Weber GmbH v Jürgen Wittmer (C - 65/09) and Ingrid Putz v Medianess Electronics GmbH (C - 87/09).

of the thing sold. The absolute disproportionality objection could also be raised if the good, in order to be brought to conformity, needed to be removed and re-installed, and related costs were higher than the price of the good in question (Art. 561¹ § 2). In contrast, in case of consumer sales, the consumer could demand removal and installation of the good even in such circumstances, provided that he or she covers some part of removal and/or installation costs (Article 561¹ § 3 PCC). The SGD has solved the matter of absolute disproportionality differently: stating in Article 13.2 – 3 that *the seller may refuse to bring the goods into conformity if repair and replacement are impossible or would impose costs on the seller that would be disproportionate*. The directive-friendly interpretation driven by the requirement of the full-harmonization in this case had to lead to the teleological reduction of the provision supported by the historical interpretation. Since the provision of Polish law was based on CJEU judicature, when EU law and jurisprudence changed, also the interpretation of Polish law should change accordingly. Then, the objection of the absolute disproportionality should be admissible in all consumer cases except for those not covered by the directive (like concerning the immovables or rights), where the Polish law should still upkeep the exclusion of this objection in consumer cases.

D. Conclusion

26 Delayed implementation of the SGD caused severe problems during the application of the existing law. This alone undermined the certainty of the law. Even if in several cases a directive-friendly interpretation of the existing national sales law could be achieved, the parties would not be able to really rely on the European law, and this state will continue with regard to contracts concluded in 2022 following the interim provision. The infringement of the duty to implement the European law was obvious. The situation was of course even more problematic in case of contracts on the supply of digital content and services, as the regulation of the above was missing from in the Polish legal system[60] and, therefore, the level of legal uncertainty was higher. Actually, from the perspective of the Polish legal system and legal certainty, there was only one scenario which could be worse than the state of the non-implementation of the both directives existing between 1.01.2022 and 1.01.2023: that is implementing both directives in the way proposed in governmental draft. This happened when the Act of 4 November 2022 amending the Act on Consumer Rights, the Act – Civil Code and the Act – Private International Law was adopted. In this manner Polish legislator destroyed the achievements of the Codification Commission. An incoherent system was created again, but this time with no legitimate rationale as PCC was already prepared to incorporate changes brought by the new EU consumer sales law. Particularly worrying is also the fact that Polish legislator used EU law to disintegrate the private law system at the national level.

---

[60] Wiewiórowska-Domagalska, Zoll, Południak-Gierz, Bańczyk, 'Transpozycja dyrektywy Parlamentu Europejskiego i Rady UE 2019/771 z dnia 20 maja 2019 w sprawie niektórych aspektów umów sprzedaży towarów' (2021) 4 *Kwartalnik Prawa Prywatnego* 926; Jagielska, 'Od konsumenta do użytkownika (o istotnej zmianie współczesnego prawa konsumenckiego)' (2021) 11 *Państwo i Prawo* 39; Namysłowska, Jabłonowska, Wiaderek, 'Implementation of the Digital Content Directive in Poland: A Fast Ride on a Tandem Bike against the Traffic' (2021) 12.2 *Journal of Intellectual Property, Information Technology and E-Commerce Law*, No. 13.

Bibliography

'Akademicki projekt zmiany kodeksu cywilnego' (2021) 2 *Kwartalnik Prawa Prywatnego*

Ewa Bagińska, 'Prawo umów konsumenckich w strukturze kodeksu cywilnego' (2017) 2 *Transformacje Prawa Prywatnego*

Wojciech Bańczyk, *Alokacja ryzyka zmiany okoliczności w czasie wykonywania długoterminowej umowy o dzieło i o roboty budowlane* (Wydawnictwo Uniwersytetu Jagiellońskiego, Kraków 2017)

Wojciech Bańczyk, 'Zmiany przesłanek odpowiedzialności sprzedawcy w prawie polskim (od wady rzeczy sprzedanej do jej niezgodności z umową)' (2018) 3 *Acta Iuris Stetinensis*

Mariusz Baran, 'Dyrektywa', in Stanisław Biernat (ed), *Podstawy i źródła prawa Unii Europejskiej. System Prawa Unii Europejskiej. Tom 1* (C.H. Beck, Warszawa 2020)

Adam Brzozowski, 'Art. 556' in Krzysztof Pietrzykowski (ed), *Kodeks cywilny, Komentarz*, Edn 10, Legalis 2021

Draft act amending the act on consumer rights and certain other acts, Sejm of the 9th term, print No. 2425, https://orka.sejm.gov.pl/Druki9ka.nsf/0/09EDF5F3C31EE7B9C12588770039AC4F/%24File/2425.pdf (accessed: 10/09/2022).

Ernst Ulrich, 'Poleń', in Karl Riesenhuber (ed), *Europäische Methodenlehre Handbuch für Ausbildung und Praxis* (De Gruyter Berlin-New York 2010)

Bogusława Gnela, Uwagi na temat wybiórczego rozszerzania ochrony konsumenckiej na niektórych przedsiębiorców będących osobami fizycznymi (2022) 334 *Acta Universitatis Wroclaviesis*

Mateusz Grochowski, 'Art. 56' in Piotr Machnikowski (ed), Kodeks cywilny. Komentarz, Legalis 2022

Ewa Habryn-Chojnacka, 'Art. 548', '556' and '556(1)', in Maciej Gutowski (ed) *Kodeks cywilny. Komentarz*, Edn 3, Legalis 2022

Monika Jagielska, 'Nowelizacja przepisów o odpowiedzialności za wady fizyczne rzeczy', in: Tadeusz Skoczny, Dorota Karczewska, Monika Namysłowska (ed), *Ustawa o prawach konsumenta. Komentarz*, (CH Beck, Warszawa, 2015)

Monika Jagielska, 'Od konsumenta do użytkownika (o istotnej zmianie współczesnego prawa konsumenckiego)' (2021) 11 *Państwo i Prawo*

Julian Jezioro, 'Art. 558' in Edward Gniewek, Piotr Machnikowski (ed), *Kodeks cywilny. Komentarz*, Legalis 2021.

Anastazja Kołodziej, 'Wpływ zastosowania metody harmonizacji pełnej w zakresie uprawnień konsumenta w dyrektywie 2019/771 na przyszłą zmianę kodeksowego poziomu ochrony konsumenta z rękojmi (część I)', (2021) 127 *Przegląd Prawa i Administracji*

Anna Kurowska, 'Implementacja dyrektywy o sprzedaży konsumenckiej do porządków prawnych wybranych państw członkowskich', (2008) 6 *Problemy Współczesnego Prawa Międzynarodowego, Europejskiego i Porównawczego*

Ewa Łętowska *Europejskie prawo umów konsumenckich*, (CH Beck Warszawa 2004)

Ewa Łętowska, *Prawo umów konsumenckich* (CH Beck Warszawa 2002)

Monika Namysłowska, Agnieszka Jabłonowska, Filip Wiaderek, Implementation of the Digital Content Directive in Poland: A Fast Ride on a Tandem Bike against the Traffic (2021) 12.2 *Journal of Intellectual Property, Information Technology and E-Commerce Law*

Bibliography

Marlena Pecyna, 'Implementacja dyrektywy o umowach o dostarczanie treści cyfrowych lub usługi cyfrowej — wyzwania dla ustawodawcy krajowego' (2021) 3 *Kwartalnik Prawa Prywatnego*

Marlena Pecyna, 'Wprowadzenie' in Marlena Pecyna (ed), *Szczególne warunki sprzedaży konsumenckiej oraz zmiana Kodeksu cywilnego. Komentarz*, LEX 2003.

Jerzy Pisuliński, 'Sprzedaż konsumencka' in Jerzy Rajski (ed), *Prawo zobowiązań. - część szczegółowa. System Prawa Prywatnego, Tom 7* (CH Beck, Warszawa 2011)

Katarzyna Południak-Gierz, *Wpływ regulacji dyrektyw 2019/770 oraz 2019/771 z zakresu rękojmi na poziom ochrony polskich konsumentów względem rozwiązań w tym zakresie obowiązujących w Kodeksie cywilnym. Implementacja do polskiego porządku prawnego dyrektyw konsumenckich na przykładzie dyrektyw 2019/770 i 2019/771*, Report for Instytut Wymiaru Sprawiedliwości 2022.

'Projekt ustawy o zmianie ustawy o prawach konsumenta i kodeksu cywilnego' (2021) 1 *Kwartalnik Prawa Prywatnego*

Zbigniew Radwański (ed), *Zielona księga. Optymalna wizja Kodeksu cywilnego w Polsce* (Ministerstwo Sprawiedliwości, Warszawa 2006)

Karl Riesenhuber, 'Die Auslegung' in Karl Riesenhuber (ed), *Europäische Methodenlehre Handbuch für Ausbildung und Praxis* (De Gruyter Berlin-New York 2010)

Ewa Rott-Pietrzyk, 'Art. 65', in Piotr Machnikowski (ed), *Kodeks cywilny. Komentarz*, Legalis 2022

Wojciech Rowiński, 'Nakaz dokonywania wykładni prounijnej jako dyrektywa wykładni systemowej' (2016) 1 Ruch Prawniczy, Ekonomiczny i Socjologiczny

Anne Röthel, 'Die Konkretisierung von Generalklauseln' in Karl Riesenhuber (ed), *Europäische Methodenlehre Handbuch für Ausbildung und Praxis* (De Gruyter Berlin-New York 2010)

Martin Schmidt-Kessel, 'Europäisches Vertragsrecht' in Karl Riesenhuber (ed), *Europäische Methodenlehre Handbuch für Ausbildung und Praxis* (De Gruyter Berlin-New York 2010)

Rainer Schulze, Fryderyk Zoll, *European Contract Law* (CH Beck, München 2021)

Karin Sein, Gerald Spindler, 'The new Directive on Contracts for Supply of Digital Content and Digital Services – Conformity Criteria, Remedies and Modifications – Part 2' (2019) 15.4 European Review of Contract Law

Maria Siemaszkiewicz, 'Zmiany w regulacji odpowiedzialności za jakość rzeczy sprzedanej dotyczące sprzedaży między profesjonalistami' (2016) 1 *Acta Iuris Stetinensis*

Agnieszka Sołtys, *Obowiązek wykładni prawa krajowego zgodnie z prawem unijnym jako instrument zapewniania efektywności prawa Unii Europejskiej* (Wolters Kluwer, Warszawa 2015)

Magdalena Tulibacka, 'Art. 556(1)', in Konrad Osajda (ed), Witold Borysiak (ed. of the volume), *Kodeks cywilny. Komentarz*, Legalis 2022, Edn 30

Uzasadnienie rządowego projektu ustawy o szczególnych warunkach sprzedaży konsumenckiej, druk nr 465 Sejmu IV kadencji, https://orka.sejm.gov.pl/Druki4ka.nsf/wgdruku/465/$file/465.pdf (accessed: 3.10.2022)

Jonathon Watson, *Das Right to Reject im Consumer Rights Act 2015* (Europaisches Privatrecht), Nomos 2019

Jacek Widło, 'Rękojmia za wady fizyczne w świetle nowelizacji Kodeksu cywilnego' (2015) 4 *Monitor Prawniczy*

Aneta Wiewiórowska-Domagalska, 'O celu i metodzie transpozycji dyrektyw unijnych – na przykładzie projektu ustawy o prawach konsumenta' (2014) 1 *Kwartalnik Prawa Prywatnego*

Aneta Wiewiórowska-Domagalska, 'Refleksje na tle orzecznictwa sądów powszechnych w zakresie sprzedaży konsumenckiej' (2014) 20 *Prawo w działaniu. Sprawy cywilne*

Aneta Wiewiórowska-Domagalska, Fryderyk Zoll, Katarzyna Południak-Gierz, Wojciech Bańczyk, 'Transpozycja dyrektywy Parlamentu Europejskiego i Rady UE 2019/771 z dnia 20 maja 2019 w sprawie niektórych aspektów umów sprzedaży towarów' (2021) 4 *Kwartalnik Prawa Prywatnego*

Roth Wulf-Hemming, 'Die richtlinien-konforme Auslegung' in Karl Riesenhuber (ed), *Europäische Methodenlehre Handbuch für Ausbildung und Praxis* (De Gruyter Berlin-New York 2010)

Fryderyk Zoll, 'Akademicki Projekt Kodeksu Cywilnego – O nowym sposobie prac kodyfikacyjnych – rozwiązanie doraźne czy stały element architektury stanowienia prawa?' (2017) 3 *Krajowa Rada Sądownictwa*

Fryderyk Zoll, 'Problem negatywnego uzgodnienia cech rzeczy sprzedanej — w oczekiwaniu na wspólne europejskie prawo sprzedaży' (2012) 2 *Transformacje Prawa Prywatnego*

Fryderyk Zoll, *Rękojmia. Odpowiedzialność sprzedawcy* (CH Beck, Warszawa 2018)

Fryderyk Zoll, Katarzyna Południak-Gierz, Wojciech Bańczyk, *Primacy of EU law and jurisprudence of Polish Constitutional Tribunal*, https://www.europarl.europa.eu/RegData/etudes/STUD/2022/732475/IPOL_STU(2022)732475_EN.pdf (accessed 1.10.2022)

Fryderyk Zoll, Katarzyna Południak-Gierz, Wojciech Bańczyk, 'The Struggle on Implementation of the Acquis Communautaire into Polish Civil Code' (2022) 20 *Nederlands Tijdschrift voor Burgerlijk Recht*.

Fryderyk Zoll, Leah Wortham, 'Judicial Independence and Accountability: Withstanding Political Stress in Poland' (2019) 42 *Fordham Int'l L.J.*

Fryderyk Zoll, Leah Wortham, 'Weaponizing judicial discipline: Poland', in Richard Devlin, Sheila Wildeman (ed), *Disciplining judges: Contemporary challenges and controversies* (Edward Elgar, Northampton-Cheltenham 2021)

Portugal

A.	Introduction	1
B.	Guided Tour of Decree-Law 84/2021	7
C.	Scope and Definitions	16
D.	Conformity	22
E.	Liability of the Trader and Burden of Proof	26
F.	Remedies for Lack of Conformity	34
G.	After-Sales Service and Parts Availability	51
H.	Commercial Guarantees	53
I.	Direct Liability of the Producer	55
J.	Direct Liability of the Online Marketplace Provider	64
K.	Right of Redress	71
L.	Conclusion	83
	Bibliography	89

A. Introduction

1 In Portugal, the long-awaited implementation of the EU Directives 2019/770 (DCD)[1] and 2019/771 (SGD)[2]/[3] finally saw the light of day with Decree-Law no. 84/2021, of 18 October 2021[4]. As expected, considering the previously presented draft (DL 1049/XXII/2021, of 1 July 2021), the transposition of both directives was done in a single legal regime. It also transposes Articles 18 and 20 of Directive 2011/83/EU on delivery and the passing of risk.

2 The fact that the entire process took place in the secrecy of the offices, without the necessary public discussion of the solutions enshrined in the legal regime, is worthy of criticism.

---

[1] Directive (EU) 2019/770 of the European Parliament and of the Council of 20 May 2019 on certain aspects concerning contracts for the supply of digital content and digital services.

[2] Directive (EU) 2019/771 of the European Parliament and of the Council of 20 May 2019 concerning contracts for the sale of goods, amending Regulation (EU) 2017/2394 and Directive 2009/22/EC, and repealing Directive 1999/44/EC.

[3] On the impact of the Directives in Portuguese law, before the transposition, see Morais Carvalho, *Manual de Direito do Consumo* (2020), 364; Morais Carvalho, "Venda de Bens de Consumo e Fornecimento de Conteúdos e Serviços Digitais – As Diretivas 2019/771 e 2019/770 e o seu Impacto no Direito Português" (2019) 3 *Revista Electrónica de Direito*, 63; Morais Carvalho and Farinha, "Goods with Digital Elements, Digital Content and Digital Services in Directives 2019/770 and 2019/771" (2020) 2 *Revista de Direito e Tecnologia*, 257; Pinto Oliveira, "O Direito Europeu da Compra e Venda 20 Anos Depois – Comparação entre a Directiva 1999/44/CE, de 25 de Maio de 1999, e a Directiva 2019/771/UE, de 20 de Maio de 2019" (2020) *Revista de Direito Comercial*, 1217; P. Mota Pinto, "Venda de bens de consumo – apontamento sobre a transposição da Diretiva (UE) 2019/771 e o Direito Português" (2021) 17 *Estudos de Direito do Consumidor*, 511; Dias Pereira, "Os direitos do consumidor de conteúdos e serviços digitais segundo a Diretiva 2019/770" (2020) 1 *Revista Electrónica de Direito*, 135; Dias Pereira, "Contratos de fornecimento de conteúdos e serviços digitais" (2019) 15 *Estudos de Direito do Consumidor*, 9; Miranda Barbosa, "O Futuro da Compra e Venda (de Coisas Defeituosas)" (2019) 79 *Revista da Ordem dos Advogados*, 723.

[4] Morais Carvalho, *Compra e Venda e Fornecimento de Conteúdos e Serviços Digitais – Anotação ao Decreto-Lei n.º 84/2021, de 18 de Outubro* (2022); Passinhas, "O novo regime da compra e venda de bens de consumo – exegese do novo regime legal" (2021) *Revista de Direito Comercial*, 1463; P. Duarte, "O novo regime da compra e venda de bens de consumo: (apenas) algumas (das) diferenças entre a lei antiga e a lei nova" (2021) 222 *Vida Judiciária*, 34; Falcão, "Análise à Nova Lei das Garantias" (2021) 81 *Revista da Ordem dos Advogados*, 493.

3   The Decree-Law also regulates some matters which did not result from the directives, such as the sales of immovable property, the direct liability of the producer or the liability of online marketplace providers.

4   The connection with other legislations that interact with those enshrined in the Decree-Law, such as those relating to intellectual property rights or the personal data protection, is almost ignored. The references to special legislation, namely in Article 52, do not solve the problems of interaction between regimes. For instance, what is the fate of the contract that has as a consideration the processing of personal data and in which the consumer withdraws consent for its processing? This is a question that remains unanswered.

5   The statement in Article 1-1-a) that it strengthens consumer rights is questionable. The legal regime is more protective of the consumer in some respects, but less so in others. In an overview, the statute is fundamentally less clear and rigorous than its predecessor[5], which in many cases imposes a more demanding task of interpretation.

6   This chapter is organised into eleven sections. It begins with a guided tour of Decree-Law 84/2021, which allows for an understanding of its systematic organisation and to frame the issues included in the regime. We then move on to an analysis of the aspects in which the Portuguese law establishes different rules in comparison with the directives. The main new features relate to the liability of the trader and the burden of proof, the after-sales service and parts availability, the direct liability of the producer, and the direct liability of online platforms providers.

B. Guided Tour of Decree-Law 84/2021

7   The Decree-Law has five chapters: (i) general provisions; (ii) legal regime applicable to the sale of consumer goods; (iii) legal regime applicable to the supply of digital content and digital services; (iv) common provisions; (v) complementary and final provisions.

8   The first contains general provisions, part of which essentially defines the scope of the two following chapters.

9   The second chapter deals with the sale of tangible goods, transposing in essence the SGD. It is divided into three sections, the first dealing with subjective and objective conformity requirements, the second with the liability of the trader, time limits, burden of proof and remedies, and the third with immovable property.

10 In the section dedicated to the conformity requirements, the topics of delivery and the passing of risk (provided for in Directive 2011/83/EU and previously included in Articles 9B and 9C of the Consumer Protection Act, repealed by the Decree-Law 84/2021) are also regulated. Admitting the adequacy of a solution that includes in the same legal regime the obligation of delivery and the obligation of conformity, the legislative technique is quite unfortunate. In fact, Article 11, which is entitled "delivery of the goods to the consumer" and deals jointly with delivery and the passing of risk, is, as noted, included in a section entitled "objective and subjective requirements of conformity". This provision comes after those that deal with conformity requirements, a problem that logically follows delivery.

11 The second section of the chapter brings together a series of diverse and hardly groupable topics, as is evident from the length of the title, with succession of topics.

---

[5] Decree-Law no. 67/2003, of 8 April 2003, amended by Decree-Law no. 84/2008, of 21 May 2008, and Decree-Law no. 9/2021, of 29 January 2021, and repealed by Decree-Law 84/2021.

The third section deals with the obligation of conformity for immovable property. It is not known why it was decided to have a different legal regime for movable and immovable goods. The provisions of Decree-Law 67/2003, which previously regulated the sale of consumer goods and did not distinguish between movable and immovable goods, were essentially maintained. It cannot be said that this regime is more suitable for immovable goods, since Decree-Law 67/2003 resulted from the transposition of a EU directive that only applied to movable goods (Directive 1999/44/EC[6]). The solution is not logical. On the one hand, the conformity criteria are now less demanding for immovables than for movables. Secondly, there is still no hierarchy of remedies in the event of lack of conformity of the immovable property, with the consumer being able to terminate the contract immediately, unlike in the case of movable goods.

The third chapter is devoted to contracts for the supply of digital content and digital services. It is divided into two sections. The first deals with the obligation to supply and the obligation to supply a digital content or a digital service that meets the conformity requirements. Contrary to the previous chapter, the logical sequence supply-conformity is followed in this context. The title of the second section points to the regulation of the liability of the trader, burden of proof and remedies, but is also includes the important matter of the modification of the digital content or digital service.

The fourth chapter contains several provisions which apply both to contracts for the sale of goods and to contracts for the supply of digital content or digital services. Section 1 regulates the liability of the producer, the right of redress and the commercial guarantees. Section 2 is both innovative and problematic, providing quite extensively for the direct liability of online marketplaces towards the consumer. Section 3 deals with the compliance with the rules of the statute and the applicable administrative offences in case of non-compliance. There is here a very significant difference in relation to the previous legal regime since most of the provisions of the statute have an associated administrative offence penalty in case of non-compliance.

The fifth chapter contains a set of final provisions, including diversified topics such as the concept of consumer, the mandatory nature of the legal regime and its application in time.

C. Scope and Definitions

The Decree-Law applies only to consumer contracts, *i.e.* contracts concluded between a consumer ("consumidor") and a trader ("profissional").

The concept of consumer corresponds to the narrow concept of consumer in EU law, the protection being limited to natural persons. In practice, in comparison with the broader concept of Articles 2-1 of the Consumer Protection Act[7] and of 1B-a) of Decree-Law 67/2003, associations and foundations, the only legal persons that can act for purposes that do not fall within the scope of a professional activity (a concept that is used in this text in a broad sense, also covering any commercial, business, industrial or craft activity), are no longer qualified as consumers.

---

[6] Directive 1999/44/EC of the European Parliament and of the Council of 25 May 1999 on certain aspects of the sale of consumer goods and associated guarantees.

[7] Law no. 24/96, of 31 July 1996, amended by Law no. 85/98, of 16 December 1998, Decree-Law no. 67/2003, of 8 April 2003, Laws no. 10/2013, of 28 January 2013, 47/2014, of 28 July 2014, and 63/2019, of 16 August 2019, and by Decree-Laws no. 59/2021, of 14 July 2021, 84/2021, of 18 October 2021, and 109-G/2021, of 10 December 2021.

18   In the case of mixed use of the goods, the digital content or the digital service, the predominant use should be considered (Article 49). If the use is predominantly professional, the person cannot be qualified as a consumer. If the use is predominantly private, the person can be qualified as a consumer.

19   The concept of trader does not bring significant novelties. However, following the tradition of EU law, which is different from that of Portuguese law (Articles 2 of the Consumer Protection Act and 1B-a) of Decree-Law 67/2003), the concepts of consumer and trader are separated.

20   In addition to the contracts covered by the Directives, the Act also applies to goods supplied under a contract for the provision of services or a lease contract. It also applies to movable goods and immovable property. The Decree-Law is not applicable to goods sold by authority of a court or public authority and to the sale of animals.

21   In line with the second paragraph of Article 3–1, paragraph 3(b) DCD extends the application of the legal regime to cases where the consumer provides personal data to the trader, considering that these contracts are not free of charge. Unlike the DCD, the concept of personal data is not included in the transposing act. This is not particularly problematic as it refers to the definition in the GDPR, which is the definition that would always be used at national level in the absence of a separate explicit delimitation. The provisions on personal data add nothing to what the Directives imposed.

D. Conformity

22   There are no major innovations in Portuguese law regarding the conformity requirements.

23   One difference is that it is also established in the sale of goods section (and not only in the section on the supply of digital content and digital services) that unless otherwise agreed by the parties, the goods shall be delivered in the most recent version on the date of conclusion of the contract. It does not seem to call into question the maximum harmonisation of the SGD, since it is an interpretative provision which points in the direction most suited to the intention of the parties.

24   The conformity requirements are included in the scope of maximum harmonisation of the directives. Portugal has therefore been obliged to provide for the exclusion of the liability of the trader for public statements (particularly advertising and labelling) in the cases where the trader was not and could not have been aware of the public statement, the public statement had already been corrected at the time of the conclusion of the contract or the decision of the consumer could not have been influenced by the public statement. There is a decrease in consumer protection in comparison with Decree-Law 67/2003, which did not provide for any of these exclusions[8].

25   The provision regarding third-party rights is transposed *ipsis verbis* including the caveat set out in the final part.

E. Liability of the Trader and Burden of Proof

26   The main novelty of the new legal regime is the extension of the period of the liability of the trader to three years (instead of the previous two years) in the sale of movable goods. In the contracts for the sale of immovable property the period is extended to ten years in the case of structural construction elements (instead of the previous five years).

---

[8] Ferreira de Almeida, *Contratos I* (2021), 68.

E. Liability of the Trader and Burden of Proof

In the case of second-hand goods, the period may be reduced to up to one and a half year if agreed by the parties, whereas under the previous legal regime, this reduction could, if there was an agreement, be up to one year. These are relevant provisions that may constitute instruments, even if timid, against planned obsolescence.

27 The reduction of the liability period by agreement is not permitted in the case of a reconditioned good, defined in Article 2(e) as a good which has been "previously used or returned and which, after inspection, preparation, checking and testing by a professional" is put back on the market as such. The reconditioned good is therefore considered to be a new good, in which case a liability period of three years applies. The law requires express mention on the invoice of the quality of the goods as reconditioned. Pursuant to Article 48-1-b), the failure to mention the quality of the reconditioned goods constitutes an administrative offence.

28 The second major innovation is related to the first. Contrary to what has been the case since the first time the topic was the object of specific legislative treatment in consumer relations in Portugal, in the Consumer Protection Act (1996), the period of the liability of the trader (in the sale of movable goods and in the supply of digital content or digital services) is not the same as the period during which the burden of proof that the lack of conformity already existed at the time of delivery is reversed. The first period is now of three years, while the second is of two years. After the first two years from delivery, the consumer must prove not only the lack of conformity, but also that the lack of conformity existed at the time of delivery.

29 This is a paradigm shift, difficult to explain to consumers and businesses who deal mainly with the concept of "legal guarantee" and are not used with operating different regimes depending on the moment when the lack of conformity appears. If the use of the expression "legal guarantee" was already questionable in the previous legal regime, it is even more misleading with the new regime.

30 The previous statute (Decree-Law 67/2003) imposed an obligation to notify. In the case of movable goods, the consumer had to notify the trader within two months of the detection of the lack of conformity.

31 After the communication of the lack of conformity, the law imposes a time limit for the consumer to judicially exercise his or her rights. The limitation period of two years previously included in article 5-A-3 of Decree-Law 67/2003 is maintained.

32 The limitation period is suspended in two cases.

> Firstly, the period is suspended "from the moment the good has been made available to the trader for the purpose of carrying out the repair or replacement operations until the lack of conformity is remedied and the good is made available to the consumer". Like the trader's liability period (Article 12-4), the limitation period is also suspended while the consumer waits for the trader to bring the goods into conformity.
>
> Secondly, the deadline is suspended "for the duration of the out-of-court settlement of the consumer dispute between the consumer and the trader or producer". This is a very important provision, not only because it allows the attempt to resolve the dispute to be unimpeded by the limitation period, but also because of the educational nature of the reference, informing the consumer of the existence of faster, cheaper, and more effective ways of resolving the dispute compared to the courts.

33 In the field of digital content or digital services, Decree-Law 84/2021 follows the provisions of DCD.

F. Remedies for Lack of Conformity

34 The establishment of a hierarchy of remedies in the event of lack of conformity is one of the main changes in the Portuguese legal regime[9]. Unlike in the previous statute, only after an attempt is made to bring the goods into conformity by repair or replacement will it be possible to terminate the contract (or reduce the price).

35 An exception is made in cases where the lack of conformity occurs within the first thirty days. Portugal has therefore made use of the possibility offered by Article 3-7 of the SGD.

36 To the lists provided for in DCD and SGD, the Portuguese law adds as grounds for the possibility of exercising the remedies to price reduction and termination of the contract *the manifestation of a new lack of conformity*. This is an important clarification, but it seems that there is no incompatibility with the EU law, since it is still a lack of conformity that appears despite the seller having attempted to bring the goods, the digital content, or the digital services into conformity.

37 The rights of the consumer are transmitted to a third party purchasing the good (free of charge or for consideration). The transfer of the right does not imply a change in the legally prescribed time limits for exercising it, and the relevant moments in the relationship between the consumer and the trader continue to apply. A restrictive interpretation of Article 15-10 must, however, be made, since its *ratio* covers only the third party who could be qualified as a consumer if he or she had been a party to the first contract. Thus, the professional who buys the good from the original consumer cannot benefit from the protection afforded by the statute.

38 As regards repair and replacement, the main novelty of the Portuguese law concerns the introduction of a fixed deadline. Article 18-3 states that "the period for repair or replacement shall not exceed 30 days, except in situations where the nature and complexity of the goods, the seriousness of the lack of conformity and the effort necessary to complete the repair or replacement justify a longer period". This provision is particularly unfortunate. Under the guise of improving the position of the consumer by providing for a fixed period, this period is in fact presented as a minimum, allowing it to be extended in the situations indicated therein. In fact, little is added in relation to the general clause of the reasonable period, which loses effect. We even doubt that the Directive is thinking of providing for both the clause on the reasonable period and the provision of a fixed period. Professionals who do not wish to comply with the 30-day deadline will always invoke one of the exceptions contained in the provision, which will also increase litigation considerably.

39 Article 18-4 establishes that the repaired good shall benefit from an additional "guarantee" period of six months for each repair, up to a maximum of four repairs. The problem is that the law does not provide for any "guarantee" period. It provides for a period of liability of the seller (three years) and a period of release or discharge from the burden of proof that the lack of conformity already existed at the time of delivery (two years). The *ratio* of the legal regime leads to the conclusion that the best solution to solve this problem is to consider that the trader is liable for an additional period of six months, where, in the first four months, the rule of release or waiver of the burden of proof of the lack of conformity at the time of delivery applies.

---

[9] Passinhas, "O novo regime da compra e venda de bens de consumo – exegese do novo regime legal" (2021) *Revista de Direito Comercial*, 1463 (1493).

F. Remedies for Lack of Conformity

The same logic should apply to cases of replacement of the good, provided for in paragraph 6. Without using the word "guarantee", reference is made in this provision to a new liability period applicable to the new good. 40

The consumer is also entitled to several rights resulting from a lack of conformity. 41

Firstly, he or she must be able to refuse to receive the good, the digital content or the digital service. This possibility is not expressly provided for in the legislation but is derived from the general rules. As long as the trader has not offered to perform his obligation to deliver a good, digital content or digital service in conformity, the consumer may refuse to perform the contract, thereby placing the trader in default. 42

Secondly, he or she may invoke the *exceptio non adimpleti contractus*. This possibility is foreseen in Article 15-7. 43

The provision in Article 15-8 is an innovation of Portuguese law and contains an incomprehensible solution ("the previous paragraph does not give the consumer the right to refuse to pay benefits which are in default"). There is no reason, in the case of a lack of conformity, to consider the consumer to be in default. The lack of conformity is assessed by reference to the moment of delivery, so that, even if it appears at a later moment, it is considered to have existed at that moment (by way of a release or discharge of the burden of proof, under the terms of Article 13, or by way of proof of its existence at the moment of delivery, if the aforementioned release or discharge does not apply). Now, if there is a lack of conformity, the trader is in default and the consumer may refuse to pay any instalment. Even if the consumer was in default before the lack of conformity was detected, the mere fact that he or she has detected the lack of conformity has the effect that the consumer is no longer in default. An abrogating interpretation of paragraph 8 is therefore required. 44

The consumer has the right to compensation, a right which, however, should not be configured as a substitute for the rights provided for in the statute[10]. Member States had wide freedom in regulating this right (Article 3-10 DCD). In Portugal, it was decided to expressly provide for it, but referring to the general legal regime (Article 52-4). 45

In the case of immovable property, the previous provision of Decree-Law 67/2003 remains in force, whereby the consumer may exercise any of the four rights (repair, replacement, price reduction or termination of the contract), unless this proves to be impossible or constitutes an abuse of rights, under the terms of Article 334 of the Civil Code (Article 24 of Decree-Law 84/2021). 46

In contracts for the supply of digital content and digital services, the Portuguese legal regime does not introduce any innovation regarding remedies (see Article 35 of Decree-Law 84/2021). 47

As in European law, no distinction is made between repair and replacement as regards the means of restoring conformity. It is therefore assumed, arguably, that the concepts of repair and replacement are appropriate only for goods. 48

The consumer is primarily entitled to have the digital content or digital service brought into conformity, a right which is limited by the impossibility or disproportionate nature of the costs. For the analysis of the disproportionate nature of the costs, account should be taken of the value the digital content or digital service would have if there were no lack of conformity and of the significance of the lack of conformity. 49

In contracts where personal data constitute a consideration, this threshold may be particularly problematic. Indeed, in such cases, the consumer is not entitled to a price reduction, since he has not paid a price, and the right of termination is not an appro- 50

---

[10] De Franceschi, "Consumer's Remedies for Defective Goods with Digital Elements" (2021) 2 *JIPITEC*, 143 (143).

priate remedy since there is nothing that the trader can refund to the consumer for exercising the right. That leaves the restoration of conformity, which will as a general rule involve disproportionate costs. A restrictive interpretation of the provision is therefore required, to the effect that the disproportionality must be significant if the consumer cannot claim that right where he has not paid a price.

G. After-Sales Service and Parts Availability

51   Article 21 imposes two post-contractual obligations on the trader: (i) to guarantee after-sales assistance in the case of movable goods subject to public registry (cars, motorbikes, boats); (ii) to inform the consumer of a duty on the part of the producer to make parts available and of the obligation to provide after-sales assistance (paragraphs 3 and 4).

52   The article also imposes a duty to make parts available to the producer (paragraph 1). The producer must make the parts needed for the repair of the goods available for a period of 10 years after the last unit of the good has been placed on the market. This means that if the good is supplied by the trader 10 years after the producer placed the last unit of the good on the market, the consumer will not be able to benefit from the protection afforded by this provision.

H. Commercial Guarantees

53   In this field, there are no significant innovations in relation to what was imposed by EU law.

54   The statement of guarantee must be issued in writing (on paper or via a computerised document). This results from the requirement that it must be "*written in* Portuguese, in a clear and intelligible language", as stated in the introductory part of Article 43-6.

I. Direct Liability of the Producer

55   The final part of Recital 63 of SGD states that "whether the consumer can also raise a claim directly against a person in previous links of the chain of transactions should not be regulated by this Directive, except in cases where a producer offers the consumer a commercial guarantee for the goods". Recital 12 of DCD points in the same direction.

56   Member States are therefore free to regulate this matter. Portugal has done so, thus maintaining the option set out in Article 6 of Decree-Law 67/2003, with variations. It should be noted that the regime now extends to contracts for the supply of digital content or digital services.

57   Producer is defined in Article 2(p) as "the manufacturer of goods, digital content or digital services, the importer of goods into the European Union or any other person purporting to be a producer by indicating on the goods his name, trademark or other distinctive sign".

58   The aim of applying the regime also to the supply of digital content and digital services is understandable, but the mention of a *manufacturer of services* is perhaps a little excessive. Recital 78 of DCD refers to a chain "from the *original designer* to the final trader".

59   Faced with a lack of conformity of the good (movable or immovable) or of the digital content or digital service, the consumer may address either the trader or the producer

and may even simultaneously require both to satisfy his or her claim. If the producer is the trader, this rule does not apply.

The fact that the producer remedies the lack of conformity does not prevent the consumer from subsequently requiring the trader to remedy the remaining lack of conformity (by means of a new repair or replacement). The same should apply where it is the trader who first attempts to remedy the lack of conformity. In this case, the consumer, when faced with a new manifestation of a lack of conformity, may turn to the producer. In short, the consumer may at any time address either the trader or the producer, provided that the conditions giving rise to liability on the part of both parties are met.

The liability of the producer is, however, still not as extensive as the liability of the trader, thus making it more advantageous for the consumer to exercise his rights *vis-à-vis* the latter. Indeed, the consumer can only exercise the rights of repair or replacement of the good. This wording should be corrected as the rule also applies to the supply of digital content or digital services. Thus, the consumer can only exercise the right to have the good or the digital content or digital service brought into conformity. The rights to have the price reduced and the contract terminated cannot be exercised against the producer, which is understandable given that there is no contract between the consumer and the producer.

In the case of reconditioned goods, the consumer cannot, as a rule, turn directly to the producer. The exception is the case where the producer is responsible for the reconditioning of the good.

In addition to the producer, the representative of the producer in the place of residence of the consumer is also liable for lack of conformity. The applicable regime is that of joint liability, so that the consumer can claim from any of them the satisfaction of his right (Article 512 of the Civil Code). He may also address both, and if one of them satisfies the claim, the other is released from liability.

J. Direct Liability of the Online Marketplace Provider

The direct liability of online marketplaces[11] is foreseen in Decree-Law 84/2021 in very broad terms.

Article 44-1 states that "the online marketplace provider that, acting for purposes related to its activity, is a contractual partner of the trader that provides the good, the digital content or the digital service is jointly liable for the lack of conformity". Paragraph 2 clarifies that "the online marketplace provider is considered to be a contractual partner of the trader whenever it exercises a predominant influence on the conclusion of the contract, which is verified, namely, in the following situations: a) the contract is concluded exclusively through the means offered by the online marketplace provider; b) payment shall be made exclusively through the means provided by the online marketplace provider; c) the terms of the contract concluded with the consumer are mainly determined by the online marketplace provider or the price to be paid by the consumer

---

[11] For an analysis of the issue of the liability of online marketplaces under Portuguese law prior to this legal regime, see Campos Carvalho, "Online Platforms: Concept, Role in the Conclusion of Contracts and Current Legal Framework in Europe" in Arroyo Amayuelas and Cámara Lapuente (eds), *El Derecho Privado en el Nuevo Paradigma Digital* (2020), 239; Campos Carvalho, "From Bilateral to Triangular: Concluding Contracts in the Collaborative Economy" in Regina Redinha et al. (eds), *The Sharing Economy: Legal Problems of a Permutations and Combinations Society* (2019), 196; Campos Carvalho, "A Proteção do Consumidor na *Sharing Economy*" in Morais Carvalho (ed), *I Congresso de Direito do Consumo* (2016), 115.

is likely to be influenced by the marketplace provider; or d) the associated advertising is focused on the online marketplace provider rather than the traders". Paragraph 3 emphasises that "for the purposes of assessing the existence of a predominant influence of the online marketplace provider in the conclusion of the contract, any facts likely to give rise to consumer confidence that the latter has a dominant influence over the trader providing the good, the digital content or the digital service may be considered".

66 Unlike most other Member States, Portugal has used the possibility provided by Recitals 23 of SGD and 18 of DCD.

67 It might have been more prudent to avoid the expression "contractual partner" (concerning the relationship between the online marketplace operator and the trader), which is used in the recitals of the Directives to refer to another relationship (between the online marketplace provider and the consumer).

68 The scheme is strongly influenced by the ELI Model Rules on Online Platforms[12]. The decisive criterion for the liability of the online marketplace provider is the predominant influence on the contract concluded between consumer and trader.

69 Article 45 imposes a special duty to inform on online marketplaces providers, partially transposing Directive 2019/2161[13] into Portuguese law[14].

70 It states that the online marketplace provider who is not the contractual partner of the professional providing the good, the digital content or the digital service must, prior to the conclusion of the contract, inform consumers in a clear and unambiguous manner that the contract will be concluded with a professional and not with the online marketplace provider, the identity of the professional, as well as his or her quality as a professional or, if this is not the case, the non-application of the rights provided for in the decree-law, and the contact details of the professional for the purposes of exercising the rights provided for in the legal regime. The online marketplace provider may rely on the information provided to it by the trader, unless the online marketplace provider knows or should know, based on the available data relating to transactions on the platform, that this information is incorrect. The consequence in case of failure to comply with this provision is the liability of the online marketplace provider as if it was a contractual partner of the professional.

K. Right of Redress

71 Decree-Law 84/2021 grants a right of redress both to the trader vis-à-vis the producer or other "person at earlier stages of the contractual chain" (arts. 41 and 42) and to the online marketplace provider vis-à-vis the trader (art. 46).

72 The justification for a right of redress for the trader vis-à-vis another person in the contractual chain is that the legislation has chosen to always hold the trader liable vis-à-vis the consumer, even though in many cases the lack of conformity is not attributable to the trader, or it is difficult to determine exactly who is liable (by action or omission).

---

[12] <https://www.europeanlawinstitute.eu/projects-publications/completed-projects-old/online-platforms> accessed 12 December 2021. See also Busch et al., "An Introduction to the ELI Model Rules on Online Platforms" (2020) 2 *EuCML*, 61.

[13] Directive (EU) 2019/2161 of the European Parliament and of the Council of 27 November 2019 amending Council Directive 93/13/EEC and Directives 98/6/EC, 2005/29/EC and 2011/83/EU of the European Parliament and of the Council as regards the better enforcement and modernisation of Union consumer protection rules.

[14] The main act transposing Directive 2019/2161 into Portuguese law is the Decree-Law no. 109-G/2021, of 10 December 2021.

K. Right of Redress

73 Thus, the trader is always liable towards the consumer, and the question of determining the person liable for the failure to supply and the lack of conformity in relations between the trader and the other links in the contractual chain is resolved[15].

74 There are relevant differences in relation to the previous regime, set out in Article 7 of Decree-Law 67/2003, all of which point in the direction of less protection for the trader vis-à-vis the other members of the contractual chain.

75 In the first place, the trader must address the person liable, by action or omission, and not the person who sold him the good or provided him with the digital content or the digital service. This solution reflects a paradigm shift in the exercise of the right of redress, since the right of redress used to be provided between the contracting parties at each link of the contractual chain (Article 7-1 of Decree-Law 67/2003) and now it is established that the right of redress must be exercised against the person liable, a person who may not have a contractual relationship with the trader.

76 Secondly, the person against whom the right of redress has been invoked does not appear in turn to have a right of redress against any other person. If the trader addresses the liable person directly, it is understandable that the liable person no longer has a right of redress against someone else. Article 7-3 of Decree-Law 67/2003 also provided for the interruption of the contractual chain from the moment the person responsible for the lack of conformity was reached.

77 Thirdly, in order to facilitate the exercise of the right of redress, Article 7-2 of Decree-Law 67/2003 provided for the application of the presumption of the existence of lack of conformity at the moment of delivery. A trader who satisfied a right of a consumer based on the presumption of lack of conformity at the moment of delivery benefited from this same presumption during the same period against the person from whom he had acquired the goods. If proving the lack of conformity in advance is difficult for the consumer, it is no less difficult for the trader, which justifies its application in the relationship between the various links in the contractual chain. This provision is not provided for in the Decree-Law 84/2021, which leads to the conclusion that the trader is currently much less protected in relation to the previous links in the contractual chain.

78 Fourthly, the provision according to which "the agreement whereby the exercise of the right of redress is excluded or limited in advance will only be effective if adequate compensation is awarded to its holder" (Article 7-4 of Decree-Law 67/2003) is not retained. The position of the trader may also be particularly weakened on this point. However, Decree-Law 446/85[16] (the legal regime on standard terms, which implements the Unfair Terms Directive and applies both to B2C and to B2B contracts) may be applied to this agreement and questions as to the inclusion and validity of clauses included in contracts entered into between the trader and the person or persons in the contractual chain may be analysed in the light of this legal regime.

79 The right of redress of the online marketplace provider vis-à-vis the trader (Article 46) is limited to the "general terms". This is a reference to the common rules of private law.

80 The online marketplace provider is not, therefore, given a new right, nor is life made easier for it in this action for redress. It does not even seem to benefit from the time limits and reversals of the burden of proof that the consumer can use against it. This

---

[15] See recitals 78 of Directive 2019/770 and 63 of Directive 2019/771 and Articles 20-2 of Directive 2019/770 and 18 of Directive 2019/771.

[16] Decree-Law no. 446/85, of 25 October, amended by Decree-Laws no. 220/95, of 31 August (rectified by Amendment Statement no. 114-B/95, of 31 August), 249/99, of 7 July, and 323/2001, of 17 December, by Law no. 32/2021, of 27 May, and by Decree-Laws no. 108/2021, of 7 December, and 109-G/2021, of 10 December.

means that in order to hold the trader liable, it will have to prove, for instance, that the lack of conformity already existed at the time of delivery.

81 In another context, addressing a possible provision that provides for the right of redress "under the general terms of the law", Rui Pinto Duarte points out that "such a provision could, in practice, lead to nothing, because the general law (especially the sale of goods general legal regime) is much more restrictive, especially as regards deadlines, of the rights of the buyer than the regime imposed by the Directive for the relations between the consumer and the final seller"[17].

82 Although not expressly stated in the regulation, nothing seems to prevent the online marketplace provider from taking direct action against the producer (or other person in the contractual chain) whenever the lack of conformity is attributable to it.

L. Conclusion

83 The overwhelming majority of the provisions of the Directives have been transposed without major novelties. This is particularly clear when it comes to digital content and digital services.

84 There are, however, significant new features.

85 The most relevant innovation from a comparative law perspective is the express and fairly broad provision for the liability of online marketplaces providers.

86 Regarding the practical and daily application of the statute in Portugal, there is a major paradigm shift, since the liability period no longer corresponds to the period of release from the burden of proof that the lack of conformity already existed at the time of delivery. The liability period is extended to three years. The period relating to the release of the burden of proof remains at two years.

87 The protection of the consumer is diminished compared to the previous regime as regards the hierarchy of remedies, the deadline to bring the goods into conformity, and the possibility for the trader to limit its liability for public statements issued by third parties. Until now, under Portuguese law, the consumer could immediately terminate the contract in case of lack of conformity. The deadline to bring the goods into conformity was always of 30 days. In relation to advertising, the grounds for exclusion of liability provided for in Directive 1999/44/EC had not been transposed into Decree-Law 67/2003.

88 With a view to strengthening consumer protection, the main innovations consist of the extension of the liability period to three years, the extension of the liability period when the good is repaired, the right to an after-sales service and availability of spare parts, and the liability of online marketplaces providers.

89 Within the Portuguese context, the application of the decree-law in practice will be decisive to understand its real impact. It is not uncommon for regulations enshrined in the legal system to have little or no practical application.

Bibliography

Carlos Ferreira de Almeida, *Contratos I* (7th edn, Almedina, Coimbra 2021)

Mafalda Miranda Barbosa, "O Futuro da Compra e Venda (de Coisas Defeituosas)" (2019) 79 *Revista da Ordem dos Advogados*, 723

---

[17] Pinto Duarte, O Direito de Regresso do Vendedor Final na Venda para Consumo" (2001) 4 *Themis*, 173.

Bibliography

Christoph Busch, Gerhard Dannemann, Hans Schulte-Nölke, Aneta Wiewiórowska-Domagalska and Fryderyk Zoll, "An Introduction to the ELI Model Rules on Online Platforms" (2020) 2 *EuCML – Journal of European Consumer and Market* Law, 61

Joana Campos Carvalho, "Online Platforms: Concept, Role in the Conclusion of Contracts and Current Legal Framework in Europe" in Esther Arroyo Amayuelas and Sergio Cámara Lapuente (eds), *El Derecho Privado en el Nuevo Paradigma Digital* (Marcial Pons, Madrid 2020), 239

Joana Campos Carvalho, "From Bilateral to Triangular: Concluding Contracts in the Collaborative Economy" in Maria Regina Redinha, Maria Raquel Guimarães and Francisco Liberal Fernandes (eds), *The Sharing Economy: Legal Problems of a Permutations and Combinations Society* (Cambridge Scholars Publishing, UK 2019), 196

Joana Campos Carvalho, "A Proteção do Consumidor na *Sharing Economy*" in Jorge Morais Carvalho (ed), *I Congresso de Direito do Consumo* (Almedina, Coimbra 2016) 115

Jorge Morais Carvalho, *Compra e Venda e Fornecimento de Conteúdos e Serviços Digitais – Anotação ao Decreto-Lei n.º 84/2021, de 18 de Outubro* (Almedina,, Coimbra 2022)

Jorge Morais Carvalho, *Manual de Direito do Consumo* (7th edn, Almedina, Coimbra 2020) 364

Jorge Morais Carvalho and Martim Farinha, "Goods with Digital Elements, Digital Content and Digital Services in Directives 2019/770 and 2019/771" (2020) 2 *Revista de Direito e Tecnologia*, 257

Jorge Morais Carvalho, "Venda de Bens de Consumo e Fornecimento de Conteúdos e Serviços Digitais – As Diretivas 2019/771 e 2019/770 e o seu Impacto no Direito Português" (2019) 3 *Revista Electrónica de Direito*, 63

Paulo Duarte, "O novo regime da compra e venda de bens de consumo: (apenas) algumas (das) diferenças entre a lei antiga e a lei nova" (2021) 222 *Vida Judiciária*, 34

Rui Pinto Duarte, O Direito de Regresso do Vendedor Final na Venda para Consumo" (2001) 4 *Themis – Revista da Faculdade de Direito da Universidade Nova de Lisboa*, 173

David Falcão, "Análise à Nova Lei das Garantias" (2021) 81 *Revista da Ordem dos Advogados*, 493

Alberto De Franceschi, "Consumer's Remedies For Defective Goods With Digital Elements" (2021) 2 *JIPITEC – Journal of Intellectual Property, Information Technology and Electronic Commerce Law*, 143

Nuno Manuel Pinto Oliveira, "O Direito Europeu da Compra e Venda 20 Anos Depois – Comparação entre a Directiva 1999/44/CE, de 25 de Maio de 1999, e a Directiva 2019/771/UE, de 20 de Maio de 2019" (2020) *Revista de Direito Comercial*, 1217

Sandra Passinhas, "O novo regime da compra e venda de bens de consumo – exegese do novo regime legal" (2021) *Revista de Direito Comercial*, 1463

Alexandre L. Dias Pereira, "Os direitos do consumidor de conteúdos e serviços digitais segundo a Diretiva 2019/770" (2020) 1 *Revista Electrónica de Direito*, 135

Alexandre Dias Pereira, "Contratos de fornecimento de conteúdos e serviços digitais" (2019) 15 *Estudos de Direito do Consumidor*, 9

Paulo Mota Pinto, "Venda de bens de consumo – apontamento sobre a transposição da Diretiva (UE) 2019/771 e o Direito Português" (2021) 17 *Estudos de Direito do Consumidor*, 511

Romania

A. Introduction. General Framework 1
 I. Special legal regulations applicable to B2C sale contracts and to the compliance of digital content and products with embedded digital content ... 1
  1. General guidelines for determining the scope of legal regulations 1
  2. Situations exempted from the scope of application of the special legal provisions 3
  3. Synopsis of the main specific obligations' incumbent on professionals ... 4
  4. Trader's liability for non-compliant delivery of autonomous and embedded digital content 10
 II. Reverberations of the transposition of the Directives on the structure of the existing general and specialised law 13
 III. Implications of compliance within the contractual force of advertising documents 16
  1. Reversing the general rule of the non-contractual nature of advertising content 16
  2. Situations exempted from the binding force of the professional trader's statements 19
 IV. Consumer's (procedural) obligation to cooperate with the trader in establishing technically available means 23

B. Definitions and scope of application 25

C. Conformity of goods 30
 I. Hybrid product conformity assessment: objective vs. subjective compliance ... 30
  1. Interconnected levels of conformity 30
  2. Subjective (atypical) criteria for assessing the conformity of products 37
  3. Expressly agreed introduction of atypical features in the contractual content 40
  4. Objective criteria for assessing conformity compliance in B2C contracts ... 42
  5. Conformity assessed in relation to consumer's legitimate / reasonable expectations 44
 II. Specific information on omitted characteristics 45
 III. Availability of spare parts and corresponding duty of information 46
 IV. Non-conformity resulting from incorrect installation of products 52
 V. Conformity remedies in hypotheses of personal data provided as a counter-performance 55
 VI. Trader's attempt to unilaterally modify the contractual content 58

D. Trader's liability for non-conformity 66
 I. Exonerating effects of fortuitous events 66
 II. Remedies for the failure to supply and remedies for the lack of conformity .. 72
 III. Consumer's right to withhold payment 80
 IV. Repair and replacement of products 85
 V. Contractual consequences of consumer's withdrawal of consent for processing personal data 89
 VI. Environmental sustainability issues and fighting premature or planned obsolescence of products 91
 VII. Transfer of consumer's rights to subsequent parties 93

E. Commercial Guarantees 96

F. Time limits and temporality bars 104

G. Seller's right of redress 113

H. Reverberations on other legal remedies 114

I. Concluding remarks 116

 Bibliography 121

A. Introduction. General Framework

I. Special legal regulations applicable to B2C sale contracts and to the compliance of digital content and products with embedded digital content

1. General guidelines for determining the scope of legal regulations

1   The provisions of Directive (EU) 2019/771 on certain aspects concerning contracts for the sale of goods (hereinafter: SGD), amending Regulation (EU) 2017/2394 and Directive 2009/22/EC, and repealing Directive 1999/44/EC were integrated into Romanian legal system though the adopting of the Governmental Extraordinary Ordinance no. 140/2021 on certain legal aspects concerning the contracts for the sale of goods, the substantial sphere of which includes specific provisions establishing the legal framework for sales contracts concluded between professional traders and consumers, particularly rules on objective and subjective criteria for establishing product conformity, corrective measures in case of non-compliance, procedural aspects concerning the implementing of the corrective measures, as well as the efficiency of commercial guarantees.

2   The Governmental Extraordinary Ordinance no. 141/2021 on certain legal aspects concerning the providing of digital content and digital services, which marks the transposition into national law of the provisions of Directive (EU) 2019/770 on certain aspects of contracts for the provision of digital content and digital services (hereinafter: DCD), entered into force on January 9h, 2022 and governs the salient aspects of the performing of B2C contracts for the provision of digital content and digital services between professional traders and consumers, such as: the compliance of digital content or digital service with B2C contractual provisions; the availability of corrective measures in case of non-compliance or in case of non-compliant provision of digital content and modalities for the implementation of these remedial or restorative measures; legal limitations on the possibility of unilaterally modifying the characteristics of digital content or the digital service provided to consumers. With regard to determining the sphere of the situations to which the provisions of the G.E.O no. 141/2021, it should be noted that, according to the provisions of the ordinance, its content applies: (i) in the perimeter of B2C contracts in which the trader provides or undertakes to provide the consumer with digital content or a digital service, and the consumer pays or undertakes to pay a price (the onerous character of the transaction being decisive)[1]; (ii) in hypotheses in which, should the professional trader provided or undertook to provide the consumer with digital content or a digital service, the consumer provides or undertakes to provide the trader with personal data, as a counter-performance, unless the personal data provided by the consumer are processed exclusively by to the trader for the provision of digital content or digital service or to enable the trader to comply with the legal requirements to which the professional is subject, and the latter does not process such personal data for any other purpose[2]; (iii) in circumstances in which the digital content or digital service was developed, calibrated[3], conceived, personalized or designed in accordance with the consumer's specifications; (iv) in cases that involve the delivery of any material which serves exclusively as a medium for digital content.

---

[1] Suciu, 'Conformitatea conținutului digital. Noi instrumente legislative europene 2.0' (2022) 1 *Revista Română de Drept Privat*, 206.

[2] Verteș-Olteanu, 'Considerații privind regimul juridic aplicabil bunurilor digitale' (2017) 3 *Revista Română de Drept Privat*, 377.

[3] *Ibidem.*

A. Introduction. General Framework

2. Situations exempted from the scope of application of the special legal provisions

It is worth noting that the provisions of the G.E.O. no. 141/2021 are not applicable *inter alia* in cases in which the digital content or digital service is incorporated into or interconnected to a product and was provided under a contract of sale relating to the main product, whether the digital content or the digital service in question is provided by the seller or by a third party. In this case, the normative provisions regarding the general legal framework concerning the guarantee of conformity will be applied, namely the provisions of the G.E.O. no. 140/2021 on certain legal aspects related to the contracts for the sale of goods. In order to reduce the perimeter of any inconsistent application of the legal provisions, it is provided that, in case of doubt as to whether the provision of embedded or interconnected digital content or digital service is part of the sales contract, the digital content or digital service is to be presumably covered by the B2C sales contract.

3. Synopsis of the main specific obligations' incumbent on professionals

At the first stage of the discussion, the first essential obligation for the trader is describable as residing in the providing of the digital content or digital service without undue delay after the conclusion of the B2C contract, unless otherwise agreed with the consumer; the supply obligation is considered to have been performed at the moment in which the digital content or any appropriate means of accessing or downloading it, or the digital service, becomes available or accessible to the consumer or is integrated into the physical or virtual equipment chosen by the consumer for this purpose. The trader is also obliged to provide the digital content or digital service in the latest version available at the time of the conclusion of the contract, preserving the possibility for the parties to agree, by express contractual clauses, on derogations from the mentioned suppletive rule (while establishing that the object of the B2C contract is represented, for example, by an earlier version / a previous version of the digital content).

In terms of conformity of delivery, the digital content or digital service provided must meet certain subjective requirements (a) in the sense of derogatory, atypical, expressly agreed requirements, and, on the other hand, objective compliance requirements (b) understood as referring to typical conformity requirements for products from the same category. Additionally, where the B2C contract provides for the continuous provision of digital content or digital service over a suitable period, the digital content delivered or the digital service provided must comply with the objective and subjective requirements of compliance throughout the contractual period.

Subsequently, in terms of compliance, the digital service or digital content is considered to meet the objective requirements[4] of compliance, despite the fact that a particular feature does not meet the objective requirements of compliance, if the consumer was explicitly informed at the time of conclusion of the contract, in clear and plain language which allows the consumer to understand the economic and legal consequences of

---

[4] As it has been emphasized under specialized scholarly analysis, "(…) the objective conformity criteria were treated as an eminently subsidiary standard to the conventional one, activated only when the contractual provisions would have been incomplete or lacking in transparency. The solution has been intensely criticized, since, giving paramount importance to contractual provisions, the consumer's vulnerability remains unaddressed in hypotheses in which the professional designed a set of standardized clauses to promote the examination of transparency. Following the amendments to the initial view, the objective criteria have become complementary to the subjective ones, applicable *de plano* regardless of the clarity issues of the contractual terms": Suciu, 'Conformitatea conținutului digital. Noi instrumente legislative europene 2.0', *loc. cit. supra* (our translation, J.G.).

that non-compliance, and the consumer has expressly and separately accepted this type of derogatory clauses (based on a granular, explicit consent to the derogations from certain objective, typical compliance requirements, which would have been incidental otherwise).

7 On the other versant of the discussion, it should be noted that the digital content or digital service is considered non-compliant if the non-compliance is caused by incorrect integration of digital content or digital service into the consumer's digital environment, should (i) the digital content or digital service have been integrated by the trader or under the trader's control or should (ii) the digital content or service were intended to be integrated by the consumer, and incorrect integration is the result of deficiencies in the integration instructions provided by the trader.

8 With regard to updates available for digital content or digital service, it can be noted that the new regulatory framework establishes the obligation for the trader to inform the consumer that updates are being provided, as well as the obligation to actually provide these updates, including security updates, stating that these B2C obligations are maintained for as long as: (i) the digital content or digital service must be provided in accordance with the contract, if the contract provides for continuous supply over a period of time; (ii) the consumer can reasonably expect this continuity if the contract provides for a single act of supply or a series of individual supply acts.

9 Where the contract stipulates for the provision of digital content or making available to the consumer of digital content or digital service over a suitable period, the provisions of G.C.O. no. 141/2021 regulate the possibility for the trader to modify the digital content or the digital service in order to keep them in compliance, should the restrictive conditions set by the normative act were cumulatively fulfilled. However, in order to provide adequate legal protection to the consumer, in relation to any unilateral changes made by the professional trader, which would have a major negative impact (especially of an economic nature) on the consumer, the latter's right to unilaterally terminate the B2C contract to supply is exercisable to the extent that the unilateral change proposed by the professional has a major adverse impact on access to or use of the digital content or digital service, unless the professional trader allows the consumer to maintain the digital content or service at no additional costs or without changes, and the digital content or digital service remains to meet the objective (typical) compliance requirements.

4. Trader's liability for non-compliant delivery of autonomous and embedded digital content

10 As follows from the provisions of the G.E.O. no. 141/2021 governing the trader's liability for the non-compliant supply of digital content or digital service, where the contract provides for a single supply act or a series of individual supply acts, the trader is considered to be liable for any non-conformity which exists at the time of supply and which is ascertained within 5 years from the date of supply; in other cases, where the B2C contract provided for continuous supply over a period of time, the trader would be liable for any non-compliance that occurs or is found to be manifesting within the time limit within which the digital content or digital service must be provided in accordance with the contractual specifications.

11 In the event of reporting deficiencies[5], the provisions of the G.E.O. no. 141/2021 recognize the right of the consumer to request at least one of the triptychs of remedies listed

---

[5] Under the provisions of Article 1708, second para. of the Romanian Civil Code. It is affected by absolute nullity the clause that removes trader's liability for damages caused by defects which were known or that should have been known by the seller at the date of concluding the contract; therefore,

A. Introduction. General Framework

by the provisions of the normative act: (i) non-contentious, out-of-court compliance with digital content or digital service (free repair or replacement of products that do not comply with expressly agreed objective, typical or subjective standards of compliance; (ii) a proportionate price reduction; (iii) unilateral termination of the B2C contract (which might be contested in court).

The consumer has the right to have the digital content or digital service complied with out of court, unless this would be impossible or would impose disproportionate costs on the trader. In this case, the trader is obliged to bring the digital content or digital service into compliance, within a period not exceeding 15 calendar days from the moment the trader was informed of the non-compliance and which is expressly agreed upon with the consumer, without causing significant costs or significant inconveniences to the consumer. The phrase 'compliance of the products' describes, in the plan of hierarchical legal remedies, the free repair / free replacement of the products or the proportional reduction of the price / termination of the contract.

II. Reverberations of the transposition of the Directives on the structure of the existing general and specialised law

The adopting of the Governmental Extraordinary Ordinances no. 140/2021 and no. 141/2021 particularly impacted the Law of obligations and contracts, through the prismatic of consecrating consumer's prerogative of opting for the unilateral termination[6] of the B2C contract, in the hypotheses in which the manifesting of lacunary objective or subjective conformity has not been followed by the seller's adopting of palliative measures, such as having the products brought into conformity and the consumer has not chosen to receive a proportionate reduction in the price. The pre-existing general legal provisions concerning the unilateral termination of contracts, especially Article 1552 of the Romanian Civil Code, provided for the termination of the contract which may take place by written notification of the debtor when the parties have so agreed, when the debtor is legally considered in delay of due performance or when the party has not fulfilled the obligation within the time limit set by contingent notification. Subsequently, it must be mentioned that, in accordance to the general legal provisions (the second thesis of Article 1552 of the Romanian Civil Code), the declaration of resolution or contractual termination must be made within the limitation period provided by law for their corresponding action; in all cases, the declaration of resolution or termination will be inserted, as the case may be, in other public registers, in order to be opposable to third parties; the declaration of unilateral termination of contract becomes irrevocable from the date of its communication to the debtor or, as the case may be, from the date of expiration of the term provided in the first paragraph of Article 1.552 of the Romanian Civil Code. The ineffectiveness of civil and business contracts subsumes all

---

a clause generating the exemption from liability for simultaneous defects of digital products triggers the adjacent remedy of compensatory damages, according to Suciu, 'Conformitatea conținutului digital. Noi instrumente legislative europene 2.0', *loc. cit. supra*.

[6] Suciu, 'Conformitatea conținutului digital. Noi instrumente legislative europene' (2021) 1 *Revista Română de Drept Privat*, 704; Popa, 'Soluții jurisdicționale cu efecte substanțiale. Un comentariu pe marginea unor hotărâri «radiante» ale Curții de Justiție a Uniunii Europene' (2021) 1 *Revista Română de Drept Privat*, 201; Țiț, 'Rolul activ al judecătorului în identificarea și calificarea actelor și faptelor deduse judecății. Câteva considerații' (2021) 1 *Revista Română de Drept Privat*, 174; Goicovici, 'The Traders' Liability for Lack of Conformity of the Digital Content and of the Digital Services, as Regulated by Directive (EU) 2019/770' (2020) L LXVI *Analele Științifice ale Universității „Alexandru Ioan Cuza" din Iași, Seria Științe Juridice*, 79.

those legal situations in which, for various reasons, the agreement does not produce its effects or stops producing those effects; there is no general regulation in the Romanian civil legislation on the matter of unilateral termination of contracts, the regulation of the ineffectiveness of civil legal acts being dispersed in the Civil Code provisions. The Civil Code regulates in a limited manner the three cases in which the party can unilaterally declare the resolution / termination, the judicial intervention modality remaining under the regulation of common law. The unilateral resolution / termination by notifying the debtor (art. 1552 of the Romanian Civil Code) is introduced as a special provision, yet without excluding the use of contractual dissolution pacts.

14   From the perspective of Data Protection law, the adopting of the G.E.O. no. 141/2021 multiplied the practical interrogations concerning the reverberations of the onerous character of the B2C transaction on consumer's right to obtain indemnification based on the professional seller's contractual liability, notably in the hypotheses in which the digital content or digital services were supplied while engaging the consumer, as a counter-performance, to provide personal data or to consent to the collecting and use of the personal data outside the purpose of contractual performance, although not implying the payment of a price in a pecuniary expression. The consumer's prerogatives of control, when exercised over the personal data processing mainly concern the active participation of the data subject in updating consumer's preferences in terms of consenting to personal data processing, including the decision to port the personal data to another controller. The mentioned prerogatives find their normative expression in the binomen represented by the data subject's right of access and the right of data portability[7], the intricacies of which require the implementing of pertinent technical standards, in terms of adequacy and appropriateness of mechanism aimed at the facilitating of the transfer from one data controller to another, such as the ability to export user data into a user-accessible local file, thus promoting interoperability, as well as facilitating searchability and data subject's effective control over data processing. The G.E.O. no. 141/2021 does not specifically address the issue of the personal data portability, in the perimeter of the exercising of consumer's right of access to personal data collected and processed in the perimeter of B2C contracts for the sale of digital content. Nevertheless, these prerogatives remain available as outlined in the text of article 15 of Regulation no. 679 of 27 April 2016 on the protection of individuals regarding the processing of personal data and on the free movement of such data. Another salient observation concerns the fact that the exercise of the right of personal data portability does not imply merely insular effects, since it consequentially engages multifaceted effects, as it is at the forefront of the effective exercise of other essential rights of the data subject, in the light of the GDPR and DCD provisions, implicitly conditioning, to a considerable extent, the exercise of the right of access to personal data, the right to rectification of personal data and the right to oppose the processing of personal data.

15   Notably, it must be observed that the G.E.O. contains mostly a series of succinct provisions on the existing cases in which the consumer's counter-performance resides in the consenting to the collecting and processing of personal data, leaving several questions unanswered, such as: (i) through the prismatic figure of the specific contractual qualification to be given to contracts for the exchange of personal data for digital content or services, are these contractual species entirely onerous and, therefore, generating the transfer of personal data into the property of the digital services provider?; (ii) are these contracts merely incorporating an agreement on the lease of personal data to the

---

[7] Goicovici, 'Portabilitatea datelor cu caracter personal, prin prisma dispozițiilor RGDP și ale Directivei 2019/770: este gambitul reginei mutarea de deschidere adecvată?' (2021) LXVII (2) *Analele Științifice ale Universității „Alexandru Ioan Cuza" din Iași, Seria Științe Juridice*, 57.

data controller (the digital services provider) and, if so, the effects of the exercise of the right of withdrawal and revocation of consent to the processing of personal data by the consumer or the consequences of breach of contract by both the entrepreneur and the consumer; (iii) what would be the most adequate matrix for the temporal sequence and contractual form in which the transfer of personal data takes place, and the special features of the exercise of pre-contractual information duties by the digital services provider?; (iv) are there distinct mechanisms describing the remedies available to consumers and the subject of modifications made on digital services and digital content by the professional trader (the provisions on the latter being further scrutinized and developed)? The crucial question remains the one referring to the establishing under which conditions such a consent may be given within the framework of a B2C contract for the providing of digital content or digital services; besides all these legal precautions, the subsequent onerous nature of the contract in which the price payment was replaced by the consumer's providing of personal data as a counter-performance reverberates on the liability regimen, including the consumer's possibility of invoking the *exceptio non adimpleti contractus* while suspending or even withdrawing the consent to the collecting and processing of personal data, in the hypotheses of manifested non-conformity of the digital content or digital services.

III. Implications of compliance within the contractual force of advertising documents

1. Reversing the general rule of the non-contractual nature of advertising content

As opposed to the general rule applicable under the Civil Code provisions to the non-contractual efficiency of advertising documents in the form of leaflets, catalogues, labels, advertising messages, the remittances / communications to consumers concerning the commercial guaranty for conformity receive contractual force in terms of compliance requirements that will be applied to the delivered product, the public statements of the professional becoming an integral part of the contract with the consumer, automatically and often in spite of clauses to the contrary indicated by to the supplier of the products, so that compliance with their content is mandatory for the trader concerned; the trader's contractual liability in case of non-performance of the obligations thus assumed regarding the substantial and functional conformity of the products may be invoked by the consumer. According to the provisions of art. 6 para. (1) lit. (d), the conformity of the delivered products, in relation to the objective criteria of conformity, will be assessed considering the content of any public statement made by or on behalf of the seller or other chain of transactions, including by the manufacturer, particularly in advertisements or on the label of the product. 16

As it has been already mentioned in the previous sections, exceptions are made where (a) any changes have been clearly communicated to the consumer before the conclusion of the contract (which excludes their tacit inclusion in the text of the offer) or (b) the changes have been made with the consumer's consent, after the conclusion of the contract (which implies, for example, either a *mutual consensus* or a novation of the obligations by change of object). In order for public statements, conformity declarative documents or advertising messages to become an integral part of the offer, several conditions may be forged, such as: (i) the advertising document must present a sufficiently firm, precise and detailed content to borrow the characters of the offer (as defined by the provisions of Article 1188 of the Romanian Civil Code), as a proposal 17 the object of which was expressed in a firm, precise and complete manner); (ii) the advertising document / public commercial statements of the professional concerning the characteristics of the product have been delivered directly to the consumer or have been publicly expressed, in the terminology used by the national legislator; (iii) the commercial document / advertising message or the public statement made by the professional had the potential to have a decisive influence on the formation of consumer consent (in principle, if the public statement included explicit references to essential characteristics of the product, according to its typical use, the decisive influence on the formation of consumer consent is presumed); (iv) the advertising document, product label or public statement made by or on behalf of the seller or other participants upstream in the chain of transactions, including the manufacturer or the distributor, has given the consumer a set of legitimate expectations as regarding the professional's allegations concerning conformity of the product in relation to the objective criteria of conformity.

18 It should be noted that, in terms of the subjective sphere of conformity assessment, the public statements are taken as a benchmark for analysing the conformity of products delivered by reference to the objective criteria set out in Article 7 of G.E.O. no. 140/2021 which may in principle belong to: (a) the professional seller or the direct distributor of the products; (b) the creator of the advertising message who acted on behalf of the professional seller or the direct distributor of the products; (c) the commercial agent, the authorized regional distributor or the persons in a subordinate relationship or contractual mandate relationship with the professional seller or the direct distributor of the products; (d) other participants upstream in the chain of transactions, including the manufacturer, regardless of whether or not there is a right of recourse between the mentioned participants (right of redress which remains relevant in B2B contracts, yet not in the B2C contract, under which the consumer reports a lack of conformity, since the seller is directly liable towards the consumer for any lack of conformity).

2. Situations exempted from the binding force of the professional trader's statements

19 As it expressly results from the provisions of Article 6, para. (2) of G.E.O. no. 140/2021, the seller is not required to comply with public statements in accordance with paragraph 1 (d) if the seller demonstrates that: (a) the trader did not know the existence or the content of the public statement and could not reasonably have been aware of the public statement in question; (b) by the time the B2C contract was concluded, the public statement has been rectified in the same way or in a manner similar to that in which it was previously made; or (c) the consumer's decision to purchase the goods could not have been influenced by the public statement.

20 It is essentially important to note, in connection with the quoted text, that it establishes three categories of exceptions to the rule postulated in art. 6 para. (1), which operates the inclusion in the contractual field, as sources of effective contractual obligations, of public statements made by or on behalf of the seller or by other persons upstream in the chain of transactions, including by the manufacturer, which generated for the consumer a legitimate confidence in the allegations of the professional provider. As mentioned in the previous section, it is necessary that the document / advertising message, respectively the public statement made by the professional had the potential to exert a decisive influence on the formation of consumer consent; otherwise, if from the evidence administered the court establishes that, for the consumer, the decision to purchase the goods could not have been influenced by the public statement, the consumer will not benefit from remedies for non-compliance resulting from the discrepancy between the public

A. Introduction. General Framework

statements of the professional trader and the qualities or actual characteristics of the delivered product.

Also, in cases where, until the conclusion of the B2C contract, the professional statement of the professional (which could result in objective criteria for determining the conformity of the products and containing inaccurate statements) was rectified in the same or similar way to the one in which it was issued, the consumer will not be able to rely on the content of the initial declaration of the professional trader when introducing consumer's request in initiating the remedies of non-compliance. It should also be noted that professional contracts which are not intended to be communicated to consumers and which may contain statements issued in the context of B2B relations or at various stages of the production or commercial distribution process are not considered to be included in the contractual content unless proven that they have been influential on consumer's consent, therefore, it must be proven that these statements were aimed at informing, retaining or persuading consumers, although having other professionals as recipients.

Nevertheless, it can be concluded, as it is resulting from the mentioned legal text, that, in so far as, in the light of the evidence administered, the courts find that the consumer did not know and could not reasonably have been aware of the public statement in question, the consumer's decision to purchase the products could not have been influenced by the public statement of the professional, the consumer will not be able to invoke remedies for non-compliance resulting from the discrepancy between those statements of the professional and the actual characteristics of the delivered product. In our opinion, the exception provided in art. 6 para. (2) lit. (a) of G.E.O. no. 141/2021 should be retained, in practice, only for statements made by professionals who have targeted other professionals in B2B relationships; on the other hand, we consider that the phrase '(the consumer) did not know and could not reasonably have known the public statement in question' should not involve, for the professional, the proof of subjective elements relating to the actual acknowledgment by the consumer who is a party to the dispute, of the content of that commercial statement; thus, we believe that the professional should provide objective evidence, consisting in the nature (respectively the content) of the business statement that is the subject of the dispute or, more precisely, related to the identification of other professionals as business partners or subordinates / collaborators / commercial agents of the issuer, as recipients of that commercial statement, or as the case may be, a scientific communication related to the state of research in a particular field etc. The decisive factor, in this view, is the elimination, on the basis of the evidence administered, of the category of consumers from the sphere of persons to whom the commercial declaration in question was addressed, in the context in which the burden of proving these elements lies with the professional trader; therefore, it is not for the consumer to prove that the trade statement in question had a decisive influence on the latter's consent, this aspect being presumed until proven otherwise by the professional trader.

IV. Consumer's (procedural) obligation to cooperate with the trader in establishing technically available means

As it results textually from the provisions of art. 11 para. (5) of the G.E.O. no. 141/2021, the obligation to cooperate with the trader is incumbent on the consumer insofar as this is reasonably possible and necessary to determine whether the non-compliance of the digital content or the digital service, at the time provided in art. 10

para. (2) or (3) was caused by the consumer's digital environment. The obligation to cooperate between the consumer and the trader is limited to technically available means which are more favourable to the consumer and involves, in principle, the assertive providing of accurate information by the consumer, which results in establishing the type or category of digital environment used and the aspects of incompatibility of digital content reported.

24   The legal reverberations of the party's failure to fulfil the obligation to cooperate (the consequences of consumer's recalcitrant behaviour or of unreasonable reluctance shown by the consumer) are described in para. (6) of art. 11, from which it results that the refusal of the consumer to cooperate for the procurement of conclusive evidence will entail the reversal of the burden of proof, which will continue to be the responsibility of the consumer, and not on the professional trader. However, the reversal effect on the burden of proof, of consumer's non-cooperation occurs, as it results from the final thesis of art. 11 para. (6) of the G.E.O. no. 141/2021, only insofar as the professional trader has properly fulfilled the pre-contractual obligation to inform the consumer on the incidence of specific compatibility and interoperability features concerning consumer's pre-existing digital medium, relevant in the event of impossibility of compliant integration of delivered digital content; on the contrary, if the professional has failed to inform the consumer of such a requirement in a clearly and easily intelligible manner, before concluding the contract, the burden of proof as to the existence of non-compliance at the time referred to in Art. 10 para. (2)-(3), remains the responsibility of the professional trader.

B. Definitions and scope of application

25   By adopting G.E.O. no. 140/2021 and 141/2021, the legislator introduced specific definitions for notions such as 'digital content', 'digital service', 'goods with digital elements', 'integration', 'digital environment', 'compatibility', 'functionality', 'interoperability', 'durable medium', which were lacking in the existing legislation and jurisprudence. Notably, the characteristic of interoperability or the compatibility with certain operating systems or the right to upgrade, as specific compliance criteria were regulated for the first time by the national legislator in the mentioned normative texts. Important clarifications on the meaning of the term 'interoperability' can be found in the text of Article 5, para. 1(a) of G.E.O no. 141/2021, according to which the concept of functionality should be understood as referring to the ways in which goods can perform their functions, correlated to their purpose. The notion of interoperability indicates whether and to what extent the digital content goods may operate with hardware or software other than that normally used for goods of the same type. Successful operation could involve, for example, the ability of goods to exchange information with such software or hardware and to use the exchanged information. According to the definition provided in the text of art. 2, pt. 13 of the G.E.O. no. 140/2021, interoperability describes the ability of products to operate with hardware or software components other than those normally (usually) used for products of the same type.

26   The impact produced in national legislation / doctrinal debate by the introduction of a provision on data as a counter-performance is describable as a significant shift from the perspective of unilaterally and gratuitously provided digital services, reverberating on the liability regimen applicable to the professional provider. The national legislator did not introduce new rules on contract formation/existence/validity in this respect. The

B. Definitions and scope of application

onerous paradigm was already queried in legal literature[8]; however, in B2C commercial practices, the digital services for the providing of which the consumer undertakes the obligation to provide personal data as a counter-performance continue being described as offered for free, while the "terms of use" and the "privacy statements" are often drafted as separate documents adjacent to B2C contracts. Therefore, the admitting of the onerous character of these digital services in G.E.O. no. 141/2021 appeared as an innovative approach, the new set of rules being applicable to the supply and conformity of digital content and digital services both on paid services and on services where the consumer provides "a counter-performance other than money in the form of personal data or any other data". Under scholarly approaches[9], the idea to treat money consideration and personal data equally was already expressed; therefore, when the concept reappeared in the regulatory framework, it would help clarifying the contractual liability regimen (as 'imported' from the sphere of onerous contracts and not from the one of unilateral, gratuitous acts). Accordingly, the provisions of Article 1481 of the Civil Code will become applicable, according to which '(1) In the case of the assuming of an obligation of result, the debtor is obliged to procure to the creditor the promised result. (2) In the case of obligations of means, the debtor is obliged to use all the necessary means to achieve the promised result. (3) In determining whether an obligation has as an object a means or an outcome, account shall be taken particularly of: a) the manner under which the obligation is stipulated in the contract; b) the existence and nature of the consideration and the other elements of the contract; c) the degree of risk involved in achieving the result; d) the influence that the other party has on the execution of the obligation.'

Article 1481 of the Civil Code regulates, as a legislative novelty, the classification of contractual obligations into obligations of means and obligations of result, by reference to the specifics of their execution and by presenting the demarcation criteria. According to para. (1), in case of the obligation of result, the debtor is obliged to procure to the creditor the promised result. The doctrine calls this obligation a determined obligation and defines it as the obligatory legal relationship in which the debtor is obliged, through his positive or negative conduct, to obtain a certain result, in favour of the creditor; the mentioned concept becomes relevant also in cases where the digital services provider undertakes an obligation to provide for a certain result to the consumer's benefit while obtaining as a counterpart consumer's personal data and, at a later moment, the result promised by the professional provider is not accomplished (the latter's liability would be treated as a strict liability for compliance to contractual obligations of determined result).

Theoretically, due to the lapsing, in the applicable legal text, of a narrowing distinction, personal data as a counter-performance could include preponderantly "actively provided" data, but also automatically generated data and collected by cookies, as well as data "necessary for the digital content to function in conformity with the contract, for example geographical location where necessary for a mobile application to function properly", and data collected "for the sole purpose of meeting legal requirements".

Most of the provisions of the implementing normative acts are not suitable to be applied to the B2B contracts, in their consistent expression under positivist law, since they are pivoting around protectionist legal mechanisms which are meant to re-equilibrate the contractual paradigm of inequalities between the contractual parties, namely the

---

[8] Șandru, 'Principiul echității în prelucrarea datelor cu caracter personal' (2018) 3 *Pandectele Române*, 36.
[9] *Ibidem*.

professional trader and the consumer[10] (the intrinsic vulnerabilities of whom are of an economic and informational nature[11]). Yet, some of these mechanisms could be adapted *de lege ferenda* to become applicable to B2B contracts concluded between professionals from distinctive domains of activity, provided that the buyer (although acting in its professional capacity) does not share the same field of speciality with the trader[12], in which case the latter may be held to offer a conformity warranty of similar traits as those characterising the conformity guaranty owed to consumers, in B2C contracts.

C. Conformity of goods

I. Hybrid product conformity assessment: objective vs. subjective compliance

1. Interconnected levels of conformity

30   The content of G.E.O. no. 140/2021 is referring to the assessment of the conformity of products delivered under B2C contracts debuting with a mixture of objective and subjective conformity criteria, broken down into four interconnected levels and nested at multiple levels:

(i) subjective criteria extracted from the express contractual clauses (in particular regarding the atypical purposes printed on the product by the consumer with the agreement of the seller or regarding the exclusion from the contractual field of typical product features, at the seller's proposal which obtained the consumer's consent);

(ii) objective criteria for assessing the conformity of the delivered products in relation to the typical functionalities, the normal characteristics of the products in that specific category and the typical nature of the accessories which should have been delivered;

(iii) the reasonable expectations of the consumer regarding the qualities and typical characteristics, the content of the installation instructions that came with the product;

(iv) the public statements of the professional resulting in specific references to certain technical features or characteristics of the product.

31   It is also apparent from the provisions of G.E.O. no. 140/2021 that, in order to be compliant to conformity requirements, goods must comply not only with the subjective requirements of conformity but also with the objective requirements of conformity. Saliently, conformity would be assessed taking into account, *inter alia*, the purpose for which the goods of the same type would normally be used, their delivery with the accessories and instructions that the consumer can reasonably expect to receive or the correspondence between them and the sample or the model made available by the seller to the consumer; goods should also have the qualities and characteristics that are normally (typically) required for goods of the same type and that the consumer can reasonably expect, given the nature of the goods and taking into account any public statement of the seller or in its name or that of other participants upstream in the chain

---

[10] Goicovici, *Dreptul relațiilor dintre profesioniști și consumatori* (2022), 126.
[11] *Ibidem*.
[12] *Idem*, p. 128.

C. Conformity of goods

of B2B transactions. The following assertions can be made on the essential provisions of G.E.O. no. 140/2021:

(a) the legal provisions draw a clear line between the subjective criteria of conformity (based on express contractual stipulations, including those incorporating in the contractual field the purpose / atypical use of the products) and the objective criteria for assessing conformity, starting from the typical purposes and functionalities of the product. This feature is describable as one of the major innovations brought about by the legal text on product conformity assessment in B2C contracts, albeit for the most part (except in the case of references to product interoperability and non-conformity resulting from incorrect installation of products), G.E.O. no. 140/2021 substantially maintains the compliance criteria previously forged in judicial practice and to which the previous regulation referred (the product delivered to correspond to the one ordered in terms of identity, quality, quantity, technical characteristics and functionality etc.);

(b) one of the atypical features of civil liability for non-compliance in B2C contracts, as its coordinates are set out in the provisions of G.C.O. no. 140/2021, is the inclusion in the contractual field, as sources of effective contractual obligations, of public statements made by the seller or on the latter's behalf or by other participants upstream in the chain of transactions, including the manufacturer, who have generated for the consumer legitimate expectations based on the professional's allegations regarding the conformity of the product with respect to objective conformity criteria;

(c) with the notable exception represented by the integrating in the contractual field of the public statements made by the professional traders, in terms of product conformity in B2C contracts, the public statements do not give rise to contractual obligations in relations with the consumer (the seller would not be bound by public statements on conformity), to the extent that the seller proves that the seller was not, and could not reasonably have been, aware of the public statement in question; or consumer's decision to order the goods could not have been influenced by the public statement; another exception to the contractual force of advertising messages / public statements related to product conformity is the situation where, until the full formation of the B2C contract, the public statement has been rectified in the same way or in a manner similar to that in which the was made;

(d) seller's previous statements are also exempt from binding force to the extent to which certain sections of the professional trader's public statement have been established not having influenced the consumer's decision to purchase those products, the non-compliance of which is reported by the consumer.

While proposing a dual assessment of the product conformity, which incorporates both subjective elements of assessment, extracted from the presence of the special purpose for which the consumer contracted (referred to as a purpose on which the consumer informed the seller at the latest contract and which the seller has specifically accepted), as well as objective elements of conformity assessment (such as correspondence with the purposes for which products of the same type or category would normally be used), the legislator draws the outlines of a hybrid system, at the confluence of the objective rigors applicable to product compliance in B2C contracts and the subjective compliance requirements, correlated with the legitimate expectations of the consumer. Succinctly, it must be noted that the G.E.O. no. 140/2021 introduces a distinction between the subjective criteria for assessing the conformity of digital content provided (Article 5) and objective compliance requirements (Article 6) to which it is added a third category of non-compliances, namely non-compliance caused by the absence of updates agreed in the B2C contract or caused, for digital goods, by the incorrect integration of digital content or digital service in the digital environment of the consumer (Article 7). The express introduction in the contractual content of the atypical characteristics benefits from an express regulation in the content of art. 5 lit. (b) of G.E.O. no. 140/2021, which states that for a consumer to be able to allege non-conformity of the delivered product in relation to the special (atypical) purpose for which the consumer contracted / purchased that product, specific contractual provisions are needed.

2. Subjective (atypical) criteria for assessing the conformity of products

37   Conformity of product designates the manner in which the product sold and delivered meets the legitimate expectations of the consumer (a), any mandatory provisions of the law on the standardization of the production process (b) or contractual specifications (c), both materially and in terms of identity of the delivered product as compared with the features agreed in the sales contract, in terms of quality and quantity requirements (i), as well as in terms of functionally, in relation to the functions, attributes, characteristics and technical limits initially agreed (ii). The consumer's legitimate expectations regarding the conformity of the product may be incidental, including tacit, in the case of technical characteristics or qualities of the product that are typical / usual for the same category of products. Instead, the atypical qualities / functions of a product must be expressly agreed in the contract (it must be expressly stipulated in the contract), so that their absence in respect of the delivered product would justify a consumer's request for repair or redress, in the hypotheses of non-compliance.

38   The recently transposed rules on product conformity seem to establish a hierarchical conformity assessment system, which gives priority to subjective conformity criteria (expressly agreed with the professional seller), while allowing courts to resort to objective conformity criteria (typical conformity that characterizes that type of product), if the text of the contract (concluded by the professional trader and consumer) does not contain contractual provisions derogating from the typical conformity standards or is unclear in this respect. In addition to the references to the requirements of conformity contained in the contractual text, the performance of the obligations of traders arising out of commercial declarations of conformity is, in turn, specifically regulated.

39   An important aspect of the concept of compliance relates to placing the burden of proof of delivery on the shoulders of the trader, the latter being called upon to provide sufficient evidence that the product delivered or the digital content provided or the digital service provided does not have deficiencies. As the burden of proof is in principle on the direct supplier / seller of the product, as provided for in the provisions of G.E.O. no. 140/2021, in cases where the consumer claims that the delivered product, digital content provided or digital service provided presents deficiencies from the category of conformity non-compliance, to attempt to prove otherwise in court.

3. Expressly agreed introduction of atypical features in the contractual content

40   Assessing the conformity of the delivered products according to the subjective conformity criteria described in the texts of G.E.O. no. 140/2021 relates essentially to the express terms of the B2C contract, including the possibility for the parties to incorporate in the scope of the contract specific specifications on the atypical purposes agreed between the consumer and the professional trader for that product, or the personalization of the product according to the consumer's preferences expressly accepted by the professional seller. In the meaning retained in the content of the legal provisions, 'subjective compliance criteria' refers to the criteria set out in the specific contractual terms, which take precedence over the objective characteristics or the typical purposes which the products in the same range / category would fulfil. Briefly, one can deduct from the legal text that,

C. Conformity of goods

by reference to the express contractual clauses detailing, customizing the characteristics of the products to be delivered, their conformity will be assessed in the light of the atypical purposes which the consumer has requested, and the seller expressly accepted by including those features in the object of the B2C contract.

In order for a consumer to be able to allege non-conformity of the delivered product in relation to the special (atypical) purpose for which the consumer contracted / purchased the product, it is necessary for the circumstances to meet three conditions simultaneously: (i) the consumer has communicated / made known to the trader the special (atypical) purpose or the atypical (intentional use) of the product; (ii) the communication of the atypical purpose must have taken place in the pre-contractual stage, at the latest at the time of concluding the contract, as expressly results from the legal text; (iii) the trader has explicitly accepted this atypical purpose (it has been introduced by the parties in the contractual field, through express clauses inserted for this purpose). The atypical purpose imprinted on the product cannot be determined unilaterally by the consumer, not even under the guise of consumer's 'legitimate expectations' related to the technical configuration of the ordered product, since for the atypical characteristics to be inserted into the contractual perimeter it is necessary for the consumer to express the intention to select an atypical use of the product and for the professional seller to have been accepted the incidence of these derogatory terms, subject to the B2C contract parties' consensus on the including of the atypical purposes in the object of the contract.

4. Objective criteria for assessing conformity compliance in B2C contracts

The provisions of G.E.O. no. 140/2021 do not ostensibly postulate the pre-eminence of subjective criteria for assessing the conformity of products in relation to objective ones, nor does it explicitly configure the architecture of a hierarchical system in which subjective conformity criteria are higher than compared to the subjective criteria, rather leaving place for the interpretation according to which the two sets of criteria will be used in a complementary manner; deficiencies of conformity in the light of the subjective criteria mentioned in article 5 or through the prism of the objective criteria enunciated in article 6, for the remedies for non-compliance to become incidental. From the wording of the first thesis of art. 7, according to which, "In addition to complying with the subjective compliance requirements", the products will also be evaluated in terms of objective conformity, applying the paradigms outlined in art. 7, it is not possible to deduce with certainty the existence of such a hierarchy, having at the top of the pyramid the objective criteria, and based on the subjective criteria of conformity from which it starts to establish the existence of possible deficiencies or discrepancies of conformity of delivered products; it is equally true, however, that the pre-eminence (partial and / or conjunctural) of subjective criteria of conformity over objective ones can be deduced from their fundamental nature; thus, while the objective conformity criteria focus on the correspondence (perfect or imperfect) between the actual characteristics of the delivered product and those of the product configured under the contractual clauses, in relation to the typical use of the products in the same range or the typical characteristics of the products category to which the delivered product belongs, the parties have the possibility to derogate from the typical characteristics or purposes of the use of that product, while inserting, through express contractual clauses, atypical purposes in connection with which the consumer has obtained the explicit consent of the professional seller and thus generating for the seller the obligation of conformity as well as for the typical purposes of the product.

Legal provisions dichotomise between the conformity of the delivered product with respect to the correspondence of its attributes with the destination for which it was purchased by the consumer, which will be assessed on the basis of the incidence of subjective conformity criteria (the atypical and strictly subjective destinations or functions of the product must be expressly included in the contractual field, by explicit specifications in this respect) and the objectively-assessed conformity, while the legitimate / reasonable expectations regarding the typical purposes of the products are considered to be intrinsic to the nature of the product, to the extent that the existence of an express contractual clause specifying them is superfluous in the case of typical purposes / uses. Conformity of product identity *lato sensu*, on the other hand, refers to the conformity of the delivered product as deduced from the contractual stipulations relative to the technical category of the ordered product, to the functional or aesthetic characteristics etc., so that the buyer is delivered the same goods as the one originally agreed with the professional seller in the B2C contract.

5. Conformity assessed in relation to consumer's legitimate / reasonable expectations

44   Express references to 'reasonable consumer expectations' as an additional (or even alternative) benchmark for assessing the conformity of digital content products are found in the text of Article 6 of G.E.O. no. 140/2021, according to which the determining of the extent to which the providing of digital content (autonomous or embedded) or interconnected digital services does form part of the B2C sales contract should depend on the content of the contract, the latter would include digital content or embedded or interconnected digital services whose provision is explicitly provided for in the contract. The latter would also include sales contracts which can be understood as having as their object the providing of specific digital content or specific digital services the functionalities of which are typical for goods of the same range and which the consumer might expect as reasonable, given the nature of the goods and taking into account any public statement made by or on behalf of the seller or other participants upstream in the chain of transactions, including the manufacturer or the importer.

II. Specific information on omitted characteristics

45   The national legislator expressly specified the provision regarding the exclusion of existence of a lack of conformity in the case provided by Article 8, para. 5 DCD and Article 7, para. 5 SGD (with regard to the concept of "particular characteristic"). In accordance with the provisions of Article 6, para. (5) of G.E.O. no. 140/2021 and, similarly, those of Article 5, para. (6) of G.E.O. no. 141/2021, there shall be no lack of conformity within the meaning of paragraph 1 or 2 if, at the time of the conclusion of the contract, the consumer was specifically informed that a particular characteristic of the digital content or digital service was deviating from the objective requirements for conformity laid down in paragraph 1 or 2 and the consumer expressly and separately accepted that deviation when concluding the contract. As explicitly resulting from the legal text, the meeting of the consumer's granularly given consent is needed for the legal exception from the objective requirements of conformity to be eligible; thus, it is only the explicit and granularly-obtained consumer's content which is considered valid in these cases, not including the tacitly expressed consent to such a deviation from the objective standards of conformity[13].

---

[13] According to specialized scholarly analyses, „This is the case where the digital content is ancillary to the good to be delivered – *e.g.* the situation of goods with digital elements (*e.g.* goods that incorporate

C. Conformity of goods

III. Availability of spare parts and corresponding duty of information

When transposing the provisions of Article 7, 1st para., Lett. d), SGD into internal law, the national legislator did not specifically address the issue of further implementing the "durability" requirement; this requirement is expressly mentioned among the objective prerequisites of product conformity.

The implementing of the requirements in product-specific Union legislation, especially the exigencies relating to durability and repairability should include durability as an objective criterion for the assessment of conformity of goods. Specifically, the G.E.O. no. 140/2021 is addressing consumer's possibility to rely on durability exigencies in order to obtain an adequate remedy for lack of objectively-assessed conformity, durability been seen as referring to the ability of the products to maintain their required functions and performance through normal use. As stated in Article 6, para. 1(d) of G.E.O. nr. 140/2021, the goods are expected to 'respect the quantity and have the qualities and other characteristics, including durability, functionality, compatibility and safety, which are normal for goods of the same type and which the consumer can reasonably expect, given the nature of the goods and taking into account any public statement made by or on behalf of the seller or by other persons in the earlier stages of the transaction chain, including by the manufacturer, in particular in advertisements or on the label'. For products to be in (objectively-assessed) conformity, these should possess the durability which is normal for goods of the same type and which the consumer can reasonably expect given the nature of the specific goods, including the possible need for reasonable maintenance of the goods, as well as any public statement made by or on behalf of any person constituting a link in the transactions chain. This type of conformity assessment is expected to also consider all other relevant circumstances, such as the price of the goods and the intensity or frequency of the use that the consumer makes of the product. Adjacently, insofar as specific durability information is indicated in any pre-contractual statement which forms part of the B2C sales contract, the consumer should be able to rely on them as a part of the subjective requirements for conformity as well.

When drafting the provisions of G.E.O. no. 140/2021 and no. 141/2021, the national legislator had not addressed the issue of availability of spare parts and corresponding information obligations, nor are these aspects foreseen in currently applicable Consumer Law regulations at national level; thus, the adopted regulations do not impose an obligation on sellers to ensure the availability of spare parts throughout a period of time as an objective requirement for conformity or to specifically inform consumers about such availability.

At the starting point of their entering into force, on January 9th, 2022, the provisions of G.E.O. no. 140/2021 and of G.E.O. no. 141/2021 were not coordinated with those of Directive 2009/125/EC establishing a framework for the setting of eco-design require-

---

digital content / service or are interconnected with these elements). However, DCD provisions point out that, in this regard, the logic of accessory may lead to a really complicated disjoint application of the rules of law on supply and compliance. Specifically, when dealing with a product presenting a built-in digital element (which involves embedded digital content or embedded interconnectivity), the compliance rules established by DCD will also apply to the delivered digital content; also, if we are dealing with an express digital content integrated in the sold good, through a contractual provision, the DCD provisions will again be applicable, yet only in terms of conformity compliance; the same rule is virtually applicable if the provision of digital content / service is performed by a third-party; finally, if there are doubts persisting on the adequate qualification (i.e. doubts on the implicit inclusion of digital content in the object of the contract for the supply of the goods), the provisions of Directive 2019/771 remain applicable.": Popa, 'Furnizarea și conformitatea conținutului digital sau serviciului digital' (2022) 1 *Revista Română de Drept Privat*, 232 – (our translation, J.G.).

ments for energy-related products, which was transposed into internal legislation by the Governmental Decision no. 55 from January 19th, 2011.

50 The penalties which were implemented according to Art. 20 of Directive 2009/125/EC do not specifically include private law sanctions, although the engaging of tort liability (for unjustifiable gross negligence, maleficent conduct, or illicit conduct, including illicit omissions or illicit actions) remains possible for the third-parties affected by these actions, under the general provisions of the Civil Code. Under the provisions of Public Law (as Public Law remedies), the acts committed by legal persons which constitute contraventions under the provisions of Article 17 of the Governmental Decision no. 55/2011 are sanctioned primarily by inflicting a pecuniary penalty and / or withdrawal from the market or with a ban on the placing on the market of non-compliant products; suspension of the sale of non-compliant products. Sanctions and penalties for failure to comply with the provisions of the G.D. no. 55/2011 pursuant to the transposition of Directive 2009/125/EC are expected to be effective, proportionate, and dissuasive under each set of circumstances, 'taking into account the degree of non-compliance and the number of units of non-compliant products placed on the market'. In case of non-compliance with the provisions of art. 8 para. (8) of G.D. no. 55/2011, the market surveillance authority can prohibit the placing on the market of the non-compliant product.

51 The national legislator did not adopt specific measures for enhancing environmental sustainability / circular economy in way of implementation of DCD and SGD into internal law by the G.E.O. no. 140/2021 and G.E.O. no. 141/2021.

IV. Non-conformity resulting from incorrect installation of products

52 Saliently, one of the major virtues of the new regulation stems from the introducing of concrete legal provisions on non-conformity resulting from incorrect installation of products, which is considered to be a non-conformity of the delivered products insofar as the installation obligation is explicitly incumbent on the professional seller from the clauses of the B2C sales contract and was made by the seller or by a third-party collaborator / supervisor / subcontractor under the contractual liability of the seller; non-compliance may also result from the failure of the correct installation of the products, even in cases where the installation of the delivered products was intended to be performed not by the seller, but by the consumer and was carried out by the latter, and the incorrect installation was due to deficiencies (lacunary aspects) in the installation instructions provided by the seller or, in the case of goods with digital elements, by the seller or supplier of the digital content or digital service; under this aspect, art. 7, para (4),(b) of G.E.O. no. 141/2021 states explicitly that non-compliance or lack of conformity may be resulting from information deficiencies of the installing instructions or from the existence of gaps or inaccuracies in the installation instructions provided by the professional for which the latter may be held liable.

53 Non-compliance resulting from incorrect installation of products, as stated in the legal provisions, concerns the non-conformity caused by the incorrect installation of the goods, which will be considered to constitute a non-conformity case when: (a) the installation is part of the contract of sale and was carried out by the seller or under the responsibility of the seller; or (b) the installation, intended to be performed by the consumer, was indeed carried out by the consumer, while the incorrect installation was due to deficiencies in the installation instructions provided by the seller or, in the case of digital goods, by the supplier of the digital content or digital service.

C. Conformity of goods

Innovative aspects of the new regulation include the introduction of concrete legal provisions on non-conformity resulting from incorrect installation of products, which is seen as non-conformity of delivered products to the extent that the installation obligation is explicitly incumbent on the professional seller under the terms of the contract. B2C sale and was made by the seller or by a third-party collaborator / supervisor / subcontractor, etc. under the contractual liability of the seller; non-compliance may also result from the failure of the correct installation of the products, even in cases where the installation of the delivered products was intended to be carried out by the consumer and was carried out by the latter. In cases where the consumer has performed the incorrect installation, the seller remains liable for the deficiencies of conformity resulting from the failed installation, as long as this was due to deficiencies in the installation instructions provided by the seller or, in the case of goods with digital elements, by the seller or provider of the digital content or service; under this aspect, as resulting from the content of art. 7 of G.E.O. no. 141/2021, it explicitly states that the non-compliance / non-compliance may take the form of information non-compliance or that it may arise in the form of gaps or inaccuracies in the installation instructions provided by the professional trader.

V. Conformity remedies in hypotheses of personal data provided as a counter-performance

Consumer's duty to provide personal data as a counter-performance in terms of its enforceability is centred on the principle that the specific legal provisions would apply only if the relationship between trader and consumer "is considered to be a contract under national law"; therefore, consumers must be party to a B2C contract in order to benefit from the consumer protection remedies enumerated by the G.E.O. no. 141/2021 in the perimeter of offering personal data as a counter-performance (based on the implicit onerous nature of the transaction) and the enforceability regimen will by one of a contractual nature (contractual liability for determined obligations). 'Concluding a contract' is expected to include the cases in which the word "contract" is used less regularly and instead consumer's consent is collected through the means of accepting the general 'terms and conditions' which are typical for contractual relationships that imply the consumer's agreement to provide personal data as a counter-performance for beneficiating from the correlative providing of digital services.

Indeed, as we have shown above, individuals seem to give their personal data a certain pecuniary value or, at the very least, to be aware that these data could have such a pecuniary value. However, this does not automatically lead to consumer's awareness that the personal data may be the subject, possibly negotiable, of a service on their part. Definitely, the analysis is placed in the perimeter of non-negotiated contractual relations, seen as adhesion contracts, which were configured through standardization; yet, the lack of a correct representation of juridical and economic effects would not be imputable to consumers; the voluntary transfer of personal data as a counterpart of the digital services presents an intrinsic economic value for the professional trader, thus accentuating the onerous character of the contractual relationship, despite the fact that the consumer is encouraged to believe in the non-onerous nature of the provided digital services. However, the General Regulation (EU) 2016/679 provisions, although it aims to regulate the free movement of personal data, ignore the transactional side of the contractual relationship, while the provisions of Article 13, 1st para, Lett. c) of GDPR do not impose on the data controllers a specific duty to inform the data subject on the manners of capitalizing the personal data, while only imposing towards the data controller an obligation to inform the data subject on the purposes and legal basis of the processing.

57 The asymmetry of the informational relationship between the digital services provider or professional trader and the consumer of digital content and digital services is accentuated by the strong tendencies of non-transparency towards consumers that are manifested by the professional traders. Therefore, if the informational asymmetry persists, the consumer does not have the representation of the extent to which personal data is economically exploited and the pecuniary benefits that the professional traders and data controllers[14] extract from this type of exploitation, since it is illusory to consider that the consumer may fully negotiate the terms of the economic exploitation of personal data[15].

VI. Trader's attempt to unilaterally modify the contractual content

58 Where the B2C contract stipulates for the provision of digital content or making available to the consumer of digital content or digital service over the specified period, the provisions of G.C.O. no. 141/2021 regulate the possibility for the trader to modify the digital content or the digital service in order to keep them in compliance, should the restrictive conditions set by the normative act were cumulatively fulfilled. However, in order to provide adequate legal protection to the consumer, in relation to any unilateral changes made by the professional trader, which would have a major negative impact (especially of an economic nature) on the consumer, the latter's right to unilaterally terminate the B2C contract to supply is exercisable to the extent that the unilateral change proposed by the professional has a major adverse impact on access to or use of the digital content or digital service, unless the professional trader allows the consumer to maintain the digital content or service at no additional costs or without changes, and the digital content or digital service remains to meet the objective (typical) compliance requirements.

59 Restrictions incumbent on the exercise of the right to unilateral modification of digital content or digital service are also worth mentioning; according to the provisions of art. 18 of the G.E.O. no. 141/2021, where the B2C contract provides for making available to the consumer the digital content or digital service over a period of time, the trader may modify the digital content or digital service beyond what is necessary to maintain the performance in accordance with the digital content or the digital service, in accordance with art. 6 and 7, if the following conditions are cumulatively met: (a) the contract allows such an amendment and provides a valid justification for it; (b) *the modification is made without additional costs for the consumer;* (c) the consumer is clearly informed, using a plain language and terms that can be easily understood, on the object of the modifications; (d) in the cases mentioned in para. (2), the consumer has the right to be informed sufficiently in advance, on a durable medium, of the characteristics and date of the implementing of the modifications and subsequently enjoys the right to unilaterally terminate the contract in accordance with para. (2); similarly, the consumer has the right to be informed regarding the possibility to refuse the modifications and to maintain the performance digital content or the digital service without the modification in question in accordance with para. (5) of the legal text.

---

[14] Goicovici, 'Clauzele privind drepturile consumatorilor în contractele de servicii cloud computing' (2019) 2 *Revista Română de Drept Privat*, 399.

[15] *Idem*, 412.

C. Conformity of goods

As resulting from the provisions of art. 18 para. (2) of the G.E.O. no. 141/2021, the consumer has the right to unilaterally terminate the contract should the modifications be considered to have negatively impacted the consumer's access to the use of digital content or digital services, unless such negative impact is of a minor value.

In the case provided in par. (2), the consumer has the right to terminate the contract free of charge, within 30 days of receiving the information or from the moment the digital content or digital service has been modified by the trader, whichever comes later. It is also worth recalling that, according to the provisions of the third paragraph of Article 18, in the hypotheses in which the consumer obtains the termination of the contract in accordance with para. (2) and (3), the provisions of art. 14 to17 will apply accordingly. Subjacent to these rules, the provisions of para. (2)-(4) remain unapplicable in cases where the trader has allowed the consumer to maintain, at no additional cost, the use of the digital content or digital service without modification, and the digital content or digital service remains in compliance.

It follows from the legal text that, congruently to the mentioned rules, the unilateral modifying by the trader, during the course of the contractual effects, of the digital content or services provided can take place only within the limits specified in the text of the normative act and is always accompanied by consumer' right to unilaterally terminate the B2C contract in the event that such a unilateral change in the digital content generated substantial negative (economic) consequences for the consumer; the assessment of the substantial nature of the negative consequences remains in the competency of the courts of law, in the event of a litigious dispute which would have as object the contestation by the professional of the meeting of the legal conditions for exercising the consumer's right to unilaterally terminate the contract.

Third-party rights were addressed in Article 8 of G.E.O. no. 140/2021 and, respectively in Article 9 of G.E.O. no. 141/2021, stating that, in cases where a restriction resulting from a violation of any right of a third party, particularly adjacent intellectual property rights, prevents or limits the use of the delivered products or the use of digital content or digital service in accordance with Articles 6 and 7, the consumer remains entitled to the remedies for lack of conformity provided for in Article 11, unless the provisions of Law no. 287/2009 on the Civil Code, republished, with subsequent amendments, stipulate for the nullity or rescission of the B2C contract for the supply of goods (including goods with embedded digital content) or for the supply of digital content or digital service in such cases. Special relevance is given to the general provisions of Article 1872 of the Romanian Civil Code on termination of the contract, which is attributable (imputable) to the contractor's culpable (inexcusable) behaviour, stating that the beneficiary has the right to obtain the payment of damages or, as the case may be, the termination of the contract in cases where, without reasonable justification: (a) the observance of the agreed term for the reception of the goods or services has become clearly impossible; (b) the goods or services are not performed in the agreed manner and within the period established by the beneficiary's agreement according to the circumstances, the contractor does not remedy the shortcomings which were found and is in impossibility to adapt the future performance; (c) specific obligations incumbent on the contractor have not been performed according to the legal provisions or under the contractual specific terms (which include the cases in which the professional provider of the digital content or digital services is in breach of the legal obligations deriving from Intellectual Property regulations[16]).

---

[16] Şandru, 'Unele consideraţii cu privire la relaţia dintre protecţia datelor (în special Regulamentul general privind protecţia datelor) şi proprietatea intelectuală' (2019) 3 *Revista Română de Drept European (Comunitar)*, 41.

64 Adjacently, according to the provisions or Article 207, 2nd para. of the Romanian Civil Code, the acts and operations in which professionals engage without possessing the authorizations regulated by mandatory legal provisions are struck by absolute nullity (*ope legis* nullity), and the professional traders who committed to these acts are unlimitedly, jointly, and severally liable for all damages caused to third-parties, regardless of the application of other sanctions provided by law.

65 The provisions of G.E.O. no. 141/2021 have not particularly addressed the legal issue of consumer's right to "resell" digital contents and contain no adjacent provisions addressing the concerns of intellectual property rights, which remain covered by the general provisions of existing Intellectual Property Law[17], where applicable.

D. Trader's liability for non-conformity

I. Exonerating effects of fortuitous events

66 The problematics of the objectively-assessed conformity of the single act / long term supply of digital content / digital services were regulated in Article 6, para. (3), Lett. (a) and (b) of G.E.O. no. 141/2021, according to which 'a) the digital content or the digital service must be provided in accordance with the contract, when the contract provides for continuous supply during a certain period; b) the consumer can reasonably expect this continuity, given the type and purpose of the digital content or digital service and taking into account the circumstances and nature of the contract, when the contract provides for a single act of supply or a series of individual acts of supply.'

67 As accentuated by the provisions of Article 7, para. (5) of G.E.O. no. 141/2021, it is necessary for the professional seller or provider to ensure that the digital content or digital service is in conformity throughout the entire duration of the contract. Short-term interruptions of the supply of digital content or a digital service are thus treated as instances of lack of conformity where those interruptions are more than negligible or they are recurrent; therefore, 'in cases where the contract provides for the continuous provision of digital content or digital service over a period of time, the digital content or digital service must be compliant to the objective criteria of conformity for the entire duration stipulated in the contractual terms.'

68 Under national law provisions, the consequences of a failure to deliver/supply with respect to obstacles like impossibility or force majeure are regulated by Article 1351 of the Civil Code on the effects of 'Force majeure and fortuitous event', according to which '(1) Unless otherwise provided by law or unless the parties have agreed otherwise, the contractual liability shall be waived when the damage is caused by force majeure or fortuitous event. (2) Force majeure is any external event, completely unpredictable, invincible and inevitable. (3) The fortuitous event is an event that cannot be foreseen or prevented by the liable person in the circumstances which characterised the liable person's sphere of activity. (4) If, according to the legal provisions, the debtor is exonerated from contractual liability for a fortuitous event, this person is also considered to be exonerated in case of force majeure.' The fortuitous case involves the meeting of fewer exigencies: unpredictability and impossibility of preventing the event are both analysed by reference to the person who would have been called to answer if the fortuitous event had not occurred, as opposed to force majeure, the conditions of which are set by approaching an abstract etalon of diligence.

---

[17] *Ibidem.*

D. Trader's liability for non-conformity

The unpredictable change of circumstances[18] impacting contractual performance is regulated under the provisions of Article 1271 of the Civil Code, according to which '(1) The parties are expected to execute their obligations, even if the performance has become more onerous than previously expected, either due to the increase of the costs of the performance of party's obligation, or due to the decrease of the value of the consideration.
(2) However, if the performance of the contract has become excessively onerous due to an exceptional change in circumstances which would make it manifestly unfair to oblige the debtor to perform the obligation, the court may order:

a) the adapting of the contract, in order to distribute equitably between the parties, the losses and the benefits resulting from the change of circumstances;
b) termination of the contract, at the time and under the conditions it establishes.

(3) The provisions of par. (2) are applicable only if:

a) the change of circumstances occurred after the conclusion of the contract;
b) the change of circumstances, as well as its extent were not and could not have been reasonably foreseen by the debtor, at the time of concluding the contract;
c) the debtor did not assume the risk of changing circumstances and could not reasonably be considered to have assumed this type of risk;
d) the debtor has tried, within a reasonable time and in good faith, to negotiate the reasonable and equitable adapting of the contractual obligations.'

The national legislator did not regulate early termination of Number-Independent Interpersonal Communication Service (NI-ICS).

When drafting the provisions of G.E.O. no. 140/2021 and G.E.O. no. 141/2021, the national legislator did not specifically address the issues related to the coordination of the provisions of Article 107, para. 2 of the European Electronic Communications Code on bundles and those of the new regulation on B2C contracts on the providing of digital content and digital services.

II. Remedies for the failure to supply and remedies for the lack of conformity

Among the remedies listed in the normative act, it can be mentioned that, in principle, the consumer has the right (i) either to a proportional reduction of the price (ii) or to the termination of the contract, if one of the following situations is registered: the corrective action to bring the digital content or service into conformity is considered impossible or disproportionate; the trader has not brought the digital content or digital service into conformity[19]; a non-conformity is recurrently found, despite the trader's attempt to bring the digital content or the digital service in accordance with the legal or contractual provisions or with the legitimate (reasonable) expectations[20] of the consumer; the seriousness of the non-compliance to the conformity criteria justifies an immediate reduction of the price or the immediate termination of the B2C contract[21];

---

[18] Goicovici, *Dreptul relațiilor dintre profesioniști și consumatori* (2022), 328.
[19] *Idem*, p. 416.
[20] *Ibidem*.
[21] *Idem*, p. 418.

the trader has stated that it will not bring the digital content or digital service into conformity or that this refusal is clearly resulting[22] from the circumstances of the case.

73 In the hierarchy of remedies for non-compliance, as established, extrajudicial remedies, free repair / replacement of non-compliant product take precedence (with the notable exception of conformity deficiencies manifested during the first 30 days from the delivery date, in which case the consumer can freely choose between the available remedies, no remedial hierarchy being in place), while consumer initiation of legal remedies (judicial termination of the B2C sales contract or action to recalculate the price) depends on the meeting of one of the following alternative sets of conditions: the seller has not completed the repair or replacement or, as the case may be, has not completed the repair or replacement in accordance with the provisions of the normative text or the seller has explicitly refused to bring the delivered products into conformity; recurrent non-compliance is noted, despite the seller's efforts to remedy it; the seriousness of the lack of conformity justifies a price reduction or the consumer's right to an immediate termination of the contract of sale; the professional seller has stated that he will not remedy the non-conformity of the products within a reasonable time or without significant inconvenience to the consumer, or this is clear from the circumstances of the case that the bringing of the products into conformity will not be implemented by the trader.

74 However, the consumer does not have the right to obtain the termination of the contract if the gravity of non-compliance is minor, lacking the scope that would justify the termination of the contract for non-performance of obligations by the professional trader; it is important to note that the burden of proving the minor nature of the non-compliance lies with the trader; these provisions regarding the unilateral termination of the contract at the initiative of the consumer for non-conformity of the delivered product are not only applicable within the scope of B2C contracts which are onerous or where the digital content or digital service is provided in exchange for payment of a price (explicit, ostensible onerous nature), but also if the consumer's consideration consisted in providing the trader with a set of personal data, while authorizing the trader to exploit these data for commercial interest (implicit onerous nature).

75 It is also recognized, as it will be underlined in the following sections, that the consumer has the right to suspend payment of a remaining part of the price of the digital content or digital service until the trader has brought the digital content or digital service into conformity, provided that the suspended payment is not related to digital content or digital service already provided by the merchant and which has been complied with the conformity criteria.

76 Corrective remedies in case of non-conformity of products during the minimum legal guarantee period refer to consumer's right:

(i) to benefit from the bringing into compliance of the products, including the digital content, unless this would be impossible or would impose disproportionate costs on the trader; the out-of-court remedy for non-compliance should be able to take place within a reasonable time from the date on which the professional seller was informed by the consumer of the non-compliance, free of charge (at no additional cost) and without any significant inconvenience to the consumer;

(ii) to benefit from a proportionate price reduction (recalibration of counter-performance);

(iii) to obtain the termination of the contract (unilateral resolution for non-performance of the seller's obligation to deliver the products in accordance with the

---

[22] *Idem*, p. 419.

D. Trader's liability for non-conformity

objective and subjective criteria of conformity or failure to bring the products into conformity). In principle, the consumer has the right to obtain a proportionate reduction in the price if the product, including in the case of B2C contracts on digital content, if the latter has been provided for consideration or to terminate the contract in the following cases:

(a) the corrective action to bring the product or digital content into conformity is considered impossible or disproportionate;

(b) the trader did not bring the product into conformity according to the subjective / objective criteria of conformity (the consumer, despite notifying the professional of the lack of conformity, did not obtain the remedy of the non-conformity / resumption of the compliant delivery of the products);

(c) recurrent non-compliance is found despite the trader's attempt to bring the digital product or content into conformity;

(d) the non-compliance is so serious as to justify an immediate price reduction or termination of the contract;

(e) the trader has stated (there is the express refusal of the trader) that it will not bring the digital content or the digital service into conformity or this is clear from the circumstances of the case that there is a tacit or implicit refusal, on the part of the seller, to bring the products into conformity.

It should be noted that the termination of the B2C contract for non-compliance with the obligation to deliver the products properly may be requested by the consumer only if the non-compliance is not minor; the burden of proof on the minor nature of the non-conformity falls on the professional seller.

The taxonomy of redress categories and remedial measures that may be requested by the consumer in the event of the manifesting of a lack of conformity (which was established on the basis of subjective and / or objective criteria) which are ranked in the text of art. 11 of the G.C.O. no. 140/2021 include the following: (i) non-onerous repair or replacement of the product, unless such a measure is considered impossible or disproportionate; it is worth recalling that a remedial measure is considered 'impossible' if the seller cannot provide identical products to replace the non-compliant product or maintenance services to repair it, including due to exhaustion / inability to renew the stock, lack of technology required by the specific repairing process etc.; (ii) the obtaining of a proportionate price reduction; (iii) termination of the contract under the conditions provided in the text of Article 11. As it results from the content of Article 11, para. (1) of G.E.O. no.140/2021, in the event of non-compliance to conformity requirements, the consumer would have the right to benefit from the non-onerous bringing into conformity of the goods or to benefit from a proportionate reduction in the price, alternatively to the termination[23] of the contract under the conditions laid down in Article 11. In order for the goods to be brought into conformity, the consumer may choose between repair and replacement, unless the corrective measure chosen is impossible or disproportionate (for instance, implies exorbitant costs or unreasonable efforts for the seller, the attributes of which remain censurable under the decision of the courts of law) or, in comparison with the other available corrective measures, would impose disproportionate costs on the seller, taking into account all circumstances, including the value of the goods in the event of non-compliance, the seriousness of the non-compliance and whether the alternative remedy could be implemented without any significant inconvenience to the consumer.

---

[23] *Idem*, p. 422.

79   It is also worth noticing that the seller may refuse to bring the goods into conformity, as already mentioned, if the repair or replacement is impossible or would incur disproportionate costs, considering all the circumstances, including those referred to in points (a) and (b) of Article 11, para. (2) of G.E.O. no. 140/2021.

III. Consumer's right to withhold payment

80   The right to withhold payment in hypotheses in which the trader failed to comply to the exigencies of conformity is recognised by the provisions of Article 9, para. (6) of G.E.O. no. 140/2021, according to which 'The consumer has the right to suspend the payment of the price or of a remaining part of the price of the goods until the seller has fulfilled its obligations'. Similarly, if the reduction of the benefit is invoked in a reciprocally-generating obligations contract by the seller, who refuses to perform its own contractual obligations, the other contractual party is placed in the hypothesis of invoking the exception of non-performance. In this respect, it has rightly been pointed out that by refusing to perform its own obligations under the contract[24], the excipient does nothing but benefit from the effects of invoking the exception of non-performance[25], consisting in obtaining a reduction in its own performance, proportionally with the debtor not fulfilling the obligation.

81   Considering the general normative character of art. 1516, para. (2) of the Civil Code, it follows that the invocation of the remedy of reducing the benefits remains possible regardless of the nature of the contractual obligation, whenever a non-compliant non-execution of the respective obligation occurs; notably, the reduction therefore covers, in principle, all contracts and all types of non-performance of contractual obligations. Although the legislator does not expressly provide for the fulfilment of such prerequisites, there must be a reciprocal interdependence of mutual obligations, as a rule which is inferred from the regulation of the benefit reduction in Section 5 'Resolution, termination and reduction of the benefit', in Chapter II 'Execution of obligations', of Title V 'Execution of obligations' of the Civil Code.

82   From the topography of art. 1551, para. (2) the Civil Code one could conclude that this remedy can be accessed by the party only if there is a significant non-execution within the contracts of *uno ictu* performance or a single non-execution in the case of contracts with successive sequences of performance; however, considering the phasing of the provisions of art. 1516 of the Civil Code, it can be considered that the creditor

---

[24] Belu-Magdo, 'Buna-credință în negocierea, încheierea și executarea contractului' (2020) 7 *Dreptul*, 23; Goicovici, 'Executarea coactivă, buna-credință versus culpa creditorului în materia obligației de moderare a prejudiciului' (2019) 3 *Revista Română de Drept Privat*, 183; Nicolae, 'Buna-credință și echitatea în Noul Cod civil' (2020) 4 *Revista Română de Drept Privat*, 70; Pop, 'Excepția de neexecutare remediu natural al neexecutării contractului în reglementarea Noului Cod civil' (2015) 3 *Dreptul*, 14; Ionuț-Florin Popa, 'Rolul vinovăției în funcționarea remediilor pentru neexecutarea contractului' (2020) 4 *Revista Română de Drept Privat*, 340; Rizoiu, 'Între credință și încredere: despre standarde de bună-credință în materie de garanții' (2020) 4 *Revista Română de Drept Privat*, 111; Stoica, 'Considerații comparative privind noțiunile de bună-credință, diligență, eroare, dol, fraudă, rea-credință, vinovăție (intenție și culpă)' (2020) 4 *Revista Română de Drept Privat*, 15; Terzea, 'Reducerea prestațiilor' (2020), 6 *Revista Română de Jurisprudență*, 136; Terzea, 'Buna-credință în negocierile contractuale' (2020) 4 *Revista Română de Drept Privat*, 207.

[25] in hypotheses where the party who has not performed its contractual obligations requests the counter-performance or is prevailing of the right to unilateral termination, the other party may invoke the exception of non-performance. This exception to non-performance, which is closely linked to the good faith incumbent on both parties to the contract (art. 1556 Civil Code), is a principle that the jurisprudence recognizes in the case of reciprocally-generating obligations contract and according to which the two obligations must be executed simultaneously, as each of the mutual obligations is the legal cause of the other and may be invoked by either contracting party.

can resort to this remedy regardless of the gravity of the non-execution of the contractual obligation or even in case of repeated non-compliant executions. Therefore, the consumer's possibility of resorting to the reduction of benefits remains eligible as a remedy in the case of non-performance of contracts with a single performance action or to the existence of a single non-performance in the case of contracts with successive sequences of performance[26].

In this sense, it should be mentioned that the provisions of art. 1516, para. (2), pt. 2 of the Civil Code do not establish a hierarchical order for exercising the remedies of the resolution and respectively the reduction of the benefit, the creditor having a right of option between the two remedies, the premise being that of the existence of a non-execution of the contractual obligations.

In addition, the desiderate behind the norm of art. 1551, 1st para. of the Romanian Civil Code is to establish the requirements of non-performance of the contractual obligation, the fulfilment of which allows the creditor to exercise the remedy of the resolution, without being able to consider that, implicitly, establishes a limitation of the scope of the remedy. Also, the reduction of benefits may occur even in the event of insignificant non-execution, only to establish the proportion in which the respective reduction will occur. The reduction of the benefit may occur both should the consumer had not accomplished his / her own counter-performance (*e.g.* the creditor will perform its own service only in proportion to the part of the service performed by the debtor) and if the creditor has performed its counterpart (*e.g.* the creditor requests a refund of part of the price paid corresponding to the amount by which the price was reduced).

IV. Repair and replacement of products

The national legislator did not adopt specific rules in order to define the place of delivery and the place of repair and replacement; in the absence of specific stipulations[27], the provisions of Article 1494 of the Civil Code remain applicable, according to which: '(1) In the absence of a contrary stipulation or if the place of performance cannot be established according to the nature of the service or on the basis of the contract, of the practices established between the parties or of the customs: a) the monetary obligations must be executed at the residence or, as the case may be, the creditor's headquarters from the date of payment; b) the obligation to hand over certain individual goods must be executed in the place where the goods were situated at the date of concluding the contract; c) the other obligations are executed at the residence or, as the case may be, the debtor's headquarters at the date of concluding the contract. (2) The party that, after concluding the contract, changes its place of residence or changes the determined headquarters, according to the provisions of para. (1), as a place of performance, shall bear the additional costs caused by these changes.'

The costs of transport for the case of repair/replacement are incumbent upon the professional trader, according to the rule stated in Article 12 para (3) of G.E.O. no. 140/2021

---

[26] According to the provisions of Article 1556 of the Romanian Civil Code on the 'Exception of non-execution', '(1) Where the obligations arising from a reciprocally-generating obligations contract are due and one of the parties does not perform or does not offer the performance of the obligation, the other party may, to an appropriate extent, refuse to perform its obligation, unless otherwise provided by law or as it results from the will of the parties or from the usages that the other party is obliged to execute its counterpart first. (2) The execution may not be refused if, according to the circumstances and considering the small significance of the non-executed performance, this refusal would be contrary to good faith.'

[27] Terzea, 'Reducerea prestațiilor', *cit. supra*, 136; Terzea, 'Buna-credință în negocierile contractuale', *loc. cit. supra*.

('The seller transports the replaced goods at its own expense.'). Should these expenses have been advanced by the consumer, the latter enjoys a right to be fully reimbursed.

87 The provision of the right of withdrawal (regarding the consent for the processing of personal data) and the right of termination through declaration, instead of representing a deviation from the general structure of the right of withdrawal under national law, it rather follows an already existing doctrinal and jurisprudential tendency, according to which consumer's right to obtain the erasure of personal data[28] and consumer's right to withdraw consent for the processing of personal data should apply fully also in connection with the B2C contracts for the providing of (autonomous or embedded) digital content or of digital services; similarly, it has been retained that consumer' right to terminate the contract based on the manifesting of non-conformity in accordance with the provisions of G.E.O. no. 141/2021 should be without prejudice to the consumer's right under Regulation (EU) 2016/679 to withdraw any consent given to the processing of user's personal data[29]; this principle of the pre-eminence of specific regulations on personal data protection is also explicitly reminded in Article 3, para. (8) and (9) of G.E.O. no. 141/2021[30].

88 Moreover, in the perimeter of the exercising of consumer's right to unilaterally terminate the contract for conformity non-compliance, it should be reminded that, according to the aspects mentioned in Recital (48) DCD, facts leading to a lack of compliance with requirements provided for by Regulation (EU) 2016/679, including core principles such as the requirements for data minimisation, data protection by design and data protection by default, may, depending on the circumstances of the case, also be considered to constitute a lack of conformity of the digital content or digital service with subjective or objective requirements for conformity provided for in DCD (although the national legislator did not insert specific provisions on these aspects); additionally, there could be hypotheses where the trader's non-compliance with its obligations under Regulation (EU) 2016/679 can also constitute a lack of conformity of the digital content or digital service with the objective requirement for conformity which requires the digital content or digital service to possess the features which are normal for digital content or digital services of the same type and which the consumer can reasonably expect, thus representing legally justified motifs for consumer's choice to terminate the contract.

---

[28] Șandru, 'Principiul transparenței în protecția datelor cu caracter personal' (2018) 4 *Pandectele Române*, 12; Șandru, 'Dreptul de acces al persoanei vizate în jurisprudența relevantă' (2018) 4 *Revista Română de Drept al Afacerilor*, 18;

[29] Șchiopu, 'Perspective ale dreptului de a fi uitat' (2019) 5 *Dreptul*, 46; Șchiopu, 'Privire generală asupra măsurilor tehnice și organizatorice necesare pentru implementarea efectivă a Regulamentului general privind protecția datelor' (2019) 2 *Revista Română de Drept al Afacerilor*, 32; Șchiopu, 'Considerații asupra rectificării și restricționării prelucrării datelor cu caracter personal' (2018) 3 *Revista Română de Drept European (Comunitar)*, 27; Șchiopu, 'Date cu caracter personal având funcție de identificare. Prelucrarea codului numeric personal sau a altui identificator cu aplicabilitate generală. Lipsa consimțământului pentru predarea unei copii a actului de identitate' (2017) 3 *Revista Română de Jurisprudență*, 38.

[30] According to the provisions of Article 3, para. (8) and (9) of G.E.O. no. 141/2021, '(8) The legal provisions in force regarding the protection of personal data shall apply to any personal data processed in connection with the contracts provided in para. (1) lit. a) and b). (9) The provisions of this Ordinance are without prejudice to Regulation (EU) 2016/679 of the European Parliament and of the Council of 27 April 2016 and to Law no. 506/2004 on the processing of personal data and the protection of privacy in the electronic communications sector, with subsequent amendments. Where a provision of this Ordinance conflicts with a provision of another act of national law transposing or establishing measures for the implementation of an E.U. regulation on the protection of personal data, the provisions of the latter will prevail'.

D. Trader's liability for non-conformity

V. Contractual consequences of consumer's withdrawal of consent for processing personal data

The national legislator did not introduce specific rules regarding the contractual consequences of withdrawal of consent for processing personal data; instead, general contract law rules remain applicable[31]; consumer's discretionary right to withdraw his / her consent to data processing founds its conceptual foundations in the assertions according to which the consent given by the consumer for personal data processing may be withdrawn at any stage, without the application of penalties and without risking the issuance of other pecuniary sanctions, and without limitation as to the reasons for the withdrawal. Generally, the exercise of the right to withdraw consent should be made comparably easy or simplified as for the consent collecting by the data controller; the consent withdrawal for the processing of personal data may, in turn, be sequential, and may target one or more of the purposes of processing initially stated, while maintaining consent for one or more of these purposes, depending on the consumer's decision. Likewise, the sequencing of the withdrawal of consent may target all processing operations or only a range of these processing activities (withdrawal of consent to data processing for commercial profiling purposes, for instance).

Restitution in cases in which the trader supplied digital content and/or digital services and the consumer provided personal data as a counter-performance is not specifically addressed by the G.E.O. no. 141/2021, despite the need for clearer regulation on these legal issues; it is a common observation, almost truistical, that those services appeared as if they would be gratuitous for the consumer, whereas the service providers earned their revenues on the other side of the market by selling personalised advertisements to business customers. The processing of the personal data, either based on user's consent or on the other legal grounds of Article 6, 1st para. of the General Data Protection Regulation (GDPR), was previously interpreted as an ancillary unilateral legal act besides the service contract, instead of seeing it as a legal component of the contractual object, in a synallagmatic paradigm. The reciprocity and interdependence of contractual obligations in a bilateral B2C contract would imply, accordingly, as far as common provisions as those of Articles 1635 to1649 of the Romanian Civil Code are concerned, that: (i) all other legal acts done in favour of a *bona fide* third party are opposable to the true owner or to the one entitled to restitution; contracts with successive performance, under the condition of observing the publicity formalities provided by law, will continue to produce effects for the duration stipulated by the parties, but not more than one year from the date of abolition of the title of the constituent party; (ii) when the goods subject to restitution have been alienated, the restitution action may be exercised against the acquiring third party, subject to the mandatory rules or the effect of the good faith acquisition of movable property or, as the case may be, the application of acquisitive prescription; (iii) the person who does not possess full capacity to exercise legal rights, is not required to reimburse the benefits attained from exploiting the resituated goods, or to reimburse them only within the limit of the benefit realized, assessed at the date of the request for reimbursement; the burden of proving the existence of this enrichment rests with the claimant; it may be subject to full restitution where, intentionally or through gross negligence, it has rendered the restitution impossible.

---

[31] Goicovici, 'Consimțământul consumatorului la prelucrarea datelor personale în contractele *business to consumer* – condiția consimțământului granular' (2019) 2 *Analele Universității de Vest din Timișoara. Seria Drept*, 6.

VI. Environmental sustainability issues and fighting premature or planned obsolescence of products

91   The national legislator did not choose to prioritize repair over replacement in order to enhance environmental sustainability (as mentioned in recital 48 SGD); instead, the desiderate of enhancing environmental stability might be rather difficult to combine with the national legislator's desiderate of maintaining consumer's free choice when selecting the means of repair for the conformity deficiencies manifested during the first 30 days from the delivery date, as stated in Article 11, para. (7) of G.E.O. no. 140/2021.

92   In terms of fighting premature / planned obsolescence of goods and the relationship with the internal rules on unfair commercial practices, it must be pointed out that the national legislator did not expressly prohibit the practices of programming the technical obsolescence of products; there are no specific legal provisions, under current legislative framework, banning the use of scheduled obsolescence practices or providing a legal definition of planned obsolescence or incriminating those practices as unfair in B2C relations, as referring to techniques by which the professional responsible for placing a product on the market seeks to deliberately reduce its shelf life in order to increase its replacement rate.

VII. Transfer of consumer's rights to subsequent parties

93   General legal norms provide for an automatic transfer of the rights against the initial seller from the initial consumer to a subsequent buyer[32], this transfer being regulated by the provisions of Article 1706 of the Civil Code. In the hypotheses in which the product has been the object of several subsequent sales contracts, at first glance, situations of this type follow the classical scheme of pledging civil liability, since the last buyer beneficiates of a conformity warranty, on a contractual basis, against its direct seller, as well as against the former seller from the transactions chain[33]. In this context, two shortcomings may arise: (i) either effective redress and the recovery of the price is blocked by the fact that the intermediary seller proves to be insolvent[34]; (ii) the intermediary buyer proves that the non-conformity motifs are prior to the latest sales contract, thus respectively justifying the entraining of the guarantee against to the first seller(s). The action of the sub-acquirer referred to in art. 1706 of the Civil Code is identical to the action obtained by its author, who is the intermediary seller; this type of action will be submitted under the conditions set in the original sales contract, to which the first seller (portrayed as defendant in this action) consented; the transmission of the guarantee to the sub-acquirer can be based on the idea of a transfer as an accessory (ancillary warranty) of product ownership.

94   Legal provisions also allow the initial consumer and a subsequent buyer to contractually agree that the rights against the initial seller are transferred to the subsequent buyer. In this perimeter, it must be noted that national law allows the initial seller to exclude the transferability of the rights under the legal guarantee or a commercial guarantee in its general terms and conditions in B2B transactions only, and not in a B2C agreement,

---

[32] Goicovici, 'Vânzările succesive ale bunului – Garanțiile ascendente în ambianța Noului Cod civil' (2016) 3 *Revista Universul Juridic*, 24; Juanita Goicovici, 'Matricea răspunderii civile extracontractuale pentru prejudiciile cauzate de produsele cu defecte de manufacturare, între testul riscuri-beneficii și testul așteptărilor legitime ale consumatorului' (2022) 1 *Studia Universitatis Babes-Bolyai Iurisprudentia*, 106.

[33] *Ibidem*.

[34] *Idem*, 26.

at least not for the mandatory conformity warranty for non-conformity manifested during the two-year period from the delivery date. Therefore, a B2C agreement of this type would only be legally efficient as regarding the commercial guarantee of conformity, for obligations voluntarily taken by the professional trader which offer a higher level of consumer protection as compared to the minimal mandatory legal guarantee. Summarising these aspects, it should be accentuated that, in B2C sales contracts, national law allows the initial professional seller to exclude the transferability of the rights under a commercial guarantee (more favourable by design than the mandatory legal guarantee, which remains latently applicable), in its general terms and conditions, while stipulating that that the rights against the initial seller based on the commercial guarantee cannot be transferred to the subsequent buyer.

In cases when the consumer bought the product, after which the initial buyer moved to another country, general legal provisions would apply, since this particular subject was not addressed in G.E.O. no. 140/2021 and G.E.O. no. 141/2021, nor was tackled the subject of establishing specific rules for the cases in which the seller delivered the goods in accordance with the Geo-Blocking Regulation and is now obliged to carry our repair or replacement in a country the seller does not offer delivery to.

E. Commercial Guarantees

The commercial guarantee (concerning the conformity of the product) is described as referring to the commitment on the part of the guarantor to the consumer, provided in the guarantee certificate or in the advertising available at or before the conclusion of the contract, in addition to the legal obligations of the seller regarding the guarantee of conformity (supplementary to the minimal set of legal obligations incumbent on the trader), to reimburse the price paid or to replace, repair or provide maintenance for the goods, if these do not meet the specifications or any other conformity requirements (art. 2 pt. 12 from G.E.O. no. 140/2021). The accent is placed on the attributes of the commercial guarantee, which is defined as referring to any voluntary commitment of the trader towards the consumer, without requesting additional costs, provided in the guarantee certificate or in the relevant advertising available at the time or before the conclusion of the contract, in addition to the legal obligation of the trader's liability for the conformity of digital content or digital services (art. 1 pt. 8 of G.E.O. no. 141/2021). The mandatory legal guarantee of conformity, operating for deficiencies that appear (that are manifesting) within a period of two years from the date of delivery of the product, takes precedence over any conventional commercial guarantees that duplicate it, the first being a minimum mandatory guarantee for the professional seller, regardless of any conventional commercial safeguards applicable in B2C relations. As it results from the text of art. 15 of G.E.O. no. 140/2021, any commercial guarantee gives rise to a legal obligation for the guarantor under the conditions laid down in the commercial guarantee certificate and the associated advertisements available at the time of the conclusion of the previous contract. If a manufacturer offers the consumer a guarantee of durability for certain goods for a specified period of time, the manufacturer will be directly liable to the consumer for the entire period covered by the guarantee of durability for the repair or replacement of the goods in accordance with Article 15; yet, through the means of a commercial guarantee, the seller can only offer the consumer more favourable conditions as compared to those already incidental in the B2C contract based on the legal provisions on the conformity mandatory warranty[35].

---

[35] *Idem*, 27.

97   Should the conditions set out in the commercial guarantee certificate be less favourable to the consumer[36] than those set out in the legal texts, the latter prevail; additionally, the commercial guarantee gives rise to legal obligations under the conditions set out in the advertising texts on commercial guarantee[37], unless the associated advertisements were corrected in the same way or in a manner comparable to that in which they were previously made.

98   The informative formalism applicable to conventional guarantees of conformity results from the content of Article 15, para. (7) of G.E.O. no. 140/2021, according to which certain mandatory provisions must be included by the professional seller in the conventional guarantee of conformity, the legislator also imposing the need to establish the conventional guarantee certificate 'on a durable medium' in writing or in digital format ('The commercial guarantee certificate shall be provided to the consumer, on a durable medium, at the latest at the time of delivery of the goods. The commercial guarantee certificate is worded in plain, intelligible language'.)

99   It is worth mentioning that the text of Article 15, para. (8) of G.E.O. no. 140/2021 expressly states that non-compliance with the informative formalities by the trader when drawing up the contractual guarantee certificate (omission of some of the mandatory particularly mentioned clauses) is not sanctioned with the nullity of the conventional guarantee nor with its ineffectiveness, since this type of formalism is not being a validating formalism (imposed *ad substantiam*), yet it is considered to be an informative formalism, intended to facilitate, for the consumer, the knowledge of certain legal prerogatives; therefore, for omitting to comply with the requirements of the informative formalism imposed on the certificate of commercial guarantee, the professional trader bears the penalty of a fine (applicable, in accordance with the provisions of national law) or may be required to pay compensation and remedy the situation in B2C relations; as a summarising observation, it must be noticed that the non-compliance with the exigencies of the informative formalism does not release the professional trader from its contractual obligations assumed on the basis of the certificate of commercial guarantee; thus, according to Article 17, 3rd para., 'Non-compliance with the 2nd paragraph shall not affect the binding nature of the commercial guarantee for the guarantor'.

100   B2C clauses that recognise to the consumer additional prerogatives above the minimum level described in the mandatory legal guarantee are valid; for example, the establishment of a 3 to 5-year warranty period or the maintenance of a 2 year legal warranty period, with the clause that for 6 months after delivery of the product, for the deficiencies of conformity manifested, and which make the product unusable according to its typical purposes, the trader undertakes, for example, to fully reimburse the price received without the consumer having to go through the preliminary stage of selecting a more temperate measure, such as product replacement / repair.

101   The pre-eminence of the minimum legal guarantee and the authorization of clauses meant to increase the prerogatives assigned to consumers remain the major features of the national regulation on commercial guarantees. The imperative character of the minimum legal guarantee of conformity for the deficiencies manifested within 2 years from the date of delivery of the products results from the wording of Article 19 of G.E.O. no. 140/2021, which provides that no contractual agreement will be binding on the consumer when, to the detriment of the consumer, precludes the application of the provisions transposing the Directive into national law, derogates from the minimal legal

---

[36] *Ibidem.*
[37] *Ibidem.*

E. Commercial Guarantees

protection prerogatives or modifies their effects when the non-conformity of the goods is brought to the notice of the seller by the consumer.

Therefore, the legal minimum guarantee of conformity cannot be removed or restricted by contractual clauses, even if they have been accepted by the consumer (those contractual provisions are seen as a part of the 'black list' of unfair terms); obviously, expressly inserted clauses can offer consumers a more advantageous contractual guarantee than the legal one. As resulting from the provisions of Article 15, 2nd para. of G.E.O. no. 140/2021, 'Under the conditions laid down in this Article and without prejudice to any other legal provisions, where a manufacturer offers the consumer a guarantee of durability for certain goods for a specified period, the manufacturer shall be directly liable to the consumer for the entire period covered by the durability guarantee, for the repair or replacement of the goods in accordance with the provisions of Article 12. (3) The manufacturer may offer to the consumer more favourable conditions in the certificate of commercial guarantee of sustainability. (4) In cases where the conditions set out in the commercial guarantee certificate are less favourable to the consumer than those set out in the associated advertisements, the commercial guarantee will give rise to legal obligations under the conditions laid down in the commercial guarantee advertising, unless, prior to the conclusion of the contract, the associated advertisements were corrected in the same way or in a manner comparable to that in which they were made. (5) The commercial guarantee certificate is offered to the consumer, on a durable medium, at the latest at the time of delivery of the product. (6) The commercial guarantee certificate shall be worded in plain, intelligible language. (7) The commercial guarantee certificate shall contain the following elements: (a) a clear statement that the consumer is entitled to remedial action by the seller, free of charge, in the event of non-conformity of the goods and that such remedies are not affected by the commercial guarantee; (b) the name and address of the guarantor; (c) the procedural steps that the consumer must follow in order to obtain the implementation of the commercial guarantee; (d) indication of the goods to which the commercial guarantee applies; (e) the conditions of the commercial guarantee. (8) Failure to comply with the provisions of para. (5)-(7) does not affect the binding nature of the commercial guarantee for the guarantor. (9) The commercial guarantee certificate must be written in Romanian, without excluding its presentation in other languages. (10) If the non-conformity is remedied by repair, the period provided for in the commercial guarantee of durability shall be extended by the time of non-functioning of the good, from the moment when the non-compliance was brought to the notice of the guarantor by the consumer. (11) If the non-conformity is remedied by replacement, for the goods replacing the non-compliant goods, the period provided for in the commercial guarantee of durability shall begin to run from the date of replacement. (12) Repairs or replacements during the commercial warranty period shall be carried out within a reasonable time which may not exceed 15 calendar days from the time the seller was informed by the consumer of the non-conformity and which is agreed in writing, between the seller and the consumer, considering the nature and complexity of the goods, the nature and gravity of the non-conformity and the effort required to complete the repair or replacement.'

As it must be observed form the cited normative text, when drafting the certificate of commercial guaranty for conformity, the professionals are expected (under the penalty of contravention fines) to use the national linguistical version (the commercial guarantee certificate will be drafted in Romanian, as a mandatory rule), the professionals being allowed to choose, as supplementary linguistical versions, the languages in which the commercial guarantee statement is to be made available to the consumer.

F. Time limits and temporality bars

104   The seller's liability for deficiencies of conformity is regulated by the provisions of Article 9 of the G.E.O. no. 140/2021, stating that the seller may be held liable for any non-conformity existing at the time of delivery of the goods and which is established within two years from this date. Without prejudice to the provisions of Article 6, 3rd para., the provisions of par. (1) also apply to goods with digital elements (embedded digital content).

105   When the B2C contract provides for the continuous supply of digital content or digital services for a certain period, the seller will also be held liable for any non-conformity of the digital content or digital service that occurs or is found within two years from the delivery date, the mentioned rule remaining applicable to products with an average use duration of up to five years, and within five years from that date for products with an average duration of use. When the B2C contract provides for continuous supply for a period of more than five years, the seller will be held liable for any non-compliance of the digital content or digital service that occurs or is found during the period in which the digital content or digital service is expected to be provided, according to the sales contract terms[38].

106   In the case of second-hand or refurbished products, the consumer and the seller may agree on contractual conditions stipulating for a shorter period of contractual liability than those provided in para. (1)-(4), provided that such periods or shorter terms have a duration of at least one year from the date of delivery.

107   It is also worth noticing that, according to the provisions of Article 10 of the G.E.O. no. 140/2021 on the burden of proof, "(1) Any non-conformity which is found to have manifested within one year from the date on which the goods were delivered is presumed to have already existed at the time of delivery, unless proven otherwise or unless this presumption is incompatible with the nature of the goods or with the nature of the non-compliance. (2) The provisions of para. (1) also apply to embedded digital content."

108   When regulating on the duration of professional trader's or digital services provider's liability for conformity compliance of repetitively supplied digital content, the legislator introduced a five-years term calculated from the digital content delivery date, respectively from the date the digital services provider started the performance, the legal (imperative) conformity guarantee thus covering the non-conformity manifesting within the 5 years period from the moment the consumer entered into the possessing of the digital content; yet, the legal provision is only applicable if, given the nature of the products and consumer's reasonable expectations, it could be established, in each particular case, that the five-year term is pertinent. Congruently, one could conclude that, beside the classicized two-year term for the conformity warranty, in the perimeter of the B2C contracts for the providing of autonomous (non-embedded) digital content, there is a five-year term (the standardized two-year term and an additional period of 3 years) during which the provider may be held liable for the manifested non-conformity, but only if, according to the circumstances, it is reasonable to appreciate that it was under consumer's legitimate expectations that the delivered digital contend would meet the conformity criteria during such a period of time; therefore, the legal nature of the

---

[38] Popa, 'Furnizarea și conformitatea conținutului digital sau serviciului digital' (2022) 1 *Revista Română de Drept Privat*, 229; Popa, Suciu, 'Transpunerea directivelor europene privind furnizarea de conținut digital și de servicii digitale, respectiv privind vânzările de consum – O.U.G. nr. 141/2021 și O.U.G. nr. 140/2021' (2022) 1 *Revista Română de Drept Privat*, 196; Goicovici, 'Unilateral Termination and Adjustment of the Consumer Contract on Digital Content' (2021) *Regional Law Review*, 283.

F. Time limits and temporality bars

five-year term would be a permissive (non-compulsory, non-mandatory) one, operating more like a guiding criterion for the courts of law, while the two-year term minimal duration for the conformity warranty still applies.

Saliently, it must be noticed that, in cases in which the B2C contract contains a stipulated term regarding the period during which the digital services will be provided, the professional provider remains liable for the non-conformity of the digital services for the entire duration of the performance period, as contractually stipulated. As stated in the text of art. 10 para. (2) and (3) of the G.E.O. no. 141/2021, "(2) When a contract provides for a single act of supply or a series of individual supply acts, the trader shall be liable for any non-conformity, pursuant to art. 6 to8, which exists at the time of supply and which is established within five years from the date of supply, without prejudice to the applicability of the provisions of art. 7 para. (3) lit. b)" (correlated with consumer's reasonable expectations, given the type and purpose of the digital content or digital service and taking into account the circumstances and nature of the contract, where the contract provides for a single act of supply or a series of individual acts of supply); "(3) When the contract provides for the continuous supply of the digital content or digital services during a certain period of time, the trader is liable for any non-conformity, pursuant to art. 6 to8, which takes place or is found during the period on which the digital content or the digital service must be provided according to the contract."

The analysis of the legal text shows that the standard duration of the guarantee of conformity for the digital content is of 5 years from the date of supply, the mentioned guarantee covering the deficiencies of conformity that would manifest in this interval of five years, and whose cause is pre-existing to the product delivery. However, the duration of the guarantee of conformity is calibrated according to the manner in which the parties have resolved, in the content of the contractual clauses, the issue of continuous supply of digital content, the above rule being applicable to the delivering of digital content; for cases involving a successive or a sequential supply, which, by hypothesis, would imply a longer or a shorter contractual period than the 5-year period, the guarantee of conformity remains due to the consumer throughout the duration set for the providing of the digital service or for the gradual providing of digital content.

The national legislator did not intend to maintain or introduce provisions on interruption or suspension of the liability period or limitation period; as stated by a classicized procedural[39] principle, the main common feature of warranty terms is, according to the general acceptance, that they are not subject to suspension or interruption. Execution of the term without the defect having manifested itself, entails the extinction of the subjective right[40] to invoke the guarantee for hidden defects.

The "obligation to notify", the introducing of which was allowed by Art. 12 SGD, has not been stipulated in the national regulation on product conformity; neither the provisions of G.E.O no. 140/2021, nor the provisions of G.E.O. no. 141/2021 contain an obligation on consumer's behalf, to notify the seller of a lack of conformity within a period of at least 2 months of the date on which the consumer detected such lack of conformity.

---

[39] Țiț, 'Încuviințarea executării silite a debitorului consumator – exigențe europene, realități naționale' (2020) 2 (66) *Analele Științifice ale Universității Alexandru Ioan Cuza din Iași, seria Științe Juridice*, 91.

[40] Țiț, 'Situații particulare referitoare la exercitarea rolului activ al judecătorului în procesul civil' (2019) 2 (45) *Analele Științifice ale Universității Alexandru Ioan Cuza din Iași, seria Științe Juridice*, 29; Țiț, 'O posibilă problemă de legalitate a procedurii de executare silită: prorogarea competenței executorului judecătoresc' (2022) 68 *Analele Stiintifice Ale Universitatii Alexandru Ioan Cuza Din Iași, seria Stiinte Juridice*, 145

G. Seller's right of redress

113   As stated by Article 16 of G.E.O. no. 140/2021, where the seller is liable to the consumer based on the manifesting of a lack of conformity which results from an act or omission, including omitting to provide updates to goods with digital elements in accordance with Article 7(3), by a participant in previous links of the chain of transactions, the seller will be entitled to pursue remedies against the person or persons liable in the chain of transactions. Similar provisions were inserted in Article 19 of G.E.O. no. 141/2021, according to which if the trader is liable to the consumer for a case of non-provision of digital content or digital service or for a non-compliance resulting from an act or omission of a person in the earlier stages of the chain of transactions, the trader will have the right to bring an action in regress against the person or persons who have the responsibility in the chain of commercial transactions, based on the provisions of Law no. 287/2009 (Civil Code, in force starting with October 1st, 2011), republished, with subsequent amendments. According to the new regulation, the compensation includes reimbursement of expenses necessary in order to fulfil the consumer's rights, in particular expenses associated with replacing or removing defects in the product sold, its disassembly, transport and re-assembly[41], as well as the amount by which the price of the product has been reduced in the B2C contractual relationship[42] and, consequently, the loss of profits for the final seller connected to the lack of conformity which has its cause in a previous link of the commercial chain. The compensation includes reimbursement of expenses necessary for fulfilment of the consumer's rights, which in practice may cover a broad range of costs. These facets are particularly important, since the parties may not modify the conditions of liability or modify the extent of the compensation when there is detriment to a consumer[43] (any contractual provisions aimed at limiting or excluding this liability in any way are invalid and completely unopposable to the consumer[44]).

H. Reverberations on other legal remedies

114   Compensation remains eligible under the conditions set in Article 1617 of the Civil code, according to which: (1) the compensation will automatically operate (in a *ope legis* manner) in cases where there are two reciprocal debts, which will be both liquidated, independently of their source, and which have as object a sum of money or a certain amount of fungible goods of the same nature; (2) each party may request the judicial liquidation of a debt in order to oppose the compensation; (3) either party may expressly or tacitly waive compensation.

115   As established in Article 1617, 1st para. of the Civil Code, should the reciprocal debts have a certain nature, in terms of existence and liquidity, the compensation automatically operates by the effect of law, the reciprocal debts being extinguished until the competition of the smallest of sums. Thus, should the conditions of legal compensation be met, a double (reciprocal) payment will no longer be possible, the compensation being considered as being a legal benefit with extinctive, retroactive effects. On the one

---

[41] Goicovici, *Dreptul relațiilor dintre profesioniști și consumatori* (2022), cit. supra, 484.
[42] Ibidem.
[43] Idem, 491. See also Mona-Lisa Belu-Magdo, 'Buna-credință în negocierea, încheierea și executarea contractului', loc. cit. supra.
[44] Goicovici, 'Executarea coactivă, buna-credință *versus* culpa creditorului în materia obligației de moderare a prejudiciului', loc. cit. supra. See also Nicolae, 'Buna-credință și echitatea în Noul Cod civil', loc. cit. supra.

hand, the compensation mechanism becomes automatically applicable, *ope legis*, while, on the other hand, by regulating the possibility of waiving compensation, the legislator linked the effect of compensation and the manifestation of will of the parties, giving the debtors the possibility to repudiate the compensatory effect (benefit), which means that, in practice, a right of option is established for each party to invoke or waive the effect of compensation. The existence of such a right of option and the possibility of waiving the compensation is justified, despite its automatically enforceable nature, by the extinctive effect of the compensation on the right of claim from the patrimony of each creditor (reciprocal debtor) which cannot be completely evaded from the legal will of the parties. Saliently, it also means that the mechanism of compensation does not emerge from the concept of public order; on the contrary, it presupposes the manifestation of the will of the parties in the sense of accepting or repudiating the extinctive effect that the law establishes as a compensatory benefit.

I. Concluding remarks

116 The *rationae personae* sphere of applicability of the new regulations has not been massively innovated by the national legislator, who mainly maintained the professional trader – consumer matrix characterising the SGD and DCD; according to recital (18), the platform providers should be considered as professionals (traders), if they acted for purposes related to their own business and in the capacity of the consumer's direct contractual partner. At the same time, the Directive allows Member States to extend its scope to those platform providers that cannot be considered as traders; as it has been noted, in the view of the European legislator, platforms are usually only intermediaries, an aspect which should exclude them from the personal scope of the Directive. However, a determinant element will be the way in which the provider (operator or controller) of the platform behaves or acts towards the consumer; if, for example, it checks and controls the bidding providers that use its platform to interact with consumers, and this commercial purpose is visible or intelligible to the consumer, then the platform operator should be considered a trader within the meaning of the DCD.

117 Recital (17) also appears to seek to extend the concept of 'consumer', in order to be able to include in the scope of the Directive also the contracts concluded for the obtaining of a dual use or hybrid use of the products, which are concluded for purposes partially limited to commercial activity and partly outside it, if the commercial purpose had been limited to the extent that it has no predominant weight in the general context of the contract. However, the preamble of the Directive can only serve as an explanatory tool for the rules contained therein, and the desideratum expressed in Recital (17) is not found in the definition provided in the 2nd Article, pt. 6 of the Directive. As regards the national legislator's (unexercised) possibility to extend the scope of the Directive to persons who do not fall within the traditional concept of 'consumer', Recital (17) is not, however, clear to this regard, since the same possibility is also mentioned in the previous recital, in which the Union legislator gives clear examples of such persons: non-governmental organizations, start-ups and small and medium-sized enterprises.

118 The following remarks may be extracted from the previous assertions:

119 (a) consumer's right to request for the repeat of performance remains a key element of the new regulation on conformity lapses; where the professional trader failed to provide a digital or to deliver a product in line with information they gave to the consumer beforehand, the seller may be requested to repeat performance carried out within a reasonable time, without significant inconvenience and at no cost to consumer,

who is also entitled to a price reduction, if repeat performance of a service is impossible or it cannot be carried out within a reasonable time or without causing the consumer significant inconvenience; consumers are also entitled to a price reduction if the digital service is not carried out within a reasonable time and where the traders are in breach of their obligations relating to information they provided the consumer with at the pre-contractual stage and which is deemed to be part of the B2C contract;

120 (b) any quantitative, qualitative, or functional inadvertence of the digital content / service no longer belongs to the sphere of non-performance remedies, if the professional had been able to prove that the supply, according to Article 13, 1st para. DCD, has been delivered; the timing of the manifesting of the non-conformity lapse is crucial for changing the burden of proof, since, up to that point, it is the professional who must prove both the elements (the fact that the supply has been performed and the compliance to the objective and subjective criteria of conformity);

121 (c) typically, it is the consumer who must prove the existence of non-conformity and, if this is established within one year form the moment of the performing of the supply, the national courts may operate with the presumption that the conformity lapse is attributable to the professional trader; therefore, should the latter intend to be released from liability, the professional seller will be required to prove that the non-conformity is not attributable to the seller (*e.g.*, proving that the consumer's digital environment is not compatible with the technical requirements of the digital content and that the professional transparently informed the consumer on these particular aspects at the pre-contractual stage).

Bibliography

Mona-Lisa Belu-Magdo, 'Buna-credință în negocierea, încheierea și executarea contractului' (2020) 7 *Dreptul*, 23.

Juanita Goicovici, 'Matricea răspunderii civile extracontractuale pentru prejudiciile cauzate de produsele cu defecte de manufacturare, între testul riscuri-beneficii și testul așteptărilor legitime ale consumatorului' (2022) 1 *Studia Universitatis Babes-Bolyai Iurisprudentia*, 106.

Juanita Goicovici, 'Unilateral Termination and Adjustment of the Consumer Contract on Digital Content' (2021) *Regional Law Review*, 283.

Juanita Goicovici, 'The Traders' Liability for Lack of Conformity of the Digital Content and of the Digital Services, as Regulated by Directive (EU) 2019/770' (2020) L LXVI *Analele Științifice ale Universității "Alexandru Ioan Cuza" din Iași, Seria Științe Juridice*, 79.

Juanita Goicovici, 'Portabilitatea datelor cu caracter personal, prin prisma dispozițiilor RGPD și ale Directivei 2019/770: este gambitul reginei mutarea de deschidere adecvată?' (2021) LXVII (2) *Analele Științifice ale Universității "Alexandru Ioan Cuza" din Iași, Seria Științe Juridice*, 57.

Juanita Goicovici, 'Consimțământul consumatorului la prelucrarea datelor personale în contractele business to consumer – condiția consimțământului granular' (2019) 2 *Analele Universității de Vest din Timișoara. Seria Drept*, 6.

Juanita Goicovici, 'Executarea coactivă, buna-credință *versus* culpa creditorului în materia obligației de moderare a prejudiciului' (2019) 3 *Revista Română de Drept Privat*, 183.

Juanita Goicovici, 'Vânzările succesive ale bunului – Garanțiile ascendente în ambianța Noului Cod civil' (2016) 3 *Revista Universul Juridic*, 24.

Juanita Goicovici, 'Clauzele privind drepturile consumatorilor în contractele de servicii cloud computing' (2019) 2 *Revista Română de Drept Privat*, 399.

Bibliography

Juanita Goicovici, *Dreptul relațiilor dintre profesioniști și consumatori* (Hamangiu, Bucharest 2022).

Marian Nicolae, 'Buna-credință și echitatea în Noul Cod civil' (2020) 4 *Revista Română de Drept Privat*, 70.

Liviu Pop, 'Excepția de neexecutare – remediu natural al neexecutării contractului în reglementarea Noului Cod civil' (2015) 3 *Dreptul*, 14.

Ionuț-Florin Popa, 'Soluții jurisdicționale cu efecte substanțiale. Un comentariu pe marginea unor hotărâri ‹‹radiante›› ale Curții de Justiție a Uniunii Europene' (2021) 1 *Revista Română de Drept Privat*, 201.

Ionuț-Florin Popa, 'Furnizarea și conformitatea conținutului digital sau serviciului digital' (2022) 1 *Revista Română de Drept Privat*, 229.

Ionuț-Florin Popa, Sorana Suciu, 'Transpunerea directivelor europene privind furnizarea de conținut digital și de servicii digitale, respectiv privind vânzările de consum – O.U.G. nr. 141/2021 și O.U.G. nr. 140/2021' (2022) 1 *Revista Română de Drept Privat*, 196.

Ionuț-Florin Popa, 'Rolul vinovăției în funcționarea remediilor pentru neexecutarea contractului' (2020) 4 *Revista Română de Drept Privat*, 340.

Radu Rizoiu, 'Între credință și încredere: despre standarde de bună-credință în materie de garanții' (2020) 4 *Revista Română de Drept Privat*, 111.

Valeriu Stoica, 'Considerații comparative privind noțiunile de bună-credință, diligență, eroare, dol, fraudă, rea-credință, vinovăție (intenție și culpă)' (2020) 4 *Revista Română de Drept Privat*, 15.

Sorana Suciu, 'Conformitatea conținutului digital. Noi instrumente legislative europene' (2020) 1 *Revista Română de Drept Privat*, 704.

Sorana Suciu, 'Conformitatea conținutului digital. Noi instrumente legislative europene 2.0' (2022) 1 *Revista Română de Drept Privat*, 206.

Daniel-Mihail Șandru, 'Unele considerații cu privire la relația dintre protecția datelor (în special Regulamentul general privind protecția datelor) și proprietatea intelectuală' (2019) 3 *Revista Română de Drept European (Comunitar)*, 41.

Daniel-Mihail Șandru, 'Principiul transparenței în protecția datelor cu caracter personal' (2018) 4 *Pandectele Române*, 12.

Daniel-Mihail Șandru, 'Dreptul de acces al persoanei vizate în jurisprudența relevantă' (2018) 4 *Revista Română de Drept al Afacerilor*, 18.

Daniel-Mihail Șandru, 'Principiul echității în prelucrarea datelor cu caracter personal' (2018) 3 *Pandectele Române*, 36.

Silviu-Dorin Șchiopu, 'Perspective ale dreptului de a fi uitat' (2019) 5 *Dreptul*, 46.

Silviu-Dorin Șchiopu, 'Privire generală asupra măsurilor tehnice și organizatorice necesare pentru implementarea efectivă a Regulamentului general privind protecția datelor' (2019) 2 *Revista Română de Drept al Afacerilor*, 32.

Silviu-Dorin Șchiopu, 'Considerații asupra rectificării și restricționării prelucrării datelor cu caracter personal' (2018) 3 *Revista Română de Drept European (Comunitar)*, 27.

Silviu-Dorin Șchiopu, 'Date cu caracter personal având funcție de identificare. Prelucrarea codului numeric personal sau a altui identificator cu aplicabilitate generală. Lipsa consimțământului pentru predarea unei copii a actului de identitate' (2017) 3 *Revista Română de Jurisprudență*, 38.

Viorel Terzea, 'Reducerea prestațiilor' (2020), 6 *Revista Română de Jurisprudență*, 136.

Viorel Terzea, 'Buna-credință în negocierile contractuale' (2020) 4 *Revista Română de Drept Privat*, 207.

Nicolae-Horia Țiț, 'O posibilă problemă de legalitate a procedurii de executare silită: prorogarea competenței executorului judecătoresc' (2022) 68 *Analele Stiintifice Ale Universitatii Alexandru Ioan Cuza Din Iași, seria Stiinte Juridice*, 145.

Nicolae-Horia Țiț, 'Rolul activ al judecătorului în identificarea și calificarea actelor și faptelor deduse judecății. Câteva considerații' (2021) 1 *Revista Română de Drept Privat*, 174.

Nicolae-Horia Țiț, 'Încuviințarea executării silite a debitorului consumator – exigențe europene, realități naționale' (2020) 2 (66) *Analele Științifice ale Universității Alexandru Ioan Cuza din Iași, seria Științe Juridice*, 91.

Nicolae-Horia Țiț, 'Situații particulare referitoare la exercitarea rolului activ al judecătorului în procesul civil' (2019) 2 (45) *Analele Științifice ale Universității Alexandru Ioan Cuza din Iași, seria Științe Juridice*, 29.

Andreea Verteș-Olteanu, 'Considerații privind regimul juridic aplicabil bunurilor digitale' (2017) 3 *Revista Română de Drept Privat*, 377.

Slovakia

A. Introduction and General Framework 4
B. Definitions and Scope of Application 8
C. Conformity of Goods and Conformity of the Digital Performance 17
    I. Information Obligation 24
    II. Service Life and Spare Parts 30
    III. Compliance with the Ecodesign Directive 37
    IV. Incorrect Installation of Digital Content or Digital Service 42
    V. Providing of Personal Data as a Counterperformance 47
    VI. Changing (Modifying) Digital Performance 52
    VII. Rights of Third Parties 54
    VIII. Resale Right 59
D. Liability of the Seller (trader) 64
    I. Single Performance, Set of Single Performances and Continuous Performance over a Period of Time 64
    II. Obstacles 71
    III. Premature Termination of a Number-independent Interpersonal Communication Service 73
    IV. Service Packages and the Impact of the European Electronic Communications Code on Slovak Civil Law 80
E. Remedies for Non-delivery and Non-compliance 84
    I. Right to Refuse to Pay the Price 88
    II. Personal Data as a Consideration 89
    III. Pointing out a Defect 93
    IV. The Impact of Environmental Sustainability on the Choice of Entitlements 96
F. Commercial Guarantees 97
G. Time Limits 101
H. Right to Compensation 104
    Bibliography 108

1   In Slovakia, the transposition of the Directive on Contracts for the Sale of Goods[1] and the Directive on Contracts for the Supply of Digital Content and Services[2] falls within the agenda of the Ministry of Economy. The Ministry has been considering how and in which legislation to transpose the Directives and it has decided to prepare a completely new broadly conceived Consumer Protection Act and to amend the Civil Code[3] and other related legislation. The plans were bold, but they have not yet been realized. Neither DCD nor SGD has yet been transposed into Slovak law and the Slovak Republic is the last EU Member State which did not transpose the "twin directives".

2   On 26 January 2022, the first phase of the legislative procedure, the so-called inter-ministerial comment procedure, started and was completed in mid-February.[4] A completely new Consumer Protection Act was introduced, but almost 800 comments and objections from different subjects and stakeholders were submitted and evaluated. On 14 April 2023, i. e. at the time this publication was submitted for printing, the draft

---

[1] Directive (EU) 2019/771 of the European Parliament and of the Council of 20 May 2019 on certain aspects concerning contracts for the sale of goods, amending Regulation (EU) 2017/2394 and Directive 2009/22/EC, and repealing Directive 1999/44/EC. OJ L 136/28 (hereinafter referred to as Sale of Goods Directive or SGD).
[2] Directive (EU) 2019/770 of the European Parliament and of the Council of 20 May 2019 on certain aspects concerning contracts for the supply of digital content and digital services. OJ L 136/1 (hereinafter referred to as Digital Content Directive or DCD).
[3] Act No. 40/1964 Coll. Civil Code as amended (hereinafter referred to as Civil Code or CC)
[4] SLOV-LEX. LP/2022/39. [online] https://www.slov-lex.sk/legislativne-procesy/SK/LP/2022/39.

law was approved by the Government of the Slovak Republic. In the next phase, the Parliament will discuss the proposal. However, the text of this publication is based on the original wording of the proposal and on the legal status as of 15 January 2023.

3   This contribution will therefore be mainly an analysis of the draft of the new legislation and its comparison with the current legislation applicable in Slovakia. The issue of SGD and DCD has received only marginal scientific attention in Slovakia since the time of their drafting.[5] Moreover, there has not been a major public debate on the draft of the new Consumer Protection Act and the related amendment to the Civil Code.[6] This contribution is therefore based primarily on an analysis of the individual provisions of the applicable and proposed legislation, with the support of selected bibliographic sources.

A. Introduction and General Framework

4   Consumer protection legislation in Slovakia is currently covered by a number of pieces of legislation. The draft of the new Consumer Protection Act is intended to introduce new general consumer protection legislation to replace

- the Consumer Protection Act of 2007 (Act No. 250/2007 Coll.),
- the Act on Consumer Protection in the Sale of Goods or the Provision of Services under a Distance or Off-Premises Contract of 2014 (Act No. 102/2014 Coll.),
- the Alternative Dispute Resolution for Consumer Disputes Act of 2015 (Act No. 391/2015 Coll.), as well as
- the Supervision and Assistance in Resolving Unjustified Geographical Discrimination against Customers in the Internal Market Act of 2019 (Act No. 299/2019 Coll.).

5   The Decree of the Ministry of Justice on the composition, decision-making, organisation of work and procedure of the commission for the assessment of terms and conditions in consumer contracts is also to be repealed (decree No. 406/2008 Coll.). In addition, other legislation should be amended, in particular the Civil Code, the Act on Financial Market Supervision (Act No. 747/2004 Coll.) and the Electronic Communications Act (Act No. 452/2021 Coll.). The fragmented consumer legislation should be brought together in a new Consumer Protection Act, thus strengthening legal certainty for both the consumer and the trader[7]. With the new legislation, the legislator wants to eliminate duplications, application problems, internal contradictions of individual provisions and terminological differences. Last but not least, the proposed regulation is intended to modernise the current consumer protection legislation and bring it into line with EU law.

6   However, our primary focus for the purposes of analysing the transposition of the SGD and the DCD will be on the proposed amendment of the Civil Code ('the CC-amnd.'), in particular with regard to the changes relating to the consumer contract of sale and the proposed new regulation of the consumer contract with digital performance. However, we will also aim at the proposed amendments to the general provisions relating to the law of obligations, in particular liability for defects.

---

[5] Jurčová et al., 'Kúpne zmluvy uzatvárané on-line a kúpa digitálneho obsahu – úvahy o novej regulácii' (2017) 2 *Právny obzor*, 143.

[6] The exception is, for example, Dulaková Jakúbeková, 'Predaj tovaru v obchode v kontexte s novou spotrebiteľskou smernicou o predaji tovaru č. 2019/701' (2019) 2 *Paneurópske právnické listy* [online] https://www.paneuropskepravnickelisty.sk/index.php/dulakova-d-3/.

[7] This is a new term to replace the currently used term 'seller'.

On the other hand, the focus of this contribution is not on the analysis of the draft new Consumer Protection Act itself. This should regulate not only the general aspects of consumer protection, but also the issue of distance or off-premises contracts, alternative dispute resolution, consumer organisations, public administration in the field of consumer protection and others. This is a wide-ranging agenda which is beyond the scope of this contribution, which is oriented purely on SGD and DCD transposition.

B. Definitions and Scope of Application

The most significant changes brought about by the forthcoming legislation of the new Consumer Protection Act are the unification of the terms used in line with EU legislation, the update of information requirements for contracts concluded at a distance or off-premises in connection with digitalisation and the new regulation of the information obligations of operators of online marketplaces. The proposal of the Act also sets out the conditions for compatibility and interoperability of digital content or digital services. In response to market developments and changes in European consumer legislation, the proposal of the Civil Code amendment (new Sec. 119a) introduces into the Slovak legal order definitions of the terms – digital object, digital content and digital service.

For all terms, the definitions in the DCD are the starting point, which do not leave much room for legislative creativity. An item with digital elements means *'any item that contains digital content or a digital service or is connected to digital content or a digital service in such a way that their absence would prevent the item from fulfilling its functions'* (Sec. 119a para. 1 DCD). An example of such goods is, for example, a smartwatch, which can only perform its functions through an app that the consumer has to install on his smartphone. The app would then be a connected digital element (rec. 15 SGD and rec. 21 DCD).

With respect to *digital content*, the current Payment Services Act (Act No. 492/209 Coll.) provides that digital content, for the purposes of (exclusively only) this Act, means goods or services that are created and delivered in digital form, the use or consumption of which is limited to the use of a technical device, and which do not in any way involve the use or consumption of tangible goods or services. The new (general) definition of digital content proposed for the amended Civil Code is that digital content means *'data which are created and supplied in digital form'* (Sec. 119a CC-amnd.).

There is also a definition of digital service in the current legislation, but only in the context of the specific regulation of cybersecurity. The Cybersecurity Act [Sec. 3 n) of the Act No. 69/2018 Coll.] classifies three types of services as digital services, namely online marketplace, internet search engine and cloud computing. Section 119a para. 3 CC-amnd. proposes a definition that a digital service is *'a service that enables the creation, processing or storage of, or access to, data in digital form, or that enables the exchange or any interaction of data in digital form that is uploaded or created by users of the service'*.

The proposed legislation then addresses further new terminology. The term integration is introduced in the context of the liability of a trader for a defect caused by *'the incorrect integration of a digital performance with the components of the consumer's digital environment or the integration of a digital performance into the components of the consumer's digital environment'* (Sec. 852h para. 3 CC-amnd.). The English term 'update' is translated in the proposal as 'actualization' (e.g. Sec. 617 CC-amnd.). Another new concept is the digital environment, which is understood as *'the hardware, software and any network connection used by the consumer to access or use the digital performance'*

(Sec. 852h para 4 CC-amnd.). The Civil Code should also provide for the concepts of compatibility, interoperability and functionality. Compatibility means the ability of an item or digital performance to function with hardware or software with which the item of the same kind is commonly used, without the need to modify the sold item, hardware or software [Sec. 616 d) CC-amnd.]. Interoperability is the ability of a sold item or digital performance to function with hardware or software different from those with which the item of the same kind is commonly used [Sec. 616 d) CC-amnd.]. Functionality, in turn, means that the sold item is characterised by the contractually defined ability to perform functions with respect to its purpose [Sec. 616 c) CC-amnd.].

13 The draft amendment to the Civil Code should thus change the legal regulation of the consumer sale contract (Sec. 612 CC-amnd.) and introduce a completely new regulation of the consumer contract with digital performance (Sec. 852a et seq. CC-amnd.). A consumer sale contract is a contract of sale concluded between a trader as a seller and a consumer as a buyer provided that the object of the purchase is any movable item, including goods with digital elements (Sec. 119a para 1 CC-amnd.), water, gas or electricity sold in a limited volume or in a specified quantity, even if the item is yet to be manufactured or produced, *inter alia,* also according to the buyer's specifications. According to Section 612 para 2 CC-amnd., in case of doubt applies, that, *'the subject matter of a consumer sale contract for the purchase of an item with digital elements shall also include the supply of digital content or providing of a digital service'*.

14 A digital performance contract is *'any consumer contract under which the trader supplies or undertakes to supply digital content or provide a digital service (digital performance) and the consumer pays or undertakes to pay the price, including the digitally expressed value, or provides or undertakes to provide the trader with his personal data, even if the digital performance is developed according to the consumer's specifications'* (Sec. 852a para 1 CC-amnd.). Digitally expressed value means, for example, electronic vouchers, electronic coupons or virtual currencies. In these cases, it is therefore neither digital content nor a digital service, but only a digital expression of value for the purpose of making a payment (*cf.* rec. 23 DCD).

15 According to Section 852a para 2 CC-amnd., a digital performance contract *'shall not be deemed to be a contract under which the trader supplies or undertakes to supply digital content or a digital service and the consumer provides or undertakes to provide only personal data which the trader processes solely for the purpose of providing the digital performance or fulfilling a legal obligation'*.

16 One of the fundamental questions is which entities are to be covered by the proposed legislation, in particular whether it is only entities that are in a B2C relationship or others as well. As mentioned above, the basis for the transposed regulation is the amendment of the consumer sale contract in the Civil Code and the introduction of a new consumer contract with digital performance in the Civil Code. In these cases, based on the proposed basic definition [Sec. 2 a) of the draft new Consumer Protection Act], a consumer is a natural person who (in the course of a commercial practice or in connection with a contract) is not acting in the course of a business, profession or occupation. It follows that, where the regulation of a consumer contract is concerned, the regulation will apply only to B2C relationships. Thus, the Slovak Republic does not plan to use the option provided in the directives to apply the new legal regulation to other than B2C relationships.

C. Conformity of Goods and Conformity of the Digital Performance

The proposed legislation primarily concerns consumer sales contracts (including the supply of goods with digital elements) and consumer digital performance contracts. Both the DCD and the SGD deal in some detail with issues of conformity of the supplied performance, distinguishing between subjective and objective requirements for conformity. This terminology should be reflected in the proposed legislation by regulating compliance with general (objective) requirements on the one hand and agreed (subjective) requirements on the other. 17

In relation to consumer sales contracts where the performance is an object or goods with digital elements, the regulation is to be included in the amended Civil Code. The requirements relating to the quality and quantity of the goods are to be regulated in the amended Section 615 Civil Code, but do not apply if the seller has expressly informed the buyer at the conclusion of the contract that a certain characteristic of the item does not comply with the general requirements and the buyer has expressly and specifically agreed to the non-compliance. 18

Additional requirements relating to compliance with the general requirements (Sec. 617 CC-amnd.) and compliance with the agreed requirements (Sec. 616 CC-amnd.) are then regulated separately. Among the agreed requirements are, for example, the requirements of functionality, compatibility and operability, or the requirement that the sold item is suitable for a specific purpose, which the buyer has informed the seller of at the latest at the conclusion of the contract and to which the seller has agreed. 19

In the case of an item with digital elements, both agreed and general requirements must be met by the digital content and digital service, regardless of whether they are supplied or provided by the seller or by another person (Sec. 615 *in fine* CC-amnd.). A specific agreed requirement that will commonly arise in the case of an item with digital elements is the requirement to deliver updates as defined in the contract [Sec. 616 h) CC-amnd.]. The buyer must also be notified of updates, including security updates, and the updates that are necessary to maintain compliance must be also supplied (Sec. 617 para. 3 CC-amnd.). 20

The question is how long the sold item must be in compliance. If it is a one-time delivery of a digital performance, it is the period of time during which the buyer can reasonably expect that the sold item will comply with the agreed (subjective) and general (objective) requirements, taking into account the type and purpose of the item and the digital elements, the nature and circumstances of the conclusion of the contract. However, if the digital performance is supplied continuously over an agreed period of time, the sold goods must comply for the agreed period of time, but at least two years after the delivery of the item with the digital elements. 21

A similar concept applies to the legal regulation of digital performance contracts, where the compliance of the digital performance is defined in the same way with respect to agreed (subjective) requirements (Sec. 852e CC-amnd.), e.g. compatibility requirements or requirements for delivery with assistance services, and general (objective) requirements (Sec. 852f CC-amnd.), which is, for example, that the digital performance corresponds to a trial version or a demonstration of the digital performance. A general requirement that the digital performance must also meet is that 22

- it is delivered in a quantity and
- it has the characteristics and performance, including functionality, compatibility, accessibility, continuity and security,

that are normal for digital performances of the same kind and that the consumer can reasonably expect, taking into account

- the nature of the digital performance and
- any public statement made by or on behalf of the trader or any other person in the supply chain, in particular in the promotion of or on the labelling of the digital performance.

23   Again, the period at which a digital performance must comply depends on whether it is delivered as a one-time, as a set of individual performances or on a continuous basis. In the first two cases, it is the period of time during which the consumer can reasonably expect the digital performance to comply with the compliance requirements, taking into account the type and purpose of the digital performance and the nature and circumstances of the conclusion of the contract (Sec. 852f para. 5 CC-amnd.). However, if the digital performance under the contract is to be delivered continuously for an agreed period of time, it must comply during the agreed period (Sec. 852f para 6 CC-amnd.).

I. Information Obligation

24   One of the fundamental rights of the consumer is his right to information within the scope and under the conditions of the Consumer Protection Act and other special regulations [Sec. 3 para. 1 b) Consumer Protection Act]. The proposed legislation then specifies the general information obligations of the trader (Sec. 5 Consumer Protection Act) as well as other aspects. The trader is obliged to communicate to the consumer in a clear and comprehensible manner the information referred to in the (proposed) Consumer Protection Act before the conclusion of the contract or, if the contract is concluded on the basis of an order from the consumer, before the consumer sends the order, unless a special regulation provides otherwise or if the information is not obvious in view of the circumstances of the conclusion of the contract or the nature of the product.

25   In relation to the performance, which is an item (including goods with digital elements), the seller must, *inter alia*, ensure that the buyer is notified of updates, including security updates, and that the buyer is supplied with the updates that are necessary to maintain the compliance of the sold item (Sec. 617 para. 3 CC-amnd.).

26   In relation to the digital performance, a similar information obligation is then laid down in Section 852f CC-amnd. The trader shall ensure that the consumer is notified of updates, including security updates, and that the updates necessary to maintain the conformity of the digital performance are delivered to the consumer.

27   This also entails certain exemptions from liability that apply both in the case of the sale of the item and the delivery of the digital performance. According to Section 619 para 5 CC-amnd., the seller is not liable for a defect in a digital item that is caused solely by the failure to install an update pursuant to Section 617 para. 3 if the buyer has not installed the update within a reasonable time after it has been delivered and

(a) the seller has notified the buyer of the availability of the update and the consequences of not installing it; and
(b) the buyer's failure to install or incorrect installation of the update was not caused by deficiencies in the installation instructions provided.

C. Conformity of Goods and Conformity of the Digital Performance

In the case of digital performance contracts (Sec. 852h para 5 CC-amnd.), the trader is not liable for a defect in the digital performance that is caused solely by the failure to install an update pursuant to Section 852f para 4 CC-amnd., if the consumer has not installed the update within a reasonable time after it has been delivered and

(a) the trader has informed the consumer of the availability of the update and the consequences of not installing it; and
(b) the consumer's failure to install or incorrect installation was not caused by deficiencies in the installation instructions provided.

The question then is whether there are also cases where the compliance requirement is excluded. An item (including goods with digital elements) does not have to comply with the general requirements if the seller has expressly informed the buyer at the conclusion of the contract that a certain feature of the item does not comply with the general requirements and the buyer has expressly and specifically agreed to the non-compliance (Sec. 615 para 2 CC-amnd).

Similarly, in the case of the delivery of a digital performance (Sec. 852d para 2 CC-amnd), such performance does not have to comply with the general requirements if the trader has expressly informed the consumer at the conclusion of the contract that a certain characteristic of the digital performance does not comply with the general requirements and the consumer has expressly and specifically agreed to the non-compliance.

II. Service Life and Spare Parts

The Slovak legislation in force does not specifically regulate the total life in use of sold items (service life). However, this aspect follows from other provisions of the Civil Code, e.g. from the general provision that if the quality is not expressly agreed, the debtor is obliged to perform a certain quantity of items determined in the average medium quality (Sec. 496 para. 2 CC). For consumer contracts, the agreement on the characteristics, purpose and quality is, in turn, deemed to be a performance in which the consumer has expressed an interest and which corresponds to the description given by the supplier, manufacturer or agent in any publicly available form (Sec. 496 para 1 CC). The criteria for the quality and quantity of the sold items are, in turn, laid down in Section 616 *et seq.* CC. The basic rule is that the sold item must be of the quality, quantity, measure or weight required or laid down by law and it must be free from defects, in particular it must comply with the binding technical standards.

In the proposed legislation, durability is included among the general requirements of the sold item within the meaning of Section 617 para 1 d) CC-amnd. This is a broader provision, which provides that a sold item complies with the general requirements if it is supplied in quantity, quality and with characteristics including functionality, compatibility, safety and the ability to retain its functionality and performance (durability) in normal use, that are normal for an item of the same kind and that the buyer can reasonably expect, having regard to the nature of the sold item and to any public statement made by or on behalf of the seller or any other person in the supply chain, including the manufacturer,[8] in particular in advertising the item or on its labelling.

---

[8] The manufacturer shall be deemed to be the producer of the item, the importer of the item on the market of the European Union from a third country or any other person who identifies himself as the manufacturer by affixing his name, trademark or other distinctive sign to the item.

32 The durability aspect shall also be taken into account in the context of a consumer guarantee. The current legislation is based on the basic concept that the law, its implementing regulation, an agreement between the parties or a unilateral declaration by the grantor may determine in which cases liability for defects occurring up to a specified or agreed period after performance (Sec. 502 CC) is to be assumed. In addition, the parties to the contractual relationship may also agree on liability for defects occurring within a specified or agreed period of time after performance or on liability according to stricter principles than those laid down by law. The obligee shall issue a written confirmation of such an agreement to the beneficiary (i. e. warranty).

33 The proposed legislation follows this concept with a provision called Consumer Guarantee (Sec. 626 CC-amnd.). According to this provision, the manufacturer or the seller (warranty provider) may undertake to refund the purchase price to the buyer, to replace or repair the sold item or to ensure its maintenance even beyond the scope of the rights arising from liability for defects. In such a case, the buyer shall have the right to claim from the warranty provider *'the performance of the consumer warranty under the terms and conditions set out in the warranty certificate or in the related advertising'*. According to paragraph 2 of this provision, if the manufacturer offers a consumer guarantee for the lifetime of the item, the buyer has rights against the manufacturer to have the defect rectified during the duration of the consumer guarantee, unless the manufacturer has provided more favourable terms in the consumer guarantee for the lifetime.

34 With regard to the durability of products, there is no specific legislation in Slovakia addressing the durability of products, but some references to this aspect can be identified in legal regulation. For example, under Government Regulation No. 404/2007 Coll. on general product safety, various aspects may be considered to determine whether a product is safe, including, but not limited to, the characteristics of the product, its composition and its durability. The obligation of the manufacturer and importer to inform the consumer in order to ensure the optimum durability of the product arises from Act No. 529/2010 Coll. on the environmental design and use of products (Ecodesign Act). Further regulation can be found, for example, in Act No. 79/2015 Coll. on waste or Act No. 55/2018 on the provision of information on technical regulation and on obstacles to the free movement of goods, which regulates the requirements that must be complied with when making a product available on the market or when using the product.

35 The Civil Code contains only a general provision on liability for defects, according to which, if the defect cannot be rectified and if the item cannot be used in the agreed manner or properly because of it, the purchaser is entitled to claim cancellation of the contract. Otherwise, the purchaser may claim either a reasonable discount on the price, replacement, or repair or completion of what is missing. The assignee shall have the rights referred to in this provision if the Civil Code for the particular contract or the agreement of the parties to the contract does not provide otherwise. The Civil Code in force contains a special regulation of claims arising from defective performance, *inter alia*, in the case of consumer sales contracts pursuant to Sections 622 to 624. These provisions of the Civil Code on liability claims for defects are special provisions in relation to Section 507 para. 1 Civil Code, which take precedence over the general provision of Section 507 para. 1 Civil Code.[9]

36 However, the minimum availability of spare parts and the time for which spare parts are available are partly regulated in the Ecodesign Act, which is explained in more detail in the following section.

---

[9] Czirfusz, in Števček et al., *'Občiansky zákonník II. § 451 – 880. Komentár'* (2015), § 507, 1744.

III. Compliance with the Ecodesign Directive

One of the topics to be addressed is the coordination of the provisions of the SGD with Directive 2009/125/EC establishing a framework for the setting of ecodesign requirements for energy-related products.[10] The Ecodesign Directive has been transposed in Slovakia into Act No. 529/2010 Coll. on Environmental Design and Use of Products (Ecodesign Act). Before placing a product on the market or putting a product into service, the manufacturer or his authorised representative is obliged to ensure that the conformity of the product's characteristics with the technical requirements is assessed. If the characteristics of the product comply with the technical requirements, he shall issue a declaration of conformity and affix the CE marking to the product.

Pursuant to Section 3 para 5 of this Act, the manufacturer or his authorised representative and the importer are obliged to provide information on the handling, use or recycling of the product in the national language or another official language of the European Union. Where possible, that information shall be provided directly on the product, otherwise it shall be attached to the product so that the consumer can compare the information on the product. This information includes, according to Section 3 para 6 c) of the Ecodesign Act, information for the consumer on how to install, use and maintain the product in order to minimise its impact on the environment and to ensure its *'optimum durability'*, as well as on how to return the product when it is no longer in use and, where appropriate, *'information on the period of time for which spare parts are available and the possibility of upgrading the product'*.

The intersection between the ecodesign regulation and consumer protection is also evident in the context of the activities of the Slovak Trade Inspection Authority, which carries out market control. The Slovak Trade Inspection Authority verifies compliance with consumer protection obligations and respect for consumer rights. It also verifies, among other things, compliance with obligations in making products available on the market and in providing services and compliance with requirements for products and services under specific regulations. It is at this point that the draft of the new Consumer Protection Act refers (in the form of a footnote) to special regulations, among which the legislator also includes the Ecodesign Act.

Article 20 of the Ecodesign Directive requires Member States to lay down rules for infringements of national provisions adopted pursuant to the Directive and to take all measures necessary to ensure their implementation. The penalties provided for must be effective, proportionate and dissuasive, taking into account the extent of non-compliance and the number of non-compliant products placed on the Community market. The Ecodesign Act provides that a natural person – entrepreneur or a legal person shall be guilty of an administrative offence if

- affixes to a product a marking which, by its meaning or form, misleads consumers and is liable to cause confusion with the CE marking,
- fails to provide information pursuant to Section 3 para. 5 of the Ecodesign Act (i.e. including the period of availability of spare parts and the possibility of updating the product),
- fails to carry out the conformity assessment procedure.

The information referred to in Section 3 para. 5 of the Ecodesign Act includes, *inter alia*, information for the consumer:

---

[10] Directive 2009/125/EC of the European Parliament and of the Council of 21 October 2009 establishing a framework for the setting of ecodesign requirements for energy-related products. OJ L 285/10.

- on the important environmental aspects and characteristics of the product in such a way that the consumer can compare the product with other products,
- how to install, use and maintain the product in order to minimise its environmental impact and to ensure its optimum lifetime, how to return the product after use and, *if appropriate, information on the period of time for which spare parts are available* and the possibility of upgrading the product,
- how to dispose of the product safely if it is to be discarded as waste; and
- the environmental profile of the product and the benefits of eco-design, if required by technical requirements.

It follows from the above that the obligation to inform the consumer of the time for which spare parts are available is rather relativized in the Ecodesign Act by the addition of *'if appropriate'*. For an administrative offence, the supervisory authority (the Slovak Trade Inspection Authority in accordance with the Act No. 128/2002 Coll.) shall impose a fine of between EUR 200 and EUR 200 000.

IV. Incorrect Installation of Digital Content or Digital Service

42   The proposed legislation specifically addresses issues related to the incorrect installation of digital content or digital services. In the case of a consumer sale contract, the Section 619 of the applicable Civil Code governs liability for defects in the sold goods. However, it is proposed to refine and supplement this regulation to specifically address cases of incorrect installation.

43   The basis of the proposed legislation is that the seller is liable for any defect in the sold goods at the time of delivery which becomes apparent within two years of delivery (Sec. 619 para. 1 CC-amnd.). If the object of the purchase is an item with digital elements, where the digital content or digital service is to be supplied continuously for an agreed period, the seller is liable for any defect in the digital content or digital service that occurs or manifests itself during the entire agreed period, but at least within two years of the delivery of the item with digital elements (Sec. 619 para. 2 CC-amnd.).

44   The draft of the Civil Code amendment also provides (Sec. 619 para. 4 CC-amnd.) that the seller is liable for a defect caused by incorrect assembly or installation of the item, digital content or digital service if

(a) the assembly or installation was part of the contract of sale and was carried out by or under the responsibility of the seller; or
(b) the assembly or installation which should have been carried out by the buyer was incorrectly carried out by the buyer as a result of deficiencies in the assembly or installation instructions provided to the buyer by the seller or the supplier of the digital content or digital service.

45   On the other hand, the seller is not liable for a defect in a digital good that is caused solely by the failure to install an update if the buyer did not install the update within a reasonable time after it was delivered and

(a) the seller has notified the buyer of the availability of the update and the consequences of not installing it; and
(b) the buyer's failure to install or incorrect installation of the update was not caused by deficiencies in the installation instructions provided.

46   Similar regulation can be found in the draft amendment to the Civil Code in the context of defects in digital performance within digital performance consumer contracts.

C. Conformity of Goods and Conformity of the Digital Performance

According to Section 852g, a digital performance is defective if it does not comply with the agreed (subjective) or general (objective) requirements or if its use is prevented or restricted by the rights of a third party, including intellectual property rights. However, according to Section 852h para. 5 CC-amnd., the trader is not liable for a defect in the digital performance which is caused solely by the failure to install an update pursuant to Section 852f para. 4 if the consumer has not installed the update within a reasonable period of time after its delivery and

(a) the trader has informed the consumer of the availability of the update and the consequences of not installing it; and
(b) the consumer's failure to install or incorrect installation was not caused by deficiencies in the installation instructions provided.

V. Providing of Personal Data as a Counterperformance

The draft amendment to the Civil Code in the context of the definition of a contract with a digital performance reflects the situation when the consumer does not pay a price for digital performance, but provides the trader with his personal data. According to the proposed Section 852a para. 1 of the Civil Code, a digital performance contract is 'any consumer contract under which the trader supplies or undertakes to supply digital content or a digital service (digital performance) and the consumer pays or undertakes to pay the price, including the digitally expressed value, or provides or undertakes to provide the trader with his personal data, even if the digital performance is developed according to the consumer's specifications'. It follows that even in the cases, where the consumer provides only his personal data as a counter value for the digital performance delivered, it is a digital performance consumer contract and the consumer thus enjoys a privileged position guaranteed by the Civil Code and by the related consumer protection.

Thus, the Slovak Republic intends to become one of the countries with special legislation on digital performance consumer contracts where the counterperformance is personal data. No specific rules are introduced regarding the formation, duration or validity of such contracts, however defects liability claims are regulated differently, as discussed in more detail below.

It should also be mentioned that a digital performance contract is not to be considered such a contract under which the trader supplies or undertakes to supply a digital performance and the consumer provides or undertakes to provide only personal data which the trader processes solely for the purpose of providing the digital performance or fulfilling a legal obligation.

According to a proposed Section 852a para. 3 f) of the Civil Code, the special provisions on consumer contracts with digital performance are also not to apply to a contract whose subject matter is software offered by the trader 'free of charge' under 'free of charge' open source licence, if the trader processes the consumer's personal data solely for the purpose of enhancing the security, compatibility or interoperability of that software. We will briefly discuss this provision, as we do not believe that its wording is appropriate. The starting point is recital 32 DCD, which describes the importance of free and open source software, which contributes to research and innovation in the marketplace. Therefore, barriers should not be created to hinder this market development, provided that such software is 'not supplied in exchange for a price and that the consumer's personal data are exclusively used for improving the security, compatibility or interoperability of the software'. Article 3(5)(f) DCD provides that the Directive does not apply to contracts relating to *'software offered by the trader under a free and open-source licence, where the consumer does not pay a price'*.

51 The duplication of the word 'free of charge' in the Slovak draft amendment to the Civil Code is misleading and does not reflect the exact wording of the Directive. Although the use of the software is to be free of charge, the licence itself is either an open source licence or a free licence. In Slovakia, the term 'public licence', which is regulated in Section 76 of the Copyright Act (Act No. 185/2015 Coll.), has been used for these cases. However, it is also possible to find statutory references to open source computer programs [e.g. Sec. 20 para 7 b) of Act No. 343/2015 Coll. on Public Procurement, Sec. 15 para. 2 d) of Act No. 95/2019 Coll. on Information Technologies in Public Administration]. We would therefore propose to align this provision with the wording of the Directive.[11]

VI. Changing (Modifying) Digital Performance

52 The draft amendment to the Civil Code also regulates the modification of such performance in the context of specific provisions on digital performance consumer contracts (Sec. 852c CC-amnd). In particular, it provides that if the digital performance is to be delivered or made available to the consumer for a certain period of time, the trader may, for justified reasons agreed in the contract, change the digital performance beyond what is necessary to maintain compliance with the requirements for the digital performance. However, this is only possible if:

(a) the consumer does not incur additional costs,
(b) the consumer has been notified of the change in a clear and comprehensible manner; and
(c) where the change adversely affects the consumer's access to (or use of) the digital performance and the adverse effect is not negligible, the consumer has been provided well in advance on a durable medium with information about the characteristics and timing of the change and about the right to withdraw from the contract or to keep the digital performance unchanged.

53 *'If the change adversely affects the consumer's access to or use of the digital performance, the consumer may withdraw from the contract free of charge, unless the adverse effect is negligible. If the consumer does not withdraw from the contract within 30 days from the date of receipt of the notification'* or from the date of the change to the digital performance, whichever is later, the consumer's right to withdraw from the contract is extinguished (Sec. 852c para. 2 CC-amnd.). The consumer does not have such right of withdrawal *'if the trader allows the consumer to keep the digital performance unchanged at no additional cost to the consumer and the failure to make the change will not lead to a defect in the digital performance'* (Sec. 852c para. 3 CC-amnd.).

VII. Rights of Third Parties

54 Both the conformity of goods (including goods with digital elements) and the conformity of a digital performance cover material and legal defects. In fact, limitations resulting from infringement of third party rights, in particular intellectual property rights,

---

[11] Similarly see Limbergová 'Směrnice o digitálním obsahu a jejich implementace v právním řádu ČR' (2022) 25 *Revue pro právo a technologie*, p. 241.

C. Conformity of Goods and Conformity of the Digital Performance

could prevent or restrict the use of the goods or digital performance in accordance with the contract. EU Member States should therefore ensure that the consumer has a remedy for non-compliance in such cases, unless national law provides for the nullity or rescission of the contract in such cases. This follows from recital 35 SGD and recital 54 DCD, as well as Articles 9 SGD and 10 DCD.

55 In the proposed amendment to the Civil Code, the European regulation is reflected in Section 618 of the Civil Code, which, in the context of a consumer sale contract, regulates defects in the sold goods. According to this provision, a sold item is defective if it does not comply with the agreed (subjective) or general (objective) requirements for the sold item or if its use is prevented or restricted by the rights of a third party, including intellectual property rights. Similarly, it is proposed to transpose Article 10 DCD into the provision of Sec. 852g of the CC-amnd. concerning digital performance consumer contracts and liability for defects in such performance. According to this provision, a digital performance is defective if it does not comply with the agreed (subjective) or general (objective) requirements or if its use is prevented or restricted by the rights of a third party, including intellectual property rights. The consumer has rights of liability for defects which he can exercise based on this regulation. Section 852j of the proposed amendment to the Slovak Civil Code provides that if the trader is liable for a defect in the digital performance, the consumer has the right to have the defect rectified (Sec. 852k CC-amnd.), to receive a reasonable price reduction (Sec. 852l CC-amnd.) or to withdraw from the contract (Sec. 852m CC-amnd.). As also stated in the explanatory memorandum to the proposed amendment, the removal of the defect is often the least invasive solution for both the trader and the consumer. Once a defect has been pointed out, the consumer has the right to have the defect in the digital performance rectified free of charge and without this rectification causing him serious inconvenience. Where it is not possible to remedy the defect or where such remedy would involve disproportionate costs, the provision gives the trader the right to refuse to remedy such defect.

56 The price reduction already constitutes a higher step in relation to the rectification of the defect. The price reduction must be proportionate and, in the case of continuous supply, the consumer is only entitled to a price reduction for the time during which the digital performance did not meet the requirements. For example, if a digital performance on a streaming platform is provided on a monthly fee basis and the digital performance was not available for a certain number of hours or days, the consumer should be entitled to a price reduction in the form of an aliquot part of the monthly fee corresponding to the time during which the defect persisted. However, short-term interruptions should basically not be considered as defects. According to recital 51 DCD, short-term interruptions of the supply of digital content or a digital service should be treated as instances of lack of conformity where those interruptions are more than negligible or recur.

57 Withdrawal from the contract should be seen as the *ultima ratio* solution among the three options. The extreme nature of this option is taken into account and, in the case of a digital performance for which the consumer has paid the price, the consumer is given the option to withdraw only if the defect is not negligible.

58 The answer to the question whether Slovakia prioritises repair over replacement is therefore in the affirmative. It is also partly related to the sustainability of the environment, however, mainly it follows from the logic of the matter and it is also linked to the existing legislation.

VIII. Resale Right

59 Apart from the regulation on defects in goods and digital performance described above, neither the proposed Consumer Protection Act nor the related amendment to the Civil Code regulate other intellectual property law issues. However, these are often related to the sale of goods and the delivery of a digital performance. One of the fundamental topics of intellectual property law is the so-called resale right. The issue is that if the holder of the intellectual property right has the exclusive right to decide on every use of the intellectual property object (including sale of goods), whether his consent must be obtained when selling intellectual property objects on secondary markets (e.g. selling books in an antique shop, donating CDs, selling perfumes from one EU country to another, etc.). We will then be particularly interested in how a secondary sale of goods with digital elements (e.g. the sale of a car in which software is installed) or the sale of a digital performance (e.g. the sale of a digital copy of a computer program) is carried out.

60 These situations are governed by the so-called exhaustion principle and its purpose is to protect the free movement of goods. For this reason, specific cases where the right holder does not have the exclusive right to decide on the dissemination or circulation of intellectual property objects on the market are regulated both in copyright and industrial property legal regulation. The right of the rightholder to decide on the distribution of his subject-matter on the market in the EU and within the EEA Contracting States exhausts, while the exhaustion is triggered by the first legitimate transfer of ownership or the first placing of products on that market. Authorised transfer/placement means disposal with the consent of the rightholder. Thereafter, any subsequent transfer/placement of the product on the market shall take place without the consent of the rightholder. Exhaustion of rights at EU level does not apply in the case of trade in counterfeit products or products marketed outside the European Economic Area (Article 6 TRIPS).

61 The question is whether the exhaustion principle applies also to digital copies of the work. The CJEU has commented on this issue in its landmark decision in Case C-128/11 *UsedSoft*,[12] but only in relation to computer programs. It ruled that the distribution right in a computer program is exhausted under certain conditions even if the copyright holder has authorised the downloading of a copy from the Internet onto a data carrier.

62 In Case C-263/18 *Tom Kabinet*,[13] the CJEU in turn addressed the application of the principle of exhaustion of rights to e-books (digital copies of books) and their use that takes place by online downloading. The gist of the judgment was that, when e-books are resent over the Internet with the help of a secondary market organiser, that organiser is actually making the copies in question available to the public and thus infringing copyright. The court stated that the supply of e-books for permanent use online by downloading does not fall under the right of distribution (distribution right), but under the right of public transmission. Therefore, the principle of exhaustion cannot apply in this case (only the distribution right is exhausted, all other rights remain).

63 The Slovak legislation regulates the principle of exhaustion of rights in individual intellectual property laws. In view of the CJEU's decision in *UsedSoft*, the Copyright Act uses a slightly different wording in relation to computer programs compared to other copyright works. However, the resale of digital reproductions other than computer programs without the consent of the rightholder is not possible.[14]

---

[12] CJEU, Case C-128/11, 3.7.2012, *UsedSoft GmbH v Oracle International Corp.*, ECLI:EU:C:2012:407.

[13] CJEU, Case C-263/18, 19.12.2019, *Nederlands Uitgeversverbond and Groep Algemene Uitgevers v Tom Kabinet Internet BV and Others*, ECLI:EU:C:2019:1111.

[14] Adamová and Hazucha, 'Autorský zákon. Komentár' (2018) 172.

D. Liability of the Seller (trader)

I. Single Performance, Set of Single Performances and Continuous Performance over a Period of Time

In determining the trader's liability, the rules may differ depending on whether the transaction is a single transaction, a set of single transactions or a continuous transaction. In a consumer sale contract, the basic rule is that the seller is liable for any defect in the sold goods at the time of delivery and which is apparent within two years of delivery (Sec. 619 para. 1 CC-amnd.).

If the object of the purchase is an item with digital elements, where the digital content or digital service is to be supplied *continuously* for an agreed period, the seller is liable for any defect in the digital content or digital service that occurs or manifests itself during the entire agreed period, but at least within two years of the delivery of the goods with digital elements.

In the case of a digital performance consumer contract, a distinction is also made as to whether it is a contract for a single performance, a contract for a single repeated performance or a contract for the continuous providing of digital performance, whether concluded for a fixed or indefinite period (see rec. 56 DCD).

Pursuant to Section 852h draft amendment to the Slovak Civil Code dealing with digital performance consumer contracts, the trader is liable for any defect that the digital performance has at the time of its delivery and that becomes apparent within two years of its delivery if it is a digital performance that is delivered in a *single* delivery or as a *set of individual* performances (para. 1). However, where the digital performance is supplied *continuously* over an agreed period, the trader is liable for any defect in the digital performance that manifests itself during that agreed period (para. 2).

The draft amendment to the Civil Code also reflects European legislation on the burden of proof (rec. 59 DCD). The trader bears the burden of proving that the digital performance was delivered in compliance with the general (objective) and agreed (subjective) requirements (Sec. 852i CC-amnd.). As far as the burden of proof is concerned, it then applies that if, within one year after the delivery of a digital performance that is delivered as a *single* delivery or as a *set of individual* performances, a defect becomes apparent, the trader bears the burden of proving that the performance did not have such a defect at the time of delivery. If the digital performance is delivered *continuously* over the agreed period, the trader bears the burden of proving that the digital performance is free from defects over the agreed period.

The draft amendment to the Slovak Civil Code then also provides that the trader does not bear the burden of proof if he proves that the consumer's digital environment is incompatible with the technical requirements of the digital performance, if the trader made them known to the consumer in a clear and comprehensible manner prior to the conclusion of the contract (Sec. 852i para. 4 CC-amnd.).

Pursuant to Section 852i para. 5 of the draft amendment to the Civil Code, the consumer shall provide the trader with the reasonable assistance necessary to establish whether the reason for the defect in the digital performance is in the consumer's digital environment. The consumer's obligatory cooperation is limited to the technically available means which are least burdensome for the consumer. If the trader informs the consumer in a clear and comprehensible manner of the obligation to provide cooperation before the conclusion of the contract and the consumer fails to provide cooperation, the consumer must prove that the digital performance was defective at the time of delivery, if the digital performance is a digital performance that is delivered in a single delivery or as a set of individual deliveries, or within the agreed period, if the digital performance is a digital performance that is delivered continuously over an agreed period, in order to enforce the rights of liability for defects.

II. Obstacles

71   The draft amendment to the Civil Code does not specifically address the consequences of a failure to deliver or to perform with respect to specific obstacles, such as impossibility of performance or force majeure. In this respect, same as at present, the general legislation will be relied upon. The concept of force majeure is not currently regulated in the Slovak legal order, but the case law shows that it is an unusual event which often does not occur and cannot be foreseen or averted, even with the greatest care of any contracting party. In some cases, force majeure may cause an obligation to be extinguished by impossibility of performance. However, performance is not impossible if it can be carried out even under difficult conditions, at greater expense or after an agreed time (Sec. 575 para. 2 CC).

72   The only case envisaged in the draft amendment to the Slovak Civil Code is the regulation of general (objective) conditions in relation to a digital service or digital performance. According to the proposed Section 852f para 1 d), a digital performance complies with the general conditions if it is supplied in the quantity and has the characteristics and performance, including functionality, compatibility, accessibility, continuity and security, which are normal for digital performances of the same kind and which the consumer can reasonably expect in view of the nature of the digital performance and taking into account any public statement made by or on behalf of the trader or other person in the supply chain, in particular in the promotion of the digital performance or on its labelling. However, according to Section 852f para. 2, the trader is not bound by such a statement,

- if he was not and could not reasonably have been aware of the public statement,
- by the time the contract is concluded, the public statement has been corrected in the same or comparable manner as it was made, or
- where the consumer's decision to conclude the contract could not have been influenced by the public statement.

According to the draft amendment to the Civil Code, the burden of proof of these facts is to be borne by the seller.

III. Premature Termination of a Number-independent Interpersonal Communication Service

73   A digital performance contract is any consumer contract under which a trader supplies or undertakes to supply digital content or a digital service (digital performance) and the consumer pays or undertakes to pay the price (or alternative personal data). Such a contract should therefore include also a contract under which the trader supplies an electronic communication service. The proposed amendment to the Civil Code should exempt these services from regulation, with the exception of the interpersonal communication service independent of numbers [Sec. 852a para. 3 b) CC-amnd.).

74   As regards electronic communication services, their regulation can be found in the Electronic Communications Act (Act No. 452/2021 Coll.). Such a service is a service

(usually provided for remuneration) over networks, which includes an internet access service, an interpersonal communication service or services consisting (wholly or mainly) of the transmission of signals, such as transmission services used for the provision of machine-to-machine (M2M) communication services and for radio and television broadcasting.

According to Section 2 para. 19 of this Act, an interpersonal communication service is *'a service, usually provided for remuneration, which enables the direct interpersonal and interactive exchange of information over networks between a finite number of persons, whereby the persons initiating or participating in the communication determine the recipient of the communication; this service does not include services which enable interpersonal and interactive communication only as an ancillary component inseparably linked to another service'*. The term interpersonal communication service thus includes services such as traditional calls between two individuals as well as all types of email, messaging or group chat services. Such a service refers only to communications between a certain, i.e. not potentially unlimited, number of natural persons, which is defined by the sender of the communication. Communications involving legal persons should be covered by the definition where natural persons are acting on behalf of legal persons or are involved on at least one side of the communication. Interactive communication means that the service allows the recipient of the information to respond. Services that do not fulfil these conditions, such as linear broadcasting, video-on-demand, websites, social networks, blogs or machine-to-machine (M2M) communication, should not be considered as interpersonal communication services.

In the context of the digital contract law, it is relevant that a distinction is made between interpersonal communication service

– based on numbers[15] and
– number-independent.

In terms of the scope of the DCD, this is significant in that the Directive does not apply to contracts relating to electronic communications services as defined in the European Electronic Communications Code,[16] with the exception of number-independent interpersonal communications services. Thus, if it concerns such interpersonal communication services which are not number-dependent, the DCD will already apply. In general, otherwise, number-independent interpersonal communications services should only be subject to obligations where the public interest requires that specific regulatory obligations apply to all types of interpersonal communications services, regardless of whether numbers are used to provide them.[17]

The Electronic Communications Act currently regulates rights and obligations in the provision of services, including the provision of a publicly available interpersonal communications service. One of the regulated areas is the duration of the service contract and its termination. According to Section 87 para. 1 of this Act, if a consumer undertakes to use an undertaking's publicly available service for a certain minimum period (commitment period), the commitment period may not exceed 24 months when the service contract is first concluded. However, this restriction does not apply to contracts for providing of number-independent interpersonal communication services

---

[15] I.e. a service using numbers from a national or international numbering plan that is associated with publicly allocated numbering resources.

[16] Directive (EU) 2018/1972 of the European Parliament and of the Council of 11 December 2018 establishing the European Electronic Communications Code. OJ L 321/36.

[17] Dôvodová správa k návrhu zákona o elektronických komunikáciách. [online] https://www.nrsr.sk/web/Dynamic/DocumentPreview.aspx?DocID=499157

or to transmission services used for providing the machine-to-machine (M2M) communication services.

78 In general, then applies that a subscriber has the right to terminate a service contract concluded for an indefinite period of time at any time for any reason or for no reason at all (Sec. 87 para. 4 Electronic Communications Act).

79 According to Section 87 para. 9 Electronic Communications Act, the subscriber also has the right, in the event of a change in the service contract by the undertaking, to withdraw from the service contract within one month of the date of notification of the change in the service contract to the subscriber, without penalty and without incurring any additional costs; this does not apply if the changes to the service contract

(a) are solely for the benefit of the subscriber,
(b) are of a purely administrative nature,
(c) do not adversely affect the subscriber; or
(d) arise from a specific regulation.

Thus, the transposition of the DCD is intended to create a situation where, in addition to the provisions of the Electronic Communications Act, the provisions on digital performance contracts (Sec. 852b – 852n CC-amnd.) will apply to contracts for providing the number-independent interpersonal communications service.

IV. Service Packages and the Impact of the European Electronic Communications Code on Slovak Civil Law

80 Article 107 of the European Electronic Communications Code regulates bundled offers, i. e. situations where either a bundle of services or a joint bundle of services and terminal equipment offered to a consumer includes at least an internet access service or a publicly available interpersonal communications service based on numbering. Pursuant to paragraph 2 of this Article, where a consumer has the right under Union law or national law in accordance with Union law to terminate any element of a bundle of services or of a bundle of services and terminal equipment before the end of the agreed contractual period as a result of a lack of compliance or non-delivery of the service, Member States shall provide that the consumer has the right to terminate the contract in respect of all elements of the bundle.

81 This provision has been reflected in the Electronic Communications Act (Act No. 452/2021 Coll.). Pursuant to Sec. 90 para. 1 of this Act, where a package of services or a package of services and terminal equipment offered to a consumer includes at least an internet access service or a publicly available number-based interpersonal communications service or both and is provided by the same undertaking under a single service contract or under a closely related or connected contract, the nature of which, when concluded, implies that these contracts are interdependent, the selected provisions of this Act shall apply to all elements of the package, including those to which the above provisions do not otherwise apply.

82 Under Section 90 para. 2 Electronic Communications Act, then, if the consumer has the right to terminate the subscription of any element of the package before the expiry of the period for which any of the contracts was concluded, as a result of a breach of contract or failure to deliver the service or goods, he has the right to terminate the contract in respect of all the elements of the package.

83 A specific regulation concerning bundles can also be found in Article 3 para. 6(3) DCD, which provides, *inter alia*, that the effects that the termination of one element of

a combined contract may have on the other elements of the combined contract shall be governed by national law, without prejudice to Article 107 para. 2 of the European Electronic Communications Code. Thus, the above-mentioned legislation is maintained and, in the context of bundled services, the amendment to the Civil Code proposes only to provide that, where another performance in addition to the digital performance is the subject-matter of the same contract, the provisions on consumer contracts with a digital performance apply only to the part of the contract relating to the digital performance. The termination of the contract in respect of a part of the digital performance in a manner other than by performance also causes the termination of the contract in respect of the other performance if it cannot reasonably be expected that the consumer would be interested in being bound by the contract further only in respect of the other performance (Sec. 852a para. 5 CC-amnd.).

E. Remedies for Non-delivery and Non-compliance

The amendment of the Civil Code also affects the area of liability for defects following the change in consumer law and the transposition of the DCD and the SGD. From the point of view of the current legislation in Slovakia, two different regimes apply: 84

(a) regulation of liability for defects according to the Civil Code and,
(b) regulation of complaints procedure according to the Consumer Protection Act.

This situation is not very satisfactory from the point of view of consumer protection due to its opacity and duplication. The basic general provision is the current Section 499 of the Civil Code, according to which *'Whoever transfers a thing to another for consideration is liable for the fact that the thing at the time of performance has the characteristics expressly mentioned or customary, that it can be used according to the nature and purpose of the contract or according to what the parties have agreed, and that the thing is free from legal defects'*. According to Section 502 of the Civil Code *'The parties may also agree on liability for defects that occur within a specified or agreed period of time after performance or liability according to stricter principles than those provided for by law. The obligee shall issue a written confirmation (warranty) to the person entitled to such an agreement.'* The special provisions on the sale of goods in the store in the context of consumer sales contracts then also apply to liability for defects in the sold goods (Sec. 619 CC-amnd.). In addition, the Consumer Protection Act provides for a special procedure for claiming liability for defects in a product or service, which it refers to as a complaint (Sec. 18 Consumer Protection Act). 85

In order to simplify, consolidate and align the regulation of liability for defects in goods, digital services and digital content with EU law, it is proposed that only the Civil Code as amended should be retained. In this context, the major change concerns the buyer's right to assert rights under liability for defects. According to Section 599 of the applicable Civil Code, in the case of a contract of sale, the buyer must claim defects from the seller without undue delay. According to the proposed amendment to the Civil Code, it is no longer required that the defect be pointed out without delay, but it is sufficient if the buyer points out the defect to the seller within 24 months of taking delivery of the goods. Such a change may be perceived rather negatively by traders, as it further favours the position of the consumer in asserting liability claims for defects. In the case of a consumer sale contract under the proposed Section 621 para. 3 of the draft amendment to the Civil Code, the buyer may only assert liability rights if he/she 86 has raised (pointed out) a defect within two months of the expiry of the period during which the seller is liable for defects in the sold goods.

87 The rights of the buyer in case of defects in the goods or of the consumer in case of defects in the digital performance are set out in Section 621 and Section 852j of the draft amendment to the Civil Code. In particular

- the right to remedy the defect (Sec. 623 and 852k CC-amnd.),
- the right to an appropriate price reduction (Sec. 624 and 852l CC-amnd.), or
- the right to withdraw from the contract (Sec. 624 and 852m CC-amnd.).

The same rights are also enshrined in applicable law in relation to consumer sales contracts. In addition to these primary claims, which seek to remedy the defective performance, there are also secondary claims which seek to satisfy the related performances, namely the right to compensation for the necessary costs incurred in connection with the exercise of the right of liability for defects, the right to compensation for non-pecuniary damage (the so-called right to adequate financial compensation) and the right to compensation for damages caused by the defective performance.[18]

I. Right to Refuse to Pay the Price

88 Recital 15 DCD provides that *'Member States should also remain free, for example, to regulate the rights of parties to withhold the performance of their obligations or part thereof until the other party performs its obligations. For example, Member States should be free to regulate whether a consumer, in cases of a lack of conformity, is to be entitled to withhold payment of the price or part thereof until the trader has brought the digital content or digital service into conformity, or whether the trader is to be entitled to retain any reimbursement due to the consumer upon termination of the contract until the consumer complies with the obligation provided for in this Directive to return the tangible medium to the trader'.* The proposed legislation reflects this requirement. Under the proposed Section 852j para. 2 of the draft amendment to the Civil Code, *'the consumer may refuse to pay the price or any part thereof until the trader has fulfilled his obligations under the liability for defects. The consumer shall pay the price within a reasonable time after the trader has fulfilled his obligations.'* A similar regulation in relation to the rights of liability for defects in the sold goods can be found also in the proposed Section 621 para. 3 of the draft amendment to the Civil Code.

II. Personal Data as a Consideration

89 The applicable Slovak legislation has not yet provided for a specific regulation of contracts in which only data would be the consideration. However, as mentioned above, the amendment to the Civil Code should introduce a new Section 852a, which regulates also this type of contract with digital performance. This rule provides that a digital performance contract is also a consumer contract under which the trader supplies or undertakes to supply digital content or a digital service (digital performance) and the consumer provides or undertakes to provide the trader with his personal data.

90 The DCD strengthens the position of the consumer also with regard to those cases where the digital performance is not provided to the consumer in exchange for a price, but where the counterperformance is personal data. It states that where digital content

---

[18] Jurčová, *'Spotrebiteľské právo'* (2021), 207.

or a digital service is supplied in exchange for a price, the consumer should only be entitled to terminate the contract if the non-compliance is not negligible. However, if the digital content or digital service is not delivered in exchange for a price but the consumer provides personal data, the consumer should be entitled to terminate the contract even where the non-compliance is negligible, because the remedy of a price discount is not available to the consumer.

The question then is to what extent the consumer's rights differ in the case of liability for defects in such digital performance. Generally, if the trader is liable for a defect in a digital performance, the consumer has a right against the trader to have the defect rectified, to receive a reasonable price reduction or to withdraw from the contract. However, in the case of a digital performance for which the consumer has not provided consideration in the form of payment of the price, but in the form of personal data, a price discount is not practically possible. In such a case, the consumer only has the right to have the defects rectified or to withdraw from the contract on the grounds set out in Section 852l para 1, as if it were a price discount. 91

In general, where a digital performance is supplied for consideration consisting of payment of the purchase price, the consumer may only withdraw from the contract if the defect is not negligible. The negligibility of the defect is therefore not a criterion for the exercise of the right of withdrawal where the counterperformance is personal data. The consumer may withdraw from such a contract even in the case of completely negligible defects. 92

III. Pointing out a Defect

A number of comments made in the context of the draft new Consumer Protection Act and the related amendment to the Civil Code concerned the fact that in the case of claims arising from the provision of defective digital content or services, it will not be a condition for their application that the defect be reproached to the supplier. This is therefore a fundamental change from the system of liability for defects applicable in Slovakia. Today, the situation is such that a defect must always be pointed out. This is a general rule enshrined in the Civil Code (Sec 504 and 505 CC). 93

Under the proposed new legislation, this would not apply to a consumer contract for digital performance. This change is necessitated by the requirement of full transposition of the DCD. 94

On the contrary, in relation to a consumer sale contract, it should apply that the buyer can only exercise the rights of liability for defects if the defect has been pointed out by the buyer no later than two months after the expiry of the period pursuant to Section 619 para. 1 to 3 of the draft amendment to the Civil Code. 95

IV. The Impact of Environmental Sustainability on the Choice of Entitlements

Recital 48 SGD supports sustainable consumption and the greater durability of products. The trend of the environmental sustainability is also followed by the proposed amendment to the Civil Code (Sec. 623 CC-amnd.), which encourages the (environmentally-minded) buyer to choose between remedying the defect by replacing the item or repairing it. The buyer may not choose only a method of removing the defect which is not possible or which would cause the seller disproportionate costs compared to the other method, taking into account all the circumstances, in particular the value the item 96 would have had without the defect, the severity of the defect and whether the other method would cause the buyer significant difficulties. On the other hand, the seller may refuse to remedy the defect if neither repair nor replacement is possible or would involve disproportionate costs having regard to all the circumstances.

F. Commercial Guarantees

97 In the applicable Civil Code, Section 502 para 2 provides that the parties may agree on liability for defects occurring within a specified or agreed period of time after performance or liability according to stricter criteria than those provided for by law. The obliged person shall issue a written confirmation of such an agreement to the authorised person (warranty certificate). This is a general provision concerning liability for defects. In relation to consumer sales contracts, the Civil Code then provides for a special regime concerning liability for defects in goods subject to a guarantee period (Sec. 626 CC).

98 Commercial warranties are also regulated in Article 17 SGD. Member States may lay down rules on other aspects of commercial warranties not covered by this Article, including rules on the language or languages in which the warranty is to be provided to the consumer. This Article is to be transposed into Section 626 of the draft amendment to the Civil Code entitled *Consumer Guarantee*. According to paragraph 1 of this provision, the manufacturer or the seller (warranty provider) may undertake to refund the purchase price to the buyer, to replace or repair the sold goods or to ensure its maintenance beyond the scope of the rights arising from liability for defects (consumer warranty). In such a case, the buyer has the right to demand from the warranty provider the performance of the consumer warranty under the terms and conditions stated in the warranty certificate or in the related advertising.

99 According to Section 496 para. 1 of the applicable Civil Code, *'an agreement on the characteristics, purpose and quality in consumer contracts shall be deemed to be a performance in which the consumer has expressed an interest and which coincides with the description given by the supplier, manufacturer or his representative in any publicly accessible form, in particular advertising, promotion and labelling of the goods'*. As Jurčová also states, not only by agreement of the parties, but also by unilateral statement, or even by a statement in an advertisement, a seller may provide a guarantee exceeding the scope of the guarantee provided for in the Civil Code. The proposed legislation then further specifies that if the terms of the consumer guarantee in the related advertisement are more favourable to the buyer than the terms under the guarantee letter, the terms stated in the advertisement shall apply. This does not apply if, before concluding the contract with the buyer, the warranty provider has aligned the related advertisement with the warranty certificate in the same or similar way as the advertisement was made.

100 The language of the guarantee letter is also specifically addressed. Pursuant to Section 626 para. 3 of the draft amendment to the Civil Code, the warranty provider shall provide the purchaser with a warranty certificate in a durable medium in the national language or, with the consumer's consent, in another language at the latest at the time of delivery. The warranty provider shall indicate in the warranty certificate in a clear and comprehensible manner the particulars pursuant to Section 502 para. 3 and the instruction that the buyer has rights against the seller under liability for defects pursuant to Section 621, which are not affected by the consumer warranty.

G. Time Limits

Article 11 para. 1 DCD provides that the trader shall be liable for any failure to deliver digital content or a digital service in accordance with Article 5. According to the proposal of the new Slovak regulation (Sec. 852h para. 1 and 2 CC-amnd.) the trader should be liable for any defect in the digital performance which is present at the time of delivery and which becomes apparent within two years of delivery, if the digital performance is delivered in a *single* performance or as a *set of individual performances*. If the digital performance is delivered *continuously* over an agreed period, the trader should be liable for any defect in the digital performance that manifests itself during that agreed period.

As regards the sale of goods, the Article 10 SGD should be transposed into Section 619 para. 2 of the draft amendment to the Civil Code so that if the object of the purchase is a digital item for which the digital content or digital service is to be supplied continuously during the agreed period, the seller is liable for any defect in the digital content or digital service that occurs or manifests itself during the entire agreed period, but at least for a period of two years from the delivery of the digital item.

With regard to liability for defects (Sec. 508 CC-amnd.), such a claim must be brought before the court within the general limitation period, which starts to run from the date on which the purchaser complained of the defect to the seller. However, it is proposed that if the Civil Code provides that the transferee may assert rights under liability for defects even without having pointed out the defect, the limitation period shall start to run from the date of performance. However, if the performance is continuous, the limitation period runs from the date of the manifestation of the defect and does not expire until two months after the performance has ceased.

H. Right to Compensation

Article 18 SGD establishes a right of redress, which is that if the seller is liable to the consumer for a non-conformity caused by an act or omission of a person upstream in the chain of transactions, including a failure to provide updates for goods with digital elements, the seller has the right to pursue a claim for redress against the responsible person or persons in the chain of transactions. The person against whom the seller may seek remedies, as well as the appropriate measures and the conditions for enforcement, shall be determined by national law.

The article in question should be transposed into Section 625 of the draft amendment to the Civil Code, entitled *'Seller's compensation for costs'*. According to this provision, if a defect for which the seller is liable is the result of an act or omission of another person in the supply chain, including a failure to supply updates for an item with digital elements, the seller is entitled to recover from that person the costs reasonably incurred as a result of the defect being brought to his attention and the buyer exercising his right of liability for defects.

Similarly, Article 20 SGD should be transposed into Section 852n of the draft amendment to the Civil Code in relation to the supply of digital performance.

In conclusion it should be emphasised once again that even at the beginning of the 2023 the fate of the transposition of the "twin directives" in Slovakia is unclear (both in terms of timing and content) and the future version of the legislation approved by the National Council of the Slovak Republic may differ substantially from the version analysed in this publication.

108 Despite the fact that a number of EU Member States had problems meeting the transposition deadline, Slovakia remained the only state of the European twenty-seven that, as of the date of submission of this contribution for publication, has not transposed SGD and DCD into national legal order. Due to the fact that the work on the transposition of the mentioned directives is still at the stage of evaluating comments to the proposal of the new legislation, it is difficult to estimate not only when the correction will be made in relation to the delay in transposition, but also how on the basis of the comment procedure, the text of the proposed amendment will be changed and in what wording the proposed amendment, which we have processed at this point, will finally be adopted during the future legislative process.

Bibliography

Zuzana Adamová and Branislav Hazucha, *'Autorský zákon. Komentár'* (C.H. Beck, Bratislava, 2018).

Zuzana Adamová and Marianna Novotná, 'Harmonizácia digitálneho zmluvného práva a nároky pri vadách digitálneho plnenia' (2022) *Právo, obchod, ekonomika*, 9 – 28.

Dulaková Jakúbeková, 'Predaj tovaru v obchode v kontexte s novou spotrebiteľskou smernicou o predaji tovaru č. 2019/701' (2019) 2 *Paneurópske právnické listy*, available at <https://www.paneuropskepravnickelisty.sk/index.php/dulakova-d-3/> accessed 15 December 2022.

Monika Jurčová, *'Spotrebiteľské právo'* (Wolters Kluwer, Praha, 2021), 207.

Monika Jurčová, Marianna Novotná, Zuzana Adamová, and Róbert Dobrovodský, 'Kúpne zmluvy uzatvárané on-line a kúpa digitálneho obsahu – úvahy o novej regulácii' (2017) 2 *Právny obzor*, 143 – 161.

Zuzana Limbergová, 'Směrnice o digitálním obsahu a jejich implementace v právním řádu ČR' (2022) 25 *Revue pro právo a technologie*, p. 241.

Števček Marek et al., *'Občiansky zákonník II. § 451 – 880. Komentár'* (C.H. Beck, Praha, 2015).

Slovenia

A.	Introduction	1
B.	Definitions and scope of application	2
	I. Scope of application	2
	II. Suitability for application to the B2B contracts	3
C.	Conformity of goods	5
	I. Transposed regime in the CPA-1	5
	II. Third party rights	6
	III. Durability requirement	8
	IV. Modification of digital content or digital service	9
D.	Liability of the Seller/Trader	10
E.	Remedies	14
	I. Remedies for the failure to supply and remedies for the lack of conformity	14
	II. Remedies for lack of conformity	16
	1. General	16
	2. Rejection and/or termination?	20
	3. Repair or replacement	21
	4. Place of delivery and place of repair or replacement	23
	5. Price reduction and termination	25
	6. Restitution after termination in contract for the supply of digital content and services	32
	7. Damages	34
	III. Consumer's obligation to provide personal data – enforceability and trader's right to terminate the contract	40
	IV. Transfer of the rights against the initial seller from the initial consumer to a subsequent buyer	45
F.	Guarantees	46
	I. Commercial guarantees	46
	II. Mandatory guarantee	49
G.	Time Limits	56
	I. Warranty period	57
	II. Further time period for the exercise of remedies	61
	III. Notification requirement	62
H.	Right of Redress	65
I.	Conclusions	68
	Bibliography	77

A. Introduction

On September 29, 2022, Slovenia has transposed the Directives 2019/770 ("DCD") and 2019/771 ("SGD") in the new Consumer Protection Act, hereinafter referred to as the "CPA-1".[1] In this paper, we are trying to present the contours of this transposition as well as to discuss some of its implications from the viewpoint of the general contract law (Obligations Code, hereinafter referred to as the "OC")[2] as well as the previous Consumer Protection Act (hereinafter referred to as "CPA").[3]

---

[1] *"Zakon o varstvu potrošnikov"*, Official Gazette of the Republic of Slovenia No. 130/22).

[2] *"Obligacijski zakonik"*, Official Gazette of the Republic of Slovenia, No. 83/01 with subsequent amendments.

[3] *"Zakon o varstvu potrošnikov"*, Official Gazette of the Republic of Slovenia, No. 20/98, with subsequent amendments;

B. Definitions and scope of application

I. Scope of application

2   The CPA-1, like the DCD, does not regulate the performance of a contract in the form of personal data as a type of contractual obligation of the consumer, but merely refers to a more detailed definition of the scope of application of the implemented regime for contracts for the supply of digital content and services.

II. Suitability for application to the B2B contracts

3   Member States are free to extend the application of the transposed rules of the SGD and DCD to B2B contracts as well.[4] The legislator limited the scope of application of the transposed rules to the B2C contracts only. However, nothing stands in the way of the analogous application of the transposed rules when the subject of the contract concluded between the two business entities is digital content, digital service, or goods with digital elements, although only those rules that do not have a specifically consumer-protective character could be considered.[5] In particular, the objective standards of conformity with the contract, e.g. those relating to updates,[6] could be used as a standard of reasonable expectations of the buyer also in B2B contracts. The same is true for the modification of the digital content or digital service, for example.[7]

4   With regard to the remedies for the lack of conformity, the situation is different, as there is already national legislation in place in OC. It is based on a slightly different remedial structure and a different approach to time limits, particularly regarding the sale of goods.[8] In this respect, the directives and their implementation offer, above all, an opportunity to reflect on the possibilities of further development. It will have to be analysed as to whether there are compelling reasons for the existence of differences between the approaches of consumer and non-consumer contract law.

C. Conformity of goods

I. Transposed regime in the CPA-1

5   Both directives bring a new description of the requirements for the conformity of the subject of contract. They are synchronised with each other and characterised by transparency and clarity, which derive in particular from the explicit separation of the subjective and objective requirements for conformity. With regard to the requirements for conformity in the SGD and DCD, the implementation was straightforward; there

---

[4] See Recital 21 SGD and Recital 16 DCD.
[5] Metzger, in Säcker, Rixecker, Oetker and Limperg (eds), *MüKoBGB*, 3rd Volume, 9. ed.(2022), BGB vor § 327 Rn. 39.
[6] Arts. 74 and 112 CPA-1.
[7] Art. 126 CPA-1. For further reading with emphasis on German implementation of DCD see Metzger, in Säcker, Rixecker, Oetker and Limperg (eds), *MüKoBGB*, 3rd Volume, 9. ed. (2022), BGB vor § 327 Rn. 38–40.
[8] On the remedial structure in the general contract law, see e.g., Možina, "Breach of Contract and Remedies in the Yugoslav Obligations Act: 40 Years Later" (2020), *ZEuP*, 135.

C. Conformity of goods

were no deviations or further specifications. As the room for the discretion for the Member States on this matter was limited, such approach was expected.

II. Third party rights

The provisions regarding third party rights were transposed without any specifications or detailed elaborations[9]. The formulation "unless the law provides for termination or nullity" was kept. Indeed, an *ipso facto* termination is foreseen in (non-consumer) sales law in the event the goods are "taken away"[10] from the buyer due to a third party right,[11] raising the question of which rules are applicable: CPA-1 or OC. Although it seems that the legislator has overlooked the OC, it nevertheless appears that the use of the remedies of the CPA-1 (SGD, DCD) was intended. It would have been rather odd to have different requirements[12] and time limits[13] for the remedies due to third party rights and for the remedies due to (other kinds of) a lack of conformity.

The CPA-1 also does not regulate the relationship with intellectual property law. It also remains silent with regard to the right to resell digital contents. Another problem that has been raised, and which DCD has implicitly circumvented with the above regime, is that the conclusion of an End-User Licence Agreement ("EULA") with the intellectual property right holder (when the intellectual property right holder is not also the trader) often represents a precondition for the installation of digital content.[14] Thus, the consumers would be entitled to remedies for the non-conformity of digital content if they were not warned by the trader at the conclusion of contract that the conclusion of EULA is a precondition for the use of that digital content when and the consumer accepted this waiver of rights in accordance with Article 8(5) DCD.[15] Unfortunately, the legislator did not make any step in the direction of clarifying the problem.

III. Durability requirement

The CPA-1 does not dwell further on the durability requirement as an objective requirement for conformity,[16] but mentions the durability as an objective pursued by the

---

[9] See Art. 77 CPA-1 as to the transposition of Art. 9 SGD and Art. 115 CPA-1 as to the transposition of Art. 10 DCD.

[10] That the goods are "taken away" should be interpreted as "the buyer is prevented from using them" due to a third party right.

[11] Art. 490 (1) OC. In such case, the buyer may choose between termination and price reduction. In the absence of special regulations, the rules on the liability of the seller for "legal mistakes" apply accordingly to all mutual contracts., Art. 100 (2) OC. If the use of the goods is merely limited (and not entirely prevented), the buyer may choose to terminate the contract (or reduce the price), Art. 490 (1), (2) and (3) OC.

[12] E.g. notification is not an absolute requirement for remedies due to legal defects, see Art. 491 OC.

[13] The time limit for the exercise of remedies due to legal defects under general contract law is one year, since the buyer has become aware of the third party right, see Art. 495 (1) OC.

[14] Metzger, "Verträge über digitale Inhalte und digitale Dienstleistungen: Neuer BGB-Vertragstypus oder punktuelle Reform?" (2019), JuristenZeitung 74(12), 577, 581.

[15] See also Statement of the European Law Institute on the European Commission's proposed Directive on the supply of digital content to consumers COM (2015) 634 final, 25, and Beale, "Conclusion and Performance of Contracts: An Overview" in Schulze, Staudenmayer, Lohsse (eds), *Contracts for the Supply of Digital Content: Regulatory Challenges and Gaps, Münster Colloquia on EU Law and the Digital Economy*, 33, 43.

[16] See 73 para. 1, and 4 CPA-1 as a transposition of Art. 7, para. 1, subpara. b. SGD.

IV. Modification of digital content or digital service

9   The legislator transposed the provisions on the modification of digital content or digital service to Art. 126 CPA-1.[18] It is intended to apply only to the regime on contracts for the supply of digital content or digital service, as it is sorted under the corresponding chapter of the legal act.[19] The applicability of this provision was not extended to the chapter where the transposed regime of SGD[20] is regulated, nor was there any special provision on the modification of digital content or digital service adopted.

D. Liability of the Seller/Trader

10   In Slovenian contract law, the seller is liable for any lack of conformity existing at the time of delivery (transfer of risk)[21] regardless of their fault or knowledge of the lack of conformity (strict liability).[22] The same principally holds true for the liability of the provider of digital content or service – the provider owes a certain result, not just their best efforts.[23]

11   There are several possibilities to address the obstacles to performance. Firstly and most importantly, there is the general exemption clause of Art. 240 OC. The debtor is not liable for damages if their non-performance is due to "circumstances arising after the conclusion of the contract that they could not have overcome or avoided". The prevailing view in Slovenian law today is that the liability is strict.[24] The debtor is liable for circumstances under their control and for the work of the persons involved in performance on his side as well.[25] However, in some contracts for services, such as the mandate, it is not the specific result that is owed (as in the contract of sale), but the exercise of diligence (best efforts).[26] The latter does not appear to be relevant, however, in the context of contracts for the supply of digital content and services (specific result).

12   If the performance becomes objectively impossible, the debtor can also rely on the rules on supervening impossibility (Arts. 329 and 116–117 OC).[27] However, the concept of impossibility is only applicable to specific obligations, as the generic obligations are considered imperishable. Furthermore, the debtor cannot rely on impossibility when they are already in delay.[28] In fact, the notion of (objective) impossibility is not operative

---

[17] See the explanatory memorandum in the Government draft CPA-1 of 12 July 2022 (EVA: 2015-2130-0005), p. 141.
to Art. 73 CPA-1.
[18] Transposition of Art. 19 DCD.
[19] Part III, Chapter III (Arts. 103–127) CPA-1.
[20] Part III, Chapter I (Arts. 66–98) CPA-1.
[21] For the transfer of risk, see Art. 436 and 437 OC.
[22] Art. 458 (1) OC.
[23] See Arts. 633 ff (contract for work).
[24] See: Plavšak, in Juhart and Plavšak, *OZ s komentarjem* (2003-4), Art. 490, 214; Higher Court in Ljubljana, Cpg 59/2011 of 22 March.2010 and I Cpg 603/2011 of 24.2.2012. Cf. Art. 79 (1) CISG and Art. 8:108(1) PECL.
[25] See Art. 244 OC, Art. 630 OC (contracts for work).
[26] See e.g., Supreme Court of Slovenia, III Ips 38/2019 of 10 March 2020, No. 18.
[27] See: Možina, "Breach of Contract and Remedies in the Yugoslav Obligations Act: 40 Years Later" (2020), *ZEuP*, 135, 142.
[28] Art. 239 (4) OC.

for the discharge of the debtor at all; only (objective) impossibility for which the debtor is not liable discharges them of performance; whether or not they are liable is resolved according to the general exemption clause of Art. 240 OC.

If the performance becomes extremely onerous for the debtor or the purpose of the contract is impossible to achieve,[29] the debtor can ask the Court to dissolve the contract due to the change of circumstances.[30] As in the general exemption clause, only the unforeseeable circumstances beyond the control of the debtor are relevant.[31] The court has to take into account the purpose of the contract, the normal risks in comparable contracts and the balance of interests of the parties.[32] If the Court decides to dissolve the contract, it may also equitably distribute the loss due to change of circumstances between the parties.[33] So far, the cases of judicial dissolution due to a change of circumstances have been extremely rare.

E. Remedies

I. Remedies for the failure to supply and remedies for the lack of conformity

Somewhat uncoordinated, the CPA-1 governs the consequences of non-delivery in a very similar way in two different places. Firstly, Arts. 26–34 CPA-1 contain a kind of "general part" of the consumer contract law.[34] Art. 108 CPA-1, implementing Art. 13 DCD, contains essentially the same basic mechanism. The consumer may request delivery; if the trader does not deliver without undue delay or in additional reasonable time (on which, however, the parties must explicitly agree), the consumer may terminate the contract.[35] Immediate termination is possible if it is obvious that the provider will not deliver with the additional time provided or timely delivery was of the essence for the contract, as was agreed between the parties or obvious from the circumstances.[36] The provisions on the effects of termination apply accordingly.

If the provider does not deliver, the consumer – if they had not already paid – has a right to withhold payment based on general contract law, as long as payment on delivery was agreed.[37] If the consumer has to pay first, they may withhold payment if the financial circumstances of the provider deteriorate to such an extent that it is uncertain whether they will be able to perform, or it is uncertain for other serious reasons.[38]

---

[29] In principle, the concept of frustration of purpose also covers supervening impossibility, but the latter was nevertheless regulated separately.
[30] Art. 112–115 OC.
[31] Art. 112 (2) OC.
[32] Art. 114 OC.
[33] See Art. 133 (5) OC.
[34] Art. 27 and 28 CPA-1 regulate some consequences of non-delivery: The consumer may request performance in additional time and can, if it expires unsuccessfully, terminate the contract. Immediate termination is possible if it is obvious from the circumstances that the business will not perform with the given additional time or if the time of performance is of the essence for the contract, based on the agreement or on the circumstances, Art. 28 CPA-1. These provisions actually only repeat the content of general contract law from the Obligations Code which would have applied any way, see Arts. 103–106 OC.
[35] Art. 108 (2) CPA-1.
[36] Art. 108 (3) CPA-1.
[37] Art. 101 (1) OC.
[38] Art. 102 (1) OC.

II. Remedies for lack of conformity

1. General

16 The provisions of the SGD on remedies for non-conformity were transposed into CPA-1 in a relatively straightforward way, i.e. the text of Art. 13 – 16 was transposed into Art. 81, 82, 83 and 86 CPA-1 almost without any changes, albeit with a different distribution of contents. However, the legislator has, – continuing the approach under the current law – added compensation of damage to the list of remedies for non-conformity.[39]

17 The remedial structure from Art. 13 and 14 SGD is a novelty in Slovenia, as the differentiation between primary (repair and replacement) and secondary remedies (termination and price reduction) was so far unknown. When the Directive 99/44/EC (hereinafter referred to as the "CSD") was being implemented (2002), its Art. 3 (3) and (5) were simply left out.[40] Instead, the legislator relied on the remedial structure from the Yugoslav Obligations Act (now Obligations Code), where the buyer can freely choose between repair, replacement and price reduction; only if they intend to terminate the contract, they must first leave the seller a reasonable additional period.[41] Thus, the seller's right to cure was limited as the buyer could reduce the price without giving them a chance to bring the goods into conformity. The existing CPA did not mention the disproportionality-criterion at all, and it was an open issue whether and how it was possible to follow the judgment of the CJEU in the case *Putz/Weber*.[42]

18 The described remedial structure is still in force in the general contract law.[43] It is rather different from the one in the regime of consumer sales contracts and consumer contracts for the supply of digital content or digital service. Moreover, the legislator had also maintained the old approach in the CPA-1 – regarding the regulation of general liability for services, which was previously regulated in the same way as liability of the seller.[44] However, the time limits of the liability of the seller in the CPA-1 are applicable to the liability of the service provider.[45] The regulation of general liability for services does not apply to services, which are subject to special regulation, such as the digital services (DCD).

19 The CPA-1 did not regulate whether and to what extent a contribution of the consumer to the lack of conformity affects their remedies as allowed by Art. 13 (7) SGD. The seller is strictly[46] liable for a lack of conformity existing upon delivery. It is a principle of general contract law that the creditor may only rely on remedies for breach of contract to the extent that it does not (or, in terms of damage, its amount) arise from their own actions.[47]

---

[39] Art. 81 (3) for sale of goods and Art 118 (2) CPA-1 for digital content or services. For the current law, see Art. 37c (2) CPA.
[40] See Možina, "Breach of Contract and Remedies in the Yugoslav Obligations Act: 40 Years Later" (2020), *ZEuP*, 135, 149.
[41] Ibid. and Art. 37c (1) CPA.
[42] CJEU, joined Cases C-65/09 and C-87/09 of 16 June 2011, Weber & Putz, ECLI:EU:C:2011:396.
[43] See Art. 468 (1) and (2) and Art. 100 (2) OC.
[44] See Art. 38 (1) CPA and Art. 100 CPA-1.
[45] Art. 100 (2) CPA-1.
[46] See the general exemption clause (Art 240 OC), based on unforeseeable circumstances beyond the control of the debtor.
[47] See Art 244 OC regarding the damages due to breach of contract.

E. Remedies

2. Rejection and/or termination?

A special right of the consumer to terminate the contract immediately (i.e. without giving the possibility of the seller to repair/replace the goods) was introduced for the event that the non-conformity becomes apparent within the first 30 days after delivery.[48] The possibility to reject the non-conforming goods already exists in Slovenian law, including consumer contract law; it is a principle of contract law that the debtor must offer performance in full conformity with the contract and the creditor is not obliged to accept performance, which does not conform to the contract.[49] It appears that Art. 3 (7) SGD and Recital 19 SGD take into account just such a right of rejection (refusal). However, the legislator explained that the aim was to limit the impact of the hierarchy of remedies from Art. 13 and 14 SGD in the interest of a higher level of consumer protection.[50] Rejection and termination are different remedies; rejection results in default (non-delivery), while termination dissolves the contract. As Recital 19 mentions rejection together with repudiation, the legislator opted for termination. It's introduction in addition to rejection does not appear to be a well thought-out solution.

3. Repair or replacement

Regarding the repair and replacement, the modification with regard to Art. 13 (1) and (2) and Art. 14 SGD is the provision, according to which the maximum duration of reasonable time in which the seller has to comply with the chosen remedy is 30 days.[51] When determining the duration of reasonable time, the nature and the purpose of goods are to be taken into account.[52] The reasonable time-limit may be further extended by a maximum of 15 days if it is necessary for the completion of repair or replacement.[53] Of course, the consumer needs not specify the reasonable time-limit when requesting repair or replacement. When determining the extension, factors to be taken into account are not just the nature, complexity and the purpose of the goods, but also the nature and severity of the non-conformity and the effort required to complete the repair or replacement.[54] The seller is obliged to inform the consumer before the expiry of the initial time-limit of the length and of the reasons for the extension.[55] As there is no need for the different criteria with regard to determination of reasonable time for repair or replacement and its extension the difference can probably be attributed to the clumsiness of the drafter. In addition, the seller who does not comply with the remedy within a reasonable time and without significant inconvenience for the consumer is punishable by a fine.[56]

If the consumer had not already paid the price, they are entitled to withhold the price or any outstanding part of it until the seller has fulfilled their obligations; the consumer exercises this right by a statement to the seller.[57] The provision on the exercise of this right, although in accordance with the principles of civil law, is nevertheless somewhat ambiguous; although all remedies are exercised by a statement, the CPA-1 says so only

---

[48] Art. 83 (2) CPA-1 and Art. 3 (7) SGD.
[49] See Art 282 (1) OC and Juhart, in Juhart and Plavšak, *OZ s komentarjem* (2003–4), Art. 101, p. 555.
[50] See the explanatory memorandum in the Government draft CPA-1 of 12 July 2022 (EVA: 2015-2130-0005), p. 146.
[51] Art. 82 (1) CPA-1.
[52] Ibid.
[53] Art. 82 (2) CPA-1.
[54] Ibid.
[55] Art. 82 (2) CPA-1.
[56] Art. 240 (1) (29) CPA-1.
[57] Art. 81 (2) CPA-1.

here and with regard to termination, implying that the exercise of other remedies might perhaps be different.[58]

4. Place of delivery and place of repair or replacement

23 Since the DCD leaves the determination of the place of delivery and place of repair to national law[59], the rules of general law of obligations that govern the place of performance are applicable. Accordingly, the debtor is obliged to perform the obligation and the creditor to accept it at a place defined by the contract and the law (Art. 294 (1) OC). If the place of performance is not defined and cannot be defined according to the purpose of the transaction, the nature of the obligation or any other circumstances, the obligation must be performed in the place where the debtor had a registered office or residence at the time when the obligation arose.[60] The considerations of the CJEU in the matter C-52/18 – *Fülla* are to be taken into account, as the place of performance is determined in a similar way as in German law. It is to be assessed whether the place of the seller is appropriate for bringing the goods into conformity free of charge, within a reasonable time and without significant inconvenience to the consumer, taking into account the nature of the goods and the purpose for which the consumer required the goods.[61]

24 With regard to the transportation costs, the legislator did not deviate from Art 14 para. 2 SGD nor did they further specify the provision.[62] If the consumer is obliged to send the non-conforming goods to the seller, they should be reimbursed for the cost of transport of the goods by the seller according to the general provision that bringing the goods into conformity should be done free of charge[63], which includes the costs of postage and carriage[64]. Bringing the goods into conformity with the contract should also be carried out without any significant inconvenience to the consumer. However, the seller is not bound to advance the costs of transport, unless the fact that the consumer must advance those costs would constitute such a burden as to deter them from asserting their rights.[65]

5. Price reduction and termination

25 The provisions of Art. 15, 16 and 17 SGD were transposed to CPA-1 more or less verbatim.[66] As aforementioned, the conditions under which the consumer can terminate the contract or reduce the price from Art. 13 (4) SGD are a novelty in Slovenia. In addition, the possibility of relying on a "serious nature of the breach" which can justify immediate termination or a price reduction from Art. 13 (4) (c) SGD is different from the general contract law, where termination is available regardless of the weight of the

---

[58] The issue is relevant in Slovenia, because according to some, the price may only be reduced by a court and not by a simple statement from one party to another, see Supreme Court of Slovenia, II Ips 38/2012 from 12.10.2013 and II Ips 288/2014 from 5.5.2015. For a critical view of this approach, see: Možina, "Problem uveljavljanja znižanja pogodbene cene" (2014), *Pravna praksa* 43/2014, 16.
[59] Recital 56 DCD.
[60] Art. 294 (2) OC.
[61] CJEU, Case C-52/18 of 23 May 2019, Fülla, ECLI:EU:C:2019:447, Fn. 48.
[62] Art. 82 (7) CPA-1.
[63] Art. 14, para. 1 subpara a. as transposed in Art. 81 1(1) CPA-1.
[64] Art. 2 (14) SGD as transposed into Art. 82 (3) CPA-1.
[65] CJEU, Case C-52/18 of 23 May 2019, Fülla, ECLI:EU:C:2019:447, Fn. 55f.
[66] For Art. 15 SGD, see Art. 83 (3) CPA-1; for Art. 16 para. 1 SGD, see Art. 83 (4) CPA-1; for Art. 16 para.2 SGD, see Art. 83 (5) CPA-1; for Art. 16 para. 3 SGD, see Art. 83 (6) CPA-1; for 16 para. 3 SGD, see Art. 83 (6) and 86 (1) CPA-1.

E. Remedies

breach (as long as the latter is not minor); the only exception being a situation where the time of performance is of essence.[67]

With regard to the effects of price reduction, a provision was added according to which the seller must return the reduced part of the price in eight days from the receipt of the claim to reduce the price.[68] A similar provision was added to the effects of termination; however, here, the time limit is "without hesitation and at the latest within eight days" from receipt of the returned goods or evidence of their dispatch.[69]

The exercise of termination (by a statement) in both directives is different from the general contract law[70] where in many situations there is an *ipso facto* termination.[71] The new approach is welcome, as *ipso facto* termination is an outdated approach, which can cause uncertainty and is particularly unsuitable for consumer contracts.[72]

A further condition to termination under general sales law, that the buyer must be able to return the goods in substantially the same condition as when they received them (albeit with several exceptions, including the deterioration due to a lack of conformity or normal use) does not apply in consumer sales.[73] As an additional condition for termination, it would be contrary to SGD.

The legislator also regulated the effects of the termination of one element of a bundle contract on other elements of the bundle contract as provided for in Art. 3, para. 6, subpara. 3 DCD.[74] Accordingly, the consumer who terminates from one element of the bundle contract consisting of digital content or digital services may terminate the other elements of that bundle contract if the consumer cannot reasonably be expected to retain the other elements of that bundle contract.[75] In such case, they are relieved from payment of any termination charges or other administrative charges, contractual penalties, amounts of benefits received or other additional charges.[76]

A consumer who has received goods at the time of conclusion of a bundle contract and who has terminated the bundle contract, before the expiry of the duration of the contract, can either choose to reimburse the trader for an amount corresponding to a proportionate part of the total value of the goods received and to keep the received goods or to return the goods to the trader at the trader's expense in the condition in which they were delivered to the consumer and the trader shall reimburse the purchase price to the consumer.[77]

The reimbursement of the trader may not exceed the value of the goods as determined at the time of the conclusion of the bundle contract or the remainder of the

---

[67] Art. 104 and 105 OC.
[68] Art. 86 (2) CPA-1.
[69] Art. 86 (1) CPA-1.
[70] See Art. 16 para. 1 SGD and Art. 83 (4) CPA-1 and Art. 15 DCD and Art 120 (5) CPA-1.
[71] Ipso facto termination is foreseen for contracts where time is of the essence, see Art. 104 (1) OC. However, even in contracts, where time is not of the essence and the creditor must first set an additional reasonable time to the debtor, termination occurs ipso facto with the lapse of additional time, see Art. 105 (3) OC. In sales contracts, the buyer who wants to terminate the contract, must first set an additional time for the seller to effect repair or replacement; if it lapses unsuccessfully, the contract is terminated *ipso facto*, see Art. 471 OC. The buyer may keep the contract in force if he immediately declares this to the seller.
[72] On the mechanics of termination in the OC, see Možina, "Breach of Contract and Remedies in the Yugoslav Obligations Act: 40 Years Later" (2020), *ZEuP*, 135, 153.
[73] See Art. 475 OC. For the view, that this condition does not apply in the present consumer sale law, too, see: Možina, "Pravice kupca na podlagi stvarne napake pri prodajni pogodbi" (2012), *Pravni letopis 2012*, 85, 99.
[74] See Art. 106 CPA-1.
[75] Art. 106 CPA-1 (2).
[76] Art. 106 (3) CPA-1.
[77] Art. 106 (4) CPA-1.

monthly payments for the goods received until the end of the term of the contract, whichever is the lesser amount.[78]

6. Restitution after termination in contract for the supply of digital content and services

32   The CPA-1 did not introduce any specific rules regarding the restitution in cases where the trader supplies digital content or digital services nor in cases where consumer provides personal data in exchange for the digital content or digital service.[79]

33   The restitution of payments under Art. 122 CPA-1[80] encompasses only those situations where consumers paid a monetary purchase price, which leaves out the consumers that provide their personal data as a counter-performance to the trader. To that end, the general reference to GDPR in Art. 16, para. 2 DCD does not offer much assistance, as the GDPR does not provide for a corresponding reimbursement claim.[81] The legislator has refrained from regulating the restitution of money for the use of consumer's personal data by the trader, although the DCD does not oppose to the enactment of such restitution mechanism.[82] However, such mechanism would mean another big step towards evaluating personal data merely through the prism of its monetary value, which could be problematic from the general point of view of data protection as a fundamental right[83].

7. Damages

34   The consumer may also demand the compensation for loss due to a lack of conformity both in contracts for the sale of goods[84] and contracts for the supply of digital content and services.[85]

35   The provision on damages in consumer sales contracts enumerates examples of the loss covered: Costs for the material, spare parts, work and transport "due to the exercise of the remedies by the consumer".[86] As repair and replacement must be free of charge for the consumer anyway,[87] the provision can only be understood in the sense of recovery of costs in the event that the consumer organises the repair or replacement themselves (damages *in lieu* of performance). Damages may also be awarded for other kinds of damages, such as damages for delay, e.g. the cost of bridging measures. In consumer contracts, lost profit will be rare, but it cannot be ruled out from the outset. Also, loss to other categories of property of the consumer cannot be ruled out.

36   In case of lack of conformity of digital content or services the CPA-1 enumerates different examples of loss: Here, the loss covered is the loss to hardware and to other digital content or service that is the property of the consumer and "was not caused by the consumer".[88] The exclusion of loss caused by the consumer is self-evident, also in sales contracts.

---

[78] Art. 106 (5) CPA-1.
[79] For obligations of the trader in the event of termination see Art. 122 and 124 CPA-1; for obligations of the consumer in the event of termination see Art. 125 CPA-1.
[80] The transposition of Art. 16, para. 1 DCD.
[81] Metzger, in Säcker, Rixecker, Oetker and Limperg (eds), *MüKoBGB*, 3rd Volume, 9. ed. (2022), BGB § 327o Rn. 9.
[82] Ibid.
[83] See Art. 8 of Charter of Fundamental Rights of the European Union (2000/C 364/01).
[84] Art. 81 (3) CPA-1.
[85] Art. 118 (2) CPA-1.
[86] Art. 81 (3) CPA-1.
[87] Art. 14 para. 1, subpara. a. SGD.
[88] Art. 118 (2) CPA-1.

E. Remedies

General rules on contract damages from the Obligations Code apply, in particular the general exemption clause (Art. 240 OC) and the full compensation as well as the foreseeability of loss to the debtor (provider) as the general measure of damages.[89]

It appears that the notification of a lack of conformity is a condition for all remedies of the consumer, including the damages claim.[90] However, the time limits seem to be different: Art. 87 CPA-1, limiting the exercise of remedies to two years from the notification of the lack of conformity, explicitly only refers to the remedies from Art. 81 (1) CPA-1 (repair, replacement, price reduction, termination). As there is no explanation, some doubt exists whether this was really the intention of the legislator. If it was, the situation is somewhat odd; the cut-off period of two years applies to all remedies except damages, which are subject to the general prescription period of five years.[91] Nevertheless, this was also the position in previous CPA.[92] The situation with regard to damages to non-conforming digital content or services is the same.[93] The different treatment regarding the time limits is all the more unusual, as the damages can, in some situations, substitute repair or replacement. If the buyer demands repair or replacement and the seller does not comply within reasonable time or without significant inconvenience, the buyer may also remedy the non-conformity himself (or have it remedied) in a reasonable way and recover the costs with damages claim (damages *in lieu* of performance). Such is at least the situation in the general contract law[94] and the SGD does not seem to prohibit it.

A general condition for damages *in lieu* of performance is, that the debtor (seller) had a reasonable opportunity to cure their non-conforming performance (reasonable time). An exception applies to the situations from Art. 13 (4) (a) and (d) SGD). Furthermore, the costs of this transaction must be reasonable. Depending on circumstances (e.g. where the transport costs are disproportionally high), such self-(organised)-repair (or replacement) might be indicated from the point of view of the duty to mitigate loss.[95]

III. Consumer's obligation to provide personal data – enforceability and trader's right to terminate the contract

In connection with the enforceability of the consumer's duty to provide personal data as a counter-performance, *Klink-Straub* establishes that the German legislator failed to classify the consumer's provision of personal data in legal terms, specifically in its relationship with the trader's obligation to deliver/supply the digital content or digital services.[96] The same reproach can be addressed to the Slovenian legislator. Should the trader have an enforceable claim against the consumer for the provision of its personal data? Such questions arise even more so after the deletion of the term data as counter-

---

[89] See Art. 243 (1) OC and Možina, "Breach of Contract and Remedies in the Yugoslav Obligations Act: 40 Years Later" (2020), *ZEuP*, 135, 157ff.
[90] Art. 84 (1) CPA-1. For time limits, see Chapter VII.
[91] Art. 346 OC.
[92] As Art. 36c (3) CPA does not explicitly mention damages, the courts held that a general prescription period applies. See e.g., High Court of Ljubljana, VSL II Cp 154/2012 of 28 August 2012.
[93] See Art. 116 (4) CPA-1: The two-year time limit only applies to other remedies and not to damages.
[94] See e.g. Možina, "Pravice kupca na podlagi stvarne napake pri prodajni pogodbi" (2012), *Pravni letopis 2012*, 85, 101; and Supreme Court of Slovenia, II Ips 348/2013 of 20 August 2015, No. 18.
[95] Art. 244 OC.
[96] Klink-Straub, Do ut des data – Bezahlen mit Daten im digitalen Vertragsrecht (2021), *NJW 2021*, 3217, 3219.

performance from the final text of the DCD at the request of European Data Protection Supervisor[97].

41 The only clear signal from the Slovenian legislator on how to resolve the situation in which the trader does lose access to processing the consumer's personal data as a result of the consumer's withdrawal of their consent to the processing of personal data or their objection to the further use thereof is stipulated in Art. 121 CPA-1. Therein, it intends to enact the right of the trader to withdraw from the contract for the supply of digital content or digital services if consumer withdraws consent to the processing of personal data or objects to the further use of personal data. The provision is based on the § 327q German Civil Code (BGB) that foresees the same right of withdrawal for the trader.

42 In a similar manner as the rule in § 327q German Civil Code (BGB) from which it drew its inspiration, Art. 121 CPA-1 does not foresee a notice period after a trader has withdrawn from the contract if the statutory or contractual notice period would impose a disproportionate burden on the trader.

43 Moreover, damage claims by the trader against the consumer for his withdrawal of consent to the processing of personal data are excluded.[98]

44 Furthermore, Art. 121 (3) CPA-1 stipulates that the consumer's personal data shall be returned to the consumer or, in agreement with the consumer, deleted or otherwise destroyed after the consumer's withdrawal of consent.

IV. Transfer of the rights against the initial seller from the initial consumer to a subsequent buyer

45 In Slovenian law, an automatic transfer of the rights against the initial seller from the initial consumer to a subsequent buyer is not regulated. Of course, the parties (i.e. initial consumer and his buyer) may agree on an assignment of claims.[99] In principle, it is also possible to agree on the non-transferability of claims in the contract between the seller (trader) and consumer.[100] However, if such agreement (*pactum de non cedendo*) is a part of the non-individual negotiated terms in a B2C contract, it can be subject to a judicial fairness review and would likely be considered unfair (and null).[101]

F. Guarantees

I. Commercial guarantees

46 The regulation of guarantees in the CPA-1 is rather complex (10 articles), the reason being the previous extensive regulation of commercial and mandatory guarantee for proper functioning.[102] Until now, Slovenia had two mandatory systems for the protection of the buyer's interest: In addition to the mandatory two-year liability of the seller based on the CSD, there was also a system of a mandatory one-year warranty for the proper functioning of technical goods, a remnant of socialist law from the times of

---

[97] European Data Protection Supervisor (EDPS), Opinion 4/2017 on the Proposal for a Directive on certain aspects concerning contracts for the supply of digital content, str. 21, para 83.
[98] Art. 121 (2) CPA-1.
[99] Art. 417 (1) OC.
[100] Art. 417 (2) OC.
[101] See Art. 24 CPA (23 CPA-1).
[102] On which see Možina, Garancija za brezhibno delovanje in odgovornost za stvarne napake (2009), *Zbornik znanstvenih razprav PF LJ*, 143.

F. Guarantees

Yugoslavia. The guarantee-liability was regulated by the OC and the CPA-1 as a kind of parallel system to the system of liability of the seller, with two important differences: Firstly, that the warranty could be enforced not only against the seller but also against the producer and, secondly, that it was not limited to B2C relationships.[103]

Art. 89 CPA-1 defines the guarantee in the sense of Art. 2 (12) SGD. The guarantee is binding under the conditions laid down in the guarantee statement or advertising (Art. 90 CPA-1). The contents of the guarantee document are regulated in Art. 91 CPA-1 for both commercial and mandatory guarantees. In addition to the contents of Art. 17 (2) SGD, some other requirements were introduced: The guarantee document must contain the date of delivery, the time limit for the resolving of complaints, territorial scope of the guarantee as well as the remedies of the consumer. 47

Art. 92 CPA-1 regulates the "commercial guarantee of durability" irrespectively of any other provision of the law of Republic of Slovenia or the EU.[104] If the producer offers a commercial guarantee of durability, they are directly liable to the consumer within the time period of the guarantee for the repair or replacement of the goods in conformity with Art. 82 (1), (2) (7), (8) and (9) CPA-1 (i.e. the provisions regulating repair and replacement). Thus, the producer must effectuate a repair or replacement within a reasonable time, at the latest within 30 days. They have no defence if the cost of the chosen remedy is disproportionate in comparison with the other remedy or in general (these provisions are not included in the reference). On the other hand, the producer must carry out or reimburse the costs of removal of the non-functioning goods (intended to be installed) and of the installation of replacement goods. The consumer shall not be liable to pay for the normal use of the goods. They shall also enable the producer to inspect the goods. 48

II. Mandatory guarantee

The CPA-1 retains the mandatory guarantee relying on an apparent high level of protection of consumers in Slovenia. As the full harmonisation principle prevented a parallel system of liability against the seller, the mandatory guarantee now only applies against the producer.[105] 49

As under the previous CPA, the guarantee is not limited to B2C contracts; it applies to B2B contracts too, raising a question as to its compatibility with the free movement of goods.[106] 50

As under the previous CPA, the Ministry for Economy shall publish a list of products which may only be sold with a guarantee; the minimum duration being one year.[107] In the first place, these are electrical products. However, in the area where the guarantee is mandatory, little sense exists for the offering of commercial guarantees. In this respect, mandatory guarantee may also be seen as depriving the commercial guarantee of its full effect. Also, the transparency requirement with regard to commercial guarantee, i.e. that the consumer is to be informed of the remedies provided by the law, should cover the remedies based on mandatory guarantee, too, but this is not the case. 51

---

[103] Ibid.
[104] See Art 17, para. 1 SGD.
[105] See See the explanatory memorandum in the Government draft CPA-1 of 12 July 2022 (EVA: 2015–2130–0005), p. 149.
[106] Art. 98 CPA-1.
[107] Art. 94 CPA-1.

52   The producer – although normally not in direct contact with the consumer – should "provide the consumer with the guarantee document", together with instructions for use and the list of authorised service providers (unless the producer carries out the service).[108] Their main duty is to bring the products into conformity by repair or replacement within 30 days during the guarantee period. The 30-day time limit can be extended to up to 15 days, in the same manner as when applying remedies for non-conformity pursuant to Art. 82 (2) CPA-1.[109]

53   A hierarchy of the remedies is prescribed by Art. 97 CPA-1: The consumer may first only claim repair; if the goods are not repaired within 30 days (or within the maximum of 45 days if the time limit is extended), they may ask for a replacement; if the goods are not replaced within a period of 30 days, the consumer may choose between price reduction or the reimbursement of the entire price.[110] If the goods malfunction within the first 30 days from delivery, the consumer may demand the reimbursement of the price paid regardless of the hierarchy of remedies.[111] These provisions, the remnants of the previous regulation of mandatory guarantee, are somewhat odd: The duties to reimburse the price in whole or in part are the effects of termination and price reduction; however, the producer normally has no contract with the consumer. Thus, the producer should reimburse the price in whole or in part (in case of price reduction), but the contract between the seller and the consumer should remain untouched. Unfortunately, the legislator provided no explanation of the structure of non-contractual liability of the producer in this situation.

54   Furthermore, the producer is liable to pay damages for the loss of use of the goods (from the moment they receive the buyer's claim until repair/replacement); they can avoid this liability by providing the consumer the use of a substitute goods.[112]

55   The producer also has duties after the expiry of the guarantee period: They shall (for a fee) provide for repair, maintenance, spare parts and connecting parts in the period of at least three years after the expiry of the guarantee period.[113] The CPA-1 sanctions the breach of these duties by a fine.[114] Although these after sales duties can be understood as contributing to a more permanent use of goods (sustainability), their practicability is limited. The producer can escape the fine by providing for service and spare parts for *any* fee.

G. Time Limits

56   Regarding the time limits for the liability of the seller/trader the CPA-1 maintains the system of combination of the warranty period and the further period for exercising rights, which has been in force since the time of the Yugoslav Act on Obligations (1978).[115]

---

[108] Art. 95 CPA-1.
[109] Art. 97 (2) CPA-1
[110] Art. 97 (3) CPA-1.
[111] Art. 97 (5) CPA-1.
[112] Art. 97 (7) and (8) CPA-1.
[113] See Art. 95 CPA-1.
[114] See Art. 240 (1) (34), (35) and (36) CPA-1.
[115] See Možina, "Breach of Contract and Remedies in the Yugoslav Obligations Act: 40 Years Later" (2020), *ZEuP*, 135, 146.

G. Time Limits

I. Warranty period

With regard to the warranty period (i.e. the period in which a non-conformity for which the seller is liable, may arise), the CPA-1 follows the directives: In principle, the seller is liable for the non-conformity existing at the time of delivery, which becomes apparent within two years after delivery.[116] The warranty period is not a prescription period but a kind of cut-off period: On the one hand, interruption and suspension are not foreseen, but on the other hand, it can be prolonged (and, outside of B2C sales, also shortened) by the parties.[117] 57

Slovenia has made use of the option in Art. 10 (6) SGD in connection with used goods: Here, the seller and the consumer may agree on a shorter warranty period; the minimum being one year.[118] 58

In case of goods with digital elements where the contract provides for the continuous supply of digital content or service over a period of time, the seller is liable for any non-conformity that occurs or becomes apparent within two years after the delivery (regardless of whether it existed at the time of the delivery), unless the contract provides for a continuous supply for a period of more than two years in which case the seller is liable for this period.[119] 59

Where a contract provides for a single act of supply or a series of individual acts of the supply of digital content or digital services, the trader is liable for any non-conformity which exists at the time of the delivery and becomes apparent within two years.[120] In case the contract provides for the continuous supply of digital content or digital services over a period of time, the trader is liable for any non-conformity with becomes apparent within this period.[121] 60

II. Further time period for the exercise of remedies

After the non-conformity becomes apparent, the consumer is obliged to notify the seller/provider about it. The moment of notification triggers a further cut-off time period for the exercise of remedies. In the CPA-1, this time period is two years.[122] A cut-off time should be taken into account by the court ex officio and it runs without the possibility of interruption and suspension.[123] It would be much more appropriate to subject the buyer's (consumer's) remedies to a prescription period. 61

---

[116] See Art. 78 (1) CPA-1 and Article 116 CPA-1.

[117] There is some controversy as to whether the court must take this period into account on its own motion (*ex officio*) or only if the party relies on it. See e.g. Možina, Predpostavke in časovni okviri odgovornosti prodajalca za stvarne napake (2008), *Podjetje in delo*, Year. 34, No. 3/4, 407. However, the jurisprudence seems to hold on to the *ex officio* approach, see Supreme Court of Slovenia, II Ips 67/2014. of 18 September 2014.

[118] Art 78 (5) CPA-1.

[119] See Art. 78 (3) and (4) CPA-1.

[120] Art. 116 (2) CPA-1.

[121] Art. 116 (3) CPA-1.

[122] Ser Art. 93 CPA-1 with regard to sale of goods and Art. 118 (4) with regard to the supply of digital content or services.

[123] For a critical view, see: Možina, Predpostavke in časovni okviri odgovornosti prodajalca za stvarne napake (2008), *Podjetje in delo*, Year. 34, No. 3/4, 407; and Možina, "Breach of Contract and Remedies in the Yugoslav Obligations Act: 40 Years Later" (2020), *ZEuP*, 135, 146.

III. Notification requirement

62   In Slovenian general sales law, the buyer's notification of defects within strict time limits is a condition for all remedies due to non-conformity.[124] This is why Slovenia used the option in Art. 5 (2) Consumer Sales Directive (99/44/EC) and introduced the notification requirement within two months also in consumer sales.[125] This approach is now being continued in conformity with Art. 12 SGD. However, the consumer should not just notify the seller of the non-conformity within two months after they had discovered it but should also provide a "precise description of the non-conformity".[126] This requirement goes beyond Art. 12 SGD and might be contrary to the jurisprudence of the CJEU based on CSD.[127] Furthermore, the CPA-1 retains a somewhat odd provision of the previous CPA on how the notification requirement should be fulfilled.[128]

63   The CPA-1 contains a further odd requirement for the seller: Upon the receipt of the consumer's notification of non-conformity, they must notify the consumer in writing within eight days if they dispute the non-conformity.[129] The breach of this duty is sanctioned by a fine.[130] The duty to dispute seems to have little sense; the same is true for the requirement that it shall be made "in writing";[131] particularly from the viewpoint that there are no general formal requirements for consumer sales contracts and also no other formal requirements for the exercise of the buyer's remedies. The existence of the provision, which is a remnant of the provision from the previous CPA,[132] is a sign of drafting shortcomings. As the provision burdens the seller with a duty which the SGD does not provide for, its conformity with the SGD is questionable. No such duty is provided for regarding the contracts for digital content or services. However, it is contained in the general rules on B2C services (Art. 101 CPA-1) which are applicable as long as there is no special regulation.[133]

64   Regarding the notification requirement in contracts for the supply of digital content and digital services the situation is not quite clear. Unlike in consumer sales, the notification requirement is not directly foreseen here. However, as it is expressly provided for that the consumer can only exercise their remedies within two years following the notification,[134] the notification requirement is implicit. It is not explicitly stated that the consumer's remedies depend on the notification, but it appears so in the light of the (parallel) regulation of consumer sales contract and general contract law. The explanatory memorandum of the draft law explains that the notification requirement

---

[124] See Arts 461, 462 and 468(1) OC. For a critical view, see: Možina, Predpostavke in časovni okviri odgovornosti prodajalca za stvarne napake (2008), *Podjetje in delo,* Year. 34, No. 3/4, 407.

[125] For a critical view of this option by the CSD and SGD, see Staudenmayer, Kauf von Waren mit digitalen Elementen – Die Richtlinie zum Warenkauf (2019), *NJW* 2019, 2889, 2893.

[126] Art. 84 (2) CPA-1.

[127] CJEU, C-497/13, 4 June 2015, *Froukje Faber,* ECLI:EU:C:2015:357, No. 62.

[128] According to Art. 84 (3) CPA-1, the consumer may notify the seller "in person" (i.e. live) of which the seller must issue a confirmation, "send it to the shop" where the goods were bought or notify the seller's agent. The rather clumsy provision must not be interpreted as providing an exhaustive regulation (and it is, in fact, meaningless).

[129] Art. 85 CPA-1.

[130] Art- 241 (1) (9) CPA-1.

[131] The notion of "in writing" is not defined by the CPA-1. However, as e.g., Art. 91 (3) CPA-1, laying down rules for guarantees, refers to a "durable medium" it appears that the "writing is to be understood as paper form".

[132] According to Art. 39 of the existing CPA, the seller must comply with the remedy chosen by the consumer within eight days or sent a written notice that the non-conformity is disputed.

[133] Art. 99 (2) CPA-1.

[134] See Art. 118 (4) CPA-1.

exists but has no time limit, relying on Recital 11 DCD prohibiting the introduction of the obligation to notify the seller "within a specific period".[135] It seems, however, that the legislator might have misunderstood Recital 11; since the DCD does not allow for additional requirements, the introduction of a notification requirement appears to be contrary to the directive.[136] The approach of the legislator appears to have been motivated by the desire to keep the system of time limits for the exercise of remedies known from general sales law and consumer sales law also for contracts for the supply of digital content and services, i.e. to regulate consumer sales and contracts for the supply of digital content in a parallel way. Without the notification requirement, the reference point for the beginning of the (cut-off) period would have been missing. However, the notification requirement without a time limit has little sense. In most cases, it can be considered fulfilled when the consumer exercises any of their remedies for non-conformity (making the further two-year cut-off period for the exercise of remedies obsolete).

H. Right of Redress

65 The regulation of the redress is a novelty the law of Slovenia, as the legislator did not adopt any provisions on the transposition of the Art. 4 of the Consumer Sales Directive into the old CPA. The redress was possible along the chain of contracts, as long as the contractual remedies could be used. Now, the seller who fulfilled the claim by the consumer, may seek reimbursement of its value either from the previous business in the chain of contracts, Art. 88 (1) CPA-1, or directly from the "business responsible", Art. 88 (5) CPA-1. The provisions on the burden of proof (in the sense of Arts. 11 SGD and 12 DCD) are applicable to the redress claim.[137] The provisions on redress cannot be modified by a contract.[138] In the first version of the draft CPA-1 only redress along the chain of contracts was foreseen. No explanation was given for the direct claim introduced additionally.

66 The reimbursement claim is subject to an extremely short prescription period of only three months starting from the fulfilment of the consumer's claim, Art. 88 (6) CPA-1. This is a serious limitation of the final seller's right of redress. No explanation was given for its introduction. The legislator seemingly attempted to protect the business responsible (direct redress) as well as all businesses in the chain of contracts (redress along the chain), possibly as a kind of counterbalance for two different options of redress. However, the prescription claim of three months limits the recourse claim of the final seller (and of the business in the chain of contracts against whom the seller may have succeeded with a recourse claim) in a rather disproportionate way. Such a short prescription period is not common in Slovenian law where the general prescription period (applicable e.g. also to restitution claims) is five years.[139]

67 Art. 127 CPA-1 is an almost identical provision for the redress in contracts for the supply of digital content or services with one difference: There is no right of redress against the previous trader or another person in the contractual chain, who has supplied, gratuitously and on the basis of a free and open source licence, software from which digital content or a digital service is composed or constructed.[140] The provision seems

---

[135] See the explanatory memorandum in the Government CPA-1 from 12 July 2022 (EVA: 2015–2130–0005), p. 159.
[136] Schulze, in: Schulze and Staudenmayer (eds), *EU Digital Law* (2020), Art. 1, No. 24, p. 38.
[137] Art. 88 (3) and 127 (3) CPA-1.
[138] Art. 88 (7) CPA-1.
[139] Art. 346 OC.
[140] Art. 127 (8) CPA-1.

somehow odd having in mind that the DCD is not applicable to the software offered by the trader under a free and open source software for which the consumer does not pay the price – Art. 3 (5) (f) DCD.

I. Conclusions

68   As the SGD and DCD aim at full harmonisation, the Member States were left with relatively little discretion as to their transposition. Still, some options were given to the Member States and Slovenia made use of most of them. The basic characteristics of the Slovene transposition could be summarised as follows:

69   Damages are an additional remedy of the consumer in case of lack of conformity. They are mandatory and cannot be excluded or limited by a contract. However, the damages appear to be subject to different time limits than other remedies. While the warranty time limit of two years from delivery is the same, the further time limit is different: A general prescription period of five years rather than a two-year (cut-off) time limit (from the notification of a lack of conformity) for the exercise of right to repair, replacement, price reduction or termination. Whether this was indented or a drafting mistake is difficult to say, as no explanation is provided on this point. The general rules on contractual damages apply, particularly the principle of foreseeability as the limitation of the amount.

70   In accordance with the approach in the previous CPA and all its general contract law – Slovenia has kept the notification of non-conformity as a condition of all consumer remedies due to a lack of conformity. Interestingly, the notification requirement is also prescribed in contracts for the supply of digital content or services – albeit without a time limit, thereby raising questions as to the reasonableness of such requirement.

71   In addition to immediate termination or a price reduction due to the "serious nature of the breach" from Art. 13 (4) (c) SGD, Slovenia introduced a further right to termination if the lack of conformity becomes apparent within the first 30 days following delivery (rejection).

72   A further characteristic of the Slovenian consumer sales law is the mandatory guarantee of the producer for the durability (proper functioning) of "technical goods" for a duration of one year.

73   A system of mandatory guarantee has long been a part of Slovenian sales law and was parallel to the mandatory liability of the seller introduced by the CSD. It could be invoked against the seller and producer and was not limited to B2C relationships. As full harmonisation prevents a parallel system of the liability of the seller, the legislator – who wanted to stay with the old system as much as possible – introduced a (non-contractual) liability of the producer. The guarantee liability can also be invoked in B2B contracts. Whether a mandatory guarantee (for technical goods) in addition to a commercial guarantee of the producer for durability is a good solution is questionable.

74   An overall feature of the CPA-1 is relatively poor drafting quality; it contains some poorly thought-out solutions and examples of overlooked links to general contract law as well as to other parts of CPA-1.

75   However, it should be emphasised that the directives bring about an important refreshment of consumer law and its alignment with technological development. In this regard, it is necessary to highlight the objective standards of conformity with the contract, particularly regarding goods with digital elements and digital content and services. Standards of conformity, e.g. with regard to updates of software, could and

should be taken as a basis for the reasonable expectations of the buyers also outside of B2C contracts.

It is also worth pointing out that the DCD regulates some aspects of a long-standing practice where the consumer does not pay for digital content or services with money but allows the use of their personal data (data as counter performance). Regarding the transposition of the DCD the legislator's decision to follow the approach of Germany in regulating the consequences of the revocation of the consent to the processing of the consumer's personal data in a contract for the supply of digital content or a digital service, is to be welcomed.

The remedial structure of both SGD and DCD represents a novelty in Slovenia, as the hierarchy of remedies in the general contract law and in the previous Consumer Protection Act was different. The consequence of the legislator's fundamental approach to the implementation of EU consumer law since joining the EU, which is to change as little as possible, is a growing tension between the national general contract law and consumer contract law. In this sense, the SGD and DCD can offer an opportunity to reflect on the future of contract law in Slovenia.

Bibliography

Axel Metzger, ‚Verträge über digitale Inhalte und digitale Dienstleistungen: Neuer BGB-Vertragstypus oder punktuelle Reform?' (2019), *JuristenZeitung* 74(12), 577.

Damjan Možina, 'Breach of Contract and Remedies in the Yugoslav Obligations Act: 40 Years Later' (2020), *ZEuP*, 135.

Damjan Možina, 'Pravice kupca na podlagi stvarne napake pri prodajni pogodbi' (2012), *Pravni letopis 2012*, 85.

Damjan Možina, 'Problem uveljavljanja znižanja pogodbene cene' (2014), *Pravna praksa* 43/2014, 16.

Damjan Možina, 'Garancija za brezhibno delovanje in odgovornost za stvarne napake' (2009), *Zbornik znanstvenih razprav PF LJ*, 143.

Damjan Možina, 'Predpostavke in časovni okviri odgovornosti prodajalca za stvarne napake' (2008), *Podjetje in delo*, Year. 34, No. 3/4, 407.

Dirk Staudenmayer, 'Kauf von Waren mit digitalen Elementen – Die Richtlinie zum Warenkauf' (2019), *NJW* 2019, 2889.

European Data Protection Supervisor (EDPS), Opinion 4/2017 on the Proposal for a Directive on certain aspects concerning contracts for the supply of digital content, URL: <https://edps.europa.eu/sites/edp/files/publication/17-03-14_opinion_digital_content_en.pdf> (16.9.2022).

Franz Jürgen Säcker, Roland Rixecker, Hartmut Oetker and Bettina Limperg (eds), *Münchener Kommentar zum Bürgerlichen Gesetzbuch*, 9th Edition, (Verlag C.H.BECK München, München 2022).

Hugh Beale, 'Conclusion and Performance of Contracts: An Overview' in: Reiner Schulze, Dirk Staudenmayer, Sebastian Lohsse, (eds) *Contracts for the Supply of Digital Content: Regulatory Challenges and Gaps, Münster Colloquia on EU Law and the Digital Economy* (Nomos, Baden-Baden, 2017), 33.

Judith Klink-Straub, 'Do ut des data – Bezahlen mit Daten im digitalen Vertragsrecht' (2021), *NJW 2021*, 3217.

Miha Juhart and Nina Plavšak (eds), 'Obligacijski zakonik (OZ) s komentarjem (GV Založba, Ljubljana 2003–4)'.

Reiner Schulze and Dirk Staudenmayer (eds), *'EU Digital Law Article-by-Article Commentary'* (Nomos, Baden-Baden 2020).

European Law Institute, 'Statement of the European Law Institute on the European Commission's proposed Directive on the supply of digital content to consumers COM (2015) 634 final'.

Spain

A. Introduction	1
B. Overview of the reform	2
I. Legislative technique	2
II. Some new developments	4
C. The legislative framework	5
I. The relationship between consumer law and general contract law	5
II. The relationship of consumer contract law with other matters	6
D. Material scope of the reform	8
I. The contractual types	8
II. In particular, Sales of goods	10
III. Mixed contracts	11
IV. Data as consideration	14
E. Subjective scope of application	17
F. Some objective conformity criteria	20
I. Durability	21
II. Updates	24
G. The modification of the digital content and digital services contract	26
H. Time Periods	27
I. Periods of liability	27
II. Identifying the day of delivery or supply	29
III. The reversal of the burden of proof	31
IV. Suspension of the liability period	34
V. Prescription of claims	35
I. Remedies for non-conformity	38
I. General points	38
II. Repair and replacement	39
III. Price reduction	44
IV. Termination	45
V. Withholding payment and damages	49
J. Redress and direct claim	50
K. Overall assessment	52
Bibliography	55

A. Introduction

As a result of the transposition of Directive (EU) 2019/770 (DCD)[1], Spain has new provisions concerning contracts for the supply of digital content and digital services. However, the transposition of Directive 2019/771 (SGD)[2] only adapts the sales contract to the changes brought about by technological advances and sustainable consumption. Both European rules have been incorporated into the *Texto Refundido de la Ley General de Defensa de los Consumidores y Usuarios* (TR-LGDCU) by means of Royal Decree-Law (RDL) 7/2021 of 27 April 2021.[3] The reform broadens the list of definitions, sets out the scope of the new rules (in accordance with the exclusions provided for in the directives) and divides the new articles between, on the one hand, the general part of consumer contracts (Book II, Title I, Chapter I) and, on the other, guarantees and after-sales services (Book II, Title IV, Chapters I-V). No specific book has been created for the

1

---

[1] OJ L 136, of 22.5.2019.
[2] OJ L 136, of 22.5.2019.
[3] BOE 101, of 28.04.2021.

new contract for the supply of digital content and digital services. Catalonia has its own norms, which have been incorporated into the Catalan Civil Code (CC Cat), and to which only *ad hoc* reference will be made here.[4]

B. Overview of the reform

I. Legislative technique

2   RDL 7/2021 amends, once again, the TR-LGDCU. The Generalitat of Catalonia has also used a Decree-Law to transpose the two directives, although transposition has taken place into Catalonia's Civil Code and not into its Consumer Code. This difference in approach is important because in a civil code the rules are general for all contracting parties, notwithstanding the fact that they may also include special features specific to consumer contracts (e.g. regarding knowledge of the defect that prevents a claim; or presumptions of lack of conformity).[5]

3   There are good reasons to support the extension to contracts other than consumer contracts. A strictly consumer-centric view forgets that along with the rights and duties of the consumer, it is also necessary to cover those of the trader or business. However, the Spanish legislator is silent on the entitlement of the seller or supplier of digital content to claim payment, withhold performance, or request interest when the consumer does not comply with the incumbent duties and, in particular, the obligation to pay the price. Even worse, the duty placed on the trader by Art. 16.3 DCD to refrain from using the data provided by the consumer when the consumer terminates the contract (Art. 119 *ter* 1 and 5 TR-LGDCU) does not apply when it is the trader who terminates it.[6]

II. Some new developments

4   The Spanish legislator has increased consumer protection at several points where the directives were of minimum harmonisation, in particular with regard to the lengthening of the liability periods in the sale of goods (from 2 to 3 years, Art. 120 TR-LGDCU), the extension of the presumption of non-conformity (now 2 years, Art. 121 TR-LGDCU)[7], or the suppression of the burden of notifying the lack of conformity within a certain period as a requirement for the consumer to exercise the remedies for lack of conformity. On the other hand, the Spanish legislator has retained provisions not covered by the directives, such as direct claim against the producer (Art. 125.1 TR-LGDCU); moreover, the suspension of the liability period has been regulated *ex novo* (Art. 122.1 and 2 TR-LGDCU); and prescription has been extended to 5 years. The legislator has also provided for generous after-sales services and availability of spare parts (Art. 127 *bis* TR-LGDCU). Furthermore, personal data collected by the trader for commercial purposes are the

---

[4] Decret Llei 27/2021, of 14.12.2021 (DOGC 8564, of 16.12.2021). See Arnau Raventós and Gramunt Fombuena, "Cap a un dret català conforme a les directives (UE) 2019/770 i 2019/771" (2022) 2 *InDret*, 171.

[5] See art. 621-26.2, 621-73.3 and 621-74.2 CC Cat (but see, for all types of sales, art. 621-24.1 and 2 CC Cat).

[6] Warning of the need to go beyond the directive, Sein and Spindler "The New Directive on Contracts for the Supply of Digital Content and Digital Services – Scope of Application and Trader's Obligation to Supply – Part 2", (2019) 4 *ERCL* 365 (379-380).

[7] In the case of second-hand goods, see below H. I (periods of liability) and III (The reversal of the burden of proof).

price or consideration for digital content or services (Art. 59.4, 119 *ter* 2 TR-LGDCU). Consequently, new rules on the contractual effects of the withdrawal of consent to data processing needed to be adopted (Art. 119 *ter* 7 TR-LGDCU).

C. The legislative framework

I. The relationship between consumer law and general contract law

Preamble IX 12 of the DL 7/2021 emphasises that the artificial distinctions between defect and *aliud pro alio* should not persist, which means that the consumer should not be able to choose between the rules of lack of conformity set out in the TR-LGDCU and those of non-performance contained in the Spanish Civil Code, which is congruent with the fact that consumer remedies are fully harmonised (Recital 47 SGD). It is therefore striking that the directives still allow a supplementary general regime on hidden defects to be maintained in national laws (Art. 3.7 SGD; Recital 12 DCD). Nevertheless, Art. 116 TR-LGDCU declares the non-compatibility between the conformity regime and the regime of *saneamiento*.[8] This reference in Art. 116 TR-LGDCU to *saneamiento* not only includes remedies for hidden defects, but also remedies for eviction, since the lack of conformity is now extended to legal defects (Art. 117.1 TR-LGDCU).[9] However, Art. 117.2 TR-LGDCU allows recourse to corrective measures other than those provided for lack of conformity when a law so declares. This is the same as provided for in the Directives (Art. 9 SGD and 10 DCD) because some Member States wanted to preserve the possibility existing in their legislation to consider contracts that violate copyright law as null and void.[10] The problem is that, in Spain, it is not clear what the reason for this reference is.[11] Certainly that law should not be the Spanish Civil Code, despite the unfortunate reference to the legal guarantee for eviction in Recital 54 DCD, because it would be of no advantage to the consumer to have to wait to be defeated in court before being able to claim against the trader and because it would undermine the directives' *effet utile* to impose a regime that is clearly less favourable for the consumer.

5

II. The relationship of consumer contract law with other matters

Digitalisation makes it necessary to harmonise contract law with other areas, such as data protection or copyright. Regulation (UE) 2016/679 of 27.4.2016, on the protection of natural persons with regard to the processing of personal data (GDPR)[12] must be applied in full and infringement of basic principles such as data minimisation or data protection by design and privacy (Art. 25 GDPR) may constitute a lack of conformity if it contravenes one or more of the conformity criteria set out in the DCD; for example, if a software bug allows identity theft, or discloses payment data (Recital 48 DCD).[13] This is a significant change of perspective, which should have been emphasised by the Spanish legislator.

6

---

[8] For more details on the understanding of the rule, see Arroyo Amayuelas, "The Implementation of EU Directives 2019/770 and 771 in Spain" (2022) 11 *EuCML*, 35 (36).
[9] Castilla Barea, *La nueva regulación europea de la venta de bienes muebles a consumidores* (2021), 336.
[10] Thus, Staudenmayer, "Die Richtlinien zu den digitalen Verträgen" (2019) 4 *ZEuP*, 663 (685).
[11] Same criticism, Castilla Barea (fn 9) 334.
[12] OJ L 119, of 4.5.2016.
[13] See Staudenmayer, Art. 8 Dir (UE) 2019/770, in Schulze and Staudenmayer (eds.), *EU Digital Law. Article by Article Commentary* (2020), 131 (137).

7 Moreover, personal data collected by the trader for commercial purposes are the price or consideration for digital content or services (Art. 59.4, 119 ter 2 TR-LGDCU). This has forced the Spanish legislator to address the consequences of the withdrawal of consent to data processing for the contract and whether the trader is entitled to be compensated in such a case (Art. 119 ter 7 TR-LGDCU).[14] By contrast, no progress has been made in enshrining the rights of consumers as opposed to those of authors. It remains unclear to what extent the consumer can claim against the trader for lack of conformity when the licence of the digital content s/he acquires for unlimited use prevents her/him from making copies, including back-up copies, using the content on different devices, sharing it with family or friends, or accessing the content already acquired once the platform that markets it stops offering it.[15] Under Directive EC 99/44, the Spanish intellectual property doctrine considered that the consumer who did not legally have those rights could not have any expectations and therefore no lack of conformity can be claimed.[16] However, consumers' reasonable expectations are not only normative expectations, and it is therefore legitimate for them to aspire to have the same rights in the digital and analogue worlds.[17] Even so, it must be acknowledged that, in the absence of concrete legislative expression of protected rights or interests of consumers acquiring copyrighted digital content,[18] it is not easy to identify what parameters serve to establish that there is an objective lack of conformity, because of the diversity of content, because the consumer does not always know what to expect, or because it is the industry that ultimately establishes at any given moment what is possible.[19] It is surprising that neither the DCD nor the SGD clearly answer the question of whether this more than probable deficit in consumer protection can be mitigated by the application of Directive EEC 93/13 on unfair terms.[20]

D. Material scope of the reform

I. The contractual types

8 Directive EU 2011/83 of 25.10.2011, on consumer rights (CRD)[21] echoes the dichotomy between (tangible) goods and (intangible) services and reserves the contract of sale for the former.[22] The SGD also applies only to tangible goods (Art. 2.1) – even if they incorporate digital elements – and the DCD, on the other hand, to intangible goods –

---

[14] See below D.IV (Data as consideration) and I (Remedies for non-conformity).
[15] In this regard, Oprysk and Sein, "Limitations in End-User Licensing Agreements: Is There A Lack of Conformity Under the New Digital Content Directive?" (2020) 51 IIC, 594; Spindler, "Digital Content Directive and Copyright-related Aspects" (2021) 2 JIPITEC, 111 (119 ff, 124 ff).
[16] See the discussion in Cabeda Serna, "Los consumidores y las medidas tecnológicas de protección incorporadas en soportes digitales", in Moreno Martínez (ed.), Límites a la propiedad intelectual y nuevas tecnologías (2008), 66 (103–105) (consulted via V-Lex).
[17] Based on an empirical study showing that restrictions on the use of digital content often interfere with consumers' reasonable expectations, Oprysk and Sein (fn 15) 611 ff.
[18] However, see Art. 5.2 Directive 2009/24/EC of 23.04.2009 (OJ L 111, of 5.5.2009) on the legal protection of computer programs: "[T]he making of a back-up copy by a person entitled to use the program may not be prevented by contract in so far as it is necessary for such use". In Spanish Law, see Art. 100.2 of Real Decreto Legislativo 1/1996, of 12.04.1996 (BOE 97, of 22.04.1996).
[19] Spindler (fn 15) 118–119; Oprysk and Sein (fn 15) 598.
[20] OJ L 95, of 21.4.1993.
[21] OJ L 304, of 22.11.2011.
[22] Art. 2.5 and 2.6 CRD. See CJEU C-583/18, of 12.03.2020, Verbraucherzentrale Berlin (§ 22); CJEU C-208/19, of 14.05.2020, NK (§ 62).

even if they are embodied in a medium. However, these intangibles are no longer classified as service contracts (as a category, as opposed to sales), since they are both the subject of digital services as such (Art. 2.2 a and b DCD) and of other, distinct digital content contracts (Art. 2.1 DCD). From the point of view of the classification of contracts on the basis of their subject matter, this raises the question of when exactly each case is involved. Software, for example, can be a type of digital content as well as a service (Recital 19 DCD).[23] In fact, the answer matters little, because the distinction between content and services mainly serves to emphasise that the DCD extends to any form of digital supply.[24]

What is relevant in the DCD is the form of access, i.e. whether there is a permanent and unlimited supply over time or whether limited temporary access to the digital content or service is provided. And it is theoretically on the basis of this distinction that national laws may provide for different contractual types (Art. 12 DCD). The Spanish legislator has not followed this path. The types of contracts subject to new rules in the TR-LGDCU are sales and a generic contract for the supply of digital content and services. In view of the huge number of access modalities, this decision does not merit any reproach.[25]

9

II. In particular, Sales of goods

Art. 59 *bis* 2 TR-LGDCU establishes that sales can only relate to tangible movable goods, thus excluding the acquisition of ownership (of a copy) of the digital content, even in cases where the consumer is granted a licence for indefinite use.[26] In contrast, Art. 59.4 TR-LGDCU does refer to the possibility of digital content or services being the subject matter of a sales contract. Art. 59 *bis* 1 letter f TR-LGDCU removes the mention of the price in the definition of the sale of goods, but it is evident that it cannot be dispensed with. According to the Spanish CC, the price must be in money or a sign representing it (Art. 1445 CC). The SGD does not refer to the fact that the price may be the consumer's personal (or other) data, although this is perhaps simply because, in practice, it is not the most frequent situation in transactions that take place in the offline world that involve tangible goods. However, the reasoning is no longer relevant if the goods are smart goods, as personal data are usually provided along with a monetary consideration. In fact, the same could happen in any other online sale with a different object and, for this reason, there should be no objection to Art. 59.4 TR-LGDCU also being applicable

10

---

[23] However, see Savin, "Harmonising Private Law in Cyberspace: The New Directives in the Digital Single Market Context", in Durovic and Tridimas (eds), *New Directions in European Private Law* (2021), 211 (221): "while content refers to raw data, services refer to a product or a platform". For a more complete analysis, Mischau, "The Concept of Digital Content and Digital Services in European Contract Law" (2022) 1 *EuCML*, 6.

[24] Schulze, "Die Digitale-Inhalte-Richtlinie-Innovation und Kontinuität im europäischen Vertragsrecht" (2019) 4 *ZEuP*, 695 (700–702).

[25] Ramberg, "Digital Content – A digital CESL II- A paradigm for contract law via the backdoor?", in Grundmann (ed), *European Contract Law in the Digital Age* (2018), 315 (326): "The efforts to categorise the legal nature of various contract types are not a viable way for the future".

[26] Cf. CJEU C-128/11, of 3.07.2012, *UsedSoft* (§§ 44–49); Cf. CJEU C-410/19, of 16.09.2021, *The Software Incubator* (§§ 37–42).

in this hypothesis.²⁷ Nor does the TR-LGDCU address payment by means of a representation of value (Art. 2.7 DCD) or with virtual currencies (Recital 23 DCD).²⁸

III. Mixed contracts

11   How the contract should be qualified when it is a package with different elements does not receive a homogeneous answer in the EU directives. Art. 3.6 I DCD stipulates that insofar as goods or other services (e.g. provision of digital television and the purchase of electronic equipment, Art. 33 DCD) are contracted together with the digital content or services, each element is governed by its own rules. In the context of the sale of tangible goods, however, the opposite is true. Thus, according to Art. 2.5 CRD, a contract that has as its object both the transfer of ownership of the goods and the provision of related services offered by the seller, such as installation or maintenance, is qualified as a sales contract. This means that, in principle, its rules also apply to performance that is not typical of such a contract. The advantage for the consumer is that this avoids having to resort to a different liability regime (objective/fault-based).

12   In the SGD the view is different. Indeed, although installation is part of the sales contract if it has to be carried out by or under the responsibility of the seller (Art. 8.1 letter a SGD), Recital 17 SGD warns that otherwise, where a contract includes elements of both goods and supply of services, it is up to Member States to decide whether the whole contract can be classified as a sales contract. Art. 59 *bis* letter f TR-LGDCU does not clearly adopt one solution or the other. The provision merely stipulates that sales "may include the provision of services", but does not specify on what basis the classification as a sale is to be retained in any such case. In interpreting the provision, it will certainly be necessary to take into account what was established in CJEU C-247/16, of 7.09.2017, *Schottelius* (§§ 38, 44) which, under Directive EC 99/44, specified that for the transaction to be considered a sale, the provision of services had to be ancillary²⁹ or, in other words, that the main purpose or predominant element of the contract should be the transfer of ownership.³⁰

13   On the other hand, when defining a service contract, Art. 59 *bis* 1 letter g stipulates that it can also be of a digital nature. Therefore, if the above criteria are also to be applied, it is possible that a contract that includes the provision of digital services (e.g. the purchase of a bicycle and a training app) should also be classified as a contract for the sale of goods in accordance with Art. 59 *bis* letter f TR-LGDCU. However, unless the services are services that are to be embedded in goods, without which the goods would not be able to fulfil their function – for then the sale will have *vis attractiva* (Recital 15 SGD) – such an interpretation would clash with Art. 3.6 I DCD, which requires each provision to be governed by its own rules. If, therefore, the mixed nature of the contract is to be preserved, it would have been reasonable for the Spanish legislator to foresee the consequences if the consumer terminates the contract due to lack of supply or lack of confor-

---

²⁷ Different opinion, Cámara Lapuente, "Un primer balance de las novedades del RDL 7/2021, de 27 de abril, para la defensa de los consumidores en el suministro de contenidos y servicios digitales (La transposición de las Directivas 2019/770 y 2019/771)", *Diario La Ley*, of 29 June 2021, 1 (20 and 30 fn 55), who also highlights the lower level of consumer protection offered by the SGD on this issue. Same criticism, De Franceschi, *La vendita di beni con elementi digitali* (2019), 60.
²⁸ See Art. 1170.1 of the Spanish CC; Arroyo Amayuelas (fn 8) 36.
²⁹ See Arnau Raventós, "Transmisión onerosa de un producto y su conformidad con el contrato: una relectura de la STJUE de 7 de septiembre de 2017 (Asunto 247/16, Schottelius)" (2018) 2 *RED*, 42.
³⁰ See Commission notice Guidance on the interpretation and application of Directive 2011/83/EU of the European Parliament and of the Council on consumer rights (OJ C 525, of 29.12.2021) 7–9.

mity of one or the other of the two elements of the bundle, or because of the unilateral modification of the digital elements by the trader. Indeed, according to Art. 3.6 III DCD, the legislator should have provided whether the termination of any of the elements affects the contract with respect to all elements or whether the contract is preserved in respect of the non-affected elements. Exceptionally, and only in the case that the contract contains at least one internet access service or number-based interpersonal communications services, Art. 107.2 of the Electronic Communications Code establishes that the termination affects the entire contract.[31]

IV. Data as consideration

When regulating the purchase or use of digital content or services, the DCD allows consumers to transfer their personal data for purposes that go beyond those that would be necessary to comply with the law or to perform the service. Since the conditions that the supplier attaches to access to the good or service exceed what would be required to agree to a donation and, furthermore, there is never a generous intention on behalf of the traders, the contract thus shaped can never be deemed to be gratuitous. However, this payment with the consumer's personal data is not called a price (see Art. 2.7 DCD), and the reason is to be found in the opinion expressed by the European Data Protection Supervisor, according to whom personal data can never be considered as consideration.[32] Even so, Spanish law does consider them as such (Art. 119 *ter* 2 TR-LGDCU). The only exception is the scenario provided for in Recital 32 and Art. 3.5 letter f DCD regarding free and open software where personal data are used exclusively to improve security, compatibility and interoperability without being a price (Art. 114.2 letter h TR-LGDCU).[33]

14

The DCD should apply when the trader provides digital content or services, and the consumer provides personal data that are used by the trader for purposes other than the mere provision of the digital content or digital service or the fulfilment of legal requirements. RDL 7/2021 welcomes the idea that there can indeed be a contract in such a case, after recalling that the traditional understanding did not contemplate such a hypothesis.[34] This means that the grounds for the transaction must be lawful, and consent must be freely given (Arts. 1261, 1262.1 CC).

15

Regulation EU 2016/679 (GDPR) is relevant in this case because the processing of personal data must be consented to by the consumer (Art. 6.1 letter a). Consent should not be considered freely given if the data subject does not have a genuine or free choice (Recital 32, Arts. 4.11 and 7.4 GDPR). The Spanish Data Protection Agency (AEPD) has recently rejected that browsing a website is a valid form of consent.[35] However, the DCD does not settle whether or not the consent to conclude the contract must be given in accordance with the GDPR. It is sensible to answer this question in the negative in order to

16

---

[31] Directive (EU) 2018/1972, of 11.12.2018 (OJ L 321, of 17.12.2018).
[32] Opinion dated 14.03.2017. However, see Recitals 15, 16 of the European Electronic Communications Code (fn 31).
[33] Sein and Spindler, "The New Directive on Contracts for the Supply of Digital Content and Digital Services – Scope of Application and Trader's Obligation to Supply – Part 1" (2019) 3 *ERCL*, 257 (268).
[34] Preamble IX 20 of the RDL 7/2021.
[35] Asociacion Española de Proteccion de Datos (AEPD), *Guidance on the use of cookies*, July 2020, pp. 21, 23. Available at: https://www.aepd.es/es/prensa-y-comunicacion/notas-de-prensa/aepd-actualiza-g uia-cookies (last visited 30 June 2022). Also CJEU C-673/17, of 1.10.2019, *Planet49* (§§ 70–71). Previously, see Aparicio Vaquero, "La protección de datos personales en las redes sociales. Apuntes desde los ordenamientos europeos y español" (2020) 1 *Tecnologia e Diritto*, 209 (236–237).

prevent non-compliance with the requirements of the GDPR from leading the trader to deprive the consumer of the protection afforded to him by the TR-LGDCU.[36] In any event, consumer law always requires express consent to enter into any payment obligation (Art. 66 *quater*, Art. 101 TR-LGDCU), which should certainly not be excluded when this is not in money. In fact, since Art. 59.4 TR-LGDCU declares the applicability of Book II to any contract in which the consideration is paid with personal data,[37] it is obvious that Arts. 60.1 letter c, 60 *bis* TR-LGDCU, on the clarity and comprehensibility of the price and additional payments that must be expressly accepted, also apply in this case. All this would lead to the conclusion that when it comes to economically exploiting the data of users of digital services, *browse agreements*, which are characterised by requiring implicit consent through access to websites, should not be permitted under Spanish consumer law.[38]

E. Subjective scope of application

17 Both directives limit their personal scope of application to consumer contracts and deal exceptionally – and very sparingly – with B2B relations, only regarding the right of redress.[39] This is so even though online platforms are the main entry point to markets for most small businesses in the digital economy and this leads to asymmetries and disadvantages when trading. The rationale for removing barriers in the internal market also applies here. It is thus a step backwards to limit the scope of application to B2C contracts, even if the explicit *caveat* is included that national laws can go further.[40] Spanish law does not offer such a broad scope, even though the definition of consumer provided by Art. 3 TR-LGDCU is more comprehensive than in European law, because it covers entities without legal personality[41] and non-profit legal persons.

18 Furthermore, in the digital environment it can be very difficult to distinguish between personal and professional use and this is maybe the reason why the Directives no longer define when a person concluding a dual-purpose contract should be considered a consumer (Recital 17 DCD, 22 SGD). The Spanish legislator has not done so either, but Spanish case law has expanded the notion of consumer to mixed contracts, and *a priori* it is not realistic to think that it will abandon this approach, sometimes somewhat erratic in determining whether the test of the main purpose of the contract or that of the resid-

---

[36] García Pérez, "Interacción entre protección del consumidor y protección de datos personales en la Directiva 770/2019: licitud del tratamiento y conformidad de los contenidos y servicios digitales", in Arroyo Amayuelas and Cámara Lapuente (dirs), *El Derecho privado en el nuevo paradigma digital* (2020), 175 (191–192); Milà Rafel, "Datos personales como contraprestación en la directiva de contenidos y Servicios digitales", in Gómez Pomar and Fernández Chacón (dirs), *Estudios de Derecho Contractual Europeo: Nuevos problemas, nuevas reglas* (2022), 407 (442–443).

[37] On this, Cámara Lapuente (fn 27) 18–20.

[38] It is nevertheless sensible to claim for a clear regulation at European level. See Cámara Lapuente "Nuevos perfiles del consentimiento en la contratación digital en la Unión Europea: ¿navegar es contratar (servicios digitales «gratuitos»)?", in Gómez Pomar and Fernández Chacón (fn 36), 331 (384).

[39] For criticism, Schulze (fn 24) 702–703; Beale, "Digital Content Directive and Rules For Contracts on Continuous Supply" (2021) 2 *JIPITEC*, 96 (105).

[40] Recital 16 DCD; Recital 21 SGD. Formerly, Recital 13 CRD; Recital 29 Dir. 2002/65, of 23.11.2002 (OJ L 271, of 09.10.2002) concerning the distance marketing of consumer financial services: "[...] extension by Member States [...] of the protection provided by this Directive to non-profit organisations and persons making use of financial services in order to become entrepreneurs".

[41] Judgement of the Spanish Supreme Court (STS) of 13.04.2021 (RJ 2021\1710). Cf. CJEU C-329/19 of 2.04.2020, *Condominio di Milano* (§§ 34–37).

ual commercial activity should be given priority.⁴² However, on the one hand, new and changing online activities are leading to a development of the notion of consumer that is very different from the traditional one⁴³ and, on the other hand, it is difficult to distinguish between professional and personal use when acquiring certain types of digital content (e.g. software). In Catalonia, the category of consumer is retained for those who primarily act for purposes unrelated to their profession (Art. 621–2 CC Cat).

It would have been appropriate to broaden the subjective scope of application of the directives, especially considering that some of their rules are naturally addressed to businesses. For example, it is mainly businesses that will require digital content adapted to their needs (Recital 26, Art. 3.2 DCD).⁴⁴ Moreover, it is provisions designed for the B2B context, such as the CISG, that can help to understand certain aspects of these directives; in particular, how the acceptance of the individual purpose expressed by the buyer to the trader should be interpreted.⁴⁵ Lastly, it is extremely easy to circumvent the protection provided to the consumer by the directives with regard to the potential exclusion of specific requirements of objective conformity, as if it were a contract between traders, who can always freely waive the protection provided to them by the law. It seems, therefore, that there is not much of a difference between the rules governing the one type of contract and the other.

F. Some objective conformity criteria

One of the objective conformity criteria is the durability or ability of the goods to maintain their required functions and performance through normal use (Art. 2.13 SGD; Art. 59 *bis* 1 letter i TR-LGDCU). It is a feature that can also relate to updates of digital content, which are due irrespective of whether there are any agreements on this point (Art. 8.2 DCD, Art. 115 *ter* 2 TR-LGDCU).⁴⁶

I. Durability

The consumer's expectation when buying a good is that it will not become obsolete prematurely and also that it can be repaired if it suffers from wear and tear. This approach has not been adequately reflected in the SGD. Despite Recital 48 SGD, repair is not enforced on a preferential basis, even if the consumer wants to keep the good.⁴⁷ Nor does the SGD impose a duty on sellers to ensure the availability of spare parts (Recital 33), even though nothing prevents the manufacturer from undertaking to sup-

---

⁴² STS of 3.06.2016 (RJ\2016\2300); STS of 5.04.2017 (RJ\2017\2669); STS of 7.11.2017 (RJ\2017\4763); STS of 28.01.2020 (RJ\2020\114).

⁴³ Concerning social media, CJEU C-498/16, of 25.01.2018, *Maximilian Schrems*. Concerning a poker player, CJEU C-774/19, of 10.12.2020, *Personal Exchange International*.

⁴⁴ Schmitt, Thomas R., "A new warranty law for digital content ante portes" (2018) 2 *University of Vienna Law Review*, 1 (5).

⁴⁵ Regarding the interpretation of Art. 7 letter b DCD in accordance with Art. 35.2 letter b CSIG (but the same would apply to art. 6 letter b SGD), see Beale (fn 39) 97–98, fn 20. But see for the opposite opinion, Marco Molina, "Los criterios legales de la conformidad con el contrato en el futuro Libro VI del Codi Civil de Catalunya: la llamada conformidad subjetiva o adecuación de lo entregado al fin individual del comprador", in Llàcer Matacàs (ed), *La codificación del Derecho Contractual de Consumo en el Derecho Civil Catalán* (2015), 193 (197–200).

⁴⁶ Twigg-Flessner, "Conformity of Goods and Digital Content/Digital Services", in Arroyo Amayuelas and Cámara Lapuente (fn 36) 49 (75); De Franceschi (fn 27) 17–18.

⁴⁷ See Terryn, "A Right to Repair? Towards Sustainable Remedies in Consumer Law" (2019) 4 *ERPL*, 851 (857–858).

ply them in the commercial guarantee (Art. 17.1 SGD). Moreover, the SGD does not provide for a minimum lifetime for goods, though it acknowledges that Member States may go further, because longer periods encourage the production of more durable goods, allow easier repair and, in short, encourage businesses to make more sustainable decisions.[48] It is paradoxical that the European legislator allows the reduction of the guarantee period for second-hand goods to a minimum of one year (Art. 10.6 SGD), regardless of the previous use that has been made of them, as if second-hand goods necessarily were always expected to last for a shorter period. In fact, the agreement excluding the seller's liability (Art. 7.5 SGD) seems to have been envisaged precisely with the durability of these goods in mind (Recital 36 SGD). These are certainly not measures that encourage their acquisition.[49]

22   In the context of the Spanish Circular Economy Strategy 2030,[50] the TR-LGDCU does indeed go somewhat further than the SGD. First of all, it preserves and reinforces the current legislation and ensures the existence of an adequate technical support service, as well as the necessary spare parts, for a minimum period of time, which is now 10 years instead of the previous 5 years, from the date on which the good ceases to be manufactured (Art. 127 *bis* 1 TR-LGDCU).[51] The aim is thus to ensure that goods are kept for as long as possible. Even so, it is clear that the requirement for manufacturers to ensure the existence of spare parts for 10 years should have been placed in relation to the expected useful life of each type of good according to the sector to which they belong (e.g. household appliances, automobiles, electronic devices), in line with the provisions of other European Regulations, which provide for periods of 7, 8 and 10 years and which, in any case, are preferentially applicable precisely because of their origin.[52]

23   Ensuring adequate technical service and spare parts is a provision that certainly contributes to maintaining the goods' value for as long as possible and helps to reduce waste (DL 7/2021 Recital IX 18). However, it is a provision independent of the statutory liability period. Although the TR-LGDCU also tries to guarantee the durability of goods by broadening the minimum warranty periods (3 years instead of 2) and the presumption of lack of conformity (2 years instead of 1), the fact is that the right to repair the good, thanks to the availability of a technical repair service and spare parts, does not mean that it does not have to be paid for if it breaks down after those three years, even if the reasonable period of use is much longer. A longer seller's or trader's liability period would have been preferable or, even better, one adapted to the foreseeable maintenance of the functions of the goods (depending on the type of good) throughout their useful life.[53] If the duration depends on the type of good, why not also the legal guarantee? If obsolescence is programmed so that the good stops working in the fourth year, just one year after the expiry of the warranty, this does not contribute to responsible consumption either. On the contrary, reinforcing the legal warranty helps to produce more robust

---

[48] Van Gool and Michel, "The New Consumer Sales Directive 2019/771 and Sustainable Consumption: a Critical Analysis" (2021) 4 *EuCML*, 136 (141).

[49] Against, Pazos García, "Sustainability, the Circular Economy and Consumer Law in Spain" (2020) 5 *EuCML*, 212 (215).

[50] Referred to in Preamble IX 18 of DL 7/2021, available at: https://www.miteco.gob.es/es/calidad-y-evaluacion-ambiental/temas/economia-circular/estrategia/ (last visited 30 June 2022).

[51] The Spanish legislator claims to have been inspired by the European Parliament Resolution of 25 November 2020: "Towards a more sustainable single market for bussiness and consumers" (P9 TA(2020)0318. 2020/2021(INI) (OJ C, of 20.10.2021) and does not mention Recital 33 SGD (Recital IX 17 of DL 7/2021).

[52] Avilés García, "El nuevo derecho a la reparación de bienes de consumo en los Servicios técnicos postventa de una economia circular", *Diario LaLey*, 2 July 2021, 1.

[53] In this sense, Van Gool and Michel (fn 48) 142.

products. For the time being, however, greater consumer protection depends entirely on what the seller may have declared (Art. 7.1 letter d SGD, Preamble IX 16, of DL 7/2021, Art. 115 *ter* d TR-LGDCU) and, where applicable, on the manufacturer's commercial guarantee (Art. 17.1 SGD; Art. 127.1 TR-LGDCU). The government's future regulation on new labelling including a repairability index for electronic devices has not yet materialised.

II. Updates

Conformity extends to the updates available for digital content or digital services. 24 These may be security updates (to fix bugs, flaws and defects in the software), or they may be in response to new operating systems and market-imposed changes,[54] but they should not be mistaken for a duty to provide upgraded versions of the product.[55] Updates are never indefinite,[56] and it is precisely the nature of the contract that governs the time during which the seller or the trader must provide them. Thus, if the supply of digital elements is continuous (Art. 8.2 letter a, Art. 8.4 DCD), the duty extends throughout the life of the contract (Art. 115 *ter* 4 TR-LGDCU). This is also the case in the sale of goods with continuous supply of digital elements, though here it is clarified that the seller must provide updates for a minimum of two years even if the contract lasts for less than two years (Art. 7.3 letter b SGD which refers to Art. 10.2 SGD).[57] In the TR-LGDCU, that period is three years (Art. 115 *ter* 2 letter b TR-LGDCU) because the legislator has made use of the scope for discretion allowed by Art. 10.3 SGD (Art. 120.2 TR-LGDCU). The intention is not to undermine the liability period that applies to the good, but it would have been reasonable to make the provision of updates dependent on the durability foreseen for each type of good.[58]

If the contract is based on the scheme of single acts of supply of digital content or 25 digital services, then the duty to update lasts for as long as the consumer can reasonably expect. On that point, there is no difference from the sales contract (Recital 31 SGD, Art. 7.3 letter a SGD and 8.2 letter b DCD). There is no longer a fixed period during which the trader must fulfil his/her obligation, nor is the use of the digital elements limited by a hypothetical duration of the contract (Art. 57 DCD). This is also the case in Spanish law (Art. 115 *ter* 2 letter a TR-LGDCU), although a period of liability of the trader of two or three years is expressly provided for (Art. 120.1 TR-LGDCU). Consequently, the consumer's reasonable expectations may coincide with the trader's liability period, but also go beyond it (e.g. regarding security updates, Recital 47 DCD) and, in the case of goods with digital elements, judges may take into account the durability of the good.[59] In any case, it is risky for the national legislator to transform this unspecified period into a fixed one, i.e. to concretise the reasonable expectations into a specific time limit.[60]

---

[54] Wendehorst, "Aktualisierungen und andere Digitale Inhalte", in Stabentheiner, Wendehorst and Zöchling-Jud (Hrsg.), *Das neue europäische Gewährleistungsrecht* (2019), 111 (122–123).

[55] Twigg-Flessner (fn 46) 69; Staudenmayer (fn 13) 154–155; Wendehorst (fn 54) 123.

[56] Against this possibility, Staudenmayer (fn 13) 160.

[57] Schulze and Zoll, *European Contract Law* (2021), 227.

[58] See European Parliament Resolution of 25.11.2020 (P9 TA(2020)0318. 2020/2021(INI), paragraph 7(a): "corrective updates – i.e. security and conformity updates – must continue throughout the estimated lifespan of the device, according to product category".

[59] Schulze and Zoll (fn 57) 227; Wendehorst (fn 54) 130.

[60] Bach, "Neue Richlinien zum Verbrauchgüterkauf und zu Verbraucherverträgen über Digital Inhalte" (2019) 24 *NJW*, 1705 (1711).

G. The modification of the digital content and digital services contract

26   For technological reasons, the trader could be obliged to modify the features of the digital content and digital services provided over a period of time (e.g. cloud storage or access to social networks), beyond what is necessary to maintain conformity – i.e. beyond updates – and in order to improve them (Recital 75 DCD). A unilateral change of contractual terms and conditions is not possible (Art. 3.1 letter j Directive EEC 93/13), and therefore Art. 19.1 DCD requires that the modification be provided for in the contract. The failure to extend the rule to the supply of individual acts is unclear.[61] Chapter IV TR-LGDCU (Arts. 126 and 126 *bis*) only implements Art. 19 DCD because of maximum harmonisation,[62] but if, as seems to be the case, the drafting of these rules is flawed, the Spanish legislator should have gone further.[63]

H. Time Periods

I. Periods of liability

27   Art. 120.1 TR-LGDCU sets a period of liability for the seller of three years from the delivery of the goods (Art. 10.1 and 3 SGD) – extended by one year with respect to the provisions of the SGD – although Art. 120.1 II TR-LGDCU allows a period of no less than one year to be agreed when the goods are second-hand (according to Art. 10.6 SGD). If the former aims to guarantee durability, the latter is clearly contrary to that purpose. If the good embodies digital elements of continuous supply, Art. 120.2 TR-LGDCU provides for a distinction according to the duration of the contract: if it is less than three years, the seller is liable for any lack of conformity of the digital content or services that occurs or manifests itself within a period of three years (it is in accordance with Art. 10.3 and 10.2 I SGD). If the contract lasts longer than three years, the liability extends to the whole duration of the contract for any lack of conformity that occurs or becomes apparent during that period (this is in line with Art. 10.2 II SGD). In a contract for the supply of digital content or digital services, the period of liability is two years from each individual act or acts of supply (Art. 120.1 TR-LGDCU, Art. 11.2 II DCD).

28   Where there is a continuous supply (Art. 11.3 DCD), the liability period coincides with the duration of the contract (Art. 120.2 TR-LGDCU), which significantly reduces the liability of the trader when the contract lasts less than three years.

II. Identifying the day of delivery or supply

29   To facilitate the calculation of the time periods, Art. 123.1 TR-LGDCU establishes that, in the absence of proof to the contrary, the delivery or supply is understood to have been made on the day that appears on the invoice or purchase receipt, or on the corresponding delivery note if this is later. This rule, now adapted to the digital context, is derived from the previous legislation, but it is no longer appropriate in the event that the

---

[61] Critical, Bach (fn 60) 1707; Wendland, Art. 19 Dir (EU) 2019/770, in Schulze and Staudenmayer (fn 13), 317 (321).

[62] Only possible option, according to Wendland (fn 62) 321. Agreeing, Cámara (fn 27) 7, 15.

[63] Sein, "Goods With Digital Elements and the Interplay With Directive 2019/771 on the Sale of Goods (January 30, 2020), 1 (8). Available at: https://ssrn.com/abstract=3600137 (last visited 30 June 2022); De Franceschi (fn 27), 41, 99–100.

H. Time Periods

goods sold are not simple goods, but goods with digital elements embedded, if it turns out that these are supplied after the delivery of the physical component.[64] In line with Recital 39 SGD, delivery can only be deemed to have taken place when the physical component has been delivered and, furthermore, the single act of supply of the digital content or services has taken place or the continuous supply has been initiated. This makes sense, because the consumer is not in a position to assess the lack of conformity of the good until the digital content or services are supplied, if this occurs later.

On the other hand, it is not possible to establish a presumption as to the time of delivery in the contract for the supply of digital content and services, ex Recital 11 DCD.[65] Indeed, Art. 12.1 DCD provides that the burden of proof of supply *under the conditions set out in Art. 5 DCD* (my italics) lies with the trader. A delivery note or invoice only shows the time of purchase (and the price) but does not prove the effective supply if it is not supported by, for instance, the access key to the digital content. Such documents cannot fulfil the function required by Art. 5 DCD. To understand otherwise by means of a legal presumption, leaving it to the consumer to prove that the content or service was not supplied to him, is certainly contrary to Art. 12.1 DCD, which clearly states that the proof of supply lies with the trader.

III. The reversal of the burden of proof

The period of presumption of lack of conformity from the time of delivery of the goods (with or without embedded digital elements) is extended to two years (it was previously 6 months) unless the opposite is proved, or unless this presumption is inconsistent with the nature of the goods or with the nature of the lack of conformity (Art. 11.2 SGD). The period is one year from the supply in the contract of digital content and digital services made by means of an individual act or a series of individual acts of supply (Art. 12.2 DCD; Art. 121.1 TR-LGDCU). The new Art. 121.1 II TR-LGDCU extends the presumption to two years for second-hand goods, but it can be reduced to one year by agreement.

In the case of continuous supply of digital content and services (whether or not embedded in the goods), the burden of proof is reversed for the entire period of liability of the seller or supplier (Art. 11.3 SGD, Art. 12.3 DCD, Art. 121.2 TR-LGDCU) because in this case, unlike in the case of a single delivery or individual acts of supply, it cannot be said that the supply leaves the sphere of influence of the trader to enter that of the consumer.[66]

Art. 121.3 and 4 TR-LGDCU render the presumption inoperative in the very same cases as Art. 12.3 and 4 DCD. The SGD is silent on the issue and Art. 121.5 TR-LGDCU excludes the application of these rules in contracts concerning goods with embedded digital elements, perhaps because it is supposed that in this scenario the idea that the trader does not have access to or is not aware of the consumer's digital environment does not fit well.[67] However, this digital environment does not necessarily refer only to the hardware in which the digital content is integrated – which the trader is aware of – but

---

[64] Cámara (fn 27) 16–17.
[65] Cámara (fn 27) 30, fn 45.
[66] Gsell and Araldi, "Plazos de las medidas correctoras en caso de vicios ocultos según la Directiva (UE) 2019/770 sobre contratos de suministro de contenidos y servicios digitales y la Directiva (UE) 2019/771 sobre el contrato de compraventa de bienes" (2020) 2 *CDT*, 475 (495). He considers a presumption unnecessary, Zoll, Art. 12 Dir (EU) 2019/770, in Schulze and Staudenmayer (fn 13), 212 (218, 221).
[67] But see Agüero Ortiz, "Nuevo régimen de garantías de los bienes de consumo y otras novedades introducidas por el RDLey 7/2021 en el TRLGDCU" (2021) 11 *AC*, 1 (4).

also extends to the installation that makes this supply possible (Art. 59 *bis* 1 letter j TR-LGDCU: "any network connection")[68] and, consequently, there will be cases in which the same differentiated approach to the burden of proof should also be imposed. This is also logical if it appears that the consumer has not taken all the measures available to him/her to ensure the compatibility of the digital environment when the trader had informed her/him of this.

IV. Suspension of the liability period

34   The liability period can be suspended in the case of repair or replacement (Art. 122.1 and 2 TR-LGDCU) but not, for example, while an out-of-court settlement of the conflict is being sought, or when the consumer exercises her/his right to suspend payments. Such a suspension implies, in fact, an extension of the liability period. Even though only Recital 44 SGD refers to this possibility, the Spanish legislator has decided to extend the rule to contracts for the supply of digital content or digital services. Moreover, the seller/trader is liable within one year after the delivery of the good or the supply of the digital content or service if the same lack of conformity appears again, which also means an extension to the liability period if it occurs in the last year. It is presumed that it is the same lack of conformity when defects with the same origin as those initially manifested recur (Art. 122.3 TR-LGDCU).

V. Prescription of claims

35   The two directives distinguish between liability periods and prescription for claims to enforce this liability. Both admit that the Member States may decide not to transpose the liability periods, and that only prescription periods apply (Art. 11.2 II and 11.3 II DCD; Art. 10.5 SGD). The Spanish legislator's option has been to combine liability and prescription periods. Correct transposition requires that the trader's/seller's liability period should not be circumvented through the prescription period (Recital 42 and Art. 10.4 SGD; Recital 58 and Art. 11.2 III DCD). Nothing is expressly said either in the directives or in the TR-LGDCU, but this double term model is not possible in cases of legal conformity.[69] There can be no liability period because the buyer's claim against the trader or seller depends on an event over which s/he has no control, such as the exercise of third party rights. It is therefore only possible to consider the prescription periods for such a claim.

36   Art. 124 TR-LGDCU establishes a prescription period of five years whose starting date is subjective, i.e. the calculation starts from the manifestation of the lack of conformity, which is what allows awareness of it (presumed awareness must be admitted if the ignorance is negligent). The objective prescription period, which in the previous regulation was three years from the delivery of the good, has been abandoned. The latter would have been consistent with the presumption that the defect already existed at the time of delivery and would have favoured legal certainty but, if the model had been maintained, it would have been necessary to create an *ad hoc* rule for the hypothesis of continuous supply of digital content. Be that as it may, it is striking that in addition to

---

[68] Cámara (fn 27) 6, 7 and fn 21.
[69] See art. 621–6.3 CC Cat.

following a subjective approach, the limitation period is also extended by two years. The latter was certainly not necessary.[70]

The fact that the *dies a quo* of the limitation period is fixed from the manifestation of the lack of conformity and that it is not added that this manifestation must take place during the liability period may excessively lengthen the time during which the trader is exposed to the consumer's action. Indeed, it could be the case that a lack of conformity that occurs during the period of supply of the digital content only becomes apparent after the termination of the contract and, consequently, it would be from that moment that the 5-year period would start. Art. 124 TR-LGDCU deserves to be re-read for corrective purposes.[71]

I. Remedies for non-conformity

1. General points

The consumer has the well-known remedies at her/his disposal: repair and replacement (primary remedies) – although the DCD omits this distinction – and price reduction and termination (secondary remedies), whose exercise requires a simple notification that no Directive requires to be made on a durable medium (Art. 2.3 DCD, 2.11 SGD). In certain situations, a direct transition to secondary remedies is possible without first going through primary remedies. Thus, if the non-conformity is serious or it is clear that the trader will not solve the problem, it is possible to directly request a price reduction or termination of the contract. This is a very important novelty in both directives that neither the European nor the Spanish legislator emphasises sufficiently.[72]

II. Repair and replacement

Bringing into conformity must be free of charge (Art. 14.1 letter a SGD; Art. 14.3 DCD, Art. 118.4 letter a TR-LGDCU), but no provision of the TR-LGDCU obliges the seller to bear the transport or delivery costs in advance (e.g. by means of the provision of postage-paid packaging). CJEU C-52/18, of 23 May 2019, *Fülla*, does not impose this as a rule either, although it admits there will be cases in which it will be necessary so as not to dissuade consumers from filing a claim (§§ 54, 56). In the sale of goods, the elimination of any charge includes the costs of removing and installing goods (Art. 14.3 SGD, Art. 118.6 TR-LGDCU), and this is the case whether they are to be replaced or only repaired, which goes beyond the provisions of CJEU C-65/09 and C-87/09, *Weber and Putz*.[73] Art. 118.4 letter a TR-LGDCU does not clarify the meaning of what complying

---

[70] For a different opinion, see Tur Faúndez, "El régimen de la falta de conformidad tras la reforma de la Ley general para la defensa de los consumidores y usuarios por el Real Decreto Ley 7/2021, de 27 de abril" (2021) 83 *La Ley Mercantil*, 1 (7). In Catalonia the subjective approach is followed and the limitation period of three years has remained unchanged (art. 621–44.1 – 3 CC Cat).

[71] The regulation is also unclear in the directives. For criticism, see Gsell and Araldi (fn 66) 489, 491.

[72] Concerning European directives, Koch, "Das System der Rechtsbehelfe", in Stabentheiner, Wendehorst and Zöchling-Jud (fn 54) 162.

[73] Zöchling-Jud "Das neue Europäische Gewährleistungsrecht für den Warenhandel" (2019) 3 *GPR*, 115 (129).

with free-of-charge conformity in the case of digital content and digital services contract actually involves.[74]

40 In accordance with CJEU C-404/06, of 17.04.2008, *Quelle* (§§ 41, 43), Art. 14.4 SGD provides that the consumer shall not be liable for the normal use of the goods replaced during the period prior to their replacement (Recital 57 SGD). This rule is not paralleled in the DCD. Consequently, Art. 118.7 TR-LGDCU only refers to the goods replaced.

41 The Spanish legislator does not set a specific timeframe for bringing the goods or the digital elements into conformity. It was not advised by Recital 64 DCD (not appropriate, given the diversity of digital content), but it was suggested by Recital 55 SGD (even with regard to certain categories of products).[75] Art. 118.4 letter b TR-LGDCU does not provide either for the consumer to establish such a period (as seems to be inferred from Recital 50 SGD) or for the parties to agree on a specific one (as suggested by Recital 64 DCD).[76] Consequently, it does not lay down any further requirements for the validity of such a hypothetical agreement. It must be understood, however, that the applicability of the rules on unfair terms would not be prevented if the period unilaterally imposed by the trader were longer than would be reasonable in view of the characteristics of the service (nature of the goods, complexity of the digital elements, seriousness of the defect, etc.).[77] According to Art. 118.4 letter b TR-LGDCU, the period starts from the moment the consumer informs the trader of the lack of conformity, which corresponds to both Art. 14.1 letter b SGD and Art. 14.3 DCD.

42 Art. 118.5 TR-LGDCU requires the consumer to place the goods to be repaired or replaced at the disposal of the seller (Art. 14.3 SGD). This can mean either that the latter must collect them from the place where they are located – so that the consumer must provide him/her with access – or that the consumer must send or take them to the place of business for repair or replacement, or to the place of business of a third party who does it on his/her behalf (e.g. the technical service workshop). The SGD does not specify where the seller must fulfil his/her obligation to repair/replace, and the TR-LGDCU also fails to do so, although this was a matter for the national legal systems to determine (Recital 56 SGD). The circumstances of each case can help to specify the rule;[78] therefore, non-negotiated clauses that *a priori* provide that the remedy must always take place at the domicile or registered office of the debtor (trader/seller), as established by default in the CC (Art. 1171), could be considered abusive.

43 Member States were also free to establish under what conditions the consumer could repair at his own expense and then pass on the costs to the seller (Recital 54 SGD). The Spanish legislator has not taken any such action either, so it is still up to the judges to determine when this is possible.[79]

III. Price reduction

44 Nothing is said in the directives about how the right to a price reduction can be exercised. It may be the unilateral exercise of a right by means of a statement (*Gestal-*

---

[74] A restrictive interpretation, Koch (fn 72) 166–167. Against, Gsell, Art. 14 Dir (EU) 2019/770, in Schulze and Staudenmayer (fn 13), 241 (250–251).

[75] Gsell (fn 74) 249. In France, the timeframe cannot exceed thirty days (art. L217–10 *Code de la consommation*). In favour of setting different timeframes, Castilla Barea (fn 9) 220, 237.

[76] For criticism of the wording of Recital 50 SGD, Koch (fn 72) 184, fn 143.

[77] Gsell (fn 74) 250.

[78] CJEU C-52/18, of 23.05.2019, *Fülla*.

[79] For the cases and conditions under which it is admitted in the case law, Arroyo Amayuelas (fn 8) 39.

tungsrecht, derecho potestativo),⁸⁰ which could also be exercised in court by means of the *exceptio non rite adimpleti contractus*. Or it can be exercised in the form of a claim for reimbursement of what has already been paid, in which case Art. 119 *quater* TR-LGDCU (common to the remedies of price reduction and termination) generalises for the sales contract what Art. 18 DCD provides for digital content and digital services contracts regarding the time limits and form of reimbursement by the trader. This is not an incorrect transposition because Art. 16.3 II SGD refers the determination of these issues to the Member States.

IV. Termination

The out-of-court exercise of remedies avoids having to resort to Art. 1124 CC in the case of termination.⁸¹ Termination is not possible when the lack of conformity is minor (Art. 119 *ter* 2 TR-LGDCU) unless the consumer pays with personal data in a contract for the supply of digital content or digital services (Art. 119 *ter* 2 in fine TR-LGDCU; Art. 14.6 DCD). However, it has been said that in some cases direct termination is possible, i.e. if the lack of conformity is of a serious nature, i.e. severe, substantial. 45

There are special features to the termination of a contract for the supply of digital content and digital services. In a contract of continuous supply, according to Art. 16.1 II DCD, the trader must refund only the part of the price paid corresponding to the period during which the digital content or services were not in conformity and any other payment made in advance corresponding to the service not received because of termination. It is unclear whether this period during which the performance was not in conformity should be calculated from the time when the lack of conformity occurs, or only from the time when the lack of conformity becomes apparent, which will be less detrimental to the trader.⁸² Art. 119 *ter* 5 letter a TR-LGDCU does not provide any solution either. 46

If the consumer has paid with personal data (e.g. name, address), termination of the contract prevents the trader from making further use of them (Art. 7.2 II GDPR, Art. 16.2 DCD, Art. 119 *ter* letter b GDPR), and the consumer also has the right to be forgotten (Art. 17.1 letter b GDPR). Consumers can also withdraw their consent to the processing of their data at any time. Withdrawal of consent is a fundamental right (Recital 42 RGPD Art. 4.11, 7.3 and 7.4, 21 RGDP) and therefore Art. 119 *ter* 7 TR-LGDCU prohibits any kind of penalty. Accordingly, it also does not seem appropriate to give the trader a right to terminate the contract, as if there were a cause of non-performance by the consumer. The balancing of interests justifies that in this scenario the trader should stop offering the digital elements, but it would have been more appropriate to grant the trader a right of denunciation, withdrawal or rescission of the contract rather than a right to terminate it.⁸³ 47

Following termination, the trader must refrain from using any content created or provided by the consumer other than personal data (photos, messages, graphics, poems), but, as already mentioned, such a requirement only applies, incorrectly, when it is the consumer who terminates the contract (Art. 119 *ter* 1 and 5 TR-LGDCU) and not also the trader.⁸⁴ The consumer should be able to retrieve such content (with exceptions), but 48

---

⁸⁰ *Vid.* Zöchling-Jud (fn 73) 130; Gsell (fn 74) 264; Sein and Spindler (fn 6) 377; Koch (fn 73) 174, 191.
⁸¹ Art. 621–42.4 CC Cat.
⁸² Different opinions, Bach (fn 60) 1710 (no exceptions for latent defects) and Twigg-Flessner, Art. 16 Dir (EU) 2019/770, in Schulze and Staudenmayer (fn 13), 278 (283) (art. 16.1 II is not intended to apply to latent defects).
⁸³ See now Art. 621–78.1 CC Cat ("desistir"). Cf. § 327 q BGB ("kündigen"). Milà Rafel (fn 36) 441.
⁸⁴ See Sein and Spindler (fn 6).

neither the European nor the Spanish legislator specifies when the consumer must request the retrieval, how long s/he has to do so, how long the trader must keep it, or within what period of time the trader must fulfil this obligation (Art. 16.4 II DCD, Art. 119 *ter* letter e TR-LGDCU).

V. Withholding payment and damages

49   Art. 117 TR-LGDCU grants the consumer the right to withhold payment (Art. 117 TR-LGDCU), but then does not establish the requirements for exercising this remedy and the question remains in the hands of courts.[85] The same Art. 117.1 TR-LGDCU acknowledges the consumer's claim to damages, in addition to other remedies. Such damages include the costs of removing and installing the good, as expressly provided for in Art. 14.3 SGD (Art. 118.6 TR-LGDCU). Otherwise, the trader must compensate the consumer only if fault is involved, by application of the rules on contractual liability in Art. 1101 CC ff, to which Art. 116.2 TR-LGDCU refers.[86] It is questionable whether damages can be claimed even if the trader's/seller's liability period has expired. There is nothing in the directives to suggest that this cannot be the case, since the European rules do not concern those matters that are not covered, and compensation for damages is one of them (Recital 8 and Art. 3.6 SGD, Recital 73 and Art. 3.10 DCD). Furthermore, the DCD does not even establish a time limit for the trader's liability. Since Art. 116.2 TR-LGDCU refers to the general civil law for the conditions for exercising the remedy, this suggests that the only limit is prescription. Art. 1106 CC establishes full compensation, with the limit of the foreseeability of the damage (Art. 1107 CC) (Recital 61 SGD, Recital 73 DCD).

J. Redress and direct claim

50   Both directives deal with the right of redress of the trader/seller who is liable to the consumer against the party who is liable for the lack of conformity (Art. 20 DCD, Art. 18 SGD). The European legislator does not interfere with B2B agreements, which is why Recital 63 SGD explicitly leaves open the option for the parties to restrict this right. The point of view of Recital 78 DCD seems to be different ("[...] it is important to ensure that the trader has appropriate rights [...]"), but it does not seem reasonable to disregard the size of the companies complaining or being complained about before imposing a mandatory rule.[87] On the other hand, Art. 125.2 TR-LGDCU does not prohibit clauses limiting or excluding liability. Nor does the provision attribute specific rights or state against whom the claim should be brought.

51   The Directives do not foresee direct claims by the consumer against the producer either, but Art. 125.1 TR-LGDCU does recognise the consumer's right to directly request the conformity against them, in the same terms and conditions as against the contractual party. However, this is only in a very restricted manner when it is impossible or excessively burdensome for the consumer to take action against the other party to the contract. The direct claim is a contractual claim against the producer when the lack of con-

---

[85] Further detail, Arroyo Amayuelas (fn 8) 39.
[86] STS of 11.03.2020 (RJ 2020752). For criticism of this non-regulation of damages in the TR-LGDCU, see Castilla Barea (fn 9) 251–254.
[87] In the same vein, other arguments, Mozina, Art. 20 Dir (EU) 2019/770, in Schulze and Staudenmayer (fn 13), 321 (328–329). Staudenmayer (fn 13) 156, clarifies that it was not intended to interfere with B2B contracts.

formity relates to the origin, identity or suitability of the goods or digital content or services, in accordance with their nature and purpose and the rules governing them. Neither termination nor price reduction can be exercised against the producer, and it has always been understood that the direct claim did not allow the consumer to make a claim for any damages that may have been suffered either, so that these should be undertaken through other channels (Art. 1902 CC, Arts. 128, 142 TR-LGDCU). More recently, though, case law on Dieselgate has accepted that they can claim contractual damages from the manufacturer, on the understanding that this is a basic consumer right that could be frustrated by the difficulty of claiming them from a seller who could be insolvent, or who could be harmed in the event that the seller was in good faith and, in contrast, the manufacturer was fraudulent (Art. 1107 CC).[88]

K. Overall assessment

What is the overall assessment of the reform? In a manifesto addressed to the European Commission in June last year,[89] the European digital industry already complained about what it considers to be disproportionate regulation. It denounces three years of warranty instead of two (which makes the product more expensive) as excessive; and suggests that the imposition of the duty to make available spare parts for 10 years, without distinguishing according to the nature of the goods, durability or price, generates an excessive burden for manufacturers, who will be forced to produce parts for all that time without knowing what the real demand is. It should be added that this time provision contradicts some European regulations and that it does not correspond at all with the seller's liability period, which is only 3 years for most goods, even though durability is an objective criterion of conformity (Art. 115 *ter* 1 letter d TR-LGDCU). In addition, such a short period of liability is at odds with the consumer's reasonable expectation that the good – at least certain types of goods – will last longer. In any case, the industry assumes that the sector innovates rapidly and that new products are better adapted to consumers' wishes. For the industry, consumer protection is best left to commercial guarantees.

Leaving aside considerations of legal policy, from a strictly technical legislative point of view, things could have been done in a more convenient and more comprehensible way. To begin with, the legislative framework is not very clear, the relationship with other topics is not explored in depth, and the structure and systematics of the norm could be much improved. The reform has given rise to very long articles that are difficult to work with, which in different paragraphs of the same provision reiterate identical or very similar rules for contracts whose subject matter is goods and for others whose subject matter is digital content and services. Furthermore, it is not always clear who the contractual partner of the consumer, generally referred to as "the business", is. There are serious errors, such as the fact that "price" is not included in the list of definitions, that the need for this in the sales contract is omitted, and that some articles establish that this contract can only cover tangible movable goods (Art. 59 *bis* 2 TR-LGDCU) whereas other articles contradict this idea by stating that digital content can be the object of the contract (Art. 59.4 TR-LGDCU).[90] Furthermore, it is not made sufficiently clear that the term "goods" used throughout the articles also refers to those that embody digital elements, and this has consequences because it does not correctly convey the idea that the

---

[88] STS of 11.07.2021 (RJ 2020752); STS of 23.07.2021 (RJ 20213583).
[89] https://www.digitaleurope.org/resources/digital-industrys-concerns-with-the-spanish-transposition-of-the-sales-of-goods-directive-2019-771/ (last visited 30 June 2022).
[90] See above D II (In particular, Sales of Goods)

digital element embedded in the good may also form part of the seller's performance, and that it is the seller who will have to respond to the consumer for the lack of supply or the lack of conformity of the digital element (e.g. for omission of updates) even if the ultimate party liable is a third party. In the same vein, is also missing a rule which specifies that, when the object of the contract is a good with digital elements, in the case of doubt it is presumed that this supply is included in the contract of sale, regardless of who executes it.[91]

54 On the other hand, the legislator does not explain the seller's grounds for relief when he warns the consumer about the inadequacy of the materials or instructions provided (Recital 20 SGD) because, instead of improving the defective rule contained in the former Art. 116.3 TR-LGDCU, it has eliminated it.[92] It has also eliminated the consumer's burden of notifying the lack of conformity within a specific period of time (Art. 123.5 TR-LGDCU), and therefore the consumer's duty to respond for the damages that late notification could cause the trader (former Art. 123.5 TR-LGDCU) has also disappeared.[93] Art. 115 *ter* 5 TR-LGDCU does not specify either how acceptance of the divergence from the objective requirements of conformity (Art. 7.5 SGD, Art. 8.5 DCD) should take place. It seems that it would not be sufficient to impose the waiver in the general terms and conditions of the contract,[94] but if it is only a matter of providing knowledge to the consumer, this would not require the clause to be negotiated either.[95] Moreover, the Spanish legislator does not incorporate the requirement of active and unequivocal behaviour on the part of the consumer (Recital 49 DCD, Recital 36 SGD), nor does it expressly exclude the validity of an oral statement.[96] Other very relevant aspects remain unregulated, such as the moment at which the calculation of the period of liability for lack of conformity begins in the case of installation of the goods;[97] the modalities and requirements for the exercise of certain remedies; or the liability of intermediary platforms.

55 In short, RDL 7/2021 illustrates well the central role of digitalisation in private law in such a classic area of civil law as contract law; yet the task of implementing such important European directives could have been handled much better and much more could have been achieved.

Bibliography

Alicia Agüero Ortiz, "Nuevo régimen de garantías de los bienes de consumo y otras novedades introducidas por el RDLey 7/2021 en el TRLGDCU" (2021) 11 *AC*, 1.

Juan Pablo Aparicio Vaquero, "La protección de datos personales en las redes sociales. Apuntes desde los ordenamientos europeos y español" (2020) 1 *Tecnologia e Diritto*, 209.

---

[91] By contrast, see art. 621–3.3 CC Cat.
[92] On the contrary, art. 621–27. Cf. furthermore, art. 621–37.3 and 4 CC Cat.
[93] *Vid.* the critique of Sánchez Lería, "Mercado digital y protección del consumidor: a propósito de la Directiva 770/2019 y su transposición al ordenamiento jurídico español" (2021) 4 *InDret*, 33 (79).
[94] Zöchling-Jud (fn 73) 120; De Franceschi (fn 27), 103: Graf von Westphalen, "Some Thoughts on the Proposed Directive on Certain Aspects Concerning Contracts for the Sales of Goods" (2018) 2 *EuCML*, 66 (70). On Art. 16.1 letter a CRD, see also Commission CRD Guidance (fn 31) 59.
[95] Sánchez Lería (fn 93) 62. But see, Graf von Westphalen (fn 94) 70. He points out the role that transparency control should play, Cámara (fn 28) 21; Beale (fn 39) 98, indicates that the meaning of "express" is that of "clear".
[96] Thus, Zöchling-Jung (fn 73) 120. Critical of this possibility, Artz, Markus, "Pactos sobre no conformidad en las Directivas 2019/770 y de franceschi 2019/771" (2019) 2–3 *LaNotaria*, 120 (121).
[97] Cf. art. 621–23.1 and art. 621–24.4 CC Cat.

Bibliography

Lidia Arnau Raventós, "Transmisión onerosa de un producto y su conformidad con el contrato: una relectura de la STJUE de 7 de septiembre de 2017 (Asunto 247/16, Schottelius)" (2018) 2 *RED*, 42.

Lidia Arnau Raventós and Mariló Gramunt Fombuena, "Cap a un dret català conforme a les directives (UE) 2019/770 i 2019/771" (2022) 2 *InDret*, 171.

Esther Arroyo Amayuelas, "The Implementation of EU Directives 2019/770 and 771 in Spain" (2022) 11 *EuCML*, 35.

Markus Artz, "Pactos sobre la falta de conformidad en las Directivas 2019/770 y 2019/771" (2019) 2–3 *LaNotaria*, 120.

Javier Avilés García, "El nuevo derecho a la reparación de bienes de consumo en los Servicios técnicos postventa de una economía circular", *Diario LaLey*, of 2 July 2021, 1.

Ivo Bach, "Neue Richlinien zum Verbrauchgüterkauf und zu Verbrucherverträgen über Digital Inhalte" (2019) 24 *NJW*, 1705.

Hugh Beale, "Digital Content Directive and Rules For Contracts on Continuous Supply" (2021) 2 *JIPITEC*, 96.

Llanos Cabeda Serna, "Los consumidores y las medidas tecnológicas de protección incorporadas en soportes digitales", in Juan Antonio Moreno Martínez (ed.), *Limites a la propiedad intelectual y nuevas tecnologías* (Dykinson, Madrid 2008), 66.

Sergio Cámara Lapuente, "Un primer balance de las novedades del RDL 7/2021, de 27 de abril, para la defensa de los consumidores en el suministro de contenidos y servicios digitales (La transposición de las Directivas 2019/770 y 2019/771)", *Diario La Ley*, of 29 June 2021, 1.

Cámara Lapuente "Nuevos perfiles del consentimiento en la contratación digital en la Unión Europea: ¿navegar es contratar (servicios digitales «grauitos»)?", in Fernando Gómez Pomar and Ignacio Fernández Chacón (dirs), *Estudios de Derecho Contractual Europeo: Nuevos problemas, nuevas reglas* (Aranzadi, Cizur Menor 2022), 331.

Margarita Castilla Barea, *La nueva regulación europea de la venta de bienes muebles a consumidores* (Aranzadi, Cizur Menor 2021).

Alberto De Franceschi, *La vendita di beni con elementi digitali* (ESI, Napoli 2019).

Rosa García Pérez, "Interacción entre protección del consumidor y protección de datos personales en la Directiva 770/2019: licitud del tratamiento y conformidad de los contenidos y servicios digitales", in Esther Arroyo Amayuelas and Sergio Cámara Lapuente (dirs.), *El Derecho privado en el nuevo paradigma digital* (Barcelona-Madrid, Marcial Pons 2020), 175.

Friedrich Graf von Westphalen, "Some Thoughts on the Proposed Directive on Certain Aspects Concerning Contracts for the Sales of Goods" (2018) 2 *EuCML*, 66.

Beate Gsell, Art. 14 Dir (EU) 2019/770, in Reiner Schulze and Dirk Staudenmayer (eds.), *EU Digital Law. Article by Article Commentary* (Baden-Baden, Hart-Beck-Nomos 2020), 241.

Beate Gsell and Rodrigo Araldi, "Plazos de las medidas correctoras en caso de vicios ocultos según la Directiva (UE) 2019/770 sobre contratos de suministro de contenidos y servicios digitales y la Directiva (UE) 2019/771 sobre el contrato de compraventa de bienes" (2020) 2 *CDT*, 495.

Juana Marco Molina, "Los criterios legales de la conformidad con el contrato en el futuro Libro VI del Codi Civil de Catalunya: la llamada conformidad subjetiva o adecuación de lo entregado al fin individual del comprador", in Mª Rosa Llàcer Matacàs (ed.), *La codificación del Derecho Contractual de Consumo en el Derecho Civil Catalán* (Madrid, Dykinson 2015), 193.

Bernhard A. Koch, "Das System der Rechtsbehelfe", in Johannes Stabentheiner, Christiane Wendehorst and Brigitta Zöchling-Jud (Hrsg.), *Das neue europäische Gewährleistungsrecht* (Wien, Manz 2019), 157.

Rosa Milà Rafel, "Datos personales como contraprestación en la directiva de contenidos y servicios digitales", in Fernando Gómez Pomar and Ignacio Fernández Chacón (dirs.), *Estudios de Derecho Contractual Europeo: Nuevos problemas, nuevas reglas* (Cizur menor, Aranzadi 2022), 407.

Lena Mischau, "The Concept of Digital Content and Digital Services in European Contract Law" (2022) 1 *EuCML*, 6.

Damjan Mozina, Art. 20 Dir (EU) 2019/770, in Reiner Schulze and Dirk Staudenmayer (eds.), *EU Digital Law. Article by Article Commentary* (Baden-Baden, Hart-Beck-Nomos 2020), 321.

Liliia Oprysk and Karin Sein, "Limitations in End-User Licensing Agreements: Is There A Lack of Conformity Under the New Digital Content Directive?" (2020) 51 *IIC*, 594.

Ricardo Pazos García, "Sustainability, the Circular Economy and Consumer Law in Spain" (2020) 5 *EuCML*, 212.

Cristina Ramberg, "Digital Content – A digital CESL II- A paradigm for contract law via the backdoor?", in Stefan Grundmann (ed.), *European Contract Law in the Digital Age* (Cambridge, Intersentia 2018), 315.

Reyes Sánchez Lería, "Mercado digital y protección del consumidor: a propósito de la Directiva 770/2019 y su transposición al ordenamiento jurídico español" (2021) 4 *InDret*, 33.

Andrej Savin, "Harmonising Private Law in Cyberspace: The New Directives in the Digital Single Market Context", in Mateja Durovic and Takis Tridimas (eds.), *New Directions in European Private Law* (Hart, Oxford 2021), 213.

Thomas R. Schmitt, "A new warranty law for digital content ante portes" (2018) 2 *University of Vienna Law Review*, 1.

Reiner Schulze, "Die Digitale-Inhalte-Richtlinie-Innovation und Kontinuität im europäischen Vertragsrecht" (2019) 4 *ZEuP*, 695.

Reiner Schulze and Fryderyck Zoll, *European Contract Law* (3rd edn, Hart-Beck-Nomos, Baden-Baden 2021).

Karen Sein, "Goods With Digital Elements and the Interplay With Directive 2019/771 on the Sale of Goods" (January 30, 2020), 1. Available at: https://ssrn.com/abstract=3600137.

Karin Sein and Gerald Spindler, "The New Directive on Contracts for the Supply of Digital Content and Digital Services – Scope of Application and Trader's Obligation to Supply – Part 1" (2019) 3 *ERCL*, 257.

Karen Sein and Gerald Spindler, "The New Directive on Contracts for the Supply of Digital Content and Digital Services – Scope of Application and Trader's Obligation to Supply – Part 2" (2019) 4 *ERCL*, 365.

Gerald Spindler, "Digital Content Directive and Copyright-related Aspects" (2021) 2 *JIPITEC*, 111.

Dirk Staudenmayer, "Die Richtlinien zu den digitalen Verträgen" (2019) 4 *ZEuP*, 663.

Dirk Staudenmayer, Art. 8 Dir (UE) 2019/770, in Reiner Schulze and Dirk Staudenmayer (eds.), *EU Digital Law. Article by Article Commentary* (Hart-Beck-Nomos, Baden-Baden 2020), 131.

Evelyn Terryn, "A Right to Repair? Towards Sustainable Remedies in Consumer Law" (2019) 4 *ERPL*, 851.

Mª Nélida Tur Faúndez, "El régimen de la falta de conformidad tras la reforma de la Ley general para la defensa de los consumidores y usuarios por el Real Decreto Ley 7/2021, de 27 de abril" (2021) 83 *La Ley Mercantil*, 1.

Christian Twigg-Flessner, "Conformity of Goods and Digital Content/Digital Services", in Esther Arroyo Amayuelas and Sergio Cámara Lapuente (dirs.), *El Derecho privado europeo en el nuevo paradigma digital* (Madrid, Marcial Pons 2020), 49.

Bibliography

Elias Van Gool and Anaïs Michel, "The New Consumer Sales Directive 2019/771 and Sustainable Consumption: a Critical Analysis" (2021) 4 *EuCML*, 136.

Christiane Wendehorst, "Aktualisierungen und andere Digitale Inhalte", in Johannes Stabentheiner, Christiane Wendehorst and Brigitta Zöchling-Jud (Hrsg.), *Das neue europäische Gewährleistungsrecht* (Wien, Manz 2019), 111.

Matthias Wendland, Art. 19 Dir (EU) 2019/770 in Reiner Schulze and Dirk Staudenmayer (eds.), *EU Digital Law. Article by Article Commentary* (Hart-Beck-Nomos, Baden-Baden 2020), 317.

Brigitta Zöchling-Jud, "Das neue Europäische Gewährleistungsrecht für den Warenhandel" (2019) 3 *GPR*, 115.

Fryderyk Zoll, Art. 12 Dir (EU) 2019/770, in Reiner Schulze and Dirk Staudenmayer (eds.), *EU Digital Law. Article by Article Commentary* (Hart-Beck-Nomos, Baden-Baden 2020), 212.

Abbreviations

AC	*Actualidad Civil*
CDT	*Cuadernos de Derecho Transnacional*
ERCL	*European Review of Contract Law*
ERPL	*European Review of Private Law*
EuCML	*Journal of European Consumer and Market Law*
GPR	*Zeitschrift für das Privatrecht der Europäischen Union*
IIC	*International Review of Intellectual Property and Competition Law*
JIPITEC	*Journal of Intellectual Property, Information Technology and Electronic Commerce Law*
NJW	*Neue Juristische Wochenschrift*
RED	*Revista Electrónica de Direito*
ZEuP	*Zeitschrift für Europäisches Privatrecht*

Sweden

A. Introduction 1
   I. The Transpositions of the Twin Directives 1
   II. Statutory Structure 8

B. Definitions and Scope of Application 12

C. Formation of Contract with Personal Data as Counter-Performance 23
   I. Digital Supply as Performance 23
   II. Personal Data as Sufficient Counter-Performance Outside of The Twin Directives 27
   III. Personal Data as Counter-Performance in B2B Contracts 28

D. Delivery and Conformity of Products 29
   I. Delivery 29
   II. Subjective and Objective Requirements for Conformity 33
   III. The Durability Requirement 39
   IV. Duties to Inform about and to Supply Necessary Updates 42
   V. The Consumer's Duty to Install Updates 45
   VI. Restricted Use Due to the Trader's Infringement of Third-Party Rights 47
   VII. The Consumer's Acceptance of Specific Characteristics of the Product 48
   VIII. Incorrect Installation 49

E. Liability of the Trader 57
   I. The Distinction of Liability between Single Acts of Supply and Continuous Supply 57
   II. Impossibility, Force Majeure and Changed Circumstances 66
   III. Electronic Communication Services 72
   IV. The GDPR and the Twin Directives 74

F. Remedies for the Trader's Breach of Contract 75
   I. The Remedies 75
   II. Withholding Payment 76
   III. Repair and Redelivery 80
   IV. Termination 84
   V. Damages 88
   VI. Passing on Rights to Subsequent Buyers 90

G. Commercial Guarantees 92

H. Intermediaries and Online Platforms 97

I. Time Limits 100
   I. Obligation to Notify of Defects 100
   II. The Trader's Right of Redress 107

J. Final Words 109

   Bibliography 112

A. Introduction

I. The Transpositions of the Twin Directives

The Digital Content Directive, shortened "DCD",[1] and the Sale of Goods Directive, shortened "SGD",[2] jointly named the "Twin Directives", were enacted in 2019 with the

---

[1] Directive (EU) 2019/770 of the European Parliament and of the Council of 20 May 2019 on certain aspects concerning contracts for the supply of digital content and digital services.

[2] Directive (EU) 2019/771 of the European Parliament and of the Council of 20 May 2019 on certain aspects concerning contracts for the sale of goods, amending Regulation (EU) 2017/2394 and Directive 2009/22/EC, and repealing Directive 1999/44/EC.

2 In Sweden, the transpositions of the Twin Directives were foremost accomplished by the enactment of the Consumer Sales Act of 2022 (hereinafter "CSA", or "CSA of 2022"),[3] by which the former Consumer Sales Act of 1990 (hereinafter "CSA of 1990")[4] was repealed.[5]

3 The legislative inquiry on the implementation of the Twin Directives, the first legislative step of introducing any important statute or statutory amendment in Swedish law, suggested that the directives should be enacted in a joint single act of parliament, under a name signalling its broader applicability, translatable to "the Act on Consumer Protection of Sale of Movables and Some Other Types of Contract".[6] The idea of transposing the Twin Directives in a single act was mostly met with acceptance by the majority of stakeholders[7] and by Parliament, but not the name of the act suggested by the inquiry. Instead, it was decided to keep the old name, the Consumer Sales Act,[8] but with a new number of enactment, due to the restructuring made.

4 Amendments were also made in five already existing acts. In four of these acts the amendments were of purely editorial character, just replacing the citations of the act of 1990 with the act of 2022.[9] In the fifth of the acts, the Marketing Practices Act of 2008,[10] some minor clarifications were made for increased linguistic coherence[11] with another provision in the Marketing Practices Act[12] and the Distance and Off-Premises Contracts Act of 2005,[13] (in both of these respects being amendments resulting from the transposition of the Consumer Rights Directive, CRD),[14] however without the intention to introduce any changes in substance.[15]

5 The Swedish implementation was not particularly "gold-plating", i.e. offensive in terms of consumer protection where the directives left room for that. Unless the directives demanded more, the already existing level of protection was mostly kept, which sometimes already afforded better protection, but sometimes a lower level of protection than the default solution in the directives (such as placing a duty of notification of breaches of contract on consumers in the case of sale of goods). However, some gold-plating was made, whereof some measures are worth special mention due to their importance.

6 The period of a reversed burden of proof concerning lack of conformity in goods was extended from six months to two years, with the exception of the sale of living

---

[3] Konsumentköplagen (2022:260).
[4] Konsumentköplagen (1990:932).
[5] CSA of 2022, Transitional provisions, Item 3.
[6] Legislative inquiry, SOU 2020:51, En ny lag om konsumentskydd vid köp och vissa andra avtal, p. 31 ff. A legislative inquiry is an official body, and has to assume a name for itself. The name chosen was Utredningen om nya konsumentregler [The Inquiry on New Consumer Rules], SOU 2020:51, p. 4.
[7] Governmental bill, Prop. 2021/22:85, En ny konsumentköplag, p. 40 and 41 ff.
[8] Prop. 2021/22:85, p. 40 and 44.
[9] 4 § köplagen (1990:931) [§ 4 of the Sale of Goods Act of 1990; SGA], 1 § lagen (1964:528) om tillämplig lag beträffande internationella köp av lösa saker [§ 1 of the Applicable Law (International Sale of Goods) Act of 1964], 11 § produktansvarslagen (1992:18) [§ 11 of the Product Liability Act of 1992], 25 § kommissionslagen (2009:865) [§ 25 of the Commission Agency Act of 2009].
[10] 22 § marknadsföringslagen (2008:486) [§ 22 of the Marketing Practices Act of 2008].
[11] Prop. 2021/22:85, p. 105 and 300.
[12] 22 a § marknadsföringslagen [§ 22 a of the Marketing Practices Act].
[13] 2 kap. 3 och 5 §§ lagen (2005:59) om distansavtal och avtal utanför affärslokaler [2:3 and 2:5 of the Distance and Off-Premises Contracts Act of 2005].
[14] Directive 2011/83/EU.
[15] Prop. 2021/22:85, p. 300, and cf. Prop. 2001/02:134, Ändringar i konsumentköplagen, p. 90.

A. Introduction

animals.[16] For goods with digital elements it is even longer, namely three years or the longer period that the digital supply continues to run. The period of a reversed burden of proof concerning lack of conformity in digital content and digital services was locked to one year in the DCD, and therefore not extendable to two years.[17]

The period of the trader's liability for lack of conformity was extended from a definitive three years from delivery to three years and two months in cases where the defect appears at the end of the three-year period.

II. Statutory Structure

The transposition of the Directives did not require any major restructuring of the statutes in the field of contract law, and none in intellectual property law or data protection law. The choice was between a special act on digital supply or a combined act comprising sale of goods and digital supply. As explained above, the combined one was chosen.

The CSA of 2022 is structurally very close to the act of 1990. The major difference is that the provisions in the new act were placed into separate chapters but without shifting the order of the provisions to any considerable extent. In this report, I will refer to provisions in the CSA of 2022 and other statutes in a condensed format.[18]

There is no civil code in Sweden. This feature admits that one does not necessarily have to take that rules might have applicability on different hierarchical levels into account. Instead there are contract specific statutes with provisions more or less placed on a string. The CSA (and the Sale of Goods Act of 1990, hereinafter "SGA") are somewhat reminding of Part III in the 1980 UN Convention on Contracts for the International Sale of Goods (hereinafter "CISG"), however even less abstract and less deductive, and thus more situation specific and inductive. (The structure looks like this: Provisions on applicability, provisions on delivery and passing of risk, provisions on defining defects, provisions on defining late delivery and remedies to that, provisions on remedies for defects, *et cetera*.) Therefore, any major restructuring was not called for. In addition, the rules of the DCD were put in the last chapter of the CSA of 2022 and the specific themes were put in the same order as for sale of goods, mostly referring to which provisions in the previous chapters apply to supply of digital content and digital services. The technique has the advantage of avoiding repetition but it also makes the chapter on DCD-implementation hard to read and hard to figure out what the rules for digital supply actually are,[19] but the method used was in a legislative sense technically correct.

The system has become rather complex. There are these two directives that are similar, SGD and DCD, but not at all identical. There is a third directive, CRD, that comes

---

[16] The sale of living animals is within the scope of the SGD, but Member States were free to leave that out, Art. 3(5)(b). In Sweden the CSA of 1990 included sale of living animals and this approach was maintained in the CSA of 2022, however with adjustments in relation to other goods. The reversed burden of proof concerning conformity of six months was kept for living animals. The SGD, Art. 11(1) and (2), seems only to offer either one year or two years of a reversed burden of proof. On the other hand, the sale of living animals could have been left out altogether, which probably give the Member States the mandate to freely deviate from SGD in this regard.

[17] Prop. 2021/22:85, p. 162. The inquiry had proposed a reversed burden of proof of only one year for goods, partly to satisfy the objective of synchronised rules, SOU 2020:51, p. 114 f.

[18] The reference 1:1 CSA means Chapter 1 § 1 of the CSA. The reference 1:3(1) CSA means Chapter 1 § 3 subpara. 1 of the CSA. The reference 1:1.1 CSA means Chapter 1 § 1 1st sentence of the CSA. The reference 1:3(2).1 CSA means Chapter 1 § 3 subpara. 2 1st sentence of the CSA. The reference 1:8–1 CSA means Chapter 1 § 8 Item 1 of the CSA.

[19] Cf. Prop. 2021/22:85, p. 41 and 43, referring to some stakeholders' responses.

into play at times. In SGD there are three types of goods. Goods with no digital elements, goods with digital elements with a single act of digital supply and goods with digital elements with continuous digital supply. In DCD there are also three types, namely contracts for continuous supply, for single acts of supply without a tangible medium and for single acts of supply on a tangible medium, and beside of these distinctions there is the dichotomy between payment and supply of personal data. One has to be very alert when searching for the relevant rules. On top of that, there is the Directive establishing the European Electronic Communications Code, (EU) 2018/1972, that include some contract law rules on the right to exercise termination and the effects of termination, Art. 105–107.[20] In addition, there is unique domestic rules. It has indeed become a complex field of law. So far, the CJEU adjudication in consumer sales, mostly represented by some few incremental cases on CSD and CRD matters, has been rather modest in volume. If SGD and DCD would boost CJEU case law, it would create a need for an increase of experts in the field.

B. Definitions and Scope of Application

12 The Twin Directives potentially pose some conceptual challenges. The following notions represent the most apparent ones, since they are introduced either by the Twin Directives or by some other acts of late: digital content, digital service, goods with digital elements, integration, updates, price, digital environment, compatibility, functionality, interoperability, durable medium. The enumerated notions have been dealt with in a directive compliant fashion, by simple enumeration. One cannot see any immediate impact on the surrounding law as it comes to these new notions.

13 Debate on the Twin Directives is not abundant in Sweden. These directives are mere drops in a large flow of laws. Nonetheless, there are two recent major doctrinal contributions concerning the interface between personal data protection law and private law.[21] Apart from a discussion with respect to the definition of 'price', which is to be described later on, there has not been any recent debate concerning the notions enumerated above. One of the reasons for the lack of debate is that most of the notions are not as problematic to assess as one could suppose. Some of these notions or themes have been encountered in earlier legislative inquiries, which probably has raised the awareness of the notions and themes and thus contributed to the adaptation in the Swedish legal community.[22]

14 'Functionality', one of the notions mentioned, has been central in the building of the Swedish concept of defects since the introduction of the SGA and the CSA of 1990. If the product does not function it is in non-conformity, unless the malfunction depends on the buyer. The product must work during the prescription period (three years in CSA and two years in SGA) unless its expected life-span is objectively shorter, like groceries and products intended for few uses. The word functionality has been used alongside with the word durability, the latter now not in the sense of environmental ef-

---

[20] Implemented through 7 kap. lagen (2022:482) om elektronisk kommunikation [Chapter 7 of the Electronic Communications Act]. Some of these rules overlap with the previously adopted lagen (2014:1449) om konsumentskydd vid automatisk avtalsförlängning [Act on Consumer Protection Concerning Automatic Prolongation].

[21] Chamberlain, Integritet och skadestånd [Privacy Torts: On the Protection of Personal Information of Swedish Law], diss. Uppsala 2021, and Kotsios, Paying with Data. A Study on EU Consumer Law and the Protection of Personal Data, diss. Uppsala 2022.

[22] Ds 2008:55, Bör konsumenttjänstlagen utvidgas?, and Ds 2012:31, App to date. Konsumenternas rättsliga ställning när varor eller tjänster betalas via telefonräkningen, m.m.

B. Definitions and Scope of Application

fect but in the meaning of mere functionality over time, in short endurable functionality. 'Compatibility' and 'interoperability', however, which are close to functionality, have not been discussed particularly, but deviations from normal expectations would at least fall under the type of defect called 'reasonable assumption' or 'subjective abstract standard', described more in detail later.

'Integration' might be seen as a demanding concept. In this context, apart from its connection with compatibility and interoperability, integration strongly denotes functionality after installation. Installation defects have been dealt with since the SGA and the CSA of 1990. § 21(2).1 SGA reads: "If the goods deteriorate after the risk has passed to the buyer, the goods shall be deemed to be defective if the deterioration is a consequence of a breach of contract by the seller."[23] This was intended to cover installation defects, making the provisions on defects in the SGA applicable, instead of rules on service contracts.[24] A similar provision, § 20(2), was inserted in the CSA of 1990. In order to fully implement the Consumer Sales Directive 1999/44/EC, CSD,[25] it was thought better to express the installation defect category in a separate provision, § 16 a of the CSA of 1990: "Where, in conjunction with completion of the sale, the seller has undertaken to install the goods and such installation has been performed by the seller or a third party on the seller's behalf, the goods shall be deemed defective as a result of defects in installation if they deviate from the provision set forth in § 16(1)–(2) or otherwise deviate from the buyer's reasonable expectations."[26] A similar wording is now found in 2:14(1).2 CSA of 2022.[27] The trader's incorrect installation will be discussed more in detail later on.

The notion of durable medium is readily understandable, and has been treated as such since long. When the trader has to give the consumer information or a confirmation of a contract/guarantee and its content, it is a duty to do so on a durable medium. This might be given on paper, but if it is given in digital form this has to be durable, and readable as long as is necessary to enable the consumer to ensure the rights of the consumer. If this duty is not fulfilled, there is a breach of duty. What type of foresight the trader must show concerning the spread and durability of the technology necessary to read the information is still to be seen. Probably it will be sufficient to show that the technology at the time of contracting was well spread and free for most non-commercial uses, and that it was possible to print or otherwise secure the information at that time. In time the trader might be considered obligated to save and at request at any time deliver all contractually relevant documents. We are most likely not there yet, compare Art. 5 of the Consumer Rights Directive 2011/83/EU, CRD, but it is a low-hanging fruit for the EU legislature to pick.

One of the subjects that probably are hardest to pinpoint conceptually is the distinction between 'supply of digital content' and 'sale of goods with digital elements'. DCD recital 21 expresses that the SGD should apply in case of "doubt as to whether the supply of the digital content or the digital service forms part of the sales contract". Goods with digital elements, taken by themselves, is however not that problematic. It is about movables that contain digital elements but does not entirely consist thereof, not including

---

[23] Unofficial translation.
[24] Prop. 1988/89:76 om ny köplag, p. 96 and 139. Prop. 1989/90:89 om ny konsumentköplag, p. 109.
[25] Directive 1999/44/EC of the European Parliament and of the Council of 25 May 1999 on certain aspects of the sale of consumer goods and associated guarantees.
[26] Unofficial translation.
[27] Unofficial translation: "If the trader has undertaken to install the goods in conjunction with completion of the sale, the liability for defects is applicable from when the installation has been performed by the seller or a third party on the seller's behalf."

the "package". If the content entirely is of a digital character, it is a digital content, falling under DCD and Chapter 9 CSA. This is so also if it is placed on a tangible medium, such as a USB stick, CD, DVD or similar.[28] However, it is challenging to figure out why the rules in the CRD should apply partially, namely concerning delay of digital content delivered on tangible media only and passing of risk concerning all products. Why, on the legal-technical level as well as in substance, were both the Twin Directives seen unfit to regulate the issue? Probably this was because the EU legislature would not like to reiterate any already existing rules, and the same rules were already at place, in CRD. However, that type of legal-technical logic is less convincing considering the obvious internal correlation between the DCD and the SGD, the non-existing primacy of the CRD over the DCD and the SGD, and the confusion this will cause within any relevant target group. It was less of a problem in the Swedish transposition, the rules on delay and passing of risk concerning sale of goods apply, but the Union must also consider the general public if it really wants to be embraced by it. A move towards self-sufficient acts, also including consolidation rather than confusing referrals, would be a step in the right direction.

18 Another issue to contemplate is the synchronisation between the rules on the sale of goods and the supply of digital content or digital services when the contract provides the consumer ownership of hardware, such as a phone or a router, and the seller at the same time supplies digital content or digital services.

19 Let say that a router is defect, which makes the digital supply impossible or disturbed. The consumer seems to have to solely rely on the rules on goods, since there is no digital component that would make the rules on digital supply applicable. Let say that the following attempts to repair or redeliver the router are fruitless. The consumer may eventually terminate the sale of the router, but what of the digital supply? In the Swedish preparatory works it was suggested – with a comparative reference to DCD Art. 3.6 – that, unless the issue is regulated in the terms of contract or in any other statute, general principles of contract law should apply.[29] In Swedish law that would probably give the consumer the right to terminate also the contract on digital supply. However, the legislator seems to have accepted that contract terms that prescribe severability, i.e. that the goods and the services should be handled apart, are to be tolerated. There is always a possibility to revise contract terms due to unfair terms or unfair results on the basis of § 36 of the Contracts Act[30] in conjunction with § 11 of the Act on Contract Terms in Consumer Relations,[31] but the threshold of unfairness is high even in consumer contracts. This type of gap, if used by the traders, might defeat much of the purpose of protecting ordinary contractual expectations.

20 In accordance with normal legislative procedure an inquiry was established to propose how to transpose the Twin Directives into Swedish law. The inquiry delivered its report. In accordance with normal procedure, the report was remitted to stakeholders, including courts, state authorities, universities and NGO:s. After having processed the replies, the Ministry of Justice amended the proposal given in the inquiry report, in accordance with normal procedure, and remitted the amended proposal to the Council of Legislation, also in course of normal procedure, consisting of three present or former Justices of the Supreme Court and the Supreme Administrative Court. The Council scrutinised the proposal and delivered its report. The Ministry of Justice then amended its proposal and issued a governmental bill before the parliament. There were many

---

[28] 1:7(2).2 CSA. DCD recital 20, most probably referring to CRD Art. 18.
[29] Prop. 2021/22:85, p. 241.
[30] 36 § lagen (1915:218) om avtal och andra rättshandlingar på förmögenhetsrättens område.
[31] 11 § lagen (1994:1512) om avtalsvillkor i konsumentförhållanden.

parliamentary motions not to accept the bill in its entirety. Most of the motions were concerning sale of living animals. The parliamentary Committee on Justice proposed Parliament to accept the bill and to make an announcement that the Government should investigate the issue of sale of living animals further.[32] Parliament voted in favor of the committee's proposal, which is most common.

The Council of Legislation criticised the proposed definition of 'price', and suggested it be left out altogether.[33] The Ministry of Justice let the definition of 'price' be stricken in the bill. In the CSA of 2022 there is thus no definition of the concept 'price'. The Council of Legislation had namely argued that a definition of 'price' including other types of currency would be superfluous and that the proposed definition was not suitable. It would according to the council be alien – at least as of today – that an evaluation would be made in other value units than national currencies. The fact that payment may be made in crypto currencies would not mean that the product would be evaluated in this currency; that payment may be made with a digital representation of value must be distinguished from money (currency) as means of evaluation. In short: Payment in other kinds is not price, since it is not 'money', it is only 'payment'. 21

One might add that some of the digitalisation issues have been dealt with in the Nordic commercial environments through self-regulatory measures, such as the theme of the seller's liability in case of programme updates. The mostly spread Nordic standard form contracts in the field of sale of machinery, industrial equipment and other goods used in mechanical industries, NL 17 and NLM 19, and some others either in the NL-family or using the NL-contracts as models, have in their latest generation specifically addressed the issues of the buyer's potential right to source code and potential right to updates.[34] The principles followed there, concerning goods with digital elements, is that any duty to provide source codes or updates does not follow. However, the goods sold must have at least the agreed functionality also without the updates if updates are not agreed upon. If the goods do not meet these standards without the updates, the seller has to "repair" the goods, in practice by delivering the updates without cost. The same is applicable in case of sublicensing. The buyer also has the right to make such changes in software that are consistent with the intended use, but for sublicensed programmes any change of delivered software requires special agreement.[35] 22

---

[32] Civilutskottets betänkande, 2021/22:CU3, En ny konsumentköplag, p. 1 and 26 ff. See SOU 2020:51, p. 179 ff. for an account of legislative initiatives since 2008 concerning the appropriateness to let the CSA encompass the sale of living animals.

[33] Lagrådet, Utdrag ur protokoll från sammanträde 2021-12-02, p. 2.

[34] "NL" is an acronym for "Nordiska leveransbestämmelser" (in the Swedish language version; there are Danish, Finnish, Norwegian, and English language versions as well), meaning Nordic Terms of Delivery in a popularised version of the name of the contract. The official name for NL 17 is however, in the English version, General Conditions for the Supply of Machinery and other Mechanical, Electrical and Electronic Equipment in Denmark, Finland, Norway and Sweden, NL 17 E. There are also sector specific standard form contracts that lean heavily on the NL-contracts, such as ALV 21, Allmänna leveransvillkor för leverans av grafiska maskiner samt annan mekanisk, elektrisk och elektronisk grafisk utrustning [General terms of delivery of graphic machinery and other mechanical, electrical and electronical graphic equipment], which very closely coincides with NLM 19.

[35] NL 17 # 5–7. NLM 19 # 7–8.

C. Formation of Contract with Personal Data as Counter-Performance

I. Digital Supply as Performance

23   Relationships for the supply of digital content or digital services or the supply of goods with digital elements did not emerge with the issuing of the Twin Directives. However, there were most probably difficulties in deciding what rules would apply when the consumer's contribution consisted only in letting the trader gather the consumer's personal data. Were the relationships contracts at all? And even if so, were they not unilateral, or non-synallagmatic?

24   The fact that the content, service or element is digital is not at all the problematic issue in defining the relationship as contractual or bilateral/synallagmatic. In cases of monetary counter-performance there is obviously no difficulty to put the relationship into the patterns of formation of contract. Instead the challenging aspect here would have been to accept that the gathering of personal data, with or without the buyer's knowledge or consent, was adequate counter-performance on the part of the consumer. However, once it is accepted that personal data is adequate counter-performance, it is less troublesome as regards formation. Other issues arise in relation to remedies for breach of contract, which are to be discussed later on in this report.

25   In that sense the Twin Directives themselves have not created any need of restructuring private law that was not present already. However, until the DCD, or at least the discussions leading up to the DCD,[36] there would have been doubts whether these relations would classify as contracts, and the DCD has clearly made its point: Apart from the mere accepting of cookies, consumers' more or less voluntary transmissions of personal data are sufficient to be considered to create full-fledged contracts.

26   As already concluded it is sufficient to provide personal data to establish a contract. However, if the consumer would have promised to deliver its personal data but would fail to do so, it may be discussed whether that could be considered as a question of aborted contracting or a breach of contract. Probably this distinction will be of no practical importance. The trader will most probably not be able to enforce the consumer's promise to hand over its correct personal data. However, the trader may reclaim its performance to the extent that it has already been delivered and refuse to continue to perform.

II. Personal Data as Sufficient Counter-Performance Outside of The Twin Directives

27   The DCD (and the SGD, but of less factual importance) made it necessary to embrace the idea of personal data as a sole adequate remuneration for the formation of a bilateral/synallagmatic contract. However, so far this idea has rather been confined. It exists only in case of the supply of digital content/services/elements to consumers. It does not yet exist in B2B-relations, or in other parts of the contract law regime. For certain, with the Twin Directives, the idea exists when it comes to pure digital supply, when the consumer engages in internet activity. And for certain, the idea exists in sale of goods when the consumer has or has not paid money or any equivalent to receive goods with digital elements, or when supply has a tangible carrier. However, in other types of contract, such as non-intellectual services, supply of telephone services, electricity,

---

[36] Ds 2008:55. Ds 2012:31.

household gas or tenancy, it is probably the opposite, when no other payment than the gathering of personal data has been done. In time, maybe soon, this may change.

III. Personal Data as Counter-Performance in B2B Contracts

The potential to enlarge the idea of personal data as sufficient counter-performance to create a contract in B2B relations is low. One could however, as in the provisions on end-user protection in the European Electronic Communications Code Directive (EU) 2018/1972, consider if this would be suitable for end-users in the categories microenterprises, small enterprises and not-for-profit organisations. Without any EU initiative on the matter this is most unlikely to happen in Sweden.

D. Delivery and Conformity of Products

I. Delivery

The place of delivery of goods is at the seller's place of business, unless otherwise would follow from the contract, 2:1 CSA. However, this rule only states what the parties have to expect before delivery has taken place and in the absence of a subsequent agreement on the matter. If the goods are actually handed over somewhere else, that place will be deemed to be the place of delivery.

Delivery occurs when the consumer has taken possession of the goods. Possession can be immediate, in the meaning that the consumer itself has physical possession. Possession can also be mediate. If the consumer has given someone an assignment to fetch or to receive the goods (e.g. a family member or a transporter), that mediate possession will constitute delivery.[37] If the consumer has asked the seller to leave the goods in the mailbox of the consumer or on the property of the consumer, and the seller does that, delivery is deemed to have taken place.[38] Would the seller leave the goods by the consumer's apartment door in an apartment building, delivery has according to the preparatory works not taken place, even if this is done in accordance with the consumer's instructions.[39]

For delivery of goods with digital elements supplied in a single act it is required that the goods are handed over and that the digital elements have been supplied, 2:4(1).1 CSA. If the digital supply is continuous, delivery is achieved when the supply has begun, 2:4(1).2 CSA.

For contracts of supply of digital content the equivalent of delivery is "supply". Supply is accomplished when the content is made available or accessible or a means suitable for access to or download of the content. A digital service is supplied when it is made available for the consumer, 9:1(2) CSA. However, for digital content on tangible media, the rules on delivery for goods without digital elements and goods with digital elements with a single act of supply apply instead, 9:1(3).

---

[37] Cf. CRD Art. 20.
[38] Prop. 1989/90:89, p. 70. NJA 2013 s. 524 (Den skadade dörren).
[39] Prop. 1989/90:89, p. 70. Cf. Håstad, p. 235.

II. Subjective and Objective Requirements for Conformity

33 The possibility for the buyer to make a claim of lack of conformity on merely objective grounds is old in Sweden. Subjective and objective requirements were already in place in the CSA of 1990, and it can be traced back to the older Consumer Sales Act of 1973.[40] These elements were in the doctrine called concrete and abstract requirements (or concrete and abstract defects or similar notions).

34 Before the implementation, the objective/abstract standard was, loosely translated, formulated as follows: "*Unless something else has been agreed upon*, the product shall comply with [the following enumeration]". Now it is, again loosely translated, stated in the following way: "The product shall, *in addition to* what follows from § 1 [i.e. the subjective/concrete requirements], comply with [the following enumeration]".

35 The new wording might pose problems when the consumer has knowingly bought an inferior product, such as in cases of second-hand goods not sold in auction. The subjective/concrete standard might be interpreted to be a subsidiary norm, only activated if and when the subjective/concrete standard is set higher than the objective/abstract norm. This would risk that courts and others would have to find a defect either in a deviation in the objective criteria or a deviation from a proven individual specification. Probably, however, the application in Swedish courts and consumer adjudication boards will not follow such a strict lexical interpretation, but rather still place the common intention of the parties in the forefront.

36 Swedish contract law has three broadly captioned main measures of defects. A defect is at hand if the product does not fit the specifications of the contract (concrete defect), is not suitable for its normally intended use (objective abstract defect) or is of lower quality than the buyer had reason to assume (subjective abstract defect). The subjective abstract standard is under the influence of the concrete standard. If the concrete standard seems to suggest lower quality than the general, the subjective abstract standard is lowered as well. The subjective abstract standard has the function of a general clause to the aid of the buyer. If nothing else is enough to show non-conformity, this might. The existence of the broad measures of contract compliance have had the positive systematic effect that there has been a less immediate need for specific standards, for example for the events of third parties' claims of infringements of third parties claims of infringements of intellectual property rights or authorities' decisions limiting the buyer's use of the product.

37 The subjective abstract standard has been put to display in the core of Swedish law of contracts, namely in the main defect defining provisions of the SGA,[41] the rules on sale of real property in the Land Code of 1970,[42] amended in 1990 to lexically match the wording of the SGA, and the now repealed CSA of 1990.[43] The subjective abstract standard has been applied either *ex analogia* or by virtue of being a general principle by the Supreme Court in a commercial construction contract dispute in which the parties unusually enough had neglected to incorporate any standard form agreement.[44] Commercial construction contracts are under no statutory contract regulation and are almost without exception regulated with standard form contracts provided by the Swedish

---

[40] NJA 2020 p. 951 (Badrummet i radhuset), p. 24, referring to konsumentköplagen (1973:877), i.e. the Consumer Sales Act of 1973, and its preparatory works, probably concerning § 9.2, see prop. 1973:138 med förslag till konsumentköplag, m.m., p. 241.
[41] § 17(3).
[42] 4 kap. 19 § jordabalken (1970:994). [4:19 of the Land Code of 1970.]
[43] § 16(3)-3.
[44] NJA 2013 p. 1174, Syrisk-Ortodoxa kyrkan.

construction business.⁴⁵ These well-balanced agreed documents do not contain any close equivalents to the subjective abstract standard.⁴⁶ Nevertheless, or maybe therefore, the subjective abstract standard was applied. The subjective abstract standard has been applied by the Supreme Court also in a consumer construction contract dispute,⁴⁷ where the then commonly used standard form consumer construction contract had been incorporated.⁴⁸ This standard form contract was the result of negotiations between the construction business and the Swedish Consumer Agency. This standard form contract, or even the closely related Consumer Services Act of 1985,⁴⁹ does not contain any direct equivalent to the subjective abstract standard. Nonetheless, by construing the standard form contract in the light of the Consumer Services Act, the SGA, the CSA of 1990 and the Land Code concerning conveyancing of real property, the Supreme Court found that the consumers could invoke defects based on the subjective abstract standard.

The SGD and the DCD do not contain any exact equivalent to the subjective abstract standard. However, the objective requirement that the products shall "be of the quantity and possess the qualities and other features … which the consumer may reasonably expect" in SGD Art. 7(1)(d) and DCD Art. 8(1)(b) is close. Especially after the Council of Legislation's opinion and the government's response to that, the wording of the subjective abstract standard was more or less restored, 4:2–3 and 9:4(1) CSA.⁵⁰ If this would not be the case one could argue that buyers in commercial or private relations are afforded better protection than consumers in this particular aspect. In that negative case, it would be a systemic error.

III. The Durability Requirement

The durability requirement is enumerated alongside other objective requirements on products in the Swedish CSA.⁵¹ As explained above, the durability requirement is of central importance, and has been so for decades in Swedish consumer contract law. As a standard, nowadays a durability of three years is expected. This does not apply to fresh produce or other products of obviously low durability, by common sense rather than statute.

When it comes to durability in the sense of environmental concerns and sustainability, it is different. In the transposition Sweden definitely paid attention to the durability requirement in the sense of sustainability, without over-emphasising the potency of

---

⁴⁵ The current versions of these are Allmänna Bestämmelser för byggnads-, anläggnings- och installationsentreprenader, AB 04, and Allmänna Bestämmelser för totalentreprenader avseende byggnads-, anläggnings- och installationsarbeten, ABT 06.

⁴⁶ The standards may rather be summarised as follows: In accordance with the contract or later modifications (the concrete standard), in accordance with the professional diligence of contractors in general (the objective abstract standard) and in accordance with statutory requirements (a specification of the objective abstract standard).

⁴⁷ NJA 2015 p. 1040, De enstegstätade fasaderna II.

⁴⁸ Allmänna Bestämmelser om småhusentreprenad, ABS 95. The current version is Allmänna Bestämmelser om småhusentreprenad, ABS 18.

⁴⁹ Consumer Services Act (1985:716).

⁵⁰ The Council of Legislation's statement of opinion 2021-12-02, p. 12 ff. and 35 f., maintaining that the subjective abstract measure is a well-established standard, and proposing the insertion of provisions very similar to the one that formerly stated the subjective abstract standard. In the bill, Prop. 2021/22:85, especially p. 197, the government explained that it would be better to use the wording from the CSA of 1990, and to use the expression throughout the whole act.

⁵¹ 4:2(3) CSA for goods and 9:4(1) CSA for supply of digital content and digital services. The durability requirement is elaborated in the same manner as in SGD Art. 2(13) and recitals 24 and 32, Prop. 2021/22:85, p. 250.

contract law. A former inquiry on circular economy had concluded that a longer period of liability – arguing for an extension from three to five years – and a longer period of reversed burden of proof – arguing for an extension from six months to two years – could enhance durability and at the same time enhance sustainability and a circular economy.[52] The general period of reversed burden of proof was in the transposition of the Twin Directives prolonged to two years, even if the former inquiry on circular economy had proposed an extension to only one year,[53] and the already existing liability period that was three years sharp from delivery was extended to a maximum om three years and two months.

41 In Sweden there are no rules on availability of spare parts and corresponding information obligations apart from the public law statutes on eco design.[54] There is no coordination between the CSA and these statutes. The eco-design penalties are public law-based only. The only type of sanction mentioned is reimbursement of public expenditures concerning testing of the products.[55]

IV. Duties to Inform about and to Supply Necessary Updates

42 SGD Art. 7(3) and DCD Art. 8(2) places a duty on the trader to inform about necessary updates, which is implemented in 4:4 and 9:4 CSA. The industries will probably use standard automated reminders and replies, and this will most probably be considered to be enough on the whole. If there will be any at all consumer benefit of this requirement is still to be assessed.

43 The duty to also supply updates necessary to maintain the functionality will be interpreted in a sterner way. According to SGD Art. 6(d) and DCD Art. 7(d), as well as 4:1(1) and 9:4 CSA, the digital element, content or service shall "be updated as stipulated by the contract". Since *pacta sunt servanda* rules, this is not novelty, but it places the burden to make the supply possible to be updated on the trader in a contract law fashion. Furthermore, in SGD Art. 7(3) and DCD Art. 8(2), implemented by 4:4 and 9:4 CSA, it is required that the trader shall ensure that the conformity of any digital element, content or service is maintained by supplying updates even if there is no mention of updates in the contract.

44 If no necessary update is made, or if an update made available is insufficient to render the product into conformity, there is a defect that the seller is accountable of. It is as simple as that,[56] and has been so in Swedish law for a long time. It becomes more difficult when the consumer changes its contact information during the lifetime of the contract. What will be required by any of the parties in this respect is still to be seen.

V. The Consumer's Duty to Install Updates

45 If the trader has informed of and made an update ready to be supplied, but the consumer fails to install the update, the consumer would lose its right to invoke non-conformity according to the SGD Art. 7(4), the DCD Art. 8(3), and 4:8 and 9:4(1) CSA. One could expect that this could occur quite often, especially during and after vacation sea-

---

[52] SOU 2017:22, Från värdekedja till värdecykel – så får Sverige en mer cirkulär ekonomi, p. 337 ff.
[53] SOU 2020:51, p. 113 ff.
[54] See first and foremost lagen (2008:112) om ekodesign [Act on Eco Design] and förordningen (2016:187) om ekodesign [Regulation on Eco Design].
[55] 17 § lagen om ekodesign [§ 17 of the Act on Eco Design].
[56] Prop. 2021/22:85, p. 200.

sons, but that the solution nonetheless will not be that the consumer has forfeited its rights. Rather the solution will in practice probably be that the trader will have to give the current customer enough support to bring the product up to date. If the product is so frail that failure to update would render the product beyond repair, the product is probably to be considered to be defective.

The legal consequences of update failures due to the consumer's unstable connection, poor bandwidth, insufficient memory, server error, router malfunction *et cetera* are not clearly answered. The wordings of the directives seem to imply that the consumer bears the risk of all failures not attributable to the trader.

VI. Restricted Use Due to the Trader's Infringement of Third-Party Rights

The product is in lack of conformity if the consumer's use of the product is restricted due to any right that a third party may have over the product, including intellectual property rights. Legal defects like this are treated as other defects, rendering the consumer the same range of remedies, 4:12 and 9:4(1) CSA. However, the consumer is also entitled to invoke rules on invalidity, such as fraud or dishonesty in accordance with Sections 30 and 33 of the Contracts Act.[57] This will however probably not be more advantageous for the consumer than making a claim based on lack of conformity, and the provisions on invalidity generally require that the consumer can show that the trader acted in bad faith.

VII. The Consumer's Acceptance of Specific Characteristics of the Product

According to SGD Art. 7(5) SGD and DCD Art. 8(5), and 4:6 and 9:4(1) CSA, the consumer's express and separate acceptance of a deviation from the objective requirements on products will result in that the product is in conformity as far that the acceptance goes. Apart from explaining that this order allows sale of second-hand products to be compliant, the governmental bill of CSA especially gives one example of a deviation from the objective requirements, namely damage on the paint of a new car.[58] If the consumer is informed about the damage and accepts it, the damage is not considered to constitute a defect. The bill also exemplified the trader's duty of information by referring to the Supreme Court case NJA 2001 p. 155.[59] The case concerned the consumer sale of a second-hand sailing boat marketed to be of "Scandinavian design". However, the boat was predominantly manufactured outside of Scandinavia, and since this particular characteristic was shown to have an impact on the market value, the boat was considered to be defective, and the consumer was granted a price reduction. By referring to previous preparatory works,[60] it was highlighted that the trader's duty encompasses clarifications on utility limits of the product as well as legal restrictions on use and risks connected to the use of the product.[61] For second-hand goods, all flaws cannot be expected to be de-

---

[57] 30 and 33 §§ lagen (1915:218) om avtal och andra rättshandlingar på förmögenhetsrättens område.
[58] Prop. 2021/22:85, p. 253.
[59] Prop. 2021/22:85, p. 70.
[60] Prop. 1989/90:89, p. 100.
[61] Prop. 2021/22:85, p. 70 f.

scribed in detail. This was in the bill exemplified with that it would not be necessary with an informed express consent of every single scratch among several scratches.⁶²

VIII. Incorrect Installation

49   If the trader, or someone on the trader's behalf, in the contract has undertaken to install the goods sold or something enabling the digital supply, and the installation is incorrect, the trader is liable for lack of conformity. The consequences are as any other lack of conformity, i.e. withholding payment, repair, redelivery, price reduction, termination and damages.

50   As already pointed out above discussing the notions of 'integration' and 'installation', installation defects were regulated already by the adoption of SGA, § 21(2), and CSA of 1990, § 20(2). However, this was not obvious for most readers, since these provisions did not mention installation at all and it only appeared indirectly, unless one consulted the preparatory works.⁶³ According to these provisions the normally critical point of time for assessing conformity, delivery (or rather the passing of risk, but which always coincides with delivery in consumer sales), should not be decisive if the goods had deteriorated after the passing of risk as a consequence of the seller's breach of contract. Incorrect installation was given as the prime example of such a breach of contract. The solution is that the risk passes to the buyer if the buyer takes possession before the seller begins the installation, but the seller is nonetheless liable under sales law for defects caused by the incorrect installation.

51   In order to loyally implement CSD Art. 2(5) it was considered better to lay down this rule in a more straightforward provision, § 16 a of the CSA of 1990, regulating installation defects singularly.⁶⁴ Furthermore, § 2(2) of the CSA of 1990 stated that the CSA of 1990 would not apply if the element of service was predominant in comparison with the element of sale of goods, and this was thought to risk confusion as to the applicability of the CSA in case of the seller's installation of the sold product.⁶⁵ In § 2–2 of the Consumer Services Act it was, and is still, stated that the act is not applicable when installation or other work is provided in order to fulfil a contract of sale of goods.

52   This has by some been construed as that the similar provision, 4:6 CSA, always results in that contracts combining sale of goods and installing the goods are to be regulated by rules on sale of goods, with no exception. So, when the contract supposes a transfer of ownership of goods combined with an "installation" of any kind, CSA is to be applied even if the element of installation is predominant.⁶⁶ However, this opinion might be questioned on several grounds.⁶⁷

---

⁶² Prop. 2021/22:85, p. 72 and 253.
⁶³ Prop. 1988/89:76 om ny köplag, p. 96. Prop. 1989/90:89, p. 109.
⁶⁴ Prop. 2001/02:134, p. 45 ff. and 83.
⁶⁵ E.g. NJA 2001 p. 138, concerning a seller's delivery and installation of a boiler ordered by a consumer, and whether the CSA of 1990 or the Consumer Services Act of 1985 would apply.
⁶⁶ Håstad, *Köprätt och annan kontraktsrätt* (2022), 233, and at 232 fn. 15 claiming that NJA 2001 s. 138 since the enactment of § 16 a of the CSA of 1990 is no longer relevant in consumer sales.
⁶⁷ Cf. Herre, *Konsumentköplagen. En kommentar* (2019), para. 2.2.2, and Johansson, *Konsumenttjänstlagen. En kommentar* (2020), para. 2.1, which do not express that all consumer contracts combining transfer of ownership of goods and instalment of the goods to be governed by the CSA (of 1990), and which do not deem NJA 2001 s. 138 to have lost its relevance.

D. Delivery and Conformity of Products

In 1:6(2) CSA it is – as before – stated that the CSA is not applicable if the element of service is predominant. This line of reasoning is in harmony with the case law of the Court of Justice of the European Union.[68]

In consumer construction contracts there is always an element of delivery of building material apart from "installing" the building material. The element of delivery of goods is however usually considered to be of lesser importance than the construction services provided by the contractor. The Consumer Services Act of 1985 apply to all consumer construction contracts,[69] whereas some provisions apply to the construction of new one- or two-family dwellings or extensions of such dwellings.[70] These latter provisions were adopted in 2004 and turned into force 2005, i.e. after the introduction in 2002 of the specific provision on installation defects, § 16 a of the CSA of 1990.[71]

Apart from the installation of goods that naturally comes with construction contracts there is repair of vehicles, that may include substitution of parts, which the repairer will charge for. In the original preparatory works of the Consumer Services Act, it was stated that substitutions of the motor and the gearbox of a car ought to be considered to be services rather than sale of goods.[72]

In SGD recital 38 it is stated that the concept of delivery is to be regulated by domestic law only, with regard to the CRD (Art. 20). The same is stated about the place of delivery, SGD recital 56. In SGD recital 40, however, it is stated that delivery is considered to be effectuated first when the seller has completed the installation. The CSA does not exactly follow this recommendation. It renders nonetheless a similar degree of protection, not directly by modifying the time of delivery but by other means. If the seller is in continuous control of the goods from the sale till the completion of the installation, delivery takes place first thereafter, which happens to be in line with the recommendation in SGD recital 40. On the other hand, if the consumer gains exclusive possession sometime between the sale and the seller's commencement of the installation, delivery has occurred before the installation and the risk has then passed to the consumer, 2:3 and 2:6 CSA. However, if the goods are to be installed by the seller, the liability period of three years starts to run from when the installation is completed, 4:14(1).2 CSA.[73] Furthermore, if the goods deteriorate after the delivery (and thus after the passing of risk) due to a breach of contract by the seller, the seller is liable for the deterioration, 4:14(3).2 CSA. If the goods deteriorate under the control of the seller, the deterioration is presumed to be caused by the seller. The seller's liability is strict, due to that the rules on lack of conformity in the CSA become applicable. The seller bears the burden of proof of that the deterioration is not caused by deficiencies in the installation but instead by something for which the consumer bears the risk.

---

[68] CJEU, Case C-247/16, *Schottelius*, EU:C:2017:638, where the CSD was considered inapplicable in case of a renovation of a swimming pool even if the contract included minor elements of delivery of goods.

[69] 1 § första stycket 2 konsumenttjänstlagen (1985:716) [§ 1(1)-2 of the Consumer Services Act].

[70] 1 § andra och tredje stycket och 51–61 §§ konsumenttjänstlagen [§ 1(2)–(3), and §§ 51–61 of the Consumer Services Act].

[71] Cf. Prop. 2003/04:45, Stärkt konsumentskydd vid småhusbyggande, where there was no mention at all of the then rather newly adopted § 16 a of the CSA of 1990, although other synchronising measures between the CSA of 1990 and the Consumer Services Act were contemplated, see inter alia p. 27 ff. and 77 ff. On the contrary, discussing the Supreme Court case NJA 2001 p. 138, it was assumed that in only few cases the element of sale of goods will outweigh the element of service when a sale of a house building kit is combined with the service to assemble the kit, p. 81.

[72] Prop. 1984/85:110 om konsumenttjänstlag, p. 153. See also SOU 1979:36, Konsumenttjänstlag, p. 413.

[73] Prop. 2021/22:85, p. 89 and 258 f.

E. Liability of the Trader

I. The Distinction of Liability between Single Acts of Supply and Continuous Supply

57 The regulation of liability of supply of digital content and digital services, including sale of goods with digital elements, differ in multiple respects, depending on if it is a single act of supply or a continuous supply. Supply of digital content on tangible media only is mostly handled as a single act of supply. These rules are of course mostly based on the Twin Directives, but with some deviations due to explicit options and pre-supposed domestic modalities.

58 For delivery of goods with digital elements it is required that not only the physical goods are handed over. The digital elements must also have been supplied to accomplish delivery, 2:4(1).1 CSA. This, however, only applies to single acts of supply. If the supply is supposed to be continuous, delivery is achieved when the supply has begun, 2:4(1).2 CSA. How this will function, considering delay and passing of risk for the future supply, has been questioned.[74] In my view, delays of either agreed-upon or necessary updates are thought to be solved by using the rules on lack of conformity, 4:1(1) and 4:4 CSA and SGD Art. 6(d) and 7(3). Also, since the absence of a necessary update will hamper functionality, the seller would be liable for the deterioration after delivery in accordance with 4:14(3).2 CSA. However, there is no nearby legal-technical solution available to tackle the problem of the liability for costs that arise after the initial delivery. If one would follow the normal rule, 4:5 CSA, the consumer would bear all costs that arise after delivery, which in these cases would include the costs for updates. Since this is obviously not the intention of the legislator – the underlying idea implied in 4:4 CSA and SGD Art. 7(3) must be that updates are to be supplied without cost for the consumer unless agreed otherwise – one must disregard from the usual implications of delivery in this particular respect.

59 As explained above, for contracts of supply of digital content, "supply", i.e. delivery, is accomplished when the content is made available or accessible, or a means suitable for access to or download of the content. A digital service is supplied when it is made available for the consumer, 9:1(2) CSA. However, for digital content on tangible media, the rules on delivery for goods without digital elements and goods with digital elements with a single act of supply apply instead, 9:1(3) CSA.

60 The seller shall inform of and supply the consumer with updates for goods with digital elements. In cases of single acts of supply this obligation is present as long as the consumer reasonably can expect updates. In cases of continuous supply, the obligation exists for at least three years from delivery or as long as the contract runs, if that would become longer than three years, 4:4(2) CSA. In contracts for the supply of digital content and digital services these obligations remain as long as the contract runs, 9:4(2).

61 The period of liability for lack of conformity in goods is three years from delivery (and up to three years and two months as described above, and later in detail), 4:14(1) CSA. For goods with digital parts with continuous digital supply the liability might extend even longer, if the digital supply carries on longer, 4:14(2) CSA. For contracts for the supply of digital content or digital services the liability is three years for lack of conformity, concerning defects that were there originally but that appeared later, 9:7(1) CSA. This applies only to the supply on tangible media and other single acts of supply.

---

[74] Håstad (2022), 236 fn. 28.

E. Liability of the Trader

For continuous supply, the liability period is as long as the contract of supply is in force, 9:7(2) CSA. The trader is liable for lack of conformity due to insufficient updates for as long as the trader is obliged to supply updates, 9:7(3) CSA.

The Twin Directives reverses the burden of proof for lack of conformity by placing it on the trader. In sale of goods in Sweden the period of reversed burden of proof is two years, but for goods with digital elements it is three years, 4:17 CSA.[75] For digital elements with continuous digital supply the reversed burden of proof applies during the whole contract period but at least for three years. For contracts on supply of digital content and digital services the period is one year, 9:8 CSA. For continuous supply, however, the reversed burden of proof applies during the contract period, and not shorter or any longer.

In case of termination of sale of goods due to a breach of contract, already performed parts shall be returned to the other party, 8:2(2).1–4 CSA. In contracts for the supply of digital content and digital services the trader shall – with exceptions soon to be accounted for – repay any payment made, 9:15(1).1 CSA. The consumer shall refrain from using the content or service, 9:17(1) CSA. Digital content supplied on a tangible medium shall be returned at the request of the trader, 9:17(2) CSA.

In case of termination of sale of goods with digital elements with continuous digital supply, the seller shall return any part of the price paid in advance for any period of contract that would have remained had the contract not been terminated, 8:2(2).5 with reference to 9:15(1) CSA. If the termination is due to a breach on the part of the seller, repayment shall be made for periods when the digital supply was not in conformity. This seems to oblige the seller to repay the whole payment for periods when the goods were in a state of lack of conformity, notwithstanding that the goods might have been in continued use by the consumer. However, according to 9:8(3) CSA, the consumer shall hand over any so-called natural return that the goods may have given (which is unusual in consumer cases) and pay reasonable remuneration for any other benefit that the consumer has had from the goods. Furthermore, as a general rule with many exceptions, the consumer shall pay for the decreased value of the goods if the consumer is unable to return the goods substantially unaltered and undiminished, 8:4 CSA. To sum up, in cases of termination of sale of goods with digital elements where the digital supply is continuous, the seller may make a deduction for the consumer's use. This is in coherence with general sales law, § 65(1) SGA and CISG Art. 84(2).

In cases of termination of contracts for supply of digital content or digital services, the trader shall reimburse payments made in advance for periods remaining after the termination, 9:15(1) CSA. Just as in terminated sales of goods due to the seller's fault, the trader must repay the payment for periods of lack of conformity if the contract of supply is terminated due to a breach by the trader. Here, however, there is no possibility to make any deductions for the consumer's use during periods when the quality of the supply was under the level of conformity. Chapter 9 CSA makes no reference to 8:3 or 8:4 CSA.[76] This is in a way coherent with the rules on redelivery, SGD Art. 14(4), which leaves no room for deductions for use even in periods when the product functioned as it was supposed to,[77] but it is hard to explain why the effects of *termination* should differ. The Swedish legislator would probably have preferred to let the provisions on deduction for use apply to contracts for the supply of digital content and digital services, but DCD

---

[75] Prop. 2021/22:85, p. 260.
[76] 9:21 CSA refers to 8:1, 8:5(1)–(2) and 8:7 CSA.
[77] Cf. CJEU, Case C-404/06, *Quelle*, EU:C:2008:231, and Munukka, 'EG-domstolen om omleverans: Konsument ska inte betala nyttoersättning för utbytt vara' (2008–09), 20 *Juridisk Tidskrift vid Stockholms universitet*, 311.

Art. 16(1) and, especially, 17(3) seems to prevent that, whereas the Swedish legislator at the same time would have been unwilling to abolish the deduction for use altogether.

II. Impossibility, Force Majeure and Changed Circumstances

66   In case of unforeseen events, the trader may be excused for its inability to perform without disturbances. The Twin Directives do not regulate matters on general contract law or damages, SGD Art. 3(10) and DCD Art. 3(6). Instead domestic rules apply.

67   As a point of departure, a party is not exempted from all of its obligations even if a burdensome event has occurred. The failure to perform is still to be treated as a breach of contract.

68   If the seller of goods proves that the failure to perform was due to an impediment beyond its control and that the trader could not reasonably be expected to have taken the impediment into account, or to have avoided or overcome the impediment or its consequences, the seller will be relieved from having to pay damages, 6:1 CSA. Relief is not possible if the damage is caused by a legal defect or when the performance deviates from a (commercial) guarantee, 6:1. The same applies for contracts for supply of digital content and digital services, 9:3 and 9:10.

69   The consumer may require the trader to make delivery. The trader is however relieved from the duty to deliver when there is an impediment which the trader is unable to overcome or if the performance would be unreasonably burdensome. If the impediment seizes to exist within a reasonable time, the consumer may again require delivery, 3:4 and 9:3(1) CSA.

70   These exemptions do not have the effect of relieving the trader from the breaches of contract as such.

71   Apart from rules in the CSA there is a doctrine of assumptions, which may give the trader relief. However, the prerequisites for the application of the doctrine are very narrow. § 36 of the Contracts Act may also give relief in burdensome cases, but the threshold is set high.

III. Electronic Communication Services

72   Electronic communication services fall outside of the scope of the CSA, except number-independent interpersonal communication services, 1:8–1 CSA.

73   When electronic communication services outside of the scope of CSA are bundled together with the supply of digital content or digital services that fall within the CSA, the CSA is applicable, but only to the part that would otherwise fall within the CSA. However, this does not apply for changes of terms of contract when the electronic communication service is an internet connection service or a generally accessible number-based communication service, 9:19(3) CSA. Changes of terms of contract in those bundles are exclusively regulated by the Electronic Communication Services Act.[78] Also, a breach of contract that would give the consumer the right to terminate a part of the bundle prematurely will entitle the consumer to terminate the whole bundle, 7:26 of the Electronic Communications Act, irrespective of if the breach directly concerns something regulated by Chapter 9 CSA or not.

---

[78] Prop. 2021/22:85, p. 185 f. Prop. 2021/22:136, p. 287 ff.

IV. The GDPR and the Twin Directives

In Sweden the synchronisation of the consumer contract rules in the Twin Directives with the GDPR[79] is seen in 1:9 CSA, where it is noticed that there are provisions on processing of personal data in the GDPR, in the Swedish act on complementary measures,[80] and in provisions adopted in conjunction thereof. The fact that a trader fails to comply with GDPR does not in itself activate the CSA.

F. Remedies for the Trader's Breach of Contract

I. The Remedies

The consumer has a range of remedies to resort to. In case of delay the consumer may withhold payment, demand performance, terminate and claim damages. In case of lack of conformity the consumer may withhold payment, demand repair or redelivery, demand price reduction, terminate and claim damages. In the following, only some of these remedies will be dealt with specifically.

II. Withholding Payment

The DCD leaves it to Member States to decide whether there should be a right to withhold performance.[81] The SGD Art. 13(6) requires that the consumer should have such a right in case of the seller's breach of contract but allows the member States to regulate the conditions and modalities for exercising the remedy.[82]

Both parties have a right to withhold performance. This applies as a general rule 1) in the original exchange, 2) in case of the other party's breach of contract and 3) after termination. I will here only give an account of the consumer's right in case of the trader's breach of contract, i.e. only 2), and only concerning the consumer's right.

The consumer may withhold payment to secure a claim due to a breach of contract. This right is afforded both in cases of delay and lack of conformity, and both in the sale of goods and digital supply, 3:3, 5:3, 9:3(1) and 9:10(1).3 CSA. The right to withhold payment extends to as much as is necessary in order to afford the consumer security for its claim on the basis of the breach of contract. The wording of the provision has been interpreted to give the consumer a somewhat wider margin concerning the sum of monies withheld than the one that buyers have under § 42 SGA, amounting (only) to the claim.[83]

It is probable that the consumer must dispatch a notice of breach before withholding payment due to a lack of conformity. The structure of the provisions seems to support that, and 5:2 CSA states that the consumer is entitled to invoke a lack of conformity only if notice is given. However, the consumer is under no obligation to make a monetary

---

[79] Regulation (EU) 2016/679 of the European Parliament and of the Council of 27 April 2016 on the protection of natural persons with regard to the processing of personal data and on the free movement of such data, and repealing Directive 95/46/EC (General Data Protection Regulation).

[80] Lagen (2018:218) med kompletterande bestämmelser till EU:s dataskyddsförordning.

[81] DCD recital 15.

[82] See also SGD recital 18.

[83] Prop. 1989/90:89, p. 75. E.g. Herre (2019), para. 6.3.2 and 8.5.2. Håstad (2022), 238, puts into question whether the wording of the CSA of 2022 (and of 1990) really give consumers a wider margin but contends that case law will probably accept the statement in the preparatory works.

claim before withholding payment. For delays, on the other hand, it is different. The consumer has no obligation to give notice of the delay as such, why the consumer most probably is entitled to withhold payment without notice of any kind.

III. Repair and Redelivery

80   Repair and redelivery are the primary remedies in case of lack of conformity, in relation to the secondary remedies price reduction and termination, 5:8 and 9:12 CSA. This is in line with general sales law, § 37 SGA. If these remedies are not available in the specific case, for instance concerning the sale of a pet that has deceased, the secondary remedies are available. In the large majority of the cases, though, the consumer must refrain from immediately requiring price reduction or termination. The consumer may, however, resort to price reduction or termination after having given the trader the opportunity to cure the breach. A novelty in Swedish law is that the consumer has the right to price reduction or termination without any previous attempt to cure, if the lack of conformity in the light of all the circumstances is of a serious nature, 5:8(1).3 and 9:12(1).3 CSA. The consumer has the right to price reduction or termination if attempts of repair or redelivery fails, 5:8(1).2 and 9:12(1).2 CSA. The wording of the provisions might give the impression that the consumer should always have the right to secondary remedies if the first attempt to cure would fail. However, in the preparatory works of the CSA of 1990 it was declared that the consumer normally would be entitled to resort to the secondary remedies only after two failed attempts,[84] and the preparatory works of CSA of 2022 declare that no deviation from that reasoning has been intended, specifying the need to take SGD recitals 50 and 52 into account.[85]

81   The seller has the primary prerogative to choose between repair and redelivery of goods in the general SGA, whereas it has been the opposite in the CSA of 1990 since the implementation of CSD.[86] The consumer still has the primary prerogative in sale of goods, which is expressly stated in 5:4(1).2 CSA.[87] In contracts for the supply of digital content or digital services it is instead the trader that has the prerogative to choose between the two types of cure, 9:11(1).2 CSA.[88]

82   The Twin Directives leave it to the Member States to decide on the places for repair and redelivery. The places of repair and redelivery are not expressly determined in the CSA. In both sale of goods and supply of digital content and digital services it must be left to the trader to decide how these remedies should be executed, as long as it is done without cost or significant inconvenience for the consumer, 5:4(3) and 9:11(3) CSA.

83   Repair and redelivery shall be performed without cost for the consumer, 5:4(3) and 9:11(3) CSA. This includes costs for postage, carriage, labour and material.[89] At the execution of redelivery in sale of goods, a seller is according to 5:6(1) CSA obliged to take the goods back at its own expense. This is supposed to clarify that the seller must not only deliver a new product but also has the duty to arrange for the return of the product and to pay for the expenses.[90] If needed to enable repair or redelivery,

---

[84] Prop. 1989/90:89, p. 122.
[85] Prop. 2021/22:85, p. 267 and 269.
[86] Prop. 2001/02:134, p. 51 ff. and 85 f. Cf. the preparatory works to the CSA of 1990 before the CSD-amendments, Prop. 1989/90:89, p. 119 and 121 f., stating that the seller has (had) the right to choose between repair and redelivery.
[87] Prop. 2021/22:85, p. 107, 109 f. and 266.
[88] Prop. 2021/22:85, p. 171 f. and 287.
[89] Prop. 2021/22:85, p. 266 and 288.
[90] Prop. 2021/22:85, p. 288.

the seller shall remove the defect product and install a new one or bear the costs for the removal and the installation, 5:6(2).1 CSA. This obligation only applies if the goods were installed before the defect appeared and in a manner that was consistent with their nature and purpose, 5:6(2).2 CSA. In contracts for the supply of digital content or digital services, the same is likely to apply *mutatis mutandis*, however less elaborately expressed in statute and preparatory works, 9:11(3) CSA.[91]

IV. Termination

The Twin Directives' rules on termination differ from general contract law in some aspects, at least lexically, namely the threshold for the right to terminate, the right to terminate in case of a serious breach of contract without having to give the trader any opportunity to cure, and the burden of proof on whether the threshold is reached. 84

Based on SGD Art. 13(5) and DCD Art. 14(6) the consumer has a right to terminate the contract in case of lack of conformity, unless the trader shows that the defect is minor. The same is stated in 5:10(1) CSA. In case of supply of digital content or digital services against payment in money the rules are the same, 9:12(2) CSA. If there is no payment in money, any lack of conformity enables the consumer to terminate.[92] 85

According to § 39(1) SGA the buyer has to prove that the defect is of substantial importance for the buyer, and that the seller knew or should have known about the importance. In § 29 CSA of 1990 the threshold was also formulated as substantial importance but without the requirement that the seller must or should have known about the importance for the buyer. Also here, the burden of proof was laid on the buyer. It is not only in sales law that the threshold for termination has been formulated as substantial importance. It is described as a general principle in the law of contracts.[93] The threshold "not minor" might lexically seem lower than the threshold "substantial importance".[94] However, at the implementation of the CSD Art. 3(6), where the threshold "minor" was also used, the preparatory works found the expressions to be practically interchangeable,[95] which was confirmed at the implementation of the Twin Directives.[96] This is also supported by the fact that the expression "not minor" was often used in older statutes, such as §§ 21, 42 and 43 SGA of 1905 and §§ 3–5 CSA of 1973, and the expression was interpreted to state the same threshold as "substantial importance".[97] 86

It might be that there is no real difference between the termination thresholds, why there would be no deviation from the general law of contracts in this respect. However, the reversed burden of proof concerning the gravity of the breach is a clear deviation from the general order. 87

---

[91] Prop. 2021/22:85, p. 267.
[92] Prop. 2021/22:85, p. 289.
[93] E.g. Bengtsson, 'Hävningsrätten i nytt läge?' (1990–91) 2 *Juridisk Tidskrift vid Stockholms universitet*, 579, with references. Hellner et al., *Speciell avtalsrätt II. Kontraktsrätt. 2 häftet. Allmänna ämnen* (2020), 191 ff. and 197. See also NJA 1999 s. 71 (Ambulansentreprenaden) and NJA 2001 s. 241.
[94] Håstad (2022), 263.
[95] Prop. 2001/02:134, p. 54 f.
[96] Prop. 2021/22:85, p. 119 f.
[97] Cf. Hellner et al. (2020), 192.

V. Damages

88 The consumer has a right to damages if any damage would occur, notwithstanding that the trader finally has performed in case of delay or that the trader has cured any lack of conformity within a reasonable time. The consumer may also combine the monetary remedies damages and price reduction, but over-compensation is not possible. Whatever damage that would remain after the price reduction is to be compensated.

89 The trader may avoid damages only if the breach of contract – delay or lack of conformity – was due to an impediment out of the trader's control, which the trader should not reasonably have expected. Once the impediment is detected the trader must try to avoid or overcome the consequences of the impediment, and relief is given only if the consequences are found to be too economically onerous to bear, 6:1 CSA. However, in cases of legal defects and deviations from commercial guarantees, the right to damages is absolute, 6:2 CSA.

VI. Passing on Rights to Subsequent Buyers

90 In Swedish legislation there is nothing providing for a subsequent buyer to have rights against the trader, apart from some rights to damages when the subsequent buyer happens to be a member of the original buyer's household, 6:3(2) CSA. On the other hand, case law strongly supports the rights of the subsequent buyer. In three judgments, delivered in 2015–2016, the Supreme Court found that contract terms prohibiting parties to a contract from conveying their contractual rights should not affect the acquirer of those rights, and not even if the acquirer had knowledge (was in bad faith) of that prohibition.[98] Two of these cases concerned the acquisition of guarantees, one concerning several guarantees B2C passed on to subsequent consumers,[99] and one concerning a guarantee B2B passed on to a subsequent trader.[100] Even if the guarantee statements did not provide any rights to subsequent buyers and, to the opposite, prohibited such acquisitions, the subsequent buyers of the properties to which the guarantees had been attached could invoke the guarantees against the guarantors. In these two cases there were no explicit transfers of the guarantees. Instead, the guarantees seem to have followed automatically with the transfers of property. In the consumer case the rights transferred was a right of repair or damages corresponding to the costs of repair.

91 From this case law one can assume that at least guarantees may be invoked by subsequent buyers. The subsequent buyer does not seem to be obliged to show an explicit acquisition of the guarantee or the rights attached to it. However, if a transfer of the guarantee or the rights within that guarantee is made explicitly, the trader will with utmost certainty not be able to avoid the claims of the subsequent buyer.[101] One can also assume that subsequent buyers of goods should be able to invoke the statutory rights of the original buyers.

---

[98] NJA 2015 s. 1040 (De enstegstätade fasaderna II). NJA 2016 s. 51 (Pippi på is). NJA 2016 s. 288 (Betalingserklæringen). See Munukka, 'Avtalade överlåtelseförbud', in Bernitz et al. (eds), *Festskrift till Lars Pehrson* (2016), 285.

[99] NJA 2015 s. 1040.

[100] NJA 2016 s. 288.

[101] Cf. NJA 1993 s. 222 (Fullwood) and NJA 2021 s. 622 (Länna Marks fordran).

G. Commercial Guarantees

Nordic legal thinking opposes the idea of a "legal guarantee". The correct concept would instead be the "liability for defects", not having to turn to fictions. Since the decisive part of EU seems to think otherwise, Nordic lawyers are given the role to accept this terminology. Real guarantees will here therefore be called 'commercial guarantees', as the decisive part of EU wishes to call them.

Commercial guarantees are frequent in Sweden, and often not on par with the current legislative rules on liability for defects. The guarantees cannot diminish rights, only extend them. However, the Swedish consumer community is rather cynical in this respect. It does not trust guarantees, since it puts trust in the consumer legislation. Of course, a consumer might invoke a 10-year or a life-time guarantee, but the real faith is put on the legislation.

On the whole, there is little statutory regulation of commercial guarantees in Swedish legislation. The option in the Twin Directives to implement rules on languages in guarantee statements was not used.

From 4:21 CSA it follows that there is a lack of conformity if the goods do not meet the requirements in the guarantee during the period given in the guarantee statement unless the seller can show that the deviation is due to an accident or the consumer's maltreatment or abnormal use or similar. If someone else than the seller has given the guarantee, the consumer may claim that person for the remedies stipulated in the guarantee, 4:22 CSA. However, if a producer has offered the consumer a guarantee of durability, the consumer always has the right to demand repair or redelivery. If the terms of the guarantee are less advantageous than what was advertised, the terms stipulated in the advertising have priority, unless the advertising have been adjusted before the sale, 4:23 CSA. In § 22 of the Marketing Practices Act of 2008 it is *inter alia* required that guarantees are formulated in a clear and intelligible manner, and that the guarantee statement and the information is given at the time of the sale, at the latest by the time of delivery.

In § 23(3) of the CSA of 1990 it was also stated that the outer time limit of three years might be longer if that would follow from a guarantee or a similar commitment. The same kind of reminder is found in § 32(2) SGA. The absence of such a (redundant) statement in the CSA of 2022 makes no difference, since the same result is achieved with 4:21(1) CSA of 2022, as was already the case with § 21(1) CSA of 1990. Promises are promises, and promises are to be kept. If not kept, there will be consequences.

H. Intermediaries and Online Platforms

Sweden did not specifically address online sale platforms in the legislation, but platforms may be seen as sellers of goods or traders supplying digital content or digital services within the scope of the CSA. Some platforms in Sweden voluntarily assume responsibility as sellers within their terms of contract, such as the largest second-hand intermediary for motor vehicles.[102]

Apart from that, businesses may fall under the scope of the CSA even if they are not deemed to be acting on their own behalf, under what is called *förmedlingsköp*, "intermediary sale". Business intermediaries have joint and several liability with the seller, if the seller is a private person. This is the case when a private person sells to another private person with a business as an intermediary, 1:4 CSA, with the effect that

---

[102] https://www.kvd.se/villkor/privatperson, last visited 2022-08-20.

the CSA in its entirety applies. The intermediary does not need to act in the capacity of a mandatary, i.e. having authority to sell on the behalf of the private seller.[103] The brokerage itself is sufficient, but if the intermediary only has put the parties in contact with each other, without having any impact on the terms of contract, the CSA does not apply.[104] Not only the intermediary is liable under the mandatory rules of the CSA, but also the private seller. The intermediary will most often have a right of redress against the private seller.[105]

99 The "intermediary sale" phenomenon might only be applicable to sale of goods, where it absolutely also has its greatest importance. The actual provision speaks only of a "seller", i.e. a private person acting as a seller, and not as a "supplier". However, the sale of digital content in tangible media, such as second-hand CD:s and DVD:s, would probably be deemed to fall under the CSA, if brokered by a professional.

I. Time Limits

I. Obligation to Notify of Defects

100 Consumers have had an obligation to give notice of defects since the Sale of Goods Act of 1905, § 52(1).[106] Since the implementation of the CSD, Art. 5(2), a minimum time limit of two months from when the consumer detected the lack of conformity applies, § 23(1).2 CSA of 1990.

101 In compliance with the option given in SGD Art. 12, it was considered best to keep the notification duty without major modifications in the CSA of 2022, 5:2(1).3 CSA.[107] In fact, case law confirms that consumers have a duty to notify of breaches also in the absence of directly applicable statutory support.[108] However, there was no room for adopting an obligation to notify in case of supply of digital content or digital services, including digital content on a tangible medium. The legislator stated that this was "unfortunate".[109] In electronic communication service contracts, with the exception of number-independent interpersonal communication services, the consumer has a duty to notify of breach of contract, 7:17(2) of the Electronic Communications Act.[110]

102 The consumer must in sale of goods, including sale of goods with digital elements, give notice within a reasonable time from when the consumer ought to have discovered the defect, 5:2(1).1 CSA. The period of notice may therefore start to run even if the consumer has not yet discovered the defect. However, the minimum period of two months starts to run only after the consumer has in fact discovered the defect. This means that the consumer's right may be time-barred only when both of these time-limits have been passed, i.e. the reasonable time from when the defect objectively should

---

[103] Prop. 1989/90:89, p. 30 f. and 61. The current rule is the same as § 1(2) CSA of 1990, Prop. 2021/22;85 p. 54 and 238. Its origin is § 1(2) CSA of 1973, but then it was required that the business actually acted in the capacity of mandatary, SOU 1972:28, Konsumentköplag, p. 8 and 60, and Prop 1973:138, p. 162 f.
[104] Prop. 1989/90:89, p. 61.
[105] Prop. 1989/90:89, p. 61.
[106] 52 § första stycket lagen (1905:38 s. 1) om köp och byte av lös egendom.
[107] Prop. 2021/22:85, p. 94 ff.
[108] NJA 2018 p. 127 (Flyget från Antalya). For an analysis and comparison with opposing Norwegian case law, see Rødvei Aagaard, 'Om att (inte) uppställa reklamationsregler på okodifierat område och om nordisk rätts(o)likhet' (2020–21) 32 *Juridisk Tidskrift vid Stockholms universitet*, 711.
[109] Prop. 2021/22:85, p. 167 f., where a reference to DCD recital 11 is made.
[110] 7 kap. 17 § andra stycket lagen (2022:482) om elektronisk kommunikation.

I. Time Limits

have been discovered and two months from when the consumer actually discovered the defect.

The consumer is relieved from its obligation to give notice if the seller has acted dishonestly or with gross negligence, 5:2(3) CSA. This does not mean that the consumer may wait with its complaints for an indefinite time,[111] but it certainly means that the time-limit is prolonged. 103

The outer time limit for the seller's liability for defects of three years after delivery in the CSA of 1990 was kept for sale of goods, 4:14(1)–(2) CSA. If goods with digital elements have a continuous digital supply the liability period is at least three years, but longer if the supply extends past that. In contracts for the supply of digital content or digital services the period is also three years, 9:7(1) CSA, but this only applies to single acts of supply. For continuous supply the liability period ends with the end of contract unless agreed otherwise, 9:7(2) CSA. 104

Even if the three-year period was kept, a prolonging modification was made. The three-year time limit in § 23 CSA of 1990 was construed as an absolute time bar, even when the defect did not appear until the very end of the period of liability. However, in the CSA of 2022 the absolute time limit is two months after the expiry of the liability period. This means that a claim must not be made within the liability period, but instead within two months of the expiry of the liability period, 5:2(2) and 9:10(2) CSA. This two-months rule applies to all liability periods for defects. 105

In case of the trader's dishonesty or gross negligence the outer time limits do not apply, 5:2(3) and 9:10(2).2 CSA. These rules will not give the consumer the right to wait with its claims in eternity, but they will break through the statutory time limits. 106

II. The Trader's Right of Redress

A right of redress is considered to follow from the general law of obligations of Sweden,[112] as a general principle.[113] Therefore no provision was deemed necessary at the implementations of the CSD[114] or the Twin Directives.[115] 107

As pointed out earlier, the key question is rather whether the seller's period of notice toward the seller's supplier should be linked to the consumer's notice of breach of contract.[116] As of now, there are no rules on this, and none are to be expected in the near future. 108

---

[111] Cf. Prop. 2004/05:13, Distans- och hemförsäljningslag m.m., p. 103 f., Prop. 1989/90:89, p. 116, and NJA 2017 s. 1195 (Skogssällskapet).

[112] A provision on redress is found in 2 § andra stycket lagen (1936:81) om skuldebrev [§ 2(2) of the Act on Promissory Notes]. The provision is considered to express the main rule in Swedish law, NJA 2009 p. 221. It states that if one of several debtors has paid the creditor more than the debtor owed visavi another debtor, the debtor that has paid may claim the other debtors for what they are due to pay.

[113] Cf. Unnersjö, Regress, 2021, p. 188, and NJA 2012 p. 804.

[114] SOU 1995:11, Nya konsumentregler. Preskriptionstid. Garantier m.m. Borgenärsskydd, p. 181. Prop. 2001/02:134, p. 55. See however dissenting inquiry expert Inger Soldéus, arguing for a mandatory right for sellers to exercise redress, SOU 1995:11, p. 201 f.

[115] SOU 2020:51, p. 162 f. Prop. 2021/22:85, p. 220 f.

[116] Cf. Sandstedt, 'Artikel 4 konsumentköpsdirektivet och skandinavisk export – om oväntade och tvingande regressfällor' (2005) 141 *Tidskrift utgiven av Juridiska Föreningen i Finland*, 295.

J. Final Words

109 The Twin Directives bring a multitude of achievements for the European collective of consumers. In some aspects the Twin Directives are forwarding even Nordic consumers' positions. It has happened before that EU consumer contract law achieve more than the existing Nordic consumer contract law, especially through the CSD's rules on a reversed burden of proof and, very much so, the minimum notice period of two months.

110 The first and foremost achievement is of course that the contracts of digital supply of any kind has been dealt with in a contract law fashion. When looking back twenty years from now, we will not be able to understand how we could do without this set of rules.

111 Another novelty this time is that a termination of contract may be acceptable even if the consumer has not given the trader the opportunity to cure the breach of contract, if the performance of the trader has been seriously bad. I believe that this idea is already a part of Swedish law, but with no hard evidence thereof outside of long-term contracts. Must you, is the question, give the performing party a second chance after a failed attempt that give the impression that the performing party is lacking in its ability, without invoking rules on invalidity or the like?[117] Hopefully the surrounding Swedish law of contracts will adapt to this, and announce that the right to terminate exists as a primary remedy in cases of lost trust in the counter-party also in momentary contracts.

112 The Twin Directives are on the same march that CSD and CRD and its forerunners started. However, the Union's goal of creating clear-cut and simple rules[118] has, to a deep level of disappointment, not been met. Ask any of the involved EU legislators, besides possibly some few civil servants at the EU Commission, and they will not know what provision will be applicable on what type of consumer contract.

Bibliography

Swedish statutes

förordningen (2016:187) om ekodesign [Regulation on Eco Design]

jordabalken (1970:994) [Land Code]

kommissionslagen (2009:865) [Commission Agency Act]

konsumentköplagen (1973:877) (repealed) [Consumer Sales Act of 1973]

konsumentköplagen (1990:932) (repealed) [Consumer Sales Act of 1990]

konsumenttjänstlagen (1985:716) [Consumer Services Act]

köplagen (1990:931) [Sale of Goods Act]

---

[117] Compare NJA 2016 s. 222, where a contractor had both used wrong material for flooring and failed to plaster the sub-floor in a professional manner, works performed when the consumer and his family wvacation. After returning home, the consumer notified the contractor of its complaints. The contractor admitted the defects and promised to cure them. Early in the morning, unannounced, the contractor's craftsmen rang the door-bell, ready to cure. The consumer explained that it was not possible to let the craftsmen in at that time. The consumer also demanded guarantees of that the cure would be safe for him and his family and that the works would be performed correctly this time. The Supreme court found that the consumer was in its right to waive cure at that unannounced point of time. However, the latter demands for guarantees were seen as ill-founded, and the consumer lost the right to remedies. With a right to direct termination in case of serious breaches, the consumer would probably have won the case.

[118] SGD recital 13. DCD recital 20.

Bibliography

lagen (1915:218) om avtal och andra rättshandlingar på förmögenhetsrättens område [Contracts Act]

lagen (2005:59) om distansavtal och avtal utanför affärslokaler [Distance and Off-Premises Contracts Act]

lagen (2008:112) om ekodesign [Act on Eco Design]

lagen (1905:38 s. 1) om köp och byte av lös egendom (repealed) [Sale of Goods Act of 1905]

lagen (1964:528) om tillämplig lag beträffande internationella köp av lösa saker [Applicable Law (International Sale of Goods) Act]

marknadsföringslagen (2008:486) [Marketing Practices Act]

produktansvarslagen (1992:18) [Product Liability Act]

EU acts

Directive 1999/44/EC of the European Parliament and of the Council of 25 May 1999 on certain aspects of the sale of consumer goods and associated guarantees, OJ L 171, 7.7.1999, p. 12–16 (repealed) ["CSD"]

Directive 2011/83/EU of the European Parliament and of the Council of 25 October 2011 on consumer rights, amending Council Directive 93/13/EEC and Directive 1999/44/EC of the European Parliament and of the Council and repealing Council Directive 85/577/EEC and Directive 97/7/EC of the European Parliament and of the Council, OJ L 304, 22.11.2011, p. 64–88 (consolidated 28.05.2022) ["CRD"]

Directive (EU) 2018/1972 of the European Parliament and of the Council of 11 December 2018 establishing the European Electronic Communications Code (consolidated 17.12.2018)

Regulation (EU) 2016/679 of the European Parliament and of the Council of 27 April 2016 on the protection of natural persons with regard to the processing of personal data and on the free movement of such data, and repealing Directive 95/46/EC (General Data Protection Regulation), OJ L 119, 4.5.2016, p. 1–88 (consolidated 04.05.2016) ["GDPR"]

Conventions

United Nations' Convention on Contracts for the International Sale of Goods, Vienna 1980 ["CISG"]

Swedish preparatory works

Civilutskottets betänkande, 2021/22:CU3, En ny konsumentköplag

Prop. 1973:138 med förslag till konsumentköplag, m.m.

Prop. 1984/85:110 om konsumenttjänstlag

Prop. 1988/89:76 om ny köplag

Prop. 1989/90:89 om ny konsumentköplag

Prop. 2001/02:134, Ändringar i konsumentköplagen

Prop. 2003/04:45, Stärkt konsumentskydd vid småhusbyggande

Prop. 2004/05:13, Distans- och hemförsäljningslag m.m.

Prop. 2021/22:85, En ny konsumentköplag

SOU 1972:28, Konsumentköplag

SOU 1979:36, Konsumenttjänstlag

SOU 1995:11, Nya konsumentregler. Preskriptionstid. Garantier m.m. Borgenärsskydd

SOU 2017:22, Från värdekedja till värdecykel – så får Sverige en mer cirkulär ekonomi

SOU 2020:51, En ny lag om konsumentskydd vid köp och vissa andra avtal

Ds 2008:55, Bör konsumenttjänstlagen utvidgas?

Ds 2012:31, App to date. Konsumenternas rättsliga ställning när varor eller tjänster betalas via telefonräkningen, m.m.

Literature

Marianne M. Rødvei Aagaard, 'Om att (inte) uppställa reklamationsregler på okodifierat område och om nordisk rätts(o)likhet' (2020–21) 32 *Juridisk Tidskrift vid Stockholms universitet*, 711

Bertil Bengtsson, 'Hävningsrätten i nytt läge?' (1990–91) 2 *Juridisk Tidskrift vid Stockholms universitet*, 579

Johanna Chamberlain, *Integritet och skadestånd [Privacy Torts: On the Protection of Personal Information of Swedish Law]*, (diss., Iustus Förlag, Uppsala 2021)

Jan Hellner, Richard Hager and Annina H. Persson, *Speciell avtalsrätt II. Kontraktsrätt. 2 häftet. Allmänna ämnen* (7th edn, Norstedts Juridik, Stockholm 2020)

Johnny Herre, *Konsumentköplagen. En kommentar* (version 5, Juno, 2019)

Torgny Håstad, *Köprätt och annan kontraktsrätt* (7th edn, Iustus Förlag, Uppsala 2022)

Svante O. Johansson, *Konsumenttjänstlagen. En kommentar* (version 2, Juno, 2020)

Andreas Kotsios, *Paying with Data. A Study on EU Consumer Law and the Protection of Personal Data* (diss., Iustus Förlag, Uppsala 2022)

Jori Munukka, 'Avtalade överlåtelseförbud', in Bernitz, Kleineman, Munukka and van der Sluijs (eds), *Festskrift till Lars Pehrson* (Jure Förlag, Stockholm 2016), 285

Jori Munukka, 'EG-domstolen om omleverans: Konsument ska inte betala nyttoersättning för utbytt vara' (2008–09) 20 *Juridisk Tidskrift vid Stockholms universitet*, 311

Johan Sandstedt, 'Artikel 4 konsumentköpsdirektivet och skandinavisk export – om oväntade och tvingande regressfällor' (2005) 141 *Tidskrift utgiven av juridiska föreningen i Finland*, 295

Alexander Unnersjö, *Regress. Begreppet regressrätt och solidarregress [Recourse. The concept of the right of recourse and joint and several liability]* (diss., Jure Förlag, Stockholm 2021)

Case Law
The Supreme Court (Sweden)

NJA 1993 s. 222 (Fullwood)

NJA 1999 s. 71 (Ambulansentreprenaden)

NJA 2001 s. 138 (Värmepannan)

NJA 2001 s. 241

NJA 2007 s. 68 (Motocrossbanan)

NJA 2009 s. 221

NJA 2012 s. 804

NJA 2013 s. 524 (Den skadade dörren)

NJA 2013 s. 1174 (Syrisk-Ortodoxa kyrkan)

NJA 2015 s. 1040 (De enstegstätade fasaderna II)

NJA 2016 s. 51 (Pippi på is)

NJA 2016 s. 222

NJA 2016 s. 288 (Betalingserklæringen)

NJA 2017 s. 1195 (Skogssällskapet)

NJA 2018 s. 127 (Flyget till Antalya)

NJA 2020 s. 951 (Badrummet i radhuset)

NJA 2021 s. 622 (Länna Marks fordran)

Court of Justice of the European Union

Case C-404/06, 17.04.2008, *Quelle AG v. Bundesverband der Verbraucherzentralen und Verbraucherverbände*, EU:C:2008:231

Case C-247/16, 07.09.2017, *Heike Schottelius v. Falk Seifert*, EU:C:2017:638

II.
DIGITAL SERVICES AND THE NEW PLATFORMS REGULATION

Some major issues of EU Regulation 2019/1150 on promoting fairness and transparency for business users of online intermediation services

A. Effect of Art. 1.4 second sentence – validity test	2
I. National Law Rules on Validity of General Contract Terms	4
1. Art. 305 sequ. BGB	4
2. Special Rules on Interpretation	5
3. Rules on Unfair Terms	8
a) Art. 307 Sec. 2 No. 1 BGB	8
b) Restrictions on the validity of disclaimers	11
4. Interim Conclusion	12
II. Scope of Art. 2 No. 10	14
III. Scope of the unfairness test of Art. 8	19
B. Transparency – the overriding issue – Art. 3 Sec. 1 lit. a	20
I. Definition	20
II. Analysis	21
1. Recital 15	21
2. Up-front analysis	22
3. Art. 5 of Directive 93/13/EEC as guidance	24
4. Transparency of the language actually used	25
5. Application of Art. 307 Sec. 1 second sentence BGB	26
a) Incorporation of Art. 5 of Directive 93/13/EEC	26
b) Three principles established by German Courts as guidelines	28
III. Interim Conclusion	29
IV. Consequences of a violation of Art. 3 Sec. 1 lit. a) – Art. 3 Sec. 3	30
1. On the basis of Art. 3 Sec. 3	
2. On the basis of Art. 306 Sec. 2 BGB	30
C. Effect of Art. 1.4 – first sentence – unfair commercial practice test	33
I. Outline	33
II. Indications within this Regulation concerning consumer protection	35
1. Within the text	36
2. Within the Recitals	40
III. Protection of the vested interests of a third party within the legal regime of German law ("Vertrag mit Schutzwirkung zugunsten Dritter")	45
1. Requirements and Consequences	45
2. Outline of main issues to be resolved	47
IV. Unfairness control to the benefit of the consumer	48
V. Unfair commercial practice due to the supply of unfair contract terms (Art. 3a UWG)	50
VI. Interim conclusion	51
D. Main issues – Art. 4 – restriction, suspension and termination of the services	52
I. Outline	52
II. Essence of Art. 3 Sec. 1 lit. c) and Art. 4 Sec. 1	53
1. Art. 3 Sec. 1 lit. c)	53
2. Art. 4 Sec. 1	54
3. Interim conclusion	56
III. Unfairness test of unilateral actions – restriction and suspension ("delisting")	57
1. Perspective of the business user	57
2. Perspective of the consumer	59
IV. Termination clauses – Art. 4 Sec. 2	62
1. Outline	62
2. Test of this rule	63
a) No conflict with Union law	63
b) Possible conflict with Art. 307 Sec. 2 No. 1 BGB	65
E. Summary	69
Bibliography	69

1   This Regulation, being in force as from July 12, 2020, is the first EU-regulation covering b2b-transactions, namely between the provider of online intermediation services (online search engines which will not covered hereunder) and the business user.[1] This relation is dominated by market strength of the providers and the relative weakness of the business users, offering their services and products on the platforms administered by the providers to the general public, i.e. the ordinary consumer. Thus, the main issue of Regulation 2019/1150, to be dealt with in this paper and to be answered in some detail, is whether its effect is really such to promote fairness and transparency, thereby also giving due respect to fostering fair commercial practices. In other words: The main (political) issue, to be addressed, is whether the European lawmakers are about to successfully restrict the overwhelming economic power of the providers of such intermediation services to the benefit of the business users and – furthermore – to the overall benefit and of the welfare of the consumers.

A. Effect of Art. 1.4 second sentence – validity test

2   Already at the outset an important reservation must be set out straight forward: The question to be addressed hereunder cannot and shall not be answered solely on the level of the rules set forth in this Regulation, as due regard must be given whether and to what extent this Regulation also opens the door to apply relevant national legal rules of the Member States. Thus, the answer to be sought is based on the rules of this Regulation as the first layer and, second, on the (applicable) rules of national law, be it in relation to b2b-transactions, be it based on consumer law, which by itself is again – to a vast extent – European Law, namely Directive 93/13/EEC[2] (unfair contract terms) and Directive 2005/29/EC[3] (unfair commercial practices).

3   In this respect the interpretation of Art. 1 Sec. 4 – second sentence – of Regulation 2019/1150[4] is of utmost importance. Sentence 2 states: *"This Regulation shall not affect national civil law, in particular contract law, such as the rules on the validity, formation, effects of termination of a contract, in so far as the national civil law rules are in conformity with Union law, and to the extent that the relevant aspects are not covered by this Regulation".*[5]

I. National Law Rules on Validity of General Contract Terms

1. Art. 305 sequ. BGB

4   There is need to stress that German Civil Contract Law provides special legal rules for interpretation[6] and validity[7] of general terms of contract in b2b-transactions (Art. 305c sequ. BGB). As there is no Union law directly or indirectly covering any of these aspects of German law, Art. 1 Sec. 4 will not be violated, provided these (national) legal rules are held to be applicable with regard to any general contract terms supplied by the provider of intermediation services to the respective business user.

---

[1] Official Journal of the European Union, July 11, 2019 – L 186/57.
[2] Official Journal of the European Communities, April 11, 1993 – L 95/29.
[3] Official Journal of the European Union, June 11, 2005 – L 149/22.
[4] All citations of „Articles" hereafter shall refer to Regulation 2019/1150, unless stated otherwise.
[5] Official Journal of the European Union, July 11, 2019 – L 186/68.
[6] Art. 305b and 305c BGB.
[7] Art. 307 to Art. 310 BGB.

A. Effect of Art. 1.4 second sentence – validity test

2. Special Rules on Interpretation

Art. 305c Sec. 2 BGB holds that general terms of contract shall be interpreted to the detriment of the supplier, there is any doubt as to the proper meaning of any such term. However, the German Courts have gone much further in defining the border lines of this general legal rule. First of all, all general terms of contract may not be interpreted in view of the will of the respective parties to the contract, as provided for by Art. 133, 157 BGB.[8] As the terms so supplied are designed to generally be incorporated into a contract, any interpretation of such terms must be based on an objective understanding of the words used in such contract term, giving them a typical meaning, being based on the reasonable understanding of such parties, as are generally involved in such transactions.[9] Thus, the interpretation must be based on the reasonable understanding of an average customer.[10]

However, a special rule developed by the German Supreme Court on Civil Matters (BGH) in line with Art. 305c Sec. 2 BGB must be taken into consideration for a wider and better understanding:[11] If the interpretation of a specific contract term does not lead to a clear-cut answer as to its proper meaning, but leaves the door open to an alternative understanding, then such interpretation shall be accepted as the only relevant result which is most favourable to the customer, as it will lead to invalidate the respective contract term pursuant to the rules of Art. 307 sequ. BGB.

There are many precedents showing that the BGH is extremely strict in applying the legal rule of Art. 305c Sec. 2 BGB. This result must be taken into account, as only the rigid interpretation will then become the basis for applying the rules of the unfairness test of Art. 307 sequ. BGB in b2c and very similar also in b2b-transaction.[12] Therefore, to conclude: The unfairness test as the second step in invalidating any contract term always rests on the result of the respective interpretation of any contract term, being the first step to go.

3. Rules on Unfair Terms

a) Art. 307 Sec. 2 No. 1 BGB

The most important legal rule dealing with unfairness is embodied in Art. 307 Sec. 2 No. 1 BGB. The essence of this rule is straight and forward: If a contract term supplied to a customer deviates from the legal rule, applicable if there were no such clause, then there is a legal assumption that it will be held to be unfair and to the detriment of the respective customer.[13] If this finding is warranted, then such clause will be held to be invalid and will, therefore, be substituted pursuant to Art. 306 Sec. 2 of the BGB by the respective legal rule.[14]

The legal purpose of so protecting the customer, having had no opportunity to individually negotiate the respective contract term, is that the legal rules, as enacted by the

---

[8] For further details vide Grüneberg/*Grüneberg, Commentary on the BGB*, 81st ed., 2022, § 305c Note 16.
[9] BGH 04.07.2017 – XI ZR 562/15, NJW 2017, 426 Note 17 – further references.
[10] BGH 18.07.2012 – VIII ZR 337/2011, NJW 2013, 291 Note 16.
[11] BGH 29.04.2008 – KZR 2/07, NJW 2008 p. 2172.
[12] Grüneberg/*Grüneberg, Commentary on the BGB*, 81st ed., 2022, § 307 Note 8.
[13] BGH 04.07.2017 – XI ZR 562/15, NJW 2017 p. 2986 Note 37 sequ.
[14] Just recently, the rule of Art. 306 Sec. 2 BGB has come under considerable fire by two rulings of the ECJ, namely ECJ, dated Sept. 8, 2023 – C-80/21 – C-82/21, NJW 2022, 3489 – D.B.P.; ECJ 8.12.2022 – C-625/21, BeckRS 2022, 34901 – Gupfinger. But these judgements are based on the interpretation of Art. 6 1993/13/EEC – Unfair Terms – and are only applicable in b2c-transactions, not directly dealt with herein; for further understanding *Wendehorst/Graf von Westphalen, Auswirkungen neuer EuGH-Urteile auf § 306 II BGB – mehr neue Vorlagefragen als Antworten*, EuZW 2021, 229.

lawmakers, represent the essence of justice and fair dealing, thereby balancing the interests of both parties in a fair manner.[15] Consequently, it must be kept in mind that – in this respect – the German law in line with the precedents established by the BGH, does not make any difference in invalidating general contract terms to be unfair pursuant to the rule of Art. 307 Sec. 2 No. 1 BGB, regardless, whether the customer is a business user, i.e. a trader or a consumer.[16] But, in legal literature there is much dispute whether this approach of the BGH is not unreasonably restricting the freedom of contract in b2b-transactions.[17] The writers supporting such view also hold that the parallelism between the protection of the consumer and of the trader is not acceptable[18] due to the underlying consideration that a consumer needs more protection against unfair contract terms than a trader. Consequently, such view maintains also that many German traders are trying to evade German law and thus derogate the applicability of the legal rules of Art. 305 sequ. BGB by either agreeing to arbitration clauses[19] or by accepting Swiss law instead of German law in national and international transactions.[20] Whether this avenue, especially with regard to arbitration clauses, can safely be taken has not yet been decided by the BGH. The answer rests on the question whether such clauses, derogating the application of German law in a domestic transaction, are held to be valid (Art. 1059 Sec. 2 No. 1 a) ZPO), despite of the fact that they in themselves are general contract terms, being subject to the unfairness test of Art. 307 BGB.

10 In this respect it must be noted that the BGH holds that the legal rules covering the specific aspects of consumer protection pursuant to the rigid catalogue of unfair terms listed in 309 BGB are nothing but an emanation of the general unfairness test of Art. 307 BGB.[21] Thus, the specific legal rules of consumer protection, as laid down in Art. 309 BGB are applied by "analogy" also to respective general contract terms in b2b-transactions. This reasoning is supported by most legal writers,[22] but there is also some criticism.[23] However, the jurisdiction of the BGH stands firm.

b) Restrictions on the validity of disclaimers

11 In following this route, one has to note that the application of Art. 309 No. 7 BGB by "analogy" within the framework of b2b-transactions renders any disclaimers null and void, if there are breaches of contract based on a willful act or on gross negligence. But the main aspect in practice is that any disclaimers of liability for breaches of contract are

---

[15] BGH 07.07.1976 – IV ZR 229/74, NJW 1976 p. 2345; for further details vide Graf von Westphalen, *Wiederentdeckte Grundpfeiler der Rechtsprechung zur AGB-Kontrolle*, NJW 2022, 1409.

[16] BGH 04.07.2017 – XI ZR 562/15, NJW 2017 p. 2786 Note 66.

[17] For a detailed debate of this issue vide Wendland, *Vertragsfreiheit und Vertragsgerechtigkeit*, Tübingen 2019, p. 691 sequ.

[18] Finkelmaier, *Über die (Un-)möglichkeit der Haftungsbegrenzung im internationalen Handel – § 307 Abs. 1 BGB als faktische Grenze der Vertragsfreiheit*, ZIP 2022, 563; Maier-Reimer, *AGB-Recht im unternehmerischen Rechtsverkehr – der BGH überdreht die Schraube*, NJW 2017, 1; for further details vide Wendland, *Vertragsfreiheit und Vertragsgerechtigkeit*, Tübingen 2019, p. 713 sequ.

[19] Ostendorf, *Abwahl des AGB-Rechts per Rechtswahl und Schiedsvereinbarung: Problem oder Problemlöser?* ZIP 2022, 730; Graf von Westphalen, *Schiedsvereinbarungen und Ausschluss der §§ 305–310 BGB, aber Aufrechterhaltung der Geltung des § 242 BGB – was gilt?* ZIP 2022, 245 – holding such arbitration clauses null and void.

[20] Sommerfeld, *Rechtsflucht in Ausland wegen des deutschen AGB-Rechts im B2B-Verkehr?* RIW 2018, 741; Sommerfeld, *Wie sinnvoll ist eine Rechtsflucht ins Schweizerische Recht vor der deutschen AGB-Kontrolle im Handelsverkehr?* IWRZ 2022, 64.

[21] BGH 19.09.2007 – VIII ZR 141/06, NJW 2007, 3774.

[22] Grüneberg/Grüneberg, *Commentary on the BGB*, 81. edi. 2022, § 309 Note 55; Erman/Roloff/Looschelders, *Commentary on the BGB*, 16th edi. 2020, § 309 Note 76; Staudinger/Coester-Waltjen, *Commentary on the BGB*, 2019, § 309 Nr. 7 Note 42.

[23] Leuschner/Leuschner, *AGB-Recht im unternehmerischen Verkehr*, 2021, § 309 Nr. 7 Note 14 sequ.

A. Effect of Art. 1.4 second sentence – validity test

considered to be inoperable also in cases of mere negligence (Art. 307 Sec. 2 No. 2 BGB), provided that there is evidence of a severe breach of contract. There is a long list of precedents holding this result to be warranted dating back to 1956.[24] At that time this issue first was raised by the BGH the legal basis of so holding was nothing but the general concept of trust and confidence, as laid down in the general rule of Art. 242 BGB.[25] Thereafter this rule was developed further by finally establishing the principle, now laid down in Art. 307 Sec. 2 No. 2 BGB, that any disclaimer shall be rendered null and void in case of a negligent breach of contract, if the obligation so breached was fundamental for the proper fulfillment of the contractual obligations entered into by the supplier of such general terms of contract and the customer could reasonably expect that such obligation, based on a contractual quid pro quo, would correctly be fulfilled.[26] Moreover, the legal concept of fundamental breach of contract is nothing new, as it can also be found in Art. 35 CISG.[27] However, the same principle is held to be applicable pursuant to Art. 307 Sec. 2 No. 2 BGB with regard to any clauses limiting the amount of damages negligently caused by a fundamental breach of contract.[28] Moreover, the question what actually will be considered to amount to such fundamental breach is rather vague, as it also will come into operation, if the breach relates to an ancillary obligation.[29] Therefore, speaking in practical terms: Any limitation clause will only be held to be operative, if the amount is such that it will cover the foreseeable amount of such damages.[30] Needless to say: Such limitation of liabilities does not serve any commercial purpose, as it is equivalent to simply applying the German legal rules on calculating the amount of damages caused pursuant to Art. 249 BGB. But, exactly this is part of German Contract Law since long.[31]

4. Interim Conclusion

To sum up, on the basis of the existing precedents established by the BGH during the last 40 years,[32] there is no possibility to disclaim or limit the amount of damages falling due in case of a negligent breach of contract,[33] unless such breach is of minor importance.[34] In other words: German law prohibits in line with Art. 307 BGB any reasonable limitation of liabilities within the framework of supplying general terms of contract to a business user. This finding, however, represents only a general statement.[35] But, as a general rule, it must be held that German law pursuant to Art. 307 BGB is extremely hostile to the validity of any clauses that deviate from the legal rules, established by the lawmakers within the framework of the BGB.[36] Therefore, such clauses will be replaced by the

12

---

[24] BGH 6.3.1956 – I ZR 154/54, BGHZ 20, 164.
[25] BGH 13.03.1956 – I ZR 133/54, NJW 1956, 1065 (1067).
[26] BGH 20.07.2005 – VIII ZR 121/04, NJW-RR 2005, 1496 (1505) with further references.
[27] *Graf von Westphalen*, Festschrift für Grunewald, *Können Art. 25 und Art. 74 CISG für eine Konkretisierung der richterlichen Inhaltskontrolle bei Haftungsfreizeichnungs- und Haftungsbegrenzungsklauseln (§ 307 Abs. 2 Nr. 2 BGB) eingesetzt werden?* 2021, 1313.
[28] BGH 12.05.1980 – VII ZR 166/79, NJW 1980, 1953.
[29] Vertragsrecht und AGB-Klauselwerke/*Graf von Westphalen*, 2020, Munich, Freizeichnungs- und Haftungsbegrenzungsklauseln Note 43 sequ.
[30] BGH 11.11.1992 – VIII ZR 238/91, NJW 1993, 335.
[31] BGH 29.1.1968 – II ZR 18/65, NJW 1968, 1567.
[32] For a detailed analysis vide *Graf von Westphalen*, *Wiederentdeckte Grundpfeiler der Rechtsprechung zur AGB-Kontrolle*, NJW 2022, 1409.
[33] For a debate in detail vide *Graf von Westphalen*, *Vertragsrecht und AGB-Klauselwerke*, 2020, Munich, Freizeichnungs- und Haftungsbegrenzungsklauseln, Note 43 sequ.
[34] So far there is no precedent clearly establishing this rule as a helpful guide in practice.
[35] Staudinger/*Wendland*, *Commentary on the BGB*, Berlin 2019, § 307 Note 348 sequ.
[36] The latest landmark decisions are BGH 27.4. 2021, NJW 2021, 2273 – invalidity of the term in general banking terms allowing a change of the respective terms by simply informing the customer, provided that

operation of Art. 306 Sec. 2 BGB, i.e. by applying the legal rules of the Civil Law in their stead.

13   Hence, within the framework of Art. 1 Sec. 4 there is a large playing field left to the German national law in order to hold general terms of contract in b2b-transactions to be invalid pursuant to the general rule of Art. 307 Sec. 2 No. 1 and No. 2 BGB.

II. Scope of Art. 2 No. 10

14   On first glance, Art. 2 No. 10 seems to be very favourable to the interests of the business user, as the definition of general terms of contract is very broad. It reads as follows:

> "'terms and conditions' means all terms and conditions or specifications, irrespective of their name or form, which govern the contractual relationship between the provider of online intermediation services and its business users and are unilaterally determined by the provider of online intermediation services, that unilateral determination being evaluated on the basis of an overall assessment, for which the relative size of the parties concerned, the fact that a negotiation took place, or that certain provisions thereof might have been subject to such a negotiation and determined together by the relevant provider and business user is not, in itself, decisive;"[37]

15   Usually, general terms of contract are defined by the simple fact that the supplier has preformulated such terms and then has presented them to the business user upon conclusion of a contract without at the same time offering him the opportunity to negotiate their content or even change them. This aspect is covered by using the words of "unilateral determination" within the above citation.

16   But there are two aspects which do need some deliberation. First, Art. 2 No. 10 states that the "fact that a negotiation took place" has to be considered as "not, in itself, decisive". This implies, as a general rule, that any negotiations between a provider of intermediation services (and the supplier of such general terms) and the respective business user will not affect the (preliminary) conclusion that the respective clause will fall under the regime of Art. 2 No. 10. By literally interpreting this section, the same should (and could) be true, if the content of any such clause, having been negotiated between the two parties, has finally been changed in its wording or content, as long as it has been "determined together". In such instance it also will be qualified as a general contract term.

17   In comparison with German law standards the results will be different: Whilst the first alternative that "negotiations" between the parties had taken place in relation to a specific contract term will also be qualified as a general contract term (Art. 305 Sec. 1, 3rd sentence BGB).[38] This finding is based on the legal rule that mere "negotiations" between the parties in relation to a general contract term will not be considered to satisfy the legal requirement of an "individually negotiated" contract term.[39] The latter, as a general rule, requires that such negotiations will lead to a (verbal) alteration of the general contract term in line with the reasonable interests of the other party.[40] But this gen-

---

such customer will not actively contradict; the other one has invalidated a term asking of yearly payments in a home savings contract BGH, 15.11.2022, ZIP 2022, 2536.

[37] Official Journal of the European Union, July 11 2019 – L 186/57 (69).

[38] BGH 22.11.2012 – VII ZR 222/12, NJW 2013, 856 (858).

[39] The term "negotiation" can safely be translated as "Verhandung" which is less than the requirement of "im Einzelnen ausgehandelt", as laid down in Art. 305 Sec. 1, 3rd sentence BGB (BGH 19.3.2019 – XI ZR 9/18, NJW 2019, 2080 Note 14). The latter term requires that due to the influence of the other party there will be a different result and that, as a general rule, the respective contract term has been altered or changed (BGH 3.11.1999 – VIII ZR 269/98, NJW 2000, 1110, 1111).

[40] BGH 22.11.2012 – VII ZR 222/12, NJW 2013, 856 Note 10; BGH 23.1.2003 – VII ZR 210/01, NJW 2003, 1805, 1807.

eral rule will not come into operation with regard to the second alternative. If there is evidence that there were negotiations between the parties and that the content of a respective clause has been "determined together", then such clause will be taken as being individually negotiated and thus will fall outside of the scope of Art. 305 sequ. BGB.[41] The main reason for so arguing rests on the interpretation of Art. 305 Sec. 1, 1st sentence BGB. General contract terms, by their definition, must be unilaterally presented by the supplier of such terms without granting the other party the chance to present its own term.[42] But, if both parties enter into negotiations and agree that specific general terms shall be used for their transaction, then such voluntary acceptance of a general contract term, "determined together", will not satisfy the requirement of Art. 305 Sec. 1, 1st sentence BGB.[43] Thus, there will be no basis to apply the validity test of Art. 307 BGB.

Contrary to this finding and due to the priority of Union Law, Art. 1 Sec. 4 would prevail and will hold that even such clauses, having been "determined together", will be qualified as general contract terms within the scope of the definition of Art. 2 No. 10. They will be subject to the validity test of Art. 8 and to the test of transparency pursuant to Art. 3 Sec. 1 lit. a. 18

III. Scope of the unfairness test of Art. 8

Even though there are references to the principles of good faith and fair dealing within the recitals, Art. 8 lit. a states the following as one of the main point in this respect: *"In order to ensure that contractual relations between providers of online intermediation services and business users are conducted in good faith and based on fair dealing, providers of online intermediation services shall (a) not impose retroactive changes to terms and conditions, except when they are required to respect a legal or regulatory obligation or when the retroactive changes are beneficial for the business users".*[44]

By all means, such obligation is simply abundant: Any legal regime would nullify any "retroactive change" of the applicable terms and conditions, agreed before between the provider of intermediation services and the respective business user. Such verdict has actually almost nothing to do with "good faith and fair dealing"; it stands on its own feet as a legal principle being self-evident.

This leads to the interim conclusion: Even though not all of the provisions listed in Art. 8 are dealt with herein,[45] it may safely be held that this Regulation covers only a very, very small aspect of the overriding principles of fair dealing and good faith with regard to the validity test of general contract terms.

However, this cannot be the final answer in order to determine the actual scope of Art. 1 Sec. 4 with regard to the validity test of general contract terms, covered by this Regulation, especially in view of the fact that Art. 3 seems to be the decisive legal provision, covering amongst other aspects the issue of transparency. This cornerstone of the Regulation shall now be analyzed. 19

---

[41] BGH 19.03.2019 – XI ZR 9/18, NJW 2019, 2080.
[42] BGH 17.2.2010 – VIII ZR 67/09, NJW 2010, 1131, 1133.
[43] This is the essence of the rule established in the judgement of BGH 17.2.2009 – VIII ZR 67/09, NJW 2010, 1131, 1133.
[44] Official Journal of the European Union, July 11, 2019 – L 186, 57 (73).
[45] For further information vide Busch/*Graf von Westphalen*, P2B-VO, *Commentary on Regulation 2019/1150*, 2021, Art. 8 Note 4 sequ.

B. Transparency – the overriding issue – Art. 3 Sec. 1 lit. a

I. Definition

20   This Regulation, dealing primarily with the requirement of transparency regarding the language of general terms of contract, stipulates that all such clauses must be "drafted in plain and intelligible language" (Art. 3 Sec. 1 lit a). Recital 18 maintains that "ensuring transparency…can be essential to promoting sustainable business relations and to preventing unfair behaviour to the detriment of business users."

II. Analysis

1. Recital 15

21   The legal purpose of this rule of transparency is to achieve "predictability" to the benefit of the business user, as has been laid down in Recital 15. Therefore, such general terms are considered to be not transparent, provided they are "vague, unspecific or lack detail on important commercial issues". Moreover, the drafters hold that "misleading language should not be considered to be plan and intelligible".[46] In this respect, the average business user should be considered to be the "test person",[47] in determining whether the general terms comply with these standards, being a user being reasonably informed, reasonably intelligent and attentive.[48]

2. Up-front analysis

22   In applying these explanations of Recital 15 as a guide, there does not seem to be too much doubt to hold that the volume of general terms covering more than 20 pages could be deemed to be hardly transparent in view of Art. 3 Sec. 1 lit. a).[49] This conclusion rests on the general experience that general terms are hardly ever read or even analyzed; usually they are accepted without any further consideration in any detail. Thus, if the volume of such general terms exceeds the quantum of – let's say – more than 12 pages, then the conclusion seems to be warranted that Art. 3 Sec. 1 lit. a) will come into operation. The same reasoning will apply, if these general terms are simply translated into another language, whilst, on the basis of the general contract terms, the ruling language for any purposes of legal interpretation shall remain English.[50] Any discrepancies or even mistakes in the draft of such terms will then become meaningless, provided that the English text is sufficiently clear. This is simply not acceptable. No one can reasonably expect an ordinary business user to compare both versions of the general terms and find out whether and to what extent the English text, in case of any discrepancies, should prevail.[51] Lack of transparency may also be argued, if the outline of such general terms misses the level of reasonable systematic aspects.[52] Such drafting of general contract

---

[46] Official Journal of the European Union, July 11, 2019 – L 186, 57 (60).
[47] Busch, Mehr Transparenz und Fairness in der Plattformökonomie? GRUR 2019, 788 (790).
[48] *Alexander* in Köhler/Bornkamm/Feddersen, *Commentary on Competition Law (UWG)*, 40th edi. 2022, Art. 3 Note 10.
[49] Busch/*Graf von Westphalen*, P2B-VO, *Commentary on Regulation 2019/1150*, 2021, Art. 3 Note 31.
[50] Busch/*Graf von Westphalen*, P2B-VO, *Commentary on Regulation 2019/1150*, 2021, Art. 3 Note 37.
[51] *Alexander* in Köhler/Bornkamm/Feddersen, *Commentary on Competition Law (UWG)*, 40th edi. 2022, Art. 3 Note 11.
[52] Busch/*Graf von Westphalen*, P2B-VO, *Commentary on Regulation 2019/1150*, 2021, Art. 3 Note 38.

terms causes too many foreseeable misunderstandings and by no means will fulfill the requirement of being written in "plain language".

Furthermore, a rather technical aspect needs to be considered. "Technical specifications" are also part of the definition of Art. 2 No. 10. It goes without saying that any business user must understand the technical background of the operation of the intermediation services offered, as such services generally are very complex.[53] Hence, the requirement of transparency will not be met, if there is a hard to analyze and even harder to understand the usual strange mixture of technical specifications and legalese.

3. Art. 5 of Directive 93/13/EEC as guidance

It has been noted that Art. 5 of Directive 93/13/EEC on unfair terms in consumer contracts[54] uses the same definition of transparency as Art. 3 Sec. 1 lit. a) does. Whether the courts will utilize this aspect and the respective interpretation of the ECJ[55] in transforming the elements of Art. 5 of Directive 93/13/EEC into the interpretation of Art. 3 Sec. 1 lit. a) remains to be seen. But one aspect, taken from these rulings, should be taken into account: The consumer and the general business user are both in the weaker position and should therefore be protected. Recital 2 clearly states that the growing use of intermediation services and platforms – data driven as they are – "leads to an increased dependance of such business users,"[56] especially with regard to SMEs. GAFA, on the other hand, is the code name of the big players. Thus, there is no barrier in at least reading and analyzing the respective rulings of the ECJ on the issue of transparency pursuant to Art. 5 Directive 93/13/EEC and taking their reasonings as a persuasive guidance in interpreting the same term – transparency – in Art. 3 Sec. 1 lit. a).

4. Transparency of the language actually used

Even though the rulings of the ECJ require to apply an autonomous method of interpretation of any Directive or Regulation,[57] it may be hard to find out whether any contract term is such as to properly stand the test of transparency in line with Art. 3 Sec. 1 lit. a). The determination of this issue, however, cannot be isolated from the language used within the framework of general contract terms. The legal requirement of "plain and intelligible language" must always be seen against the background of the respective language and the corresponding understanding of such contractual term by the respective (ordinary and average) business user. The answer to this question becomes even more troublesome, if the provider of intermediation services has chosen a law to govern this transaction which is different from the actual language used (Irish law and German language). It seems questionable whether a court being confronted with such a case will really be able to adjudicate the issue of transparency with regard to a foreign language without requiring assistance by a qualified interpreter. If, however, any provider supplies its general terms of contract in the language of the market place whilst stipulating at the same time that a foreign forum shall rule on any dispute and that the version of the language, corresponding with the mother tongue of the court should prevail, then such

---

[53] *Alexander* in Köhler/Bornkamm/Feddersen, UWG, 40th edi. 2022, Art. 3 Note 11.
[54] Official Journal of the European Communities, April 21, 1993 – L 95, 29.
[55] ECJ 18.11.2021 – C- 212/20 – ClientEarth/EIB, WM 2022, 73 Note 38; ECJ 30.04.2014 – C 26/13 NJW 2014, 2335 Note 69 – Kásler.
[56] Official Journal of the European Union, July 11, 2019 – L 186, 57.
[57] ECJ C-21.03.2019 – C-465/17, NZBau 2019, 314 Note 28 – Falck Rettungsdienste; ECJ 04.06.2020 – C-429/19 NZBau 2020, 457 Note 24 – Remondis – both judgements with further references.

practice should not stand as not misleading and as being compliant with the issue of transparency of Art. 3 Sec. 1 lit. a).

5. Application of Art. 307 Sec. 1 second sentence BGB

a) Incorporation of Art. 5 of Directive 93/13/EEC

26 Returning to the reservation of Art. 1 Sec. 4, the question needs to be answered whether the interpretation of the term transparency in Art. 3 Sec. 1 lit a) could also be based on the legal rule of Art. 307 Sec. 1, 2nd sentence BGB, as this provision is nothing but the incorporation of Art. 5 of Directive 93/13/EEC.[58] This being accepted as a starting point and as a reasonable basis to establish some guidelines for the interpretation what constitutes a "plain and intelligible language" in general contract terms supplied by an intermediate.

27 Having no dogmatic difficulties in accepting this approach as being in line with Art. 1 Sec. 4, one has to take into account hat the German lawmakers have decided that the rule of Art. 5 of Directive 93/13/EEC should not be restricted to consumer contracts, but should also be applicable in b2b-transactions. The terms describing the requirement of transparency in Art. 307 Sec. 1, 2nd sentence BGB are the same as are used in the Union law ("intelligible and plain"), namely "klar und verständlich". Therefore, there is uniformity in the use of the term "transparency" within the Union and the German national law and, thus, no violation of the priority rule in Art. 1 Sec. 4 can be found, if one decides to refer to the interpretation of the requirement "plain and intelligible language" in Art. 3 Sec. 1 second sentence BGB and the respective rulings of the BGH, relating to Art. 307 Sec. 1, 2nd sentence BGB.

b) Three principles established by German Courts as guidelines

28 There are three basic principles developed by the BGH during the last 40 years, specifying the requirements of transparency. First, the BGH stresses the requirement of "intelligible language" ("Verständlichkeitsgebot").[59] The simple test here is whether the customer has been made aware of what he will and has to expect in consideration of the contract concluded and the aspects governed by the general contract terms.[60] Therefore, the rights and obligations of the respective customer must be defined as clearly and as reasonably understandable in the respective contract terms to the extent possible.[61] Second, transparency requires predictability.[62] This implies that the contractual preconditions of any right or obligation of the customer and their consequences (in case of breach) in a specific clause and its connection with other clauses must be so clearly outlined that the supplier of such general terms has no unjustified room of divergent (beneficial for himself) interpretation of the contractual conditions and any actions to be taken in accordance therewith (in case of breach).[63] Finally, a general term of contract may not be drafted in any misleading manner.[64] In order to fulfill this requirement it must be noted that there is no need to evidence that the respective customer actually has been

---

[58] For a detailed analysis vide Busch/*Graf von Westphalen*, P2B-VO, *Commentary on Regulation 2019/1150*, 2021, Art. 3 Note 59 sequ.
[59] For further information vide Grüneberg/*Grüneberg*, *Commentary on the BGB*, 81st edi. 2022, § 307 Note 25.
[60] BGH 25.02.2106 – VIIZR 156/13, NJW 2016, 1575 Note 31.
[61] BGH 03.12.2015 – VII ZR 100/15, NJW 2016, 401 Note 16.
[62] Grüneberg/*Grüneberg*, *Commentary on the BGB*, 81st edi. 2022, § 307 Note 26.
[63] BGH 19.05.2016 – III ZR 274/15, NJW-RR 2016, 842 Note 26; BGH 10.02.2016 – VIII ZR 137/15, NJW 2016, 1308 Note 18.
[64] Grüneberg/*Grüneberg*, *Commentary on the BGB*, 81st edi. 2022, § 307 Note 27.

misled. It suffices, if the interpretation of such clause, based on an objective method of interpretation pursuant to Art. 305c Sec. 2 BGB, could in itself be held to be misleading.[65] In this respect it has been held that the false presentation of the applicable law in the general contract terms supplied amounts to a violation of the duty to draft them in a transparent manner.[66]

III. Interim Conclusion

It seems acceptable to interpret the term transparency in Art. 3 Sec. 1 lit. a) in the same way as the BGH has interpreted this topic, based on the same language (of Art. 5 Directive 93/13/EEC) in Art. 307 Sec. 1, 2nd sentence BGB. Such approach may not be interpreted as being a violation of the priority rule of Union law in Art. 1 Sec. 4.

29

IV. Consequences of a violation of Art. 3 Sec. 1 lit. a) – Art. 3 Sec. 3

1. On the basis of Art. 3 Sec. 3

Provided there is any breach of the transparency requirement pursuant to Art. 3 Sec. 1 lit. a) (or any further provisions listed in Section 1), then the legal consequences are set out in Art. 3 Sec. 3. Any non-compliance of a general term of contract will render the respective clause "null and void". However, this is only half of the picture. In reading these words, one immediately believes that such nullification will affect only the parties, actually involved in any court proceedings or legal dispute, holding that such clause lacks the necessary transparency, as it is not "drafted in plain and intelligible language". But this assumption proves to be wrong. In reading Recital 20 the solution offered therein is quite different. It states: *"In order to protect business users and to provide legal certainty for both sides, non-compliant terms and conditions should be null and void, that is, deemed to have never existed, with effects erga omnes and ex tunc."*[67]

The legal consequence of any such non-compliance, therefore, is not restricted to the inter-partes-relation, but rather has been taken from the shelf of the rules dealing with unfair commercial practices. This is exactly the place where the German lawmakers have incorporated this regulation, namely in Art. 8a UWG (Code on unfair commercial practices). The legal instrument to arrive at an effect operating "erga omnes" is a claim for total elimination of any such clause, violating Art. 3 Sec. 1 lit. a) ("Beseitigung" – § 8 UWG).

2. On the basis of Art. 306 Sec. 2 BGB

In line with the reservation of Art. 1 Sec. 4, calling for full respect of the priority of Union law, the legal consequences of Art. 3 Sec. 3 must fully be taken into account, regardless of whether any such interpretation has been arrived at by looking at the principles as guidelines that have been established by the BGH in applying the German legal rule of transparency pursuant to Art. 307 Sec. 1, 2nd sentence BGB.

30

Any non-compliance of a general contract term violating the principle of Art. 3 Sec. 1 lit. a) will lead to the consequence to be null and void erga omnes and ex tunc.

31

---

[65] BGH 27.09.2000 – VIII ZR 155/99, NJW 2000, 292 (296).
[66] For further case law vide Grüneberg/*Grüneberg*, Commentary on the BGB, 81st edi. Munich 2022, § 307 Note 27.
[67] Official Journal of the European Union, July 11, 2019 – L 186/57 (60).

32 On the other hand, if there is evidence that a general contract term is held to be invalid pursuant to the fairness test of Art. 307 BGB, then it will be held to be null and void in accordance with Art. 306 Sec. 2 BGB. But such nullification will be restricted to the respective parties, unless there is a class action in line with the rules of the UKlaG,[68] being, however, limited to the use of general terms in consumer transactions.

C. Effect of Art. 1.4 – first sentence – unfair commercial practice test

I. Outline

33 This part of the reservation of Art. 1.4 refers to two issues, thereby claiming the priority of union law. First, it must be noted that this rule states the following in its first sentence: *"This Regulation shall be without prejudice to national rules which, in conformity with Union law, prohibit or sanction unilateral conduct or unfair commercial practices, to the extent that the relevant aspects are not covered by this Regulation."*[69] A literal interpretation of this provision opens the door to the applicability of the rules on unfair commercial practises, insofar they are not covered by this Regulation. This link refers to Directive 2005/29/EC,[70] covering only unfair commercial practises in consumer contracts. Therefore, the application of the provisions of this Directive stands on its own feet. Second, one has to take into account that on the basis of Union law there are no harmonized rules relating to unfair commercial practises in b2b-transactions. Of course, there are national rules covering these issues (UWG)[71]. Therefore, insofar the provisions of this Regulation are held to be applicable in a b2b-transaction, they will have priority pursuant to the general reservation of priority of Union law set forth in Art. 1.4. From a German viewpoint, one has to consider that the legal rules provided for in this Regulation have been made part of the law on unfair competition, namely the UWG (§ 8a UWG).

34 This then will lead to the question whether there is any room left to apply Directive 2005/29/EC within the framework of this Regulation, even though it concerns unfair commercial practises in business-to-consumer transactions.[72] If one accepts this question to be of any relevance, then one has to find out whether this Regulation in itself has any relevance to issues of consumer protection, whilst mainly dealing with b2b-issues, i.e. the contractual relation between the provider of intermediation services to the respective business users. It falls into the same category to extent the question and its respective answer also to the applicability of Directive 93/13/EEC on unfair contract terms between a trader and a consumer.[73] However, on first glance this will lead to problems of validity, unless it can be established that both Directives are interrelated with one another and are held applicable at the same time in order to improve consumer protection to its most extent.

---

[68] Unterlassungsklagegesetz ("Injunctive Relief Act"), dated 26.11.2001 (Federal Law Gazette I 3138).
[69] Official Journal of the European Union, July 17, 2019 L 186 p. 57 (68).
[70] Official Journal of the European Union, June 6, 2005 l 149 p. 22.
[71] Act against Unfair Competition, dated March 3, 2010 (Federal Law Gazette I p. 254)
[72] Official Journal of the European Union, June 6, 2005 l 149 p. 22.
[73] Official Journal of the European Communities, April 21, 1993 L 95 p. 29.

II. Indications within this Regulation concerning consumer protection

Therefore, the first question to be addressed is whether this Regulation opens the door for interpretation concerning the goals of consumer protection against unfair commercial practices being an integral part of its legal purpose. 35

1. Within the text

The strongest reference to the role of the consumer is contained in the definition of "online intermediation services", namely in Art. 2 Sec. 2 lit. b). There it is said: *"They allow business users to offer goods or services to consumers, with a view to facilitating the initiating of direct transactions between those business users and consumers, irrespective of where those transactions are ultimately concluded".*[74] In reading this section, it becomes crystal-clear that the consumer is the ultimate beneficiary of any contractual relation between the provider of such services and the business user. 36

This fact is underlined by the next section which holds concerning the definition of a provider of "online intermediation services": *"They are provided to business users on the basis of contractual relationships between the provider of those services and business users which offer goods or services to consumers."*[75] 37

Hence, it may safely be concluded from these citations that the drafters of this Regulation were fully aware of the decisive role to be played by the consumer in the context of his relation to the business user and to the contract concluded between him and the provider of online intermediation services. 38

Thus, it may be safely derived therefrom that the incorporation of the consumer as a third (integrated) party will become entitled to be legally protected by the general terms of contract supplied by the provider of these services to the business user. Therefore, it is Union law that supports the argument that the assumption is well founded: The service contract entered into by the provider of online intermediation services and the respective business user also shall and will encompass its general protective mechanism to the benefit of the consumer in the same way as provided for by the German case-law on the basis of a "Vertrag mit Schutzwirkung zugunsten Dritter"[76] which will be argued later in some detail. 39

2. Within the Recitals

Before arriving at a preliminary conclusion there is need to now address the Recitals in order to find out whether the aim of this Regulation has been correctly interpreted so far, i.e. also covering relevant aspects of consumer protection within the framework of the contract (and its general contract terms) between the provider of intermediation services and the respective business user. 40

The first sentence of Recital 3 states a general, but well accepted fact: The services offered by the providers of online platform services are not only designed to satisfy the interests of its contract partners, i.e. the business users, but also those of the consumers as the buyer of the products or services offered on an online platform. In this respect one will find Recital 3 reading as follows: *"Consumers have embraced the use of online intermediation services."*[77] But the next two sentences are even more important in 41

---

[74] Official Journal of the European Union, July 17, 2019 L 186 p. 57 (68).
[75] Official Journal of the European Union, July 17, 2019 L 186 p. 57 (68).
[76] A contract being designed (by virtue of interpretation) to offer protection also a third party being integrated into such contract.
[77] Official Journal of the European Union, July 17, 2019 L 186 p. 57.

42 Thus, it seems fair to conclude that the requirement of transparency of Art. 3 Sec. 1 lit. a) as the relevant protection scheme for business users may also be considered as an appropriate vehicle being "indirectly" designed to further trust and confidence of the consumer "in the online platform economy".[79]

43 But it seems even more important to note that this Regulation qualifies the intermediation services of the provider as a "gateway" "*to consumers in the form of natural persons, the notion of consumer used to delineate the scope of this Regulation should be understood as referring solely to natural persons ...*"[80] Regardless of such delineation it must be taken into account that the operation of an online platform necessarily implies that the business user enters into a (sales) transaction with a consumer. His products and services offered and displayed on the platform are placed there solely for the reason to be bought by an ordinary consumer. Thus, his role as purchaser is vital and indispensable in order to enable the business user to act as a "gateway"[81] to the general public.

44 Therefore, the essence of this review of important Recitals of this Regulation is that they open the door to the legal regime of German law, provided German Law is held to be applicable as the governing contract law between the provider of intermediation services and the business user. The relevant question therefore is whether this contract could reasonably be construed as incorporating also the protection of the interests of the consumer, being the ordinary purchaser of the goods and services offered on the respective platform. Therefore, a very important issue of "formation" of such contract is at stake here which as such has been reserved to the national law of a Member State pursuant to the general rule of Art. 1 Sec. 4 – 2nd sentence of this Regulation.

III. Protection of the vested interests of a third party within the legal regime of German law ("Vertrag mit Schutzwirkung zugunsten Dritter")

1. Requirements and Consequences

45 It does not really support a better understanding, if this writer would outline here the intricacies of German law, its preconditions and legal consequences for establishing a contract protecting the interests of a third party ("Vertrag mit Schutzwirkung für Dritte").[82] It would be too abundant to cover the main principles and also their exceptions. But, there is need to outline the main line of arguments of this feature being mandatory for an understanding of the main thesis of this paper: The debtor in cases arguing the requirement to also protect the interests of third parties is deemed to have a duty to take care of the interests of such third party. Therefore, this party must be "integrated" into the contractual scheme of protection. Whether this is so, is a question of interpretation,[83] as only the creditor remains entitled to claim proper fulfillment of

---

[78] Official Journal of the European Union, July 17, 2019 L 186 p. 57.
[79] Recital 3 vide Official Journal of the European Union, July 17, 2019 L 186 p. 57.
[80] Recital No. 12 vide Official Journal of the European Union, July 17, 2019 L 186 p. 57 (59).
[81] Recital No. 12 vide Official Journal of the European Union, July 17, 2019 L 186 p. 57 (59).
[82] For an insight vide Busch/*Graf von Westphalen*, P2B, *Commentary on Regulation 2019/1150*, 2021, Art. 3 Note 78 sequ.
[83] BGH 24.4.2014 – III ZR 156/13, NJW 2014, 2345 Note 10 sequ.

C. Effect of Art. 1.4 – first sentence – unfair commercial practice test

the contractual obligation of the debtor.[84] Thus, the salient question is whether the creditor is considered being obliged to properly protect the vested interests of third parties,[85] coming into a rather close relationship with the proper fulfillment of the main contractual obligations to be fulfilled by the debtor.[86] If such duty can reasonably be derived from the circumstances in view of the scope of the respective contractual obligations and if such duty has negligently been breached by the debtor, thereby causing damages (injury, damage, or loss) to such third party, then established rules of German case-law will grant a claim for compensation directly to such (third) party, provided that such damage – apart from any direct tort action – would not otherwise be recoverable under German Law.[87] Furthermore, precedents underline that the application of these rules should be based on proper fulfillment of the above requirements, however, to be narrowly interpreted.[88]

Thus, if the provider of intermediation service on an online platform has violated any of the obligations embodied in this Regulation and such breach would cause damage or loss not only to the business user, but also to the consumer in its capacity as (prospective) buyer of the goods or services offered on the platform, then such contract scheme of protection to the benefit of a third party will come into play. The best and most persuasive examples in this respect are listed in Art. 4 Sec. 1, enabling the provider of such intermediation services to "suspend", "restrict" or even "terminate" the services to the detriment of the business user. The same goes in cases of a "delisting" of the services or products to be presented on the online platform by the business user or to downgrade its "ranking" (Art. 5) or just decide to "dim" ("Google prison" – front pages and all of a sudden placed on page 25) the respective offers. 46

2. Outline of main issues to be resolved

In alle these cases it seems equitable to the benefit of the consumer to open the door for satisfactory redress of the interests of the consumer as a (protected) third party, as it is very likely that its rights will be impaired, if the respective offers and market activities of the business user will be " suspended" or even "terminated". Moreover, the protection granted to the business user under the rules of the Regulation must be seen as being insufficient, as it is mainly based on the sole answer whether the respective general contract terms were drafted in "plain and intelligible language". But on the basis of the ideas presented so far in this paper it seems essential and also mandatory to extent the protection scheme granted to the business user above the border lines of the (European) transparency requirements of Art. 3 Section 1 by taking recourse to the – much wider – unfairness test offered by the German Law rule embodied in Art. 307 Sec. 2 No. 1 BGB. Therefore, the next – salient – question is whether the protection of the consumer pursuant to the rules of unfair commercial practices could be applied in these instances and, finally, may also include the protection mechanism offered by Directive 93/13/EEC. 47

IV. Unfairness control to the benefit of the consumer

There are reliable precedents to be found in German law that the protective mechanism concerning unfair contract terms will not be adjudicated in order to protect the 48

---

[84] Vide Grüneberg/*Grüneberg*, Commentary on the BGB, 81st edit., Munich 2022, Art. 328 Note 13.
[85] BGH 17.11.2016 – III ZR 139/14, NJW-RR 2017, 888 Note 15.
[86] BGH 2.7.1996 – X ZR 104/94, NJW 1996, 2927 – covering also aspects of commercial loss.
[87] BGH 02.07.1996 X ZR 104/94, NJW 1996, 2927 (2928).
[88] BGH 17.11.2016 – III ZR 139/14, NJW-RR 2017, 888 Note 15.

interests of the business user as the contracting party, but would rather take into account the interests of the consumer as the third party to be properly protected.[89] But offering such extended protection to a third party requires some further explanation of German Law.

49 In accepting the vehicle of a "Vertrag mit Schutzwirkungen zugunsten Dritter" two distinct consequences will follow. First, the test of the fairness control of the general contract terms supplied by the provider of intermediation services will to the benefit of the so protected interests of the consumer as the third party will be based on the rules of consumer law. This implies that the entire regime of Art. 307, 308 and 309 of the BGB will come into play in adjudicating whether the general contract terms supplied by the provider of intermediation services to the business user will stand or will be deemed to be null and void. Thus, consumer protection becomes dominant in these cases. This is the first consequence.

V. Unfair commercial practice due to the supply of unfair contract terms (Art. 3a UWG)

50 The second consequence may be developed along the following line of arguments: If there is evidence that the provider of such intermediation services has supplied unfair terms to the detriment of the business user/consumer, then Art. 3a UWG (unfair competition law) will come into operation. There are persuasive precedents established by the BGH holding that the supply of illegal and unfair contract terms in a consumer transaction is to be considered also as violation of the standards of fair commercial practices.[90] The reasoning of these judgments takes into account that a consumer, being confronted with general contract terms held to violate Art. 307, 308 or 309 BGB, will not lodge any claim against the supplier of such illegal contract terms,[91] as he will be confused by only reading unfair contract terms, being, however, illegal which he will not be aware of. Hence, such consumer will not take due recourse to his legal remedies. Thus, they will be impaired due to the use of such unfair general contract terms.[92] Moreover, the BGH bases its reasoning also on aspects of Union law: Directive 2009/25/EC comes into play, as having fully harmonized the law on unfair commercial practices within b2c-transactions.[93] This effect will lead to the further consequence: Any violation of national legal rules governing such unfair commercial practices of a trader against a consumer could only be based on a violation of Union law rules.[94] By the same token, such unfair general terms in consumer contracts will then also violate the rules of Directive 93/13/EEC dealing with unfair contract terms. So there will be a doubled standard, both being found in Union Law.

---

[89] BGH 15.06.1989 – VII ZR 205/88, NJW 1989, 2750 (2751); BGH 30.03.2010 – XI ZR 200/09, NJW 2010, 2041 Note 31; Grüneberg/Grüneberg, Commentary on the BGB, 81st edi., 2022 § 307 Note 11.
[90] BGH 31.05.2012 – I ZR 45/11, GRUR 2012, 949 Note 46 – missbräuchliche Vertragsstrafe; BGH 31.03.2010 – I ZR 34/08, GRUR 2010, 1117 Note 16 – Gewährleistungsausschluss im Internet.
[91] BGH 31.05.2012 – I ZR 45/11, GRUR 2012, 949 Note 46 – missbräuchliche Vertragsstrafe.
[92] BGH 31.05.2012 – I ZR 45/11, GRUR 2012, 949 Note 46 – missbräuchliche Vertragsstrafe.
[93] ECJ 14.01.2010 C-304/08, GRUR 2010, 244 Note 41 – Plus Warenhandelsgesellschaft.
[94] BGH 31.05.2012 – I ZR 45/11, GRUR 2012, 949 Note 467 – missbräuchliche Vertragsstrafe.

VI. Interim conclusion

Thus, the protection scheme established in this Regulation by operation of Union law to the benefit of the consumer is two-fold: It is based on contract law (Art. 307, 308, 309 BGB) and on the law on unfair commercial practices (§ 3a UWG). Consumer organizations, therefore, will be entitled to base their claims for elimination and for cease and desist against the provider of illegal contract terms on both legal grounds.[95] This is important to note, as this result, relating only to the claim for elimination, is in line with Art. 4 Sec. 3 of Regulation 2019/1150 holding that contract terms, violating the principle of transparency pursuant to the rule stated in Art. 3 Sec. 1 lit. a), shall be null and void, not only between the parties, but erga omnes and ex tunc.[96] Thus, the remedial structure and the protection scheme offered by operation of Union Law will be enlarged by the application of the German Law on unfair contract terms in consumer transactions. 51

D. Main issues – Art. 4 – restriction, suspension and termination of the services

I. Outline

It is self-evident that clauses empowering the provider of intermediation online services to restrict, suspend, or delist the presentation of products and services of the business user on the respective platform or even to terminate the contract forthwith are of extreme commercial importance. But the question needs to be addressed, whether the protection scheme offered to the business user (and to the consumer) in this Regulation may be considered as sufficiently effective or whether only the legal rules provided by the national law provide satisfactory remedies. The answer has to embark on the following route. 52

II. Essence of Art. 3 Sec. 1 lit. c) and Art. 4 Sec. 1

1. Art. 3 Sec. 1 lit. c)

Art. 3 Sec. 1 lit. c) states the following, based on the requirement of transparency ("plain and intelligible language"): "*(c) set out the grounds for decisions to suspend or terminate or impose any other kind of restriction upon, in whole or in part, the provision of their online intermediation services to business users*".[97] In this respect, it needs to be underlined that Recital 23 clarifies that such reasons to restrict, delist, suspend or terminate the services contracted by the business user, could be "legitimate reasons". But, this requirement, clearly relating to the category of fairness and good faith, is in itself not part of Art. 3 Sec. 1 lit c).[98] Therefore, the conclusion seems to be warranted that the "grounds" pursuant to this article to be listed in the respective general contract term, supplied by the provider of intermediation services, must simply satisfy the requirement of transparency, as established in Art. 3 Sec. 1 lit. a). 53

---

[95] BGH 14.12.2017 – I ZR 184/15, GRUR 2018, 423 – Klauselersetzung.
[96] Recital 20 Official Journal of the European Union, July 11, 2019 L 189 p. 57 (60).
[97] Official Journal of the European Union, July 11, 2019 L 189 p. 57 (70).
[98] For further details Busch/*Graf von Westphalen*, P2B, *Commentary on Regulation 2019/1150*, 2021, Art. 3 Note 187 sequ.

2. Art. 4 Sec. 1

54 But, a further answer might be embodied in Art. 4 Sec. 1. This provision reads as follows: *"Where a provider of online intermediation services decides to restrict or suspend the provision of its online intermediation services to a given business user in relation to individual goods or services offered by that business user, it shall provide the business user concerned, prior to or at the time of the restriction or suspension taking effect, with a statement of reasons for that decision on a durable medium."*[99] The salient term of this article is that the provider of intermediation online services shall supply a "statement of reasons" to the business user why and due to which reasons he has decided to "restrict, suspend" or "delist" the services contracted for to the detriment of the business user. However, it needs to be noted at this point that this term has not been qualified in any manner by the drafters of this Regulation. A "statement of reasons" can rest on legitimate reasons or on reasons not to be accepted as legally valid by the applicable law at all. To leave this issue unanswered, is somewhat more than unsatisfactory.

55 Even though the business user, so affected by an unilateral action of the provider of online intermediation services, may take resort in these cases (and others) to an internal complaint management system in accordance with Art. 11, initiate a mediation procedure in line with Art. 12 or even go to court according to 14 Sec. 9, the conclusion cannot be set aside: Neither Art. 3 Sec. 1 lit. c) nor Art. 4 Sec. 1 offer any indication that the drafters of this Regulation wanted to establish a validity test or restrict such unilateral actions of suspension, restriction or alike to those cases where there is no violation of the standards of good commercial practices. The door of interpretation seems to be extremely wide open, lacking any solid foundation for a valid legal argument in its support.

3. Interim conclusion

56 Therefore, the door left open to the application of the national law by Art. 1.4, 2nd sentence – priority of Union law – is now open to invoke the general validity test of German law. As we have seen, this fairness test, applicable to protect business users, is established by Art. 307 BGB. But one can go one step further and take into account that this writer opines (and has demonstrated) that also the issue of proper consumer protection is at stake here in accordance with the general principle of unfair contract terms in such contractual undertakings pursuant to Art. 3 Sec. 1 of Directive 93/13/EEC. If this assumption proves to be correct in these cases, then there will also an infringement of Art. 3a UWG, i.e. a violation of the standards of good and fair commercial practices in b2c-transactions.

III. Unfairness test of unilateral actions – restriction and suspension ("delisting")

1. Perspective of the business user

57 The decisive question to be answered here is whether such unilateral action taken against the business user, based on respective general contract terms pursuant to Art. 2 No. 10, is held to be valid. In view of German law, it is generally accepted that the rule of Art. 308 No. 4 BGB is per analogy applicable in b2b-transactions pursuant to the general

---

[99] Official Journal of the European Union, July 11, 2019 L 189 p. 57 (71).

fairness test of Art. 307 BGB.[100] Art. 308 No. 4 BGB states that unilateral changes of the obligations to be performed by the supplier of general contract terms are – lacking any express consent by the customer – subject to the criterion of reasonableness. This implies a number of requirements must be met by the respective clause, to be evaluated as being valid on the basis of precedents established by the BGH.[101] First, the preconditions of such unliteral right to change the content of the contract must be sufficiently concrete and transparent so that the business user is fully aware of what might happen. Second, there must be serious and legitimate reasons claimed by the supplier of such general contract terms in order to legitimately change the content of the agreement without the consent of the business user. Third and finally, due regard must be given to reasonably safeguard the interests of the business user in respect of the existing equivalence of rights and obligations under a given contract.

It goes without saying that these preconditions for a unilateral suspension, restriction or delisting of the services to be rendered by the provider of intermediate online services by far go beyond the border lines of Art. 3 Sec. 1 lit. c) and Art. 4 Sec. 1. Moreover, one has to taken into account: If the business user is in breach of its contractual obligations, the provider of such intermediation services – by mere operation of the applicable law – will be entitled to ask for respective (legal) remedies, including a compensation of damages incurred, be in case of a delay of payment, be it in case of delivering non-conforming goods. These remedies, as a general rule, are deemed to be satisfactory to cure any breach of contract in a legally accepted and adequate manner. Therefore, it seems very doubtful whether the application of the fairness test, based Art. 307 Sec. 2 No. 1 BGB, will not immediately come into operation, simply due to the fact that the enactment of any further remedy, such as suspending or restricting the services to be rendered, will be considered to be an illegal double sanction to the detriment of the business user. 58

2. Perspective of the consumer

There is agreement in German legal literature that the rule of Art. 308 No. 4 BGB corresponds to the clause listed in the Annex of Art. 3 Sec. 3 of Directive 93/13/EEC (lit. j).[102] Therefore, the validity test of this Article, allowing an unilateral change of the content of the contract, depends on the (legally accepted) existence of a serious ground to be expressly named in the respective contract clause.[103] However, whether such clause finally will stand the validity test of fairness depends, at the final end, on an evaluation of the (general) interests of the parties involved in such a contractual undertaking, resulting in the finding that the interests of the supplier of such general terms, entitled to unilaterally change the content of the contract, are held to prevail over the interests of the consumer.[104] 59

Neither Art. 3 Sec. 1 lit. c) nor Art. 4 Sec. 1 require the provider of intermediation online services to indicate within the respective clauses serious and legitimate reasons for doing so, whilst granting the right of suspension, restriction, delisting or "dimming" of the products or services to be displayed on the online platform to be purchased by the 60

---

[100] Grüneberg/*Grüneberg*, *Commentary on the BGB*, 81st edi., 2022, § 308 Note 26; Erman/*Roloff/ Looschelders*, *Commentary on the BGB*, 16th edi., 2020, § 308 Note 37; *Dammann* in Wolf/Lindacher/Pfeiffer, *AGB-Recht*, 7th edi., 2020, § 308 No. 4 Note 70 sequ.; Staudinger/*Coester-Waltjen*, *Commentary on the BGB*, 2019, § 308 No. 4 Note 11.

[101] BGH 12.01.1994 – VIII ZR 165/92, NJW 1994, 1060 (1063); BGH 06.10.1999 – VIII ZR 125/98, NJW 2000, 515 (520); BGH 20.07.2005 – VIII ZR 121/04, NJW-RR 2005, 1496 (1501).

[102] *Pfeiffer* in Wolf/Lindacher/Pfeiffer, *Commentary on the AGB-Recht*, 7th edi. 2020, Annex Note 92.

[103] *Pfeiffer* in Wolf/Lindacher/Pfeiffer, *Commentary on the AGB-Recht*, 7th edi. 2020, Annex Note 91.

[104] *Pfeiffer* in Wolf/Lindacher/Pfeiffer, *Commentary on the AGB-Recht*, 7th edi. 2020, Annex Note 90.

user fort the purpose of reselling them to the consumer. Moreover, Art. 4 Sec. 1 does not even require the provider of such online services to indicate that there is any rule of proportionality to be observed by the provider of such online services in choosing either a unilateral suspension or a respective restriction or in order to clear the ground which preconditions will apply if the decision will be taken to delist or suspend any of the products or services to be presented on the online platform by the business user.

61 Hence, the are valid reasons to hold that the exercise of these unilateral rights of the provider of online intermediation services pursuant to Art. 4 Sec. 1 will infringe the consumer rights in line with Art. 3 Sec. 3 of Directive 93/13/EEC (Annex clause j). If this reasoning is accepted, then one has to remember that such breach will also be considered to amount to a breach of Art. 3a UWG within the framework of unfair commercial practices. Such infringement will then grant the consumer organizations – this is of utmost practical importance – to claim elimination of such illegal clauses (erga omnes and ex tunc) and to also claim the right against the provider of these services to desist and cease the use of such (illegal) clauses (Art. 8 UWG).[105]

IV. Termination clauses – Art. 4 Sec. 2

1. Outline

62 Ordinary termination clauses hardly ever cause legal difficulties, as they are more or less self-executing. But the story is quite different, if an immediate termination of the contract with cause has to be addressed. In this respect Art. 4 Sec. 2 provides: *"Where a provider of online intermediation services decides to terminate the provision of the whole of its online intermediation services to a given business user, it shall provide the business user concerned, at least 30 days prior to the termination taking effect, with a statement of reasons for that decision on a durable medium."*[106] But, the requirement to grant a grace period of 30 days can be disregarded in line with Art. 4 Sec. 4 lit. b), as it is stated there that the provider of such services shall not be bound to respect such period, if he *"exercises a right of termination under an imperative reason pursuant to national law which is in compliance with Union law."*[107]

2. Test of this rule

a) No conflict with Union law

63 Given the fact that the contract to provide online intermediation services to a business user can be qualified as a contract to render services to the benefit of the business user, as the products or services presented on the platform will be sold by him to the consumer pursuant to the rules of Art. 675, 611 BGB, then Art. 626 BGB relating to an immediate termination will come into operation. The precondition for the exercise of such right requires that the party being entitled to so terminate the agreement cannot be reasonably be expected to further continue its contractual obligations until the projected final end of such contract, thereby giving due regard to all circumstances of the case and in view of a proper evaluation of the interests of the parties. Whether Art. 626 Sec. 2 BGB is applicable in the contract here at hand, is open to doubt, as this rule requires that the right to terminate the contract forthwith may only exercised within a period of two weeks, running form the date the party so entitled to terminate has become aware of the

---

[105] 14.12.2017 – I ZR 184/15, GRUR 2018, 423 – Klauselersetzung.
[106] Official Journal of the European Union, July 11, 2019 L 189 p. 57 (71).
[107] Official Journal of the European Union, July 11, 2019 L 189 p. 57 (71).

relevant facts granting the right of termination.[108] But, it is doubtful whether this rule will be applicable in contracts of intermediation services offered on platforms,[109] a final decision of the BGH is still outstanding.

However, the salient point here is that Art. 626 Sec. 1 BGB is a mandatory rule.[110] Therefore, Art. 4 Sec. 4 lit. b) will come into play, allowing to take resort to the legal rules of German law, being mandatory, provided they are not in conflict with Union law. In evaluating this issue, it is safe to conclude: There is no indication of the existence of any legal instrument of Union law, possibly being in conflict with the right of immediate termination of a service contract pursuant to Art. 626 Sec. 1 BGB.

b) Possible conflict with Art. 307 Sec. 2 No. 1 BGB

But this answer does not cover all possible issues in connection with an immediate termination with cause. As clauses of termination are generally covered by the wide-ranging definition of "terms and conditions", as listed in Art. 2 No. 10, the question to be answered here is whether and to what extent the supplier of such general terms of contract is entitled to deviate from the mandatory legal rule of Art. 626 Sec. 1 BGB. The general answer is precise: General contract terms supplied to the business user may interpret the meaning of Art. 626 Sec. 1 BGB in line with the case-law, established by the BGH. But they may not deviate therefrom in a manner being to the detriment of the business user by entitling the supplier of such general terms to exercise its right of immediate termination without being validly supported in this respect by the precedents established by the BGH.[111]

This strict interpretation of the rule on immediate termination has a consequence listed in Art. 4 Sec. 4 lit. c). There it is said that the right of termination with cause may rest on the fact that the provider of intermediation services *"(c) can demonstrate that the business user concerned has repeatedly infringed the applicable terms and conditions, resulting in the termination of the provision of the whole of the online intermediation services in question."*[112] As this rule has been drafted without giving due regard to the problem whether it will or will not be in conflict with mandatory national legal rules, the issue arising therefrom must be resolved along the following lines: In view of the mandatory rule of Art. 626 Sec. 1 BGB it seems very improbable that a repeated infringement of general contract terms by the business user will fall into the category of this mandatory rule of Art. 626 Sec. 1 BGB.

This view may be supported by the finding that such contravention by the business user against general contract terms is not at all qualified, whether it amounts to a fundamental breach or only of a breach of an ancillary obligation, causing or not at all causing substantial damages. Hence, the interpretation rule of Art. 305c Sec. 2 BGB will come into play, holding that the interpretation, being most favorable to the user will come into play,[113] implying that there is a clear violation of Art. 307 Sec. 2 No. 1 BGB: If one assumes that the business user had breached an obligation listed in the general contract terms twice or even three times (during which period?), the interpretation rule of Art. 305 Sec. 2 BGB will hold that such breaches lack any substantial damage to the interests of the provider of online intermediation services. If there is even the smallest

---

[108] For a detailed debate vide Busch/*Graf von Westphalen*, P2B, *Commentary on Regulation 20129/1150*, 2021, Art. 3 Note 222.
[109] BGH 15.12.1993 – VIII ZR 157/92, NJW 1994, 722.
[110] Grüneberg/*Weidenkaff*, *Commentary on the BGB*, 81st edi. 2022, § 626 Note 2.
[111] BGH 08.02.2012 – XII ZR 42/10, NJW 2012, 1431 Note 27.
[112] Official Journal of the European Union, July 11, 2019 L 189 p. 57 (71).
[113] BGH 29.4.2008 – KZR 2/07, NJW 2008, 2172 – leading precedent.

room for a divergent interpretation of contract clause, the courts will always apply the interpretation which is most disadvantageous to the supplier of such clause.[114]

68 But whether the result so arrived at will and can be considered as final depends (again) on the interpretation of the priority rule of Art. 1.4. One may argue that Art. 4 Sec. 4 lit. c) is part of this Regulation and therefore supersedes the application of the validity test that has given way to the application of national law. But here it is different, as Art. 4 Sec. 4 lit. c) allows any immediate termination of the contract in case of a repeated infringement of the general contract terms. Hence, the sounder approach seems to be that Art. 4 Section 4 lit. c will stand on its own feet as part of the applicable Union law regime.[115]

E. Summary

69 1. The protection against unfair contract terms granted by this Regulation to the business user is restricted (inter alia) to the test whether the specific clauses have been drafted in "plain and intelligible language" (Art. 3 Abs. 1 lit. a). Such protection is rather limited, as there is practically no test of unfairness or unfair dealing.
2. The scope of protection, however, will be considerably enlarged to the benefit of the business user by applying the fairness test of German national law, as embodied in Art. 307 BGB. Art. 1.4 opens the door to so argue, as issues of validity have been left to the national law regimes of the Member States. In this regard, German law by far offers the most effective and comprehensive protection shield in b2b-transactions. Its established case law goes back for more than 50 years.[116]
3. The protection shield will even be considerably enlarged, if one accepts that this Regulation provides protection against unfair contract terms not only to the business user, but also to the benefit of the consumer, being the ultimate purchaser of the products and services displayed on the online platform for sale. There are reliable indications within the text and within the Recitals of this Regulation to hold by virtue of interpretation that such protection to the consumer can be made available in line with established German law principles ("Vertrag mit Schutzwirkung zugunsten Dritter").
4. On this basis the fairness test of general contract terms, supplied to the business user, will be construed from the view-point of the consumer to be protected by the full range of Art. 307, 308, 309 BGB. This operation still can be seen as being secured by the interpretation of the validity test pursuant to Art. 1.4, 2nd sentence, left to the law regimes of the Member States.
5. If general contract terms supplied by the provider of online intermediation services are violating Art. 307, 308, 309 BGB, as being the rules protecting the consumer, then there is, by the same token, a violation of the rules of Directive 93/13/EEC. Such breach then will call Directive 2005/29/EC into operation, as illegal contract terms are considered to violate the principles of fair commercial practices (Art. 3a UWG).
6. Therefore, the consumer organizations will be entitled to sue the provider of online intermediation online services and ask for elimination of such illegal contract terms

---

[114] For further examples vide Grüneberg/*Grüneberg,* Commentary on the BGB, 81st edit., Munich 2022, § 305c Note 18 sequ.
[115] For further details vide Busch/*Graf von Westphalen,* P2B, *Commentary on Regulation 2019/1150,* 2021, Art. 4 Note 16.
[116] For a detailed analysis vide *Graf von Westphalen, Wiederentdeckte Grundpfeiler der Rechtsprechung zur AGB-Kontrolle,* NJW 2022, 1409.

and also for desist and cease the further use of them.[117] Thus, the remedial structure of Regulation 2019/1150 is considerably enlarged.
7. It seems likely that any clauses, based on the rights established in Art. 4 Sec. 1 to suspend, restrict, delist or dim the rights of the business user, are violating Art. 307 in line with the requirements set forth in Art. 308 No. 4 BGB, generally lacking the requirement of reasonableness and due regard to the interests of the business user (Art. 307 Sec. 2 No. 1 BGB).
8. The right to terminate a contract with immediate effect is embodied in the mandatory rule of Art. 626 Sec. 1 BGB which is respected by virtue of Art. 4 sec. 4. b) as being applicable. Any general contract term shall not be valid if it changes or alters any of the aspects being relevant as precedents established by the BGH in interpreting the mandatory provision of Art. 626 Sec. 1 BGB.
9. Finally, it may be taken for granted that the practical use of this (new) Regulation proves to be complex and complicated due to the multi-layer-system of Union law.

Bibliography

Alexander in Köhler/Bornkamm/Feddersen, *Commentary on Competition Law (UWG)*, 40th edi. 2022;

Busch, Mehr Transparenz und Fairness in der Plattformökonomie? GRUR 2019, 788 (790);

Busch/*Graf von Westphalen*, P2B-VO, *Commentary on Regulation 2019/1150*, 2021;

Dammann in Wolf/Lindacher/Pfeiffer, *Commentary on the AGB-Recht*, 7th edi., 2020;

Erman/*Roloff/Looschelders, Commentary on the BGB*, 16th edi. 2020;

Finkelmaier, Über die (Un-)möglichkeit der Haftungsbegrenzung im internationalen Handel – § 307 Abs. 1 BGB als faktische Grenze der Vertragsfreiheit, ZIP 2022, 563;

Graf von Westphalen, Festschrift für Grunewald, *Können Art. 25 und Art. 74 CISG für eine Konkretisierung der richterlichen Inhaltskontrolle bei Haftungsfreizeichnungs- und Haftungsbegrenzungsklauseln (§ 307 Abs. 2 Nr. 2 BGB) eingesetzt werden?* 2021, 1313;

Graf von Westphalen, *Schiedsvereinbarungen und Ausschluss der §§ 305–310 BGB. aber Aufrechterhaltung der Geltung des § 242 BGB – was gilt?* ZIP 2022, 245;

Graf von Westphalen, *Wiederentdeckte Grundpfeiler der Rechtsprechung zur AGB-Kontrolle*, NJW 2022, 1409;

Grüneberg/*Grüneberg, Commentary on the BGB*, 81st ed., 2022;

Leuschner/*Leuschner, AGB-Recht im unternehmerischen Verkehr*, 2021;

Maier-Reimer, AGB-Recht im unternehmerischen Rechtsverkehr – der BGH überdreht die Schraube, NJW 2017, 1;

Ostendorf, Abwahl des AGB-Rechts per Rechtswahl und Schiedsvereinbarung: Problem oder Prolemlöser? ZIP 2022, 730;

Pfeiffer in Wolf/Lindacher/Pfeiffer, *Commentary on the AGB-Recht*, 7th edi. 2020;

Sommerfeld, Rechtsflucht in Ausland wegen des deutschen AGB-Rechts im B2B-Verkehr? RIW 2018, 741;

---

[117] BGH 14.12.2017 – I ZR 184/15, GRUR 2018, 423 – Klauselersetzung.

Sommerfeld, Wie sinnvoll ist eine Rechtsflucht ins Schweizerische Recht vor der deutschen AGB-Kontrolle im Handelsverkehr? IWRZ 2022, 64;

Staudinger/Coester-Waltjen, Commentary on the BGB, 2019, § 309 Nr. 7;

Wendland, Vertragsfreiheit und Vertragsgerechtigkeit, Tübingen 2019.

The EU Digital Services Act and EU Consumer Law

A. Overview of the DSA: History and main content 3
   I. Quick adoption 3
   II. Scope and main content of the DSA 4

B. Consumer Law in the DSA 6
   I. Article 6 DSA: Liability of online platforms 7
   II. Article 14 DSA: Terms and Conditions 11
   III. Article 30 DSA: Traceability of traders 20

C. The (now filled?) enforcement gap in the DSA 25

D. Conclusions: The DSA as 'regulatory private law' with potentially far-reaching consequences 29

   Bibliography 30

Since the e-Commerce Directive was enacted in 2000, the number of digital services has risen immensely. However, the rules generally regulating digital services at the EU level has not changed to match. In order to mitigate the potential risks and create a safer and more open digital space, the European Commission proposed the Digital Services Act Package, consisting of two legislative acts: the Digital Services Act (DSA) and the Digital Markets Act (DMA).[1] The scope of these acts goes far beyond the specific consumer contract law for digital services in the Digital Content and Services Directive (DCD).[2] While the DMA aims to regulate the strong market power of large online platforms ("gatekeepers"), the DSA mainly focuses on setting fairness and transparency rules on online platforms of various sizes in order to strengthen the fundamental rights of users on the internet.

This paper focuses on the DSA. Despite the fact that the DSA is not genuine consumer law, some provisions contain consumer protection elements nevertheless. The aim of this paper is to identify traces of consumer law in the DSA and provide some thoughts on the interplay of EU consumer legislation and the enforcement of the consumer protection rules in the DSA. This paper was written while the final text of the DSA was still being finalised.[3] The manuscript had to be completed just a few days after the publication of the DSA in the Official Journal, and it turned out that the articles from the proposal of the DSA presented in the oral version were significantly changed at the last minute. This means that the considerations made here are only sketchy and could not yet benefit from the numerous legal writings on the finally adopted text of the DSA, which will certainly appear very soon.[4]

---

[1] https://digital-strategy.ec.europa.eu/en/policies/digital-services-act-package.
[2] Directive (EU) 2019/770 on certain aspects concerning contracts for the supply of digital content and digital services.
[3] The presentation was given at the Conference on "Harmonising Digital Contract Law" in Ferrara on 9 and 10 June 2022.
[4] On the proposal, see, for example, Christoph Busch, Vanessa Mak, Putting the Digital Services Act in Context: Bridging the Gap Between EU Consumer Law and Platform Regulation, EuCML 2021, 109; Ruth Janal, Haftung und Verantwortung im Entwurf des Digital Services Acts, ZEuP 2021, 227; Matthias Berberich, Fabian Seip, Der Entwurf des Digital Services Act, GRUR-Prax 2021, 4; cf. also the other authors cited in the following footnotes.

A. Overview of the DSA: History and main content

I. Quick adoption

3   As part of the Digital Services Package mentioned above, the Commission published the proposal of the DSA in December 2020. The Council agreed in November 2021, with some amendments made to the text. In January 2022, the Parliament approved the proposal and suggested amendments before reaching a political agreement on the text with the Council in April 2022. The DSA was finally adopted – with further amendments – in July 2022 and was published in the Official Journal of the European Union in October 2022. According to Article 93 DSA, it entered into force on 16 November 2022 and will apply from 17 February 2024.

II. Scope and main content of the DSA

4   For the purpose of this paper, it should be sufficient to sketch out the scope of the DSA, which is structured like a Russian matryoshka doll. The provisions of the act are directed towards various kinds of platforms, differentiating between four sizes and functions: (1) intermediary services, (2) hosting services, (3) online platforms, and (4) very large online platforms (known as "Vlops"). The number of rules applicable to the respective addressees increases with size. Only certain rules apply to the intermediary services category, while "Vlops", the narrowest category, are generally covered by all the rules of the DSA.[5]

5   The DSA consists of five chapters. The provisions address a rather long list of regulatory issues, using the described matryoshka technique to direct some of the provisions at all categories of intermediary services, while directing some provisions only to hosting services and the narrower categories. After the general provisions in Chapter I, the DSA provides liability provisions in its Chapter II, addressing all providers of intermediary services. Chapter III sets out obligations for a transparent and safe online environment. It has five sub-sections addressing the four described categories of platforms before concluding in section five, where provisions containing due diligence obligations. Chapter IV regulates sanctions and enforcement before Chapter V provides final provisions.

B. Consumer Law in the DSA

6   The DSA is not strictly consumer law, but is rather a general market regulation instrument that imposes obligations on certain actors in the market. In this case to concerns the four groups of addressees mentioned above: intermediary services, hosting services, online platforms and "Vlops". Nevertheless, the DSA includes some provisions that expressly deal with consumers,[6] of which Articles 6, 14 and 30 DSA are the most significant examples.

---

[5] https://ec.europa.eu/info/strategy/priorities-2019-2024/europe-fit-digital-age/digital-services-act-ensuring-safe-and-accountable-online-environment_en.

[6] On this see, for example, Christoph Busch, Vanessa Mak, Putting the Digital Services Act in Context: Bridging the Gap Between EU Consumer Law and Platform Regulation, EuCML 2021, 109, Bram Duivenvoorde, The Liability of Online Marketplaces under the Unfair Commercial Practices Directive, the E-commerce Directive and the Digital Services Act, EuCML 2022, 43 (52); Ukrow, Impulse aus dem EMR: Die Vorschläge der EU-Kommission für einen Digital Services Act und einen Digital Markets Act, 2021, 45.

B. Consumer Law in the DSA

I. Article 6 DSA: Liability of online platforms

The first provision relating to consumers can be found in Article 6 (3) DSA, addressing online platforms. Since Article 6 (3) refers to Article 6 (1), a slightly broader extract from Article 6 DSA is quoted here:

Article 6 DSA: Hosting
1. Where an information society service is provided that consists of the storage of information provided by a recipient of the service, the service provider shall not be liable for the information stored at the request of a recipient of the service on condition that the provider:
(a) does not have actual knowledge of illegal activity or illegal content and, as regards claims for damages, is not aware of facts or circumstances from which the illegal activity or illegal content is apparent; or
(b) upon obtaining such knowledge or awareness, acts expeditiously to remove or to disable access to the illegal content.
(...)
3. Paragraph 1 shall not apply with respect to the liability under consumer protection law of online platforms that allow consumers to conclude distance contracts with traders, where such an online platform presents the specific item of information or otherwise enables the specific transaction at issue in a way that would lead an average consumer to believe that the information, or the product or service that is the object of the transaction, is provided either by the online platform itself or by a recipient of the service who is acting under its authority or control.
(...)

Article (6) DSA presupposes a three-tier structure that can be generally characterised as rule, exception and counter-exception. The rule itself is not contained in the DSA but is implicitly presumed. It is that online platforms (according to other EU legislation or the applicable national law) are liable for breaches of their duties by which they caused damage. The exception to this liability is set out in Article 6 (1), from which Article 6 (3) in turn forms a counter-exception for the protection of consumers. The provision in Article 6 (1) DSA, exempting hosting services from liability (e.g. under national law) for information provided by a recipient of the service, is already known from the e-Commerce Directive.[7] Not included in the e-Commerce Directive, however, was the counter-exception in Article 6 (3) DSA, stating that the exemption in (1) does not apply to the liability of online platforms under consumer protection law.

The provision addresses cases where online platforms allow consumers to conclude distance contracts with traders without disclosing who the trader actually is, and so give the consumer the impression that they are contracting with the platform itself, which might not actually be the case. The provision obviously has similarities with the ECJ's very well-known *Wathelet*[8] case. The case dealt with a used car sold by an intermediary who did not disclose to the buyer that he was contracting on behalf of a third party. The ECJ ruled that the intermediary was liable for the remedies that the actual seller would have to provide for non-conformity under the Consumer Sales Directive. This means that failing to sufficiently inform a consumer about the actual contractual partner may lead to the intermediary's own liability.

The same legal idea can be found in Article 6 (3) DSA concerning online platforms. The DSA does not grant a positive claim to consumers. However, when read together with the Digital Content Directive (DCD), for example, the *Wathelet* ruling could lead to a consumer claim against the provider of an online platform, which falls under the

---

[7] Caroline Cauffman, Catalina Goanta, A New Order: The Digital Services Act and Consumer Protection, European Journal of Risk Regulation (2021), 12:4, 758 (764).
[8] ECJ C-149/15, ECLI:EU:C:2016:840 – Wathelet.

counter-exception in Article 6(3) DSA. The result could be that a consumer who enters into a contract for services on an online platform that does not properly inform them of the identity of the service provider can use all the remedies under the DCD (which are actually against the service provider only) also against the platform provider. The platform provider's liability under the DCD would even be strict liability, since the remedies granted by the DCD do not require fault. The idea of the platform provider's liability under the DCD is supported by Recital (23) of the DSA.[9]

II. Article 14 DSA: Terms and Conditions

11 Article 14 DSA stipulates some requirements on the terms and conditions of the providers of intermediary services that overlap with the Unfair Terms in Consumer Contracts Directive (UCTD).[10] The article reads (in extracts):

> Article 14 DSA: Terms and conditions
> 1. *Providers of intermediary services shall include information on any restrictions that they impose in relation to the use of their service in respect of information provided by the recipients of the service, in their terms and conditions. That information shall include information on any policies, procedures, measures and tools used for the purpose of content moderation, including algorithmic decision-making and human review, as well as the rules of procedure of their internal complaint handling system. It shall be set out in clear, plain, intelligible, user-friendly and unambiguous language, and shall be publicly available in an easily accessible and machine-readable format.*
> 2. *Providers of intermediary services shall inform the recipients of the service of any significant change to the terms and conditions....*

12 In the list of definitions in Article 3 DSA, the notion of 'terms and conditions' is defined in letter (u) as follows:

> (u) *'terms and conditions' means all clauses, irrespective of their name or form, which govern the contractual relationship between the provider of intermediary services and the recipients of the service;*

13 Since the recipients of the service will often be consumers and the service provider will always be a business, Article 14 DSA covers standard terms that may also fall under the UCTD.

14 The UCTD partly contains similar rules. The first sentence of Article 5 UCTD also deals with the language and presentation of terms. It reads:

> Article 5 UCTD
> *In the case of contracts where all or certain terms offered to the consumer are in writing, these terms must always be drafted in plain, intelligible language. ...*

15 Comparing the adjectives in the first sentence of Article 5 UCTD with the second sentence of Article 14 (1) DSA, gives the following picture:

UCTD: "... *drafted in plain, intelligible language* ..."
DSA: "... *set out in clear, plain, intelligible, user-friendly and unambiguous language, and shall be publicly available in an easily accessible and machine-readable format.*"

---

[9] Recital (23) of the DSA reads: "The exemption of liability should not apply where the recipient of the service is acting under the authority or the control of the provider of a hosting service. For example, where the provider of an online platform that allows consumers to conclude distance contracts with traders determines the price of the goods or services offered by the trader, it could be considered that the trader acts under the authority or control of that online platform."

[10] Directive 93/13/EEC of 5 April 1993 on unfair terms in consumer contracts.

B. Consumer Law in the DSA

This conflict of rules is easy to solve by classical methods. It could be a case of *"lex specialis"* in the sense that the more specific DSA rule prevails. Strictly speaking, there is even no conflict at the level of EU law at all, since Article 5 UCTD is part of a directive that is not horizontally applicable and therefore cannot conflict with a provision in a regulation that is, of course, directly applicable. Where a provision of national law (e.g. one that transposes the UCTD) conflicts with the transparency requirements in Article 14 (1) DSA, the EU Regulation prevails due to the priority of application of EU law over conflicting national law.

Another overlap can be observed with the right of the provider to alter their terms and conditions, which seems to be presupposed in Article 14 (1) DSA. In cases falling under the UCTD, letters (j) and (k) of the annex to the UCTD could lead a court to hold that a service provider may not alter the terms, or any characteristics of the service, "without a valid reason."[11] In other words, it may be that terms providing for restrictions of service in the sense of Article 14 (1) DSA are already invalid because of a violation of the UCTD. In this case, the question of the legal consequences of a violation of the transparency rules in Article 14 DSA no longer arises.

It may, nevertheless, be a problem that the DSA leaves completely open the question of what consequences a violation of Article 14 DSA can have for the validity of the terms and conditions. It is worth noting that, in the position of the European Parliament, an express provision was suggested saying that terms not complying with the requirements set out in this article of the DSA *"shall not be binding on recipients."*[12] This clarification proposed by the European Parliament did not make it into the final text of the DSA; it was dropped during the trilogue negotiations. The reason for this decision is not known. One of the problems of the proposed radical solution whereby terms contradicting the requirements of the DSA should be invalid could be that this would also cover non-transparent terms simply due to their non-transparency, regardless of their content. If understood literally, non-transparent terms would be invalid even if they are favourable to the consumer.

However, this gap will have to be filled because in litigation and administrative proceedings it will often have to be decided whether the terms are effective or not. A pragmatic solution, probably not only for the area of consumer law, might be to take Article 6 UTCD as a model. Article 6 (1) UCTD reads:

> Article 6 UCTD
> 1. Member States shall lay down that unfair terms used in a contract concluded with a consumer by a seller or supplier shall, as provided for under their national law, not be binding on the consumer and that the contract shall continue to bind the parties upon those terms if it is capable of continuing in existence without the unfair terms.

One can conclude from this that any terms sufficiently non-transparent to be unfair are invalid. This example again shows that the DSA, as far as it is applicable to consumer cases, has to be read together with EU consumer contract law. The model of Article 6

---

[11] Cf. the annex to the UCTD letters (j) and (k), which read: *(j) enabling the seller or supplier to alter the terms of the contract unilaterally without a valid reason which is specified in the contract; (k) enabling the seller or supplier to alter unilaterally without a valid reason any characteristics of the product or service to be provided.*

[12] Amendments adopted by the European Parliament on 20 January 2022 on the proposal for a regulation of the European Parliament and of the Council on a Single Market For Digital Services (Digital Services Act) and amending Directive 2000/31/EC, Document P9_TA(2022)0014, Amendment 539: Insertion of a new para which reads: "Terms that do not comply with this Article shall not be binding on recipients."

UCTD has the advantage that terms cannot be declared invalid regardless of which party invokes invalidity, but only if this is favourable to the consumer.

III. Article 30 DSA: Traceability of traders

20   Another example of an overlap with EU consumer law can be found in Article 30 DSA. The provision reads:

> Art. 30: Traceability of traders
> 1. Providers of online platforms allowing consumers to conclude distance contracts with traders shall ensure that traders can only use those online platforms to promote messages on or to offer products or services to consumers located in the Union if, prior to the use of their services for those purposes, they have obtained the following information, where applicable to the trader:
> (a) the name, address, telephone number and email address of the trader;
> (b) a copy of the identification document of the trader …;
> (c) the payment account details of the trader;
> (d) where the trader is registered in a trade register or similar public register, the trade register in which the trader is registered and its registration number or equivalent means of identification in that register;
> (e) a self-certification by the trader committing to only offer products or services that comply with the applicable rules of Union law.

21   Following this para (1) of Article 30 DSA comes para (2) which obliges the provider of an online platform to make its best efforts to assess whether the information given under para (1) is reliable and complete. Para (3) obliges the provider of an online platform, if it obtains sufficient indications or has reasons to believe that any item of information given by the trader is inaccurate, to make the trader correct any incomplete information and, if the trader fails to correct that information, to swiftly suspend the provision of any service to this trader.

22   Article 30 DSA is intended to lay down a "Know Your Business Customer" rule.[13] It obliges online platforms that allow consumers to conclude distance contracts with traders to collect information from the traders. The information to be collected is listed in the five letters in Article 30 (1) DSA. They mainly concern the trader's personal data, contact and payment account details as well as the trader's self-certification that it will only offer products and services that comply with applicable rules of Union law. In this way, Article 30 (2) and (3) DSA oblige online platforms to make their best efforts to check the information collected from traders for accuracy and completeness.

23   The original proposal of the DSA did not include any sanction for a breach of these obligations; in particular, no claims, e.g. for damages, were brought against the platform operator. The question arising from this was whether a consumer would have individual remedies against an online platform at all, in the event that the platform did not (fully) comply with the obligations from Article 30 DSA.

24   A partial solution to this gap could already be found in the revised Unfair Commercial Practices Directive (UCPD).[14] The newly introduced Article 11a UCPD obliges Member States' legislators add a claim for damages for consumers into national laws.[15] In cases where a violation of Article 30 DSA is also a violation of the UCPD, EU con-

---

[13] Cf., also on the inconsistencies with the pre-existing obligations of platforms to inform consumer about traders, Caroline Cauffman, Catalina Goanta, A New Order: The Digital Services Act and Consumer Protection, European Journal of Risk Regulation (2021), 12:4, 758 (762).

[14] Directive 2005/29/EC concerning unfair business-to-customer commercial practices in the internal market, amended by Directive (EU) 2019/2161.

[15] Cf. Article 11a UCPD, of which the first sentences read: "*Redress. (1) Consumers harmed by unfair commercial practices, shall have access to proportionate and effective remedies, including compensation for*

sumer law in principle provides for a claim for damages. However, it is doubtful whether the Member States would actually create effective claims for damages for breaches of obligations resulting from the UCPD in their national legislation, and whether courts would apply such national legislation to breaches of Article 30 DSA.[16] It is therefore to be welcomed that, at the last moment in the trilogue negotiations of the EU legislative bodies, a claim for damages against the user for a breach of the obligations under the DSA was introduced in Article 54 DSA. This provision will be briefly discussed here.

C. The (now filled?) enforcement gap in the DSA

25 The DSA provides a well-developed administrative enforcement system. In Article 49, the DSA obliges Member States to designate coordinators responsible for supervising the providers of intermediary services and enforcing the regulation. Article 52 DSA then obliges Member States to lay down rules on penalties applicable to infringements of the regulation. In its consolidated text, the DSA stipulates that the fines are 1 %, 5 % or 6 % of the platform's annual global turnover, depending on the nature of the infringement of the regulation. In addition, the DSA contains a rather innovative collective enforcement system involving researchers and trusted flaggers.

26 The proposal of the DSA, however, did not contain any provision regarding individual remedies for consumers in cases of infringement, in particular no claims for damages. Both the literature[17] and the European Parliament[18] called for the introduction of individual consumer remedies for breaches of the obligations under the DSA. The rights of users (i.e. including consumers) against intermediary platforms have since been significantly improved within the published final text of the DSA. In Article 54, the DSA now contains the following provision:

> Article 54 DSA: Compensation
> Recipients of the service shall have the right to seek, in accordance with Union and national law, compensation from providers of intermediary services, in respect of any damage or loss suffered due to an infringement by those providers of their obligations under this Regulation.

27 According to Recital (121), this claim is without prejudice to the exemptions of liability regulated by the DSA concerning information transmitted or stored at the request of a user. As previously explained regarding Article 6 DSA, however, this exemption of liability does not apply in cases referred to in Article 6 (3) DSA when consumers are involved. Therefore, at least consumer users should benefit from this provision in any case. Because of this, the claim may be a valuable addition to consumer rights.

28 However, it is already foreseeable that the application of this claim for damages in Article 54 DSA, which was introduced late into the DSA and is only sketchily formulated, will give rise to numerous questions in the courts. An example of this can already be seen in the parliamentary documents. In its report, the Internal Market and Consumer

---

damage suffered by the consumer and, where relevant, a price reduction or the termination of the contract. Member States may determine the conditions for the application and effects of those remedies ..."

[16] See further scepticism from Christoph Busch and Vanessa Mak in Putting the Digital Services Act in Context: Bridging the Gap Between EU Consumer Law and Platform Regulation, EuCML 2021, 109 (112).

[17] Christoph Busch, Vanessa Mak, Putting the Digital Services Act in Context: Bridging the Gap Between EU Consumer Law and Platform Regulation, EuCML 2021, 109 (112); Gerald Spindler, Der Vorschlag für ein neues Haftungsregime für Internetprovider – der EU-Digital Services Act, GRUR 2021, 653 (661).

[18] European Parliament legislative resolution of 5 July 2022 on the proposal for a regulation of the European Parliament and of the Council on a Single Market For Digital Services (Digital Services Act), Document P9_TA(2022)0269, Recital (83a).

Protection Committee (IMCO) had proposed that only a claim for compensation for "direct damage or loss" should be introduced.[19] This restriction to direct damage was finally dropped, which indicates that indirect damage, such as consequential damage, can now also be compensable in principle. In particular, it will have to be decided whether damages for pain and suffering can be claimed, which, in view of the possible violations of rights under the DSA and in light of the *Simone Leitner* decision of the ECJ,[20] is at any rate suggestible.

D. Conclusions: The DSA as 'regulatory private law' with potentially far-reaching consequences

29   The DSA embodies a type of EU legislation that has recently appeared more frequently, regulates large market sectors and contains predominantly market regulation law. The original proposal of the DSA only provided for an administrative enforcement of the numerous obligations imposed on intermediary services. The provisions of the draft DSA were, at this stage, public law only. The proposal almost completely ignored the fact that EU consumer law and national law would, in principle, also allow recipients of digital services to make claims under private law and that the DSA would create great uncertainty as to whether such claims can actually be enforced in parallel to the administrative enforcement. The introduction of the very broad claim for damages in Article 54 DSA has now made it clear that the DSA is hybrid law, which is still predominantly public law, but also has effects in private law and in particular in consumer law. Even if the proportion of private law provisions is very small, the DSA can still have far-reaching consequences for consumer law. In particular, where platform providers act in a non-transparent manner, e.g. do not make it clear who the consumer's contractual partner is, they now run the risk of being liable themselves towards the recipients, in particular consumers, under private law. It is particularly striking that, in the DSA, the EU appears to have given up the reluctance observed in the SGD[21] and the DCD to also regulate claims for damage.

30   The dynamics of EU legislation seem to be shifting significantly. EU private and consumer law is now being developed less in the traditional specific consumer contract law instruments, such as the SGD and the DCD, but in broad, predominantly public law market regulation legislation[22] such as the DSA. In these legal acts, private law is only a subordinate aspect, but one that has an impact on the entire EU private law and national private law. The discussion about this 'regulatory EU private law',[23] which is new at least in its scope, is only just beginning.[24]

---

[19] Report of the Committee on the Internal Market and Consumer Protection (IMCO) of 20.12.2021 on the proposal for a regulation on a Single Market for Digital Services (Digital Services Act) and amending Directive 2000/31/EC, Document A9–0356/2021, Amendment 398.

[20] ECJ C-168/00, ECLI:EU:C:2002:163 – *Simone Leitner*

[21] Directive (EU) 2019/771 of 20 May 2019 on certain aspects concerning contracts for the sale of goods.

[22] For a critical look at the (over)emphasis on market integration in EU law and the enforcement deficits in consumer law, see Geraint Howells, Christian Twigg-Flesner, Thomas Wilhelmsson, Rethinking EU Consumer Law (2017).

[23] This term was probably minted by Hans Micklitz, The Visible Hand of European Regulatory Private Law, European University Institute (EUI), Department of Law, EUI-LAW Working Papers Law (2008/01/01).

[24] Olha Cherednychenko, Islands and the Ocean: Three Models of the Relationship between EU Market Regulation and National Private Law, Modern Law Review 2021, 84(6), 1294; see also the forthcoming

Bibliography

Matthias Berberich and Fabian Seip, 'Der Entwurf des Digital Services Act' (2021) GRUR-Prax 4 ff.

Christoph Busch and Vanessa Mak, 'Putting the Digital Services Act in Context: Bridging the Gap Between EU Consumer Law and Platform Regulation' (2021) EuCML 109.

Caroline Cauffman and Catalina Goanta, 'A New Order: The Digital Services Act and Consumer Protection, European Journal of Risk Regulation' (2021) European Journal of Risk Regulation 758 ff.

Olha Cherednychenko, 'Islands and the Ocean: Three Models of the Relationship between EU Market Regulation and National Private Law' (2021) Modern Law Review 1294 ff.

Bram Duivenvoorde, 'The Liability of Online Marketplaces under the Unfair Commercial Practices Directive, the E-commerce Directive and the Digital Services Act' (2022) EuCML 2022, p. 42 ff.

Ruth Janal, 'Haftung und Verantwortung im Entwurf des Digital Services Acts' (2021) ZEuP 2021, 227.

Geraint Howells, Christian Twigg-Flesner and Thomas Wilhelmsson, Rethinking EU Consumer Law (Routledge 2017).

André Janssen, Matthias Lehmann and Reiner Schulze (eds), 'The Future of European Private Law' forthcoming.

Hans-Wolfgang Micklitz, 'The Visible Hand of European Regulatory Private Law' (2008) EUI-LAW Working Papers Law.

Gerald Spindler, 'Der Vorschlag für ein neues Haftungsregime für Internetprovider – der EU-Digital Services Act' (2021) GRUR 653 ff.

Jörg Ukrow, 'Impulse aus dem EMR: Die Vorschläge der EU-Kommission für einen Digital Services Act und einen Digital Markets Act' (2021) 45, available at <https://emr-sb.de/wp-content/uploads/2021/01/Impulse-aus-dem-EMR_DMA-und-DSA.pdf> accessed on 30 November 2022.

---

contributions in the conference volume "The Future of European Private Law" of a conference organised by André Janssen, Matthias Lehmann and Reiner Schulze 3 and 4 November 2022 at Nijmegen.

The Impact of the EU Digital Markets Act on Contract Law

A. Introduction 1
B. An Overview of the DMA. Relevant aspects 10
   I. Core platform services 11
   II. The gatekeeper status 14
   III. Prohibited practices 19
   IV. Public enforcement 30
   V. Summary 36
C. The impact of the DMA on the Drafting of Gatekeeper's Terms and Conditions. Some general observations 37
   I. Focus on practices, not contracts 40
   II. Contractual and non-contractual practices 44
   III. Mostly negative obligations 47
   IV. Contracting party status and group of companies 50
   V. Adjusting to changes in the regulatory situation 54
D. Private enforcement of the DMA? Some common issues and principles 59
   I. Availability of private law remedies 64
   II. 'Shield-actions' 68
   III. 'Sword-actions' 90

    Bibliography 96

A. Introduction

In the current discussion about so-called digital contract law, the question arises of how the recently enacted Digital Market Act (DMA) may impact on the European harmonization of contract law. [1]

The DMA is a piece of market regulation, and is not intended to regulate contracts as such. This may explain why this question has not been given much attention so far. As we shall see, many contract law issues arising in the context of the DMA are similar to those that are found in the neighbouring areas of antitrust, unfair competition and sectoral competition regulation. [2]

The DMA has already been approved by the European Parliament and the Council, and is expected to be implemented by 2023. Essentially, the DMA is a piece of ex ante regulation of digital markets[1], based to a large extent on the experience gained by the European Commission in its enforcement of general antitrust law regarding big tech firms. [3]

The DMA is directed at large online platforms, acting as so-called gatekeepers in eight sectors, called core platform services (CPS), among them search engines, intermediation services, social networks, etc. acting as so-called gatekeepers in various sectors. The aim of the DMA is to prevent practices that are likely to reduce competition in such markets, which are already highly concentrated, and/or to prevent practices resulting in unfair trading conditions to the disadvantage of business users as well as end users. [4]

---

[1] See also Schweitzer, 'The Art to Make Gatekeeper Positions Contestable and the Challenge to Know What is Fair: A Discussion of the Digital Markets Act Proposal' (2021), 509 ff., suggesting that the DMA should be interpreted as having the same fundamental objectives as antitrust law; similarly, Podszun, Philipp Bongartz and Langestein, 'The Digital Market Act: Moving from Competition Law to Regulation for Large Gatekeepers' (2021), 62, stressing the central role in this context of consumer sovereignty and competition on the merits; Petit, 'The Proposed Digital Markets Act (DMA): A Legal and Policy Review' (2021), partly views the DMA as an exercise in simplifying traditional antitrust law rules. See also Heimann, 'The Digital Markets Act – We gonna catch 'em all?' (2022).

Philipp Fabbio

5   The question, here, is how this piece of market regulation may contribute to the harmonization of digital contract law in Europe. Briefly, here are some thoughts on this issue.

6   The DMA is directed at a very limited number of big players. Unlike consumer Directives 2019/770/EU and 2019/771/EU or Regulation (EU) 2019/1150, the DMA is not exactly about contracts. The focus, instead, is on business practices. Nonetheless, the DMA will affect an immense number of transactions, thereby shaping current business practices and thus the competitive landscape in most digital markets.

7   In my opinion, the obligations imposed by the DMA upon gatekeepers cannot easily be extended by analogy to online platforms other than gatekeepers, whether through general competition law or through general contract law. Perhaps, though, we can expect some degree of spontaneous alignment to market practices, including contractual practices, which might later be adopted by gatekeepers under the influence of the DMA.

8   Apart from that, the DMA does of course have some implications in terms of contract law, of the kind that are familiar to the competition lawyer, but not necessarily to contract law specialists. Therefore, what I shall try to do here is to introduce a competition lawyer's perspective.

9   This chapter will be structured in three parts. First, I will provide an overview of the DMA, focusing on the features that are more relevant to our question of how the DMA impacts on contract law. Second, I shall try to make some general observation on how the DMA may reflect itself onto the terms and conditions used by gatekeepers. Third, I will discuss possible remedies. What are the private law remedies available when a gatekeeper's terms and conditions or contractual behaviour violate the DMA? More generally, what is the role of private enforcement in the context of the DMA?

B. An Overview of the DMA. Relevant aspects

10   Here are presented the salient features of the DMA, with a special attention to those elements that can be more relevant to our analysis.

I. Core platform services

11   Which are the sectors concerned? Which are the relevant digital markets?

12   The DMA is directed at large online platforms, acting as so-called gatekeepers in certain digital sectors. To be precise there are currently eight sectors under the rubric 'core platforms services' or CPS: i) search engines; ii) intermediation services; iii) social networks; iv) video sharing platforms; v) communication platforms; vi) operating systems; vii) cloud services; viii) advertising services (Art. 2(2) DMA).

13   For the sake of legal certainty, the list of CPS, although broadly termed, is meant to be exhaustive. But at the same time it is subject to review (Art. 17 DMA). This introduces a dynamic factor, which, from a contract law perspective, poses the issue of what happens with contracts that relate to newly identified CPS, but are already in place when the new CPS are added to the list.

II. The gatekeeper status

14   How does a CPS provider become (or cease to qualify as) a gatekeeper?

B. An Overview of the DMA. Relevant aspects

CPS Providers are designated by the European Commission as gatekeepers in one or more sectors if they meet certain qualitative criteria (Art. 3(1) DMA). However, to make things easier for all parties involved, when a CPS provider reaches certain quantitative thresholds (turnover and number of active end users over a significant period of time) a rebuttable presumption applies (Art. 3(2) DMA). Otherwise, the burden to prove that the relevant provider can qualify as a gatekeeper lies with the Commission itself.

The Commission may identify a CPS provider as a gatekeeper also in view of foreseeable future developments (Art. 3(6.3) DMA). Also in this case a formal act of designation by the Commission is required (Art. 3(7) DMA).

Finally, the status of gatekeepers can be revoked at any time and is subject to periodical review (Art. 4 DMA).

In conclusion, the gatekeeper status is a formal status requiring a corresponding act of designation by the Commission. At the same time, it is a dynamic factor, meaning that a CPS provider may acquire and/or lose its gatekeeper status over time. Both aspects, as we shall see, have implications in terms of contract law.

III. Prohibited practices

The obligations which Gatekeepers must comply with are laid down in Art. 5 and 6 DMA.

A number of listed practices are clearly inspired by the recent European experience with enforcing general antitrust law in digital markets[2]. The list would include tying, bundling, self-preferencing, MFN clauses and others. Other prohibitions could lead to controls on fair pricing.

The Commission's approach has been criticized for being somewhat random (a 'salad' of obligation as one critic wrote[3]) and also as being 'too custom-made'[4].

However, the European Commission has a long-standing tradition of using Art. 101 and 102 TFEU to establish precedents or to pave the way for block exemptions under Art. 101 or sectoral ex ante regulation of certain markets (energy, telecom etc.). Even the list of prohibited practices in Art. 101 and 102 TFEU is a 'salad' of prohibitions.

The difference lies in that in Art. 101 and 102 TFEU the lists of prohibited practices add to a general clause (of anti-competitive agreements and abuse of a dominant position, respectively), while in the DMA, the European Commission is given the power to update the list of prohibited practices and to further specify those contained in Art. 6 DMA by engaging in a 'dialogue' with the concerned gatekeeper.

The declared objectives are 'contestability' and 'fairness'. The precise meaning of these terms is, of course, a source of debate[5]. As far as we here are concerned, suffice it to say that the DMA seeks to prevent business practices that may reduce the contestability of markets that are already highly concentrated, and/or practices that may result in unfair trading conditions for the gatekeepers' counterparts, as well as for business users and, to a more limited extent, end users. In both cases, Art. 5 and 6 should be interpreted in a way that is consistent with the objectives of EU competition law[6].

---

[2] Caffarra and Scott Morton, 'The European Commission Digital Markets Act …' (2021).
[3] Podszun, Bongartz and Langestein, 'The Digital Market Act …' (2021), 65.
[4] Caffarra and Scott Morton, 'The European Commission Digital Markets Act …' (2021).
[5] Schweitzer, 'The Art to Make Gatekeeper Positions …' (2021), 512 ff., 517. Nicholas Petit, 'The Proposed Digital Markets Act …' (2021).
[6] Schweitzer, 'The Art to Make Gatekeeper Positions …' (2021), 517; and, to some extent, Podszun, Bongartz and Langestein, 'The Digital Market Act …' (2021), 62.

25 Some of the prohibitions, namely those set out in Art. 5 DMA, can be considered, without doubt, to be self-executing and thus directly applicable, even for the purpose of private enforcement before national courts. While some other prohibitions can be further specified by the Commission within a regulatory dialogue with concerned gatekeepers (Art. 6 and 7 DMA). As a consequence, their direct applicability for the purpose of private enforcement must be excluded[7].

26 In general, the level of detail is such that one can say that the DMA provides for a rules-based regulation, and not a principles-based regulation[8]. For the sake of legal certainty, the DMA does not contain any general clauses, such as those found, for instance, in Art. 101 and 102 TFEU or in the European directive on unfair commercial practices 2005/29/EC.

27 However, the Commission may adopt regulatory acts under the DMA to expand the list of prohibited practices (Art. 10 DMA). This adds another element of dynamism, with possible consequences on gatekeepers' contracts.

28 In both Art. 5 and 6 we are confronted with what antitrust law specialists would call per-se-rules[9]. These are rules that apply with no need (or little need) to carry out a context-dependent and effect-oriented analysis of the relevant practices[10]. In this way, the DMA departs from the approach that currently prevails in European antitrust, and thus results in an authentic piece of *ex-ante* regulation.

29 Nonetheless, there remains ample room for interpreting these legal provisions, including the ones that are contained in Art. 5 DMA. This may become more problematic in the context of private enforcement, and may call for some correction of the kind that are found in antitrust law, such as guidelines or amicus curiae briefs by the European Commission.

IV. Public enforcement

30 The enforcement mechanism laid down in the DMA is largely inspired by public antitrust enforcement, with additional measures such as structural remedies (Art. 18 ff. DMA).

31 Generally, the focus is on corporate fines. As in antitrust law, these fines can be quite high – up to ten per cent of the overall annual turnover (Art. 26(1) DMA). Based on established case-law in the neighbouring field of antitrust law, the basis for calculating fines in the case of a group of companies will likely be the group turnover, which can enormously increase the final amount of the fine.

32 This focus on fines reflects a European as well as, perhaps, an international trend. By now, this approach is found not only in competition law, but also in European data protection law. It relies on the assumption that in market regulation deterrence is fundamental, and can be achieved only by means of heavy corporate fines.

33 In reality, this punitive ex post approach is often questionable, but currently the European competition law discourse seems to pay little attention to its collateral effects, not to speak of its actual effectiveness. This, in turn, results in a systematic underestimation of both proportionality concerns and of the comparative advantages of a more regula-

---

[7] Similarly, Podszun, Bongartz and Langestein, 'Proposals on how to Improve the Digital Markets Act' (2021), 9.
[8] Schweitzer, 'The Art to Make Gatekeeper Positions …' (2021), 532.
[9] A. Witt, 'Platform Regulation in Europe – Per se Rules to the Rescue' (2022), 12.
[10] *Ibid.*, 512. N. Petit, 'The Proposed Digital Markets Act …' (2021), 2.

tory approach. A correction would require adequate analysis of likely future market developments, and making more use of behavioural remedies.

Apart from fines, other enforcement tools are also available under the DMA. They include, among others, interim measures (Art. 22 DMA), commitment decisions (Art. 23 DMA), behavioural and even structural remedies (Art. 7 and 16 DMA). Except for structural remedies, they are the common tools of public antitrust enforcement.

Yet, the DMA says nothing, not even in the recitals, about private enforcement. Nonetheless, in legal literature it has been advocated that there should be room here for private enforcement[11], possibly in the way it is applied in general competition law. We will return to this point in the last part of this chapter.

V. Summary

To sum up, the DMA provides for a piece of ex ante regulation of competition in digital markets. The DMA regulates practices, not contracts, but may have significant implications on contracts, namely on the terms and conditions and the contractual behaviour of gatekeepers in very large numbers of transactions. The DMA does not consider private remedies at all. Nonetheless, private remedies may still play some role in enforcing the DMA, a possibility which will now be examined.

C. The impact of the DMA on the Drafting of Gatekeeper's Terms and Conditions. Some general observations

We now turn our attention to the impact of the DMA on contract law. Here, the initial and fundamental dimension is the drafting of contracts.

It is, of course, the service provider who drafts its contracts both with business users and end users. Given the high level of fines that can be imposed under the DMA, gatekeepers can be expected to make strenuous efforts to avoid violating Art. 5 and 6, even when drafting their terms and conditions.

The details of finding how every single obligation imposed on gatekeepers under the DMA may translate into a gatekeeper's terms and conditions will, here, not be delved into. Instead, some general aspects will be highlighted, which are quite familiar to competition lawyers, but may not be so obvious to contract law specialists.

I. Focus on practices, not contracts

First of all, the obligations that apply to gatekeepers under Art. 5 and 6 are, so to speak, contract-neutral.

They relate to business practices, irrespective of their nature or, to quote Art. 11 DMA, *"regardless of whether this behaviour is of contractual, commercial, technical or any other nature"*. To put it another way, Art. 5 and 6 DMA do not relate to contractual terms and conditions or contractual behaviour as such.

There are, however, at least two exceptions to this. Under the DMA, business users must be granted access to data relative to their positioning in online searches (Art. 6, lit. j DMA) and to software application stores (Art. 6, lit. k DMA) on fair, reasonable and

---

[11] Schweitzer, 'The Art to Make Gatekeeper Positions ...' (2021), 541.

non-discriminatory terms. Such terms must necessarily be spelled out in explicit contractual provisions.

43 This means that most of the obligations imposed on gatekeepers under Art. 5 and 6 DMA may, but do not necessarily, affect the gatekeepers' contracts by positively requiring specific contractual provisions.

II. Contractual and non-contractual practices

44 A second general aspect to point out is that prohibited practices may result from a combination of contractual provisions and technical arrangements and/or behaviour of other nature.

45 This implies that, at least in principle, a contractual provision could be deemed to be in violation of the DMA, not in itself, but rather in combination with some other behaviour on the part of the gatekeeper. This further means that a certain contractual provision may become illegal or stop being illegal, depending on the gatekeeper's behaviour.

46 In conclusion, the illegality of contractual provisions under the DMA can be, so to speak, a dynamic illegality. This notion of dynamic illegality is quite familiar to competition lawyers, but is, perhaps, less accepted among contract law specialists.

III. Mostly negative obligations

47 All of the obligations set out in Art. 5 DMA and most of those set out in Art. 6 DMA are negative ones. In most cases, gatekeepers must only refrain from adopting the listed business practices.

48 It follows then that, as a matter of principle, most obligations laid down in Art. 5 and 6 DMA do not need to be translated into contractual provisions. It is up to the gatekeeper to adopt (or not to adopt) corresponding contractual clauses.

49 The question arises, however, if gatekeepers should be required under the DMA, for the sake of transparency, to flesh out their terms and conditions, by explicitly stating what their counterparts are already implicitly allowed to do. This is all but obvious, and the Commission would have to adopt some formal act, guidelines or the like, to achieve such an outcome.

IV. Contracting party status and group of companies

50 A fourth point, perhaps not so obvious for contract law specialists, has to do with the status of the contracting party, when the gatekeeper is a group of companies.

51 When the gatekeeper is structured as or belongs to a group of companies, there will likely be only one company of the group entering the contract with the business user or the end user, and from a contract law perspective that one company is the contracting party with all the contract law consequences deriving thereof.

52 If the contract in question results in a violation of the DMA, it is, however, the gatekeeper as a group of companies that will likely be held liable under the DMA, following principles that have so far been established in antitrust law. Although, even in antitrust law these principles may still need some refinement at EU level. One wonders if the implementation of the DMA might be an opportunity for some fine-tuning.

In conclusion and more generally, contract law categories do not help elude liability under the DMA, which is in fact centered not on contracts, but on business practices.

V. Adjusting to changes in the regulatory situation

A fifth and final point – The DMA provides for quite a dynamic regulatory scheme.

The gatekeeper status, although based on a formal designation procedure, can be acquired and lost over time. Some of the obligations imposed on gatekeepers can be further specified within a regulatory dialogue with the Commission. The Commission may even adopt specific procedures to update and extend the list of obligations applying to gatekeepers.

On the level of contract drafting and management, this implies that over time the need may arise to adjust terms and conditions, for instance because a CPS provider has been designated as a gatekeeper, or because designated gatekeepers must comply with new obligations.

This dynamic feature of the DMA requires gatekeepers to be highly attentive when drafting their terms and conditions and to adopt mechanisms that preserve the contractual relationship, while adjusting the contractual terms to any potential changes in the regulatory situation.

From a more general perspective, one could consider an interpretation of general contract law rules that is in line with the objective of keeping the contractual relationship alive, but without putting into question the contestability of the markets concerned.

D. Private enforcement of the DMA? Some common issues and principles

The DMA does not contain a single reference to private law remedies, not even in its recitals. The focus is put solely on public enforcement, and the reasons for that are quite obvious.

In the context of this new piece of ex ante regulation, concerned with a handful of big international players and featuring a dynamic approach, a public enforcement system administered by the European Commission ensures legal certainty and effectiveness at the same time.

The whole dimension of private law remedies is thus left to national contract law, and the choice of applicable law made in gatekeepers' contracts becomes decisive in this respect.

Nonetheless, it is possible here to make some general observations and state some principles that follow from them regarding the role of private enforcement as well as the fashioning of the single types of remedies.

In this respect, the European experience with private antitrust enforcement provides perspectives, conceptual categories and solutions that can be usefully deployed also in the context of the DMA.

I. Availability of private law remedies

64 In general there should be no doubt that, when the gatekeeper violates a directly applicable prohibition, this will gives rise to private law remedies, based on general contract and tort law[12] principles.

65 However, the role of private enforcement in the context of the DMA should not be overstated nor overused. There is no need here to employ what Americans call a 'private attorney general', the idea of which is deeply rooted in the US antitrust law experience[13]. In recent years it has even had some influence over the development of this area of the law in the EU as well, as it shows in the Directive on antitrust damages 2004/104/EU.

66 However, the recent European experience also suggests that strong private enforcement combined with a punitive approach to public enforcement may often go too far. Such combination, although widely supported by academicians and competition authorities, springs from an ideal of deterrence, which may not be fully aligned with social and economic reality, especially in the European context. It does not consider, most importantly, that antitrust enforcement is directed at business organizations (and not, or not primarily, at individuals), and that in terms of dynamic efficiency the costs of draconian corporate fines combined with extensive private enforcement could prove excessive, especially in comparison to the alternative option of a more lenient fining policy and a more regulatory approach in public enforcement.

67 That said, the DMA relies on the continuous monitoring of relevant markets and strong public enforcement, and it does not need to be supplemented with private enforcement to better achieve its objectives[14]. This does not mean that private enforcement should not be available, which will be described here in more detail.

II. 'Shield-actions'

68 A main distinction that is made in the context of private antitrust enforcement is between shield-actions and sword-actions. That is, private plaintiffs may use antitrust law as a 'shield' or as a 'sword'. A so-called shield-action occurs when a private plaintiff invokes competition law as a 'shield' to get rid of a single contractual provision or even of a contract in its entirety, on the grounds that they infringe on competition law[15].

69 In the context of the DMA, shield-actions (or just the threat of them) are certainly the easiest form of private enforcement from the plaintiff's perspective, especially in the case where the European Commission has already found a certain contractual practice to be in violation of the DMA.

70 The DMA, unlike Art. 101 TFEU, does not provide for the invalidity of contract provisions violating Art. 5 and 6. Nonetheless, contractual counterparts, especially business users, as well as third parties, particularly competitors, should be entitled to invoke the unenforceability of illegal contract clauses, whether contained in an individual contract

---

[12] Schweitzer, 'The Art to Make Gatekeeper Positions ...' (2021), 541.
[13] See, most recently, Davis and Lande, 'Restoring the Legitimacy of Private Antitrust Enforcement' (2018), *University of Baltimore School of Law Legal Studies* Research Paper No. 2018–02.
[14] Some, on the contrary, seem to assume that private enforcement should be used to enhance the effectiveness of the DMA, but without giving details of how this idea this should reflect onto the shaping of private law remedies under the DMA. See, for instance, the position expressed by the Governments of France, Germany and the Netherlands: Wiggers and Struijlaart, 'Germany, France and the Netherlands call for a tougher Digital Markets Act' (2021).
[15] For a recent critical assessment, Ullrich, 'Private Enforcement of the EU Rules on Competition – Nullity Neglegted' (2021), 52 *IIC*, 606 ff.

D. Private enforcement of the DMA? Some common issues and principles

or in the gatekeeper's general terms and conditions, based on general contract law and/or tort law principles.

In fact, a common equation in Member States' domestic contract law is that illegality (meaning here violating mandatory rules or being contrary to public policy or good morals) makes a contract null and void. This equation may have become more nuanced over time, due to efforts to fine-tune the remedies available in the case of contracts "tainted with illegality"[16].

Nonetheless, a legal provision explicitly stating that contractual arrangements in violation of DMA are void is not necessary. In the neighbouring area of EU antitrust law, it has been long accepted that not only contractual arrangements contrary to Art. 101 TFEU, but also those contrary to Art. 102 TFEU (abuse of a dominant position) can be null and void, although the former – unlike Art. 101(2) TFEU – does not provide for such invalidity[17].

It has also been long recognized in EU antitrust law that national courts may declare agreements that violate Art. 101 or 102 TFUE to be null and void, with no need for a previous finding of infringement by the European Commission. The prohibitions contained in Art. 101 and 102 TFEU are, in fact, directly applicable. The same conclusion, therefore, applies to the prohibitions contained in the DMA, in so far as they are self-executing, or have been further specified by the European Commission in its regulatory dialogue with gatekeepers.

This being clarified, the problem arises of how such invalidity should work in detail, absent any explicit indications within the DMA. The matter is, to a large extent, left to Member States' domestic laws.

Notwithstanding the existing differences between national regimes, it seems quite obvious that the rules governing such invalidity should be construed in a way that is consistent with the objectives and the context of the DMA. This is also what has happened so far, at least to some extent, with contract invalidity in EU competition law.

In this respect relevant issues include, among others: severability, ex tunc and ex nunc effect, standing of third parties, and follow-on transactions.

1. The gatekeeper's counterpart usually has an interest in preserving the contractual relationship, and might be prevented from challenging clauses in violation of the DMA should they put the entire contract at risk. Also, the effectiveness of the relevant EU law prohibitions is not put into question, if the contract is not voided in its entirety. Severability should therefore be the preferred option.

In the same logic, one should consider the possibility of reducing the substance of contractual clauses setting prices, duration and other quantities. This mechanism is known in German contract law as *geltungserhaltende Reduktion*, but is not generally accepted in all Member States (for example, not in Italy).

2. The invalidity of contracts contrary to public order generally has an ex tunc effect. However, in the context of the DMA, a contractual provision can be legal at the onset, and become illegal at a later point of time, when, for instance, the CPS provider is designated as a gatekeeper, a new CPS is added to the list, or a new prohibition is introduced etc. Insofar, one could say that the invalidity deriving from a violation of the DMA may under certain circumstances have an ex nunc effect.

---

[16] Cerchia, *A Comparative Viewpoint on Illegal Contracts: in Favour of Flexibility and Proportionality* (2021), 21 *Global Jurist*, 447 ff.

[17] CJEU, Case C-66/86, 11.4.1989, *Ahmed Saeed Flugreisen et al. v Zentrale zur Bekämpfung Unlauteren Wettbewerbs*, ECLI:EU:C:1989:140, para. 45: 'judicial authorities must … rule, where appropriate, that the agreement is void on the basis … of their national legislation'.

79   To contract law specialists, the idea of invalidity deriving from supervening circumstances could appear somehow problematic, and might appear difficult to reconcile with traditional contract law categories.

80   The very same idea, however, is well accepted in antitrust law. For instance, a company may increase its market share over time and thus be confronted at some point with the inapplicability of a block exemption under Art. 101(3) TFEU to agreements, that had till then been exempted.

81   On this point, a difference from antitrust law could be that under the DMA most (although not all) supervening circumstances, which can turn a gatekeeper's legal practice into an illegal one, require the European Commission to adopt a corresponding formal act.

82   On the other hand, it could also be the case that a contractual provision, that violates the DMA at the onset, at some point becomes legal. Which poses an issue of qualification under contract law and, especially, with respect to invalidity.

3. In the same vein, one can observe that a contractual provision may result in a prohibited practice not in itself, but in combination with technical limitations, business practices or behaviour of any other nature (see Art. 11(1) DMA).

83   Again, it may not be obvious to contract law specialists that the invalidity of contractual clauses could depend, to such an extent, on external circumstances.

4. In antitrust law, whether third parties should be entitled to challenge the validity of an anti-competitive agreement is still controversial, but is, again, a matter of domestic law.

84   With respect to the DMA, the rationale of the prohibitions contained in Art. 5 and 6 suggests that some sort of remedy, ensuring the unenforceability of illegal contract clauses, should be made available to third parties as well.

85   This especially applies to the prohibitions that are mainly aimed at preventing market foreclosure to the detriment of competitors.

86   It could also apply, at a closer look, to exploitative practices, which are those that cause an immediate detriment to business users and/or end users. Such practices may affect competitors as well, although in a less obvious way, insofar as they drain financial resources from the gatekeeper's clients, thereby reinforcing the gatekeeper's position on the market and preventing its clients from possibly investing part of their resources for alternative uses.

87   In such cases, the appropriate remedy may be found, depending on the peculiarities of each Member State's domestic law, in contract law (standing to challenge the validity of the illegal contract clause) and/or tort law (as with an injunction[18] intended to prevent the illegal clause from being executed).

5. A controversial issue in competition law is how the invalidity of an anti-competitive agreement affects follow-on transactions.

88   Follow-on transactions are those entered into by a company's participation in an anti-competitive agreement (for instance, a horizontal price cartel) with a third party (typically, a client), and somehow replicating the contents of the anti-competitive agreement (in the aforementioned example, by setting prices at a level agreed upon by the cartelists).

89   In the context of the DMA, posing this issue may make little sense. For reasons of legal certainty, the list of prohibited practices in Art. 5 and 6 DMA is meant to be exhaustive. As a consequence, follow-on transactions, including those entered into with end-users, can be deemed in violation of the DMA and thus declared invalid, only if

---

[18] Schweitzer, 'The Art to Make Gatekeeper Positions …' (2021), 541.

D. Private enforcement of the DMA? Some common issues and principles

they fit into one or another category of prohibited practices, and not just because their contents somehow reflect that of an 'upstream' illegal practice.

III. 'Sword-actions'

Competition law can also be invoked as a 'sword', in the form of damage actions and, more generally, as a way to seek monetary compensation or injunctive relief.

Absent any explicit indications in Art. 101 and 102 TFEU and long before Directive 2014/104/EU on antitrust damages was enacted, the European Court of Justice decided that antitrust infringements can give rise to damage actions under Member States' domestic tort law, given the EU law principles of direct applicability and effectiveness[19]. The same, in principle, applies to the DMA[20].

Should such actions ever occur in the context of the DMA, it will most likely be what can be called 'follow-on actions', that is private actions based on a previous infringement decision made by the European Commission.

As in antitrust matters, infringement decisions made by the European Commission under the DMA are also to be deemed binding on national courts, for the sake of legal certainty and due to the obligation of sincere cooperation resting on national courts[21]. As a consequence, the plaintiff would be basically be left to prove only causation and actual damages.

Also stand-alone actions are permitted under the DMA, at least in principle, although they are unlikely to occur. This applies to both the prohibitions of the DMA that are directly applicable (Art. 5 DMA) and those that have been further specified by the Commission (Art. 6 DMA). Both are, in fact, directly applicable to EU law.

Unlike in antitrust law, and in the context of damage actions based on the DMA, there should be no room for an 'unclean hands' defense. In antitrust law, the party of an anti-competitive agreement may seek damages from its counterpart only under certain conditions, namely when the agreement has been unilaterally imposed by the defendant[22]. Under the DMA, instead, only the gatekeeper is held responsible and can be sanctioned by the European Commission for violations of Art. 5 and 6, under the assumption that contractual arrangements violating the DMA are imposed by the gatekeeper on business as well as end users.

No matter whether follow-on or stand-alone actions, it should be further considered that in the domain of competition law, the antitrust damages directive 2014/104/EU and its relative soft law lays down principles, rules and presumptions that could, at least to some degree, be extended by means of interpretation to damage actions brought under the DMA.

---

[19] Most prominently, CJEU, Case C-453/99, 20.9.2001, *Courage v Crehan Ltd*, ECLI:EU:C:465, para. 26.
[20] Nonetheless, G. Monti, 'The Digital Markets Act Institutional Design and Suggestions for Improvement' (2021), 11 and Podszun, Bongartz and Langestein, 'The Digital Market Act ...' (2021), 66, suggest that the DMA should also clarify that infringements of Art. 5 and 6 DMA can give rise to damage actions.
[21] CJEU, Case C-234/89, 28.2.1991, *Delimitis v. Henninger Bräu AG*, ECLI:EU:C:1991:9, para. 47 and CJEU, Case C-344/98, 14.12.2000, *Masterfood Ltd v HB Ice Cream Ltd*, ECLI:EU:C:2000:689, para. 56 e 57. The binding effect of infringement decisions adopted by the European Commission has been further specified in Art. 16 Regulation (EU) No 1/2003, and Art. 9 Directive 2014/104/EU later extended it to infringement decisions adopted by national competition authorities.
[22] CJEU, Case C-453/99, 20.9.2001, *Courage v Crehan Ltd*, ECLI:EU:C:465, para. 31 and 32.

Bibliography

Cristina Caffarra and Fiona Scott Morton, 'The European Commission Digital Markets Act: A translation' (2021), available at <https://voxeu.org/Art./european-commission-digital-markets-acttranslation> accessed on 15 December 2022.

Rossella Esther Cerchia, 'A Comparative Viewpoint on Illegal Contracts: In Favor of Flexibility and Proportionality' (2021), 21 *Global Jurist*, 447–479.

Filomena Chirico, 'Digital Markets Act: A Regulatory Perspective' (2021), 12 *JECLP*, 493–499.

Josh P. Davis and Robert H. Lande, 'Restoring the Legitimacy of Private Antitrust Enforcement (May 3, 2017). A Report to the 45th President (American Antitrust Institute, 2017 Forthcoming)' (2018), *University of Baltimore School of Law Legal Studies* Research Paper No. 2018–02, available at <https://ssrn.com/abstract=2962579> accessed on 15 December 2022.

Alexandre de Streel *et al.*, 'The European Proposal for a Digital Markets Act. A First Assessment' (2021), Centre on Regulation in Europe, Brussels, 1–27.

Florian Heimann, 'The Digital Markets Act – We gonna catch 'em all?' (2022), *Kluwer Competition Law Blog*.

Giorgio Monti, 'The Digital Markets Act Institutional Design and Suggestions for Improvement' (2021), TILEC Discussion Paper No. 2021–04, available <https://ssrn.com/abstract=3797730> accessed on 15 December 2022.

Nicholas Petit, 'The Proposed Digital Markets Act (DMA): A Legal and Policy Review' (2021), 12 *JECLP*, 529–541.

Rupprecht Podszun, Philipp Bongartz and Sarah Langestein, 'Proposals on how to Improve the Digital Markets Act' (2021), available at <https://ssrn.com/abstract=3788571> accessed on 15 December 2022.

Rupprecht Podszun, Philipp Bongartz and Sarah Langestein, 'The Digital Market Act: Moving from Competition Law to Regulation for Large Gatekeepers' (2021), *EuCML*, 60–67.

Heike Schweitzer, 'The Art to Make Gatekeeper Positions Contestable and the Challenge to Know What is Fair: A Discussion of the Digital Markets Act Proposal' (2021), *ZEuP*, 503–543.

Heike Schweitzer and Kai Woeste, 'Der 'Private Attorney General': Ein Modell für die private Rechtsdurchsetzung des Marktordnungsrechts?' (2020), available at <https://ssrn.com/abstract=3695965> accessed on 15 December 2022.

Hans Ullrich, 'Private Enforcement of the EU Rules on Competition – Nullity Neglegted' (2021), 52 *IIC*, 606–635.

Marc Wiggers and Robin Struijlaart, 'Germany, France and the Netherlands call for a tougher Digital Markets Act' (2021), *Kluwer Competition Law Blog*.

Anne Witt, 'Platform Regulation in Europe – Per se Rules to the Rescue' (2022), forthcoming in *JCLE*, currently available at <https://ssrn.com/abstract=4017504> accessed on 15 December 2022.

III.
RESHAPING CONTRACTS IN THE DIGITAL AGE

Digital Content Regulation as Building Block of the Private Law Harmonization

A. Introductory Remarks 1
B. Conventional and Unconventional Tendencies 3
   I. Conventional Tendencies – Remedies 4
   II. Unconventional Tendencies – Deviating from contract types, expansive tendency, replacing market standards 5
C. Progress Factors – Gain Points 8
   I. Tackling the Digital Age – Specific Common Market Relevance 9
   II. "Issue-related approach" as a Tool to Focus Rules 12
   III. Comprehensive Legislation 14
D. Concerns – Pain Points 17
   I. Tendency towards Mandatory Legislation 18
   II. Breaking the Chains of Consumer Protection? 20
   III. The Issue of Multi-Layerism 22
   IV. The Mystery of Maximum Harmonization 28
   V. The Procedural Gap 29
E. Concluding Remarks 32
   Bibliography 32

A. Introductory Remarks

By the *Digital Content Directive*[1] (DCD) – in part complemented by the *Sale of Goods Directive* (SGD)[2] – the EU regulates the law of contracts, as far as it relates to digital content. On the one hand, these two directives seem to mark another major step towards the harmonization of private law. On the other hand, however, the directives are not based on a comprehensive overall conception, but rather fit into the EU's "salami tactics" approach on contract law harmonization. Significant previous steps of these "salami tactics" endeavors include numerous acts of consumer protection (introducing withdrawal rights; information requirements; mandatory rules)[3] and the *Consumer Sales Directive*[4]. The *Draft Common Frame of Reference*[5] – a comprehensive model code developed as an academic project – has not been put into legal force. It is sometimes called a toolbox and it may serve as a source of inspiration but does not have the authoritative status of a binding law. The same applies to the *Common European Sales Law*[6], which was

---

[1] Directive (EU) 2019/770 of the European Parliament and of the Council of 20 May 2019 on certain aspects concerning contracts for the supply of digital content and digital services.
[2] Directive (EU) 2019/771 of the European Parliament and of the Council of 20 May 2019 on certain aspects concerning contracts for the sale of goods, amending Regulation (EU) 2017/2394 and Directive 2009/22/EC, and repealing Directive 1999/44/EC.
[3] See, in particular, Directive 2011/83/EU of the European Parliament and of the Council of 25 October 2011 on consumer rights, amending Council Directive 93/13/EEC and Directive 1999/44/EC of the European Parliament and of the Council and repealing Council Directive 85/577/EEC and Directive 97/7/EC of the European Parliament and of the Council. Cf. those Directives amended or repealed by the aformentioned Directive.
[4] Directive 1999/44/EC of the European Parliament and of the Council of 25 May 1999 on certain aspects of the sale of consumer goods and associated guarantees (Note: No longer in force, repealed by the SGD).
[5] V. Bar et al., *Principles, Definitions and Model Rules of European Private Law. Draft Common Frame of Reference (DCFR)* (2009).
[6] See European Commission, *Communication from the commission to the European Parliament, the Council, the European Economic and Social Committee and the Committee of the Regions. A common European Sales Law to Facilitate Cross-Border Transactions in the Single Market*, 11 October 2011,

developed on behalf of the EU, intended to act as a second, uniform opt-in regime alongside national sales laws – but it also never entered into force.

2   In any case, the DCD and the SGD introduce a new phase of harmonization that shows significant conventional and unconventional tendencies (II.) and some progress factors (III.), but they also raise some serious concerns (IV.).

B. Conventional and Unconventional Tendencies

3   Taking a closer look at the DCD and SGD-provisions, one may notice some conventional and some unconventional tendencies.

I. Conventional Tendencies – Remedies

4   With regard to remedies, the directives' approach is quite conventional. Art. 13–16 DCD as well as SGD provide for conventional legal remedies for irregularity in performance (*Leistungsstörungsrecht*), namely supplementary performance, reduction of price and termination of contract.[7] Also in line with earlier EU legislation, the regulations once again leave wide gaps regarding the design of the remedies in detail.[8] There is, for example, still no regulation on compensation for damages; instead, national rules apply (cf. Art. 3 (10) and recital 73 DCD as well as Art. 3 (6) and recital 18 SGD).[9]

II. Unconventional Tendencies – Deviating from contract types, expansive tendency, replacing market standards

5   On the unconventional side, one may observe a complete decoupling from the traditional structure of contract law systems in so far as the DCD adopts a "subject-matter-based" ("digital-feature-based") rather than a "contract-types-based" approach: The application of the directive is to be determined – in contrast to traditional contract law – predominantly with regard to the quality of the subject matter of the contract, and not with regard to the character of the respective main performance obligations, cf. Art. 3 (1)-(3) DCD.[10]

6   Also in a rather unconventional manner, the DCD shows a clearly expansive tendency. By including contracts with a merely partially digital character, the new rules extend to a large number of everyday items. They do not only apply to the sales-based download of software or video and music files, but also to the rent or purchase of smartphones and laptops or "smart" cars, refrigerators, toothbrushes etc.[11] It goes without saying that the dynamic process of digitalization has an obvious tendency to increase the scope of digital content law ever further (cf. "internet of things").

COM(2011)636 final; European Commission, *Proposal for a regulation of the European Parliament and of the Council on a Common European Sales Law*, 11 October 2011, COM/2011/635 final.

[7] For details Gsell, 'Rechtsbehelfe bei Vertragswidrigkeit in den Richtlinienvorschlägen zum Fernabsatz von Waren und zur Bereitstellung digitaler Inhalte' in Artz and Gsell (eds), *Verbrauchervertragsrecht und digitaler Binnenmarkt* (2018) 143 (146–160).

[8] Schulze, in: Schulze and Staudenmayer (eds), *EU Digital Law* (2020) Art. 1 DCD, mn. 25-33.

[9] Schulze, in: Schulze and Staudenmayer (eds), *EU Digital Law* (2020) Art. 1 DCD, mn. 28.

[10] Gansmeier and Kochendörfer, 'Digitales Vertragsrecht – Anwendungssystematik, Regelungsprinzipien und schuldrechtliche Integration der §§ 327 ff. BGB' (2022) 8 *ZfPW*, 1 (2 and 5).

[11] Schulze, 'Die Digitale Inhalte Richtlinie – Innovation und Kontinuität im europäischen Vertragsrecht' (2019) 27 *ZEuP*, 695 (701 seq.).

Moreover, while traditional contract law tends to tie in with market standards and refers to such standards, the DCD and the SGD aim at setting market standards. This holds true, in particular, for the provisions on follow-up-duties of businesses (traders) concerning the updating of digital goods (Art. 7 (d), Art. 8 (2) DCD, Art. 7 (3) SGD). Even though the context is somewhat vague, the requirements are inclined to replace the mere reference to market standards with mandatory standards of law which will eventually have to be spelled out by the judiciary.

C. Progress Factors – Gain Points

The new phase of harmonization introduced by the adoption of the DCD and the SGD shows some progress factors and gain points.

I. Tackling the Digital Age – Specific Common Market Relevance

With "digital contents", the directives address matters of specific relevance to the Common Market. In doing so, they also tackle several "big issues of our time", e.g. "paying with data" and – quite generally – the specifics of digital contents and services in the private law context.[12]

The digital form of the contractual subject matter serves as a reference point for the justification of the specific Common Market relevance[13] because specific digital features render digital content predestined for cross-border exchange – especially via online distribution. Those digital features include that digital goods can be copied, reproduced, changed and transferred quickly and largely without effort (e.g. video or music files).[14] At the same time, digital goods are dependent on machines that read them and are therefore particularly sensitive to disruption and frequently threatened by rapid technological "overhaul".[15]

Even more clearly than in relation to digital goods, the Common Market relevance becomes visible in relation to digital marketing and e-commerce, which naturally overcome traditional spatial constraints. Therefore, harmonized rules on distance marketing[16], e-commerce[17] and consumer sales[18] predate the DCD. The marginal "Common-Market-value" of the DCD lies in its objective to overcome the limitations of traditional sales contracts and adapting the harmonized body of law to the specific characteristics of digital features.

---

[12] Staudenmayer, 'Digitale Verträge: Die Richtlinienvorschläge der Europäischen Kommission' (2016) 24 ZEuP, 801 (803–805).

[13] On the criterion of specific Common Market relevance and its critical function for establishing EU competency see with more detail Grigoleit, 'Abstraktion und Willensmängel – Die Anfechtbarkeit des Verfügungsgeschäfts' (1999) 199 AcP, 354 (364–377).

[14] Wendlandt, 'Dogmatische Grundlagen des Rechts der Digitalisierung' in Weller and Wendland (eds), Digital Single Market (2019), 71 (73 and 115).

[15] Gansmeier and Kochendörfer, 'Digitales Vertragsrecht – Anwendungssystematik, Regelungsprinzipien und schuldrechtliche Integration der §§ 327 ff. BGB' (2022) 8 ZfPW, 1 (6).

[16] Directive 2002/65/EC of the European Parliament and of the Council of 23 September 2002 concerning the distance marketing of consumer financial services and amending Council Directive 90/619/EEC and Directives 97/7/EC and 98/27/EC.

[17] Directive 2000/31/EC of the European Parliament and of the Council of 8 June 2000 on certain legal aspects of information society services, in particular electronic commerce, in the Internal Market ('Directive on electronic commerce').

[18] See above, fn. 4.

II. "Issue-related approach" as a Tool to Focus Rules

12 The digital-feature-related-approach and the neglect of the traditional order of contract types (above II.2.) may open up a specific harmonization potential. On the grounds of the issue-related-approach, there is no need to level national differences in contract type related doctrines because these are no longer a relevant point of reference.[19] Also, the test of applicability appears to be relatively straightforward ("digital feature" or "no digital feature"?) – if one for the moment ignores the complexities of multi-layerism (below IV.3).

13 In addition, the digital-feature-related-approach – by decoupling "digital rules" from contract types – serves to improve the legal focus and potentially also the legal quality of the rules in question. The respective provisions can be tailored to the requirements of digital features without having to fit for other fact patterns according to the demands of abstract contract classifications. A good example of such a tailoring is the duty to update digital contents that is set out in Art. 8 (2) DCD, Art. 7 (3) SGD. By its legislative foundation and the judicial specifications to be expected, the duty to update can be shaped in accordance with the technical and market-wise conditions of digital features.

III. Comprehensive Legislation

14 To tackle digitalization, the EU-legislation envisages a comprehensive approach reaching beyond the tools of traditional private law. While the two directives may be seen as providing an impulse for the fundamental legal management of Big Data issues, an impulse that may reach beyond the details of the DCD and the SGD, the comprehensive approach manifests itself in the EU-legislative context of the two directives: The EU pursues to address digital issues from a multidimensional perspective including civil law (DCD, SGD), competition and antitrust law (Digital Services Act[20] and Digital Markets Act[21]), data protection law (General Data Protection Regulation[22]) and the law pertaining to artificial intelligence (e.g. AI Act, AI Liability Directive and the "AI-Modernization" of the Product Liability Directive[23]).

15 While this approach is plausible in the abstract, the reforms so far fail to actually leverage significant synergies, as there is no sufficient linkage and not enough coherence

---

[19] Staudenmayer, 'Digitale Verträge: Die Richtlinienvorschläge der Europäischen Kommission' (2016) 24 ZEuP, 801 (805).

[20] European Commission, *Proposal for a Regulation of the European Parliament and of the Council on a Single Market For Digital Services (Digital Services Act) and amending Directive 2000/31/EC*, 15 December 2020, COM(2020)825 final.

[21] Regulation (EU) 2022/1925 of the European Parliament and of the Council of 14 September 2022 on contestable and fair markets in the digital sector and amending Directives (EU) 2019/1937 and (EU) 2020/1828 (Digital Markets Act) (Text with EEA relevance).

[22] See the fundamental and comprehensive approach in Regulation (EU) 2016/679 of the European Parliament and of the Council of 27 April 2016 on the protection of natural persons with regard to the processing of personal data and on the free movement of such data, and repealing Directive 95/46/EC (General Data Protection Regulation).

[23] See e.g. European Commission, *Proposal for a Regulation of the European Parliament and of the Council laying down harmonised rules on artificial intelligence (Artificial Intelligence Act) and amending certain Union legislative Acts*, 22 April 2022, COM(2021)206 final; European Commission, *Proposal for a Directive of the European Parliament and of the Council on adapting non-contractual civil liability rules to artificial intelligence (AI Liability Directive)*, 28 September 2022, COM(2022)496 final; European Commission, *Proposal for a Directive of the European Parliament and of the Council on liability for defective products*, 25 March 2022, COM(2022)495 final.

between the different regulatory approaches and tools.²⁴ For example, the DCD focuses on the retail level – the entity that must provide the digital product. The effects on the manufacturing level are only briefly touched and remain obscure (Art. 20 DCD on redress), even though generally only the manufacturer controls the quality of the digital content. Moreover, there is still no legal certainty as to the relative – and meaningful – scope of private enforcement and public enforcement, private law and public law etc.

A worthwhile goal for the future development should therefore be a greater focus on sanctions and fine-tuning. In this context, fine-tuning means that private law sanctions need to be addressed more comprehensively and at the same time with more specificity, *inter alia* regarding damages, statutes of limitation, preclusion, estoppel, etc.²⁵ Regarding sanctions, the potential of private enforcement should be thoroughly compared with the potential of public enforcement, for example in the context of consumer protection, as a satisfactory degree of harmonization can only be achieved if the sanctions context is addressed comprehensively.²⁶

D. Concerns – Pain Points

Besides the progress factors, the digital content regulation activates and stresses some of the (traditional) pain points of EU private law regulation.

I. Tendency towards Mandatory Legislation

EU private law legislation has so far had a tendency towards mandatory regulation. This tendency is upheld by the recent acts of digital content regulation. Stipulations on quality deviations or deficiencies of digital goods ("negative supply agreement", "*negative Beschaffenheitsvereinbarung*"), for instance, are permissible (i.e.: suspend liability) only under quite prohibitive formal requirements (cf. Art. 8 (5) DCD, Art. 7 (5) SGD).²⁷ The resulting restrictions create an undue obstacle to free trade and jeopardize legal certainty. Even B2B-contracts are subjected to mandatory provisions, as exemplified by the right of redress laid down in Art. 20 DCD. In addition, "spillover effects" are likely, as legal limitations to contractual stipulations on the B2C-level necessarily also limit the practical leeway of B2B-stipulations.

To a certain extent, the tendency of EU-regulation towards mandatory regulation may be referred to and justified by the general ideas of consumer protection. However, it is conspicuous that the utilization of mandatory provision is also – and arguably: foremost – a tool to bolster harmonizing effects:²⁸ The principle of freedom of contracts

---

²⁴ Critically Lehmann, 'Binnenkohärenz des europäischen Verbrauchervertragsrechts' in: Artz and Gsell (eds), *Verbrauchervertragsrecht und digitaler Binnenmarkt* (2018) 1 (19 seq.); Riehm, 'Regelungsbereich und Harmonisierungsintensität des Richtlinienentwurfs zum Waren-Fernabsatz' in: Artz and Gsell (eds), *Verbrauchervertragsrecht und digitaler Binnenmarkt* (2018) 73 (76–79).

²⁵ In more detail Grigoleit, 'Der Verbraucheracquis und die Entwicklung des Europäischen Privatrechts' (2010) 210 *AcP*, 354 (380–385).

²⁶ Adressing the issue from a general perspective Poelzig, *Normdurchsetzung durch Privatrecht* (2012), 568 seq.

²⁷ Riehm and Abold, 'Rechtsbehelfe von Verbrauchern bei Verträgen über digitale Produkte' (2021) CR, 530 (534 seq.); Gsell, 'Informationspflichten im Europäischen Verbraucherrecht' (2022) 8 ZfPW, 130 (144–149); Rachlitz, Kochendörfer and Gansmeier, 'Mangelbegriff und Beschaffenheitsvereinbarung' (2022) 77 JZ, 705 (705 seq.).

²⁸ For the issues concerning mandatory rules and harmonization Grigoleit, 'Der Verbraucheracquis und die Entwicklung des Europäischen Privatrechts' (2010) 210 *AcP*, 354 (412 seq.); Grigoleit, 'Mandatory Law –

naturally gives rise to a variety of contractual and therefore legal norms. Mandatory laws set limits to this variety and thereby may be expected to strengthen harmonization. However, vague expectations of promoting harmonization do not necessarily justify any restriction on contractual freedom. The critical test should be whether the marginal value of the harmonization effect (by mandatory rules) justifies the marginal loss of contractual freedom. It is, for example, more than doubtful if the restrictions on negative supply agreements can pass this test.

II. Breaking the Chains of Consumer Protection?

20   For competency reasons, the recent reforms have linked the idea of regulating digital products with consumer protection goals. For some time, the EU legislator has presumed to have a stable basis of competency in contract law with respect to consumer protection.[29] Furthermore, there is a (reliable) political expectation that consumer protection is always easy to sell to the public – regardless of the concrete merits of the legislative product.

21   However, the limitation of digital content regulation to B2C-contracts *is not compelling* (in principle), if and because digital features of goods, i.e.: *specific kinds of products*, provide for a specific relevance to the Common Market. This specific nexus between digital goods and the Common Market is a crucial premise of the reform (cf. recital 1 and 4 DCD and above III.1.). The reasons for the nexus are predominantly rooted in the quality of the goods and not in the inequality of the parties. The digital content regulation may thus well be the nucleus of EU-contract-law-legislation beyond the scope of consumer contract law.

III. The Issue of Multi-Layerism

22   Due to the multi-level system of the EU, EU regulation "naturally" produces additional layers of law that need to be coordinated in the course of adjudication. The "multi-layerism" caused by EU contract law legislation has always raised serious complexity concerns.

23   Within the scope of digital content regulation, there are numerous potentially overlapping layers of law that must be considered in the course of resolving legal issues.[30] To mention some of those potentially overlapping layers: general contract law (mainly national), general consumer contract law (mainly EU-rooted), the law of sales (EU-rooted and national), the law of "other types" of contracts (mainly national), the law of remedies (EU-rooted and national), tort law (mainly national), the law of restitution (mainly national) and, as of lately, also the rules of digital content law (EU-rooted).

Specific regulation in European Private Law', in: Basedow et al. (eds), *Max Planck Encyclopedia of European Private Law* (2012).

[29] Which is debatable, see the reservation of positive effects on "the establishment and functioning of the internal market" in Art. 114, 169 TFEU. See Krebber, in: Calliess and Ruffert (eds), *EUV/AEUV* (2022) Art. 169, mn. 18. On the position of the author Grigoleit, 'Der Verbraucheracquis und die Entwicklung des Europäischen Privatrechts (2010) 210 AcP, 354 (372–374).

[30] For the complexity concerning the implementation of the DCD into national law Riehm, 'Regelungsbereich und Harmonisierungsintensität des Richtlinienentwurfs zum Waren-Fernabsatz' in: Artz and Gsell (eds), *Verbrauchervertragsrecht und digitaler Binnenmarkt* (2018), 73 (79 seq.); Gansmeier and Kochendörfer, 'Digitales Vertragsrecht – Anwendungssystematik, Regelungsprinzipien und schuldrechtliche Integration der §§ 327 ff. BGB' (2022) 8 ZfPW, 1 (19–38).

D. Concerns – Pain Points

The *multi-layerism* under the digital content regulation is particularly critical because it does not only result from the sheer number of layers but also from the hybrid character – digital and non-digital – of some of the goods covered (e.g. think of the rent of a "smart" refrigerator). In line with the hybrid character of such goods, Art. 3 (6) DCD provides that different sets of rules apply to the digital and non-digital elements of such a contract. 24

In spite of the obviousness of *multi-layerism*, not even the demarcation issues between the simultaneously enacted DCD and SGD have been resolved. The areas of application of the DCD and the SGD are difficult to delineate legally (due to unclear legal terms, e.g. "goods with digital elements" according to Art. 2 (5) b SGD) and sometimes also as a practical matter (due to the close interlocking of digital and non-digital elements of products).[31] This leads to considerable uncertainty in the context of divergent provisions. As an example, one may have a look at the different regulations of compensation for use (cf. under German law Sec. 346 et seq. vs. Sec. 327o et seq. German Civil Code (BGB)).[32] 25

One may add that the neglect of contract types by the "digital-layer" (cf. above II.2. and III.2.) ignores the fact that the traditional contract law regimes take, by their reference to different types of contracts, account of diverse party interests (e.g. concerning the termination of contract or contract reversal in contexts of continuing obligations vs. single exchange of services). Such specifications tend to get lost under the new "digital layer". 26

While the complexity of EU *multi-layerism* has always been significant, the digital content regulation adds to the phenomenon of "multi-layerism" and exacerbates it significantly. Complexity raises issues of transaction costs in the form of legal enforcement costs. And complexity ultimately calls into question the goal of harmonization. 27

IV. The Mystery of Maximum Harmonization

The principle of maximum harmonization and the far-reaching scope of the digital content regulation does not overcome their fragmentary character (see above: *multi-layerism*). The result is that maximum or "full" harmonization – as pursued by the digital content regulation – remains a mystery. Evidently, the maximum harmonization principle does not cover a legal relationship as a whole, but addresses only certain aspects of it, like its formation, validity, remedies, details of sales law or tort law (cf. Art. 3 (10) DCD, Art. 3 (6) SGD). Any aspired "exhaustive" quality of "fully" harmonized rules is always relative and needs to be specified in its dimension (full in which respect?). Therefore, from the outset, parties can only partially rely on a uniform regulatory regime. Maximum harmonization is not a solution to *multi-layerism*, but rather another problem of it. "Full" harmonization will not actually cause fully uniform regimes.[33] 28

---

[31] For criterias of delimitation Gansmeier and Kochendörfer, 'Digitales Vertragsrecht – Anwendungssystematik, Regelungsprinzipien und schuldrechtliche Integration der §§ 327 ff. BGB' (2022) 8 *ZfPW*, 1 (7–16).

[32] Cf. Gansmeier and Kochendörfer, 'Leistungsstörungen im Kontext des Internet of Things. Zur Totallösung vom Paketvertrag nach § 327a Abs. 1 BGB' (2022) 2 *ZfDR*, 261 (274–284).

[33] Cf. Strasser, *Wege der Rechtsangleichung im Vertragsrecht: Vollharmonisierung, Mindestharmonisierung, optionales Instrument* (2014), 266–270 and 270–304 for a possible solution.

V. The Procedural Gap

29   Private law cannot work without an effective private law court system. It is obvious that developing a reliable structure of contract law greatly depends on a well-performing civil justice system. The judiciary carries out a crucial function with regard to fine-tuning contract law rules. The legislation – typically and sensibly – restrains itself to standards and quite abstract rules and thereby refers the fine-tuning to the courts who are confronted with the infinite variety of cases and better suited to define practicable and timely solutions to concrete legal problems.

30   In the context of the digital content legislation, the function of the judiciary is particularly crucial, due to the wide-ranging encroachment on core areas of private law, the principle of maximum harmonization, the relevance of vague standards and the extreme complexity resulting from the *multi-layerism* issue (above IV.3.). It follows that the realization of harmonizing effects greatly depends upon a *successful judicial processing* of the digital content regulation.

31   However, the procedural gap that is characteristic for the EU legal system will significantly impair the judicial specification of the reformed digital content law: The national court systems may professionally process the reform provisions but they are not suitable to effectively implement the objectives of harmonization. The ECJ cannot reliably step in. According to Art. 267 TFEU (preliminary ruling procedure), the ECJ is only responsible for construing EU law, but not for applying it. Its task basically consists of supplying legal opinions on abstract questions. It is therefore not within the ECJ's power to decide a concrete dispute and to develop all relevant norms pertaining to contract law disputes. Moreover, it is beyond the functions of the ECJ to interpret and apply national law which would be essential to comprehensively resolve the *multi-layerism* issues (above IV.3.). Finally, the ECJ lacks the institutional equipment to act as a competent appellate court for private law matters (no specialized expertise, insufficient manpower etc.).[34]

E. Concluding Remarks

32   The digital content regulation pursues important targets. From a general perspective, it is reasonable to address the issues of digital contracts specifically and with a comprehensive plan. However, the institutional background of the EU, the restraints, and intricacies of the multi-level system, greatly impede beneficial effects and may even create legal costs that well exceed any benefits. This critical assessment basically rests upon two issues: The tendency of the digital content legislation towards mandatory provisions and – foremost – the enormous complexity caused by the phenomenon of *multi-layerism*, the obscure and unparalleled interplay between numerous layers of EU-rooted and national laws. With a view to this interplay, the demand of maximum harmonization is an empty promise. Due to the procedural gap that is characteristic for the EU legal system, it is not very likely that the issues of *multi-layerism* can be resolved on the judicial level. Overall, the digital content regulation is another striking example for the proposition that contract law harmonization will not be achieved on the EU-level in a satisfactory

---

[34] In more detail on the procedural gap Strasser, *Wege der Rechtsangleichung im Vertragsrecht: Vollharmonisierung, Mindestharmonisierung, optionales Instrument* (2014), 252–259; Grigoleit, 'Der Verbraucheracquis und die Entwicklung des Europäischen Privatrechts' (2010) 210 AcP, 354 (388–391); Grigoleit, 'Against the Background of DCFR and CESL: Developing Quality Standards for Future Harmonization of European Contract Law', in: Universidade Católica Porto (ed), *A European Law of Obligations? The influence of the DCFR* (2015).

quality, unless the essential (and still lacking) background conditions will have been secured. Not even the magic of digital products will conjure up an operable contract law system against the demands of reason.

Bibliography

Johannes Gansmeier and Luca Kochendörfer, 'Digitales Vertragsrecht – Anwendungssystematik, Regelungsprinzipien und schuldrechtliche Integration der §§ 327 ff. BGB' (2022) 8 *ZfPW*, 1.

Johannes Gansmeier and Luca Kochendörfer, 'Leistungsstörungen im Kontext des Internet of Things. Zur Totallösung vom Paketvertrag nach § 327a Abs. 1 BGB' (2022) 2 *ZfDR*, 261.

Hans Christoph Grigoleit, 'Abstraktion und Willensmängel – Die Anfechtbarkeit des Verfügungsgeschäfts' (1999) 199 *AcP*, 354.

Hans Christoph Grigoleit, 'Against the Background of DCFR and CESL: Developing Quality Standards for Future Harmonization of European Contract Law', in: Universidade Católica Porto (ed), *A European Law of Obligations? The influence of the DCFR* (2015), available at SSRN: <http://ssrn.com/abstract=2636960>.

Hans Christoph Grigoleit, 'Mandatory Law – Specific regulation in European Private Law', in: Jürgen Basedow et al. (eds), *Max Planck Encyclopedia of European Private Law* (2012), available at SSRN: <http://ssrn.com/abstract=1950686>.

Hans Christoph Grigoleit, 'Der Verbraucheracquis und die Entwicklung des Europäischen Privatrechts' (2010) 210 *AcP*, 354.

Beate Gsell, 'Informationspflichten im Europäischen Verbraucherrecht' (2022) 8 *ZfPW*, 130.

Beate Gsell, 'Rechtsbehelfe bei Vertragswidrigkeit in den Richtlinienvorschlägen zum Fernabsatz von Waren und zur Bereitstellung digitaler Inhalte' in Artz and Gsell (eds), *Verbrauchervertragsrecht und digitaler Binnenmarkt* (2018) 143.

Sebastian Krebber, in: Christian Calliess and Matthias Ruffert (eds), *EUV/AEUV* (2022) Art. 169, mn. 18.

Matthias Lehmann, 'Binnenkohärenz des europäischen Verbrauchervertragsrechts' in: Markus Artz and Beate Gsell (eds), *Verbrauchervertragsrecht und digitaler Binnenmarkt* (2018) 1.

Dörte Poelzig, *Normdurchsetzung durch Privatrecht* (2012).

Richard Rachlitz, Luca Kochendörfer and Johannes Gansmeier, 'Mangelbegriff und Beschaffenheitsvereinbarung' (2022) 77 *JZ*, 705.

Thomas Riehm, 'Regelungsbereich und Harmonisierungsintensität des Richtlinienentwurfs zum Waren-Fernabsatz' in: Artz and Gsell (eds), *Verbrauchervertragsrecht und digitaler Binnenmarkt* (2018) 73.

Thomas Riehm and Metawi Adrian Abold, 'Rechtsbehelfe von Verbrauchern bei Verträgen über digitale Produkte' (2021) *CR*, 530.

Reiner Schulze, in: Reiner Schulze and Dirk Staudenmayer (eds), *EU Digital Law* (2020) Art. 1 DCD.

Reiner Schulze, 'Die Digitale Inhalte Richtlinie – Innovation und Kontinuität im europäischen Vertragsrecht' (2019) 27 *ZEuP*, 695.

Dirk Staudenmayer, 'Digitale Verträge: Die Richtlinienvorschläge der Europäischen Kommission' (2016) 24 *ZEuP*, 801.

Constanze Strasser, *Wege der Rechtsangleichung im Vertragsrecht: Vollharmonisierung, Mindestharmonisierung, optionales Instrument* (2014).

Christian von Bar et al., *Principles, Definitions and Model Rules of European Private Law. Draft Common Frame of Reference (DCFR)* (2009).

Matthias Wendland, 'Dogmatische Grundlagen des Rechts der Digitalisierung' in Weller and Wendland (eds), *Digital Single Market* (2019), 71.

Smart Contracts

A. The culture shock of 'code is law' 1
B. Smart contracts: Notion or definition? 4
C. The ELI project on blockchains and smart contracts 7
    I. Overview of the ELI project 7
    II. Legal relevance of transactions on a blockchain 8
    III. A typology of smart contracts 9
    IV. Smart contracts and consumer protection 10
    V. Duties to (re)code 12
D. Concluding remarks 14
    Bibliography 19

A. The culture shock of 'code is law'

After the first culture shock that computer code might be the new law and that computer programmers were to be the new 'oracles of the law', gradually it became apparent that this could only result in a chaotic anarchy where some would win, but most – especially those not initiated in the world of programming and not taking part in this 'brave new world' – would lose. A new elite – so the self-image of software developers – would arise, unfettered by the acquired wisdom to be found in centuries of law making by courts, legislatures and academic scholars. They would be a group of IT specialists not aimed at analysing human problems in a nuanced and balanced way and not looking for fair and just solutions, thus not following the old Roman saying: 'ius est ars boni et aequi', but leaving it to a by software created 'community' to decide. This was to have enormous consequences, as – at least until now – software is built in on a 'yes' or 'no' answer to questions, with no 'maybe's' or doubts. They could, so it was thought, develop a 'truth machine' and a 'single source of truth'.[1] Human relationships, however, are not binary, they are multi-coloured, facetious and show spectra of emotions and rationality. 1

Distributed Ledger Technology (DLT), with its decentralised storage of shared information, became the basis of blockchain technology, allowing for storing information immutably and pseudonymously while avoiding the 'double spending problem', thus doing away with the value decreasing possibility of copying data and instead creating unique data clusters ('blocks', 'coins' or 'tokens') which could represent money, objects and rights. The machinery driving blockchains became 'smart contracts': self-executing computer programmes. Smart contracts are the steam engines of this new Industrial Revolution. As long as all of this resembled more a computer game than 'real world' transactions, with real world (economic and social) consequences, any protentional legal implications were not immediately realised, let alone understood. But with the quick rise of Bitcoin as a cryptocurrency, followed by other blockchains with their own currency, the development of private blockchains next to public blockchains, this began to change drastically. 2

A now steadily growing legal literature, beginning case law and first legislative measures show attempts to begin controlling what was happening in the world of IT and 3

---

[1] Cf. T.J. de Graaf, From old to new: From internet to smart contracts and from people to smart contracts, Computer Law & Security Review 35 (2019) 105322, p. 2 and 5.

re-claim the precedence of the law over computer code.² In the following paragraphs I will briefly describe how within a long running project of the European Law Institute, after extensive and fundamental debate, proposals are made as to Principles which can be seen as a framework for further legal development by both courts and legislatures, both in European and globally.

B. Smart contracts: Notion or definition?

4   After the first shock was over, it began to become clear that 'smart contracts' were neither smart, nor contracts in the legal sense of the word. They were not thought to be smart, as they could not think for themselves, although in the meantime some smart contracts are no longer qualified as 'dumb', the latter meaning that they only react to a 'yes' or 'no' response, but driven by Artificial Intelligence (AI) and in that sense become more autonomous and hence 'smart'. Smart contracts are computer code that upon the answer 'yes' or 'no' to a particular question containing a condition precedent will yes or no proceed to the next step and thus may result in actions which could have an impact either inside or outside an algorithmic environment. By inside is meant that any transaction only has algorithmic consequences, outside meaning that consequences will follow in the real world. An example of an inside transaction is selling and buying cryptocurrencies, an example of the latter is the actual delivery of physical goods. That smart contracts cannot think like human beings might not be so certain anymore in the future, given the rapid development of Artificial Intelligence and quantum computing. How fast these developments will go is uncertain. However, what can be predicted with certainty is that the law will be running behind. For the time being we are trying to resolve the question whether a smart contract, or more generally: a transaction on a blockchain, can be seen as legally relevant, perhaps even as a binding agreement: contracts in the legal sense of the word. If the answer positive, then a whole spectrum of follow-up questions appears. What about the traditional distinction between formation, content and performance, the way we until looked at the average life cycle of a contract? Whenever a smart contract is used, formation and performance occur in a pre-coded way and frequently coincide. If they do not coincide, the smart contract will in any case execute automatically. So can there still be non-performance? Another problem concerns the legal consequences of nullities. In case a contract might be considered to be legally void, still the smart contract performed on a blockchain that creates immutable transactions. Void then no longer means void, but an entitlement and a corresponding duty to a reverse transaction. I can only mention here some of the more general questions which arise.

5   Of course there has been debate about such legal consequences, if any, of smart contracts, but as could be expected given the fairly recent development of this type of algorithm, no final conclusions have been reached yet. Furthermore, developments go on, as we now also see that smart contracts are in fact a type of Automated Decision Making (ADM), which next to so-called "dumb" smart contracts that only use pre-set criteria, includes smart contracts which use Artificial Intelligence (AI). ADM also covers automatic and autonomous (not necessarily 'smart') contracts (which may, again, be

---

² See, for example, Martin Hanzl, Handbuch Blockchain und Smart Contracts (Vienna: Linde Verlag, 2020) and Andrea Stazi, Smart Contracts and Comparative Law. A Western Perspective (Cham: Springer Nature and G. Giappichelli Editore, 2021).

using AI) and what is called 'profiling'.[3] It also matters who the actual or potential parties are: Business to Business (B2B), Business to Consumer (B2C), Business to Government (B2G) etc., and whether contracting takes place without direct human involvement, as can be found in Peer to Peer (P2P) or Machine to Machine (M2M) transactions.

It seems as if it is really difficult giving a clear and concise legal definition of smart contracts, because the definition implies an answer to the question of their legal effectiveness. Offering a notion rather than a definition, together with a typology of various types of smart contracts from a legal perspective, might be a more productive way of looking at smart contracts. Definitions are more characteristic of a dogmatic structure, which locks reality into pre-defined concepts, thus limiting our view. Definitions, particularly in an area as rapidly developing as IT, run the risk of over and under inclusion. You either regulate too much and create stumbling blocks for future development or you regulate poorly and new developments that should have been regulated are left unfettered. Offering a facade of legal certainty (even 'truth') is precisely what software developers do when they say that code is law: narrowing their view. This is a mistake that we should not make when trying to legally qualify and regulate smart contracts. A notion presents an open-ended description of a phenomenon, such that we all understand what we are talking about and leaving open that at the margins it might not be so clear what a smart contract precisely does. Because we are here at the borderline of (Internet) technology and law, we should also be prepared to describe the notion of smart contracts as a mixture of technical applications and legal constructs. It is the technology – whether we as lawyers like it, or not – that drives developments, including legal developments. So, first we should look at how smart contracts are defined from a technical point of view and then see whether this technical approach provides with a tool for legal development. We could still call this a definition, but it would in fact be the description of an open-ended notion. This is why the project of the European Law Institute (ELI) in Vienna on blockchains, smart contracts and consumer protection – which will be discussed in more detail in the next part of this contribution – gives the following description of a smart contract, as a: "Computer programme that upon the occurrence of pre-defined conditions runs automatically and executes pre-defined actions. A smart contract may or may not be intended to represent terms in a contract in law or be legally recognised. This definition considers smart contracts only in the context of distributed ledger systems. It is recognised that smart contracts are not restricted to distributed ledger systems and the term may have a different meaning in other contexts." When further on in this contribution the term 'smart contract' is used, it is this description that is referred to.

C. The ELI project on blockchains and smart contracts

I. Overview of the ELI project

Already in 2018 the European Law Institute in Vienna (an independent non-profit organisation established to initiate, conduct and facilitate research, make recommendations and provide practical guidance in the field of European legal development: in short aimed at improved law making in Europe) initiated a project to provide guid-

---

[3] As such ADM is particularly a privacy problem, but not only, as it may result in relationships which we would qualify as binding legal agreements. See on ADM: Guiding Principles for Automated Decision-Making in the EU, ELI Innovation Paper (Vienna: 2022). On algorithmic contracting see Lauren Henry Scholz, Algorithmic Contracts, Stanford Technology Law Review 2017, p. 128 ff.

ance regarding the legal aspects of blockchains and smart contracts. Later consumer protection aspects were added to be dealt with separately. Within the project team very fundamental discussions took place on the nature of transactions on a blockchain and how to approach smart contracts from a legal viewpoint. Could what happens in a coded environment at all be seen as legally relevant or should legal effects only be attached to 'off-chain' acts expressing a human will? Another question that was faced concerned consumer protection, or more general: the protection of weaker parties (for example employees or self-employed persons, private persons renting goods, micro, small or medium-sized enterprises, etc.). Given the absolute nature, so it was feared, of a transaction on a blockchain and the self-executing force of a smart contract, would not this result in taking away from weaker parties, and in particular consumers, any right to self-determination and protection? Or, to approach the question regarding the legal implications of blockchains and smart contracts from a different and more pragmatic angle, should we accept that the technology is there, is used in practice, that data is becoming an object of contract law (and perhaps even a form of property), is traded on markets and that blockchains and smart contracts are becoming a widely used tool that is replacing more traditional types of software? We do accept that a contract can be concluded by e-mail or by ticking a box on the website of a web shop. Why should it matter whether behind the mouse click there is old or new technology? That does absolutely not, however, imply that weaker parties should not be protected. On the contrary. Given the use of new technology and its absolute nature and because of the 'black box' nature of what happens behind what we see and do on a screen, weaker parties – and the project team focussed particularly on consumers – must not only be given the same protection on-chain as off-chain, but sometimes it must even be more. Once a consumer is considered to be bound by a transaction on a blockchain ('on-chain'), the tools for a consumer to be protected must be at least equivalent to any tools which the consumer has 'off-chain'. Finally the latter approach was chosen, considering that the new technology was already widely used, experimented with and rapidly further developed for example by adding Artificial Intelligence. Not accepting any legal consequences of the use of blockchain and smart contracts would have left such use unregulated and, in practice, would have resulted in leaving weaker parties unprotected. A consequence that was seen by all as undesirable and even unacceptable.

II. Legal relevance of transactions on a blockchain

8   The Principles, as proposed, now state the following. First of all, Principle 5, which is the centre piece of the general part of the Principles makes clear that a transaction on a blockchain could have legally relevant consequences. The Principle states: "The triggering of transactions, or of elements of transactions, performed on a blockchain may amount to an offer, acceptance or any other contractual declaration where, depending on the specific nature of the smart contract, such triggering can reasonably be understood as a declaration of will and is attributable to the relevant party." Principle 6 then builds on this by giving guidelines as to when an on-chain declaration of will becomes effective: "The point in time at which a contractual declaration as mentioned in Principle 5 becomes effective should be contractually agreed upon between the parties. In the absence of such agreement between the parties, an on-chain declaration of intent may only trigger legal consequences if (i) the recipient has actually received it or (ii) the transactions are securely stored in the blockchain (i.e. cannot vanish in an orphan block)." Almost unavoidably these Principles use technical language, some of which

has already been explained. To make clear what is meant within their framework, the Principles expressly describe what a 'transaction' on a 'blockchain' means and give the following definitions, which precede the actual text of the Principles themselves. First of all: What is a blockchain? This is defined as a "method of operating a distributed ledger. Data are typically stored in blocks organised in an append-only, sequential chain using cryptographic links to validate the integrity of historic data, with algorithmic validation of transaction logic and confirmation of the records by a defined mechanism for consensus among the nodes that process transactions." Nodes are, to put it in simple terms, computers, so a blockchain is a system where computers interact and the persons behind the nodes remain hidden. Secondly: What does the term transaction mean? This is defined as "an action on the blockchain which results in a change of state on the blockchain (eg a transfer of cryptocurrency comprising a reduction of the amount of cryptocurrency the owner of private key A can dispose of and an increase of the amount of cryptocurrency the owner of private key B can dispose of)." Cryptocurrency (or virtual currency) is a digital representation of value. It could be representing money, but also any other object, such as a car, or a right, such as the right of ownership. Cryptocurrency itself can also be seen as an object, as to which rights can be claimed. A private key could be explained – again in rather simplified terms – as your password to access files that are stored in a digitally protected and secured environment (a 'wallet') which others may approach by using the file's publicly known name (the 'public key').[4] Further, in these Principles the terms 'on-chain' and 'orphan block' are referred to. The Principles define 'on-chain', as this is a term that is essential to decide if rules on a coded environment apply or not. In the Principles 'on-chain' means "located, performed or run inside a blockchain system". Legally binding agreements can be laid down in coded language, but they only become 'on-chain' when they are embedded within a blockchain. The Principles, therefore, do not apply, at least not directly, to the legal implications of using computer code as such when contracting ('algorithmic contracts'), but it will be obvious that if, for example, consumers are given the same protection against the use of smart contracts 'on-chain' as 'off-chain', this will have a spill-over effect on 'off-chain' agreements in a coded format, either completely, in part or when it comes to execution and performance. The same policy considerations which apply to consumer protection 'on-chain', the most important of which being that the application of code is like a 'black box' of which consumers have no understanding let alone control, *mutatis mutandis* also applies to consumer transactions in other coded environments. And then, finally, the term 'orphan block'. That term is, like private and public key, also not defined, but refers to a block that is lost in the process.

III. A typology of smart contracts

Another centre-piece of the Principles concerns the offering of a typology as a guide to distinguish legally relevant from non-legally relevant smart contracts. Based upon the definition of smart contracts as discussed earlier, Principle 2 offers the following guidance. A smart contract can be (1) mere code and no legal agreement exists, the situation is a mere transaction (in the technical sense of the word, above explained), (2) a tool to execute a legal agreement, the legal agreement exists off-chain; (3) a legally binding declaration of will, such as an offer or acceptance; or constitute a legal agreement itself;

9

---

[4] It could be compared with an e-mail address (publicly known) and a password (privately known) for the user of that particular e-mail address, which allows others to send messages to the in-box which the user after logging in can read.

(4) merged with the legal agreement and therefore exists simultaneously both on-chain and off-chain. The latter refers to so-called 'Ricardian contracts', which exist both in computer code and in readable text. Added to this typology, Principle 2 adds that if the smart contract is merged with the legal agreement, it ought to be determined by the parties whether the agreement should be treated as on-chain or off-chain. However, as we will see later, this is less relevant in the case of a consumer contract, as in consumer law a final, third, centre-piece of the Principles applies, i.e. Principle 13 that consumer protection prevails over and fully governs coded transactions. In other words: consumers are protected in a coded environment as they would be in a more traditional, non-coded environment. Merging a smart contract with a legal agreement will therefore have no consequences from the perspective of the consumer. Finally, Principle 2 states that the Principles focus on smart contracts as a legally binding declaration (such as an offer or acceptance) and on smart contracts as a legal agreement.

IV. Smart contracts and consumer protection

10   To summarise what was discussed previously, the following three statements can be made. (1) The Principles take as their starting point that a transaction on a blockchain can be legally relevant. (2) Smart contracts can result in legally binding agreements (either as part of a more traditional agreement or as a legal agreement by itself). (3) Weaker parties, particularly consumers, but also micro, small or medium-sized enterprises, shall be given the same or at least equal protection on-chain as they are entitled to off-chain, which protection must be adequate from a perspective of both technological neutrality and functional equivalence considering the algorithmic nature of a transaction. More specifically for consumers this means that they must be given a protective shield which is at least equivalent to the protection which a consumer would have had if no such technology or smart contract would have been used. The latter can be found in Principle 13 (b). Principle 13 (c) reiterates this in relation to the use of a platform. Irrespective of the legal nature and contractual structure of a platform, the use of blockchain technology or a smart contract shall not deprive consumers of any rights they might have had if the platform had not been used. Principle 13 (d) adds that the immutability of a blockchain transaction or the automatic performance and execution of a smart contract shall not deprive consumers of any right they would have had if an equivalent legally binding agreement had been concluded off-chain. Building upon this, Principle 16 (a) makes clear that as regards information duties of a seller consumers shall always have the same or functionally equivalent rights to information towards their counterparts (including platform operators or similar service providers) as they would have had if no transaction on a blockchain or smart contract had been used. A considerable problem here is who the addressees of such information duties might be. In any case addressees are the contractual counterparties of the consumer, especially the seller, but also a platform operator with whom a consumer has a contractual relationship.[5] It should also not be forgotten that platform operators may have several types of duties towards their users, customers and suppliers. They may be more of a broad nature and result in a general duty which applies outside a contractual relationship and the violation of which may result in a tort claim or a claim based on a breach of (pre- and/or post-contractual) good faith. Rather innovative is Principle 16 under (d) and (e). Consumers are entitled to, what with regard to financial transactions is called, a Key

---

[5] See the Report of the European Law Institute 'Model Rules on Online Platforms' (Vienna: European Law Institute, 2019).

C. The ELI project on blockchains and smart contracts

Information Document: a clear, concise overview of what the smart contract contains and implies. Such a document must be natural, plain, intelligible and for the consumer understandable language.[6] That consumers must be informed in natural language builds upon Principle 15 and deviates from Principle 8 (a) stating that contracts between businesses and between private parties can be concluded on-chain; they can also agree that the contractual language is a programming language. Principle 8 (a) takes as its starting point that between businesses and between private parties sufficient bargaining power exists, unless one of the parties is a natural person who is acting for purposes which are outside their trade, business, craft or profession, in other words: a consumer. It should, however, be borne in mind that the Principles in their general part (Principle 12) express that they are not only are aimed at protecting consumers, but more generally weaker parties. Such parties can also be micro, small or medium-sized enterprises. The consumer law principles do not directly apply to such other weaker parties, but for each Principle it could be considered whether it might also apply by analogy. This entails that transactions between businesses are not always to be considered as strictly B2B, but in fact B2C equivalent, with the resulting protection by analogy flowing from the Principles focussing on consumer law.

At the heart of consumer protection is restoring the unequal bargaining position between consumer and business. There is a huge information a-symmetry and the consumer does not have the resources to analyse their legal position when concluding a contract. This is why one of the first European measures to protect consumers was the Unfair Terms Directive.[7] Around this directive a considerable amount of case law, particularly by the Court of Justice of the European Union, developed. For this reason it can come as no surprise that Principle 18 (a), following the overall guiding Principle 13, declaring that consumer protection prevails over and fully governs coded transactions, affirms that the protection of consumers against unfair terms shall be as effective on-chain as off-chain. However, it is also expressly provided in Principle 18 (b) that a standard term that any agreement can only be concluded in digital format is, as such, not an unfair term. However, Principle 18 (b) should certainly not be interpreted *a contrario*, implying that such a term would always be valid. It could still be an unfair clause, and its use against good faith, in the circumstances of a particular case. Principle 18 (a) is further elaborated upon in Principle 18 (d), which adds that in case the unfair term is a self-enforceable part of a smart contract, the consumer is entitled to immediate redress by having the contract re-coded.

---

[6] Cf. the Key Information Document (KID) as prescribed in Regulation (EU) No 1286/2014 of the European Parliament and of the Council of 26 November 2014 on key information documents for packaged retail and insurance-based investment products (PRIIPs) [2014] OJ L352/1. Principles 16 (d) and (e) read as follows: "d) Consumers are, in advance, entitled to a translation and explanation of Smart Contracts (both regarding procedure and substance) in natural, plain, intelligible and for the consumer understandable language, updated whenever the Smart Contract is updated, which must also be made available on a durable medium and publicly available on the user's website. If such translation and explanation are not made available, no legally binding agreement results from the Smart Contract, or, in the case of an update, the agreement can be terminated. e) If the explanation deviates from the terms and conditions which apply once the contract has been concluded, the information contained in the explanation prevails or, if the deviation concerns essential characteristics of the contract, may result in the contract being avoided."

[7] Council Directive 93/13/EEC on unfair terms in consumer contracts [1993] OJ L95/29.

V. Duties to (re)code

12   It has been argued that in the world of code it is code that creates the law. In some sense this is correct. When using software the code decides what happens. For example it does not make much sense wanting to type a 'b' in a word processing programme, when pressing the 'a'. But this is law in the meaning of technical rules, command lines in a computer programme, as if we are talking about a (virtual) engine. Does this also mean that computer code can make the law when 'law' refers to the whole system and complex of rules governing a society, trying to reach a fair and reasonable balance of interests between those living in that society? Keven Werbach has argued that what we should try to do is make the law more 'code-like' and code more 'law-like'.[8] What he means is that the 'oracles of the law' should understand that computer code, with its own version of 'oracles' in the sense of outside sources delivering input into a running programme, is a form of expressing rules and these could include legal rules. At the same time computer programmers as well as those using their software should understand that they are involved in rule making at a, first of all, technical level, but with potentially enormous legal implications which they should not deny.

13   It is from the latter perspective that the Principles contain several duties as to how coding should be done. One example (Principle 18 (d)) was already discussed above. In Principle 18 (e), it is stated that whenever a clause has been declared unfair in collective proceedings (such as under the Injunctions Directive or the Representative Actions Directive) there should be a duty on the relevant business to re-code all contracts affected.[9] Another example can be found in Principle 17 that affirms a consumer's right to a cooling-off or right to withdrawal period. The Principle is very strict in stressing that not only consumer protection prevails over and fully governs coded transactions, but that such protection must be seen to be done by coding it into the smart contract. According to Principle 17 (a) smart contracts must be must be programmed in such a way that any right which a consumer has regarding a cooling-off period or a right to withdrawal can be used as effectively on-chain as off-chain.[10] In Principle 17 (c) this duty to code is made further explicit. The smart contract shall be programmed in such a way that when a consumer exercises its right to withdrawal, the exercise of such right by itself results in a reverse transaction, taking into consideration the nature of the performance. If the nature of the performance prevents a reverse transaction, the consumer is entitled to a monetary claim representing the value of the transaction. The consumer should also be informed about this and, therefore, Principle 17 (d) adds an extra duty to inform resting on the counterparty of the consumer. The smart contract shall be programmed in such a way that the consumer is informed that the reverse

---

[8] Kevin Werbach, The Blockchain and the New Architecture of Trust (Cambridge, MA: MIT Press, 2018), p. 203 ff.

[9] Directive 2009/22/EC of the European Parliament and of the Council of 23 April 2009 on injunctions for the protection of consumers' interests (Codified version) [2009] OJ L110/30, to be replaced by Directive (EU) 2020/1828 of the European Parliament and of the Council of 25 November 2020 on representative actions for the protection of the collective interests of consumers and repealing Directive 2009/22/EC [2020] OJ L409/1.

[10] Principle 17 (b) further elaborates on this: "A cooling-off period shall be coded in such a way that the Smart Contract (1) only begins to perform and execute once the cooling-off period ended, unless (2) the consumer has explicitly and validly requested that the contract be performed and executed before the expiry of the cooling-off period."

transaction has taken place and about any other of its rights following from a cooling-off period or the right to withdraw.[11]

D. Concluding remarks

Smart contracts are sometimes only software, needed to keep a computer system running, and sometimes they are legally relevant and might even constitute as such a binding legal agreement. This diversity, which makes ex ante qualification of smart contracts sometimes very difficult, is the background why the Principles in Principle 3 urge that the legal aspects of smart contracts are to be analysed on a case-by-case basis and, consequently, a case specific approach is followed.

The Principles explicitly do not deal with the creation of rights in rem, such as a security right, the proprietary effect of contracts, legal or judicial enforcement, questions regarding access to digital assets in succession, matrimonial property or registered partnership property matters. How to create a security right in a digital asset is dealt with in another ELI report.[12] Legal or judicial enforcement is part of a project that is still going on and that will also deal with succession, matrimonial property or registered partnership property. What remains as a topic deliberately left out are the property aspects of smart contracts.

Regarding property aspects several problems can be detected. First of all, the very debated question whether 'ownership' of data is at all possible. The approach that in my view is the most pragmatic and efficient is to accept that data are to be part of a new legal area: data law, which is on the borderline of public law (the General Data Protection Regulation or GDPR, to give but one example) and private law, and with regard to private law being a mixture of (1) contract law (particularly the possibility that contracts may have third party effect), (2) property law (should the Civil Law perhaps accept that one unitary concept of ownership no longer functions properly in a coded environment?), (3) tort law (where there is no contract in the traditional sense, still duties might arise resting for example on platform operators) and (4) unjustified enrichment law (to complement the other traditional sources of obligations). Data law is about data rights and the content of these rights might therefore be in part looking at privacy protection, in part at the circulation of data as a result of, to given but one example, a duty to share such data as can be found in the recently proposed Data Act.[13]

In earlier writings I defended that as to a person's right concerning data our view should no longer be based on the rather static approach to property law which is so characteristic of the Civil Law, but that we should consider following a more dynamic approach and be inspired by the ongoing acceptance of fragmented ownership rights

---

[11] Also this Principle has an exception, Principle 17 (e): "Coding a cooling-off period or a reverse transaction following the exercise of the right to withdrawal as part of the Smart Contract will not be necessary, if (1) the performance has begun with the consumer's prior express consent or (2)in case a right to withdrawal exists, the nature of the good, product or service is such that the performance cannot be undone."

[12] ELI Principles on the Use of Digital Assets as Security, Report of the European Law Institute (Vienna: European Law Institute, 2022).

[13] Proposal for a Regulation of the European Parliament and of the Council on harmonised rules on fair access to and use of data (Data Act), COM(2022) 68 final. As regards data rights see also the ALI-ELI Principles for a Data Economy – Data Transactions and Data Rights, to be found at: https://www.europea nlawinstitute.eu/fileadmin/user_upload/p_eli/Projects/Data_Economy/Principles_for_a_Data_Economy _Final_Council_Draft.pdf.

as can be found in the Common Law tradition.[14] Rights to data, so it could be argued, change over time, depending upon, among several other policy weighing factors, how many copies exist and who have access. Questions that should be asked are: Who are the stakeholders involved, are they natural persons or legal persons, are the data of a personal nature or not? The more copies of data exist, the more any rights to control the use of these copies vanishes in thin air. As to access, a debate has arisen as to what it really means, whether it can be defined at all or should rather be approached as a notion. This is, methodologically speaking, a discussion of the same nature as we saw earlier regarding how to define a smart contract. In any case, access may comprise (1) being informed about the existence of data, (2) knowing not just their existence, but knowing the content of the data, a right to (3) change, (4) port or transfer data (such as take data with you from one provider to another) and to (5) delete data (such as the right to be forgotten, known from privacy law). In essence, access is more like management of data than rights to data and is therefore, what is advocated above, an approach that is both making code more law-like and law more code-like.

18 With regard, specifically, to smart contracts, answering property law questions seems to be avoided. Not only because of the unresolved debate about the nature of rights to data, but also because, so it looks, the impact of using a smart contract in actual practice is not fully realised. If a smart contract can be qualified as (part of) a binding legal agreement, what are then the consequences of such a contract in a legal system as the French where a contract of sale has from the moment of its conclusion a proprietary effect or a legal system as the German where the passing of ownership requires a separate legal act? Given that smart contracts are self-executing, the outcome is that formation and performance take place at the same moment. This fits rather well with French law, but does it fit with German law? At the same time, in cases of, for example, avoidance, any nullity cannot change the immutable nature of the transaction. This is why a reverse transaction is needed to undo the consequences. This fits more with the German abstract system of transfer, than the French causal system. All of these consequences will have to be considered both at a national and a European level.

19 Analysing the legal consequences of, more generally, the Digital Revolution and, more specifically, transactions on a blockchain and the use of smart contracts has only just begun. And the same applies to the quest towards finding adequate legal solutions.

Bibliography

T.J. de Graaf, 'From old to new: From internet to smart contracts and from people to smart contracts' (2019) 35 Computer Law & Security Review 2 ff.

Martin Hanzl, 'Handbuch Blockchain und Smart Contracts' (Vienna: Linde Verlag, 2020).

Andrea Stazi, 'Smart Contracts and Comparative Law. A Western Perspective' (Cham: Springer Nature and G. Giappichelli Editore, 2021).

Lauren Henry Scholz, 'Algorithmic Contracts' (2017) Stanford Technology Law Review 128 ff.

Kevin Werbach, 'The Blockchain and the New Architecture of Trust' (Cambridge, MA: MIT Press, 2018) 203 ff.

---

[14] Sjef van Erp, Management as Ownership of Data, in: Sebastian Lohsse, Reiner Schulze and Dirk Staudenmayer (eds.), Data as Counter-Performance: Contract Law 2.0? (Hart/Nomos:), p. 77 ff. and Sjef van Erp, COVID-19 Apps, Corona Vaccination Apps and Data "Ownership"(2022) China-EU Law Journal 45 ff. .

Bibliography

Sjef van Erp, 'Management as Ownership of Data', in: Sebastian Lohsse, Reiner Schulze and Dirk Staudenmayer (eds.), Data as Counter-Performance: Contract Law 2.0? (Hart/Nomos: 2020), p. 77 ff.

Sjef van Erp, Covid-19 apps, Corona vaccination apps and data "ownership" (2022) China-EU Law Journal 45 ff.

The Impact on Private Law of the Product Policy Initiatives under the European Green Deal

Since the early days of European environmental policy, there has been a tension between the objective of protecting the environment and society's ambition for growth and prosperity. This tension was already clearly expressed in 1987 by the so-called "Brundtland Report" in the definition of sustainable development prior to the second World Conference on the Environment[1] in Rio de Janeiro in 1992 (UNCED 1992). The report describes sustainable development as a development that meets the needs of the present without risking that future generations will not be able to meet their own needs. The tension is addressed by two key words. On the one hand, the concept of meeting the *needs* of the present in the context of the need to preserve the capacity of the environment to meet future needs.

Against that background it must be pointed out that for many years, environmental policy worldwide has focused on correcting the consequences of economic development.[2] This is best exemplified by scientists and people becoming aware of the harmful effects of emissions and use of chemicals in industry and pesticides in agriculture during the 1950s and '60s. The Minamata disease in 1956 in Japan and the publication of the book "Silent Spring" (1962) by American biologist Rachel Carson were important steps in the development of a public interest. Numerous legislative and policy measures have been put in place at the global, international, and domestic level, however mostly without calling into question the fundamental drivers behind the problem – the fact that current patterns of development far exceed the limits of the planet. The concept of the Earth's ecological boundaries was developed and presented in 2009 by a team of scientists led by Johan Rockström from the Stockholm Resilience Centre.[3] The basic idea is that our planetary system needs to find a so-called "safe space" in which society can meet its needs without sudden or irreversible changes in the environment.

This perception of a tension increased even more in Europe and globally, as growth and job creation continued to be a political priority in the context of the global economic crisis after 2008. To resolve this tension, the international community sought to find economic concepts that could combine the two priorities. In 2011, the European Commission published a Communication on a "Roadmap to a Resource Efficient Europe".[4] On the basis of this roadmap, the European Resource Efficiency Platform – a group of high-level economic and environmental experts – prepared a report by 2014 containing a number of recommendations for action in the economy.[5] This report was the basis for further reflection by the European Commission on how to turn these general recommendations into concrete proposals for implementation. At the same time, the Ellen McArthur Foundation also worked intensively on the concept of transition to a circular economy. A number of studies analysed and presented the challenges and

---

[1] Our Common Future, Report, from the United Nations World Commission on Environment and Development
Oxford University Press, 1987, Oxford University Press.

[2] Peter N. Kinga and Hideyuki Mori, 'The Development of Environmental Policy' (2007) 7 International Review for Environmental Strategies pp. 7–16.

[3] Will Steffen, 'Planetary boundaries: Guiding human development on a changing planet' (2015) Science 347 (6223): 1259855, available at <https://www.science.org/doi/10.1126/science.1259855> accessed on 29 November 2022.

[4] Communication from the Commission to the European Parliament, the Council, the European Economic and Social Committee and the Committee of the Regions. Roadmap to a Resource Efficient Europe. COM (2011) 571.

[5] EREP – Manifesto and policy recommendations, European Commission, 31st March 2014.

opportunities of the transition, not least a 2013 study carried out by McKinsey for the Ellen McArthur Foundation[6]. These and other studies have strongly influenced the policy discussion on the circular economy. A visual presentation of the circular economy as developed by the Ellen McArthur Foundation clearly shows the complexity, but also the opportunities of this new economic approach, covering all sectors of the economy and society, both on the biotic as well as on the abiotic side.

4   In the face of these developments, the European Commission presided by Jose Manuel Barroso in 2014 adopted a first circular economy package.[7] This package consisted of a Communication developing a narrative on the transition to a circular economy, together with a legislative proposal to revise the targets in a number of waste management directives as well as several Communications[8]. However, this package was subsequently reviewed by the new Commission, led by Jean-Claude Juncker, as regards its consistency with the 10 EU policy priorities established for this Commission. It was deemed to be at the same time too ambitious, especially since it contained a proposal for an overall "resource efficiency target" for the EU; but also not specific or concrete enough as it didn't contain a specific list of proposed measure and initiatives. It was also criticized for focusing too much on the downstream part of the economic cycle. In addition, it initially was also seen to be incompatible with the overall priorities of the European Commission and was therefore withdrawn. This led to very intensive discussions with the Council of Ministers, the European Parliament, and relevant stakeholders and the Commission announced in February 2015 that it would present a new, more ambitious action plan in the course of 2015.

---

[6] Ellen Mac Arthur Foundation, Towards the Circular Economy – Economic and business rationale for an accelerated transition, 2013.

[7] Towards a circular economy: A zero waste programme for Europe COM (2014) 398 final Brussels, 2.7.2014.

[8] Proposal for a Directive of the European Parliament and of the Council amending Directives 2008/98/EC on waste, 94/62/EC on packaging and packaging waste, 1999/31/EC on the landfill of waste, 2000/53/EC on end-of-life vehicles, 2006/66/EC on batteries and batteries and waste batteries and pools, and 2012/19/EU on waste electrical and electronic equipment; COM(2014) 397 final, 2014/0201 (COD); Communication from the Commission to the European Parliament, the Council, the European Economic and Social Committee and the Committee of the Regions on Resource Efficiency Opportunities in the Building Sector; COM/2014/0445 final; Communication from the Commission to the European Parliament, the Council, the European Economic and Social Committee and the Committee of the Regions Green Action Plan for SMEs enabling SMEs to turn environmental challenges into business opportunities; COM/2014/0440 final.

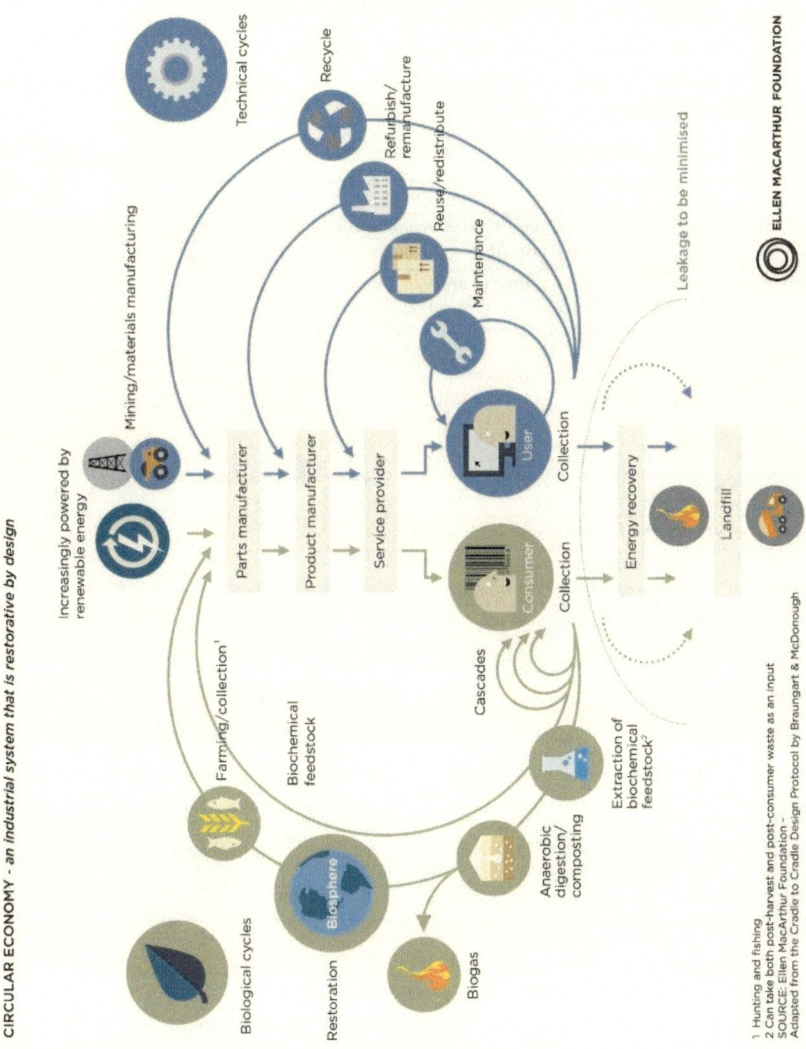

After intensive work, the European Commission adopted on 2nd December 2015, the first EU action plan for the transition to a circular economy[9] aimed at supporting the transition to a more circular economy in the EU where resources are used more sustainably, and their value is kept longer in the economy. This action plan included legislative proposals to revise European waste legislation, as well as a list of 54 specific measures

---

[9] Closing the loop – An EU action plan for the Circular Economy. Closing the loop, Brussels, 2.12.2015. COM (2015) 614 final. Proposal for a Directive of the European Parliament and of the Council amending Directive 2008/98/EC on waste; COM/2015/0595 final – 2015/0275 (COD); Proposal for a Directive of the European Parliament and of the Council amending Directive 94/62/EC on packaging and packaging waste; COM/2015/0596 final – 2015/0276 (COD); Proposal for a Directive of the European Parliament and of the Council amending Directive 1999/31/EC on the landfill of waste; COM/2015/0594 final – 2015/0274 (COD); Proposal for a Directive of the European Parliament and of the Council amending Directives 2000/53/EC on end-of-life vehicles, 2006/66/EC on batteries and accumulators and waste batteries and batteries, and 2012/19/EU on waste electrical and electronic equipment; COM/2015/0593 final – 2015/0272 (COD).

covering the whole life cycle of products and materials. This plan was presented as part of the European Commission's priorities and as an essential contribution to the EU's comprehensive agenda for growth and jobs. It was a first package of concrete measures as listed on the table below.

Actions	Timetable
Production	
Emphasis on circular economy aspects in future **product requirements under the Eco-design directive.**	2016 onwards
Eco-design work plan 2015-2017 and **request to European standardisation organisations** to develop standards on material efficiency for setting future Eco-design requirements on durability, reparability and recyclability of products.	December 2015
Proposal for an **implementing regulation** on televisions and displays	End 2015 or beginning 2016
Examine options and actions for a more coherent policy framework of the different strands of work of EU product policy in their contribution to the circular economy	2018
Include guidance on circular economy into **Best Available Techniques reference documents (BREFs)** for several industrial sectors	2016 onwards
Guidance and promotion of best practices in the mining waste management plans	2018
Establishing an open, **pan-European network of technological infrastructures for SMEs** to integrate advanced manufacturing technologies into their production processes	2016
Examine **how to improve the efficiency and uptake** of the EU Eco-Management and Audit Scheme (EMAS) and the pilot programme on environmental technology verification (ETV)	2017
Develop an improved **knowledge base and support to SMEs** for the substitution of hazardous substances of very high concern	2018
Consumption	
Better enforcement of existing guarantees on tangible products, accompanied by a **reflection on improvements** (upcoming Commission proposal for online sales of goods, and Fitness Check of consumer legislation)	2015-2017
Action on false green claims, including **updated guidance** on unfair commercial practices	2016
Analysis of the possibility to propose horizontal requirements on repair information provision in the context of Eco-design	2018
REFIT of Ecolabel, to be followed by actions to enhance its effectiveness	2016
Assessment of the possibility of an **independent testing programme** on planned obsolescence	2018
Subject to evaluation of the current ongoing pilots, explore the possible uses of the Product Environmental Footprint to measure and communicate environmental information	2016 onwards
Action on Green Public Procurement: enhanced integration of circular economy requirements, support to higher uptake including through training schemes, reinforcing its use in Commission procurement and EU funds	2016 onwards

Waste management	
Revised legislative proposal on waste	Dec 2015
Improved cooperation with Member States for better implementation of EU waste legislation, and combat illicit shipment of end of life vehicles	2015 onwards
Stepping up **enforcement** of revised Waste Shipment regulation	2016 onwards
Promotion of industry-led **voluntary certification** of treatment facilities for key waste/recyclate streams	2018 onwards
Initiative on waste to energy in the framework of the Energy Union	2016
Identification and dissemination of good practices in waste collection systems	2016 onwards

Market for secondary raw materials	
Development of **quality standards** for secondary raw materials (in particular for plastics)	2016 onwards
Proposal for a revised fertilisers regulation	Early 2016
Proposed legislation setting minimum requirements for reused water for irrigation and groundwater recharge	2017
Promotion of safe and cost-effective water reuse, including **guidance** on the integration of water reuse in water planning and management, **inclusion of best practices in relevant BREFs**, and support to innovation (through the European Innovation Partnership and Horizon 2020) and investments	2016-2017
Analysis and policy options to address the interface between chemicals, products and waste legislation, including how to reduce the presence and improve the tracking of chemicals of concern in products	2017
Measures to facilitate waste shipment across the EU, including **electronic data exchange** (and possibly other measures)	2016 onwards
Further development of the EU **raw materials information system**	2016 onwards

Sectorial action	
Plastics	
Strategy on plastics in the circular economy	2017
Specific action to reduce marine litter implementing the 2030 Sustainable Development Goals	2015 onwards

Food waste	
Development of a **common methodology and indicators** to measure food waste	2016
Stakeholders platform to examine how to achieve SDGs goals on food waste, share best practice and evaluate progress	2016
Clarify relevant EU legislation related to waste, food and feed in order to facilitate food donation and utilisation of former foodstuffs for animal feed	2016
Explore options for more effective use and understanding of date marking on food	2017

Critical raw materials	
Report on critical raw materials and the circular economy	2017
Improve **exchange of information** between manufacturers and recyclers on electronic products	2016 onwards
European standards for material-efficient recycling of electronic waste, waste batteries and other relevant complex end-of-life products	2016 onwards
Sharing of best practice for the recovery of critical raw materials from mining waste and landfills	2017

Construction and demolition	
Pre-demolition assessment **guidelines** for the construction sector	2017
Voluntary industry-wide **recycling protocol** for construction and demolition waste	2016
Core indicators for the assessment of the lifecycle environmental performance of a building, and incentives for their use	2017 onwards

Biomass and bio-based materials	
Guidance and dissemination of best practice on the cascading use of biomass and support to innovation in this domain through Horizon 2020	2018- 2019
Ensuring coherence and synergies with the circular economy when examining the sustainability of bioenergy under the Energy Union	2016
Assessment of the contribution of the 2012 Bio-economy Strategy to the circular economy and possible review	2016

Innovation and investments	
Initiative "Industry 2020 and the circular economy" under **Horizon 2020**	October 2015
Pilot project for "innovation deals" to address possible regulatory obstacles for innovators	2016
Targeted outreach to encourage applications for funding under EFSI, and support the development of projects and investment platforms relevant to the circular economy	2016 onwards
Targeted outreach and communication activities to assist Member States and regions for the uptake of Cohesion Policy funds for the circular economy	2016 onwards
Support to Member States and regions to strengthen innovation for the circular economy through smart specialisation	2016 onwards
Assessment of the possibility of launching a **platform together with the EIB and national banks** to support the financing of the circular economy	2016
Engagement with stakeholders in the implementation of this action plan through existing fora in key sectors	2016 onwards
Support to a range of stakeholders through actions on public-private partnerships, cooperation platforms, support to voluntary business approaches, and exchanges of best practices	2015 onwards

Monitoring	
Development of a **monitoring framework** for the circular economy	2017

6   The Circular Economy Action Plan was the starting point for a development in Europe that moves away from a linear economic model that is highly resource intensive. Its adoption was a recognition of the fact that meeting the needs of the population associated with a huge increase in pressure on resources such as land, water, food, feed, raw materials, and energy, it was no longer possible to continue to rely on an economic approach based on the principle of 'taking, producing, using, throwing away'. Such an approach was not only deemed inappropriate from an environmental sustainability perspective, but also from an economic point of view. Indeed, the transition to a circular economy was also recognized as a tool to strengthen European competitiveness by reducing the scarcity of resources and price volatility of raw materials and by creating additional incentives to develop new business models, innovative and more efficient production methods and sustainable consumption models. The proposed measures were also closely linked to the EU's energy and climate policies. A transition to a circular economy therefore also seen as important in supporting the implementation of the Paris Agreement on Climate Change and the achievement of the 17 Sustainable Development Goals agreed by the global community in the United Nations 2030 Agenda for Sustainable Development.

Implementing the measures contained in the Circular Economy Action Plan was 7 there a first step towards a fundamental transformation of the EU economy, based not just an environmental, but also an economic imperative. The circular economy is the only model that makes sense for the European society and economy in the long term. Europe does not have the same natural resources as many other parts of the world and cannot (and does not want to) compete for lower labour costs. Europe can only be at the forefront of a global competition if natural resources are used and reused in a smarter and more sustainable way. This approach can help European business and industry remain competitive and become a market leader in green technologies and approaches.

Actions under the first action plan aimed at the entire economic cycle covering 8 primary and secondary raw materials, the design, production and provision of products and services, distribution and consumption, the proper disposal and reuse of materials and, ultimately, the generation and use of secondary raw materials . The 54 actions at EU level of course covered only areas where action at European level makes sense. The European single market provides a good legal framework for this.

A significant part of the plan has been from the outset focused on measures that 9 would support the development of products that are "circular economy proof". Such products should be more durable, easier to repair and to disassemble, re-use and better recycle their material. This was to be done through the development of technical standards, but also through better implementation of existing regulatory frameworks, such as the Eco-design Directive and other Directives and Regulations.

A range of tools are designed to enable consumers to make purchasing decisions on 10 the basis of clear and independent information. The tools range from the EU Ecolabel, the sustainability criteria in public procurement (GPP), the methodology for calculating the environmental footprint of products and organisations, consumer protection tools, such as the directives to combat misleading environmental claims, to an EU program to test products for elements of premature obsolescence.

Waste management continues to play a central role in the transition to a circular 11 economy. The supply and demand of secondary raw materials should be developed in such a way that material cycles in the EU are largely closed. Based on the European Commission's proposals, the European Parliament and the Council of Ministers agreed on ambitious new targets for waste management in Europe. This framework will be the basis for a better and more efficient supply of secondary raw materials in Europe. It also includes the development of quality standards for secondary raw materials, but also improvements in the monitoring of the economic cycle regarding the occurrence of substances of concern.

The measures also included proposals for the economic sectors considered important 12 for the transition to a circular economy: for example, the construction sector, the so-called bioeconomy, and the raw materials sector. At the beginning of 2018, the Commission presented another comprehensive package of measures in the field of plastics and chemicals, largely implementing the measures of the first Action Plan.[10] However, it was clear from the outset that the first action plan would only be a step in longer development.

When the current European Commission, led by President von der Leyen, took office 13 it was of course important to see whether the new Commission would continue the path that its predecessor had embarked upon. Frans Timmermans who had been a main driving force behind the first Action Plan remained in the Commission. Early in the tenure of the new Commission it became clear that the development would continue to

---

[10] http://ec.europa.eu/environment/circular-economy/index_en.htm.

gain momentum. Shortly after taking office, Ms von der Leyen said that one of the main objectives of her term of office would be to ensure that Europe can face the challenge of global environmental crises. She announced a new EU wide strategy saying that, "The European Green Deal is our new growth strategy – for growth that brings us more than it costs us. It shows how to transform our way of living and working, of producing and consuming so that we live healthier and make our businesses innovative".[11]

14   The European Green Deal includes a comprehensive roadmap of actions to promote resource efficiency by moving towards a clean and circular economy, halting climate change, tackling biodiversity loss and reducing pollution. It outlines investments needed and financing tools available and explains how to ensure a just and inclusive transition. It covers a range of policies and sectors relevant for the sustainability transition proposing measures addressing the triple environment crisis of climate change, biodiversity loss and pollution, while aiming at ensuring a just transition for all.

15   One of the main initiatives in this context is the continuation and expansion of work towards the transition to a circular economy in Europe and at global level. As part of the 2015 package, the European Commission had already committed to present a comprehensive implementation report five years after the adoption of the 2015 Action Plan. This report was presented as a working document of the European Commission in spring 2020.[12] It took a first stock of developments since 2015 and provided the basis for further reflection on measures for the transition to a circular economy. It was also the basis for the new Circular Economy Action Plan presented by the European Commission on the same day.[13]

---

[11] https://ec.europa.eu/commission/presscorner/detail/de/ip_19_6691.
[12] Commission Staff Working Document "Leading the way to a global circular economy: State of play and outlook", Brussels, 11.3.2020, SWD (2020) 100 final.
[13] Communication from the European Commission, A new Circular Economy Action Plan – For a cleaner and more competitive Europe, Brussels, 11.3.2020, COM (2020) 98 final.

Like its predecessor this Action Plan announced a wide range of proposals and actions in areas where action at EU level brings real added value, in particular by focusing on issues such as: 16

- Promoting sustainable product design;
- Promoting sustainable consumption;
- Ensure that used resources remain in the EU economy for as long as possible.

The specific measures were designed to ensure that:

- Sustainable products become the norm in Europe;
- Users and consumers are enabled to make sustainable choices;
- They include the sectors that consume the most resources and where the "circular potential" is greatest, such as electronics and ICT, batteries and vehicles, plastics and packaging, textiles of all kinds, construction and buildings, food, water and nutrients;
- Waste generation is further reduced;
- Waste exports from the EU are better controlled and further restricted;
- circularity in a toxic-free environment is strengthened;
- The creation of a well-functioning EU market for secondary raw materials is promoted; and
- The EU can play a leading role in global efforts.

The comprehensive list of measure illustrates the complexity and size of the task. For the purpose of this contribution I will focus on a few of these initiatives. 17

Key actions	Date
A SUSTAINABLE PRODUCT POLICY FRAMEWORK	
Legislative proposal for **a sustainable product policy initiative**	2021
Legislative proposal **empowering consumers in the green transition**	2020
Legislative and non-legislative measures establishing a new **"right to repair"**	2021
Legislative proposal on substantiating **green claims**	2020
Mandatory Green Public Procurement (GPP) criteria and targets in sectoral legislation and phasing-in **mandatory reporting on GPP**	as of 2021
Review of the **Industrial Emissions Directive**, including the integration of circular economy practices in upcoming Best Available Techniques reference documents	as of 2021
Launch of an **industry-led industrial symbiosis reporting and certification system**	2022
KEY PRODUCT VALUE CHAINS	
Circular Electronics Initiative, **common charger solution**, and **reward systems to return old devices**	2020/ 2021
Review of the Directive on the **restriction of the use of certain hazardous substances in electrical and electronic equipment** and guidance to clarify its links with REACH and Ecodesign requirements	2021
Proposal for a new **regulatory framework for batteries**	2020
Review of the rules on **end-of-life vehicles**	2021
Review of the rules on proper treatment of **waste oils**	2022
Review to reinforce the **essential requirements for packaging** and reduce (over)packaging and packaging waste	2021
Mandatory requirements on **recycled plastic content** and **plastic waste reduction measures** for key products such as packaging, construction materials and vehicles	2021/ 2022
Restriction of **intentionally added microplastics** and measures on **unintentional release of microplastics**	2021
Policy framework for **bio-based plastics and biodegradable or compostable plastics**	2021
EU Strategy for Textiles	2021
Strategy for a Sustainable Built Environment	2021
Initiative to **substitute single-use packaging, tableware and cutlery by reusable products in food services**	2021
LESS WASTE, MORE VALUE	
Waste reduction targets for specific streams and other measures on **waste prevention**	2022
EU-wide **harmonised model for separate collection of waste and labelling** to facilitate separate collection	2022

Methodologies to track and minimise the presence of substances of concern in recycled materials and articles made thereof	2021
Harmonised information systems for the presence of substances of concern	2021
Scoping the development of further **EU-wide end-of-waste and by-product criteria**	2021
Revision of the rules on **waste shipments**	2021
Making the circular economy work for people, regions and cities	
Supporting the circular economy transition through the **Skills Agenda**, the forthcoming **Action Plan for Social Economy, the Pact for Skills** and the **European Social Fund Plus.**	as of 2020
Supporting the circular economy transition through **Cohesion policy funds, the Just Transition Mechanism** and **urban initiatives**	as of 2020
CROSSCUTTING ACTIONS	
Improving measurement, modelling and policy tools to capture **synergies between the circular economy and climate change mitigation and adaptation** at EU and national level	as of 2020
Regulatory framework for the **certification of carbon removals**	2023
Reflecting circular economy objectives in the revision of the guidelines on **state aid in the field of environment and energy**	2021
Mainstreaming circular economy objectives in the context of the rules on **non-financial reporting**, and initiatives on **sustainable corporate governance** and on **environmental accounting**	2020/ 2021
Leading efforts at global level	
Leading efforts towards reaching a **global agreement on plastics**	as of 2020
Proposing a **Global Circular Economy Alliance** and initiating discussions on an **international agreement on the management of natural resources**	as of 2021
Mainstreaming circular economy objectives in **free trade agreements**, in other **bilateral, regional and multilateral** processes and agreements, and in **EU external policy funding instruments**	as of 2020
MONITORING THE PROGRESS	
Updating the **Circular Economy Monitoring Framework** to reflect new policy priorities and develop further **indicators on resource use**, including **consumption and material footprints**	2021

Since March 2020, the European Commission has already put forward several proposals to help achieve these goals. These are proposals aimed at:

- Ensuring that products placed on the EU market are designed to last longer and are easier to repair, retrofit, recycle and reuse;
- Improving the sorting, reuse and recycling of textiles, making it easier for consumers to choose sustainable textiles, and applying the eco-design principle also to clothing;
- Phasing out single-use products are where possible and replacing them by durable or reusable products;

- Incentivising the product-as-a-service model;
- Limiting and ultimately eliminating the targeted addition of microplastics to products and materials and avoiding the unplanned separation of microplastics at all relevant stages of the life cycle of products.

19   In a dense sequence, the European Commission has therefore proposed new regulations on sustainable batteries[14], to lower the limit values for highly harmful chemicals in waste,[15] on shipments of waste,[16] on Eco-design [17] a Construction Products [18] a Directive to strengthen consumer rights for the green transition,[19] an EU strategy for sustainable and circular textiles[20] the revision of the Industrial Emissions and Landfill Directive[21] including the establishment of an Industrial Emissions Portal.[22]

20   A few of the proposals listed above were put forward in the context of the so called "Sustainable Product Policy Framework", an idea in the making in the EU since at least 2003, when the European Commission adopted a first Communication on that topic.[23] This was the first result of a policy development that had started in 1998, when Integrated Product Policy was first discussed with stakeholders at a conference. The following year, IPP was considered at the Weimar Informal Meeting of EU Environment Ministers, where the German Presidency concluded that the meeting welcomed the Commission's intention to adopt a Green Paper and emphasized that improving the market conditions for greener products on the European market would also help to strengthen the competitiveness of European industries. The Commission adopted a Green Paper in February 2001 following the priority themes in the 6th Environmental Action Programme.[24] In the area of managing natural resources more responsibly the European Council in adopting the EAP had agreed, "that the EU Integrated Product Policy aimed at reducing resource use and the environmental impact of waste should be implemented in co-operation with business".

---

[14] Proposal for a Regulation of the European Parliament and of the Council concerning batteries and waste batteries, repealing Directive 2006/66/EC, and amending Regulation (EU) 2019/1020 COM/2020/798 final.

[15] COM (2021) 656: Proposal for a Regulation of the European Parliament and of the Council amending Annexes IV and V to Regulation (EU) 2019/1021 of the European Parliament and of the Council on persistent organic pollutants.

[16] COM (2021) 709 Final, Proposal for a Regulation of the European Parliament and of the Council on shipments of waste and amending Regulations (EU) No 1257/2013 and (EU) 2020/1056.

[17] COM (2022) 142 final, Proposal for a Regulation of the European Parliament and of the Council establishing a framework for setting eco-design requirements for sustainable products and repealing Directive 2009/125/EC.

[18] COM (2022) 144: Proposal for a Regulation of the European Parliament and of the Council laying down harmonised conditions for the marketing of construction products, amending Regulation (EU) 2019/1020 and repealing Regulation (EU) No 305/2011.

[19] COM (2022) 143 final, Proposal for a Directive of the European Parliament and of the Council amending Directives 2005/29/EC and 2011/83/EU as regards empowering consumers for the green transition through better protection against unfair practices and better information.

[20] COM (2022) 141 final, Communication from the Commission to the European Parliament, the Council, the European Economic and Social Committee and the Committee of the Regions: EU strategy for sustainable and circular textiles.

[21] COM (2022) 156 final, Proposal for a Directive of the European Parliament and of the Council amending Directive 2010/75/EU of the European Parliament and of the Council of 24 November 2010 on industrial emissions (integrated pollution prevention and control) and Council Directive 1999/31/EC of 26 April 1999 on the landfill of waste.

[22] COM (2022) 157 Final, Proposal for a Regulation of the European Parliament and of the Council on the reporting of environmental data from industrial installations and the establishment of an Industrial Emissions Portal.

[23] https://ec.europa.eu/environment/ipp/ippcommunication.htm.

[24] https://ec.europa.eu/environment/archives/action-programme/intro.htm.

The next step in the development was the adoption of a Sustainable Consumption 21
and Production and Sustainable Industrial Policy (SCP/SIP) Action Plan in 2008[25]
which led to a fundamental review of certain legislative and policy instruments. The
changes included notably the extension of the scope of the Directive on Eco-design,
the revision of product labelling provisions under the Energy Labelling Directive and a
further development of the Ecolabel Regulation. All this was made with the intention
of incentivizing producers to move towards more sustainable products and materials
and providing consumers with information about the energy and/or environmental
performance of products. These proposals were also made to establish a harmonised
base for public procurement and incentives provided by the EU and its Member States.

These measures however stopped short of establishing binding design rules for prod- 22
ucts, except in the area of energy efficiency. This was over the years recognized as a
major shortcoming of the policy framework.

The challenge had already been recognised in the action table resulting from the first 23
Circular Economy Action Plan, which included an action point calling for examining
options for a coherent product policy framework. While some preparatory work had
been done already, the real commitment for action only came with the adoption of
the second Action Plan that included a clear commitment from the Commission for
the development of legislative proposals in that regard. This was the starting point of
the development of a comprehensive package that is based on the vision of a policy
framework as depicted in the image below.

---

[25] Communication from the Commission to the European Parliament, the Council, the European Economic and Social Committee and the Committee of the Regions on the Sustainable Consumption and Production and Sustainable Industrial Policy Action Plan {SEC (2008) 2110} {SEC (2008) 2111.

Making sustainable products the norm in a more resilient Single Market

Complementary sectoral rules on construction and other product categories (e.g. batteries, chemicals, packaging)

Strategy for Sustainable and Circular Textiles
→ Binding eco-design requirements, incl. durability, reparability, and recycled fiber content
→ Stop microplastics pollution
→ Tackle fast fashion, textile waste, and the destruction of unsold products
→ Accurate green claims
→ Sustainable global value chains

New rules to empower consumers for the green transition
→ Protection against greenwashing and the deliberate planning or design of products with limited lifespans
→ Information on product durability and reparability

Ecodesign for Sustainable Products Regulation
→ Performance and information requirements for greener products
→ Tackle the destruction of unsold goods
→ Waste prevention and reduction
→ Mandatory criteria for green public procurement
→ Digital Product Passport and new labelling rules
→ Stronger market surveillance

Global action
→ Global sustainable consumption and production forum
→ Corporate sustainability due diligence

Support for circular business models
↑ European circular business hub
↑ Guidance to businesses

Ecodesign Working Plan 2022-2024
→ Higher energy efficiency and circularity for energy-related products
→ New rules for consumer electronics (smartphones, tablets, solar panels)

24 This led to the adoption of the Product Policy Package in March 2020 at which occasion Executive Vice President Frans Timmermans said that "It's time to end the model of 'take, make, break, and throw away' that is so harmful to our planet, our health and our economy. Today's proposals will ensure that only the most sustainable products are sold in Europe. They allow consumers to save energy, repair and not replace broken products, and make smart environmental choices when they are shopping for new ones."

25 The Package comprised a range of measures as pictured below.

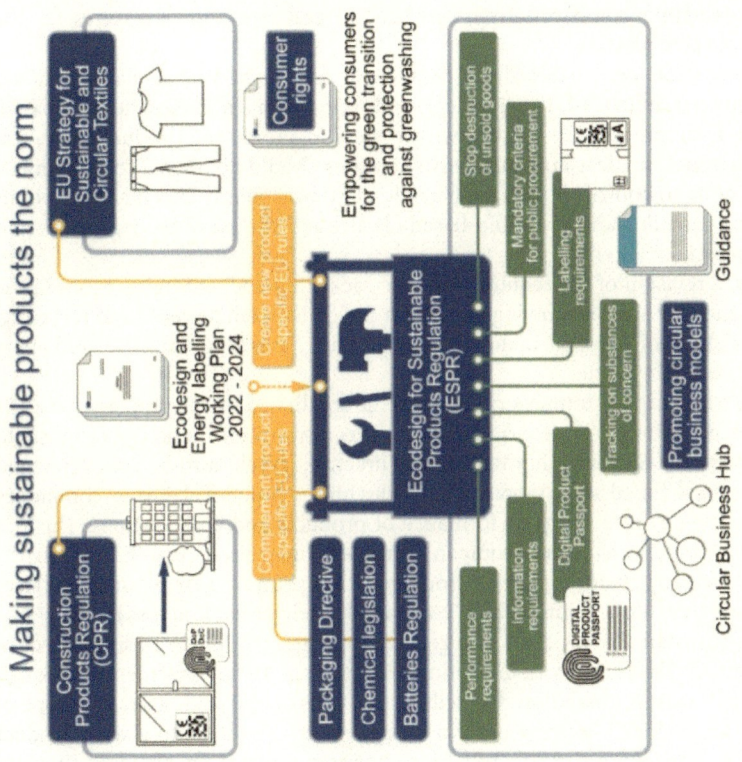

For the purpose of this article, I will focus on two of the initiatives notably the proposals for:

1) An Eco-design for Sustainable Products Regulation (ESPR);
2) Consumer Rights and Sustainability Reporting.

Further Proposals are planned for the near future. An initiative on microplastic pollution will aim to tackle microplastics unintentionally released into the environment. It will focus on labelling, standardisation, certification and regulatory measures for the main sources of these plastics.

27   A Communication on bio-based, biodegradable and compostable plastics should clarify the understanding of the impacts and opportunities linked to bio-based, biodegradable and compostable plastics with a view to promoting products with real environmental benefits. Clear and trustworthy options should be offered to consumers. The initiative aims to contribute to a sustainable plastics economy and make proposals on the sourcing, labelling and use of bio-based plastics and the use of biodegradable and compostable plastics.

28   And finally, a revision of the requirements for packaging and packaging waste in the EU should include rules for improving packaging design to promote reuse and recycling, increasing the share of recycled materials in packaging, avoiding excessive packaging and reducing packaging waste.

29   Finally, the transparency framework, already[26] strengthened by the proposal for a Directive on strengthening consumer rights for the green transition[27] and the proposal to amend the Corporate Sustainability Reporting Directive, should also be complemented by another proposal aimed at harmonising the rules on the proof of claims by companies with regard to the environmental performance of products and organisations. The aim of this proposal would be to require companies to use standardised quantification methods to substantiate any claims on the environmental footprint of their products/services in order to make this information reliable, comparable and verifiable across the EU.

30   In the area of sustainable products, the general approach of the Eco Design Directive will be maintained. The framework legislation will continue to be implemented through product-specific measures based on detailed impact assessments. However, the scope of measures will be extended, moving beyond energy-related products to a wide product scope. It will be possible to develop and adopt horizontal requirements in addition to product-specific requirements. There will also be a stronger focus on product information such as through tools such as the "Digital Product Passport" and the increased use of labels. Under the ESPR mandatory GPP criteria become possible through delegated acts. The proposal also foresees additional transparency requirements for those choosing to discard unsold goods and the possibility to ban their destruction for relevant product groups. One of the weaknesses of the existing system, notably the market surveillance will also be addressed by proposals to reinforce controls on regulated products, including market surveillance implementing plans, possible targets on checks, support to common projects and investments.

31   The proposal on improved transparency aims at empowering consumers to make informed and environment-friendly choices when buying products. Consumers will have the right to be better informed about how long the product is made to last and if it can be repaired. They will have more rights against misleading practices related to greenwashing or to premature obsolescence of products. Sellers will have to provide information whether the producer of a consumer good offers a commercial guarantee of durability of 2+ years, whether software updates are provided, for goods with digital elements, digital content and digital services. Information about a product's reparability score, where applicable, or other repair information given by the producer (availability of spare parts, repair manual, etc.) must be made available.

---

[26] COM (2021) 189 final Proposal for a Directive of the European Parliament and of the Council amending Directives 2013/34/EU, 2004/109/EC and 2006/43/EC and Regulation (EU) No 537/2014 as regards corporate sustainability reporting.

[27] See footnote 18 above.

The new rules will therefore ensure that traders do not mislead consumers about environmental and social impacts, durability and reparability of products. They ban making vague claims where environmental excellence cannot be demonstrated ('eco', 'green', etc.), environmental claims about the entire product when they only concern parts of the product and claiming that a good has a certain durability when it does not.

These will be powerful rules complementing the transparency legislation explained above. Together with the enhanced system for market surveillance it will also be possible for consumer representatives to engage in collective legal action as initially proposed by the European Commission in 2018.[28] This was agreed among the co-legislators in 2020 and Member States had until December 2022 to amend their domestic law to meet the minimum requirements[29] under the EU Directive 2020/1828, "Representative actions for the protection of the collective interests of consumers", which was adopted in late 2020. This will be a major step forward, putting huge pressure on EU Member States regarding the enforcement of all these requirements. As the website of an international law office proclaimed "The Representative Actions Directive: Get set for a New Wave of European Class Actions".[30]

It is now up to the EU Member States to implement and transpose existing legislation and together with the European Parliament to speed up the decision-making process on pending proposals. It is also clear, however, that the transition to a circular economy will not be achieved through Commission packages alone; the transition requires a joint effort by all. There is a need to mobilise all actors in the European Union, including Member States, regional and local authorities, businesses and NGOs. The role of local and regional authorities is of utmost importance. Business and civil society initiatives are essential for the continued success of the joint efforts to move towards a circular economy in Europe and globally. Further legal developments at all levels will follow.

The EU is also active internationally in the field of the circular economy, initiating and supporting proposals in international negotiations. At global level, the EU has created an alliance of states and stakeholders working together to promote the circular economy, the so-called Global Alliance on Circular Economy and Resource Efficiency (GACERE).[31] The EU also supports the extension of controls on hazardous waste, materials and chemical substances in multilateral environmental conventions such as the Basel Convention,[32] the Rotterdam Convention,[33] the Stockholm Convention[34] and the Minamata Convention.[35] A further concern for the EU since the adoption of the European Plastics Strategy in 2018 has been to enshrine the principles of the circular economy at global level in the context of a global agreement to combat plastic damage to the environment. In this regard, the EU has played a crucial role in taking a decisive step forward at the 5th session of the World Environment Assembly in Nairobi (UNEA 5)

---

[28] Brussels, 11.4.2018 COM (2018) 184 final Proposal for a Directive of the European Parliament and of the Council on Representative Actions for the Protection of the Collective Interests of Consumers, and repealing Directive 2009/22/EC.

[29] Directive (EU) 2020/1828 of the European Parliament and of the Council of 25 November 2020 on representative actions for the protection of the collective interests of consumers and repealing Directive 2009/22/EC.

[30] https://www.herbertsmithfreehills.com/insight/the-representative-actions-directive-get-set-for-a-new-wave-of-european-class-actions.

[31] https://ec.europa.eu/environment/international_issues/gacere.html.

[32] Basel Convention on the Control of Transboundary Movements of Hazardous Wastes and Their Disposal.

[33] Rotterdam Convention on the Prior Informed Consent Procedure for Certain Hazardous Chemicals and Pesticides in International Trade.

[34] Stockholm Convention on Persistent Organic Pollutants.

[35] Minamata Convention on Mercury.

in March 2022. UNEA has a decisive role to establish an International Negotiating Committee (INC) to negotiate an agreement by 2024.[36] The first meeting of the INC did take place at the end of November 2022.[37]

Bibliography

Peter N. Kinga and Hideyuki Mori, 'The Development of Environmental Policy' (2007) 7 International Review for Environmental Strategies p. 7–16.

Ellen Mac Arthur Foundation, Towards the Circular Economy – Economic and business rationale for an accelerated transition, 2013.

Will Steffen, 'Planetary boundaries: Guiding human development on a changing planet' (2015) Science 347 (6223): 1259855, available at <https://www.science.org/doi/10.1126/science.1259855> accessed on 29 November 2022.

---

[36] https://www.unep.org/news-and-stories/press-release/un-environment-assembly-concludes-14-resolutions-curb-pollution.

[37] https://www.unep.org/events/conference/inter-governmental-negotiating-committee-meeting-inc-1.